INTERNATIONAL AWARD WINNING
HARRIS REFERENCE
CATALOG

POSTAGE
STAMP
PRICES

UNITED STATES
UNITED NATIONS
CANADA & PROVINCES

Confederate States, U.S. Possessions,
U.S. Trust Territories, and
Comprehensive U.S. Stamp Identifier

H.E. Harris & Co.®
Serving the Collector Since 1916

I

2021 US/BNA POSTAGE STAMP CATALOG

H.E. Harris & Company was founded by Henry Ellis Harris. Harris began the business in 1916 at an early age of fourteen and took advantage of free advertising in the Washington Post to begin his mail-order business. He built an enormously successful stamp company and garnered the support and confidence of the philatelic community. This annual US/BNA Catalog began publication in 1935 and was 64 pages.

ISBN: 0794848257

Copyright ©2020 Whitman Publishing, LLC.
1974 Chandalar Drive • Suite D • Pelham AL 35124
Designed in U.S.A. / Printed in China

ABOUT OUR CATALOG PRICES

The prices quoted in this catalog are the prices for which H.E. Harris offers stamps for retail sale at the time of publication. (*Harris no longer offers first day covers for sale.*)

These prices are based on current market values as researched by our staff, but, more importantly, on our day-to-day buying and selling activities in the stamp market.

Although you may certainly use this catalog as a guide to current market prices, you must keep in mind the fact that prices can change in response to varying levels of collector demand, or dealer promotions, and/or special purchases. We are not responsible for typographical errors.

You should also remember that condition is always the key factor in determining the value and price of a given stamp or set of stamps. Unlike some other stamp catalogs, we price U.S. stamps issued up to 1935 in three different condition grades for unused and used examples. For these earlier issues, we have also shown the percentage premium that would apply to Never Hinged Mint examples.

Our illustrated definitions of condition grades are presented on pages XII-XIII.

We have not found it possible to keep every stamp in stock that is listed in this catalog, and we cannot guarantee that we can supply all of the stamps in all conditions that are listed.

However, we will search for any stamp in any condition that a customer may want if that stamp is not in our stock at the time the customer places an order for it.

H.E. Harris & Co.®
Serving the Collector Since 1916

I N D E X

In this section we will attempt to define and explain some of the terms commonly used by stamp collectors. Instead of listing the terms in an alphabetical dictionary or glossary format, we have integrated them. In this way, you can see how an individual term fits within the total picture.

PRODUCTION

The manufacture of stamps involves a number of procedures. We will discuss the major steps here, with emphasis on their implications for stamp collectors. Although we present them separately, modern printing presses may combine one or more operations so that the steps tend to blend together. There also are steps in the process that we do not cover here. While they may be important to the production process, their direct implications for most collectors are minimal.

PLATE MAKING

Before anything can be printed, a printing plate must be made. Using the intaglio printing process (which is explained under **printing**) as an example, the steps involved in plate production are as follows:

- A **master die** is made. The design is recess engraved in a reverse mirror-image. Most master dies consist of only one impression of the design.
- The next step is to prepare a **transfer roll**. The soft steel of the transfer roll is rocked back and forth under pressure against the hardened master die and a series of multiple impressions, called **reliefs**, are created in the transfer roll. Note that the impression on the transfer roll will be raised above the surface, since the roll was pressed into the recesses of the master die.
- Once the transfer roll has been made and hardened, it is used to impress designs in to the soft steel of a **printing plate** that can fit up to 400 impressions of small, definitive-sized stamps or 200 impressions of large, commemorative-sized stamps. This time, the raised design on the transfer roll impresses a recessed design into the plate.

The process is much more complex than this, but these are the basics. Once the printing plate is hardened, it is almost ready to be used to create printed sheets of stamps. Depending on the printing equipment to be used, the printing plate will be shaped to fit around a cylinder for rotary press printing or remain flat for flat-bed press printing. In either form, the plate is then hardened and is ready for use in printing.

DESIGN VARIETIES

The complexity of the platemaking process can result in major or minor flaws. The inspection process will catch most of these flaws, but those that escape detection will result in **plate varieties**.

The early United States Classic issues have been examined in minute detail over the decades. Through **plating** studies, minor differences in individual stamps have been used to identify the position on the printing plate of each design variety. Sometimes called **"flyspeck philately"** because it involves the detection of minute "flyspeck" differences, such plating work has resulted in the identification of some of our greatest rarities. Compare the prices for the one cent blue issues of 1851 and 1857 (#s 5-9 and 18-24) and you will see the tremendous dollar difference that can result from minute design variations. (The Harris Stamp Identifier in this catalog explains the design differences.)

During the plate making or subsequent printing process, plate flaws that are detected will be corrected, sometimes incompletely or incorrectly. Corrections or revisions in an individual die impression or in all plate impressions include the following:

- **Retouching**—minor corrections made in a plate to repair damage or wear.
- **Recutting or re-engraving**—similar to, but more extensive than, retouching. Recutting usually applies to changes made before a plate has been hardened, while re-engraving is performed on a plate that has had to be tempered (softened) after hardening.
- **Redrawing**—the intentional creation of a slightly different design. The insertion of secret marks on the National Bank Notes plates when they were turned over to the Continental Bank Note Company in 1873 can be considered redrawings.
- **Reentry**—the reapplication of a design from a transfer roll to the plate, usually to improve a worn plate. If the reentry is not done completely, or if it is not done precisely on top of the previous design, a double transfer will result. Such double transfers will show on the printed stamp as an extra line at one or more points on the stamp.

Other design varieties may result from undetected plate flaws. A **plate crack** (caused by the hardened plate cracking under wear or pressure) or a **plate scratch** (caused by an object cutting into the plate) will show as an ink line on the printed stamp.

One other group that can be covered here to avoid possible confusion includes **reissues, reprints, special printings and reproductions**. None of these are design varieties that result from plate flaws, corrections or revisions. In fact, reissues, reprints and special printings are made from the same, unchanged plates as the originals. They show no differences in design and usually can be identified only by variations in paper, color or gum. Reproductions (such as U.S. #3 and #4), on the other hand, are made from entirely new plates and, therefore, can be expected to show some variation from the originals.

ERRORS, FREAKS, ODDITIES

"EFOs", as they are called, are printed varieties that result from abnormalities in the production process. They are design varieties, but of a special nature because the result looks different from the norm. When you see them, you know something went wrong. Basically, freaks and oddities can be loosely defined as minor errors. They include the following:

- **Misperforations**, that is, the placement of the perforations within the design rather than at the margins.
- **Foldovers**, caused by a sheet being turned, usually at a corner, before printing and/or perforating. The result is part of a design printed on the reverse of the sheet or placement of perforations at odd angles. Such freaks and oddities may be of relatively minor value, but they do make attractive additions to a collection. Truly major errors, on the other hand, can be of tremendous value. It would not be overstating the case to argue that many collectors are initially drawn to the hobby by the publicity surrounding discoveries of valuable errors and the hope that they might someday do the same. Major errors include the following:
- **Inverts.** These are the most dramatic and most valuable of all major errors and almost always result from printing processes that require more than one pass of a sheet through the presses. If the sheet inadvertently gets "flipped" between passes, the portion printed on the second pass will emerge inverted.

Two definitions we should introduce here are **"frame" and "vignette"**. The vignette is the central design of the stamp; the frame encloses the vignette and, at its outer edges, marks the end of the printed stamp design. Oftentimes, stamps described as inverted centers (vignettes) actually are inverted frames. The center was properly printed in the first pass and the frame was inverted in the second pass.

- **Color errors.** The most noticeable color errors usually involve one or more omitted colors. The sheet may not have made it through the second pass in a two-step printing process. In the past such errors were extremely rare because they were obvious enough to be noticed by inspectors. In modern multi-color printings, the chances of such errors escaping detection have increased. Nonetheless, they still qualify as major errors and carry a significant premium. *Other color errors involve the use of an incorrect color. They may not seem as dramatic as missing colors, but the early issues of many countries include some very rare and valuable examples of these color errors. Although technically not a color error, we can include here one of the most unusual of all errors, the United States 1917 5-cent stamps that are supposed to be blue, but are found in the carmine or rose color of the 2-cent stamps. The error was not caused by a sheet of the 5-centers being printed in the wrong color, as you might expect. Rather, because a few impressions on a 2-cent plate needed reentry, they were removed. But an error was made and the 5-cent design was entered. Thus it is a reentry error, but is described in most catalogs as a color error because that is the apparent result. Whatever the description, the 5-cent denomination surrounded by 2-cent stamps is a real showpiece.
- **Imperfs.** A distinction should be drawn here between imperforate errors and intentionally imperforate stamps. When the latter carry a premium value over their perforated counterparts, it is because they were printed in smaller quantities for specialized usages. They might have been intended, for example, for sale to vending machine manufacturers who would privately perforate the imperforate sheets

On the other hand, errors in which there is absolutely no trace of a perforation between two stamps that were supposed to be perforated carry a premium based on the rarity of the error. Some modern United States coil imperforate errors have been found in such large quantities that they carry little premium value. But imperforate errors found in small quantities represent tremendous rarities.

Be they intentional or errors, imperforate stamps are commonly collected in pairs or larger multiples because it can be extremely difficult—often impossible, to distinguish them from stamps that have had their perforations trimmed away in an attempt to pass them off as more valuable imperfs. Margin singles that show the stamp and a wide, imperforate selvage at one of the edges of the sheet are another collecting option.

PRINTING

There are three basic printing methods:

1. Intaglio, also known as **recess** printing. Line engraved below the surface of the printing plate (that is, in recess) accept the ink and apply it to damp paper that is forced into the recesses of the plate. Intaglio methods include **engraved** and **photogravure (or rotogravure)**. Photogravure is regarded by some as separate from intaglio because the engraving is done by chemical etching and the finished product can be distinguished from hand or machine engraving.

2. Typography. This is similar to intaglio, in that it involves engraving, but the action is in reverse, with the design left at the surface of the plate and the portions to be unprinted cut away. Ink is then applied to the surface design, which is imprinted onto paper. **Typeset** letterpress printing is the most common form of typography.

3. Lithography. This method differs from the previous two in that it involves **surface printing**, rather than engraving. Based on the principle that oil and water do not mix, the design to be printed is applied with a greasy ink onto a plate that is then wet with a watery fluid. Printing ink run across the plate is accepted only at the greased (oiled) points. The ink applies the design to paper that is brought in contact with the plate. **Offset** printing, a modern lithographic method, involves a similar approach, but uses a rubber blanket to transfer the inked design to paper.

PRINTING, CONTINUED

The printing method that was used to produce a given stamp can be determined by close inspection of that stamp.

1. Because the paper is pressed into the grooves of an intaglio plate, when viewed from the surface the design appears to be slightly raised. Running a fingernail lightly across the surface also will reveal this raised effect. When viewed from the back, the design will appear to be recessed (or pressed out toward the surface). Photogravure stamps have a similar appearance and feel, but when viewed under a magnifier, they reveal a series of dots, rather than line engravings.

2. Because the raised design on a plate is pressed into the paper when the typograph process is used, when viewed from the surface, the printing on the stamp does not have the raised effect of an intaglio product. On the other hand, when viewed from the reverse, a raised impression will be evident where the design was imprinted. Overprints often are applied by typography and usually show the raised effect on the back of the stamp.

3. Unlike either of the previous two methods, lithographed stamps look and feel flat. This dull, flat effect can be noticed on any of the United States 1918-20 offset printings, #s 525-536.

"EFOs", as they are called, are printed varieties that result from abnormalities in the production process. They are design varieties, but of a special nature because the result looks different from the norm. When you see them, you know something went wrong. Basically, freaks and oddities can be loosely defined as minor errors. They include the following:

WATERMARKS

This actually is one of the first steps in the stamp production process because it is part of paper manufacturing. A watermark is a slight thinning of the paper pulp, usually in the form of a relevant design. It is applied by devices attached to the rolls on papermaking machines. Without getting involved in the technical aspects, the result is a watermark that can sometimes be seen when held to the light, but more often requires watermark detector fluid.

A word of caution here. Such detector fluids may contain substances that can be harmful when inhaled. This is particularly true of lighter fluids that often are used by collectors in lieu of specially made stamp watermark detector fluids.

Watermarks are used to help detect counterfeits. Although it is possible to reproduce the appearance of a watermark, it is extremely difficult. The authorities have at times been able to identify a counterfeit by the lack of a watermark that should be present or by the presence of an incorrect watermark.

On the other hand, there are occasions when the incorrect or absent watermark did not indicate a counterfeit, but a printing error. The wrong paper may have been used or the paper may have been inserted incorrectly (resulting in an inverted or sideways watermark). The United States 30 cent orange red that is listed among the 1914-17 issues on unwatermarked paper (#467A) is an example of a printing error. It was produced on watermarked paper as part of the 1914-15 series, but a few sheets were discovered without watermarks.

Unfortunately, the difficulty encountered in detecting watermarks on light shades, such as orange or yellow, makes experts very reluctant to identify single copies of #476A. Although not visible, the watermark just might be there.

Because an examination of a full sheet allows the expert to examine the unprinted selvage and all stamps on that sheet at one time, positive identification is possible and most of the stamps that come down to us today as #476A trace back to such full sheets.

GUMMING

Gumming once was almost always applied after printing and before perforating and cutting of sheets into panes. Today, pregummed paper may be used, so the placement of this step in the process cannot be assured—nor is it the sequence of much significance.

The subject of gum will be treated more fully in the **Condition** section of this catalog. At this point, we will only note that certain stamps can be identified by their gum characteristics. Examples include the identification of rotary press stamps by the presence of gum breaker ridges or lines and the detection of the presence of original gum on certain stamps that indicates they can not be a rarer issue that was issued without gum, such as #s 40-47. Others, such as #s 102-111 can be identified in part by their distinctive white, crackly original gum.

PERFORATING

We have already discussed the absence of perforations in the **Errors** section. Here we will concentrate on the perforating process itself.

All perforating machines use devices to punch holes into the printed stamp paper. The holes usually are round and are known as perforations. When two adjacent stamps are separated, the semicircular cutouts are the **perforations**; the remaining paper between the perforations forms **perf tips**, or "**teeth**".

Most perforations are applied by perforators that contain a full row of punches that are driven through the paper as it is fed through the perforating equipment. **Line Perforators** drive the punches up and down; **rotary perforators** are mounted on cylinders that revolve. There are other techniques, but these are the most common.

To clear up one point of confusion, the **perforation size** (for example, "perf 11") is not the size of the hole or the number of perforations on the side of a given stamp. Rather, it describes the number of perforations that could be fit within two centimeters.

A perf 8 stamp will have visibly fewer perforations than a perf 12 stamp, but it is much harder to distinguish between perf 11 and perf 10-1/2. **Perforation gauges** enable collectors to make these distinctions with relative ease.

∽ TAGGING ∾

Modern, high-speed, mechanical processing of mail has created the need for "tagging" stamps by coating them with a luminescent substance that could be detected under ultraviolet (U.V.) light or by printing them on paper that included such substances. When passed under a machine capable of detecting these substances, an envelope can be positioned and the stamp automatically cancelled, thereby eliminating time-consuming and tedious manual operations. The tagged varieties of certain predominantly untagged stamps, such as #s 1036 and C67, do carry modest premiums. There also are technical differences between phosphorescent and fluorescent types of luminescent substances. But these details are primarily of interest to specialists and will not be discussed in this general work.

∽ PAPER ∾

The fact that we have not devoted more attention to paper should not be an indication of any lack of interest or significance. Books have been written on this one subject alone, and a lack of at least a rudimentary knowledge of the subject can lead to mis-identification of important varieties and result in financial loss.

The three most common categories of paper on which stamps are printed are **wove, laid, and India.** The most frequently used is machine-made **wove paper**, similar to that used for most books. The semiliquid pulp for wove paper is fed onto a fine wire screen and is processed much the same as cloth would be woven. Almost all United States postage stamps are printed on wove paper.

Laid paper is formed in a process that uses parallel wires rather than a uniform screen. As a result, the paper will be thinner where the pulp was in contact with the wires. When held to the light, alternating light and dark lines can be seen. Laid paper varieties have been found on some early United States stamps.

India paper is very thin and tough, without any visible texture. It is, therefore, more suited to obtaining the sharp impressions that are needed for printers' pre-production proofs, rather than to the high-volume printing of stamps.

Other varieties include **bluish** paper, so described because of the tone created by certain substances added to the paper, and silk paper, which contains threads or fibers of silk that usually can be seen on the back of the stamp. Many United States revenue stamps were printed on silk paper.

∽ COLLECTING FORMATS ∾

Whatever the production method, stamps reach the collector in a variety of forms. The most common is in sheet, or more correctly, pane form.

Sheets are the full, uncut units as they come from a press. Before distribution to post offices, these sheets are cut into **panes**. For United States stamps, most regular issues are printed in sheets of 400 and cut into panes of 100; most commemoratives are printed in sheets of 200 and cut into panes of 50. There are numerous exceptions to this general rule, and they are indicated in the mint sheet listings in this catalog. Sheets also are cut in **booklet panes** for only a few stamps—usually four to ten stamps per pane. These panes are assembled in complete booklets that might contain one to five panes, usually stapled together between two covers. An intact booklet is described as **unexploded**; when broken apart it is described as exploded.

Coils are another basic form in which stamps reach post offices. Such stamps are wound into continuous coil rolls, usually containing from 100 to 5,000 stamps, the size depending on the volume needs of the expected customer. Almost all coils are produced with perforations on two opposite sides and straight edges on the remaining two sides. Some serious collectors prefer collecting coils in pairs or strips—two or more adjacent stamps—as further assurance of genuineness. It is much easier to fake a coil single that shows only portions of each perforation hole than a larger unit that shows the complete perf hole.

A variation on this theme is the **coil line pair**—adjacent stamps that show a printed vertical line between. On rotary press stamps the line appears where the two ends of a printing plate meet on a rotary press cylinder. The joint is not complete, so ink falls between the plate ends and is transferred onto the printed coil. On flat plate stamps the guideline is the same as that created for sheet stamps, as described below. **Paste-up** coil pairs are not as popular as line pairs. They were a necessary by-product of flat plate printings in which the coil strips cut from separate sheets had to be pasted together for continuous winding into roll form.

The modern collecting counterpart to coil line pairs is the **plate number strip**—three or five adjacent coil stamps with the plate number displayed on the middle stamp. Transportation coil plate strips have become particularly sought after. On most early coil rolls, the plate numbers were supposed to be trimmed off. Freaks in which the number remains are interesting, but do not carry large premiums since they are regarded as examples of miscut oddities rather than printing errors.

Miniature sheets and souvenir sheets are variations on one theme—small units that may contain only one or at most a much smaller quantity of stamps than would be found on the standard postal panes. Stamps may be issued in miniature sheet format for purposes of expedience, as for example the Bret Harte $5 issue (#2196), which was released in panes of 20 to accommodate the proportionately large demand by collectors for plate blocks rather than single stamps. As the name implies, a souvenir sheet is a miniature sheet that was released as a souvenir to be saved, rather than postally used—although such sheets or the stamps cut out from them can be used as postage. **Note: souvenir cards** are created strictly for promotional and souvenir purposes. They contain stamp reproductions that may vary in size, color or design from the originals and are not valid for postal use.

Often, a common design may be produced in sheet, coil and booklet pane form. The common design is designated by collectors as one **type**, even though it may be assigned many different catalog numbers because of variations in color, size, perforations, printing method, denomination, etc. On the other hand, even minor changes in a basic design represent a new type.

Sheet stamps offer the greatest opportunity for format variation and collecting specialization. Using the following illustration for reference, the varieties that can be derived include the following:

Block (a)—this may be any unit of four stamps or more in at least 2 by 2 format. Unless designated as a different size, blocks are assumed to be blocks of four.

Specialized forms of blocks include:

Arrow block (b)—adjacent stamps at the margin of a sheet, showing the arrow printed in the margin for registration in the printing process, as, for example, in two-color printings. When the arrow designates the point at which a sheet is cut into panes, the result will appear as one leg of the arrow, or V, on each pane. **Guideline block (c)**—similar to arrow block, except that it can be any block that shows the registration line between two rows of two stamps each. **Gutter block**—similar to guideline block, except that an uncolored gutter is used instead of a printed line. The best known United States gutter blocks are those cut from full-sheet "Farley printings". Pairs of stamps from adjacent panes on each side of the gutter form the gutter block. **Imprint, or inscription blocks (d)**—include **copyright, mail early, and ZIP (e) blocks**. On most modern United States sheets, the **selvage (f)**, that is, the margin that borders the outer rows of stamps (f), includes one or more inscriptions in addition to the plate numbers. It may be a copyright protection notice or an inscription that encourages mail users to post their mail early or to use the ZIP code on their mail. Because the inscription appears along the margin, rather than in one of the corners, it is customary to collect copyright blocks and mail early blocks in two rows of three stamps each, with the inscription centered in the margin. The ZIP inscription appears in one of the corners of each pane, so it is collected in corner margin blocks of four. **Plate number block (g)**—this is by far the most popular form of block collecting. On each sheet of stamps, a plate number (or numbers) is printed to identify the printing plate(s) used. Should a damage be discovered, the plate can easily be identified. On flat plate sheets, where the plate number appeared along the margin, the format usually is in plate blocks of six, with the plate number centered in the margin. On rotary press and other sheets where a single plate number appears in one of the four corners of the margin, the customary collecting format is a **corner margin block of four (h)**. This also is true for plate blocks with two plate numbers in two adjacent corner stamps and for modern plates where single digits are used to designate each plate number and the complete series (containing one digit for each printing color) appears in the corner. Before single digits were adopted for modern multi-color printings, the five-digit numbers assigned to each plate might run down a substantial portion of the sheet margin. **Plate strips (i)** are collected in such instances. Their size is two rows times as many stamps as are attached to the margin area that shows all plate numbers. Because a sheet of stamps is cut into separate panes, printing plates include plate numbers that can be seen on each of the cut panes. On modern sheets the plate numbers would be located in each of the four corners of the uncut sheet. Once cut, each of the four panes would show the same plate number in one of its corners. The position of the plate number, which matches the position of the pane on the uncut sheet, is designated as upper left or right and lower left or right. Some specialists seek matched sets. A **matched set** is one of each of the four positions for a given plate number. A **complete matched set** is all positions of all plate numbers for a given issue.

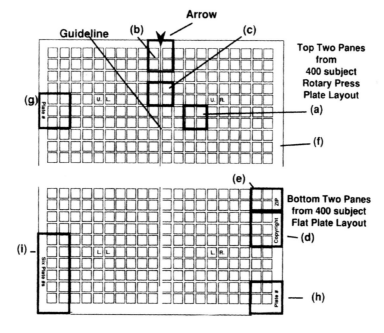

**This diagram is for placement purposes only, and is not an exact reproduction of margin markings.

Other definitions that relate in one way or another to the format in which stamps are produced include:

Se-tenant—from the French, meaning joined together. A pair, block, or larger multiple that contains different designs. The 1967 Space Twins issue is an example of a se-tenant pair in which the two different stamps are part of an integral design. The 1968 Historic Flags se-tenant strip contains ten separate designs, each of which can stand alone.

Tete-beche pair—from the French, meaning head-to-tail. Such pairs show adjacent stamps, one of which is upside down in relation to the other.

Proof—any trial impression used in the evaluation of prospective or final designs. Final die proofs—that is, those made from a completed die preparatory to its being used in the production of printing plates—are the standard proof collecting form.

Essay—a partial or complete illustration of a proposed design. In the strict philatelic sense, essays are printed in proof form.

Color trials—a preliminary proof of a stamp design in one or more colors. Trial color proofs are used to select the color in which the stamp will be printed.

Grill—a pattern of embossed cuts that break the stamp paper. See the information at the head of the 1861-67 Issue listings and the section of grills in the Harris Stamp Identifier.

POSTAL MARKINGS

The extensive subject of cancellations and postal markings on stamps and covers is too specialized to present in detail here. Volumes have been written on individual categories of markings—straight line markings, ship cancels, foreign mail cancels, flight covers, etc. In this section we will limit ourselves to the basic definitions related to the stamp and the manner in which it is cancelled, rather than the specialized usage of the envelope to which the stamp is affixed.

• **Manuscript,** or **pen cancels** were the earliest form of "killing" a stamp—that is, marking it to indicate it had been postally used.
• **Handstamps** were created shortly after the first stamps were issued. The early devices might only show a pattern such as a grid and often were carved from cork.
• **Fancy cancels** were an extension of the handstamp. Local postmasters carved cork cancelers that depicted bees, kicking mules, flowers, and hundreds of other figures. Stamps with clear strikes of such fancy cancels usually carry hefty premiums over those with standard cancels.
• **Machine cancels** are applied by mechanical rather than manual means.
• A stamp is **tied** to a cover (or piece) when the cancellation, whatever its form, extends beyond the margins of the stamp onto the cover. Such a tie is one indication of the authenticity of the cover.
Specialized cancellations include the following:
• **Cut cancel**—as the name implies, a cancel that actually cuts the stamp, usually in the form of a thin, straight incision. The most common usage of cut cancels on United States stamps is on Revenue issues.
• **Perfin,** or **perforated initial**—usually not a cancellation as such, but rather a privately administered punching into the stamp of one or more initials. Most often, the initials were those of a large firm that wished to prevent personal use of their stamps by employees.
• **Precancel**—a cancellation printed on stamps in advance of their sale. The primary purpose of precancels is for sale to large volume mailers, whose mail is delivered to post offices and processed in bulk without necessarily receiving further cancellation.
• **Non-contemporary cancel**—a cancellation applied to a stamp long after the normal period of use for that stamp. A stamp that is worth more used than unused or a damaged unused stamp that would be worth more on cover are examples of candidates for non-contemporary markings.
• **Cancel-to-order,** or **C.T.O.**—a cancel that is printed on a stamp by an issuing country to give it the appearance of having been used, or to render it invalid for postage in that country. Special fancy cancels or "favor cancels" have been applied at various times in the countries for philatelic reasons.

CATEGORIES

The number of specialized categories into which stamps can be slotted is limited only by the imagination of the individual collector. Some collectors have attempted to collect one of each and every stamp ever issued by every nation that ever existed. Other collectors have concentrated on all the possible varieties and usages of only one stamp. Between these two extremes, stamps can be divided into certain generally accepted categories, whether or not they are used as boundaries for a collection. These categories are as follows:

• **Definitives,** or **regulars**—stamps that are issued for normal, everyday postage needs. In the United States, they are put on sale for a period limited only by changing rate needs or infrequent issuance of a new definitive series. Post offices can requisition additional stocks of definitives as needed.
• **Commemoratives**—stamps issued to honor a specific event, anniversary, individual or group. They are printed in a predetermined quantity and are intended for sale during a limited period. Although they can be used indefinitely, once stocks are sold out at a local post office, commemoratives usually are not replenished unless the issue has local significance.
• **Pictorials**—stamps that depict a design other than the portrait of an individual or a static design such as a coat of arms or a flag. While some collectors think of these strictly as commemoratives (because most commemoratives are pictorials), some definitives also can be pictorials. Any number of definitives that depict the White House are examples.
• **Airmails,** or **air posts**—stamps issued specifically for airmail use. Although they do not have to bear a legend, such as "airmail", they usually do. Airmail stamps usually can be used to pay other postage fees. When air flights were a novelty, airmail stamp collecting was an extremely popular specialty. Part of this popularity also can be ascribed to the fact that the first airmail stamps usually were given special attention by issuing postal administrations. Produced using relatively modern technology, they often were among the most attractive of a nation's issues.
• **Zeppelin stamps**—although these do not rate as a major category, they deserve special mention. Zeppelin issues were primarily released for specific use on Zeppelin flights during the 1920s and 1930s. They carried high face values and were issued during the Great Depression period, when most collectors could not afford to purchase them. As a result, most Zeppelin issues are scarce and command substantial premiums. United States "Zepps" are the Graf Zeppelins (C13-C15) and the Century of Progress issue (C18).
• **Back-of-the-book**—specialized stamps that are identified as "back-of-the-book" because of their position in catalogs following the listings of regular and commemorative postal issues. Catalogs identified them with a prefix letter. Some collectors include airmail stamps in this category, in part because they carry a prefix letter (C) and are listed separately. Most collectors treat the airmails as part of a standard collection and begin the back-of-the-book section with semi-postals (B) or, for the United States, special deliveries (E). Other frequently used "b-o-b" categories include postage dues (J), offices in China, or Shanghais (K), officials (O), parcel posts (Q), newspapers (PR), and revenues (R), the latter including "Duck" hunting permit stamps (RW).

∼ CATEGORIES, CONTINUED ∽

Postal stationery and postal cards are the major non-stamp back-of-the-book categories. A complete envelope or card is called an **entire**; the cutout corner from such a piece, showing the embossed or otherwise printed design, is described as a **cut square**.

Some collecting categories do not relate to the intended use of the stamps. Examples include **topicals** (stamps collected by the theme of the design, such as sports, dance, paintings, space, etc.) and **first day covers**. Modern first day covers show a stamp or stamps postmarked in a designated first day city on the official first day of issue. The cancel design will relate to the issue and the cover may bear a privately-printed cachet that further describes and honors the subject of the stamp.

One of the oddities of the hobby is that **stampless covers** are an accepted form of "stamp" collecting. Such covers display a usage without a stamp, usually during the period before stamps were required for the payment of postage. They bear manuscript or handstamps markings such as "due 5," "PAID," etc. to indicate the manner in which postage was paid.

Although they do not constitute a postal marking, we can include **bisects** here for want of a better place. A bisect is a stamp cut in half and used to pay postage in the amount of one-half of the stamp's denomination. The 1847 ten cent stamp (#2) cut in half and used to pay the five cent rate is an example.

Bisects should be collected only on cover and properly tied. They also should reflect an authorized usage, for example, from a post office that was known to lack the proper denomination, and sould pay an amount called for by the usuage shown on the cover.

Not discussed in detail here is the vast subject of **covers**, or postal history. Envelopes, usually but not necessarily showing a postal use, are described by collectors as covers. Early "covers" actually were single letter sheets with a message on one side and folded into the form of an enclosing wrapper when viewed from the outside. The modern aerogramme or air letter is similar in design to these early folded letters.

∼ USED STAMPS ∽

For used stamps, the presence of gum would be the exception, since it would have been removed when the stamp was washed from the envelope, so gum is not a factor on used stamps. The centering definitions, on the other hand, would be the same as for unused issues. In addition, the cancellation would be a factor. We should point out here that we are not referring to the type of cancellation, such as a fancy cancel that might add considerably to the value of a stamp, or a manuscript cancel that reduces its value. Rather, we are referring to the degree to which the cancellation covers the stamp. A **lightly cancelled** used stamp, with all of the main design elements showing and the usage evidenced by an unobtrusive cancel, is the premier condition sought by collectors of used stamps. On the other hand, a stamp whose design has been substantially obliterated by a **heavy cancel** is at best a space filler that should be replaced by a moderate to lightly cancelled example.

∼ PERFORATIONS ∽

The condition of a stamp's perforations can be determined easily by visual examination. While not necessarily perfect, all perforations should have full teeth and clean perforation holes. A **blunt perf** is one that is shorter than it should be, while a **pulled perf** actually shows a portion of the margin or design having been pulled away. **Blind perfs** are the opposite: paper remains where the perforation hole should have been punched out. One irony of the demand for perforation is that **straight edges**, that is, the normal sheet margin straight edge that was produced when flat-plate sheets were cut into panes, are not acceptable to many collectors. In fact, many collectors will prefer a reperforated stamp to a straight edge. (Technically, **"re"perforated** can only apply to a stamp that is being perforated again, as when a damaged or excessive margin has been cut away and new perforations are applied, but we will follow the common practice of including the perforation of normal straight edges in this category). As a result of this preference, many straight edges no longer exist as such. When one considers that they were in the minority to start with (a pane of 100 flat plate stamps would include 19 straight edges) and that even fewer come down to us today, an argument could be made that they may someday be rarities...although it is hard to conceive of anyone paying a premium for straight edges.

∼ FAKES, FAULTS, AND EXPERTISING ∽

Below the first quality level—stamps free of defects—a range of stamps can be found from attractive **"seconds"** that have barely noticeable flaws to **space fillers** that may have a piece missing and which ought to be replaced by a better copy— unless we are talking about great rarities which would otherwise be beyond the budget of most collectors. The more common flaws include **thins, tears, creases, stains, pulled perfs, pinholes** (some dealers and collectors used to display their stamps pinned to boards), **face scuffs** or erasures, and **fading**. Stamps with faults sometimes are **repaired**, either to protect them from further damage or to deceive collectors. While the terms that are applied to stamps that are not genuine often are used interchangeably, they do have specific meaning, as follows:

- **fakes** (in French, faux; in German, falsch)—stamps that appear to be valuable varieties, but which were made from cheaper genuine stamps. Trimming away the perforations to create an imperforate is a common example of a fake.
- **bogus stamps, phantoms, labels**—outright fantasies, usually the product of someone's imagination, produced for amusement rather than deception.

While most stamps are genuine, and the average collector need not be concerned about the possibility of repairs, **expertizing** services do exist for collectors who are willing to pay a fee to obtain an independent opinion on their more valuable stamps.

H.E. Harris Pictorial Guide to Centering

Cat #	Very Fine	Fine	Average
1 to 293 1847 to 1898	Perfs clear of design on all four sides. Margins may not be even.	Perfs well clear of design on at least three sides. But may almost touch design on one side.	Perfs cut into design on at least one side.
294 to 749 1901 to 1934	Perfs clear of design. Margins relatively even on all four sides.	Perfs clear of design. Margins not even on all four sides.	Perfs touch design on at least one side.
750 to Date 1935 to Present	Perfs clear of design. Centered with margins even on all four sides.	Perfs clear of design. Margins may be uneven.	Perfs may touch design on at least one side.

Note: Margins are the area from the edges of stamp to the design. Perfs are the serrations between stamps that aid in separating them.

CENTERING

One major factor in the determination of a stamp's fair value is its **centering**, the relative balance of the stamp design within its margins. Whether the stamp has perforations or is imperforate, its centering can be judged. Because the stamp trade does not have an established system for grading or measuring centering, "eyeballing" has become the standard practice. As a result, one collector's definition may vary from another's. This can create some confusion, but the system seems to work, so it has remained in force. Centering can range from poor to superb, as follows:

- **Poor**—so far off center that a significant portion of the design is lost because of bad centering. On a poorly centered perforated stamp, the perforations cut in so badly that even the perf tips may penetrate the design.
- **Average**—a stamp whose frame or design is cut slightly by the lack of margins on one or two sides. On a perforated stamp, the perf holes might penetrate the stamp, but some margin white space will show on the teeth. Average stamps are accepted by the majority of collectors for 19th century stamps and early 20th century stamps, as well as for the more difficult later issues.
- **Fine**—the perforations are clear of the design, except for those issues that are known to be extremely poorly centered, but the margins on opposite sides will not be balanced, that is, equal to each other. (Note: a stamp whose top and bottom margins are perfectly balanced may still be called fine if the left and right margins differ substantially from each other.)
- **Very fine**—the opposite margins may still appear to differ somewhat, but the stamp is closer to being perfectly centered than it is to being fine centered. Very fine stamps are sought by collectors who are particularly interested in high quality and who are willing to pay the premiums such stamps command.
- **Superb**— perfect centering. They are so scarce that no comprehensive price list could attempt to include a superb category. Superb stamps, when they are available, command very high premiums.
- **"Jumbo"**—an abnormal condition, in which the stamp's margins are oversized compared to those of the average stamp in a given issue. Such jumbos can occur in the plate making process when a design is cut into the printing plate and excessive space is allowed between that design and the adjacent stamps.

Note: Some collectors also define a "fine to very fine" condition, in which the margin balance falls into a mid-range between fine and very fine. In theory it may be an attractive compromise, but in practice the range between fine and very fine is too narrow to warrant a separate intermediate category.

Quality and Condition Definitions

In determining the value of a given stamp, a number of factors have to be taken into consideration. For mint stamps, the condition of the gum, whether or not it has been hinged, and the centering are all major factors that determine their value. For used stamps, the factors to consider are cancellation and centering. The following H.E. Harris guidelines will enable you to determine the quality standards you may choose from in acquiring stamps for your collection.

Mint Stamp Gum

Unused—A stamp that is not cancelled (used), yet has had all the original gum removed. On early U.S. issues this is the condition that the majority of mint stamps exist in, as early collectors often soaked the gum off their stamps to avoid the possibility of the gum drying and splitting.

Original Gum (OG)—A stamp that still retains the adhesive applied when the stamp was made, yet has been hinged or has had some of the gum removed. Mint stamps from #215 to date can be supplied in this condition.

Never Hinged (NH)—A stamp that is in "post office" condition with full gum that has never been hinged. For U.S. #215 to #715 (1935), separate pricing columns or percentages are provided for "Never Hinged" quality. From #772 (1935) to date, all stamps are priced as Never Hinged.

Cancellations

The cancellations on Used stamps range from light to heavy. A lightly cancelled stamp has the main design of the stamp clearly showing through the cancel, while a heavy cancel usually substantially obliterates the design elements of the stamp. In general it should be assumed that Very fine quality stamps will have lighter cancels than Average cancellation stamps.

Heavy Cancel   **Light Cancel**

∽ GUM ∾

The impact of the condition of the back of an unused stamp (i.e. the **gum**) upon that stamp's value in today's market needs careful consideration. The prices for 19th century stamps vary widely based on this element of condition. Some traditional collectors feel that modern collectors pay too much attention to gum condition. Around the turn of the century, some collectors washed the gum off the stamps to prevent it from cracking and damaging the stamp themselves. But that generation has passed and the practice not only is no longer popular, it is almost unheard of. To some extent the washing of gum is no longer necessary, since modern gums are not as susceptible to cracking. A more important development, however, has been the advent of various mounts that allow the collector to place a stamp in an album without the use of a hinge. With that development, "never hinged" became a premium condition that could be obtained on stamps issued from the 1930s to date. As a result, gum took on added significance, and its absence on 20th century stamps became unacceptable.

The standard definitions that pertain to gum condition are as follows:

• **Original gum, or o.g.**—the gum that was applied when the stamp was produced. There are gradations, from "full" original gum through "partial" original gum, down to "traces". For all intents and purposes, however, a stamp must have most of its original gum to be described as "o.g."

• **Regummed**— the stamp has gum, but it is not that which would have been applied when the stamp was produced. Many collectors will avoid regummed stamps because the gum may hide some repair work. At best, regumming may give the stamp an appearance of completeness, but a premium should not be paid for a stamp that lacks its original gum.

• **Unused**—while many collectors think of this as any stamp that is not used, the narrow philatelic definition indicates a stamp that has no gum or is regummed.

• **Unhinged**—as with "unused", the term has a specific meaning to collectors: a regumming that shows no traces of a hinge mark. Unfortunately, in their confusion some collectors purchase stamps described as "unused" and "unhinged" as if they bore original gum.

• **No gum**—the stamp lacks its gum, either because it was intentionally produced without gum (also described as **ungummed**) or had the gum removed at a later date. It is customary to find 19th century stamps without gum, and the condition is acceptable to all but the most fastidious collectors. On 20th century stamps, original gum is to be expected.

• **Hinged**—the gum shows traces of having been mounted with a hinge. This can range from **lightly hinged** (the gum shows traces, but none of the hinge remains) to **heavily hinged** (a substantial portion of one or more hinge remnants is stuck to the stamp, or a significant portion of the gum has been lost in the removal of a hinge).

• **Thinned**— not only has the gum been removed, but a portion of the stamp paper has been pulled away. A thin usually will show when the stamp is held to a light. One of the faults that may be covered over on regummed stamps is a thin that has been filled in.

• **Never hinged**—as the name implies, the stamp has its original gum in post office condition and has never been hinged. Although some collectors think of **"mint"** stamps as any form of unused, o.g. stamps, the more accepted "mint" definition is never hinged.

UNITED STATES STAMP IDENTIFIER

Shows you how to distinguish between the rare and common U.S. stamps that look alike.

Types of 1¢ Franklin Design of 1851-60

TYPE I has the most complete design of the various types of stamps. At top and bottom there is an unbroken curved line running outside the bands reading "U.S. POSTAGE" and "ONE CENT". The scrolls at bottom are turned under, forming curls. The scrolls and outer line at top are complete.

TYPE Ia is like Type I at bottom but ornaments and curved line at top are partly cut away.

TYPE Ib (not illustrated) is like Type I at top but little curls at bottom are not quite so complete nor clear and scroll work is partly cut away.

TYPE II has the outside bottom line complete, but the little curls of the bottom scrolls and the lower part of the plume ornament are missing. Side ornaments are complete.

TYPE III has the outside lines at both top and bottom partly cut away in the middle. The side ornaments are complete.

TYPE IIIa (not illustrated) is similar to Type III with the outer line cut away at top or bottom, but not both.

TYPE IV is similar to Type II but the curved lines at top or bottom (or both) have been recut in several different ways, and usually appear thicker than Type IIs.

TYPE V is similar to Type III but has the side ornaments parlty cut away. Type V occurs only on perforated stamps.

Types of 3¢ Washington & 5¢ Jefferson Designs of 1851-60

3¢ WASHINGTON

TYPE I has a frame line around the top, bottom and sides.

TYPE III has the frame line removed at top and bottom, while the side frame lines are continuous from the top to bottom of the plate.

TYPE IV is similar to Type III, but the side frame lines were recut individually, and therefore are broken between stamps.

5¢ JEFFERSON

TYPE I is a complete design with projections (arrow) at the top and bottom as well as at the sides.

TYPE II has the projections at the top or bottom partly or completely cut away.

Types of the 10¢ Washington Design of 1851-60

TYPE I has the "shells" at the lower corners practically complete, while the outer line below "TEN CENTS" is very nearly complete. At the top, the outer lines above "U.S. POSTAGE" above the "X" in each corner are broken.

TYPE II has the design complete at the top, but the outer line at the bottom is broken in the middle and the "shells" are partially cut away.

TYPE III has both top and bottom outer lines cut away; similar to Type I at the top and Type II at the bottom.

TYPE IV has the outer lines at the top or bottom of the stamp, or at both place, recut to show more strongly and heavily.

Types I, II, III and IV have complete ornaments at the sides and three small circles or pearls (arrow) at the outer edges of the bottom panel.

TYPE V has the side ornaments, including one or two of the small "pearls" partly cut away. Also, the outside line, over the "X" at the right top, has been partly cut away.

Types of the 12¢ Washington issues of 1851-60

PLATE 1 has stronger, more complete outer frame lines than does Plate 3. Comes imperforate (#17 or perf #36).

PLATE 3 has uneven or broken outer frame lines that are particularly noticeable in the corners. The stamps are perf 15. (#36b)

The 1875 REPRINT plate is similar to plate 1, but the Reprint stamps are greenish black and slightly taller than plate 1 stamps (25mm from top to bottom frame lines versus 24.5 mm) The paper is whiter and the perforations are 12 gauge.

Shows you how to distinguish between the rare and common U.S. stamps that look alike.

Types of the 1861 Issue, Grills & Re-Issues

Shortly after the outbreak of the Civil War in 1861, the Post Office demonitized all stamps issued up to that time in order to prevent their use by the Confederacy. Two new sets of designs, consisting of six stamps shown below plus 24¢ and 30¢ demonitized, were prepared by the American Bank Note Company. The first designs, except for the 10¢ and 24¢ values, were not regularly issued and are extremely rare and valuable. The second designs became the regular issue of 1861. The illustrations in the left column show the first (or unissued) designs, which were all printed on thin, semi- transparent paper. The second (or regular) designs are shown at right.

Types of the 1861 Issues

1st

SECOND DESIGN shows a small dash (arrow) under the tip of the ornaments at the right of the figure "1" in the upper left-hand corner of the stamp.

2nd

1st

SECOND DESIGN, 3¢ value, shows a small ball (arrow) at each corner of the design. Also, the ornaments at the corners are larger than in the first design.

2nd

1st

SECOND DESIGN, 5¢ value has a leaflet (arrow) projecting from the scrolled ornaments at each corner of the stamp.

2nd

1st

FIRST DESIGN has no curved line below the row of stars and there is only one outer line of the ornaments above them.
SECOND DESIGN has a heavy curved line below the row of stars (arrow); ornaments above the stars have double outer line.

2nd

1st

FIRST DESIGN has rounded corners.
SECOND DESIGN has a oval and a scroll (arrow) in each corner of the design

2nd

Types of the 15¢ "Landing of Columbus" Design of 1869

Type I

Type II

TYPE I has the central picture without the frame line shown in Type II.
TYPE II has a frame line (arrows) around the central picture; also a diamond shaped ornament appears below the "T" of "Postage".
TYPE III (not illustrated) is like Type I except that the fringe of brown shading lines which appears around the sides and bottom of the picture on Types I and II has been removed.

IDENTIFIER CHART
1861-1867 Bank Notes

Description and Identifying Features				1¢	2¢	3¢	5¢	10¢	12¢	15¢	24¢	30¢	90¢
1861. National. First designs. Thin, semi-transparent paper. No grill.				55		56	57	58[1], 62B	59		60	61	62
1861-62. National. Modified designs[3]. Thicker, opaque paper. No grill.				63		64[2], 65[2], 66[2]	67	68	69		70[2]	71	72
1861-66. National. Thicker, opaque paper. No grill. a. New designs.					73					77			
b. Same designs, new shades.						74[2]		75[2], 76[2]		78[2]			
1867. National. Grills. All on thick, opaque paper.													
Grills	Pts. as seen from stamp face	Area of covered Horiz. x Vert.	# of rows of Pts.										
A	Up	All over	—				79	80				81	
B	Up	18 x 15 mm	22 x 18				82						
C	Up	c. 13 x 16 mm	16-17 x 18-21				83						
D	Down	c. 12 x 14 mm	15 x 17-18			84	85						
Z	Down	c. 11 x 14 mm	13-14 x 17-18	85A	85B	85C			85D	85E 85F			
E	Down	c. 11 x 13 mm	14 x 15-17	86	87	88			89	90 91			
F	Down	c. 9 x 13 mm	11-12 x 15-17	92	93	94	95	96	97	98	99	100	101
1875. National. Re-issues. Hard, white paper. White crackly gum. No grill.				102	103	104	105	106	107	108	109	110	111

FOOTNOTES:
1. #58 does not exist used. Unused, it cannot be distinguished from #62B.
2. Different from corresponding 1861-66 issues only in color.
3. See diagrams for design modification.

UNITED STATES STAMP IDENTIFIER

Shows you how to distinguish between the rare and common U.S. stamps that look alike.

Types of the 1870-71 Through 1887 Bank Notes

The stamps of the 1870-71 issue were printed by the National Bank Note Company. The similar issue of 1873 was printed by the Continental Bank Note Company. When Continental took over the plates previously used by National, they applied the so-called "secret marks" to the designs of the 1¢ through 15¢ denominations by which the two issues can be distinguished as shown below. The illustrations at the left show the original designs of 1870-71; those at the right show secret marks applied to the issue of 1873.

 1¢ Secret mark is a small curved mark in the pearl at the left of the figure "1".

 7¢ Secret mark is two tiny semicircles drawn around the end of the lines which outline the ball in the lower right-hand corner.

 2¢ 1870-71 are red brown. The 1873 issue is brown and in some copies has a small diagonal line under the scroll at the left of the "U.S." (arrow).

 10¢ Secret mark is a small semicircle in the scroll at the right-hand side of the central design.

 3¢ Secret mark is the heavily shaded ribbon under the letters "RE".

 12¢ Secret mark shows the "balls" at the top and bottom on the figure "2" crescent-shaped (right) instead of nearly round as at the left.

 6¢ Secret mark shows the first four vertical lines of shading in the lower part of the left ribbon greatly strengthened.

 15¢ Secret mark shows as strengthened lines (arrow) in the triangle in the upper left-hand corner, forming a "V".

IDENTIFIER CHART
1870-1887 Bank Notes

Description and Identifying Features	1¢	2¢	3¢	5¢	6¢	7¢	10¢	12¢	15¢	21¢	30¢	90¢
1870-71. National. No secret marks. White wove paper, thin to medium thick. With grills.	134	135	136		137	138	139	140	141	142	143	144
1870-71. National. As above, except without grills.	145	146	147		148	149	150	151	152	153	154[2]	155[2]
1873. Continental. White wove paper, thin to thick. No grills.												
a. With secret marks.	156	157	158		159	160	161	162	163			
b. No secret marks.											165[2]	166[2]
1875. Continental. Special Printing. Same designs as 1873 Continental. Hard, white wove paper. No gum.	167	168	169		170	171	172	173	174	175	176	177
1875. Continenal. New color or denomination. Hard yellowish, wove paper.		178		179								
1875. Continental. Special printing. Same designs as 1875 Continental. Hard, white wove paper. No gum.		180		181								
1879. American. Same designs as 1873-75. Continental. Soft, porous paper.	182	183[3]	184[3]	185	186[3]		188		189[3]		190[3]	191[3]
a. Without secret mark.							187[3]					
1880. American. Special printing. Same as 1879 issue. Soft, porous paper. No gum.	192	193, 203[3]	194[3]	204	195[3]	196	197[3]	198	199[3]	200	201[3]	202[3]
1881-82. American. Designs of 1873. Re-engraved[4]. Soft, porous paper.	206		207[5]		208		209					
1887. American. Same designs as 1881-82. New colors.		214[5]									217	218

FOOTNOTES:
1. See diagrams for secret marks.
2. Corresponding denominations differ from each other only in color.
3. Corresponding denominations differ from each other only in color and gum. The special printings are slightly deeper and richer. The lack of gum is not positive identifier because it can be washed from the 1879 issues.
4. See diagrams for re-engravings.
5. Corresponding denominations differ from each other in color.

UNITED STATES STAMP IDENTIFIER

Shows you how to distinguish between the rare and common U.S. stamps that look alike.

Re-Engraved Designs 1881-82

1¢ has strengthened vertical shading lines in the upper part of the stamp, making the background appear almost solid. Lines of shading have also been added to the curving ornaments in the upper corners.

3¢ has a solid shading line at the sides of the central oval (arrow) that is only about half the previous width. Also a short horizontal line has been cut below the "TS" of "CENTS".

6¢ has only three vertical lines between the edge of the panel and the outside left margin of the stamp. (In the preceding issues, there were four such lines.)

10¢ has only four vertical lines between the left side of the oval and the edge of the shield. (In the preceding issues there were five such lines.) Also, the lines in the background have been made much heavier so that these stamps appear more heavily linked than previous issues.

2¢ Washington Design of 1894-98

TYPE I has horizontal lines of the same thickness within and without the triangle.

TYPE II has horizontal lines which cross the triangle but are thinner within it than without.

TYPE III has thin lines inside the triangle and these do not cross the double frame line of the triangle.

2¢ Columbian "Broken Hat" Variety of 1893

231

As a result of a plate defect, some stamps of the 2¢ Columbian design show a noticeable white notch or gash in the hat worn by the third figure to the left of Columbus. This "broken hat" variety is somewhat less common than the regular 2¢ design.

Broken Hat variety, 231c

4¢ Columbian Blue Error

Collectors often mistake the many shades of the normal 4¢ ultramarine for the rare and valuable blue error. Actually, the "error" is not ultramarine at all, but a deep blue, similar to the deeper blue shades of the 1¢ Columbian.

$1 Perry Design of 1894-95

TYPE I shows circles around the "$1" are broken at point where they meet the curved line below "ONE DOLLAR" (arrows).

TYPE II shows these circles complete.

10¢ Webster design of 1898

TYPE I has an unbroken white curved line below the words "TEN CENTS".

TYPE II shows white line is broken by ornaments at a point just below the "E" in "TEN" and the "T" in "CENTS" (arrows).

2¢ Washington Issue of 1903

Die I
319, 319g, 320

The rounded inner frame line below and to the left "T" in "TWO" has a dark patch of color that narrows, but remains strong across the bottom.

Die II
319f, 320a

2¢ "cap of 2" Variety of 1890

Cap on left "2"

Plate defects in the printing of the 2¢ "Washington" stamp of 1890 accounts for the "Cap of left 2" and "Cap on both 2s" varieties illustrated.

Cap on right "2"

UNITED STATES STAMP IDENTIFIER

Shows you how to distinguish between the rare and common U.S. stamps that look alike.

FRANKLIN AND WASHINGTON ISSUES OF 1908-22

Perforation	Watermark	Other Identifying Features		1¢	2¢	1¢	2¢	3¢ thru $1 denominations	8¢ thru $1 denominations
PERF. 12	USPS	White paper		331	332			333-42	422-23
		Bluish gray paper		357	358			359-66	
	USPS	White paper		374	375	405	406	376-82, 407	414-21
COIL 12	USPS	Perf. Horizontal		348	349			350-51	
		Perf. Vertical		352	353			354-56	
	USPS	Perf. Horizontal		385	386				
		Perf. Vertical		387	388			389	
IMPERF.	USPS			343	344			345-47	
	USPS	Flat Plate		383	384	408	409		
		Rotary Press					459		
	Unwmkd.	Flat Plate				481	482-82A	483-85	
		Offset				531	532-34B	535	
COIL 8-1/2	USPS	Perf. Horizontal		390	391	410	411		
		Perf. Vertical		392	393	412	413	394-96	
PERF. 10	USPS								460
	USPS					424	425	426-30	431-40
	Unwmkd.	Flat Plate				462	463	464-69	470-78
		Rotary Press				543			
COIL 10	USPS	Perf. Horizontal	Flat			441	442		
			Rotary			448	449-50		
		Perf. Vertical	Flat			443	444	445-47	
			Rotary			452	453-55	456-58	
	Unwmkd.	Perf. Horizontal				486	487-88	489	
		Perf. Vertical				490	491-92	493-96	497
PERF. 11	USPS				519				
	USPS						461		
	Unwmkd.	Flat Plate				498	499-500	501-07	508-18
		Rotary Press				*544-45	546		
		Offset				525	526-28B	529-30	
Perf. 12-1/2	Unwkmd.	Offset				536			
11 x 10	Unwkmd.	Rotary				538	539-40	541	
10 x 11	Unwkmd.	Rotary				542			

* Design of #544 is 19 mm wide x 22-1/2 mm high. #545 is 19-1/2 to 20 mm wide x 22 mm high.

Size of Flat Plate Design

22mm

18-1/2 to 19mm

Stamps printed by rotary press are always slightly wider or taller on issues prior to 1954. Measurements do not apply to booklet singles.

HOW TO USE THIS IDENTIFICATION CHART

Numbers referred to herein are from Scott's Standard Postage Stamp Catalog. To identify any stamp in this series, first check the type by comparing it with the illustrations at the top of the chart. Then check the perforations, and whether the stamp is single or double line watermarked or unwatermarked. With this information you can quickly find out the Standard Catalog number by checking down and across the chart. For example, a 1¢ Franklin, perf. 12, single line watermark, must be Scott's #374.

UNITED STATES STAMP IDENTIFIER

Shows you how to distinguish between the rare and common U.S. stamps that look alike.

Types of The 2¢ Washington Design of 1912-20

Type I

Type I where the ribbon at left above the figure "2" has one shading line in the first curve, while the ribbon at the right has one shading line in the second curve. Bottom of toga has a faint outline. Top line of toga, from bottom to front of throat, is very faint. Shading lines of the face, terminating in front of the ear, are not joined. Type I occurs on both flat and rotary press printings.

Type Ia is similar to Type I except that all of the lines are stronger. Lines of the Toga button are heavy. Occurs only on flat press printings.

Type Ia

Type II

Type II has ribbons shaded as in Type I. Toga button and shading lines to left of it are heavy. Shading lines in front of ear are joined and end in a strong vertically curved line (arrow). Occurs only on rotary press printings.

Type III where ribbons are shaded with two lines instead of one; otherwise similar to Type II. Occurs on rotary press printings only.

Type III

Type IV

Type IV where top line of toga is broken. Shading lines inside the toga bottom read "Did". The Line of color in the left "2" is very thin and usually broken. Occurs on offset printings only.

Type V in which top line of toga is complete. Toga button has five vertical shaded lines. Line of color in the left "2" is very thin and usually broken. Nose shaded as shown in illustration. Occurs on offset printings only.

Type V

Type Va

Type Va is same as Type V except in shading dots of nose. Third row of dots from bottom has four dots instead of six. Also, the Overall height of Type Va is 1/3 millimeter less than Type V. Occurs on offset printings only.

Type VI is same as Type V except that the line of color in left "2" is very heavy (arrow). Occurs in offset printings only.

Type VI

Type VII

Type VII in which line of color in left "2" is clear and continuous and heavier than Types V or Va, but not as heavy as in Type VI. There are three rows of vertical dots (instead of two) in the shading of the upper lip, and additional dots have been added to hair at top of the head. Occurs on offset printings only.

Types of The 3¢ Washington Design of 1908-20

Type I

TYPE I in which the top line of the toga is weak, as are the top parts of the shading lines that join the toga line. The fifth shading line from the left (arrow) is partly cut away at the top. Also the line between the lips is thin. Occurs on flat and rotary press printings.

Type II

TYPE II where top line of toga is strong and the shading lines that join it are heavy and complete. The line between the lips is heavy. Occurs on flat and rotary press printings.

Type III

TYPE III in which top line of toga is strong, but the fifth shading line from the left (arrow) is missing. The center line of the toga button consists of two short vertical lines with a dot between them. The "P" and "O" of "POSTAGE" are separated by a small line of color. Occurs on offset printings only.

Type IV

TYPE IV in which the shading lines of the toga are complete. The center line of the toga button consists of a single unbroken vertical line running through the dot in the center. The "P" and the "O" of "POSTAGE" are joined. Type IV occurs only in offset printings.

Types of 5¢ Franklin, 10¢ Washington 1847-1947

In the original 5¢ design, the top edge of Franklin's shirt touches the circular frame about at a level with the top of the "F" of "FIVE", while in the 1875 reproduction it is on a level with the top of the figure "5".

In the original 10¢ design, the left edge of Washington's coat points to the "T" of "TEN", and the right edge points between the "T" and "S" of "CENTS". In the reproductions, the left and right outlines of the coat point to the right edge of "X" and to the the center of the "S" of "CENTS" respectively. Also, on the 1875 reprints, the eyes have a sleepy look and the line of the mouth is straighter.

The 1947 "Cipex" Souvenir Sheet, issued on the hundredth anniversary of United States stamps, features reproductions of the two original designs. Stamps cut out of souvenir sheet are, of course, valid postage. However, no difficulty in identification should be encountered since the 1947 reproductions are light blue (5¢) instead of the original red brown, and brownish orange (10¢) instead of the original black.

GROW YOUR STAMP COLLECTION

WITH THESE GREAT PRODUCTS FROM *H.E. Harris & Co.*

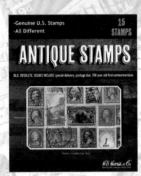

Antique Stamp Collection
$3.49 • Item #0794847676
15 genuine U.S.
postage stamps.

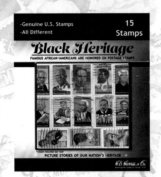

**Black Heritage
Stamp Collection**
$3.49 • Item #0794847684
15 genuine U.S.
postage stamps.

**American Entertainers
Stamp Collection**
$3.49 • Item #90922176
15 genuine U.S.
postage stamps.

**Arts & Culture
Stamp Collection**
$3.49 • Item #0794844596
15 genuine U.S.
postage stamps.

Stamps of Love Collection
$3.49 • Item #0794847668
14 genuine U.S.
postage stamps.

**Famous American Women
Stamp Collection**
$3.49 • Item #90922051
20 genuine U.S.
postage stamps.

**Famous American Men
Stamp Collection**
$3.49 • Item #0794823939
20 genuine U.S.
postage stamps.

Flower Stamp Collection
$3.49 • Item #0794839207
14 genuine U.S.
postage stamps.

**United We Stand U.S.
Stamp Collection**
$3.49 • Item #9TRT3403
15 genuine U.S.
postage stamps.

**Birds and Flowers
Stamp Collection**
$3.49 • Item #9TRT2978
25 genuine worldwide
postage stamps.

Dinosaurs Stamp Collection
$3.49 • Item #0794839223
22 genuine worldwide
postage stamps.

Wildlife Stamp Collection
$3.49 • Item #0794847692
50 genuine worldwide
postage stamps.

MENTION USBNA 21 TO RECEIVE FREE SHIPPING
ON YOUR ORDER OF $10 OR MORE

COMMEMORATIVE IDENTIFIER

The following handy identifier is a list of commemoratives organized alphabetically by key words on the stamp, which are the most prominent after "U.S. Postage," and matches the stamp with its corresponding Scott number.

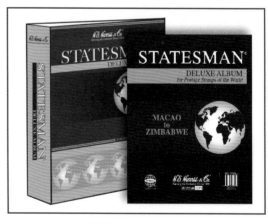

GENERAL ISSUES

1847 – THE FIRST ISSUE
Imperforate

"For every single letter in manuscript or paper of any kind by or upon which information shall be asked or communicated in writing or by marks or signs conveyed in the mail, for any distance under three hundred miles, five cents; and for any distance over three hundred miles, ten cents . . . and every letter or parcel not exceeding half an ounce in weight shall be deemed a single letter, and every additional weight of half ounce, shall be charged with an additional single postage."

With these words, the Act of March 3, 1845, authorized, but not required, the prepayment of postage effective July 1, 1847, and created a need for the first United States postage stamps. Benjamin Franklin, as the first Postmaster General of the United States and the man generally regarded as the "father" of the postal system, was selected for the 5 cent stamp. As the first President of the United States, George Washington was designated for the 10 cent issue.

The 1847 stamps were released July 1, 1847, but were available only in the New York City post office on that date. The earliest known usages are July 7 for the 5 cent and July 2 for the 10 cent.

The best estimates are that 4,400,000 of the 5 cent and 1,050,000 of the 10 cent stamps reached the public. The remaining stocks were destroyed when the stamps were demonetized and could no longer be used for postage as of July 1, 1851.

Like most 19th century United States stamps, the first Issue is much more difficult to find unused than used. Stamps canceled by "handstamp" marking devices—usually carved from cork—are scarcer than those with manuscript, or "pen", cancels.

Issued without gum, the Reproductions of the 1847 issue were printed from entirely new dies for display at the 1876 Centennial Exposition and were not valid for postal use. The issue also was reproduced on a souvenir sheet issued in 1947 to celebrate the centenary of the First Issue. Differences between the 1847 issue, 1875 Reproductions and 1948 stamps are described in the Stamp Identifier at the front of this catalog. (Page XIX)

1, 3
Franklin

2, 4
Washington

SCOTT NO.	DESCRIPTION	UNUSED VF	UNUSED F	AVG	USED VF	USED F	AVG
		1847 Imperforate (OG + 100%)					
1	5¢ red brown	3500.00	2000.00	1200.00	600.00	475.00	300.00
1	— Pen cancel	....	....	....	475.00	300.00	200.00
2	10¢ black . . .	20000.00	13000.00	7000.00	1200.00	900.00	700.00
2	— Pen cancel	....	....	....	800.00	700.00	600.00
		1875 Reprints of 1847 Issues, without gum					
3	5¢ red brown	1000.00	800.00	650.00	....	....	....
4	10¢ black	1250.00	1000.00	800.00	....	....	....

1851-61 – THE CLASSIC ISSUES

An act of Congress approved March 3, 1851, enacted new, reduced postage rates, introduced additional rates and made the prepayment of additional postage compulsory. Although the use of postage stamps was not required, the 1851 Act stimulated their use and paved the way for their required usage from July 1, 1855 on.

Under the Act of 1851, the basic prepaid single letter rate (defined as one-half ounce or less) was set at 3 cents. As this would be the most commonly used value, it was decided that a likeness of George Washington should grace the 3 cent stamp. Benjamin Franklin was assigned to the 1 cent stamp, which, among other usages, met the newspaper and circular rates.

Washington also appears on the 10, 12, 24 and 90 cent stamps and Franklin on the 30 cent value. Thomas Jefferson was selected for the new 5 cent stamp that was issued in 1856.

By 1857, improved production techniques and the increasing usage of stamps led to the introduction of perforated stamps that could be more easily separated. The result was the 1857-61 series whose designs are virtually identical to the 1851 set. The 1857-61 perforated stamps were set in the printing plates with very little space between each stamp. As a result, insufficient space was allowed to accommodate the perforations, which often cut into the design on these stamps. In fact, stamps with complete designs and wide margins on all four sides are the exception and command very substantial premiums.

The most fascinating—and most challenging—feature of the 1851-61 stamps is the identification of many major and minor types. An extremely slight design variation can mean a difference of thousands of dollars and collectors even today can apply their knowledge to discover rare, misidentified types.

The various "Types", identified below by Roman numerals in parentheses, resulted from minor changes in the printing plates caused by wear or plate retouching. The 1851-57 one-cent blue stamp may be the most studied of all the United States issues and is found in seven major catalog-listed Types (14, if we count imperforate and perforated stamps separately), plus countless minor listed and unlisted varieties. A thorough explanation of the differences in the major types for all denominations of the 1857-61 series is contained in the Harris Stamp Identifier in this catalog.

Shortly after the outbreak of the Civil War, the 1851-61 stamps were demonetized to prevent Southern post offices from selling the stamps in the North to raise cash for the Confederate States. After the war, large supplies of unused 1857-61 stamps were located in Southern post offices and purchased by stamp dealers and collectors. This explains the relatively large supply of unused 1857-61 issues that still exist today. The short life and limited use of 90 cent high value, which was issued in 1860, and the 5 cent orange brown, released May 8, 1861, explains why those stamps sell for more used than unused.

5-9, 18-24, 40
Franklin

10, 11, 25, 26, 41
Washington

12, 27-30A, 42
Jefferson

13-16, 31-35, 43
Washington

17, 36, 44
Washington

SCOTT NO.	DESCRIPTION	UNUSED VF	UNUSED F	AVG	USED VF	USED F	AVG
		1851-57 Imperforate (OG + 100%)					
5	1¢ blue (I)	....	....	....	....	69000.00	....
5A	1¢ blue (Ib)	13000.00	10750.00	8900.00	9500.00	6425.00	4475.00
6	1¢ dark blue (Ia)	22000.00	16700.00	12250.00	11000.00	8000.00	5275.00
7	1¢ blue (II)	500.00	375.00	250.00	250.00	175.00	100.00
8	1¢ blue (III)	9500.00	6000.00	4200.00	2500.00	1500.00	1000.00
8A	1¢ blue (IIIa)	5000.00	3400.00	2100.00	1725.00	1100.00	800.00
9	1¢ blue (IV)	350.00	270.00	175.00	200.00	125.00	85.00
10	3¢ orange brown (I) . .	2000.00	1200.00	800.00	225.00	140.00	180.00
11	3¢ deep claret (I)	200.00	185.00	75.00	30.00	17.25	15.00
12	5¢ red brown (I)	13650.00	10250.00	6750.00	1100.00	600.00	450.00
13	10¢ green (I)	11050.00	8500.00	6000.00	1175.00	650.00	475.00
14	10¢ green (II)	2300.00	1750.00	1350.00	300.00	200.00	180.00
15	10¢ green (III)	2500.00	1800.00	1300.00	300.00	200.00	180.00
16	10¢ green (IV)	18900.00	12500.00	10000.00	2000.00	1500.00	1150.00
17	12¢ black	3250.00	2500.00	1750.00	300.00	200.00	150.00

NOTE: For further details on the various types of similar appearing stamps please refer to our U.S. Stamp Identifier.

37, 45
Washington

38, 46
Franklin

39, 47
Washington

73, 84, 85B, 87,
93, 103
Jackson

77, 85F, 91, 98, 108
Lincoln

SCOTT NO.	DESCRIPTION	UNUSED VF	F	AVG	USED VF	F	AVG
	1857-61 Same design as preceding Issue, Perf. 15-1/2 (†) (OG + 75%)						
18	1¢ blue (I)	1500.00	950.00	700.00	1000.00	550.00	300.00
19	1¢ blue (Ia)	22000.00	12500.00	9125.00	9000.00	5900.00	3790.00
20	1¢ blue (II)	750.00	525.00	400.00	400.00	290.00	160.00
21	1¢ blue (III)	8150.00	5500.00	4200.00	3000.00	1700.00	1200.00
22	1¢ blue (IIIa)	1350.00	950.00	650.00	795.00	425.00	300.00
23	1¢ blue (IV)	4900.00	3400.00	2400.00	1500.00	925.00	600.00
24	1¢ blue (V)	95.00	60.00	35.00	70.00	40.00	30.00
25	3¢ rose (I)	1750.00	1300.00	1000.00	230.00	153.50	97.25
26	3¢ dull red (III)	45.00	25.00	15.00	20.00	7.50	5.00
26a	3¢ dull red (IV)	350.00	265.00	185.00	170.00	120.00	85.00
27	5¢ brick red (I)	22000.00	15750.00	10750.00	2250.00	1685.00	900.00
28	5¢ red brown (I)	20000.00	13000.00	8500.00	2000.00	1350.00	825.00
28A	5¢ Indian red (I)	40000.00	20000.00	13000.00	3600.00	2800.00	2000.00
29	5¢ brown (I)	1800.00	975.00	725.00	590.00	325.00	200.00
30	5¢ orange brown (II) . .	925.00	650.00	500.00	2100.00	1400.00	800.00
30A	5¢ brown (II)	1250.00	975.00	650.00	475.00	275.00	180.00
31	10¢ green (I)	12000.00	9500.00	6000.00	1500.00	1100.00	650.00
32	10¢ green (II)	3200.00	2200.00	1650.00	450.00	220.00	150.00
33	10¢ green (III)	3200.00	2200.00	1650.00	375.00	295.00	190.00
34	10¢ green (IV)	22500.00	15750.00	12500.00	2600.00	2100.00	1650.00
35	10¢ green (V)	180.00	75.00	50.00	120.00	65.00	45.00
36	12¢ black, Plate I	1100.00	800.00	600.00	550.00	375.00	200.00
36b	12¢ black, Plate III . . .	550.00	380.00	250.00	400.00	275.00	185.00
37	24¢ gray lilac	800.00	500.00	300.00	500.00	400.00	200.00
38	30¢ orange	1250.00	700.00	500.00	700.00	400.00	275.00
39	90¢ blue	1700.00	1100.00	600.00	10000.00	7750.00	5750.00
	1875 Reprints of 1857-61 Issue. Perf. 12 Without Gum						
40	1¢ bright blue	700.00	550.00	300.00	....	....	....
41	3¢ scarlet	5000.00	3200.00	2800.00	....	....	....
42	5¢ orange brown	3000.00	1700.00	1200.00	....	....	....
43	10¢ blue green	4300.00	3200.00	2200.00	....	....	....
44	12¢ greenish black . . .	4500.00	3500.00	2000.00	....	....	....
45	24¢ blackish violet . . .	5600.00	3800.00	2200.00	....	....	....
46	30¢ yellow orange . . .	5400.00	3800.00	2200.00	....	....	....
47	90¢ deep blue	3500.00	1700.00	1200.00	....	....	....

THE 1861-67 ISSUE

The 1861-66 Issue and its 1867 Grilled varieties are among the most interesting and controversial of all stamps. Born out of the need to demonetize previously-issued stamps in the possession of Southern post offices, they were rushed into service shortly after the outbreak of the Civil War.

The controversy begins with the "August Issues", catalog #s 55-62B. It is now generally accepted that all but the 10 and 24 cent values never were issued for use as postage. The set is more aptly described as "First Designs", because they were printed by the National Bank Note Company and submitted to the Post Office Department as fully gummed and perforated sample designs.

63, 85A, 86,
92, 102
Franklin

64-65, 79, 82,
83, 85, 85C, 88,
94, 104
Washington

67, 75, 76, 80,
95, 105
Jefferson

62B, 68, 85D, 89,
96, 106
Washington

69, 85E, 90,
97, 107
Washington

70, 78, 99, 109
Washington

71, 81, 100, 110
Franklin

72, 101, 111
Washington

(†) means Issue is actually very poorly centered.
Perforations may touch the design on "Fine" quality.

SCOTT NO.	DESCRIPTION	UNUSED VF	F	AVG	USED VF	F	AVG
	1861 First Design (†) Perf. 12 (OG + 75%)						
62B	10¢ dark green	3600.00	2200.00	1325.00	1900.00	1325.00	875.00
	1861-62 Second Design (†) Perf. 12 (OG + 75%)						
63	1¢ blue	160.00	85.00	60.00	55.00	40.00	25.00
64	3¢ pink	5500.00	3900.00	2800.00	750.00	575.00	400.00
64b	3¢ rose pink	325.00	250.00	190.00	165.00	115.00	90.00
65	3¢ rose	60.00	40.00	28.00	4.50	3.00	2.00
66	3¢ lake	2850.00	2100.00	1500.00	....		....
67	5¢ buff	11550.00	7250.00	5500.00	975.00	700.00	550.00
68	10¢ yellow green	500.00	300.00	220.00	85.00	50.00	38.00
69	12¢ black	825.00	600.00	380.00	125.00	80.00	50.00
70	24¢ red lilac	1400.00	800.00	500.00	400.00	200.00	135.00
71	30¢ orange	1280.00	775.00	500.00	250.00	180.00	100.00
72	90¢ blue	1600.00	900.00	600.00	650.00	480.00	325.00
	1861-66 (†) (OG + 75%)						
73	2¢ black	200.00	120.00	75.00	115.00	75.00	45.00
75	5¢ red brown	2800.00	2200.00	1450.00	600.00	475.00	300.00
76	5¢ brown	700.00	450.00	275.00	170.00	120.00	70.00
77	15¢ black	2000.00	1325.00	850.00	220.00	185.00	115.00
78	24¢ lilac	1200.00	725.00	450.00	350.00	175.00	120.00

From 1867 to 1870, grills were embossed into the stamp paper to break the fiber and prevent the eradication of cancellations. The first "A" grilled issues were grilled all over. When postal clerks found that the stamps were as likely to separate along the grill as on the perforations, the Post Office abandoned the "A" grill and tried other configurations, none of which proved to be effective. The Grilled Issues include some of our greatest rarities. The most notable is the 1 cent "Z", only two of which are known to exist. One realized $935,000 in a 1998 auction, making it the most valuable United States stamp. The grills are fully explained and identified in the Harris Stamp Identifier.

SCOTT NO.	DESCRIPTION	UNUSED VF	F	AVG	USED VF	F	AVG
	1867 Grill with Points Up **A. Grill Covering Entire Stamp (†)** **(OG + 75%)**						
79	3¢ rose	....	5000.00	3500.00	....	1400.00	975.00
80	5¢ brown	....	....	....	....	270000.00	
81	30¢ orange	....	....	....	....	....	250000.00
	B. Grill about 18 x 15 mm. **(OG + 75%)**						
82	3¢ rose	....	....	....	....	1000000.00	....
	C. Grill About 13 x 16 mm. (†) **(OG + 75%)**						
83	3¢ rose	2500.00	1400.00	1000.00	1200.00	800.00	500.00
	1867 Grill with Points Down **D. Grill About 12 x 14 mm. (†)** **(OG + 75%)**						
84	2¢ black	12000.00	8000.00	6000.00	8000.00	5000.00	3000.00
85	3¢ rose	3200.00	1800.00	1200.00	1200.00	800.00	500.00
	Z. Grill About 11 x 14 mm. (†) **(OG + 75%)**						
85A	1¢ blue	....		....	....		....
85B	2¢ black	7000.00	5000.00	3000.00	1350.00	1050.00	700.00
85C	3¢ rose	9500.00	6750.00	4800.00	3500.00	3050.00	2075.00
85D	10¢ green	....	....	....	650000.00	475000.00	....
85E	12¢ black	8400.00	6250.00	4700.00	2500.00	1900.00	1500.00
85F	15¢ black	....	....	....	2000000.00	....	....
	E. Grill About 11 x 13 mm. (†) **(OG + 75%)**						
86	1¢ blue	1600.00	1100.00	650.00	775.00	400.00	200.00
87	2¢ black	800.00	615.00	450.00	325.00	190.00	130.00
88	3¢ rose	495.00	375.00	250.00	45.00	30.75	20.50
89	10¢ green	2400.00	1500.00	900.00	375.00	220.00	150.00
90	12¢ black	2200.00	1200.00	850.00	500.00	250.00	160.00
91	15¢ black	5200.00	3000.00	2000.00	750.00	550.00	325.00

SCOTT NO.	DESCRIPTION	UNUSED VF	UNUSED F	AVG	USED VF	USED F	AVG
			F. Grill About 9 x 13 mm. (†) (OG + 75%)				
92	1¢ blue	1250.00	775.00	500.00	600.00	375.00	200.00
93	2¢ black	375.00	180.00	140.00	100.00	60.00	40.00
94	3¢ red.	220.00	150.00	90.00	15.00	10.00	6.00
95	5¢ brown	1800.00	1400.00	950.00	1125.00	775.00	475.00
96	10¢ yellow green . .	1300.00	700.00	400.00	350.00	240.00	135.00
97	12¢ black	1600.00	1000.00	580.00	320.00	275.00	160.00
98	15¢ black	2100.00	1300.00	800.00	400.00	300.00	190.00
99	24¢ gray lilac	4300.00	2500.00	1900.00	2000.00	1200.00	750.00
100	30¢ orange.	4500.00	2600.00	2000.00	1000.00	800.00	500.00
101	90¢ blue	7000.00	4000.00	3000.00	3000.00	2000.00	1200.00

The Re-Issues of the 1861-66 Issue were issued with gum and, while scarce, are found used. They can be distinguished by their bright colors, sharp printing impressions, hard paper and white, crackly original gum.

SCOTT NO.	DESCRIPTION	UNUSED VF	UNUSED F	AVG	USED VF	USED F	AVG
			1875. Re-Issue of 1861-66 Issue. Hard White Paper (OG + 75%)				
102	1¢ blue	450.00	325.00	225.00	1600.00	1225.00	850.00
103	2¢ black	2000.00	1200.00	875.00	13000.00	9500.00	7000.00
104	3¢ brown red	2200.00	1500.00	1000.00	17000.00	14785.00	10000.00
105	5¢ brown	1400.00	900.00	650.00	7200.00	5000.00	3000.00
106	10¢ green.	1800.00	1400.00	950.00	125000.00	95000.00	77250.00
107	12¢ black	2200.00	1500.00	1100.00	15000.00	12000.00	9250.00
108	15¢ black	2300.00	1800.00	1175.00	35000.00	28000.00	22000.00
109	24¢ deep violet. . .	3200.00	2200.00	1400.00	20000.00	16000.00	13000.00
110	30¢ brownish orange	3400.00	2600.00	1500.00	25000.00	20000.00	16875.00
111	90¢ blue	4200.00	2400.00	1700.00	225000.00	. . . .	130000.00

THE 1869 PICTORIALS

As the first United States series to include pictorial designs, the 1869 issue is one of the most popular today. They were so unpopular that they were removed from sale less than a year after issue. Most protests were directed toward their odd size and the tradition-breaking pictorial designs.

The 1869 issue broke important new ground in the use of two color designs. Not only does this add to their attractiveness; it also is the source for the first United States "Inverted Centers". These inverted errors appear on the bi-colored 15, 24 and 30 cent values. The printing technology of the time required a separate printing pass for each color. On the first pass, the central designs, or vignettes, were printed. The second pass applied the frames.

In a very few instances, the sheets with their central designs already printed were passed upside down through the printing press. As a result, the frames were printed upside down. So the description "inverted center" for the 15 and 24 cent errors is technically incorrect, but the form in which these errors are photographed and displayed is with the center, rather than the frame, inverted.

Used copies of the 1869 Pictorials are not as scarce as might be expected. Any of the stamps above the 3 cent denomination were used on mail to Europe and were saved by collectors overseas. When stamp collecting became popular in the United States and Americans were able to purchase stamps abroad at relatively low prices, many of these used 1869 Pictorials found their way back to this country. On the other hand, because of the short life of the issue in post offices and their sudden withdrawal, unused stamps—particularly the high values—are quite rare.

All values of the 1869 Pictorials are found with the "G" grill. Ungrilled varieties are known on all values except the 6, 10, 12 and type II 15 cent stamps. (The Harris Stamp Identifier describes the difference in the three 15 cent types.)

The 1869 Pictorials were re-issued in 1875 in anticipation of the 1876 Centennial Exposition. Most collectors who had missed the original 1869 issue were delighted to have a second chance to purchase the stamps, which explains why the high value re-issues carry lower prices today than do the original 1869 pictorials. At the time, most collectors did not realize they were buying entirely different stamps. The same designs were used, but the re-issues were issued on a distinctive hard, white paper without grills.

The 1 cent stamp was re-issued a second time, in 1880. This re-issue can be distinguished by the lack of a grill and by the soft, porous paper used by the American Bank Note Company.

112, 123, 133,133a
Franklin

113, 124
Pony Express
Rider

114, 125
Locomotive

115, 126
Washington

116, 127
Shield & Eagle

117, 128
S.S. Adriatic

118, 119, 129
Landing of Columbus

120, 130
Signing of Declaration

121, 131
Shield, Eagle & Flags

122, 132
Lincoln

SCOTT NO.	DESCRIPTION	UNUSED VF	UNUSED F	AVG	USED VF	USED F	AVG
			1869 G. Grill measuring 9-1/2 x 9-1/2 mm. (†) (OG + 75%)				
112	1¢ buff	375.00	190.00	120.00	200.00	150.00	90.00
113	2¢ brown	320.00	195.00	115.00	115.00	90.00	60.00
114	3¢ ultramarine . . .	150.00	80.00	50.00	25.00	18.00	12.00
115	6¢ ultramarine . . .	1300.00	900.00	500.00	220.00	175.00	100.00
116	10¢ yellow	1200.00	750.00	400.00	150.00	120.00	80.00
117	12¢ green.	1200.00	750.00	400.00	150.00	120.00	80.00
118	15¢ brown & blue (I)	4600.00	3000.00	2500.00	950.00	650.00	400.00
119	15¢ brown & blue (II)	1700.00	1000.00	650.00	275.00	190.00	120.00
120	24¢ green & violet	4000.00	2200.00	1500.00	700.00	490.00	320.00
121	30¢ blue & carmine	2000.00	1400.00	1000.00	550.00	350.00	250.00
122	90¢ carmine & black	4500.00	3500.00	2000.00	2400.00	1800.00	1200.00
			1875 Re-Issue of 1869 Issue. Hard White Paper. Without Grill (OG + 75%)				
123	1¢ buff	390.00	275.00	175.00	450.00	325.00	230.00
124	2¢ brown	390.00	275.00	175.00	900.00	650.00	450.00
125	3¢ blue	3000.00	1800.00	1200.00	. . . .	25000.00	. . . .
126	6¢ blue	900.00	550.00	450.00	3500.00	2200.00	1200.00
127	10¢ yellow	950.00	650.00	450.00	2400.00	2000.00	1300.00
128	12¢ green.	1600.00	850.00	550.00	3500.00	2400.00	1350.00
129	15¢ brown & blue (III)	950.00	600.00	400.00	1300.00	900.00	600.00
130	24¢ green & violet	1300.00	850.00	600.00	1900.00	1200.00	900.00
131	30¢ blue & carmine	1400.00	900.00	675.00	3200.00	2300.00	1500.00
132	90¢ carmine & black	2000.00	1550.00	1250.00	6500.00	4800.00	3600.00
			1880 Re-Issue. Soft Porous Paper, Issued Without Grill (†) (#133 OG +50%)				
133	1¢ buff	200.00	150.00	95.00	500.00	400.00	285.00
133a	1¢ brown orange . (issued w/o gum)	325.00	195.00	150.00	400.00	300.00	220.00

THE 1870-88 BANK NOTE ISSUES

The "Bank Notes" are stamps that were issued between 1870 and 1888 by the National, Continental and American Bank Note Companies.

The myriad of varieties, secret marks, papers, grills, re-engravings and special printings produced by the three companies resulted in no less than 87 major catalog listings for what basically amounts to 16 different designs. For collectors, what seems to be the very difficult task of properly identifying all these varieties can be eased by following these guidelines:

1. The chronological order in which the three Bank Note companies produced stamps is their reverse alphabetical order: National, Continental, American.

2. "3, 6, 9" identifies the number of years each of the companies printed stamps within the 18-year Bank Note period. Starting in 1870, National continued its work for 3 more years, until 1873, when the Continental Company began printing stamps. That company served for the next 6 years, until 1879, when American took over the Continental company. Although American printed some later issues, the "Bank Note" period ended 9 years later, in 1888.

3. The first Bank Note issue, the Nationals of 1870-71, continued the practice of grilling stamps. Although some specialists contend there are grilled Continental stamps, for all intents and purposes, if a Bank Note stamp bears a genuine grill, it must be from the 1870-71 National issue.

4. The secret marks on values through the 12 cent, and possibly the 15 cent value, were added when the Continental Company took over. They enabled the government to distinguish between National's work and that of its successor. If a Bank Note stamp did not show a secret mark, the Post Office could identify it as the work of the National Bank Note Company. You can do the same.

5. The paper used by the National and Continental companies is similar, but that of the American Bank Note company is noticably different from the first two. When held to the light, the thick, soft American paper shows its coarse, uneven texture, while that of its two predecessors is more even and translucent. The American Bank Note paper also reveals a yellowish hue when held to the light, whereas the National and Continental papers are whiter.

6. Experienced collectors also apply a "snap test" to identify American Bank Note paper by gently flexing a Bank Note stamp at one of its corners. The American Bank Note paper will not "snap" back into place. The National and Continental stamps, on the other hand, often give off a noticeable sound when the flex is released.

7. By purchasing one Bank Note design put into use after 1882 (which can only be an American) and one early Bank Note stamp without the secret mark, (which can only be a National), the collector has a reference point against which to compare any other Bank Note stamp. If it is a soft paper, it is an American Bank Note issue; if a harder paper, it is either a National or a Continental—and these two can be classified by the absence (National) or presence (Continental) of the secret marks or other distinguishing features or colors. The Harris Stamp Identifier in this catalog provides illustrations of the secret marks and further information on the distinguishing features of the various Bank Notes. With two reference stamps, some practice and the use of the information in this catalog, collectors can turn the "job" of understanding the Bank Notes into a pleasant adventure.

134, 145, 156, 167, 182, 192, 206	135, 146, 157, 168, 178, 180, 183, 193, 203	136, 147, 158, 169, 184, 194, 207, 214
Franklin	*Jackson*	*Washington*

NOTE: For further details on the various types of similar appearing stamps please refer to our U.S. Stamp Identifier.

137, 148, 159, 170, 186, 195, 208	138, 149, 160, 171, 196	139, 150, 161, 172, 187, 188, 197, 209
Lincoln	*Stanton*	*Jefferson*

140, 151, 162, 173, 198	141, 152, 163, 174, 189, 199	142, 153, 164, 175, 200
Clay	*Webster*	*Scott*

143, 154, 165, 176, 190, 201, 217	144, 155, 166, 177, 191, 202, 218
Hamilton	*Perry*

SCOTT NO.	DESCRIPTION	UNUSED VF	UNUSED F	UNUSED AVG	USED VF	USED F	USED AVG
\multicolumn{8}{c}{**1870 National Bank Note Co., without Secret Marks.**}							
\multicolumn{8}{c}{**With H Grill about (10 x 12 mm. or 8-1/2 x 10 mm.) Perf 12. (†)**}							
\multicolumn{8}{c}{**(OG +75%)**}							
134	1¢ ultramarine . . .	850.00	650.00	500.00	300.00	200.00	110.00
135	2¢ red brown	450.00	360.00	275.00	110.00	85.00	50.00
136	3¢ green	300.00	200.00	150.00	45.00	30.00	15.00
137	6¢ carmine	2000.00	1700.00	1000.00	600.00	450.00	250.00
138	7¢ vermillion	1800.00	1250.00	900.00	650.00	450.00	300.00
139	10¢ brown	3000.00	2500.00	1750.00	1300.00	800.00	525.00
140	12¢ dull violet	16800.00	11500.00	6500.00	3800.00	2800.00	1800.00
141	15¢ orange	4750.00	2700.00	1850.00	1500.00	1100.00	650.00
142	24¢ purple	....	....	....	7500.00	6000.00	4300.00
143	30¢ black	10000.00	6750.00	4800.00	4000.00	2800.00	1800.00
144	90¢ carmine	12100.00	7250.00	4500.00	2600.00	1800.00	1200.00
\multicolumn{8}{c}{**1870-71. National Bank Note Co., without Secret Marks.**}							
\multicolumn{8}{c}{**Without Grill. Perf 12. (†)**}							
\multicolumn{8}{c}{**(OG +75%)**}							
145	1¢ ultramarine . . .	400.00	275.00	150.00	30.00	20.00	15.00
146	2¢ red brown	250.00	155.00	100.00	25.00	16.00	10.50
147	3¢ green	275.00	170.00	112.00	4.00	2.75	1.60
148	6¢ carmine	675.00	400.00	225.00	50.00	31.00	19.00
149	7¢ vermillion	700.00	450.00	250.00	165.00	92.00	56.00
150	10¢ brown	850.00	600.00	395.00	63.00	43.00	27.00
151	12¢ dull violet	1500.00	1000.00	600.00	325.00	215.00	135.00
152	15¢ bright orange . .	1500.00	1000.00	600.00	350.00	235.00	150.00
153	24¢ purple	1250.00	800.00	550.00	300.00	180.00	120.00
154	30¢ black	4000.00	2800.00	1600.00	450.00	300.00	175.00
155	90¢ carmine	3000.00	2000.00	1150.00	500.00	350.00	200.00
\multicolumn{8}{c}{**1873. Continental Bank Note Co.**}							
\multicolumn{8}{c}{**Same designs as 1870-71, with Secret Marks, on thin hard grayish white paper. Perf 12 (†)**}							
\multicolumn{8}{c}{**(OG + 75%)**}							
156	1¢ ultramarine . . .	110.00	90.00	65.00	5.00	3.75	2.25
157	2¢ brown	150.00	125.00	75.00	30.00	21.00	12.00
158	3¢ green	75.00	40.00	25.00	1.25	.75	.50
159	6¢ dull pink	150.00	125.00	85.00	35.00	20.00	14.00
160	7¢ orange vermillion	400.00	325.00	250.00	150.00	105.00	68.00
161	10¢ brown	500.00	250.00	195.00	40.00	28.00	17.00
162	12¢ black violet . .	800.00	600.00	400.00	200.00	130.00	86.00
163	15¢ yellow orange	800.00	600.00	400.00	225.00	150.00	90.00
165	30¢ gray black . . .	1450.00	1250.00	700.00	200.00	130.00	83.00
166	90¢ rose carmine .	1000.00	850.00	500.00	475.00	300.00	175.00
\multicolumn{8}{c}{**1875 Special Printing–On Hard White Wove Paper–Without Gum**}							
\multicolumn{8}{c}{**Perf. 12**}							
167	1¢ ultramarine . . .	20000.00	13250.00	7500.00	....	....	....
168	2¢ dark brown . . .	10000.00	6500.00	4400.00	....	....	....
169	3¢ blue green	25000.00	16750.00	11250.00	....	....	....
170	6¢ dull rose	25000.00	16750.00	11250.00	....	....	....
171	7¢ reddish vermillion	6500.00	4300.00	3000.00	....	....	....
172	10¢ pale brown . . .	23500.00	15750.00	10500.00	....	....	....
173	12¢ dark violet . . .	8000.00	5250.00	3800.00	....	....	....
174	15¢ bright orange .	23000.00	15500.00	10250.00	....	....	....
175	24¢ dull purple . . .	5750.00	3800.00	2600.00	....	....	....
176	30¢ greenish black .	20000.00	13500.00	9250.00	....	....	....
177	90¢ violet carmine .	32500.00	21500.00	15000.00	....	....	....

179, 181, 185, 204
Taylor

205, 205C, 216
Garfield

SCOTT NO.	DESCRIPTION	UNUSED VF	F	AVG	USED VF	F	AVG

1875 Continental Bank Note Co.
Hard yellowish paper, Perf 12. (†)
(OG + 50%)

SCOTT NO.	DESCRIPTION	VF	F	AVG	VF	F	AVG
178	2¢ vermillion.....	145.00	100.00	75.00	20.00	14.00	9.50
179	5¢ blue	350.00	225.00	150.00	45.00	28.00	15.00

1875 Continental Bank Note Co., Special Printings.
Same as 1875, on hard white paper, without gum. Perf 12.

| 180 | 2¢ carmine vermillion | 80000.00 | 60000.00 | 36500.00 | .... | .... | .... |
| 181 | 5¢ bright blue .... | 500000.00 | 375000.00 | 235000.00 | .... | .... | .... |

1879 American Bank Note Co.
Same designs as 1870-71 Issue (with Secret Marks) and 1875 Issue on soft, porous, coarse, yellowish paper. Perf 12. (†)
(OG + 60%)

182	1¢ dark ultramarine	150.00	100.00	80.00	8.00	5.00	3.00
183	2¢ vermilion	60.00	40.00	25.00	5.50	4.00	3.00
184	3¢ green.........	45.00	35.00	27.00	1.00	.70	.50
185	5¢ blue	185.00	130.00	100.00	26.00	18.00	12.00
186	6¢ pink	350.00	275.00	195.00	45.00	32.50	19.50
187	10¢ brown (no secret mark)..	1500.00	1000.00	600.00	70.00	50.00	30.00
188	10¢ brown (secret mark)	900.00	600.00	450.00	50.00	36.50	21.95
189	15¢ red orange...	100.00	85.00	50.00	40.00	30.00	17.25
190	30¢ full black	400.00	350.00	200.00	150.00	100.00	67.00
191	90¢ carmine	900.00	700.00	525.00	500.00	320.00	230.00

1880 American Bank Note Co., Special Printings.
Same as 1879 Issue, on soft, porous paper, without gum. Perf 12.

192	1¢ dark ultramarine	75000.00	47000.00	28000.00	....	....	....
193	2¢ black brown...	28000.00	19750.00	12750.00	....	....	....
194	3¢ blue green	120000.00	75000.00	48000.00	....	....	....
195	6¢ dull rose......	90000.00	55000.00	34000.00	....	....	....
196	7¢ scarlet vermillion	9000.00	6250.00	4200.00	....	....	....
197	10¢ deep brown ..	55000.00	35000.00	21000.00	....	....	....
198	12¢ black purple ..	15000.00	10500.00	7000.00	....	....	....
199	15¢ orange......	35000.00	25000.00	18000.00	....	....	....
200	24¢ dark violet ...	15000.00	10500.00	7000.00	....	....	....
201	30¢ greenish black	35000.00	18000.00	12000.00	....	....	....
202	90¢ dull carmine..	35000.00	26000.00	18000.00	....	....	....
203	2¢ scarlet vermillion	120000.00	90000.00	60000.00	....	....	....
204	5¢ deep blue	260000.00	200000.00	145000.00	....	....	....

1882 American Bank Note Company Perf 12.
(OG + 60%)

| 205 | 5¢ yellow brown .. | 110.00 | 85.00 | 65.00 | 15.00 | 11.00 | 7.00 |

1882 American Bank Note Co., Special Printing.
Same as in 1882 Issue, on soft, porous Paper. Perf 12.

| 205C | 5¢ gray brown ... | .... | 50000.00 | .... | .... | .... | .... |

210, 211B, 213
Washington

211, 211D, 215
Jackson

212
Franklin

SCOTT NO.	DESCRIPTION	UNUSED VF	F	AVG	USED VF	F	AVG

1881-82 American Bank Note Co.
Same designs as 1873, Re-Engraved. On soft, porous paper. Perf 12. (†)
(OG + 100%)

206	1¢ gray blue	45.00	30.00	25.00	1.50	.95	.70
207	3¢ blue green	35.00	25.00	18.00	1.25	.75	.55
208	6¢ rose.........	250.00	170.00	100.00	130.00	100.00	70.00
208a	6¢ brown red	175.00	150.00	120.00	175.00	130.00	87.50
209	10¢ brown	75.00	65.00	50.00	10.00	7.50	4.50
209b	10¢ black brown..	1100.00	950.00	600.00	350.00	250.00	150.00
210	2¢ red brown	25.00	17.00	12.00	.75	.45	.35
211	4¢ blue green	100.00	80.00	60.00	32.50	23.00	17.00

SCOTT NO.	DESCRIPTION	UNUSED VF	F	AVG	USED VF	F	AVG

1883 American Bank Note Co. Special Printing.
Same design as 1883 Issue, on soft porous paper. Perf 12.

| 211B | 2¢ pale red brown | 175.00 | 100.00 | 80.00 | .... | .... | .... |
| 211D | 4¢ deep blue green | 65000.00 | .... | .... | .... | .... | .... |

1887 American Bank Note Co.
New designs or colors. Perf 12.
(OG + 60%)

212	1¢ ultramarine ...	50.00	40.00	30.00	3.00	2.15	1.25
213	2¢ green........	30.00	18.00	10.00	.60	.40	.30
214	3¢ vermillion.....	60.00	40.00	25.00	100.00	64.00	40.00

SCOTT NO.	DESCRIPTION	UNUSED O.G. VF	F	AVG	USED VF	F	AVG

1888 American Bank Note Company.
New Colors Perf 12.
(NH + 100%)

215	4¢ carmine	290.00	187.50	125.00	35.00	25.00	15.00
216	5¢ indigo........	300.00	195.00	130.00	22.50	16.00	3.75
217	30¢ orange brown	400.00	200.00	150.00	125.00	100.00	55.00
218	90¢ purple	1400.00	700.00	500.00	345.00	250.00	150.00

THE 1890-93 SMALL BANK NOTE ISSUES

Unlike the complex Large Bank Notes, the 1890-93 series is the simplest of the 19th century definitive issues. They were printed by the American Bank Note Company and what few printing varieties there are can easily be determined by using the Harris Stamp Identifier.

The two major printing varieties are the 2 cent carmine with a "cap" on the left 2 (#219a) or both 2s (#219c).

The "cap" appears to be just that—a small flat hat just to the right of center on top of the denomination numeral 2. It was caused by a breakdown in the metal of the transfer roll that went undetected while it was being used to enter the designs into a few printing plates.

219 *Franklin* | **219D, 220** *Washington* | **221** *Jackson* | **222** *Lincoln*

223 *Grant* | **224** *Garfield* | **225** *Sherman* | **226** *Webster*

227 *Clay* | **228** *Jefferson* | **229** *Perry*

SCOTT NO.	DESCRIPTION	UNUSED O.G. VF	F	AVG	USED VF	F	AVG

(NH +100%)

219	1¢ dull blue......	45.00	25.00	20.50	.60	.45	.35
219D	2¢ lake	250.00	180.00	110.00	5.00	3.50	1.85
220	2¢ carmine	35.00	19.00	14.00	.55	.40	.30
220a	Cap on left "2" ..	250.00	140.00	90.00	....	....	....
220c	Cap on both "2"s .	750.00	400.00	275.00	40.00	25.00	18.50
221	3¢ purple	95.00	60.00	45.00	13.50	8.00	6.00
222	4¢ dark brown ...	135.00	80.00	60.00	6.50	4.95	3.50
223	5¢ chocolate.....	120.00	78.00	54.00	6.50	4.90	3.25
224	6¢ brown red	110.00	70.00	50.00	34.00	23.00	16.00
225	8¢ lilac	95.00	65.00	47.50	20.00	13.00	9.00
226	10¢ green........	250.00	160.00	110.00	5.75	3.75	2.25
227	15¢ indigo........	350.00	210.00	150.00	42.00	30.00	19.00
228	30¢ black	550.00	350.00	245.00	58.00	38.00	23.00
229	90¢ orange......	700.00	425.00	300.00	175.00	100.00	70.00

230	231	232	233
In Sight of Land	*Landing of Columbus*	*Flagship*	*Fleet of Columbus*

234	235	236	237
Soliciting Aid	*At Barcelona*	*Restored To Favor*	*Presenting Natives*

238	239	240	241
Discovery	*At La Rábida*	*Recall of Columbus*	*Pledging Jewels*

242	243	244	245
Columbus in Chains	*Describing Third Voyage*	*Isabella & Columbus*	*Portrait of Columbus*

THE COLUMBIANS

Perhaps the most glamorous of all United States issues is the 1893 Columbians set. Consisting of 16 denominations, the set was issued to celebrate the 1893 World's Columbian Exposition.

Even then, the Post Office Department was aware that stamps could be useful for more than just the prepayment of postage. We quote from an internal Post Office Department report of November 20, 1892:

"During the past summer the determination was reached by the Department to issue, during the progress of the Columbian Exposition at Chicago, a special series of adhesive postage stamps of such a character as would help to signalize the four hundredth anniversary of the discovery of America by Columbus. This course was in accordance with the practice of other great postal administrations on occasions of national rejoicing.

The collecting of stamps is deserving of encouragement, for it tends to the cultivation of artistic tastes and the study of history and geography, especially on the part of the young. The new stamps will be purchased in large quantities simply for the use of collections, without ever being presented in payment of postage; and the stamps sold in this way will, of course, prove a clear gain to the department."

As it turned out, the Columbians issue did sell well, being purchased in large quantities not only by collectors, but by speculators hoping to capitalize on the expected demand for the stamps and the fact that they were supposed to be on sale for only one year, from January 2 to December 31, 1893. (The 8 cent stamp was issued March 3, 1893 to meet the new, reduced Registration fee.)

Although sales of the stamps were brisk at the Exposition site in Chicago, speculation proved less than rewarding. The hordes that showed up on the first day of sale in Chicago (January 3rd) and purchased large quantities of the issue ended up taking losses on most of the stamps.

The set was the most expensive postal issue produced to date by the Post Office. The lower denominations matched those of the previous, "Small" Bank Note issue and the 50 cent Columbian replaced the 90 cent Bank Note denomination. But the $1 through $5 denominations were unheard of at that time. The reason for their release was explained in the

November 20, 1892 report: "...such high denominations having heretofore been called for by some of the principal post offices".

The Columbians were an instant success. Businesses did not like the wide size, but they usually could obtain the smaller Bank Note issue. Collectors enjoyed the new stamps, although at least one complained that some of the high values purchased by him had straight edges—and was quickly authorized to exchange "the imperfect stamps" for perfect ones.

The one major variety in this set is the 4 cent blue error of color. It is similar to, but richer in color than, the 1 cent Columbian and commands a larger premium over the normal 4 cent ultramarine color.

The imperforates that are known to exist for all values are proofs which were distributed as gifts and are not listed as postage stamps. The only exception, the 2 cent imperforate, is believed to be printers' waste that was saved from destruction.

SCOTT NO.	DESCRIPTION	UNUSED O.G. VF	F	AVG	USED VF	F	AVG
	1893 COLUMBIAN ISSUE (NH + 100%)						
230	1¢ deep blue	22.00	15.00	12.75	.70	.50	.30
231	2¢ brown violet...	22.00	18.00	12.75	.30	.25	.20
231C	2¢ "broken hat"...	65.00	45.00	35.00	3.50	2.50	1.50
232	3¢ green........	65.00	45.00	35.00	25.00	15.00	10.00
233	4¢ ultramarine . .	85.00	55.00	30.00	11.00	7.50	4.50
234	5¢ chocolate.....	85.00	55.00	30.00	11.00	7.50	4.75
235	6¢ purple	85.00	55.00	30.00	45.00	25.00	12.00
236	8¢ magenta	75.00	45.00	35.00	25.00	14.00	10.00
237	10¢ black brown ..	135.00	85.00	60.00	13.00	8.50	5.50
238	15¢ dark green...	320.00	225.00	150.00	115.00	70.00	50.00
239	30¢ orange brown .	320.00	225.00	150.00	115.00	70.00	50.00
240	50¢ slate blue.....	700.00	450.00	350.00	220.00	180.00	140.00
241	$1 salmon.......	1450.00	925.00	725.00	700.00	500.00	400.00
242	$2 brown red	1475.00	975.00	775.00	700.00	500.00	400.00
243	$3 yellow green ..	2200.00	1350.00	900.00	900.00	700.00	500.00
244	$4 crimson lake ..	3000.00	1800.00	1500.00	1375.00	1000.00	725.00
245	$5 black	3400.00	2200.00	1700.00	1400.00	1100.00	750.00

246, 247, 264, 279
Franklin

248-252, 265-267, 279B
Washington

253, 268
Jackson

254, 269, 280
Lincoln

255, 270, 281
Grant

256, 271, 282
Garfield

257, 272
Sherman

258, 273, 282C, 283
Webster

259, 274, 284
Clay

260, 275
Jefferson

261, 261A, 276, 276A
Perry

262, 277
Madison

263, 278
Marshall

1894-98 THE FIRST BUREAU ISSUES

In 1894, the United States Bureau of Engraving and Printing replaced the American Bank Note Company as the contractor for all United States postage stamps. The "First" Bureau issues, as they are commonly known, actually consist of three series, as follows:

The 1894 Series. In order to expedite the transfer of production to the Bureau, the plates then being used by the American Bank Note Company for the 1890-93 Small Bank Notes were modified, small triangles being added in the upper corners. The 1 cent through 15 cent stamps are otherwise essentially the same as the 1890-93 issue although minor variations have been noted on some values. The 30 cent and 90 cent 1890-93 denominations were changed to 50 cents and $1, respectively, and new $2 and $5 denominations were added.

The 1895 Series. To protect against counterfeiting of United Sates stamps, the Bureau adopted the use of watermarked paper. (A scheme for counterfeiting 2 cent stamps had been uncovered around the same time the watermarked paper was being adopted. Some of these counterfeits are known postally used.) This series is almost exactly the same as the 1984 series except for the presence of watermarks. The watermarks can be difficult t detect on this series, particularly on the light-colored stamps, such as the 50 cent, and on used stamps. Since the 1894 unwatermarked stamps (with the exception of the 2 cent carmine type I) are worth more than the 1895 watermarked stamps, collectors will want to examine their 1894 stamps carefully. (Some collectors feel they can recognize the 1894 stamps by their ragged perforations, caused by difficulties the Bureau encountered when it first took over the produciton of postage stamps. This is not a reliable method.)

The 1898 "Color Changes." With the adoption of a Universal Postal Union code that recommended standard colors for international mail, the United States changed the colors for the lower values in the 1895 Series. The stamps were printed on the same watermarked paper as that used for the 1895 Series. Except for the 2 cent, which was changed from carmine to red, the colors of the 1898 Series are easily differentiated from the 1895 set. The 2 cent value is the most complicated of the First Bureau Issues. In addition to the color changes that took place, three different triangle types are known. The differences are attributed to the possibility that the work of engraving the triangles into the American Bank Note plates was performed by several Bureau engravers.

The 10 cent and $1 types I and II can be distinguished by the circles surrounding the numeral denominations. The Type IIs are identical to the circles of the 1890-93 Small Bank Notes.

All stamps in these series are perf. 12. The Harris Stamp Identifier at the front of this catalog provides additional information on the major types and watermarks of all three series.

SCOTT NO.	DESCRIPTION	UNUSED O.G. VF	F	AVG	USED VF	F	AVG
	1894 Unwatermarked (†) (NH + 100%)						
246	1¢ ultramarine . . .	50.00	32.75	23.75	10.50	6.75	4.25
247	1¢ blue	90.00	53.00	37.00	4.00	2.50	1.75
248	2¢ pink (I)	35.00	22.00	16.00	12.50	8.00	5.00
249	2¢ carmine lake (I)	275.00	160.00	110.00	10.00	6.75	4.00
250	2¢ carmine (I)	50.00	32.75	23.00	2.00	1.00	.75
251	2¢ carmine (II) . . .	400.00	250.00	150.00	18.00	12.75	8.00
252	2¢ carmine (III) . . .	165.00	90.00	60.00	20.00	14.50	9.00
253	3¢ purple	145.00	85.00	60.00	17.50	9.75	6.50
254	4¢ dark brown . . .	195.00	110.00	80.00	16.00	9.75	6.25
255	5¢ chocolate	160.00	90.00	70.00	14.00	8.50	5.50
256	6¢ dull brown	210.00	125.00	85.00	39.00	28.00	19.00
257	8¢ violet brown. . .	200.00	130.00	94.00	35.00	21.25	16.95
258	10¢ dark green. . .	375.00	240.00	160.00	20.00	10.00	7.00
259	15¢ dark blue . . .	385.00	240.00	180.00	96.00	58.00	38.00
260	50¢ orange.	725.00	425.00	315.00	185.00	115.00	70.00
261	$1 black (I)	1300.00	800.00	550.00	625.00	375.00	260.00
261A	$1 black (II)	2700.00	1750.00	1200.00	1000.00	675.00	450.00
262	$2 bright blue . . .	3600.00	2300.00	1850.00	1500.00	1100.00	725.00
263	$5 dark green	5050.00	3700.00	2900.00	3000.00	2100.00	1500.00
	1895 Double Line Watermark "USPS" (†) (NH + 75%)						
264	1¢ blue	8.50	5.50	3.75	.50	.35	.25
265	2¢ carmine (I) . . .	55.00	35.00	25.00	4.00	2.65	1.75
266	2¢ carmine (II) . . .	60.00	38.50	25.00	6.00	4.20	2.75
267	2¢ carmine (III). . .	6.50	4.00	3.00	.35	.30	.25
268	3¢ purple	50.00	31.25	22.25	3.00	1.90	1.25
269	4¢ dark brown . . .	65.00	38.00	26.00	4.25	2.85	1.50
270	4¢ dark brown. . . .	52.50	36.00	22.00	4.25	2.75	1.75
271	6¢ dull brown	165.00	90.00	65.00	9.00	6.00	4.50
272	8¢ violet brown. . .	85.00	50.00	35.00	3.50	2.00	1.25
273	10¢ dark green. . .	125.00	70.00	50.00	2.75	1.75	1.00
274	15¢ dark blue . . .	300.00	170.00	110.00	27.50	18.00	12.25
275	50¢ orange	375.00	225.00	160.00	75.00	52.50	32.00
276	$1 black (I)	775.00	450.00	310.00	155.00	100.00	64.00
276A	$1 black (II)	1500.00	1000.00	700.00	275.00	195.00	135.00
277	$2 bright blue	1100.00	825.00	625.00	625.00	450.00	305.00
278	$5 dark green. . . .	2500.00	1800.00	1050.00	925.00	600.00	425.00
	1898 New Colors (NH + 75%)						
279	1¢ deep green . . .	15.00	9.00	6.50	.50	.35	.25
279B	2¢ red (IV)	13.00	7.50	5.00	.50	.30	.25
279Bc	2¢ rose carmine (IV)	325.00	195.00	120.00	200.00	125.00	95.00
279Bd	2¢ orange red (IV)	17.50	10.00	7.00	2.00	1.50	1.00
280	4¢ rose brown . . .	55.00	37.25	24.75	4.00	2.65	1.75
281	5¢ dark blue	48.00	29.00	18.00	2.75	1.85	1.00
282	6¢ lake	80.00	52.50	40.00	8.00	5.50	3.25
282C	10¢ brown (I)	265.00	180.00	125.00	7.00	4.65	3.00
283	10¢ orange brown (II)	210.00	125.00	78.00	9.00	5.75	3.50
284	15¢ olive green. . .	190.00	115.00	80.00	20.00	12.50	8.75

1898 THE TRANS-MISSISSIPPI ISSUE

Issued for the Trans-Mississippi Exposition in Omaha, Nebraska, the "Omahas", as they also are known, did not receive the same welcome from collectors as that accorded the first commemorative set, the 1893 Columbians. Although the uproar was ascribed to the fact that collectors felt put upon by another set with $1 and $2 values, had the $1 to $5 values in the Columbian series appreciated in value, no doubt the protests would have been muted.

On the other hand, the public at large enjoyed the new issue. The Trans-Mississippi issues depict various works of art and are among the most beautiful stamps ever issued by the United States. The 8 and 10 cent values reproduce works by Frederic Remington and the $1 "Western Cattle in Storm", based on a work by J.A. MacWhirter, is regarded as one of our finest examples of the engraver's art.

As appealing as these stamps are in single colors, the set might have been even more beautiful. The original intent was to print each stamp with the vignette, or central design, in black and the frame in a distinctive second color that would be different for each denomination. That plan had to be dropped when the Bureau was called upon to produce large quantities of revenue stamps at the outbreak of the Spanish-American War.

285
Marquette on the Mississippi

286
Farming in the West

287
Indian Hunting Buffalo

288
Fremont on the Rocky Mountains

289
Troops Guarding Train

290
Hardships of Emigration

291
Western Mining Prospector

292
Western Cattle in Storm

293
Eads Bridge over Mississippi River

SCOTT NO.	DESCRIPTION	UNUSED O.G. VF	F	AVG	USED VF	F	AVG
		1898 Trans-Mississippi Exposition Issue (†) (NH + 100%)					
285	1¢ dark yellow green	55.00	36.75	25.75	10.00	6.50	4.00
286	2¢ copper red	35.00	23.00	17.50	3.00	2.00	1.25
287	4¢ orange	225.00	135.00	95.00	59.00	35.00	22.00
288	5¢ dull blue	240.00	135.00	92.00	32.00	20.00	11.00
289	8¢ violet brown	310.00	200.00	125.00	85.00	55.00	32.00
290	10¢ gray violet	260.00	165.00	100.00	56.00	33.00	19.00
291	50¢ sage green	950.00	575.00	475.00	250.00	180.00	140.00
292	$1 black	2000.00	1150.00	850.00	990.00	775.00	600.00
293	$2 orange brown	2500.00	1600.00	1000.00	1200.00	950.00	700.00

1901 THE PAN-AMERICAN ISSUE

Issued to commemorate the Pan-American Exposition in Buffalo, N.Y., this set depicts important engineering and manufacturing achievements. The beautiful engraving is showcased by the bicolored printing.

294, 294a
Fast Lake Navigation

295, 295a
Fast Express

296, 296a
Automobile

297
Bridge at Niagara Falls

298
Canal at Sault Ste. Marie

299
Fast Ocean Navigation

SCOTT NO.	DESCRIPTION	UNUSED O.G. VF	F	AVG	USED VF	F	AVG
		1901 Pan-American Issue (NH + 75%)					
294-99	1¢-10¢ (6 varieties, complete)	530.00	370.00	300.00	190.00	125.00	80.00
294	1¢ green & black	25.00	16.00	12.00	3.00	2.20	1.50
294a	same, center inverted	...	12500.00	...	...	16000.00	...
295	2¢ carmine & black	22.00	14.00	11.00	1.30	.90	.40
295a	same, center inverted	...	45000.00	...	...	60000.00	...
296	4¢ deep red brown & black	90.00	70.00	60.00	24.00	14.00	11.00
296a	same, center inverted	...	40000.00	...	...	...	...
296aS	same, center inverted (Specimen)	...	7500.00	...	...	...	...
297	5¢ ultramarine & black	90.00	70.00	60.00	24.00	14.00	11.00
298	8¢ brown violet & black	150.00	90.00	70.00	95.00	60.00	40.00
299	10¢ yellow brown & black	175.00	130.00	90.00	45.00	35.00	20.00

	UNUSED PLATE BLOCKS OF 6 NH F	AVG	OG F	AVG	UNUSED ARROW BLOCKS NH F	AVG	OG F	AVG
294	475.00	340.00	285.00	215.00	165.00	105.00	72.50	57.50
295	475.00	340.00	280.00	215.00	160.00	100.00	65.00	50.00
296	3750.00	2750.00	2100.00	1650.00	825.00	575.00	375.00	315.00
297	4200.00	3250.00	2600.00	2000.00	825.00	550.00	400.00	325.00
298	7500.00	5500.00	4000.00	3200.00	1050.00	700.00	500.00	375.00
299	10500.00	8000.00	6000.00	4800.00	1500.00	900.00	695.00	500.00

THE 1902-03 SERIES

The Series of 1902-03 was the first regular issue designed and produced by the United States Bureau of Engraving and Printing, most of the work on the 1894-98 series having been performed by the American Bank Note Company. (When the Bureau was awarded the contract to produce the 1894 series, they added triangles in the upper corners of the American Bank Note designs.)

The new series filled a number of gaps and was the first United States issue to feature a woman—in this case Martha Washington, on the 8 cent value.

Modern collectors consider the 1902-03 issue one of the finest regular series ever produced by the Bureau.

The intricate frame designs take us back to a period when such work still was affordable. In its time, however, the 1902-03 set was looked upon with disdain. The 2 cent Washington, with its ornate frame design and unflattering likeness of George Washington, came in for particular scorn. Yielding to the clamor, in 1903, less than one year after its release, the Post Office recalled the much criticized 2 cent stamp and replaced it with an attractive, less ornate design that cleaned up Washington's appearance, particularly in the area of the nose, and used a shield design that was less ornate.

The issue marked the first time United States stamps were issued in booklet form, the 1 and 2 cent values being printed in panes of six stamps each. Also for the first time since perforating was adopted in 1857, United States stamps were once again deliberately issued in imperforate form for postal use. The intent was to have such stamps available in sheet and coil form for use in vending machines. The manufacturers of such machines could purchase the imperforate stamps and perforate them to fit their equipment. One of these imperforate issues, the 4 cent brown of 1908 (#314A), ranks as one of the great rarities of 20th century philately. It is found only with the private perforations of the Schermack Mailing Machine Company.

Coil stamps intended for use in stamp affixing and vending machines also made their inaugural appearance with this issue. Their availability was not widely publicized and few collectors obtained copies of these coils. All genuine coils from this series are very rare and extremely valuable. We emphasize the word "genuine" because most coils that are seen actually have been faked by trimming the perforated stamps or fraudulently perforating the imperfs.

The only major design types are found on the 1903 2 cent, catalog #s 319 and 320. Identified as Die I and Die II, the differences are described in the Harris Stamp Identifier.

300, 314, 316, 318
Franklin

301
Washington

302
Jackson

303, 314A
Grant

304, 315, 317
Lincoln

305
Garfield

306
Martha Washington

307
Webster

308
Harrison

309
Clay

310
Jefferson

311
Farragut

312, 479
Madison

313, 480
Marshall

319-22
Washington

SCOTT NO.	DESCRIPTION	UNUSED O.G.			USED		
		VF	F	AVG	VF	F	AVG
	1902-03 Perf. 12 (†) **(NH + 75%)**						
300	1¢ blue green....	16.00	9.00	6.00	.35	.25	.20
300b	1¢ booklet pane of 6	....	550.00	375.00	....	....	....
301	2¢ carmine......	19.50	13.00	8.00	.35	.25	.20
301c	2¢ booklet pane of 6	....	475.00	335.00	....	....	....
302	3¢ brown violet...	75.00	43.00	30.00	6.00	3.95	2.25
303	4¢ brown	75.00	43.00	30.00	2.50	1.50	1.00
304	5¢ blue.........	82.50	50.00	35.00	3.50	1.75	.90
305	6¢ claret........	90.00	50.00	35.00	9.00	5.00	3.00
306	8¢ violet black ...	65.00	35.00	27.00	5.00	2.75	1.75
307	10¢ pale red brown	85.00	50.00	36.00	4.00	2.25	1.50
308	13¢ purple black..	60.00	35.00	25.00	17.00	11.00	6.50
309	15¢ olive green...	225.00	140.00	98.00	17.00	11.00	7.00
310	50¢ orange......	625.00	375.00	260.00	52.00	33.00	23.00
311	$1 black	800.00	525.00	360.00	120.00	73.00	46.00
312	$2 dark blue.....	1000.00	900.00	550.00	325.00	250.00	180.00
313	$5 dark green....	2500.00	2000.00	1500.00	1000.00	750.00	525.00
	1906 Imperforate **(NH + 75%)**						

This and all subsequent imperforate issues can usually be priced as unused pairs at double the single price.

SCOTT NO.	DESCRIPTION	VF	F	AVG	VF	F	AVG
314	1¢ blue green....	20.00	15.00	10.00	35.00	20.00	15.00
314A	4¢ brown	....	100000.00	....	....	50000.00	....
315	5¢ blue.........	600.00	400.00	300.00	1500.00	900.00	650.00
	1908 Coil Stamps. Perf 12 Horizontally						
316	1¢ blue green, pair	....	....	....	....	....	....
317	5¢ blue, pair.....	....	5800.00	....			
	1908 Coil Stamps. Perf 12 Vertically						
318	1¢ blue green, pair	....	5500.00	....			
	1903. Perf. 12 (†) **(NH + 60%)**						
319	2¢ carmine, Die I .	10.00	6.00	4.75	.50	.30	.20
319f	2¢ lake, Die II....	17.50	11.00	7.50	1.00	.70	.50
319g	2¢ carmine, Die I, booklet pane of 6 .	....	160.00	....			
	1906 Imperforate **(NH + 75%)**						
320	2¢ carmine, Die I .	55.00	40.00	28.00	79.00	45.00	31.00
320a	2¢ lake, Die I	80.00	65.00	45.00	58.00	40.00	28.00
	1908 Coil Stamps. Perf 12 Horizontally						
321	2¢ carmine, pair ..	....	....	....	....	....	....
	1908 Coil Stamps. Perf 12 Vertically						
322	2¢ carmine, pair ..	....	5500.00	....			

SCOTT NO.	UNUSED NH		UNUSED OG		SCOTT NO.	UNUSED NH		UNUSED OG	
	F	AVG	F	AVG		F	AVG	F	AVG
	PLATE BLOCKS OF 6					**CENTER LINE BLOCKS**			
300	350.00	200.00	215.00	137.50	314	300.00	200.00	180.00	145.00
301	425.00	220.00	235.00	155.00	320	335.00	235.00	200.00	175.00
314	425.00	315.00	290.00	215.00		**ARROW BLOCKS**			
319	295.00	200.00	160.00	115.00	314	235.00	185.00	140.00	110.00
320	415.00	290.00	225.00	175.00	320	250.00	200.00	135.00	100.00

1904 THE LOUISIANA PURCHASE ISSUE

Issued to commemorate the Louisiana Purchase Exposition held in St. Louis in 1904, these stamps were not well received. Collectors at the time did not purchase large quantities of the stamps, and the series was on sale for only seven months. As a result, well centered unused stamps are extremely difficult to locate.

323
Robert R. Livingston

324
Jefferson

325
Monroe

326
McKinley

327
Map of Louisiana Purchase

SCOTT NO.	DESCRIPTION	UNUSED O.G.			USED		
		VF	F	AVG	VF	F	AVG

1904 Louisiana Purchase Issue
(NH + 75%)

SCOTT NO.	DESCRIPTION	VF	F	AVG	VF	F	AVG
323-27	1¢-10¢ (5 varieties, complete)	460.00	325.00	185.00	120.00	70.00	52.00
323	1¢ green	45.00	25.00	20.00	8.00	6.00	3.00
324	2¢ carmine	30.00	22.00	16.00	2.75	2.25	1.25
325	3¢ violet	120.00	80.00	50.00	40.00	20.00	15.00
326	5¢ dark blue	120.00	80.00	50.00	30.00	20.00	15.00
327	10¢ red brown . . .	150.00	120.00	100.00	40.00	25.00	20.00

1907 THE JAMESTOWN EXPOSITION ISSUE

This set may be the most difficult United States 20th century issue to find well centered. Issued in April, 1907 for the Jamestown Exposition at Hampton Roads, Virginia, the set was removed from sale when the Exposition closed on November 30th of that year. Very fine copies carry hefty premiums.

328
Capt. John Smith

329
Founding of Jamestown

330
Pocahontas

1907 Jamestown Exposition Issue
(NH + 75%)

SCOTT NO.	DESCRIPTION	VF	F	AVG	VF	F	AVG
328-30	1¢-5¢ (3 varieties, complete)	220.00	155.00	100.00	50.00	35.00	22.00
328	1¢ green	35.00	20.00	15.00	6.00	4.00	3.00
329	2¢ carmine	40.00	20.00	14.00	6.00	4.00	2.00
330	5¢ blue	150.00	120.00	80.00	40.00	30.00	20.00

	UNUSED PLATE BLOCKS OF 6				UNUSED ARROW BLOCKS			
SCOTT NO.	NH		OG		NH		OG	
	F	AVG	F	AVG	F	AVG	F	AVG
323	550.00	415.00	275.00	220.00	200.00	120.00	130.00	85.00
324	550.00	412.50	290.00	220.00	160.00	100.00	95.00	65.00
325	1750.00	1325.00	1120.00	840.00	550.00	355.00	400.00	265.00
326	1750.00	1150.00	965.00	845.00	675.00	380.00	375.00	250.00
327	3000.00	1950.00	1500.00	1150.00	1100.00	715.00	650.00	530.00
328	700.00	490.00	400.00	300.00	150.00	95.00	100.00	75.00
329	700.00	475.00	415.00	285.00	195.00	110.00	120.00	95.00
330	5000.00	3000.00	2750.00	1950.00	800.00	475.00	400.00	300.00

THE WASHINGTON-FRANKLIN HEADS

The Washington-Franklin Heads—so called because all stamps in the regular series featured the busts of George Washington and Benjamin Franklin—dominated the postal scene for almost two decades. Using a variety of papers, denominations, perforation sizes and formats, watermarks, design modifications and printing processes, almost 200 different major catalog listings were created from two basic designs.

The series started modestly, with the issuance of 12 stamps (#331-342) between November 1908 and January 1909. The modest designs on the new set replaced the ornate 1902-03 series. Their relative simplicity might have relegated the set to a secondary position in 20th century United States philately had it not been for the complexity of the varieties and the years of study the Washington-Franklin Heads now present to collectors.

The first varieties came almost immediately, in the form of imperforate stamps (#343-347) and coils, the latter being offered with horizontal (#348-351) or vertical (#352-356) perforations. The imperfs were intended for the fading vending machine technology that required private perforations while the coils were useful in standardized dispensers that were just coming into their own.

Then, in 1909, the Post Office began its experimentation. In this instance, it was the paper. As noted in our introduction to the 1909 Bluish Papers which follows, the Post Office Department and the Bureau of Engraving and Printing hoped that the new paper would reduce losses due to uneven shrinkage of the white wove paper used at the time. The experimental Washington-Franklin Bluish Papers (#357-66) are now among the most valuable in the series and the 8 cent Bluish Paper (#363) is the highest priced of the major listed items.

Attention was next directed to the double line watermark as the cause of the uneven shrinkage, as well as for weakness and thinning in the paper. As a result, a narrower, single line watermark was adopted for sheet stamps (#374-82), imperforates (#383-84), and coils with horizontal perfs (#385-86) and vertical perfs (#387-89).

Even as these experiments were being conducted, the perforation size was being examined to determine if a change was in order. Up until now, the perf 12 gauge had been used on all Washington-Franklin Heads.

The first perforation change was necessitated by the development of new coil manufacturing equipment. Under the increased pressure of the new equipment, the coil strips with the closely-spaced perf 12 gauge were splitting while being rolled into coils. To add paper between the holes, a perf 8-1/2 gauge was adopted for coil stamps and two new major varieties were created: with horizontal perfs (#390-91) and vertical perfs (#392-396).

Necessity was the driving force behind still more changes in 1912, when stamps with numeral denominations were issued to replace the "ONE CENT" and "TWO CENTS" stamps. This responded to the need for numeral denominations on foreign mail and created new sheets (#410-11) and vertically perforated (#412-13) coils. At the same time, a 7 cent value (#407) was issued to meet changing rate requirements.

In conjunction with the introduction of numerals on the 1 and 2 cent stamps, the design of the 1 cent was changed, with the bust of Washington replacing that of Franklin. Meanwhile, the bust of Franklin, which had been used only on the 1 cent stamp, was placed on all values from 8 cents to the $1 (#414-21) and a ribbon was added across their top to make the high value stamp even more noticeable to postal clerks.

As if to add just a little more variety while all the other changes were being made—but in actuality to use up a supply of old double-line watermark paper—50 cent and $1 issues with double-line watermarks (#422-23) were introduced.

The work with perforation changes on coil stamps carried over to sheet stamps in 1914 with the release of a perf 10 series (#424-40). The perf 10 size was then adapted to coils perforated horizontally (#441-42) and vertically (#443-47).

The transition to Rotary Press printing created new coils perforated 10 horizontally (#448-50) and vertically (#452-58). An imperforate Rotary coil (#459) for vending machine manufacturers also was produced.

A perf 10 double-line watermark $1 (#460) and a perf 11 two-cent sheet stamp (#461) added only slightly to the variety, but were followed by completely new runs on unwatermarked paper: perf 10 sheet stamps (#462-478) and imperforates (#481-84) were produced on the flat plate presses, while the Rotary press was used for coils perforated horizontally (#486-489) and vertically (#490-97).

While all this was taking place, the amazing 5 cent carmine error of color (#485) appeared on certain imperf 2 cent sheets. That same error (in rose, #505) was found when perf 11 sheet stamps (#498-518) were issued. The stamps turned out to be too hard to separate. Another strange issue, a 2 cent stamp on double-line watermark paper but perforated 11 (#519), came about when a small supply of old imperfs (#344) were discovered and put into the postal stream.

New $2 and $5 Franklins (#523-24), the former using an erroneous color, were released. To compensate for plate damage being caused by poor quality offset printings, perf 11 (#525-530) and imperforate (#531-535) were tried—and quickly resulted in a whole new series of "types" that had collectors spending more time with their magnifying glasses than with their families.

Odd perf sizes and printings (#538/546) came about as the Bureau cleaned out old paper stock. Then, in one final change, the Bureau corrected the color of the $2 from orange red and black to carmine and black. Almost 200 different stamps, all from two basic designs!

1909 THE BLUISH PAPERS

The Bluish Paper varieties are found on the 1 through 15 cent Washington-Franklin series of 1908-09 and on the 1909 Commemoratives. According to Post Office notices of the period, the experimental paper was a 30% rag stock that was intended to reduce paper waste. After being wet, a preliminary operation in the printing process, the standard white wove paper often would shrink so much that the perforators would cut into the designs. The rag paper did not solve the problem, the experiment was quickly abandoned and the 1909 Bluish Papers became major rarities.

The Harris Stamp Identifier provides further information on identifying the Washington-Franklin Heads.

331, 343, 348, 352, 357, 374, 383, 385, 387, 390, 392
Franklin

332, 344, 349, 353, 358, 375, 384, 386, 388, 391, 393
Washington

333, 345, 359, 376, 389, 394
Washington

334, 346, 350, 354, 360, 377, 395
Washington

335, 347, 351, 355, 361, 378, 396
Washington

336, 362, 379
Washington

337, 363, 380
Washington

338, 356, 364, 381
Washington

339, 365
Washington

340, 366, 382
Washington

341
Washington

342
Washington

NOTE: *For further details on the various types of similar appearing stamps please refer to our U.S. Stamp Identifier.*

SCOTT NO.	DESCRIPTION	UNUSED O.G. VF	F	AVG	USED VF	F	AVG
	1908-09 Double Line Watermark "USPS" Perf. 12 (NH + 75%)						
331-42	1¢-$1 (12 varieties, complete)	1600.00	960.00	620.00	300.00	200.00	115.00
331	1¢ green	11.25	6.50	4.00	1.00	.70	.60
331a	1¢ booklet pane of 6	200.00	145.00	95.00	......	......	......
332	2¢ carmine	11.25	7.00	4.25	.75	.50	.40
332a	2¢ booklet pane of 6	185.00	120.00	85.00	......	......	......
333	3¢ deep violet (I)	52.50	29.00	18.00	6.50	4.25	2.50
334	4¢ orange brown	55.00	34.00	22.00	2.00	1.25	.80
335	5¢ blue	72.00	40.00	24.00	3.75	2.60	1.75
336	6¢ red orange	80.00	50.00	30.00	8.50	5.00	3.25
337	8¢ olive green	60.00	38.00	24.00	5.50	3.25	2.25
338	10¢ yellow	85.00	58.00	43.00	4.75	2.50	1.50
339	13¢ blue green	60.00	34.00	23.00	80.00	50.00	29.00
340	15¢ pale ultramarine	82.00	50.00	35.00	12.00	8.00	5.00
341	50¢ violet	400.00	235.00	145.00	45.00	30.00	18.00
342	$1 violet brown	675.00	400.00	260.00	145.00	100.00	63.00
	1908-09 Imperforate (NH + 75%)						
343-47	1¢-5¢ (5 varieties, complete)	90.00	65.00	50.00	100.00	75.00	50.00
343	1¢ green	6.00	4.00	3.00	5.75	4.50	2.75
344	2¢ carmine	6.50	4.50	4.00	5.00	4.00	2.75
345	3¢ deep violet (I)	16.00	14.00	12.00	28.00	19.00	11.00
346	4¢ orange brown	18.00	15.00	10.00	28.00	20.00	18.00
347	5¢ blue	45.00	30.00	24.00	42.00	30.00	20.00
	1908-10 Coil Stamps Perf. 12 Horizontally (NH + 75%)						
348	1¢ green	48.00	30.00	28.00	55.00	35.00	25.00
349	2¢ carmine	115.00	80.00	55.00	150.00	80.00	65.00
350	4¢ orange brown	150.00	100.00	85.00	240.00	160.00	140.00
351	5¢ blue	150.00	100.00	85.00	350.00	220.00	160.00

NOTE: **Counterfeits are common on #348-56 and #385-89**

SCOTT NO.	DESCRIPTION	UNUSED O.G. VF	F	AVG	USED VF	F	AVG
	1909 Coil Stamps Perf. 12 Vertically (NH + 75%)						
352	1¢ green	140.00	80.00	70.00	250.00	175.00	90.00
353	2¢ carmine	175.00	125.00	82.50	240.00	150.00	70.00
354	4¢ orange brown	275.00	170.00	110.00	290.00	175.00	110.00
355	5¢ blue	300.00	180.00	120.00	350.00	250.00	175.00
356	10¢ yellow	3500.00	2500.00	2000.00	6000.00	4000.00	3000.00

SCOTT NO.	UNUSED NH F	AVG	UNUSED OG F	AVG	SCOTT NO.	UNUSED NH F	AVG	UNUSED OG F	AVG
	PLATE BLOCKS OF 6					**CENTER LINE BLOCKS**			
331	140.00	110.00	100.00	70.00	343	80.00	60.00	60.00	45.00
332	140.00	110.00	100.00	70.00	344	105.00	90.00	87.50	55.00
333	450.00	325.00	290.00	210.00	345	250.00	185.00	190.00	155.00
334	635.00	415.00	400.00	280.00	346	325.00	285.00	275.00	200.00
335	950.00	700.00	600.00	475.00	347	450.00	315.00	325.00	230.00
336	1250.00	900.00	700.00	495.00					
337	700.00	495.00	375.00	275.00					
338	1000.00	790.00	735.00	475.00		**ARROW BLOCKS**			
339	750.00	615.00	430.00	320.00					
343	125.00	115.00	80.00	60.00	343	57.50	52.00	52.00	37.50
344	175.00	140.00	152.50	110.00	344	100.00	87.50	85.00	55.00
345	330.00	250.00	320.00	240.00	345	240.00	180.00	185.00	150.00
346	600.00	450.00	465.00	390.00	346	295.00	260.00	250.00	175.00
347	650.00	525.00	555.00	400.00	347	390.00	300.00	320.00	210.00

		(NH + 75%)					
	COIL LINE PAIRS UNUSED OG				**COIL PAIRS UNUSED OG**		
	VF	F	AVG		VF	F	AVG
348	365.00	235.00	160.00		180.00	125.00	80.00
349	675.00	450.00	310.00		300.00	215.00	130.00
350	1300.00	1000.00	725.00		650.00	420.00	310.00
351	2250.00	1675.00	1225.00		600.00	400.00	270.00
352	1050.00	765.00	540.00		350.00	250.00	175.00
353	700.00	500.00	350.00		330.00	230.00	165.00
354	1650.00	1100.00	775.00		800.00	570.00	395.00
355	1650.00	1100.00	775.00		800.00	625.00	445.00
356	17500.00	12000.00	9000.00		10000.00	6800.00	4500.00

SCOTT NO.	DESCRIPTION	UNUSED O.G. VF	F	AVG	USED VF	F	AVG
	1909 Bluish Gray paper Perf. 12 (NH + 75%)						
357	1¢ green	105.00	80.00	55.00	175.00	140.00	100.00
358	2¢ carmine	100.00	75.00	50.00	175.00	140.00	100.00
359	3¢ deep violet (I)	2400.00	1800.00	1300.00	9800.00	7000.00	6000.00
360	4¢ orange brown	......	27000.00	18000.00	......	......	......
361	5¢ blue	7000.00	3900.00	2800.00	20000.00	15000.00	11500.00
362	6¢ red orange	2000.00	1200.00	800.00	22500.00	15500.00	11350.00
363	8¢ olive green	......	30000.00	20000.00	......	......	......
364	10¢ yellow	2500.00	1500.00	1100.00	12000.00	9000.00	8000.00
365	13¢ blue green	3500.00	2200.00	1500.00	4000.00	2700.00	1850.00
366	15¢ pale ultramarine	1900.00	1400.00	1100.00	13000.00	10000.00	7000.00

THE 1909 COMMEMORATIVES

After the 16-value Columbian commemorative set, the Post Office Department began gradually reducing the number of stamps in subsequent series. The 1909 commemoratives were the first to use the single-stamp commemorative approach that is now the common practice.

The Lincoln Memorial issue was released on the 100th anniversary of the birth of America's 16th President. The Alaska-Yukon was issued for the Alaska-Yukon Exposition held in Seattle to publicize the development of the Alaska territory. The Hudson-Fulton stamp commemorated Henry Hudson's 1609 discovery of the river that bears his name, the 1809 voyage of Robert Fulton's "Clermont" steamboat and the 1909 celebration of those two events.

As noted earlier, the 1909 Commemoratives were issued on experimental "bluish" paper in addition to the white wove standard. The stamps on white wove paper also were issued in imperforate form for private perforation by vending and stamp-affixing machine manufacturers.

367-369
Lincoln

370, 371
William H. Seward

372, 373
S.S. Clermont

SCOTT NO.	DESCRIPTION	UNUSED O.G. VF	F	AVG	USED VF	F	AVG
		1909 LINCOLN MEMORIAL ISSUE (NH + 50%)					
367	2¢ carmine, perf. .	8.00	5.50	3.50	2.00	1.50	1.00
368	2¢ carmine, imperf.	25.00	15.00	12.00	28.00	18.00	15.00
369	2¢ carmine (bluish paper)	200.00	165.00	115.00	270.00	180.00	140.00
		1909 ALASKA-YUKON ISSUE					
370	2¢ carmine, perf. .	11.00	8.00	5.50	3.00	2.20	1.40
371	2¢ carmine, imperf.	20.00	12.00	10.00	25.00	16.00	10.00
		1909 HUDSON-FULTON ISSUE					
372	2¢ carmine, perf. .	12.50	8.00	6.00	5.00	3.20	2.00
373	2¢ carmine, imperf	22.00	15.00	11.00	30.00	18.00	13.00
		1910-11 Single Line Watermark "USPS" Perf. 12 (NH + 50%)					
374-82	1¢-15¢ (9 varieties, complete)	700.00	495.00	398.00	60.00	40.00	28.00
374	1¢ green	15.00	9.50	6.00	.30	.30	.20
374a	1¢ booklet pane of 6	225.00	145.00	100.00	......	......	......
375	2¢ carmine	14.50	9.00	6.00	.30	.30	.20
375a	2¢ booklet pane of 6	150.00	105.00	66.00	......	......	......
376	3¢ deep violet (I) .	32.50	18.00	12.00	4.25	2.50	1.50
377	4¢ brown	47.50	28.50	21.50	1.25	.85	.55
378	5¢ blue	40.00	24.00	18.00	1.50	1.10	.75
379	6¢ red orange	60.00	36.00	23.00	2.25	1.25	.85
380	8¢ olive green	115.00	90.00	70.00	22.00	15.00	11.00
381	10¢ yellow	125.00	95.00	75.00	7.00	5.50	3.75
382	15¢ pale ultramarine	255.00	190.00	170.00	25.00	16.00	11.00
		1911 Imperforate					
383	1¢ green	3.25	2.70	1.50	2.75	1.75	1.10
384	2¢ carmine	4.20	3.25	2.10	3.00	2.20	1.80

SCOTT NO.	UNUSED NH F	AVG	UNUSED OG F	AVG	SCOTT NO.	UNUSED NH F	AVG	UNUSED OG F	AVG
	PLATE BLOCKS OF 6					**CENTER LINE BLOCKS**			
367	225.00	155.00	160.00	110.00	368	225.00	165.00	165.00	125.00
368	385.00	270.00	300.00	220.00	371	300.00	200.00	200.00	150.00
370	320.00	220.00	220.00	150.00	373	365.00	265.00	265.00	200.00
371	475.00	330.00	345.00	235.00	383	45.00	30.00	30.00	25.00
372	400.00	250.00	290.00	200.00	384	90.00	55.00	65.00	40.00
373	475.00	330.00	345.00	235.00					
374	150.00	90.00	85.00	60.00		**ARROW BLOCKS**			
375	150.00	85.00	95.00	70.00					
376	350.00	230.00	245.00	220.00	368	180.00	130.00	120.00	110.00
377	390.00	250.00	285.00	185.00	371	235.00	190.00	180.00	135.00
378	325.00	245.00	245.00	185.00	373	265.00	200.00	200.00	160.00
383	100.00	68.75	62.50	35.00	383	42.00	30.00	30.00	20.00
384	210.00	150.00	140.00	95.00	384	50.00	45.00	45.00	36.00

Very Fine Plate Blocks from this period command premiums.

SCOTT NO.	DESCRIPTION	UNUSED O.G. VF	F	AVG	USED VF	F	AVG
		COIL STAMPS **1910 Perf. 12 Horizontally** (NH + 75%)					
385	1¢ green	60.00	45.00	30.00	48.00	30.00	20.00
386	2¢ carmine	165.00	100.00	70.00	100.00	70.00	55.00
		1910-11 Perf. 12 Vertically (†)					
387	1¢ green	240.00	180.00	130.00	145.00	110.00	70.00
388	2¢ carmine	1650.00	1200.00	875.00	2100.00	800.00	600.00
389	3¢ deep violet (I) .	......	110000.00	......	......	12500.00	......
		1910 Perf. 8-1/2 Horizontally					
390	1¢ green	7.00	4.00	3.00	15.00	11.00	8.00
391	2¢ carmine	65.00	38.00	22.00	60.00	42.00	28.00
		1910-13 Perf. 8-1/2 Vertically					
392	1¢ green	35.00	24.00	15.00	60.00	39.00	25.00
393	2¢ carmine	55.00	38.00	22.00	50.00	30.00	20.00
394	3¢ deep violet (I) .	75.00	55.00	45.00	70.00	45.00	30.00
395	4¢ brown	75.00	55.00	45.00	80.00	75.00	52.00
396	5¢ blue	70.00	50.00	40.00	98.00	68.00	45.00

	(NH + 75%)					
SCOTT NO.	COIL LINE PAIRS UNUSED OG VF	F	AVG	COIL PAIRS UNUSED OG VF	F	AVG
385	450.00	300.00	195.00	200.00	125.00	87.50
386	1300.00	800.00	550.00	330.00	225.00	130.00
387	1200.00	825.00	585.00	700.00	460.00	310.00
390	50.00	35.00	22.50	25.00	16.50	9.00
391	330.00	235.00	140.00	150.00	100.00	60.00
392	225.00	140.00	95.00	120.00	82.00	48.00
393	325.00	210.00	150.00	155.00	100.00	60.00
394	600.00	395.00	265.00	200.00	135.00	85.00
395	475.00	315.00	225.00	220.00	150.00	95.00
396	450.00	295.00	200.00	210.00	136.00	90.00

THE PANAMA-PACIFIC ISSUE

The Panama-Pacific stamps were issued to commemorate the discovery of the Pacific Ocean in 1513 and the opening of the 1915 Panama-Pacific Exposition that celebrated the completion of the Panama Canal. Released in perf 12 form in 1913, the set of four denominations was changed to perf 10 in 1914. Before the perf change, the 10 cent orange yellow shade was determined to be too light. It was changed to the deeper orange color that is found both perf 12 and perf 10.

Because many collectors ignored the perf 10 stamps when they were issued, these stamps are scarcer than their perf 12 predecessors. In fact, #404 is the rarest 20th century commemorative issue.

397, 401
Balboa

398, 402
Panama Canal

399, 403
Golden Gate

400, 400A, 404
Discovery of San Francisco Bay

SCOTT NO.	DESCRIPTION	UNUSED O.G. VF	F	AVG	USED VF	F	AVG
		1913 Perf. 12 (NH + 75%)					
397-400A	1¢-10¢ (5 varieties, complete)	510.00	380.00	260.00	70.00	48.50	34.00
397	1¢ green	25.00	14.00	10.00	2.50	1.70	1.00
398	2¢ carmine	28.00	16.00	12.00	1.75	.90	.75
399	5¢ blue	85.00	65.00	45.00	12.00	8.00	6.00
400	10¢ orange yellow	140.00	114.00	80.00	30.00	22.00	16.00
400A	10¢ orange	240.00	180.00	118.00	25.00	18.00	12.00
		1914-15 Perf. 10 (NH + 75%)					
401-04	1¢-10¢ (4 varieties, complete)	1240.00	995.00	745.00	115.00	72.00	55.00
401	1¢ green	35.00	25.00	18.00	9.00	7.00	5.00
402	2¢ carmine	90.00	65.00	52.00	4.50	2.75	1.75
403	5¢ blue	220.00	170.00	120.00	24.00	15.00	10.00
404	10¢ orange	900.00	740.00	560.00	80.00	50.00	40.00

405/545
Washington

406/546
Washington

426/541
Washington

427, 446, 457, 465, 495, 503
Washington

428, 447, 458, 466, 467, 496, 504, 505
Washington

429, 468, 506
Washington

407, 430, 469, 507
Washington

414, 431, 470, 508
Franklin

415, 432, 471, 509
Franklin

416, 433, 472, 497, 510
Franklin

434, 473, 511
Franklin

417, 435, 474, 512
Franklin

513
Franklin

418, 437, 475, 514
Franklin

419, 438, 476, 515
Franklin

420, 439, 476A, 516
Franklin

421, 422, 440, 477, 517
Franklin

423, 478, 518, 460
Franklin

SCOTT NO.	DESCRIPTION	UNUSED O.G. VF	F	AVG	USED VF	F	AVG
		1912-14 Single Line Watermark Perf. 12 (NH + 60%)					
405	1¢ green......	16.50	9.50	5.50	1.00	.80	.65
405b	1¢ booklet pane of 6	95.00	65.00	45.00	......	......	......
406	2¢ carmine (I)..	11.00	7.00	4.25	.75	.65	.50
406a	2¢ booklet pane of 6	95.00	65.00	45.00	......	......	......
407	7¢ black	125.00	75.00	50.00	25.00	16.00	10.50
		1912 Imperforate					
408	1¢ green......	2.75	2.00	1.50	1.50	.95	.65
409	2¢ carmine (I)..	3.95	3.00	2.00	1.50	1.15	.85

SCOTT NO.	UNUSED NH F	AVG	UNUSED OG F	AVG	SCOTT NO.	UNUSED NH F	AVG	UNUSED OG F	AVG
	PLATE BLOCKS OF 6					**CENTER LINE BLOCKS**			
397	350.00	237.50	260.00	167.50	408	15.50	11.00	11.00	8.50
398	450.00	350.00	290.00	200.00	409	17.00	11.95	14.50	9.50
401	425.00	250.00	275.00	195.00					
405	160.00	120.00	100.00	70.00		**ARROW BLOCKS**			
406	160.00	120.00	100.00	70.00					
408	32.00	24.00	19.00	14.00	408	10.00	9.00	7.50	6.00
409	56.00	40.00	35.00	25.00	409	12.00	10.00	10.00	8.00

SCOTT NO.	DESCRIPTION	UNUSED O.G. VF	F	AVG	USED VF	F	AVG
		COIL STAMPS 1912 Perf. 8-1/2 Horizontally (NH + 60%)					
410	1¢ green......	8.95	5.50	3.75	17.50	10.00	5.75
411	2¢ carmine (I)..	14.00	8.50	5.50	14.00	9.00	5.50
		1912 Perf. 8-1/2 Vertically					
412	1¢ green......	32.00	22.00	15.00	20.00	12.75	9.00
413	2¢ carmine (I)..	75.00	43.00	28.00	35.00	25.00	15.00

	(NH + 60%)					
SCOTT NO.	**COIL LINE PAIRS UNUSED OG** VF	F	AVG	**COIL PAIRS UNUSED OG** VF	F	AVG
410	48.00	29.00	18.00	19.00	12.50	8.00
411	70.00	45.00	30.00	30.00	20.00	12.50
412	150.00	100.00	65.00	80.00	60.00	40.00
413	375.00	250.00	170.00	150.00	100.00	65.00

SCOTT NO.	DESCRIPTION	VF	F	AVG	VF	F	AVG
		1912-14 Perf. 12 Single Line Watermark (NH + 60%)					
414	8¢ pale olive green	70.00	45.75	30.00	3.50	2.00	1.50
415	9¢ salmon red .	80.00	51.00	30.00	40.00	25.00	16.00
416	10¢ orange yellow	70.00	38.00	24.00	.75	.50	.35
417	12¢ claret brown	70.00	46.00	30.00	7.50	5.00	3.25
418	15¢ gray......	140.00	77.00	50.00	7.00	4.25	3.00
419	20¢ ultramarine	275.00	185.00	115.00	39.00	23.00	16.00
420	30¢ orange red.	160.00	105.00	65.00	40.00	24.00	17.00
421	50¢ violet	575.00	340.00	225.00	51.00	33.00	22.00
		1912 Double Line Watermark "USPS" Perf 12					
422	50¢ violet	350.00	225.00	150.00	58.00	38.00	25.00
423	$1 violet black .	675.00	425.00	250.00	185.00	110.00	70.00

1914-15 Single Line Watermark, "USPS" Perf. 10 (NH + 60%)

SCOTT NO.	DESCRIPTION	VF	F	AVG	VF	F	AVG
424-40	1¢-50¢ (16 varieties, complete)	2220.00	1375.00	925.00	185.00	110.00	78.00
424	1¢ green......	6.50	4.00	2.50	.25	.20	.15
424d	1¢ booklet pane of 6	8.00	4.00	3.00	......	......	......
425	2¢ rose red....	5.00	2.50	1.75	.25	.20	.15
425e	2¢ booklet pane of 6	30.00	23.00	16.00	......	......	......
426	3¢ deep violet (I)	32.50	20.00	13.00	5.50	3.00	2.00
427	4¢ brown	55.00	34.00	24.00	1.25	.75	.50
428	5¢ blue........	55.00	39.00	28.00	1.25	.75	.50
429	6¢ red orange..	70.00	45.00	30.00	4.25	2.75	1.50
430	7¢ black	135.00	79.00	59.00	12.00	7.50	4.25
431	8¢ pale olive green	75.00	48.75	30.00	4.50	3.25	2.25
432	9¢ salmon red .	77.50	42.00	27.00	25.00	17.00	10.00
433	10¢ orange yellow	72.50	43.00	29.00	2.75	2.00	1.25
434	11¢ dark green.	42.50	28.00	20.00	26.00	16.00	11.00
435	12¢ claret brown	40.00	26.00	18.00	10.00	7.00	4.00
437	15¢ gray......	170.00	105.00	80.00	15.00	9.00	6.00
438	20¢ ultramarine	275.00	165.00	115.00	12.00	8.25	5.25
439	30¢ orange red.	400.00	220.00	170.00	35.00	23.00	15.00
440	50¢ violet	800.00	500.00	325.00	58.00	38.00	25.00

	UNUSED PLATE BLOCKS OF 6								
SCOTT NO.	**NH** F	AVG	**OG** F	AVG	SCOTT NO.	**NH** F	AVG	**OG** F	AVG
414	600.00	400.00	450.00	285.00	429	525.00	315.00	340.00	200.00
415	875.00	612.50	600.00	437.50	430	1350.00	950.00	900.00	615.00
416	700.00	450.00	430.00	300.00	431	650.00	500.00	500.00	360.00
417	875.00	595.00	562.50	375.00	432	875.00	630.00	650.00	465.00
418	900.00	650.00	600.00	450.00	433	800.00	575.00	600.00	425.00
424 (6)	75.00	55.00	40.00	27.25	434	400.00	260.00	290.00	165.00
424 (10)	225.00	140.00	155.00	95.00	435	400.00	225.00	270.00	170.00
425 (6)	75.00	40.00	37.50	30.00	437	1200.00	850.00	850.00	625.00
425 (10)	225.00	150.00	145.00	100.00	438	3850.00	2950.00	2500.00	1950.00
426	350.00	275.00	250.00	150.00	439	6000.00	4275.00	3700.00	2850.00
427	600.00	415.00	445.00	315.00	440	20000.00	13500.00	14500.00	10500.00
428	500.00	315.00	350.00	210.00					

SCOTT NO.	DESCRIPTION	VF	F	AVG	VF	F	AVG
		COIL STAMPS 1914 Perf. 10 Horizontally (NH + 60%)					
441	1¢ green......	2.75	1.50	1.00	2.50	1.90	1.25
442	2¢ carmine (I)..	17.50	11.00	7.00	35.00	23.00	13.00
		1914 Perf.10 Vertically (NH + 60%)					
443	1¢ green......	50.00	33.00	21.00	40.00	24.00	14.00
444	2¢ carmine (I)..	75.00	44.00	27.00	30.00	21.75	13.50
445	3¢ violet (I)....	400.00	255.00	180.00	315.00	200.00	125.00
446	4¢ brown	300.00	200.00	150.00	150.00	90.00	65.00
447	5¢ blue........	72.50	47.00	33.00	120.00	80.00	50.00

SCOTT NO.	DESCRIPTION	UNUSED O.G. VF	F	AVG	USED VF	F	AVG

ROTARY PRESS COIL STAMPS 1915-16 Perf. 10 Horizontally
(NH + 60%)

448	1¢ green......	9.50	7.00	4.00	20.00	13.50	8.50
449	2¢ red (I)	3500.00	2100.00	1450.00	725.00	550.00	335.00
450	2¢ carmine (III).	27.50	20.00	14.00	25.00	16.50	8.25

1914-16 Perf. 10 Vertically
(NH + 60%)

452	1¢ green......	22.50	16.00	12.00	25.00	17.75	12.50
453	2¢ carmine rose (I)	200.00	137.50	93.75	20.00	13.00	10.00
454	2¢ red (I)	145.00	100.00	65.00	25.00	14.25	10.00
455	2¢ carmine (III).	14.00	10.00	6.50	4.50	3.35	1.70
456	3¢ violet (I)	450.00	300.00	190.00	365.00	200.00	140.00
457	4¢ brown	60.00	31.00	22.00	56.00	35.00	21.00
458	5¢ blue.......	45.00	30.00	20.00	60.00	38.00	23.00

1914 Imperforate Coil
(NH + 60%)

| 459 | 2¢ carmine (I).. | 675.00 | 575.00 | 450.00 | 1100.00 | 800.00 | .... |

1915 Flat Plate Printing Double Line Watermark Perf. 10
(NH + 60%)

| 460 | $1 violet black . | 1250.00 | 750.00 | 525.00 | 250.00 | 150.00 | 100.00 |

1915 Single Line Watermark "USPS" Perf. 11
(NH + 60%)

| 461 | 2¢ pale carmine red (I) .... | 250.00 | 130.00 | 73.00 | 550.00 | 285.00 | 170.00 |

1916-17 Unwatermarked Perf. 10
(NH + 60%)

462	1¢ green......	17.50	12.00	8.00	1.25	.60	.40
462a	1¢ booklet pane of 6	25.00	16.00	9.50	....	....	....
463	2¢ carmine (I)..	7.95	5.50	3.50	.50	.30	.20
463a	2¢ booklet pane of 6	110.00	80.00	55.00	....	....	....
464	3¢ violet (I)	130.00	70.00	52.00	40.00	25.00	16.50
465	4¢ orange brown	80.00	50.00	30.00	3.25	2.25	1.25
466	5¢ blue.......	120.00	65.00	40.00	5.00	3.50	2.00
467	5¢ carmine (error)	1395.00	845.00	515.00	1000.00	650.00	450.00
468	6¢ red orange..	155.00	83.00	50.00	33.00	19.00	10.50
469	7¢ black	210.00	115.00	80.00	52.00	32.00	18.00
470	8¢ olive green .	135.00	75.00	50.00	18.00	10.50	7.00
471	9¢ salmon red .	150.00	83.00	53.00	53.00	35.00	21.00
472	10¢ orange yellow	180.00	94.00	69.00	13.50	10.00	6.00
473	11¢ dark green .	85.00	54.00	31.50	66.00	38.00	25.00
474	12¢ claret brown	140.00	90.00	65.00	21.00	13.00	8.50
475	15¢ gray......	325.00	225.00	130.00	41.00	23.00	16.00
476	20¢ light ultramarine	400.00	220.00	160.00	42.00	25.00	16.00
476A	30¢ orange red.	.....	4800.00	....	....	....	....
477	50¢ light violet .	1600.00	950.00	625.00	175.00	110.00	72.00
478	$1 violet black..	1200.00	690.00	510.00	48.00	33.00	19.00

Design of 1902-03

| 479 | $2 dark blue ... | 485.00 | 335.00 | 245.00 | 120.00 | 68.00 | 54.00 |
| 480 | $5 light green .. | 425.00 | 270.00 | 160.00 | 145.00 | 83.00 | 59.00 |

1916-17 Imperforate
(NH + 60%)

481	1¢ green......	2.50	1.75	.75	1.50	1.00	.50
482	2¢ carmine (I).	2.50	2.00	1.00	3.75	2.25	1.50
483	3¢ violet (I)	35.00	25.00	17.00	28.00	23.00	17.00
484	3¢ violet (II) ...	22.50	19.00	13.00	24.00	19.00	14.00

(NH + 60%)

SCOTT NO.	COIL LINE PAIRS UNUSED OG VF	F	AVG	COIL PAIRS UNUSED OG VF	F	AVG
441	12.50	8.75	5.00	5.75	3.75	2.50
442	90.00	48.00	30.00	40.00	25.00	16.00
443	180.00	120.00	75.00	100.00	66.00	42.00
444	425.00	300.00	185.00	150.00	88.00	54.00
445	1600.00	900.00	600.00	750.00	495.00	350.00
446	900.00	500.00	350.00	550.00	370.00	275.00
447	325.00	185.00	125.00	175.00	110.00	75.00
448	62.00	39.00	25.00	32.00	18.00	12.00
450	90.00	65.00	40.00	58.00	40.00	28.00
452	115.00	65.00	40.00	47.50	35.00	24.00
453	850.00	500.00	350.00	400.00	250.00	174.00
454	750.00	425.00	325.00	350.00	200.00	140.00
455	90.00	50.00	35.00	32.00	20.00	13.00
456	1350.00	900.00	550.00	900.00	625.00	380.00
457	240.00	130.00	90.00	120.00	80.00	52.00
458	250.00	145.00	95.00	115.00	85.00	50.00
459	1800.00	1250.00	900.00	1350.00	1150.00	900.00

NOTE: *For further details on the various types of similar appearing stamps please refer to our U.S. Stamp Identifier.*

UNUSED PLATE BLOCKS OF 6

SCOTT NO.	NH F	AVG	OG F	AVG	SCOTT NO.	NH F	AVG	OG F	AVG
462	195.00	125.00	125.00	80.00	472	2000.00	1500.00	1500.00	1000.00
463	175.00	110.00	110.00	67.50	473	550.00	400.00	375.00	275.00
464	1500.00	1100.00	1150.00	825.00	474	950.00	600.00	600.00	400.00
465	800.00	500.00	600.00	425.00	481	35.00	25.00	25.00	16.50
466	1100.00	850.00	950.00	565.00	482	35.00	22.00	22.50	17.00
470	750.00	550.00	600.00	350.00	483	200.00	160.00	160.00	110.00
471	850.00	675.00	595.00	400.00	484	150.00	95.00	125.00	85.00

CENTER LINE BLOCKS					**ARROW BLOCKS**				
481	10.00	6.00	5.00	4.00	481	8.00	5.00	4.00	3.00
482	13.50	8.00	8.50	5.50	482	11.00	7.00	7.75	4.75
483	130.00	95.00	97.50	72.50	483	125.00	90.00	95.00	70.00
484	80.00	55.00	70.00	55.00	484	75.00	50.00	65.00	50.00

SCOTT NO.	DESCRIPTION	UNUSED O.G. VF	F	AVG	USED VF	F	AVG

ROTARY PRESS COIL STAMPS 1916-19 Perf. 10 Horizontally
(NH + 60%)

486	1¢ green......	1.75	1.00	.50	1.00	.75	.50
487	2¢ carmine (II) .	32.50	19.00	12.00	30.00	21.00	12.50
488	2¢ carmine (III).	5.95	3.75	2.50	5.00	3.50	2.00
489	3¢ violet (I)	7.00	4.50	3.00	2.75	1.95	1.00

1916-22 Perf. 10 Vertically (NH + 60%)

490	1¢ green......	1.00	.50	.50	.35	.25	.20
491	2¢ carmine (II) .	2750.00	1750.00	1100.00	800.00	550.00	375.00
492	2¢ carmine (III).	16.00	9.00	6.00	.50	.25	.20
493	3¢ violet (I)	37.50	21.00	16.00	7.00	4.25	2.75
494	3¢ violet (II) ...	22.50	13.00	8.50	1.50	1.00	.80
495	4¢ orange brown	27.50	15.75	11.00	10.50	6.00	4.00
496	5¢ blue.......	7.00	4.00	3.00	1.60	1.00	.75
497	10¢ orange yellow	35.00	20.00	15.00	25.00	16.50	9.25

(NH + 60%)

SCOTT NO.	COIL LINE PAIRS UNUSED OG VF	F	AVG	COIL PAIRS UNUSED OG VF	F	AVG
486	6.50	4.50	3.50	3.50	2.00	1.25
487	160.00	105.00	75.00	67.50	42.00	25.00
488	28.00	18.00	12.00	12.50	9.00	5.75
489	40.00	30.00	24.00	16.00	10.00	7.00
490	6.00	3.75	1.90	2.50	1.50	1.00
491	......	10000.00	6000.00	6450.00	4500.00	3000.00
492	70.00	50.00	35.00	36.00	20.00	14.00
493	160.00	100.00	70.00	78.75	60.00	35.00
494	90.00	60.00	48.00	47.00	35.00	19.50
495	100.00	75.00	55.00	55.00	35.00	22.00
496	40.00	28.00	19.50	15.00	9.00	7.00
497	160.00	115.00	75.00	75.00	45.00	35.00

1917-19 Flat Plate Printing Perf. 11 (NH + 60%)

498/518	(498-99, 501-04, 506-18) 19 varieties	680.00	410.00	270.00	45.00	25.00	19.00
498	1¢ green......	.90	.50	.50	.35	.25	.20
498e	1¢ booklet pane of 6	7.50	4.50	3.25	....	....	....
498f	1¢ booklet pane of 30.........	1300.00	800.00	550.00	....	....	....
499	2¢ rose (I).....	.90	.50	.25	.35	.25	.20
499e	2¢ booklet pane of 6	7.00	4.50	3.50	....	....	....
500	2¢ deep rose (Ia)	400.00	225.00	165.00	300.00	200.00	125.00
501	3¢ light violet (I)	25.00	15.00	10.00	1.00	.70	.50
501b	3¢ booklet pane of 6	95.00	65.00	45.00	....	....	....
502	3¢ dark violet (II)	26.00	15.00	10.00	2.25	1.50	.95
502b	3¢ booklet pane of 6	100.00	56.00	38.00	....	....	....
503	4¢ brown	17.00	10.00	6.00	1.25	.85	.50
504	5¢ blue	15.00	8.50	5.50	1.00	.75	.45
505	5¢ rose (error) .	895.00	525.00	360.00	700.00	475.00	300.00
506	6¢ red orange..	22.00	13.00	8.00	.75	.50	.35
507	7¢ black	42.00	25.00	17.00	2.75	2.00	1.10
508	8¢ olive bistre..	25.00	15.00	9.00	1.50	1.20	.80
509	9¢ salmon red .	24.00	14.00	9.00	4.75	2.95	2.00
510	10¢ orange yellow	30.00	17.00	10.50	.30	.25	.20
511	11¢ light green .	22.50	13.00	4.75	7.50	4.75	3.25
512	12¢ claret brown	22.50	13.00	4.75	1.25	.75	.60
513	13¢ apple green .	25.00	14.00	9.00	17.00	10.00	9.00
514	15¢ gray......	64.00	38.00	26.00	2.50	1.50	1.25
515	20¢ light ultramarine	85.00	46.00	34.00	.75	.50	.35
516	30¢ orange red	70.00	40.00	30.00	2.50	1.50	1.25
517	50¢ red violet ..	100.00	75.00	50.00	1.50	.80	.75
518	$1 violet black .	110.00	75.00	50.00	4.25	2.75	1.75

1917 Design of 1908-09
Double Line Watermark Perf. 11

| 519 | 2¢ carmine .... | 715.00 | 385.00 | 255.00 | 1800.00 | 1400.00 | 800.00 |

UNUSED PLATE BLOCKS OF 6

SCOTT NO.	NH F	NH AVG	OG F	OG AVG	SCOTT NO.	NH F	NH AVG	OG F	OG AVG
498	25.00	18.75	17.95	15.50	511	225.00	125.00	165.00	100.00
499	25.00	18.75	17.95	15.50	512	220.00	125.00	155.00	100.00
501	200.00	150.00	165.00	115.00	513	220.00	150.00	145.00	90.00
502	225.00	200.00	195.00	150.00	514	835.00	465.00	595.00	385.00
503	215.00	165.00	150.00	130.00	515	975.00	565.00	675.00	425.00
504	165.00	100.00	135.00	80.00	516	800.00	475.00	640.00	375.00
506	275.00	200.00	195.00	135.00	517	2000.00	1350.00	1300.00	900.00
507	375.00	285.00	265.00	225.00	518	1750.00	1080.00	1225.00	800.00
508	375.00	255.00	300.00	200.00	519	5000.00	2785.00	3575.00	2150.00
509	220.00	150.00	175.00	120.00			**ARROW BLOCK**		
510	325.00	270.00	200.00	155.00	518	450.00	280.00	300.00	225.00

523, 547
Franklin

524
Franklin

SCOTT NO.	DESCRIPTION	UNUSED O.G. VF	F	AVG	USED VF	F	AVG
		1918 Unwatermarked (NH + 60%)					
523	$2 orange red & black	775.00	650.00	400.00	350.00	200.00	125.00
524	$5 deep green & black	300.00	200.00	150.00	60.00	40.00	20.00
		1918-20 Offset Printing Perf. 11 (NH + 60%)					
525	1¢ gray green . .	6.00	4.00	2.50	1.25	.85	.50
526	2¢ carmine (IV)	42.50	30.00	16.00	7.00	5.00	3.25
527	2¢ carmine (V) .	35.00	23.00	14.00	2.25	1.50	.85
528	2¢ carmine (Va)	17.00	11.00	8.00	1.00	.75	.55
528A	2¢ carmine (VI)	72.50	55.00	36.00	2.00	1.50	1.00
528B	2¢ carmine (VII)	38.50	25.00	18.00	.60	.50	.35
529	3¢ violet (III) . . .	7.50	5.50	4.50	.50	.35	.25
530	3¢ purple (IV) . .	2.50	1.75	1.25	.50	.30	.20
		1918-20 Offset Printing Imperforate					
531	1¢ gray green . .	22.50	14.00	10.50	41.00	25.00	19.00
532	2¢ carmine rose (IV)	100.00	71.00	54.00	120.00	83.00	56.00
533	2¢ carmine (V) .	425.00	320.00	235.00	210.00	150.00	110.00
534	2¢ carmine (VI)	42.50	33.00	19.00	47.00	35.00	23.00
534A	2¢ carmine (VI)	130.00	73.00	53.00	44.00	29.00	22.00
534B	2¢ carmine (VII)	2500.00	1800.00	1350.00	1350.00	1175.00	770.00
535	3¢ violet (IV) . . .	18.50	13.00	9.00	22.00	14.00	8.50
		1919 Offset Printing Perf. 12-1/2					
536	1¢ gray green . .	40.00	28.00	18.00	65.00	40.00	26.00

537
"Victory" and Flags

SCOTT NO.	DESCRIPTION	UNUSED O.G. VF	F	AVG	USED VF	F	AVG
		1919 VICTORY ISSUE (NH + 50%)					
537	3¢ violet	18.50	10.50	6.50	7.50	4.50	2.75
		1919-21 Rotary Press Printings—Perf. 11 x 10 (†) (NH + 50%)					
538	1¢ green	25.00	14.00	9.50	32.00	22.00	16.00
538a	Same, imperf. horizontally	80.00	50.00	36.00	. . . . . .	. . . . . .	. . . . . .
539	2¢ carmine rose (II)	3300.00	2700.00	1800.00	. . . . . .	22000.00	. . . . . .
540	2¢ carmine rose (III)	17.50	10.00	6.00	25.00	15.00	10.50
540a	Same, imperf. horizontally	85.00	48.00	38.00	. . . . . .	. . . . . .	. . . . . .
541	3¢ violet (II) . . .	80.00	48.00	37.00	95.00	55.00	41.00
		Perf. 10 x 11					
542	1¢ green	17.00	11.00	7.00	2.25	1.35	1.00
		Perf. 10					
543	1¢ green	1.35	.75	.50	.75	.40	.20

SCOTT NO.	DESCRIPTION	UNUSED O.G. VF	F	AVG	USED VF	F	AVG
		Perf. 11					
544	1¢ green (19 x 22-1/2mm)	. . . . . .	18000.00	14200.00	. . . . . .	3700.00	. . . . . .
545	1¢ green (19-1/2 x 22mm)	300.00	200.00	130.00	300.00	185.00	125.00
546	2¢ carmine rose (III)	165.00	110.00	68.25	300.00	185.00	125.00
		1920 Flat Plate Printing Perf. 11					
547	$2 carmine & black	335.00	225.00	130.00	79.00	50.00	38.00

SCOTT NO.	NH F	NH AVG	OG F	OG AVG	SCOTT NO.	NH F	NH AVG	OG F	OG AVG
	UNUSED PLATE BLOCKS OF 6					**UNUSED PLATE BLOCKS OF (—)**			
525 (6)	45.00	30.00	25.00	20.00	535 (6)	105.00	85.00	85.00	65.00
526 (6)	400.00	275.00	250.00	200.00	536 (6)	250.00	175.00	175.00	135.00
527 (6)	300.00	200.00	180.00	150.00	537 (6)	250.00	175.00	165.00	125.00
528 (6)	150.00	100.00	95.00	60.00	538 (4)	135.00	97.50	90.00	60.00
528A (6)	700.00	450.00	490.00	315.00	540 (4)	130.00	80.00	80.00	50.00
528B (6)	300.00	200.00	195.00	145.00	541 (4)	500.00	350.00	330.00	225.00
529 (6)	100.00	67.50	65.00	45.00	542 (6)	195.00	135.00	135.00	90.00
530 (6)	40.00	26.50	25.00	17.00	543 (6)	35.00	20.00	15.00	10.00
531 (6)	150.00	112.50	110.00	85.00	543 (6)	55.00	32.00	30.00	20.00
532 (6)	650.00	500.00	485.00	375.00	545 (4)	1200.00	800.00	950.00	675.00
533 (6)	2100.00	1800.00	1575.00	1175.00	546 (4)	1000.00	700.00	700.00	475.00
534 (6)	275.00	200.00	435.00	150.00	547 (8)	6000.00	4575.00	4350.00	3150.00
534A (6)	800.00	550.00	525.00	415.00	548 (6)	100.00	65.00	67.50	50.00
					549 (6)	110.00	70.00	75.00	55.00
					550 (6)	725.00	525.00	475.00	330.00

	CENTER LINE					**ARROW BLOCKS**			
531	80.00	50.00	55.00	35.00	531	60.00	45.00	50.00	40.00
532	325.00	200.00	225.00	145.00	532	275.00	170.00	195.00	120.00
533	2000.00	1250.00	1000.00	650.00	533	1000.00	700.00	700.00	500.00
534	95.00	55.00	70.00	50.00	534	90.00	55.00	60.00	45.00
534A	275.00	200.00	185.00	125.00	534A	220.00	160.00	160.00	120.00
535	90.00	65.00	55.00	40.00	535	85.00	60.00	52.50	37.50
547	1400.00	975.00	1175.00	835.00	547	1275.00	900.00	1100.00	825.00

548
The "Mayflower"

549
Landing of the Pilgrims

550
Signing of the Compact

SCOTT NO.	DESCRIPTION	UNUSED O.G. VF	F	AVG	USED VF	F	AVG
		1920 PILGRIM TERCENTENARY ISSUE (NH + 50%)					
548-50	1¢-5¢ (3 varieties, complete)	75.00	48.00	37.00	42.00	21.00	18.50
548	1¢ green	9.50	6.50	4.75	7.00	3.75	2.50
549	2¢ carmine rose	12.00	7.50	4.25	4.50	2.50	2.00
550	5¢ deep blue . .	70.00	40.00	32.00	37.00	20.00	18.00

For Your Convenience in Ordering, Complete Sets are Listed Before Single Stamp Listings!

551, 653
Nathan Hale

552, 575, 578, 581, 594, 596, 597, 604, 632
Franklin

553, 576, 582, 598, 605, 631, 633
Harding

554, 577, 579, 583, 595, 599-99A, 606, 634-34A
Washington

555, 584, 600, 635
Lincoln

556, 585, 601, 636
Martha Washington

557, 586, 602, 637
Roosevelt

558, 587, 638, 723
Garfield

559, 588, 639
McKinley

560, 589, 640
Grant

561, 590, 641
Jefferson

562, 591, 603, 642
Monroe

563, 692
Hayes

564, 693
Cleveland

565, 695
American Indian

566, 696
Statue of Liberty

567, 698
Golden Gate

568, 699
Niagara Falls

569, 700
Bison

570, 701
Arlington Amphitheatre

571
Lincoln Memorial

572
U.S. Capitol

573
"America"

SCOTT NO.	DESCRIPTION	UNUSED O.G. VF	F	AVG	USED VF	F	AVG
	THE 1922-25 ISSUE Flat Plate Printings Perf. 11 (NH + 60%)						
551-73	1/2¢-$5 (23 varieties, complete)	1145.00	760.00	555.00	74.00	40.00	28.00
551	1/2¢ olive brown (1925)	.60	.50	.25	.25	.20	.15
552	1¢ deep green (1923)	4.25	3.00	2.25	1.00	.80	.60
552a	1¢ booklet pane of 6	17.50	13.00	9.00	....	....	....
553	1-1/2¢ yellow brown (1925).	5.25	3.25	2.50	2.00	1.35	.95
554	2¢ carmine (1923)	4.50	3.00	2.00	1.00	.80	.60
554c	2¢ booklet pane of 6	12.00	9.00	5.50	....	....	....
555	3¢ violet (1923)	32.50	23.00	15.00	2.00	1.50	1.00
556	4¢ yellow brown (1923).	33.50	24.00	15.00	1.00	.65	.50
557	5¢ dark blue . . .	33.50	24.00	15.00	1.00	.65	.50
558	6¢ red orange. .	60.00	38.00	28.00	2.75	1.75	1.25
559	7¢ black (1923)	17.50	12.00	9.00	2.25	1.25	.90
560	8¢ olive green (1923)	65.00	44.00	31.00	2.00	1.25	.95
561	9¢ rose (1923) .	30.00	18.00	12.00	4.00	2.25	1.50
562	10¢ orange (1923)	35.00	23.00	15.00	.30	.20	.15
563	11¢ light blue . .	4.25	3.00	2.00	.75	.50	.30
564	12¢ brown violet (1923).	15.00	8.00	5.00	.75	.50	.40
565	14¢ blue (1923)	9.00	5.00	3.00	2.50	2.00	1.25
566	15¢ gray	40.00	23.00	18.00	.25	.20	.15
567	20¢ carmine rose (1923).	40.00	25.00	20.00	.25	.20	.15
568	25¢ yellow green	33.50	21.00	15.00	2.25	1.50	1.25
569	30¢ olive brown (1923).	60.00	39.00	28.00	1.00	.60	.40
570	50¢ lilac	95.00	56.00	45.00	.50	.25	.20
571	$1 violet black (1923)	72.50	48.00	37.00	2.00	1.25	.75
572	$2 deep blue (1923)	165.00	105.00	88.00	18.00	11.00	6.50
573	$5 carmine & blue (1923).	300.00	220.00	160.00	29.00	18.00	12.00
	1923-25 Imperforate						
575	1¢ green	16.50	12.00	9.00	14.00	8.00	5.50
576	1-1/2¢ yellow brown (1925).	3.25	2.00	1.25	4.75	2.50	2.00
577	2¢ carmine	3.25	2.25	1.25	4.25	2.50	1.75
	Rotary Press Printings 1923 Perf. 11 x 10 (†) (NH + 60%)						
578	1¢ green	100.00	85.00	60.00	250.00	180.00	130.00
579	2¢ carmine . . .	150.00	87.00	62.50	225.00	140.00	100.00
	1923-26 Perf. 10 (†)						
581-91	1¢-10¢ (11 varieties, complete)	285.00	175.00	125.00	49.00	29.00	18.00
581	1¢ green	18.25	12.00	7.50	1.25	.85	.60
582	1-1/2¢ brown (1925)	6.00	4.00	3.00	1.25	.90	.65
583	2¢ carmine (1924)	4.00	2.00	1.25	.25	.20	.15
583a	2¢ booklet pane of 6 (1924).	110.00	70.00	50.00	....	....	....
584	3¢ violet (1925)	40.00	24.00	17.00	5.00	3.50	2.00
585	4¢ yellow brown (1925).	24.00	16.00	11.00	1.50	1.15	.75
586	5¢ blue (1925) .	24.00	16.00	11.00	1.00	0.50	0.30
587	6¢ red orange (1925)	18.50	10.00	6.50	1.50	.90	.60
588	7¢ black (1926)	25.00	16.00	10.50	18.00	12.00	8.00
589	8¢ olive green (1926)	40.00	24.00	15.00	13.00	8.50	5.00
590	9¢ rose (1926) .	8.00	4.00	3.00	10.00	5.00	3.25
591	10¢ orange (1925)	90.00	55.00	42.00	.55	.45	.35
	Perf. 11 (†)						
594	1¢ green	....	65000.00	....	....	11000.00	8800.00
595	2¢ carmine	275.00	225.00	170.00	550.00	350.00	225.00
	Perf. 11						
596	1¢ green	....	....	....	.... 200000.00		....

SCOTT NO.	PLATE BLOCKS (6)	UNUSED NH VF	F	AVG.	UNUSED OG VF	F	AVG.
551	1/2¢ olive brown (1923)	25.00	20.00	15.00	15.00	12.00	9.00
552	1¢ deep green (1923)	52.00	30.00	25.00	32.50	20.00	14.00
553	1-1/2¢ yellow brown (1923)	95.00	80.00	65.00	65.00	55.00	35.00
554	2¢ carmine (1923)	50.00	30.00	22.50	32.50	21.50	15.00
555	3¢ violet (1923)	350.00	225.00	180.00	195.00	150.00	110.00
556	4¢ yellow brown (1923)	365.00	235.00	185.00	205.00	150.00	110.00
557	5¢ dark blue	375.00	240.00	200.00	210.00	160.00	125.00
558	6¢ red orange	750.00	450.00	400.00	500.00	350.00	250.00
559	7¢ black (1923)	150.00	100.00	70.00	100.00	65.00	45.00
560	8¢ olive green (1923)	1100.00	740.00	650.00	750.00	500.00	375.00
561	9¢ rose (1923)	340.00	225.00	160.00	195.00	160.00	130.00
562	10¢ orange (1923)	400.00	290.00	200.00	300.00	200.00	160.00
563	11¢ light blue	55.00	38.00	32.00	45.00	28.00	18.50
564	12¢ brown violet (1923)	250.00	145.00	100.00	175.00	100.00	80.00
565	14¢ blue (1923)	120.00	80.00	57.50	85.00	52.50	42.50
566	15¢ grey	500.00	350.00	240.00	350.00	225.00	175.00
567	20¢ carmine rose (1923)	475.00	320.00	240.00	400.00	220.00	190.00
568	25¢ yellow green	420.00	260.00	200.00	325.00	190.00	125.00
569	30¢ olive brown (1923)	550.00	375.00	295.00	325.00	225.00	160.00
570	50¢ lilac	1350.00	1000.00	750.00	850.00	600.00	450.00
571	$1 violet black (1923)	800.00	520.00	400.00	550.00	400.00	300.00
572	$2 deep blue (1923)	1750.00	1300.00	1000.00	1100.00	850.00	650.00
573(8)	$5 carmine + blue (1923)	5000.00	3750.00	2800.00	3500.00	2250.00	1750.00

SCOTT NO.	CENTER LINE BLOCKS	F/NH	F/OG	AVG/OG	ARROW BLOCKS F/NH	F/OG	AVG/OG
571	$1 violet black	....	....	....	310.00	210.00	140.00
572	$2 deep blue	....	....	....	650.00	450.00	360.00
573	$5 carmine & blue	1100.00	925.00	775.00	1050.00	900.00	750.00
575	1¢ imperforate	58.00	50.00	40.00	55.00	47.50	38.00
576	1-1/2¢ imperforate	19.50	15.00	10.50	11.00	8.00	5.00
577	2¢ imperforate	22.50	17.50	12.00	12.00	9.00	7.00

SCOTT NO.	PLATE BLOCKS	UNUSED NH VF	F	AVG.	UNUSED OG VF	F	AVG.
575 (6)	1¢ green	160.00	110.00	75.00	110.00	70.00	50.00
576 (6)	1-1/2¢ yellow brown (1925)	50.00	33.00	25.00	35.00	22.00	16.00
577 (6)	2¢ carmine	50.00	34.00	25.00	42.00	25.00	18.00
578	1¢ green	2100.00	1200.00	950.00	1300.00	900.00	675.00
579	2¢ carmine	1100.00	700.00	525.00	695.00	450.00	350.00
581	1¢ green	225.00	140.00	100.00	160.00	100.00	70.00
582	1-1/2¢ brown (1925)	85.00	55.00	35.00	60.00	38.00	25.00
583	2¢ carmine (1923)	75.00	45.00	28.50	55.00	33.00	20.00
584	3¢ violet (1925)	400.00	260.00	190.00	260.00	190.00	150.00
585	4¢ yellow green (1925)	300.00	200.00	157.50	220.00	160.00	115.00
586	5¢ blue (1925)	375.00	240.00	170.00	275.00	170.00	120.00
587	6¢ red orange (1925)	225.00	145.00	95.00	150.00	95.00	65.00
588	7¢ black (1926)	250.00	155.00	100.00	175.00	110.00	70.00
589	8¢ olive green (1926)	400.00	260.00	190.00	275.00	190.00	125.00
590	9¢ rose (1926)	115.00	70.00	45.00	80.00	50.00	30.00
591	10¢ orange (1925)	1050.00	700.00	500.00	650.00	475.00	380.00

SCOTT NO.	DESCRIPTION	UNUSED VF	F	AVG	USED VF	F	AVG
	1923-29 Rotary Press Coil Stamps (NH + 50%)						
597/606	597-99, 600-06 (10 varieties)..	34.25	23.50	15.50	3.50	2.45	1.65
	Perf. 10 Vertically						
597	1¢ green......	.60	.25	.25	1.00	.80	.60
598	1-1/2¢ deep brown (1925).......	1.35	1.00	.75	1.00	.65	.50
599	2¢ carmine (I) (1923)	.60	.50	.25	1.00	.80	.60
599A	2¢ carmine (II) (1929).......	210.00	115.00	73.50	25.00	15.25	9.75
600	3¢ violet (1924)	13.75	9.00	5.50	1.00	.70	.45
601	4¢ yellow brown	8.25	5.50	4.25	1.50	.75	.45
602	5¢ dark blue (1924)	2.95	1.75	1.25	1.00	.75	.50
603	10¢ orange (1924)	7.25	5.00	3.50	1.00	.75	.50
	Perf. 10 Horizontally						
604	1¢ yellow green (1924)	.60	.50	.25	1.00	.75	.50
605	1-1/2¢ yellow brown (1925).......	.75	.50	.25	1.00	.75	.50
606	2¢ carmine	.65	.50	.25	1.00	.75	.50

SCOTT NO.	UNUSED OG (NH + 40%)	COIL LINE PAIRS VF	F	AVG.	COIL PAIRS VF	F	AVG.
597	1¢ green	2.55	1.95	1.40	1.20	.65	.50
598	1-1/2¢ brown (1925)	6.75	5.25	4.00	2.70	2.00	1.50
599	2¢ carmine (I)	2.15	1.65	1.20	1.25	1.00	.55
599A	2¢ carmine (II) (1929)	825.00	557.50	375.00	450.00	247.50	157.50
600	3¢ deep violet (1924)	40.00	30.00	23.75	28.00	18.00	11.50
601	4¢ yellow brown	35.75	27.50	22.00	16.50	12.00	8.50
602	5¢ dark blue	11.75	9.00	6.00	6.25	4.25	2.75
603	10¢ orange (1924)	35.00	27.00	20.00	15.00	10.00	7.00
604	1¢ green (1924)	3.40	2.60	1.65	1.25	1.00	.50
605	1-1/2¢ yellow brown (1925)	4.25	3.00	2.00	1.50	1.00	.75
606	2¢ carmine	2.75	2.00	1.35	1.30	1.00	.50

610-613
Harding

SCOTT NO.	DESCRIPTION	UNUSED VF	F	AVG	USED VF	F	AVG
	1923 HARDING MEMORIAL ISSUE (NH + 50%)						
610	2¢ black, perf 11 flat	1.50	1.00	.75	1.00	.75	.50
611	2¢ black, imperf	17.50	10.50	8.00	15.00	10.00	8.00
612	2¢ black, perf 10 rotary ..	27.00	14.00	12.00	6.00	3.50	2.50
613	2¢ black perf 11 rotary	......	......	......	......	45000.00	36500.00

614
Ship "New Netherlands"

615
Landing at Fort Orange

616
Monument at Mayport, Fla.

1924 HUGUENOT-WALLOON ISSUE (NH + 40%)

SCOTT NO.	DESCRIPTION	UNUSED VF	F	AVG	USED VF	F	AVG
614-16	1¢-5¢ (3 varieties, complete)	69.00	51.00	39.00	45.00	32.00	20.00
614	1¢ dark green..	6.50	4.75	3.50	6.50	3.75	3.00
615	2¢ carmine rose	10.00	6.00	4.00	5.50	3.75	2.75
616	5¢ dark blue...	60.00	47.00	37.00	37.00	29.00	20.00

617
Washington at Cambridge

618
Birth of Liberty

619
The Minute Man

1925 LEXINGTON-CONCORD SESQUICENTENNIAL (NH + 40%)

SCOTT NO.	DESCRIPTION	UNUSED VF	F	AVG	USED VF	F	AVG
617-19	1¢-5¢ (3 varieties, complete)	76.00	56.00	42.25	41.00	30.00	20.00
617	1¢ deep green .	8.75	5.50	4.75	9.50	6.00	4.25
618	2¢ carmine rose	13.50	9.00	6.00	10.50	8.00	6.00
619	5¢ dark blue ...	60.00	46.00	34.00	29.00	22.00	14.00

NOTE: For further details on the various types of similar appearing stamps please refer to our U. S. Stamp Identifier.

SCOTT NO.	DESCRIPTION	VF	UNUSED O.G. F	AVG	VF	USED F	AVG

620
Sloop "Restaurationen"

621
Viking Ship

1925 NORSE-AMERICAN ISSUE (NH + 40%)

SCOTT NO.	DESCRIPTION	VF	UNUSED O.G. F	AVG	VF	USED F	AVG
620-21	2¢-5¢ (2 varieties, complete)	45.00	28.50	19.25	40.00	27.00	19.00
620	2¢ carmine & black	10.25	7.00	5.50	8.00	6.00	4.50
621	5¢ dark blue & black	39.50	24.00	16.00	36.00	24.00	17.00

622, 694
Harrison

623, 697
Wilson

1925-26 Flat Plate Printings, Perf. 11

SCOTT NO.	DESCRIPTION	VF	UNUSED O.G. F	AVG	VF	USED F	AVG
622	13¢ green (1926)	25.00	16.00	11.00	1.25	.75	.60
623	17¢ black	31.50	19.00	15.00	.75	.50	.40

		PLATE BLOCKS					
SCOTT NO.		UNUSED NH			UNUSED OG		
		VF	F	AVG	VF	F	AVG
610 (6)	2¢ black perf 11 flat	45.00	30.00	22.00	33.00	23.00	18.00
611 (6)	2¢ black imperf	210.00	140.00	90.00	160.00	105.00	80.00
611 (4)	2¢ black center line block	110.00	85.00	60.00	77.50	60.00	45.00
611 (4)	2¢ black arrow block	58.00	45.00	32.50	45.00	35.00	25.00
612 (4)	2¢ black perf 10 rotary	500.00	370.00	300.00	390.00	275.00	210.00
614 (6)	1¢ dark green	80.00	54.00	40.00	60.00	39.00	25.00
615 (6)	2¢ carmine rose	150.00	90.00	65.00	110.00	75.00	55.00
616 (6)	5¢ dark blue	620.00	450.00	350.00	510.00	325.00	250.00
617 (6)	1¢ deep green	90.00	50.00	40.00	65.00	40.00	30.00
618 (6)	2¢ carmine rose	160.00	95.00	75.00	115.00	72.00	55.00
619 (6)	5¢ dark blue	510.00	395.00	300.00	410.00	315.00	220.00
620 (8)	2¢ carmine black	325.00	250.00	175.00	235.00	180.00	125.00
621 (8)	5¢ dark blue+black	1050.00	800.00	550.00	815.00	625.00	435.00
622 (6)	13¢ green (1926)	280.00	215.00	150.00	190.00	145.00	105.00
623 (6)	17¢ black	325.00	250.00	175.00	255.00	195.00	136.50

627
Liberty Bell

628
John Ericsson Statue

629, 630
Hamilton's Battery

1926-27 COMMEMORATIVES (NH + 40%)

SCOTT NO.	DESCRIPTION	VF	UNUSED O.G. F	AVG	VF	USED F	AVG
627/644	627-29, 643-44 (5 varieties, complete)	32.00	25.00	17.00	17.00	12.00	7.50

1926 COMMEMORATIVES

627	2¢ Sesquicentennial	5.75	4.25	3.25	1.00	.80	.55
628	5¢ Ericsson Memorial	16.25	13.00	9.00	7.00	5.00	3.50
629	2¢ White Plains	3.75	2.75	2.00	3.25	2.50	1.50
630	White Plains Sheet of 25	425.00	300.00	250.00	550.00	425.00	300.00
630V	2¢ Dot over "S" variety	450.00	350.00	300.00	600.00	475.00	350.00

Rotary Press Printings Designs of 1922-25 1926 Imperforate

631	1-1/2¢ yellow brown	4.95	3.75	2.75	6.00	4.25	3.00
631	1-1/2¢ center line block	26.00	20.00	13.50	....	....	....
631	1-1/2¢ arrow block	12.25	9.50	6.50	....	....	....

SCOTT NO.	DESCRIPTION	VF	UNUSED O.G. F	AVG	VF	USED F	AVG

1926-28 Perf. 11 x 10 1/2

632/42	1¢-10¢ (632-34, 635-42 11 varieties) . . .	41.00	33.00	25.00	2.60	2.10	1.55
632	1¢ green (1927)	.50	.25	.25	.25	.20	.15
632a	1¢ booklet pane of 6	7.00	5.00	3.50	....	....	....
633	1-1/2¢ yellow brown (1927).	3.75	2.75	2.00	.25	.20	.15
634	2¢ carmine (I). .	.40	.25	.25	.25	.20	.15
634	Electric Eye Plate	5.50	4.25	2.75	....	....	....
634d	2¢ booklet pane of 6	2.15	1.75	1.25	....	....	....
634A	2¢ carmine (II) (1928).	550.00	395.00	255.00	25.00	17.00	11.00
635	3¢ violet (1927)	1.00	.75	.50	.25	.20	.15
636	4¢ yellow brown (1927)	4.25	3.25	2.75	.50	.30	.25
637	5¢ dark blue (1927)	3.95	3.00	2.25	25	.20	.15
638	6¢ red orange (1927)	6.25	4.75	3.50	25	.20	.15
639	7¢ black (1927)	6.00	4.50	3.25	25	.20	.15
640	8¢ olive green (1927)	6.00	4.50	3.25	25	.20	.15
641	9¢ orange red (1931)	4.50	3.50	2.50	25	.20	.15
642	10¢ orange (1927)	6.75	5.50	4.00	.25	.20	.15

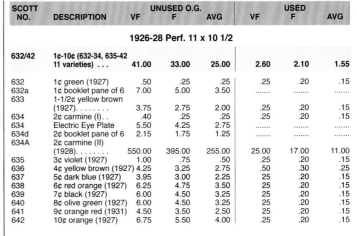

643

644

1927 COMMEMORATIVES

643	2¢ Vermont. . . .	3.25	2.50	1.75	2.75	2.15	1.50
644	2¢ Burgoyne. . .	6.95	5.50	3.75	5.00	3.95	2.50

645

646

647

648

649

650

1928 COMMEMORATIVES (NH + 40%)

645-50	6 varieties, complete	61.00	42.00	30.00	52.00	34.00	25.00
645	2¢ Valley Forge	2.50	2.00	1.50	1.50	1.10	.80
646	2¢ Molly Pitcher	2.35	2.00	1.50	2.75	2.25	1.50
647	2¢ Hawaii	7.75	5.00	3.25	7.50	6.00	3.50
648	5¢ Hawaii	32.50	23.00	16.75	33.00	25.00	17.00
649	2¢ Aeronautics .	4.00	2.50	2.00	4.00	2.25	1.50
650	5¢ Aeronautics .	13.50	9.00	7.00	9.00	5.00	3.75

651

654-656

657

1929 COMMEMORATIVES (NH + 40%)

651/81	651, 654-55, 657, 680-81 (6 varieties) . . .	10.25	8.25	5.25	5.00	3.70	2.75
651	2¢ George R. Clark	2.25	1.25	1.25	1.75	1.10	.90
	Same, arrow block of 4	4.50	3.35	2.35	....	....	....

1929 Design of 1922-25 Rotary Press Printing Perf. 11x10-1/2

| 653 | 1/2¢ olive brown | .60 | .50 | .50 | .25 | .20 | .15 |

SCOTT NO.	DESCRIPTION	UNUSED O.G. VF	F	AVG	USED VF	F	AVG
	1929 COMMEMORATIVES						
654	2¢ Edison, Flat, Perf 11	2.15	1.75	1.25	1.75	1.40	1.00
655	2¢ Edison, Rotary, 11x10-1/2	1.50	1.25	1.00	.50	.45	.35
656	2¢ Edison, Rotary Press Coil, Perf. 10 Vertically	28.50	22.00	15.00	3.00	2.35	1.50
657	2¢ Sullivan Expedition	1.60	1.25	1.00	1.75	1.40	1.10

1929. 632-42 Overprinted Kansas
(NH + 50%)

SCOTT NO.	DESCRIPTION	VF	F	AVG	VF	F	AVG
658-68	1¢-10¢ (11 varieties, complete)	250.00	200.00	165.00	200.00	160.00	110.00
658	1¢ green.	3.00	1.75	1.25	2.10	1.60	1.20
659	1-1/2¢ brown . .	4.25	3.25	2.25	3.25	2.00	1.40
660	2¢ carmine	4.25	3.00	2.00	1.75	1.25	.75
661	3¢ violet	20.00	16.00	14.00	20.00	15.00	12.00
662	4¢ yellow brown	22.00	17.00	12.00	15.00	10.00	7.00
663	5¢ deep blue . .	15.00	12.00	9.00	12.00	9.00	6.00
664	6¢ red orange. .	30.00	25.00	20.00	22.00	18.00	12.00
665	7¢ black	30.00	25.00	20.00	28.00	22.00	18.00
666	8¢ olive green .	80.00	70.00	60.00	70.00	62.00	40.00
667	9¢ light rose . . .	18.00	12.50	10.00	13.00	11.00	7.00
668	10¢ orange yellow	28.00	22.00	18.00	14.00	12.00	10.00

1929. 632-42 Overprinted Nebraska
(NH + 50%)

SCOTT NO.	DESCRIPTION	VF	F	AVG	VF	F	AVG
669-79	1¢-10¢, 11 varieties, complete	330.00	240.00	185.00	210.00	164.00	120.00
669	1¢ green.	3.75	3.00	2.20	3.10	2.20	1.60
670	1-1/2¢ brown . .	4.00	2.50	2.00	3.20	2.50	1.80
671	2¢ carmine	4.00	2.50	2.00	2.00	1.50	1.00
672	3¢ violet	12.00	10.50	8.00	17.50	12.00	8.00
673	4¢ yellow brown	22.00	15.00	12.00	18.00	15.50	11.00
674	5¢ deep blue . .	20.00	14.00	11.00	18.00	15.50	11.00
675	6¢ red orange. .	38.00	26.00	22.00	30.00	22.00	16.00
676	7¢ black	28.00	21.00	16.00	22.00	18.00	14.00
677	8¢ olive green .	35.00	26.00	18.00	35.00	24.00	18.00
678	9¢ light rose . . .	40.00	35.00	25.00	38.00	30.00	25.00
679	10¢ orange yellow	125.00	88.00	77.00	32.00	22.00	15.00

SCOTT NO.		PLATE BLOCKS UNUSED NH VF	F	AVG.	UNUSED OG VF	F	AVG.
627 (6)	Sesquicentennial.	65.00	50.00	35.00	49.50	38.00	26.00
628 (6)	5¢ Ericsson Memorial.	145.00	110.00	77.50	110.00	85.00	60.00
629 (6)	2¢ White Plains	67.50	52.00	35.00	52.00	40.00	30.00
631	1-1/2¢ yellow brown	93.00	71.50	50.00	70.00	55.00	40.00
632	1¢ green.	3.25	2.50	1.75	2.60	2.00	1.40
633	1-1/2¢ yellow brown (1927)	120.00	92.50	65.00	90.00	70.00	48.00
634	2¢ carmine (1)	2.60	1.95	1.40	2.10	1.70	1.25
635	3¢ violet.	15.00	12.50	9.00	10.50	7.50	4.50
636	4¢ yellow brown (1927)	130.00	95.00	70.00	105.00	80.00	55.00
637	5¢ dark blue (1927).	29.50	22.50	15.75	22.75	17.50	12.75
638	6¢ red orange (1927)	29.50	22.50	15.75	22.75	17.50	12.75
639	7¢ black (1927)	29.50	22.50	15.75	22.75	17.50	12.75
640	8¢ olive green (1927)	29.50	22.50	15.75	22.75	17.50	12.75
641	9¢ orange red (1931)	30.00	23.00	16.00	23.00	18.00	13.00
642	10¢ orange (1927).	43.50	33.50	23.00	34.00	26.00	18.25
643 (6)	2¢ Vermont.	65.00	50.00	35.00	58.00	42.00	28.00
644 (6)	2¢ Burgoyne	80.00	57.00	42.00	60.00	45.00	30.00
645 (6)	2¢ Valley Forge	58.00	40.00	28.00	41.00	30.00	19.50
646	2¢ Molly Pitcher	60.00	42.50	32.00	42.00	33.00	25.00
647	2¢ Hawaii	205.00	140.00	110.00	145.00	110.00	77.00
648	5¢ Hawaii	425.00	315.00	225.00	335.00	260.00	185.00
649 (6)	2¢ Aeronautics	24.00	18.00	12.00	19.50	14.00	10.00
650 (6)	5¢ Aeronautics	115.00	90.00	65.00	85.00	65.00	47.50
651 (6)	2¢ George R. Clark	19.50	15.00	10.00	14.50	11.00	7.50
653	1/2¢ olive brown	2.75	2.00	1.25	1.95	1.50	.95
654 (6)	2¢ Edison	51.00	39.50	28.00	40.00	31.50	22.50
655	2¢ Edison	70.00	55.00	40.00	58.00	45.00	30.50
657 (6)	2¢ Sullivan Expedition.	45.00	35.00	26.50	39.50	30.00	22.50
	LINE PAIR						
656	2¢ Edison, coil.	125.00	95.00	65.00	80.00	62.50	45.00

SCOTT NO.		PLATE BLOCKS UNUSED NH VF	F	AVG.	UNUSED OG VF	F	AVG.
658	1¢ green.	65.00	40.00	30.00	45.00	30.00	20.00
659	1-1/2¢ brown	80.00	50.00	35.00	60.00	38.00	25.00
660	2¢ carmine	80.00	50.00	35.00	60.00	38.00	25.00
661	3¢ violet.	425.00	265.00	200.00	275.00	200.00	225.00
662	4¢ yellow brown	375.00	225.00	150.00	250.00	165.00	115.00
663	5¢ deep blue	275.00	165.00	125.00	185.00	120.00	90.00
664	6¢ red orange	850.00	550.00	400.00	525.00	325.00	225.00
665	7¢ black	850.00	550.00	400.00	525.00	325.00	225.00
666	8¢ olive green	1500.00	900.00	750.00	1000.00	625.00	475.00
667	9¢ light rose	450.00	300.00	200.00	295.00	200.00	125.00
668	10¢ orange yellow	650.00	425.00	295.00	425.00	285.00	195.00
669	1¢ green.	85.00	50.00	40.00	55.00	35.00	25.00
670	1-1/2¢ brown	100.00	60.00	40.00	60.00	35.00	25.00
671	2¢ carmine	80.00	50.00	35.00	55.00	35.00	25.00
672	3¢ violet.	350.00	200.00	140.00	225.00	135.00	95.00
673	4¢ yellow brown	475.00	300.00	200.00	325.00	200.00	140.00
674	5¢ deep blue	500.00	300.00	200.00	350.00	210.00	150.00
675	6¢ red orange	1000.00	550.00	450.00	650.00	375.00	265.00
676	7¢ black	550.00	325.00	225.00	335.00	215.00	155.00
677	8¢ olive green	750.00	450.00	315.00	475.00	350.00	250.00
678	9¢ light rose	1000.00	550.00	400.00	600.00	375.00	265.00
679	10¢ orange yellow	2000.00	1200.00	850.00	1200.00	750.00	550.00

SCOTT NO.	DESCRIPTION	UNUSED O.G. VF	F	AVG	USED VF	F	AVG

680

681

1929 COMMEMORATIVES
(NH + 30%)

680	2¢ Fallen Timbers	2.50	2.00	1.25	2.00	1.50	1.00
681	2¢ Ohio River Canal	1.50	1.25	1.00	1.25	1.00	.75

682

683

684, 686

685, 687

1930-31 COMMEMORATIVES

682/703	(682-83, 688-90, 702-03) 7 varieties, complete	5.50	4.10	3.10	5.35	4.15	2.85

1930 COMMEMORATIVES

682	2¢ Massachusetts Bay	1.50	1.25	1.00	1.25	1.00	.65
683	2¢ Carolina-Charleston	2.50	2.00	1.50	3.25	2.50	1.75

1930 Rotary Press Printing Perf. 11 x 10-1/2
(NH + 30%)

684	1-1/2¢ Harding .	.75	.50	.50	.25	.20	.15
685	4¢ Taft	1.50	1.25	.75	.25	.20	.15

1930 Rotary Press Coil Stamps Perf. 10 Vertically

686	1-1/2¢ Harding .	2.95	2.25	1.50	.25	.20	.15
687	4¢ Taft	4.75	3.75	2.50	1.00	.75	.50

688

689

690

1930 COMMEMORATIVES

688	2¢ Braddock's Field	1.95	1.50	1.00	2.50	1.80	1.25
689	2¢ Von Steuben	1.10	1.00	.75	1.25	.90	.65

1931 COMMEMORATIVES

690	2¢ Pulaski	.75	.50	.50	.50	.40	.30

SCOTT NO.	PLATE BLOCKS					
	UNUSED NH			UNUSED OG		
	VF	F	AVG.	VF	F	AVG.
680 (6) 2¢ Fallen Timbers..........	48.00	35.00	22.50	36.00	27.50	21.00
681 (6) 2¢ Ohio River Canal.........	33.75	25.00	15.75	26.00	20.00	12.00
682 (6) 2¢ Massachusetts Bay......	58.50	40.00	27.00	39.00	30.00	18.00
683 (6) 2¢ Carolina-Charleston.....	85.00	60.00	40.00	64.50	49.50	36.00
684 1-1/2¢ Harding	3.65	2.50	1.70	2.90	2.25	1.65
685 4¢ Taft.......................	17.00	12.00	9.00	13.00	10.00	6.00
686		15.00	10.75	7.50	10.00	8.00	6.00
687		30.00	22.50	15.00	20.00	15.00	10.00
688 (6) 3¢ Braddock's Field...........	71.50	47.50	33.00	52.00	40.00	24.00
689 (6) 2¢ Von Steuben..........	40.00	31.50	18.00	32.50	25.00	15.00
690 (6) 2¢ Pulaski.................	23.50	17.00	10.75	18.25	14.00	8.50

SCOTT NO.	DESCRIPTION	UNUSED			USED		
		VF	F	AVG	VF	F	AVG

1931 Designs of 1922-26. Rotary Press Printing.
(NH + 35%)

692-701	11¢ to 50¢ (10 varieties, complete)	184.00	140.00	105.00	3.25	2.75	2.25

Perf. 11 x 10-1/2

692	11¢ light blue . .	5.50	4.25	3.50	.25	.20	.15
693	12¢ brown violet	10.50	8.00	5.50	.25	.25	.20
694	13¢ yellow green	4.00	3.00	2.25	1.00	.75	.50
695	14¢ dark blue . .	10.50	8.00	5.50	3.00	2.50	1.90
696	15¢ gray......	16.00	12.00	9.00	.25	.20	.15

Perf. 10-1/2 x 11

697	17¢ black	12.50	9.50	6.50	.50	.40	.30
698	20¢ carmine rose	16.50	13.00	9.00	.25	.20	.15
699	25¢ blue green.	16.00	12.00	9.00	.25	.20	.15
700	30¢ brown	36.50	28.00	21.00	.25	.20	.15
701	50¢ lilac	65.00	50.00	41.00	.25	.20	.15

702

703

1931 COMMEMORATIVES
(NH + 30%)

702	2¢ Red Cross..	.50	.25	.25	.25	.25	.20
702	2¢ arrow block .	1.50	1.00	.65	....	....	....
703	2¢ Yorktown . . .	.60	.50	.50	.75	.50	.40
703	2¢ center line block	3.00	2.15	1.75	....	....	....
703	2¢ arrow block .	2.75	1.95	1.45	....	....	....

1932 WASHINGTON BICENTENNIAL ISSUE

Planning for this set, which celebrated the 200th anniversary of the birth of George Washington, began more than eight years before its release. Despite many suggestions that a pictorial series be created, the final set depicted 12 portraits of Washington at various stages of his life. For reasons of economy, the stamps were produced in single colors and in the same size as regular issues. Nevertheless, the set was an instant success and it was reported that more than a million covers were mailed from Washington, D.C. on January 1, 1932, the first day of issue.

704

705

706

707

708

709

710

711

712

713

714

715

SCOTT NO.	DESCRIPTION	UNUSED			USED		
		VF	F	AVG	VF	F	AVG

(NH + 40%)

704-15	1/2¢ to 10¢ (12 varieties, complete)	32.00	21.00	16.00	4.50	3.40	2.50
704	1/2¢ olive brown	.35	.25	.25	.25	.20	.15
705	1¢ green......	.40	.25	.25	.25	.20	.15
706	1-1/2¢ brown . .	.75	.50	.25	.25	.25	.20
707	2¢ carmine rose	.40	.25	.25	.25	.20	.15
708	3¢ deep violet..	.90	.70	.40	.25	.20	.15
709	4¢ light brown..	.75	.50	.50	.25	.20	.20
710	5¢ blue......	2.20	1.70	1.20	.50	.25	.20
711	6¢ red orange..	5.00	3.00	2.00	.25	.20	.15
712	7¢ black	.95	.75	.50	.50	.30	.20
713	8¢ olive bistre..	5.00	2.50	2.00	1.50	1.00	.75
714	9¢ pale red....	3.00	2.00	1.20	.30	.25	.20
715	10¢ orange yellow	15.00	10.00	8.00	.25	.20	.15

716

717

718

719

1932 COMMEMORATIVES
(NH + 30%)

716/25	(716-19, 724-25) 6 varieties	12.75	9.50	7.50	2.10	1.55	1.25
716	2¢ Winter Olympics	.95	.75	.50	.50	.40	.35
717	2¢ Arbor Day . .	.40	.25	.25	.25	.20	.15
718	3¢ Summer Olympics	4.00	3.00	2.50	.25	.20	.15
719	5¢ Summer Olympics	6.00	4.50	3.50	.75	.50	.40

720-722

723

724

725

726

1932 Rotary Press

720	3¢ deep violet..	.50	.25	.25	.25	.20	.15
720b	3¢ booklet pane of 6	60.00	40.00	28.00	....	....	....
721	3¢ deep violet coil perf 10 vertically	3.95	3.00	2.00	.25	.20	.15
722	3¢ deep violet coil perf 10 horizontally	2.95	2.25	1.50	1.00	.80	.65
723	6¢ Garfield, coil perf 10 vertically	17.50	13.00	9.00	.75	.75	.65

1932 COMMEMORATIVES

724	3¢ Penn	1.10	.75	.50	.50	.30	.25
725	3¢ Webster....	1.30	.75	.50	.55	.40	.30

SCOTT NO.		UNUSED OG (NH + 30%)					
		COIL LINE PAIRS			COIL PAIRS		
		VF	F	AVG.	VF	F	AVG.
686	1-1/2¢ Harding	10.00	8.00	5.50	5.90	4.50	3.00
687	4¢ Taft..............................	20.00	15.00	10.00	9.50	7.50	5.00
721	3¢ deep violet perf 10 vertically	10.75	8.25	5.50	7.90	6.00	4.00
722	3¢ deep violet perf 10 horizontally............	7.75	6.00	4.15	5.90	4.50	3.00
723	6¢ Garfield perf 10 vertically	71.50	55.00	33.00	35.00	26.00	18.00

SCOTT NO.	DESCRIPTION	UNUSED VF	F	AVG	USED VF	F	AVG

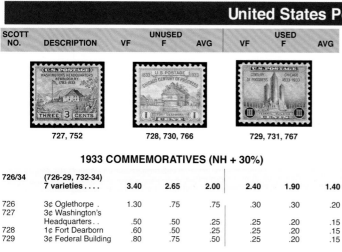

727, 752   728, 730, 766   729, 731, 767

1933 COMMEMORATIVES (NH + 30%)

726/34	(726-29, 732-34) 7 varieties	3.40	2.65	2.00	2.40	1.90	1.40
726	3¢ Oglethorpe .	1.30	.75	.75	.30	.30	.20
727	3¢ Washington's Headquarters . .	.50	.50	.25	.25	.20	.15
728	1¢ Fort Dearborn	.60	.50	.25	.25	.20	.15
729	3¢ Federal Building	.80	.75	.50	.25	.20	.15

Special Printing for A.P.S. Convention
Imperforate: Without Gum

730	1¢ yellow green, sheet of 25	....	42.50	....	....	43.00	....
730a	1¢ yellow green single	1.25	1.00	.75	.75	1.00	.65
731	3¢ violet, sheet of 25	....	33.50	....	....	34.00	....
731a	3¢ violet, single	1.25	1.25	.75	.60	1.25	.90

732   733, 735, 753, 768   734   736

732	3¢ N.R.A.	.40	.25	.25	.25	.20	.15
733	3¢ Byrd.	1.50	1.25	1.00	1.75	1.25	.95
734	5¢ Kosciuszko .	1.50	1.25	1.00	1.50	1.25	.90

1934 NATIONAL PHILATELIC EXHIBITION
Imperforate Without Gum

735	3¢ dark blue, sheet of 6	....	21.50	....	....	17.00	....
735a	3¢ dark blue, single	4.50	4.25	....	2.75	2.50	....

737, 738, 754   739, 755

1934 COMMEMORATIVES (NH + 30%)

736-39	4 varieties	1.95	1.45	.85	1.15	.90	.75
736	3¢ Maryland . . .	.55	.50	.25	.30	.30	.25
737	3¢ Mother's Day, rotary, perf 11 x 10-1/2	.50	.25	.25	.30	.25	.20
738	3¢ Mother's Day, flat, perf 11	.60	.50	.25	.50	.35	.30
739	3¢ Wisconsin . .	.60	.50	.25	.30	.25	.20

For Your Convenience in Ordering, Complete Sets are Listed Before Single Stamp Listings!

740, 751, 756, 769

741, 757

742, 750, 758, 770

743, 759

745, 761

744, 760

747, 763

746, 762

748, 764

749, 765

SCOTT NO.	DESCRIPTION	UNUSED VF	F	AVG	USED VF	F	AVG

1934 NATIONAL PARKS ISSUE (NH + 30%)

740-49	1¢-10¢ (10 varieties, complete)	22.25	16.00	12.75	9.25	7.95	5.35
740	1¢ Yosemite . . .	.30	.25	.25	.25	.20	.15
741	2¢ Grand Canyon	.30	.25	.25	.25	.20	.15
742	3¢ Mt. Rainier. .	.50	.25	.25	.25	.20	.15
743	4¢ Mesa Verde. .	1.60	1.25	1.00	.75	.65	.45
744	5¢ Yellowstone .	2.00	1.50	1.25	1.75	1.35	.95
745	6¢ Crater Lake. .	3.35	2.25	1.75	2.50	1.95	1.25
746	7¢ Acadia	1.75	1.25	1.00	2.00	1.65	1.10
747	8¢ Zion.	4.50	3.50	2.50	4.75	3.65	2.50
748	9¢ Glacier.	4.25	3.00	2.50	1.75	1.30	.90
749	10¢ Great Smoky Mountains	6.50	5.00	4.00	2.50	2.00	1.25

Special Printing for the A.P.S. Convention & Exhibition of Atlantic City
Imperforate Souvenir Sheet
(NH + 30%)

750	3¢ deep violet, sheet of 6	....	45.00	....	....	43.00	....
750a	3¢ deep violet, single	7.25	6.50	....	6.00	5.00	....

Special Printing for Trans-Mississippi Philatelic Exposition and Convention at Omaha
Imperforate Souvenir Sheet
(NH + 30%)

751	1¢ green, sheet of 6	....	16.50	....	....	17.00	....
751a	1¢ green, single	3.25	2.75	....	2.75	2.25	....

SCOTT NO.		PLATE BLOCKS UNUSED NH			UNUSED OG		
		VF	F	AVG.	VF	F	AVG.
692	11¢ light blue	22.50	16.50	10.00	16.50	12.75	9.50
693	12¢ brown violet	47.50	32.50	20.00	33.00	25.00	19.75
694	13¢ yellow green	21.50	16.50	10.00	16.50	12.75	9.50
695	14¢ dark blue	50.00	33.50	26.50	37.50	25.00	23.50
696	15¢ grey	65.00	50.00	35.00	49.75	36.00	27.00
697	17¢ black	65.00	47.50	30.00	40.00	30.00	20.00
698	20¢ carmine rose	75.00	55.00	40.00	55.00	43.00	30.00
699	25¢ blue green	75.00	60.00	40.00	55.00	45.00	30.00
700	30¢ brown	145.00	100.00	75.00	105.00	75.00	55.00
701	50¢ lilac	350.00	275.00	155.00	250.00	195.00	115.00
702	2¢ Red Cross	4.00	3.00	2.00	3.00	2.50	1.75
703	2¢ Yorktown (4)	5.75	4.00	2.70	4.25	3.35	2.65
704-15	Washington Bicentennial	590.00	435.00	290.00	445.00	335.00	248.50
704	1/2¢ olive brown	7.50	5.00	3.50	5.50	4.00	3.00
705	1¢ green	7.50	5.00	3.50	5.75	4.50	3.25
706	1-1/2¢ brown	34.50	23.50	17.00	25.00	18.00	13.25
707	2¢ carmine rose	3.00	2.00	1.25	2.25	1.60	1.10
708	3¢ deep violet	25.00	18.50	12.50	21.00	15.00	10.50
709	4¢ light brown	11.50	8.00	6.00	8.50	6.00	4.50
710	5¢ blue	30.00	20.00	16.00	23.50	18.00	14.00
711	6¢ red orange	105.00	80.00	49.50	78.00	60.00	46.50
712	7¢ black	12.00	8.50	6.00	9.00	7.00	5.50
713	8¢ olive bistre	105.00	80.00	49.50	78.00	60.00	40.00
714	9¢ pale red	80.00	55.00	40.00	57.50	42.50	30.00
715	10¢ orange yellow	200.00	150.00	100.00	155.00	115.00	90.00
716 (6)	2¢ Winter Olympics	22.00	16.00	11.00	16.95	13.00	9.50
717	2¢ Arbor Day	14.00	10.50	6.50	10.75	8.25	6.00
718	3¢ Summer Olympics	30.00	22.50	15.00	21.00	15.00	11.00
719	5¢ Summer Olympics	45.00	35.00	25.00	35.00	28.00	20.00
720	3¢ deep violet	2.95	2.00	1.40	2.15	1.65	1.10
724 (6)	3¢ Penn	20.00	14.00	9.50	14.00	11.00	9.00
725 (6)	3¢ Daniel Webster	35.75	26.00	14.00	28.00	22.00	16.00
726 (6)	3¢ Oglethorpe	23.50	16.50	11.00	18.00	14.00	10.00
727	3¢ Washington Hdqrs	10.00	7.00	4.50	7.95	6.00	4.50
728	1¢ Fort Dearborn	3.55	2.75	1.65	2.95	2.25	1.65
729	3¢ Federal Building	6.00	4.00	2.75	4.25	3.35	2.25
732	3¢ N.R.A.	2.95	2.00	1.40	2.55	1.95	1.40
733 (6)	3¢ Byrd	27.50	20.00	13.00	21.00	16.00	13.00
734 (6)	5¢ Kosciuszko	60.00	45.00	28.00	42.95	33.00	25.00
736 (6)	3¢ Maryland	17.50	12.50	8.25	13.00	10.00	8.25
737	3¢ Mother's Day, rotary perf. 11 x 10-1/2	2.95	2.00	1.30	2.40	1.75	1.40
738 (6)	3¢ Mother's Day, flat, perf. 11	8.50	6.50	3.95	6.50	5.00	3.85
739 (6)	3¢ Wisconsin	9.50	7.50	5.00	7.00	5.50	4.00
740-49	10 varieties complete	210.00	160.00	96.50	160.00	125.00	94.00
740 (6)	1¢ Yosemite	3.75	2.65	1.70	2.85	2.00	1.60
741 (6)	2¢ Grand Canyon	4.50	3.25	2.00	3.35	2.50	1.90
742 (6)	3¢ Mt. Rainier	3.50	2.75	1.65	3.00	2.30	1.55
743 (6)	4¢ Mesa Verde	15.50	12.00	7.25	13.00	10.00	7.00
744 (6)	5¢ Yellowstone	19.50	15.00	9.00	14.00	11.00	8.25
745 (6)	6¢ Crater Lake	33.50	26.00	15.50	26.50	20.50	15.50
746 (6)	7¢ Acadia	21.50	16.50	10.00	17.25	13.25	10.00
747 (6)	8¢ Zion	33.50	26.00	15.50	26.50	20.50	15.50
748 (6)	9¢ Glacier	33.50	26.00	15.50	26.50	20.50	15.50
749 (6)	10¢ Great Smoky Mountains	53.50	41.25	24.75	39.00	30.00	23.50

SELECTED U.S. COMMEMORATIVE MINT SHEETS

SCOTT NO.	F/NH SHEET	SCOTT NO.	F/NH SHEET
610 (100)	175.00	709 (100)	72.50
614 (50)	350.00	710 (100)	400.00
615 (50)	500.00	711 (100)	800.00
617 (50)	400.00	712 (100)	90.00
618 (50)	650.00	713 (100)	925.00
620 (100)	1175.00	714 (100)	675.00
627 (50)	275.00	715 (100)	2450.00
628 (50)	775.00	716 (100)	90.00
629 (100)	350.00	717 (100)	45.00
643 (100)	335.00	718 (100)	365.00
644 (50)	325.00	719 (100)	600.00
645 (100)	275.00	724 (100)	100.00
646 (100)	265.00	725 (100)	125.00
647 (100)	895.00	726 (100)	115.00
648 (100)	3895.00	727 (100)	50.00
649 (50)	175.00	728 (100)	55.00
650 (50)	650.00	729 (100)	72.50
651 (50)	95.00	732 (100)	35.00
654 (100)	225.00	733 (50)	135.00
655 (100)	200.00	734 (100)	155.00
657 (100)	175.00	736 (100)	55.00
680 (100)	250.00	737 (50)	22.50
681 (100)	130.00	738 (50)	26.50
682 (100)	145.00	739 (50)	30.00
683 (100)	275.00	740-49 set	925.00
688 (100)	225.00	740 (50)	12.00
689 (100)	110.00	741 (50)	12.00
690 (100)	70.00	742 (50)	20.00
702 (100)	42.50	743 (50)	65.00
703 (50)	28.00	744 (50)	80.00
704-15 set	4975.00	745 (50)	140.00
704 (100)	35.00	746 (50)	75.00
705 (100)	30.00	747 (50)	175.00
706 (100)	95.00	748 (50)	170.00
707 (100)	37.50	749 (50)	300.00
708 (100)	125.00		

THE FARLEY PERIOD

The 1933-35 period was one of great excitement for the hobby. With a stamp collector in the White House, in the person of President Franklin Delano Roosevelt, it was a period during which special Souvenir Sheets were issued for the A.P.S. Convention in 1933 (catalog #730) and the National Philatelic Exhibition in 1934 (#735). Collectors gloried in the limelight.

But there was a darker side, in the form of rare imperforate sheets that were being released to then Postmaster General James A. Farley, President Roosevelt himself, and a few other prominent personages. The protests against the practice grew to unmanageable proportions when word got around that one of the imperforate sheets of the 1934 Mother's Day issue had been offered to a stamp dealer for $20,000. Adding insult to injury, it was learned shortly thereafter that not only were there individual sheets floating around, but full, uncut sheets also had been presented as gifts to a fortunate few.

The outcry that followed could not be stifled. Congress had become involved in the affair and the demands were mounting that the gift sheets be recalled and destroyed. This being deemed impractical or undesirable, another solution was found—one that comes down to us today in the form of "The Farleys".

The solution was to let everyone "share the wealth", so to speak. Instead of recalling the few sheets in existence, additional quantities of the imperforates were issued in the same full sheet form as the gift sheets. Naturally, this step substantially reduced the value of the original, very limited edition, but it satisfied most collectors and left as its legacy "The Farley Issues".

The Farleys were issued March 15, 1935, and consisted of reprints of 20 issues. They remained on sale for three months, a relatively short time by most standards, but more than enough time for collectors who really cared. Although purists felt then—and some still do now—that President Roosevelt would have saved collectors a considerable sum by having the first few sheets destroyed, the issue has provided us with a wondrous selection of Gutters and Lines, arrow blocks, single sheets and full panes.

The collector on a limited budget can fill the spaces in an album with single imperforates. But the Farleys are such an interesting study that owning and displaying at least one of each variety of any one issue is a must. We illustrate here one of the full sheets of the 1 cent Century of Progress Farley Issue. The full sheets consisted of nine panes of 25 stamps each. The individual panes were separated by wide horizontal (**A**) or vertical (**B**) gutters and the gutters of four adjacent sheets formed a cross gutter (**C**).

NOTE: For #s 753-765 and 771, lines separated the individual panes. The lines ended in arrows at the top, bottom and side margins.

1935 "FARLEY SPECIAL PRINTINGS"
Designs of 1933-34 Imperforate (#752, 753 Perf.) Without Gum

SCOTT NO.		PLATE BLOCK	CENTER LINE BLOCK	ARROW BLOCK T OR B	L OR R	PAIR WITH V. LINE	H. LINE	FINE UNUSED	USED
752-71	20 varieties, complete ..	....	470.00	....	....	135.00	91.50	35.00	29.75
752	3¢ Newburgh	27.00	50.00	16.50	9.50	8.50	5.00	.45	.40
753	3¢ Byrd	(6)19.00	95.00	90.00	4.00	42.50	1.80	.75	.75
754	3¢ Mother's Day......	(6)19.00	9.50	4.00	4.25	1.80	2.00	.75	.65
755	3¢ Wisconsin	(6)19.00	9.50	4.00	4.25	2.00	2.25	.75	.65
756-65	1¢-10¢ Parks (10 varieties, complete)..	295.00	150.00	140.00	140.00	42.25	43.50	19.50	17.00
756	1¢ Yosemite	(6) 5.00	4.00	1.40	1.10	.60	.50	.30	.25
757	2¢ Grand Canyon....	(6) 6.50	5.50	1.55	1.45	.65	.85	.40	.30
758	3¢ Mt. Rainier	(6)16.50	6.50	3.60	4.00	1.55	1.75	.75	.65
759	4¢ Mesa Verde	(6)22.00	11.00	6.00	7.00	2.50	3.10	1.50	1.35
760	5¢ Yellowstone	(6)27.50	16.50	12.00	10.50	5.25	4.75	2.50	2.00
761	6¢ Crater Lake	(6)45.00	22.00	15.00	16.50	6.50	7.50	3.00	2.75
762	7¢ Acadia ..	(6)36.00	18.00	10.50	12.25	4.50	5.50	2.25	2.00
763	8¢ Zion	(6)45.00	20.00	14.50	12.00	7.00	5.50	2.75	2.25
764	9¢ Glacier ..	(6)50.00	22.00	13.00	5.75	5.75	6.50	3.00	2.50
765	10¢ Great Smoky Mountains ..	(6)57.50	33.00	25.00	22.00	11.00	10.00	5.00	4.25
766a-70a	5 varieties, complete ..	....	95.00	....	....	40.00	35.50	9.45	7.75
766a	1¢ Fort Dearborn	....	20.00			9.00	6.50	.85	.65
767a	3¢ Federal Building....	....	21.50			9.00	6.50	.75	.65
768a	3¢ Byrd	....	19.00			8.25	7.25	3.00	2.75
769a	1¢ Yosemite	....	12.00			7.75	5.50	1.85	1.60
770a	3¢ Mt. Rainier	....	28.00			11.50	13.00	3.60	3.05
771	16¢ Air Post Special Delivery....	(6)80.00	82.50	15.00	16.50	6.75	8.25	3.50	3.20

U.S. FARLEY ISSUE COMPLETE MINT SHEETS

SCOTT NO.	F/NH SHEET	SCOTT NO.	F/NH SHEET
752-71 set	7500.00	761 (200)	650.00
752 (400)	440.00	762 (200)	500.00
753 (200)	635.00	763 (200)	550.00
754 (200)	190.00	764 (200)	600.00
755 (200)	190.00	765 (200)	950.00
756-65 set	4100.00	766 (225)	400.00
756 (200)	75.00	767 (225)	400.00
757 (200)	90.00	768 (150)	550.00
758 (200)	160.00	769 (120)	275.00
759 (200)	280.00	770 (120)	600.00
760 (200)	450.00	771 (200)	600.00

SCOTT NO.	DESCRIPTION	FIRST DAY COVERS SING	PL. BLK.	MINT SHEET	PLATE BLOCK F/NH	UNUSED F/NH	USED F

772, 778a

773, 778b

774

775, 778c

1935-36 COMMEMORATIVES

SCOTT NO.	DESCRIPTION	FIRST DAY COVERS SING	PL. BLK.	MINT SHEET	PLATE BLOCK F/NH	UNUSED F/NH	USED F
772/84	(772-77, 782-84) 9 varieties.......	....	....	....	....	3.60	1.75
772	3¢ Connecticut........	12.00	19.50	18.50 (50)	2.25	.40	.25
773	3¢ San Diego...	12.00	19.50	18.50 (50)	1.85	.40	.25
774	3¢ Boulder Dam..	12.00	19.50	25.00 (50)	(6)3.50	.50	.25
775	3¢ Michigan..........	12.00	19.50	22.00 (50)	3.00	.50	.25

776, 778d

777

1936 COMMEMORATIVE

SCOTT NO.	DESCRIPTION	FIRST DAY COVERS SING	PL. BLK.	MINT SHEET	PLATE BLOCK F/NH	UNUSED F/NH	USED F
776	3¢ Texas	15.00	25.00	22.00 (50)	2.55	.50	.25
777	3¢ Rhode Island	12.00	19.50	24.00 (50)	3.00	.50	.25

778

782

783

784

1936 THIRD INTERNATIONAL PHILATELIC EXHIBITION
"TIPEX" Imperforate Souvenir Sheet
Designs of 772, 773, 775, 776

SCOTT NO.	DESCRIPTION	FIRST DAY COVERS SING	PL. BLK.	MINT SHEET	PLATE BLOCK F/NH	UNUSED F/NH	USED F
778	red violet, sheet of 4	16.50	....	....	....	3.50	3.00
778a	3¢ Connecticut.	....	....	....	....	1.00	.75
778b	3¢ San Diego.	....	....	....	....	1.00	.75
778c	3¢ Michigan.	....	....	....	....	1.00	.75
778d	3¢ Texas.	....	....	....	....	1.00	.75
782	3¢ Arkansas Statehood ..	12.00	19.50	24.00 (50)	3.00	.55	.25
783	3¢ Oregon Territory	12.00	19.50	22.00 (50)	1.85	.45	.25
784	3¢ Suffrage for Women ..	12.00	19.50	31.00 (100)	1.75	.40	.25

FIRST DAY COVERS:

First Day Covers are envelopes cancelled on the "First Day of Issue" of the stamp used on an envelope. Usually they also contain a picture (cachet) on the left side designed to go with the theme of the stamp. From 1935 to 1949, prices listed are for cacheted, addressed covers. From 1950 to date, prices are for cacheted, unad-dressed covers. *While we list values for these, H.E. Harris no longer sells them.

SCOTT NO.	DESCRIPTION	FIRST DAY COVERS SING	PL. BLK.	MINT SHEET	PLATE BLOCK F/NH	UNUSED F/NH	USED F

785   786

787   788

789

1936-37 ARMY AND NAVY ISSUE

| 785-94 | 10 varieties, complete.. | 57.50 | ...... | ...... | 59.00 | 5.50 | 2.30 |

ARMY COMMEMORATIVES

785	1¢ green	6.00	12.00	15.00 (50)	1.60	.40	.25
786	2¢ carmine	6.00	12.00	17.00 (50)	1.75	.40	.25
787	3¢ purple	6.00	12.00	24.00 (50)	3.00	.60	.25
788	4¢ gray	6.00	14.50	40.00 (50)	12.00	.60	.30
789	5¢ ultramarine	7.00	14.50	43.00 (50)	13.50	.75	.35

790   791

792   793

794

NAVY COMMEMORATIVES

790	1¢ green	6.00	12.00	14.00 (50)	1.75	.30	.25
791	2¢ carmine	6.00	12.00	14.00 (50)	1.85	.35	.25
792	3¢ purple	6.00	12.00	22.00 (50)	2.50	.50	.25
793	4¢ gray	6.00	14.50	42.00 (50)	12.25	.75	.30
794	5¢ ultramarine	7.00	14.50	50.00 (50)	13.25	1.25	.35

SCOTT NO.	DESCRIPTION	FIRST DAY COVERS SING	PL. BLK.	MINT SHEET	PLATE BLOCK F/NH	UNUSED F/NH	USED F

795   796

1937 COMMEMORATIVES

795/802	(795-96, 798-802) 7 varieties	....	....	....	....	3.25	2.10
795	3¢ Northwest Ordinance	8.50	16.00	19.00 (50)	2.00	.45	.25
796	5¢ Virginia Dare	8.50	16.00	25.00 (48)	8.50(6)	.45	.30

797

1937 S.P.A. CONVENTION ISSUE
Design of 749 Imperforate Souvenir Sheet

| 797 | 10¢ blue green | 8.50 | .... | .... | .... | 1.00 | .80 |

798   799

800   801

802

798	3¢ Constitution	10.00	16.00	34.00 (50)	4.00	.75	.25
799	3¢ Hawaii	10.00	16.00	26.00 (50)	2.75	.50	.25
800	3¢ Alaska	10.00	16.00	23.00 (50)	2.75	.50	.25
801	3¢ Puerto Rico	10.00	16.00	29.00 (50)	3.00	.55	.25
802	3¢ Virgin Islands	10.00	16.00	29.00 (50)	3.00	.55	.25

1938 PRESIDENTIAL SERIES

In 1938 a new set of definitive stamps was issued honoring the first 29 presidents, Ben Franklin, Martha Washington, and the White House. These were regular issues that effectively replaced the previous definitive issues of the 1922-25 series.

The "Presidential Series" contained 32 denominations ranging from 1/2¢-$5.00. It is an interesting series because various printing methods were employed. The 1/2¢-50¢ values were printed in single colors on rotary presses using both normal and "electric eye" plates. The $1.00 to $5.00 values were printed in two colors on flat plate presses.

The $1.00 value was reprinted twice, once in 1951 on revenue paper watermarked "USIR" (#832b) and again in 1954. The 1954 issue was "dry printed" on thick white paper, with an experimental colorless gum (832c).

This series in regular and coil form was used for 16 years until it was replaced by the new definitive issues of 1954.

823   824   825   826

827   828   829

830   831

832   833   834

803

804, 839, 848   805, 840, 849   806, 841, 850

807, 842, 851   808, 843   809, 844   810, 845

811, 846   812   813   814

815, 847   816   817   818

819   820   821   822

SCOTT NO.	DESCRIPTION	FIRST DAY COVERS SING	FIRST DAY COVERS PL. BLK.	MINT SHEET	PLATE BLOCK F/NH	UNUSED F/NH	USED F
	1938 PRESIDENTIAL SERIES						
803-34	1/2¢-$5, 32 varieties, complete.........	520.00	....	....	900.00	200.00	17.50
803-31	1/2¢-50¢, 29 varieties	110.00	....	....	225.00	50.00	6.50
803	1/2¢ Franklin	2.50	5.50	17.00(100)	1.00	.25	.25
804	1¢ G. Washington . . .	2.50	5.50	22.00(100)	1.15	.25	.25
804b	1¢ booklet pane of 6 .	14.00	....	....	....	2.25	....
805	1-1/2¢ M. Washington	2.50	5.50	23.00(100)	1.15	.25	.25
806	2¢ J. Adams.	2.50	5.50	32.00(100)	1.50	.30	.25
806	E.E. Plate Block of 10				7.00	....	....
806b	2¢ booklet pane of 6 .	14.00	....	....	....	6.25	....
807	3¢ Jefferson.	2.50	5.50	30.00(100)	1.50	.30	.25
807	E.E. Plate Block of 10	....	....	....	125.00	....	....
807a	3¢ booklet pane of 6 .	14.00	....	....	....	9.25	....
808	4¢ Madison	2.50	5.50	90.00(100)	5.25	1.00	.25
809	4-1/2¢ White House..	2.50	5.50	43.00(100)	2.00	.50	.25
810	5¢ J. Monroe	2.50	5.50	52.00(100)	2.50	.50	.25
811	6¢ J.Q. Adams.	2.50	5.50	75.00(100)	3.50	.75	.25
812	7¢ A. Jackson	2.50	5.50	56.00(100)	3.00	.60	.25
813	8¢ Van Buren.	2.50	5.50	75.00(100)	3.75	.80	.25
814	9¢ Harrison	2.50	5.50	66.00(100)	4.00	.75	.25
815	10¢ Tyler	2.50	5.50	58.00(100)	3.00	.60	.25
816	11¢ Polk.	3.75	6.75	94.00(100)	5.00	1.00	.25
817	12¢ Taylor	3.75	6.75	130.00(100)	7.00	1.75	.25
818	13¢ Fillmore.	3.75	6.75	158.00(100)	8.50	1.75	.25
819	14¢ Pierce	3.75	6.75	143.00(100)	7.00	1.75	.25
820	15¢ Buchanan	3.75	6.75	124.00(100)	5.00	1.35	.25
821	16¢ Lincoln	4.50	8.25	194.00(100)	8.75	2.00	.55
822	17¢ Johnson	4.50	8.25	158.00(100)	7.75	2.00	.25
823	18¢ Grant.	4.50	8.25	325.00(100)	17.00	4.00	.25
824	19¢ Hayes	4.50	8.25	214.00(100)	9.00	2.00	.75
825	20¢ Garfield.	4.75	11.25	228.00(100)	9.75	2.25	.25
826	21¢ Arthur	5.25	11.25	215.00(100)	12.00	2.75	.25
827	22¢ Cleveland	5.25	11.25	196.00(100)	12.00	2.00	.75
828	24¢ B. Harrison	6.25	11.25	440.00(100)	20.00	4.00	.30
829	25¢ McKinley.	6.25	13.75	173.00(100)	9.50	1.75	.25
830	30¢ T. Roosevelt	8.50	13.75	670.00(100)	26.00	6.50	.25
831	50¢ Taft	15.00	30.00	895.00(100)	36.00	8.00	.25
	Flat Plate Printing Perf. 11						
832	$1 Wilson.	70.00	150.00	1225.00(100)	55.00	12.00	.25
832	$1 center line block . .	....	....	....	55.00	....	....
832	$1 arrow block"	....	....	....	50.00	....	....
832b	$1 Watermarked "USIR"	....	....	....	....	300.00	70.00
832c	$1 dry print thick paper (1954)	35.00	75.00	1100.00(100)	40.00	8.50	.25
833	$2 Harding.	135.00	275.00	....	140.00	25.00	5.50
833	$2 center line block . .	....	....	....	130.00	....	....
833	$2 arrow block	....	....	....	130.00	....	....
834	$5 Coolidge	225.00	400.00	....	600.00	125.00	5.25
834	$5 center line block . .	....	....	....	600.00	....	....
834	$5 arrow block	....	....	....	625.00	....	....

SCOTT NO.	DESCRIPTION	FIRST DAY COVERS SING	PL. BLK.	MINT SHEET	PLATE BLOCK F/NH	UNUSED F/NH	USED F

835   836

837   838

1938-39 COMMEMORATIVES

SCOTT NO.	DESCRIPTION	SING	PL. BLK.	MINT SHEET	PLATE BLOCK F/NH	UNUSED F/NH	USED F
835/58	(835-38, 852-58) 11 varieties, complete	....	....	....	....	7.00	2.15
835	3¢ Ratification	10.00	14.00	35.00(50)	6.00	.70	.25
836	3¢ Swedes-Finns	10.00	14.00	20.00(48)	(6)4.00	.40	.25
837	3¢ Northwest Territory	10.00	14.00	40.00(100)	9.00	.40	.25
838	3¢ Iowa Territory	10.00	14.00	40.00(50)	8.50	.70	.25

1939 PRESIDENTIALS ROTARY PRESS COIL

SCOTT NO.	DESCRIPTION	SING	LINE PAIR		LINE PAIR	UNUSED F/NH	USED F
839-51	13 varieties, complete	67.50	120.00	....	148.50	36.75	5.30

Perforated 10 Vertically

839	1¢ G. Washington	5.00	8.50	....	1.75	.40	.25
840	1-1/2¢ M. Washington	5.00	8.50	....	1.75	.40	.25
841	2¢ J. Adams	5.00	8.50	....	1.85	.45	.25
842	3¢ T. Jefferson	5.00	8.50	....	2.00	.70	.25
843	4¢ J. Madison	5.75	10.50	....	35.00	8.00	.70
844	4-1/2¢ White House	5.75	10.50	....	6.25	.75	.50
845	5¢ J. Monroe	5.75	11.00	....	32.00	5.75	.50
846	6¢ J.Q. Adams	5.75	11.00	....	8.25	1.50	.40
847	10¢ J. Tyler	8.50	16.00	....	56.00	12.00	1.00

Perforated 10 Horizontally

848	1¢ G. Washington	5.00	8.50	....	3.25	1.10	.30
849	1-1/2¢ M. Washington	5.00	8.50	....	5.00	1.50	.70
850	2¢ J. Adams	5.00	8.50	....	9.00	3.00	.80
851	3¢ T. Jefferson	5.00	8.50	....	8.75	3.00	.80

852   853   854

855   856

1939 COMMEMORATIVES

852	3¢ Golden Gate	12.00	19.50	20.00(50)	2.00	.40	.25
853	3¢ World's Fair	12.00	19.50	20.00(50)	2.50	.40	.25
854	3¢ Inauguration	12.00	19.50	40.00(50)	(6)7.00	.75	.25
855	3¢ Baseball	37.50	60.00	110.00(50)	12.00	2.00	.30
856	3¢ Panama Canal	17.50	25.00	25.00(50)	(6)5.00	.60	.25

857   858

1939 COMMEMORATIVES

857	3¢ Printing	12.00	19.50	20.00(50)	2.35	.40	.25
858	3¢ Four States	10.00	14.50	30.00(50)	3.75	.75	.25

859   860   861

862   863

1940 FAMOUS AMERICANS ISSUES

859-93	35 varieties, complete	130.00	....	....	475.00	43.00	19.95

American Authors

859	1¢ Washington Irving	3.00	4.00	20.00(70)	1.75	.35	.25
860	2¢ James F. Cooper	3.00	4.00	25.00(70)	2.00	.35	.25
861	3¢ Ralph W. Emerson	3.00	4.00	24.00(70)	2.00	.35	.25
862	5¢ Louisa May Alcott	4.00	6.00	45.00(70)	13.00	.60	.35
863	10¢ Samuel L. Clemens	7.50	13.50	180.00(70)	49.50	2.25	1.75

864   865   866

867   868

American Poets

864	1¢ Henry W. Longfellow	3.00	4.00	26.00(70)	3.50	.35	.25
865	2¢ John Whittier	3.00	4.00	24.00(70)	3.50	.35	.25
866	3¢ James Lowell	3.00	4.00	29.00(70)	4.25	.35	.25
867	5¢ Walt Whitman	4.00	6.00	60.00(70)	15.00	.80	.35
868	10¢ James Riley	7.50	11.50	195.00(70)	42.00	2.75	1.75

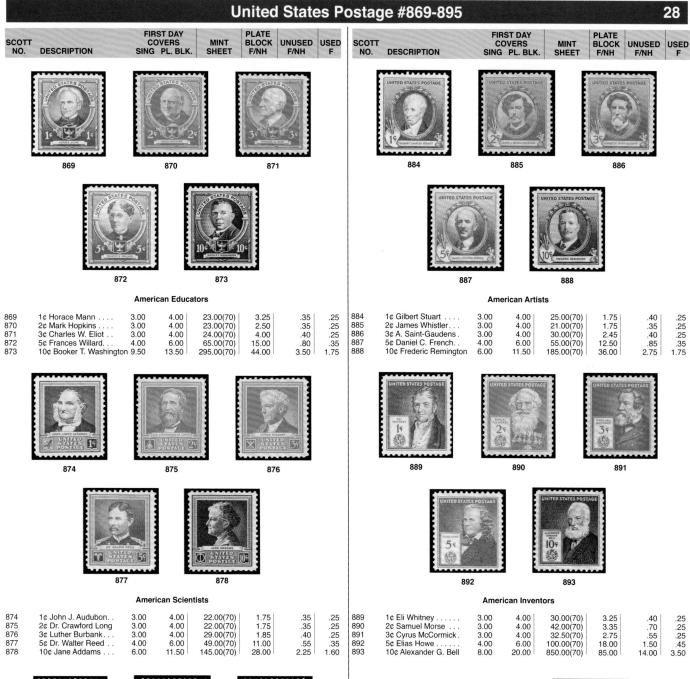

SCOTT NO.	DESCRIPTION	FIRST DAY COVERS SING	PL. BLK.	MINT SHEET	PLATE BLOCK F/NH	UNUSED F/NH	USED F

American Educators

869	1¢ Horace Mann	3.00	4.00	23.00(70)	3.25	.35	.25
870	2¢ Mark Hopkins	3.00	4.00	23.00(70)	2.50	.35	.25
871	3¢ Charles W. Eliot ..	3.00	4.00	24.00(70)	4.00	.40	.25
872	5¢ Frances Willard. . .	4.00	6.00	65.00(70)	15.00	.80	.35
873	10¢ Booker T. Washington	9.50	13.50	295.00(70)	44.00	3.50	1.75

American Scientists

874	1¢ John J. Audubon..	3.00	4.00	22.00(70)	1.75	.35	.25
875	2¢ Dr. Crawford Long	3.00	4.00	22.00(70)	1.75	.35	.25
876	3¢ Luther Burbank...	3.00	4.00	29.00(70)	1.85	.40	.25
877	5¢ Dr. Walter Reed ..	4.00	6.00	49.00(70)	11.00	.55	.35
878	10¢ Jane Addams ...	6.00	11.50	145.00(70)	28.00	2.25	1.60

American Composers

879	1¢ Stephen Foster...	3.00	4.00	22.00(70)	1.75	.35	.25
880	2¢ John Philip Sousa.	3.00	4.00	22.00(70)	1.75	.35	.25
881	3¢ Victor Herbert	3.00	4.00	26.00(70)	1.85	.40	.25
882	5¢ Edward A. MacDowell	4.00	6.00	70.00(70)	14.00	.75	.35
883	10¢ Ethelbert Nevin..	6.00	11.50	360.00(70)	50.00	5.50	2.00

American Artists

884	1¢ Gilbert Stuart	3.00	4.00	25.00(70)	1.75	.40	.25
885	2¢ James Whistler...	3.00	4.00	21.00(70)	1.75	.35	.25
886	3¢ A. Saint-Gaudens .	3.00	4.00	30.00(70)	2.45	.40	.25
887	5¢ Daniel C. French..	4.00	6.00	55.00(70)	12.50	.85	.35
888	10¢ Frederic Remington	6.00	11.50	185.00(70)	36.00	2.75	1.75

American Inventors

889	1¢ Eli Whitney	3.00	4.00	30.00(70)	3.25	.40	.25
890	2¢ Samuel Morse ...	3.00	4.00	42.00(70)	3.35	.70	.25
891	3¢ Cyrus McCormick .	3.00	4.00	32.50(70)	2.75	.55	.25
892	5¢ Elias Howe	4.00	6.00	100.00(70)	18.00	1.50	.45
893	10¢ Alexander G. Bell	8.00	20.00	850.00(70)	85.00	14.00	3.50

1940 COMMEMORATIVES

894-902	9 varieties, complete	....	....	....	....	3.80	1.80
894	3¢ Pony Express	7.00	11.00	30.00(50)	4.75	.70	.25
895	3¢ Pan Am Union. ...	5.00	11.00	22.00(50)	4.50	.45	.25

MINT SHEETS: From 1935 to date, we list prices for standard size Mint Sheets in Fine, Never Hinged condition. The number of stamps in each sheet is noted in ( ).

FAMOUS AMERICANS: Later additions to the Famous American series include #945 Edison, #953 Carver, #960 White, #965 Stone, #975 Rogers, #980 Harris, #986 Poe, and #988 Gompers.

SCOTT NO.	DESCRIPTION	FIRST DAY COVERS SING	PL. BLK.	MINT SHEET	PLATE BLOCK F/NH	UNUSED F/NH	USED F

896

897

898

1940 COMMEMORATIVES

896	3¢ Idaho Statehood . .	6.00	11.00	29.00(50)	3.50	.60	.25
897	3¢ Wyoming Statehood	6.00	11.00	28.00(50)	3.25	.60	.25
898	3¢ Coronado Expedition	6.00	11.00	32.00(52)	3.75	.75	.25

899   900   901   902

NATIONAL DEFENSE ISSUE

899	1¢ Liberty	4.00	7.00	20.00(100)	1.25	.30	.25
900	2¢ Gun	4.00	7.00	20.00(100)	1.25	.30	.25
901	3¢ Torch	4.00	7.00	24.00(100)	1.50	.30	.25
902	3¢ Emancipation	9.00	11.00	27.50(50)	4.75	.60	.35

903

1941-43 COMMEMORATIVES

| 903-08 | 3¢-5¢ 6 varieties . . . . | . . . . | . . . . | . . . . | . . . . | 4.75 | 1.00 |

1941 COMMEMORATIVES

| 903 | 3¢ Vermont . . . . | 7.00 | 10.75 | 30.00(50) | 3.00 | .55 | .25 |

904

905

906

1942 COMMEMORATIVES

904	3¢ Kentucky	5.00	10.75	22.00(50)	2.50	.50	.25
905	3¢ Win The War	4.50	7.50	52.00(100)	2.25	.55	.25
906	5¢ China Resistance .	12.00	20.00	400.00(50)	36.00	3.50	.45

907

908

1943 COMMEMORATIVES

| 907 | 2¢ Allied Nations . . . . | 6.00 | 7.50 | 16.00(100) | 1.25 | .30 | .25 |
| 908 | 1¢ Four Freedoms . . . | 6.00 | 10.50 | 15.00(100) | 1.25 | .30 | .25 |

909   910

911   912

913   914

915   916

917   918

919   920

921

1943-44 OVERRUN COUNTRIES SERIES

| 909-21 | 13 varieties, complete | 50.00 | . . . . | . . . . | 75.00 | 6.50 | 3.50 |

909	5¢ Poland	5.00	10.00	24.00(50)	9.00	.40	.25
910	5¢ Czechoslovakia . .	5.00	10.00	20.00(50)	4.00	.40	.25
911	5¢ Norway	5.00	10.00	19.00(50)	2.75	.40	.25
912	5¢ Luxembourg	5.00	10.00	18.00(50)	2.00	.40	.25
913	5¢ Netherlands	5.00	10.00	18.00(50)	2.00	.40	.25
914	5¢ Belgium	5.00	10.00	18.00(50)	2.00	.40	.25
915	5¢ France	5.00	10.00	20.00(50)	2.00	.75	.25
916	5¢ Greece	5.00	10.00	47.00(50)	16.00	.75	.40
917	5¢ Yugoslavia	5.00	10.00	27.50(50)	8.00	.60	.30
918	5¢ Albania	5.00	10.00	25.00(50)	8.00	.60	.30
919	5¢ Austria	5.00	10.00	24.00(50)	6.00	.60	.30
920	5¢ Denmark	5.00	10.00	34.00(50)	8.00	.75	.30
921	5¢ Korea (1944)	5.00	10.00	30.00(50)	8.55	.60	.30

SCOTT NO.	DESCRIPTION	FIRST DAY COVERS SING	PL. BLK.	MINT SHEET	PLATE BLOCK F/NH	UNUSED F/NH	USED F

922   923

924   925

926   927

1944 COMMEMORATIVES

922-26	5 varieties........	......	......	......	......	1.90	1.00
922	3¢ Railroad	9.00	12.00	32.00(50)	3.50	.55	.25
923	3¢ Steamship.......	9.00	12.00	20.00(50)	2.50	.40	.25
924	3¢ Telegraph	9.00	12.00	18.00(50)	2.25	.40	.25
925	3¢ Corregidor.......	9.00	12.00	17.50(50)	2.50	.40	.25
926	3¢ Motion Picture....	9.00	12.00	15.00(50)	2.00	.40	.25

928

929

1945-46 COMMEMORATIVES

927-38	1¢-5¢ (12 varieties, complete)	......	......	......	......	4.00	2.50
927	3¢ Florida.........	10.00	15.00	17.00(50)	2.00	.40	.25
928	5¢ Peace Conference	10.00	15.00	16.00(50)	1.75	.35	.25
929	3¢ Iwo Jima	17.00	20.00	29.00(50)	3.50	.60	.25

930   931

932   933

930	1¢ FDR & Hyde Park	4.00	6.00	7.50(50)	1.10	.30	.25
931	2¢ FDR & "Little White House"..	4.00	6.00	8.50(50)	1.10	.30	.25
932	3¢ FDR & White House	4.00	6.00	13.00(50)	1.50	.30	.25
933	5¢ FDR & Globe (1946)	4.00	6.00	17.00(50)	1.75	.35	.25

934   935

936   937   938

934	3¢ Army...........	10.00	14.00	18.50(50)	2.00	.35	.25
935	3¢ Navy...........	10.00	14.00	18.50(50)	2.00	.35	.25
936	3¢ Coast Guard....	10.00	14.00	14.00(50)	1.75	.35	.25
937	3¢ Al Smith	10.00	14.00	27.00(100)	1.75	.35	.25
938	3¢ Texas Statehood..	10.00	14.00	18.00(50)	2.25	.50	.25

939   940

941   942

943   944

1946-47 COMMEMORATIVES

939/52	(939-47, 949-52) 13 varieties........	......	......	......	......	4.50	2.50
939	3¢ Merchant Marine..	10.00	12.00	15.00(50)	1.50	.35	.25
940	3¢ Honorable Discharge	10.00	12.00	26.00(100)	1.50	.35	.25
941	3¢ Tennessee Statehood	3.00	5.00	15.00(50)	1.50	.35	.25
942	3¢ Iowa Statehood...	3.00	5.00	15.00(50)	1.50	.40	.25
943	3¢ Smithsonian Institute	3.00	5.00	15.00(50)	1.50	.40	.25
944	3¢ Kearny Expedition	3.00	5.00	15.00(50)	1.50	.40	.25

945   946   947

1947 COMMEMORATIVES

945	3¢ Thomas A. Edison	3.00	5.00	19.00(70)	1.40	.30	.25
946	3¢ Joseph Pulitzer...	3.00	5.00	14.00(50)	1.40	.30	.25
947	3¢ Stamp Centenary .	3.00	5.00	15.00(50)	1.50	.30	.25

NEVER HINGED: From 1888 to 1935, Unused OG or Unused prices are for stamps with original gum that have been hinged. If you desire Never Hinged stamps, refer to the NH listings.

SCOTT NO.	DESCRIPTION	FIRST DAY COVERS SING	FIRST DAY COVERS PL. BLK.	MINT SHEET	PLATE BLOCK F/NH	UNUSED F/NH	USED F

"CIPEX" SOUVENIR SHEET

948	5¢ & 10¢ Sheet of 2. .	4.00	....	....	....	1.25	1.00
948a	5¢ blue, single stamp	....	....	....	....	.65	.50
948b	10¢ brown orange, single stamp	....	....	....	....	.65	.50

949   **950**

951   **952**   **953**

949	3¢ Doctors	8.00	12.00	15.50(50)	1.50	.35	.25
950	3¢ Utah Centennial . .	3.00	5.00	18.00(50)	1.85	.50	.25
951	3¢ "Constitution"	8.00	12.00	13.50(50)	1.50	.40	.25
952	3¢ Everglades National Park.	4.00	6.00	15.50(50)	1.85	.45	.25

954   **955**

956   **957**

1948 COMMEMORATIVES

953-80	3¢-5¢ (28 varieties, complete)	....	....	....	....	9.25	5.50
953	3¢ George Washington Carver	6.00	10.00	19.00(70)	1.60	.35	.25
954	3¢ Gold Rush.	2.40	5.00	16.00(50)	1.60	.35	.25
955	3¢ Mississippi Territory	2.40	5.00	16.00(50)	1.60	.35	.25
956	3¢ Chaplains	3.00	5.00	16.00(50)	1.60	.35	.25
957	3¢ Wisconsin Statehood	2.40	5.00	16.00(50)	1.75	.45	.25

958   **959**

960   **961**

962   **963**

958	5¢ Swedish Pioneer. .	2.40	5.00	16.00(50)	1.80	.35	.25
959	3¢ Women's Progress	2.40	5.00	15.00(50)	1.25	.40	.25
960	3¢ William White	2.40	5.00	18.00(70)	1.50	.35	.25
961	3¢ U.S.-Canada Friendship	2.40	5.00	13.00(50)	1.50	.35	.25
962	3¢ Francis S. Key . . .	2.40	5.00	13.00(50)	1.50	.35	.25
963	3¢ Salute to Youth . . .	2.40	5.00	13.00(50)	1.50	.35	.25

964   **965**   **966**

967   **968**

969   **970**

964	3¢ Oregon Territory . .	2.40	5.00	18.00(50)	2.00	.50	.25
965	3¢ Harlan Stone.	2.40	5.00	18.00(70)	1.50	.35	.25
966	3¢ Mt. Palomar	3.00	5.00	19.00(70)	1.75	.35	.25
967	3¢ Clara Barton	3.00	5.00	13.00(50)	1.60	.35	.25
968	3¢ Poultry	2.40	5.00	16.00(50)	1.75	.35	.25
969	3¢ Gold Star Mothers	2.40	5.00	12.50(50)	1.60	.35	.25
970	3¢ Fort Kearny.	2.40	5.00	17.00(50)	2.00	.45	.25

PLATE BLOCKS: are portions of a sheet of stamps adjacent to the number(s) indicating the printing plate number used to produce that sheet. Flat plate issues are usually collected in plate blocks of six (number opposite middle stamp) while rotary issues are normally corner blocks of four.

SCOTT NO.	DESCRIPTION	FIRST DAY COVERS SING	PL. BLK.	MINT SHEET	PLATE BLOCK F/NH	UNUSED F/NH	USED F

971

972

973

974

971	3¢ Volunteer Firemen	5.00	7.00	14.00(50)	1.50	.35	.25
972	3¢ Indian Centennial .	2.40	5.00	14.00(50)	1.50	.35	.25
973	3¢ Rough Riders	2.40	5.00	16.00(50)	1.50	.35	.25
974	3¢ Juliette Low.	7.00	10.00	14.00(50)	1.70	.35	.25

975

976

977

978

979

980

975	3¢ Will Rogers	2.40	5.00	20.00(50)	1.70	.40	.25
976	3¢ Fort Bliss.	2.40	5.00	22.00(50)	1.70	.40	.25
977	3¢ Moina Michael . . .	2.40	5.00	13.00(50)	1.50	.35	.25
978	3¢ Gettysburg Address	3.00	5.00	16.00(50)	1.75	.35	.25
979	3¢ American Turners .	2.40	5.00	13.00(50)	1.40	.35	.25
980	3¢ Joel C. Harris	2.40	5.00	19.00(70)	1.40	.35	.25

981

982

983

984

1949-50 COMMEMORATIVES

981-97	17 varieties, complete	. . . .	. . . .	. . . .	. . . .	5.70	3.40
981	3¢ Minnesota Territory	2.40	4.25	17.00(50)	1.60	.40	.25
982	3¢ Washington & Lee University.	2.40	4.25	12.50(50)	1.35	.35	.25
983	3¢ Puerto Rico.	3.00	4.25	18.00(50)	2.00	.45	.25
984	3¢ Annapolis	3.00	4.25	12.50(50)	1.40	.35	.25

985

986

| 985 | 3¢ G.A.R. . . . . | 3.00 | 4.25 | 18.00(50) | 1.65 | .35 | .25 |
| 986 | 3¢ Edgar A. Poe . . . . | 3.00 | 4.25 | 20.00(70) | 1.85 | .45 | .25 |

987

988

989

1950 COMMEMORATIVES

987	3¢ Bankers Association	2.40	4.25	14.00(50)	1.50	.35	.25
988	3¢ Samuel Gompers .	2.40	4.25	18.00(70)	1.50	.35	.25
989	3¢ Statue of Freedom	2.40	4.25	15.00(50)	1.50	.35	.25

990

991

992

993

994

995

996

997

990	3¢ Executive Mansion	2.40	4.25	18.00(50)	1.75	.50	.25
991	3¢ Supreme Court . . .	2.40	4.25	16.00(50)	1.75	.35	.25
992	3¢ United States Capitol	2.40	4.25	16.00(50)	1.75	.35	.25
993	3¢ Railroad	4.00	5.25	16.00(50)	1.75	.35	.25
994	3¢ Kansas City	2.40	4.25	16.00(50)	1.60	.35	.25
995	3¢ Boy Scouts	7.00	10.00	16.00(50)	1.60	.35	.25
996	3¢ Indiana Territory . .	2.40	4.25	18.00(50)	2.00	.50	.25
997	3¢ California Statehood	2.40	4.25	18.00(50)	2.00	.50	.25

BUY COMPLETE SETS AND SAVE!

SCOTT NO.	DESCRIPTION	FIRST DAY COVERS SING	PL. BLK.	MINT SHEET	PLATE BLOCK F/NH	UNUSED F/NH	USED F

998

999

1000

1001

1002

1003

1951-52 COMMEMORATIVES

998-1016 19 varieties, complete	....	....	....	....	6.40	3.95	

Scott	Description	Sing	Pl. Blk.	Mint Sheet	Plate Block	Unused	Used
998	3¢ Confederate Veterans	3.00	4.25	21.00(50)	2.25	.40	.25
999	3¢ Nevada Settlement	2.00	4.25	15.00(50)	1.75	.35	.25
1000	3¢ Landing of Cadillac	2.00	4.25	15.00(50)	1.50	.35	.25
1001	3¢ Colorado Statehood	2.00	4.25	17.00(50)	1.50	.35	.25
1002	3¢ Chemical Society	2.00	4.25	16.00(50)	1.50	.35	.25
1003	3¢ Battle of Brooklyn	2.00	4.25	12.50(50)	1.50	.35	.25

1004

1005

1006

1007

1008

1009

1010

1952 COMMEMORATIVES

Scott	Description	Sing	Pl. Blk.	Mint Sheet	Plate Block	Unused	Used
1004	3¢ Betsy Ross	2.50	5.50	13.50(50)	1.40	.40	.25
1005	3¢ 4-H Club	6.00	10.00	14.00(50)	1.40	.40	.25
1006	3¢ B. & O. Railroad	4.00	6.50	17.50(50)	2.25	.40	.25
1007	3¢ AAA	2.00	4.25	14.00(50)	1.60	.40	.25
1008	3¢ NATO	2.00	4.25	24.00(100)	1.60	.40	.25
1009	3¢ Grand Coulee Dam	2.00	4.25	18.00(50)	1.75	.40	.25
1010	3¢ Lafayette	2.00	4.25	13.50(50)	1.40	.40	.25

1011

1012

1013

1014

1015

1016

Scott	Description	Sing	Pl. Blk.	Mint Sheet	Plate Block	Unused	Used
1011	3¢ Mt. Rushmore	2.00	4.25	19.00(50)	2.25	.50	.25
1012	3¢ Civil Engineers	2.00	4.25	12.50(50)	1.40	.35	.25
1013	3¢ Service Women	2.25	4.25	13.50(50)	1.40	.35	.25
1014	3¢ Gutenburg Press	2.00	4.25	13.50(50)	1.40	.35	.25
1015	3¢ Newspaper Boys	2.00	4.25	12.50(50)	1.40	.35	.25
1016	3¢ Red Cross	3.00	6.25	12.50(50)	1.40	.35	.25

1017

1018

1019

1020

1021

1022

1953-54 COMMEMORATIVES

1017/63 (1017-29, 1060-63) 17 varieties, complete	....	....	....	....	5.55	3.55	

Scott	Description	Sing	Pl. Blk.	Mint Sheet	Plate Block	Unused	Used
1017	3¢ National Guard	2.00	4.25	12.50(50)	1.40	.35	.25
1018	3¢ Ohio Statehood	2.00	4.25	17.50(70)	1.40	.35	.25
1019	3¢ Washington Territory	2.00	4.25	18.00(50)	2.25	.50	.25
1020	3¢ Louisiana Purchase	4.00	6.00	13.50(50)	1.85	.40	.25
1021	5¢ Opening of Japan	3.00	4.25	14.00(50)	1.50	.40	.25
1022	3¢ American Bar Association	5.00	6.25	14.00(50)	1.50	.40	.25

SCOTT NO.	DESCRIPTION	FIRST DAY COVERS SING	FIRST DAY COVERS PL. BLK.	MINT SHEET	PLATE BLOCK F/NH	UNUSED F/NH	USED F
1023	3¢ Sagamore Hill	2.00	4.25	12.50(50)	1.40	.35	.25
1024	3¢ Future Farmers. . .	2.00	4.25	12.50(50)	1.40	.35	.25
1025	3¢ Trucking Industry .	2.50	4.50	12.50(50)	1.40	.35	.25
1026	3¢ Gen. George S. Patton	3.00	4.75	12.50(50)	1.40	.35	.25
1027	3¢ New York City	2.00	4.25	12.50(50)	1.40	.35	.25
1028	3¢ Gadsden Purchase	2.00	4.25	15.00(50)	1.60	.35	.25

1954 COMMEMORATIVE

1029	3¢ Columbia University	2.00	4.25	12.50(50)	1.40	.35	.20

1954-68 LIBERTY SERIES

SCOTT NO.	DESCRIPTION	FIRST DAY COVERS SING	FIRST DAY COVERS PL. BLK.	MINT SHEET	PLATE BLOCK F/NH	UNUSED F/NH	USED F
1030-53	1/2¢-$5, 27 varieties, complete.	110.00	235.00	. . . .	385.00	100.00	12.50
1030-51	1/2¢-50¢, 25 varieties	55.00	115.00	. . . .	85.00	19.00	5.50
1030	1/2¢ Benjamin Franklin (1955)	2.00	4.25	13.00(100)	1.00	.25	.25
1031	1¢ George Washington	2.00	4.25	20.00(100)	1.25	.25	.25
1031A	1-1/4¢ Palace of Governors (1960) . . .	2.00	4.25	16.00(100)	1.25	.25	.25
1032	1-1/2¢ Mount Vernon .	2.00	4.25	20.00(100)	2.50	.25	.25
1033	2¢ Thomas Jefferson .	2.00	4.25	19.00(100)	1.25	.25	.25
1034	2-1/2¢ Bunker Hill (1959)	2.00	4.25	18.00(100)	1.25	.25	.25
1035	3¢ Statue of Liberty . .	2.00	4.25	23.00(100)	1.25	.35	.25
1035a	3¢ booklet pane of 6 .	3.50	. . . .	. . . .	. . . .	6.00	. . . .
1036	4¢ Abraham Lincoln . .	2.00	4.25	25.00(100)	1.50	.25	.25
1036a	4¢ booklet pane of 6 .	3.00	. . . .	. . . .	. . . .	3.75	. . . .
1037	4-1/2¢ Hermitage (1959)	2.00	4.25	30.00(100)	2.00	.40	.25
1038	5¢ James Monroe . . .	2.00	4.25	30.00(100)	2.00	.40	.25
1039	6¢ T. Roosevelt (1955)	2.00	4.25	40.00(100)	2.25	.60	.25
1040	7¢ Woodrow Wilson (1956)	2.00	4.25	48.00(100)	2.75	.55	.25
1041	8¢ Statue of Liberty (flat plate).	2.00	4.25	30.00(100)	2.50	.40	.25
1041B	8¢ Statue of Liberty . .	2.00	4.25	120.00(100)	6.00	.70	.25
1042	8¢ Liberty re-engraved (1958)	2.00	4.25	35.00(100)	2.00	.45	.25
1043	9¢ Alamo (1956)	2.25	5.00	52.00(100)	3.00	.65	.25
1044	10¢ Independence Hall (1956)	2.25	5.00	52.00(100)	3.00	.60	.25
1044A	11¢ Statue of Liberty (1961)	2.25	5.00	52.00(100)	3.50	.75	.25
1045	12¢ Benjamin Harrison (1959)	2.25	5.00	88.00(100)	4.00	.85	.25
1046	15¢ John Jay (1958) .	2.50	5.25	90.00(100)	5.50	1.25	.25
1047	20¢ Monticello (1956)	2.50	5.25	125.00(100)	6.50	1.30	.25
1048	25¢ Paul Revere (1958)	2.50	5.25	200.00(100)	10.00	2.50	.25
1049	30¢ Robert E. Lee (1955)	3.75	6.00	243.00(100)	17.00	3.00	.25
1050	40¢ John Marshall (1955)	3.75	7.00	280.00(100)	16.00	3.50	.25
1051	50¢ Susan B. Anthony (1955)	5.50	8.50	280.00(100)	15.00	3.00	.25
1052	$1 Patrick Henry (1955)	9.25	17.50	615.00(100)	35.50	7.00	.25
1053	$5 Alexander Hamilton (1956)	50.00	110.00	. . . .	350.00	85.00	10.00

1954-65 COIL STAMPS
Perf. 10 Vertically or Horizontally

SCOTT NO.	DESCRIPTION	FIRST DAY COVERS SING	FIRST DAY COVERS LINE PAIR	MINT SHEET	PLATE BLOCK LINE PAIR	UNUSED F/NH	USED F
1054-59A	1¢-25¢ (8 varieties, complete).	16.00	29.75	. . . .	32.00	4.65	2.75
1054	1¢ George Washington	2.00	3.75	. . . .	1.25	.30	.25
1054A	1-1/4¢ Palace of Governors(1960)	2.00	3.75	. . . .	3.00	.30	.25
1055	2¢ Thomas Jefferson(1957)	2.00	3.75	. . . .	2.75	.50	.25
1056	2-1/2¢ Bunker Hill Mon. (1959)	2.00	3.75	. . . .	5.00	.45	.30
1057	3¢ Statue of Liberty(1956)	2.00	3.75	. . . .	.85	.25	.25
1058	4¢ Abraham Lincoln (1958)	2.00	3.75	. . . .	1.00	.35	.25
1059	4-1/2¢ Hermitage (1959)	2.00	3.75	. . . .	19.00	2.00	2.00
1059A	25¢ Paul Revere (1965)	2.50	5.00	. . . .	3.50	1.25	.25

NOTE: Pairs of the above can be priced at two times the single price.

SCOTT NO.	DESCRIPTION	FIRST DAY COVERS SING	PL. BLK.	MINT SHEET	PLATE BLOCK F/NH	UNUSED F/NH	USED F

1060

1061

1062

1063

1954 COMMEMORATIVES

1060	3¢ Nebraska Territory	2.00	4.25	13.00(50)	1.50	.35	.25
1061	3¢ Kansas Territory . .	2.00	4.25	14.00(50)	1.50	.50	.25
1062	3¢ George Eastman .	2.00	4.25	17.00(70)	1.50	.35	.25
1063	3¢ Lewis & Clark	4.00	6.00	16.00(50)	2.25	.65	.25

1064

1065

1066

1067

1068

1069

1955 COMMEMORATIVES

1064-72	3¢-8¢ (9 varieties, complete)	....	....	....	....	2.95	1.95
1064	3¢ Pennsylvania Academy	2.00	4.25	16.00(50)	1.50	.40	.25
1065	3¢ Land Grant Colleges	2.50	4.50	17.00(50)	1.85	.50	.25
1066	8¢ Rotary International	5.00	7.00	20.00(50)	2.00	.55	.25
1067	3¢ Armed Forces Reserve	2.00	4.25	13.00(50)	1.55	.35	.25
1068	3¢ Great Stone Face .	2.00	4.25	19.00(50)	1.75	.45	.25
1069	3¢ Soo Locks.	2.00	4.25	13.00(50)	1.35	.50	.25

1070

1071

1072

1070	3¢ Atoms for Peace . .	2.00	4.25	12.50(50)	1.35	.35	.25
1071	3¢ Fort Ticonderoga .	2.00	4.25	14.00(50)	1.50	.40	.25
1072	3¢ Andrew Mellon . . .	2.00	4.25	19.00(70)	1.75	.40	.25

SCOTT NO.	DESCRIPTION	FIRST DAY COVERS SING	PL. BLK.	MINT SHEET	PLATE BLOCK F/NH	UNUSED F/NH	USED F

1073

1074

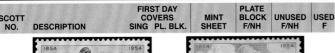

1075

1956 COMMEMORATIVES

1073/85	(1073-74, 1076-85) 12 varieties.	....	....	....	....	4.00	2.00
1073	3¢ Benjamin Franklin.	2.00	4.25	14.00(50)	1.40	.35	.25
1074	3¢ Booker T. Washington	3.50	5.50	14.00(50)	1.40	.35	.25
1075	3¢ & 8¢ FIPEX Sheet of 2	6.00	....	....	....	3.25	3.25
1075a	3¢ deep violet, single.	....	....	....	....	1.25	1.05
1075b	8¢ violet blue & carmine, single	....	....	....	....	1.75	1.25

1076

1077

1078

1079

1076	3¢ FIPEX	2.00	4.25	12.50(50)	1.30	.35	.25
1077	3¢ Wild Turkey.	2.75	4.50	14.00(50)	1.55	.35	.25
1078	3¢ Antelope	2.75	4.50	14.00(50)	1.55	.35	.25
1079	3¢ Salmon	2.75	4.50	14.00(50)	1.55	.35	.25

PLATE BLOCKS: are portions of a sheet of stamps adjacent to the number(s) indicating the printing plate number used to produce that sheet. Flat plate issues are usually collected in plate blocks of six (number opposite middle stamp) while rotary issues are normally corner blocks of four.

SCOTT NO.	DESCRIPTION	FIRST DAY COVERS SING	FIRST DAY COVERS PL. BLK.	MINT SHEET	PLATE BLOCK F/NH	UNUSED F/NH	USED F

1080   **1081**   **1082**

1080	3¢ Pure Food & Drug Act	2.00	4.25	13.50(50)	1.35	.35	.25
1081	3¢ "Wheatland"	2.00	4.25	13.50(50)	1.35	.35	.25
1082	3¢ Labor Day.	2.00	4.25	13.50(50)	1.35	.35	.25

1083

1084

1085

1083	3¢ Nassau Hall	2.00	4.25	13.50(50)	1.35	.35	.25
1084	3¢ Devil's Tower	2.00	4.25	16.00(50)	1.75	.50	.25
1085	3¢ Children of the World	2.00	4.25	13.00(50)	1.50	.35	.25

1086

1087

1088

1089

1090

1091

1957 COMMEMORATIVES

1086-99	14 varieties, complete	. . . .	. . . .	. . . .	. . . .	4.35	3.00
1086	3¢ Alexander Hamilton	2.00	4.25	17.00(50)	1.85	.45	.25
1087	3¢ Polio	2.25	4.50	13.00(50)	1.35	.35	.25
1088	3¢ Coast & Geodetic Survey	2.00	4.25	13.00(50)	1.35	.35	.25
1089	3¢ Architects	2.00	4.25	13.00(50)	1.35	.35	.25
1090	3¢ Steel Industry	2.00	4.25	13.00(50)	1.35	.35	.25
1091	3¢ International Naval Review.	2.00	4.25	13.00(50)	1.35	.35	.25

1092   **1093**

1094   **1095**

1096   **1097**

1092	3¢ Oklahoma Statehood	2.00	4.25	15.00(50)	2.00	.50	.25
1093	3¢ School Teachers. .	2.25	4.50	12.50(50)	1.35	.45	.25
1094	4¢ 48-Star Flag	2.00	4.25	12.50(50)	1.35	.35	.25
1095	3¢ Shipbuilding Anniversary	2.00	4.25	17.00(70)	1.50	.35	.25
1096	8¢ Ramon Magsaysay	2.50	4.25	17.00(48)	1.75	.40	.25
1097	3¢ Birth of Lafayette .	2.00	4.25	12.50(50)	1.35	.35	.25

1098   **1099**   **1100**

| 1098 | 3¢ Whooping Cranes. | 2.25 | 4.50 | 12.50(50) | 1.35 | .35 | .25 |
| 1099 | 3¢ Religious Freedom | 2.00 | 4.25 | 12.50(50) | 1.35 | .35 | .25 |

1104   **1105**

1106   **1107**

1958 COMMEMORATIVES

1100-23	21 varieties, complete	. . . .	. . . .	. . . .	. . . .	7.00	4.40
1100	3¢ Gardening & Horticulture.	2.00	4.25	12.50(50)	1.35	.35	.25
1104	3¢ Brussels Exhibition	2.00	4.25	12.50(50)	1.35	.35	.25
1105	3¢ James Monroe . . .	2.00	4.25	25.00(70)	2.00	.35	.25
1106	3¢ Minnesota Statehood	2.00	4.25	14.00(50)	1.75	.40	.25
1107	3¢ Int'l. Geophysical Year	2.00	4.25	12.50(50)	1.35	.35	.25

SCOTT NO.	DESCRIPTION	FIRST DAY COVERS SING	FIRST DAY COVERS PL. BLK.	MINT SHEET	PLATE BLOCK F/NH	UNUSED F/NH	USED F

1108

1109

1110, 1111

1112

1108	3¢ Gunston Hall.	2.00	4.25	12.50(50)	1.30	.35	.25
1109	3¢ Mackinac Bridge. .	2.00	4.25	13.00(50)	1.30	.40	.25
1110	4¢ Simon Bolivar	2.00	4.25	17.00(70)	1.30	.35	.25
1111	8¢ Simon Bolivar	2.00	4.50	28.00(72)	2.50	.40	.25
1112	4¢ Atlantic Cable Centenary	2.00	4.25	14.00(50)	1.30	.35	.25

1113

1114

1115

1116

1113	1¢ Abraham Lincoln (1959)	2.00	4.25	8.00(50)	1.00	.30	.25
1114	3¢ Bust of Lincoln (1959)	2.00	4.25	13.50(50)	1.75	.40	.25
1115	4¢ Lincoln-Douglas Debates.	2.00	4.25	15.00(50)	1.75	.40	.25
1116	4¢ Statue of Lincoln (1959)	2.00	4.25	19.00(50)	2.15	.45	.25

1117, 1118

1119

1120

1117	4¢ Lajos Kossuth. . . .	2.00	4.25	18.00(70)	1.35	.35	.25
1118	8¢ Lajos Kossuth. . . .	2.00	4.50	20.00(72)	1.75	.35	.25
1119	4¢ Freedom of Press.	2.00	4.25	12.50(50)	1.35	.35	.25
1120	4¢ Overland Mail	2.00	4.25	12.50(50)	1.35	.35	.25

1121

1122

1123

1121	4¢ Noah Webster. . . .	2.00	4.25	17.00(70)	1.25	.35	.25
1122	4¢ Forest Conservation	2.00	4.25	14.00(50)	1.50	.35	.25
1123	4¢ Fort Duquesne . . .	2.00	4.25	12.50(50)	1.25	.35	.25

1124

1125, 1126

1127

1128

1129

1959 COMMEMORATIVES

1124-38	4¢-8¢, 15 varieties . .	. . . . . .	. . . .	. . . .	. . . .	4.95	3.25
1124	4¢ Oregon Statehood	2.00	4.25	17.00(50)	1.70	.35	.25
1125	4¢ José de San Martin	2.00	4.25	17.00(70)	1.40	.35	.25
1126	8¢ José de San Martin	2.00	4.25	19.50(72)	1.75	.35	.25
1127	4¢ NATO	2.00	4.25	17.00(70)	1.40	.35	.25
1128	4¢ Arctic Exploration .	2.00	4.25	12.50(50)	1.40	.35	.25
1129	8¢ World Peace & Trade	2.00	4.25	19.00(50)	1.95	.40	.25

1130

1131

1132

1133

1134

1135

Plate blocks will be blocks of 4 stamps unless otherwise noted.

SCOTT NO.	DESCRIPTION	FIRST DAY COVERS SING	FIRST DAY COVERS PL. BLK.	MINT SHEET	PLATE BLOCK F/NH	UNUSED F/NH	USED F

1136, 1137

1138

1130	4¢ Silver Centennial .	2.00	4.25	19.00(50)	1.95	.50	.25
1131	4¢ St. Lawrence Seaway	2.00	4.25	12.50(50)	1.35	.35	.25
1132	4¢ 49-Star Flag	2.00	4.25	12.50(50)	1.35	.35	.25
1133	4¢ Soil Conservation .	2.00	4.25	13.00(50)	1.40	.35	.25
1134	4¢ Petroleum	2.00	4.25	15.00(50)	1.40	.40	.25
1135	4¢ Dental Health	5.00	7.00	15.00(50)	1.40	.40	.25
1136	4¢ Ernst Reuter	2.00	4.25	17.00(70)	1.40	.35	.25
1137	8¢ Ernst Reuter	2.00	4.25	20.00(72)	1.75	.35	.25
1138	4¢ Dr. Ephraim McDowell	2.00	4.25	18.00(70)	1.50	.35	.25

1139

1140

1141

1142

1143

1144

1960-61 CREDO OF AMERICA SERIES

1139-44	6 varieties, complete	. . . .	. . . .	. . . .	. . . .	1.85	1.15
1139	4¢ Credo—Washington	2.00	4.25	14.00(50)	1.35	.50	.25
1140	4¢ Credo—Franklin . .	2.00	4.25	12.50(50)	1.35	.35	.25
1141	4¢ Credo—Jefferson .	2.00	4.25	14.00(50)	1.35	.50	.25
1142	4¢ Credo—Key	2.00	4.25	12.50(50)	1.35	.35	.25
1143	4¢ Credo—Lincoln . . .	2.00	4.25	12.50(50)	1.35	.35	.25
1144	4¢ Credo—Henry (1961)	2.00	4.25	15.00(50)	1.50	.35	.25

1145

1146

1147, 1148

1149

WATER CONSERVATION
1150

SCOTT NO.	DESCRIPTION	FIRST DAY COVERS SING	FIRST DAY COVERS PL. BLK.	MINT SHEET	PLATE BLOCK F/NH	UNUSED F/NH	USED F

1151

1152

1153

1960 COMMEMORATIVES

1145-73	4¢-8¢, 29 varieties . .	. . . .	. . . .	. . . .	. . . .	8.85	5.25
1145	4¢ Boy Scouts	8.50	10.50	14.00(50)	1.75	.40	.25
1146	4¢ Winter Olympics . .	2.00	4.25	12.50(50)	1.35	.35	.25
1147	4¢ Thomas Masaryk .	2.00	4.25	17.00(70)	1.35	.35	.25
1148	8¢ Thomas Masaryk .	2.00	4.25	21.00(72)	1.75	.40	.25
1149	4¢ World Refugee Year	2.00	4.25	12.50(50)	1.35	.35	.25
1150	4¢ Water Conservation	2.00	4.25	12.50(50)	1.35	.35	.25
1151	4¢ SEATO	2.00	4.25	17.00(70)	1.50	.35	.25
1152	4¢ American Women .	2.00	4.25	12.50(50)	1.35	.35	.25
1153	4¢ 50-Star Flag	2.00	4.25	15.00(50)	1.50	.35	.25

1154

1155

1156

1157

1158

1159, 1160

1161

1162

1163

1154	4¢ Pony Express	2.00	4.25	15.00(50)	1.70	.45	.25
1155	4¢ Employ the Handicapped	2.00	4.25	12.00(50)	1.35	.35	.25
1156	4¢ World Forestry Congress	2.00	4.25	15.00(50)	1.50	.40	.25
1157	4¢ Mexican Independence	2.00	4.25	12.00(50)	1.35	.35	.25
1158	4¢ U.S.-Japan Treaty	2.00	4.25	17.00(50)	1.70	.35	.25
1159	4¢ Ignacy Paderewski	2.00	4.25	17.00(70)	1.75	.35	.25
1160	8¢ Ignacy Paderewski	2.00	4.25	20.00(72)	1.75	.35	.25
1161	4¢ Robert A. Taft	2.00	4.25	19.00(70)	1.75	.35	.25
1162	4¢ Wheels of Freedom	2.00	4.25	15.00(50)	1.50	.35	.25
1163	4¢ Boys' Club of America	2.25	4.25	12.00(50)	1.40	.35	.25

BUY COMPLETE SETS AND SAVE!

SCOTT NO.	DESCRIPTION	FIRST DAY COVERS SING PL. BLK.		MINT SHEET	PLATE BLOCK F/NH	UNUSED F/NH	USED F

1164

1165, 1166

1167

1168, 1169

1170

1171

1172

1173

1164	4¢ Automated Post Office	2.00	4.25	16.00(50)	1.50	.45	.25
1165	4¢ Gustaf Mannerheim	2.00	4.25	17.00(70)	1.40	.30	.25
1166	8¢ Gustaf Mannerheim	2.00	4.25	19.50(72)	1.60	.35	.25
1167	4¢ Camp Fire Girls	5.00	7.25	17.00(70)	1.40	.60	.25
1168	4¢ Giuseppe Garibaldi	2.00	4.25	17.00(70)	1.40	.30	.25
1169	8¢ Giuseppe Garibaldi	2.00	4.25	19.50(72)	1.50	.35	.25
1170	4¢ Walter George	2.00	4.25	20.00(70)	1.50	.50	.25
1171	4¢ Andrew Carnegie	2.00	4.25	17.50(70)	1.25	.35	.25
1172	4¢ John Foster Dulles	2.00	4.25	17.50(70)	1.25	.35	.25
1173	4¢ "ECHO I" Satellite	3.00	6.50	17.00(50)	1.40	.70	.25

1174, 1175

1176

1177

1961 COMMEMORATIVES

1174/90	(1174-77, 1183-90) 12 varieties	....	....	....	....	5.75	2.55
1174	4¢ Mahatma Gandhi	2.00	4.25	20.00(70)	1.35	.50	.25
1175	8¢ Mahatma Gandhi	2.00	4.25	20.00(72)	1.75	.50	.25
1176	4¢ Range Conservation	2.00	4.25	17.00(50)	1.75	.50	.25
1177	4¢ Horace Greeley	2.00	4.25	20.00(70)	1.75	.50	.25

1178

1179

1180

1181

1182

1183

1961-65 CIVIL WAR CENTENNIAL SERIES

1178-82	4¢-5¢, 5 varieties, complete	....	....	....	....	2.75	1.05
1178	4¢ Fort Sumter	7.50	10.00	20.00(50)	2.00	.60	.25
1179	4¢ Shiloh (1962)	7.50	10.00	22.00(50)	1.75	.40	.25
1180	5¢ Gettysburg (1963)	7.50	10.00	22.00(50)	2.25	.60	.25
1181	5¢ Wilderness (1964)	7.50	10.00	22.00(50)	1.75	.55	.25
1181	Zip Code Block	....	....	....	1.40	....	....
1182	5¢ Appomattox (1965)	7.50	10.00	25.00(50)	3.00	.75	.25
1182	Zip Code Block	....	....	....	3.50	....	....

1184

1185

1186

1187

1188

1189

1190

1961 COMMEMORATIVES

1183	4¢ Kansas Statehood	2.00	4.25	17.00(50)	1.50	.60	.25
1184	4¢ George W. Norris	2.00	4.25	12.00(50)	1.30	.35	.25
1185	4¢ Naval Aviation	2.00	4.25	14.00(50)	1.30	.35	.25
1186	4¢ Workmen's Compensation	2.00	4.25	13.00(50)	1.30	.35	.25
1187	4¢ Frederic Remington	2.00	4.25	15.00(50)	1.30	.35	.25
1188	4¢ Sun Yat-sen	6.00	10.00	34.00(50)	3.75	.85	.25
1189	4¢ Basketball	9.00	12.00	17.00(50)	1.30	.65	.25
1190	4¢ Nursing	13.50	20.00	17.00(50)	1.30	.65	.25

NOTE: To determine the VF price on stamps issued from 1941 to date, add 20% to the F/NH or F (used) price (minimum .03 per item). All VF unused stamps from 1941 date priced as NH.

SCOTT NO.	DESCRIPTION	FIRST DAY COVERS SING	PL. BLK.	MINT SHEET	PLATE BLOCK F/NH	UNUSED F/NH	USED F

1191

1192

1193

1194

1962 COMMEMORATIVES

1191-1207	17 varieties	....	....	....	....	5.40	3.40
1191	4¢ New Mexico Statehood	1.75	4.00	15.00(50)	1.50	.40	.25
1192	4¢ Arizona Statehood	1.75	4.00	15.00(50)	1.50	.35	.25
1193	4¢ Project Mercury	5.00	7.50	14.00(50)	1.40	.35	.25
1194	4¢ Malaria Eradication	1.75	4.00	14.00(50)	1.40	.35	.25

1195

1196

1197

1195	4¢ Charles Evans Hughes	2.00	4.00	13.00(50)	1.40	.35	.25
1196	4¢ Seattle World's Fair	2.00	4.00	15.00(50)	2.00	.35	.25
1197	4¢ Louisiana Statehood	2.00	4.00	15.00(50)	1.50	.40	.25

1198

1199

1200

1201

1202

1203

1205

1206

1207

1198	4¢ Homestead Act.	2.00	4.00	14.00(50)	1.40	.35	.25
1199	4¢ Girl Scouts	7.00	10.00	14.00(50)	1.40	.35	.25
1200	4¢ Brien McMahon	2.00	4.00	14.00(50)	1.50	.35	.25
1201	4¢ Apprenticeship .	2.00	4.00	14.00(50)	1.40	.35	.25
1202	4¢ Sam Rayburn . .	2.00	4.00	17.00(50)	1.50	.35	.25
1203	4¢ Dag Hammarskjold	2.00	4.00	12.00(50)	1.40	.35	.25
1204	same, yellow inverted	5.00	10.25	12.00(50)	1.50	.35	.25
1205	4¢ Christmas 1962	2.00	4.00	23.00(50)	2.00	.35	.25
1206	4¢ Higher Education	2.00	4.00	12.00(50)	1.40	.35	.25
1207	4¢ Winslow Homer	2.00	4.00	12.50(50)	1.40	.35	.25

1208

1209, 1225

1213, 1229

1214

1962-66 REGULAR ISSUE

1208	5¢ Flag & White House (1963)	2.00	4.25	22.00(100)	1.35	.30	.25
1209	1¢ Andrew Jackson (1963)	2.00	4.00	20.00(100)	2.00	.30	.25
1213	5¢ Washington . . .	2.00	4.00	27.50(100)	1.50	.30	.25
1213a	5¢ b. pane of 5—Slog. I	2.50	....			6.50	....
1213a	5¢ b. pane of 5—Slog. II (1963)					20.00	
1213a	5¢ b. pane of 5—Slog. III (1964)					3.50	
1213c	5¢ Tagged pane of 5 Slogan II (1963). . .	....	....			105.00	
1213c	5¢ b. p. of 5—Slog. III (1963)	....	....	....		2.50	
1214	8¢ John J. Pershing (1961)	2.25	5.00	40.00(100)	2.95	.65	.25

Slogan I—Your Mailman Deserves Your Help · Keep Harmful Objects Out of...
Slogan II—Add Zip to Your Mail · Use Zone Numbers for Zip Code.
Slogan III—Add Zip to Your Mail · Always Use Zip Code.

1962-66 COIL STAMPS Perf. 10 Vertically

			LINE PAIRS		LINE PAIRS		
1225	1¢ Andrew Jackson (1963)	2.00	3.00	....	3.00	.50	.25
1229	5¢ Washington (1963)	2.00	3.00	....	4.00	1.25	.25

1230

1231

1232

1233

1963 COMMEMORATIVES

1230-41	12 varieties.	....	....	....	....	3.85	2.00
1230	5¢ Carolina Charter	2.00	4.00	14.00(50)	1.50	.40	.25
1231	5¢ Food for Peace	2.00	4.00	12.00(50)	1.40	.35	.25
1232	5¢ West Virginia Statehood	2.00	4.00	15.00(50)	1.70	.50	.25
1233	5¢ Emancipation Proclamation	4.00	6.00	12.50(50)	1.70	.35	.25

SCOTT NO.	DESCRIPTION	FIRST DAY COVERS SING	PL. BLK.	MINT SHEET	PLATE BLOCK F/NH	UNUSED F/NH	USED F

1234

1235

1236

1237

1238

1239

1240

1241

1242

1243

1963 COMMEMORATIVES

Scott No.	Description	Sing	Pl. Blk.	Mint Sheet	Plate Block	Unused	Used
1234	5¢ Alliance for Progress	2.00	4.00	12.00(50)	1.30	.30	.25
1235	5¢ Cordell Hull. . . .	2.00	4.00	12.00(50)	1.75	.40	.25
1236	5¢ Eleanor Roosevelt	2.00	4.00	12.50(50)	1.30	.35	.25
1237	5¢ The Sciences . .	2.00	4.00	12.00(50)	1.30	.30	.25
1238	5¢ City Mail Delivery	2.00	4.00	12.00(50)	1.30	.30	.25
1239	5¢ International Red Cross.	2.00	4.00	12.00(50)	1.30	.30	.25
1240	5¢ Christmas 1963	2.00	4.00	25.00(100)	1.50	.35	.25
1241	5¢ John J. Audubon	2.00	4.00	12.00(50)	1.30	.30	.25

SCOTT NO.	DESCRIPTION	FIRST DAY COVERS SING	PL. BLK.	MINT SHEET	PLATE BLOCK	UNUSED F/NH	USED

1244

1245

1964 COMMEMORATIVES

1242-60	19 varieties.	. . . . . .	. . . . . .	. . . . . .	. . . . . .	6.95	3.90
1242	5¢ Sam Houston	4.00	6.00	17.50(50)	1.75	.70	.25
1243	5¢ Charles M. Russell	2.00	4.00	15.00(50)	1.75	.35	.25
1244	5¢ New York World's Fair	2.00	4.00	12.50(50)	1.30	.35	.25
1245	5¢ John Muir	2.00	4.00	18.00(50)	2.00	.50	.25

SCOTT NO.	DESCRIPTION	FIRST DAY COVERS SING	PL. BLK.	MINT SHEET	PLATE BLOCK F/NH	UNUSED F/NH	USED F

1246

1247

| 1246 | 5¢ John F. Kennedy. . | 2.50 | 5.00 | 17.00(50) | 1.75 | .50 | .25 |
| 1247 | 5¢ New Jersey Tercentenary . . . . | 1.75 | 4.00 | 12.00(50) | 1.35 | .35 | .25 |

1248

1249

1250

1251

1252

1248	5¢ Nevada Statehood	2.00	4.00	16.00(50)	1.50	.35	.25
1249	5¢ Register and Vote. .	2.00	4.00	14.00(50)	1.50	.30	.25
1250	5¢ Shakespeare	2.00	4.00	12.00(50)	1.35	.30	.25
1251	5¢ Mayo Brothers . . .	5.00	7.00	14.00(50)	1.50	.60	.25
1252	5¢ American Music . .	2.00	4.00	12.00(50)	1.35	.30	.25

1253

1254

1255

1256

1257

1253	5¢ Homemakers	2.00	4.00	15.00(50)	1.50	.30	.25
1254-57	5¢ Christmas, 4 varieties, attached .	5.25	7.50	42.00(100)	2.50	2.00	1.50
1254	5¢ Holly	2.75	. . . .	. . . .	. . . .	.40	.25
1255	5¢ Mistletoe	2.75	. . . .	. . . .	. . . .	.40	.25
1256	5¢ Poinsettia	2.75	. . . .	. . . .	. . . .	.40	.25
1257	5¢ Pine Cone.	2.75	. . . .	. . . .	. . . .	.40	.25

COMMEMORATIVES: Commemorative stamps are special issues released to honor or recognize persons, organizations, historical events or landmarks. They are usually issued in the current first class denomination to supplement regular issues.

SCOTT NO.	DESCRIPTION	FIRST DAY COVERS SING	FIRST DAY COVERS PL. BLK.	MINT SHEET	PLATE BLOCK F/NH	UNUSED F/NH	USED

1258   **1259**   **1260**

1258	5¢ Verrazano-Narrows. Bridge	2.00	4.00	12.50(50)	1.30	.35	.25
1259	5¢ Modern Art	2.00	4.00	12.00(50)	1.30	.35	.25
1260	5¢ Radio Amateurs	8.00	10.00	23.50(50)	2.50	.60	.25

1271   **1272**   **1273**

1266	5¢ International Cooperation Year	2.00	4.00	12.50(50)	1.25	.30	.25
1267	5¢ Salvation Army	3.00	4.00	12.50(50)	1.25	.30	.25
1268	5¢ Dante Alighieri	2.00	4.00	12.50(50)	1.25	.30	.25
1269	5¢ Herbert Hoover	2.00	4.00	14.00(50)	1.75	.50	.25
1270	5¢ Robert Fulton	2.00	4.00	14.00(50)	1.20	.45	.25
1271	5¢ Florida Settlement	2.00	4.00	14.00(50)	1.75	.40	.25
1272	5¢ Traffic Safety	2.00	4.00	14.00(50)	1.75	.40	.25
1273	5¢ John S. Copley	2.00	4.00	12.00(50)	1.20	.30	.25

1261   **1262**   **1263**

1274   **1275**   **1276**

1274	11¢ Telecommunication	2.00	4.00	30.00(50)	5.00	.75	.40
1275	5¢ Adlai Stevenson	2.00	4.00	12.00(50)	1.20	.30	.25
1276	5¢ Christmas 1965	2.00	4.00	28.00(100)	2.00	.30	.25

1265

1264

1965 COMMEMORATIVES

1261-76	5¢-11¢, 16 varieties	....	....	....	....	5.15	3.30
1261	5¢ Battle of New Orleans	2.00	4.00	14.00(50)	1.75	.40	.25
1262	5¢ Physical Fitness	2.00	4.00	14.00(50)	1.35	.30	.25
1263	5¢ Crusade Against Cancer	4.00	6.00	12.00(50)	1.35	.30	.25
1264	5¢ Winston Churchill	2.00	4.00	12.00(50)	1.35	.40	.25
1265	5¢ Magna Carta	2.00	4.00	12.00(50)	1.35	.30	.25

1266   **1267**   **1268**

1269   **1270**

STAMP HISTORY

THATCHER FERRY BRIDGE

In 1962, during the regular course of business H.E. Harris purchases, at their 4 cent face value, a pane of 50 stamps honoring the Canal Zone's Thatcher Ferry Bridge. Due to a printing error, the silver bridge has been omitted. Harris discovers that his is the only pane from the sheet of 200 printed that has reached the public. Because a recent error in a Dag Hammerskjold stamp prompted the U.S. Postal Service to reprint thousands in order to make the error worthless, Harris questions how the Canal Zone will handle the bridge error. Flooding the market, he insists, would blunt the fun and excitement of stamp collecting. When the Canal Zone says it will reprint the error, Harris sues. March 25, 1965, The Federal District Court in Washington rules in Harris' favor, stopping the Canal Zone authorities from reprinting the stamp error. Viewed as a precedent-setting event in philately, the effort won Harris the respect and awards of his fellow collectors.

SCOTT NO.	DESCRIPTION	FIRST DAY COVERS SING	FIRST DAY COVERS PL. BLK.	MINT SHEET	PLATE BLOCK F/NH	UNUSED F/NH	USED

1278, 1299   1279   1280   1281, 1297

1282, 1303   1283, 1304   1283B, 1304C   1284, 1298

1285   1286   1286A   1287

1288, 1288B, 1288d, 1305E, 1305Ei   1289   1290   1291

1292   1293   1294, 1305C

1295   1305

1965-78 PROMINENT AMERICAN SERIES

SCOTT NO.	DESCRIPTION	SING	PL. BLK.	MINT SHEET	PLATE BLOCK	UNUSED	USED
1278-95	1¢-$5, 20 varieties, complete (No #1288B or 1288d).	91.50	....	....	150.00	32.50	7.75
1278	1¢ T. Jefferson (1968) .	1.75	4.00	12.00(100)	1.00	.25	.25
1278a	1¢ bklt.pane of 8	2.50	....	....		1.55	....
1278ae	1¢ test gum	90.00	....	....		2.00	....
1278b	1¢ bklt pane of 4 (1971)	18.00	....	....		1.00	....
1279	1¹⁄₄¢ A. Gallatin (1967)	1.75	4.00	18.00(100)	12.00	.25	.25
1280	2¢ F.L. Wright (1966). .	1.75	4.00	15.00(100)	.90	.25	.25
1280a	2¢ bklt pane of 5 (1968)	2.50	....	....		1.00	....
1280c	2¢ bklt pane of 6 (1971)	18.00	....	....		1.00	....
1280ce	2¢ test gum	125.00	....	....		1.00	....
1281	3¢ F. Parkman (1967) .	1.75	4.00	14.00(100)	1.15	.25	.25
1282	4¢ A. Lincoln	1.75	4.00	22.00(100)	1.15	.25	.25
1283	5¢ G. Washington (1966)	1.75	4.00	23.00(100)	1.15	.25	.25
1283B	5¢ Washington, redrawn (1967)	1.75	4.00	21.00(100)	1.25	.30	.25
1284	6¢ F. D. Roosevelt(1966)	1.75	4.00	24.00(100)	1.35	.35	.25
1284b	6¢ bklt pane of 8 (1967)	3.00	....	....		1.75	....
1284c	6¢ bklt pane of 5 (1968)	150.00	....	....		1.60	....
1285	8¢ A. Einstein (1966). .	4.00	6.00	40.00(100)	2.25	.50	.25
1286	10¢ A. Jackson (1967).	2.00	4.25	48.00(100)	2.25	.50	.25
1286A	12¢ H. Ford (1968) . . .	2.00	4.25	46.00(100)	2.25	.50	.25
1287	13¢ J.F. Kennedy (1967)	2.50	4.50	52.00(100)	3.50	.70	.25
1288	15¢ O.W. Holmes, die I (1968)	2.25	4.50	48.00(100)	2.25	.60	.25
1288d	15¢ Holmes, die II (1979)	....	....	90.00(100)	14.00	1.10	.45

SCOTT NO.	DESCRIPTION	FIRST DAY COVERS SING	FIRST DAY COVERS PL. BLK.	MINT SHEET	PLATE BLOCK F/NH	UNUSED F/NH	USED
1288B	same, from bklt pane (1978).	2.25	....	....	....	.60	.25
1288Bc	15¢ bklt pane of 8 . . .	3.75	....	....	....	4.75	....
1289	20¢ G.C. Marshall (1967)	2.25	4.50	65.00(100)	5.00	.70	.25
1290	25¢ F. Douglass (1967)	5.00	6.00	96.00(100)	5.50	1.20	.25
1291	30¢ J. Dewey (1968) . .	2.50	5.00	130.00(100)	7.00	1.25	.25
1292	40¢ T. Paine (1968) . .	2.50	5.00	155.00(100)	6.50	1.50	.25
1293	50¢ L. Stone (1968) . .	3.75	7.25	210.00(100)	8.00	2.00	.25
1294	$1 E. O'Neil (1967) . . .	6.00	12.50	395.00(100)	18.00	5.00	.25
1295	$5 J. B. Moore (1966)	50.00	115.00	....	70.00	16.00	3.50

BOOKLET PANE SLOGANS

Slogan IV : Mail Early in the Day.   #1278b–Slogans IV and V
Slogan V: Use Zip Code.   #1280a, 1284c–Slogans IV or V

1966-81 COIL STAMPS

SCOTT NO.	DESCRIPTION	SING	PL. BLK.	LINE PAIR	PLATE BLOCK / LINE PAIR	UNUSED	USED
1297/1305C	1¢-$1, 9 varieties, (No #1305Ei).	....	....	....	15.00	6.80	2.75
	Perf. 10 Horizontally						
1297	3¢ F. Parkman (1975) .	1.75	2.75	....	.70	.25	.25
1298	6¢ F.D. Roosevelt (1967)	1.75	2.75	....	1.70	.40	.25
	Perf. 10 Vertically						
1299	1¢ T. Jefferson (1968) .	1.75	2.75	....	.65	.35	.25
1303	4¢ A. Lincoln	1.75	2.75	....	1.00	.35	.25
1304	5¢ G. Washington	1.75	2.75	....	1.00	1.00	.25
1304C	5¢ Washington, redrawn (1981)	1.75	2.75	....	2.75	.30	.25
1305	6¢ F.D. Roosevelt (1968)	1.75	2.75	....	.85	.50	.25
1305E	15¢ O.W. Holmes, die I (1978)	2.00	3.25	....	1.40	.50	.25
1305Ei	15¢ O.W. Holmes, die II (1979)	....	....	....	4.50	1.25	.30
1305C	$1 E. O'Neil (1973) . . .	5.00	9.50	....	10.00	3.95	1.50

1306   1307

1308   1309   1310

1312   1313   1314

1966 COMMEMORATIVES

SCOTT NO.	DESCRIPTION	SING	PL. BLK.	MINT SHEET	PLATE BLOCK	UNUSED	USED
1306/22	(1306-10, 1312-22) 16 varieties.	....	....	....	....	5.10	3.35
1306	5¢ Migratory Bird Treaty	2.00	4.25	17.00(50)	1.50	.35	.25
1307	5¢ A.S.P.C.A.	2.00	4.00	14.00(50)	1.50	.35	.25
1308	5¢ Indiana Statehood .	2.00	4.00	14.00(50)	1.95	.35	.25
1309	5¢ American Circus . . .	3.00	4.25	14.00(50)	1.60	.35	.25
1310	5¢ SIPEX (single)	2.00	4.00	12.50(50)	1.25	.35	.25
1311	5¢ SIPEX, Imperf Souvenir Sheet	2.00	....	....	....	.35	.25
1312	5¢ Bill of Rights	2.25	4.00	15.00(50)	1.60	.35	.25
1313	5¢ Polish Millennium . .	2.00	4.00	12.50(50)	1.25	.35	.25
1314	5¢ National Park Service	2.00	4.00	22.00(50)	2.40	.55	.25

SCOTT NO.	DESCRIPTION	FIRST DAY COVERS SING PL. BLK.	MINT SHEET	PLATE BLOCK F/NH	UNUSED F/NH	USED

1315   1316   1317

1318   1319   1320

SCOTT NO.	DESCRIPTION	SING	PL. BLK.	MINT SHEET	PLATE BLOCK F/NH	UNUSED F/NH	USED
1315	5¢ Marine Corps Reserve	2.00	4.00	18.00(50)	2.00	.30	.25
1316	5¢ Women's Clubs. . .	2.00	4.00	12.50(50)	1.25	.30	.25
1317	5¢ Johnny Appleseed	2.00	4.00	22.00(50)	1.50	.40	.25
1318	5¢ Beautification . . .	2.00	4.00	15.00(50)	1.50	.55	.25
1319	5¢ Great River Road .	2.00	4.00	15.00(50)	1.50	.40	.25
1320	5¢ Servicemen–Bonds.	2.00	4.00	12.50(50)	1.20	.30	.25

1321   1322   1323

| 1321 | 5¢ Christmas 1966 . . | 1.75 | 4.00 | 24.00(100) | 1.50 | .35 | .25 |
| 1322 | 5¢ Mary Cassatt . . . . | 1.75 | 4.00 | 12.00(50) | 1.20 | .30 | .25 |

1324   1325

1326   1327

1967 COMMEMORATIVES

1323-37	15 varieties, complete.	....	....	....	....	7.50	3.25
1323	5¢ National Grange . . .	2.00	4.00	12.00(50)	1.25	.35	.25
1324	5¢ Canada Centennial.	2.00	4.00	12.00(50)	1.25	.30	.25
1325	5¢ Erie Canal.	2.00	4.00	14.00(50)	1.50	.40	.25
1326	5¢ Search for Peace . .	2.00	4.00	12.00(50)	1.25	.30	.25
1327	5¢ Henry D. Thoreau. .	2.00	4.00	14.00(50)	1.75	.40	.25

1328   1330   1329

1328	5¢ Nebraska Statehood	2.00	4.00	20.00(50)	2.00	.30	.25
1329	5¢ Voice of America . .	4.00	6.00	12.00(50)	1.25	.30	.25
1330	5¢ Davy Crockett.	2.50	4.25	12.00(50)	1.25	.30	.25

1331   1332

1331-32	5¢ Space, attached, 2 varieties	12.50	25.00	30.00(50)	3.50	1.75	1.20
1331	5¢ Astronaut	4.00	....	....	....	1.50	.40
1332	5¢ Gemini 4 Capsule. .	4.00	....	....	....	1.50	.40

1333   1334

| 1333 | 5¢ Urban Planning. . . . | 2.00 | 4.00 | 12.00(50) | 1.20 | .30 | .25 |
| 1334 | 5¢ Finland Independence . . . . | 2.00 | 4.00 | 12.00(50) | 1.20 | .30 | .25 |

1335   1336   1337

1335	5¢ Thomas Eakins . . .	2.00	4.00	12.00(50)	1.20	.30	.25
1336	5¢ Christmas 1967 . . .	2.00	4.00	12.00(50)	1.20	.30	.25
1337	5¢ Mississippi Statehood	2.00	4.00	17.00(50)	1.75	.45	.25

SCOTT NO.	DESCRIPTION	FIRST DAY COVERS SING	PL. BLK.	MINT SHEET	PLATE BLOCK	UNUSED F/NH	USED

1338, 1338A, 1338D   **1338F, 1338G**

GIORI PRESS
1868 Design size: 18¹/₂ x 22 mm Perf.11

| 1338 | 6¢ Flag & White House | 1.75 | 4.00 | 24.00(100) | 1.20 | .30 | .25 |

HUCK PRESS Design size: 18 x 21 mm
1969 Coil Stamp Perf. 10 Vertically

| 1338A | 6¢ Flag & White House | 1.75 | .... | .... | 5.75 | .30 | .25 |

1970 Perf. 11 x 10¹/₂

| 1338D | 6¢ Flag & White House | 2.00 | 4.25 | 23.00(100) | 5.25(20) | .30 | .25 |

1971 Perf. 11 x 10¹/₂

| 1338F | 8¢ Flag & White House | 2.00 | 4.25 | 33.00(100) | 8.00(20) | .45 | .25 |

Coil Stamp Perf. 10 Vertically

| 1338G | 8¢ Flag & White House | 2.00 | .... | .... | .... | .45 | .25 |

1339   **1340**

1968 COMMEMORATIVES

1339/64	(1339-40, 1342-64) 25 varieties.........	....	....	....	....	11.75	5.95
1339	6¢ Illinois Statehood ..	2.00	4.00	15.00(50)	1.50	.50	.25
1340	6¢ Hemisfair '68......	2.00	4.00	12.00(50)	1.25	.30	.25

1341

| 1341 | $1 Airlift to Servicemen | 8.50 | 17.50 | 165.00(50) | 15.00 | 3.95 | 2.75 |

1342   **1343**   **1344**

1342	6¢ Support our Youth..	2.00	4.00	12.00(50)	1.25	.30	.25
1343	6¢ Law and Order	4.00	6.00	19.00(50)	1.95	.45	.25
1344	6¢ Register and Vote..	2.00	4.00	12.00(50)	1.25	.30	.25

SCOTT NO.	DESCRIPTION	FIRST DAY COVERS SING	PL. BLK.	MINT SHEET	PLATE BLOCK	UNUSED F/NH	USED

1345   **1346**

1347   **1348**

1349   **1350**

1351   **1352**

1353   **1354**

1968 HISTORIC AMERICAN FLAGS

1345-54	10 varieties, complete, attached	10.00	....	20.00(50)	10.00	5.25	....
1345-54	Same, set of singles .	57.50	....	....	....	4.25	3.25
1345	6¢ Fort Moultrie Flag ..	6.00	....	....	....	.55	.45
1346	6¢ Fort McHenry Flag .	6.00	....	....	....	.55	.45
1347	6¢ Washington's Cruisers	6.00	....	....	....	.55	.45
1348	6¢ Bennington Flag ...	6.00	....	....	....	.55	.45
1349	6¢ Rhode Island Flag .	6.00	....	....	....	.55	.45
1350	6¢ First Stars & Stripes	6.00	....	....	....	.55	.45
1351	6¢ Bunker Hill Flag ...	6.00	....	....	....	.55	.45
1352	6¢ Grand Union Flag ..	6.00	....	....	....	.55	.45
1353	6¢ Philadelphia Light Horse	6.00	....	....	....	.55	.45
1354	6¢ First Navy Jack....	6.00	....	....	....	.55	.45

NOTE: All ten varieties of 1345-54 were printed on the same sheet; therefore, plate and regular blocks are not available for each variety separately. Plate blocks of four will contain two each of #1346, with number adjacent to #1345 only; Zip blocks will contain two each of #1353 and #1354, with inscription adjacent to #1354 only; Mail Early blocks will contain two each of #1347-49 with inscription adjacent to #1348 only. A plate strip of 20 stamps, with two of each variety will be required to have all stamps in plate block form and will contain all marginal inscription.

1355   **1356**

1357   1358

1359   1360   1361

1968 COMMEMORATIVES

SCOTT NO.	DESCRIPTION	FIRST DAY COVERS SING	PL. BLK.	MINT SHEET	PLATE BLOCK	UNUSED F/NH	USED
1355	6¢ Walt Disney	40.00	50.00	40.00(50)	4.75	1.25	.30
1356	6¢ Father Marquette	2.00	4.00	15.00(50)	2.25	.50	.25
1357	6¢ Daniel Boone	2.00	4.00	15.00(50)	1.50	.50	.25
1358	6¢ Arkansas River	2.00	4.00	15.00(50)	1.75	.50	.25
1359	6¢ Leif Erikson	2.00	4.00	12.00(50)	1.25	.50	.25
1360	6¢ Cherokee Strip	2.00	4.00	25.00(50)	2.50	.70	.25
1361	6¢ Trumbull Art	4.00	6.00	14.00(50)	1.30	.40	.25

1362   1363   1364

1362	6¢ Waterfowl Conservation	2.00	4.00	15.00(50)	1.70	.40	.25
1363	6¢ Christmas 1968	2.00	....	12.00(50)	3.25(10)	.30	.25
1364	6¢ Chief Joseph	2.00	4.00	17.00(50)	1.70	.40	.25

1365   1366

1367   1368

1969 COMMEMORATIVES

1365-86	22 varieties, complete	....	....	....	....	10.25	5.00
1365-68	Beautification, 4 varieties, attached	6.00	8.50	20.00(50)	3.00	2.50	2.00
1365	6¢ Azaleas & Tulips	3.00	....	....	....	1.00	.25
1366	6¢ Daffodils	3.00	....	....	....	1.00	.25
1367	6¢ Poppies	3.00	....	....	....	1.00	.25
1368	6¢ Crabapple Trees	3.00	....	....	....	1.00	.25

1369   1370   1371

1369	6¢ American Legion	2.00	4.00	12.00(50)	1.40	.30	.25
1370	6¢ Grandma Moses	2.00	4.00	12.00(50)	1.40	.30	.25
1371	6¢ Apollo 8 Moon Orbit	2.50	5.00	22.00(50)	2.40	.50	.25

1372   1373

1374   1375

1372	6¢ W.C. Handy–Musician	3.50	5.00	13.00(50)	1.50	.40	.25
1373	6¢ California Settlement	2.00	4.00	13.00(50)	1.50	.40	.25
1374	6¢ Major J.W. Powell	2.00	4.00	13.00(50)	1.50	.40	.25
1375	6¢ Alabama Statehood	2.00	4.00	13.00(50)	1.50	.40	.25

1376   1377

1378   1379

1376-79	Bontanical Congress, 4 varieties, attached	7.00	9.50	24.00(50)	3.75	2.50	2.25
1376	6¢ Douglas Fir	3.00	....	....	....	1.00	.25
1377	6¢ Lady's-slipper	3.00	....	....	....	1.00	.25
1378	6¢ Ocotillo	3.00	....	....	....	1.00	.25
1379	6¢ Franklinia	3.00	....	....	....	1.00	.25

AVERAGE QUALITY: From 1935 to date, deduct 20% from the Fine price to determine the price for an Average quality stamp.

MINT SHEETS: From 1935 to date, we list prices for standard size Mint Sheets in Fine, Never Hinged condition. The number of stamps in each sheet is noted in ( ).

SCOTT NO.	DESCRIPTION	FIRST DAY COVERS SING	PL. BLK.	MINT SHEET	PLATE BLOCK	UNUSED F/NH	USED

1380

1381

1382

 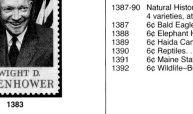

1383

1380	6¢ Dartmouth College .	2.00	4.00	12.00(50)	1.50	.40	.25
1381	6¢ Professional Baseball	16.00	25.00	30.00(50)	3.00	.60	.30
1382	6¢ College Football . . .	7.00	13.50	20.00(50)	2.00	.40	.25
1383	6¢ Eisenhower.	2.00	4.00	12.00(32)	1.75	.40	.25

1384   1385   1386

1384	6¢ Christmas 1969 . . .	2.00	....	14.00(50)	3.50(10)	.30	.25
1384a	6¢ precancelled set of 4 cities	....	....	280.00(50)	150.00(10)	4.50	....
1385	6¢ Rehabilitation	2.00	4.00	12.00(50)	1.20	.30	.25
1386	6¢ William M. Harnett .	2.00	4.00	8.00(32)	1.20	.30	.25

1387

1388

1389

1390

1391

1392

1970 COMMEMORATIVES

1387/1422	(1387-92, 1405-22) 24 varieties, (No precancels). . . .	....	....	....	....	11.85	5.75
1387-90	Natural History, 4 varieties, attached . .	5.00	7.00	12.00(32)	2.25	1.95	1.50
1387	6¢ Bald Eagle	2.50	....	....	....	.50	.25
1388	6¢ Elephant Herd.	2.50	....	....	....	.50	.25
1389	6¢ Haida Canoe.	2.50	....	....	....	.50	.25
1390	6¢ Reptiles.	2.50	....	....	....	.50	.25
1391	6¢ Maine Statehood . .	2.00	4.00	14.00(50)	1.75	.40	.25
1392	6¢ Wildlife–Buffalo. . . .	2.00	4.00	17.00(50)	2.00	.40	.25

1393, 1401   1393D

1394   1395, 1402   1396

1397   1398   1399   1400

1970-74 REGULAR ISSUE

1393/1400	6¢-21¢, 8 varieties, complete (No #1395)	....	....	....	....	3.85	1.30
1393	6¢ D. Eisenhower	1.75	4.00	23.00(100)	1.50	.30	.25
1393a	6¢ bklt pane of 8	2.75	....	....	....	1.95	....
1393ae	6¢ test gum	90.00	....	....	....	1.90	....
1393b	6¢ bklt pane of 5– Slogan IV or V	3.75	....	....	....	1.75	....
1393D	7¢ B. Franklin (1972) . .	1.75	4.00	28.00(100)	1.75	.35	.25
1394	8¢ Ike–black, blue, red (1971)	1.75	4.00	32.00(100)	1.60	.30	.25
1395	same, deep claret bklt single (1971)	2.50	....	....	....	.45	.25
1395a	8¢ bklt pane of 8	2.50	....	....	....	2.40	....
1395b	8¢ bklt pane of 6	2.25	....	....	....	1.90	....
1395c	8¢ bklt pane of 4, VI & VII (1972).	2.00	....	....	....	1.95	....
1395d	8¢ bklt pane of 7 II or V (1972)	2.50	....	....	....	3.75	....
1396	8¢ Postal Service Emblem (1971)	1.75	4.00	24.00(100)	3.75(12)	.35	.25
1397	14¢ F. LaGuardia (1972)	1.75	4.00	50.00(100)	3.50	.75	.25
1398	16¢ E. Pyle (1971). . . .	2.50	4.50	60.00(100)	3.75	.85	.25
1399	18¢ E. Blackwell (1974)	2.00	4.25	60.00(100)	3.50	.75	.25
1400	21¢ A.P. Giannini (1973)	2.50	4.50	70.00(100)	3.75	.75	.30

1970-71 COIL STAMPS–Perf. 10 Vertically

		LINE PAIR			LINE PAIR		
1401	6¢ D. Eisenhower	1.75	2.75	....	.90	.30	.25
1402	8¢ Eisenhower, claret (1971)	1.75	2.75	....	1.00	.35	.25

| | 1415 | 1416 |
| | 1417 | 1418 |

SCOTT NO.	DESCRIPTION	FIRST DAY COVERS SING	PL. BLK.	MINT SHEET	PLATE BLOCK	UNUSED F/NH	USED
1415-18	Christmas Toys, 4 varieties, attached . .	5.50	....	20.00(50)	5.50(8)	3.75	2.25
1415	6¢ Locomotive	3.00	....	....	....	1.00	.30
1416	6¢ Horse	3.00	....	....	....	1.00	.30
1417	6¢ Tricycle	3.00	....	....	....	1.00	.30
1418	6¢ Doll Carriage.	3.00	....	....	....	1.00	.30

Precancelled

SCOTT NO.	DESCRIPTION	FIRST DAY COVERS SING	PL. BLK.	MINT SHEET	PLATE BLOCK	UNUSED F/NH	USED
1414a	6¢ Nativity (precancelled)	4.00	....	14.00(50)	2.75(8)	.30	.25
1415a-18a	Christmas Toys, precancelled, 4 varieties attached .	45.00	....	40.00(50)	8.50(8)	4.25	3.75
1415a	6¢ Locomotive	7.00	....	....	....	1.50	.25
1416a	6¢ Horse	7.00	....	....	....	1.50	.25
1417a	6¢ Tricycle	7.00	....	....	....	1.50	.25
1418a	6¢ Doll Carriage.	7.00	....	....	....	1.50	.25

NOTE: Unused precancels are with original gum, while used are without gum.

1408   **1409**

1970 COMMEMORATIVES

SCOTT NO.	DESCRIPTION	FIRST DAY COVERS SING	PL. BLK.	MINT SHEET	PLATE BLOCK	UNUSED F/NH	USED
1405	6¢ E.L. Master–Poet . .	2.00	4.00	13.00(50)	1.50	.40	.25
1406	6¢ Woman Suffrage. . .	2.00	4.00	14.00(50)	1.75	.70	.25
1407	6¢ South Carolina Tercentenary	2.00	4.00	12.50(50)	1.50	.50	.25
1408	6¢ Stone Mountain Memorial	2.00	4.00	14.00(50)	1.75	.50	.25
1409	6¢ Fort Snelling	2.00	4.00	19.50(50)	2.00	.50	.25

1412   **1413**

| | 1410 | 1411 |

SCOTT NO.	DESCRIPTION	FIRST DAY COVERS SING	PL. BLK.	MINT SHEET	PLATE BLOCK	UNUSED F/NH	USED
1410-13	Anti-Pollution, 4 varieties, attached . .	5.00	7.00	15.00(50)	4.00(10)	2.00	1.75
1410	6¢ Globe & Wheat	2.50	....	....	....	.40	.25
1411	6¢ Globe & City	2.50	....	....	....	.40	.25
1412	6¢ Globe & Bluegill . . .	2.50	....	....	....	.40	.25
1413	6¢ Globe & Seagull . . .	2.50	....	....	....	.40	.25

1414

SCOTT NO.	DESCRIPTION	FIRST DAY COVERS SING	PL. BLK.	MINT SHEET	PLATE BLOCK	UNUSED F/NH	USED
1414	6¢ Nativity	1.75	....	12.00(50)	2.75(8)	.30	.25

1419

1420

SCOTT NO.	DESCRIPTION	FIRST DAY COVERS SING	PL. BLK.	MINT SHEET	PLATE BLOCK	UNUSED F/NH	USED
1419	6¢ U.N. 25th Anniversary	2.00	4.00	18.00(50)	1.95	.45	.25
1420	6¢ Pilgrim Landing	2.00	4.00	12.00(50)	1.35	.35	.25

1421   **1422**

SCOTT NO.	DESCRIPTION	FIRST DAY COVERS SING	PL. BLK.	MINT SHEET	PLATE BLOCK	UNUSED F/NH	USED
1421-22	D.A.V. Servicemen, 2 varieties, attached . .	3.00	5.00	15.00(50)	2.25	.75	.60
1421	6¢ Disabled Veterans .	2.00	....	....	....	.35	.30
1422	6¢ Prisoners of War . . .	2.00	....	....	....	.35	.30

FIRST DAY COVERS: First Day Covers are envelopes cancelled on the "First Day of Issue" of the stamp used on the envelope. Usually they also contain a picture (cachet) on the left side designed to go with the theme of the stamp. From 1935 to 1949, prices listed are for cacheted, addressed covers. From 1950 to date, prices are for cacheted, unaddressed covers.

SE-TENANTS: Beginning with the 1964 Christmas issue (#1254-57), the United States has issued numerous Se-Tenant stamps covering a wide variety of subjects. Se-Tenants are issues where two or more different stamp designs are produced on the same sheet in pair, strip or block form. Mint stamps are usually collected in attached blocks, etc.; used are generally saved as single stamps.

1423

1424

1425

1426

1434　　　　1435

SCOTT NO.	DESCRIPTION	FIRST DAY COVERS SING	PL. BLK.	MINT SHEET	PLATE BLOCK	UNUSED F/NH	USED
1434-35	Space Achievements, 2 varieties, attached	3.50	4.50	13.50(50)	1.75	.75	.55
1434	8¢ Moon, Earth, Sun & Landing Craft	2.00	....	....	....	.45	.30
1435	8¢ Lunar Rover	2.00	....	....	....	.45	.30

1436

1437

1971 COMMEMORATIVES

SCOTT NO.	DESCRIPTION	FIRST DAY COVERS SING	PL. BLK.	MINT SHEET	PLATE BLOCK	UNUSED F/NH	USED
1423-45	6¢-8¢, 23 varieties complete	....	....	....	....	9.75	4.95
1423	6¢ Sheep	1.75	4.00	14.00(50)	1.60	.50	.25
1424	6¢ General D. MacArthur	1.75	4.00	14.00(50)	1.60	.50	.25
1425	6¢ Blood Donors	1.75	4.00	12.00(50)	1.35	.30	.25
1426	8¢ Missouri Statehood	1.75	4.00	17.00(50)	5.50(12)	.50	.25

1438

1439

1427　　　　1428

1429　　　　1430

SCOTT NO.	DESCRIPTION	FIRST DAY COVERS SING	PL. BLK.	MINT SHEET	PLATE BLOCK	UNUSED F/NH	USED
1436	8¢ Emily Dickinson	2.00	4.00	14.00(50)	1.70	.40	.25
1437	8¢ San Juan	2.00	4.00	28.00(50)	2.50	.65	.25
1438	8¢ Drug Addiction	2.00	4.00	13.00(50)	2.25(6)	.35	.25
1439	8¢ CARE	2.00	4.00	14.00(50)	2.70(8)	.45	.25

SCOTT NO.	DESCRIPTION	FIRST DAY COVERS SING	PL. BLK.	MINT SHEET	PLATE BLOCK	UNUSED F/NH	USED
1427-30	Wildlife Conservation, 4 varieties, attached	5.00	9.00	12.50(32)	2.50	2.00	1.50
1427	8¢ Trout	2.50	....	....	....	.40	.25
1428	8¢ Alligator	2.50	....	....	....	.40	.25
1429	8¢ Polar Bear	2.50	....	....	....	.40	.25
1430	8¢ Condor	2.50	....	....	....	.40	.25

1440　　　　1441

1442　　　　1443

1431

1432

1433

SCOTT NO.	DESCRIPTION	FIRST DAY COVERS SING	PL. BLK.	MINT SHEET	PLATE BLOCK	UNUSED F/NH	USED
1440-43	Historic Preservation, 4 varieties, attached	5.00	6.00	12.50(32)	2.00	1.75	1.00
1440	8¢ Decatur House	2.50	....	....	....	.40	.25
1441	8¢ Whaling Ship	2.50	....	....	....	.40	.25
1442	8¢ Cable Car	2.50	....	....	....	.40	.25
1443	8¢ Mission	2.50	....	....	....	.40	.25

SCOTT NO.	DESCRIPTION	FIRST DAY COVERS SING	PL. BLK.	MINT SHEET	PLATE BLOCK	UNUSED F/NH	USED
1431	8¢ Antarctic Treaty	2.00	4.00	14.00(50)	1.75	.40	.25
1432	8¢ American Revolution	2.00	4.00	12.00(50)	1.50	.40	.25
1433	8¢ John Sloan–Artist	2.00	4.00	12.00(50)	1.50	.35	.25

SCOTT NO.	DESCRIPTION	FIRST DAY COVERS SING	FIRST DAY COVERS PL. BLK.	MINT SHEET	PLATE BLOCK	UNUSED F/NH	USED

1444

1445

| 1444 | 8¢ Christmas Nativity. . | 2.00 | 4.00 | 12.00(50) | 4.25(12) | .35 | .25 |
| 1445 | 8¢ Christmas Patridge. | 2.00 | 4.00 | 12.00(50) | 4.25(12) | .35 | .25 |

1446

1447

1972 COMMEMORATIVES

1446/74	29 varieties, complete.	....	....	....	....	10.15	6.00
1446	8¢ Sidney Lanier–Poet	2.00	4.00	14.00(50)	1.75	.50	.25
1447	8¢ Peace Corps.	2.00	4.00	12.50(50)	2.25(6)	.40	.25

1448   1449

1450   1451

1452

1454

1453

1972 NATIONAL PARKS CENTENNIAL

1448-54	2¢-15¢, 7 varieties, complete	....	....	....	....	2.50	1.50
1448-51	Cape Hatteras, 4 varieties, attached.	6.00	7.00	13.00(100)	1.15	1.00	.65
1448	2¢ Ship's Hull.	....	....	....	....	.25	.25
1449	2¢ Lighthouse	....	....	....	....	.25	.25
1450	2¢ Three Seagulls	....	....	....	....	.25	.25
1451	2¢ Two Seagulls	....	....	....	....	.25	.25
1452	6¢ Wolf Trap Farm Park	2.00	4.00	13.00(50)	1.75	.50	.25
1453	8¢ Yellowstone Park . .	2.00	4.00	16.00(32)	2.75	.50	.25
1454	15¢ Mount McKinley . .	2.00	4.00	24.00(50)	2.75	.60	.35

1455

1972 COMMEMORATIVES

| 1455 | 8¢ Family Planning . . . | 2.00 | 4.00 | 14.00(50) | 1.50 | .35 | .25 |

1456   1457

1458   1459

1456-59	Colonial Craftsmen, 4 varieties, attached . .	3.75	4.75	15.00(50)	1.75	1.50	1.20
1456	8¢ Glassmaker	2.25	....	....	....	.45	.25
1457	8¢ Silversmith	2.25	....	....	....	.45	.25
1458	8¢ Wigmaker	2.25	....	....	....	.45	.25
1459	8¢ Hatter	2.25	....	....	....	.45	.25

1460

1461

1462

1460	6¢ Olympics–Cycling. .	2.10	4.25	12.00(50)	3.25(10)	.30	.25
1461	8¢ Olympics–Bob Sled Racing.	2.10	4.25	12.25(50)	3.25(10)	.35	.25
1462	15¢ Olympics–Foot Racing.	2.10	4.25	22.00(50)	6.00(10)	.50	.45

1463

| 1463 | 8¢ Parent Teacher Association . . . . | 2.00 | 4.00 | 14.00(50) | 1.50 | .40 | .25 |
| 1463a | Same, Reversed Plate Number . . . . | 2.00 | 4.00 | 15.00(50) | 1.75 | .... | .... |

SCOTT NO.	DESCRIPTION	FIRST DAY COVERS SING	FIRST DAY COVERS PL. BLK.	MINT SHEET	PLATE BLOCK	UNUSED F/NH	USED

1464   1465

1466   1467

1464-67	Wildlife Conservation, 4 varieties, attached . .	4.00	6.00	17.00(32)	3.25	2.00	1.50
1464	8¢ Fur Seal	2.00	....	....	....	.50	.25
1465	8¢ Cardinal	2.00	....	....	....	.50	.25
1466	8¢ Brown Pelican.	2.00	....	....	....	.50	.25
1467	8¢ Bighorn Sheep	2.00	....	....	....	.50	.25

1468

1469   1470

1468	8¢ Mail Order Business	2.00	4.00	13.00(50)	4.25(12)	.35	.25
1469	8¢ Osteopathic Medicine	2.00	4.25	15.00(50)	2.75(6)	.45	.25
1470	Tom Sawyer–Folklore .	2.00	4.00	14.00(50)	2.25	.35	.25

1473

1471   1472

1471	8¢ Christmas–Virgin Mother	1.75	4.00	13.00(50)	4.50(12)	.35	.25
1472	8¢ Christmas–Santa . . Claus	1.75	4.00	13.00(50)	4.50(12)	.35	.25
1473	8¢ Pharmacy	8.00	10.00	13.00(50)	1.75(4)	.35	.25

1474   1475

| 1474 | 8¢ Stamp Collecting . . | 2.00 | 4.25 | 10.00(40) | 1.50(4) | .35 | .25 |

SCOTT NO.	DESCRIPTION	FIRST DAY COVERS SING	FIRST DAY COVERS PL. BLK.	MINT SHEET	PLATE BLOCK	UNUSED F/NH	USED

1476   1477

1478   1479

1973 COMMEMORATIVES

| 1475-1508 | 34 varieties, complete | .... | .... | .... | .... | 12.00 | 7.60 |
| 1475 | 8¢ "Love" . . . . | 2.25 | 5.00 | 12.50(50) | 2.25(6) | .35 | .25 |

COLONIAL COMMUNICATIONS

1476	8¢ Pamphlet Printing . .	2.00	4.00	12.50(50)	1.50	.35	.25
1477	8¢ Posting Broadside .	2.00	4.00	12.50(50)	1.50	.35	.25
1478	8¢ Colonial Post Rider.	2.00	4.00	12.50(50)	1.50	.35	.25
1479	8¢ Drummer & Soldiers	2.00	4.00	12.50(50)	1.50	.35	.25

1480   1481

1482   1483

1480-83	Boston Tea Party, 4 varieties, attached . .	4.50	6.50	16.00(50)	1.85	1.60	1.25
1480	8¢ Throwing Tea	2.25	....	....	....	.45	.25
1481	8¢ Ship	2.25	....	....	....	.45	.25
1482	8¢ Rowboats	2.25	....	....	....	.45	.25
1483	8¢ Rowboat & Dock. . .	2.25	....	....	....	.45	.25

1484

1485

1488

1486   1487

SCOTT NO.	DESCRIPTION	FIRST DAY COVERS SING	PL. BLK.	MINT SHEET	PLATE BLOCK	UNUSED F/NH	USED
		AMERICAN ARTS					
1484	8¢ George Gershwin–Composer	2.00	4.00	10.25(40)	4.00(12)	.35	.25
1485	8¢ Robinson Jeffers–Poet	2.00	4.00	10.25(40)	4.25(12)	.35	.25
1486	8¢ Henry O. Tanner–Artist	5.00	6.00	10.25(40)	4.00(12)	.35	.25
1487	8¢ Willa Cather–Novelist	2.00	4.00	14.00(40)	7.00(12)	.60	.25
1488	8¢ Nicolaus Copernicus	2.00	4.00	12.25(40)	1.50	.35	.25

1489

1490

1491

1492

1493

1494

1495

1496

1497

1498

1973 POSTAL SERVICE EMPLOYEES

SCOTT NO.	DESCRIPTION	SING	PL. BLK.	MINT SHEET	PLATE BLOCK	UNUSED F/NH	USED
1489-98	10 varieties, complete, attached . .	6.50	. . . .	18.00(50)	9.00(20)	4.50	3.60
1489-98	Set of singles, complete	22.00	. . . .	. . . .	. . . .	4.25	3.25
1489	8¢ Window Clerk	2.25	. . . .	. . . .	. . . .	.45	.35
1490	8¢ Mail Pickup	2.25	. . . .	. . . .	. . . .	.45	.35
1491	8¢ Conveyor Belt	2.25	. . . .	. . . .	. . . .	.45	.35
1492	8¢ Sacking Parcels	2.25	. . . .	. . . .	. . . .	.45	.35
1493	8¢ Mail Cancelling	2.25	. . . .	. . . .	. . . .	.45	.35
1494	8¢ Manual Sorting	2.25	. . . .	. . . .	. . . .	.45	.35
1495	8¢ Machine Sorting	2.25	. . . .	. . . .	. . . .	.45	.35
1496	8¢ Loading Truck	2.25	. . . .	. . . .	. . . .	.45	.35
1497	8¢ Letter Carrier	2.25	. . . .	. . . .	. . . .	.45	.35
1498	8¢ Rural Delivery	2.25	. . . .	. . . .	. . . .	.45	.35

1499

1500

1501

1502

1503

1973 COMMEMORATIVES

SCOTT NO.	DESCRIPTION	SING	PL. BLK.	MINT SHEET	PLATE BLOCK	UNUSED F/NH	USED
1499	8¢ Harry S. Truman . . .	2.00	4.00	12.00(32)	2.25	.50	.25
1500	6¢ Electronics	2.00	4.00	12.00(50)	1.50	.35	.25
1501	8¢ Electronics	2.00	4.00	14.00(50)	1.75	.35	.25
1502	15¢ Electronics	2.00	4.00	25.00(50)	2.50	.60	.40
1503	8¢ Lyndon B. Johnson .	2.00	4.00	12.00(32)	5.50(12)	.50	.25

1504

1505

1506

1973-74 RURAL AMERICA

SCOTT NO.	DESCRIPTION	SING	PL. BLK.	MINT SHEET	PLATE BLOCK	UNUSED F/NH	USED
1504	8¢ Angus Cattle	2.00	4.00	16.50(50)	1.85	.45	.25
1505	10¢ Chautauqua (1973)	2.00	4.00	16.50(50)	1.85	.45	.25
1506	10¢ Winter Wheat (1974)	2.00	4.00	14.00(50)	1.85	.45	.25

1507

1508

1973 CHRISTMAS

SCOTT NO.	DESCRIPTION	SING	PL. BLK.	MINT SHEET	PLATE BLOCK	UNUSED F/NH	USED
1507	8¢ Madonna	2.25	3.25	13.00(50)	4.25(12)	.40	.25
1508	8¢ Christmas Tree	2.25	3.25	13.00(50)	4.25(12)	.40	.25

SCOTT NO.	DESCRIPTION	FIRST DAY COVERS SING	PL. BLK.	MINT SHEET	PLATE BLOCK	UNUSED F/NH	USED

1509, 1519   **1510, 1520**   **1511**   **1518**

1973-74 REGULAR ISSUES

Scott	Description	Sing	Pl.Blk	Mint Sheet	Plate Block	Unused	Used
1509	10¢ Crossed Flags . . .	2.25	4.00	32.00(100)	7.75(20)	.40	.25
1510	10¢ Jefferson.Memorial	2.25	4.00	34.00(100)	2.50	.50	.25
1510b	10¢ bklt pane of 5– Slogan VIII.	2.25	......	......	......	1.85	......
1510c	10¢ bklt pane of 8	2.25	......	......	......	3.50	......
1510d	10¢ bklt pane of 6 (1974)	2.25	......	......	......	8.75	......
1511	10¢ Zip Code Theme (1974)	2.25	4.00	29.50(100)	2.75(8)	.35	.25

BOOKLET PANE SLOGANS

VI– Stamps in This Book....   VII– This Book Contains 25....   VIII–Paying Bills....

COIL STAMPS Perf.10 Vertically

Scott	Description	Sing	LINE PAIR	LINE PAIR	Unused	Used
1518	6.3¢ Liberty Bell.	2.25	2.75	.90	.40	.25
1519	10¢ Crossed Flags . . .	2.25	......	......	.50	.25
1520	10¢ Jefferson Memorial	2.25	2.75	1.25	.40	.25

1525

1526

1527

1528

1529

1974 COMMEMORATIVES

Scott	Description	Sing	Pl.Blk	Mint Sheet	Plate Block	Unused	Used
1525-52	28 varieties, complete.	......	......	......	......	11.00	6.00
1525	10¢ Veterans of Foreign Wars	2.25	4.00	14.00(50)	1.50	.40	.25
1526	10¢ Robert Frost	2.25	4.00	16.50(50)	1.85	.40	.25
1527	10¢ Environment— EXPO '74.	2.25	4.00	16.00(40)	6.00(12)	.40	.25
1528	10¢ Horse Racing	2.25	4.00	19.50(50)	6.00(12)	.40	.25
1529	10¢ Skylab Project. . . .	2.25	4.00	14.25(50)	1.75	.40	.25

1530

1531

1532

1533

1534

1535

1536   **1537**

1974 UNIVERSAL POSTAL UNION

Scott	Description	Sing	Pl.Blk	Mint Sheet	Plate Block	Unused	Used
1530-37	8 varieties, attached .	6.00	......	13.00(32)	7.50(16)	3.50(8)	2.95
1530-37	Set of singles, complete	17.50	......	......	......	3.25	2.25
1530	10¢ Raphael	2.75	......	......	......	.50	.35
1531	10¢ Hokusai.	2.75	......	......	......	.50	.35
1532	10¢ J.F. Peto	2.75	......	......	......	.50	.35
1533	10¢ J.E. Liotard	2.75	......	......	......	.50	.35
1534	10¢ G. Terborch.	2.75	......	......	......	.50	.35
1535	10¢ J.B.S. Chardin . . .	2.75	......	......	......	.50	.35
1536	10¢ T. Gainsborough . .	2.75	......	......	......	.50	.35
1537	10¢ F. de Goya	2.75	......	......	......	.50	.35

1538

1540   **1539**

1541

1974 COMMEMORATIVES

Scott	Description	Sing	Pl.Blk	Mint Sheet	Plate Block	Unused	Used
1538-41	Mineral Heritage, 4 varieties, attached . .	3.50	5.00	18.00(48)	2.25	1.75	1.25
1538	10¢ Petrified Wood . . .	2.25	......	......	......	.50	.25
1539	10¢ Tourmaline	2.25	......	......	......	.50	.25
1540	10¢ Amethyst.	2.25	......	......	......	.50	.25
1541	10¢ Rhodochrosite . . .	2.25	......	......	......	.50	.25

SCOTT NO.	DESCRIPTION	FIRST DAY COVERS SING	PL. BLK.	MINT SHEET	PLATE BLOCK	UNUSED F/NH	USED
1542	10¢ Fort Harrod Bicentennial	2.25	4.00	15.00(50)	1.75	.40	.25
1543-46	Continental Congress, 4 varieties, attached	4.50	6.00	17.00(50)	2.25	1.75	1.25
1543	10¢ Carpenter's Hall	2.25	....	....	....	.40	.25
1544	10¢ Quote–First Congress	2.25	....	....	....	.40	.25
1545	10¢ Quote–Declaration– of Independence	2.25	....	....	....	.40	.25
1546	10¢ Independence Hall	2.25	....	....	....	.40	.25
1547	10¢ Energy Conservation	2.25	4.00	17.00(50)	1.90	.45	.25
1548	10¢ Sleepy Hollow	2.25	4.00	15.00(50)	1.75	.40	.25
1549	10¢ Retarded Children	2.25	4.00	19.00(50)	1.90	.40	.25
1550	10¢ Christmas–Angel	2.25	4.00	14.00(50)	4.50(10)	.35	.25
1551	10¢ Christmas–Currier & Ives	2.25	4.00	14.00(50)	5.00(12)	.35	.25
1552	10¢ Christams– Dove of Peace	2.25	4.00	18.00(50)	9.50(20)	.40	.25
1552	same	....	....	....	5.50(12)	....	....

1975 COMMEMORATIVES

SCOTT NO.	DESCRIPTION	FIRST DAY COVERS SING	PL. BLK.	MINT SHEET	PLATE BLOCK	UNUSED F/NH	USED
1553-80	8¢-10¢, 28 varieties, complete	....	....	....	....	12.00	6.25
1553	10¢ Benjamin West– Arts	2.25	4.00	16.00(50)	5.00(10)	.45	.25
1554	10¢ Paul Dunbar–Arts	2.25	4.00	18.00(50)	5.00(10)	.45	.25
1555	10¢ D.W. Griffith–Arts	2.25	4.00	17.00(50)	2.00	.45	.25
1556	10¢ Pioneer 10	2.25	4.00	16.00(50)	2.00	.45	.25
1557	10¢ Mariner 10	2.25	4.00	16.00(50)	2.00	.45	.25
1558	10¢ Collective Bargaining	2.25	4.00	16.00(50)	3.25(8)	.40	.25
1559	8¢ Sybil Ludington	2.25	4.00	14.00(50)	4.00(10)	.35	.25
1560	10¢ Salem Poor	2.25	4.00	16.00(50)	5.00(10)	.45	.25
1561	10¢ Haym Salomon	2.25	4.00	16.00(50)	5.00(10)	.45	.25
1562	18¢ Peter Francisco	2.25	4.00	27.50(50)	8.00(10)	.70	.40
1563	10¢ Lexington-Concord	2.25	4.00	15.00(40)	5.75(12)	.45	.25
1564	10¢ Battle of Bunker Hill	2.25	4.00	16.00(40)	5.50(12)	.45	.25

1542

1543   **1544**

1545   **1546**

1547   **1548**   **1549**

1550   **1551**   **1552**

1553   **1554**   **1555**

1556   **1557**

1558

1559   **1560**

1561   **1562**

1563   **1564**

SCOTT NO.	DESCRIPTION	FIRST DAY COVERS SING	PL. BLK.	MINT SHEET	PLATE BLOCK	UNUSED F/NH	USED

1565   1566   1567   1568

1565-68	Military Uniforms, 4 varieties, attached	4.00	6.00	17.00(50)	5.75(12)	1.75	1.30
1565	10¢ Continental Army	2.25	....	....	....	.50	.25
1566	10¢ Continental Navy	2.25	....	....	....	.50	.25
1567	10¢ Continental Marines	2.25	....	....	....	.50	.25
1568	10¢ American Militia	2.25	....	....	....	.50	.25

1569

1570

1569-70	Apollo-Soyuz Mission, 2 varieties, attached	3.00	4.50	11.00(24)	5.75(12)	.95	.65
1569	10¢ Docked	2.25	....	....	....	.50	.30
1570	10¢ Docking	2.25	....	....	....	.50	.30

1571

| 1571 | 10¢ International Women's Year | 2.25 | 4.00 | 14.00(50) | 2.40(6) | .35 | .25 |

1572   1573

1574   1575

1572-75	Postal Service Bicentennial, 4 varieties, attached	4.00	5.00	19.00(50)	5.50(12)	1.85	1.50
1572	10¢ Stagecoach & Trailer	2.25	....	....	....	.50	.25
1573	10¢ Locomotives	2.25	....	....	....	.50	.25
1574	10¢ Airplanes	2.25	....	....	....	.50	.25
1575	10¢ Satellite	2.25	....	....	....	.50	.25

SCOTT NO.	DESCRIPTION	FIRST DAY COVERS SING	PL. BLK.	MINT SHEET	PLATE BLOCK	UNUSED F/NH	USED

1576

1577   1578

1576	10¢ World Peace through Law	2.25	4.00	15.00(50)	2.00	.45	.25
1577-78	Banking & Commerce, 2 varieties, attached	2.50	3.75	15.00(40)	2.25	1.00	.70
1577	10¢ Banking	2.25	....	....	....	.60	.25
1578	10¢ Commerce	2.25	....	....	....	.60	.25

1579   1580

1579	(10¢) Madonna	2.25	4.00	15.00(50)	5.00(12)	.45	.25
1580	(10¢) Christams Card	2.25	4.00	15.00(50)	5.00(12)	.45	.25
1580b	(10¢) Christmas Card, perf. 10½ x 11	....	....	66.00(50)	19.00(12)	1.40	.80

1581, 1811   1582   1584   1585

1590, 1591, 1616   1592, 1617   1593   1594, 1816

1595, 1618   1596   1597, 1598, 1618C   1599, 1619

1603   1604   1605   1606

SCOTT NO.	DESCRIPTION	FIRST DAY COVERS SING	PL. BLK.	MINT SHEET	PLATE BLOCK	UNUSED F/NH	USED

1608   1610   1611   1612

1975-81 AMERICANA ISSUE

1581/1612	1¢-$5, (No #1590, 1590a, 1595, or 1598) 19 varieties, complete	51.50	....	....	155.00	33.50	6.95
1581	1¢ Inkwell & Quill (1977)	2.25	4.00	10.00(100)	1.25	.35	.25
1582	2¢ Speaker's Stand (1977)	2.25	4.00	10.00(100)	2.00	.25	.25
1584	3¢ Ballot Box (1977)	2.25	4.00	17.00(100)	2.00	.30	.25
1585	4¢ Books & Eyeglasses (1977)	2.25	4.00	18.00(100)	2.00	.30	.25
1590	9¢ Capitol, from bklt pane (1977)	15.00	....	....	....	1.25	1.00
1590a	same, perf 10 (1977)	....	....	....	....	33.00	....
1590,1623	Attached pair, from bklt pane	....	....	....	....	1.75	....
1590a, 1623b	Attached pair, perf. 10	....	....	....	....	35.00	....
1591	9¢ Capitol, grey paper	2.25	4.00	30.00(100)	1.75	.40	.25
1592	10¢ Justice (1977)	2.25	4.00	32.00(100)	1.75	.40	.25
1593	11¢ Printing Press	2.25	4.00	36.00(100)	2.25	.50	.25
1594	12¢ Torch (1981)	2.25	4.00	38.50(100)	2.50	.50	.25
1595	13¢ Liberty Bell from bklt pane	2.25	....	....	....	.50	.25
1595a	13¢ bklt pane of 6	2.25	....	....	....	3.25	....
1595b	13¢ bklt pane of 7– Slogan VIII	2.50	....	....	....	3.50	....
1595c	13¢ bklt pane of 8	2.50	....	....	....	3.75	....
1595d	13¢ bklt pane of 5– Slogan IX (1976)	2.25	....	....	....	3.50	....

VIII–Paying Bills... IX–Collect Stamps...

1596	13¢ Eagle & Shield	2.25	4.00	40.00(100)	7.00(12)	.50	.25
1597	15¢ Fort McHenry Flag (1978)	2.25	4.00	43.00(100)	12.00(20)	.50	.25
1598	same, from bklt pane (1978)	2.25	....	....	....	.90	.25
1598a	15¢ bklt pane of 8	3.00	....	....	....	8.50	....
1599	16¢ Statue of Liberty (1978)	2.25	4.00	52.00(100)	3.00	.60	.30
1603	24¢ Old North Church	2.25	4.00	72.00(100)	4.50	.95	.25
1604	28¢ Fort Nisqually (1978)	2.25	4.00	92.00(100)	5.75	1.10	.35
1605	29¢ Lighthouse (1978)	2.25	4.00	100.00(100)	5.75	1.20	.50
1606	30¢ School House (1979)	2.25	4.00	100.00(100)	6.00	1.20	.30
1608	50¢ "Betty" Lamp (1979)	2.50	5.25	150.00(100)	9.00	2.00	.30
1610	$1 Rush Lamp (1979)	3.50	17.50	305.00(100)	16.00	3.50	.30
1610c	Same, candle flame inverted	....	....	....	....	14500.00	....
1611	$2 Kerosene Lamp (1978)	7.00	14.50	600.00(100)	32.50	7.25	.85
1612	$5 Conductor's Lantern (1979)	15.00	31.50	1375.00(100)	74.00	16.00	3.00

1613   1614   1615   1615C

1975-79 COIL STAMPS Perforated Vertically

1613-19	3.1¢-16¢, 9 varieties, complete	....	....	....	LINE PR. 12.50	3.75	1.80
1613	3.1¢ Guitar (1979)	2.25	2.75	....	1.20	.45	.25
1614	7.7¢ Saxhorns (1976)	2.25	2.75	....	1.50	.60	.40
1615	7.9¢ Drum (1976)	2.25	2.75	....	1.40	.60	.40
1615C	8.4¢ Piano (1978)	2.25	2.75	....	5.00	.60	.40
1616	9¢ Capitol (1976)	2.25	2.75	....	1.30	.60	.40
1617	10¢ Justice (1977)	2.25	2.75	....	1.25	.50	.25
1618	13¢ Liberty Bell	2.25	2.75	....	1.50	.60	.30
1618C	15¢ Fort McHenry Flag (1978)	2.25	....	....	....	.85	.25
1619	16¢ Statue of Liberty (1978)	2.25	2.75	....	2.50	.75	.60

1622, 1625   1623, 1623b

1975-77 REGULAR ISSUES

1622	13¢ Flag & Independence Hall, 11 x 10½	2.25	4.00	40.00(100)	12.00(20)	.55	.25
1622c	same, perf. 11 (1981)	....	....	150.00(100)	90.00(20)	1.20	....
1623	13¢ Flag & Capitol from bklt pane, perf 11 x 10½ (1977)	3.00	....	....	....	.50	.50
1623a	bklt pane of 8 (one–1590, seven–1623)	30.00	....	....	....	4.00	3.75
1623b	13¢ Flag & Capitol from bklt pane, perf. 10	2.25	....	....	....	.90	.75
1623c	bklt pane of 8 (one–1590a, seven–1623b)	17.00	....	....	....	38.00	....

1975 COIL STAMP

1625	13¢ Flag & Independence Hall	2.25	....	....	3.75	.55	.25

1629   1630   1631

1632

1976 COMMEMORATIVES

1629/1703	(1629-32, 1683-85, 1690-1703) 21 varieties	....	....	....	....	12.80	3.50
1629-31	Spirit of '76 , 3 varieties, attached	3.00	6.00	22.00(50)	7.25(12)	1.75	1.25
1629	13¢ Boy Drummer	2.00	....	....	....	.60	.25
1630	13¢ Older Drummer	2.00	....	....	....	.60	.25
1631	13¢ Fifer	2.00	....	....	....	.60	.25
1632	13¢ Interphil	2.25	4.00	19.00(50)	2.25	.50	.25

1633   1682

1976 BICENTENNIAL STATE FLAGS
Complete Set Printed in One Sheet of 50 Stamps

1633	Delaware	1650	Louisiana	1667	West Virginia
1634	Pennsylvania	1651	Indiana	1668	Nevada
1635	New Jersey	1652	Mississippi	1669	Nebraska
1636	Georgia	1653	Illinois	1670	Colorado
1637	Connecticut	1654	Alabama	1671	North Dakota
1638	Massachusetts	1655	Maine	1672	South Dakota
1639	Maryland	1656	Missouri	1673	Montana
1640	South Carolina	1657	Arkansas	1674	Washington
1641	New Hampshire	1658	Michigan	1675	Idaho
1642	Virginia	1659	Florida	1676	Wyoming
1643	New York	1660	Texas	1677	Utah
1644	North Carolina	1661	Iowa	1678	Oklahoma
1645	Rhode Island	1662	Wisconsin	1679	New Mexico
1646	Vermont	1663	California	1680	Arizona
1647	Kentucky	1664	Minnesota	1681	Alaska
1648	Tennessee	1665	Oregon	1682	Hawaii
1649	Ohio	1666	Kansas		

COIL LINE PAIRS: are two connected coil stamps with a line the same color as the stamps printed between the two stamps. This line usually appears every 20 to 30 stamps on a roll depending on the issue.

SCOTT NO.	DESCRIPTION	FIRST DAY COVERS SING	PL. BLK.	MINT SHEET	PLATE BLOCK	UNUSED F/NH	USED

1976 BICENTENNIAL STATE FLAGS
Complete Set Printed in One Sheet of 50 Stamps
Continued

SCOTT NO.	DESCRIPTION	SING	PL. BLK.	MINT SHEET	PLATE BLOCK	UNUSED F/NH	USED
1633-82	13¢ State Flags, 50 varieties, attached...........	....	....	29.00(50)	....	29.00	....
	Set of 50 singles	95.00	....	....	....	....	18.75
	Singles of above	2.50	....	....	....	1.00	.50

1683

1684

1685

1683	13¢ Telephone.......	2.25	4.00	28.00(50)	2.75	.60	.25
1684	13¢ Aviation.........	2.25	4.00	20.00(50)	8.50(10)	.75	.25
1685	13¢ Chemistry.......	2.25	4.00	25.00(50)	7.50(12)	.60	.25

1686

1687

1976 BICENNTENNIAL SOUVENIR SHEETS

1686-89	4 varieties, complete ..	32.50	....	....	....	30.00	27.00
1686	13¢ Cornwallis Surrender	6.00	....	....	....	5.00	4.75
1686a-e	13¢ singles, each.....	3.50	....	....	....	1.20	1.10
1687	18¢ Independence....	7.50	....	....	....	7.00	6.50
1687a-e	18¢ singles, each.....	3.75	....	....	....	1.60	1.50
1688	24¢ Washington Crossing Delaware.........	9.50	....	....	....	9.00	8.25
1688a-e	24¢ singles, each.....	4.25	....	....	....	1.90	1.80
1689	31¢ Washington at Valley Forge..............	11.50	....	....	....	12.00	10.50
1689a-e	31¢ singles, each.....	5.25	....	....	....	2.40	2.30

1690

1691   1692   1693   1694

1690	13¢ Benjamin Franklin.	2.25	4.00	21.00(50)	2.25	.50	.25
1691-94	Declaration of Independence, 4 varieties, attached ..	5.00	10.00	26.00(50)	12.00(16)	3.50	3.00
1691	13¢ Delegation members	2.25	....	....	....	1.10	.25
1692	13¢ Adams, etc..	2.25	....	....	....	1.10	.25
1693	13¢ Jefferson, Franklin, etc.	2.25	....	....	....	1.10	.25
1694	13¢ Hancock, Thomson, etc.	2.25	....	....	....	1.10	.25

1695   1696   1697   1698

1695-98	Olympic Games, 4 varieties, attached ..	4.00	6.00	24.00(50)	7.50(12)	2.40	1.95
1695	13¢ Diving..........	2.25	....	....	....	.75	.25
1696	13¢ Skiing..........	2.25	....	....	....	.75	.25
1697	13¢ Running........	2.25	....	....	....	.75	.25
1698	13¢ Skating.........	2.25	....	....	....	.75	.25

1699

1700

| 1699 | 13¢ Clara Maass..... | 2.25 | 4.00 | 17.00(40) | 7.00(12) | .60 | .25 |
| 1700 | 13¢ Adolph S. Ochs... | 2.25 | 4.00 | 16.00(32) | 2.50 | .60 | .25 |

1701

1702, 1703

1701	13¢ Nativity.........	2.25	....	20.00(50)	6.50(12)	.55	.25
1702	13¢ "Winter Pastime" (Andreati)...........	2.25	....	20.00(50)	5.50(10)	.55	.25
1703	13¢ "Winter Pastime" (Gravure Int.)........	2.25	....	22.00(50)	13.00(20)	.55	.25

1704

1705

1977 COMMEMORATIVES

SCOTT NO.	DESCRIPTION	FIRST DAY COVERS SING	PL. BLK.	MINT SHEET	PLATE BLOCK	UNUSED F/NH	USED
1704-30	27 varieties, complete	....	....	....	....	13.00	5.00
1704	13¢ Princeton	2.25	4.00	16.00(40)	5.50(10)	.60	.25
1705	13¢ Sound Recording .	2.25	4.00	20.00(50)	2.25	.60	.25

1708   1709

1706   1707

1706-09	Pueblo Art, 4 varieties, attached ..	4.00	....	19.00(40)	6.50(10)	3.00	2.50
1706	13¢ Zia.	2.25	....	....	....	.75	.25
1707	13¢ San Ildefonso	2.25	....	....	....	.75	.25
1708	13¢ Hopi	2.25	....	....	....	.75	.25
1709	13¢ Acoma.	2.25	....	....	....	.75	.25

1710

1711

1710	13¢ Transatlantic Flight	3.00	5.00	22.00(50)	7.50(12)	.50	.25
1711	13¢ Colorado Statehood	2.25	4.00	22.00(50)	7.50(12)	.50	.25

1712   1713

Mint Sheets: From 1935 to date, we list prices for standard size Mint Sheets Fine, Never Hinged condition. The number of stamps in each sheet is noted in ( ).

1714   1715

1716

1712-15	Butterflies, 4 varieties, attached ..	4.00	6.00	22.00(50)	7.50(12)	3.00	2.50
1712	13¢ Swallowtail	2.25	....	....	....	.60	.25
1713	13¢ Checkerspot	2.25	....	....	....	.60	.25
1714	13¢ Dogface	2.25	....	....	....	.60	.25
1715	13¢ Orange-Tip	2.25	....	....	....	.60	.25
1716	13¢ Lafayette........	2.25	6.00	17.00(40)	2.25	.50	.25

1717   1718

1719   1720

1717-20	Skilled Hands, 4 varieties, attached ..	4.00	....	22.00(50)	7.25(12)	2.50	2.00
1717	13¢ Seamstress......	2.25	....	....	....	.60	.25
1718	13¢ Blacksmith	2.25	....	....	....	.60	.25
1719	13¢ Wheelwright	2.25	....	....	....	.60	.25
1720	13¢ Leatherworker. ...	2.25	....	....	....	.60	.25

1721

1722

1723

1724

1721	13¢ Peace Bridge	2.25	4.00	21.00(50)	3.00	.50	.25
1722	13¢ Herkimer at Oriskany	2.25	4.00	17.50(40)	5.25(10)	.50	.25
1723-24	Energy, 2 varieties, attached ..	2.50	....	18.00(40)	7.25(12)	1.10	.85
1723	13¢ Conservation	2.25	....	....	....	.60	.25
1724	13¢ Development	2.25	....	....	....	.60	.25

SCOTT NO.	DESCRIPTION	FIRST DAY COVERS SING	FIRST DAY COVERS PL. BLK.	MINT SHEET	PLATE BLOCK	UNUSED F/NH	USED

1725

1726

1727

1728

1729

1730

1725	13¢ Alta California	2.25	4.00	20.00(50)	2.25	.45	.25
1726	13¢ Articles of Confederation	2.25	4.00	20.00(50)	2.25	.45	.25
1727	13¢ Talking Pictures . .	2.25	4.00	20.00(50)	2.25	.45	.25
1728	13¢ Surrender at Saratoga	2.25	....	17.50(40)	5.25(10)	.45	.25
1729	13¢ Washington, Christmas	2.50	....	48.00(100)	13.00(20)	.60	.25
1730	13¢ Rural Mailbox, Christmas	2.50	....	39.00(100)	5.25(10)	.50	.25

1731

1732

1733

1978 COMMEMORATIVES

1731/69	(1731-33, 1744-56, 1758-69) 28 varieties .	....	....	....	....	19.50	7.00
1731	13¢ Carl Sandburg . . .	2.25	4.00	22.00(50)	2.50	.50	.25
1732-33	Captain Cook, 2 varieties, attached . .	2.00	....	24.00(50)	12.00(20)	1.50	1.20
1732	13¢ Captain Cook (Alaska)	2.25	4.00	....	2.50	.55	.25
1733	13¢ "Resolution" (Hawaii)	2.25	4.00	....	2.50	.55	.25

NOTE: The Plate Block set includes #1732 & 1733 Plate Blocks of four.

1734

1735, 1736, 1743

1737

1978-80 DEFINITIVES

1734	13¢ Indian Head Penny	2.25	4.00	58.00(150)	2.50	.60	.25
1735	(15¢) "A" Definitive (Gravure)	2.25	4.00	45.00(100)	2.50	.60	.25
1736	same (Intaglio), from bklt pane	2.25	....	....	....	.60	.25
1736a	15¢ "A" bklt pane of 8 .	3.50	....	....	....	4.50	....
1737	15¢ Roses	2.25	....	....	....	.60	.25
1737a	same, bklt pane of 8 . .	4.00	....	....	....	4.50	....

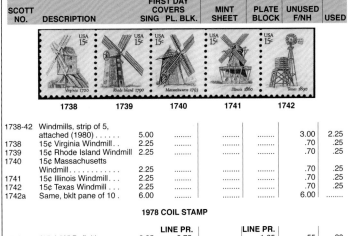

1738

1739

1740

1741

1742

1738-42	Windmills, strip of 5, attached (1980)	5.00	....	....	....	3.00	2.25
1738	15¢ Virginia Windmill. .	2.25	....	....	....	.70	.25
1739	15¢ Rhode Island Windmill	2.25	....	....	....	.70	.25
1740	15¢ Massachusetts Windmill	2.25	....	....	....	.70	.25
1741	15¢ Illinois Windmill . . .	2.25	....	....	....	.70	.25
1742	15¢ Texas Windmill . . .	2.25	....	....	....	.70	.25
1742a	Same, bklt pane of 10 .	6.00	....	....	....	6.00	....

1978 COIL STAMP

			LINE PR.		LINE PR.		
1743	(15¢) "A" Definitive	2.25	2.75	....	1.65	.55	.20

1745

1744

1746

1747

1748

1744	13¢ Harriet Tubman. . .	5.00	7.00	29.00(50)	9.50(12)	.65	.25
1745-48	Quilts, 4 varieties, attached	3.50	....	30.00(48)	12.00(12)	3.00	2.00
1745	13¢ Flowers.	2.25	....	....	....	.75	.25
1746	13¢ Stars.	2.25	....	....	....	.75	.25
1747	13¢ Stripes	2.25	....	....	....	.75	.25
1748	13¢ Plaid	2.25	....	....	....	.75	.25

1750

1749

1752

1751

1749-52	American Dance, 4 varieties, attached . .	5.00	....	22.00(48)	7.75(12)	3.00	2.00
1749	13¢ Ballet.	2.25	....	....	....	.75	.25
1750	13¢ Theater	2.25	....	....	....	.75	.25
1751	13¢ Folk.	2.25	....	....	....	.75	.25
1752	13¢ Modern	2.25	....	....	....	.75	.25

SCOTT NO.	DESCRIPTION	FIRST DAY COVERS SING	PL. BLK.	MINT SHEET	PLATE BLOCK	UNUSED F/NH	USED

1753 **1754** **1755** **1756**

1753	13¢ French Alliance...	2.25	4.00	16.00(40)	2.25	.50	.25
1754	13¢ Dr. Papanicolaou .	2.25	4.00	20.00(50)	2.25	.60	.25
1755	13¢ Jimmie Rodgers ..	2.25	4.00	23.00(50)	8.00(12)	.75	.25
1756	15¢ George M. Cohan.	2.25	4.00	23.00(50)	8.00(12)	.75	.25

1757

1978 CAPEX SOUVENIR SHEET

1757	$1.04 CAPEX	4.25	....	19.00(6)	4.00	3.50	3.00
1757a	13¢ Cardinal	2.25	....			.45	.40
1757b	13¢ Mallard	2.25	....			.45	.40
1757c	13¢ Canada Goose ...	2.25	....			.45	.40
1757d	13¢ Blue Jay	2.25	....			.45	.40
1757e	13¢ Moose..........	2.25	....			.45	.40
1757f	13¢ Chipmunk.......	2.25	....			.45	.40
1757g	13¢ Red Fox	2.25	....			.45	.40
1757h	13¢ Raccoon	2.25	....			.45	.40

1759

1758

| 1758 | 15¢ Photography ..... | 2.25 | 4.00 | 17.00(40) | 7.25(12) | .60 | .25 |
| 1759 | 15¢ Viking Mission.... | 2.25 | 4.00 | 23.00(50) | 3.00 | .60 | .25 |

1760 **1761** **1762** **1763**

1760-63	American Owls, 4 varieties, attached...........	5.00	6.00	30.00(50)	3.50	3.00	2.00
1760	15¢ Great Gray	2.25	....			.70	.25
1761	15¢ Saw-Whet......	2.25	....			.70	.25
1762	15¢ Barred Owl	2.25	....			.70	.25
1763	15¢ Great Horned	2.25	....			.70	.25

SCOTT NO.	DESCRIPTION	FIRST DAY COVERS SING	PL. BLK.	MINT SHEET	PLATE BLOCK	UNUSED F/NH	USED

1764 **1765**

1766 **1767**

1764-67	Trees, 4 varieties, attached...........	5.00	....	28.00(40)	12.00(12)	3.25	2.00
1764	15¢ Giant Sequoia....	2.25	....	....	....	.70	.25
1765	15¢ Pine	2.25	....	....	....	.70	.25
1766	15¢ Oak...........	2.25	....	....	....	.70	.25
1767	15¢ Birch...........	2.25	....	....	....	.70	.25

1768 **1769**

| 1768 | 15¢ Madonna, Christmas | 2.25 | 4.00 | 44.00(100) | 7.25(12) | .60 | .25 |
| 1769 | 15¢ Hobby Horse, Christmas | 2.25 | 4.00 | 44.00(100) | 8.25(12) | .60 | .25 |

1770 **1771**

1979 COMMEMORATIVES

1770/1802	(1770-94, 1799-1802) 29 varieties, complete	....	....	....	....	17.50	6.00
1770	15¢ Robert F. Kennedy	2.25	4.00	25.00(48)	2.75	.65	.25
1771	15¢ Martin L. King, Jr. .	3.00	5.00	25.00(50)	8.50(12)	.75	.25

1772 **1773** **1774**

1772	15¢ International Year of the Child	2.25	4.00	23.50(50)	2.75	.65	.25
1773	15¢ John Steinbeck....	2.25	4.00	25.00(50)	2.75	.65	.25
1774	15¢ Albert Einstein.	3.00	5.00	25.00(50)	3.25	.75	.25

U.S. BICENTENNIAL: The U.S.P.S. issued stamps commemorating the 200th anniversary of the struggle for independence from 1775 through 1783. These include numbers: 1432, 1476-83, 1543-46, 1559-68, 1629-31, 1633-82, 1686-89, 1691-94, 1704, 1716-20, 1722, 1726, 1728-29, 1753, 1789, 1826, 1937-38, 1941, 2052 and C98.

SCOTT NO.	DESCRIPTION	FIRST DAY COVERS SING	PL. BLK.	MINT SHEET	PLATE BLOCK	UNUSED F/NH	USED

1775　1776

1779　1780

1781　1782

1777　1778

1775-78	Pennsylvania Toleware, 4 varieties, attached	5.00	....	20.00(40)	6.75(10)	2.50	2.00
1775	15¢ Coffee Pot	2.25	....			.75	.25
1776	15¢ Tea Caddy	2.25	....			.75	.25
1777	15¢ Sugar Bowl	2.25	....			.75	.25
1778	15¢ Coffee Pot	2.25	....			.75	.25
1779-82	Architecture, 4 varieties, attached	5.00	6.00	27.00(48)	4.00	3.50	2.75
1779	15¢ Virginia Rotunda	2.25	....			1.00	.25
1780	15¢ Baltimore Cathedral	2.25	....			1.00	.25
1781	15¢ Boston State House	2.25	....			1.00	.25
1782	15¢ Philadelphia Exchange	2.25	....			1.00	.25

1783　1784　1785　1786

1783-86	Endangered Flora, 4 varieties, attached	5.00	....	25.00(50)	8.25(12)	2.75	2.25
1783	15¢ Trillium	2.25	....			.75	.25
1784	15¢ Broadbean	2.25	....			.75	.25
1785	15¢ Wallflower	2.25	....			.75	.25
1786	15¢ Primrose	2.25	....			.75	.25

1787　1788　1789, 1789a　1790

1787	15¢ Guide Dog	2.25	....	24.00(50)	12.00(20)	.70	.25
1788	15¢ Special Olympics	2.25	....	24.00(50)	6.00(10)	.65	.25
1789	15¢ John Paul Jones perf. 11 x 12	2.25	....	24.00(50)	6.00(10)	.65	.25
1789a	same, perf. 11	2.25	....	35.00(50)	9.00(10)	1.00	.30

NOTE: #1789a may be included in year date sets and special offers and not 1789.

1790	10¢ Summer Olympics, Javelin Thrower	2.25	4.00	15.00(50)	5.25(12)	.40	.25

1791　1792

1793　1794

1791-94	Summer Olympics, 4 varieties, attached	5.00	....	24.00(50)	8.25(12)	2.50	2.00
1791	15¢ Runners	2.25	....			.70	.25
1792	15¢ Swimmers	2.25	....			.70	.25
1793	15¢ Rowers	2.25	....			.70	.25
1794	15¢ Equestrian	2.25	....			.70	.25

1795　1796

1797　1798

1980

1795-98	Winter Olympics, 4 varieties, attached	5.00	....	25.00(50)	8.25(12)	2.75	2.00
1795	15¢ Skater	2.25	....			.70	.25
1796	15¢ Downhill Skier	2.25	....			.70	.25
1797	15¢ Ski Jumper	2.25	....			.70	.25
1798	15¢ Hockey	2.25	....			.70	.25
1795a-98a							
	same, perf. 11, attached	....	....	45.00(50)	15.00(12)	4.50	3.50
1795a	15¢ Skater	....	....			1.20	.75
1796a	15¢ Downhill Skier	....	....			1.20	.75
1797a	15¢ Ski Jumper	....	....			1.20	.75
1798a	15¢ Hockey	....	....			1.20	.75

SCOTT NO.	DESCRIPTION	FIRST DAY COVERS SING	PL. BLK.	MINT SHEET	PLATE BLOCK	UNUSED F/NH	USED

1799

1800

1979 COMMEMORATIVES

1799	15¢ Christmas–Madonna	2.25	....	44.00(100)	7.25(12)	.60	.25
1800	15¢ Christmas–Santa Claus	2.25	....	49.00(100)	8.00(12)	.70	.25

1801

1802

1801	15¢ Will Rogers......	3.00	....	25.00(50)	8.00(12)	.70	.25
1802	15¢ Vietnam Veterans .	3.00	5.25	27.00(50)	8.00(10)	.70	.25

1803

1804

1980 COMMEMORATIVES

1795/1843	(1795-98, 1803-10, 1821-43) 35 varieties, complete	....	....	....	....	23.00	7.50
1803	15¢ W.C. Fields......	2.25	4.00	24.00(50)	7.25(12)	.60	.25
1804	15¢ Benjamin Banneker	2.25	4.00	27.00(50)	8.75(12)	.70	.25

1805   **1806, 1808, 1810**   **1807**   **1809**

1805-10	6 varieties, attached ..	4.50	....	32.00(60)	24.00(36)	4.25	2.75
1805-06	2 varieties, attached ..	2.50	....	....	....	....	....
1807-08	2 varieties, attached ..	2.50	....	....	....	....	....
1809-10	2 varieties, attached ..	2.50	....	....	....	....	....
1805	15¢ "Letters Preserve Memories"	2.25	....	....	....	.75	.35
1806	15¢ claret & multicolor.	2.25	....	....	....	.75	.35
1807	15¢ "Letters Lift Spirits"	2.25	....	....	....	.75	.35
1808	15¢ green & multicolor.	2.25	....	....	....	.75	.35
1809	15¢ "Letters Shape Opinions"	2.25	....	....	....	.75	.35
1810	15¢ red, white & blue..	2.25	....	....	....	.75	.35

1813

1818, 1819, 1820

1980-81 Coil Stamps, Perf. 10 Vertically

			LINE PR.		LINE PR.		
1811	1¢ Inkwell & Quill.....	2.25	2.75	....	.60	.20	.25
1813	3.5¢ Two Violins	2.25	2.75	....	1.40	.30	.25
1816	12¢ Torch (1981)	2.25	2.75	....	2.25	.50	.40
1818	(18¢) "B" definitive....	2.50	3.50	55.00(100)	3.25	.70	.25
1819	(18¢) "B" definitive, from bklt pane	2.25	....	....	....	.70	.25
1819a	(18¢) "B" bklt pane of 8	4.00	....	....	....	5.25	....

1981 Coil Stamp Perf. Vertically

1820	(18¢) "B" definitive	2.25	2.75	....	2.00	.75	.25

1821   **1822**   **1823**

1824   **1825**   **1826**

1821	15¢ Frances Perkins ..	2.25	4.00	23.00(50)	2.50	.55	.25
1822	15¢ Dolley Madison...	2.25	4.00	72.00(150)	2.75	.60	.25
1823	15¢ Emily Bissell	2.25	4.00	23.00(50)	2.50	.60	.25
1824	15¢ Helen Keller & Anne Sullivan........	2.25	4.00	27.00(50)	3.00	.60	.25
1825	15¢ Veterans Administration	2.25	4.00	25.00(50)	2.50	.60	.25
1826	15¢ General Bernardo. deGalvez...........	2.25	4.00	25.00(50)	3.50	.60	.25

1827   **1828**   **1829**   **1830**

1827-30	Coral Reefs, 4 varieties, attached ..	5.00	....	40.00(50)	13.00(12)	4.00	2.75
1827	15¢ Brain Coral, Virgin Is.	2.25	....	....	....	1.00	.30
1828	15¢ Elkhorn Coral, Florida	2.25	....	....	....	1.00	.30
1829	15¢ Chalice Coral, American Samoa.....	2.25	....	....	....	1.00	.30
1830	15¢ Finger Coral, Hawaii	2.25	....	....	....	1.00	.30

1831   **1832**   **1833**

1831	15¢ Organized Labor..	2.25	4.00	29.00(50)	10.00(12)	.65	.25
1832	15¢ Edith Wharton....	2.25	4.00	25.00(50)	2.75	.65	.25
1833	15¢ Education	2.25	4.00	25.00(50)	3.75(6)	.65	.25

SCOTT NO.	DESCRIPTION	FIRST DAY COVERS SING	PL. BLK.	MINT SHEET	PLATE BLOCK	UNUSED F/NH	USED

1834   1835

1836   1837

	American Folk Art,						
1834-37	4 varieties, attached . .	5.00	....	24.00(40)	9.00(10)	3.25	2.00
1834	15¢ Bella Bella Tribe . .	2.25	....	....	....	1.00	.25
1835	15¢ Chilkat Tlingit Tribe	2.25	....	....	....	1.00	.25
1836	15¢ Tlingit Tribe	2.25	....	....	....	1.00	.25
1837	15¢ Bella Coola Tribe .	2.25	....	....	....	1.00	.25

1838   1839

1840   1841

	American Architecture,						
1838-41	4 varieties, attached . .	4.00	5.00	25.00(40)	3.50	3.00	2.00
1838	15¢ Smithsonian Inst. .	2.25	....	....	....	1.00	.25
1839	15¢ Trinity Church	2.25	....	....	....	1.00	.25
1840	15¢ Penn Academy . . .	2.25	....	....	....	1.00	.25
1841	15¢ Lyndhurst	2.25	....	....	....	1.00	.25

1842   1843

1842	15¢ Madonna	2.25	4.00	22.50(50)	7.00(12)	.55	.25
1843	15¢ Christmas Wreath & Toy	2.25	4.00	23.50(50)	12.00(20)	.55	.25

SE-TENANTS: Beginning with the 1964 Christmas issue (#1254-57), the United States has issued numerous Se-Tenant stamps covering a wide variety of subjects. Se-Tenants are issues where two or more different stamp designs are produced on the same sheet in pair, strip or block form. Mint stamps are usually collected in attached blocks, etc.; used are generally saved as single stamps.

SCOTT NO.	DESCRIPTION	FIRST DAY COVERS SING	PL. BLK.	MINT SHEET	PLATE BLOCK	UNUSED F/NH	USED

1844   1845   1846   1847

1848   1849   1850   1851

1852   1853   1854   1855

1856   1857   1858   1859

1860   1861   1862   1863

1864   1865   1866   1867

1868   1869

1980-85 GREAT AMERICANS

1844-69	1¢-50¢, 26 varieties, complete	....	....	....	....	17.50	6.40
1844	1¢ Dorothea Dix, 11.2, (1983)	2.25	4.00	13.00(100)	5.00(20)	.25	.25
1844c	1¢ Dorothea Dix, 10.9, small block tagging . . .	....	....	16.00(100)	5.00(20)	.25	.25
1844d	1¢ Dorothea Dix, 10.95 large block tagging . . .	....	....	17.00(100)	7.00(20)	.85	.45
1845	2¢ Igor Stravinsky (1982)	2.25	4.00	13.00(100)	1.25	.25	.25
1846	3¢ Henry Caly (1983) .	2.25	4.00	21.00(100)	2.25	.25	.25
1847	4¢ Carl Schurz (1983) .	2.25	4.00	22.00(100)	1.35	.25	.25
1848	5¢ Pearl Buck (1983) . .	2.25	4.00	38.00(100)	3.00	.70	.25
1849	6¢ Walter Lippmann (1985)	2.25	4.00	23.00(100)	6.25(20)	.40	.25
1850	7¢ Abraham Baldwin (1985)	2.25	4.00	33.00(100)	7.75(20)	.60	.25
1851	8¢ Henry Knox (1985) .	2.25	4.00	29.00(100)	1.75	.30	.25
1852	9¢ Sylvanus Thayer (1985)	2.25	4.00	33.00(100)	8.00(20)	.40	.25
1853	10¢ Richard Russell (1984)	2.25	4.00	53.00(100)	15.00(20)	.60	.25
1854	11¢ Partridge (1985) . .	2.25	4.00	64.00(100)	4.00	.65	.25
1855	13¢ Crazy Horse (1982)	2.25	4.00	49.00(100)	3.00	.50	.40
1856	14¢ Sinclair Lewis (1985)	2.25	4.00	66.00(100)	17.00(20)	.80	.25
1857	17¢ Rachel Carson (1981)	2.25	4.00	53.00(100)	3.25	.60	.25
1858	18¢ George Mason (1981)	2.25	4.00	58.00(100)	3.75	.60	.25
1859	19¢ Sequoyah	2.25	4.00	65.00(100)	3.75	.75	.40
1860	20¢ Ralph Bunche (1982)	2.25	4.00	79.00(100)	4.00	.80	.25
1861	20¢ T. H. Gallaudet (1983)	2.25	4.00	80.00(100)	4.75	1.00	.25

SCOTT NO.	DESCRIPTION	FIRST DAY COVERS SING	FIRST DAY COVERS PL. BLK.	MINT SHEET	PLATE BLOCK	UNUSED F/NH	USED
1862	20¢ Harry Truman (1984)	2.25	4.00	65.00(100)	17.50(20)	.80	.25
1862a	same, Bullseye perf. .				6.50	.95	
1863	22¢ J. Audubon (1985)	2.25	4.00	75.00(100)	18.00(20)	.80	.25
1863a	same, Bullseye perf. .				28.00	1.00	
1864	30¢ F.C. Laubach (1984)	2.25	4.00	98.00(100)	24.00(20)	1.00	.25
1864a	same, Bullseye perf. .				7.00	1.25	
1865	35¢ Charles Drew (1981)	2.25	4.50	140.00(100)	8.00	1.50	.40
1866	37¢ Robert Millikan (1982)	2.25	4.50	125.00(100)	7.00	1.20	.25
1867	39¢ Grenville Clark(1985)	2.25	4.50	125.00(100)	33.00(20)	1.50	.25
1867c	Large Block Tagging Perf 10.9			365.00(100)	85.00	4.25	0.70
1867d	Large Block Tagging Perf 11.2			200.00(100)	11.00	2.25	0.35
1868	40¢ Lillian Gilbreth (1984)	2.25	4.50	125.00(100)	31.00(20)	1.50	.25
1868a	same, Bullseye perf. .			170.00(100)	8.50	1.60	
1869	50¢ Chester Nimitz (1985)	2.25	4.50	155.00(100)	13.00	1.80	.25
1869a	same, Bullseye perf. .			205.00(100)	13.00	2.25	0.35

USA 15c Everett Dirksen

1874

Whitney Moore Young — Black Heritage USA 15c

1875

1981 COMMEMORATIVES

1874/1945	(1874-79, 1910-45) 42 varieties, complete	....	....	....	....	32.00	10.50
1874	15¢ Everett Dirksen. . .	2.25	4.00	22.00(50)	2.50	.60	.25
1875	15¢ Whitney Moore Young	2.25	4.00	26.00(50)	3.00	.70	.25

1876   **1877**

Rose USA 18c — Camellia USA 18c — Dahlia USA 18c — Lily USA 18c

1878   **1879**

1876-79	Flowers, 4 varieties, attached . .	5.00	6.00	30.00(48)	3.50	3.25	2.60
1876	18¢ Rose.	2.25	....	....	....	.80	.25
1877	18¢ Camellia	2.25	....	....	....	.80	.25
1878	18¢ Dahlia	2.25	....	....	....	.80	.25
1879	18¢ Lily	2.25	....	....	....	.80	.25

1880   **1881**   **1882**   **1883**   **1884**

1885   **1886**   **1887**   **1888**   **1889**

1981 WILDLIFE DEFINITIVES

1880-89	Wildlife, set of singles .	17.00	....	....	....	11.00	2.75
1880	18¢ Bighorned Sheep .	2.25	....	....	....	1.25	.30
1881	18¢ Puma	2.25	....	....	....	1.25	.30
1882	18¢ Seal	2.25	....	....	....	1.25	.30
1883	18¢ Bison.	2.25	....	....	....	1.25	.30
1884	18¢ Brown Bear.	2.25	....	....	....	1.25	.30
1885	18¢ Polar Bear.	2.25	....	....	....	1.25	.30
1886	18¢ Elk.	2.25	....	....	....	1.25	.30
1887	18¢ Moose.	2.25	....	....	....	1.25	.30
1888	18¢ White-tailed Deer .	2.25	....	....	....	1.25	.30
1889	18¢ Pronghorned Antelope	2.25	....	....	....	1.25	.30
1889a	Wildlife, bklt pane of 10 .	6.50	....	....	....	12.75	....

1890   **1891**   **1892**

1893

1894, 1895, 1896

1981 FLAG AND ANTHEM ISSUE

SCOTT NO.	DESCRIPTION	FIRST DAY COVERS SING	FIRST DAY COVERS PL. BLK.	MINT SHEET	PLATE BLOCK	UNUSED F/NH	USED
1890	18¢ "Waves of Grain" .	2.25	4.00	58.00(100)	15.00(20)	.75	.25

1981 Coil Stamp Perf. 10 Vertically

			PLATE# STRIP 3		PLATE# STRIP 3		
1891	18¢ "Shining Sea"	2.25	....	....	6.00	.80	.25

1981

1892	6¢ Stars, from bklt pane	2.25				1.20	1.00
1893	18¢ "Purple Mountains" from bklt pane	2.25				.75	.25
1892-93	6¢ & 18¢ as above, attached pair	....				2.75	2.00
1893a	2-1892, 6-1893 bklt pane of 8	5.25				5.00	5.00

			PLATE BLOCK		PLATE BLOCK		
1894	20¢ Flag & Supreme Court	2.25	4.00	85.00(100)	22.50(20)	1.10	.25

			PLATE# STRIP 3		PLATE# STRIP 3		
1895	20¢ Flag & Supreme Court	2.25	5.00	....	5.25	.75	.25
1896	20¢ Flag & Supreme Court, from bklt pane	2.25	....			.80	.25
1896a	20¢ bklt pane of 6	3.50	....			4.25	....
1896b	20¢ bklt pane of 10 . . .	5.50	....			8.00	....

Note: **For plate number strips of 5, see page 194**

Omnibus 1880s USA 1c — Locomotive 1870s USA 2c — Handcar 1880s USA 3c

1897   **1897A**   **1898**

Stagecoach 1890s USA 4c — Motorcycle 1913 USA 5c — Sleigh 1880s USA 5.2c Auth. Nonprofit Org

1898A   **1899**   **1900**

Bicycle 1870s USA 5.9c Auth. Nonprofit Org. — Baby Buggy 1880s USA7.4c — Mail Wagon 1880s USA 9.3c Bulk Rate

1901   **1902**   **1903**

Hansom Cab 1890s USA 10.9c Bulk Rate — RR Caboose 1890s USA 11c Bulk Rate — Electric Auto 1917 USA 17c

1904   **1905**   **1906**

SCOTT NO.	DESCRIPTION	FIRST DAY COVERS SING	PL. BLK.	MINT SHEET	PLATE BLOCK	UNUSED F/NH	USED

1907

1908

NOTE: #1898A—"Stagecoach 1890s" is 19-1/2 mm long.

1981-84 Perf. 10 Vertically
TRANSPORTATION COILS

Scott No.	Description	FDC SING	PLATE# STRIP 3		PLATE# STRIP 3	4.50	3.10
1897-1908	1¢-20¢, 14 varieties, complete	29.50	. . . .	. . . .	. . . .		
1897	1¢ Omnibus (1983) . . .	2.25	17.50	. . . .	.70	.25	.25
1897A	2¢ Locomotive (1982) .	2.25	25.00	. . . .	.75	.25	.25
1898	3¢ Handcar (1983). . . .	2.25	25.00	. . . .	1.05	.25	.25
1898A	4¢ Stagecoach (1982) .	2.25	22.50	. . . .	1.80	.25	.25
1899	5¢ Motorcycle (1983). .	2.25	25.00	. . . .	1.25	.25	.25
1900	5.2¢ Sleigh (1983)	2.25	37.50	. . . .	5.00	.35	.25
1901	5.9¢ Bicycle (1982) . . .	2.25	37.50	. . . .	5.00	.50	.40
1902	7.4¢ Baby Buggy (1984)	2.25	25.00	. . . .	5.00	.50	.40
1903	9.3¢ Mail Wagon	2.25	42.50	. . . .	4.00	.50	.40
1904	10.9¢ Hansom Cab (1982)	2.25	40.00	. . . .	8.00	.50	.40
1905	11¢ Caboose (1984) . .	2.25	40.00	. . . .	4.00	.50	.25
1906	17¢ Electric Car	2.25	37.50	. . . .	3.75	.70	.25
1907	18¢ Surrey	2.25	55.00	. . . .	4.00	.75	.25
1908	20¢ Fire Pumper	2.25	55.00	. . . .	3.75	.75	.25

NOTE: Plate # Strips of 3 and 5 have plate number under center stamp. Some issues have lines between two of the stamps.

PRECANCELLED COILS

The following are for precancelled, unused, never hinged stamps.
Stamps without gum sell for less.

SCOTT NO.		PL# STRIP 3	UNUSED
1895b	20¢ Supreme Court	45.00	1.00
1898Ab	4¢ Stagecoach	5.00	.35
1900a	5.2¢ Sleigh	6.00	.30
1901a	5.9¢ Bicycle	36.00	.45
1902a	7.4¢ Baby Buggy	7.00	.40
1903a	9.3¢ Mail Wagon	4.50	.40
1904a	10.9¢ Hansom Cab	24.00	.50
1905a	11¢ Caboose	4.50	.45
1906a	17¢ Electric Car	5.00	.55

1909

1983 EXPRESS MAIL BOOKLET SINGLE

1909	$9.35 Eagle & Moon . .	75.00	. . . .	. . . .	. . . .	35.00	22.50
1909a	$9.35 bklt pane of 3 . . .	200.00	. . . .	. . . .	. . . .	105.00	. . . .

1910

1911

1981 COMMEMORATIVES (Continued)

1910	18¢ American Red Cross	2.25	4.00	27.75(50)	3.25	.60	.25
1911	18¢ Savings & Loans Assoc.	2.25	4.00	25.75(50)	3.00	.60	.25

1912

1913

1914

1915

1916

1917

1918

1919

1912-19	Space Achievement, 8 varieties, attached . .	6.00	9.00	32.00(48)	7.25(8)	5.75	5.50
1912-19	same, set of singles . . .	15.50	. . . .	. . . .	. . . .		2.50
1912	18¢ Exploring the Moon	2.00	. . . .	. . . .	. . . .	1.00	.35
1913	18¢ Releasing Boosters	2.00	. . . .	. . . .	. . . .	.80	.35
1914	18¢ Cooling Electric Systems	2.00	. . . .	. . . .	. . . .	.80	.35
1915	18¢ Understanding the Sun	2.00	. . . .	. . . .	. . . .	.80	.35
1916	18¢ Probing the Planets	2.00	. . . .	. . . .	. . . .	.80	.35
1917	18¢ Shuttle and Rockets	2.00	. . . .	. . . .	. . . .	.80	.35
1918	18¢ Landing	2.00	. . . .	. . . .	. . . .	.80	.35
1919	18¢ Comprehending the Universe	2.00	. . . .	. . . .	. . . .	.80	.35

1920

1920	18¢ Professional Management	2.25	4.00	26.50(50)	3.25	.65	.25

1921

1922

1923

1924

1921-24	Wildlife Habitats, 4 varieties, attached . .	5.00	6.00	38.00(50)	5.00	4.00	3.00
1921	18¢ Blue Heron	2.25	. . . .	. . . .	. . . .	.90	.25
1922	18¢ Badger	2.25	. . . .	. . . .	. . . .	.90	.25
1923	18¢ Grizzly Bear	2.25	. . . .	. . . .	. . . .	.90	.25
1924	18¢ Ruffled Grouse . . .	2.25	. . . .	. . . .	. . . .	.90	.25

SCOTT NO.	DESCRIPTION	FIRST DAY COVERS SING	PL. BLK.	MINT SHEET	PLATE BLOCK	UNUSED F/NH	USED

1925 **1926** **1927**

1925	18¢ Disabled Persons .	2.25	4.00	26.00(50)	3.25	.75	.25
1926	18¢ Edna St. Vincent Millay	2.25	4.00	26.00(50)	3.25	.75	.25
1927	18¢ Alcoholism	4.50	7.00	60.00(50)	47.50(20)	.75	.25

1928 **1929**

1930 **1931**

1928-31	American Architecture, 4 varieties, attached . .	5.00	6.00	26.00(40)	4.25	3.75	3.00
1928	18¢ New York Univ. Library	2.25	....	....		1.00	.25
1929	18¢ Biltmore House . . .	2.25	....	....		1.00	.25
1930	18¢ Palace of the Arts .	2.25	....	....		1.00	.25
1931	18¢ National Farmers Bank	2.25	....	....		1.00	.25

1932 **1933**

| 1932 | 18¢ Babe Zaharias . . . | 12.00 | 15.00 | 30.00(50) | 4.50 | .90 | .30 |
| 1933 | 18¢ Bobby Jones . . . . . | 15.00 | 18.00 | 39.00(50) | 6.00 | 1.20 | .30 |

1934

1935 **1936**

1937 **1938**

1934	18¢ Coming Through the Rye	2.25	4.50	32.00(50)	3.75	.80	.25
1935	18¢ James Hoban	2.25	4.00	29.00(50)	3.25	.70	.25
1936	20¢ James Hoban	2.25	4.00	33.00(50)	3.25	.70	.30
1937-38	Yorktown/Virginia Capes, 2 varieties, attached . .	2.00	4.00	34.00(50)	3.50	1.75	1.25
1937	18¢ Yorktown	2.25	....	....		1.00	.30
1938	18¢ Virginia Capes . . .	2.25	....	....		1.00	.30

1939 **1940** **1941**

1939	(20¢) Madonna & Child	2.25	4.00	54.00(100)	3.25	.75	.25
1940	(20¢) Christmas Toy . .	2.25	4.00	28.00(50)	3.25	.75	.25
1941	20¢ John Hanson	2.25	4.00	29.50(50)	3.25	.75	.25

1943

1942 **1944** **1945**

1942-45	Desert Plants, 4 varieties, attached . .	5.00	6.00	29.00(40)	4.00	3.75	3.00
1942	20¢ Barrel Cactus	2.25	....	....		1.00	.25
1943	20¢ Agave	2.25	....	....		1.00	.25
1944	20¢ Beavertail Cactus .	2.25	....	....		1.00	.25
1945	20¢ Saguaro	2.25	....	....		1.00	.25

1946, 1947, 1948 **1949**

1981-1982 Regular Issues

| 1946 | (20¢) "C" Eagle, 11x10¹/2 | 2.25 | 4.00 | 65.00(100) | 3.75 | .75 | .25 |

			LINE PAIR		LINE PAIR		
1947	(20¢) "C" Eagle, coil. . .	2.25	2.75		2.75	.95	.25
1948	(20¢) "C" Eagle, from pane	2.25	....			.95	.25
1948a	same, bklt pane of 10 .	6.00	....			8.00	....
1949	20¢ Bighorned Sheep, blue, from bklt pane (1982) .	2.25				.95	.25
1949a	same, bklt pane of 10 .	6.00	....			8.50	....
1949c	Type II, from bklt pane .					2.25	.40
1949d	same, bklt pane of 10 .	....				20.00	

SCOTT NO.	DESCRIPTION	FIRST DAY COVERS SING	PL. BLK.	MINT SHEET	PLATE BLOCK	UNUSED F/NH	USED

1950

1951

1952

1982 COMMEMORATIVES

1950/2030	(1950-52, 2003-04, 2006-30)						
	30 varieties	....	....	....	....	26.00	7.00
1950	20¢ Franklin D. Roosevelt	2.25	4.00	31.00(48)	3.25	.80	.25
1951	20¢ LOVE, perf. 11 . . .	1.85	4.25	31.00(50)	3.25	.65	.25
1951a	same, perf. 11x 10½ . .	....	....	48.00(50)	5.50	1.10	.75

NOTE: Perforations will be mixed on Used #1951.

| 1952 | 20¢ George Washington | 2.25 | 4.00 | 30.00(50) | 3.75 | .80 | .25 |

1982 STATE BIRDS AND FLOWERS

1953

1953	Alabama	1978	Montana
1954	Alaska	1979	Nebraska
1955	Arizona	1980	Nevada
1956	Arkansas	1981	New Hampshire
1957	California	1982	New Jersey
1958	Colorado	1983	New Mexico
1959	Connecticut	1984	New York
1960	Delaware	1985	North Carolina
1961	Florida	1986	North Dakota
1962	Georgia	1987	Ohio
1963	Hawaii	1988	Oklahoma
1964	Idaho	1989	Oregon
1965	Illinois	1990	Pennsylvania
1966	Indiana	1991	Rhode Island
1967	Iowa	1992	South Carolina
1968	Kansas	1993	South Dakota
1969	Kentucky	1994	Tennessee
1970	Louisiana	1995	Texas
1971	Maine	1996	Utah
1972	Maryland	1997	Vermont
1973	Massachusetts	1998	Virginia
1974	Michigan	1999	Washington
1975	Minnesota	2000	West Virginia
1976	Mississippi	2001	Wisconsin
1977	Missouri	2002	Wyoming

1973 (Massachusetts)

1966 (Indiana)

2002 (Wyoming)

Perf. 10½ x 11

1953-2002	20¢, 50 varieties, attached......		....	38.00(50)	....	38.00	....
	set of singles.	86.00	....		....	40.00	25.00
	singles of above	2.00	....		....	1.25	.65
1953a-2002a	same, perf. 11.	....	....	48.00(50)	....	48.00	....
	singles of above	....	....		....	50.00	

NOTE: Used singles will not be sorted by perf. sizes.

2003

2004

2005

2003	20¢ USA/Netherlands .	2.25	4.00	32.00(50)	17.00(20)	.70	.25
2004	20¢ Library of Congress	2.25	4.00	49.00(50)	5.00	1.25	.25

			PLATE# STRIP 3		PLATE# STRIP 3		
2005	20¢ Consumer Education, Coil	2.25	60.00	....	18.00	1.20	.25

2006   2007

2008   2009

2006-09	World's Fair, 4 varieties, attached . .	5.00	6.00	36.00(50)	4.50	4.00	2.00
2006	20¢ Solar Energy.	2.25	....	....	....	1.00	.25
2007	20¢ Synthetic Fuels . .	2.25	....	....	....	1.00	.25
2008	20¢ Breeder Reactor. .	2.25	....	....	....	1.00	.25
2009	20¢ Fossil Fuels	2.25	....	....	....	1.00	.25

2010

2011

2012

2010	20¢ Horatio Alger.	2.25	4.00	29.00(50)	3.25	.70	.25
2011	20¢ Aging Together . . .	2.25	4.00	29.00(50)	3.25	.70	.25
2012	20¢ Barrymores.	2.25	4.00	30.00(50)	3.25	.70	.25

2013

2014

2015

2013	20¢ Dr. Mary Walker . .	2.25	4.00	29.50(50)	3.25	.70	.25
2014	20¢ Peace Garden . . .	2.25	4.00	48.00(50)	6.00	1.20	.25
2015	20¢ America's Libraries	2.25	4.00	29.00(50)	3.25	.60	.25

2016

2017

2018

2016	20¢ Jackie Robinson . .	7.00	13.50	90.00(50)	11.00	2.50	.25
2017	20¢ Touro Synagogue .	3.00	4.00	40.00(50)	18.00(20)	.85	.25
2018	20¢ Wolf Trap Farm. . .	2.25	4.00	29.00(50)	3.25	.75	.25

PLATE BLOCKS: are portions of a sheet of stamps adjacent to the number(s) indicating the printing plate number used to produce that sheet. Flat plate issues are usually collected in plate blocks of six (number opposite middle stamp) while rotary issues are normally corner blocks of four.

SCOTT NO.	DESCRIPTION	FIRST DAY COVERS SING	PL. BLK.	MINT SHEET	PLATE BLOCK	UNUSED F/NH	USED

2019   **2020**

2021   **2022**

SCOTT NO.	DESCRIPTION	FIRST DAY COVERS SING	PL. BLK.	MINT SHEET	PLATE BLOCK	UNUSED F/NH	USED
2019-22	American Architecture, 4 varieties, attached ..	5.00	6.00	32.00(40)	4.50	4.00	3.25
2019	20¢ Fallingwater Mill Run	2.25	....	....	....	1.25	.25
2020	20¢ Illinois Inst. Tech ..	2.25	....	....	....	1.25	.25
2021	20¢ Gropius House ...	2.25	....	....	....	1.25	.25
2022	20¢ Dulles Airport	2.25	....	....	....	1.25	.25

2023   **2024**

2025   **2026**

SCOTT NO.	DESCRIPTION	FIRST DAY COVERS SING	PL. BLK.	MINT SHEET	PLATE BLOCK	UNUSED F/NH	USED
2023	20¢ St. Francis of Assisi	2.25	4.00	30.00(50)	3.25	.75	.25
2024	20¢ Ponce de Leon ...	2.25	4.00	39.00(50)	20.00(20)	1.00	.25
2025	13¢ Kitten & Puppy, Christmas	2.25	4.00	25.00(50)	2.50	.60	.25
2026	20¢ Madonna & Child, Christmas	2.25	4.00	30.00(50)	17.00(20)	.75	.25

2027   **2028**

2029   **2030**

SCOTT NO.	DESCRIPTION	FIRST DAY COVERS SING	PL. BLK.	MINT SHEET	PLATE BLOCK	UNUSED F/NH	USED
2027-30	Winter Scenes, Christmas, 4 varieties, attached ..	4.00	5.00	38.00(50)	5.00	4.25	3.50
2027	20¢ Sledding	2.25	....	....	....	1.25	.25
2028	20¢ Snowman	2.25	....	....	....	1.25	.25
2029	20¢ Skating	2.25	....	....	....	1.25	.25
2030	20¢ Decorating	2.25	....	....	....	1.25	.25

2031

1983 COMMEMORATIVES

SCOTT NO.	DESCRIPTION	FIRST DAY COVERS SING	PL. BLK.	MINT SHEET	PLATE BLOCK	UNUSED F/NH	USED
2031-65	13¢-20¢, 35 varieties, complete..........	....	....	....	....	28.40	7.70
2031	20¢ Science & Industry	2.25	4.00	29.00(50)	3.25	.75	.25

2033

2032   **2034**   **2035**

SCOTT NO.	DESCRIPTION	FIRST DAY COVERS SING	PL. BLK.	MINT SHEET	PLATE BLOCK	UNUSED F/NH	USED
2032-35	20¢ Ballooning, 4 varieties, attached ..	5.00	6.00	33.00(40)	4.00	3.55	2.50
2032	20¢ Intrepid	2.25	....	....	....	1.10	.25
2033	20¢ Red, white, & blue balloon.............	2.25	....	....	....	1.10	.25
2034	20¢ Yellow, gold & green balloon.............	2.25	....	....	....	1.10	.25
2035	20¢ Explorer II	2.25	....	....	....	1.10	.25

2036   **2037**   **2038**

SCOTT NO.	DESCRIPTION	FIRST DAY COVERS SING	PL. BLK.	MINT SHEET	PLATE BLOCK	UNUSED F/NH	USED
2036	20¢ USA/Sweden	2.25	4.00	29.00(50)	3.25	.70	.25
2037	20¢ Civilian Conservation Corps..............	2.25	4.00	29.00(50)	3.25	.70	.25
2038	20¢ Joseph Priestley ..	2.25	4.00	29.00(50)	3.25	.70	.25

2039

2040   **2041**

SCOTT NO.	DESCRIPTION	FIRST DAY COVERS SING	PL. BLK.	MINT SHEET	PLATE BLOCK	UNUSED F/NH	USED
2039	20¢ Volunteerism.....	2.25	4.00	34.50(50)	18.00(20)	.70	.25
2040	20¢ German Immigrants	2.25	4.00	29.00(50)	3.00	.70	.25
2041	20¢ Brooklyn Bridge ..	3.00	5.00	30.00(50)	3.00	.70	.25

SCOTT NO.	DESCRIPTION	FIRST DAY COVERS SING	PL. BLK.	MINT SHEET	PLATE BLOCK	UNUSED F/NH	USED

2042

2043

2044

2042	20¢ Tennessee Valley Authority	2.25	4.00	30.00(50)	16.00(20)	.70	.25
2043	20¢ Physical Fitness . .	2.25	4.00	30.00(50)	16.00(20)	.70	.25
2044	20¢ Scott Joplin.	2.25	4.00	35.00(50)	4.00	.75	.25

2045

2046

2047

2045	20¢ Medal of Honor. . . .	6.00	8.00	35.00(40)	4.50	1.00	.25
2046	20¢ Babe Ruth.	8.00	16.00	75.00(50)	10.00	2.00	.25
2047	20¢ Nathaniel Hawthorne	2.25	4.00	32.50(50)	4.00	.75	.25

2048   2049

2050   2051

2048-51	Olympics, 4 varieties, attached . .	5.00	6.00	29.00(50)	3.50	3.00	2.75
2048	13¢ Discus.	2.25	. . . .	. . . .	. . . .	1.00	.30
2049	13¢ High Jump	2.25	. . . .	. . . .	. . . .	1.00	.30
2050	13¢ Archery	2.25	. . . .	. . . .	. . . .	1.00	.30
2051	13¢ Boxing.	2.25	. . . .	. . . .	. . . .	1.00	.30

2052

2053

2054

2052	20¢ Treaty of Paris . . .	2.25	4.00	24.00(40)	3.25	.75	.25
2053	20¢ Civil Service	2.25	4.00	32.00(50)	18.00(20)	.75	.25
2054	20¢ Metropolitan Opera	2.25	4.00	30.00(50)	3.25	.75	.25

2055   2056

2057   2058

2055-58	Inventors, 4 varieties, attached . .	5.00	6.00	38.00(50)	4.50	4.00	3.00
2055	20¢ Charles Steinmetz	2.25	. . . .	. . . .	. . . .	1.35	.25
2056	20¢ Edwin Armstrong .	2.25	. . . .	. . . .	. . . .	1.35	.25
2057	20¢ Nikola Tesla	2.25	. . . .	. . . .	. . . .	1.35	.25
2058	20¢ Philo T. Farnsworth	2.25	. . . .	. . . .	. . . .	1.35	.25

2059   2060

2061   2062

2059-62	Streetcars, 4 varieties, attached . .	5.00	6.00	40.00(50)	4.50	4.00	3.00
2059	20¢ First Streetcar. . . .	2.25	. . . .	. . . .	. . . .	1.25	.25
2060	20¢ Electric Trolley . . .	2.25	. . . .	. . . .	. . . .	1.25	.25
2061	20¢ "Bobtail"	2.25	. . . .	. . . .	. . . .	1.25	.25
2062	20¢ St. Charles Streetcar	2.25	. . . .	. . . .	. . . .	1.25	.25

2063

2064

| 2063 | 20¢ Madonna. . . . . . . | 2.25 | 4.00 | 32.00(50) | 3.75 | .75 | .25 |
| 2064 | 20¢ Santa Claus . . . . . | 2.25 | 4.00 | 32.00(50) | 16.00(20) | .85 | .25 |

2065

| 2065 | 20¢ Martin Luther . . . . | 2.25 | 4.00 | 33.00(50) | 3.75 | .85 | .25 |

SCOTT NO.	DESCRIPTION	FIRST DAY COVERS SING	PL. BLK.	MINT SHEET	PLATE BLOCK	UNUSED F/NH	USED

2066

1984 COMMEMORATIVES

SCOTT NO.	DESCRIPTION	SING	PL. BLK.	MINT SHEET	PLATE BLOCK	UNUSED F/NH	USED
2066-2109	44 varieties, complete	. . . .	. . . .	. . . .	. . . .	37.50	9.30
2066	20¢ Alaska Statehood .	2.25	4.00	32.00(50)	3.25	.70	.25

2067 **2068** **2069** **2070**

SCOTT NO.	DESCRIPTION	SING	PL. BLK.	MINT SHEET	PLATE BLOCK	UNUSED F/NH	USED
2067-70	Winter Olympics, 4 varieties, attached . .	5.00	6.00	36.00(50)	4.50	3.50	3.00
2067	20¢ Ice Dancing.	2.25	. . . .	. . . .	. . . .	1.10	.30
2068	20¢ Downhill Skiing. . .	2.25	. . . .	. . . .	. . . .	1.10	.30
2069	20¢ Cross Country Skiing	2.25	. . . .	. . . .	. . . .	1.10	.30
2070	20¢ Hockey	2.25	. . . .	. . . .	. . . .	1.10	.30

2071 **2072** **2073** **2074**

SCOTT NO.	DESCRIPTION	SING	PL. BLK.	MINT SHEET	PLATE BLOCK	UNUSED F/NH	USED
2071	20¢ Federal Deposit Insurance Corporation	2.25	4.00	29.00(50)	3.25	.75	.25
2072	20¢ Love	1.95	4.00	29.00(50)	16.50(20)	.75	.25
2073	20¢ Carter G. Woodson	3.00	4.00	32.00(50)	3.50	.75	.25
2074	20¢ Conservatiion	2.25	4.00	29.00(50)	3.25	.75	.25

2076

2078

2075

2077

2079

SCOTT NO.	DESCRIPTION	SING	PL. BLK.	MINT SHEET	PLATE BLOCK	UNUSED F/NH	USED
2075	20¢ Credit Union	1.95	4.50	29.00(50)	3.25	.70	.25
2076-79	Orchids, 4 varieties, attd.	4.00	5.00	34.00(48)	3.75	3.25	2.75
2076	20¢ Wildpink	2.25	. . . .	. . . .	. . . .	.95	.25
2077	20¢ Lady's-slipper	2.25	. . . .	. . . .	. . . .	.95	.25
2078	20¢ Spreading Pogonia	2.25	. . . .	. . . .	. . . .	.95	.25
2079	20¢ Pacific Calypso . . .	2.25	. . . .	. . . .	. . . .	.95	.25

2080 **2081**

SCOTT NO.	DESCRIPTION	SING	PL. BLK.	MINT SHEET	PLATE BLOCK	UNUSED F/NH	USED
2080	20¢ Hawaii Statehood .	2.25	4.00	32.00(50)	3.50	.75	.25
2081	20¢ National Archives .	2.25	4.00	34.00(50)	3.75	.85	.25

2082 **2083** **2084** **2085**

SCOTT NO.	DESCRIPTION	SING	PL. BLK.	MINT SHEET	PLATE BLOCK	UNUSED F/NH	USED
2082-85	Olympics, 4 varieties, attached.	5.00	6.00	37.00(50)	5.00	4.50	4.00
2082	20¢ Men's Diving.	2.25	. . . .	. . . .	. . . .	1.20	.25
2083	20¢ Long Jump	2.25	. . . .	. . . .	. . . .	1.20	.25
2084	20¢ Wrestling.	2.25	. . . .	. . . .	. . . .	1.20	.25
2085	20¢ Women's Kayak . .	2.25	. . . .	. . . .	. . . .	1.20	.25

2086 **2087** **2088**

SCOTT NO.	DESCRIPTION	SING	PL. BLK.	MINT SHEET	PLATE BLOCK	UNUSED F/NH	USED
2086	20¢ Louisiana Exposition	2.25	4.00	36.00(40)	4.50	.95	.25
2087	20¢ Health Research. .	2.25	4.00	32.00(50)	3.50	.70	.25
2088	20¢ Douglas Fairbanks	2.25	4.00	49.00(50)	26.00(20)	1.30	.30

2089 **2090** **2091**

SCOTT NO.	DESCRIPTION	SING	PL. BLK.	MINT SHEET	PLATE BLOCK	UNUSED F/NH	USED
2089	20¢ Jim Thorpe	4.50	8.00	66.00(50)	8.50	2.00	.30
2090	20¢ John McCormack .	3.00	4.00	30.00(50)	3.25	.65	.25
2091	20¢ St. Lawrence Seaway	3.00	4.00	30.00(50)	3.25	.65	.25

SE-TENANTS: Beginning with the 1964 Christmas issue (#1254-57), the United States has issued numerous Se-Tenant stamps covering a wide variety of subjects. Se-Tenants are issues where two or more different stamp designs are produced on the same sheet in pair, strip or block form. Mint stamps are usually collected in attached blocks, etc.—Used are generally saved as single stamps. Our Se-Tenant prices follow in this collecting pattern.

SCOTT NO.	DESCRIPTION	FIRST DAY COVERS SING	FIRST DAY COVERS PL. BLK.	MINT SHEET	PLATE BLOCK	UNUSED F/NH	USED

2092

2093

| 2092 | Preserving Wetlands .. | 1.95 | 4.00 | 34.00(50) | 3.50 | .80 | .25 |
| 2093 | Roanoke Voyages .... | 2.25 | 4.00 | 34.00(50) | 3.50 | .80 | .25 |

2094   **2095**   **2096**   **2097**

2094	20¢ Herman Melville .	2.25	4.00	29.00(50)	3.25	.70	.25
2095	20¢ Horace Moses ..	2.25	4.00	31.00(50)	19.00(20)	.90	.25
2096	20¢ Smokey Bear ...	2.25	4.00	34.00(50)	3.50	.90	.25
2097	20¢ Roberto Clemente	12.00	20.00	95.00(50)	10.00	2.00	.50

2098   **2099**

2100   **2101**

2098-2101	American Dogs, 4 varieties, attached .	5.00	6.00	32.50(40)	4.75	4.25	3.75
2098	20¢ Beagle, Boston Terrier	2.25				1.25	.25
2099	20¢ Chesapeake Bay Retriever, Cocker Spaniel	2.25				1.25	.25
2100	20¢ Alaskan Malamute, Collie	2.25				1.25	.25
2101	20¢ Black & Tan Coonhound, American Foxhound ..	2.25				1.25	.25

2102   **2103**   **2104**

2102	20¢ Crime Prevention .	2.25	4.00	29.00(50)	3.25	.60	.25
2103	20¢ Hispanic Americans	3.00	4.00	28.00(40)	4.00	.60	.25
2104	20¢ Family Unity	2.25	4.00	36.00(50)	20.00(20)	1.00	.25

2105   **2106**   **2107**

2105	20¢ Eleanor Roosevelt	2.25	4.00	28.00(40)	3.25	.70	.25
2106	20¢ Nation of Readers	2.25	4.00	33.00(50)	4.00	1.10	.30
2107	20¢ Madonna & Child .	2.25	4.00	29.00(50)	3.25	.60	.25

2108   **2109**

| 2108 | 20¢ Santa Claus . . . . . | 1.35 | 4.00 | 30.00(50) | 3.25 | .60 | .30 |
| 2109 | 20¢ Vietnam Veterans . | 5.00 | 4.00 | 32.00(40) | 4.65 | 1.00 | .30 |

2110

1985 COMMEMORATIVES

| 2110/2166 | (2110, 2137-47, 2152-66) 27 varieties . . . . . . | | | | | 33.50 | 7.50 |
| 2110 | 22¢ Jerome Kern. . . . . | 2.25 | 4.00 | 32.00(50) | 3.25 | .70 | .25 |

2111-2113   **2114, 2115**   **2116**

1985 REGULAR ISSUES

2111	(22¢) "D" Eagle	2.25	4.00	72.00(100)	25.00(20)	.90	.25
			PLATE# STRIP 3		PLATE# STRIP 3		
2112	(22¢) "D" Eagle, coil. . .	2.25	21.00		6.75	.75	.25
2113	(22¢) "D" Eagle from bklt pane	2.25				1.25	.25
2113a	same, bklt pane of 10 .	7.50				12.00	
			PLATE BLOCK		PLATE BLOCK		
2114	22¢ Flag over Capitol	2.25	4.00	75.00(100)	4.00	.80	.25
			PLATE# STRIP 3		PLATE# STRIP 3		
2115	22¢ Flag over Capitol, coil	2.25	27.50		3.75	.85	.25
2115a	same, narrow block tagging				4.50	.85	.25
2115b	same, wide & tall block tagging				65.00	2.00	
2115c	22¢ Flag over Capitol "T" Coil (1985-87)	2.90			4.50	.90	.75
2116	22¢ Flag over Capitol from booklet pane	2.25				1.00	.25
2116a	same, bklt pane of 5 . . .	2.90				5.25	

SCOTT NO.	DESCRIPTION	FIRST DAY COVERS SING	PL. BLK.	MINT SHEET	PLATE BLOCK	UNUSED F/NH	USED

2235 2236 2237 2238

1986 COMMEMORATIVES (continued)

2235-38	Navajo Art, 4 varieties, attached ..	4.00	5.00	51.00(50)	6.50	6.00	3.50
2235	22¢ Navajo Art......	2.25	....	....	....	1.75	.25
2236	22¢ Navajo Art......	2.25	....	....	....	1.75	.25
2237	22¢ Navajo Art......	2.25	....	....	....	1.75	.25
2238	22¢ Navajo Art......	2.25	....	....	....	1.75	.25

2239

| 2239 | 22¢ T.S. Eliot........ | 2.25 | 4.00 | 38.00(50) | 4.00 | 1.00 | .25 |

2240 2241 2242 2243

2240-43	Woodcarved Figurines, 4 varieties, attached ..	4.00	5.00	39.00(50)	4.50	4.25	3.00
2240	22¢ Highlander Figure.	2.25	....	....	....	1.10	.30
2241	22¢ Ship Figurehead..	2.25	....	....	....	1.10	.30
2242	22¢ Nautical Figure ...	2.25	....	....	....	1.10	.30
2243	22¢ Cigar Store Figure	2.25	....	....	....	1.10	.30

2244 2245

| 2244 | 22¢ Madonna........ | 2.25 | 4.00 | 66.00(100) | 4.00 | .75 | .25 |
| 2245 | 22¢ Village Scene .... | 2.25 | 4.00 | 66.00(100) | 4.00 | .75 | .25 |

2246 2247 2248

2249 2250 2251

1987 COMMEMORATIVES

2246/2368	(2246-51, 2275, 2336-38, 2349-54, 2360-61, 2367-68) 20 varieties	....	....	....	....	18.50	5.25
2246	22¢ Michigan Statehood	2.25	4.00	39.00(50)	4.50	1.00	.25
2247	22¢ Pan American Games	2.25	4.00	38.00(50)	4.00	.95	.25
2248	22¢ LOVE	3.00	4.50	68.00(100)	4.00	.95	.25
2249	22¢ Jean Baptiste Pointe du Sable......	2.25	4.00	36.00(50)	4.00	.95	.25
2250	22¢ Enrico Caruso....	2.25	4.00	36.00(50)	4.00	.95	.25
2251	22¢ Girls Scouts	2.25	4.00	36.00(50)	4.00	.95	.25

2252 2253 2254 2255

2256 2257 2258 2259

2260 2261 2262 2263

2264 2265 2266

1987-93 TRANSPORTATION COILS

SCOTT	DESCRIPTION	PLATE# STRIP 3		PLATE# STRIP 3		
2252	3¢ Conestoga Wagon (1988)	2.25	9.00	....	1.25	.25	.25
2252a	same, untagged (1992)		9.00	....	1.75	.25	.25
2253	5¢ Milk Wagon......	2.25	9.00	....	1.90	.25	.25
2254	5.3¢ Elevator,precancel ('88)	2.25	9.00	....	1.90	.40	.25
2255	7.6¢ Carreta, precancel ('88)	2.25	9.00	....	3.25	.40	.25
2256	8.4¢ Wheel Chair, precancel (1988)	2.25	9.00	....	3.50	.40	.25
2257	10¢ Canal Boat	2.25	9.00	....	3.50	.40	.25
2257a	same, overall tagging (1993)		9.00	....	18.00	3.00	.25
2258	13¢ Police Wagon, precancel (1988)	2.25	9.00	....	8.50	.90	.25
2259	13.2¢ Railroad Coal Car, precancel (1988)	2.25	9.00	....	3.50	.40	.25
2260	15¢ Tugboat (1988) ...	2.25	9.00	....	3.50	.50	.25
2260a	same, overall tagging (1990)		9.00	....	5.25	.75	.25
2261	16.7¢ Popcorn Wagon, precancel (1988)	2.25	9.00	....	4.25	.60	.25
2262	17.5¢ Racing Car.....	2.25	9.00	....	5.25	1.25	.35
2262a	17.5¢ Racing Car, precancel (1988)	2.25	9.00	....	5.25	.90	.55
2263	20¢ Cable Car (1988) .	2.25	9.00	....	4.50	.70	.25
2263b	same, overall tagging (1990)		9.00	....	11.00	1.85	.40
2264	20.5¢ Fire Engine, precancel (1988)	2.25	9.00	....	8.00	1.50	.55
2265	21¢ Railroad Mail Car, precancel (1988)	2.25	9.00	....	5.50	.80	.45
2266	24.1¢ Tandem Bicycle, precancel (1988)	2.25	9.00	....	6.50	1.20	.90

SCOTT NO.	DESCRIPTION	FIRST DAY COVERS SING	PL. BLK.	MINT SHEET	PLATE BLOCK	UNUSED F/NH	USED

2267

2268   2269

2270   2271   2272

2273   2274

1987 SPECIAL OCCASIONS BOOKLET PANE

2267	22¢ Congratulations! ..	2.25	....	....	....	2.00	.55
2268	22¢ Get Well!	2.25	....	....	....	2.00	.55
2269	22¢ Thank You!	2.25	....	....	....	2.00	.55
2270	22¢ Love You, Dad! ...	2.25	....	....	....	2.00	.55
2271	22¢ Best Wishes!	2.25	....	....	....	2.00	.55
2272	22¢ Happy Birthday! ...	2.25	....	....	....	2.00	.55
2273	22¢ Love You, Mother!	2.25	....	....	....	2.00	.55
2274	22¢ Keep in Touch! ...	2.25	....	....	....	2.00	.55
2274a	Special Occasions bklt pane of 10, attached ..	17.00	....	....	....	17.50	....

NOTE: #2274a contains 1 each of #2268-71, 2273-74 and 2 each of #2267 and 2272.

2275

1987 COMMEMORATIVES (continued)

2275	22¢ United Way	2.25	4.00	34.00(50)	3.50	1.00	.25

2276   2277, 2279, 2282, 2282a   2278, 2285A, 2285Ac

1987-88 REGULAR ISSUE

2276	22¢ Flag & Fireworks ..	2.25	4.00	68.00(100)	4.00	1.00	.25
2276a	bklt pane of 20	12.50	....	....	....	13.50	....
2277	(25¢) "E" Earth (1988) .	2.25	4.00	72.00(100)	4.50	.95	.25
2278	25¢ Flag with Clouds (1988)	2.25	4.00	72.00(100)	5.00	1.00	.25

2280   2281   2283, 2283a

2284   2285, 2285b

		PLATE # STRIP 3		PLATE# STRIP 3			
2279	(25¢) "E" Earth coil (1988)	2.25	7.50	....	4.50	.80	.25
2280	25¢ Flag over Yosemite, coil (1988)	2.25	7.50	....	4.50	.90	.25
2280a	25¢ Flag over Yosemite, phosphor (1989)	2.25	....	....	5.00	.95	.25
2281	25¢ Honey Bee, coil (1988)	2.25	7.50	....	4.00	.85	.25
2282	(25¢) "E" Earth, bklt single (1988)	2.25	....	....	....	.85	.25
2282a	(25¢) "E" Earth, bklt pane of 10	7.25	....	....	....	9.75	....
2283	25¢ Pheasant bklt single (1988)	2.25	....	....	....	1.50	.25
2283a	25¢ Pheasant, bklt pane of 10	7.25	....	....	....	10.00	....
2283b	25¢ Pheasant, (red omitted) bklt single	....	....	....	....	11.00	....
2283c	25¢ Pheasant, (red omitted) bklt pane of 10	....	....	....	....	105.00	....
2284	25¢ Grosbeak, bklt single (1988)	2.25	....	....	....	1.00	.25
2285	25¢ Owl bklt single ...	2.25	....	....	....	1.00	.25
2285b	25¢ Owl/Grosbeck, bklt pane of 10	7.25	....	....	....	8.75	....
2285A	25¢ Flag with Clouds, bklt single	2.25	....	....	....	.95	.25
2285Ac	as above, bklt pane of 6 (1988)	4.00	....	....	....	5.75	....

2286   2310   2335

1987 AMERICAN WILDLIFE

2286	Barn Swallow	2302	Ringtail	2319	Pika
2287	Monarch Butterfly	2303	Red-winged Blackbird	2320	Bison
2288	Bighorn Sheep	2304	American Lobster	2321	Snowy Egret
2289	Broad-tailed Hummingbird	2305	Black-tailed Jack Rabbit	2322	Gray Wolf
		2306	Scarlet Tanager	2323	Mountain Goat
2290	Cottontail	2307	Woodchuck	2324	Deer Mouse
2291	Osprey	2308	Roseate Spoonbill	2325	Black-tailed Prairie Dog
2292	Mountain Lion	2309	Bald Eagle	2326	Box Turtle
2293	Luna Moth	2310	Alaskan Brown Bear	2327	Wolverine
2294	Mule Deer	2311	Iiwi	2328	American Elk
2295	Gray Squirrel	2312	Badger	2329	California Sea Lion
2296	Armadillo	2313	Pronghorn	2330	Mockingbird
2297	Eastern Chipmunk	2314	River Otter	2331	Raccoon
2298	Moose	2315	Ladybug	2332	Bobcat
2299	Black Bear	2316	Beaver	2333	Black-footed Ferret
2300	Tiger Swallowtail	2317	White-tailed Deer	2334	Canada Goose
2301	Bobwhite	2318	Blue Jay	2335	Red Fox

2286-2335	22¢, 50 varieties, attached	70.00	....	60.00(50)	....	60.00	....
	set of singles	86.00	....	....	....	65.00	25.00
	singles of above, each	2.00	....	....	....	1.55	1.00

2336   2337   2338   2339

SCOTT NO.	DESCRIPTION	FIRST DAY COVERS SING	PL. BLK.	MINT SHEET	PLATE BLOCK	UNUSED F/NH	USED

2340

2341

2342

2343

2344

2345

2346

2347

2348

1987-90 COMMEMORATIVES

Scott No.	Description	Sing	Pl. Blk.	Mint Sheet	Plate Block	Unused F/NH	Used
2336	22¢ Delaware Statehood	2.25	4.00	40.00(50)	4.00	1.00	.25
2337	22¢ Pennsylvania Statehood	2.25	4.00	40.00(50)	4.00	1.00	.25
2338	22¢ New Jersey Statehood	2.25	4.00	40.00(50)	4.00	1.00	.25
2339	22¢ Georgia Statehood (1988)	2.25	4.00	40.00(50)	4.00	1.00	.35
2340	22¢ Connecticut Statehood (1988)	2.25	4.00	40.00(50)	4.00	1.00	.25
2341	22¢ Massachusetts Statehood (1988)	2.25	4.00	40.00(50)	4.00	1.00	.40
2342	22¢ Maryland Statehood (1988)	2.25	4.00	40.00(50)	4.00	1.00	.40
2343	25¢ South Carolina Statehood (1988)	2.25	4.00	40.00(50)	4.00	1.00	.25
2344	25¢ New Hampshire Statehood (1988)	2.25	4.00	40.00(50)	4.00	1.00	.25
2345	25¢ Virginia Statehood (1988)	2.25	4.00	40.00(50)	4.00	1.00	.25
2346	25¢ New York Statehood (1988)	2.25	4.00	40.00(50)	4.00	1.00	.25
2347	25¢ North Carolina Statehood (1989)	2.25	4.00	45.00(50)	5.50	1.50	.25
2348	25¢ Rhode Island Statehood (1990)	2.25	9.00	45.00(50)	5.50	1.50	.25

2349

2350

Scott No.	Description	Sing	Pl. Blk.	Mint Sheet	Plate Block	Unused F/NH	Used
2349	22¢ Morocco	2.25	4.00	35.00(50)	3.75	.80	.25
2350	22¢ William Faulkner	2.25	4.00	37.00(50)	4.75	1.25	.25

SCOTT NO.	DESCRIPTION	FIRST DAY COVERS SING	PL. BLK.	MINT SHEET	PLATE BLOCK	UNUSED F/NH	USED

2351   2352
2353   2354

Scott No.	Description	Sing	Pl. Blk.	Mint Sheet	Plate Block	Unused F/NH	Used
2351-54	Lacemaking, 4 varieties, attached	4.00	5.00	38.00(40)	5.00	4.50	3.50
2351	22¢ Lace, Ruth Maxwell	2.25	....	....	....	1.25	.30
2352	22¢ Lace, Mary McPeek	2.25	....	....	....	1.25	.30
2353	22¢ Lace, Leslie K. Saari	2.25	....	....	....	1.25	.30
2354	22¢ Lace, Trenna Ruffner	2.25	....	....	....	1.25	.30

2355   2356

2357   2358

2359

Scott No.	Description	Sing	Pl. Blk.	Mint Sheet	Plate Block	Unused F/NH	Used
2355	22¢ "The Bicentennial"	2.25	....	....	1.50	.30
2356	22¢ "We the people"	2.25	....	....	1.50	.30
2357	22¢ "Establish justice"	2.25	....	....	1.50	.30
2358	22¢ "And secure"	2.25	....	....	1.50	.30
2359	22¢ "Do ordain"	2.25	....	....	1.50	.30
2359a	Drafting of Constitution bklt pane, 5 varieties, attached	4.60	....	....	....	7.75	6.50

2360

2361

Scott No.	Description	Sing	Pl. Blk.	Mint Sheet	Plate Block	Unused F/NH	Used
2360	22¢ Signing of U.S. Constitution	2.25	4.00	45.00(50)	4.50	1.00	.25
2361	22¢ Certified Public Accountants	12.00	15.00	75.00(50)	7.50	1.75	.25

SCOTT NO.	DESCRIPTION	FIRST DAY COVERS SING	FIRST DAY COVERS PL. BLK.	MINT SHEET	PLATE BLOCK	UNUSED F/NH	USED

2362

2363

2364

2365

2366

LOCOMOTIVES ISSUE

SCOTT NO.	DESCRIPTION	SING	PL. BLK.	MINT SHEET	PLATE BLOCK	UNUSED F/NH	USED
2362	22¢ "Strourbridge Lion, 1829"	2.25	....	....	....	1.25	.25
2363	22¢ "Best Friend of Charleston, 1830"	2.25	....	....	....	1.25	.25
2364	22¢ "John Bull, 1831"	2.25	....	....	....	1.25	.25
2365	22¢ "Brother Jonathan, 1832"	2.25	....	....	....	1.25	.25
2366	22¢ "Gowan + Marx, 1839"	2.25	....	....	....	1.25	.25
2366a	Locomotives, bklt pane, 5 varieties, attached	4.60	....	....	....	6.00	4.75

2367

2368

| 2367 | 22¢ Madonna | 2.25 | 4.00 | 68.00(100) | 4.00 | .90 | .25 |
| 2368 | 22¢ Ornament | 2.25 | 4.00 | 68.00(100) | 4.00 | .90 | .25 |

2369

2370

2371

2372   2373

2374   2375

2376

2377

2378

1988 COMMEMORATIVES

SCOTT NO.	DESCRIPTION	SING	PL. BLK.	MINT SHEET	PLATE BLOCK	UNUSED F/NH	USED
2339/2400	(2339-46, 2369-80, 2386-93, 2399-2400) 30 varieties	....	....	....	....	29.00	9.00
2369	22¢ Winter Olympics	2.25	4.00	47.00(50)	7.00	1.50	.25
2370	22¢ Australia Bicentennial	2.25	4.00	28.00(50)	3.50	.75	.25
2371	22¢ James Weldon Johnson	2.25	4.00	44.00(50)	5.00	1.00	.30
2372-75	Cats, 4 varieties, attached	8.00	12.00	40.00(40)	6.50	5.00	4.00
2372	22¢ Siamese, Exotic Shorthair	2.25	....	....	....	1.50	.75
2373	22¢ Abyssinian, Himalayan	2.25	....	....	....	1.50	.75
2374	22¢ Maine Coon, Burmese	2.25	....	....	....	1.50	.75
2375	22¢ American Shorthair, Persian	2.25	....	....	....	1.50	.75
2376	22¢ Knute Rockne	4.00	6.00	45.00(50)	4.75	1.20	.50
2377	25¢ Francis Ouimet	8.00	10.00	48.00(50)	7.00	1.25	.30
2378	25¢ LOVE	2.25	4.00	72.00(100)	4.00	.85	.25

2379

2380

| 2379 | 45¢ LOVE | 2.25 | 4.00 | 67.50(50) | 7.00 | 1.50 | .25 |
| 2380 | 25¢ Summer Olympics | 2.25 | 4.00 | 46.00(50) | 4.75 | 1.00 | .25 |

2381

2382

2383

2384

2385

2381	25¢ Locomobile	2.25	....	....	....	2.00	.40
2382	25¢ Pierce-Arrow	2.25	....	....	....	2.00	.40
2383	25¢ Cord	2.25	....	....	....	2.00	.40
2384	25¢ Packard	2.25	....	....	....	2.00	.40
2385	25¢ Duesenberg	2.25	....	....	....	2.00	.40
2385a	Classic Automobiles bklt pane, 5 varieties, attached	4.60	....	....	....	10.50	7.00

BOOKLET PANE SINGLES: Traditionally, booklet panes have been collected only as intact panes since, other than the straight edged sides, they were identical to sheet stamps. However, starting with the 1971 8¢ Eisenhower stamp, many issues differ from the comparative sheet stamp or may even be totally different issues (e.g. #1738-42 Windmills). These newer issues are now collected as booklet singles or panes—both methods being acceptable.

SCOTT NO.	DESCRIPTION	FIRST DAY COVERS SING	PL. BLK.	MINT SHEET	PLATE BLOCK	UNUSED F/NH	USED

2386 2387
2388 2389

SCOTT NO.	DESCRIPTION	SING	PL. BLK.	MINT SHEET	PLATE BLOCK	UNUSED F/NH	USED
2386-89	Antarctic Explorers, 4 varieties, attached . .	4.00	5.00	48.00(50)	6.00	5.75	4.00
2386	25¢ Nathaniel Palmer .	2.25	....	....	....	1.50	.45
2387	25¢ Lt. Charles Wilkes.	2.25	....	....	....	1.50	.45
2388	25¢ Richard E. Byrd . .	2.25	....	....	....	1.50	.45
2389	25¢ Lincoln Ellsworth. .	2.25	....	....	....	1.50	.45

2390 2391 2392 2393

2390-93	Carousel Animals, 4 varieties, attached . .	4.00	5.00	52.50(50)	6.75	6.00	4.00
2390	25¢ Deer	2.25	....	....	....	1.60	.30
2391	25¢ Horse	2.25	....	....	....	1.60	.30
2392	25¢ Camel	2.25	....	....	....	1.60	.30
2393	25¢ Goat	2.25	....	....	....	1.60	.30

2394

2394	$8.75 Express Mail . . .	32.00	70.00	535.00(20)	125.00	30.00	10.00

2395 2396

2397 2398

2395-2398	Special Occasions, bklt singles.	7.00	....	....	....	4.50	1.85
2396a	Bklt pane (6) with gutter 3–#2395 + 3–#2396 . .	4.60	....	....	....	6.00	5.00
2398a	Bklt pane (6) with gutter 3–#2397 + 3–#2398 . .	4.60	....	....	....	6.00	5.00

2399 2400

2399	25¢ Madonna and Child	2.25	4.00	36.00(50)	3.75	1.00	.25
2400	25¢ One Horse Sleigh .	2.25	4.00	36.00(50)	3.75	1.00	.25

2401 2402

1989 COMMEMORATIVES

2347/2437	(2347, 2401-04, 2410-14, 2416-18, 2420-28, 2434-37) 26 varieties	....	....	....	....	27.75	6.25
2401	25¢ Montana Statehood	2.25	4.00	60.00(50)	7.00	1.50	.25
2402	25¢ A.P. Randolph	3.00	4.00	55.00(50)	5.00	1.20	.25

2403 2404

2403	25¢ North Dakota Statehood	2.25	4.00	65.00(50)	7.00	1.50	.25
2404	25¢ Washington Statehood	2.25	4.00	60.00(50)	7.00	1.50	.25

2405 2406

2407 2408

2409

2405	25¢ "Experiment,1788-90"	2.25	....	....	....	1.40	.35
2406	25¢ "Phoenix, 1809" . .	2.25	....	....	....	1.40	.35
2407	25¢ "New Orleans, 1812"	2.25	....	....	....	1.40	.35
2408	25¢ "Washington, 1816"	2.25	....	....	....	1.40	.35
2409	25¢ "Walk in the Water,1818"	2.25	....	....	....	1.40	.35
2409a	Steamboat, bklt pane, 5 varieties, attached . .	6.00	....	....	....	7.50	4.00
2409av	same, bklt pane, unfolded	....	....	....	....	12.00	....

SCOTT NO.	DESCRIPTION	FIRST DAY COVERS SING	PL. BLK.	MINT SHEET	PLATE BLOCK	UNUSED F/NH	USED

2410

2411

| 2410 | 25¢ World Stamp Expo '89 | 2.25 | 4.00 | 36.00(50) | 3.75 | 1.00 | .25 |
| 2411 | 25¢ Arturo Toscanini .. | 2.25 | 4.00 | 38.00(50) | 3.75 | 1.00 | .25 |

2412

2413

2414

2415

2412	25¢ U.S. House of Representatives......	2.25	4.00	45.00(50)	4.50	1.00	.25
2413	25¢ U.S. Senate	2.25	4.00	58.00(50)	5.25	1.15	.25
2414	25¢ Executive Branch .	2.25	4.00	40.00(50)	4.00	1.00	.25
2415	25¢ U.S. Supreme Court (1990)	2.25	4.00	40.00(50)	4.00	1.00	.25

2416

| 2416 | 25¢ South Dakota Statehood .... | 2.25 | 4.00 | 55.00(50) | 6.00 | 1.50 | .25 |

2417

2418

| 2417 | 25¢ Lou Gehrig ...... | 5.00 | 8.00 | 55.00(50) | 6.00 | 1.20 | .30 |
| 2418 | 25¢ Ernest Hemingway | 2.25 | 4.00 | 42.50(50) | 4.50 | 1.00 | .25 |

2419

| 2419 | $2.40 Moon Landing .. | 7.50 | 15.75 | 165.00(20) | 40.00 | 10.00 | 5.00 |

2420

2421

| 2420 | 25¢ Letter Carriers.... | 2.25 | 4.00 | 29.00(50) | 4.00 | 1.00 | .25 |
| 2421 | 25¢ Bill of Rights ..... | 2.25 | 4.00 | 43.00(50) | 5.00 | 1.25 | .25 |

2422   2423

2424   2425

2422-25	Prehistoric Animals, 4 attached	5.00	7.00	38.00(40)	5.50	5.00	3.75
2422	25¢ Tyrannosaurus Rex	2.50	....	....	....	1.40	.25
2423	25¢ Pteranodon.......	2.50	....	....	....	1.40	.25
2424	25¢ Stegosaurus	2.50	....	....	....	1.40	.25
2425	25¢ Brontosaurus	2.50	....	....	....	1.40	.25

2426

| 2426 | 25¢ Kachina Doll ..... | 2.25 | 4.00 | 38.00(50) | 4.00 | 1.00 | .25 |

2427

2428, 2429

2431

2427	25¢ Madonna & Child .	1.75	4.00	40.00(50)	4.00	1.00	.25
2427a	same, bklt pane of 10 .	7.25	....	....	....	9.00	....
2427av	same, bklt pane, unfolded	....	....	....	....	15.00	....
2428	25¢ Sleigh full of Presents	2.25	4.00	40.00(50)	4.00	.85	.25
2429	25¢ Sleigh full of Presents, bklt single...........	2.25	....	....	....	.90	.25
2429a	same, bklt pane of 10 .	7.25	....	....	....	9.00	....
2429av	same, bklt pane, unfolded	....	....	....	....	19.00	....
2431	25¢ Eagle & Shield, self-adhesive	1.95	....	....	....	1.25	.75
2431a	same, bklt pane of 18 .	32.00	....	....	....	19.50	....
2431	same, coil	....	....	....	3.00(3)	1.25	....

SCOTT NO.	DESCRIPTION	FIRST DAY COVERS SING	PL. BLK.	MINT SHEET	PLATE BLOCK	UNUSED F/NH	USED

2433

The classic 1869 U.S. Abraham Lincoln stamp is reborn in these four larger versions commemorating World Stamp Expo'89, held in Washington, D.C. during the 20th Universal Postal Congress of the UPU. These stamps show the issued colors and three of the trial proof color combinations. ©USPS 1988

| 2433 | $3.60 World Stamp Expo, Imperf. Souvenir Sheet | 15.00 | .... | .... | .... | 22.00 | 18.00 |

2434   **2435**

2436   **2437**

2434-37	Classic Mail Delivery, 4 attached	5.00	7.00	40.00(40)	5.75	5.00	4.00
2434	25¢ Stagecoach	2.25	....	....	....	1.50	.40
2435	25¢ Paddlewheel Steamer	2.25	....	....	....	1.50	.40
2436	25¢ Biplane	2.25	....	....	....	1.50	.40
2437	25¢ Automobile	2.25	....	....	....	1.50	.40
2438	$1.00 Classic Mail Delivery Imperf. Souvenir Sheet	4.50	....	....	....	8.00	6.50

2439   **2440, 2441**   **2442**

1990 COMMEMORATIVES

2348/2515	(2348, 2415, 2439-40, 2442, 2444-49, 2496-2500, 2506-15, 26 varieties	....	....	....	....	32.00	6.25
2439	25¢ Idaho Statehood	2.25	4.00	60.00(50)	5.00	1.50	.25
2440	25¢ LOVE	2.25	4.00	44.00(50)	4.00	1.50	.25
2441	25¢ LOVE, bklt single	2.25	....	....	....	1.25	.25
2441a	25¢ LOVE bklt pane of 10	8.65	....	....	....	12.00	....
2441av	same, bklt pane, unfolded	....	....	....	....	50.00	....
2442	25¢ Ida B. Wells	3.00	4.00	60.00(50)	5.00	1.50	.25

2443   **2444**

2445   **2449**   **2446**

2447   **2448**

2443	15¢ Umbrella, bklt single	2.25	....	....	....	.60	.25
2443a	15¢ Umbrella, bklt pane of 10	5.75	....	....	....	5.00	3.40
2443av	same, bklt pane, unfolded	....	....	....	....	10.00	....
2444	25¢ Wyoming Statehood	8.00	10.00	60.00(50)	6.00	1.75	.25
2445-48	Classic Films, 4 varieties, attached	8.00	7.00	65.00(40)	8.00	7.50	5.00
2445	25¢ Wizard of OZ	4.00	....	....	....	2.25	.35
2446	25¢ Gone with the Wind	4.00	....	....	....	2.25	.35
2447	25¢ Beau Geste	4.00	....	....	....	2.25	.35
2448	25¢ Stagecoach	4.00	....	....	....	2.25	.35
2449	25¢ Marianne Craig Moore	2.25	4.00	48.00(50)	5.00	1.50	.20

2451   **2452, 2452B, 2452D**   **2453, 2454**   **2457, 2458**

2463   **2464**   **2466**   **2468**

1990-95 TRANSPORTATION COILS

SCOTT NO.	DESCRIPTION	PLATE# STRIP 3		PLATE# STRIP 3		UNUSED F/NH	USED
2451	4¢ Steam Carriage (1991)	2.25	6.50	....	1.50	.25	.25
2451b	4¢ Steam Carriage, untagged	....	....	....	1.50	.25	.25
2452	5¢ Circus Wagon	2.25	6.50	....	1.75	.25	.25
2452a	5¢ Circus Wagon, untagged	....	....	....	2.50	.25	.25
2452B	5¢ Circus Wagon, Gravure (1992)	2.25	6.50	....	2.50	.35	.25
2452D	5¢ Circus Wagon, coil (Reissue, 1995 added)	3.00	10.00	....	1.85	.35	.25
2453	5¢ Canoe, precancel, brown (1991)	2.25	6.50	....	1.85	.35	.25
2454	5¢ Canoe, precancel, red (1991)	2.25	6.50	....	2.50	.35	.25
2457	10¢ Tractor Trailer (1991)	2.25	6.50	....	3.00	.45	.25
2458	10¢ Tractor Trailer, Gravure (1994)	2.25	6.50	....	7.50	.70	.50
2463	20¢ Cog Railway Car, coil	1.95	10.00	....	5.00	.70	.25
2464	23¢ Lunch Wagon (1991)	2.25	6.50	....	4.50	.85	.25
2466	32¢ Ferryboat, coil	1.95	10.00	....	7.75	1.25	.25
2468	$1 Seaplane, coil	3.00	10.00	....	15.00	4.00	1.00

BUY COMPLETE SETS AND SAVE!

SCOTT NO.	DESCRIPTION	FIRST DAY COVERS SING	FIRST DAY COVERS PL. BLK.	MINT SHEET	PLATE BLOCK	UNUSED F/NH	USED

2470   **2471**   **2472**   **2473**   **2474**

2470	25¢ Admiralty Head Lighthouse..........	2.25	....			2.25	.25
2471	25¢ Cape Hatteras Lighthouse..........	2.25	....			2.25	.25
2472	25¢ West Quoddy Head Lighthouse.....	2.25	....			2.25	.25
2473	25¢ American Shoals Lighthouse..........	2.25	....			2.25	.25
2474	25¢ Sandy Hook Lighthouse..........	2.25	....			2.25	.25
2474a	Lighthouse, bklt pane, 5 varieties	4.60	....			12.00	6.50
2474av	Same, bklt pane, unfolded	....	....			18.00	....

2475

| 2475 | 25¢ ATM Plastic Stamp, single........ | 2.25 | .... | .... | .... | 1.75 | 1.25 |
| 2475a | Same, pane of 12 .... | 20.00 | .... | .... | .... | 13.00 | .... |

2476   **2477**   **2478**   **2479**

2480   **2481**   **2482**   **2483**

1990-95 REGULAR ISSUE

2476	1¢ Kestrel (1991).....	2.25	4.00	10.00(100)	.90	.25	.25
2477	1¢ Kestrel (redesign 1¢, 1995)	2.25	4.00	10.00(100)	.90	.25	.25
2478	3¢ Bluebird (1993)....	2.25	4.00	15.00(100)	1.50	.25	.25
2479	19¢ Fawn (1993).....	2.25	4.00	58.00(100)	5.00	.75	.25
2480	30¢ Cardinal (1993)...	2.25	4.00	85.00(100)	5.25	1.10	.80
2481	45¢ Pumpkinseed Sunfish (1992)	2.00	4.50	135.00(100)	7.75	1.50	.75
2482	$2 Bobcat	6.00	14.00	110.00(20)	28.00	6.50	1.15
2483	20¢ Blue Jay, bklt single (1991)	1.95	....	....	....	.85	.30
2483a	same, bklt pane of 10 .	9.00	....	....	....	9.00	....
2483av	same, bklt pane, unfolded	....	....	....	....	11.00	....

2484, 2485   **2486**   **2487, 2493, 2495**   **2488, 2494, 2495A**

SCOTT NO.	DESCRIPTION	FIRST DAY COVERS SING	FIRST DAY COVERS PL. BLK.	MINT SHEET	PLATE BLOCK	UNUSED F/NH	USED

2489   **2490**   **2491**   **2492**

2484	29¢ Wood Duck, bklt single (BEP) (1991)	2.25	....	....	....	.95	.25
2484a	same, bklt pane of 10 (BEP)	9.00	....	....	....	9.50	....
2484av	same, bklt pane, unfolded	....	....	....	....	13.00	....
2485	29¢ Wood Duck, bklt single (KCS) (1991)	2.25	....	....	....	1.20	.25
2485a	same, bklt pane of 10 (KCS).	9.00	....	....	....	10.50	....
2485av	same, bklt pane, unfolded	....	....	....	....	14.00	....
2486	29¢ African Violet, bklt single.............	2.25	....	....	....	1.10	.25
2486a	same, bklt pane of 10 .	9.00	....	....	....	12.00	....
2486av	same, bklt pane, unfolded	....	....	....	....	14.00	....
2487	32¢ Peach, bklt single .	1.95	....	....	....	1.25	.25
2488	32¢ Pear, bklt single ..	1.95	....	....	....	1.25	.25
2488a	32¢ Peach & Pear, bklt pane of 10.......	7.25	....	....	....	12.00	....
2488av	same, bklt pane, unfolded	....	....	....	....	15.00	....
2489	29¢ Red Squirrel, self-adhesive (1993) ..	2.25	....	....	....	1.10	.45
2489a	same, bklt pane of 18 .	13.50	....	....	....	20.00	....
2489v	same, coil	....	....	....	3.00(3)	1.10	....
2490	29¢ Rose, self-adhesive (1993)	2.25	....	....	....	1.10	.40
2490a	same, bklt pane of 18 .	13.50	....	....	....	20.00	....
2491	29¢ Pine Cone, self-adhesive........	2.25	....	....	....	1.10	.40
2491a	same, bklt pane of 18 .	13.50	....	....	....	19.00	....
2492	32¢ Pink Rose, self-adhesive........	1.95	....	....	....	1.10	.30
2492a	same, bklt pane of 20 .	14.50	....	....	....	21.00	....
2492b	same, bklt pane of 15 .	11.50	....	....	....	18.00	....
2493	32¢ Peach, self-adhesive........	1.95	....	....	....	1.10	.30
2494	32¢ Pear, self-adhesive	1.95	....	....	....	1.10	.30
2494a	32¢ Peach & Pear, self-adhesive, bklt pane of 20 .	14.50	....	....	....	22.00	....
2495	32¢ Peach, self-adhesive coil (1993)	1.95	....	....	15.00(3)	3.50	....
2495A	32¢ Pear, self-adhesive coil	1.95	....	....	....	3.50	....

2496   **2497**

2498   **2499**

2500

2496-2500	Olympians, strip of 5, attached..........	7.50	10.00	35.00(35)	12.00(10)	7.00	5.00
2496	25¢ Jesse Owens....	2.40	....	....	....	1.75	.50
2497	25¢ Ray Ewry	2.40	....	....	....	1.75	.50
2498	25¢ Hazel Wightman ..	2.40	....	....	....	1.75	.50
2499	25¢ Eddie Eagan	2.40	....	....	....	1.75	.50
2500	25¢ Helene Madison ..	2.40	....	....	....	1.75	.50

SCOTT NO.	DESCRIPTION	FIRST DAY COVERS SING	PL. BLK.	MINT SHEET	PLATE BLOCK	UNUSED F/NH	USED

2501

2502

2503

2504

2505

2501-05	25¢ Headdresses strip of 5					9.00	
2501	25¢ Assiniboine	2.40	. . . .	. . . .	. . . .	2.00	.40
2502	25¢ Cheyenne	2.40	. . . .	. . . .	. . . .	2.00	.40
2503	25¢ Comanche	2.40	. . . .	. . . .	. . . .	2.00	.40
2504	25¢ Flathead	2.40	. . . .	. . . .	. . . .	2.00	.40
2505	25¢ Shoshone	2.40	. . . .	. . . .	. . . .	2.00	.40
2505a	25¢ bklt pane of 10 . . .	7.85	. . . .	. . . .	. . . .	18.00	. . . .
2505av	same, bklt pane, unfolded	. . . .	. . . .	. . . .	. . . .	25.00	. . . .

2506   2507

2506-07	Micronesia + Marshall Islands 2 varieties, attached . .	5.00	6.00	48.00(50)	5.00	2.00	1.30
2506	25¢ Micronesia	2.50	. . . .	. . . .	. . . .	1.00	.25
2507	25¢ Marshall Islands . .	2.50	. . . .	. . . .	. . . .	1.00	.25

2508   2509

2510   2511

1990 REGULAR ISSUES

2508-11	Sea Creatures, ... 4 varieties, attached . .	5.00	6.00	37.00(40)	6.00	5.50	3.50
2508	25¢ Killer Whales	2.50	. . . .	. . . .	. . . .	1.40	.40
2509	25¢ Northern Sea Lions	2.50	. . . .	. . . .	. . . .	1.40	.40
2510	25¢ Sea Otter	2.50	. . . .	. . . .	. . . .	1.40	.40
2511	25¢ Common Dolphin .	2.50	. . . .	. . . .	. . . .	1.40	.40

SCOTT NO.	DESCRIPTION	FIRST DAY COVERS SING	PL. BLK.	MINT SHEET	PLATE BLOCK	UNUSED F/NH	USED

2512

2513

2514

2515, 2516

2512	25¢ Americas Issue (Grand Canyon)	2.25	4.00	42.00(50)	5.00	1.25	.25
2513	25¢ Dwight D. Eisenhower	2.25	4.00	38.00(40)	5.00	1.25	.25
2514	25¢ Madonna & Child– Antonello	2.25	4.00	38.00(50)	3.50	.95	.25
2514a	same, bklt pane of 10 .	6.50	. . . .	. . . .	. . . .	10.00	. . . .
2514av	same, bklt pane, unfolded	. . . .	. . . .	. . . .	. . . .	15.00	. . . .
2515	25¢ Christmas Tree . . .	2.25	4.00	38.00(50)	4.00	.75	.25
2516	25¢ Christmas Tree bklt single	2.25	. . . .	. . . .	. . . .	1.50	.25
2516a	same, bklt pane of 10 .	6.00	. . . .	. . . .	. . . .	13.00	. . . .
2516av	same, bklt pane, unfolded	. . . .	. . . .	. . . .	. . . .	19.50	. . . .

2517- 2519, 2520

1991 REGULAR ISSUES

| 2517 | (29¢) 'F" Flower . . . . . . | 2.25 | 4.25 | 90.00(100) | 4.25 | .95 | .25 |

		FIRST DAY COVERS SING	PLATE # STRIP 3		PLATE# STRIP 3		
2518	(29¢) "F" Flower, coil . .	2.25	10.00	. . . .	5.00	.95	.25
2519	(29¢) "F" Flower, bklt single (BEP)	2.25				1.00	.25
2519a	same, bklt pane of 10 (BEP)	6.50	. . . .	. . . .	. . . .	11.00	. . . .
2520	(29¢) "F" Flower, bklt single (KCS)	3.00				3.50	.70
2520a	same, bklt pane of 10 (KCS)	6.50	. . . .	. . . .	. . . .	33.00	. . . .

2521

2522

2521	(4¢) "F" Make-up Rate .	2.25	4.25	17.00(100)	1.00	.20	.25
2522	(29¢) "F" ATM Plastic Stamp, single	2.25				1.75	.50
2522a	same, pane of 12	9.00	. . . .	. . . .	. . . .	18.00	. . . .

2523, 2523A

		FIRST DAY COVERS SING	PLATE# STRIP 3		PLATE# STRIP 3		
2523	29¢ Flag over Mt. Rushmore, coil	2.25	10.00	. . . .	6.00	1.50	.25
2523A	29¢ Falg over Mt. Rushmore, photogravure coil	2.25	10.00	. . . .	7.50	1.50	1.00

SCOTT NO.	DESCRIPTION	FIRST DAY COVERS SING	FIRST DAY COVERS PL. BLK.	MINT SHEET	PLATE BLOCK	UNUSED F/NH	USED

2524-27

| 2524 | 29¢ Flower. . . . . | 2.25 | 4.25 | 90.00(100) | 5.00 | 1.00 | .25 |
| 2524A | 29¢ Flower, perf. 13. . . | . . . . | . . . . | 155.00(100) | 55.00 | 1.40 | .50 |

			PLATE# STRIP 3		PLATE# STRIP 3		
2525	29¢ Flower, coil rouletted	2.25	10.00	. . . .	5.50	1.20	.25
2526	29¢ Flower, coil, perf (1992)	2.25	10.00	. . . .	5.50	1.30	.25
2527	29¢ Flower, bklt single	2.25	. . . .	. . . .	. . . .	1.20	.25
2527a	same, bklt pane of 10 .	6.50	. . . .	. . . .	. . . .	9.50	. . . .
2527av	same, bklt pane, unfolded	. . . .	. . . .	. . . .	. . . .	12.00	. . . .

2528   **2529, 2529C**   **2530**

2531   **2531A**

			PLATE# STRIP 3		PLATE# STRIP3		
2528	29¢ Flag with Olympic Rings, bklt single.	2.25	. . . .	. . . .	. . . .	1.10	.25
2528a	same, bklt pane of 10 .	6.50	. . . .	. . . .	. . . .	10.00	. . . .
2528av	same, bklt pane, unfolded	. . . .	. . . .	. . . .	. . . .	12.00	. . . .
2529	19¢ Fishing Boat Type I	2.25	10.00	. . . .	4.50	.75	.25
2529a	same, Type II (1993) . .	. . . .	. . . .	. . . .	4.50	.75	.40
2529C	19¢ Fishing Boat (reengraved)	2.25	10.00	. . . .	9.00	1.25	.60
2530	19¢ Hot-Air Balloon bklt single.	2.25	. . . .	. . . .	. . . .	.70	.25
2530a	same, bklt pane of 10 .	10.00	. . . .	. . . .	. . . .	6.75	.25
2530av	same, bklt pane, unfolded	. . . .	. . . .	. . . .	. . . .	8.00	. . . .
2531	29¢ Flags on Parade . .	2.25	4.25	95.00(100)	5.00	1.25	.25
2531A	29¢ Liberty Torch ATM Stamp	2.25	. . . .	. . . .	. . . .	1.25	.30
2531Ab	same, pane of 18	15.00	. . . .	. . . .	. . . .	20.00	. . . .

2532

1991 COMMEMORATIVES

2532/2579	(2532-35, 2537-38, 2550-51, 2553-61, 2567, 2578-79) 29 varieties	. . . .	. . . .	. . . .	. . . .	32.00	11.50
2532	50¢ Switzerland	2.25	5.00	58.00(40)	7.00	1.75	.40

2533   **2534**   **2535, 2536**

2537   **2538**   **2539**

2533	29¢ Vermont Statehood	2.25	4.25	56.00(50)	6.00	1.50	.25
2534	29¢ Savings Bonds . . .	2.25	4.25	45.00(50)	4.75	1.00	.25
2535	29¢ Love	2.25	4.25	43.00(50)	4.75	1.00	.25
2535a	29¢ Love, perf 11. . . .	2.25	4.25	65.00(50)	8.50	1.50	.25
2536	29¢ Love, bklt single. .	2.25	. . . .	. . . .	. . . .	1.00	.25
2536a	same, bklt pane of 10 .	6.50	. . . .	. . . .	. . . .	10.00	. . . .
2536av	same, bklt pane, unfolded	. . . .	. . . .	. . . .	. . . .	13.00	. . . .
2537	52¢ Love	2.25	5.00	80.00(50)	8.50	1.75	.35
2538	29¢ William Saroyan . .	2.25	4.25	45.00(50)	5.00	1.00	.25
2539	$1 USPS/Olympic Rings	3.00	6.50	58.00(20)	15.00	3.50	1.50

2540

2540	$2.90 Eagle and Olympic Rings	10.00	16.50	210.00(20)	55.00	13.00	5.50

2541   **2542**

2541	$9.95 Express Mail . . .	27.00	50.00	600.00(20)	150.00	33.00	11.00
2542	$14.00 Express Mail . .	35.00	67.50	825.00(20)	200.00	45.00	23.00

2543   **2544**

2544A

2543	$2.90 Space Vechicle, priority mail	8.00	17.50	375.00(40)	45.00	10.00	2.75
2544	$3 Challenger Shuttle, priority mail (1995)	8.00	17.50	170.00(20)	42.00	9.00	3.00
2544A	$10.75 Endeavour Shuttle, express mail (1995) . . .	27.50	57.50	625.00(20)	155.00	30.00	10.00
2544b	Challenger Shuttle, Priority Mail (1996)	. . . .	. . . .	180.00(20)	42.00	10.00	3.50

SCOTT NO.	DESCRIPTION	FIRST DAY COVERS SING	PL. BLK.	MINT SHEET	PLATE BLOCK	UNUSED F/NH	USED

2545

2546

2547

2548

2549

SCOTT NO.	DESCRIPTION	FIRST DAY COVERS SING	PL. BLK.	MINT SHEET	PLATE BLOCK	UNUSED F/NH	USED
2545	29¢ "Royal Wulff"	2.25	....	....	....	2.00	.25
2546	29¢ "Jock Scott"	2.25	....	....	....	2.00	.25
2547	29¢ "Apte Tarpon"	2.25	....	....	....	2.00	.25
2548	29¢ "Lefty's Deceiver"	2.25	....	....	....	2.00	.25
2549	29¢ "Muddler Minnow"	2.25	....	....	....	2.00	.25
2549a	Fishing Flies, bklt pane, 5 varieties, attached	4.50	....	....	....	12.00	9.00
2549av	same, bklt pane, unfolded	....	....	....	....	18.00	....

2550

2551, 2552

2550	29¢ Cole Porter	2.25	4.25	50.00(50)	5.00	1.10	.25
2551	29¢ Desert Storm	2.25	4.25	50.00(50)	4.75	1.10	.25
2552	29¢ Desert Storm, bklt single	2.25	....	....	....	2.50	.25
2552a	same, bklt pane of 5	4.75	....	....	....	5.50	....
2552av	same, bklt pane, unfolded	....	....	....	....	7.50	....

2553

2554

2555

2556

2557

2558

2553-57	Summer Olympics, 5 varieties, attached	4.50	....	38.00(40)	12.00(10)	5.25	4.50
2553	29¢ Pole Vault	2.25	....	....	....	1.10	.60
2554	29¢ Discus	2.25	....	....	....	1.10	.60
2555	29¢ Sprinters	2.25	....	....	....	1.10	.60
2556	29¢ Javelin	2.25	....	....	....	1.10	.60
2557	29¢ Hurdles	2.25	....	....	....	1.10	.60
2558	29¢ Numismatics	2.25	4.25	60.00(50)	6.00	1.30	.60

2559

2559	$2.90 World War II, 1941, souvenir sheet of 10	14.00	....	22.00(20)	....	14.00	11.00
2559a	29¢ Burma Road	3.00	....	....	....	1.35	.75
2559b	29¢ Peacetime Draft	3.00	....	....	....	1.35	.75
2559c	29¢ Lend-Lease Act	3.00	....	....	....	1.35	.75
2559d	29¢ Atlantic Charter	3.00	....	....	....	1.35	.75
2559e	29¢ "Arsenal of Democracy"	3.00	....	....	....	1.35	.75
2559f	29¢ Destroyer "Reuben James"	3.00	....	....	....	1.35	.75
2559g	29¢ Civil Defense	3.00	....	....	....	1.35	.75
2559h	29¢ Liberty Ship	3.00	....	....	....	1.35	.75
2559i	29¢ Pearl Harbor	3.00	....	....	....	1.35	.75
2559j	29¢ Declaration of War on Japan	3.00	....	....	....	1.35	.75

2560

| 2560 | 29¢ Basketball | 3.00 | 4.50 | 65.00(50) | 6.50 | 1.50 | .25 |

2561

| 2561 | 29¢ District of Columbia | 2.25 | 4.25 | 45.00(50) | 4.50 | 1.30 | .25 |

SCOTT NO.	DESCRIPTION	FIRST DAY COVERS SING	PL. BLK.	MINT SHEET	PLATE BLOCK	UNUSED F/NH	USED

2562

2564

2565

2566

2562	29¢ Laurel and Hardy .	2.25	....	....	....	1.50	.35
2563	29¢ Bergen and McCarthy	2.25	....	....	....	1.50	.35
2564	29¢ Jack Benny......	2.25	....	....	....	1.50	.35
2565	29¢ Fanny Brice	2.25	....	....	....	1.50	.35
2566	29¢ Abbott and Costello	2.25	....	....	....	1.50	.35
2566a	Comedians, bklt pane of 10......	8.00	....	....	....	13.00	9.50
2566av	same, bklt pane, unfolded	....	....	....	....	17.00	....

2567

2567	29¢ Jan Matzeliger ...	2.25	4.25	45.00(50)	4.75	1.20	.25

2568

2569

2570

2572

2574

2575

2576

2577

2568	29¢ Mercury and Mariner 10.........	2.25	....	....	....	1.50	.40
2569	29¢ Venus and Mariner 2...........	2.25	....	....	....	1.50	.40
2570	29¢ Earth and Landsat	2.25	....	....	....	1.50	.40
2571	29¢ Moon and Lunar Orbiter	2.25	....	....	....	1.50	.40
2572	29¢ Mars and Viking Orbiter	2.25	....	....	....	1.50	.40
2573	29¢ Jupiter and Pioneer 11	2.25	....	....	....	1.50	.40
2574	29¢ Saturn and Voyager 2	2.25	....	....	....	1.50	.40
2575	29¢ Uranus and Voyager 2	2.25	....	....	....	1.50	.40
2576	29¢ Neptune and Voyager 2	2.25	....	....	....	1.50	.40
2577	29¢ Pluto, "Not Yet Explored"	2.25	....	....	....	1.50	.40
2577a	Space Explorations, bklt pane of 10.......	9.00	....	....	....	14.00	12.00
2577av	same, bklt pane, unfolded	....	....	....	....	20.00	....

2578

2579-81

2582

2583

2584

2585

2578	(29¢) Christmas– Traditional	2.25	4.25	45.00(50)	4.75	1.00	.25
2578a	same, bklt pane of 10 .	7.00	....	....	....	12.00	....
2578av	same, bklt pane, unfolded	....	....	....	....	15.00	....
2579	(29¢) Christmas– Contemporary	2.25	4.25	45.00(50)	4.75	.95	.25
2580-85	(29¢) Santa & Chimney set of 6 singles......	12.00	....	....	....	13.50	3.50
2581b-85a	same, bklt pane of 4 .	....	....	....	....	28.00	....
2581-85av	same, bklt pane of 4, unfolded............	20.00	....	....	....	32.50	....

NOTE: The far left brick from the top row of the chimney is missing from Type II, No. 2581

2587

2590

1992-95 Regular Issues

2587	32¢ James K. Polk (1995)	1.95	4.75	120.00(100)	7.00	1.75	.25
2590	$1 "Surrender at Saratoga" (1994)	4.00	6.50	60.00(20)	15.00	3.50	1.00

2592

2592	$5 Washington & Jackson (1994)	22.00	30.00	300.00(20)	68.00	16.50	3.00

SCOTT NO.	DESCRIPTION	FIRST DAY COVERS SING	FIRST DAY COVERS PL. BLK.	MINT SHEET	PLATE BLOCK	UNUSED F/NH	USED

2593, 2594

2593	29¢ Pledge of Allegiance (black) bklt single	2.25	....	....	....	1.00	.25
2593a	same, bklt pane of 10 .	7.00	....	....	....	10.00	....
2593av	same, bklt pane, unfolded	....	....	....	....	14.00	....
2594	29¢ Pledge of Allegiance (red) bklt single (1993).	2.25	....	....	....	1.50	.25
2594a	same, bklt pane of 10 .	7.00	....	....	....	11.00	....
2594av	same, bklt pane, unfolded	....	....	....	....	14.00	....

2595-97   **2598**   **2599**

1992-94 Self-Adhesive Stamps

2595	29¢ Eagle & Shield (brown) bklt single	2.25	....	....	....	1.20	.30
2595a	same, bklt pane of 17 .	12.00	....	....	....	19.00	....
2595v	same, coil	2.50	....	....	....	1.20	.30
2596	29¢ Eagle & Shield (green) bklt single	1.75	....	....	....	1.20	.30
2596a	same, bklt pane of 17 .	12.00	....	....	....	20.00	....
2596v	same, coil	2.50	....	....	....	1.20	.30
2597	29¢ Eagle & Shield (red) bklt single	2.25	....	....	....	1.20	.30
2597a	same, bklt pane of 17 .	12.00	....	....	....	20.00	....
2597v	same, coil	2.50	....	....	....	1.20	.30
2598	29¢ Eagle (1994)	2.25	....	....	....	1.20	.30
2598a	same, bklt pane of 18 .	13.50	....	....	....	22.00	....
2598v	29¢ Eagle, coil	2.50	....	....	9.50(3)	1.20	....
2599	29¢ Statue of Liberty (1994)	2.25	....	....	....	1.20	.30
2599a	same, bklt pane of 18 .	13.50	....	....	....	22.00	....
2599v	29¢ Statue of Liberty, coil	2.50	....	....	12.00(3)	1.20	....

2602   **2603, 2604**   **2605**

2606-08   **2609**

1991-93 Regular Issue

SCOTT NO.	DESCRIPTION	FIRST DAY COVERS SING	PLATE# STRIP 3		PLATE# STRIP 3	UNUSED F/NH	USED
2602	(10¢) Eagle, Bulk-Rate coil	2.25	10.00	....	3.75	.40	.25
2603	(10¢) Eagle, Bulk-Rate coil (orange-yellow) (BEP)	2.25	10.00	....	4.25	.40	.25
2604	(10¢) Eagle, Bulk-Rate coil (Stamp Ventures) (gold) (1993)	2.25	10.00	....	3.00	.40	.25
2605	23¢ Flag, Presort First-Class	2.25	10.00	....	5.00	.75	.30
2606	23¢ USA, Presort First-Class (ABN) (1992)	2.25	10.00	....	5.75	.75	.30
2607	23¢ USA, Presort First-Class (BEP) (1992)	2.25	10.00	....	5.75	.75	.30
2608	23¢ USA, Presort First-Class (Stamp Ventures) (1993)	2.25	10.00	....	7.00	1.40	.30
2609	29¢ Flag over White House, coil (1992)	2.25	10.00	....	6.00	1.20	.25

2611   **2612**

2613   **2614**

2615

1992 COMMEMORATIVES

SCOTT NO.	DESCRIPTION	FIRST DAY COVERS SING	FIRST DAY COVERS PL. BLK.	MINT SHEET	PLATE BLOCK	UNUSED F/NH	USED
2611/2720	(2611-23, 2630-41, 2697-2704, 2710-14, 2720) 48 varieties	....	....	....	....	50.00	16.50
2611-15	Winter Olympics, 5 varieties, attached . .	6.00	....	40.00(35)	12.00(10)	5.75	4.50
2611	29¢ Hockey	2.25	....	....	....	1.30	.25
2612	29¢ Figure Skating . . .	2.25	....	....	....	1.30	.25
2613	29¢ Speed Skating . . .	2.25	....	....	....	1.30	.25
2614	29¢ Skiing	2.25	....	....	....	1.30	.25
2615	29¢ Bobsledding	2.25	....	....	....	1.30	.25

2616   **2617**

| 2616 | 29¢ World Columbian Expo . . . . | 2.25 | 4.25 | 45.00(50) | 4.75 | 1.50 | .25 |
| 2617 | 29¢ W.E.B. Du Bois . . . | 3.00 | 4.25 | 52.00(50) | 5.50 | 1.50 | .25 |

2618   **2619**

| 2618 | 29¢ Love . . . . | 2.25 | 4.25 | 45.00(50) | 4.50 | .95 | .25 |
| 2619 | 29¢ Olympic Baseball . | 3.75 | 5.50 | 52.00(50) | 6.50 | 1.25 | .25 |

ORDER BY MAIL, PHONE (800) 546-2995
OR FAX (256) 246-1116

SCOTT NO.	DESCRIPTION	FIRST DAY COVERS SING	PL. BLK.	MINT SHEET	PLATE BLOCK	UNUSED F/NH	USED

2620   2621

2622   2623

2620-23	First Voyage of Columbus	4.00	5.00	40.00(40)	5.50	4.25	4.00
2620	29¢ Seeking Isabella's Support	2.25	....	....	....	1.25	.35
2621	29¢ Crossing the Atlantic	2.25	....	....	....	1.25	.35
2622	29¢ Approaching Land	2.25	....	....	....	1.25	.35
2623	29¢ Coming Ashore...	2.25	....	....	....	1.25	.35

2624

2625

2626

2627

2628

2629

| 2624-29 | 1¢-$5 Columbian Souvenir Sheets (6)... | 55.00 | .... | .... | .... | 50.00 | 40.00 |
| 2624a-29a | same, set of 16 singles | 105.00 | .... | .... | .... | 54.00 | 39.00 |

SCOTT NO.	DESCRIPTION	FIRST DAY COVERS SING	PL. BLK.	MINT SHEET	PLATE BLOCK	UNUSED F/NH	USED

2630

| 2630 | 29¢ NY Stock Exchange | 4.00 | 6.00 | 35.00(40) | 4.75 | 1.00 | .25 |

2631   2632   2633   2634

2631-34	Space, US/Russian Joint Issue	4.00	5.00	48.00(50)	5.50	5.00	3.50
2631	29¢ Cosmonaut & Space Shuttle	2.50	....	....	....	1.30	.40
2632	29¢ Astronaut & Mir Space Station	2.50	....	....	....	1.30	.40
2633	29¢ Apollo Lunar Module & Sputnik	2.50	....	....	....	1.30	.40
2634	29¢ Soyuz, Mercury & Gemini Space Craft...	2.50	....	....	....	1.30	.40

2635   2636

| 2635 | 29¢ Alaska Highway.. | 2.25 | 4.75 | 45.00(50) | 4.75 | 1.20 | .25 |
| 2636 | 29¢ Kentucky Statehood | 2.25 | 4.75 | 45.00(50) | 4.75 | 1.20 | .25 |

2637

2638   2639

2640   2641

SCOTT NO.	DESCRIPTION	FIRST DAY COVERS SING	PL. BLK.	MINT SHEET	PLATE BLOCK	UNUSED F/NH	USED

2783

2784

SCOTT NO.	DESCRIPTION	FIRST DAY COVERS SING	PL. BLK.	MINT SHEET	PLATE BLOCK	UNUSED F/NH	USED
2779-82	National Postal Museum, 4 varieties, attached . .	4.00	5.00	27.00(20)	7.75	6.50	5.00
2779	29¢ Ben Franklin	2.25	....	....	....	1.75	1.00
2780	29¢ Soldier & Drum . . .	2.25	....	....	....	1.75	1.00
2781	29¢ Lindbergh	2.25	....	....	....	1.75	1.00
2782	29¢ Stamps & Bar Code	2.25	....	....	....	1.75	1.00
2783-84	American Sign Language/ Deaf Communication, 2 varieties, attached . .	2.50	4.75	22.00(20)	5.50	2.00	1.25
2783	29¢ Mother/Child	2.25	....	....	....	1.10	.35
2784	29¢ Hand Sign.	2.25	....	....	....	1.10	.35

2785   **2786**

2787   **2788**

2785-88	Youth Classics, 4 varieties, attached . .	5.00	6.00	47.00(40)	7.00	6.00	4.50
2785	29¢ Rebecca of Sunnybrook Farm	2.25	....	....	....	1.60	.45
2786	29¢ Little House on the Prairie	2.25	....	....	....	1.60	.45
2787	29¢ Adventures of Huckleberry Finn	2.25	....	....	....	1.60	.45
2788	29¢ Little Women.	2.25	....	....	....	1.60	.45

2789, 2790

2791, 2798, 2801   **2792, 2797, 2802**   **2793, 2796, 2799, 2803**   **2794, 2795, 2800**

2789	29¢ Christmas–Traditional	2.25	4.75	45.00(50)	5.25	1.00	.25
2790	29¢ Christmas–Traditional, bklt single.	2.25	....	....	....	1.00	.25
2790a	same, bklt pane of 4 . .	3.00	....	....	....	4.00	....
2790av	same, bklt pane, unfolded	....	....	....	....	6.00	....
2791-94	Christmas–Contemporary, 4 varieties, attached . .	3.00	4.75	55.00(50)	6.50	5.50	4.00

2791	29¢ Jack-in-the-Box. . .	2.25	....	....	....	1.25	.25
2792	29¢ Red-Nosed Reindeer	2.25	....	....	....	1.25	.25
2793	29¢ Snowman	2.25	....	....	....	1.25	.25
2794	29¢ Toy Soldier Blowing Horn.	2.25	....	....	....	1.25	.25
2795	29¢ Toy Soldier Blowing Horn, bklt single.	2.25	....	....	....	1.40	.25
2796	29¢ Snowman, bklt single	2.25	....	....	....	1.40	.25
2797	29¢ Red-Nosed Reindeer, bklt single.	2.25	....	....	....	1.40	.25
2798	29¢ Jack-in-the-Box, bklt single.	2.25	....	....	....	1.40	.25
2798a	same, bkle pane of 10 . .	7.00	....	....	....	14.00	....
2798av	same, bklt pane, unfolded	....	....	....	....	18.00	....
2799- 2802v	29¢ Christmas–Contemporary, coil				18.00(8)	7.50(4)	
2799	29¢ Snowman, self-adhesive (3 buttons)	2.25	....	....	....	1.25	.80
2800	29¢ Toy Soldier Blowing Horn, self-adhesive	2.25	....	....	....	1.25	.80
2801	29¢ Jack-in-the-Box, self-adhesive	2.25	....	....	....	1.25	.80
2802	29¢ Red-Nosed Reindeer, self-adhesive	2.25	....	....	....	1.25	.80
2802a	same, bklt pane of 12 . .	9.00	....	....	....	17.00	....
2803	29¢ Snowman, self-adhesive (2 buttons)	2.25	....	....	....	1.25	.80
2803a	same, bklt pane of 18 . .	13.50	....	....	....	20.00	....

2804   **2805**

2806

2804	29¢ Commonwealth of North Mariana Islands .	2.25	4.75	25.00(20)	6.00	1.75	.25
2805	29¢ Columbus Landing in Puerto Rico	2.25	4.75	48.00(50)	4.75	1.20	.25
2806	29¢ AIDS Awareness. .	2.25	4.75	45.00(50)	4.50	1.20	.25
2806a	29¢ AIDS Awareness, bklt single.	2.25	....	....	....	1.10	.25
2806b	same, bklt pane of 5 . .	9.00	....	....	....	5.00	....
2806bv	same, bklt pane, unfolded	....	....	....	....	6.50	....

2807   **2808**   **2809**

2810   **2811**

1994 COMMEMORATIVES

2807/76	(2807-12, 2814C-28, 2834-36, 2838-39, 2848-68, 2871-72, 2876) 59 varieties	....	....	....	80.00	35.50
2807-11	Winter Olympics, 5 varieties, attached . .	5.00	....	22.00(20)	12.00(10)	7.00	6.00
2807	29¢ Alpine Skiing.	2.25	....	....	....	1.50	.50
2808	29¢ Luge	2.25	....	....	....	1.50	.50
2809	29¢ Ice Dancing.	2.25	....	....	....	1.50	.50
2810	29¢ Cross Country Skiing	2.25	....	....	....	1.50	.50
2811	29¢ Ice Hockey	2.25	....	....	....	1.50	.50

SCOTT NO.	DESCRIPTION	FIRST DAY COVERS SING	PL. BLK.	MINT SHEET	PLATE BLOCK	UNUSED F/NH	USED

2812

2813

2815

2814

1994 COMMEMORATIVES (continued)

SCOTT NO.	DESCRIPTION	FIRST DAY COVERS SING	PL. BLK.	MINT SHEET	PLATE BLOCK	UNUSED F/NH	USED
2812	29¢ Edward R. Murrow	2.25	4.75	65.00(50)	8.00	1.75	.25
2813	29¢ Love (sunrise), self-adhesive	2.25	....	....	....	1.25	.30
2813a	same, bklt pane of 18	13.50	....	....	....	20.00	....
2813v	29¢ Love (sunrise), self-adhesive coil	2.50	....	....	7.00(3)	1.40	....
2814	29¢ Love (dove), bklt single	2.25	....	....	....	1.10	.30
2814a	same, bklt pane of 10	7.00	....	....	....	11.00	....
2814av	same, bklt pane, unfolded	....	....	....	....	12.00	....
2814C	29¢ Love (dove)	2.25	4.75	48.00(50)	5.00	1.20	.25
2815	52¢ Love (dove)	2.00	4.50	75.00(50)	9.00(4)	1.75	.40
....	same, plate block of 10	....	....	....	16.00(10)	....	....

2816

2817

2818

SCOTT NO.	DESCRIPTION	FIRST DAY COVERS SING	PL. BLK.	MINT SHEET	PLATE BLOCK	UNUSED F/NH	USED
2816	29¢ Allison Davis	2.25	4.75	30.00(20)	8.00	1.50	.25
2817	29¢ Chinese New Year of the Dog	2.25	4.75	29.00(20)	8.00	1.75	.25
2818	29¢ Buffalo Soldiers	4.00	5.00	20.00(20)	4.75	1.50	.25

2819

2820

2821

2822

2823

2824

2825

2826

2827

2828

SCOTT NO.	DESCRIPTION	FIRST DAY COVERS SING	PL. BLK.	MINT SHEET	PLATE BLOCK	UNUSED F/NH	USED
2819	29¢ Rudolph Valentino	2.25	....	....	....	2.00	.95
2920	29¢ Clara Bow	2.25	....	....	....	2.00	.95
2821	29¢ Charlie Chaplin	2.25	....	....	....	2.00	.95
2822	29¢ Lon Chaney	2.25	....	....	....	2.00	.95
2823	29¢ John Gilbert	2.25	....	....	....	2.00	.95
2824	29¢ Zasu Pitts	2.25	....	....	....	2.00	.95
2825	29¢ Harold Lloyd	2.25	....	....	....	2.00	.95
2826	29¢ Keystone Cops	2.25	....	....	....	2.00	.95
2827	29¢ Theda Bara	2.25	....	....	....	2.00	.95
2828	29¢ Buster Keaton	2.25	....	....	....	2.00	.95
2819-28	Silent Screen Stars, 10 varieties, attached	7.00	....	59.00(40)	22.50(10)	18.00	15.00

2829

2830

2831

2832

2833

SCOTT NO.	DESCRIPTION	FIRST DAY COVERS SING	PL. BLK.	MINT SHEET	PLATE BLOCK	UNUSED F/NH	USED
2829	29¢ Lily	2.25	....	....	....	1.25	.30
2830	29¢ Zinnia	2.25	....	....	....	1.25	.30
2831	29¢ Gladiola	2.25	....	....	....	1.25	.30
2832	29¢ Marigold	2.25	....	....	....	1.25	.30
2833	29¢ Rose	2.25	....	....	....	1.25	.30
2833a	Summer Garden Flowers, bklt pane of 5	4.50	....	....	....	7.00	6.00
2833av	same, bklt pane, unfolded	....	....	....	....	7.50	....

2834

2836

2835

2941   2942   2943

2957, 2959   2958   2960

1995-99 GREAT AMERICANS

SCOTT NO.	DESCRIPTION	FIRST DAY COVERS SING	PL. BLK.	MINT SHEET	PLATE BLOCK	UNUSED F/NH	USED
2933	32¢ Milton S. Hershey .	2.25	4.75	120.00(100)	7.50	1.40	.55
2934	32¢ Carl Farley (1996).	2.25	4.75	110.00(100)	7.00	1.30	.50
2935	32¢ Henry R. Luce (1998)	2.25	4.75	20.00(20)	5.50	1.15	.80
2936	32¢ Lila & DeWitt Wallace (1998)	2.25	4.75	20.00(20)	5.50	1.10	.90
2938	46¢ Ruth Benedict . . .	2.25	5.00	150.00(100)	8.50	1.75	1.05
2940	55¢ Alice Hamilton. . . .	2.25	5.00	155.00(100)	9.00	1.85	.35
2941	55¢ Justin Morrill (1999)	2.25	5.00	30.00(20)	8.50	1.85	.35
2942	77¢ Mary Breckenridge (1998)	2.25	5.50	48.00(20)	12.00	2.75	1.55
2943	78¢ Alice Paul	2.25	5.50	245.00(100)	14.00	2.75	.50

SCOTT NO.	DESCRIPTION	FIRST DAY COVERS SING	PL. BLK.	MINT SHEET	PLATE BLOCK	UNUSED F/NH	USED
2955	32¢ Richard M. Nixon .	2.25	4.75	65.00(50)	6.00	1.35	.30
2956	32¢ Bessie Coleman . .	2.25	4.75	60.00(50)	7.00	1.50	.30
2957	32¢ Love (Cherub). . . .	2.25	4.75	55.00(50)	6.00	1.25	.25
2958	55¢ Love (Cherub). . . .	2.50	5.00	83.00(50)	8.00	1.85	.60
2959	32¢ Love (Cherub), bklt single.	2.25	....	....	....	1.30	.30
2959a	same, bklt pane of 10 .	7.25	....	....	....	11.00	....
2959av	same, bklt pane, unfolded	....	....	....	....	13.00	....
2960	55¢ Love (Cherub), self-adhesive	2.50	....	....	....	1.85	.70
2960a	same, bklt pane of 20 .	23.50	....	....	....	33.00	9.95

2948   2949   2950

1995 COMMEMORATIVES

SCOTT NO.	DESCRIPTION	FIRST DAY COVERS SING	PL. BLK.	MINT SHEET	PLATE BLOCK	UNUSED F/NH	USED
2948/3023	(2948, 2950-58, 2961-68, 2974, 2976-92, 2998-99, 3001-07, 3019-23)						
	50 varieties	....	....	....	....	90.00	32.00
2948	(32¢) Love (Cherub) . .	2.25	4.75	46.00(50)	5.00	1.10	.25
2949	(32¢) Love (Cherub), self-adhesive	2.25	....	....	....	1.25	.25
2949a	same, bklt pane of 20 .	14.50	....	....	....	23.00	....
2950	32¢ Florida Statehood .	2.25	4.75	25.00(20)	7.00	1.60	.25

2961   2962

2963   2964

2951   2952

2953   2954

2965

SCOTT NO.	DESCRIPTION	FIRST DAY COVERS SING	PL. BLK.	MINT SHEET	PLATE BLOCK	UNUSED F/NH	USED
2961-65	Recreational Sports, 5 varieties, attached . .	7.00	....	22.00(20)	13.00(10)	6.00	4.50
2961	32¢ Volleyball	3.00	....	....	....	1.20	1.00
2962	32¢ Softball	3.00	....	....	....	1.20	1.00
2963	32¢ Bowling.	3.00	....	....	....	1.20	1.00
2964	32¢ Tennis.	3.00	....	....	....	1.20	1.00
2965	32¢ Golf.	3.00	....	....	....	1.20	1.00

SCOTT NO.	DESCRIPTION	FIRST DAY COVERS SING	PL. BLK.	MINT SHEET	PLATE BLOCK	UNUSED F/NH	USED
2951-54	Kids Care About Environment, 4 varieties, attached.	4.00	4.75	18.00(16)	5.50	4.95	3.50
2951	32¢ Earth in a Bathtub.	2.25	....	....	....	1.20	.35
2952	32¢ Solar Energy.	2.25	....	....	....	1.20	.35
2953	32¢ Tree Planting	2.25	....	....	....	1.20	.35
2954	32¢ Beach Clean-Up. .	2.25	....	....	....	1.20	.35

2966

2955   2956

2968

2967

SCOTT NO.	DESCRIPTION	FIRST DAY COVERS SING	PL. BLK.	MINT SHEET	PLATE BLOCK	UNUSED F/NH	USED
2966	32¢ POW & MIA	3.00	4.00	20.00(20)	5.00	1.20	.30
2967	32¢ Marilyn Monroe. . .	4.00	5.00	30.00(20)	6.00	1.75	.35
2967v	same as above, uncut sheet of 120 (6 panes)	....	....	180.00(120)	....	....	....
....	block of 8 with vertical gutter	....	....	....	....	50.00	....
....	cross gutter block of 8.	....	....	....	....	65.00	....
....	vertical pair with horizontal gutter.	....	....	....	....	5.50	....
....	horizontal pair with vertical gutter.	....	....	....	....	9.50	....
2968	32¢ Texas Statehood. .	3.00	4.75	28.00(20)	5.50	1.35	.35

SCOTT NO.	DESCRIPTION	FIRST DAY COVERS SING	FIRST DAY COVERS PL. BLK.	MINT SHEET	PLATE BLOCK	UNUSED F/NH	USED

2969

2970

2971

2972

2973

2974

SCOTT NO.	DESCRIPTION	SING	PL. BLK.	MINT SHEET	PLATE BLOCK	UNUSED F/NH	USED
2969	32¢ Split Rock Lighthouse	2.25	....	....	....	2.00	.40
2970	32¢ St. Joseph Lighthouse	2.25	....	....	....	2.00	.40
2971	32¢ Spectacle Reef Lighthouse.........	2.25	....	....	....	2.00	.40
2972	32¢ Marblehead Lighthouse	2.25	....	....	....	2.00	.40
2973	32¢ Thirty Mile Point Lighthouse..........	2.25	....	....	....	2.00	.40
2973a	Great Lakes Lighthouses, bklt pane of 5........	5.50	....	....	....	12.00	6.50
2973av	same, bklt pane, unfolded	....	....	....	....	14.00	....
2974	32¢ United Nations ...	1.75	4.75	19.00(20)	4.75	1.00	.25

2975

CIVIL WAR

2975a	*Monitor-Virginia*	**2975k**	*Harriet Tubman*
2975b	*Robert E. Lee*	**2975l**	*Stand Watie*
2975c	*Clara Barton*	**2975m**	*Joseph E. Johnston*
2975d	*Ulysses S. Grant*	**2975n**	*Winfield Hancock*
2975e	*Shiloh*	**2975o**	*Mary Chestnut*
2975f	*Jefferson Davis*	**2975p**	*Chancellorsville*
2975g	*David Farragut*	**2975q**	*William T. Sherman*
2975h	*Frederick Douglass*	**2975r**	*Phoebe Pember*
2975i	*Raphael Semmes*	**2975s**	*"Stonewall" Jackson*
2975j	*Abraham Lincoln*	**2975t**	*Gettysburg*

2975	32¢ Civil War, 20 varieties, attached .	....	....	45.00(20)	....	45.00	40.00
....	set of singles	35.00	....	....	....	25.00	....
....	singles of above, each..	....	....	....	....	....	1.25

2975v	32¢ Civil War, uncut sheet of 120 (6 panes)	....	....	150.00(120)	....	150.00	....
....	cross gutter block of 20	....	....	....	....	55.00	....
....	cross gutter block of 4	....	....	....	....	27.50	....
....	vertical pair with horizontal gutter	....	....	....	....	6.00	....
....	horizontal pair with vertical gutter	....	....	....	....	6.00	....

2976

2977

2978

2979

2976-79	Carousel Horses, 4 varieties, attached ..	4.00	4.75	23.00(20)	5.75	5.00	3.75
2976	32¢ Palamino.	2.25	....	....	....	1.25	.45
2977	32¢ Pinto Pony	2.25	....	....	....	1.25	.45
2978	32¢ Armored Jumper. .	2.25	....	....	....	1.25	.45
2979	32¢ Brown Jumper . . .	2.25	....	....	....	1.25	.45

2980

2980	32¢ Women's Suffrage	1.95	4.75	44.00(40)	5.00	1.10	.30

2981

2981	$3.20 World War II (1945) Souvenir Sheet of 10 . .	8.25	....	40.00(20)	....	22.00	15.00
2981a	32¢ Marines raise flag on Iwo Jima	2.25	....	....	....	2.50	1.00
2981b	32¢ Fierce fighting frees Manila	2.25	....	....	....	2.50	1.00
2981c	32¢ Okinawa, the last big battle	2.25	....	....	....	2.50	1.00
2981d	32¢ U.S. & Soviets link up at Elbe River	2.25	....	....	....	2.50	1.00
2981e	32¢ Allies liberate Holocaust survivors	2.25	....	....	....	2.50	1.00
2981f	32¢ Germany surrenders at Reims	2.25	....	....	....	2.50	1.00
2981g	32¢ By 1945, World War II has uprooted millions. .	2.25	....	....	....	2.50	1.00
2981h	32¢ Truman announces Japan's surrender	2.25	....	....	....	2.50	1.00
2981i	32¢ News of victory hits home	2.25	....	....	....	2.50	1.00
2981j	32¢ Hometowns honor their returning veterans	2.25	....	....	....	2.50	1.00

SCOTT NO.	DESCRIPTION	FIRST DAY COVERS SING PL. BLK.		MINT SHEET	PLATE BLOCK	UNUSED F/NH	USED

2982

| 2982 | 32¢ Louis Armstrong . . | 1.95 | 4.75 | 25.00(20) | 5.50 | 1.50 | .50 |

2983   **2984**

2985   **2986**

2987   **2988**

2989   **2990**

2991   **2992**

2983-92	Jazz Musicians, 10 varieties attached	8.25	....	65.00(20)	35.00(10)	32.00	24.00
2983	32¢ Coleman Hawkins.	2.25	....	....	....	3.00	2.50
2984	32¢ Louis Armstrong . .	2.25	....	....	....	3.00	2.50
2985	32¢ James P. Johnson	2.25	....	....	....	3.00	2.50
2986	32¢ "Jelly Roll" Morton.	2.25	....	....	....	3.00	2.50
2987	32¢ Charlie Parker. . . .	2.25	....	....	....	3.00	2.50
2988	32¢ Eubie Blake	2.25	....	....	....	3.00	2.50
2989	32¢ Charles Mingus. . .	2.25	....	....	....	3.00	2.50
2990	32¢ Thelonius Monk . .	2.25	....	....	....	3.00	2.50
2991	32¢ John Coltrane	2.25	....	....	....	3.00	2.50
2992	32¢ Erroll Garner.	2.25	....	....	....	3.00	2.50

ORDER BY MAIL, PHONE (800) 546-2995
OR FAX (256) 246-1116

SCOTT NO.	DESCRIPTION	FIRST DAY COVERS SING PL. BLK.		MINT SHEET	PLATE BLOCK	UNUSED F/NH	USED

2993   **2994**   **2995**   **2996**

2998   **2999**

2997

2993	32¢ Aster	2.25	....	....	....	1.25	.40
2994	32¢ Chrysanthemum . .	2.25	....	....	....	1.25	.40
2995	32¢ Dahlia	2.25	....	....	....	1.25	.40
2996	32¢ Hydrangea	2.25	....	....	....	1.25	.40
2997	32¢ Rudbeckia.	2.25	....	....	....	1.25	.40
2997a	Fall Garden Flowers, bklt pane of 5.	5.50	....	....	....	6.00	4.00
2997av	same, bklt pane, unfolded	....	....	....	....	9.00	
2998	60¢ Eddie Rickenbacker	2.25	5.00	100.00(50)	10.00	3.25	.50
2998a	Large, 1995 date (1999)	2.25	5.00	128.00(50)	16.00	2.75	1.00
2999	32¢ Republic of Palau .	2.25	4.75	46.00(50)	5.00	1.20	.25

3000
COMIC STRIPS

3000a	The Yellow Kid	3000k	Popeye
3000b	Katzenjammer Kids	3000l	Blondie
3000c	Little Nemo	3000m	Dick Tracy
3000d	Bringing Up Father	3000n	Alley Oop
3000e	Krazy Kat	3000o	Nancy
3000f	Rube Goldberg	3000p	Flash Gordon
3000g	Toonerville Folks	3000q	Li'l Abner
3000h	Gasoline Alley	3000r	Terry and the Pirates
3000i	Barney Google	3000s	Prince Valiant
3000j	Little Orphan Annie	3000t	Brenda Starr

3000	32¢ Comic Strips, 20 varieties, attached .	....	....	25.00(20)	....	25.00	20.00
....	set of singles	50.00	....	....	....	12.75	
....	single of above, each. .	....	....	....	....	....	1.00

SCOTT NO.	DESCRIPTION	FIRST DAY COVERS SING	FIRST DAY COVERS PL. BLK.	MINT SHEET	PLATE BLOCK	UNUSED F/NH	USED

COMIC STRIPS (continued)

SCOTT NO.	DESCRIPTION	SING	PL. BLK.	MINT SHEET	PLATE BLOCK	UNUSED F/NH	USED
3000v	32¢ Comic Strips, uncut sheet of 120 (6 panes)	....	....	120.00(120)	....	120.00	....
....	cross gutter block of 20	....	....	....	....	40.00	....
....	cross gutter block of 4	....	....	....	....	18.50	....
....	vertical pair with horizontal gutter	....	....	....	....	4.50	....
....	horizontal pair with vertical gutter	....	....	....	....	4.50	....

3001

3002

| 3001 | 32¢ Naval Academy. . . | 2.25 | 4.75 | 35.00(20) | 8.00 | 1.50 | .35 |
| 3002 | 32¢ Tennessee Williams | 2.25 | 4.75 | 25.00(20) | 6.00 | 1.50 | .40 |

3013

3013	32¢ Children Sledding, self-adhesive	2.25	....	....	....	1.25	.80
3013a	same, bklt pane of 18 .	13.00	....	....	....	20.00	....
3014-17	Santa & Children with Toys, self-adhesive, coil strip of 4	....	....	....	45.00(8)	20.00	....
3014	32¢ Santa working on Sled, self-adhesive coil.	2.25	....	....	....	5.50	1.35
3015	32¢ Girl holding Jumping Jack, self-adhesive coil	2.25	....	....	....	5.50	1.35
3016	32¢ Santa at Chimney, self-adhesive coil.	2.25	....	....	....	5.50	1.35
3017	32¢ Boy holding Toy Horse, self-adhesive coil.	2.25	....	....	....	5.50	1.35
3018	32¢ Midnight Angel, self-adhesive coil.	3.00	....	....	17.75(3)	1.75	1.00

3004, 3010, 3016   **3005, 3009, 3015**   **3006, 3011, 3017**   **3007, 3008, 3014**

3019

3020

3021

3022

3023

3003

3003	32¢ Madonna & Child .	2.25	4.75	47.00(50)	5.00	1.00	.25
3003a	32¢ Madonna & Child, bklt single.	2.25	....	....	....	1.10	.25
3003b	same, bklt pane of 10 .	7.25	....	....	....	10.50	....
3003bv	same, bklt pane, unfolded	....	....	....	....	11.50	....
3004-07	Santa & Children with Toys, 4 varieties, attached	4.00	4.75	50.00(50)	6.50	5.00	4.00
3004	32¢ Santa at Chimney.	2.25	....	....	....	1.65	.40
....	same, bklt single	2.25	....	....	....	1.65	.40
3005	32¢ Girl holding Jumping Jack.	2.25	....	....	....	1.65	.40
....	same, bklt single	2.25	....	....	....	1.65	.40
3006	32¢ Boy holding Toy Horse	2.25	....	....	....	1.65	.40
....	same, bklt single	2.25	....	....	....	1.65	.40
3007	32¢ Santa working on Sled	2.25	....	....	....	1.65	.40
....	same, bklt single	2.25	....	....	....	1.65	.40
3007b	32¢ Santa & Children with Toys, bklt pane of 10 (3 each of 3004-05) . . .	7.25	....	....	....	12.50	....
....	same, bklt pane unfolded	....	....	....	....	14.00	....
3007c	32¢ Santa & Children with Toys, bklt pane of 10 (3 each of 3006-07) . . .	7.25	....	....	....	12.50	....
....	same, bklt pane, unfolded	....	....	....	....	14.00	....
3008	32¢ Santa working on Sled, self-adhesive	2.25	....	....	....	1.75	.50
3009	32¢ Girl holding Jumping Jack, self-adhesive . . .	2.25	....	....	....	1.75	.50
3010	32¢ Santa at Chimney, self-adhesive	2.25	....	....	....	1.75	.50
3011	32¢ Boy holding Toy Horse, self-adhesive	2.25	....	....	....	1.75	.50
3011a	32¢ Santa & Children with Toys, self-adhesive, pane of 20	14.50	....	....	....	30.00	....
3012	32¢ Midnight Angel, self-adhesive	2.25	....	....	....	1.25	.45
3012a	same, bklt pane of 20 .	14.50	....	....	....	22.50	....

Utah 1896

3024

3019-23	Antique Automobiles, 5 varieties, attached . .	5.50	....	30.00(25)	12.50(10)	7.50	6.50
3019	32¢ 1893 Duryea.	2.25	....	....	....	1.50	.90
3020	32¢ 1894 Haynes	2.25	....	....	....	1.50	.90
3021	32¢ 1898 Columbia . . .	2.25	....	....	....	1.50	.90
3022	32¢ 1899 Winton	2.25	....	....	....	1.50	.90
3023	32¢ 1901 White	2.25	....	....	....	1.50	.90

3012, 3018

3025   **3026**   **3027**

SCOTT NO.	DESCRIPTION	FIRST DAY COVERS SING	PL. BLK.	MINT SHEET	PLATE BLOCK	UNUSED F/NH	USED

3028   **3029**

1996 COMMEMORATIVES

SCOTT NO.	DESCRIPTION	SING	PL. BLK.	MINT SHEET	PLATE BLOCK	UNUSED F/NH	USED
3024/3118	(3024, 3030, 3058-67, 3069-70, 3072-88, 3090-3104, 3106-11, 3118) 53 varieties	....		....		68.00	25.50
3024	32¢ Utah Statehood...	2.25	4.75	65.00(50)	7.00	1.85	.40
3025	32¢ Crocus	2.25	....			1.85	.40
3026	32¢ Winter Aconite . . .	2.25	....			1.85	.40
3027	32¢ Pansy	2.25	....			1.85	.40
3028	32¢ Snowdrop	2.25	....			1.85	.40
3029	32¢ Anemone	2.25	....			1.85	.40
3029a	Winter Garden Flowers, bklt pane of 5	5.50	....			6.50	5.00
3029av	same, bklt pane, unfolded	....				7.75	....

3030   **3031, 3031A, 3044**   **3032, 3045**   **3033**

3036, 3036a   **3048, 3053**   **3049, 3054**

3050, 3051, 3055   **3052, 3052E**

SCOTT NO.	DESCRIPTION	SING	PL. BLK.	MINT SHEET	PLATE BLOCK	UNUSED F/NH	USED
3030	32¢ Love (Cherub), self-adhesive	2.25	....			1.25	.25
3030a	same, bklt pane of 20 .	14.50	....			22.00	9.95
3030b	same, bklt pane of 15 .	11.50	....			17.00	
3031	1¢ Kestrel, self-adhesive	2.25	....	10.00(50)	1.15	.25	.25
3031A	1¢ Kestrel, self-adhesive (2000)	1.95	....	12.00(50)	1.15	.25	.25
3032	2¢ Red-headed Woodpecker	2.25	4.75	15.00(100)	1.25	.25	.25
3033	3¢ Eastern Bluebird (redesign 3¢)	2.25	4.75	16.00(100)	1.35	.25	.25
3036	$1 Red Fox, self-adhesive	5.00	10.00	125.00(20)	25.00	8.00	.75
3036a	$1 Red Fox, 11.75 X 11(2002)	....		130.00(20)	30.00	9.00	.85
3044	1¢ Kestrel, coil.	2.25	5.00			.25	.25
3044a	1¢ Kestrel, large date, coil(1999)	2.25	5.00			1.00	.25
3045	2¢ Red-headed Wood-pecker, coil.	2.25	....		1.00	.25	.25
3048	20¢ Blue Jay, self-adhesive	2.25	....			.75	.30
3048a	same, bklt pane of 10 .	8.00	....			7.25	
3049	32¢ Yellow Rose, self-adhesive	2.25	....			1.10	.25
3049a	same, bklt pane of 20 .	14.50	....			21.00	....
3049b	same, bklt pane of 4 . .	....				5.50	
3049c	same, bklt pane of 5 and label					6.75	
3049d	same, bklt pane of 6 . .					6.75	
3050	20¢ Ring-necked Pheasant, self-adhesive	2.25	....			.90	.25
3050a	same, bklt pane of 10 .	9.00	....			9.25	....
3050b	20¢ Pheasant, die cut 11	2.25	....			5.25	.85
3050c	same, bklt pane of 10 .	5.50	....			45.00	....

SCOTT NO.	DESCRIPTION	SING	PL. BLK.	MINT SHEET	PLATE BLOCK	UNUSED F/NH	USED
3051	20¢ Ring-necked Pheasant, die cut 10 1/2 x 11, self-adhesive	2.25	....	....	....	1.60	1.00
die cut 10 1/2		2.25	....	....	....	13.00	6.00
3051b	same, bklt pane of 5, (4 #3051, 1 #3051a) . .	3.50	....	....	....	17.50	
3052	33¢ Coral Pink Rose, self-adhesive	2.25	....			1.35	.30
3052a	same, bklt pane of 4 . .	3.00	....			5.25	....
3052b	same, bklt pane of 5 . .	3.75	....			6.50	....
3052c	same, bklt pane of 6 . .	4.50	....			7.50	....
3052d	same, bklt pane of 20 .	14.50	....			25.00	....
3052E	33¢ Coral Pink Rose, die-cut 10.75 x 10.5, self-adhesive (2000) . .	2.25	....			1.40	.30
3052Ef	same, bklt pane of 20 .	14.50	....			24.00	....
3053	20¢ Blue Jay, self-adhesive, coil (1996)	2.25	....	....	8.00	1.00	.25
3054	32¢ Yellow Rose, self-adhesive coil (1997)	2.25	....	....	9.00	1.00	.25
3055	20¢ Ring-necked Pheasant, self-adhesive coil (1998)	2.25	....	....	5.00	.80	.25

3058   **3059**   **3060**

SCOTT NO.	DESCRIPTION	SING	PL. BLK.	MINT SHEET	PLATE BLOCK	UNUSED F/NH	USED
3058	32¢ Ernest Just	3.00	4.75	22.50(20)	5.00	1.50	.25
3059	32¢ Smithsonian Institution	2.25	4.75	19.50(20)	5.00	1.20	.25
3060	32¢ Year of the Rat . . .	2.25	4.75	25.00(20)	5.50	1.40	.25

3061   **3062**

3063   **3064**

SCOTT NO.	DESCRIPTION	SING	PL. BLK.	MINT SHEET	PLATE BLOCK	UNUSED F/NH	USED
3061-64	Pioneers of Communication, 4 varieties, attached . .	4.00	4.75	22.00(20)	5.50	5.00	3.25
3061	32¢ Eadweard Muybridge	2.25	....			1.55	.65
3062	32¢ Ottmar Mergenthaler	2.25	....			1.55	.65
3063	32¢ Frederic E. Ives . .	2.25	....			1.55	.65
3064	32¢ William Dickson . .	2.25	....			1.55	.65

3066   **3065**   **3067**

SCOTT NO.	DESCRIPTION	SING	PL. BLK.	MINT SHEET	PLATE BLOCK	UNUSED F/NH	USED
3065	32¢ Fulbright Scholarships	2.25	4.75	70.00(50)	8.00	1.85	.25
3066	50¢ Jacqueline Cochran	2.25	5.00	83.00(50)	8.50	2.00	.60
3067	32¢ Marathon	3.00	4.75	20.00(20)	5.00	1.00	.25

SCOTT NO.	DESCRIPTION	FIRST DAY COVERS SING	PL. BLK.	MINT SHEET	PLATE BLOCK	UNUSED F/NH	USED

3068

1996 SUMMER OLYMPIC GAMES

3068a *Decathlon*	**3068k** *Beach volleyball*
3068b *Men's canoeing*	**3068l** *Men's rowing*
3068c *Women's running*	**3068m** *Men's sprints*
3068d *Women's diving*	**3068n** *Women's swimming*
3068e *Men's cycling*	**3068o** *Women's softball*
3068f *Freestyle wrestling*	**3068p** *Men's hurdles*
3068g *Women's gymnastics*	**3068q** *Men's swimming*
3068h *Women's sailboarding*	**3068r** *Men's gymnastics*
3068i *Men's shot put*	**3068s** *Equestrian*
3068j *Women's soccer*	**3068t** *Men's basketball*

SCOTT NO.	DESCRIPTION	SING	PL. BLK.	MINT SHEET	PLATE BLOCK	UNUSED F/NH	USED
3068	32¢ Centennial Olympic Games, 20 varieties, attached .		....	25.00(20)	....	25.00	20.00
....	set of singles	35.00	....	....	....	....	17.00
....	single of above, each. .	....	....	....	....	....	1.00
3068v	same as above, uncut sheet of 120 (6 panes)		....	135.00(120)	....	135.00	....
....	cross gutter block of 20	....	....	....	....	35.00	....
....	cross gutter block of 4 .	....	....	....	....	19.50	....
....	vertical pair with horizontal gutter	....	....	....	....	4.50	....
....	horizontal pair with vertical gutter	....	....	....	....	4.50	....

3069

3070, 3071

SCOTT NO.	DESCRIPTION	SING	PL. BLK.	MINT SHEET	PLATE BLOCK	UNUSED F/NH	USED
3069	32¢ Georgia O'Keeffe	2.25	....	23.00(15)	7.50	1.75	.25
3070	32¢ Tennessee Statehood	2.25	4.75	60.00(50)	6.00	1.25	.25
3071	32¢ Tennessee Statehood, self-adhesive	2.25	....	....	....	1.40	.40
3071a	same, bklt pane of 20 .	14.50	....	....	....	30.00	....

3072   **3073**   **3074**

3075   **3076**

SCOTT NO.	DESCRIPTION	SING	PL. BLK.	MINT SHEET	PLATE BLOCK	UNUSED F/NH	USED
3072-76	American Indian Dances, 5 varieties, attached . .	5.50	....	28.00(20)	16.00(10)	8.00	7.00
3072	32¢ Fancy Dance	2.25	....	....	....	1.50	.85
3073	32¢ Butterfly Dance. . .	2.25	....	....	....	1.50	.85
3074	32¢ Traditional Dance .	2.25	....	....	....	1.50	.85
3075	32¢ Raven Dance	2.25	....	....	....	1.50	.85
3076	32¢ Hoop Dance	2.25	....	....	....	1.50	.85

3077   **3078**

3079   **3080**

SCOTT NO.	DESCRIPTION	SING	PL. BLK.	MINT SHEET	PLATE BLOCK	UNUSED F/NH	USED
3077-80	Prehistoric Animals, 4 varieties, attached . .	4.00	4.75	22.00(20)	5.50	5.00	3.50
3077	32¢ Eohippus.	2.25	....	....	....	1.25	.40
3078	32¢ Woolly Mammoth .	2.25	....	....	....	1.25	.40
3079	32¢ Mastodon	2.25	....	....	....	1.25	.40
3080	32¢ Saber-tooth Cat . .	2.25	....	....	....	1.25	.40

3081   **3082**

SCOTT NO.	DESCRIPTION	SING	PL. BLK.	MINT SHEET	PLATE BLOCK	UNUSED F/NH	USED
3081	32¢ Breast Cancer Awareness.	2.25	4.75	20.00(20)	5.00	1.10	.25
3082	32¢ James Dean	3.00	4.75	25.00(20)	6.00	1.50	.25
....	vertical pair with horizontal gutter	....	....	....	....	4.50	....
....	horizontal pair with vertical gutter	....	....	....	....	7.00	....

SCOTT NO.	DESCRIPTION	FIRST DAY COVERS SING	PL. BLK.	MINT SHEET	PLATE BLOCK	UNUSED F/NH	USED

3083   MIGHTY CASEY   3084   PAUL BUNYAN   3085   JOHN HENRY   3086   PECOS BILL

SCOTT NO.	DESCRIPTION	SING	PL. BLK.	MINT SHEET	PLATE BLOCK	UNUSED F/NH	USED
3083-86	Folk Heroes, 4 varieties, attached	4.00	4.75	25.00(20)	7.00	6.00	4.75
3083	32¢ Mighty Casey	2.25	....	....	....	1.60	1.05
3084	32¢ Paul Bunyan.....	2.25	....	....	....	1.60	1.05
3085	32¢ John Henry......	2.25	....	....	....	1.60	1.05
3086	32¢ Pecos Bill	2.25	....	....	....	1.60	1.05

3087

3088, 3089

3087	32¢ Olympic Discus Thrower............	2.25	4.75	27.50(20)	6.00	1.50	.30
3088	32¢ Iowa Statehood...	2.25	4.75	65.00(50)	7.00	1.75	.30
3089	32¢ Iowa Statehood, self-adhesive	2.25	....	....	....	1.25	.35
3089a	same, bklt pane of 20 .	14.50	....	....	....	30.00	....

3090

3090	32¢ Rural Free Delivery	2.25	4.75	30.00(20)	7.00	1.50	.30

3091

3092

3093

3094

3095

3091-95	Riverboats, 5 varieties, attached ..	6.50	....	25.00(20)	14.00(10)	7.00	5.00
3091	32¢ Robt. E. Lee	2.25	....	....	....	1.50	.40
3092	32¢ Sylvan Dell	2.25	....	....	....	1.50	.40
3093	32¢ Far West.......	2.25	....	....	....	1.50	.40
3094	32¢ Rebecca Everingham	2.25	....	....	....	1.50	.40
3095	32¢ Bailey Gatzert....	2.25	....	....	....	1.50	.40
3091-95b	32¢ Riverboats, special die cutting, 5 attached ..	....	....	....	210.00(10)	97.00	....
3095b	same, as above, pane of 20	....	....	325.00(20)	....	325.00	....

3098   GLENN MILLER   3099   BENNY GOODMAN   3096   COUNT BASIE   3097   TOMMY & JIMMY DORSEY

3096-99	Big Band Leaders, 4 varieties, attached ..	6.00	7.00	25.00(20)	6.50	6.00	4.50
3096	32¢ Count Basie	2.25	....	....	....	1.60	.85
3097	32¢ Tommy & Jimmy Dorsey	2.25	....	....	....	1.60	.85
3098	32¢ Glenn Miller	2.25	....	....	....	1.60	.85
3099	32¢ Benny Goodman. .	2.25	....	....	....	1.60	.85

3102   DOROTHY FIELDS   3103   HOAGY CARMICHAEL   3100   HAROLD ARLEN   3101   JOHNNY MERCER

3100-03	Songwriters, 4 varieties, attached ..	6.00	7.00	25.00(20)	6.00	5.50	4.50
3100	32¢ Harold Arlen	2.25	....	....	....	1.50	.75
3101	32¢ Johnny Mercer ...	2.25	....	....	....	1.50	.75
3102	32¢ Dorothy Fields ...	2.25	....	....	....	1.50	.75
3103	32¢ Hoagy Carmichael	2.25	....	....	....	1.50	.75

3104

3104	23¢ F. Scott Fitzgerald.	2.25	4.75	45.00(50)	5.00	1.20	.25

SE-TENANTS: Beginning with the 1964 Christmas issue (#1254-57), the United States has issued numerous Se-Tenant stamps covering a wide variety of subjects. Se-Tenants are issues where two or more different stamp designs are produced on the same sheet in pair, strip or block form. Mint stamps are usually collected in attached blocks, etc.—Used are generally saved as single stamps. Our Se-Tenant prices follow in this collecting pattern.

SCOTT NO.	DESCRIPTION	FIRST DAY COVERS SING	PL. BLK.	MINT SHEET	PLATE BLOCK	UNUSED F/NH	USED

3105

ENDANGERED SPECIES

National Stamp Collecting Month 1996 highlights these 15 species to promote awareness of endangered wildlife. Each generation must work to protect the delicate balance of nature, so that future generations may share a sound and healthy planet.

3105a	*Black-footed ferret*	**3105i**	*California condor*
3105b	*Thick-billed parrot*	**3105j**	*Gila trout*
3105c	*Hawaiian monk seal*	**3105k**	*San Francisco garter snake*
3105d	*American crocodile*	**3105l**	*Woodland caribou*
3105e	*Ocelot*	**3105m**	*Florida panther*
3105f	*Schaus swallowtail butterfly*	**3105n**	*Piping plover*
3105g	*Wyoming toad*	**3105o**	*Florida manatee*
3105h	*Brown pelican*		

3105	32¢ Endangered Species, 15 varieties, attached .	15.00	....	22.00(15)	....	22.00	17.00
....	set of singles	27.50	....	....	....	....	12.00
....	singles of above, each.	....	....	....	....	....	1.25

3106

3107, 3112

3106	32¢ Computer Technology	2.25	4.75	40.00(40)	5.00	1.00	.25
3107	32¢ Madonna & Child	2.25	4.75	47.00(50)	5.00	1.00	.25

3108, 3113   **3109, 3114**   **3110, 3115**   **3111, 3116**

3108-11	Christmas Family Scenes, 4 varieties, attached .	4.00	4.75	55.00(50)	6.00	5.50	4.00
3108	32¢ Family at Fireplace	2.25	....	....	....	1.25	.35
3109	32¢ Decorating Tree .	2.25	....	....	....	1.25	.35
3110	32¢ Dreaming of SantaClaus	2.25	....	....	....	1.25	.35
3111	32¢ Holiday Shopping	2.25	....	....	....	1.25	.35
3112	32¢ Madonna & Child, self-adhesive	2.25	....	....	....	1.25	.30
3112a	same, bklt pane of 20	14.50	....	....	....	21.00	....
3113	32¢ Family at Fireplace, self-adhesive	2.25	....	....	....	1.25	.35
3114	32¢ Decorating Tree, self-adhesive	2.25	....	....	....	1.25	.35
3115	32¢ Dreaming of Santa Claus, self-adhesive	2.25	....	....	....	1.25	.35
3116	32¢ Holiday Shopping, self-adhesive	2.25	....	....	....	1.25	.35
3116a	Christams Family Scenes, self-adhesive, bklt pane of 20	14.50	....	....	....	26.00	....

3117   **3118**

3117	32¢ Skaters, self-adhesive	2.25	....	....	....	1.70	1.00
3117a	same, bklt pane of 18	13.00	....	....	....	19.00	....
3118	32¢ Hanukkah, self-adhesive	2.25	....	22.00(20)	4.50	1.00	.25

3119

3119	50¢ Cycling, sheet of 2	4.00	....	....	....	4.50	4.00
3119a-b	same, set of 2 singles	5.00	....	....	....	5.00	3.00

3120   **3121**

1997 COMMEMORATIVES

3120/75	(3120-21, 3125, 3130-31, 3134-35, 3141, 3143-50, 3152-75) 40 varieties .	....	....	....	....	50.00	26.00
3120	32¢ Year of the Ox. . . .	3.00	....	24.00(20)	5.50	1.25	.25
3121	32¢ Benjamin O. Davis, Sr.	3.00	4.75	30.00(20)	5.50	1.50	.50

3122

3122	32¢ Statue of Liberty, self-adhesive (1997) .	2.25	....	....	....	1.45	.25
3122a	same, bklt pane of 20	14.50	....	....	....	22.00	....
3122b	same, bklt pane of 4 .	4.75	....	....	....	5.00	....
3122c	same, bklt pane of 5 .	5.00	....	....	....	6.00	....
3122d	same, bklt pane of 6 .	5.75	....	....	....	12.00	....
3122E	32¢ Statue of Liberty, die cut 11.5 x 11.8 . . .	....	....	....	....	2.75	1.00
3122Ef	same, bklt pane of 20	....	....	....	....	62.00	....
3122Eg	same, bklt pane of 6 .	....	....	....	....	15.00	....

3123   **3124**

3123	32¢ Swans, self-adhesive	2.25	....	....	....	1.25	.35
3123a	same, bklt pane of 20	14.50	....	....	....	21.00	....
3124	55¢ Swans, self-adhesive	2.50	....	....	....	2.00	.60
3124a	same, bklt pane of 20	19.75	....	....	....	35.00	....

SCOTT NO.	DESCRIPTION	FIRST DAY COVERS SING	PL. BLK.	MINT SHEET	PLATE BLOCK	UNUSED F/NH	USED

3125

| 3125 | 32¢ Helping Children Learn | 2.25 | 4.75 | 19.50(20) | 5.00 | 1.10 | .30 |

3126, 3128   **3127, 3129**

3126	32¢ Citron, Moth, Larvae, Pupa, Beetle, self-adhesive (Die Cut 10.9 x 10.2) . .	2.25	....	....	....	1.15	.35
3127	32¢ Flowering Pineapple, Cockroaches, self-adhesive (Die Cut 10.9 x 10.2) . .	2.25	....	....	....	1.15	.35
3127a	same, bklt pane of 20 (10–#3126, 10–#3127)	14.50	....	....	....	21.00	....
3128	32¢ Citron, Moth, Larvae, Pupa, Beetle, self-adhesive (Die Cut 11.2 x 10.8) . .	2.25	....	....	....	1.95	1.30
3128a	same, stamp sideways	2.25	....	....	....	6.00	3.50
3128b	same, bklt pane of 5 (2–#3128 & #3129, 1–#3128a)	5.50	....	....	....	13.00	....
3129	32¢ Flowering Pineapple, Cockroaches, self-adhesive (Die Cut 11.2 x 10.8) . .	2.25	....	....	....	1.95	1.30
3129a	same, stamp sideways	2.25	....	....	....	12.00	4.00
3129b	same, bklt pane of 5 (2–#3128 & #3129, 1–#3129a)	5.50	....	....	....	19.00	....

3130

3131

3130-31	32¢ Stagecoach & Ship, (Pacific '97) 2 varieties, attached.	3.00	4.75	19.00(16)	6.00	2.75	2.00
3130	32¢ Ship	2.25	....	....	....	1.40	.35
3131	32¢ Stagecoach.	2.25	....	....	....	1.40	.35
3130-31v	same, as above, uncut sheet of 96 (6 panes)	....	....	110.00(96)	....	110.00	....
....	block of 32 with vertical or horizontal gutter between (2 panes).	....	....	37.50(32)	....	37.50	....
....	cross gutter block of 16	....	....	....	....	30.00	....
....	vertical pairs with horizontal gutter.	....	....	....	....	10.00	....
....	horizontal pairs with vertical gutter	....	....	....	....	8.00	....

3132

| 3132 | (25¢) Juke Box, self-adhesive linerless coil. . . . . | 2.25 | .... | .... | 15.00(3) | 2.35 | 1.25 |
| 3133 | 32¢ Flag Over Porch, self-adhesive, linerless coil | 2.25 | .... | .... | 11.00(3) | 2.00 | 1.10 |

3134   **3135**

| 3134 | 32¢ Thornton Wilder . . | 2.25 | 4.75 | 20.00(20) | 5.25 | 1.10 | .30 |
| 3135 | 32¢ Raoul Wallenberg . | 3.00 | 4.75 | 20.00(20) | 5.25 | 1.10 | .30 |

3136

DINOSAURS

3136a	Ceratosaurus	3136f	Stegosaurus	3136k	Daspletosaurus
3136b	Camptosaurus	3136g	Allosaurus	3136l	Palaeosaniwa
3136c	Camarasaurus	3136h	Opisthias	3136m	Corythosaurus
3136d	Brachiosaurus	3136i	Edmontonia	3136n	Ornithominus
3136e	Goniopholis	3136j	Einiosaurus	3136o	Parasaurolophus

3136	32¢ Dinosaurs, 15 varieties, attached	11.50	....	....	....	20.00	18.00
....	set of singles	26.50	....	....	....	....	12.00
....	singles of above, each	....	....	....	....	....	1.00

3137, 3138

3137	32¢ Bugs Bunny, self-adhesive, pane of 10	9.50	....	....	....	13.00	....
3137a	same, single from pane	2.50	....	....	....	1.25	.35
3137b	same, pane of 9 (#3137a)	....	....	....	....	10.00	....
3137c	same, pane of 1 (#3137a)	....	....	....	....	2.50	....
3137v	same, top press sheet (6 panes) . .	....	....	350.00	....	350.00	....
3137v	same, bottom press w/ plate# (6 panes)	....	....	800.00	....	800.00	....
....	pane of 10 from press sheet	....	....	95.00	....	95.00	....
....	pane of 10 from press sheet w/ plate#	....	....	500.00	....	500.00	....

SCOTT NO.	DESCRIPTION	FIRST DAY COVERS SING	PL. BLK.	MINT SHEET	PLATE BLOCK	UNUSED F/NH	USED
	1997 COMMEMORATIVES (continued)						
3138	32¢ Bug Bunny, self-adhesive, Die Cut, pane of 10 . . .	....	....	....	....	325.00	....
3138a	same, single from pane	....	....	....	....		....
3138b	same, pane of 9 (#3138a)	....	....	....	....		....
3138c	same, pane of 1 (#3138a)	....	....	....	....	200.00	....

3139

3140

3139	50¢ Benjamin Franklin, Souvenir Sheet of 12 (Pacific '97)	25.00	....	....	....	22.00	20.00
3139a	same, single from sheet	5.00	....	....	....	1.90	1.50
3140	60¢ George Washington, Souvenir Sheet of 12 (Pacific '97)	25.00	....	....	....	25.00	24.00
3140a	same, single from sheet	5.00	....	....	....	2.00	1.50

3141

3141	32¢ Marshall Plan	1.95	4.75	20.00(20)	5.00	1.00	.30

3142

CLASSIC AMERICAN AIRCRAFT

3142a	Mustang	**3142k**	Flying Fortress
3142b	Model B	**3142l**	Stearman
3142c	Cub	**3142m**	Constellation
3142d	Vega	**3142n**	Lightning
3142e	Alpha	**3142o**	Peashooter
3142f	B-10	**3142p**	Tri-Motor
3142g	Corsair	**3142q**	DC-3
3142h	Stratojet	**3142r**	314 Clipper
3142i	GeeBee	**3142s**	Jenny
3142j	Staggerwing	**3142t**	Wildcat

SCOTT NO.	DESCRIPTION	FIRST DAY COVERS SING	PL. BLK.	MINT SHEET	PLATE BLOCK	UNUSED F/NH	USED
3142	32¢ Classic American Aircraft, 20 varieties, attached .	....	....	25.00(20)	....	25.00	20.00
....	set of singles	35.00	....	....	....	....	14.00
....	singles of above, each.	....	....	....	....	....	1.00
3142v	same as above, uncut sheet of 120 (6 panes)	....	....	125.00(120)	....	125.00	....
....	cross gutter block of 20	....	....	....	....	28.00	....
....	cross gutter block of 4 .	....	....	....	....	18.50	....
....	vertical pair with horizontal gutter	....	....	....	....	3.50	....
....	horizontal pair with vertical gutter	....	....	....	....	3.50	....

3143, 3148   3144, 3149

3145, 3147   3146, 3150

3143-46	Legendary Football Coaches, 4 varieties, attached . .	4.00	4.75	25.00(20)	5.50	5.25	4.00
3143	32¢ Paul "Bear" Bryant	2.25	....	....	....	1.30	1.30
3144	32¢ Glenn "Pop" Warner	2.25	....	....	....	1.30	1.30
3145	32¢ Vince Lombardi. . .	2.25	....	....	....	1.30	1.30
3146	32¢ George Halas	2.25	....	....	....	1.30	1.30
3147	32¢ Vince Lombardi. . .	2.25	4.75	24.00(20)	5.50	1.30	1.30
3148	32¢ Paul "Bear" Bryant	2.25	4.75	24.00(20)	5.50	1.30	1.30
3149	32¢ Glenn "Pop" Warner	2.25	4.75	24.00(20)	5.50	1.30	1.30
3150	32¢ George Halas	2.25	4.75	24.00(20)	5.50	1.30	1.30

SCOTT NO.	DESCRIPTION	FIRST DAY COVERS SING PL. BLK.	MINT SHEET	PLATE BLOCK	UNUSED F/NH	USED

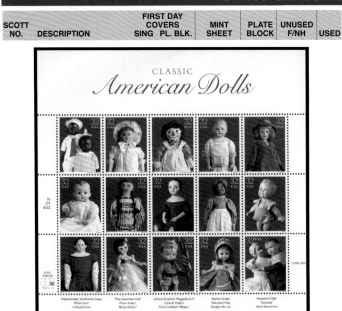

3151

CLASSIC AMERICAN DOLLS

3151a "Alabama Baby," and doll by Martha Chase	**3151i** "Babyland Rag"
3151b "Columbian Doll"	**3151j** "Scootles"
3151c Johnny Gruelle's "Raggedy Ann"	**3151k** Doll by Ludwig Greiner
3151d Doll by Martha Chase	**3151l** "Betsy McCall"
3151e "American Child"	**3151m** Percy Crosby's "Skippy"
3151f "Baby Coos"	**3151n** "Maggie Mix-up"
3151g Plains Indian	**3151o** Dolls by Albert Schoenhut
3151h Doll by Izannah Walker	

SCOTT NO.	DESCRIPTION	SING	PL. BLK.	MINT SHEET	PLATE BLOCK	UNUSED F/NH	USED
3151	32¢ Classic American Dolls, 15 varieties, attached	....	....	22.50(15)	....	22.50	18.00
....	set of singles	30.00	....	....	....	....	14.00
....	singles of above. each.	....	....	....	....	....	1.00

3152

3152	32¢ Humphrey Bogart .	3.00	....	27.00(20)	6.00	1.50	.35
3152v	same, as above, uncut sheet of 120 (6 panes)	....	....	125.00(120)	....	125.00	....
....	block of 8 with vertical gutter	....	....	....	....	18.00	....
....	cross gutter block of 8 .	....	....	....	....	21.00	....
....	vertical pair with horizontal gutter	....	....	....	....	3.50	....
....	horizontal pair with vertical gutter	....	....	....	....	5.00	....

3153

3153	32¢ "The Stars & Stripes Forever"	2.25	4.75	47.00(50)	5.00	1.00	.30

3154

3155

3156

3157

3154-57	Opera Singers, 4 varieties, attached	4.00	4.75	22.00(20)	5.50	4.75	4.00
3154	32¢ Lily Pons	2.25	....	....	....	1.25	1.00
3155	32¢ Richard Tucker	2.25	....	....	....	1.25	1.00
3156	32¢ Lawrence Tibbett	2.25	....	....	....	1.25	1.00
3157	32¢ Rosa Ponselle	2.25	....	....	....	1.25	1.00

3158

3159

3160

3161

3162

3163

3164

3165

3158-65	Composers and Conductors, 8 varieties, attached	7.00	....	39.00(20)	20.00(8)	17.00	10.00
3158	32¢ Leopold Stokowski	2.25	....	....	....	2.00	1.00
3159	32¢ Arthur Fiedler	2.25	....	....	....	2.00	1.00
3160	32¢ George Szell	2.25	....	....	....	2.00	1.00
3161	32¢ Eugene Ormandy	2.25	....	....	....	2.00	1.00
3162	32¢ Samuel Barber	2.25	....	....	....	2.00	1.00
3163	32¢ Ferde Grofé	2.25	....	....	....	2.00	1.00
3164	32¢ Charles Ives	2.25	....	....	....	2.00	1.00
3165	32¢ Louis Moreau Gottschalk	2.25	....	....	....	2.00	1.00

3166

3167

3166	32¢ Padre Félix Varela	2.25	4.75	19.00(20)	4.75	1.00	.50
3167	32¢ U.S. Air Force 50th Anniverary	4.00	6.00	19.00(20)	4.75	1.25	.30

SCOTT NO.	DESCRIPTION	FIRST DAY COVERS SING	FIRST DAY COVERS PL. BLK.	MINT SHEET	PLATE BLOCK	UNUSED F/NH	USED

3168

3169   **3170**

3171   **3172**

SCOTT NO.	DESCRIPTION	SING	PL. BLK.	MINT SHEET	PLATE BLOCK	UNUSED F/NH	USED
3168-72	Movie Monster, 5 varieties, attached ..	10.00	....	27.50(20)	15.00(10)	7.00	5.00
3168	32¢ Lon Chaney as The Phantom of the Opera .	2.25	....	....	....	1.50	1.00
3169	32¢ Bela Lugosi as Dracula	2.25	....	....	....	1.50	1.00
3170	32¢ Boris Karloff as Frankenstein's Monster	2.25	....	....	....	1.50	1.00
3171	32¢ Boris Karloff as The Mummy	2.25	....	....	....	1.50	1.00
3172	32¢ Lon Chaney Jr. as The Wolfman	2.25	....	....	....	1.50	1.00
3168-72v	same as above, uncut sheet of 180 (9 panes)			225.00(180)	....	225.00	....
....	block of 8 with vertical gutter	....	....	....	....	14.00	....
....	block of 10 with horizontal gutter	....	....	....	....	17.50	....
....	cross gutter block of 8 .	....	....	....	....	22.50	....
....	vertical pair with horizontal gutter	....	....	....	....	4.00	....
....	horizontal pair with vertical gutter	....	....	....	....	4.00	....

3173

3173	32¢ First Supersonic Flight, 50th Anniversary	3.00	4.75	20.00(20)	5.00	1.00	.30

3174

3174	32¢ Women in Military Service.	3.00	4.75	24.00(20)	6.25	1.35	.35

3175

3175	32¢ Kwanzaa	3.00	4.75	47.00(50)	5.00	1.00	.30
....	same, as above, uncut sheet of 250 (5 panes)	....	....	725.00(250)	....	....	....

3176   **3177**

3176	32¢ Madonna & Child, self-adhesive	2.25	....	....	....	1.00	.25
3176a	same, bklt pane of 20 .	14.50	....	....	....	19.50	....
3177	32¢ American Holly, self-adhesive	2.25	....	....	....	1.00	.25
3177a	same, bklt pane of 20 .	14.50	....	....	....	19.75	....
3177b	same, bklt pane of 4 . .	3.00	....	....	....	5.50	....
3177c	same, bklt pane of 5 . .	3.75	....	....	....	6.75	....
3177d	same, bklt pane of 6 . .	4.50	....	....	....	7.25	....

3178

3178	$3 Mars Rover Sojourner, Souvenir Sheet	14.00	....	....	....	9.50	5.00
....	same, as above, uncut sheet of 18 souvenir sheets .	....	....	175.00(18)	....	175.00	....
3178v	single souvenir sheet from uncut sheet of 18.	....	....	....	....	10.50	....

3179

1998 COMMEMORATIVES

3179/3252	(3179-81, 3192-3203, 3206, 3211-27, 3230-35, 3237-43, 3249-52) 50 varieties	....	....	....	....	72.00	27.00
3179	32¢ Year of the Tiger . .	3.00	4.75	22.50(20)	5.50	1.20	.30

3180   **3181**

3180	32¢ Alpine Skiing	2.25	4.75	25.00(20)	6.00	1.75	.30
3181	32¢ Madam C.J. Walker	3.00	4.75	22.50(20)	5.50	1.50	.35

SCOTT NO.	DESCRIPTION	FIRST DAY COVERS SING	PL. BLK.	MINT SHEET	PLATE BLOCK	UNUSED F/NH	USED

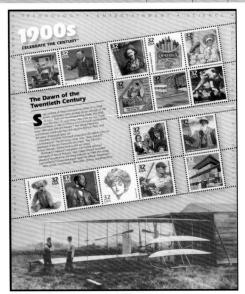

3182

CELEBRATE THE CENTURY 1900's

3182a	Model T Ford	3182i	Immigrants arrive.
3182b	Theodore Roosevelt	3182j	John Muir, preservationist
3182c	"The Great Train Robbery" 1903	3182k	"Teddy" bear created
3182d	Crayola Crayons, introduced, 1903	3182l	W.E.B. DuBois, social activist
3182e	St. Louis World's Fair, 1904	3182m	Gibson Girl
3182f	Pure Food & Drug Act, 1906	3182n	First baseball World Series, 1903
3182g	Wright Brothers first flight, 1903	3182o	Robie House, Chicago
3182h	Boxing match in painting		

SCOTT NO.	DESCRIPTION	SING	PL. BLK.	MINT SHEET	PLATE BLOCK	UNUSED F/NH	USED
3182	32¢ Celebrate the Century 1900's, 15 varieties, attached..........	17.50	....	18.00(15)	....	18.00	14.00
....	set of singles........	32.00	....	....	....	....	12.00
....	singles of above, each.	....	....	....	....	....	1.00
3182v	same as above, uncut sheet of 60 (4 panes)......	....	....	70.00(4)	....	70.00	....

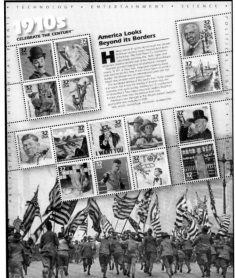

3183

CELEBRATE THE CENTURY 1910's

3183a	Charlie Chaplin as the Little Tramp	3183i	United States enters WWI
3183b	Federal Reserve system created, 1913	3183j	Boy Scouts, 1910
3183c	George Washington Carver	3183k	Woodrow Wilson
3183d	Avant-garde art, 1913	3183l	First crossword puzzle, pub., 1913
3183e	First-Transcontinental telephone line, 1914	3183m	Jack Dempsey wins title, 1919
3183f	Panama Canal opens, 1914	3183n	Construction toys
3183g	Jim Thorpe wins decathlon, 1912	3183o	Child labor reform
3183h	Grand Canyon National Park, 1913		

SCOTT NO.	DESCRIPTION	SING	PL. BLK.	MINT SHEET	PLATE BLOCK	UNUSED F/NH	USED
3183	32¢ Celebrate the Century 1910's, 15 varieties, attached..........	17.50	....	18.00(15)	....	18.00	14.00
....	set of singles........	32.00	....	....	....	....	12.00
....	singles of above, each.	....	....	....	....	....	1.00
3183v	same as above, uncut sheet of 60 (4 panes)......	....	....	70.00(4)	....	70.00	....

3184

CELEBRATE THE CENTURY 1920's

3184a	Babe Ruth	3184i	Radio entertains America
3184b	The Gatsby style	3184j	Art Deco style (Chrysler Building)
3184c	Prohibition enforced	3184k	Jazz flourishes
3184d	Electric toy trains	3184l	Four Horsemen of Notre Dame
3184e	19th Ammendment	3184m	Lindbergh flies the Atlantic
3184f	Emily Post's Etiquette	3184n	American realism
3184g	Margaret Mead, anthropologist	3184o	Stock Market crash, 1929
3184h	Flappers do the Charleston		

SCOTT NO.	DESCRIPTION	SING	PL. BLK.	MINT SHEET	PLATE BLOCK	UNUSED F/NH	USED
3184	32¢ Celebrate the Century 1920's, 15 varieties, attached..........	17.50	....	18.00(15)	....	18.00	14.00
....	set of singles........	32.00	....	....	....	....	12.00
....	singles of above, each.	....	....	....	....	....	1.00
3184v	same, as above, uncut sheet of 60 (4 panes)......	....	....	70.00(4)	....	70.00	....

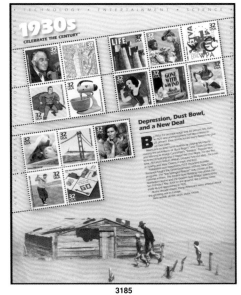

3185

CELEBRATE THE CENTURY 1930's

3185a	Franklin D. Roosevelt	3185i	"Gone with the Wind"
3185b	Empire State Building	3185j	Jesse Owens
3185c	1st Issue of Life Magazine	3185k	Streamline design
3185d	Eleanor Roosevelt	3185l	Golden Gate Bridge
3185e	FDR's New Deal	3185m	America survives the Depression
3185f	Superman arrives	3185n	Bobby Jones wins Grand Slam
3185g	Household conveniences	3185o	The Monopoly Game
3185h	"Snow White and the Seven Dwarfs"		

SCOTT NO.	DESCRIPTION	SING	PL. BLK.	MINT SHEET	PLATE BLOCK	UNUSED F/NH	USED
3185	32¢ Celebrate the Century 1930's, 15 varieties, attached..........	17.50	....	18.00(15)	....	18.00	14.00
....	set of singles........	32.00	....	....	....	....	12.00
....	singles of above, each.	....	....	....	....	....	1.00
3185v	same as above, uncut sheet of 60 (4 panes)......	....	....	70.00(4)	....	70.00	....

SCOTT NO.	DESCRIPTION	FIRST DAY COVERS SING	PL. BLK.	MINT SHEET	PLATE BLOCK	UNUSED F/NH	USED

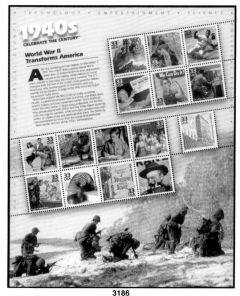

3186

CELEBRATE THE CENTURY 1940's

3186a	World War II	**3186i**	GI Bill, 1944
3186b	Antibiotics save lives	**3186j**	Big Band Sounds
3186c	Jackie Robinson	**3186k**	Intl. Style of Architecture
3186d	Harry S. Truman	**3186l**	Postwar Baby Boom
3186e	Women support war effort	**3186m**	Slinky, 1945
3186f	TV entertains America	**3186n**	"A Streetcar Named Desire" 1947
3186g	Jitterbug sweeps nation	**3186o**	Orson Welles' "Citizen Kane"
3186h	Jackson Pollock, Abstract Expressionism		

SCOTT NO.	DESCRIPTION	SING	PL. BLK.	MINT SHEET	PLATE BLOCK	UNUSED F/NH	USED
3186	33¢ Celebrate the Century 1940's, 15 varieties,						
	attached.	17.50	....	22.00(15)	....	22.00	15.00
....	set of singles	32.00	....	....	....	....	14.00
....	singles of above, each.		....	....	....	....	.85
3186v	same as above, uncut sheet of 60 (4 panes)	....	....	70.00(4)	....	70.00	1.00

3187

CELEBRATE THE CENTURY 1950's

3187a	Polio vaccine developed	**3187i**	Drive-in movies
3187b	teen fashions	**3187j**	World series rivals
3187c	The "Shot Heard Round the World"	**3187k**	Rocky Marciano, undefeated
3187d	US launches satellites	**3187l**	"I Love Lucy"
3187e	Korean War	**3187m**	Rock 'n Roll
3187f	Desegregation public schools	**3187n**	Stock car racing
3187g	Tail fins, chrome	**3187o**	Movies go 3-D
3187h	Dr. Seuss "The Cat in the Hat"		

3187	33¢ Celebrate the Century 1950's, 15 varieties,						
	attached.	17.50	....	22.00(15)	....	22.00	15.00
....	set of singles	32.00	....	....	....	....	14.00
....	singles of above, each.		....	....	....	....	1.00
3187v	same as above, uncut sheet of 60 (4 panes)	....	....	70.00(4)	....	70.00	....

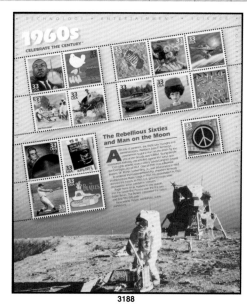

3188

CELEBRATE THE CENTURY 1960's

3188a	"I Have a Dream" Martin Luther King	**3188i**	Barbie Doll
3188b	Woodstock	**3188j**	The Integrated Circuit
3188c	Man Walks on the Moon	**3188k**	Lasers
3188d	Green Bay Packers	**3188l**	Super Bowl I
3188e	Star Trek	**3188m**	Peace Symbol
3188f	The Peace Corps	**3188n**	Roger Maris, 61 in '61
3188g	The Vietnam War	**3188o**	The Beatles "Yellow Submarine"
3188h	Ford Mustang		

3188	33¢ Celebrate the Century 1960's, 15 varieties,						
	attached.	17.50	....	22.00(15)	....	22.00	15.00
....	set of singles	32.00	....	....	....	....	14.00
....	singles of above, each.		....	....	....	....	1.00
3188v	same as above, uncut sheet of 60 (4 panes)	....	....	70.00(4)	....	70.00	....

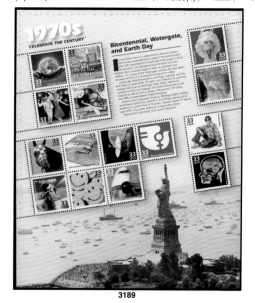

3189

CELEBRATE THE CENTURY 1970's

3189a	Earth Day Celebrated	**3189i**	Pioneer 10
3189b	"All in the Family", TV Series	**3189j**	Women's Rights Movement
3189c	Sesame Street	**3189k**	1970's Fashion
3189d	Disco Music	**3189l**	Monday Night Football
3189e	Steelers Win Four Super Bowls	**3189m**	America Smiles
3189f	U.S. Celebrates 200th Birthday	**3189n**	Jumbo Jets
3189g	Secretariat Wins Triple Crown	**3189o**	Medical Imaging
3189h	VCR's Transform Entertainment		

3189	33¢ Celebrate the Century 1970's, 15 varieties,						
	attached.	17.50	....	22.00(15)	....	22.00	15.00
....	set of singles	32.00	....	....	....	....	14.00
....	singles of above, each.		....	....	....	....	1.00
3189v	same as above, uncut sheet of 60 (4 panes)	....	....	70.00(4)	....	70.00	....

SCOTT NO.	DESCRIPTION	FIRST DAY COVERS SING	FIRST DAY COVERS PL. BLK.	MINT SHEET	PLATE BLOCK	UNUSED F/NH	USED

CELEBRATE THE CENTURY 1980's

3190a	Space Shuttle program	**3190i**	Cabbage Patch Kids
3190b	Cats, Musucal Smash	**3190j**	"The Cosby Show", Hit Comedy
3190c	San Francisco 49ers	**3190k**	Fall of the Berlin Wall
3190d	Hostages Come Home	**3190l**	Video Games
3190e	Figure Skating	**3190m**	"E.T. The Extra-Terrestrial"
3190f	Cable TV	**3190n**	Personal Computers
3190g	Vietnam Veterans Memorial	**3190o**	Hip-hop Culture
3190h	Compact Discs		

SCOTT NO.	DESCRIPTION	SING	PL. BLK.	MINT SHEET	PLATE BLOCK	UNUSED F/NH	USED
3190	33¢ Celebrate the Century 1980's, 15 varieties, attached..........	17.50	....	22.00(15)	....	22.00	15.00
....	set of singles	32.00	....	....	....	....	14.00
....	singles of above, each.	....	....	....	....	....	1.00
3190v	same as above, uncut sheet of 60 (4 panes)	....	....	70.00(4)	....	70.00	....

CELEBRATE THE CENTURY 1990's

3191a	New Baseball Records	**3191i**	Special Olympics
3191b	Gulf War	**3191j**	Virtual Reality
3191c	"Seinfield" Sitcom Sensation	**3191k**	"Jurassic Park"
3191d	Extreme Sports	**3191l**	"Titanic" Blockbuster Film
3191e	Improving Education	**3191m**	Sport Utility Vehicles
3191f	Computer Art and Graphics	**3191n**	World Wide Web
3191g	Recovering Species	**3191o**	Cellular Phones
3191h	Return to Space		

SCOTT NO.	DESCRIPTION	SING	PL. BLK.	MINT SHEET	PLATE BLOCK	UNUSED F/NH	USED
3191	33¢ Celebrate the Century 1990's, 15 varieties, attached..........	17.50	....	22.00(15)	....	22.00	15.00
....	set of singles	32.00	....	....	....	....	14.00
....	singles of above, each.	....	....	....	....	....	1.00
3191v	same as above, uncut sheet of 60 (4 panes)	....	....	70.00(4)	....	70.00	....

3192

SCOTT NO.	DESCRIPTION	SING	PL. BLK.	MINT SHEET	PLATE BLOCK	UNUSED F/NH	USED
3192	32¢ "Remember the Maine"	3.00	4.75	27.00(20)	6.75	1.50	.30

3193   **3194**   **3195**

3196   **3197**

SCOTT NO.	DESCRIPTION	SING	PL. BLK.	MINT SHEET	PLATE BLOCK	UNUSED F/NH	USED
3193-97	Flowering Trees, self-adhesive, 5 varieties, attached...........	5.75	....	26.00(20)	15.00(10)	7.00	5.00
3193	32¢ Southern Magnolia	2.25	....	....	....	1.10	.40
3194	32¢ Blue Paloverde ..	2.25	....	....	....	1.10	.40
3195	32¢ Yellow Poplar ..	2.25	....	....	....	1.10	.40
3196	32¢ Prairie Crab Apple	2.25	....	....	....	1.10	.40
3197	32¢ Pacific Dogwood.	2.25	....	....	....	1.10	.40

3198   **3199**

3200   **3201**   **3202**

SCOTT NO.	DESCRIPTION	SING	PL. BLK.	MINT SHEET	PLATE BLOCK	UNUSED F/NH	USED
3198-3202	Alexander Calder, 5 varieties, attached..........	5.75	....	27.00(20)	16.00(10)	7.50	5.50
3198	32¢ Black Cascade, 13 Verticals, 1959 ...	1.95	....	....	....	1.50	1.00
3199	32¢ Untitled, 1965 ...	1.95	....	....	....	1.50	1.00
3200	32¢ Rearing Stallion, 1928	1.95	....	....	....	1.50	1.00
3201	32¢ Potrait of a Young Man, c. 1945..........	1.95	....	....	....	1.50	1.00
3202	32¢ Un Effet du Japonais, 1945..........	1.95	....	....	....	1.50	1.00
3198-3202v	same, as above, uncut sheet of 120 (6 panes)	....	....	140.00(120)	....	....	....

SCOTT NO.	DESCRIPTION	FIRST DAY COVERS SING	FIRST DAY COVERS PL. BLK.	MINT SHEET	PLATE BLOCK	UNUSED F/NH	USED

3203

SCOTT NO.	DESCRIPTION	FIRST DAY COVERS SING	FIRST DAY COVERS PL. BLK.	MINT SHEET	PLATE BLOCK	UNUSED F/NH	USED
3203	32¢ Cinco De Mayo, self-adhesive	2.25	4.75	22.00(20)	5.75	1.10	.30
3203v	same as above, uncut sheet of 180 (9 panes)			180.00(180)	....	180.00	....
....	cross gutter block of 4 .	....	....	....	....	16.00	....
....	vertical pair with horizontal gutter	....	....	....	....	3.00	....
....	horizontal pair with vertical gutter	....	....	....	....	3.00	....

3204, 3205

SCOTT NO.	DESCRIPTION	FIRST DAY COVERS SING	FIRST DAY COVERS PL. BLK.	MINT SHEET	PLATE BLOCK	UNUSED F/NH	USED
3204	32¢ Sylvester & Tweety, self-adhesive, pane of 10	12.00	....	....	....	12.00	....
3204a	same, single from pane	2.25	....	....	....	1.35	.35
3204b	same, pane of 9 (#3204a)	....	....	....	....	9.75	....
3204c	same, pane of 1 (#3204a)	7.00	....	....	....	2.75	....
....	same, top press sheet of 60 (6 panes)	....	....	100.00(60)	....	100.00	....
....	same, bottom press sheet of 60 (6 panes)	....	....	175.00(60)	....	175.00	....
....	same, pane of 10 from press sheet	....	....	....	....	17.50	....
....	same, pane of 10 from press sheet w/ plate # .	....	....	....	....	80.00	....
....	vert. pair with horiz. gutter	....	....	....	....	10.00	....
....	horiz pair with vert. gutter	....	....	....	....	20.00	....
3205	32¢ Sylvester & Tweety, self-adhesive, Die-Cut, pane of 10	20.00	....	....	....	22.00	....
3205a	same, single from pane	....	....	....	....	1.75	....
3205b	same, pane of 9 (#3205a)	....	....	....	....	14.00	....
3205c	same, pane of 1, imperf.	12.00	....	....	....	6.00	....

3206

SCOTT NO.	DESCRIPTION	FIRST DAY COVERS SING	FIRST DAY COVERS PL. BLK.	MINT SHEET	PLATE BLOCK	UNUSED F/NH	USED
3206	32¢ Wisconsin, self-adhesive	1.95	4.75	20.00(20)	5.00	1.20	.30

3207, 3207a

3208, 3208a

SCOTT NO.	DESCRIPTION	FIRST DAY COVERS SING	FIRST DAY COVERS PLATE# STRIP 3	MINT SHEET	PLATE BLOCK PLATE# STRIP 3	UNUSED F/NH	USED
3207	(5¢) Wetlands, Nonprofit, coil	2.25	10.00	....	2.00	.25	.25

SCOTT NO.	DESCRIPTION	FIRST DAY COVERS SING	FIRST DAY COVERS PLATE# STRIP 3	MINT SHEET	PLATE BLOCK PLATE# STRIP 3	UNUSED F/NH	USED
3207A	same, self-adhesive coil .	2.25	....	....	2.00	.25	.25
....	same, plate strip of 5 . .	....	....	....	....	1.85	....
3207Ab	same, self-adhesive coil, large date.	....	....	....	3.75	.40	.25
....	same, plate strip of 5 . .	....	....	....	....	4.50	....
3208	(25¢) Diner, Presorted First-Class, coil	1.95	10.00	....	6.00	1.00	.50
3208a	same, self-adhesive coil, die cut 9.7	1.95	....	....	6.00	1.00	.50
....	same, plate strip of 5 . .	....	....	....	....	7.00	....

3209

SCOTT NO.	DESCRIPTION	FIRST DAY COVERS SING	FIRST DAY COVERS PL. BLK.	MINT SHEET	PLATE BLOCK	UNUSED F/NH	USED
3209	1¢-$2 Trans-Mississippi, Souvenir Sheet of 9 . . .	12.00	....	....	....	18.00	13.00
....	same, set of 9 singles .	18.00	....	....	....	16.00	12.00
3209v	block of 9 with horiz. gutter	....	....	....	....	60.00	....
3209v	vert. pair with horiz. gutter	....	....	....	....	12.50	....

3210

SCOTT NO.	DESCRIPTION	FIRST DAY COVERS SING	FIRST DAY COVERS PL. BLK.	MINT SHEET	PLATE BLOCK	UNUSED F/NH	USED
3210	$1 Cattle in Storm, Souvenir Sheet of 9 . . .	17.50	....	....	....	32.00	22.00
....	same, single stamp . .	....	....	....	....	3.75	2.50
3209-10	same, press sheet of 54 (6 panes, 3–#3209 & 3–#3210)	....	....	175.00(54)	....	175.00	....
3210v	cross gutter block of 12	....	....	....	....	85.00	....
3210v	vert. pair with horiz. gutter	....	....	....	....	12.50	....
3210v	horiz. pair with vert. gutter	....	....	....	....	12.50	....

3211

SCOTT NO.	DESCRIPTION	FIRST DAY COVERS SING	FIRST DAY COVERS PL. BLK.	MINT SHEET	PLATE BLOCK	UNUSED F/NH	USED
3211	32¢ Berlin Airlift, 50th Anniversary	1.95	4.75	25.00(20)	6.00	1.35	.30

SCOTT NO.	DESCRIPTION	FIRST DAY COVERS SING	PL. BLK.	MINT SHEET	PLATE BLOCK	UNUSED F/NH	USED

3212   3213

3215   3214

3212-15	Folk Musicains,						
	4 varieties, attached ..	12.00	14.00	32.00(20)	8.00	7.00	5.00
	Same, Top plate block of 8	....	....	....	15.00(8)	....	....
3212	32¢ Huddie "Leadbelly"						
	Ledbetter	3.00	....	....	....	1.75	1.00
3213	32¢ Woody Guthrie ...	3.00	....	....	....	1.75	1.00
3214	32¢ Sonny Terry	3.00	....	....	....	1.75	1.00
3215	32¢ Josh White	3.00	....	....	....	1.75	1.00

3216   3217

3218   3219

3216-19	Gospel Singers,						
	4 varieties, attached ..	12.00	14.00	36.00(20)	8.00	7.00	4.00
	Same, Top plate block of 8	....	....	....	16.00(8)	....	....
3216	32¢ Mahalia Jackson..	3.00	....	....	....	1.75	1.00
3217	32¢ Roberta Martin ...	3.00	....	....	....	1.75	1.00
3218	32¢ Clara Ward	3.00	....	....	....	1.75	1.00
3219	32¢ Sister Rosetta Tharpe	3.00	....	....	....	1.75	1.00

3220

3221

3220	32¢ Spanish Settlement of						
	the Southwest	2.25	4.75	19.50(20)	4.75	1.20	.25
3221	32¢ Stephen Vincent Benet	2.25	4.75	19.50(20)	4.75	1.20	.35

Need Supplements?
See page 98 for a complete list of U.S. Liberty I Album Supplements. Update your album today!

SCOTT NO.	DESCRIPTION	FIRST DAY COVERS SING	PL. BLK.	MINT SHEET	PLATE BLOCK	UNUSED F/NH	USED

3222   3223

3224   3225

3222-25	Tropical Birds,						
	4 varieties, attached ..	5.00	6.00	22.00(20)	6.50	6.00	4.00
3222	32¢ Antillean Euphonia	2.25	....	....	....	1.25	.75
3223	32¢ Green-throated Carib	2.25	....	....	....	1.25	.75
3224	32¢ Crested Honeycreeper	2.25	....	....	....	1.25	.75
3225	32¢ Cardinal Honeyeater	2.25	....	....	....	1.25	.75

3226

3226	32¢ Alfred Hitchcock .	2.25	....	26.00(20)	6.00	1.50	.35
3226v	same as above, uncut sheet						
	of 120 (6 panes) ...	....	....	120.00(120)	....	120.00	....
....	block of 8 with vertical gutter.....					18.00	....
....	cross gutter block of 8					25.00	....
....	vertical pair with horizontal						
	gutter					4.50	....
....	horizontal pair with vertical						
	gutter					6.00	....

3227

3228, 3229

3227	32¢ Organ & Tissue Donation,						
	self-adhesive	2.25	....	22.00(20)	5.50	1.20	.25
3228	(10¢) Modern Bicycle, self-						
	adhesive coil, die cut 9.8	2.25	....	....	3.75(3)	.40	.25
3228a	large "1998" date	....	....	....	3.50(3)	.75	.50
....	same, plate strip of 5 .	....	....	....	....	4.50	....
3229	(10¢) Modern Bicycle, coil	2.25	10.00	....	3.75(3)	.40	.25
3229a	large "1998" date	....	....	....	3.00(3)	.45	.25
....	same, plate strip of 5 .	....	....	....	....	4.50	....

3230

3231

3232

3233

SCOTT NO.	DESCRIPTION	FIRST DAY COVERS SING	PL. BLK.	MINT SHEET	PLATE BLOCK	UNUSED F/NH	USED

1998 COMMEMORATIVES (continued)

3234

3230-34	Bright Eyes, self-adhesive,						
	5 varieties, attached .	12.00	....	28.00(20)	15.00(10)	7.00	6.00
3230	32¢ Bright Eyes Dog .	3.00	....	....	....	1.50	.45
3231	32¢ Bright Eyes Fish .	3.00	....	....	....	1.50	.45
3232	32¢ Bright Eyes Cat. .	3.00	....	....	....	1.50	.45
3233	32¢ Bright Eyes Parakeet	3.00	....	....	....	1.50	.45
3234	32¢ Bright Eyes Hamster	3.00	....	....	....	1.50	.45

3235

| 3235 | 32¢ Klondike Gold Rush | 2.25 | .... | 22.00(20) | 6.00 | 1.20 | .25 |

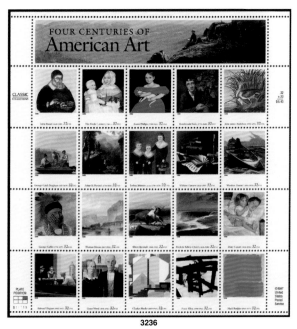

3236

AMERICAN ART

3236a "Portrait of Richard Mather," by John Foster
3236b "Mrs. Elizabeth Freake and Baby Mary," by The Freake Limner
3236c "Girl in Red Dress with Cat and Dog," by Ammi Phillips
3236d "Rubens Peale with Geranium," by Rembrandt Peale
3236e "Long-billed Curlew, Numenius Longrostris," by John James Audubon
3236f "Boatmen on the Missouri," by George Caleb Bingham
3236g "Kindred Spirits," by Asher B. Durand
3236h "The Westwood Children," by Joshua Johnson
3236i "Music and Literature," by William Harnett
3236j "The Fog Warning," by Winslow Homer
3236k "The White Cloud, Head Chief of the Iowas," by George Catlin
3236l "Cliffs of Green River," by Thomas Moran
3236m "The Last of the Buffalo," by Alfred Bierstadt
3236n "Niagara," by Frederic Edwin Church
3236o "Breakfast in Bed," by Mary Cassatt
3236p "Nighthawks," by Edward Hopper
3236q "American Gothic," by Grany Wood
3236r "Two Against the White," by Charles Sheeler
3236s "Mahoning," by Franz Kline
3236t "No. 12," by Mark Rothko

3236	32¢ American Art,						
	20 varieties, attached	....	....	32.00(20)	....	32.00	28.00
	set of singles	35.00	....	....	....	....	19.00
	same as above, uncut						
	sheet of 120 (6 panes)	....	....	175.00(120)	....	175.00	....
	block of 24 with vert. gutter	....	....	....	....	27.50	....
	block of 25 with horiz. gutter	....	....	....	....	32.50	....
	cross gutter block of 20	....	....	....	....	40.00	....
	vert. pair with horiz. gutter	....	....	....	....	7.00	....

AMERICAN ART (continued)

....	horiz. pair with vert. gutter	....	....	....	....	9.00	....
....	horiz. blk of 8 with vert. gutter	....	....	....	....	....	....
....	vert. blk of 10 with horiz. gutter	....	....	....	....	....	....

3237

3243

3237	32¢ Ballet.	1.95	....	23.00(20)	6.00	1.50	.35
....	same,uncut sheet of						
	120 (6 panes)	....	....	115.00(120)	....	115.00	....
....	cross gutter blk of 4 . .	....	....	....	....	13.00	....
....	vert. pair with horiz. gutter	....	....	....	....	3.00	....
....	horiz. pair with vert. gutter	....	....	....	....	3.00	....

3238

3239

3240

3241

3244

3242

3238-42	Space Discovery,						
	5 varieties, attached	5.75	11.00	24.00(20)	15.00(10)	7.50	6.50
3238	32¢ Space City	2.25	....	....	....	1.50	1.00
3239	32¢ Space ship landing	2.25	....	....	....	1.50	1.00
3240	32¢ Person in space suit	2.25	....	....	....	1.50	1.00
3241	32¢ Space Ship taking off	2.25	....	....	....	1.50	1.00
3242	32¢ Large domed structure	2.25	....	....	....	1.50	1.00
3238-42v	same, uncut sheet of 180						
	(9 panes)	....	....	185.00(180)	....	185.00	....
....	cross gutter blk of 10 .	....	....	....	....	27.50	....
....	vert. blk of 10 with						
	horiz. gutter	....	....	....	....	20.00	....
....	horiz. pair with vert. gutter	....	....	....	....	3.50	....
....	vert. pair with horiz. gutter	....	....	....	....	3.50	....

3245, 3249

3246, 3250

3247, 3251

3248, 3252

3243	32¢ Giving and Sharing,						
	self-adhesive	2.25	4.75	22.00(20)	5.50	1.20	.30
3244	32¢ Madonna & Child,						
	self-adhesive	2.25	....	....	....	1.50	.25
3244a	same, booklet pane of 20	14.50	....	....	....	25.00	....
3245	32¢ Evergreen Wreath,						
	self-adhesive	2.25	....	....	....	4.00	1.00
3246	32¢ Victorian Wreath,						
	self-adhesive	2.25	....	....	....	4.00	1.00
3247	32¢ Chili Pepper Wreath,						
	self-adhesive	2.25	....	....	....	4.00	1.00
3248	32¢ Tropical Wreath						
	self-adhesive	2.25	....	....	....	4.00	1.00

SCOTT NO.	DESCRIPTION	FIRST DAY COVERS SING	PL. BLK.	MINT SHEET	PLATE BLOCK	UNUSED F/NH	USED
3248a	32¢ Christmas Wreaths, self-adhesive, bklt pane of 4	4.00	....	....	....	20.00	....
3248b	same, bklt pane of 5 .	5.00	....	....	....	25.00	....
3248c	same, bklt pane of 6 .	5.50	....	....	....	30.00	....
3249-52	32¢ Christmas Wreaths, self-adhesive, 4 varieties, attached	4.00	4.75	60.00(20)	15.00	13.00	....
3249-52a	die cut 11.7x11.6	....	....	....	....	19.00	....
3249	32¢ Evergreen Wreath, self-adhesive	2.25	....	....	....	2.50	.75
3249a	32¢ Evergreen Wreath, self-adhesive, die-cut 11.7x11.6	2.25	....	....	....	4.50	1.00
3250	32¢ Victorian Wreath, self-adhesive	2.25	....	....	....	2.50	.75
3250a	32¢ Victorian Wreath, self-adhesive, die-cut 11.7x11.6	2.25	....	....	....	4.50	1.00
3251	32¢ Chili Pepper Wreath, self-adhesive	2.25	....	....	....	2.50	.75
3251a	32¢ Chili Pepper Wreath, self-adhesive, die-cut 11.7x11.6	2.25	....	....	....	4.50	1.00
3252	32¢ Tropical Wreath, self-adhesive	2.25	....	....	....	2.50	.75
3252a	32¢ Tropical Wreath, self-adhesive, die-cut 11.7x11.6	2.25	....	....	....	4.50	1.00
3252c	same, bklt pane of 20	14.50	....	....	....	55.00	....
3252e	bklt pane of 20, 5 each of 3249a-52a + label . . .	14.50	....	....	....	80.00	....

3257, 3258   **3259, 3263**   **3260, 3264, 3265, 3266, 3267, 3268, 3269**

SCOTT NO.	DESCRIPTION	FIRST DAY COVERS SING	PL. BLK.	MINT SHEET	PLATE BLOCK	UNUSED F/NH	USED
3257	(1¢) Weather Vane (white USA)	2.25	3.50	11.00(50)	1.10	.25	.25
3258	(1¢) Weather Vane (pale blue USA)	2.25	3.50	11.00(50)	1.10	.25	.25
3259	22¢ Uncle Sam, self-adhesive	2.25	4.75	14.00(20)	3.75	.75	.35
3259a	22¢ Uncle Sam, die cut 10.8	....	....	30.00(20)	12.00	3.50	1.35
3260	(33¢) Uncle Sam's Hat	2.25	4.75	50.00(50)	7.00	1.25	.35

3261

3262

SCOTT NO.	DESCRIPTION	FIRST DAY COVERS SING	PL. BLK.	MINT SHEET	PLATE BLOCK	UNUSED F/NH	USED
3261	$3.20 Space Shuttle Landing, self-adhesive	7.50	26.50	200.00(20)	46.00	11.00	5.00
3262	$11.75 Piggyback Space Shuttle, self-adhesive	28.50	95.00	695.00(20)	150.00	38.00	22.00
3263	22¢ Uncle Sam, self adhesive coil	2.25	....	....	5.75	.85	.35
....	same, plate strip of 5 .	....	....	....	....	6.50	....
3264	(33¢) Uncle Sam's Hat, coil	2.25	10.00	....	8.00	1.20	.65
....	same, plate strip of 5 .	....	....	....	....	9.50	....
3265	(33¢) Uncle Sam's Hat, self-adhesive coil, die cut 9.9	2.25	....	....	11.00	1.25	.30
....	same, plate strip of 5 .	....	....	....	....	12.00	....
3266	(33¢) Uncle Sam's Hat, self-adhesive coil, die cut 9.7	2.25	....	....	20.00	3.00	1.65
....	same, plate strip of 5 .	....	....	....	....	21.00	....
3267	(33¢) Uncle Sam's Hat, self-adhesive, die cut 9.9	2.25	....	....	....	1.25	.30
3267a	same, bklt pane of 10	7.25	....	....	....	11.00	....
3268	(33¢) Uncle Sam's Hat, self-adhesive, die cut 11.2 x 11.1	2.25	....	....	....	1.25	.30
3268a	same, bklt pane of 10	7.25	....	....	....	12.00	....
3268b	(33¢) Uncle Sam's Hat, d/c 11	....	....	....	....	1.25	.50
3268c	same, bklt pane of 20	14.50	....	....	....	23.00	....
3269	(33¢) Uncle Sam's Hat, self-adhesive, die cut 8	2.25	....	....	....	1.30	.75
3269a	same, bklt pane of 18	13.50	....	....	....	24.00	....

SCOTT NO.	DESCRIPTION	FIRST DAY COVERS SING	PL. BLK.	MINT SHEET	PLATE BLOCK	UNUSED F/NH	USED
3270	(10¢) Eagle, Presorted Std. coil, d/c 9.8, small date	2.25	....	....	4.00	.40	.25
3270a	same, large date	....	....	....	10.00(5)	.85	.50
....	plate strip of 5	....	....	....	....	10.00	....
3271	(10¢) Eagle, Presorted Std., self-adhesive coil d/c 9.9	2.25	....	....	4.00	.40	.25
....	same, plate strip of 5 .	....	....	....	....	4.50	....
3271a	same, large date	....	....	....	8.50(5)	1.25	.30

3270, 3271

3272

3273

1999 COMMEMORATIVES

SCOTT NO.	DESCRIPTION	FIRST DAY COVERS SING	PL. BLK.	MINT SHEET	PLATE BLOCK	UNUSED F/NH	USED
3272/3369	(3272-73, 3276, 3286-92, 3308-09, 3314-3350, 3352, 3354, 3356-59, 2368-69) 56 varieties	....	....	....	....	84.00	28.00
3272	33¢ Year of the Rabbit .	2.25	4.75	22.00(20)	5.00	1.25	.25
3273	33¢ Malcolm X, Civil Rights, self-adhesive	2.25	4.75	24.00(20)	6.00	1.50	.25

3274

3275

SCOTT NO.	DESCRIPTION	FIRST DAY COVERS SING	PL. BLK.	MINT SHEET	PLATE BLOCK	UNUSED F/NH	USED
3274	33¢ Love, self-adhesive	2.25	....	....	....	1.25	.25
3274a	same, bklt pane of 20	14.50	....	....	....	21.00	....
3275	55¢ Love, self-adhesive	2.50	....	30.00(20)	7.50	1.70	.50

3276

3277, 3278, 3279, 3280, 3281, 3282

3283

SCOTT NO.	DESCRIPTION	FIRST DAY COVERS SING	PL. BLK.	MINT SHEET	PLATE BLOCK	UNUSED F/NH	USED
3276	33¢ Hospice Care, self-adhesive	2.25	4.75	20.00(20)	5.00	1.00	.25
3277	33¢ Flag and City . . .	2.25	4.75	250.00(100)	48.00	2.50	.75
3278	33¢ Flag and City, self-adhesive, die cut 11.1	1.95	4.75	25.00(20)	6.00	1.10	.25
3278a	same, bklt pane of 4 .	4.00	....	....	....	5.25	....
3278b	same, bklt pane of 5 .	5.00	....	....	....	6.75	....
3278c	same, bklt pane of 6 .	5.50	....	....	....	8.00	....
3278d	same, bklt pane of 10	7.25	....	....	....	18.00	....
3278e	same, bklt pane of 20	14.50	....	....	....	21.00	....
3278F	33¢ Flag and City, self-adhesive, die cut 11.5x11.75	2.25	....	....	....	1.95	.50
3278Fg	same, bklt pane of 20	14.50	....	....	....	36.00	....
3278i	Flag and City, die cut 11.25	2.25	....	....	....	5.00	2.50
3278j	same, bklt pane of 10	7.25	....	....	....	45.00	....
3279	33¢ Flag and City, self-adhesive, die cut 9.8	2.25	....	....	....	1.25	.30
3279a	same, bklt pane of 10	7.25	....	....	....	13.00	....
3280	33¢ Flag and City, coil d/c 9.9	2.25	....	....	6.00	1.15	.25
....	same, plate strip of 5 .	....	....	....	....	7.75	....
3280a	33¢ Flag and City coil, large date	....	....	....	....	2.50	1.15
....	same, plate strip of 5 .	....	....	....	....	14.00	....
3281	33¢ Flag and City, self-adhesive coil (square corners) large date	2.25	....	....	7.00	1.25	.25
....	same, plate strip of 5 .	....	....	....	....	8.50	....
3281c	same, small date, type II	2.25	....	....	14.00	2.00	.25
....	same, plate strip of 5 .	....	....	....	....	17.00	....
3281d	same, small date, type I	....	....	....	....	7.00	....
....	plate and strip of 5 . . .	....	....	....	....	39.00	....

SCOTT NO.	DESCRIPTION	FIRST DAY COVERS SING	PL. BLK.	MINT SHEET	PLATE BLOCK	UNUSED F/NH	USED
3282	33¢ Flag and City, self-adhesive coil (round corners)	2.25	....	....	6.00	1.50	.60
......	same, plate strip of 5 .	....	....	....	....	8.00	....
3283	33¢ Flag and Chalkboard, self-adhesive	2.25	....	....	....	1.25	.50
3283a	same, bklt pane of 18	13.50	....	....	....	22.00	....

3286

3287

3286	33¢ Irish Immigration .	2.25	4.75	22.00(20)	5.50	1.20	.25
3287	33¢ Alfred Lunt & Lynn Fontanne, Actors	2.25	4.75	20.00(20)	4.75	1.20	.25

3288

3289

3290

3291   **3292**

3288-92	Arctic Animals, 5 varieties, attached .	12.00	....	20.00(15)	15.00(10)	7.50	5.00
3288	33¢ Arctic Hare	2.25	....	....	....	1.50	.75
3289	33¢ Arctic Fox	2.25	....	....	....	1.50	.75
3290	33¢ Snowy Owl	2.25	....	....	....	1.50	.75
3291	33¢ Polar Bear	2.25	....	....	....	1.50	.75
3292	33¢ Gray Wolf	2.25	....	....	....	1.50	.75

3293

SONORAN DESERT

3293a *Cactus wren, brittlebush, teddy bear cholla*
3293b *Desert tortoise*
3293c *White-winged dove, prickly pear*
3293d *Gambel quail*
3293e *Saquaro cactus*
3293f *Desert mule deer*
3293g *Desert cottontail, hedgehog cactus*
3293h *Gila monster*
3293i *Western diamondback rattlesnake, cactus mouse*
3293j *Gila woodpecker*

3293	33¢ Sonoran Desert, 10 varieties, attached, self-adhesive	....	....	16.00(10)	....	16.00	....
......	set of singles	18.50	....	....	....	....	9.00
3293v	same, uncut sheet of 60 (6 panes)	....	....	80.00(60)	....	80.00	....

3294, 3298, 3302   **3295, 3299, 3303**   **3296, 3300, 3304**   **3297, 3301, 3305**

SCOTT NO.	DESCRIPTION	FIRST DAY COVERS SING	PL. BLK.	MINT SHEET	PLATE BLOCK	UNUSED F/NH	USED
3294	33¢ Blueberries, self-adhesive, die cut 11.2 x 11.7	2.25	....	....	....	1.30	.30
3294a	same, dated "2000" . .	2.25	....	....	....	1.75	.30
3295	33¢ Raspberries, self-adhesive, die cut 11.2 x 11.7	2.25	....	....	....	1.50	.30
3295a	same, dated "2000" . .	2.25	....	....	....	1.75	.30
3296	33¢ Strawberries, self-adhesive, die cut 11.2x 11.7	2.25	....	....	....	1.50	.30
3296a	same, dated "2000" . .	2.25	....	....	....	1.75	.30
3297	33¢ Blackberries, self-adhesive, die cut 11.2 x 11.7	2.25	....	....	....	1.50	.30
3297b	same, bklt pane of 20 (3294-97 x 5 of each)	14.50	....	....	....	27.00	....
3297a	same, dated "2000" . .	2.25	....	....	....	1.75	.30
3297d	same, bklt pane of 20	14.50	....	....	....	34.00	....
3297e	same, block of 4, (#3294a-96a, 3297c).	4.00	....	....	....	8.50	....
3298	33¢ Blueberries, self-adhesive, die cut 9.5 x 10	2.25	....	....	....	1.75	.55
3299	33¢ Strawberries, self-adhesive, die cut 9.5 x 10	2.25	....	....	....	1.75	.55
3300	33¢ Raspberries, self-adhesive, die cut 9.5 x 10	2.25	....	....	....	1.75	.55
3301	33¢ Blackberries, self-adhesive, die cut 9.5 x 10	2.25	....	....	....	1.75	.55
3301a	same, bklt pane of 4 (3298-3301 x 1)	4.00	....	....	....	8.00	....
3301b	same, bklt pane of 5, (3298, 3299, 3301, 3300 x 2)	5.00	....	....	....	10.00	....
3301c	same, bklt pane of 6, (3300, 3301, 3298 x 2, 3299)	6.00	....	....	....	12.00	....
3302-05	33¢ Berries, self-adhesive coil, strip of 4, attached	4.00	....	....	....	10.00	....
3302	33¢ Blueberries, self-adhesive coil. . . .	2.25	....	....	....	2.00	.50
3303	33¢ Raspberries, self-adhesive coil. . . .	2.25	....	....	....	2.00	.50
3304	33¢ Blackberries, self-adhesive coil. . . .	2.25	....	....	....	2.00	.50
3305	33¢ Strawberries, self-adhesive coil. . . .	2.25	....	....	....	2.00	.50
3302-05	33¢ Berries, self-adhesive coil, pl# strip of 5 (3302 x 2, 3303-05 x 1)	10.00	....	....	....	12.00	....

3306, 3307   **3308**

3306	33¢ Daffy Duck, self-adhesive, pane of 10	12.00	....	....	....	12.50	....
3306a	same, single from pane	2.25	....	....	....	1.25	.45
3306b	same, pane of 9 (3306a)	....	....	....	....	9.50	....
3306c	same, pane of 1 (3306a)	7.00	....	....	....	2.50	....
3306v	same, top press sheet of 60 (6 panes)	....	....	80.00(60)	....	80.00	....
....	same, bottom press sheet of 60 w/ plate # (6 panes)	....	....	110.00(60)	....	110.00	....
....	same, pane of 10 from press sheet	....	....	....	....	15.00	....
....	same, pane of 10 from press sheet with plate #.	....	....	....	....	85.00	....
....	vert. pair with horiz. gutter	....	....	....	....	5.00	....
....	horiz. pair with vert. gutter	....	....	....	....	10.00	....
3307	33¢ Daffy Duck, self-adhesive, die cut, pane of 10	15.00	....	....	....	23.00	....
3307a	same, single from pane	....	....	....	....	2.00	....
3307b	same, pane of 9 (3307a)	....	....	....	....	16.00	....
3307c	same, pane of 1, imperf.	12.00	....	....	....	6.00	....
3308	33¢ Ayn Rand	2.25	4.75	20.00(20)	5.00	1.10	.35

SCOTT NO.	DESCRIPTION	FIRST DAY COVERS		MINT SHEET	PLATE BLOCK	UNUSED F/NH	USED
		SING	PL. BLK.				

3309

| 3309 | 33¢ Cinco De Mayo, self-adhesive . . . . | 2.25 | 4.75 | 20.00(20) | 5.00 | 1.10 | .30 |

3310 **3311**

3312 **3313**

3310-13	33¢ Tropical Flowers, self-adhesive, 4 varieties, attached	8.00	. . . .	. . . .	. . . .	5.75	5.00
3310	33¢ Bird of Paradise, self-adhesive	2.25	. . . .			1.25	.35
3311	33¢ Royal Poinciana, self-adhesive	2.25	. . . .			1.25	.35
3312	33¢ Gloriosa Lily, self-adhesive	2.25	. . . .			1.25	.35
3313	33¢ Chinese Hibiscus, self-adhesive	2.25	. . . .			1.25	.35
3313a	same, bklt pane of 20 (3310-13 x 5)	. . . .	. . . .	. . . .	. . . .	27.00	. . . .

3314 **3315** **3316**

3314	33¢ John & William Bartram, Botanists	2.25	4.75	20.00(20)	5.00	1.10	.30
3315	33¢ Prostate Cancer Awareness	2.25	4.75	20.00(20)	5.00	1.10	.30
3316	33¢ California Gold Rush	2.25	4.75	20.00(20)	5.00	1.10	.30

3317 **3318**

3319 **3320**

3317-20	Aquarium Fish, self-adhesive, 4 varieties, attached	8.00	. . . .	25.00(20)	11.00(8)	6.50	6.00
3317	33¢ Yellow fish, red fish, cleaner shrimp	2.25	. . . .	. . . .	. . . .	1.40	.35
3318	33¢ Fish, thermometer	2.25	. . . .	. . . .	. . . .	1.40	.35
3319	33¢ Red fish, blue fish	2.25	. . . .	. . . .	. . . .	1.40	.35
3320	33¢ Fish, heater.	2.25	. . . .	. . . .	. . . .	1.40	.35

3321 **3322** **3323** **3324**

3321-24	Xtreme Sports, self-adhesive, 4 varieties, attached	8.00	. . . .	22.00(20)	5.00	4.50	4.00
3321	33¢ Skateboarding . .	2.25	. . . .	. . . .	. . . .	1.25	.45
3322	33¢ BMX biking	2.25	. . . .	. . . .	. . . .	1.25	.45
3323	33¢ Snowboarding. . .	2.25	. . . .	. . . .	. . . .	1.25	.45
3324	33¢ Inline skating. . . .	2.25	. . . .	. . . .	. . . .	1.25	.45

3325 **3326** **3327** **3328**

3325-28	American Glass, 4 varieties, attached .	10.00	. . . .	30.00(15)	. . . .	10.00	5.00
3325	33¢ Freeblown glass .	3.00	. . . .	. . . .	. . . .	2.25	.45
3326	33¢ Mold-blown glass	3.00	. . . .	. . . .	. . . .	2.25	.45
3327	33¢ Pressed glass. . .	3.00	. . . .	. . . .	. . . .	2.25	.45
3328	33¢ Art glass	3.00	. . . .	. . . .	. . . .	2.25	.45

3329

| 3329 | 33¢ James Cagney . . | 1.95 | 4.75 | 28.00(20) | 7.00 | 1.50 | .35 |

3330 **3331** **3332**

3330	55¢ General William "Billy" Mitchell, self-adhesive	2.50	. . . .	32.00(20)	7.75	1.75	.75
3331	33¢ Honoring Those Who Served, self-adhesive	2.25	. . . .	25.00(20)	5.50	1.50	.30
3332	45¢ Universal Postal Union	2.25	5.00	27.00(20)	6.50	1.60	1.00

SCOTT NO.	DESCRIPTION	FIRST DAY COVERS SING	FIRST DAY COVERS PL. BLK.	MINT SHEET	PLATE BLOCK	UNUSED F/NH	USED

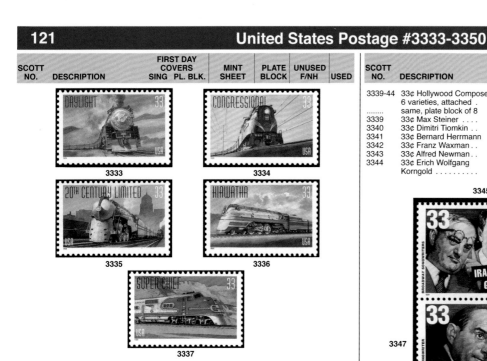

3333 3334

3335 3336

3337

3333-37	33¢ Famous Trains, 5 varieties, attached .	10.00	15.00	25.00(20)	14.00(8)	7.00	7.00
3333	33¢ Daylight.	3.00	....	....	....	1.40	.45
3334	33¢ Congressional. . .	3.00	....	....	....	1.40	.45
3335	33¢ 20th Century Limited	3.00	....	....	....	1.40	.45
3336	33¢ Hiawatha.	3.00	....	....	....	1.40	.45
3337	33¢ Super Chief.	3.00	....	....	....	1.40	.45
3333-37v	same, uncut sheet of 120 (6 panes)	....	....	175.00(120)		175.00	....
....	block of 8 with horiz. gutter	....	....	....	....	22.50	....
....	block of 10 with vert. gutter	....	....	....	....	23.50	....
....	cross gutter block of 8	....	....	....	....	25.00	....
....	horiz. pair with vert. gutter	....	....	....	....	4.00	....
....	vert. pair with horiz. gutter	....	....	....	....	4.00	....

3338

| 3338 | 33¢ Frederick Law Olmstead, Landscape Architect . | 1.95 | 4.75 | 19.50(20) | 5.00 | 1.10 | .30 |

3339 3340

3341 3342

3343 3344

3339-44	33¢ Hollywood Composers, 6 varieties, attached .	12.00	17.00	30.00(20)	14.00(6)	12.00	8.00
....	same, plate block of 8	....	....	....	18.00	....	....
3339	33¢ Max Steiner	3.00	....	....	....	1.75	.95
3340	33¢ Dimitri Tiomkin . .	3.00	....	....	....	1.75	.95
3341	33¢ Bernard Herrmann	3.00	....	....	....	1.75	.95
3342	33¢ Franz Waxman . .	3.00	....	....	....	1.75	.95
3343	33¢ Alfred Newman . .	3.00	....	....	....	1.75	.95
3344	33¢ Erich Wolfgang Korngold	3.00	....	....	....	1.75	.95

3345 3346

3347 3348

3349 3350

3345-50	33¢ Broadway Songwriters, 6 varieties, attached .	12.00	17.00	30.00(20)	14.00(6)	12.00	7.75
....	same, plate block of 8	....	....	....	18.00	....	....
3345	33¢ Ira & George Gershwin	3.00	....	....	....	1.75	1.00
3346	33¢ Lerner & Loewe .	3.00	....	....	....	1.75	1.00
3347	33¢ Lorenz Hart.	3.00	....	....	....	1.75	1.00
3348	33¢ Rodgers & Hammerstein	3.00	....	....	....	1.75	1.00
3349	33¢ Meredith Willson.	3.00	....	....	....	1.75	1.00
3350	33¢ Frank Loesser. . .	3.00	....	....	....	1.75	1.00

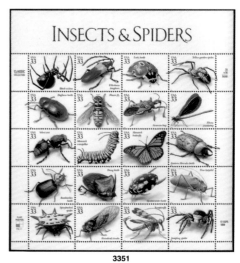

3351

INSECTS & SPIDERS

3351a	Black Widow	3351k	Monarch butterfly
3351b	Elderberry longhorn	3351l	Eastern hercules beetle
3351c	Lady beetle	3351m	Bombardier beetle
3351d	Yellow garden spider	3351n	Dung beetle
3351e	Dogbane beetle	3351o	Spotted water beetle
3351f	Flower fly	3351p	True Katydid
3351g	Assassin bug	3351q	Spinybacked spider
3351h	Ebony jewelwing	3351r	Periodical cicada
3351i	Velvet ant	3351s	Scorpionfly
3351j	Monarch caterpillar	3351t	Jumping spider

SCOTT NO.	DESCRIPTION	FIRST DAY COVERS SING	PL. BLK.	MINT SHEET	PLATE BLOCK	UNUSED F/NH	USED

3414 / **3415**

3416 / **3417**

SCOTT NO.	DESCRIPTION	FIRST DAY COVERS SING	PL. BLK.	MINT SHEET	PLATE BLOCK	UNUSED F/NH	USED
3414-17	33¢ Stampin' the Future, 4 varieties, attached . .	8.00	10.00	20.00(20)	10.00(8)	5.50	4.00
3414	33¢ Designed by Zachary Canter	2.25	....	....	....	1.40	.50
3415	33¢ Designed by Sarah Lipsey	2.25	....	....	....	1.40	.50
3416	33¢ Designed by Morgan Hill	2.25	....	....	....	1.40	.50
3417	33¢ Designed by Ashley Young	2.25	....	....	....	1.40	.50

3420 / **3422, 3436** / **3426** / **3427**

3427A / **3428** / **3430** / **3431, 3432**

3432A / **3432B** / **3433, 3434** / **3435**

2000-2009 DISTINGUISHED AMERICANS

SCOTT NO.	DESCRIPTION	SING	PL. BLK.	MINT SHEET	PLATE BLOCK	UNUSED F/NH	USED
3420	10¢ Joseph W. Stilwell	2.25	4.00	7.00(20)	1.75	.40	.25
3422	23¢ Wilma Rudolph, self-adhesive, die cut 11.25 x 10.75 .	2.25	4.75	15.00(20)	3.50	.85	.40
3426	33¢ Claude Pepper . .	2.25	4.75	20.00(20)	5.00	1.10	.55
3427	58¢ Margaret Chase Smith, self-adhesive (2007) .	2.25	5.50	32.00(20)	8.50	1.75	.65
3427a	59¢ James A. Michener	2.25	5.50	32.00(20)	8.50	1.75	.70
3428	63¢ Dr. Jonas Salk (2006)	2.25	6.00	34.00(20)	9.25	1.85	.70
3430	75¢ Harriett Beecher Stowe, self-adhesive (2007) .	2.95	6.00	38.00(20)	10.50	2.25	.95
3431	76¢ Hattie W. Caraway, die cut 11	2.95	5.50	54.00(20)	16.00	3.00	.60
3432	76¢ Hattie W. Caraway, die cut 11.5 x 11	....	....	135.00(20)	36.00	8.00	4.00
3432a	76¢ Edward Trudeau .	2.95	5.75	37.00(20)	9.50	2.50	.95
3432b	78¢ Mary Lasker (2009)	3.75	....	34.00(20)	9.50	2.25	.75
3433	83¢ Edna Ferber, die cut 11 x 11.5.	2.95	5.50	52.00(20)	14.00	3.00	.95
3434	83¢ Edna Ferber, die cut 11.25 (2003) . .	2.95	5.50	48.00(20)	13.00	2.75	.90
3435	87¢ Dr. Albert Sabin (2006)	2.95	5.50	46.00(20)	12.00	2.75	.95
3436	23¢ Wilma Rudolph, self-adhesive, die cut 11.25 x 10.75 .	2.25	....	....	....	.85	.50
3436a	same, bklt pane of 4 .	3.00	....	....	....	3.25	....
3436b	same, bklt pane of 6 .	4.00	....	....	....	4.75	....
3436c	same, bklt pane of 10	6.75	....	....	....	7.50	....

3438

SCOTT NO.	DESCRIPTION	SING	PL. BLK.	MINT SHEET	PLATE BLOCK	UNUSED F/NH	USED
3438	33¢ California Statehood, self-adhesive	2.25	....	22.00(20)	6.00	1.50	.40

3439 / **3440**

3441

3442 / **3443**

SCOTT NO.	DESCRIPTION	SING	PL. BLK.	MINT SHEET	PLATE BLOCK	UNUSED F/NH	USED
3439-43	33¢ Deep Sea Creatures, 5 varieities attached. .	5.75	11.00	20.00(15)	....	7.00	4.75
3439	33¢ Fanfin Anglerfish.	2.25	....	....	....	1.40	.85
3440	33¢ Sea Cucumber . .	2.25	....	....	....	1.40	.85
3441	33¢ Fangtooth	2.25	....	....	....	1.40	.85
3442	33¢ Amphipod	2.25	....	....	....	1.40	.85
3443	33¢ Medusa.	2.25	....	....	....	1.40	.85

3444 / **3445** / **3446**

SCOTT NO.	DESCRIPTION	SING	PL. BLK.	MINT SHEET	PLATE BLOCK	UNUSED F/NH	USED
3444	33¢ Thomas Wolfe . .	2.25	4.75	20.00(20)	4.75	1.10	.30
3445	33¢ White House	2.25	4.75	35.00(20)	9.00	2.00	.35
3446	33¢ Edward G. Robinson	2.25	4.75	49.00(20)	12.00	3.00	2.00
....	same, uncut sheet of 120 (6 panes)	....	....	175.00(120)	....	240.00	....
....	cross gutter block of 8	....	....	....	....	35.00	....
....	block of 8 with vert. gutter	....	....	....	....	24.00	....
....	horiz. pair with vert. gutter	....	....	....	....	6.00	....
....	vert. pair with horiz. gutter	....	....	....	....	4.50	....

SCOTT NO.	DESCRIPTION	FIRST DAY COVERS SING	PL. BLK.	MINT SHEET	PLATE BLOCK	UNUSED F/NH	USED

3447

3448, 3449, 3450,

3451, 3452, 3453

SCOTT NO.	DESCRIPTION	SING	PL. BLK.	MINT SHEET	PLATE BLOCK	UNUSED F/NH	USED
3447	10¢ New York Public Library Lion, coil	2.25	. . . . . .	. . . . . .	4.00	.50	.25
. . . . . .	same, pl# strip of 5 . .	. . . . . .	. . . . . .	. . . . . .	. . . . . .	5.00	. . . . . .
3447a	10¢ New York Public Library, self-adhesive, coil, die cut 11.5	2.25	. . . . . .	. . . . . .	. . . . . .	.75	.60
. . . . . .	same, pl# strip of 5 . .	. . . . . .	. . . . . .	. . . . . .	. . . . . .	5.00	. . . . . .
3448	34¢ Flag over Farm . .	2.25	4.75	27.00(20)	7.00	1.50	.75
3450	self-adhesive	2.25	4.75	25.00(20)	6.00	1.30	.30
3450	34¢ Flag over Farm, self-adhesive	2.25	. . . . . .	. . . . . .	. . . . . .	1.60	.75
3450a	same, bklt pane of 18	14.00	. . . . . .	. . . . . .	. . . . . .	29.00	. . . . . .
3451	34¢ Statue of Liberty, self-adhesive	2.25	. . . . . .	. . . . . .	. . . . . .	1.20	.35
3451a	same, bklt pane of 20	14.50	. . . . . .	. . . . . .	. . . . . .	24.00	. . . . . .
3451b	same, bklt pane of 4 .	4.00	. . . . . .	. . . . . .	. . . . . .	7.00	. . . . . .
3451c	same, bklt pane of 6 .	5.50	. . . . . .	. . . . . .	. . . . . .	10.50	. . . . . .
3452	34¢ Statue of Liberty, coil	2.25	. . . . . .	. . . . . .	7.00	1.25	.25
. . . . . .	same, pl# strip of 5 . .	. . . . . .	. . . . . .	. . . . . .	. . . . . .	9.00	. . . . . .
3453	34¢ Statue of Liberty, self-adhesive coil	1.95	. . . . . .	. . . . . .	10.00	1.25	.25
. . . . . .	same, pl# strip of 5 . .	. . . . . .	. . . . . .	. . . . . .	. . . . . .	12.00	. . . . . .
3453b	same, large date	. . . . . .	. . . . . .	15.00(3)	. . . . . .	1.80	.30

3454, 3458, 3465   3455, 3459, 3464   3456, 3460, 3463   3457, 3461, 3462

SCOTT NO.	DESCRIPTION	SING	PL. BLK.	MINT SHEET	PLATE BLOCK	UNUSED F/NH	USED
3454-57	34¢ Flowers, self-adhesive, 4 varieties attached . .	4.25	. . . . . .	. . . . . .	. . . . . .	7.50	. . . . . .
3454	34¢ Fressia, self-adhesive, die cut 10.25 x 10.75 .	2.25	. . . . . .	. . . . . .	. . . . . .	2.50	.40
3455	34¢ Symbidium Orchid, self-adhesive, die cut 10.25 x 10.75	2.25	. . . . . .	. . . . . .	. . . . . .	2.50	.40
3456	34¢ Longiflorum Lily, self-adhesive, die cut 10.25 x 10.75	2.25	. . . . . .	. . . . . .	. . . . . .	2.50	.40
3457	34¢ Asian Hybrid, self-adhesive, die cut 10.25 x 10.75	2.25	. . . . . .	. . . . . .	. . . . . .	2.50	.40
3457b	same, bklt pane of 4 (3454-57)	4.00	. . . . . .	. . . . . .	. . . . . .	8.50	. . . . . .
3457c	same, bklt pane of 6 (3456, 3457, 3454 x 2 3455 x 2)	5.50	. . . . . .	. . . . . .	. . . . . .	14.00	. . . . . .
3457d	same, bklt pane of 6 (3454, 3455, 3456 x 2 3457 x 2)	5.50	. . . . . .	. . . . . .	. . . . . .	14.00	. . . . . .
3457e	34¢ Flowers, bklt pane of 20, self-adhesive (5 each 3457a + label)	14.50	. . . . . .	. . . . . .	. . . . . .	36.00	. . . . . .
3458-61	(34¢) Flowers, self-adhesive, 4 varieties attached . .	4.25	. . . . . .	. . . . . .	. . . . . .	18.00	. . . . . .
3458	34¢ Fressia, bklt single, self-adhesive, die cut 11.5 x 11.75	2.25	. . . . . .	. . . . . .	. . . . . .	5.50	1.00
3459	34¢ Symbidium Orchid, bklt single, self-adhesive, die cut 11.5 x 11.75 . .	2.25	. . . . . .	. . . . . .	. . . . . .	5.50	1.00
3460	34¢ Longiflorum Lily, bklt single, self-adhesive, die cut 11.5 x 11.75 . .	2.25	. . . . . .	. . . . . .	. . . . . .	5.50	1.00
3461	34¢ Asian Hybrid Lily, bklt single, self-adhesive, die cut 11.5 x 11.75 . .	2.25	. . . . . .	. . . . . .	. . . . . .	5.50	1.00
3461b	same, bklt pane of 20, self-adhesive (2 each 3461a, 3 each 3457a)	14.50	. . . . . .	. . . . . .	. . . . . .	70.00	. . . . . .
3461c	same, bklt pane of 20, self-adhesive (2 each 3457a, 3 each 3461a)	14.50	. . . . . .	. . . . . .	. . . . . .	90.00	. . . . . .
3462	34¢ Longiflorum Lily, self-adhesive coil	2.25	. . . . . .	. . . . . .	. . . . . .	5.00	.60
3463	34¢ Asian Hybrid Lily, self-adhesive coil	2.25	. . . . . .	. . . . . .	. . . . . .	5.00	60
3464	34¢ Symbidium Orchid, self-adhesive coil	2.25	. . . . . .	. . . . . .	. . . . . .	5.00	.60
3465	self-adhesive coil	2.25	. . . . . .	. . . . . .	. . . . . .	5.00	.60
3462-65	34¢ Flowers, self-adhesive coil, strip of 4	4.25	. . . . . .	. . . . . .	. . . . . .	20.00	. . . . . .
. . . . . .	same, pl# strip of 5 . .	. . . . . .	. . . . . .	. . . . . .	. . . . . .	28.00	. . . . . .

3466, 3476, 3477, 3485   3467, 3468, 3475, 3484, 3484A   3468A, 3475A   3469, 3470

3471   3471A

2001 REGULAR ISSUES

SCOTT NO.	DESCRIPTION	SING	PL. BLK.	MINT SHEET	PLATE BLOCK	UNUSED F/NH	USED
3466	34¢ Statue of Liberty, self-adhesive coil, die cut 9.75 (round corners)	2.25	. . . . . .	. . . . . .	8.50	1.30	.50
. . . . . .	same, pl# strip of 5 . .	. . . . . .	. . . . . .	. . . . . .	. . . . . .	11.00	. . . . . .
3467	21¢ Buffalo	2.25	4.75	160.00(100)	37.00	1.50	.75
3468	21¢ Buffalo. self-adhesive	2.25	4.75	16.00(20)	4.50	.90	.75
3468A	23¢ George Washington, self-adhesive	2.25	4.75	15.00(20)	4.00	.90	.75
3469	34¢ Flag over Farm . .	2.25	4.75	170.00(100)	38.00	1.50	.90
3470	34¢ Flag over Farm, self-adhesive	2.25	4.75	28.00(20)	8.00	2.00	.50
3471	55¢ Eagle, self-adhesive	2.50	5.00	45.00(20)	11.00	2.25	.80
3471A	57¢ Eagle, self-adhesive	2.50	5.00	41.00(20)	11.00	2.50	80

3472   3473

SCOTT NO.	DESCRIPTION	SING	PL. BLK.	MINT SHEET	PLATE BLOCK	UNUSED F/NH	USED
3472	$3.50 Capitol Dome, self-adhesive	8.00	30.00	210.00(20)	48.00	12.00	5.00
3473	$12.25 Washington Monument, self-adhesive	30.00	98.50	700.00(20)	155.00	40.00	12.00
3475	21¢ Buffalo, self-adhesive coil	2.25	. . . . . .	. . . . . .	5.00	.75	.35
. . . . . .	same, pl# strip of 5 . .	. . . . . .	. . . . . .	. . . . . .	. . . . . .	6.00	. . . . . .
3475A	23¢ George Washington, self-adhesive coil	2.25	. . . . . .	. . . . . .	. . . . . .	1.20	.30
. . . . . .	same, pl# strip of 5 . .	. . . . . .	. . . . . .	. . . . . .	. . . . . .	9.00	. . . . . .
3476	34¢ Statue of Liberty, coil	2.25	. . . . . .	. . . . . .	7.00	1.50	.40
. . . . . .	same, pl# strip of 5 . .	. . . . . .	. . . . . .	. . . . . .	. . . . . .	9.00	. . . . . .
3477	34¢ Statue of Liberty, self-adhesive coil die cut 9.75 (square corners)	2.25	. . . . . .	. . . . . .	7.75	1.50	.25
. . . . . .	same, pl# strip of 5 . .	. . . . . .	. . . . . .	. . . . . .	. . . . . .	10.00	. . . . . .

3478, 3489   3479, 3490   3480, 3488   3481, 3487

SCOTT NO.	DESCRIPTION	SING	PL. BLK.	MINT SHEET	PLATE BLOCK	UNUSED F/NH	USED
3478	34¢ Longiflorum, self-adhesive coil	2.25	. . . . . .	. . . . . .	. . . . . .	2.50	.50
3479	34¢ Asain Hybrid Lily, self-adhesive coil	2.25	. . . . . .	. . . . . .	. . . . . .	2.50	50
3480	34¢ Symbidium Orchid, self-adhesive coil	2.25	. . . . . .	. . . . . .	. . . . . .	2.50	.50
3481	34¢ Fressia, self-adhesive coil	2.25	. . . . . .	. . . . . .	. . . . . .	2.50	.50
3478-81	34¢ Flowers, self-adhesive, coil, strip of 4	4.25	. . . . . .	. . . . . .	. . . . . .	9.00	. . . . . .
. . . . . .	same, pl# strip of 5 . .	. . . . . .	. . . . . .	. . . . . .	. . . . . .	14.00	. . . . . .

SCOTT NO.	DESCRIPTION	FIRST DAY COVERS SING	PL. BLK.	MINT SHEET	PLATE BLOCK	UNUSED F/NH	USED

3482, 3483   **3491, 3493**   **3492, 3494**   **3495**

Scott No.	Description	FDC Sing	Pl. Blk.	Mint Sheet	Plate Block	Unused F/NH	Used
3482	20¢ George Washington, self-adhesive, die cut 11.25	2.25	....	....	....	1.00	.50
3482a	same, bklt pane of 10	5.50	....	....	....	9.50	....
3482b	same, bklt pane of 4, die cut 11.25 x 11....	3.00	....	....	....	6.50	....
3482c	same, bklt pane of 6, die cut 11.25 x 11....	4.00	....	....	....	5.00	....
3483	20¢ George Washington, self-adhesive, die cut 10.5 x 11.25........	2.25	....	....	....	7.00	1.80
3483a	same, bklt pane of 4 (2 each 3482-3483)..	3.00	....	....	....	22.00	....
3483b	same, bklt pane of 6 (3 each 3482-3483)..	4.00	....	....	....	33.00	....
3483c	same, bklt pane of 10, die cut 10.5 x 11 (3482 x 5 at L, 3483 x 5 at R)..	5.50	....	....	....	38.00	....
3483d	same, bklt pane of 4 (2 each 3482-3483), die cut 11.25 x 11....	....	....	....	....	20.00	....
3483e	same, bklt pane of 6 (2 each 3482-3483), die cut 11.25 x 11....	....	....	....	....	34.00	....
3483f	same, bklt pane of 10 (5 each 3482-3483), die cut 11.25 x 11....	....	....	....	....	38.00	....
3483g	pair, 3482 at left, 3483 at right........	....	....	....	....	8.50	....
3483h	pair 3483 at left, 3482 at right........	....	....	....	....	8.50	....
3484	21¢ Buffalo, self-adhesive, die cut 11.25	2.25	....	....	....	1.00	.50
3484b	same, bklt pane of 4 .	3.00	....	....	....	4.00	....
3484c	same, bklt pane of 6 .	4.00	....	....	....	5.00	....
3484d	same, bklt pane of 10	5.50	....	....	....	9.50	....
3484A	21¢ Buffalo, self-adhesive, die cut 10.5 X 11.25...	2.25	....	....	....	7.00	2.50
3484Ae	same, bklt pane of 4 (3484 x 2 at L, 3484A x 2 at R)	....	....	....	....	22.00	....
3484Af	same, bklt pane of 6 (3484 x 3 at L, 3484A x 3 at R)	....	....	....	....	34.00	....
3484Ag	same, bklt pane of 10 (3484 x 5 at L, 3484A x 5 at R)	....	....	....	....	38.00	....
3484Ah	same, bklt pane of 4 (3484A x 2 at L, 3484 x 2 at R)	....	....	....	....	23.00	....
3484Ai	same, bklt pane of 6 (3484A x 3 at L, 3484 x 3 at R)	....	....	....	....	34.00	....
3484Aj	same, bklt pane of 10 (3484A x 5 at L, 3484 x 5 at R)	....	....	....	....	38.00	....
3484Ak	same, pair (3484 at L, 3484A at R)	....	....	....	....	7.50	....
3484Al	same, pair (3484A at L, 3484 at R)	....	....	....	....	8.00	....
3485	34¢ Statue of Liberty, self-adhesive........	2.25	....	....	....	1.45	.25
3485a	same, bklt pane of 10	7.25	....	....	....	14.00	....
3485b	same, bklt pane of 20	14.50	....	....	....	28.00	....
3485c	same, bklt pane of 4 .	4.00	....	....	....	7.00	....
3485d	same, bklt pane of 6 .	5.50	....	....	....	9.50	....
3487-90	34¢ Flowers, self-adhesive 4 varieties attached ..	4.25	....	....	....	6.00	3.50
3487	34¢ Fressia, self-adhesive, die cut 10.25 x 10.75 .	2.25	....	....	....	1.75	.35
3488	34¢ Symbidium Orchid, self-adhesive, die cut 10.25 x 10.75........	2.25	....	....	....	1.75	.35
3489	34¢ Longiflorum Lily, self-adhesive, die cut 10.25 x 10.75........	2.25	....	....	....	1.75	.35
3490	34¢ Asian Hybrid Lily, self-adhesive, die cut 10.25 x 10.75........	2.25	....	....	....	1.75	.35
3490b	same, bklt pane of 4 (3487-90 x 1)........	4.00	....	....	....	6.50	....
3490c	same, bklt pane of 6 (3489-3490, 3487 x 2, 3488 x 2)...........	5.50	....	....	....	8.50	....
3490d	same, bklt pane of 6 (3487-3488, 3498 x 2 3490 x 2)...........	5.50	....	....	....	8.50	....
3490e	same, bklt pane of 20 (3487-90 x 5 + label) .	14.50	....	....	....	28.00	....
3491	34¢ Apple, self-adhesive	2.25	....	....	....	1.75	.25
3492	34¢ Orange, self-adhesive	2.25	....	....	....	1.75	.25
3491-92	34¢ Apple & Orange, Pair	2.50	....	....	....	3.50	....
3492b	34¢ Apple & Orange, bklt pane of 20, self-adhesive	14.50	....	....	....	26.00	....
3493	34¢ Apple, self-adhesive, die cut 11.5 x 10.75 .	2.25	....	....	....	2.50	.65
3494	34¢ Orange, self-adhesive, die cut 11.5 x 10.75 .	2.25	....	....	....	2.50	.65
3493-94	34¢ Apple & Orange, Pair	2.50	....	....	....	5.00	....
3494b	same, bklt pane of 4 (3493 x 2, 3494 x 2)..	4.00	....	....	....	10.00	....

Scott No.	Description	FDC Sing	Pl. Blk.	Mint Sheet	Plate Block	Unused F/NH	Used
3494c	same, bklt pane of 6 (3493 x 3, 3494 x 3) (3493 at UL)........	5.50	....	....	....	15.00	....
3494d	same, bklt pane of 6 (3493 x 3, 3494 x 3) (3494 at UL)........	5.50	....	....	....	15.00	....
3495	34¢ Flag over Farm, self-adhesive........	1.95	....	....	....	2.00	.50
3495a	same, ATM bklt pane of 18	14.00	....	....	....	37.00	....

3496   **3497, 3498**   **3499**

Scott No.	Description	FDC Sing	Pl. Blk.	Mint Sheet	Plate Block	Unused F/NH	Used
3496	34¢ LOVE, self-adhesive, die cut 11.75	2.25	....	....	....	1.50	.30
3496a	same, bklt pane of 20	14.50	....	....	....	30.00	....
3497	34¢ LOVE, self-adhesive, die cut 11.25	2.25	....	....	....	1.50	.30
3497a	same, bklt pane of 20	14.50	....	....	....	30.00	....
3498	34¢ LOVE, self-adhesive, die cut 11.5 x 10.75	2.25	....	....	....	2.50	.30
3498a	same, bklt pane of 4 .	4.00	....	....	....	9.00	....
3498b	same, bklt pane of 6 .	5.50	....	....	....	12.00	....
3499	55¢ LOVE, self-adhesive	2.50	5.00	35.00(20)	8.50	1.85	.65

3500   **3501**

2001 COMMEMORATIVES

Scott No.	Description	FDC Sing	Pl. Blk.	Mint Sheet	Plate Block	Unused F/NH	Used
3500/3548	(3500-01, 3503-04, 3507-19, 3521, 3523-33, 3536-40, 3545-48) 38 varieties.......	....	....	....	....	49.00	13.50
3500	34¢ Year of the Snake	2.25	4.75	25.00(20)	6.00	1.50	.35
3501	34¢ Roy Wilkins, self-adhesive.......	2.25	4.75	27.00(20)	6.50	1.50	.30

3502

AMERICAN ILLUSTRATORS

3502a	Marine Corps poster	3502k	"Galahad's Departure"
3502b	"Interlude (The Lute Players)"	3502l	"The First Lesson"
3502c	Advertisement for Arrow Collars and Shirts	3502m	Illustration for cover of McCall's
3502d	Advertisement for Carrier Corp. Refrigeration	3502n	"Back Home for Keeps"
3502e	Advertisement for Luxite Hosiery	3502o	"Something for Supper"
3502f	Illustration for correspondence school lesson	3502p	"A Dash for the Timber"
3502g	"Br'er Rabbit"	3502q	Illustration for "Moby Dick"
3502h	"An Attack on a Galleon"	3502r	"Captain Bill Bones"
3502i	Kewpie and Kewpie Doodle Dog	3502s	Illustration for The Saturday Evening Post
3502j	Illustration for cover of True Magazine	3502t	"The Girl He Left Behind"

SCOTT NO.	DESCRIPTION	FIRST DAY COVERS SING	PL. BLK.	MINT SHEET	PLATE BLOCK	UNUSED F/NH	USED

AMERICAN ILLUSTRATORS (Continued)

SCOTT NO.	DESCRIPTION	SING	PL. BLK.	MINT SHEET	PLATE BLOCK	UNUSED F/NH	USED
3502	34¢ American Illustrators, 20 varieties, attached, self-adhesive	....	....	28.00(20)	....	28.00	....
....	set of singles	37.50	....	....	....	....	15.00
3502v	same, uncut sheet of 80 (4 panes)	....	....	120.00(80)	....	120.00	....
....	cross gutter block of 20	....	....	....	....	60.00	....
....	block of 8 with horiz. gutter	....	....	....	....	40.00	....
....	block of 10 with vert. gutter	....	....	....	....	40.00	....
....	vert. pair with horiz. gutter	....	....	....	....	7.00	....
....	horiz. pair with vert. gutter	....	....	....	....	7.00	....

3503

3504

3503	34¢ Diabetes Awareness	2.25	4.75	22.00(20)	5.75	1.25	.30
3504	34¢ Nobel Prize Centenary	2.25	4.75	22.00(20)	5.75	1.25	.30

3505

3505	1¢-80¢ Pan-American Expo. Invert Souvenir Sheet of 7	10.00	....	....	....	12.00	8.00
....	same, uncut sheet of 28 (4 panes)	....	....	....	....	60.00	....

3506

GREAT PLAINS PRAIRIE

3506a	Pronghorns, Canada geese	3506f	Western Meadowlark, camel cricket, prairie coneflowers, prairie wild flowers
3506b	Burrowing owls, American buffalos		Badger, Harvester ants
3506c	American buffalo, Black-tailed prairie dogs, wild alfalfa	3506g	
		3506h	Eastern short-horned lizard, plains gopher
3506d	Black-tailed prairie dogs, American Buffalo	3506i	Plains spadefoot, dung beetle, prairie roses
3506e	Painted lady butterfly, American buffalo, prairie coneflowers, prairie wild roses	3506j	Two-striped grasshopper, Ord's kangaroo rat

3506	34¢ Great Plains Prairie, 10 varieties, attached, self-adhesive	....	....	15.00(10)	....	15.00	....
....	set of singles	19.50	....	....	....	....	7.00
3506v	same, uncut sheet of 60 (6 panes)	....	....	60.00(60)	....	60.00	....

3507

3509

3508

3507	34¢ Peanuts, self-adhesive	2.25	4.75	25.00(20)	6.50	1.50	.35
3508	34¢ US Veterans, self-adhesive	2.25	4.75	34.00(20)	7.00	1.85	.35
3509	34¢ Frida Kahlo	2.25	4.75	22.00(20)	5.50	1.25	.30

3510   **3511**

3512   **3513**

3514   **3515**

3516   **3517**

3518   **3519**

BASEBALL'S LEGENDARY PLAYING FIELDS

3510	Ebbets Field	3515	Forbes Field
3511	Tiger Stadium	3516	Fenway Park
3512	Crosley Field	3517	Comiskey Park
3513	Yankee Stadium	3518	Shibe Park
3514	Polo Grounds	3519	Wrigley Field

3510-19	34¢ Baseball's Legendary Playing Fields, 10 varieties, self-adhesive	7.25	....	25.00(20)	15.00(10)	14.00	12.00
....	set of singles	25.00	....	....	....	....	6.00
3510-19v	same, uncut sheet of 160 (8 panes)	....	....	160.00(160)	....	160.00	....
....	cross gutter block of 12	....	....	....	....	25.00	....
....	block of 10 with vert. gutter	....	....	....	....	15.00	....
....	block of 4 with horiz. gutter	....	....	....	....	7.50	....
....	vert. pair with horiz. gutter	....	....	....	....	3.50	....
....	horiz. pair with vert. gutter	....	....	....	....	3.50	....

SCOTT NO.	DESCRIPTION	FIRST DAY COVERS SING	PL. BLK.	MINT SHEET	PLATE BLOCK	UNUSED F/NH	USED

3520

3521

3522

SCOTT NO.	DESCRIPTION	SING	PL. BLK.	MINT SHEET	PLATE BLOCK	UNUSED F/NH	USED
3520	10¢ Atlas Statue, coil	2.25	....	....	4.00	.35	.25
	self-adhesive, die cut 8.5						
....	same, pl# strip of 5 . .	....	....	....	....	4.50	....
3521	34¢ Leonard Bernstein	2.25	4.75	20.00(20)	5.00	1.10	.40
3522	15¢ Woody Wagon,						
	self-adhesive coil	2.25	....	....	4.00	.50	.40
....	same, pl# strip of 5 . .	....	....	....	....	5.00	....

3523

SCOTT NO.	DESCRIPTION	SING	PL. BLK.	MINT SHEET	PLATE BLOCK	UNUSED F/NH	USED
3523	34¢ Lucille Ball,						
	self-adhesive	2.25	4.75	28.00(20)	6.50	1.50	35
3523v	same, uncut sheet of						
	180 (9 panes)	....	....	185.00(180)	....	185.00	....
....	cross gutter block of 8	....	....	....	....	30.00	....
....	block of 8 with vert. gutter	....	....	....	....	22.50	....
....	vert. pair with horiz. gutter	....	....	....	....	3.00	....
....	horiz. pair with vert. gutter	....	....	....	....	4.00	....

3524   **3525**

3526   **3527**

SCOTT NO.	DESCRIPTION	SING	PL. BLK.	MINT SHEET	PLATE BLOCK	UNUSED F/NH	USED
3524-27	34¢ Amish Quilts,						
	4 varieties attached . .	4.25	5.25	22.00(20)	5.50	5.00	4.00
3524	34¢ Diamond in the Square	2.25	....	....	....	1.30	.50
3525	34¢ Lone Star	2.25	....	....	....	1.30	.50
3526	34¢ Sunshine and Shadow	2.25	....	....	....	1.30	.50
3527	34¢ Double Ninepatch Variation	2.25	....	....	....	1.30	.50

| **3528** | **3529** | **3530** | **3531** |

SCOTT NO.	DESCRIPTION	SING	PL. BLK.	MINT SHEET	PLATE BLOCK	UNUSED F/NH	USED
3528-31	34¢ Carnivorous Plants,						
	4 varieties attached . .	4.25	5.25	23.00(20)	5.25	5.00	4.00
3528	34¢ Venus Flytrap . .	2.25	....	....	....	1.30	.40
3529	34¢ Yellow Trumpet . .	2.25	....	....	....	1.30	.40
3530	34¢ Cobra	2.25	....	....	....	1.30	.40
3531	34¢ English Sundew .	2.25	....	....	....	1.30	.40

| **3532** | **3533** | **3534, 3535** |

SCOTT NO.	DESCRIPTION	SING	PL. BLK.	MINT SHEET	PLATE BLOCK	UNUSED F/NH	USED
3532	34¢ "Eid Mubarak",						
	self-adhesive	2.25	4.75	21.00(20)	5.50	1.25	.30
3533	34¢ Enrico Fermi,						
	self-adhesive	2.25	4.75	22.00(20)	5.50	1.25	.30
3534	34¢ That's All Folks,						
	self-adhesive, pane of 10	12.50	....	....	....	18.00	....
3534a	same, single from pane	2.50	....	....	....	1.50	.30
3534b	same, pane of 9 (3534a)	....	....	....	....	12.00	....
3534c	same, pane of 1 (3534a)	7.25	....	....	....	3.25	....
....	same, top press sheet of						
	60 (6 panes) w/ pl# . .	....	....	80.00(60)	....	80.00	....
....	same, bottom press sheet						
	of 60 (6 panes) w/ pl#	....	....	95.00(60)	....	95.00	....
....	same, pane of 10 from						
	press sheet	....	....	....	....	15.00	....
....	same, pane of 10 w/						
	pl# on front.	....	....	....	....	70.00	....
....	vert. pair with horiz. gutter	....	....	....	....	4.00	....
....	horiz. pair with vert. gutter	....	....	....	....	7.50	....
3535	34¢ That's All Folks, die cut,						
	self-adhesive, pane of 10	15.00	....	....	....	85.00	....
3535a	same, single form pane	....	....	....	....	8.00	....
3535b	same, pane of 9 (3435a)	....	....	....	....	65.00	....
3535c	same, pane of 1, imperf.	12.50	....	....	....	25.00	....

3536

SCOTT NO.	DESCRIPTION	SING	PL. BLK.	MINT SHEET	PLATE BLOCK	UNUSED F/NH	USED
3536	34¢ Madonna and Child,						
	self-adhesive	2.25	....	....	....	1.30	.25
3536a	same, bklt pane of 20	14.50	....	....	....	25.00	....

| **3537, 3537a, 3541** | **3538, 3538a, 3542** | **3539, 3539a, 3543** | **3540, 3540a, 3544** |

SCOTT NO.	DESCRIPTION	SING	PL. BLK.	MINT SHEET	PLATE BLOCK	UNUSED F/NH	USED
3537-40	34¢ Santas, self-adhesive,						
	4 varieties attach, large date	4.25	5.25	30.00(20)	6.50	5.75	....
3537	34¢ Santa w/ horse, large date	2.25	....	....	....	1.40	.50
3538	34¢ Santa w/ horn, large date	2.25	....	....	....	1.40	.50
3539	34¢ Santa w/ drum, large date	2.25	....	....	....	1.40	.50
3540	34¢ Santa w/ dog, large date	2.25	....	....	....	1.40	.50

SCOTT NO.	DESCRIPTION	FIRST DAY COVERS SING	PL. BLK.	MINT SHEET	PLATE BLOCK	UNUSED F/NH	USED
3537a-40a	34¢ Santas, self-adhesive, 4 varieties attach, small date	4.25	5.25	....	....	5.75	4.50
3537a	34¢ Santa w/ horse, small date	2.25	....	....	....	1.30	.60
3538a	34¢ Santa w/ horn, small date	2.25	....	....	....	1.30	.60
3539a	34¢ Santa w/ drum, small date	2.25	....	....	....	1.30	.60
3540a	34¢ Santa w/ dog, small date	2.25	....	....	....	1.30	.60
3540d	same, bklt pane of 20, 3537a-40a x 5 + label	14.50				28.00	....
3537b-40e	34¢ Santas, self-adhesive, 4 varieties attach, large date	4.25	5.25	....	....	15.00	11.00
3537b	34¢ Santa w/ horse, large date	2.25	....	....	....	4.00	.75
3538b	34¢ Santa w/ horn, large date	2.25	....	....	....	4.00	.75
3539b	34¢ Santa w/ drum, large date	2.25	....	....	....	4.00	.75
3540e	34¢ Santa w/ dog, large date	2.25	....	....	....	4.00	.75
3540g	same, bklt pane of 20, 3537b-40e x 5 + label	14.50				65.00	....
3541-44	34¢ Santas, self-adhesive, 4 varieties attach, green denom.	4.25	....	....	....	7.50	....
3541	34¢ Santa w/ horse, green denom	2.25				1.85	.50
3542	34¢ Santa w/ horn, green denom	2.25				1.85	.50
3543	34¢ Santa w/ drum, green denom	2.25				1.85	.50
3544	34¢ Santa w/ dog, green denom	2.25				1.85	.50
3544b	same, bklt pane of 4 (3541-3544)	4.00				8.00	....
3544c	same, bklt pane of 6 (3543-44, 3541-42 x 2)	5.50	....			12.00	....
3544d	same, bklt pane of 6 (3541-42, 3543-44 x 2)	5.50	....			12.00	....

3545

3545	34¢ James Madison .	2.25	4.75	25.00(20)	6.00	1.25	.30
3545v	same, uncut sheet of 120 (6 panes)	....	....	150.00(120)	....	150.00	....
....	cross gutter block of 4	....		....	....	11.00	....
....	horiz. pair with vert. gutter	....				4.50	....
....	vert. pair with horiz. gutter	....				3.50	....

3546

3547

3548

3546	34¢ We Give Thanks, self-adhesive	2.25	4.75	20.00(20)	5.00	1.10	.35
3547	34¢ Hanukkah, self-adhesive	2.25	4.75	22.00(20)	5.50	1.25	.30
3548	34¢ Kwanzaa, self-adhesive	2.25	4.75	22.00(20)	5.50	1.25	.30

3549, 3549B, 3550, 3550A

3551

3549	34¢ United We Stand, self-adhesive	2.25	....	....	....	1.75	.30
3549a	same, bklt pane of 20	14.50	....	....	....	36.00	....
3549B	34¢ United We Stand, die cut 10.5 x 10.75 on 2 or 3 sides	2.25				1.90	.30
3549Bc	same, bklt pane of 4 .	4.00				7.50	....
3549Bd	same, bklt pane of 6 .	5.50				11.00	....
3549Be	same, bklt pane of 20 (double-sided)	....				38.00	....
3550	34¢ United We Stand, self-adhesive coil (square corners)	2.25				1.40	.30
....	same, pl# strip of 5 . .	....				12.00	
3550A	34¢ United We Stand, self-adhesive coil, (round corners)	2.25				1.40	.40
....	same, pl# strip of 5 . .	....				12.00	
3551	57¢ Love, self-adhesive	2.50	5.00	32.00(20)	8.00	1.75	.50

3554　　　　**3555**

3552　　　　**3553**

2002 COMMEMORATIVES

3552/3695	(3552-60, 3650-56, 3659-74, 3676-79, 3692, 3695) 38 varieties	....	....	....	....	55.00	12.50
3552-55	34¢ Winter Olympics, self-adhesive, 4 varieties attached.	4.25	5.25	28.00(20)	7.00	6.00	4.00
3552	34¢ Ski Jumping	2.25				1.60	.40
3553	34¢ Snowboarding. . .	2.25				1.60	.40
3554	34¢ Ice Hockey	2.25				1.60	.40
3555	34¢ Figure Skating . .	2.25				1.60	.40
3552-55v	same, uncut sheet of 180 (9 panes)	....		185.00(180)		185.00	....
....	cross gutter block of 8	....				25.00	....
....	block of 4 with vert. gutter	....				8.00	....
....	block of 8 with horiz. gutter	....				11.50	....
....	vert. pair with horiz. gutter	....				3.00	....
....	horiz. pair with vert. gutter	....				2.00	....

3556　　　　**3557**　　　　**3558**

3556	34¢ Mentoring a Child, self-adhesive	2.25	4.75	22.00(20)	5.50	1.20	.30
3557	34¢ Langston Hughes, self-adhesive	2.25	4.75	25.00(20)	6.50	1.50	.30
3558	34¢ Happy Birthday, self-adhesive	2.25	4.75	20.00(20)	5.00	1.20	.30

3559

3560

3559	34¢ Year of the Horse, self-adhesive	2.25	4.75	27.00(20)	7.00	1.50	.30
3560	34¢ Military Academy Bicentennial, self-adhesive	2.25	4.75	20.00(20)	5.00	1.00	.30

H.E. Harris & Co.®
Serving the Collector Since 1916

SCOTT NO.	DESCRIPTION	FIRST DAY COVERS SING	PL. BLK.	MINT SHEET	PLATE BLOCK	UNUSED F/NH	USED

3561   3610

GREETINGS FROM AMERICA

3561	Alabama	3578	Louisiana	3595	Ohio
3562	Alaska	3579	Maine	3596	Oklahoma
3563	Arizona	3580	Maryland	3597	Oregon
3564	Arkansas	3581	Massachusetts	3598	Pennsylvania
3565	California	3582	Michigan	3599	Rhode Island
3566	Colorado	3583	Minnesota	3600	South Carolina
3567	Connecticut	3584	Mississippi	3601	South Dakota
3568	Delaware	3585	Missouri	3602	Tennessee
3569	Florida	3586	Montana	3603	Texas
3570	Georgia	3587	Nebraska	3604	Utah
3571	Hawaii	3588	Nevada	3605	Vermont
3572	Idaho	3589	New Hampshire	3606	Virginia
3573	Illinois	3590	New Jersey	3607	Washington
3574	Indiana	3591	New Mexico	3608	West Virginia
3575	Iowa	3592	New York	3609	Wisconsin
3576	Kansas	3593	North Carolina	3610	Wyoming
3577	Kentucky	3594	North Dakota		

SCOTT NO.	DESCRIPTION	SING	PL. BLK.	MINT SHEET	PLATE BLOCK	UNUSED F/NH	USED
3561-3610	34¢ Greetings from America, self-adhesive, 50 varieties attached. .	....	....	60.00(50)	....	60.00	....
....	set of singles.	120.00	....	....	....	....	45.00
	singles each			....	....	....	1.00

LONGLEAF PINE FOREST

3611

LONGLEAF PINE FOREST

3611a	Bachman's sparrow
3611b	Northern bobwhite, yellow pitcher plants
3611c	Fox squirrel, red-bellied woodpecker
3611d	Brown-headed nuthatch
3611e	Broadhead skink, yellow pitcher plants, pipeworts
3611f	Eastern towhee, yellow pitcher plants, meadow beauties, toothache grass
3611g	Gray Fox, gopher tortoise
3611h	Blind click beetle, sweetbay, pine woods freefrog
3611i	Rosebuds orchid, pipeworts, southern toad, yellow pitcher plants
3611j	Grass-pink orchid, yellow-sided skimmer, pipeworts

SCOTT NO.	DESCRIPTION	SING	PL. BLK.	MINT SHEET	PLATE BLOCK	UNUSED F/NH	USED
3611	34¢ Longleaf Pine Forest, 10 varieties, attached, self-adhesive	....	....	25.00(10)	....	25.00	....
....	set of singles	25.00	....	....	....	....	10.00
3611v	same, uncut sheet of 90 (9 panes)	....	....	100.00(90)	....	100.00	....

3612   3613, 3614, 3615   3616, 3617, 3618, 3619   3620, 3621, 3622, 3623, 3624, 3625

SCOTT NO.	DESCRIPTION	SING	PL. BLK.	MINT SHEET	PLATE BLOCK	UNUSED F/NH	USED
3612	5¢ Toleware coffee pot, coil.	2.25	....	....	....	.25	.25
....	same, pl# strip of 5 . .	....	....	....	....	2.50	....
3613	3¢ Lithographed Star (year at LL)	2.25	4.75	6.00(50)	1.20	.25	.25
3614	3¢ Photogravure Star (year of LR)	2.25	4.75	6.00(50)	1.20	.25	.25
3615	3¢ Star, coil	2.25	....	....	....	.25	.25
....	same, pl# strip of 5 . .	....	....	....	....	2.00	....
3616	23¢ George Washington .	2.25	4.75	150.00(100)	38.00	1.10	.45

SCOTT NO.	DESCRIPTION	SING	PL. BLK.	MINT SHEET	PLATE BLOCK	UNUSED F/NH	USED
3617	23¢ George Washington, self-adhesive coil. . . .	2.25	....	....	....	.75	.40
....	same pl# strip of 5. . .	....	....	....	....	5.50	....
3618	23¢ George Washington, self-adhesive die cut 11.25	2.25	....	....	....	.95	.45
3618a	same, bklt pane of 4 .	3.00	....	....	....	4.00	....
3618b	same, bklt pane of 6 .	4.00	....	....	....	6.00	....
3618c	same, bklt pane of 10	6.75	....	....	....	8.00	....
3619	23¢ George Washington, self-adhesive, die cut 10.5 x 11.25	1.95	....	....	....	6.00	2.75
3619a	same, bklt pane of 4 (3619 x 2 at L, 3618 x 2 at R).		....	....	....	13.00	....
3619b	same, bklt pane of 6 (3619 x 3 at L, 3618 x 3 at R).		....	....	....	21.00	....
3619c	same, bklt pane of 4 (3618 x 2 at L, 3619 x 2 at R).		....	....	....	14.00	....
3619d	same, bklt pane of 6 (3618 x 3 at L, 3619 x 3 at R)		....	....	....	21.00	....
3619e	same, bklt pane of 10 (3619 x 5 at L, 3618 x 5 at R).		....	....	....	30.00	....
3619f	same, bklt pane of 10 (3618 x 5 at L, 3619 at R)		....	....	....	30.00	....
3619g	same, pair (3619 at L, 3618 at R)		....	....	....	6.50	....
3619h	same, pair (3618 at L, 3619 at R)		....	....	....	6.50	....
3620	(37¢) Flag	2.25	4.75	155.00(100)	23.00	1.40	1.00
3621	(37¢) Flag, self-adhesive	2.25	4.75	30.00(20)	8.00	1.55	.35
3622	(37¢) Flag, self-adhesive coil	2.25	....	....	....	1.50	.25
....	same, pl# strip of 5 . .	....	....	....	....	11.00	....
3623	(37¢) Flag, self-adhesive, die cut 11.25	2.25	....	....	....	1.25	.25
3623a	same, bklt pane of 20	....	....	....	....	24.00	....
3624	(37¢) Flag, self-adhesive, die cut 10.5 x 10.75 . .	2.25	....	....	....	1.75	.65
3624a	same, bklt pane of 4 .	4.00	....	....	....	5.75	....
3624b	same, bklt pane of 6 .	5.50	....	....	....	8.50	....
3624c	same, bklt pane of 20	15.00	....	....	....	33.00	....
3625	(37¢) Flag, self-adhesive, die cut 8.	2.25	....	....	....	1.60	.45
3625a	same, ATM bklt pane of 18	15.00	....	....	....	32.00	....

3626   3627   3628   3629

SCOTT NO.	DESCRIPTION	SING	PL. BLK.	MINT SHEET	PLATE BLOCK	UNUSED F/NH	USED
3626	(37¢) Toy mail wagon, self-adhesive	2.25	....	....	....	1.40	.40
3627	(37¢) Toy locomotive, self-adhesive	2.25	....	....	....	1.40	.40
3628	(37¢) Toy taxicab, self-adhesive	2.25	....	....	....	1.40	.40
3629	(37¢) Toy fire pumper, self-adhesive	2.25	....	....	....	1.40	.40
3626-29	(37¢) Antique Toys, self-adhesive, 4 varieties attached . .	4.25	....	....	....	6.00	4.50
3629b	same, bklt pane of 4 (3626-29 x 1)	4.25	....	....	....	6.00	....
3629c	same, bklt pane of 6 (3627, 3629, 3626 x 2, 3628 x 2)	5.50	....	....	....	9.50	....
3629d	same, bklt pane of 6 . (3626, 3628, 3627 x 2, 3629 x 2)	5.50	....	....	....	9.50	....
3629e	same, bklt pane of 20	15.00	....	....	....	25.00	....
3629F	37¢ Flag.	2.25	4.75	135.00(100)	26.00	1.50	1.00

3629F, 3630, 3631, 3632, 3632A, 3632C, 3633, 3633A, 3633B, 3635, 3636, 3636D, 3637

SCOTT NO.	DESCRIPTION	SING	PL. BLK.	MINT SHEET	PLATE BLOCK	UNUSED F/NH	USED
3630	37¢ Flag, self-adhesive	2.25	4.75	24.00(20)	8.00	1.20	.30
3631	37¢ Flag, coil	2.25	....	....	....	1.50	.30
....	same, pl# strip of 5 . .	....	....	....	....	12.00	....
3632	37¢ Flag, self-adhesive coil, die cut 10 vert.	2.25	....	....	....	1.25	.30
....	same, pl# strip of 5 . .	....	....	....	....	10.00	....
3632A	37¢ Flag coil, die cut 10, flag lacking star point.	2.25	....	....	....	1.25	.55
....	same, pl# strip of 5 . .	....	....	....	....	10.00	....
3632C	37¢ Flag, self-adhesive coil, die cut 11.75 (2004) . .	2.25	....	....	....	1.25	.80
....	same, pl# strip of 5 . .	....	....	....	....	10.00	....
3633	37¢ Flag, self-adhesive coil, die cut 8.5 vert.	2.25	....	....	....	1.25	.60
....	same, pl# strip of 5 . .	....	....	....	....	10.00	....

SCOTT NO.	DESCRIPTION	FIRST DAY COVERS SING	PL. BLK.	MINT SHEET	PLATE BLOCK	UNUSED F/NH	USED
3633A	37¢ Flag coil, die cut 8.5, right angel corners. . .	1.95	....	....	....	3.00	1.00
....	same, pl# strip of 5 . .					20.00	....
3633B	37¢ Flag coil, die cut 9.5 (dated 2005)	2.25	....	....	....	10.00	.75
....	same, plt. strip of 5 . .					53.00	....
3634	37¢ Flag, self-adhesive, die cut 11	2.25	....	....	....	1.50	1.20
3634a	same, bklt pane of 10					16.00	....
3634b	same, self-adhesive, bklt single, dated 2003 . . .	2.25				1.60	1.20
3634c	same, bklt pane of 4 (3634b)	4.25				6.00	....
3634d	same, bklt pane of 6 (3634b)	5.50				9.00	....
3634e	same, die cut 11.3 . . .					1.35	.35
3634f	same, bklt pane of 10 of 3634e.					9.00	
3635	37¢ Flag, self-adhesive, die cut 11.25	2.25				1.25	.50
3635a	same, bklt pane of 20	....				25.00	....
3636	37¢ Flag, self-adhesive, die cut 10.5 x 10.75. .	2.25				3.00	.60
3636a	same, bklt pane of 4 .					4.00	....
3636b	same, bklt pan of 6 . .					5.00	....
3636c	same, bklt pane of 20					28.00	....
3636D	37¢ Flag, die cut 11.25 x 11, self-adhesive	2.25				1.85	.85
3636De	same, bklt pane of 20	....				37.00	....
3637	37¢ Flag, self-adhesive, die cut 8	2.25				1.50	.85
3637a	same, ATM bklt pane of 18	15.00				28.00	....
3638	37¢ Toy locomotive, self-adhesive coil, die cut 8.5 horiz.	2.25				1.75	.50
3639	37¢ Toy mail wagon, self-adhesive coil, die cut 8.5 horiz.	2.25				1.75	.50
3640	37¢ Toy fire pumper, self-adhesive coil, die cut 8.5 horiz.	2.25				1.75	.50
3641	37¢ Toy taxicab, self-adhesive coil, die cut 8.5 horiz.	2.25				1.75	.50
3638-41	37¢ Antique Toys, self-adhesive coil, strip of 4.	4.25				6.50	5.00
....	same, pl# strip of 5 . .	....	....	....		15.50	....
3642	37¢ Toy mail wagon, self-adhesive, die cut 11	2.25				1.50	.50
3642a	same, die cut 11x11.25, 2003	2.25				1.50	.50
3643	37¢ Toy locomotive, self-adhesive, die cut 11	2.25				1.50	.50
3643a	same, die cut 11x11.25, 2003	2.25				1.50	.50
3644	37¢ Toy taxicab, self-adhesive, die cut 11	2.25				1.50	.50
3644a	same, die cut 11x11.25, 2003	2.25				1.50	.50
3645	37¢ Toy fire pumper, self-adhesive, die cut 11	2.25				1.50	.50
3645f	same, die cut 11x11.25, 2003	2.25				1.50	.50
3642-45	37¢ Antique Toys, self-adhesive, 4 varieties attach.	4.25				6.00	4.00
3645b	same, bklt pane of 4 (3642-45 x 1)	4.25				9.00	....
3645c	same, bklt pane of 6 (3643, 3645, 3642 x 2, 3644 x 2)	5.50				8.00	
3645d	same, bklt pane of 6 (3642, 3644, 3642 x 2, 3645 x 2)	5.50				8.00	
3645e	same, bklt pane of 20	15.00				26.00	....
3645g	37¢ Antique Toys, self-adhesive, blk of 4 (3642a, 3643a, 3644a, 3645f)	4.25				6.00	
3645h	same, bklt pane of 20	15.00	....	....		32.00	

3649

3649	37¢ Masters of American Photography, self-adhesive, 20 varieties attached .	....	....	30.00(20)	....	30.00	....
....	same, set of singles. .	50.00	....	....		....	17.00

3650

3652

3651

3650	37¢ John James Audubon, self-adhesive	2.25	4.75	28.00(20)	6.50	1.75	.30
3651	37¢ Harry Houdini, self-adhesive	2.25	4.75	26.00(20)	6.00	1.50	.30
3652	37¢ Andy Warhol, self-adhesive	2.25	4.75	29.00(20)	7.00	1.50	.30

3653

3654

3655   **3656**

3653-56	37¢ Teddy Bears, self-adhesive, 4 varieties attached.	5.00	6.00	30.00(20)	6.75	6.00	5.00
3653	37¢ Bruin Teddy Bear	2.25	....	....		1.75	.50
3654	37¢ Stick Teddy Bear	2.25	....	....		1.75	.50
3655	37¢ Gund Teddy Bear	2.25	....	....		1.75	.50
3656	37¢ Ideal Teddy Bear.	2.25	....	....		1.75	.50

3646

3648

3647

3646	60¢ Coverlet Eagle, self-adhesive	2.75	5.50	35.00(20)	8.00	2.00	.50
3647	$3.85 Jefferson Memorial, self-adhesive	8.75	35.00	230.00(20)	52.00	13.00	7.75
3647A	same, die cut 11x10.75, dated 2003.	8.75	35.00	235.00(20)	54.00	14.00	8.75
3648	$13.65 Capitol Dome, self-adhesive	35.00	105.00	775.00(20)	175.00	44.00	12.00

MASTERS OF AMERICAN PHOTOGRAPHY

3649a	*Albert Sands Southworth & Josiah Johnson Hawes*	**3649k**	*James VanDerZee*
3649b	*Timothy H. O'Sullivan*	**3649l**	*Dorothea Lange*
3649c	*Carleton E. Watkins*	**3649m**	*Walker Evans*
3649d	*Getrude Kasebier*	**3649n**	*Eugene Smith*
3649e	*Lewis W. Hine*	**3649o**	*Paul Strand*
3649f	*Alvin Langdon Coburn*	**3649p**	*Ansel Adams*
3649g	*Edward Steichen*	**3649q**	*Imogen Cunningham*
3649h	*Alfred Steiglitz*	**3649r**	*Andre Kertesz*
3649i	*Man Ray*	**3649s**	*Garry Winogrand*
3649j	*Edward Weston*	**3649t**	*Minor White*

3657

3658

3659

3657	37¢ Love, self-adhesive	2.25				1.25	.35
....	same, bklt pane of 20	15.00	....	....		22.00	....
3658	60¢ Love, self-adhesive	2.75	5.50	35.00(20)	9.00	2.20	.75
3659	37¢ Ogden Nash, self-adhesive	2.25	4.75	22.50(20)	5.50	1.40	.35

3661   **3662**

3663   **3664**

3660

3672   **3673**   **3674**

SCOTT NO.	DESCRIPTION	FIRST DAY COVERS SING	PL. BLK.	MINT SHEET	PLATE BLOCK	UNUSED F/NH	USED
3660	37¢ Duke Kahanamoku, self-adhesive	2.25	4.75	22.00(20)	5.50	1.25	.35
3661-64	37¢ American Bats, self-adhesive, 4 varieties attached.	4.25	4.75	28.50(20)	7.25	7.00	4.00
3661	37¢ Red Bat.	2.25	. . . .	. . . .	. . . .	1.75	.45
3662	37¢ Leaf-nosed Bat . .	2.25	. . . .	. . . .	. . . .	1.75	.45
3663	37¢ Pallid Bat	2.25	. . . .	. . . .	. . . .	1.75	.45
3664	37¢ Spotted Bat.	2.25	. . . .	. . . .	. . . .	1.75	.45

SCOTT NO.	DESCRIPTION	FIRST DAY COVERS SING	PL. BLK.	MINT SHEET	PLATE BLOCK	UNUSED F/NH	USED
3672	37¢ Hanukkah, self-adhesive	2.25	4.75	25.00(20)	6.00	1.30	.40
3673	37¢ Kwanzaa, self-adhesive	2.25	4.75	21.00(20)	5.50	1.20	.40
3674	37¢ EID, self-adhesive	2.25	4.75	21.00(20)	5.50	1.20	.40

3675

SCOTT NO.	DESCRIPTION	FIRST DAY COVERS SING	PL. BLK.	MINT SHEET	PLATE BLOCK	UNUSED F/NH	USED
3675	37¢ Madonna & Child, self-adhesive	2.25	4.75	. . . .	. . . .	1.50	.30
	same, bklt pane of 20	15.00	. . . .	. . . .	. . . .	27.00	

3665   **3666**

3667   **3668**

3676, 3683, 3684, 3688   **3677, 3680, 3685, 3689**   **3678, 3681, 3686, 3690**   **3679, 3682, 3687, 3691**

SCOTT NO.	DESCRIPTION	FIRST DAY COVERS SING	PL. BLK.	MINT SHEET	PLATE BLOCK	UNUSED F/NH	USED
3665-68	37¢ Women In Journalism, self-adhesive, 4 varieties attached.	6.00	7.00	37.00(20)	9.00	8.00	5.00
3665	37¢ Nellie Bly.	2.25	. . . .	. . . .	. . . .	2.00	.50
3666	37¢ Ida M. Tarbel. . . .	2.25	. . . .	. . . .	. . . .	2.00	.50
3667	37¢ Ethel L. Payne . .	2.25	. . . .	. . . .	. . . .	2.00	.50
3668	37¢ Marguerite Higgins	2.25	. . . .	. . . .	. . . .	2.00	.50

3669

SCOTT NO.	DESCRIPTION	FIRST DAY COVERS SING	PL. BLK.	MINT SHEET	PLATE BLOCK	UNUSED F/NH	USED
3669	37¢ Irving Berlin, self-adhesive	2.25	4.75	25.00(20)	6.00	1.25	.30

SCOTT NO.	DESCRIPTION	FIRST DAY COVERS SING	PL. BLK.	MINT SHEET	PLATE BLOCK	UNUSED F/NH	USED
3676-79	37¢ Snowmen, self-adhesive, 4 varieties attached . .	6.00	7.00	32.00(20)	8.50	8.00	4.75
3676	37¢ Snowman with red and green scarf	2.25	. . . .	. . . .	. . . .	2.00	1.25
3677	37¢ Snowman with blue scarf.	2.25	. . . .	. . . .	. . . .	2.00	1.25
3578	37¢ Snowman with pipe	2.25	. . . .	. . . .	. . . .	2.00	1.25
3679	37¢ Snowman with top hat	2.25	. . . .	. . . .	. . . .	2.00	1.25
3680	37¢ Snowman with blue scarf, self-adhesive coil	2.25	. . . .	. . . .	. . . .	2.50	.75
3681	37¢ Snowman with pipe, self-adhesive coil. . . .	2.25	. . . .	. . . .	. . . .	2.50	.75
3682	37¢ Snowman with top hat, self-adhesive coil. . . .	2.25	. . . .	. . . .	. . . .	2.50	.75
3683	37¢ Snowman with red and green scarf, self-adhesive coil	2.25	. . . .	. . . .	. . . .	2.50	.75
3680-83	37¢ Snowmen, self-adhesive coil, strip of 4	4.25	. . . .	. . . .	. . . .	12.00	. . . .
	same, pl# strip of 5 . .	. . . .	. . . .	. . . .	. . . .	21.00	. . . .
3684	37¢ Snowman with red and green scarf, large design	2.25	. . . .	. . . .	. . . .	1.75	.50
3685	37¢ Snowman with blue scarf, large design. . .	2.25	. . . .	. . . .	. . . .	1.75	.50
3686	37¢ Snowman with pipe, large design.	2.25	. . . .	. . . .	. . . .	1.75	.50
3687	37¢ Snowman with top hat, large design.	2.25	. . . .	. . . .	. . . .	1.75	.50
3684-87	37¢ Snowman, self-adhesive, 4 varieties attached . .	4.25	. . . .	. . . .	. . . .	7.00	4.75
3687b	same, bklt pane of 20 (3684-87 x 5 + label) .	15.00	. . . .	. . . .	. . . .	36.00	. . . .
3688	37¢ Snowman with red and green scarf, small design	2.25	. . . .	. . . .	. . . .	2.25	.75
3689	37¢ Snowman with blue scarf, small design. . .	2.25	. . . .	. . . .	. . . .	2.25	.75
3690	37¢ Snowman with pipe, small design.	2.25	. . . .	. . . .	. . . .	2.25	.75
3691	37¢ Snowman with top hat, small design.	2.25	. . . .	. . . .	. . . .	2.25	.75
3688-91	37¢ Snowmen , self-adhesive, 4 varieties attached . .	4.25	. . . .	. . . .	. . . .	10.00	6.25
3691b	same, bklt pane of 4, (3688-91).	4.25	. . . .	. . . .	. . . .	10.00	. . . .
3691c	same, bklt pane of 6 (3690-91, 3688-89 x 2)	5.50	. . . .	. . . .	. . . .	15.00	. . . .
3691d	same, bklt pane of 6 (3688-89, 3690-91 x 2)	5.50	. . . .	. . . .	. . . .	15.00	. . . .

3670   **3671**

SCOTT NO.	DESCRIPTION	FIRST DAY COVERS SING	PL. BLK.	MINT SHEET	PLATE BLOCK	UNUSED F/NH	USED
3670-71	37¢ Neuter and Spay, self-adhesive, 2 varieties attached.	4.00	4.75	25.00(20)	6.00	3.50	2.00
3670	37¢ Kitten	2.25	. . . .	. . . .	. . . .	2.00	.40
3671	37¢ Puppy	2.25	. . . .	. . . .	. . . .	2.00	.40

3693, 3775, 3785   **3692**   **3695**

SCOTT NO.	DESCRIPTION	FIRST DAY COVERS SING	PL. BLK.	MINT SHEET	PLATE BLOCK	UNUSED F/NH	USED
3692	37¢ Cary Grant, self-adhesive	2.25	4.75	30.00(20)	7.00	1.50	.40
3693	(5¢) Sea Coast coil, self-adhesive	2.25	....	....	....	.25	.20
....	same, pl# strip of 5	....	....	....	....	2.50	....

3694

SCOTT NO.	DESCRIPTION	FIRST DAY COVERS SING	PL. BLK.	MINT SHEET	PLATE BLOCK	UNUSED F/NH	USED
3694	37¢ Hawaiian Missionary, souvenir sheet of 4	5.00	....	....	....	8.00	6.00
3694a	37¢ Hawaii 2¢ of 1851	2.25				2.00	1.00
3694b	37¢ Hawaii 5¢ of 1851	2.25				2.00	1.00
3694c	37¢ Hawaii 13¢ of 1851	2.25				2.00	1.00
3694d	37¢ Hawaii 13¢ of 1852	2.25				2.00	1.00
3695	37¢ Happy Birthday, self-adhesive	2.25	4.75	25.00(20)	6.00	1.20	.30

3696   **3745**

GREETINGS FROM AMERICA

3696	*Alabama*	3713	*Louisiana*	3730	*Ohio*
3697	*Alaska*	3714	*Maine*	3731	*Oklahoma*
3698	*Arizona*	3715	*Maryland*	3732	*Oregon*
3699	*Arkansas*	3716	*Massachusetts*	3733	*Pennsylvania*
3700	*California*	3717	*Michigan*	3734	*Rhode Island*
3701	*Colorado*	3718	*Minnesota*	3735	*South Carolina*
3702	*Connecticut*	3719	*Mississippi*	3736	*South Dakota*
3703	*Delaware*	3720	*Missouri*	3737	*Tennessee*
3704	*Florida*	3721	*Montana*	3738	*Texas*
3705	*Georgia*	3722	*Nebraska*	3739	*Utah*
3706	*Hawaii*	3723	*Nevada*	3740	*Vermont*
3707	*Idaho*	3724	*New Hampshire*	3741	*Virginia*
3708	*Illinois*	3725	*New Jersey*	3742	*Washington*
3709	*Indiana*	3726	*New Mexico*	3743	*West Virginia*
3710	*Iowa*	3727	*New York*	3744	*Wisconsin*
3711	*Kansas*	3728	*North Carolina*	3745	*Wyoming*
3712	*Kentucky*	3729	*North Dakota*		

SCOTT NO.	DESCRIPTION	FIRST DAY COVERS SING	PL. BLK.	MINT SHEET	PLATE BLOCK	UNUSED F/NH	USED
3696-3745	37¢ Greetings from America, self-adhesive, 50 varieties attached	....	....	60.00(50)	....	60.00	....
	set of singles	120.00	....	....	....	....	35.00
	singles each	....	....	....	....	....	.85

3746   **3747**   **3748**

2003 COMMEMORATIVES

SCOTT NO.	DESCRIPTION	FIRST DAY COVERS SING	PL. BLK.	MINT SHEET	PLATE BLOCK	UNUSED F/NH	USED
3746/3824	(3746-48, 3771, 3773-74, 3781-82, 3786-91, 3803, 3808-18, 3821-24) 30 varieties	....	....	....	....	45.00	10.50
3746	37¢ Thurgood Marshall, self-adhesive	2.25	4.75	28.00(20)	7.00	1.50	.30
3747	37¢ Year of the Ram, self-adhesive	2.25	4.75	25.00(20)	6.00	1.50	.30
3748	37¢ Zora Neale Hurston, self-adhesive	2.25	4.75	30.00(20)	7.50	2.00	.30

3749, 3749a, 3758, 3758a   **3750, 3751, 3752, 3753, 3758b**   **3754, 3759**   **3755, 3761**   **3756**   **3757, 3762**

AMERICAN DESIGN SERIES

SCOTT NO.	DESCRIPTION	FIRST DAY COVERS SING	PL. BLK.	MINT SHEET	PLATE BLOCK	UNUSED F/NH	USED
3749	1¢ Tiffany Lamp, self-adhesive (2007)	2.25	4.75	3.00(20)	.95	.25	.25
3749a	1¢ Tiffany Lamp	2.95	5.75	4.25(20)	1.00	.25	.25
3750	2¢ Navajo Necklace, self-adhesive	2.25	4.75	5.00(20)	.90	.25	.25
3751	same, self-adhesvie, die cut 11.25 X 11.5	2.25	4.75	8.00(20)	1.75	.40	.25
3752	same, w/ USPS micro-printing, self-adhesive, die cut 11.25 X 11	2.25	4.75	7.00(20)	1.75	.30	.25
3753	same, die cut 11.5 X 11, (2007 date)	2.25	4.75	6.00(20)	1.25	.30	.25
3754	3¢ Silver Coffeepot, self-adhesive (2007)	2.25	4.75	4.50(20)	1.25	.25	.25
3755	4¢ Chippendale Chair, self-adhesive (2004)	2.25	4.75	5.50(20)	1.20	.25	.25
3756	5¢ Toleware, self-adhesive	2.25	4.75	6.00(20)	1.40	.35	.25
3756a	5¢ Toleware, 11.25x10.75 (dated 2007)	2.25	4.75	6.00(20)	1.40	.35	.35
3757	10¢ American Clock, self-adhesive	2.25	4.75	7.00(20)	1.50	.35	.25
3758	1¢ Tiffany Lamp, coil (2003)	2.25	....	....	....	.25	.25
....	same, pl# strip of 5	....	....	....	....	2.25	....
3758a	1¢ Tiffany Lamp, coil (2008) perf 10	2.25	....	....	....	.25	.25
....	same, pl# strip of 5	....	....	....	....	2.25	....
3758b	2¢ Navajo Necklace Perf 9.75 vert. (2011)	....	....	....	3.75	.25	....
....	same, plate number strip of 5	....	....	....	....	2.25	....
3759	3¢ Silver Coffeepot, coil	2.25	....	....	....	.25	.25
....	same, pl# strip of 5	....	....	....	....	8.00	....
3761	4¢ Chippendale Chair, coil (2007)	2.25	....	....	....	.25	.25
....	same, pl# strip of 5	....	....	....	....	3.00	.25
3761A	4¢ Chippendale Chair, Chair Coil (ap) (2013 Date)	2.75	....	....	....	.30	.25
....	Same, Plate # strip of 5	....	....	....	....	1.5	....
3762	10¢ American Clock, coil	2.25	....	....	....	.30	.25
....	same, pl# strip of 5	....	....	....	....	3.00	.25
3763	10¢ American Clock (2003)	....	....	....	....	.30	.25
....	same, plate strip of 5.	....	....	....	....	4.00	....
3763A	10¢ American Clock Coil (untagged) (2008 Date)	....	....	....	....	.30	.25
....	Same, Plate # strip of 5	....	....	....	....	4	....

3766   **3769**   **3770**   **3771**

SCOTT NO.	DESCRIPTION	FIRST DAY COVERS SING	PL. BLK.	MINT SHEET	PLATE BLOCK	UNUSED F/NH	USED
3766	$1 Wisdom, self-adhesive	3.50	7.50	61.00(20)	14.50	3.25	.70
3766a	$1 Wisdom, (2008) die cut 11.25x11	3.50	7.50	60.00(20)	13.50	3.00	.70
3769	(10¢) New York Library Lion, perf. 10 vert.	2.25	....	....	4.00(3)	.30	.20
....	same, pl# strip of 5	....	....	....	....	6.00	....
3770	(10¢) Atlas Statue, self-adhesive coil, die cut 11 dated 2003	2.25	....	....	....	.30	.25
....	same, pl# strip of 5	....	....	....	....	6.00	....
3771	80¢ Special Olympics, self-adhesive	3.00	7.00	45.00(20)	12.00	2.50	1.00

SCOTT NO.	DESCRIPTION	FIRST DAY COVERS SING	PL. BLK.	MINT SHEET	PLATE BLOCK	UNUSED F/NH	USED

ART OF THE AMERICAN INDIAN

3873

ART OF THE AMERICAN INDIAN

3873a	Mimbres bowl	3873f	Mississippian dffigy
3873b	Kutenai parfleche	3873g	Acoma pot
3873c	Tlingit sculptures	3873h	Navajo weaving
3873d	Ho-Chunk bag	3873i	Seneca carving
3873e	Seminole doll	3873j	Luiseno basket

SCOTT NO.	DESCRIPTION	SING	PL. BLK.	MINT SHEET	PLATE BLOCK	UNUSED F/NH	USED
3873	37¢ Art of the American Indian, 10 varieties attached			28.00(10)		28.00	
....	set of singles	25.00					8.00
3874	(5¢) Sea Coast, coil, perf. 10 vert., self-adhesive	2.25				.55	.30
....	same, pl# strip of 5					4.75	
3874a	(5¢) Sea Coast with small date, coil, die cut 10 vert., self-adhesive	2.25				.45	.30
....	same, pl# strip of 5					3.50	
3875	(5¢) Sea Coast, coil, perf. 11.5 vert., self-adhesive	2.25				.45	.30
....	same, pl# strip of 5					3.50	

3876

3877

3876	37¢ John Wayne	2.25	4.75	31.00(20)	6.50	1.50	.40
....	same, uncut sheet of 120			120.00(20)		120.00	
....	cross gutter block of 8					21.00	
....	block of 8 with vert. gutter					13.50	
....	horizontal pair with vertical gutter					4.00	
....	vertical pair with horizontal gutter					3.00	
3877	37¢ Sickle Cell Disease Awareness	2.25	4.75	22.00(20)	5.50	1.20	.40

CLOUDSCAPES

3878

CLOUDSCAPES

3878a	Cirrus radiatus	3878i	Altocumulus castellanus
3878b	Cirrostratus fibratus	3878j	Alotcumulus lenticularis
3878c	Cirrocumulus undulatus	3878k	Stratocumulus undulatus
3878d	Cumulonimbus mammatus	3878l	Stratus opacus
3878e	Cumulonimbus incus	3878m	Cumulus humilis
3878f	Alocumulus stratiformis	3878n	Cumulus congestus
3878g	Altostratus translucidus	3878o	Cumulonimbus with tornado
3878h	Altocumulus undulatus		

SCOTT NO.	DESCRIPTION	SING	PL. BLK.	MINT SHEET	PLATE BLOCK	UNUSED F/NH	USED
3878	37¢ Cloudscapes, 15 varieties attached	35.00		24.00(15)		24.00	
....	set of singles	35.00					14.00

3879

3880

3879	37¢ Madonna & Child, self-adhesive, die cut 10.75 x 11	2.25				1.25	.30
3879a	same, bklt pane of 20					26.00	
3880	37¢ Hanukkah-Dreidel, self-adhesive	2.25	4.75	21.00(20)	5.50	1.25	.30

3881

3882

3881	37¢ Kwanzaa-People in Robes, self-adhesive	2.25	4.75	21.00(20)	5.50	1.25	.35
3882	37¢ Moss Hart, self-adhesive	2.25	4.75	21.00(20)	5.50	1.25	.40

3883, 3887, 3892   **3884, 3888, 3891**   **3885, 3889, 3894**   **3886, 3890, 3893**

3883-86	37¢ Santa Christmas Ornaments, self-adhesive, 4 attached	4.25	4.75	27.00(20)	7.00	6.00	4.25
3883	37¢ Purple Santa Ornament	2.25				1.85	.55
3884	37¢ Green Santa Ornament	2.25				1.85	.55
3885	37¢ Blue Santa Ornament	2.25				1.85	.55
3886	37¢ Red Santa Ornament	2.25				1.85	.55
3886b	same, bklt pane of 20					32.00	
3887	37¢ Purple Santa Ornament, die cut 10.25 x 10.75	2.25				1.85	.55
3888	37¢ Green Santa Ornament, die cut 10.25 x 10.75	2.25				1.85	.55
3889	37¢ Blue Santa Ornament, die cut 10.25 x 10.75	2.25				1.85	.55
3890	37¢ Red Santa Ornament, die cut 10.25 x 10.75	2.25				1.85	.55
3887-90	37¢ Santa Christmas Ornaments, self-adhesive, 4 attached die cut 10.25 x 10.75	4.25				7.75	3.50
3890b	same, bklt pane of 4	4.25				7.75	
3890c	same, bklt pane of 6 (3889-90, 3887-88 x 2)	5.50				12.00	
3890d	same, bklt pane of 6 (3887-88, 3889-90 x 2)	5.50				12.00	
3891	37¢ Green Santa Ornament, die cut 8	2.25				3.00	1.00
3892	37¢ Purple Santa Ornament, die cut 8	2.25				3.00	1.00
3893	37¢ Red Santa Ornament, die cut 8	2.25				3.00	1.00
3894	37¢ Blue Santa Ornament, die cut 8	2.25				3.00	1.00
3891-94	37¢ Christmas Ornaments, self-adhesive, 4 attached, die cut 8	4.25				14.00	4.00
3894b	same, bklt pane of 18	15.00				52.00	

SCOTT NO.	DESCRIPTION	FIRST DAY COVERS SING	PL. BLK.	MINT SHEET	PLATE BLOCK	UNUSED F/NH	USED

3895

CHINESE NEW YEAR TYPES OF 1992-2004

3895a	*Rat*	3895g	*Horse*
3895b	*Ox*	3895h	*Ram*
3895c	*Tiger*	3895i	*Monkey*
3895d	*Rabbit*	3895j	*Rooster*
3895e	*Dragon*	3895k	*Dog*
3895f	*Snake*	3895l	*Boar*

3895	37¢ Chinese New Year, self-adhesive, 24 varieties attached	....	....	....	....	30.00	....
....	set of singles	23.50	....	....	....	....	13.00

2005 COMMEMORATIVES

3896/3964	(3896-97, 3904-3909, 3911-25, 3930, 3936 3938-43, 3945-52 3961-64) 43 varieties	....	....	....	....	56.00	27.00

3896   **3897**   **3898**

3896	37¢ Marian Anderson, self-adhesive	3.00	4.75	27.00(20)	6.25	1.20	.40
3897	37¢ Ronald Reagan, self-adhesive	3.00	4.75	22.00(20)	5.50	1.35	.40
....	same, uncut sheet of 120	....	....	120.00(120)	....	120.00	....
....	cross gutter block of 4	....	....	....	....	9.50	....
....	horiz. pair with vert. gutter	....	....	....	....	4.00	....
....	vert. pair with horiz. gutter	....	....	....	....	3.00	....
3898	37¢ Love-Hand and Flower Bouquet, self-adhesive	3.00	....	....	....	1.20	.30
3898a	same, bklt pane of 20	....	....	....	....	22.00	....

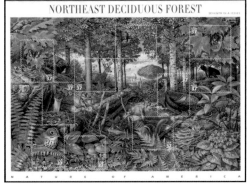

3899

NORTHEAST DECIDUOUS FOREST

3899a	*Eastern buckmouth*	3899f	*Long-tailed weasel*
3899b	*Red-shouldered hawk*	3899g	*Wild turkey*
3899c	*Eastern red bat*	3899h	*Ovenbird*
3899d	*White-tailed deer*	3899i	*Red eft*
3899e	*Black bear*	3899j	*Eastern chipmunk*

3899	37¢ Northeast Deciduous Forest, self-adhesive, 10 varieties attached	....	....	15.00(10)	....	15.00	....
....	set of singles	25.00	....	....	....	....	7.75

SCOTT NO.	DESCRIPTION	FIRST DAY COVERS SING	PL. BLK.	MINT SHEET	PLATE BLOCK	UNUSED F/NH	USED

3900   **3901**   **3902**   **3903**

3900	37¢ Hyacinth	3.00	....	....	....	1.75	.45
3901	37¢ Daffodil	3.00	....	....	....	1.75	.45
3902	37¢ Tulip	3.00	....	....	....	1.75	.45
3903	37¢ Iris	3.00	....	....	....	1.75	.45
3900-03	37¢ Spring Flowers, self-adhesive, 4 varieties attached	4.25	....	....	....	7.00	....
3903b	same, bklt pane of 20	....	....	....	....	32.00	....

3904   **3905**

3904	37¢ Robert Penn Warren, self-adhesive	3.00	4.75	22.00(20)	5.50	1.50	.35
3905	37¢ Yip Harburg, self-adhesive	3.00	4.75	22.00(20)	5.50	1.50	.35

3906   **3907**

3908   **3909**

3906-09	37¢ American Scientists, self-adhesive, 4 attached	4.25	4.75	27.00(20)	7.00	6.00	3.50
3906	37¢ Barbara McClintock	3.00	....	....	....	1.50	.60
3907	37¢ Josiah Willard Gibbs	3.00	....	....	....	1.50	.60
3908	37¢ John von Neuman	3.00	....	....	....	1.50	.60
3909	37¢ Richard Feynman	3.00	....	....	....	1.50	.60
....	same, plate blk of 8 with Top Label	....	....	....	10.00(8)	....	....

3910

MODERN AMERICAN ARCHITECTURE

3910a	*Guggenheim Museum*	3910g	*National Gallery of Art*
3910b	*Chrysler Building*	3910h	*Glass House*
3910c	*Vanna Venturi House*	3910i	*Yale Art and Architecture Bldg.*
3910d	*TWA Terminal*	3910j	*High Museum of Atlanta*
3910e	*Walt Disney Concert Hall*	3910k	*Exeter Academy Library*
3910f	*860-880 Lake Shore Drive*	3910l	*Hancock Center*

3910	37¢ Modern American Architecture, self-adhesive, 12 varieties attached	....	....	15.00(12)	....	15.00	....
....	set of singles	....	....	....	....	....	9.00

SCOTT NO.	DESCRIPTION	FIRST DAY COVERS SING	PL. BLK.	MINT SHEET	PLATE BLOCK	UNUSED F/NH	USED

3911

| 3911 | 37¢ Henry Fonda, self-adhesive | 3.00 | 4.75 | 30.00(20) | 8.00 | 1.50 | .50 |
| .... | same, uncut sheet of 180 | .... | .... | 270.00(180) | .... | 270.00 | .... |

3912   3913

3914   3915

3912-15	37¢ Disney Characters, self-adhesive, 4 attached	4.25	4.75	24.00(20)	6.50	6.00	3.50
3912	37¢ Pluto, Mickey Mouse	3.00	....	....	....	1.50	.50
3913	37¢ Mad Hatter, Alice	3.00	....	....	....	1.50	.50
3914	37¢ Flounder, Ariel. . .	3.00	....	....	....	1.50	.50
3915	37¢ Snow White, Dopey	3.00	....	....	....	1.50	.50

3916   3917

3918   3919

3920   3921

3922   3923

3924   3925

ADVANCES IN AVIATION

3916	Boeing 247	3921	Lockheed P80 Shooting Star
3917	Consolidated PBY Catalina	3922	Consolidated B24 Liberator
3918	Grumman F6F	3923	Boeing B29 Superfortress
3919	Republic P47 Thunderbolt	3924	Beechcraft 35 Bonanza
3920	E & R Corp. Ercoupe 415	3925	Northrop YB-49 Flying Wing

| 3916-25 | 37¢ Advances in Aviation, self-adhesive, 10 attached | 25.00 | .... | 25.00(20) | 16.00(10) | 15.00 | 11.00 |
| .... | set of singles | .... | .... | .... | .... | 15.00 | 9.00 |

3926   3927   3928   3929

3926	37¢ Blanket w/ yellow, orange, and red stripes	3.00	....	....	....	1.50	.85
3927	37¢ Blanket w/ black, orange red, and yellow	3.00	....	....	....	1.50	.85
3928	37¢ Blanket w/ yellow and black diamonds. .	3.00	....	....	....	1.50	.85
3929	37¢ Blanket w/ zigzag diamonds	3.00	....	....	....	1.50	.85
3926-29	37¢ Rio Grande Blankets, self-adhesive, 4 attached	4.25	....	....	....	6.50	4.00
3929b	same, bklt pane of 20	15.00	....	....	....	29.00	....

3930   3931   3936

3932   3933

3934   3935

SCOTT NO.	DESCRIPTION	FIRST DAY COVERS SING	PL. BLK.	MINT SHEET	PLATE BLOCK	UNUSED F/NH	USED
3930	37¢ Presidential Libraries Act, 50th Anniv., self-adhesive	3.00	4.75	22.00(20)	5.50	1.25	.35
3931	37¢ 1953 Studebaker Starliner	3.00	....	....	....	1.50	.50
3932	37¢ 1954 Kaiser Darren	3.00	....	....	....	1.50	.50
3933	37¢ 1953 Chevrolet Corvette	3.00	....	....	....	1.50	.50
3934	37¢ 1952 Nash Healey	3.00	....	....	....	1.50	.50
3935	37¢ 1955 Ford Thunderbird	3.00	....	....	....	1.50	.50
3935b	same, bklt pane of 20	15.00	....	....	....	30.00	....
3936	37¢ Arthur Ashe, self-adhesive	3.00	4.75	22.00(20)	5.50	1.20	.40

3937

TO FORM A MORE PERFECT UNION

3937a	1948 Executive Order 9981	3937f	1961 Freedom Riders
3937b	1965 Voting Rights Act	3937g	1964 Civil Rights Act
3937c	1960 Lunch Counter Sit-Ins	3937h	1963 March on Washington
3937d	1957 Litte Rock Nine	3937i	1965 Selma March
3937e	1955 Montgomery Bus Boycott	3937j	1954 Brown vs. Board of Education

3937	37¢ To Form A More Perfect Union, self-adhesive, 10 attached	15.00	....	18.00(10)	....	18.00	10.00
....	set of singles	....	....	....	....	18.00	8.75

3938

3939

3943

3940

3941

3942

3938	37¢ Child Health, self-adhesive	3.00	4.75	24.00(20)	6.00	1.35	.35
3939-42	37¢ Let's Dance, self-adhesive, 4 attached	4.25	4.75	30.00(20)	14.00	7.50	5.75
3939	37¢ Merengue	3.00	....	....	....	1.75	1.25
3940	37¢ Salsa	3.00	....	....	....	1.75	1.25
3941	37¢ Cha Cha Cha	3.00	....	....	....	1.75	1.25
3942	37¢ Mambo	3.00	....	....	....	1.75	1.25
3943	37¢ Greta Garbo, self-adhesive	3.00	4.75	22.00(20)	5.50	1.20	1.25

3944

JIM HENSON AND THE MUPPETS

3944a	Kermit the Frog	3944g	Animal
3944b	Fozzie Bear	3944h	Dr. Brunsen Honeydew and Beaker
3944c	Sam the Eagle and flag	3944i	Rowlf the Dog
3944d	Miss Piggy	3944j	The Great Gonzo and Camilia
3944e	Statler and Waldorf	3944k	Jim Henson
3944f	The Swedish Chef and fruit		

3944	37¢ Jim Henson and the Muppets, self-adhesive, 11 varieties attached	12.00	....	15.00(11)	....	15.00	....
....	set of singles	30.00	....	....	....	15.00	9.00

3945 **3946** **3947** **3948**

3945-48	37¢ Constellations, self-adhesive, 4 attached	4.25	4.75	28.00(20)	6.50	6.00	4.00
3945	37¢ Leo	3.00	....	....	....	1.75	.90
3946	37¢ Orion	3.00	....	....	....	1.75	.90
3947	37¢ Lyra	3.00	....	....	....	1.75	.90
3948	37¢ Pegasus	3.00	....	....	....	1.75	.90

3949, 3953, 3957 **3950, 3954, 3958** **3951, 3955, 3959** **3952, 3956, 3960**

3949-52	37¢ Christmas Cookies, self-adhesive, 4 attached	4.25	4.75	28.00(20)	6.75	6.00	4.00
3949	37¢ Santa Claus cookie	3.00	....	....	....	1.50	.55
3950	37¢ Snowmen cookie	3.00	....	....	....	1.50	.55
3951	37¢ Angel cookie	3.00	....	....	....	1.50	.55
3952	37¢ Elves cookie	3.00	....	....	....	1.50	.55
3953	37¢ Santa Claus cookie, die cut 10.75 X 11	3.00	....	....	....	1.75	.60
3954	37¢ Snowmen cookie, die cut 10.75 X 11	3.00	....	....	....	1.75	.60
3955	37¢ Angel cookie, die cut 10.75 X 11	3.00	....	....	....	1.75	.60
3956	37¢ Elves cookie, die cut 10.75 X 11	3.00	....	....	....	1.75	.60
3953-56	37¢ Christmas cookies, self-adhesive, 4 attached, die cut 10.75 X 11	4.25	....	....	....	7.50	4.00
3956b	same, bklt pane of 20	....	....	....	....	38.00	....

SCOTT NO.	DESCRIPTION	FIRST DAY COVERS SING	PL. BLK.	MINT SHEET	PLATE BLOCK	UNUSED F/NH	USED

4100

| 4100 | 39¢ Madonna and Child, self-adhesive . . . . | 3.00 | . . . . | . . . . | . . . . | 1.50 | .40 |
| 4100a | same, bklt pane of 20 | . . . . | . . . . | . . . . | . . . . | 28.00 | . . . . |

4103, 4107, 4111, 4114

4102, 4106, 4110, 4115

4101, 4105, 4109, 4113

4104, 4108, 4112, 4116

4101-04	39¢ Snowflakes, self-adhesive, die cut 11.25 x 11, 4 attached	4.25	4.75	30.00(20)	7.50	6.00	. . . .
4101	39¢ Spindly Arms and Branches	3.00	. . . .	. . . .	. . . .	1.50	.50
4102	39¢ Leafy Arms	3.00	. . . .	. . . .	. . . .	1.50	.50
4103	39¢ Large Center. . . .	3.00	. . . .	. . . .	. . . .	1.50	.50
4104	39¢ Arms w/ Wide Centers	3.00	. . . .	. . . .	. . . .	1.50	.50
4105-08	39¢ Snowflakes, self-adhesive, die cut 11.25 x 11.5, 4 attached	4.25	. . . .	. . . .	. . . .	8.50	. . . .
4105	39¢ Spindly Arms and Branches	3.00	. . . .	. . . .	. . . .	1.75	.50
4106	39¢ Leafy Arms	3.00	. . . .	. . . .	. . . .	1.75	.50
4107	39¢ Large Center. . . .	3.00	. . . .	. . . .	. . . .	1.75	.50
4108	39¢ Arms w/ Wide Centers	3.00	. . . .	. . . .	. . . .	1.75	.50
4108b	same, bklt pane of 20 (4105-08 x 5)	. . . .	. . . .	. . . .	. . . .	32.00	. . . .
4109-12	39¢ Snowflakes, self-adhesive, die cut 11.25 x 11, 4 attached	4.25	. . . .	. . . .	. . . .	7.50	. . . .
4109	39¢ Spindly Arms and Branches	3.00	. . . .	. . . .	. . . .	1.75	1.25
4110	39¢ Leafy Arms	3.00	. . . .	. . . .	. . . .	1.75	1.25
4111	39¢ Large Center. . . .	3.00	. . . .	. . . .	. . . .	1.75	1.25
4112	39¢ Arms w/ Wide Centers	3.00	. . . .	. . . .	. . . .	1.75	1.25
4112b	same, bklt pane of 4 (4109-12)	. . . .	. . . .	. . . .	. . . .	8.00	. . . .
4112c	same, bklt pane of 6 (4111-4112, 4109-4110 x 2)	. . . .	. . . .	. . . .	. . . .	12.00	. . . .
4112d	same, bklt pane of 6 (4109-4110, 4111-4112 x 2). .	. . . .	. . . .	. . . .	. . . .	12.00	. . . .
4113-16	39¢ Snowflakes, die cut 8, self-adhesive, 4 attached	4.25	. . . .	. . . .	. . . .	9.00	. . . .
4113	39¢ Spindly Arms and Branches.	3.00	. . . .	. . . .	. . . .	2.00	1.75
4114	39¢ Large Center	3.00	. . . .	. . . .	. . . .	2.00	1.75
4115	39¢ Leafy Arms.	3.00	. . . .	. . . .	. . . .	2.00	1.75
4116	39¢ Arms w/ Wide Centers	3.00	. . . .	. . . .	. . . .	2.00	1.75
4116b	same, bklt pane of 18 (4113 x 5, 4114 x 4, 4115 x 5, 4116 x 4)	. . . .	. . . .	. . . .	. . . .	30.00	. . . .

4117

4119

4118

4117	39¢ EID, self-adhesive	3.00	4.75	22.00(20)	5.50	1.50	.85
4118	39¢ Hanukkah-Dreidal, self-adhesive	3.00	4.75	22.00(20)	5.50	1.50	.40
4119	39¢ Kwanzaa-People self-adhesive	3.00	4.75	22.00(20)	5.50	1.50	.40

SCOTT NO.	DESCRIPTION	FIRST DAY COVERS SING	PL. BLK.	MINT SHEET	PLATE BLOCK	UNUSED F/NH	USED

2007 COMMEMORATIVES

| 4120/4220 | (4120, 4121, 4124, 4136, 4146-4150, 4160-4163, 4192-4197, 4199-4205, 4207-4210, 4219, 4220) 32 varieties | . . . . | . . . . | . . . . | | 44.00 | 15.00 |

4120

4121

4122

4120	39¢ Ella Fitzgerald, self-adhesive	3.00	4.75	22.00(20)	5.50	1.50	.40
4121	39¢ Oklahoma Statehood self-adhesive	3.00	4.75	22.00(20)	5.50	1.50	.40
4122	39¢ Hershey's Kiss, self-adhesive	3.00	4.75	28.00(20)	. . . .	1.50	.40
4122a	same, bklt pane of 20	. . . .	. . . .	. . . .	. . . .	28.00	. . . .

4123

4123	84¢ International Polar Year, self-adhesive, souvenir sheet of 2 . .	. . . .	. . . .	. . . .		8.00	. . . .
4123a	84¢ Aurora Borealis. .	4.00	. . . .	. . . .		5.00	2.50
4123b	84¢ Aurora Australis .	4.00	. . . .	. . . .		5.00	2.50

4124

4125, 4126, 4127, 4128, 4437

4129, 4130, 4132, 4133, 4134, 4135

4124	39¢ Henry Wadsworth Longfellow, self-adhesive	3.00	4.75	21.00(20)	5.50	1.50	.40
4125	(41¢) Forever Liberty Bell, self-adhesive, large micro print	3.50	. . . .	. . . .	. . . .	1.50	.35
4125a	same, bklt pane of 20	. . . .	. . . .	. . . .	. . . .	27.00	. . . .
4125b	(42¢) Forever, Liberty Bell, large micro print, bell 16mm wide dated 2008	3.50	. . . .	. . . .	. . . .	1.50	.35
4125c	same, bklt pane of 20	. . . .	. . . .	. . . .	. . . .	27.00	. . . .
4125f	(44¢) Forever, dated 2009, large micro, bell 16mm wide	. . . .	. . . .	. . . .	. . . .	1.50	.45
4125g	same, booklet pane of 20	. . . .	. . . .	. . . .	. . . .	27.00	. . . .
4126	(41¢) Forever, Liberty Bell, self-adhesive, small micro print	3.50	. . . .	. . . .	. . . .	1.50	.35
4126a	same, bklt pane of 20	. . . .	. . . .	. . . .	. . . .	27.00	. . . .
4126b	(42¢) Forever, Liberty Bell, small micro print, bell 16mm wide dated 2008	3.50	. . . .	. . . .	. . . .	1.50	.45
4126c	same, bklt pane of 20	. . . .	. . . .	. . . .	. . . .	27.00	. . . .
4126d	(44¢) Forever, dated 2009, small micro, bell 16mm wide	. . . .	. . . .	. . . .	. . . .	1.50	.45
4126e	same, booklet pane of 20	. . . .	. . . .	. . . .	. . . .	27.00	. . . .
4127	(41¢) Forever Liberty Bell, self-adhesive, medium micro print	3.50	. . . .	. . . .	. . . .	2.00	.35
4127a	same, bklt pane of 20	. . . .	. . . .	. . . .	. . . .	38.00	. . . .
. . . .	solid tagging	. . . .	. . . .	. . . .	. . . .	160.00	. . . .
4127b	same, bklt pane of 4 .	. . . .	. . . .	. . . .	. . . .	5.25	. . . .
4127c	same, bklt pane of 6 .	. . . .	. . . .	. . . .	. . . .	7.75	. . . .
4127d	(42¢) Forever Liberty Bell, med. micro print, bell 15 wide, mottled tagging dated 2008	3.50	. . . .	. . . .	. . . .	2.00	.65
4127e	(42¢) Forever Liberty Bell, dbl-sided, bklt pane of 20	. . . .	. . . .	. . . .	. . . .	36.00	. . . .
4127f	(42¢) Forever Liberty Bell, dated 2008, small type, solid tagging	3.50	. . . .	. . . .	. . . .	1.50	. . . .
4127g	(42¢) Forever Liberty Bell, dated 2008, small type, solid tagging, bklt pane of 4	. . . .	. . . .	. . . .	. . . .	5.25	. . . .

SCOTT NO.	DESCRIPTION	FIRST DAY COVERS SING	FIRST DAY COVERS PL. BLK.	MINT SHEET	PLATE BLOCK	UNUSED F/NH	USED
4127h	(42¢) Forever Liberty Bell, (2008), bklt pane of 6	....	....	....	....	7.75	....
	same, vending bklt of 20	....	....	....	....	29.00	....
4127i	(44¢) Forever Liberty Bell, dated 2009 in copper....	3.50	....	....	....	1.50	.65
4127j	(44¢) Forever Liberty Bell, double sided pane of 20...	....	....	....	....	27.00	....
4128	(41¢) Forever Liberty Bell, self-adhesive, ATM . .	3.50	....	....	....	1.50	.60
4128a	same, bklt pane of 18	....	....	....	....	28.00	....
4128b	(42¢) Forever, Liberty Bell large micro print, bell 16mm wide dated 2009	3.50	....	....	....	1.50	.65
4128c	same, bklt pane of 18	....	....	....	....	27.00	....
4129	(41¢) American Flag, die cut 11.25	3.50	5.00	127.00(100)	16.00	1.50	1.05
4130	(41¢) American Flag, self-adhesive, 11.25 x 10.75	3.50	5.00	24.00(20)	5.75	1.80	.45
4131	(41¢) American Flag, coil, die cut 9.75.	3.50	....	....	....	1.50	.65
	same, pl# strip of 5 . .	....	....	....	....	10.50	....
4132	(41¢) American Flag, coil, self-adhesive, die cut 9.5	3.50	....	....	....	1.50	.40
	same, pl# strip of 5	....	....	....	....	10.50	....
4133	(41¢) American Flag, coil, self-adhesive, die cut 11	3.50	....	....	....	1.50	.40
	same, pl# strip of 5 . .	....	....	....	....	10.50	....
4134	(41¢) American Flag, coil, self-adhesive, die cut 8.5	3.50	....	....	....	1.50	.40
	same, pl# strip of 5 . .	....	....	....	....	10.00	....
4135	(41¢) American Flag, coil, self-adhesive, rounded corners, die cut 11 . . .	3.50	....	....	....	1.70	1.15
	same, pl# strip of 5 . .	....	....	....	....	12.00	....

4136

4137, 4139, 4141, 4142

4138, 4140

SCOTT NO.	DESCRIPTION	FIRST DAY COVERS SING	FIRST DAY COVERS PL. BLK.	MINT SHEET	PLATE BLOCK	UNUSED F/NH	USED
4136	41¢ Settlement of Jamestown, self-adhesive . .	3.50	5.00	30.00(20)	....	1.50	.50
4137	26¢ Florida Panther, water-activated, ...	3.00	4.75	78.00(100)	13.50	.85	.35
4138	17¢ Big Horn Sheep, self-adhesive	3.00	4.00	13.00(20)	3.50	.75	.35
4139	26¢ Florida Panther, self-adhesive	3.00	4.75	16.00(20)	4.50	.85	.35
4140	17¢ Big Horn Sheep, self-adhesive, coil . . .	3.00	....	....	....	.75	.35
	same, pl# strip of 5 . .	....	....	....	....	6.75	....
4141	26¢ Florida Panther, self-adhesive, coil . . .	3.00	....	....	....	1.00	.35
	same, pl# strip of 5 . .	....	....	....	....	9.00	....
4142	26¢ Florida Panther, self-adhesive	3.00	....	....	....	1.00	.30
4142a	same, bklt pane of 10	....	....	....	....	10.00	....

STAR WARS

- **4143a** Darth Vader
- **4143b** Millennium Falcon
- **4143c** Emperor Palpatine
- **4143d** Anakin Skywalker and Obi-Wan Kenobi
- **4143e** Luke Skywalker
- **4143f** Princess Leia & R2-D2
- **4143g** C-3PO
- **4143h** Queen Padme Amidala
- **4143i** Obi-Wan Kenobi
- **4143j** Boba Fett
- **4143k** Darth Maul
- **4143l** Chewbacca and Han Solo
- **4143m** X-wing Starfighter
- **4143n** Yoda
- **4143o** Stormtroopers

4143

SCOTT NO.	DESCRIPTION	FIRST DAY COVERS SING	FIRST DAY COVERS PL. BLK.	MINT SHEET	PLATE BLOCK	UNUSED F/NH	USED
4143	41¢ Star Wars, self-adhesive, 15 attached	....	....	22.00(15)	....	22.00	....
....	same, set of singles. .	....	....	....	....	22.00	15.00

4144

4145

SCOTT NO.	DESCRIPTION	FIRST DAY COVERS SING	FIRST DAY COVERS PL. BLK.	MINT SHEET	PLATE BLOCK	UNUSED F/NH	USED
4144	$4.60 Air Force One, self-adhesive	10.00	30.00	230.00(20)	58.00	13.00	10.00
4145	$16.25 Marine One, self-adhesive	35.00	80.00	800.00(20)	200.00	46.00	30.00

4146 **4147** **4148** **4149** **4150**

SCOTT NO.	DESCRIPTION	FIRST DAY COVERS SING	FIRST DAY COVERS PL. BLK.	MINT SHEET	PLATE BLOCK	UNUSED F/NH	USED
4146-50	41¢ Pacific Lighthouses, self-adhesive, 5 attached	5.50	8.00	30.00(20)	16.00(10)	8.50	....
4146	41¢ Diamond Head . .	3.50	....	....	....	1.75	.50
4147	41¢ Five Finger	3.50	....	....	....	1.75	.50
4148	41¢ Grays Harbor . . .	3.50	....	....	....	1.75	.50
4149	41¢ Umpqua River. . .	3.50	....	....	....	1.75	.50
4150	41¢ St. George Reef .	3.50	....	....	....	1.75	.50

4151

4152

SCOTT NO.	DESCRIPTION	FIRST DAY COVERS SING	FIRST DAY COVERS PL. BLK.	MINT SHEET	PLATE BLOCK	UNUSED F/NH	USED
4151	41¢ Wedding Hearts, self-adhesive	3.50	....	....	....	1.50	.35
4151a	same, bklt pane of 20	....	....	....	....	27.00	....
4152	58¢ Wedding Hearts, self-adhesive	4.00	5.50	33.00(20)	8.00	1.85	.65

4153 **4154**

4155 **4156**

SCOTT NO.	DESCRIPTION	FIRST DAY COVERS SING	FIRST DAY COVERS PL. BLK.	MINT SHEET	PLATE BLOCK	UNUSED F/NH	USED
4153-56	41¢ Pollination, self-adhesive, 4 attached .	4.50	....	....	....	7.00	....
4153	41¢ Purple Nightshade and Morrison's Bumblebee, type I, straight edge at left . .	3.50	....	....	....	1.50	.55
4153a	same, type II, straight edge at right.	3.50	....	....	....	1.50	.55
4154	41¢ Hummingbird Trumpet and Calliope Hummingbird, type I, straight edge at right	3.50	....	....	....	1.50	.55
4154a	same, type II, straight edge at left.	3.50	....	....	....	1.50	.55
4155	41¢ Saguaro and Lesser Long-nosed Bat, type I, straight edge at left . .	3.50	....	....	....	1.50	.55
4155a	same, type II, straight edge at right.	3.50	....	....	....	1.50	.55
4156	41¢ Prairie Ironweed and Southern Dogface Butterfly, type I, straight edge at right	3.50	....	....	....	1.50	.55
4156a	same, type II, straight edge at left.	3.50	....	....	....	1.50	.55
4156b	same, blk of 4 (4153-4156)	4.50	....	....	....	6.00	....
4156c	same, blk of 4 (4153a-4156a)	4.50	....	....	....	6.00	....
4156d	same, bklt pane of 20 (4153-4156 x 3, 4153a-4156a x 2)	4.50	....	....	....	28.00	....

SCOTT NO.	DESCRIPTION	FIRST DAY COVERS SING	PL. BLK.	MINT SHEET	PLATE BLOCK	UNUSED F/NH	USED
4157	(10¢) Patriotic Banner, self-adhesive, round corners	....	....	....	....	.35	.25
....	same, pl# strip of 5 . .	....	....	....	....	3.50	....
4158	(10¢) Patriotic Banner, self-adhesive, straight corners	....	....	....	....	.35	.25
....	same, pl# strip of 5 . .	....	....	....	....	4.75	....

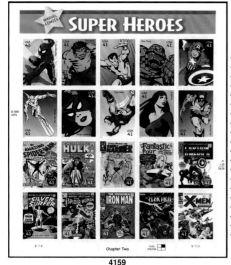

4159

MARVEL COMICS SUPER HEROES

4159a	Spider-Man
4159b	The Incredible Hulk
4159c	Sub-Mariner
4159d	The Thing
4159e	Captain America
4159f	Silver Surfer
4159g	Spider-Woman
4159h	Iron Man
4159i	Elektra
4159j	Wolverine
4159k	Spider-Man Cover
4159l	Incredible Hulk Cover
4159m	Sub-Mariner Cover
4159n	Fantastic Four Cover
4159o	Captain America Cover
4159p	Silver Surfer Cover
4159q	Spider-Woman Cover
4159r	Iron Man Cover
4159s	Elektra Cover
4159t	X-Men Cover

SCOTT NO.	DESCRIPTION	FIRST DAY COVERS SING	PL. BLK.	MINT SHEET	PLATE BLOCK	UNUSED F/NH	USED
4159	41¢ Marvel Comics Super Heroes, self-adhesive, 20 varieties attached .	....	....	29.00(20)	....	29.00	....
	same, set of singles. .	....	....			29.00	20.00

4160	4161	4162	4163

SCOTT NO.	DESCRIPTION	SING	PL. BLK.	MINT SHEET	PLATE BLOCK	UNUSED F/NH	USED
4160-63	41¢ Vintage Mahogany Speedboats, self-adhesive, 4 attached .	4.50	6.50	18.00(12)	14.00(8)	7.00	....
4160	41¢ 1915 Hutchinson	....	....	....	....	1.75	1.00
4161	41¢ 1945 Chris-Craft	....	....	....	....	1.75	1.00
4162	41¢ 1939 Hacker-Craft	....	....	....	....	1.75	1.00
4163	41¢ 1931 Gar Wood .	....	....	....	....	1.75	1.00

4157, 4158   **4165, 4165a**

4164

SCOTT NO.	DESCRIPTION	SING	PL. BLK.	MINT SHEET	PLATE BLOCK	UNUSED F/NH	USED
4164	41¢ Purple Heart, self-adhesive	3.50	5.00	24.00(20)	5.50	1.50	.40
4165	41¢ Louis Comfort Tiffany, self-adhesive	3.50	....	....	....	1.50	.40
4165a	same, bklt pane of 20	....	....	....	....	28.00	....
4166-75	41¢ Flowers Strip of 10	....	....	....	....	25.00	....
	same, plate strip of 11	....	....	....	....	35.00	....
4166	41¢ Iris S/A coil	$3.75	....	....	....	2.75	.85
4167	41¢ Dahalia S/A coil .	$3.75	....	....	....	2.75	.85
4168	41¢ Magnolia S/A coil	$3.75	....	....	....	2.75	.85
4169	41¢ Red Gerbera Daisy, S/A coil.	$3.75	....	....	....	2.75	.85
4170	41¢ Coneflower S/A coil	$3.75	....	....	....	2.75	.85
4171	41¢ Tulip S/A coil. . . .	$3.75	....	....	....	2.75	.85
4172	41¢ Water Lily S/A coil	$3.75	....	....	....	2.75	.85
4173	41¢ Poppy S/A coil . .	$3.75	....	....	....	2.75	.85
4174	41¢ Chrysanthemum, S/A coil.	$3.75	....	....	....	2.75	.85
4175	41¢ Orange Gerbera Daisy, S/A coil	$3.75	....	....	....	2.75	.85

4166, 4178   **4167, 4179**   **4168, 4180**   **4169, 4181**

4170, 4184   **4171, 4185**   **4172, 4182**

4173, 4183   **4174, 4176**   **4175, 4177**

SCOTT NO.	DESCRIPTION	SING	PL. BLK.	MINT SHEET	PLATE BLOCK	UNUSED F/NH	USED
4176	41¢ Chrysanthemum, booklet single	$3.75	....	....	....	1.50	.60
4177	41¢ Orange Gerbera Daisy, booklet single	$3.75	....	....	....	1.50	.60
4178	41¢ Iris, bklt single. . .	$3.75	....	....	....	1.50	.60
4179	41¢ Dahalia, bklt single	$3.75	....	....	....	1.50	.60
4180	41¢ Magnolia, bklt single	$3.75	....	....	....	1.50	.60
4181	41¢ Red Gerbera Daisy, booklet single	$3.75	....	....	....	1.50	.60
4182	41¢ Water Lily, bklt single	$3.75	....	....	....	1.50	.60
4183	41¢ Poppy, bklt single	$3.75	....	....	....	1.50	.60
4184	41¢ Coneflower, booklet single.	$3.75	....	....	....	1.50	.60
4185	41¢ Tulip, bklt single. .	$3.75	....	....	....	1.50	.60
4185a	41¢ Flowers dbl-sided, booklet pane . .	....	....	....	....	29.00	....
4186	41¢ Flag S/A coil, die cut 9.5, microprint, rt. side of flagpole . . .	3.75	....	....	....	1.50	.35
	same, plate strip of 5 .	....	....	....	....	12.00	....
4187	41¢ Flag S/A coil, die cut 11, microprint, left side of flagpole. . .	3.75	....	....	....	1.50	.35
	same, plate strip of 5 .	....	....	....	....	12.00	....
4188	41¢ Flag S/A coil, 8.5 perpendicular corners,	3.75	....	....	....	1.50	.35
	same, plate strip of 5 .	....	....	....	....	12.00	....
4189	41¢ Flag S/A coil, die cut 11 w/round corners,	3.75	....	....	....	1.50	.35
	same, plate strip of 5 .	....	....	....	....	12.00	....
4190	41¢ Flag bklt single, S/A die-cut 11.25x10.75, microprint rt. side of pole	3.75	....	....	....	1.50	.35
4190a	same bklt pane of 10 .	....	....	....	....	13.00	....
4191	41¢ Flag bklt single, S/A die-cut 11.25x10.75, microprint left side of pole	3.75	....	....	....	1.50	.35
4191a	same bklt pane of 20 .	....	....	....	....	27.00	....

4192   **4193**

4194   **4195**

4186-91

4196

SCOTT NO.	DESCRIPTION	SING	PL. BLK.	MINT SHEET	PLATE BLOCK	UNUSED F/NH	USED
4192-95	41¢ Magic of Disney, 4 attached, ...	4.25	4.75	24.00 (20)	6.50	6.00	....
4192	41¢ Mickey Mouse. . .	3.75	....	....	....	1.50	.50
4193	41¢ Peter Pan & Tinkerbell	3.75	....	....	....	1.50	.50
4194	41¢ Dumbo & Timothy Mouse	3.75	....	....	....	1.50	.50
4195	41¢ Aladdin & Genie .	3.75	....	....	....	1.50	.50
4196	41¢ Celebrate	3.75	4.50	22.00 (20)	5.50	1.50	.35

SCOTT NO.	DESCRIPTION	FIRST DAY COVERS SING	PL. BLK.	MINT SHEET	PLATE BLOCK	UNUSED F/NH	USED

4197

| 4197 | 41¢ James Stewart .. | 3.75 | 4.50 | 30.00 (20) | 7.50 | 1.75 | .50 |

4198

ALPINE TUNDRA

4198a	*Elk*	4198f	*Magdalena Alpine Butterfly*
4198b	*Golden Eagle*	4198g	*Big-White-Tailed Ptarmigan*
4198c	*Yellow-bellied marmot*	4198h	*Rocky Mountain Parnassian Butterfly*
4198d	*American Pike*	4198i	*Melissa Arctic Butterfly*
4198e	*Big Horn Sheep*	4198j	*Brown-Capped Rosy-Finch*

| 4198 | 41¢ Alpine Tundra, sheet of 10 .... | .... | .... | 15.00 (10) | .... | 15.00 | .... |
| | set of singles .... | 20.00 | .... | .... | .... | 15.00 | 9.00 |

4199   **4200**   **4201**

4199	41¢ Gerald R. Ford ..	3.75	4.50	24.00 (20)	6.00	1.50	.40
4200	41¢ Jury Duty.......	3.75	4.50	24.00 (20)	6.00	1.50	.40
4201	41¢ Mendez v. Westminster	3.75	4.50	24.00 (20)	6.00	1.50	.40

4202

| 4202 | 41¢ EID .... | 3.75 | 4.50 | 22.00 (20) | 5.50 | 1.40 | .35 |

4203   **4204**

4203-04	41¢ Polar Lights	4.25	4.75	32.00 (20)	9.50	3.50	....
4203	41¢ Aurora Borealis...	3.75	....	....	....	1.75	.65
4204	41¢ Aurora Australis ..	3.75	....	....	....	1.75	.65

4205   **4206**

4205	41¢ Yoda	3.75	4.50	24.00 (20)	6.00	1.50	.40
4206	41¢ Madonna of the Carnation, by Bernardino Luini ..	3.75	....	....	....	1.30	.35
4206a	same, double-sided, booklet pane of 20...	....	....	....	....	24.00	....

4207, 4211, 4215   **4208, 4212 4216**   **4209, 4213, 4217**   **4210, 4214, 4218**

4207-10	41¢ Christmas Knits, S/A, die-cut 10.75 ...	4.75	....	24.00 (20)	6.50	6.00	....
4207	41¢ Knit Reindeer, S/A, die-cut 10.75	3.75	....	....	....	1.25	.50
4208	41¢ Knit Christmas Tree, S/A, die-cut 10.75	3.75	....	....	....	1.25	.50
4209	41¢ Knit Snowman, S/A, die-cut 10.75	3.75	....	....	....	1.25	.50
4210	41¢ Knit Bear, S/A, die-cut 10.75	3.75	....	....	....	1.25	.50
4210b	41¢ Christmas Knits, booklet pane of 20...	....	....	....	....	32.00	....
4211-14	41¢ Christmas Knits, S/A, die-cut 11.25X11, block of 4 attached ..	4.75	....	....	....	7.50	....
4211	41¢ Knit Reindeer, S/A, die-cut 11.25x11 ..	3.75	....	....	....	1.75	.75
4212	41¢ Knit Christmas Tree, S/A, die-cut 11.25x11 ..	3.75	....	....	....	1.75	.75
4213	41¢ Knit Snowman, S/A, die-cut 11.25x11 ..	3.75	....	....	....	1.75	.75
4214	41¢ Knit Bear, S/A, die-cut 11.25x11 ..	3.75	....	....	....	1.75	.75
4214b	booklet pane of 4,= 4211-14	....	....	....	....	7.50	....
4214c	booklet pane of 6, 4213-14, 2 ea. 4211-12	....	....	....	....	11.00	....
4214d	booklet pane of 6, 4211-12, 2 ea. 4213-14	....	....	....	....	11.00	....
4215-18	41¢ Christmas Knits, S/A, die-cut 8.......	4.50	....	....	....	8.00	....
4215	41¢ Knit Reindeer, S/A, die-cut 8........	3.75	....	....	....	2.00	.75
4216	41¢ Knit Christmas Tree, S/A, die-cut 8........	3.75	....	....	....	2.00	.75
4217	41¢ Knit Snowman, S/A, die-cut 8........	3.75	....	....	....	2.00	.75
4218	41¢ Knit Bear, S/A, die-cut 8	3.75	....	....	....	2.00	.75
4218b	booklet pane of 18, 4 ea. of 4215, 4218, 5 ea. of 4216, 4217...	....	....	....	....	34.00	....

4219   **4220**

| 4219 | 41¢ Hanukkah S/A, die-cut 10.75x11 ..... | 3.75 | 4.50 | 22.00 (20) | 5.50 | 1.40 | .45 |
| 4220 | 41¢ Kwanza,S/A, die-cut, 11x10.75..... | 3.75 | 4.50 | 22.00 (20) | 5.50 | 1.40 | .45 |

SCOTT NO.	DESCRIPTION	FIRST DAY COVERS SING	PL. BLK.	MINT SHEET	PLATE BLOCK	UNUSED F/NH	USED

2008 COMMEMORATIVES

| 4221/4373 | (4221-4227, 4248-4252, 4265, 4266, 4334, 4335, 4336-4345, 4349-4351, 4353-4357, 4358, 4372, 4373) 37 varieties .... | | | .... | .... | 52.00 | 24.00 |

4221

4222

4223

4221	41¢ Year of the Rat, SA. .	3.75	....	17.00 (12)	....	1.50	.45
4222	41¢ Charles W. Chestnutt	3.75	....	24.00 (20)	5.50	1.50	.45
4223	41¢ Marjorie Kinnan Rawlings	3.75	4.50	24.00 (20)	5.50	1.50	.45

| 4224 | 4225 | 4226 | 4227 |

4224-27	41¢ American Scientists. .	4.50	7.50	25.00 (20)	12.00(8)	6.00	....
4224	41¢ Gerty Cori.	3.75				1.50	.90
4225	41¢ Linus Pauling. . . .	3.75				1.50	.90
4226	41¢ Edwin Hubble. . .	3.75				1.50	.90
4227	41¢ John Bardeed. . .	3.75				1.50	.90

| 4229, 4233, 4237, 4241, 4245 | 4230, 4234, 4238, 4242, 4246 | 4231, 4235, 4239, 4243, 4247 | 4228, 4232, 4236, 4240, 4244 |

4228-31	42¢ Flag 24/7, W/A coil.	6.50	....	....	....	9.00	....
	same, plate # strip of 5	....				20.00	....
	same, plate # strip of 9	....				30.00	....
4228	42¢ Flag at Dusk, W/A coil.	3.50				2.50	.85
4229	42¢ Flag at Night, W/A coil.	3.50				2.50	.85
4230	42¢ Flag at Dawn, W/A coil.	3.50				2.50	.85
4231	42¢ Flag at Midday, W/A coil.	3.50				2.50	.85
4232-35	42¢ Flag 24/7, S/A coil 9.5 (AP).	6.50				7.50	....
	same, plate # strip of 5	....				12.00	....
	same, plate # strip of 9	....				18.00	....
4232	42¢ Flag at Dusk, S/A coil 9.5 (AP). . . .	3.50				2.50	.60
4233	42¢ Flag at Night, S/A coil 9.5 (AP). . . .	3.50				2.50	.60
4234	42¢ Flag at Dawn, S/A coil 9.5 (AP) . . .	3.50				2.50	.60
4235	42¢ Flag at Midday, S/A coil 9.5 (AP).	3.50				2.50	.60
4236-39	42¢ Flag 24/7, S/A coil, 11 perpend. corners (SSP)	6.50				7.50	....
	same, plate # strip of 5	....				13.00	....
	same, plate # strip of 9	....				19.00	....
4236	42¢ Flag at Dusk, S/A coil, 11 perpend. corners (SSP)	3.50				2.50	.60
4237	42¢ Flag at Night, S/A coil, 11 perpend. corners (SSP)	3.50				2.50	.60
4238	42¢ Flag at Dawn, S/A coil, 11 perpend. corners (SSP)	3.50				2.50	.60
4239	42¢ Flag at Midday, S/A coil, 11 perpend. corners (SSP)	3.50				2.50	.60
4240-43	42¢ Flag 24/7, S/A coil, 8.5 perpend. corners (AV)	6.50				7.50	....
	same, plate # strip of 5	....				13.00	....
	same, plate # strip of 9	....				18.00	....
4240	42¢ Flag at Dusk, S/A coil, 8.5 perpend. corners (AV)	3.50				2.50	.60
4241	42¢ Flag at Night, S/A coil, 8.5 perpend. corners (AV)	3.50				2.50	.60
4242	42¢ Flag at Dawn, S/A coil, 8.5 perpend. corners (AV)	3.50				2.50	.60
4243	42¢ Flag at Midday, S/A coil, 8.5 perpend. corners (AV)	3.50				2.50	.60
4244-47	42¢ Flag 24/7, S/A coil, 11 rounded corners (AV)	6.50				7.50	....
	same, plate # strip of 5	....				13.00	....

	same, plate # strip of 9	....	....	....	....	18.00	....
4244	42¢ Flag at Dusk, S/A coil, 11 rounded corners (AV)	3.50	....	....	....	2.50	.60
4245	42¢ Flag at Night, S/A coil, 11 rounded corners (AV)	3.50	....	....	....	2.50	.60
4246	42¢ Flag at Dawn, S/A coil, 11 rounded corners (AV)	3.50	....	....	....	2.50	.60
4247	42¢ Flag at Midday, S/A coil, 11 rounded corners (AV)	3.50	....	....	....	2.50	.60

4248

4249

4250

4251

4252

4248-52	42¢ American Journalists	4.50	7.50	35.00(20)	18.00(10)	9.00	....
	same	....	....	....	12.00(8)		
4248	42¢ Martha Gellhorn. .	3.75				2.00	1.00
4249	42¢ John Hersey.	3.75				2.00	1.00
4250	42¢ George Polk. . . .	3.75				2.00	1.00
4251	42¢ Ruben Salazar. . .	3.75				2.00	1.00
4252	42¢ Eric Sevareid. . . .	3.75				2.00	1.00

| 4253,4258 | 4254,4259 | 4255,4260 | 4256,4261 | 4257,4265 |

4253-57	27¢ Tropical Fruit. . . .	4.75		19.00(20)	12.00(10)	6.00	....
4253	27¢ Pomegranate. . . .	2.50				1.25	.50
4254	27¢ Star Fruit.	2.50				1.25	.50
4255	27¢ Kiwi.	2.50				1.25	.50
4256	27¢ Papaya	2.50				1.25	.50
4257	27¢ Guava	2.50				1.25	.50
4258-62	27¢ Tropical Fruit. . . .	4.75				9.00	....
	same, plate strip of 5 .	....				15.00	....
	same, plate strip of 11	....				22.00	....
4258	27¢ Pomegranate Coil	2.50				2.00	.50
4259	27¢ Star Fruit Coil. . . .	2.50				2.00	.50
4260	27¢ Kiwi Coil.	2.50				2.00	.50
4261	27¢ Papaya Coil	2.50				2.00	.50
4262	27¢ Guava Coil.	2.50				2.00	.50

4263, 4264

| 4263 | 42¢ Purple Heart . . . . | 3.50 | 4.75 | 148.00 (100) | 40.00 | 1.70 | .70 |
| 4264 | 42¢ Purple Heart, S/A | 3.50 | 4.75 | 24.00 (20) | 6.00 | 1.50 | .45 |

4265

4266

| 4265 | 42¢ Frank Sinatra . . . | 3.75 | 4.75 | 24.00 (20) | 6.00 | 1.50 | .40 |
| 4266 | 42¢ Minnesota Statehood | 3.75 | 4.75 | 22.00 (20) | 5.50 | 1.50 | .40 |

SCOTT NO.	DESCRIPTION	FIRST DAY COVERS SING	FIRST DAY COVERS PL. BLK.	MINT SHEET	PLATE BLOCK	UNUSED F/NH	USED

4267

4268

4269

4267	69¢ Dragonfly	3.75	5.00	55.00 (20)	9.00	3.00	1.25
4268	$4.80 Mount Rushmore	12.00	....	245.00 (20)	65.00	14.00	10.00
4269	$16.50 Hoover Dam . .	35.00	....	800.00 (20)	200.00	45.00	35.00

4270

4271

4272

4270	42¢ All Heart	3.75	....	....	....	1.40	.40
4270a	42¢ All Heart, pane of 20	....	....	....	....	27.00	....
4271	42¢ Weddings	3.75	....	....	....	1.40	.40
4271a	42¢ Weddings, pane of 20	12.00	....	....	....	27.00	....
4272	59¢ Silver Heart	3.75	....	32.00(20)	9.00	2.00	.75

4273

4332

4273-82	42¢ Flags of Our Nation, coil strip of 11	....	....	....	....	14.00	....
	same, plate # strip of 10	....	....	....	....	19.00	....
4273	42¢ American Flag. .	3.75	....	....	....	1.50	.75
4274	42¢ Alabama Flag . . .	3.75	....	....	....	1.50	.75
4275	42¢ Alaska Flag.	3.75	....	....	....	1.50	.75
4276	42¢ American Samoa Flag	3.75	....	....	....	1.50	.75
4277	42¢ Arizona Flag . . .	3.75	....	....	....	1.50	.75
4278	42¢ Arkansas Flag. . .	3.75	....	....	....	1.50	.75
4279	42¢ California Flag . .	3.75	....	....	....	1.50	.75
4280	42¢ ColoradoFlag . . .	3.75	....	....	....	1.50	.75
4281	42¢ Connecticut Flag	3.75	....	....	....	1.50	.75
4282	42¢ Deleware Flag . .	3.75	....	....	....	1.50	.75
4283-92	42¢ Flags of Our Nation coil strip of 10	....	....	....	....	14.00	....
	coil strip of 10	....	....	....	....	19.00	....
4283	42¢ District of Columbia Flag	3.75	....	....	....	1.50	.75
4284	42¢ Florida Flag.	3.75	....	....	....	1.50	.75
4285	42¢ Georgia Flag. . . .	3.75	....	....	....	1.50	.75
4286	42¢ Guam Flag	3.75	....	....	....	1.50	.75
4287	42¢ Hawaii Flag.	3.75	....	....	....	1.50	.75
4288	42¢ Idaho Flag.	3.75	....	....	....	1.50	.75
4289	42¢ Illinois Flag	3.75	....	....	....	1.50	.75
4290	42¢ Indiana Flag	3.75	....	....	....	1.50	.75
4291	42¢ Iowa Flag	3.75	....	....	....	1.50	.75
4292	42¢ Kansas Flag	3.75	....	....	....	1.50	.75
4293- 4302	44¢ Flags of Our Nation, coil strip of 10	12.00	....	....	....	14.00	....
	same, plate # strip of 11	....	....	....	....	19.00	....
4293	44¢ Kentucky Flag. . .	3.75	....	....	....	1.50	.75
4294	44¢ Louisiana Flag . . .	3.75	....	....	....	1.50	.75
4295	44¢ Maine Flag	3.75	....	....	....	1.50	.75
4296	44¢ Maryland Flag. . .	3.75	....	....	....	1.50	.75
4297	44¢ Massachusetts . .	3.75	....	....	....	1.50	.75
4298	44¢ Michigan Flag. . .	3.75	....	....	....	1.50	.75
4299	44¢ Minnesota Flag . .	3.75	....	....	....	1.50	.75
4300	44¢ Mississippi Flag .	3.75	....	....	....	1.50	.75
4301	44¢ Missouri Flag . . .	3.75	....	....	....	1.50	.75
4302	44¢ American Flag & Wheat.	3.75	....	....	....	1.50	.75
4303-12	44¢ Flags of Our Nation. coil strip of 10.	12.00	....	....	....	14.00	....
	same, plate strip of 11	....	....	....	....	19.00	....
4303	44¢ American Flag and Mountains	3.75	....	....	....	1.50	.75
4304	44¢ Montana Flag . . .	3.75	....	....	....	1.50	.50
4305	44¢ Nebraska Flag . .	3.75	....	....	....	1.50	.50
4306	44¢ Nevada Flag	3.75	....	....	....	1.50	.50
4307	44¢ New Hampshire Flag	3.75	....	....	....	1.50	.50
4308	44¢ New Jersey Flag.	3.75	....	....	....	1.50	.50
4309	44¢ New Mexico Flag	3.75	....	....	....	1.50	.50
4310	44¢ New York Flag . .	3.75	....	....	....	1.50	.50
4311	44¢ North Carolina Flag	3.75	....	....	....	1.50	.50
4312	44¢ North Dakota Flag	3.75	....	....	....	1.50	.50
4313-22	(44¢) Flags of Our Nation	....	....	....	....	14.00	....
	same, plate # strip of 11	....	....	....	....	19.00	....
4313	(44¢) N. Marianas Flag .	3.75	....	....	....	1.50	.75
4314	(44¢) Ohio Flag	3.75	....	....	....	1.50	.75
4315	(44¢) Oklahoma Flag.	3.75	....	....	....	1.50	.75

SCOTT NO.	DESCRIPTION	FIRST DAY COVERS SING	FIRST DAY COVERS PL. BLK.	MINT SHEET	PLATE BLOCK	UNUSED F/NH	USED
4316	(44¢) Oregon Flag. . .	3.75	....	....	....	1.50	.75
4317	(44¢) Pennsylvania Flag	3.75	....	....	....	1.50	.75
4318	(44¢) Puerto Rico Flag	3.75	....	....	....	1.50	.75
4319	(44¢) Rhode Island Flag	3.75	....	....	....	1.50	.75
4320	(44¢) South Carolina Flag	3.75	....	....	....	1.50	.75
4321	(44¢) South Dakota Flag	3.75	....	....	....	1.50	.75
4322	(44¢) Tennessee Flag	3.75	....	....	....	1.50	.75
4323-32	(45¢) Flags of our Nation	....	....	....	....	16.00	
	same, plate strip of 11	....	....	....	....	21.00	
4323	(45¢) Texas Flag . . .	3.75	....	....	....	1.75	.50
4324	(45¢) Utah Flag	3.75	....	....	....	1.75	.50
4325	(45¢) Vermont Flag . .	3.75	....	....	....	1.75	.50
4326	(45¢) Virgin Islands Flag	3.75	....	....	....	1.75	.50
4327	(45¢)Virginia Flag . . .	3.75	....	....	....	1.75	.50
4328	(45¢) Washington Flag	3.75	....	....	....	1.75	.50
4329	(45¢) West Virginia Flag	3.75	....	....	....	1.75	.50
4330	(45¢) Wisconsin Flag .	3.75	....	....	....	1.75	.50
4331	(45¢) Wyoming Flag . .	3.75	....	....	....	1.75	.50
4332	(45¢) American Flag and Fruited Plain	3.75	....	....	....	1.75	.50

4333

CHARLES (1907-78) AND RAY (1912-88) EAMES, DESIGNERS

4333a	Christmas card depicting Charles and Ray Eames
4333b	"Crosspatch" fabric design
4333c	Stacking chairs
4333d	Case Study House #8, Pacific Palisades, CA
4333e	Wire-base table
4333f	Lounge chair and ottoman
4333g	Hang-it-all
4333h	La Chaise
4333i	Scene from film, "Tops"
4333j	Wire mesh chair
4333k	Cover of May 1943 edition of California Arts & Architecture Magazine
4333l	House of Cards
4333m	Molded plywood sculpture
4333n	Eames Storage Unit
4333o	Aluminum group chair
4333p	Molded plywood chair

4333	42¢ Charles & Ray Eames	....	....	25.00 (16)	....	25.00	....
4333a	42¢ Charles & Ray Eames	3.75	....	....	....	1.75	.75
4333b	42¢ Crosspatch Fabric Design	3.75	....	....	....	1.75	.75
4333c	42¢ Stacking Chairs .	3.75	....	....	....	1.75	.75
4333d	42¢ Case Study House No.8	3.75	....	....	....	1.75	.75
4333e	42¢ Wire Base Tables	3.75	....	....	....	1.75	.75
4333f	42¢ Lounge Chair & Ottoman	3.75	....	....	....	1.75	.75
4333g	42¢ Hang-It-All.	3.75	....	....	....	1.75	.75
4333h	42¢ La Chaise	3.75	....	....	....	1.75	.75
4333i	42¢ "Tops".	3.75	....	....	....	1.75	.75
4333j	42¢ Wire Mesh Chair	3.75	....	....	....	1.75	.75
4333k	42¢ "Arts & Architecture" Cover	3.75	....	....	....	1.75	.75
4333l	42¢ House of Cards .	3.75	....	....	....	1.75	.75
4333m	42¢ Molded Plywood Sculpture	3.75	....	....	....	1.75	.75
4333n	42¢ Eames Storage Unit	3.75	....	....	....	1.75	.75
4333o	42¢ Aluminum Group Chair	3.75	....	....	....	1.75	.75
4333p	42¢ Molded Plywood Chair	3.75	....	....	....	1.75	.75

4334

4335

| 4334 | Summer Olympics . . . | 3.75 | 4.50 | 25.00 (20) | 6.50 | 1.60 | .40 |
| 4335 | 42¢ Celebrate . . . . . . | 3.75 | 4.50 | 22.00 (20) | 6.00 | 1.50 | .40 |

| **4336** | **4337** | **4338** | **4339** | **4340** |

4336-40	42¢ Vintage Black Cinema	....	....	30.00(20)	15.00(10)	8.50	....
4336	42¢ Poster for "Black & Tan"	3.75	....	....	....	1.60	1.50
4337	42¢ Poster for "The Sport of the Gods"	3.75	....	....	....	1.60	1.50
4338	42¢ Poster for "Prinsesse Tam-Tam".....	3.75	....	....	....	1.60	1.50
4339	42¢ Poster for "Caledonia"	3.75	....	....	....	1.60	1.50
4340	42¢ Poster for "Hallelujah"	3.75	....	....	....	1.60	1.50

SCOTT NO.	DESCRIPTION	FIRST DAY COVERS SING	PL. BLK.	MINT SHEET	PLATE BLOCK	UNUSED F/NH	USED

4341

| 4341 | 42¢ Take Me Out To Ballgame | 3.75 | 4.50 | 25.00 (20) | 6.50 | 1.50 | .40 |

4342 **4343** **4344** **4345**

4342-45	42¢ Art of Disney....	4.25	4.75	24.00 (20)	7.50	7.00	....
4342	42¢ Lucky & Pongo, from 101 Dalmations ..	3.75	....	....	....	1.60	.75
4343	42¢ Steamboat Willie .	3.75	....	....	....	1.60	.75
4344	42¢ Sleeping Beauty..	3.75	....	....	....	1.60	.75
4345	42¢ Mowgli & Baloo, from Jungle Book	3.75	....	....	....	1.60	.75

4346 **4347** **4348**

4346	42¢ Albert Bierstadt ..	3.75	4.50	....	....	1.50	.45
4346a	42¢ Albert Bierstadt bklt pane of 20.....	....	....	....	....	26.00	....
4347	42¢ Sunflower	3.75	....	....	....	1.50	.35
4347a	same, bklt pane of 20	....	....	....	....	26.00	....
4348	5¢ Sea Coast, coil (2008) water-activated	....	....	....	....	.30	.25
	same, plate strip of 5..	....	....	....	....	3.75	....

4349 **4350** **4351**

4349	42¢ Latin Jazz	3.75	....	24.00(20)	5.50	1.50	.40
4350	42¢ Bette Davis	3.75	....	36.00(20)	8.00	1.85	.50
4351	42¢ EID, die cut 11 ..	3.75	....	24.00(20)	5.50	1.50	.90

4352

GREAT LAKES DUNES

4352a	Vesper Sparrow	4352f	Spotted Sandpiper
4352b	Red Fox	4352g	Tiger Beetle
4352c	Piping Plover	4352h	White Footed Mouse
4352d	Eastern Hognose Snake	4352i	Piper Plover Nestings
4352e	Common Mergansers	4352j	Red Admiral Butterfly

| 4352 | 42¢ Great Lakes Dunes, sheet of 10. .... | .... | .... | 17.00 | .... | 17.00 | .... |
| | set of singles .... | 20.00 | .... | .... | .... | .... | 9.00 |

4353 **4354** **4355**

4356 **4357**

4353-57	42¢ Automobiles of the 1950's	3.75	....	25.00(20)	15.00 (10)	7.50	....
4353	42¢ 1959 Cadillac Eldorado	....	....	....	....	1.50	.85
4354	42¢ 1957 Studebaker Golden Hawk.......	....	....	....	....	1.50	.85
4355	42¢ 1957 Pontiac Safari	....	....	....	....	1.50	.85
4356	42¢ 1957 Lincoln Premiere	....	....	....	....	1.50	.85
4357	42¢ 1957 Chrysler 300C	....	....	....	....	1.50	.85

4358 **4359**

4358	42¢ Alzheimer's Awareness	....	....	22.00	5.50	1.50	.40
4359	42¢ Virgin and Child, Botticelli	3.75	....	....	....	1.50	.40
4359a	same, bklt pane of 20	....	....	....	....	26.00	....

4360, 4364, 4368   **4361, 4365, 4369**   **4362, 4366, 4370**   **4363, 4367, 4371**

4360-63	42¢ Nutcrackers, block of 4, die cut 10.75x11	....	....	....	....	8.50	....
4360	42¢ Drummer Nutcracker, die cut 10.75x11	3.75	....	....	....	1.75	1.00
4361	42¢ Santa Claus Nutcracker, die cut 10.75x11	3.75	....	....	....	1.75	1.00
4362	42¢ King Nutcracker, die cut 10.75x11	3.75	....	....	....	1.75	1.00
4363	42¢ Soldier Nutcracker, die cut 10.75x11	3.75	....	....	....	1.75	1.00
4363b	42¢ Nutcracker, pane of 20	....	....	....	....	34.00	....
4364-67	42¢ Nutcrackers, block of 4 die cut 11.25x11.....	....	....	....	....	7.50	....
4364	42¢ Drummer Nutcracker, die cut 11.25x11.....	3.75	....	....	....	2.00	1.25
4365	42¢ Santa Claus Nutcracker, die cut 11.25x11.....	3.75	....	....	....	2.00	1.25
4366	42¢ King Nutcracker, die cut 11.25x11.....	3.75	....	....	....	2.00	1.25
4367	42¢ Soldier Nutcracker, die cut 11.25x11.....	3.75	....	....	....	2.00	1.25
4367b	42¢ Nutcracker, bklt pane of 4.......	....	....	....	....	7.50	....
4367c	42¢ Nutcracker, (2 each 4366, 4367) bklt pane of 6.......	....	....	....	....	11.00	....
4367d	42¢ Nutcracker, (2 each 4364, 4365) bklt pane of 6.......	....	....	....	....	11.00	....
4367bk	42¢ Nutcracker, bklt pane of 20, complete	....	....	....	....	34.00	....
4368-71	42¢ Nutcrackers, block of 4, die cut 8 ..	4.75	....	....	....	9.00	....
4368	42¢ Drummer Nutcracker, die cut 8.....	3.75	....	....	....	2.00	1.00
4369	42¢ Santa Claus Nutcracker, die cut 8.....	3.75	....	....	....	2.00	1.00
4370	42¢ King Nutcracker, die cut 8.....	3.75	....	....	....	2.00	1.00
4371	42¢ Soldier Nutcracker, die cut 8.....	3.75	....	....	....	2.00	1.00
4371b	42¢ Nutcracker, bklt pane of 18......	....	....	....	....	34.00	....

SCOTT NO.	DESCRIPTION	FIRST DAY COVERS SING	FIRST DAY COVERS PL. BLK.	MINT SHEET	PLATE BLOCK	UNUSED F/NH	USED

4372

4373

| 4372 | 42¢ Hanukkah | 3.75 | ...... | 24.00(20) | 6.00 | 1.50 | .75 |
| 4373 | 42¢ Kwanzaa | 3.75 | ...... | 24.00(20) | 6.00 | 1.50 | .75 |

2009 COMMEMORATIVES

| 4374/4434 | (4374-4377, 4380-83, 4386, 4406, 4407, 4408, 4409-4413, 4415, 4416, 4417-4420, 4421, 4433, 4434) 26 varieties | ...... | ...... | ...... | | 43.00 | 27.50 |

4374

4375

| 4374 | 42¢ Alaska Statehood | 3.75 | ...... | 22.00(20) | 5.50 | 1.40 | .40 |
| 4375 | 42¢ Year of the Ox | 3.75 | ...... | 14.00(12) | 5.50 | 1.40 | .40 |

4376

4377

| 4376 | 42¢ Oregon Statehood | 3.75 | ...... | 22.00(20) | 5.50 | 1.50 | .40 |
| 4377 | 42¢ Edgar Allen Poe | 3.75 | ...... | 22.00(20) | 5.50 | 1.50 | .40 |

4378

4379

| 4378 | $4.95 Redwood Forrest | 12.00 | ...... | 245.00(20) | 60.00 | 14.00 | 10.00 |
| 4379 | $17.50 Old Faithful | 35.00 | ...... | 840.00(20) | 195.00 | 48.00 | 30.00 |

4380

4381

4382

4383

4380-83	42¢ Lincoln, strip of 4	5.75	......	34.00(20)	16.00(8)	8.50	......
4380	42¢ Lincoln as Rail Splitter	4.75				2.00	.75
4381	42¢ Lincoln as Lawyer	4.75				2.00	.75
4382	42¢ Lincoln as Politician	4.75				2.00	.75
4383	42¢ Lincoln as President	4.75				2.00	.75

4384

4384	42¢ Civil Rights Pioneers	......	......	......	......	14.00	......
4384a	42¢ Mary Church Terrell & Mary White Ovington	......				2.25	1.50
4384b	42¢ J R Clifford & Joel Elias Spingarn..	......				2.25	1.50
4384c	42¢ Oswald Garrison Villard & Daisy Gatson Bates	......				2.25	1.50
4384d	42¢ Charles Hamilton Houston & Walter White	......				2.25	1.50
4384e	Medgar Evers & Fannie Lou Hamer..	......				2.25	1.50
4384f	Ella Baker & Ruby Hurley	......				2.25	1.50

4385

4386

4385	10¢ Patriotic Banner..	3.75	......	......	......	.50	.30
	same, plate strip of 5..	......	......	......	......	6.00	......
4386	61¢ Richard Wright	3.75	......	30.00	8.00	2.00	.85

4387, 4389

4388

4390

4387	28¢ Polar Bear	3.75	......	15.00(20)	4.00	.85	.45
4388	64¢ Dolphin	3.75	......	31.00(20)	8.00	1.75	.85
4389	28¢ Polar Bear, coil	3.75	......	......	......	.85	.45
	same, plate strip of 5..	......	......	......	......	8.50	......
4390	44¢ Purple Heart	3.75	......	22.50(20)	5.50	1.50	.45
4391	44¢ Flag, water-activated coil	3.75	......	......	......	1.50	.80
	same, plate strip of 5.	......	......	......	......	11.00	......
4392	44¢ Flag, s/a coil die cut 11 w/pointed corners	......	......	......	......	2.50	.45
	same, plate strip of 5 ..	......	......	......	......	13.00	......
4393	44¢ Flag, s/a coil die cut 9 1/2..	......	......	......	......	2.00	.45
	same, plate strip of 5 ..	......	......	......	......	12.00	......
4394	44¢ Flag, s/a coil die cut 8 1/2	......	......	......	......	2.00	.45
	same, plate strip of 5 .	......	......	......	......	12.00	......
4395	44¢ Flag, s/a coil die cut 11 w/rounded corners	3.75	......	......	......	2.00	.55
	same, plate strip of 5 .	......	......	......	......	12.00	......
4396	44¢ American Flag...	3.75	......	......	......	1.50	.45
	same, conv. bklt of 10	......	......	......	......	14.00	......

4391-4396

4397

4398

| 4397 | 44¢ Wedding Rings .. | 3.75 | ...... | 28.00(20) | 7.00 | 1.50 | .40 |
| 4398 | 61¢ Wedding Cake .. | 3.75 | ...... | 34.00(20) | 9.00 | 2.00 | .85 |

SCOTT NO.	DESCRIPTION	FIRST DAY COVERS SING	PL. BLK.	MINT SHEET	PLATE BLOCK	UNUSED F/NH	USED

4399

4400

4401

4402

4403

4399	44¢ Homer Simpson .	3.75	....	....	....	2.00	.85
4400	44¢ Marge Simpson .	3.75	....	....	....	2.00	.85
4401	44¢ Bart Simpson . . .	3.75	....	....	....	2.00	.85
4402	44¢ Lisa Simpson . . .	3.75	....	....	....	2.00	.85
4403	44¢ Maggie Simpson.	3.75	....	....	....	2.00	.85
4403a	Simpson's, bklt pane of 20	....	....	....	....	36.00	....

4404

4405

4404	44¢ King of Hearts. . .	3.75	....	....	....	1.75	.50
4405	44¢ Queen of Hearts .	3.75	....	....	....	1.75	.50
4405a	King and Queen of Hearts, conv. bklt of 20.	....	....	....	....	34.00	....

4406

| 4406 | 44¢ Bob Hope . . . . . . | 3.75 | .... | 35.00(20) | 8.50 | 1.75 | .50 |

4407

4408

| 4407 | 44¢ Celebrate . . . . . . | 3.75 | .... | 22.00(20) | 5.50 | 1.50 | .40 |
| 4408 | 44¢ Anna Julia Cooper | 3.75 | .... | 24.00(20) | 5.50 | 1.50 | .50 |

SCOTT NO.	DESCRIPTION	FIRST DAY COVERS SING	PL. BLK.	MINT SHEET	PLATE BLOCK	UNUSED F/NH	USED

| 4409 | 4410 | 4411 | 4412 | 4413 |

4409-13	44¢ Gulf Coast Lighthouses	6.00	....	28.00(20)	16.00	9.00	....
4409	44¢ Matagorda Island Lighthouse	2.50	....	....	....	1.75	.75
4410	44¢ Sabine Pass Lighthouse	2.50	....	....	....	1.75	.75
4411	44¢ Biloxi Lighthouse. .	2.50	....	....	....	1.75	.75
4412	44¢ Sand Island Lighthouse	2.50	....	....	....	1.75	.75
4413	44¢ Fort Jefferson Lighthouse	2.50	....	....	....	1.75	.75

4414

EARLY TV MEMORIES

4414a	Milton Berle	4414k	Kukla, Fran & Ollie
4414b	I Love Lucy	4414l	Phil Silvers Show
4414c	The Red Skelton Show	4414m	The Lone Ranger
4414d	Howdy Doody	4414n	Perry Mason
4414e	Dragnet	4414o	Alfred Hitchcock
4414f	Lassie	4414p	Burns & Allen
4414g	Hopalong Cassidy	4414q	Ozzie & Harriet
4414h	Groucho Marx	4414r	The Tonight Show
4414i	Dinah Shore Show	4414s	The Twilight Zone
4414j	The Ed Sullivan Show	4414t	The Honeymooners

4414	44¢ Early TV Memories	20.00	....	35.00 (20)	....	35.00	....
	Set of Singles		....				18.00
	Singles		....				1.00

4415

4416

| 4415 | 44¢ Hawaii Statehood . | 2.25 | 7.50 | 48.00 (20) | 10.00 | 2.50 | .50 |
| 4416 | 44¢ EID . . . . | 2.25 | .... | 22.00 (20) | 6.00 | 1.50 | .50 |

SCOTT NO.	DESCRIPTION	FIRST DAY COVERS SING	FIRST DAY COVERS PL. BLK.	MINT SHEET	PLATE BLOCK	UNUSED F/NH	USED

4417　　4418　　4419　　4420

SCOTT NO.	DESCRIPTION	SING	PL. BLK.	MINT SHEET	PLATE BLOCK	UNUSED F/NH	USED
4417-20	44¢ Thanksgiving Day Parade	5.25	....	23.00 (20)	12.00 (8)	6.50	....
4417	44¢ Crowd, Street Sign, Bear Balloon	2.25	....	....	....	1.50	.55
4418	44¢ Drum Major, Musicians	2.25	....	....	....	1.50	.55
4419	44¢ Musicians, Balloon, Horse	2.25	....	....	....	1.50	.55
4420	44¢ Cowboy, Turkey Balloon	2.25	....	....	....	1.50	.55

4421

| 4421 | 44¢ Gary Cooper . . . . . | 2.25 | .... | 35.00 (20) | 8.50 | 1.75 | .60 |

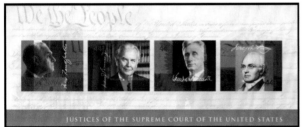

4422

4422	Supreme Court Justices S/S of 4	4.75	....	....	....	7.00	5.00
4422a	44¢ Felix Frankfurter . .	2.25	....	....	....	1.75	1.00
4422b	44¢ William J. Brennan, Jr.	2.25	....	....	....	1.75	1.00
4422c	44¢ Louis D. Brandeis .	2.25	....	....	....	1.75	1.00
4422d	44¢ Joseph Story.	2.25	....	....	....	1.75	1.00

4423

KELP FOREST

4423a　*Brown Pelican*
4423b　*Western Gull, Southern Sea Otters, Red Sea Urchin*
4423c　*Harbor Seal*
4423d　*Lion's Mane Nudibranch*
4423e　*Yellow-tail Rockfish, White-spotted Rose Anemone*
4423f　*Vermillion Rockfish*
4423g　*Copper Rockfish*
4423h　*Pacific Rock Crab, Jeweled Top Snail*
4423i　*Northern Kelp Crab*
4423j　*Treefish, Monterey Turban Snail, Brooding Sea Anemone*

| 4423 | 44¢ Kelp Forest . . . . . . | 10.00 | .... | 18.00 (10) | .... | 18.00 | .... |
| | Set of Singles . . . . | .... | .... | .... | .... | 18.00 | 8.00 |

4424

| 4424 | 44¢ Madonna & Sleeping Child | 2.25 | .... | .... | .... | 1.50 | .45 |
| 4424a | same, booklet pane of 20 | .... | .... | .... | .... | 28.00 | .... |

4425, 4429　　4426, 4430　　4427, 4431　　4428, 4432

4425-28	44¢ Winter Holidays, block of 4	5.00	....	....	....	7.50	....
4425	44¢ Reindeer, die cut 10.75x11	2.25	....	....	....	1.75	.50
4426	44¢ Snowman, die cut 10.75x11	2.25	....	....	....	1.75	.50
4427	44¢ Gingerbread Man, die cut 10.75x11	....	....	....	....	1.75	.50
4428	44¢ Toy Soldier, die cut 10.75x11	2.25	....	....	....	1.75	.50
4428b	Booklet pane of 20, 5 each 4425-28	....	....	....	....	34.00	....
4429-32	44¢ Winter Holidays, block of 4	5.00	....	....	....	7.50	....
4429	44¢ Reindeer, die cut 8	2.25	....	....	....	1.75	.60
4430	44¢ Snowman, die cut 8	2.25	....	....	....	1.75	.60
4431	44¢ Gingerbread Man, die cut 8	2.25	....	....	....	1.75	.60
4432	44¢ Toy Soldier, die cut 8	2.25	....	....	....	1.75	.60
4432b	Booklet pane of 18, 5 each: 4429, 4431 4 each: 4430, 4432	....	....	....	....	30.00	....

4433　　4434

| 4433 | 44¢ Hanukkah . . . . | 2.25 | .... | 22.00 (20) | 5.50 | 1.50 | .50 |
| 4434 | 44¢ Kwanzaa. . . . . | 2.25 | .... | 22.00 (20) | 5.50 | 1.50 | .50 |

2010 COMMEMORATIVES

| 4435/4477 | (4435, 4436, 4440-4443, 4445, 4446-61, 4463-73, 4475, 4476, 4477) 37 varieties | .... | .... | .... | 55.00 | 18.00 |

4435　　4436

4435	44¢ Year of the Tiger . .	2.25	....	15.00 (12)	....	1.75	.55
4436	44¢ 2010 Olympics Snowboarder	2.25	4.75	22.00 (20)	5.50	1.25	.45
4437	44¢ Forever Liberty Bell, dated in copper "2009", medium microprinting, bell 16mm, die-cut 11.25x10.75	2.25	....	....	....	1.50	.55
4437a	same, booklet pane of 18	....	....	....	....	26.00	....

SCOTT NO.	DESCRIPTION	FIRST DAY COVERS SING	FIRST DAY COVERS PL. BLK.	MINT SHEET	PLATE BLOCK	UNUSED F/NH	USED

4438

4439

| 4438 | $4.90 Mackinac Bridge. | 12.00 | .... | 235.00 (20) | 60.00 | 15.00 | 10.00 |
| 4439 | $18.30 Bixby Creek Bridge | 39.00 | .... | 875.00 (20) | 215.00 | 55.00 | 35.00 |

4440 **4441**
4442 **4443**

4440-43	44¢ Distinguished Sailors, block of 4	5.25	7.50	24.00 (20)	5.50 (4) 10.00 (8)	6.50	....
4440	Admiral William S. Sims	2.25	....	....	....	1.75	1.00
4441	Admiral Arleigh A. Burke	2.25	....	....	....	1.75	1.00
4442	Lt. Commander John McCloy	2.25	....	....	....	1.75	1.00
4443	Petty Officer 3rd Class Doris Miller	2.25	....	....	....	1.75	1.00

4444

ABSTRACT EXPRESSIONISTS

4444a	*The Golden Wall*	4444f	*1948-C*
4444b	*Ashville*	4444g	*Elegy to the Spanish Republic*
4444c	*Orange and yellow*	4444h	*La Grande Vallee O*
4444d	*Howdy Doody*	4444i	*Romanesque Façade*
4444e	*The Liver is the Cock's Comb*	4444j	*Achilles*

4444	Abstract Expressionists	....	20.00	....	....	20.00	....
	set of singles.........	....	....	....	....	....	10.00
	singles each	....	....	....	....	....	1.00

4445

| 4445 | 44¢ Bill Mauldin ...... | 2.25 | .... | 22.00 (20) | 5.75 | 1.50 | .45 |

SCOTT NO.	DESCRIPTION	FIRST DAY COVERS SING	FIRST DAY COVERS PL. BLK.	MINT SHEET	PLATE BLOCK	UNUSED F/NH	USED

4446 **4447**
4448 **4449**

4446-49	44¢ Cowboys of the Silver Screen	5.75	....	32.00 (20)	8.00	7.50	....
4446	44¢ Roy Rogers	2.25	....	....	....	2.00	1.00
4447	44¢ Tom Mix	2.25	....	....	....	2.00	1.00
4448	44¢ William S Hart	2.25	....	....	....	2.00	1.00
4449	44¢ Gene Autry.......	2.25	....	....	....	2.00	1.00

4450

| 4450 | 44¢ Love: Pansies in a basket | 2.25 | .... | 28.00(20) | 6.50 | 1.50 | .40 |

4451 **4452** **4453**

4454 **4455** **4456**

4457 **4458** **4459**

4460

4451-60	44¢ Adopt a Shelter Pet	11.50	....	32.00(20)	19.00(10)	17.50	....
4451	44¢ Wire-haired Jack Russell Terrier	2.25	....	....	....	1.50	.65
4452	44¢ Maltese Cat	2.25	....	....	....	1.50	.65
4453	44¢ Calico Cat	2.25	....	....	....	1.50	.65
4454	44¢ Yellow Labrador retriever	2.25	....	....	....	1.50	.65
4455	44¢ Golden retriever...	2.25	....	....	....	1.50	.65
4456	44¢ Gray, white and tan cat	2.25	....	....	....	1.50	.65
4457	44¢ Black, white and tan cat	2.25	....	....	....	1.50	.65
4458	44¢ Australian shepherd	2.25	....	....	....	1.50	.65
4459	44¢ Boston terrier.....	2.25	....	....	....	1.50	.65
4460	44¢ Orange tabby cat..	2.25	....	....	....	1.50	.65

SCOTT NO.	DESCRIPTION	FIRST DAY COVERS SING	PL. BLK.	MINT SHEET	PLATE BLOCK	UNUSED F/NH	USED

4461

4462

| 4461 | 44¢ Katherine Hepburn | 2.25 | .... | 24.00(20) | 6.00 | 1.50 | .45 |
| 4462 | 64¢ Monarch Butterfly... | 2.25 | .... | 31.00(20) | 7.50 | 2.00 | 1.15 |

KATE SMITH
4463

Oscar Micheaux
4464

| 4463 | 44¢ Kate Smith....... | 2.25 | .... | 21.00(20) | 5.75 | 1.50 | .45 |
| 4464 | 44¢ Oscar Micheaux... | 3.75 | .... | 20.00(20) | 5.75 | 1.50 | .45 |

4465   4466

4465-66	44¢ Negro Leagues Baseball, attached pair.........	4.25	7.50	22.00(20)	5.75	3.25	1.25
4465	44¢ Play at Home.....	2.50	....	....		1.50	.65
4466	44¢ Rube Foster......	2.50	....	....		1.50	.65

4467   4468   4469   4470   4471

4467-71	44¢ Sunday Funnies...	4.25	7.50	31.00(20)	18.00(10)	8.00	....
4467	44¢ Beetle Bailey.....	2.50	....	....		1.50	.75
4468	44¢ Calvin and Hobbes	2.50	....	....		1.50	.75
4469	44¢ Archie..........	2.50	....	....		1.50	.75
4470	44¢ Garfield........	2.50	....	....		1.50	.75
4471	44¢ Dennis the Menace	2.50	....	....		1.50	.75

4472

4473

| 4472 | 44¢ Scouting........ | 2.50 | 3.75 | 21.00(20) | 5.50 | 1.50 | .45 |
| 4473 | 44¢ Boys in Pasture, Winslow Homer...... | 2.50 | 3.75 | 21.00(20) | 5.50 | 1.50 | .25 |

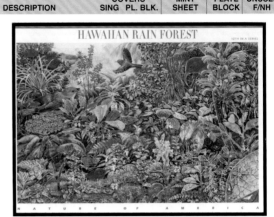

4474

HAWAIIAN RAIN FOREST

4474a	*Hawaii 'amakihi, Hawaii 'elepaio*	**4474f**	*Pulehua, kelea lau nui, 'ilihia*
4474b	*'Akepa, 'ope'ape'a*	**4474g**	*Koele Mountain damselfly, 'akala*
4474c	*I'iwi, haha*	**4474h**	*Apapane, Hawaiian Mint*
4474d	*'Oma'o, kanawao, 'ohelo kau lau nui*	**4474i**	*Jewel Orchid*
4474e	*'Oha*	**4474j**	*Happyface spider, 'ala'ala wai nui*

| 4474 | 44¢ Hawaiian Rain Forest sheet | 10.00 | 15.00(10) | .... | 15.00 | .... |
| | set of singles .... | .... | .... | .... | 15.00 | 10.00 |

4475

4476

4477

4475	44¢ Mother Teresa	2.50	3.75	22.00(20)	5.50	1.50	.45
4476	44¢ Julia de Burgos ...	2.50	3.75	21.00(20)	5.50	1.50	.45
4477	44¢ Angel with Lute ...	2.50	3.75	21.00(20)	5.50	1.50	.45

4478   4479

4480   4481

4478-81	(44¢) Forever Pine cones, die cut	11.00	5.50	....		6.00	....
4478	(44¢) Forever Ponderosa Pine	2.25	....	....		1.50	.50
4479	(44¢) Forever Easter Red Cedar	2.25	....	....		1.50	.50
4480	(44¢) Forever Balsam Fir	2.25	....	....		1.50	.50
4481	(44¢) Forever Blue Spruce	2.25	....	....		1.50	.50
4481b	(44¢) Forever pine cones, die cut 11, bklt pane of 20	....	....	....		30.00	....
4482-85	(44¢) Forever pine cones, die cut 11.25x10.75 ...	5.50		....		6.00	....
4482	(44¢) Forever Ponderosa Pine	2.25	....	....		1.50	.60
4483	(44¢) Forever Eastern Red Cedar	2.25	....	....		1.50	.60
4484	(44¢) Forever Balsam Fir	2.25	....	....		1.50	.60
4485	(44¢) Forever Blue Spruce	2.25	....	....		1.50	.60
4485b	(44¢) Forever pine cones, d/c 11.25x10.75, bklt pane of 18	....	....	....		28.00	....

SCOTT NO.	DESCRIPTION	FIRST DAY COVERS SING	FIRST DAY COVERS PL. BLK.	MINT SHEET	PLATE BLOCK	UNUSED F/NH	USED

4486, 4488, 4490

4487, 4489, 4491

4486-87	(44¢) Forever Lady Liberty & Flag (AP) D/C 9.5 (MICRO 4evR)	....	....	....		3.0	....
	same, plate strip of 5 . .	....	....	12.00		....	....
4486	(44¢) Forever Lady Liberty, (AP) D/C 9.5.	2.25	....			1.50	.45
4487	(44¢) Forever Flag, (AP) D/C 9.5.	2.25	....			1.50	.45
4488-89	(44¢) Forever Lady Liberty & Flag, (SSP) D/C 11 (MICRO 4evR)	....	....			3.50	
	same, plate strip of 5 . .	....	....	12.00		....	....
4488	(44¢) Forever Lady Liberty, (SSP) D/C 11	2.25	....			1.50	.45
4489	(44¢) Forever Flag	2.25	....			1.50	.45
4490-91	(44¢) Forever Lady Liberty & Flag, (AV) D/C 8.5 (MICRO 4EVR)			9.50		3.50	
	same, plate strip of 5 . .	....	....	12.00		....	....
4490	(44¢) Forever Lady Liberty, (AV) D/C 8.5.	2.25	....			1.50	.45
4491	(44¢)Forever Flag.	2.25	....			1.50	.45

2011 COMMEMORATIVES

| 4492/4584 | (4492-4494, 4497-4503, 4522-4523, 4525-4528, 4530, 4541-4545, 4547-4558, 4565-4569, 4583-4584) 41 varieties | .... | .... | .... | | 58.50 | 24.00 |

4492

4493

| 4492 | (44¢) Year of the Rabbit | 2.25 | .... | 13.00(12) | .... | 1.50 | .45 |
| 4493 | (44¢) Kansas Statehood | 2.25 | .... | 22.00(20) | 5.50 | 1.50 | .45 |

4495

4494

4496

4494	(44¢) Ronald Reagan . .	2.25	....	25.00(20)	6.00	1.50	.50
4495	(5¢) Art Deco Bird, Non-Profit Coil	2.25				.25	.25
	same, plate number strip of 5					1.70	
4496	44¢ Quill and Inkwell Coil	2.25				1.25	.50
	same, plate number strip of 5	....				12.00	....

4497-4501

4497-4501	Latin Music Legends	....	....	22.00(20)	13.00(10)	8.00	....
4497	(44¢) Tito Fuente	2.25				1.75	.65
4498	(44¢) Carmen Miranda .	2.25				1.75	.65
4499	(44¢) Selena.	2.25				1.75	.65
4500	(44¢) Carlos Gardel . . .	2.25				1.75	.65
4501	(44¢) Celia Cruz	2.25				1.75	.65

4502

4503

4504

4502	(44¢) Celebrate.	2.25	....	24.00(20)	5.50	1.50	.45
4503	(44¢) Jazz.	2.25	....	24.00(20)	5.50	1.50	.45
4504	20¢ George Washington	2.25	....	12.00(20)	2.50	.60	.45

4505-09

4505-09	29¢ Herbs.	....	....	16.00(20)	9.00(10)	5.00	....
4505	29¢ Oregano.	2.25	....			1.15	.55
4506	29¢ Flax	2.25	....			1.15	.55
4507	29¢ Foxglove	2.25	....			1.15	.55
4508	29¢ Lavender	2.25	....			1.15	.55
4509	29¢ Sage	2.25	....			1.15	.55

4510   4511   4512

4510	84¢ Oveta Culp Hobby .	3.75	....	39.00	9.00	3.00	.85
4511	$4.95 New River Gorge Bridge	12.00	....	235.00	55.00	14.00	6.75
4512	20¢ George Washington Coil	2.25	....	....		.50	.35
	same, plate # strip of 5 .				7.00	....	....

4513-17

4513-17	29¢ Herbs Coil	....	....			5.00	....
	same, plate # strip of 5 .	....	....		8.00		....
4513	29¢ Oregano Coil	2.25	....			1.15	.40
4514	29¢ Flax Coil.	2.25	....			1.15	.40
4515	29¢ Foxglove Coil.	2.25	....			1.15	.40
4516	29¢ Lavender Coil	2.25	....			1.15	.40
4517	29¢ Sage Coil.	2.25	....			1.15	.40

4518-19

4518-19	(44¢) Lady Liberty and Flag	3.75	....		....	3.50	....
4518	(44¢) Lady Liberty.	2.25	....			1.75	.70
4519	(44¢) Flag.	2.25	....			1.75	.70
4519b	Booklet pane of 20, (44¢) Lady Liberty & Flag	....				30.00	....

SCOTT NO.	DESCRIPTION	FIRST DAY COVERS SING	PL. BLK.	MINT SHEET	PLATE BLOCK	UNUSED F/NH	USED

4520

4521

| 4520 | (44¢) Wedding Roses.. | 2.25 | .... | 22.00(20) | 6.00 | 1.75 | .50 |
| 4521 | 64¢ Wedding Cake.... | 2.75 | .... | 31.00(20) | 8.00 | 2.50 | .90 |

4522-4523

4522-23	(44¢) Civil War Sesquicentennial	3.75	....	18.00(12)	....	18.00	....
4522	(44¢) Battle of Fort Sumter	2.25	....	....	....	1.75	.65
4523	(44¢) First Battle of Bull Run	2.25	....	....	....	1.75	.65

4524

GO GREEN

4524a	Buy local produce, reduce bags
4524b	Fix Water Leaks
4524c	Share rides
4524d	Turn off lights when not in use
4524e	Choose to walk
4524f	Go green, step by step
4524g	Compost
4524h	Let nature do the work
4524i	Recycle more
4524j	Ride a bike
4524k	Plant trees
4524l	Insulate the home
4524m	Use public transportation
4524n	Use efficient light bulbs
4524o	Adjust the thermostat
4524p	Maintain tire pressure

| 4524 | (44¢) Go Green Pane of 16 | .... | .... | 21.00(16) | .... | 21.00 | .... |
| | same, set of singles ... | .... | .... | .... | .... | .... | 14.00 |

4525

4526

| 4525 | (44¢) Helen Hayes .... | 2.25 | .... | 22.50(20) | 5.50 | 1.50 | .50 |
| 4526 | (44¢) Gregory Peck ... | 2.25 | .... | 24.00(20) | 6.50 | 1.50 | .50 |

4527   4528

4527-28	(44¢) Space Firsts....	3.75	....	22.00(20)	5.50	3.50	1.50
4527	(44¢) Alan B. Shepard, Jr.	2.25	....	....	....	1.75	.65
4528	(44¢) Messenger Mission	2.25	....	....	....	1.75	.65

4529

4530

| 4529 | (44¢) Purple Heart .... | 2.25 | .... | 22.00(20) | 5.00 | 1.50 | .45 |
| 4530 | (44¢) Indianapolis 500 . | 2.25 | .... | 22.00(20) | 5.00 | 1.50 | .45 |

4531-4540

4531-40	(44¢) Garden of Love ..	12.00	....	38.00(20)	21.00(10)	18.00	....
4531	(44¢) Pink Flower	2.25	....	....	....	1.75	.60
4532	(44¢) Red Flower	2.25	....	....	....	1.75	.60
4533	(44¢) Blue Leaves	2.25	....	....	....	1.75	.60
4534	(44¢) Butterfly........	2.25	....	....	....	1.75	.60
4535	(44¢) Green Vine Leaves	2.25	....	....	....	1.75	.60
4536	(44¢) Blue Flower	2.25	....	....	....	1.75	.60
4537	(44¢) Doves	2.25	....	....	....	1.75	.60
4538	(44¢) Orange Red Flowers	2.25	....	....	....	1.75	.60
4539	(44¢) Strawberry......	2.25	....	....	....	1.75	.60
4540	(44¢) Yellow Orange Flowers	2.25	....	....	....	1.75	.60

4541   4542

4543   4544

4541-44	(44¢) American Scientists	5.75	....	22.00(20)	12.00(8)	6.50	....
4541	(44¢) Melvin Calvin....	2.75	....	....	....	1.50	.60
4542	(44¢) Asa Gray	2.75	....	....	....	1.50	.60
4543	(44¢) Maria Goeppert Mayer	2.75	....	....	....	1.50	.60
4544	(44¢) Severo Ochoa ...	2.75	....	....	....	1.50	.60

SCOTT NO.	DESCRIPTION	FIRST DAY COVERS SING	PL. BLK.	MINT SHEET	PLATE BLOCK	UNUSED F/NH	USED

4545

| 4545 | (44¢) Mark Twain . . . . . | 2.50 | ...... | 22.00(20) | 5.50 | 1.50 | .45 |

4546

PIONEERS OF AMERICAN INDUSTRIAL DESIGN

4546a	Peter Muller-Munk	**4546g**	Norman Bel Geddes
4546b	Frederick Hurten Rhead	**4546h**	Dave Chapman
4546c	Raymond Loewy	**4546i**	Greta von Nessen
4546d	Donald Deskey	**4546j**	Eliot Noyes
4546e	Walter Dorwin Teague	**4546k**	Russel Wright
4546f	Henry Dreyfuss	**4546l**	Gilbert Rohde

| 4546 | (44¢) Pioneers of American Industrial Design . . . . . | 15.00 | ...... | 18.00(12) | ...... | 18.00 | ...... |
| | set of singles. . . . . | ...... | ...... | | | 18.00 | 12.00 |

4547

| 4547 | (44¢) Owney the Postal Dog | 2.75 | ...... | 24.00(20) | 5.50 | 1.50 | .50 |

4548   **4549**

4550   **4551**

4548-51	(44¢) U.S. Merchant Marine	4.75	......	22.00(20)	6.00	5.50	......
4548	(44¢) Clipper Ship. . . .	2.75	......	......	......	1.50	.75
4549	(44¢) Auxiliary Steamship	2.75	......	......	......	1.50	.75
4550	(44¢) Liberty Ship	2.75	......	......	......	1.50	.75
4551	(44¢) Container Ship . .	2.75	......	......	......	1.50	.75

4552

| 4552 | (44¢) EID . . . . | 2.75 | ...... | 21.00(20) | 5.00 | 1.50 | .50 |

4553-57

4553-57	(44¢) Pixar Films: Send a Hello	5.50	......	22.00(20)	13.00(10)	8.00	......
4553	(44¢) Lightening McQueen & Mater	3.25	......	......	......	1.75	.70
4554	(44¢) Remy the Rat & Linquini	3.25	......	......	......	1.75	.70
4555	(44¢) Buzz Lightyear & Two Aliens	3.25	......	......	......	1.75	.70
4556	(44¢) Carl Frederickson & Dug	3.25	......	......	......	1.75	.70
4557	(44¢) Wall-E	3.25	......	......	......	1.75	.70

4559, 4561, 4563   **4558**   **4560, 4562, 4564**

4558	(44¢) Edward Hopper . .	2.75	......	21.00(20)	5.00	1.50	.50
4559	(44¢) Lady Liberty (AP)	2.75	......	......	......	1.75	.65
4560	(44¢) American Flag (AP)	2.75	......	......	......	1.75	.65
4560A	Booklet pane of 20	......	......	......	......	28.00	......
4561	(44¢) Lady Liberty (SSP)	2.75	......	......	......	1.75	.65
4562	(44¢) American Flag (SSP)	2.75	......	......	......	1.75	.65
4562A	Booklet pane of 20	......	......	......	......	28.00	......
4563	(44¢) Lady Liberty (AV).	2.75	......	......	......	1.75	.65
4564	(44¢) American Flag (AV)	2.75	......	......	......	1.75	.65
4564A	Booklet pane of 20	......	......	......	......	28.00	......

4565   **4566**   **4567**

4570   **4568**   **4569**

4565	(44¢) Barbara Jordan . .	2.75	......	21.00(20)	5.00	1.50	.50
4566-69	(44¢) Romare Bearden.	5.50	......	19.00(16)	11.00(6)	6.00	......
4566	(44¢) Conjunction	2.75	......	......	......	1.50	1.00
4567	(44¢) Odyesseus	2.75	......	......	......	1.50	1.00
4568	(44¢) Prevalence of Ritual	2.75	......	......	......	1.50	1.00
4569	(44¢) Falling Star	2.75	......	......	......	1.50	1.00
4570	(44¢) Madonna, Raphael	2.75	......	......	......	1.50	.35
4570a	same, booklet pane of 18	......	......	......	......	24.00	......

SCOTT NO.	DESCRIPTION	FIRST DAY COVERS SING	FIRST DAY COVERS PL. BLK.	MINT SHEET	PLATE BLOCK	UNUSED F/NH	USED

4571, 4575, 4579

4572, 4576, 4580

4573, 4577, 4581

4574, 4578, 4582

SCOTT NO.	DESCRIPTION	SING	PL. BLK.	MINT SHEET	PLATE BLOCK	UNUSED F/NH	USED
4571-74	(44¢)Christmas Ornaments, bklt of 4, 10 3/4x11, microprinted on collar	5.5	......	......	......	6.00	......
4571	(44¢) Red Ornament. . .	2.75	......	......	......	1.50	.70
4572	(44¢) Blue Ornament, green ribbon	2.75	......	......	......	1.50	.70
4573	(44¢) Blue Ornament, red ribbon	2.75	......	......	......	1.50	.70
4574	(44¢) Green Ornament .	2.75	......	......	......	1.50	.70
4574b	Same, booklet pane of 20	5.50	......	......	......	25.00	......
4575-78	(44¢) Christmas Ornaments, bklt of 4, ... 10 3/4x11, microprinted not on collar	2.75	......	......	......	6.00	......
4575	(44¢) Red Ornament. . .	2.75	......	......	......	1.50	.70
4576	(44¢) Blue Ornament, green ribbon	2.75	......	......	......	1.50	.70
4577	(44¢) Blue Ornament, red ribbon	2.75	......	......	......	1.50	.70
4578	(44¢) Green Ornament .	2.75	......	......	......	1.50	.70
4578b	Same, booklet pane of 20	......	......	......	......	25.00	......
4579-82	(44¢) Christmas Ornament, bklt of 4, 11 1/4x11	5.5	......	......	......	6.00	......
4579	(44¢) Red Ornament. . .	2.75	......	......	......	1.50	.70
4580	(44¢) Blue Ornament, green ribbon	2.75	......	......	......	1.50	.70
4581	(44¢) Blue Ornament, red ribbon	2.75	......	......	......	1.50	.70
4582	(44¢) Green Ornament .	2.75	......	......	......	1.50	.70
4582bm	Same, booklet pane of 18	......	......	......	......	25.00	......

4583

4584

4583	(44¢) Hanukkah	2.75	......	21.00(20)	5.00	1.50	.45
4584	(44¢) Kwanzaa	2.75	......	21.00(20)	5.00	1.50	.45

4585-90

4585-90	(25¢) Eagles presort, strip of 6	4.75	......	......	......	4.50	......
	same, plate strip of 7 . .	......	......	......	......	8.00	......
4585	(25¢) Eagle, green	2.50	......	......	......	.80	.45
4586	(25¢) Eagle, blue green	2.50	......	......	......	.80	.45
4587	(25¢) Eagle, blue green	2.50	......	......	......	.80	.45
4588	(25¢) Eagle, red violet .	2.50	......	......	......	.80	.45
4589	(25¢) Eagle, brown orange	2.50	......	......	......	.80	.45
4590	(25¢) Eagle, yellow orange	2.50	......	......	......	.80	.45

2012 COMMEMORATIVES

4591/4705	(4591, 4623-4625, 4627-4628, 4651-4665, 4667-4671, 4677-4681, 4687-4703, 4705) 49 varieties	......	......	......	......	72.00	28.00

4591

4591	(44¢) New Mexico	2.75	5.75	21.00(20)	5.00	1.50	.50

4592-96

4592-96	32¢ Aloha Shirts, strip of 5	5.25	......	44.00(20)	22.00(10)	12.00	......
4592	32¢ Surfers and Palm Trees	2.50	......	......	......	2.25	.55
4593	32¢ Surfers	2.50	......	......	......	2.25	.55
4594	32¢ Fossil Fish	2.50	......	......	......	2.25	.55
4595	32¢ Shells	2.50	......	......	......	2.25	.55
4596	32¢ Fish and Starfish . .	2.50	......	......	......	2.25	.55
4597-							
4601	32¢ Aloha Shirts, coil strip of 5	5.25	......	......	......	7.00	......
4597	32¢ Fish and Starfish . .	2.50	......	......	......	1.50	.55
4598	32¢ Surfers and Palm Trees	2.50	......	......	......	1.50	.55
4599	32¢ Surfers	2.50	......	......	......	1.50	.55
4600	32¢ Fossil Fish	2.50	......	......	......	1.50	.55
4601	32¢ Shells	2.50	......	......	......	1.50	.55
	Same, plate # strip of 5	......	......	......	......	9.00	......
	Same, plate # strip of 11	......	......	......	......	15.00	......

4602

4603

4604   **4605**

4606   **4607**

4602	65¢ Wedding Cake	2.75	......	29.00(20)	7.00	2.00	.85
4603	65¢ Baltimore Checkerspot	2.75	......	29.00(20)	6.75	1.50	.85
4604-07	65¢ Dogs at Work, 4 attached	7.50	......	34.00(20)	10.50	10.00	......
4604	65¢ Seeing Eye Dog. . .	2.75	......	......	......	2.25	.85
4605	65¢ Therapy Dog	2.75	......	......	......	2.25	.85
4606	65¢ Military Dog	2.75	......	......	......	2.25	.85
4607	65¢ Rescue Dog.	2.75	......	......	......	2.25	.85

4608-4612

4608-12	85¢ Birds of Prey, strip of 5	10.75	......	40.00(20)	24.00(10)	12.00	......
4608	85¢ Northern Goshawk	3.50	......	......	......	2.50	1.50
4609	85¢ Peregrine Falcon . .	3.50	......	......	......	2.50	1.50
4610	85¢ Golden Eagle	3.50	......	......	......	2.50	1.50
4611	85¢ Osprey	3.50	......	......	......	2.50	1.50
4612	85¢ Northern Harrier. . .	3.50	......	......	......	2.50	1.50

4613-4617

SCOTT NO.	DESCRIPTION	FIRST DAY COVERS SING	PL. BLK.	MINT SHEET	PLATE BLOCK	UNUSED F/NH	USED
4613-17	45¢ Weather Vanes, coil strip of 5	6.75	......	......	......	8.00	......
	Same, plate # strip of 5					11.00	......
	Same, plate # strip of 11					18.00	......
4613	45¢ Rooster With Perch	2.75				1.75	.50
4614	45¢ Cow	2.75				1.75	.50
4615	45¢ Eagle	2.75				1.75	.50
4616	45¢ Rooster	2.75				1.75	.50
4617	45¢ Centaur	2.75				1.75	.50

4618

4619

4620

4621

4622

4618-22	(45¢) Bonsai, strip of 5	6.75	......	......	......	12.00	
4618	(45¢) Sierra Juniper	2.50	......	......	......	2.25	.50
4619	(45¢) Black Pine	2.50	......	......	......	2.25	.50
4620	(45¢) Banyan	2.50	......	......	......	2.25	.50
4621	(45¢) Trident Maple	2.50	......	......	......	2.25	.50
4622	(45¢) Azalea	2.50	......	......	......	2.25	.50
4622b	Booklet pane of 20	......	......	......	......	44.00	......

4623

4624

4625

4626

4627

4628

4623	(45¢) Chinese New Year	2.50	......	12.00(12)	......	1.50	.50
4624	(45¢) John H. Johnson	2.50	......	22.00(20)	5.50	1.50	.50
4625	(45¢) Heart Health	2.50	......	22.00(20)	5.50	1.50	.50
4626	(45¢) Love Ribbons	2.50	......	22.00(20)	5.50	1.50	.50
4627	(45¢) Arizona Statehood Cent.	2.50	......	22.00(20)	5.50	1.50	.50
4628	(45¢) Danny Thomas	2.75	......	22.00(20)	5.50	1.50	.50
4629-32	(45¢) Flag Strip of 4, d/c 8.5 vertical	......	......	......	......	6.50	......
4629	(45¢) Flag & Equality coil, d/c 8.5 vertical	2.50	......	......	......	1.75	.80
4630	(45¢) Flag & Justice coil, d/c 8.5 vertical	2.50	......	......	......	1.75	.80

4629, 4633, 4637, 4643, 4647 | **4630, 4634, 4638, 4644, 4648** | **4631, 4635, 4639, 4641, 4645** | **4632, 4636, 4640, 4642, 4646**

4631	(45¢) Flag & Freedom coil, d/c 8.5 vertical	2.50	......	......	......	1.75	.80
4632	(45¢) Flag & Liberty coil, d/c 8.5 vertical	2.50	......	......	......	1.75	.80
	Same, plate # strip of 5	......				9.00	......
	Same, plate # strip of 11	......				14.00	......
4633-36	(45¢) Flag strip of 4, d/c 9.5 vertical	......				6.00	
4633	(45¢) Flag & Equality coil, d/c 9.5 vertical	2.50				1.50	.80
4634	(45¢) Flag & Justice coil, d/c 9.5 vertical	2.50				1.50	.80
4635	(45¢) Flag & Freedom coil, d/c 9.5 vertical	2.50				1.50	.80
4636	(45¢) Flag & Liberty coil, d/c 9.5 vertical	2.50				1.50	.80
	Same, plate # strip of 5	......				9.00	
	Same, plate # strip of 11	......				14.00	......
4637-40	(45¢) Flag strip of 4, d/c 11 vertical	......				6.50	
4637	(45¢) Flag & Equality coil, d/c 11 vertical	2.50				1.75	.80
4638	(45¢) Flag & Justice coil, d/c 11 vertical	2.50				1.75	.80
4639	(45¢) Flag & Freedom coil, d/c 11 vertical	2.50				1.75	.80
4640	(45¢) Flag & Liberty coil, d/c 11 vertical	2.50				1.75	.80
	Same, plate # strip of 5	......				9.00	
	Same, plate # strip of 11	......				14.00	......
4641-44	(45¢) Flag block of 4 from bklt, colored dots in stars, 18.5 mm from LL to LR corners of flag	5.50				6.00	
4641	(45¢) Flag & Freedom bklt Single, colored dots in stars	2.50				1.50	.80
4642	(45¢) Flag & Liberty bklt single, colored dots in stars	2.50				1.50	.80
4643	(45¢) Flag & Equality bklt single, colored dots in stars	2.50				1.50	.80
4644	(45¢) Flag & Justice bklt single, colored dots in stars	2.50				1.50	.80
4644b	Same, bklt pane of 20	......				30.00	......
4645-48	(45¢) Flag block of 4 from bklt, dark dots in stars, 19mm from LL to LR corners of flag	5.50				6.50	
4645	(45¢) Flag & Freedom bklt single, dark dots in stars	2.50				1.75	.80
4646	(45¢) Flag & Liberty bklt single, dark dots in stars	2.50				1.75	.80
4647	(45¢) Flag & Equality bklt single, dark dots in stars	2.50				1.75	.80
4648	(45¢) Flag & Justice bklt single, dark dots in stars	2.50				1.75	.80
4648b	Same, bklt pane of 20	......				30.00	......

4649

4650

4651-4652

4649	$5.15 Sunshine Skyway Bridge	12.00	......	235.00(20)	55.00	15.00	9.00
4650	$18.95 Carmel Mission	39.00	......	425.00(20)	185.00	50.00	28.00
4651-52	(45¢) Cherry Blossom Centennial	3.75	......	21.00(20)	5.00	3.50	......
	Same, plate block of 8	......			9.00(8)		
4651	(45¢) Cherry Blossoms & Washington Monument	2.50	......	......	......	1.80	.75
4652	(45¢) Cherry Blossoms & Jefferson Memorial	2.50	......	......	......	1.80	.75

SCOTT NO.	DESCRIPTION	FIRST DAY COVERS SING	PL. BLK.	MINT SHEET	PLATE BLOCK	UNUSED F/NH	USED

4653

| 4653 | (45¢) Flowers, by William H. Johnson.... | 2.50 | .... | 24.00(20) | 6.00 | 1.50 | .50 |
| | Same .... | .... | .... | .... | 12.00(10) | .... | .... |

4654-63

4654-63	(45¢) Twentieth Century Poets	10.00	....	44.00(20)	21.00(10)	20.00	....
4654	(45¢) Joseph Brodsky..	2.50	....	....	....	2.25	1.00
4655	(45¢) Gwendolyn Brooks	2.50	....	....	....	2.25	1.00
4656	(45¢) William Carlos Williams	2.50	....	....	....	2.25	1.00
4657	(45¢) Robert Hayden ..	2.50	....	....	....	2.25	1.00
4658	(45¢) Sylvia Plath	2.50	....	....	....	2.25	1.00
4659	(45¢) Elizabeth Bishop .	2.50	....	....	....	2.25	1.00
4660	(45¢) Wallace Stevens .	2.50	....	....	....	2.25	1.00
4661	(45¢) Denise Levertov .	2.50	....	....	....	2.25	1.00
4662	(45¢) E.E. Cummings..	2.50	....	....	....	2.25	1.00
4663	(45¢) Theodore Roethke	3.75	....	....	....	2.25	1.00

4664   **4665**

4664-65	(45¢) Civil War Sesquicentennial	3.75	....	18.00(12)	....	3.00	....
4664	(45¢) Battle of New Orleans	2.50	....	....	....	1.75	.65
4665	(45¢) Battle of Antietam	2.50	....	....	....	1.75	.65

4666   **4667**

| 4666 | (45¢) Jose Ferrer ..... | 2.50 | .... | 22.00(20) | 5.50 | 1.50 | .65 |
| 4667 | (45¢) Louisiana Statehood Bicentennial .... | 2.50 | .... | 22.00(20) | 5.50 | 1.50 | .45 |

4668-4671

4672, 4672a

4668-71	(45¢) Great Film Directors	5.50	....	21.00(20)	6.50	6.00	....
	Same	....	....	....	9.00(8)	....	....
4668	(45¢) John Ford, "The Searchers", John Wayne	2.75	....	....	....	1.50	.60
4669	(45¢) Frank Capra, "It Happened One Night", Clark Gable and Claudette Colbert	2.75	....	....	....	1.50	.60
4670	(45¢) Billy Wilder, "Some Like It Hot", Marilyn Monroe.	2.75	....	....	....	1.50	.60
4671	(45¢) John Huston, "The Maltese Falcon", Humphrey Bogart	2.75	....	....	....	1.50	.60
4672	1¢ Bobcat	2.25	....	....	....	.25	.25
	Same, plate # strip of 5	....	....	....	.95	....	....
4672a	1¢ Bobcat (dated 2015)	....	....	....	....	.25	.25
	Same, Plate # Strip of 5	....	....	....	1.00	....	....

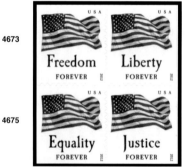

4673   **4674**   **4675**   **4676**

4673-76	(45¢) Flags, block or 4 from booklet, colored dots in stars, 19.25 mm from LL to LR corners of flag	5.25	....	....	....	6.00	....
4673	(45¢) Flag & Freedom bklt single, colored dots in stars ...	2.50	....	....	....	1.50	.45
4674	(45¢) Flag & Liberty bklt single, colored dots in stars ...	2.50	....	....	....	1.50	.45
4675	(45¢) Flag & Equality bklt single, colored dots in stars ...	2.50	....	....	....	1.50	.45
4676	(45¢) Flag & Justice bklt single, colored dots in stars ...	2.50	....	....	....	1.50	.45
4676b	Same, booklet pane of 10	....	....	....	....	13.50	....

4677-81

4677-81	(45¢) Pixar Mail a Smile	6.75	....	25.00(20)	14.00(10)	7.00	....
4677	(45¢) Flik & Dot from "A Bug's Life"	2.75	....	....	....	1.75	.65
4678	(45¢) Bob Parr & Dashiell Parr from "The Incredibles"	2.75	....	....	....	1.75	.65
4679	(45¢) Nemo & Squirt from "Finding Nemo".......	2.75	....	....	....	1.75	.65
4680	(45¢) Jessie, Woody, & Bullseye from "Toy Story 2".....	2.75	....	....	....	1.75	.65
4681	(45¢) Boo, Mike Wazowskie & James P. "Sulley" Sullivan from Monsters, Inc........	2.75	....	....	....	1.75	.65

SCOTT NO.	DESCRIPTION	FIRST DAY COVERS SING	PL. BLK.	MINT SHEET	PLATE BLOCK	UNUSED F/NH	USED

4937 | **4938** | **4939** | **4940**

4937-40	(49¢) Winter Fun.	....	....	....	....	6.50	....
4937	(49¢) Skaters	....	....	....	....	1.75	.35
4938	(49¢) Child Making Snowman	....	....	....	....	1.75	.35
4939	(49¢) Cardinal.	....	....	....	....	1.75	.35
4940	(49¢) Child Making Snow Angel	....	....	....	....	1.75	.35
4940b	Same, Booklet Pane of 20	....	....	....	....	28.00	....
4941-44	(49¢) Winter Fun.	....	....	....	....	6.50	....
4941	(49¢) Skaters	....	....	....	....	1.75	1.00
4942	(49¢) Child Making Snowman	....	....	....	....	1.75	1.00
4943	(49¢) Cardinal.	....	....	....	....	1.75	1.00
4944	(49¢) Child Making Snow Angel	....	....	....	....	1.75	1.00
4944b	Same, ATM Booklet Pane of 18	....	....	....	....	24.00	....

4946 | **4945** | **4949**

4947 | **4948**

4945	(49¢) Magi	2.75	....	....	....	1.50	.30
4945a	Same, Booklet Pane of 20	....	....	....	....	21.00	....
4946-49	(49¢) Rudolph the Red-Nosed Reindeer.	5.75	....	....	....	6.50	....
4946	(49¢) Rudolph the Red-Nosed Reindeer.	2.75	....	....	....	1.75	.35
4947	(49¢) Hermey and Rudolph	....	....	....	....	1.75	.35
4948	(49¢) Santa Claus.	....	....	....	....	1.75	.35
4949	(49¢) Bumble	....	....	....	....	1.75	.35
4949b	Same, Booklet Pane of 20	....	....	....	....	28.00	....

4950-4951

4950-51	(49¢) Wilt Chamberlain.	5.75	....	22.50(18)	6.00	3.00	....
4950	(49¢) Wilt Chamberlain in Philadelphia Warriors Uniform	2.75	....	....	....	1.75	.75
4951	(49¢) Wilt Chamberlain in Los Angelos Lakers Uniform	2.75	....	....	....	1.75	.75

2015 COMMEMORATIVES

| 4952/5020 | (4952, 4957-58, 4968-72, 4979-87, 4988a, 5003, 5008-12, 5020) 27 varieties . . . . | .... | .... | .... | .... | 40.00 | .... |

4952

| 4952 | (49¢) Battle of New Orleans | 2.75 | .... | 21.00(20) | .... | 1.50 | .30 |

SCOTT NO.	DESCRIPTION	FIRST DAY COVERS SING	PL. BLK.	MINT SHEET	PLATE BLOCK	UNUSED F/NH	USED

4953 | **4954**

| 4953 | $1 Patriotic Waves . . . . | 3.75 | .... | 22.50(10) | 9.00 | 3.00 | 1.00 |
| 4954 | $2 Patriotic Waves . . . . | 5.75 | .... | 45.00(10) | 18.00 | 5.00 | 5.00 |

4955 | **4956** | **4957**

4955-56	(49¢) Love	3.75	....	22.50(20)	5.00	3.25	....
4955	(49¢) Love, Red	2.75	....	....	....	1.75	1.00
4956	(49¢) Love, Red and Gray	2.75	....	....	....	1.75	1.00
4957	(49¢) Chinese New Year	2.75	....	14.00(12)	....	1.50	.50

4959 | **4958** | **4960**

4961 | **4962** | **4963**

4958	(49¢) Robert Robinson Taylor	2.75	....	22.50(20)	5.50	1.50	.30
4959	(49¢) Red & Black Rose & Heart	2.75	....	22.00(20)	5.50	1.50	.30
4960	70¢ Black & Red, Tulip & Heart	2.75	....	28.00(20)	6.00	2.00	.80
4961-63	(10¢) Stars and Stripes	....	....	....	....	1.00	....
	Same, Plate # Strip of 5	....	....	....	....	4.00	....
4961	(10¢) Stripes at Left, Stars at Right	....	....	....	....	.35	.25
4962	(10¢) Stars & White Stripe	....	....	....	....	.35	.25
4963	(10¢) Stars at Left, Stripes at Right	....	....	....	....	.35	.25

4964 | **4965**

4966 | **4967**

4964-67	(49¢) Water Lilies	6.50	....	....	....	6.50	....
4964	(49¢) Pale Pink Water Lily	2.75	....	....	....	1.75	.30
4965	(49¢) Red Water Lily. . .	2.75	....	....	....	1.75	.30
4966	(49¢) Purple Water Lily.	2.75	....	....	....	1.75	.30
4967	(49¢) White Water Lily .	2.75	....	....	....	1.75	.30
4967b	Same, Booklet Pane of 20	....	....	....	....	28.00	....

SCOTT NO.	DESCRIPTION	FIRST DAY COVERS SING	PL. BLK.	MINT SHEET	PLATE BLOCK	UNUSED F/NH	USED

4968   4969   4970   4971   4972

4968-72	(49¢) Art by Martin Ramirez	5.75	....	22.50(20)	14.00(10)	8.00	....
4968	(49¢) Horse and Rider with Trees	2.75	....	....		1.75	1.00
4969	(49¢) Man Riding Donkey	2.75	....	....		1.75	1.00
4970	(49¢) Trains on Inclined Tracks	2.75	....	....		1.75	1.00
4971	(49¢) Deer	2.75	....	....		1.75	1.00
4972	(49¢) Tunnel with Cars & Busses	2.75	....	....		1.75	1.00

4874, 4977   4875, 4973   4876, 4974   4877, 4975   4878, 4976

4973-77	(49¢) Ferns, date 2014, Microprinted "USPS". . .	7.75	....	....		7.00	....
	Same, Plate # Strip of 5	....	....	....		10.50	....
4973	(49¢) Soft Shield Fern .	2.75	....	....		1.75	1.00
4974	(49¢) Autumn Fern	2.75	....	....		1.75	1.00
4975	(49¢) Goldie's Wood Fern	2.75	....	....		1.75	1.00
4976	(49¢) Painted Fern	2.75	....	....		1.75	1.00
4977	(49¢) Fortune's Holly Fern	2.75	....	....		1.75	1.00
4973a-4977a	(49¢) Ferns, date 2015, Microprinted "USPS". . .	7.75	....	....		7.00	....
	Same, Plate # Strip of 5	....	....	....		10.50	....
4973a	(49¢) Soft Shield Fern .	2.75	....	....		1.75	1.00
4974a	(49¢) Autumn Fern	2.75	....	....		1.75	1.00
4975a	(49¢) Goldie's Wood Fern	2.75	....	....		1.75	1.00
4976a	(49¢) Painted Fern	2.75	....	....		1.75	1.00
4977a	(49¢) Fortune's Holly Fern	2.75	....	....		1.75	1.00

4978   4979

| 4978 | (49¢) From Me To You . | 2.75 | .... | 22.00(20) | 12.00(10) | 1.50 | .30 |
| 4979 | (49¢) Maya Angelou . . . | 2.75 | .... | 16.00(12) | .... | 1.50 | .30 |

4980   4981

4980-81	(49¢) Civil War Sheet . .	....	....	18.00(12)		3.00	....
4980	(49¢) Battle of Five Forks	2.50	....	....		1.75	1.00
4981	(49¢) Surrender at Appomattox Court House	2.50	....	....		1.75	1.00

4982   4983   4984   4985

4982-85	(49¢) Gifts of Friendship	7.75	....	18.00(12)		14.00	....
4982	(49¢) Lincoln Memorial and Cherry Blossoms	2.75	....	....		1.50	1.00
4983	(49¢) U.S. Capitol and Cherry Blossoms	2.75	....	....		1.50	1.00
4983a	Horizontal Pair, 4982-83	5.25	....	....		3.00	....
4984	(49¢) Japanese Diet, Tokyo, and Dogwood Blossoms . . .	2.75	....	....		1.50	1.00
4985	(49¢) Clock Tower, Tokyo, and Dogwood Blossoms . . .	2.75	....	....		1.50	1.00
4985a	Horizontal Pair, 4984-85	5.25	....	....		3.00	....

4987   4986   4989, 4990   4988, 4988a

4986	(49¢) Special Olympic World Games	2.75	....	22.00(20)	5.50	1.50	.35
4987	(49¢) Help Find Missing Children	2.75	....	22.00(20)	5.50	1.50	.35
4988	(49¢) Medal of Honor, Air Force, Vietnam	....	....	30.00(24)	8.50(6)	....	....
4988a	Horizontal strip of 3. . . .	4.50	....	....		4.75	....
4989	(22¢) Emperor Penguins	2.75	....	10.00(20)	2.50	.55	.30
4990	(22¢) Emperor Penguins coil	2.75	....	....		.55	.30
	same, plate number strip of 5	....	....	....		3.75	....

4991, 4997   4994, 4996   4992, 4998   4993, 4995

4991-94	(35¢) Coastal Birds. . . .	4.75	....	15.00(20)	4.25	4.00	....
4991	(35¢) Red Knot	2.75	....	....		1.25	.45
4992	(35¢) King Elder	2.75	....	....		1.25	.45
4993	(35¢) Spoonbill	2.75	....	....		1.25	.45
4994	(35¢) Frigate Bird	2.75	....	....		1.25	.45
4995-98	Coastal Birds coil	4.75	....	....		4.00	....
	same, plate number strip of 5	....	....	....		6.25	....
4995	(35¢) Spoonbill coil. . . .	2.75	....	....		1.25	.45
4996	(35¢) Frigate Bird coil . .	2.75	....	....		1.25	.45
4997	(35¢) Red Knot coil. . . .	2.75	....	....		1.25	.45
4998	(35¢) King Elder coil. . . .	2.75	....	....		1.25	.45

SCOTT NO.	DESCRIPTION	FIRST DAY COVERS SING	PL. BLK.	MINT SHEET	PLATE BLOCK	UNUSED F/NH	USED
4999	(71¢) Eastern Tiger Swallowtail Butterfly	3.25	. . . .	32.00(20)	7.50	2.00	.75
5000	(71¢) Wedding Cake. . .	3.25	. . . .	30.00(20)	7.50	2.00	1.00
5001	(71¢) Flowers and Yes, I Do	3.25	. . . .	31.00(20)	7.50	2.00	1.00
5002	(71¢) Tulip and Hearts .	3.25	. . . .	30.00(20)	7.50	2.00	1.00
5003	(93¢) Flannery O'Connor	3.75	. . . .	39.00(20)	8.50	2.50	1.00
5004-07	(49¢) Summer Harvest .	6.50	. . . .	. . . .	. . . .	6.50	. . . .
5004	(49¢) Watermelons	. . . .	. . . .	. . . .	. . . .	1.75	.35
5005	(49¢) Sweet Corn	. . . .	. . . .	. . . .	. . . .	1.75	.35
5006	(49¢) Cantaloupes	. . . .	. . . .	. . . .	. . . .	1.75	.35
5007	(49¢) Tomatoes.	. . . .	. . . .	. . . .	. . . .	1.75	.35
5007b	same, booklet pane of 20	. . . .	. . . .	. . . .	. . . .	30.00	. . . .
5008	(49¢) Coast Guard	2.75	. . . .	21.00(20)	5.00	1.50	.50
5009	(49¢) Elvis Presley	3.50	. . . .	18.00(20)	. . . .	1.25	.50
5010-11	(49¢) World Stamp Show	4.25	. . . .	22.00(20)	5.00	3.00	. . . .
5010	(49¢) World Stamp Show, red	2.75	. . . .	. . . .	. . . .	1.75	.60
5011	(49¢) World Stamp Show, blue	2.75	. . . .	. . . .	. . . .	1.75	.60
5012	(49¢) Ingrid Bergman . .	2.75	. . . .	22.00(20)	5.00	1.50	.60

SCOTT NO.	DESCRIPTION	FIRST DAY COVERS SING	PL. BLK.	MINT SHEET	PLATE BLOCK	UNUSED F/NH	USED
5013-18	(25¢) eagles, strip of 6, D/C 10.25	5.75	. . . .	. . . .	. . . .	7.00	. . . .
	same, plate number strip of 7	. . . .	. . . .	. . . .	. . . .	8.00	. . . .
5013	(25¢) Green	. . . .	. . . .	. . . .	. . . .	1.25	.30
5014	(25¢) Blue/Green	. . . .	. . . .	. . . .	. . . .	1.25	.30
5015	(25¢) Blue	. . . .	. . . .	. . . .	. . . .	1.25	.30
5016	(25¢) Red/Violet	. . . .	. . . .	. . . .	. . . .	1.25	.30
5017	(25¢) Brown/Orange. . .	. . . .	. . . .	. . . .	. . . .	1.25	.30
5018	(25¢) Yellow/Orange. . .	. . . .	. . . .	. . . .	. . . .	1.25	.30
5019	(49¢) Celebrate, 2015 date	2.75	. . . .	21.00(20)	5.00	1.50	.40
5020	(49¢) Paul Newman . . .	2.75	. . . .	21.00(20)	5.00	1.50	.60
5021-30	(49¢) Charlie Brown Christmas	12.00	. . . .	. . . .	. . . .	16.00	. . . .
5021	(49¢) Charlie Brown carrying Christmas Tree	. . . .	. . . .	. . . .	. . . .	1.50	.60
5022	(49¢) Charlie Brown, Pigpen and Dirty Snowman . . .	. . . .	. . . .	. . . .	. . . .	1.50	.60
5023	(49¢) Snoopy, Lucy, Violet, Sally and Schroder Skating	. . . .	. . . .	. . . .	. . . .	1.50	.60
5024	(49¢) Characters, Dog House and ChristmasTree	. . . .	. . . .	. . . .	. . . .	1.50	.60
5025	(49¢) Linus and Christmas Tree	. . . .	. . . .	. . . .	. . . .	1.50	.60
5026	(49¢) Charlie Brown looking in Mailbox	. . . .	. . . .	. . . .	. . . .	1.50	.60
5027	(49¢) Charlie Brown and Linus behind brick wall .	. . . .	. . . .	. . . .	. . . .	1.50	.60
5028	(49¢) Charlie Brown, Linus and Christmas Tree	. . . .	. . . .	. . . .	. . . .	1.50	.60
5029	(49¢) Charlie Brown screaming, Snoopy decorating dog house	. . . .	. . . .	. . . .	. . . .	1.50	.60
5030	(49¢) Charlie Brown hanging ornament on Christmas Tree	. . . .	. . . .	. . . .	. . . .	1.50	.60
5030b	same, booklet pane of 20	. . . .	. . . .	. . . .	. . . .	28.00	. . . .

SCOTT NO.	DESCRIPTION	FIRST DAY COVERS SING	PL. BLK.	MINT SHEET	PLATE BLOCK	UNUSED F/NH	USED

5031-34	(49¢) Geometric Snowflakes	5.75	....	....	....	6.50	....
5031	(49¢) Purple and Lilac .	2.75	....	....	....	1.75	.60
5032	(49¢) Dark blue and blue	2.75	....	....	....	1.75	.60
5033	(49¢) Dark green and green	2.75	....	....	....	1.75	.60
5034	(49¢) Crimson and pink	2.75	....	....	....	1.75	.60
5034b	same, booklet pane of 20	....	....	....	....	28.00	....
5035	(49¢) Purple Heart, "USPS" microprinted at left	....	24.00(20)	6.00	1.50	.30

2016 COMMEMORATIVES

| 5036/5153 | (5036, 5056-57, 5059-60, 5062-76, 5091-92, 5100, 5105, 5132-35, 5141-42, 5149-53) 35 varieties | .... | .... | .... | .... | 62.50 | .... |

5036	(49¢) Quilled Paper Hearts	2.75	....	21.00(20)	5.00	1.40	.50
5037	1¢ Apples coil	2.75	....	....	....	.20	.20
	same, plate strip of 5 . .	....	....	....	....	1.45	
5038	5¢ Pinot Noir Grapes coil	2.75	....	....	....	.30	.30
	same, plate number strip of 5	....	....	....	....	1.75	
5039	10¢ Red Pears coil	2.75	....	....	....	.35	.30
	same, plate number strip of 5	....	....	....	....	2.25	....

| 5040 | $6.45 La Cueva del Indio, Puerto Rico . . . . | 14.00 | .... | 140.00(10) | 55.00 | 13.50 | 8.00 |
| 5041 | $22.95 Columbia River George | 47.00 | .... | 475.00(10) | 185.00 | 47.50 | 25.00 |

5042-51	(49¢) Botanical Art	11.00	....	....	....	18.00	....
5042	(49¢) Corn Lilies	2.75	....	....	....	1.75	.45
5043	(49¢) Tulips	2.75	....	....	....	1.75	.45
5044	(49¢) Tulips	2.75	....	....	....	1.75	.45
5045	(49¢) Dahlias	2.75	....	....	....	1.75	.45
5046	(49¢) Stocks	2.75	....	....	....	1.75	.45
5047	(49¢) Roses	2.75	....	....	....	1.75	.45
5048	(49¢) Japanese Irises . .	2.75	....	....	....	1.75	.45
5049	(49¢) Tulips	2.75	....	....	....	1.75	.45
5050	(49¢) Petunias	2.75	....	....	....	1.75	.45
5051	(49¢) Jonquils	2.75	....	....	....	1.75	.45
5051b	same, booklet pane of 10	....	....	....	....	18.00	....
5051c	same, booklet pane of 20	....	....	....	....	28.00	....
5052	(49¢) Flag, d/c 11, SSP coil microprinted USPS to right of pole under flag	2.75	....	....	....	1.50	.30
	same, plate number strip of 5	....	....	....	....	9.00	
5053	(49¢) Flag, d/c 9.5, AP coil microprinted USPS on second white flag stripe	2.75	....	....	....	1.50	.30
	same, plate number strip of 5	....	....	....	....	9.00	
5054	(49¢) Flag, 11.25x10.75, SSP booklet	2.75	....	....	....	1.50	.30
	microprinted USPS to right of pole under the flag						
5054a	same, booklet pane of 10	....	....	....	....	14.00	
5054b	same, booklet pane of 20	....	....	....	....	28.00	
5055	(49¢) Flag, 11.25x10.75, AP booklet	2.75	....	....	....	1.50	.30
	microprinted USPS on second white flag stripe						
5055a	same, booklet pane of 20	....	....	....	....	28.00	....

5056	(49¢) Richard Allen	2.75	....	21.00(20)	5.00	1.40	.45
5057	(49¢) Chinese New Year Year of the Monkey	2.75	....	12.50(20)	....	1.40	.45
5058	($1.20) Moon	4.25	....	25.00(10)	12.50	3.00	1.00

SCOTT NO.	DESCRIPTION	FIRST DAY COVERS SING	PL. BLK.	MINT SHEET	PLATE BLOCK	UNUSED F/NH	USED

5163, 5169   5164, 5170   5165, 5167   5166, 5168

SCOTT NO.	DESCRIPTION	SING	PL. BLK.	MINT SHEET	PLATE BLOCK	UNUSED F/NH	USED
5163-66	(34¢) Seashells	8.00(4)	. . . . . .	15.00(20)	8.00(8)	3.90	. . . . . .
5163	(34¢) Queen Conch, die cut 11.25x10.75	. . . . . .	. . . . . .	. . . .	. . .	.85	.40
5164	(34¢) Pacific Calico Scallop, die cut 11.25x10.75	. . . . . .	. . . . . .	. . . .	. . .	.85	.40
5165	(34¢) Alphabet Cone Shell, die cut 11.25x10.75	. . . . . .	. . . . . .	. . . .	. . .	.85	.40
5166	(34¢) Zebra Nerite Shell, die cut 11.25x10.75	. . . . . .	. . . . . .	. . . .	. . .	.85	.40
5167-70	(34¢) Seashells coil . . .	8.00(4)	. . . . . .	. . . .	. . .	3.90	. . . . . .
	same, plate number strip of 5	. . . . . .	. . . . . .	. . . .	. . .	6.50	. . . . . .
5167	(34¢) Alphabet Cone Shell, die cut 9.75 vertical. . . .	. . . . . .	. . . . . .	. . . .	. . .	.85	.40
5168	(34¢) Zebra Nerite Shell, die cut 9.75 vertical	. . . . . .	. . . . . .	. . . .	. . .	.85	.40
5169	(34¢) Queen Conch, die cut 9.75 vertical	. . . . . .	. . . . . .	. . . .	. . .	.85	.40
5170	(34¢) Pacific Calico Scallop, die cut 9.75 vertical	. . . . . .	. . . . . .	. . . .	. . .	.85	.40

5171

5172

5171	(49¢) Dorothy Height . .	2.75	. . . . . .	24.00(20)	5.50	1.50	.70
5172	(5¢) USA Star Coil	2.75	. . . . . .	. . . .	. . .	.30	.30
	same, plate number strip of 5	. . . . . .	. . . . . .	. . . .	. . .	1.75	. . . . . .

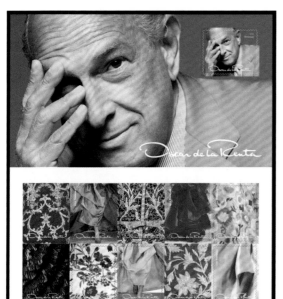

5173

OSCAR DE LA RENTA

5173a	Photograph of ODLR	5173g	Blue dress
5173b	Bright pink and gray fabric	5173h	Floral fabric with white
5173c	Green dress	5173i	Yellow dress
5173d	Black and white fabric	5173j	Pink, white and gray floral fabric
5173e	Red dress	5173k	Pink dress
5173f	Floral fabric with dull green		

| 5173 | (49¢) Oscar de la Renta | . . . . . . | . . . . | 18.00(11) | . . . | . . . . . . | . . . . . . |

5174

5175

| 5174 | (21¢) Uncle Sam's Hat . | 2.75 | . . . . . . | 8.00(20) | 2.50 | .50 | .30 |
| 5175 | (49¢) John F. Kennedy . | 2.75 | . . . . . . | 16.50(12) | 5.50 | 1.50 | .70 |

5177

5178

5179

5177	5¢ Pinot Noir Grapes . .	2.75	. . . . . .	3.80(20)	1.50	.30	.30
5178	10¢ Red Pears, die cut 11.25x11	2.75	. . . . . .	5.50(20)	1.50	.35	.30
5179	(49¢) Nebraska Statehood	2.75	. . . . . .	24.00(20)	5.50	1.50	.70

5180

5181

5182

5183

5184

5185

5186

5187

5188

5189

5180-89	(49¢) WPA Posters	22.00(10)	. . . . . .	. . . .	. . .	18.00	. . . . . .
5180	(49¢) WPA-See America Welcome to Montana . .	. . . . . .	. . . . . .	. . . .	. . .	2.00	.70
5181	(49¢) WPA-Work Pays America	. . . . . .	. . . . . .	. . . .	. . .	2.00	.70
5182	(49¢) WPA-Field Day . .	. . . . . .	. . . . . .	. . . .	. . .	2.00	.70
5183	(49¢) WPA-Discover Puerto Rico	. . . . . .	. . . . . .	. . . .	. . .	2.00	.70
5184	(49¢) WPA-City of NY Municipal Airports . .	. . . . . .	. . . . . .	. . . .	. . .	2.00	.70
5185	(49¢) WPA-Foreign Trade Zone	. . . . . .	. . . . . .	. . . .	. . .	2.00	.70
5186	(49¢) WPA-Visit the Zoo	. . . . . .	. . . . . .	. . . .	. . .	2.00	.70
5187	(49¢) WPA-Work with Care	. . . . . .	. . . . . .	. . . .	. . .	2.00	.70
5188	(49¢) WPA-National Parks Preserve Wild Life . .	. . . . . .	. . . . . .	. . . .	. . .	1.10	.70
5189	(49¢) WPA-Hiking	. . . . . .	. . . . . .	. . . .	. . .	1.10	.70
5189b	same, double sided convertible bklt of 20	. . . . . .	. . . . . .	. . . .	. . .	30.00	. . . . . .

SCOTT NO.	DESCRIPTION	FIRST DAY COVERS SING	PL. BLK.	MINT SHEET	PLATE BLOCK	UNUSED F/NH	USED

5190

Robert Panara

5191

| 5190 | (49¢) Mississippi Statehood | 2.75 | .... | 24.00(20) | 5.50 | 1.50 | .70 |
| 5191 | (70¢) Robert Panara... | 3.00 | .... | 30.00(20) | 7.50 | 2.00 | .80 |

5192

5193

5194

5195

5196

5197

5192-97	(49¢) Delicioso, Latin American Dishes .	12.00(6)	....	....	....	8.50	....
5192	(49¢) Tamales........	....	....	....	....	1.50	.70
5193	(49¢) Flan..........	....	....	....	....	1.50	.70
5194	(49¢) Sancocho	....	....	....	....	1.50	.70
5195	(49¢) Empanadas.....	....	....	....	....	1.50	.70
5196	(49¢) Chili Relleno	....	....	....	....	1.50	.70
5197	(49¢) Ceviche........	....	....	....	....	1.50	.70
5197b	same, double sided convertible bklt of 20............	....	....	....	....	28.50	....

5198

5199

5200

5198	($1.15) Echeveria Plant, Global	4.00	....	25.00(10)	12.00	3.00	.90
5199	(49¢) Boutonniere.....	2.75	....	24.00(20)	5.00	1.50	.60
5200	(70¢) Corsage........	2.75	....	30.00(20)	7.50	2.00	.80

5201

5202

5201	3¢ Strawberries coil, die cut 10 vertical	2.75	....	....	....	.30	.30
	same, plate number strip of 5	....	....	....	....	1.75	
5202	(49¢) Henry David Thoreau	2.75	....	24.00(20)	5.50	1.50	.60

5203   **5204**

5205   **5206**   **5207**

5208   **5209**   **5210**

5203-10	(49¢) Sports Balls.....	20.00(8)	.....	28.00(16)	18.50(8)	15.00	.....
5203	(49¢) Football........		.....	.....	......	2.00	0.70
5204	(49¢) Volleyball.......		.....	.....	......	2.00	0.70
5205	(49¢) Soccer.........		.....	.....	......	2.00	0.70
5206	(49¢) Golf..........		.....	.....	......	2.00	0.70
5207	(49¢) Baseball		.....	.....	......	2.00	0.70
5208	(49¢) Basketball		.....	.....	......	2.00	0.70
5209	(49¢) Tennis.........		.....	.....	......	2.00	0.70
5210	(49¢) Kickball		.....	.....	......	2.00	0.70

5211

| 5211 | (49¢) Total Eclipse | 2.75 | .... | 24.00(16) | 5.50 | 1.50 | .70 |

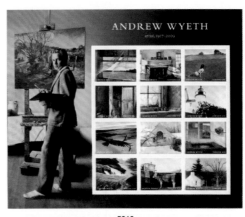

5212

ANDREW WYETH

5212a *Wind from the Sea*	5212g *Soaring*
5212b *Big Room*	5212h *North Light*
5212c *Christina's World*	5212i *Spring Fed*
5212d *Alvaro & Christin*	5212j *The Carry*
5212e *Frostbitten*	5212k *Young Bull*
5212f *Sailor's Valentine*	5212l *My Studio*

| 5212 | (49¢) Andrew Wyeth... | 25.00(12) | ..... | 18.00(12) | ..... | ..... | ..... |

SCOTT NO.	DESCRIPTION	FIRST DAY COVERS SING	PL. BLK.	MINT SHEET	PLATE BLOCK	UNUSED F/NH	USED

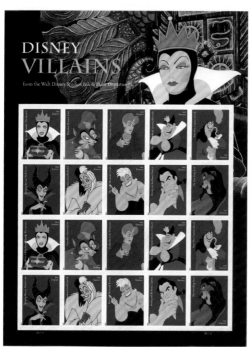

5213-5222

5213-22	(49¢) Disney Villians	22.00(10)	.....	30.00(20)	20.00(10)	18.00(10)	.....
5213	(49¢) The Queen, Snow White	.....	.....			2.00	0.80
5214	(49¢) Honest John, Pinocchio	.....	.....			2.00	0.80
5215	(49¢) Lady Tremaine, Cinderella	.....	.....			2.00	0.80
5216	(49¢) Queen of Hearts, Alice in Wonderland	.....				2.00	0.80
5217	(49¢) Captain Hook, Peter Pan	.....	.....			2.00	0.80
5218	(49¢) Maleficent, Sleeping Beauty	.....				2.00	0.80
5219	(49¢) Cruella De Vil, 101 Dalmations	.....				2.00	0.80
5220	(49¢) Ursula, Little Mermaid	.....	.....			2.00	0.80
5221	(49¢) Gaston, Beauty and the Beast	.....				2.00	0.80
5222	(49¢) Scar, The Lion King	.....	.....			2.00	0.80

5223

5224

5225

5226

5227

5223-27	(49¢) Sharks	12.00(5)	.....	30.00(20)	18.00(10)	8.50(5)	.....
5223	(49¢) Mako	.....	.....			2.00	0.70
5224	(49¢) Whale	.....	.....			2.00	0.70
5225	(49¢) Tresher	.....	.....			2.00	0.70
5226	(49¢) Hammerhead	.....	.....			2.00	0.70
5227	(49¢) Great White	.....	.....			2.00	0.70

5228

5229

5230

5231

5232

5228-32	(49¢) Protect Pollinators	12.00(5)	.....	30.00(20)	18.00(10)	8.50(5)	.....
5228	(49¢) Monarch on Purple Coneflower	.....	.....			2.00	0.70
5229	(49¢) Honeybee on Golden Ragwort	.....	.....			2.00	0.70
5230	(49¢) Monarch on Red Zinnia	.....	.....			2.00	0.70
5231	(49¢) Honeybee on Purple Aster	.....	.....			2.00	0.70
5232	(49¢) Monarch on Goldenrod	.....	.....			2.00	0.70

5233, 5237

5234, 5238

5235, 5239

5236, 5240

5233-36	(49¢) Flowers from the Garden	8.00(4)	.....	.....	.....	5.50	.....
	same, plate number strip of 5	.....	.....	.....	.....	11.00	.....
5233	(49¢) Red Camellias in Yellow Pitcher	.....	.....	.....	.....	1.50	0.70
5234	(49¢) Flowers in White Vase	.....	.....	.....	.....	1.50	0.70
5235	(49¢) Peonies in Clear Vase	.....	.....	.....	.....	1.50	0.70
5236	(49¢) Hydrangeas in Blue Pot	.....	.....	.....	.....	1.50	0.70
5237-40	(49¢) Flowers from the Garden	8.00(4)	.....	.....	.....	5.50	.....
5237	(49¢) Red Camellias in Yellow Pitcher	.....	.....	.....	.....	1.50	0.70
5238	(49¢) Flowers in White Vase	.....	.....	.....	.....	1.50	0.70
5239	(49¢) Peonies in Clear Vase	.....	.....	.....	.....	1.50	0.70
5240	(49¢) Hydrangeas in Blue Pot	.....	.....	.....	.....	1.50	0.70
5240b	same, double-sided bklt pane of 20	.....	.....			28.50	.....

5243 **5244**

5241, 5242

5245 **5246**

5241	(49¢) Father Theodore Hesburgh	2.75	.....	24.00(20)	5.50	1.50	0.60
5242	(49¢) Father Theodore Hesburgh, coil	2.75	.....	.....	.....	1.50	0.60
	same, plate number strip of 5	.....	.....	.....	.....	11.00	.....
5243-46	(49¢) The Snowy Day, Ezra Jack Keats	8.00(4)	.....	.....	.....	5.50	.....
5243	(49¢) Making Snowball	.....	.....	.....	.....	1.50	0.60
5244	(49¢) Sliding	.....	.....	.....	.....	1.50	0.60
5245	(49¢) Making Snow Angel	.....	.....	.....	.....	1.50	0.60
5246	(49¢) Leaving Footprints	.....	.....	.....	.....	1.50	0.60
5246b	same, double-sided bklt pane of 20	.....	.....			28.50	.....

SCOTT NO.	DESCRIPTION	FIRST DAY COVERS SING	PL. BLK.	MINT SHEET	PLATE BLOCK	UNUSED F/NH	USED

5247   5248   5249   5250

5247-50	(49¢) Christmas Carols.	8.00(4)	.....	.....	.....	5.50	.....
5247	(49¢) Deck the Halls...	.....	.....	.....	.....	1.50	0.60
5248	(49¢) Silent Night	.....	.....	.....	.....	1.50	0.60
5249	(49¢) Jingle Bells	.....	.....	.....	.....	1.50	0.60
5250	(49¢) Jolly Old St. Nicholas	.....	.....	.....	.....	1.50	0.60
5250b	same, double-sided bklt pane of 20	.....	.....	.....	.....	28.50	.....

5251

| 5251 | (49¢) National Museum of African American History and Culture | 2.75 | ..... | 24.00(20) | 5.50 | 1.50 | 0.70 |

5252   5253

5252-53	(49¢) History of Ice Hockey	5.00(2)	.....	19.00(20)	4.75	3.25	.....
5252	(49¢) Player Wearing Gear	.....	.....	.....	.....	2.00	0.70
5253	(49¢) Player Wearing Hat & Scraf	.....	.....	.....	.....	2.00	0.70
5253c	(49¢) History of Ice Hockey, souvenir sheet of 2......	.....	.....	.....	.....	3.25	.....
5252a	(49¢) Player Wearing Gear	.....	.....	.....	.....	2.00	0.70
5253a	(49¢) Player Wearing Hat & Scraf	.....	.....	.....	.....	2.00	0.70

2018 COMMEMORATIVES

| 5254/5338 | (5254, 5259, 5264-79, 5281-84, 5299-2305, 5307-10, 5312-16, 5321-30, 5337-38) 50 varieties | .... | .... | .... | .... | 87.00 | .... |

5254   5255   5256

5254	(49¢) Year of the Dog	2.75	.....	15.00(12)	.....	1.50	0.60
5255	(49¢) Love Flourishes	2.75	.....	24.00(20)	5.50	1.50	0.60
5256	2¢ Lemon, coil...........	.....	.....	.....	0.30	0.30	.....
	same, plate number strip of 5	.....	.....	.....	.....	1.75	.....

SCOTT NO.	DESCRIPTION	FIRST DAY COVERS SING	PL. BLK.	MINT SHEET	PLATE BLOCK	UNUSED F/NH	USED

5257   5259   5258

5260, 5261   5262, 5263

5257	$6.70 Byodo-In-Temple, Priority	15.00	.....	60.00(4)	.....	20.00	8.50
5258	$24.70 Sleeping Bear Dunes, Express	48.00	.....	240.00(4)	.....	65.00	30.00
5259	(50¢) Lena Horne	2.75	.....	24.00(20)	5.50	1.50	0.70
5260	(50¢) U.S. Flag coil, die cut 9.5 vert.	2.75	.....	.....	.....	1.50	0.70
	same, plate number strip of 5	.....	.....	.....	.....	10.00	.....
5261	(50¢) U.S. Flag coil, die cut 11 vert.	2.75	.....	.....	.....	1.50	0.70
	same, plate number strip of 5	.....	.....	.....	.....	10.00	.....
5262	(50¢) U.S. Flag, micro USPS at left of flag	2.75	.....	.....	.....	1.50	0.70
5262a	same, double-sided bklt pane of 20	.....	.....	.....	.....	28.50	.....
5263	(50¢) U.S. Flag, micro USPS at right of flag	2.75	.....	.....	.....	1.50	0.70
5263a	same, double-sided bklt pane of 20	.....	.....	.....	.....	28.50	.....

5264   5265

5266   5267

5268   5269

5270   5271

5272   5273

5264-73	(50¢) Bioluminescent Life .	45.00(20)	.....	38.00(20)	.....	20.00(10)	.....
5264	(50¢) Octopus	.....	.....	.....	.....	2.25	0.80
5265	(50¢) Jellyfish	.....	.....	.....	.....	2.25	0.80
5266	(50¢) Comb Jelly	.....	.....	.....	.....	2.25	0.80
5267	(50¢) Mushrooms	.....	.....	.....	.....	2.25	0.80
5268	(50¢) Firefly	.....	.....	.....	.....	2.25	0.80
5269	(50¢) Bamboo Coral	.....	.....	.....	.....	2.25	0.80
5270	(50¢) Marine Worm	.....	.....	.....	.....	2.25	0.80
5271	(50¢) Crown Jellyfish. ...	.....	.....	.....	.....	2.25	0.80
5272	(50¢) Marine Worm	.....	.....	.....	.....	2.25	0.80
5273	(50¢) Sea Pen...........	.....	.....	.....	.....	2.25	0.80

SCOTT NO.	DESCRIPTION	FIRST DAY COVERS SING	PL. BLK.	MINT SHEET	PLATE BLOCK	UNUSED F/NH	USED

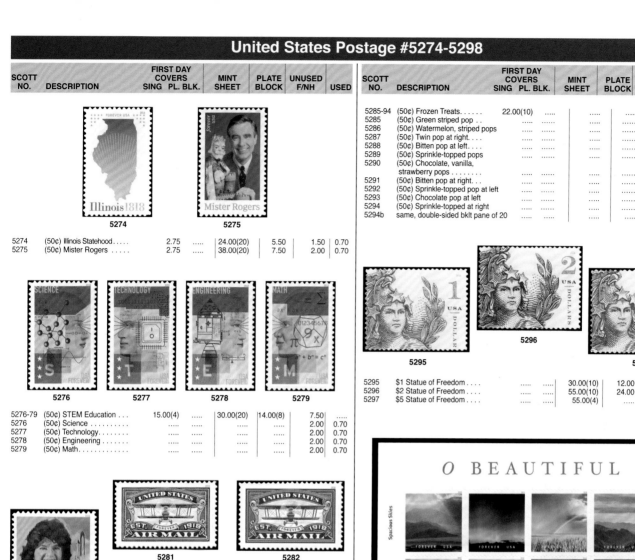

5274

5275

| 5274 | (50¢) Illinois Statehood..... | 2.75 | ..... | 24.00(20) | 5.50 | 1.50 | 0.70 |
| 5275 | (50¢) Mister Rogers ..... | 2.75 | ..... | 38.00(20) | 7.50 | 2.00 | 0.70 |

5276   **5277**   **5278**   **5279**

5276-79	(50¢) STEM Education ...	15.00(4)	.....	30.00(20)	14.00(8)	7.50	.....
5276	(50¢) Science		.....	.....	.....	2.00	0.70
5277	(50¢) Technology........		.....	.....	.....	2.00	0.70
5278	(50¢) Engineering		.....	.....	.....	2.00	0.70
5279	(50¢) Math.............		.....	.....	.....	2.00	0.70

5281   **5282**

5283   **5284**   **5280**

5280	(50¢) Peace Rose.......	2.75	.....	.....	.....	1.50	0.60
5280a	same, double-sided bklt pane of 20		.....	.....	.....	28.50	.....
5281	(50¢) Air Mail Centenary, blue	2.75	.....	24.00(20)	5.50	1.50	0.70
5282	(50¢) Air Mail Centenary, red	2.75	.....	24.00(20)	5.50	1.50	0.70
5283	(50¢) Sally Ride.........	2.75	.....	24.00(20)	5.50	1.50	0.70
5284	(50¢) Flag Act of 1818 Bicentennial	2.75	.....	24.00(20)	5.50	1.50	0.70

5285   **5286**   **5287**   **5288**

5289   **5290**   **5291**   **5292**

5293   **5294**

SCOTT NO.	DESCRIPTION	FIRST DAY COVERS SING	PL. BLK.	MINT SHEET	PLATE BLOCK	UNUSED F/NH	USED
5285-94	(50¢) Frozen Treats......	22.00(10)	.....	.....	.....	18.00(10)	
5285	(50¢) Green striped pop ..	.....	.....	.....	.....	2.00	0.70
5286	(50¢) Watermelon, striped pops	.....	.....	.....	.....	2.00	0.70
5287	(50¢) Twin pop at right....	.....	.....	.....	.....	2.00	0.70
5288	(50¢) Bitten pop at left....	.....	.....	.....	.....	2.00	0.70
5289	(50¢) Sprinkle-topped pops	.....	.....	.....	.....	2.00	0.70
5290	(50¢) Chocolate, vanilla, strawberry pops........	.....	.....	.....	.....	2.00	0.70
5291	(50¢) Bitten pop at right...	.....	.....	.....	.....	2.00	0.70
5292	(50¢) Sprinkle-topped pop at left	.....	.....	.....	.....	2.00	0.70
5293	(50¢) Chocolate pop at left	.....	.....	.....	.....	2.00	0.70
5294	(50¢) Sprinkle-topped at right	.....	.....	.....	.....	2.00	0.70
5294b	same, double-sided bklt pane of 20	.....	.....	.....	.....	34.00	.....

5295   **5296**   **5297**

5295	$1 Statue of Freedom	.....	.....	30.00(10)	12.00	3.50	1.25
5296	$2 Statue of Freedom	.....	.....	55.00(10)	24.00	6.50	3.50
5297	$5 Statue of Freedom	.....	.....	55.00(4)		15.00	8.00

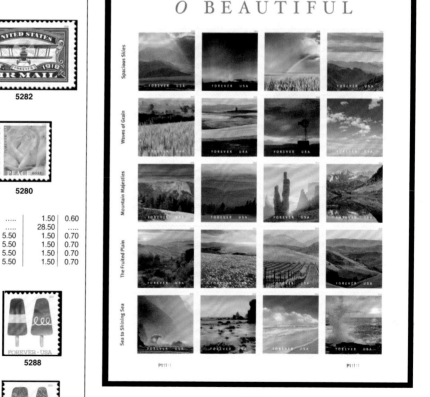

O BEAUTIFUL

Spacious Skies
Waves of Grain
Mountain Majesties
The Fruited Plain
Sea to Shining Sea

5298

O BEAUTIFUL

5298a (50¢) Death Valley National Park
5298b (50¢) Three Fingers Mountain .
5298c (50¢) Double Rainbow over Kansas Field
5298d (50¢) Great Smoky Mountains .
5298e (50¢) Field of Wheat, Wisconsin
5298f (50¢) Plowed Wheat Field .....
5298g (50¢) Grasslands Wildlife Management Area
5298h (50¢) Field of Wheat, Montana .
5298i (50¢) Yosemite National Park
5298j (50¢) Crater Lake National Park.

5298k (50¢) Monument Valley Navajo Tribal Park
5298l (50¢) Maroon Bells
5298m (50¢) Sunrise Near Orinda, California
5298n (50¢) Pigeon Point
5298o (50¢) Edna Valley
5298p (50¢) Livermore
5298q (50¢) Napali Coast State Wilderness Park
5298r (50¢) Lone Ranch Beach
5298s (50¢) Canaveral National Seashore
5298t (50¢) Bailey Island

| 5298 | (50¢) O Beautiful ..... | 45.00(20) | | 30.00(20) | ..... | ..... | ..... |

SCOTT NO.	DESCRIPTION	FIRST DAY COVERS SING	FIRST DAY COVERS PL. BLK.	MINT SHEET	PLATE BLOCK	UNUSED F/NH	USED
5299	(50¢) Scooby-Doo	2.75	. . . . .	15.00(12)	5.50	1.50	0.70
5300	(50¢) World War I, Turning the Tide	2.75	. . . . .	24.00(20)	5.50	1.50	0.70

5299

5300

5301, 5306a

5302

5303

5304

5305

SCOTT NO.	DESCRIPTION	SING	PL. BLK.	MINT SHEET	PLATE BLOCK	UNUSED F/NH	USED
5301-05	(50¢) Art of Magic	12.00(5)	. . . . .	30.00(20)	18.00(10)	9.00(5)	. . . . .
5301	(50¢) Rabbit in Hat	. . . . .	. . . . .	. . . . .	. . . . .	2.00	0.70
5302	(50¢) Fortune Teller.	. . . . .	. . . . .	. . . . .	. . . . .	2.00	0.70
5303	(50¢) Woman Hoop.	. . . . .	. . . . .	. . . . .	. . . . .	2.00	0.70
5304	(50¢) Empty Bird Cage . . .	. . . . .	. . . . .	. . . . .	. . . . .	2.00	0.70
5305	(50¢) Bird in Flower.	. . . . .	. . . . .	. . . . .	. . . . .	2.00	0.70
5306	(50¢) Art of Magic, souvenir sheet of 3	. . . . .	. . . . .	. . . . .	. . . . .	6.00	. . . . .

5307

5308

5309

5310

SCOTT NO.	DESCRIPTION	SING	PL. BLK.	MINT SHEET	PLATE BLOCK	UNUSED F/NH	USED
5307-10	(50¢) Dragons	15.00(4)	. . . . .	30.00(20)	9.00(4)	7.50	. . . . .
5307	(50¢) Green Dragon and Castle		. . . . .	. . . . .	. . . . .	2.00	0.70
5308	(50¢) Purple Dragon and Castle		. . . . .	. . . . .	. . . . .	2.00	0.70
5309	(50¢) Dragon and Ship . . .		. . . . .	. . . . .	. . . . .	2.00	0.70
5310	(50¢) Dragon and Pagoda.		. . . . .	. . . . .	. . . . .	2.00	0.70

5311

SCOTT NO.	DESCRIPTION	SING	PL. BLK.	MINT SHEET	PLATE BLOCK	UNUSED F/NH	USED
5311	($1.15) Poinsettia	4.00	. . . . .	25.00(10)	12.00(4)	3.00	1.00

5312

5313

5314

5315

SCOTT NO.	DESCRIPTION	SING	PL. BLK.	MINT SHEET	PLATE BLOCK	UNUSED F/NH	USED
5312-15	(50¢) John Lennon	15.00(4)	. . . . .	25.00(16)	. . . . .	7.50	. . . . .
5312	(50¢) Red	. . . . .	. . . . .	. . . . .	. . . . .	2.00	0.80
5313	(50¢) Red Lilac	. . . . .	. . . . .	. . . . .	. . . . .	2.00	0.80
5314	(50¢) Violet	. . . . .	. . . . .	. . . . .	. . . . .	2.00	0.80
5315	(50¢) Blue	. . . . .	. . . . .	. . . . .	. . . . .	2.00	0.80

5316

SCOTT NO.	DESCRIPTION	SING	PL. BLK.	MINT SHEET	PLATE BLOCK	UNUSED F/NH	USED
5316	(50¢) Honoring First Responders.	2.75	. . . . .	24.00(20)	5.50(4)	1.50	0.70

5317

5318

5319

5320

SCOTT NO.	DESCRIPTION	SING	PL. BLK.	MINT SHEET	PLATE BLOCK	UNUSED F/NH	USED
5317-20	(50¢) Birds in Winter	15.00(4)	. . . . .	15.00(16)	. . . . .	7.50	. . . . .
5317	(50¢) Chickadee	. . . . .	. . . . .	. . . . .	. . . . .	2.00	0.80
5318	(50¢) Cardinal	. . . . .	. . . . .	. . . . .	. . . . .	2.00	0.80
5319	(50¢) Woodpecker.	. . . . .	. . . . .	. . . . .	. . . . .	2.00	0.80
5320	(50¢) Blue Jay	. . . . .	. . . . .	. . . . .	. . . . .	2.00	0.80
5320b	same, double-sided bklt pane of 20	. . . . .	. . . . .	. . . . .	. . . . .	30.00	

5321

5322

SCOTT NO.	DESCRIPTION	FIRST DAY COVERS SING	PL. BLK.	MINT SHEET	PLATE BLOCK	UNUSED F/NH	USED

5323

5324

5325

5326

5327

5328

5329

5330

SCOTT NO.	DESCRIPTION	FIRST DAY COVERS SING	PL. BLK.	MINT SHEET	PLATE BLOCK	UNUSED F/NH	USED
5321-30	(50¢) Hot Wheels	35.00(10)	.....	30.00(20)	.....	18.00(10)	.....
5321	(50¢) Purple Passion. . . .	.....	.....	.....	.....	2.00	0.90
5322	(50¢) Rocket-Bye-Baby. . .	.....	.....	.....	.....	2.00	0.90
5323	(50¢) Rigor Motor	.....	.....	.....	.....	2.00	0.90
5324	(50¢) Rodger Dodger	.....	.....	.....	.....	2.00	0.90
5325	(50¢) Mach Speeder	.....	.....	.....	.....	2.00	0.90
5326	(50¢) Twin Mill.	.....	.....	.....	.....	2.00	0.90
5327	(50¢) Bone Shaker	.....	.....	.....	.....	2.00	0.90
5328	(50¢) HW40.	.....	.....	.....	.....	2.00	0.90
5329	(50¢) Deora II	.....	.....	.....	.....	2.00	0.90
5330	(50¢) Sharkruiser	.....	.....	.....	.....	2.00	0.90

5332

5333

5334

5335

5336

5331

5337

5338

SCOTT NO.	DESCRIPTION	FIRST DAY COVERS SING	PL. BLK.	MINT SHEET	PLATE BLOCK	UNUSED F/NH	USED
5331	(50¢) Madonna and Child .	2.75	.....	.....	.....	1.50	0.60
5331a	same, double-sided bklt pane of 20	.....	.....	.....	.....	24.00	.....
5332-35	(50¢) Sparkling Holiday Santas	8.00(4)	.....	.....	.....	5.50	.....
5332	(50¢) Santa Head	.....	.....	.....	.....	1.50	0.60
5333	(50¢) Santa and Wreath . .	.....	.....	.....	.....	1.50	0.60
5334	(50¢) Santa and Book	.....	.....	.....	.....	1.50	0.60
5335	(50¢) Santa and Card	.....	.....	.....	.....	1.50	0.60
5335b	same, double-sided bklt pane of 20	.....	.....	.....	.....	24.00	.....
5336	(50¢) Sparkling Holiday Santa, souvenir sheet	.....	.....	.....	.....	2.50	.....
5337	(50¢) Kwanzaa	2.75	.....	24.00(20)	5.50(4)	1.50	0.60
5338	(50¢) Hanukkah.	2.75	.....	24.00(20)	5.50(4)	1.50	0.60

2019 COMMEMORATIVES

SCOTT NO.	DESCRIPTION	FIRST DAY COVERS SING	PL. BLK.	MINT SHEET	PLATE BLOCK	UNUSED F/NH	USED
5254/5338	(5340, 5349, 5360, 5371-80, 5382-93, 5399-5404, 5409-14, 5420-23) 41 varieties	....	....	....	....	65.00	....

5339

5340

SCOTT NO.	DESCRIPTION	FIRST DAY COVERS SING	PL. BLK.	MINT SHEET	PLATE BLOCK	UNUSED F/NH	USED
5339	(50¢) Love Hearts	2.75	.....	24.00(20)	5.00(4)	1.50	0.60
5340	(50¢) Year of the Boar	2.75	.....	15.00(12)	.....	1.50	0.60

5342, 5343

5341

5344, 5345

5346

SCOTT NO.	DESCRIPTION	FIRST DAY COVERS SING	PL. BLK.	MINT SHEET	PLATE BLOCK	UNUSED F/NH	USED
5341	(15¢) Uncle Sam Hat, coil.....	.....	.....	.....	.....	0.30	0.30
	same, plate number strip of 5	.....	.....	.....	.....	3.00	.....
5342	(55¢) U.S. Flag coil, die cut 11	2.75	.....	.....	.....	1.50	0.60
	same, plate number strip of 5	.....	.....	.....	.....	10.50	.....
5343	(55¢) U.S. Flag coil, die cut 9.5	2.75	.....	.....	.....	1.50	0.60
	same, plate number strip of 5	.....	.....	.....	.....	10.50	.....
5344	(55¢) U.S. Flag, micro USPS at upper left	2.75	.....	.....	.....	1.50	0.60
5344a	same, double-sided bklt pane of 20	.....	.....	.....	.....	24.50	.....
5345	(55¢) U.S. Flag, micro USPS at right	2.75	.....	.....	.....	1.50	0.60
5345a	same, double-sided bklt pane of 20	.....	.....	.....	.....	24.50	.....
5346	(70¢) California Dogface Butterfly	3.00	.....	30.00(20)	7.50(4)	2.00	0.70

5347

5348

SCOTT NO.	DESCRIPTION	FIRST DAY COVERS SING	PL. BLK.	MINT SHEET	PLATE BLOCK	UNUSED F/NH	USED
5347	($7.35) Joshua Tree, Priority Mail	15.00	.....	60.00(4)	.....	15.50	8.00
5348	($25.50) Bethesda Fountain, Express Mail	48.00	.....	200.00(4)	.....	55.00	25.00

SCOTT NO.	DESCRIPTION	FIRST DAY COVERS SING	PL. BLK.	MINT SHEET	PLATE BLOCK	UNUSED F/NH	USED

5349

| 5349 | (55¢) Gregory Hines . . . . . | 2.75 | ..... | 24.00(20) | 5.50(4) | 1.50 | 0.70 |

5350

5351

5352

5353   **5354**   **5355**   **5356**

5357   **5358**   **5359**

5350-59	(55¢) Cactus Flowers	30.00(10)	.....	.....	.....	18.00	.....
5350	(55¢) Opuntia Engelmannii	.....	.....	.....	.....	2.00	0.90
5351	(55¢) Rebutia Minuscula.....	.....	.....	.....	.....	2.00	0.90
5352	(55¢) Echinocereus Dasyacanthus	.....	.....	.....	.....	2.00	0.90
5353	(55¢) Echinocereus Poselgeri	.....	.....	.....	.....	2.00	0.90
5354	(55¢) Echinocereus Coccineus	.....	.....	.....	.....	2.00	0.90
5355	(55¢) Pelecyphora Aselliformis	.....	.....	.....	.....	2.00	0.90
5356	(55¢) Parodia Microsperma	.....	.....	.....	.....	2.00	0.90
5357	(55¢) Echinocereus Horizonthalonius	.....	.....	.....	.....	2.00	0.90
5358	(55¢) Thelocactus Heterochromus	.....	.....	.....	.....	2.00	0.90
5359	(55¢) Parodia Scopa	.....	.....	.....	.....	2.00	0.90
5359b	same, double-sided bklt pane of 20	.....	.....	.....	.....	34.00	.....

5360   **5361, 5362**

5360	(55¢) Alabama Statehood..............	2.75	.....	24.00(20)	5.50(4)	1.50	0.70
5361	(55¢) Star Ribbon	2.75	.....	24.00(20)	5.50(4)	1.50	0.60
5362	(55¢) Star Ribbon coil..............	2.75	.....	.....	.....	1.50	0.60
	same, plate number strip of 5	.....	.....	.....	.....	10.50	.....

5363, 5369   **5364, 5370**   **5365, 5367**   **5366, 5368**

5363-66	(35¢) Coral Reefs	6.00(4)	.....	14.00(20)	6.00(8)	3.00	.....
5363	(35¢) French Angelfish	.....	.....	.....	.....	0.80	0.60
5364	(35¢) Spotted Moray Eel.....	.....	.....	.....	.....	0.80	0.60
5365	(35¢) Grouper and Neon Gobies	.....	.....	.....	.....	0.80	0.60
5366	(35¢) Blue-striped Grunts.....	.....	.....	.....	.....	0.80	0.60
5367-70	(35¢) Coral Reefs coil	6.00(4)	.....	.....	.....	3.00	.....
	same, plate number strip of 5	.....	.....	.....	.....	6.00	.....
5367	(35¢) Grouper and Neon Gobies coil	.....	.....	.....	.....	0.80	0.60
5368	(35¢) Blue-striped Grunts coil	.....	.....	.....	.....	0.80	0.60
5369	(35¢) French Angelfish coil.....	.....	.....	.....	.....	0.80	0.60
5370	(35¢) Spotted Moray Eel coil	.....	.....	.....	.....	0.80	0.60

5371

| 5371 | (55¢) Marvin Gaye.............. | 2.75 | ..... | 22.00(16) | ..... | 1.50 | 0.70 |

5372

5373   **5374**

5375   **5376**

5372-76	(55¢) Post Office Murals..............	15.00(5)	.....	18.00(10)	.....	9.00	.....
5372	(55¢) Piggott, Arkansas...........	.....	.....	.....	.....	2.00	0.80
5373	(55¢) Florence, Colorado...........	.....	.....	.....	.....	2.00	0.80
5374	(55¢) Rockville, Maryland..........	.....	.....	.....	.....	2.00	0.80
5375	(55¢) Anadarko, Oklahoma...........	.....	.....	.....	.....	2.00	0.80
5376	(55¢) Deming, New Mexico...........	.....	.....	.....	.....	2.00	0.80

5377

| 5377 | (55¢) Maureen Connolly Brinker... | 2.75 | ..... | 24.00(20) | 5.50(4) | 1.50 | 0.70 |

SCOTT NO.	DESCRIPTION	FIRST DAY COVERS SING	FIRST DAY COVERS PL. BLK.	MINT SHEET	PLATE BLOCK	UNUSED F/NH	USED

5378   **5379**   **5380**

SCOTT NO.	DESCRIPTION	SING	PL. BLK.	MINT SHEET	PLATE BLOCK	UNUSED F/NH	USED
5378-80	Transcontinental Railroad............	10.00(3)	.....	24.00(18)	8.00(6)	4.00	.....
5378	(55¢) Jupiter Locomotive...........	.....	.....	.....	.....	1.50	0.80
5379	(55¢) Golden Spike	.....	.....	.....	.....	1.50	0.80
5380	(55¢) No. 119 Locomotive...........	.....	.....	.....	.....	1.50	0.80

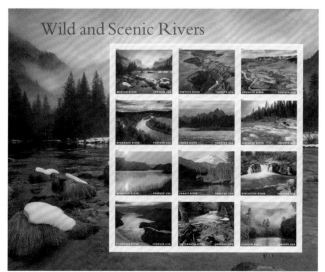

5381

WILD AND SCENIC RIVERS

5381a *Merced River*	**5381g** *Missouri River*
5381b *Owyhee River*	**5381h** *Skagit River*
5381c *Koyukuk River*	**5381i** *Deschutes River*
5381d *Niobrara River*	**5381j** *Tlikakila River*
5381e *Snake River*	**5381k** *Ontonagon River*
5381f *Flathead River*	**5381l** *Clarion River*

5381	(55¢) Wild and Scenic Rivers...	40.00(12)	.....	18.00		.....	.....

5382   **5383**   **5384**   **5385**   **5386**

5387   **5388**   **5389**   **5390**   **5391**

5382-91	(55¢) Art of Ellsworth Kelly	35.00(10)	.....	30.00(20)	20.00(10)	18.00	.....
5382	(55¢) Yellow White, 1961 .	.....	.....	.....	.....	2.00	0.80
5383	(55¢) Colors for a Large Wall, 1951	.....	.....	.....	.....	2.00	0.80
5384	(55¢) Blue Red Rocker, 1963	.....	.....	.....	.....	2.00	0.80
5385	(55¢) Spectrum I, 1953 . . .	.....	.....	.....	.....	2.00	0.80
5386	(55¢) South Ferry, 1956 . .	.....	.....	.....	.....	2.00	0.80
5387	(55¢) Blue Green, 1962. . .	.....	.....	.....	.....	2.00	0.80
5388	(55¢) Orange Red Relief, 1990	.....	.....	.....	.....	2.00	0.80
5389	(55¢) Meschers, 1951	.....	.....	.....	.....	2.00	0.80
5390	(55¢) Red Blue, 1964	.....	.....	.....	.....	2.00	0.80
5391	(55¢) Gaza, 1956	.....	.....	.....	.....	2.00	0.80

5392   **5393**

5392	(55¢) USS Missouri.............	2.75	.....	24.00(20)	5.50(4)	1.50	0.70
5393	(55¢) Pres. George H.W. Bush	2.75	.....	24.00(20)	5.50(4)	1.50	0.60

5394

SESAME STREET

5394a *Big Bird*	**5394i** *Herry Monster*
5394b *Ernie*	**5394j** *Julia*
5394c *Bert*	**5394k** *Guy Smiley*
5394d *Cookie Monster*	**5394l** *Snuffleupagus*
5394e *Rosita*	**5394m** *Elmo*
5394f *The Count*	**5394n** *Telly*
5394g *Oscar*	**5394o** *Grover*
5394h *Abby Cadabby*	**5394p** *Zoe*

5394	(55¢) Sesame Street.	50.00(16)	.....	24.00 (16)		.....	.....

5395   **5396**

5397   **5398**

5395-98	(55¢) Frogs	15.00(4)	.....	.....	.....	5.50	.....
5395	(55¢) Pacific Tree Frog.............	.....	.....	.....	.....	1.50	0.70
5396	(55¢) Northern Leopard Frog.....	.....	.....	.....	.....	1.50	0.70
5397	(55¢) American Green Tree Frog	.....	.....	.....	.....	1.50	0.70
5398	(55¢) Squirrel Tree Frog.....	.....	.....	.....	.....	1.50	0.70
5398b	same, double-sided bklt pane of 20	.....	.....	.....	.....	28.50	.....

SCOTT NO.	DESCRIPTION	FIRST DAY COVERS SING	PL. BLK.	MINT SHEET	PLATE BLOCK	UNUSED F/NH	USED

5399   **5400**

5399-5400	(55¢) 50th Anniv. First Moon Landing	6.00(2)	.....	27.00(24)	5.50(4)	2.75	.....
5399	(55¢) Adwin E. Aldrin Jr. on Moon	.....	.....	.....	.....	1.50	0.70
5400	(55¢) Moon Landing Site.....	.....	.....	.....	.....	1.50	0.70

5401   **5402**   **5403**   **5404**

5401-04	(55¢) State and County Fairs	18.00(4)	.....	25.00(20)	9.00(8)	5.50	.....
5401	(55¢) Farmers Unloading Fruits	.....	.....	.....	.....	1.50	0.70
5402	(55¢) Girl and Farm Animals.....	.....	.....	.....	.....	1.50	0.70
5403	(55¢) Parents and Children.....	.....	.....	.....	.....	1.50	0.70
5404	(55¢) Child and Candy Apple.....	.....	.....	.....	.....	1.50	0.70

5405

5406

5407

5408

5405-08	(55¢) Military Working Dogs	15.00(4)	.....	.....	.....	5.50	.....
5405	(55¢) German Shepherd.....	.....	.....	.....	.....	1.50	0.70
5406	(55¢) Labrador Retriever.....	.....	.....	.....	.....	1.50	0.70
5407	(55¢) Belgian Malinois.....	.....	.....	.....	.....	1.50	0.70
5408	(55¢) Dutch Shepherd.....	.....	.....	.....	.....	1.50	0.70
5408b	same, double-sided bklt pane of 20	.....	.....	.....	.....	28.50	.....

5409

| 5409 | (55¢) 50th Anniv. Woodstock | 2.75 | ..... | 24.00(20) | 5.50(4) | 1.50 | 0.70 |

SCOTT NO.	DESCRIPTION	FIRST DAY COVERS SING	PL. BLK.	MINT SHEET	PLATE BLOCK	UNUSED F/NH	USED

5410   **5411**

5412   **5413**

5410-13	(55¢) Tyrannosaurus Rex .	15.00(4)	.....	30.00(16)	8.00(4)	7.50	.....
5410	(55¢) Juvenile Tyrannosaurus Rex, Egg, Insect	.....	.....	.....	.....	2.00	0.80
5411	(55¢) Adult Tyrannosaurus Rex	.....	.....	.....	.....	2.00	0.80
5412	(55¢) Young Adult Tyrannosaurus Rex	.....	.....	.....	.....	2.00	0.80
5413	(55¢) Juvenile Tyrannosaurus Rex, Mammal	.....	.....	.....	.....	2.00	0.80

5414

| 5414 | Walt Whitman . . . . | 3.20 | ..... | 35.00(20) | 7.50(4) | 2.00 | 1.20 |

5415   **5416**   **5417**   **5418**

5415-18	(55¢) Winter Berries	15.00(4)	.....	.....	.....	5.50	.....
5415	(55¢) Winterberry	.....	.....	.....	.....	1.50	0.70
5416	(55¢) Juniper Berry	.....	.....	.....	.....	1.50	0.70
5417	(55¢) Beautyberry	.....	.....	.....	.....	1.50	0.70
5418	(55¢) Soapberry	.....	.....	.....	.....	1.50	0.70
5418b	same, double-sided bklt pane of 20	.....	.....	.....	.....	28.50	.....

5419

| 5419 | Purple Heart . . . . | 2.75 | ..... | 22.00(20) | 5.00(4) | 1.20 | 0.70 |

5420   **5421**   **5422**   **5423**

5420-23	(55¢) Spooky Silhouettes .	15.00(4)	.....	28.00(20)	6.00(4)	5.50	.....
5420	(55¢) Cat and Raven.....	.....	.....	.....	.....	1.50	0.80
5421	(55¢) Ghosts	.....	.....	.....	.....	1.50	0.80
5422	(55¢) Spider and Web	.....	.....	.....	.....	1.50	0.80
5423	(55¢) Bats	.....	.....	.....	.....	1.50	0.80

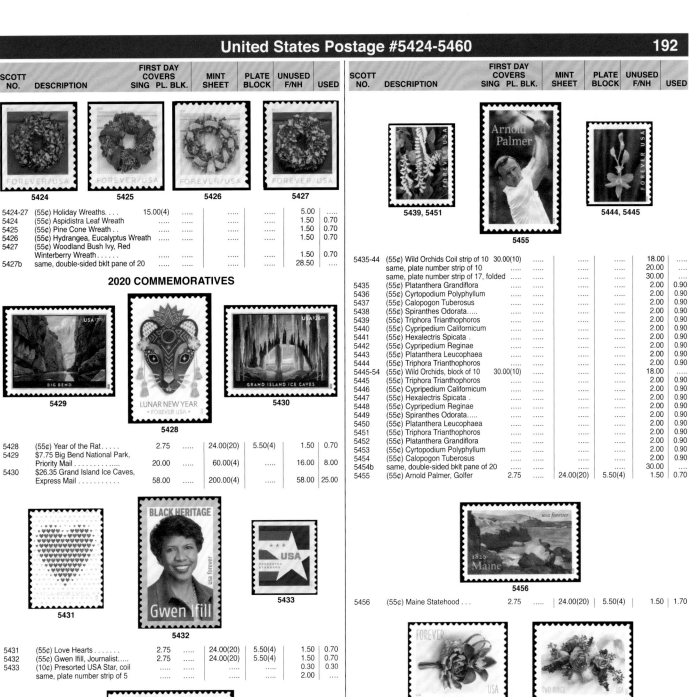

SCOTT NO.	DESCRIPTION	FIRST DAY COVERS SING	FIRST DAY COVERS PL. BLK.	MINT SHEET	PLATE BLOCK	UNUSED F/NH	USED
5424-27	(55¢) Holiday Wreaths. . . .	15.00(4)	.....	.....	.....	5.00	....
5424	(55¢) Aspidistra Leaf Wreath	.....	.....	.....	.....	1.50	0.70
5425	(55¢) Pine Cone Wreath . .	.....	.....	.....	.....	1.50	0.70
5426	(55¢) Hydrangea, Eucalyptus Wreath	.....	.....	.....	.....	1.50	0.70
5427	(55¢) Woodland Bush Ivy, Red Winterberry Wreath.	.....	.....	.....	.....	1.50	0.70
5427b	same, double-sided bklt pane of 20	.....	.....	.....	.....	28.50	....

2020 COMMEMORATIVES

SCOTT NO.	DESCRIPTION	FIRST DAY COVERS SING	FIRST DAY COVERS PL. BLK.	MINT SHEET	PLATE BLOCK	UNUSED F/NH	USED
5428	(55¢) Year of the Rat	2.75	.....	24.00(20)	5.50(4)	1.50	0.70
5429	$7.75 Big Bend National Park, Priority Mail	20.00	.....	60.00(4)	.....	16.00	8.00
5430	$26.35 Grand Island Ice Caves, Express Mail	58.00	.....	200.00(4)	.....	58.00	25.00

SCOTT NO.	DESCRIPTION	FIRST DAY COVERS SING	FIRST DAY COVERS PL. BLK.	MINT SHEET	PLATE BLOCK	UNUSED F/NH	USED
5431	(55¢) Love Hearts	2.75	.....	24.00(20)	5.50(4)	1.50	0.70
5432	(55¢) Gwen Ifill, Journalist.	2.75	.....	24.00(20)	5.50(4)	1.50	0.70
5433	(10¢) Presorted USA Star, coil	.....	.....	.....	.....	0.30	0.30
	same, plate number strip of 5	.....	.....	.....	.....	2.00	....

SCOTT NO.	DESCRIPTION	FIRST DAY COVERS SING	FIRST DAY COVERS PL. BLK.	MINT SHEET	PLATE BLOCK	UNUSED F/NH	USED
5434	Let's Celebrate	2.75	.....	24.00(20)	5.50(4)	1.50	1.70

SCOTT NO.	DESCRIPTION	FIRST DAY COVERS SING	FIRST DAY COVERS PL. BLK.	MINT SHEET	PLATE BLOCK	UNUSED F/NH	USED
5435-44	(55¢) Wild Orchids Coil strip of 10	30.00(10)	.....	.....	.....	18.00	....
	same, plate number strip of 10	.....	.....	.....	.....	20.00	....
	same, plate number strip of 17, folded	.....	.....	.....	.....	30.00	....
5435	(55¢) Platanthera Grandiflora	.....	.....	.....	.....	2.00	0.90
5436	(55¢) Cyrtopodium Polyphyllum	.....	.....	.....	.....	2.00	0.90
5437	(55¢) Calopogon Tuberosus	.....	.....	.....	.....	2.00	0.90
5438	(55¢) Spiranthes Odorata.	.....	.....	.....	.....	2.00	0.90
5439	(55¢) Triphora Trianthophoros	.....	.....	.....	.....	2.00	0.90
5440	(55¢) Cypripedium Californicum	.....	.....	.....	.....	2.00	0.90
5441	(55¢) Hexalectris Spicata .	.....	.....	.....	.....	2.00	0.90
5442	(55¢) Cypripedium Reginae	.....	.....	.....	.....	2.00	0.90
5443	(55¢) Platanthera Leucophaea	.....	.....	.....	.....	2.00	0.90
5444	(55¢) Triphora Trianthophoros	.....	.....	.....	.....	2.00	0.90
5445-54	(55¢) Wild Orchids, block of 10	30.00(10)	.....	.....	.....	18.00	....
5445	(55¢) Triphora Trianthophoros	.....	.....	.....	.....	2.00	0.90
5446	(55¢) Cypripedium Californicum	.....	.....	.....	.....	2.00	0.90
5447	(55¢) Hexalectris Spicata .	.....	.....	.....	.....	2.00	0.90
5448	(55¢) Cypripedium Reginae	.....	.....	.....	.....	2.00	0.90
5449	(55¢) Spiranthes Odorata.	.....	.....	.....	.....	2.00	0.90
5450	(55¢) Platanthera Leucophaea	.....	.....	.....	.....	2.00	0.90
5451	(55¢) Triphora Trianthophoros	.....	.....	.....	.....	2.00	0.90
5452	(55¢) Platanthera Grandiflora	.....	.....	.....	.....	2.00	0.90
5453	(55¢) Cyrtopodium Polyphyllum	.....	.....	.....	.....	2.00	0.90
5454	(55¢) Calopogon Tuberosus	.....	.....	.....	.....	2.00	0.90
5454b	same, double-sided bklt pane of 20	.....	.....	.....	.....	30.00	....
5455	(55¢) Arnold Palmer, Golfer	2.75	.....	24.00(20)	5.50(4)	1.50	0.70

SCOTT NO.	DESCRIPTION	FIRST DAY COVERS SING	FIRST DAY COVERS PL. BLK.	MINT SHEET	PLATE BLOCK	UNUSED F/NH	USED
5456	(55¢) Maine Statehood . . .	2.75	.....	24.00(20)	5.50(4)	1.50	1.70

SCOTT NO.	DESCRIPTION	FIRST DAY COVERS SING	FIRST DAY COVERS PL. BLK.	MINT SHEET	PLATE BLOCK	UNUSED F/NH	USED
5457	(55¢) Boutoniere	2.75	.....	24.00(20)	5.50(4)	1.50	0.70
5458	(70¢) Corsage	3.75	.....	30.00(20)	6.50(4)	1.75	1.00

SCOTT NO.	DESCRIPTION	FIRST DAY COVERS SING	FIRST DAY COVERS PL. BLK.	MINT SHEET	PLATE BLOCK	UNUSED F/NH	USED
5459	(55¢) Earth Day.	2.75	.....	.....	.....	1.50	0.70
5459a	same, double-sided bklt pane of 20	.....	.....	.....	.....	28.50	....

SCOTT NO.	DESCRIPTION	FIRST DAY COVERS SING	FIRST DAY COVERS PL. BLK.	MINT SHEET	PLATE BLOCK	UNUSED F/NH	USED
5460	($1.20) Global Chrysanthemum	5.00	.....	25.00(10)	12.00(4)	3.00	1.30

SCOTT NO.	DESCRIPTION	FIRST DAY COVERS SING	PL. BLK.	MINT SHEET	PLATE BLOCK	UNUSED F/NH	USED

5462

5461

5463

5464

5465

5466

5468

5467

5469

5470

SCOTT NO.	DESCRIPTION	SING	PL. BLK.	MINT SHEET	PLATE BLOCK	UNUSED F/NH	USED
5461-70	(55¢) American Gardens . .	30.00(10)	.....	24.00(20)	15.00(10)	14.00	.....
5461	(55¢) Brooklyn Botanic, New York	.....	.....	.....	1.50	.....	0.80
5462	(55¢) Stan Hywet Hall, Ohio	.....	.....	.....	.....	1.50	0.80
5463	(55¢) Dumbarton Oaks, DC	.....	.....	.....	.....	1.50	0.80
5464	(55¢) Coastal Maine Botanical, Maine	.....	.....	.....	1.50	.....	0.80
5465	(55¢) Chicago Botanic, Illinois	.....	.....	.....	.....	1.50	0.80
5466	(55¢) Winterthur, Delaware	.....	.....	.....	.....	1.50	0.80
5467	(55¢) Biltmore, North Carolina	.....	.....	.....	.....	1.50	0.80
5468	(55¢) Alfred B Maclay, Florida	.....	.....	.....	.....	1.50	0.80
5469	(55¢) Huntington Botanical, California	.....	.....	.....	.....	1.50	0.80
5470	(55¢) Norfolk Botanical, Virginia	.....	.....	.....	.....	1.50	0.80

5471

5472

5473

5474

SCOTT NO.	DESCRIPTION	SING	PL. BLK.	MINT SHEET	PLATE BLOCK	UNUSED F/NH	USED
5471-74	(55¢) Voices of the Harlem Renaissance	15.00(4)	.....	24.00(20)	10.00(8)	5.00	.....
5471	(55¢) Nella Larsen	.....	.....	.....	.....	1.20	0.80
5472	(55¢) Arturo Schomburg . .	.....	.....	.....	.....	1.20	0.80
5473	(55¢) Anne Spencer	.....	.....	.....	.....	1.20	0.80
5474	(55¢) Alain Locke	.....	.....	.....	.....	1.20	0.80

5475

5476

5477

5478

5479

SCOTT NO.	DESCRIPTION	SING	PL. BLK.	MINT SHEET	PLATE BLOCK	UNUSED F/NH	USED
5475-79	(55¢) Enjoy the Great Outdoors	18.00(5)	.....	24.00(20)	13.00(10)	7.00	.....
5475	(55¢) Child building Sandcastle	.....	.....	.....	.....	1.50	0.80
5476	(55¢) Canoeing	.....	.....	.....	.....	1.50	0.80
5477	(55¢) Hiking	.....	.....	.....	.....	1.50	0.80
5478	(55¢) Bicycling	.....	.....	.....	.....	1.50	0.80
5479	(55¢) Cross-country Skiing	.....	.....	.....	.....	1.50	0.80

5480 **5481** **5482** **5483**

SCOTT NO.	DESCRIPTION	SING	PL. BLK.	MINT SHEET	PLATE BLOCK	UNUSED F/NH	USED
5480-83	(55¢) Hip Hop	12.00(4)	.....	24.00(20)	6.00(4)	5.50	.....
5480	(55¢) MC with Microphone	.....	.....	.....	.....	1.50	0.80
5481	(55¢) B-boy Dancing	.....	.....	.....	.....	1.50	0.80
5482	(55¢) Graffiti Art	.....	.....	.....	.....	1.50	0.80
5483	(55¢) DJ at Turntable	.....	.....	.....	.....	1.50	0.80

5484 **5485** **5486** **5487**

5488 **5489** **5490** **5491**

5492 **5493**

SCOTT NO.	DESCRIPTION	SING	PL. BLK.	MINT SHEET	PLATE BLOCK	UNUSED F/NH	USED
5484-93	(55¢) Fruits and Vegetables, block of 10	30.00(10)	.....	.....	.....	14.00	.....
5484	(55¢) Plums	.....	.....	.....	.....	1.50	0.90
5485	(55¢) Tomatoes	.....	.....	.....	.....	1.50	0.90
5486	(55¢) Carrots	.....	.....	.....	.....	1.50	0.90
5487	(55¢) Lemons	.....	.....	.....	.....	1.50	0.90
5488	(55¢) Blueberries	.....	.....	.....	.....	1.50	0.90
5489	(55¢) Grapes	.....	.....	.....	.....	1.50	0.90
5490	(55¢) Lettuce	.....	.....	.....	.....	1.50	0.90
5491	(55¢) Strawberries	.....	.....	.....	.....	1.50	0.90
5492	(55¢) Eggplant	.....	.....	.....	.....	1.50	0.90
5493	(55¢) Figs	.....	.....	.....	.....	1.50	0.90
5493b	same, double-sided bklt pane of 20	.....	.....	.....	.....	28.50	.....

SCOTT NO.	DESCRIPTION	FIRST DAY COVERS SING PL. BLK.	MINT SHEET	PLATE BLOCK	UNUSED F/NH	USED

SEMI-POSTAL

B1 (1998 year date)
B5 (2014 year date)

B4

B2

B3

B6

B7

SCOTT NO.	DESCRIPTION	SING	PL. BLK.	MINT SHEET	PLATE BLOCK	UNUSED F/NH	USED
	1998						
B1	(32¢ + 8¢) Breast Cancer	2.25	5.50	30.00(20)	5.50	1.50	.50
	2002						
B2	(34¢ + 11¢) Heroes of 2001	2.50	5.50	30.00(20)	5.50	1.50	.50
	2003						
B3	(37¢ + 8¢)Stop Family Violence	2.50	5.50	30.00(20)	5.50	1.50	.50
	2011						
B4	(44¢ + 11¢) Save Vanishing Species	2.70	....	35.00(20)	7.00	2.00	.65
	2015						
B5	(49¢ + 11¢) Breast Cancer Semi-Postal (2014 date)	2.75	....	35.00(20)	7.00	2.00	.75
	2017						
B6	(49¢ + 11¢) Alzheimers	$2.75	....	35.00(20)	7.00	2.00	0.90
	2019						
B7	(55¢ + 10¢) Healing PTSD	$2.75	....	35.00(20)	6.50	1.50	0.90

PLATE NUMBER STRIPS OF 5

SCOTT NO.	UNUSED F/NH	SCOTT NO.	UNUSED F/NH
1891	7.50	2281	6.00
1895	6.00	2451	1.60
1897	.95	2451b	1.75
1897A	.85	2452	3.00
1898	1.20	2452a	3.50
1898A	2.00	2452B	3.00
1899	1.60	2452D	3.00
1900	9.00	2453	2.75
1901	9.00	2454	3.75
1902	8.00	2457	4.25
1903	9.00	2458	8.50
1904	19.00	2463	7.00
1905	5.50	2464	5.50
1906	4.00	2466	9.00
1907	5.25	2468	21.50
1908	5.00	2495Ab	20.00
1898Ab	10.00	2518	6.00
1900A	12.00	2523	8.00
1901A	42.00	2523A	7.50
1902A	9.00	2525	8.00
1903A	5.25	2526	8.50
1904A	42.00	2529	5.00
1905A	5.25	2529a	5.00
1906A	7.00	2529c	11.50
2005	165.00	2598b	11.00
2112	10.00	2599b	11.00
2115	5.50	2602	4.25
2115a	5.50	2603	4.50
2115b	85.00	2604	4.50
2115c	6.00	2605	6.50
2123	2.00	2606	6.25
2124	1.80	2607	7.50
2125	2.75	2608	11.00
2126	2.40	2609	8.00
2127	3.50	2802b	14.00
2128	2.75	2813b	12.00
2129	5.00	2886b	20.00
2130	8.50	2888	10.00
2131	3.00	2889	20.00
2132	4.50	2890	9.50
2133	4.75	2891	10.00
2134	3.50	2892	14.00
2135	6.00	2893	7.00
2136	6.50	2902	3.00
2123A	7.00	2902B	4.00
2124A	2.50	2903	2.50
2125A	3.50	2904	2.95
2126A	3.00	2904A	6.50
2127A	4.50	2904B	7.00
2127Av	3.25	2905	4.00
2128A	3.00	2906	8.00
2129A	4.50	2907	9.00
2130A	3.50	2908	4.00
2130Av	3.25	2909	4.00
2132A	4.50	2910	5.00
2132B	35.00	2911	7.50
2133A	Unused	2912	7.50
2149	4.50	2912A	8.75
2149A	4.00	2912B	9.00
2150	5.50	2913	8.00
2150A	5.25	2914	10.00
2225	1.20	2915	20.00
2225a	1.50	2915A	10.00
2226	1.10	2915B	16.50
2226a	1.35	2915C	35.00
2228	2.00	2915D	23.00
2228a	10.00	3017a	35.00
2231	12.00	3018	13.50
2252	1.40	3044	1.00
2252a	1.90	3045	1.25
2253	2.50	3053	8.50
2254	2.50	3054	10.00
2255	3.50	3055	8.00
2256	3.50	3132	17.00
2257	4.50	3133	12.00
2257a	18.00	3207	3.00
2258	7.50	3207A	2.50
2259	5.00	3208	6.00
2260	4.00	3208A	5.75
2260a	6.25	3228	4.50
2261	4.75	3229	4.50
2262	8.00	3263	9.50
2262a	8.00	3264	8.50
2263	5.00	3265	11.00
2263b	12.00	3266	10.00
2264	10.00	3270	4.50
2265	7.50	3271	4.50
2266	6.00	3280	9.00
2279	5.00	3281	12.00
2280	5.00	3282	10.00
2280a	6.00	3305A	11.00

In July of 2012, the United States Postal Service released the first self-adhesive imperforate (no die-cuts) press sheets. This section covers the imperforate press sheets, mint sheets or booklet panes, plate blocks or se-tentants, and mint singles from the press sheets.
Due to the popularity of these issues, the current prices are subject to change.

SCOTT NO.	DESCRIPTION	IMPERF PRESS SHEET	IMPERF MINT SHEET OR BOOKLET	IMPERF PLATE BLOCK	IMPERF UNUSED F/NH
2012					
4694	(45¢) Ted Williams	120.00(120)	40.00 (20)	19.50(8)	2.25
4695	(45¢) Larry Doby.	120.00(120)	40.00(20)	19.50(8)	2.25
4696	(45¢) Willie Stargell . . .	120.00(120)	40.00(20)	19.50(8)	2.25
4697	(45¢) Joe DiMaggio . . .	120.00(120)	40.00(20)	19.50(8)	2.25
4694-97a	(45¢) Major League Baseball	350.00(120)	70.00 (20)	45.00(8)	15.00
4703	(45¢) War of 1812 Bicentennial	175.00(100)	55.00(20)	9.00(4)	2.25
4704	(45¢) Purple Heart	80.00(60)	30.00(20)	9.00(4)	2.25
4710	(45¢) Earthscapes	325.00(135)	50.00(15)	....	....
4711c	(45¢) Holy Family & Donkey	250.00(200)	30.00(20)	....	2.25
	same, 3 convertible panes of 20	70.00(60)	30.00(20)	....	....
4712-15	(45¢) Christmas Santa & Sleigh	250.00(200)	30.00(20)	....	8.00
	same, 3 convertible panes of 20	70.00(60)	30.00(20)	....	....
4716	(45¢) Lady Bird Johnson	250.00(96)	16.00(6)	....	....
2013					
4721	(45¢) Emancipation Proclamation	190.00(200)	30.00(20)	9.00(4)	2.25
4726	(45¢) Chinese New Year	150.00(108)	25.00(12)	....	2.25
4727-30	33¢ Apples	150.00(200)	25.00(20)	6.75(4)	6.00
4735	66¢ Wedding Cake. . . .	295.00(200)	45.00(20)	9.00(4)	3.25
4736	66¢ Spicebush Swallowtail	295.00(200)	45.00(20)	9.00(4)	3.25
4737	86¢ Tufted Puffins. . . .	225.00(120)	45.00(20)	9.00(4)	3.25
4740	($1.10) Earth Global . .	200.00(120)	70.00(20)	10.00(4)	3.75
4741	(46¢) Envelope with wax seal	125.00(120)	30.00(20)	6.75(4)	2.25
4742	(46¢) Rosa Parks	195.00(200)	30.00(20)	6.75(4)	2.25
4743-47	(46¢) Muscle Cars	195.00(200)	30.00(20)	22.00(10)	10.00
4748	(46¢) Modern Art in America	195.00(60)	70.00(12)	....	....
4750-53	(46¢) La Florida	200.00(160)	30.00(16)	9.00(4)	8.50
4764	Where Dreams Blossom	175.00(160)	30.00(20)	9.00(4)	2.25
4765	66¢ Wedding Flowers and "Yes I Do"	285.00(180)	35.00(20)	12.00(4)	3.25
4786	(46¢) Lydia Mendoza . .	135.00(200)	25.00(16)	....	2.25
4787-88	(46¢) Civil War	85.00(72)	25.00(12)	....	4.50
4789	(46¢) Johnny Cash. . . .	150.00(128)	30.00(16)	....	2.25
4790	(46¢) West Virginia Statehood	225.00(200)	35.00(20)	9.50(4)	2.25
4791-95	(46¢) New England Lighthouses	140.00(120)	35.00(20)	22.50(10)	10.50
4800	(46¢) EID	225.00(160)	50.00(20)	9.50(4)	2.25
4801	(46¢) Made in America . .	.....(60)	....	....	....
4803	(46¢) Althea Gibson . . .	225.00(200)	35.00(20)	9.50(4)	2.25
4804	(46¢) 1963 March on Washington	225.00(200)	35.00(20)	9.50(4)	2.25
4805	(46¢) 1812 Battle of Lake Erie	150.00(120)	25.00(20)	....	2.25
4806	$2 Inverted Jenny.	500.00(36)	140.00(6)	....	15.00
4807	(46¢) Ray Charles	200.00(144)	35.00(16)	....	2.25
4813	(46¢) Holy Family & Donkey	250.00(200)	35.00(20)	9.50(4)	2.25
4814	($1.10) Christmas Wreath	150.00(60)	35.00(20)	12.00(4)	3.75
4815a	(46¢) Virgin & Child, convertible booklet of 20.	225.00(160)	40.00(20)	....	2.25
4816a	(46¢) Poinsettia, convertible booklet of 20.	225.00(160)	40.00(20)	....	2.25
4817-20	(46¢) Gingerbread Houses, convertible booklet of 20	225.00(160)	35.00(20)	....	9.50
4822-23	(46¢) Medal of Honor . .	70.00(120)	35.00(20)	9.50(4)	9.00
4824	(46¢) Hanukkah	175.00(160)	35.00(20)	9.50(4)	2.25
4825-44	(46¢) Harry Potter.	350.00(120)	....	....	....
4845	(46¢) Kawanzaa	150.00(160)	35.00(20)	9.50(4)	2.25
2014					
4822a-					
4823a	(49¢) Medal of Honor, dated 2014	70.00(60)	35.00(20)	9.50(4)	9.00
4846	(46¢) Chinese New Year	195.00(120)	30.00(12)	.....	2.25
4847	(46¢) Love	120.00(120)	30.00(20)	9.50(4)	2.25
4856	(29¢) Shirley Chisholm .	175.00(160)	30.00(20)	9.50(4)	2.25
4859	70¢ Great Spangled Fritillary	295.00(200)	45.00(20)	10.00(4)	3.75
4860	21¢ Abraham Lincoln . .	55.00(60)	25.00(20)	4.50(4)	1.50
4862-65	(49¢) Winter Flowers, convertible booklet of 20	175.00(160)	30.00(20)	.....	9.00
4866	91¢ Ralph Ellison	400.00(200)	50.00(20)	15.00(4)	4.00
4873	$19.95 USS Arizona Memorial	1300.00(30)	500.00(10)	250.00(4)	60.00
4879	70¢ Alfred "Chief" Anderson	300.00(160)	45.00(20)	9.50(4)	3.25
4880	(49¢) Jimi Hendrix	175.00(144)	30.00(16)	.....	2.25
4882-91	(49¢) Songbrids, convertible booklet of 20	180.00(160)	35.00(20)	.....	25.00
4892	(49¢) Charlton Heston .	225.00(180)	35.00(20)	9.50(4)	2.25
4893	($1.15) Map of Sea Surface Temperatures	150.00(50)	35.00(10)	18.00(4)	4.00

SCOTT NO.	DESCRIPTION	IMPERF PRESS SHEET	IMPERF MINT SHEET OR BOOKLET	IMPERF PLATE BLOCK	IMPERF UNUSED F/NH
2014, continued					
4898-					
4905	(49¢) Circus Posters. . .	150.00(96)	30.00(16)	....	....
4906	(49¢) Harvey Milk	260.00(240)	35.00(20)	9.50(4)	2.25
4907	(49¢) Nevada Statehood	260.00(240)	35.00(20)	9.50(4)	2.25
4908-09	(49¢) Hot Rods, convert. bklt of 20	160.00(140)	35.00(20)	.....	5.00
4910-11	(49¢) Civil War	105.00(72)	25.00(12)	.....	8.00
4912-15	(49¢) Farmer's Market .	150.00(100)	35.00(20)	17.50(8)	11.00
4916	(49¢) Janis Joplin	180.00(144)	30.00(16)	.....	2.25
4917-20	(49¢) Hudson River School, convertible booklet of 20	100.00(80)	35.00(20)	.....	9.50
4921	(49¢) Ft. McHenry, War of 1812	125.00(100)	35.00(20)	.....	2.25
4922-26	(49¢) Celebrity Chefs . .	225.00(180)	35.00(20)	25.00(10)	12.00
4927	$5.75 Glade Creek Grist Mill	800.00(60)	150.00(10)	90.00(4)	22.25
4928-35	(49¢) Batman	225.00(180)	35.00(20)	.....	.....
4936	($1.15) Silver Bells Wreath	155.00(60)	40.00(10)	18.00(4)	4.50
4937-40	(49¢) Winter Fun, convert. bklt of 20	150.00(120)	35.00(20)	.....	9.50
4945	(49¢) Magi, convert. bklt of 20	180.00(160)	35.00(20)	.....	2.25
4946-49	(49¢) Rudolph, convert. bklt of 20	150.00(120)	35.00(20)	.....	9.50
4950-51	(49¢) Wilt Chamberlain.	170.00(144)	30.00(18)	9.50(4)	4.50
2015					
4952	(49¢) Battle of New Orleans	125.00(100)	30.00(10)	.....	2.25
4953	$1 Patriotic Waves	300.00(140)	30.00(10)	16.00(4)	4.00
4954	$2 Patriotic Waves	425.00(100)	55.00(10)	30.00(4)	8.00
4955-56	(49¢) Hearts Forever . .	130.00(60)	30.00(20)	9.50(4)	5.00
4957	(49¢) Chinese New Year	170.00(144)	30.00(12)	.....	2.25
4958	(49¢) Robert Robinson Taylor	130.00(120)	30.00(20)	9.50(4)	2.25
4959	(49¢) Rose & Heart . . .	275.00(240)	30.00(20)	9.50(4)	2.25
4960	70¢ Tulip & Heart	375.00(240)	45.00(20)	10.00(4)	3.75
4964-67	(49¢) Water Lilies, convertible booklet of 20.	275.00(240)	30.00(20)	.....	9.50
4968-72	(49¢) Art of Martin Ramirez	275.00(240)	30.00(20)	20.00(10)	12.00
4978	(49¢) From Me To You .	225.00(240)	30.00(20)	20.00(10)	2.25
4979	(49¢) Maya Angelou . . .	120.00(96)	30.00(20)	9.50(4)	2.25
4980-81	(49¢) Civil War	.....(72)	.....	.....	.....
4982-85	(49¢) Gifts of Friendship	130.00(72)	30.00(12)	.....	.....
4986	(49¢) Special Olympics World Games	80.00(80)	25.00(20)	9.50(4)	2.25
4987	(49¢) Forget-Me-Nots Missing Children.	120.00(120)	30.00(20)	9.50(4)	2.25
4988a	(49¢) Medal of Honor, strip of 3, dated 2015 . .	80.00(72)	35.00(24)	12.00(6)	9.00
4989	(22¢) Emperor Penguins	120.00(200)	15.00(20)	5.00(4)	1.00
4991-94	(35¢) Costal Birds.	150.00(20)	20.00(20)	5.50(4)	5.00
4999	(71¢) Eastern Tiger Swallowtail	225.00(120)	50.00(20)	10.00(4)	2.25
5003	(93¢) Flannery O'Connor	225.00(120)	50.00(20)	15.00(4)	3.25
5004-07	(49¢) Summer Harvest, convertible bklt of 20. . .	170.00(160)	30.00(20)	.....	9.50
5008	(49¢) Coast Guard	120.00(120)	30.00(20)	9.50(4)	2.25
5009	(49¢) Elvis Presley	150.00(144)	25.00(20)	.....	2.25
5010-11	(49¢) 2016 World Stamp Show	120.00(120)	30.00(20)	9.50(4)	5.00
5012	(49¢) Ingrid Bergman . .	180.00(180)	30.00(20)	9.50(4)	2.25
5020	(49¢) Paul Newman . . .	120.00(120)	30.00(20)	9.50(4)	2.25
5021-30	(49¢) Charlie Brown, convertible booklet of 20.	170.00(160)	30.00(20)	.....	9.50
5031-34	(49¢) Geometric Snowflakes, convertible booklet of 20	120.00(120)	30.00(20)	.....	9.50
2016					
5036	(49¢) Quilled Paper Heart	200.00(200)	30.00(20)	9.50(4)	2.25
5040	$6.45 La Cueva del Indio	180.00(10)	180.00(10)	85.00(4)	20.00
5041	$22.95 Columbia River Gorge	....	1000.00(10)	500.00	150.00
5042-51	(49¢) Botanical Art, convertible bklt of 20.	190.00(200)	30.00(20)	.....	15.00
5056	(49¢) Richard Allen. . . .	120.00(120)	25.00(20)	9.50(4)	2.25
5057	(49¢) Chinese New Year	75.00(72)	20.00(12)	.....	2.25
Semi-Postals					
B5	(49¢ + 11¢) Breast Cancer	350.00(240)	35.00(20)	9.50(4)	2.25

SCOTT NO.	DESCRIPTION	UNUSED O.G. VF	F	AVG	USED VF	F	AVG

AIR POST

C1-C3	C4	C5	C6
Curtiss Jenny Biplane	Airplane Propeller	Badge of Air Service	Airplane

1918 (C1-6 NH + 75%)

SCOTT NO.	DESCRIPTION	VF	F	AVG	VF	F	AVG
C1-3	6¢-24¢, 3 varieties, complete.	250.00	200.00	176.00	115.00	95.00	80.00
C1	6¢ orange	75.00	60.00	55.00	35.00	29.00	23.00
C2	16¢ green	85.00	70.00	60.00	38.00	30.00	27.00
C3	24¢ carmine rose & blue	95.00	75.00	65.00	45.00	40.00	35.00
C3a	same, center inverted	....	450000.00	....	....	....	....

SCOTT NO.	DESCRIPTION	CENTER LINE BLOCKS F/NH	F/OG	A/OG	ARROW BLOCKS F/NH	F/OG	A/OG
C1	6¢ orange	800.00	425.00	280.00	550.00	385.00	255.00
C2	16¢ green	625.00	400.00	325.00	550.00	360.00	285.00
C3	24¢ carmine rose & blue	650.00	425.00	330.00	575.00	370.00	275.00

1923

C4-6	8¢-24¢, 3 varieties, complete.	225.00	165.00	145.00	85.00	68.00	50.00
C4	8¢ dark green	25.00	20.00	15.00	15.00	12.00	10.00
C5	16¢ dark blue.	95.00	80.00	70.00	35.00	28.00	20.00
C6	24¢ carmine.	110.00	70.00	65.00	38.00	30.00	22.00

C7-C9
Map of U.S. and Airplanes

1926-30 (C7-12 NH + 50%)

C7-9	10¢-20¢, 3 varieties, complete.	17.50	14.50	9.50	5.95	5.00	3.45
C7	10¢ dark blue.	3.75	3.10	2.40	.65	.50	.35
C8	15¢ olive brown	4.25	3.60	2.75	3.00	2.50	1.75
C9	20¢ yellow green (1927)	11.50	9.00	7.00	2.75	2.25	1.65

C10
Lindbergh's Airplane "Spirit of St. Louis"

1927 LINDBERGH TRIBUTE ISSUE

C10	10¢ dark blue.	10.75	8.25	6.00	2.85	2.20	1.75
C10a	same, bklt pane of 3	125.00	95.00	67.50	....	....	....

C11
Beacon and Rocky Mountains

C12, C16, C17, C19
Winged Globe

1928 BEACON

C11	5¢ carmine & blue . .	6.50	4.75	3.25	.90	.70	.50

1930 Flat Plate Printing, Perf.11

C12	5¢ violet.	12.50	9.75	8.50	.85	.65	.50

C13
Graf Zeppelin

C14	C15

1930 GRAF ZEPPELIN ISSUE (NH + 50%)

C13-15	65¢-$2.60, 3 varieties, complete.	1620.00	1465.00	1265.00	1500.00	1180.00	965.00
C13	65¢ green	300.00	250.00	200.00	275.00	210.00	175.00
C14	$1.30 brown.	425.00	370.00	320.00	450.00	375.00	295.00
C15	$2.60 blue	900.00	850.00	750.00	800.00	600.00	500.00

1931-32 Rotary Press Printing. Perf. 10¹/₂ x 11, Designs as #C12 (C16-C24 NH + 40%)

C16	5¢ violet.	8.00	6.00	5.00	.80	.55	.40
C17	8¢ olive bistre	3.25	2.75	2.15	.55	.40	.35

C18
Graf Zeppelin

1933 CENTURY OF PROGRESS ISSUE

C18	50¢ green	100.00	90.00	75.00	80.00	70.00	60.00

1934 DESIGN OF 1930

C19	6¢ dull orange	3.75	3.00	2.00	.45	.35	.25

C20-22
China Clipper

1935 TRANS-PACIFIC ISSUE

C20	25¢ blue.	1.55	1.25	1.05	1.10	.90	.80

1937. Type of 1935 Issue, Date Omitted

C21	20¢ green	12.00	10.00	7.50	2.00	1.65	1.35
C22	50¢ carmine.	12.00	10.25	7.75	5.40	4.50	3.75

C23
Eagle

1938

C23	6¢ dark blue & carmine	.65	.55	.45	.35	.30	.25

C24
Winged Globe

1939 TRANS-ATLANTIC ISSUE

C24	30¢ dull blue	12.50	11.00	10.00	1.70	1.50	1.20

AIR POST PLATE BLOCKS #C1-C24

SCOTT NO.		UNUSED NH			UNUSED O.G.		
		VF	F	AVG	VF	F	AVG
C1(6)	6¢ orange.......	1550.00	1150.00	925.00	1050.00	875.00	600.00
C2(6)	16¢ green.......	2100.00	1975.00	1575.00	1400.00	1100.00	900.00
C3(12)	24¢ carmine rose & blue	2800.00	2000.00	1825.00	1800.00	1700.00	1300.00
C4(6)	8¢ dark green.....	610.00	450.00	360.00	350.00	300.00	260.00
C5(6)	16¢ dark blue.....	3400.00	2700.00	2250.00	2200.00	2000.00	1650.00
C6(6)	24¢ carmine......	4300.00	3300.00	2825.00	2800.00	2200.00	1900.00
C7(6)	10¢ dark blue.....	77.00	55.00	49.00	54.00	41.50	30.00
C8(6)	15¢ olive brown ...	85.00	66.00	52.75	60.00	50.00	44.00
C9(6)	20¢ yellow green ..	185.00	155.00	125.00	110.00	90.00	80.00
C10(6)	10¢ dark blue	200.00	188.00	165.00	135.00	115.00	85.00
C11(6)	5¢ carmine & blue .	85.00	65.00	54.00	60.00	46.50	31.50
C12(6)	5¢ violet	285.00	220.00	175.00	215.00	165.00	120.00
C13(6)	65¢ green........	5200.00	3800.00	3000.00	3300.00	2600.00	2100.00
C14(6)	$1.30 brown......	12500.00	1100.00	8000.00	8000.00	7000.00	5500.00
C15(6)	$2.60 blue	19000.00	18000.00	13000.00	12000.00	10000.00	8000.00
C16(4)	5¢ violet	150.00	135.00	105.00	110.00	95.00	65.00
C17(4)	8¢ olive bistre.....	58.50	45.00	36.00	40.00	30.00	24.00
C18(4)	50¢ green........	1400.00	1150.00	800.00	950.00	795.00	635.00
C19(4)	6¢ dull orange	39.50	33.00	26.00	30.00	25.00	20.00
C20(6)	25¢ blue	33.00	27.50	22.00	26.50	22.00	17.50
C21(6)	20¢ green........	125.00	105.00	90.00	115.00	100.00	85.00
C22(6)	50¢ carmine......	125.00	90.00	75.00	90.00	75.00	65.00
C23(4)	6¢ dark blue & carmine	19.00	15.00	12.00	15.00	12.00	9.00
C24(6)	30¢ dull blue......	185.00	155.00	135.00	155.00	130.00	95.00

SCOTT NO.	DESCRIPTION	FIRST DAY COVERS		MINT SHEET	PLATE BLOCK	UNUSED F/NH	USED
		SING	PL. BLK.				

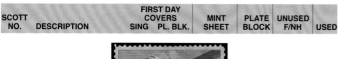

C25-C31

1941-44 TRANSPORT ISSUE

C25-31	6¢-50¢, 7 varieties, complete..........	....	....	....	127.50	23.95	5.60
C25	6¢ Transport Plane ...	7.00	10.00	15.00(50)	1.25	.30	.25
C25a	same, bklt pane of 3 ..	30.00	....	....	4.25	....	....
C26	8¢ Transport Plane ...	6.00	11.25	16.00(50)	2.20	.30	.25
C27	10¢ Transport Plane ..	8.00	15.00	82.50(50)	9.00	1.65	.25
C28	15¢ Transport Plane ..	8.00	15.00	150.00(50)	13.95	3.25	.40
C29	20¢ Transport Plane ..	10.00	20.00	125.00(50)	14.00	2.75	.40
C30	30¢ Transport Plane ..	20.00	30.00	140.00(50)	14.00	3.00	.40
C31	50¢ Transport Plane ..	28.50	68.75	575.00(50)	65.00	14.00	4.25

C32

1946

C32	5¢ DC-4 Skymaster ...	2.00	4.25	13.00(50)	1.00	.30	.25

C33, C37, C39, C41

C34

C35

C36

SCOTT NO.	DESCRIPTION	FIRST DAY COVERS		MINT SHEET	PLATE BLOCK	UNUSED F/NH	USED
		SING	PL. BLK.				
	1947						
C33-36	5¢-25¢, 4 varieties, complete..........	....	....	....	....	2.10	.70
C33	5¢ DC-4 Skymaster ...	2.00	4.25	25.00(100)	1.20	.30	.25
C34	10¢ Pan American Bldg.	2.00	4.25	19.00(50)	2.00	.45	.25
C35	15¢ New York Skyline .	2.00	4.25	26.00(50)	2.75	.60	.30
C36	25¢ Plane over Bridge.	2.00	5.00	75.00(50)	7.50	1.60	.30

1948
Rotary Press Coil–Perf. 10 Horiz.

		LINE PR.			LINE PR.		
C37	5¢ DC-4 Skymaster ...	2.00	4.25	....	12.00	1.40	1.00

C38   **C40**

C38	5¢ New York Jubliee ..	2.00	4.25	22.00(100)	5.25	.30	.25

1949

C39	6¢ DC-4 Skymaster (as #C33)...........	2.00	4.25	23.00(100)	1.50	.30	.25
C39a	same, bklt pane of 6 ..	10.00	....	....	....	14.00	....
C40	6¢ Alexandria, Virginia.	2.00	4.25	12.00(50)	1.30	.35	.25

Rotary Press Coil–Perf. 10 Horiz.

		LINE PR.			LINE PR.		
C41	6¢ DC-4 Skymaster (as#C37)	2.00	4.25	....	22.00	4.25	.25

NOTE: Unused Air Mail coil pairs can be supplied at two times the single price.

C42   **C43**

C44

1949 U.P.U. ISSUES

C42-44	10¢-25¢, 3 varieties, complete...........	....	....	....	....	1.90	1.35
C42	10¢ Post Office	2.00	4.25	17.50(50)	1.85	.40	.30
C43	15¢ Globe & Doves ...	3.00	5.00	25.00(50)	2.25	.60	.45
C44	25¢ Plane & Globe ...	4.00	6.25	42.00(50)	7.25	1.10	.75

C45

C46   **C47**

1949-58

C45-51	7 varieties, complete .	....	....		....	9.00	2.30
C45	6¢ Wright Brothers (1949)	2.00	4.25	25.00(50)	2.00	.50	.25
C46	80¢ Hawaii (1952)	15.00	35.00	350.00(50)	35.00	8.00	2.00
C47	6¢ Powered Flight (1953)	2.00	4.25	12.00(50)	1.30	.30	.25

SCOTT NO.	DESCRIPTION	FIRST DAY COVERS SING	PL. BLK.	MINT SHEET	PLATE BLOCK	UNUSED F/NH	USED

C142

C143

C144

C145

2007-12

C142	69¢ Okefenokee Swamp, self-adhesive	2.50	6.00	37.00(20)	9.00	2.25	.80
C143	90¢ Hagatna Bay, self-adhesive	2.75	6.50	49.00(20)	12.00	3.00	1.05
C144	72¢ New Hampshire River Scene	3.75	4.75	34.00(20)	9.00	2.00	1.00
C145	94¢ St. John, US Virgin Islands	3.75	4.75	47.00(20)	12.00	3.00	1.55

C146

C147

| C146 | 79¢ Zion National Park | 3.75 | .... | 35.50(20) | 9.00 | 2.25 | 1.60 |
| C147 | 98¢ Grand Teton National Park | 3.75 | .... | 45.00(20) | 11.00 | 2.75 | 1.25 |

C148

| C148 | 80¢ Voyagers National Park | 3.50 | .... | 36.00(20) | 9.50 | 2.25 | 1.75 |

C149

| C149 | 85¢ Glaciers National Park, Montana | 3.50 | .... | 41.00(20) | 9.00 | 2.25 | 1.50 |

C150

| C150 | $1.05 Amish Horse & Buggy, Lancaster County, Pennsylvania | 4.25 | .... | 50.00(20) | 12.00 | 3.00 | 1.50 |

AIR MAIL SPECIAL DELIVERY STAMPS

771, CE1, CE2

SCOTT NO.	DESCRIPTION	PLATE BLOCK F/NH	F	AVG	UNUSED F/NH	F	AVG	USED F	AVG
CE1	16¢ dark blue (1934)	25.00	18.00	14.50	1.10	.80	.60	.70	.55
CE2	16¢ red & blue (1936)	14.00	10.00	8.00	.85	.65	.50	.35	.25
CE2	same, center line block	6.00	4.00	2.00	....	....	....	....	....
CE2	same, arrow block of 4	5.00	3.50	2.75	....	....	....	....	....

SPECIAL DELIVERY STAMPS

E1

E2, E3

E4, E5

(E1-E14 for VF Centering–Fine Price + 35%)

SCOTT NO.	DESCRIPTION	UNUSED NH F	AVG	UNUSED OG F	AVG	USED F	AVG
1885 Inscribed "Secures Immediate Delivery at Special Delivery Office" Perf. 12							
E1	10¢ blue	1000.00	650.00	450.00	300.00	60.00	40.00
1888 Inscribed "Secures Immediate Delivery at any Post Office"							
E2	10¢ blue	900.00	680.00	450.00	350.00	38.00	22.00
1893							
E3	10¢ orange	580.00	400.00	250.00	175.00	40.00	25.00
1894 Same type as preceding issue, but with line under "Ten Cents" Unwatermarked							
E4	10¢ blue	1900.00	1350.00	750.00	450.00	75.00	50.00
1895 Double Line Watermark							
E5	10¢ blue	400.00	275.00	190.00	120.00	10.00	6.00

E6, E8-11

E7

SCOTT NO.	DESCRIPTION	UNUSED NH F	AVG	UNUSED OG F	AVG	USED F	AVG
1902							
E6	10¢ ultramarine	675.00	440.00	350.00	225.00	12.00	8.00
1908							
E7	10¢ green	185.00	120.00	80.00	55.00	50.00	40.00
1911 Single Line Watermark							
E8	10¢ ultramarine	275.00	175.00	125.00	75.00	12.00	9.00
1914 Perf. 10							
E9	10¢ ultramarine	500.00	300.00	200.00	130.00	14.00	11.00
1916 Unwatermarked Perf. 10							
E10	10¢ pale ultra	775.00	500.00	350.00	220.00	50.00	35.00
1917 Perf. 11							
E11	10¢ ultramarine	60.00	45.00	30.00	20.00	.95	.70
E11	same, plate block of 6	550.00	400.00	325.00	225.00	....	....

E12, E15

E14, E19

1922-25 Flat Plate Printing Perf. 11

SCOTT NO.	DESCRIPTION	PLATE BLOCK F/NH	F	AVG	UNUSED F/NH	F	AVG	USED F	AVG
E12	10¢ gray violet	(6) 950.00	700.00	550.00	75.00	50.00	30.00	1.50	1.35
E13	15¢ deep orange (1925)	(6) 800.00	650.00	475.00	85.00	60.00	40.00	2.00	1.25
E14	20¢ black (1925)	(6) 80.00	60.00	40.00	4.75	2.75	1.90	2.50	1.75

SCOTT NO.	DESCRIPTION	FIRST DAY COVERS SING	PL. BLK.	MINT SHEET	PLATE BLOCK	UNUSED F/NH	USED
1927-51 Rotary Press Printing Perf. 11 x 10½							
E15-19	10¢-20¢, 5 varieties	....	....	....	50.00	9.00	3.25
E15	10¢ gray violet	....	....	80.00(50)	7.00	1.30	.30
E16	15¢ orange (1931)	....	....	67.00(50)	6.50	1.30	.30
E17	13¢ blue (1944)	9.00	20.00	62.00(50)	5.00	1.20	.30
E18	17¢ orange yellow (1944)	12.00	28.00	245.00(50)	28.00	4.00	2.75
E19	20¢ black (1951)	5.00	12.50	105.00(50)	12.00	1.95	.25

E20

E22

SCOTT NO.	DESCRIPTION	FIRST DAY COVERS SING	PL. BLK.	MINT SHEET	PLATE BLOCK	UNUSED F/NH	USED
1954-57							
E20	20¢ deep blue	2.50	6.25	32.00(50)	3.50	.70	.20
E21	30¢ lake (1957)	2.50	6.25	43.00(50)	4.50	1.00	.20
1969-71							
E22	45¢ carmine & violet blue	2.50	6.25	74.00(50)	8.00	1.60	.35
E23	60¢ violet blue & carmine (1971)	2.75	6.75	88.00(50)	9.00	1.85	.20

REGISTRATION STAMP

F1

1911 Registration

SCOTT NO.	DESCRIPTION	UNUSED NH F	AVG	UNUSED OG F	AVG	USED F	AVG
F1	10¢ ultramarine	200.00	135.00	95.00	60.00	12.00	8.00

U.S. CERTIFIED STAMP

FA1

1955 Certified Mail

SCOTT NO.	DESCRIPTION	FIRST DAY COVERS SING	PL. BLK.	MINT SHEET	PLATE BLOCK	UNUSED F/NH	USED
FA1	15¢ red	2.50	6.25	32.00(50)	6.25	.65	.50

SCOTT NO.	DESCRIPTION	UNUSED NH F	AVG	UNUSED OG F	AVG	USED F	AVG

J1-J28 (image) J29-J68 (image)

1879 Unwatermarked Perf. 12

J1	1¢ brown	275.00	165.00	95.00		70.00	17.00	11.00
J2	2¢ brown	1200.00	900.00	450.00	450.00	20.00	14.00
J3	3¢ brown	325.00	270.00	120.00	75.00	7.50	6.00
J4	5¢ brown	1900.00	1300.00	750.00	600.00	80.00	38.00
J5	10¢ brown	2700.00	1800.00	1100.00	800.00	80.00	60.00
J6	30¢ brown	1000.00	700.00	500.00	300.00	70.00	55.00
J7	50¢ brown	1900.00	1400.00	700.00	450.00	80.00	60.00

1884-89

J15	1¢ red brown	225.00	165.00	85.00	55.00	8.00	6.50
J16	2¢ red brown	275.00	200.00	100.00	70.00	7.00	5.00
J17	3¢ red brown	2900.00	2300.00	1180.00	875.00	350.00	275.00
J18	5¢ red brown	1600.00	1200.00	750.00	475.00	50.00	36.00
J19	10¢ red brown	1600.00	1450.00	750.00	460.00	40.00	30.00
J20	30¢ red brown	385.00	350.00	275.00	185.00	70.00	60.00
J21	50¢ red brown	4400.00	3000.00	2000.00	1450.00	250.00	185.00

1891

J22	1¢ bright claret	100.00	75.00	44.00	30.00	2.25	1.25
J23	2¢ bright claret	110.00	85.00	45.00	34.00	2.25	1.25
J24	3¢ bright claret	225.00	160.00	85.00	65.00	18.00	12.00
J25	5¢ bright claret	350.00	225.00	125.00	80.00	18.00	12.00
J26	10¢ bright claret	600.00	450.00	250.00	180.00	35.00	20.00
J27	30¢ bright claret	2000.00	1600.00	800.00	550.00	300.00	175.00
J28	50¢ bright claret	2100.00	1600.00	800.00	600.00	225.00	150.00

1894 Unwatermarked Perf. 12 (†)

J29	1¢ pale vermillion	6500.00	4200.00	2850.00	2250.00	750.00	600.00
J30	2¢ dark vermillion	2250.00	1375.00	900.00	700.00	400.00	255.00
J31	1¢ deep claret	325.00	260.00	90.00	70.00	14.00	12.00
J32	2¢ deep claret	300.00	250.00	75.00	50.00	12.00	9.00
J33	3¢ deep claret	625.00	400.00	225.00	175.00	55.00	40.00
J34	5¢ deep claret	1050.00	825.00	350.00	270.00	60.00	48.00
J35	10¢ deep claret	1200.00	900.00	450.00	300.00	45.00	35.00
J36	30¢ deep claret	1450.00	925.00	650.00	425.00	250.00	150.00
J36b	30¢ pale rose	1300.00	1000.00	600.00	400.00	225.00	125.00
J37	50¢ deep claret	5000.00	3800.00	2250.00	1750.00	850.00	600.00

1895 Double Line Watermark Perf. 12 (†)

J38	1¢ deep claret	48.00	40.00	18.00	13.50	1.50	1.00
J39	2¢ deep claret	48.00	40.00	18.00	13.50	1.50	1.00
J40	3¢ deep claret	300.00	250.00	120.00	90.00	4.50	3.00
J41	5¢ deep claret	325.00	275.00	130.00	100.00	4.50	3.00
J42	10¢ deep claret	325.00	275.00	130.00	100.00	7.00	5.50
J43	30¢ deep claret	1900.00	1300.00	800.00	650.00	70.00	60.00
J44	50¢ deep claret	1300.00	900.00	500.00	350.00	55.00	48.00

1910-12 Single Line Watermark Perf. 12

J45	1¢ deep claret	135.00	105.00	50.00	40.00	6.00	4.50
J46	2¢ deep claret	125.00	95.00	45.00	35.00	3.00	2.00
J47	3¢ deep claret	1800.00	1500.00	750.00	600.00	60.00	45.00
J48	5¢ deep claret	350.00	250.00	150.00	115.00	15.00	10.00
J49	10¢ deep claret	375.00	225.00	165.00	125.00	25.00	18.00
J50	50¢ deep claret (1912)	3200.00	2300.00	1200.00	900.00	185.00	150.00

1914 Single Line Watermark Perf. 10

J52	1¢ carmine lake	275.00	150.00	95.00	65.00	16.00	12.00
J53	2¢ carmine lake	225.00	130.00	75.00	55.00	1.25	.80
J54	3¢ carmine lake	3500.00	2500.00	1200.00	900.00	85.00	60.00
J55	5¢ carmine lake	175.00	135.00	60.00	45.00	7.00	5.00
J56	10¢ carmine lake	250.00	200.00	95.00	75.00	5.00	3.00
J57	30¢ carmine lake	650.00	400.00	300.00	185.00	60.00	40.00
J58	50¢ carmine lake	....	....	18500.00	15500.00	1600.00	1300.00

1916 Unwatermarked Perf. 10

J59	1¢ rose	11000.00	7500.00	5000.00	3500.00	750.00	600.00
J60	2¢ rose	800.00	600.00	325.00	250.00	80.00	60.00

SCOTT NO.	DESCRIPTION	PLATE BLOCK (OG) F/NH	F	AVG	UNUSED (OG) F/NH	F	AVG	USED F	AVG

1917 Unwatermarked Perf. 11

J61	1¢ carmine rose (6)	85.00	53.00	35.00	11.00	5.00	3.00	.30	.25
J62	2¢ carmine rose (6)	85.00	53.00	35.00	11.00	5.00	3.00	.30	.25
J63	3¢ carmine rose (6)	170.00	95.00	70.00	45.00	17.00	10.00	.95	.45
J64	5¢ carmine rose (6)	240.00	150.00	95.00	40.00	16.00	8.00	.95	.45
J65	10¢ carmine rose (6)	450.00	190.00	145.00	75.00	30.00	18.00	1.25	.85
J66	30¢ carmine rose	....	....	....	300.00	150.00	95.00	2.50	2.00
J67	50¢ carmine rose	....	....	....	425.00	160.00	80.00	1.25	.85

1925

J68	1/2¢ dull red (6)	20.00	15.00	12.50	2.00	1.25	1.00	.30	.25

SCOTT NO.	DESCRIPTION	PLATE BLOCK (OG) F/NH	F	AVG	UNUSED (OG) F/NH	F	AVG	USED F	AVG

J69-J76, J79-J86 (image) J77, J78, J87 (image) J88-J104 (image)

1930 Perf. 11

J69	1/2¢ carmine (6)	70.00	55.00	40.00	11.00	6.00	5.00	2.00	1.50
J70	1¢ carmine (6)	80.00	60.00	45.00	7.50	3.50	2.50	.40	.30
J71	2¢ carmine (6)	55.00	60.00	50.00	10.00	6.00	4.00	.40	.25
J72	3¢ carmine (6)	450.00	300.00	250.00	55.00	35.00	25.00	3.00	2.50
J73	5¢ carmine (6)	400.00	300.00	230.00	50.00	22.00	17.00	6.00	4.00
J74	10¢ carmine (6)	675.00	300.00	350.00	100.00	75.00	60.00	2.50	1.85
J75	30¢ carmine	....	....	....	350.00	160.00	125.00	4.50	3.75
J76	50¢ carmine	....	....	....	500.00	325.00	250.00	2.50	1.75
J77	$1 scarlet (6)	325.00	260.00	210.00	75.00	60.00	40.00	.40	.30
J78	$5 scarlet (6)	350.00	295.00	220.00	95.00	50.00	38.00	.40	.30

1931 Rotary Press Printing Perf. 11 x 10½

J79-86	1/2¢-50¢, 8 varieties, complete	....	....	....	30.00	24.00	15.00	1.90	1.50
J79	1/2¢ dull carmine	28.00	20.00	18.00	1.75	1.00	.75	.30	.25
J80	1¢ dull carmine	2.25	1.80	1.25	.35	.30	.25	.30	.25
J81	2¢ dull carmine	2.25	1.80	1.25	.35	.30	.25	.30	.25
J82	3¢ dull carmine	3.10	2.50	1.75	.35	.30	.25	.30	.25
J83	5¢ dull carmine	4.75	3.75	3.00	.40	.35	.25	.30	.25
J84	10¢ dull carmine	9.75	7.50	5.50	1.90	1.25	.40	.30	.25
J85	30¢ dull carmine	60.00	45.00	33.00	12.00	8.00	6.00	.30	.25
J86	50¢ dull carmine	95.00	65.00	50.00	17.00	12.50	10.00	.30	.25

1956 Rotary Press Printing Perf. 10½ x 11

J87	$1 scarlet	260.00	210.00		50.00	40.00		.30	

SCOTT NO.	DESCRIPTION	MINT SHEET	PLATE BLOCK F/NH	F	UNUSED F/NH	F	USED F

1959

J88-101	1/2¢-$5, 14 varieties, complete	....	....	....	20.50	14.50	3.90
J88	1/2¢ carmine rose & black	400.00(100)	210.00	175.00	1.85	1.50	1.50
J89	1¢ carmine rose & black	9.50(100)	1.25	.75	.30	.25	.25
J90	2¢ carmine rose & black	13.00(100)	1.25	.75	.30	.25	.25
J91	3¢ carmine rose & black	14.00(100)	1.00	.70	.30	.25	.25
J92	4¢ carmine rose & black	20.00(100)	1.25	.85	.30	.25	.25
J93	5¢ carmine rose & black	20.00(100)	1.00	.70	.30	.25	.25
J94	6¢ carmine rose & black	20.00(100)	1.35	.90	.30	.25	.25
J95	7¢ carmine rose & black	32.00(100)	2.25	1.75	.30	.25	.25
J96	8¢ carmine rose & black	32.00(100)	2.25	1.75	.30	.25	.25
J97	10¢ carmine rose & black	32.00(100)	1.80	1.30	.45	.30	.25
J98	30¢ carmine rose & black	97.00(100)	5.25	4.25	1.55	1.00	.25
J99	50¢ carmine rose & black	155.00(100)	7.00	5.75	2.00	1.50	.25
J100	$1 carmine rose & black	310.00(100)	17.00	12.00	3.75	2.75	.25
J101	$5 carmine rose & black	1500.00(100)	72.00	60.00	17.00	13.00	.50

1978-1985

J102	11¢ carmine rose & black	37.00(100)	4.00	....	.45	....	.50
J103	13¢ carmine rose & black	42.00(100)	2.95	....	.50	....	.50
J104	17¢ carmine rose & black	116.00(100)	40.00	....	.75	....	.55

OFFICES IN CHINA

SCOTT NO.	DESCRIPTION	UNUSED NH F	AVG	UNUSED OG F	AVG	USED F	AVG

SHANGHAI
2¢
CHINA
1919
K1-16: U.S. Postage 498-518 surcharged

SHANGHAI
2 Cts.
CHINA
1922
K17-18: U.S. Postage 498-528B with local surcharge

1919

K1	2¢ on 1¢ green	75.00	50.00	35.00	25.00	50.00	40.00
K2	4¢ on 2¢ rose	75.00	50.00	35.00	25.00	50.00	40.00
K3	6¢ on 3¢ violet	160.00	125.00	75.00	50.00	115.00	85.00
K4	8¢ on 4¢ brown	160.00	135.00	75.00	50.00	115.00	85.00
K5	10¢ on 5¢ blue	180.00	145.00	75.00	50.00	115.00	85.00
K6	12¢ on 6¢ red orange	225.00	185.00	100.00	60.00	165.00	111.00
K7	14¢ on 7¢ black	230.00	190.00	90.00	60.00	180.00	120.00
K8	16¢ on 8¢ olive bister	185.00	130.00	75.00	50.00	125.00	90.00
K8a	16¢ on 8¢ olive green	165.00	125.00	75.00	50.00	110.00	95.00
K9	18¢ on 9¢ salmon red	175.00	135.00	70.00	50.00	150.00	100.00
K10	20¢ on 10¢ orange yellow	165.00	125.00	70.00	50.00	125.00	80.00
K11	24¢ on 12¢ brown carmine	225.00	175.00	70.00	50.00	130.00	70.00
K11a	24¢ on 12¢ claret brown	280.00	200.00	115.00	80.00	175.00	110.00
K12	30¢ on 15¢ gray	225.00	160.00	100.00	60.00	200.00	160.00
K13	40¢ on 20¢ deep ultra.	325.00	235.00	150.00	90.00	285.00	200.00
K14	60¢ on 30¢ orange red	300.00	200.00	150.00	90.00	240.00	180.00
K15	$1 on 50¢ light violet	1350.00	950.00	600.00	400.00	850.00	600.00
K16	$2 on $1 violet brown	1200.00	800.00	600.00	400.00	750.00	450.00

1922 LOCAL ISSUES

K17	2¢ on 1¢ green	300.00	200.00	140.00	90.00	170.00	125.00
K18	4¢ on 2¢ carmine	300.00	200.00	140.00	90.00	150.00	120.00

SCOTT NO.	DESCRIPTION	UNUSED F	UNUSED AVG	USED F	USED AVG

OFFICIAL STAMPS

O1-O9, O94, O95   **O10-O14**   **O15-O24, O96-O103**   **O25-O34, O106, O107**

Except for the Post Office Department, portraits for the various denominations are the same as on the regular issues of 1870-73

1873 Printed by the Continental Bank Note Co.
Thin hard paper
(OG + 40%)
(O1-O120 for VF Centering–Fine Price + 50%)

DEPARTMENT OF AGRICULTURE

Scott	Description	Unused F	Unused AVG	Used F	Used AVG
O1	1¢ yellow	225.00	140.00	175.00	130.00
O2	2¢ yellow	200.00	115.00	80.00	50.00
O3	3¢ yellow	180.00	110.00	18.00	13.00
O4	6¢ yellow	220.00	140.00	65.00	45.00
O5	10¢ yellow	440.00	250.00	175.00	130.00
O6	12¢ yellow	375.00	225.00	220.00	145.00
O7	15¢ yellow	345.00	240.00	200.00	160.00
O8	24¢ yellow	345.00	240.00	190.00	125.00
O9	30¢ yellow	475.00	325.00	250.00	190.00

EXECUTIVE DEPARTMENT

Scott	Description	Unused F	Unused AVG	Used F	Used AVG
O10	1¢ carmine	750.00	500.00	410.00	280.00
O11	2¢ carmine	490.00	410.00	225.00	155.00
O12	3¢ carmine	650.00	475.00	225.00	165.00
O13	6¢ carmine	800.00	675.00	450.00	350.00
O14	10¢ carmine	1100.00	800.00	700.00	500.00

DEPARTMENT OF THE INTERIOR

Scott	Description	Unused F	Unused AVG	Used F	Used AVG
O15	1¢ vermillion	65.00	50.00	11.00	8.50
O16	2¢ vermillion	65.00	50.00	13.00	11.00
O17	3¢ vermillion	70.00	55.00	7.00	5.75
O18	6¢ vermillion	65.00	50.00	11.00	9.00
O19	10¢ vermillion	65.00	50.00	22.00	18.00
O20	12¢ vermillion	80.00	60.00	13.00	10.00
O21	15¢ vermillion	180.00	140.00	26.00	22.00
O22	24¢ vermillion	160.00	130.00	21.00	18.00
O23	30¢ vermillion	240.00	200.00	21.00	17.00
O24	90¢ vermillion	290.00	250.00	48.00	38.00

DEPARTMENT OF JUSTICE

Scott	Description	Unused F	Unused AVG	Used F	Used AVG
O25	1¢ purple	230.00	210.00	100.00	85.00
O26	2¢ purple	280.00	240.00	110.00	95.00
O27	3¢ purple	290.00	240.00	38.00	24.00
O28	6¢ purple	280.00	240.00	45.00	36.00
O29	10¢ purple	290.00	240.00	90.00	70.00
O30	12¢ purple	240.00	195.00	70.00	60.00
O31	15¢ purple	420.00	360.00	185.00	165.00
O32	24¢ purple	1150.00	920.00	400.00	355.00
O33	30¢ purple	1200.00	900.00	340.00	250.00
O34	90¢ purple	1800.00	1400.00	800.00	700.00

O35-O45   **O47-O56, O108**   **O57-O67**   **O68-O71**

NAVY DEPARTMENT
(OG + 30%)

Scott	Description	Unused F	Unused AVG	Used F	Used AVG
O35	1¢ ultramarine	150.00	120.00	55.00	46.00
O36	2¢ ultramarine	155.00	125.00	30.00	26.00
O37	3¢ ultramarine	160.00	130.00	14.00	10.00
O38	6¢ ultramarine	175.00	140.00	23.00	14.00
O39	7¢ ultramarine	600.00	500.00	240.00	185.00
O40	10¢ ultramarine	200.00	160.00	38.00	25.00
O41	12¢ ultramarine	215.00	170.00	38.00	25.00
O42	15¢ ultramarine	350.00	310.00	60.00	35.00
O43	24¢ ultramarine	400.00	350.00	64.00	38.00
O44	30¢ ultramarine	300.00	280.00	45.00	26.00
O45	90¢ ultramarine	900.00	800.00	375.00	320.00

OFFICIAL STAMPS: From 1873 to 1879, Congress authorized the use of Official Stamps to prepay postage on government mail. Separate issues were produced for each department so that mailing costs could be assigned to that department's budget. Penalty envelopes replaced Official Stamps on May 1, 1879.

O72-O82, O109-O113   **O83-O93, O1140-O120**

POST OFFICE DEPARTMENT

Scott	Description	Unused F	Unused AVG	Used F	Used AVG
O47	1¢ black	22.00	17.00	12.00	8.00
O48	2¢ black	25.00	18.00	10.00	7.00
O49	3¢ black	10.00	7.00	2.50	1.00
O50	6¢ black	26.00	20.00	7.00	5.00
O51	10¢ black	120.00	85.00	52.00	40.00
O52	12¢ black	115.00	95.00	12.00	8.00
O53	15¢ black	125.00	90.00	19.00	12.00
O54	24¢ black	175.00	130.00	23.00	15.00
O55	30¢ black	185.00	135.00	24.00	16.00
O56	90¢ black	210.00	130.00	24.00	16.00

DEPARTMENT OF STATE

Scott	Description	Unused F	Unused AVG	Used F	Used AVG
O57	1¢ dark green	240.00	150.00	70.00	55.00
O58	2¢ dark green	280.00	225.00	95.00	75.00
O59	3¢ bright green	195.00	140.00	24.00	18.00
O60	6¢ bright green	195.00	145.00	30.00	20.00
O61	7¢ dark green	300.00	185.00	60.00	45.00
O62	10¢ dark green	210.00	135.00	55.00	40.00
O63	12¢ dark green	270.00	185.00	110.00	75.00
O64	15¢ dark green	285.00	225.00	95.00	78.00
O65	24¢ dark green	485.00	450.00	230.00	175.00
O66	30¢ dark green	450.00	390.00	185.00	145.00
O67	90¢ dark green	900.00	700.00	300.00	250.00
O68	$2 green & black	1450.00	1100.00	2000.00	1400.00
O69	$5 green & black	6400.00	5000.00	10000.00	7000.00
O70	$10 green & black	4450.00	3600.00	6000.00	5500.00
O71	$20 green & black	4800.00	4200.00	4450.00	2900.00

TREASURY DEPARTMENT
(OG + 30%)

Scott	Description	Unused F	Unused AVG	Used F	Used AVG
O72	1¢ brown	120.00	90.00	10.00	8.00
O73	2¢ brown	125.00	95.00	8.50	7.00
O74	3¢ brown	110.00	90.00	2.50	1.25
O75	6¢ brown	120.00	90.00	4.50	3.50
O76	7¢ brown	230.00	190.00	37.00	30.00
O77	10¢ brown	230.00	190.00	12.00	8.00
O78	12¢ brown	260.00	200.00	9.00	7.00
O79	15¢ brown	270.00	220.00	12.00	8.00
O80	24¢ brown	575.00	450.00	90.00	70.00
O81	30¢ brown	375.00	275.00	12.00	8.00
O82	90¢ brown	425.00	330.00	15.00	12.00

WAR DEPARTMENT

Scott	Description	Unused F	Unused AVG	Used F	Used AVG
O83	1¢ rose	230.00	180.00	14.00	10.00
O84	2¢ rose	230.00	180.00	14.00	10.00
O85	3¢ rose	230.00	180.00	5.00	3.50
O86	6¢ rose	600.00	475.00	11.00	9.00
O87	7¢ rose	160.00	135.00	85.00	65.00
O88	10¢ rose	140.00	110.00	24.00	18.00
O89	12¢ rose	250.00	220.00	13.00	10.00
O90	15¢ rose	85.00	70.00	16.00	13.00
O91	24¢ rose	85.00	70.00	13.00	11.00
O92	30¢ rose	125.00	110.00	13.00	11.00
O93	90¢ rose	195.00	165.00	55.00	45.00

1879 Printed by American Bank Note Co.
Soft Porous Paper
DEPARTMENT OF AGRICULTURE

Scott	Description	Unused F	Unused AVG	Used F	Used AVG
O94	1¢ yellow	6000.00	4900.00	....	....
O95	3¢ yellow	525.00	450.00	120.00	75.00

DEPARTMENT OF INTERIOR

Scott	Description	Unused F	Unused AVG	Used F	Used AVG
O96	1¢ vermillion	275.00	230.00	320.00	240.00
O97	2¢ vermillion	10.00	8.00	3.50	2.50
O98	3¢ vermillion	9.00	7.00	3.25	2.25
O99	6¢ vermillion	11.00	8.00	13.00	10.00
O100	10¢ vermillion	95.00	80.00	80.00	70.00
O101	12¢ vermillion	225.00	185.00	120.00	100.00
O102	15¢ vermillion	375.00	210.00	400.00	290.00
O103	24¢ vermillion	4200.00	3500.00	6200.00	....

DEPARTMENT OF JUSTICE

Scott	Description	Unused F	Unused AVG	Used F	Used AVG
O106	3¢ bluish purple	175.00	140.00	110.00	85.00
O107	6¢ bluish purple	450.00	385.00	260.00	195.00

POST OFFICE DEPARTMENT

Scott	Description	Unused F	Unused AVG	Used F	Used AVG
O108	3¢ black	32.00	27.00	9.00	6.00

TREASURY DEPARTMENT

Scott	Description	Unused F	Unused AVG	Used F	Used AVG
O109	3¢ brown	80.00	60.00	11.00	8.75
O110	6¢ brown	180.00	130.00	55.00	48.00
O111	10¢ brown	250.00	215.00	75.00	45.00
O112	30¢ brown	2400.00	2000.00	440.00	350.00
O113	90¢ brown	4600.00	3400.00	600.00	375.00

SCOTT NO.	DESCRIPTION	UNUSED F	UNUSED AVG	USED F	USED AVG
	WAR DEPARTMENT				
O114	1¢ rose red	8.00	5.00	4.50	3.75
O115	2¢ rose red	13.00	10.00	4.50	3.75
O116	3¢ rose red	13.00	10.00	2.25	1.50
O117	6¢ rose red	12.00	9.00	3.25	2.50
O118	10¢ rose red	64.00	44.00	45.00	30.00
O119	12¢ rose red	60.00	40.00	13.00	8.00
O120	30¢ rose red	190.00	120.00	86.00	60.00

SCOTT NO.	DESCRIPTION	UNUSED NH F	UNUSED NH AVG	UNUSED OG F	UNUSED OG AVG	USED F	USED AVG

1910-11
Double Line Watermark

SCOTT NO.	DESCRIPTION	UNUSED NH F	UNUSED NH AVG	UNUSED OG F	UNUSED OG AVG	USED F	USED AVG
O121	2¢ black	40.00	25.00	20.00	11.00	2.50	1.75
O122	50¢ dark green	380.00	250.00	175.00	135.00	65.00	48.00
O123	$1 ultramarine	460.00	350.00	225.00	175.00	17.00	12.00
	Single Line Watermark						
O124	1¢ dark violet	25.00	15.00	10.00	7.00	2.25	1.75
O125	2¢ black	130.00	75.00	60.00	35.00	7.50	5.00
O126	10¢ carmine	50.00	30.00	20.00	15.00	2.25	1.75

SCOTT NO.	DESCRIPTION	FIRST DAY COVERS SING	FIRST DAY COVERS PL. BLK.	MINT SHEET	PLATE BLOCK	UNUSED	USED

O127-O136

O138-O143

1983-89

SCOTT NO.	DESCRIPTION	SING	PL. BLK.	MINT SHEET	PLATE BLOCK	UNUSED	USED
O127	1¢ Great Seal	2.00	4.25	11.00(100)	1.20	.25	.25
O128	4¢ Great Seal	2.00	4.25	14.00(100)	1.20	.25	.25
O129	13¢ Great Seal	2.00	4.25	40.00(100)	2.50	.50	2.25
O129A	14¢ Great Seal (1985)	2.00	....	40.00(100)	....	.50	.55
O130	17¢ Great Seal	2.00	4.25	60.00(100)	3.50	.60	.50
O132	$1 Great Seal	5.75	14.25	300.00(100)	14.00	4.00	2.25
O133	$5 Great Seal	16.50	14.25	1100.00(100)	15.00	15.00	10.00

SCOTT NO.	DESCRIPTION	SING	PLATE# STRIP 3		PLATE# STRIP 3	UNUSED	USED
O135	20¢ Great Seal, coil	2.00	30.00	....	19.50	2.00	2.25
O136	22¢ Seal, coil (1985)	2.00	....		....	1.60	2.50

1985 Non-Denominated Issues

SCOTT NO.	DESCRIPTION	SING	PL. BLK.	MINT SHEET	PLATE BLOCK	UNUSED	USED
O138	(14¢) Great Seal, postcard D	2.00	30.00	640.00(100)	45.00	5.50	12.00
O138A	15¢ Great Seal, coil (1988)	2.00	....	....	....	.85	1.25
O138B	20¢ Great Seal, coil (1988)	2.00	....	....	....	.90	.75

SCOTT NO.	DESCRIPTION	SING	PLATE# STRIP 3		PLATE# STRIP 3	UNUSED	USED
O139	(22¢) Great Seal "D" coil (1985)	2.00	80.00	....	60.00	5.50	11.00
O140	(25¢) Great Seal "E" coil (1988)	2.00	....	....	....	1.30	2.25
O141	25¢ Great Seal, coil (1988)	2.00	....	....	....	1.25	.90
O143	1¢ Great Seal (1989)	2.00	....	10.00(100)	....	.25	.25

O144

O145

O146

O146A

O147

O148

1991-94

SCOTT NO.	DESCRIPTION	SING	PL. BLK.	MINT SHEET	PLATE BLOCK	UNUSED	USED
O144	(29¢) Great Seal "F" coil	2.00	....	....	....	1.75	1.10
O145	29¢ Great Seal, coil	2.00	....	....	....	1.25	.70
O146	4¢ Great Seal	2.00	....	20.00(100)	....	.40	.45
O146A	10¢ Great Seal	2.00	....	35.00(100)	....	.65	.50
O147	19¢ Great Seal	2.00	....	65.00(100)	....	.70	.95
O148	23¢ Great Seal	2.00	....	80.00(100)	....	1.10	1.10

SCOTT NO.	DESCRIPTION	FIRST DAY COVERS SING	FIRST DAY COVERS PL. BLK.	MINT SHEET	PLATE BLOCK	UNUSED	USED

O151   O152   O153   O154

O155   O156   O157, O158, O159, O160, O162   O161, 0163

1993-95

SCOTT NO.	DESCRIPTION	SING	PL. BLK.	MINT SHEET	PLATE BLOCK	UNUSED	USED
O151	$1 Great Seal	6.00	....	600.00(100)	....	6.00	4.00
O152	(32¢) Great Seal "G" coil	2.75	....	....	....	1.00	1.25
O153	32¢ Official Mail	1.95	....	....	....	3.25	2.00
O154	1¢ Official Mail	1.95	....	10.00(100)	....	.25	.35
O155	20¢ Official Mail	1.95	....	70.00(100)	....	.90	1.00
O156	23¢ Official Mail	1.95	....	90.00(100)	....	1.00	1.10
	1999-2007						
O157	33¢ Great Seal, coil	1.95	....	....	....	2.50	1.75
O158	34¢ Great Seal, coil	1.95	....	....	....	2.60	1.50
O159	37¢ Great Seal, coil	1.95	....	....	....	1.40	1.10
	same, pl# strip of 5	....	....	....	....	13.00	....
O160	39¢ Great Seal, coil	1.95	....	....	....	1.25	1.00
	same, pl# strip of 5	....	....	....	....	13.00	....
O161	$1 Great Seal	2.75	....	45.00(20)	9.00	2.25	1.25
O162	41¢ Great Seal, water-activated, coil	2.25	....	....	....	1.35	.90
	same, pl# strip of 5	....	....	....	....	15.00	....
O163	1¢ Official Stamp, s/a die cut 11.5x10.75	3.75	....	2.50(20)	....	.25	.25

PARCEL POST STAMPS

SPECIAL HANDLING STAMPS

PARCEL POST DUE STAMPS

Q1-Q12 Various Designs

QE1-QE4

JQ1-JQ5

SCOTT NO.	DESCRIPTION	UNUSED NH F	UNUSED NH AVG	UNUSED OG F	UNUSED OG AVG	USED F	USED AVG
	(Q1-QE4a for VF Centering–Fine Price + 50%)						
	1912-13 Parcel Post–All Printed in Carmine Rose						
Q1	1¢ Post Office Clerk	15.00	10.00	7.00	5.00	2.00	1.50
Q2	2¢ City Carrier	20.00	12.00	10.00	7.00	1.50	1.20
Q3	3¢ Railway Clerk	45.00	30.00	20.00	15.00	7.00	5.50
Q4	4¢ Rural Carrier	115.00	85.00	50.00	30.00	4.00	2.85
Q5	5¢ Mail Train	100.00	70.00	50.00	40.00	3.00	2.50
Q6	10¢ Steamship	170.00	120.00	80.00	50.00	4.00	3.00
Q7	15¢ Auto Service	185.00	135.00	80.00	55.00	16.00	13.00
Q8	20¢ Airplane	400.00	200.00	200.00	125.00	32.00	28.00
Q9	25¢ Manufacturing	200.00	120.00	75.00	55.00	9.00	7.00
Q10	50¢ Dairying	800.00	500.00	350.00	220.00	52.00	39.00
Q11	75¢ Harvesting	270.00	160.00	120.00	70.00	42.00	36.00
Q12	$1 Fruit Growing	1000.00	650.00	420.00	250.00	48.00	38.00
	1912 Parcel Post Due						
JQ1	1¢ dark green	30.00	20.00	12.00	8.00	5.00	4.00
JQ2	2¢ dark green	250.00	150.00	100.00	65.00	18.00	15.00
JQ3	5¢ dark green	45.00	30.00	20.00	12.00	6.00	5.00
JQ4	10¢ dark green	450.00	300.00	200.00	130.00	50.00	44.00
JQ5	25¢ dark green	300.00	200.00	120.00	80.00	6.00	5.00
	1925-29 Special Handling						
QE1	10¢ yellow green	5.00	3.75	3.00	2.50	1.50	1.20
QE2	15¢ yellow green	5.50	40.00	3.50	2.25	2.00	1.20
QE3	20¢ yellow green	8.50	6.00	5.00	4.00	1.95	1.35
QE4	25¢ deep green	50.00	30.00	21.00	16.00	8.00	5.00
QE4a	25¢ yellow green	50.00	40.00	30.00	19.00	18.00	14.00

POSTAL NOTE STAMPS
PN1-P18
All values printed in black

SCOTT NO.	DESCRIPTION	UNUSED F/NH	UNUSED F/OG	USED F
PN1-18	1¢-90¢, 18 varieties, complete	42.00	35.00	5.00

SCOTT NO.	DESCRIPTION	UNUSED ENTIRE	UNUSED CUT SQ.	USED CUT SQ.

ENVELOPES

U1-U10
Washington

U19-U24
Franklin

U26, U27
Washington

1853-55

SCOTT NO.	DESCRIPTION	UNUSED ENTIRE	UNUSED CUT SQ.	USED CUT SQ.
U1	3¢ red on white, die 1	1650.00	400.00	38.00
U2	3¢ red on buff, die 1	875.00	95.00	35.00
U3	3¢ red on white, die 2	3800.00	1000.00	52.00
U4	3¢ red on buff, die 2	3275.00	500.00	45.00
U5	3¢ red on white, die 3	26000.00	6000.00	600.00
U6	3¢ red on buff, die 3	......	5200.00	105.00
U7	3¢ red on white, die 4	......	5500.00	160.00
U8	3¢ red on buff, die 4	......	8500.00	485.00
U9	3¢ red on white, die 5	150.00	45.00	4.00
U10	3¢ red on buff, die 5	80.00	25.00	6.00
U11	6¢ red on white	400.00	325.00	100.00
U12	6¢ red on buff	365.00	150.00	100.00
U13	6¢ green on white	600.00	275.00	165.00
U14	6¢ green on buff	400.00	225.00	130.00
U15	10¢ green on white, die 1	750.00	500.00	110.00
U16	10¢ green on buff, die 1	475.00	180.00	100.00
U17	10¢ green on white, die 2	725.00	400.00	150.00
U18	10¢ green on buff, die 2	650.00	375.00	110.00

1860-61

U19	1¢ blue on buff, die 1	90.00	35.00	15.50
W20	1¢ blue on buff, die 1	130.00	70.00	55.00
W21	1¢ blue on manila, die 1	135.00	65.00	45.00
W22	1¢ blue on orange, die 1	6500.00	3200.00	......
U23	1¢ blue on orange, die 2	850.00	625.00	350.00
U24	1¢ blue on buff, die 3	725.00	365.00	110.00
U26	3¢ red on white	60.00	30.00	18.00
U27	3¢ red on buff	50.00	25.00	15.00
U28	3¢ & 1¢ red & blue on white	525.00	260.00	240.00
U29	3¢ & 1¢ red & blue on buff	525.00	260.00	260.00
U30	6¢ red on white	3500.00	2200.00	1750.00
U31	6¢ red on buff	5500.00	3700.00	1600.00
U32	10¢ green on white	10000.00	1400.00	460.00
U33	10¢ green on buff	3500.00	1500.00	420.00

U34-U37   **U40-U41**
Washington

1861

U34	3¢ pink on white	65.00	30.00	6.00
U35	3¢ pink on buff	65.00	35.00	6.50
U36	3¢ pink on blue (letter sheet)	250.00	75.00	75.00
U37	3¢ pink on orange	4500.00	3000.00	......
U38	6¢ pink on white	220.00	110.00	85.00
U39	6¢ pink on buff	225.00	65.00	65.00
U40	10¢ yellow green on white	80.00	45.00	35.00
U41	10¢ yellow green on buff	80.00	45.00	35.00
U42	12¢ brown & red on buff	480.00	185.00	185.00
U43	20¢ blue & red on buff	460.00	260.00	225.00
U44	24¢ green & red on buff	640.00	220.00	220.00
U45	40¢ red & black on buff	750.00	325.00	425.00

U46-U49   **U50-W57**
Jackson

1863-64

U46	2¢ black on buff, die 1	85.00	55.00	25.00
W47	2¢ black on dark manila, die 1	125.00	110.00	70.00
U48	2¢ black on buff, die 2	4800.00	2500.00	......
U49	2¢ black on orange, die 2	4200.00	2000.00	......
U50	2¢ black on buff, die 3	45.00	20.00	12.00
W51	2¢ black on buff, die 3	700.00	460.00	280.00
U52	2¢ black on orange, die 3	40.00	23.00	12.00
W53	2¢ black on dark manila, die 3	180.00	50.00	42.00

SCOTT NO.	DESCRIPTION	UNUSED ENTIRE	UNUSED CUT SQ.	USED CUT SQ.
U54	2¢ black on buff, die 4	40.00	20.00	10.00
W55	2¢ black on buff, die 4	170.00	100.00	70.00
U56	2¢ black on orange, die 4	38.00	25.00	12.00
W57	2¢ black on light manila, die 4	40.00	25.00	15.00

U58-1   **U66-U67**
Washington

1864-65

U58	3¢ pink on white	22.00	12.00	1.80
U59	3¢ pink on buff	22.00	12.00	3.20
U60	3¢ brown on white	140.00	70.00	40.00
U61	3¢ brown on buff	120.00	50.00	30.00
U62	6¢ pink on white	190.00	110.00	30.00
U63	6¢ pink on buff	120.00	48.00	30.00
U64	6¢ purple on white	120.00	58.00	28.00
U65	6¢ purple on buff	75.00	50.00	22.00
U66	9¢ lemon on white	600.00	400.00	255.00
U67	9¢ orange on buff	220.00	130.00	95.00
U68	12¢ brown on buff	620.00	300.00	280.00
U69	12¢ red brown on buff	185.00	130.00	60.00
U70	18¢ red on buff	185.00	90.00	98.00
U71	24¢ blue on buff	230.00	90.00	98.00
U72	30¢ green on buff	225.00	120.00	85.00
U73	40¢ rose on buff	365.00	110.00	260.00

U74-W77, U108-U121   **U78-W81, U122-W158**   **U82-U84, U159-U169**
Franklin   *Jackson*   *Washington*

U172-U180   **U85-U87, U181-U184**   **U88, U185, U186**
Taylor   *Lincoln*   *Stanton*

U89-U92, U187-U194   **U93-U95, U195-U197**   **U96-U98, U198-U200**
Jefferson   *Clay*   *Webster*

U99-U101, U201-U203   **U102-U104, U204-U210,**   **U105-U107, U211-U217,**
Scott   **U336-U341**   **U342-U347**
           Hamilton   *Perry*

NOTE: For details on die or silmilar appearing varieties of envelopes, please refer to the Scott Specialized Catalogue.

SCOTT NO.	DESCRIPTION	FIRST DAY COVER	UNUSED ENTIRE	USED CUT SQ.

U532 *Franklin*   **U533**   **U535**
Washington

1950

U532	1¢ green	2.00	8.75	2.50
U533	2¢ carmine	2.00	1.45	.35
U534	3¢ dark violet	2.00	.75	.30

1952

| U535 | 1-1/2¢ brown | ...... | 7.25 | 4.00 |

U537, U538, U552, U556   **U539, U540, U545, U553**

Surcharge on Envelopes of 1916-32, 1950, 1965, 1971

1958

U536	4¢ red violet	1.75	1.00	.30
U537	2¢ & 2¢ (4¢) carmine ....(U429)	......	5.25	2.00
U538	2¢ & 2¢ (4¢) carmine ....(U533)	......	1.25	1.50
U539	3¢ & 1¢ (4¢) purple, die1 ....(U436a)	......	18.50	12.00
U539a	3¢ & 1¢ (4¢) purple, die 7 ....(U436e)	......	15.00	10.00
U539b	3¢ & 1¢ (4¢) purple, die 9 ....(U436f)	......	36.00	17.00
U540	3¢ & 1¢ (4¢) dark violet ....(U534)	......	.70	1.25

U541 *Franklin*   **U542** *Washington*

1960

| U541 | 1-1/4¢ turquoise | 1.75 | 1.00 | .60 |
| U542 | 2-1/2¢ dull blue | 1.75 | 1.15 | .60 |

U543

| U543 | 4¢ Pony Express | 2.00 | .80 | .40 |

U544 *Lincoln*   **U546**

1962

| U544 | 5¢ dark blue | 1.75 | 1.20 | .25 |

Surcharge on Envelope of 1958

| U545 | 4¢+1¢ red violet ....(U536) | ...... | 1.80 | 1.35 |

1964

| U546 | 5¢ New York World's Fair | 1.75 | .75 | .45 |

SCOTT NO.	DESCRIPTION	FIRST DAY COVER	UNUSED ENTIRE	USED CUT SQ.

U547, U548, U548A, U566   **U549**

U550   **U551**

1965-69

U547	1-1/4¢ brown	1.75	.95	.55
U548	1-4/10¢ brown (1968)	1.75	1.25	.55
U548A	1-6/10¢ orange (1969)	1.75	1.15	.55
U549	4¢ bright blue	1.75	1.15	.25
U550	5¢ bright purple	1.75	1.00	.25
U551	6¢ light green (1968)	1.75	1.00	.25

U554

1968
1958 Type Surcharges on Envelopes of 1965

| U552 | 4¢ & 2¢ (6¢) blue ....(U549) | 9.00 | 4.25 | 2.25 |
| U553 | 5¢ & 1¢ (6¢) purple ....(U550) | 9.00 | 4.00 | 3.00 |

1970

| U554 | 6¢ Moby Dick | 1.75 | .65 | .25 |

U555   **U557**

1971

U555	6¢ Conference on Youth	1.75	.90	.25
U556	1-7/10¢ deep lilac	1.75	.40	.25
U557	8¢ ultramarine	1.75	.60	.25

U561 & U562 Surcharge

| U561 | 6¢ & (2¢) (8¢) green ....(on U551) | 4.00 | 1.25 | 1.35 |
| U562 | 6¢ & (2¢) (8¢) blue ....(on U555) | 4.00 | 3.00 | 2.75 |

U563   **U564**

| U563 | 8¢ Bowling | 1.75 | .90 | .25 |
| U564 | 8¢ Conference on Aging | 1.75 | .75 | .25 |

SCOTT NO.	DESCRIPTION	FIRST DAY COVER	UNUSED ENTIRE	USED CUT SQ.

U565

1972

U565	8¢ Transpo '72...	1.75	.80	.30

U567

1973

U566	8¢ & 2¢ ultramarine ....(on U557)	3.00	.65	1.35
U567	10¢ emerald	1.75	.65	.30

U568

U569

1974

U568	1-8/10¢ blue green...	1.75	.85	.30
U569	10¢ Tennis Centenary	2.50	.80	.30

U571

U572

U573

U574

U575

1975-76 BICENTENNIAL ERA

U571	10¢ Seafaring..	1.75	.60	.30
U572	13¢ Homemaker (1976)......................................	1.75	.60	.30
U573	13¢ Farmer (1976)..	1.75	.60	.30
U574	13¢ Doctor (1976)...	1.75	.60	.30
U575	13¢ Craftsman (1976)...	1.75	.60	.30

CUT SQUARES: From 1947 to date, Unused Envelope Cut Squares can be supplied at the Unused Entire Price.

SCOTT NO.	DESCRIPTION	FIRST DAY COVER	UNUSED ENTIRE	USED CUT SQ.

U576

1975

U576	13¢ orange brown..	1.75	.60	.30

U577

U578

U579

U581

1976-78

U577	2¢ red..	1.75	.60	.30
U578	2.1¢ green (1977)	1.75	.70	.30
U579	2.7¢ green (1978)	1.75	.95	.30
U580	(15¢) "A" orange (1978)	1.75	.65	.30
U581	15¢ red & white (1978).......................................	1.75	.65	.30

1976

U582	13¢ Bicentennial (design of U218)......................	1.75	.55	.30

U583

1977

U583	13¢ Golf	8.00	.80	.35

U584

U585

U584	13¢ Energy Conservation	1.75	.55	.30
U585	13¢ Energy Development	1.75	.55	.30

SCOTT NO.	DESCRIPTION	UNUSED ENTIRE	UNUSED CUT SQ.	USED CUT SQ.

UC1

UC2-UC7

Airplane in Circle

Die 1. Vertical rudder not semi-circular, but slopes to the left. Tail projects into "G".
Die 2. Vertical rudder is semi-circular. Tail only touches "G" Die 2a. "6" is 6-1/2mm. wide.
Die 2b. "6" is 6mm. wide.
Die 2c. "6" is 5-1/2mm. wide.
Die 3. Vertical rudder leans forward. "S" closer to "O" than to "T" of "POSTAGE" and "E" has short center bar.

1929-44

SCOTT NO.	DESCRIPTION	UNUSED ENTIRE	UNUSED CUT SQ.	USED CUT SQ.
UC1	5¢ blue, die 1	6.00	4.00	4.00
UC2	5¢ blue, die 2	16.00	12.00	10.00
UC3	6¢ orange, die 2a	2.50	1.75	1.00
UC3n	6¢, die 2a, no border	3.00	1.50	1.00
UC4	6¢, die 2b, with border	72.00	53.00	2.50
UC4n	6¢, die 2b, no border	6.00	4.00	2.50
UC5	6¢, die 2c, no border	1.55	1.00	.50
UC6	6¢ orange on white, die 3	2.25	1.25	.45
UC6n	6¢, die 3, no border	3.00	1.50	.50
UC7	8¢ olive green	21.00	14.50	4.00

REVALUED
5¢
P.O. DEPT.

Envelopes of 1916-32 surcharged

1945

UC8	6¢ on 2¢ carmine on white	(U429)	1.75	1.55	1.15
UC9	6¢ on 2¢ carmine on white	(U525)	120.00	90.00	72.50

1946

UC10	5¢ on 6¢, die 2a	(UC3n)	6.00	4.50	2.60
UC11	5¢ on 6¢, die 2b	(UC4n)	12.00	11.75	8.50
UC12	5¢ on 6¢, die 2c	(UC5)	1.50	1.15	.80
UC13	5¢ on 6¢, die 3	(UC6n)	1.15	1.15	.75

UC14: Die 1. Small projection below rudder is rounded.
UC15: Die 2. Small projection below rudder is sharp pointed.

UC14, UC15, UC18, UC26
DC-4 Skymaster

SCOTT NO.	DESCRIPTION	FIRST DAY COVER	UNUSED ENTIRE	USED CUT SQ.
UC14	5¢ carmine, die 1	2.50	1.25	.75
UC15	5¢ carmine, die 2	......	1.25	.75

UC16
DC-4 Skymaster

UC17
Washington and Franklin, Mail-carrying Vehicles

1947

UC16	10¢ red on blue, Entire "Air Letter" on face, 2-line inscription on back	6.00	9.00	10.50
UC16a	Entire, "Air Letter" on face, 4-line inscription on back	......	18.00	15.00
UC16c	Entire "Air Letter" and "Aerogramme" on face, 4-line inscription on back	......	55.00	13.50
UC16d	Entire "Air Letter" and "Aerogramme" on face, 3-line inscription on back	......	9.50	9.00

1947 CIPEX COMMEMORATIVE

UC17	5¢ carmine	3.00	.65	.60

1950 Design of 1946

UC18	6¢ carmine	1.75	.60	.35

1951 (Shaded Numeral)

UC19	6¢ on 5¢, die 1	(UC14)	......	2.40	1.60
UC20	6¢ on 5¢, die 2	(UC15)	......	1.25	1.60

1952 (Solid Numeral)

UC21	6¢ on 5¢, die 1	(UC14)	......	35.00	19.00
UC22	6¢ on 5¢, die 2	(UC15)	......	9.00	2.75
UC23	6¢ on 5¢	(UC17)	......	2100.00	......

SCOTT NO.	DESCRIPTION	FIRST DAY COVER	UNUSED ENTIRE	USED CUT SQ.

REVALUED
6¢
P. O. DEPT.

ENVELOPE of 1946 Surcharged

REVALUED
6¢
P.O. DEPT.

ENVELOPE of 1946-47 Surcharged

1956 FIPEX COMMEMORATIVE

UC25	6¢ red	1.75	1.10	.60

1958 Design of 1946

UC26	7¢ blue	1.75	1.10	.60

UC36

UC27-UC31
Surcharge on Envelopes of 1934 to 1956

UC25

1958

UC27	6¢ & 1¢ (7¢) orange, die 2a	(UC3n)	......	420.00	......
UC28	6¢ & 1¢ (7¢), die 2b	(UC4n)	......	125.00	82.50
UC29	6¢ & 1¢ (7¢) orange, die 2c	(UC5)	......	60.00	52.50
UC30	6¢ & 1¢ (7¢) carmine	(UC18)	......	1.35	.60
UC31	6¢ & 1¢ (7¢) red	(UC25)	......	1.40	.60

UC32

UC33, UC34

UC35

1958-59

UC32	10¢ blue & red Entire letter sheet, 2-line inscription on back (1959)	......	7.00	5.25
UC32a	Entire letter sheet, 3 line inscription on back	2.25	12.00	5.25

1958

UC33	7¢ blue	1.75	.80	.30

1960

UC34	7¢ carmine	1.75	.85	.30

1961

UC35	11¢ red & blue	3.25	3.00	3.75

1962

UC36	8¢ red	1.75	.85	.25

1965

UC37	8¢ red	1.75	.70	.25
UC38	11¢ J.F. Kennedy	1.75	4.00	4.50

UC37

UC38, UC39

UC40

UC41
(surcharge on UC37)

UC42

1967

UC39	13¢ J.F. Kennedy	1.75	3.50	4.50

1968

UC40	10¢ red	1.75	.85	.25
UC41	8¢ & 2¢ (10¢) red	12.00	.95	.25
UC42	13¢ Human Rights Year	1.75	11.00	8.00

SCOTT NO.	DESCRIPTION	FIRST DAY COVER	UNUSED ENTIRE	USED CUT SQ.

UC43

UC44

1971

UC43	11¢ red & blue....................................	1.75	.85	1.85
UC44	15¢ gray, red, white and blue Birds in Flight............	1.75	2.00	3.50
UC44a	Aerogramme added	1.75	2.00	3.50

UC45 (surcharge on UC40)

UC47

1971 Revalued

| UC45 | 10 & (1¢) (11¢) red................................. | 6.00 | 2.50 | .25 |

1973

| UC46 | 15¢ Ballooning .... | 1.75 | 1.25 | 1.50 |
| UC47 | 13¢ rose red .... | 1.75 | .75 | .25 |

UC48

UC49

1974

| UC48 | 18¢ red & blue... | 1.75 | 1.50 | 2.25 |
| UC49 | 18¢ NATO 25th Anniversary .... | 1.75 | 1.25 | 2.25 |

UC50

UC51

1976

| UC50 | 22¢ red, white & blue .... | 1.75 | 1.55 | 2.25 |

1978

| UC51 | 22¢ blue .... | 1.75 | 1.55 | 2.25 |

UC52

UC53, UC54

UC55

1979

| UC52 | 22¢ Moscow Olympics................................ | 1.75 | 2.25 | 2.25 |

1980-81

| UC53 | 30¢ red, blue & brown .... | 1.75 | 1.25 | 1.75 |
| UC54 | 30¢ yellow, magenta, blue & black (1981) .... | 1.75 | 1.25 | 1.25 |

1982

| UC55 | 30¢ Made in U.S.A. .... | 1.75 | 1.45 | 3.00 |

UC56

Olympics 84
USA 30c
UC57

1983

| UC56 | 30¢ Communications .... | 1.75 | 1.25 | 5.50 |
| UC57 | 30¢ Olympics .... | 1.75 | 1.25 | 5.50 |

UC58

USA 36
UC59

1985

UC58	36¢ Landsat Satellite	1.75	1.50	5.50
UC59	36¢ Travel	1.75	1.55	3.50
UC60	36¢ Mark Twain, Halley's Comet..........................	1.75	1.75	6.50

USA 36
UC60

USA 39
UC61

1986

| UC61 | 39¢ Letters .... | 1.75 | 2.00 | 6.50 |

1989

| UC62 | 39¢ Blair & Lincoln .... | 1.75 | 1.75 | 26.00 |

USA 39
UC62

USA 45
UC63

1991

| UC63 | 45¢ Eagle .... | 1.75 | 1.75 | 2.50 |

1995

| UC64 | 50¢ Thaddeus Lowe .... | 1.95 | 1.75 | 5.50 |

USA 50
UC64

USA 60
UC65

1999

| UC65 | 60¢ Voyagers National Park, Minnesota.................. | 1.95 | 2.50 | 7.75 |

SCOTT NO.	DESCRIPTION	UNUSED ENTIRE	UNUSED CUT SQ.	USED CUT SQ.

UO1-UO13 **UO14-UO17** **UO18-UO69** *Washington*

OFFICIAL ENVELOPES

NOTE: For details on similar appearing varieties please refer to the Scott Specialized Catalogue

POST OFFICE DEPARTMENT

1873 SMALL NUMERALS

UO1	2¢ black on lemon	40.00	28.00	11.00
UO2	3¢ black on lemon	38.00	21.00	7.00
UO4	6¢ black on lemon	46.00	31.00	17.00

1874-79 LARGE NUMERALS

UO5	2¢ black on lemon	19.00	13.00	5.00
UO6	2¢ black on white	255.00	150.00	40.00
UO7	3¢ black on lemon	5.00	4.00	1.00
UO8	3¢ black on lemon	5800.00	3250.00	2400.00
UO9	3¢ black on amber	180.00	155.00	42.00
UO12	6¢ black on lemon	31.00	18.00	7.00
UO13	6¢ black on white	5800.00	3250.00	......

1877 POSTAL SERVICE

UO14	black on white	12.00	8.00	5.00
UO15	black on amber	955.00	250.00	45.00
UO16	blue on amber	955.00	225.00	38.00
UO17	blue on blue	16.00	10.00	7.00

Portraits for the various denominations are the same as on the regular issue of 1870-73

WAR DEPARTMENT

1873 REAY ISSUE

UO18	1¢ dark red on white	1150.00	750.00	325.00
UO19	2¢ dark red on white	3250.00	2500.00	475.00
UO20	3¢ dark red on white	110.00	75.00	48.00
UO22	3¢ dark red on cream	1150.00	1050.00	315.00
UO23	6¢ dark red on white	480.00	350.00	95.00
UO24	6¢ dark red on cream	......	8500.00	440.00
UO25	10¢ dark red on white	......	......	2500.00
UO26	12¢ dark red on white	250.00	190.00	65.00
UO27	15¢ dark red on white	225.00	175.00	65.00
UO28	24¢ dark red on white	250.00	200.00	55.00
UO29	30¢ dark red on white	785.00	600.00	165.00
UO30	1¢ vermillion on white	455.00	225.00	......
WO31	1¢ vermillion on manila	42.00	23.00	15.00
UO32	2¢ vermillion on white	......	550.00	......
WO33	2¢ vermillion on manila	750.00	300.00	......
UO34	3¢ vermillion on white	225.00	110.00	45.00
UO35	3¢ vermillion on amber	400.00	140.00	......
UO36	3¢ vermillion on cream	45.00	20.00	14.00
UO37	6¢ vermillion on white	200.00	110.00	......
UO38	6¢ vermillion on cream	......	600.00	......
UO39	10¢ vermillion on white	655.00	375.00	......
UO40	12¢ vermillion on white	260.00	185.00	......
UO41	15¢ vermillion on white	3250.00	275.00	......
UO42	24¢ vermillion on white	690.00	475.00	......
UO43	30¢ vermillion on white	680.00	550.00	......

1875 PLIMPTON ISSUE

UO44	1¢ red on white	275.00	210.00	95.00
UO45	1¢ red on amber	......	1200.00	......
WO46	1¢ red on manila	10.00	5.25	3.00
UO47	2¢ red on white	225.00	170.00	......
UO48	2¢ red on amber	60.00	40.00	18.00
UO49	2¢ red on orange	85.00	72.00	18.00
WO50	2¢ red on manila	250.00	130.00	60.00
UO51	3¢ red on white	25.00	18.00	11.00
UO52	3¢ red on amber	32.00	26.00	11.00
UO53	3¢ red on cream	10.00	8.00	4.00
UO54	3¢ red on blue	7.00	4.50	3.00
UO55	3¢ red on fawn	12.00	7.00	3.00
UO56	6¢ red on white	125.00	75.00	35.00
UO57	6¢ red on amber	150.00	100.00	50.00
UO58	6¢ red on cream	560.00	250.00	95.00
UO59	10¢ red on white	325.00	275.00	90.00
UO60	10¢ red on amber	1600.00	1320.00	......
UO61	12¢ red on white	200.00	75.00	42.00
UO62	12¢ red on amber	1000.00	850.00	......
UO63	12¢ red on cream	1000.00	800.00	......
UO64	15¢ red on white	325.00	275.00	150.00
UO65	15¢ red on amber	1150.00	1000.00	......
UO66	15¢ red on cream	1000.00	850.00	......
UO67	30¢ red on white	250.00	200.00	150.00
UO68	30¢ red on amber	2500.00	1150.00	......
UO69	30¢ red on cream	1400.00	1100.00	......

SCOTT NO. DESCRIPTION	UNUSED ENTIRE	UNUSED CUT SQ.	USED CUT SQ.

UO70-UO72

1911 POSTAL SAVINGS

UO70	1¢ green on white	120.00	88.00	27.00
UO71	1¢ green on oriental buff	280.00	255.00	77.00
UO72	2¢ carmine on white	29.00	15.00	4.50

SCOTT NO.	DESCRIPTION	FIRST DAY COVER	UNUSED ENTIRE	USED CUT SQ.

UO73 **UO74** **UO75**

1983

| UO73 | 20¢ blue and white | 2.50 | 1.40 | 40.00 |

1985

| UO74 | 22¢ blue and white | 2.00 | 1.00 | 35.00 |

1987 Design Similar to UO74

| UO75 | 22¢ Savings Bond | 3.25 | 2.50 | 35.00 |

UO76 **UO77** **UO78**

UO81 **UO83** **UO84**

1989

UO76	(25¢) "E" black and blue Savings Bonds	2.00	1.65	35.00
UO77	25¢ black and blue	2.00	1.00	25.00
UO78	25¢ black and blue Savings Bonds	2.00	1.45	35.00

1990

UO79	45¢ black & blue seal	2.25	1.55	......
UO80	65¢ black & blue seal	3.00	1.95	......
UO81	45¢ Self-sealing Envelope	2.25	1.55	......
UO82	65¢ Self-sealing Envelope	3.00	1.95	......

UO85 **UO86, UO87** **UO88, UO89, UO90, UO91, UO92, UO93**

1991-92

UO83	(29¢) "F" black and blue Savings Bond	2.00	1.50	36.00
UO84	29¢ black and blue	2.00	1.00	25.00
UO85	29¢ black and blue Savings Bond	2.00	1.00	25.00
UO86	52¢ Consular Service	2.50	6.00	......
UO87	75¢ Consular Service	3.00	12.50	......

1995

| UO88 | 32¢ Great Seal, red and blue | 2.00 | 1.00 | 25.00 |

1999

| UO89 | 33¢ Great Seal, red and blue | 2.00 | 1.25 | 25.00 |

2001-07

UO90	34¢ Great Seal, red and blue	2.00	1.25	25.00
UO91	37¢ Great Seal, red and blue	2.00	1.25	....
UO92	39¢ Great Seal, red and blue	2.00	1.25	....
UO93	41¢ Great Seal, red and blue	2.00	1.25	....
UO94	42¢ Great Seal, official stamped envelope	2.50	1.25	....

SCOTT NO.	DESCRIPTION	MINT	UNUSED	USED

POSTAL CARDS

Prices Are For Entire Cards

MINT: As Issued, no printing or writing added.
UNUSED: Uncancelled, with printing or writing added.

UX1, UX3, U65   **UX4, UX5, UX7**   **UX6, UX13, UX16**
           Liberty

1873

UX1	1¢ brown, large watermark	425.00	95.00	27.00
UX3	1¢ brown, small watermark	90.00	26.00	4.00

1875 Inscribed "Write the Address", etc.

UX4	1¢ black, watermarked	4100.00	800.00	450.00
UX5	1¢ black, unwatermarked	92.00	9.75	.75

1879

UX6	2¢ blue on buff	42.00	15.00	38.50

1881 Inscribed "Nothing but the Address", etc.

UX7	1¢ black on buff	85.00	9.00	.50

UX8   **UX9**   **UX10, UX11**
   Jefferson   *Grant*

1885

UX8	1¢ brown on buff	60.00	15.00	1.50

1886

UX9	1¢ black on buff	31.00	3.00	.65

1891

UX10	1¢ black on buff	52.00	11.00	1.75
UX11	1¢ blue on grayish white	26.00	6.00	3.00

UX12   **UX14**   **UX15**
   Jefferson   *John Adams*

1894

UX12	1¢ black on buff Small Wreath	57.00	3.50	.75

1897

UX13	2¢ blue on cream	250.00	95.00	95.00
UX14	1¢ black on buff Large Wreath	50.00	4.00	.75

1898

UX15	1¢ black on buff	58.00	15.00	16.00
UX16	2¢ black on buff	18.00	7.00	20.00

SCOTT NO.	DESCRIPTION	MINT	UNUSED	USED

UX18   **UX19, UX20**   **UX21**
         McKinley

1902 Profile Background

UX18	1¢ black on buff	23.00	3.00	.40

1907

UX19	1¢ black on buff	65.00	4.00	.60

1908 Correspondence Space at Left

UX20	1¢ black on buff	72.00	12.00	4.50

1910 Background Shaded

UX21	1¢ blue on bluish	120.00	25.00	14.00

UX22, UX24   **UX23, UX26**   **UX25**
   Mckiny   *Lincoln*   *Grant*

White Portrait Background

UX22	1¢ blue on bluish	29.00	3.25	.85

1911

UX23	1¢ red on cream	12.00	4.00	6.00
UX24	1¢ red on cream	14.00	1.50	.40
UX25	2¢ red on cream	1.75	1.25	22.00

1913

UX26	1¢ green on cream	15.00	3.00	9.00

UX27   **UX28, UX43**   **UX29, UX30**   **UX32, UX33**
Jefferson   *Lincoln*   *Jefferson*   *surcharge*

1914

UX27	1¢ green on buff	.45	.35	.40

1917-18

UX28	1¢ green on cream	1.00	.40	.40
UX29	2¢ red on buff, die 1	52.00	11.00	4.00
UX30	2¢ red on cream, die 2 (1918)	35.00	7.00	1.80

NOTE: On UX29 end of queue slopes sharply down to right while on UX30 it extends nearly horizontally.

1920 UX29 & UX30 Revalued

UX32	1¢ on 2¢ red, die 1	68.00	22.00	15.00
UX33	1¢ on 2¢ red, die 2	18.00	4.00	3.00

UX37   **UX38**   **UX39-42 sur-**
McKinley   *Franklin*   **charge**

1926

UX37	3¢ red on buff	5.50	2.50	17.50

SCOTT NO.	DESCRIPTION	FIRST DAY COVER	MINT	USED

UX147

UX148

UX150

UX151

UX152

1990

UX145	15¢ Papermaking	1.75	.55	.50
UX146	15¢ Literacy	1.75	.55	.85
UX147	15¢ Bingham	1.75	1.75	3.00
UX148	15¢ Isaac Royall House	1.75	.55	.85
UX150	15¢ Stanford University	1.75	.55	.85
UX151	15¢ DAR Memorial Hall	1.75	1.60	2.50
UX152	15¢ Chicago Orchestra Hall	1.75	.55	.85

UX153

UX154

UX155

1991

UX153	19¢ Flag	1.75	.65	.85
UX154	19¢ Carnegie Hall	1.75	.65	.85
UX155	19¢ Old Red Administration Building	1.75	.65	.50

UX156

UX157

| UX156 | 19¢ Bill of Rights | 1.75 | .65 | .85 |
| UX157 | 19¢ University of Notre Dame, Administration Building | 1.75 | .65 | .85 |

UX158

UX159

| UX158 | 30¢ Niagara Falls | 1.75 | .90 | 10.00 |
| UX159 | 19¢ Old Mill University of Vermont | 1.75 | .65 | 1.00 |

UX160

UX161

UX162

UX163

UX164

UX165

1992

UX160	19¢ Wadsworth Atheneum	1.75	.65	.85
UX161	19¢ Cobb Hall University of Chicago	1.75	.65	.85
UX162	19¢ Waller Hall	1.75	.65	.85
UX163	19¢ America's Cup	1.75	1.95	4.00
UX164	19¢ Columbia River Gorge	1.75	.65	.85
UX165	19¢ Great Hall, Ellis Island	1.75	.65	.85

UX166

UX167

1993

| UX166 | 19¢ National Cathedral | 1.75 | .65 | .85 |
| UX167 | 19¢ Wren Building | 1.75 | .65 | .85 |

UX168

UX169

| UX168 | 19¢ Holocaust Memorial | 2.00 | 1.85 | 4.00 |
| UX169 | 19¢ Fort Recovery | 1.75 | .65 | .85 |

UX170

UX171

| UX170 | 19¢ Playmakers Theatre | 1.75 | .65 | .85 |
| UX171 | 19¢ O'Kane Hall | 1.75 | .65 | .85 |

SCOTT NO.	DESCRIPTION	FIRST DAY COVER	MINT	USED

UX172

UX173

1993 (continued)

UX172	19¢ Beecher Hall	1.75	.65	.85
UX173	19¢ Massachusetts Hall	1.75	.65	.85

UX174

UX175

UX176

UX177

1994

UX174	19¢ Abraham Lincoln Home	1.75	.65	.85
UX175	19¢ Myers Hall	1.75	.65	.85
UX176	19¢ Canyon de Chelly	1.75	.65	.85
UX177	19¢ St. Louis Union Station	1.75	.65	.85

Legends of the West

UX178

UX178	Home on the Range	UX188	Nellie Cashman
UX179	Buffalo Bill	UX189	Charles Goodnight
UX180	Jim Bridger	UX190	Geronimo
UX181	Annie Oakley	UX191	Kit Carson
UX182	Native American Culture	UX192	Wild Bill Hickok
UX183	Chief Joseph	UX193	Western Wildlife
UX184	Bill Pickett	UX194	Jim Beckwourth
UX185	Bat Masterson	UX195	Bill Tilghman
UX186	John Fremont	UX196	Sacagawea
UX187	Wyatt Earp	UX197	Overland Mail

UX178-97	19¢ Legends of the West, set of 20	35.00	35.00	65.00

UX198

UX199

UX198

1995

UX198	20¢ Red Barn	1.75	.65	.75
UX199	20¢ "G" Old Glory	1.75	4.25	3.00

Civil War

UX201

UX200	Monitor-Virginia	UX210	Tubman
UX201	Lee	UX211	Watie
UX202	Barton	UX212	Johnston
UX203	Grant	UX213	Hancock
UX204	Shiloh	UX214	Chestnut
UX205	Davis	UX215	Chancellorsville
UX206	Farragut	UX216	Sherman
UX207	Douglass	UX217	Pember
UX208	Semmes	UX218	Jackson
UX209	Lincoln	UX219	Gettysburg

UX200-19	20¢ Civil War, set of 20	35.00	60.00	65.00
UX219a	50¢ Eagle	1.75	1.75	10.00

UX220

UX241

UX220	20¢ American Clipper Ships	1.75	.65	.85

American Comic Strips

UX221

UX221	Yellow Kid	UX231	Popeye
UX222	Katzenjammer Kids	UX232	Blondie
UX223	Little Nemo	UX233	Dick Tracy
UX224	Bring Up Father	UX234	Alley Oop
UX225	Krazy Kat	UX235	Nancy
UX226	Rube Goldberg	UX236	Flash Gordon
UX227	Toonerville Folks	UX237	Li'l Abner
UX228	Gasoline Alley	UX238	Terry/Pirates
UX229	Barney Google	UX239	Prince Valiant
UX230	Little Orphan Annie	UX240	Brenda Starr

UX221-40	20¢ American Comic Strips, set of 20	35.00	68.00	80.00

1996

UX241	20¢ Winter Farm Scene	1.75	.65	.50

Centennial Olympic Games

UX242

UX242	Men's cycling	UX252	Women's softball
UX243	Women's diving	UX253	Women's swimming
UX244	Women's running	UX254	Men's sprints
UX245	Men's canoeing	UX255	Men's rowing
UX246	Decathlon	UX256	Beach volleyball
UX247	Women's soccer	UX257	Men's basketball
UX248	Men's shot put	UX258	Equestrian
UX249	Women's sailboarding	UX259	Men's gymnastics
UX250	Women's gymnastics	UX260	Men's swimming
UX251	Freestyle wrestling	UX261	Men's hurdles

UX242-61	20¢ Centennial Olympic Games, set of 20	35.00	77.00	75.00

UX262   **UX263**

UX262	20¢ McDowell Hall	1.75	.65	.85
UX263	20¢ Alexander Hall	1.75	.65	.85

Engandered Species

UX264

UX264	Florida panther
UX265	Black-footed ferret
UX266	American crocodile
UX267	Piping plover
UX268	Gila trout
UX269	Florida manatee
UX270	Schaus swallowtail butterfly
UX271	Woodland caribou
UX272	Thick-billed parrot
UX273	San Francisco garter snake
UX274	Ocelot
UX275	Wyoming toad
UX276	California condor
UX277	Hawaiian monk seal
UX278	Brown pelican

UX264-78	20¢ Endangered Species, set of 15	26.50	77.00	70.00

UX279

UX280

1997

UX279	20¢ Swans	2.50	6.00	2.00
UX279a	20¢ Swans, set of 12	20.00(8)	60.00	.....
UX280	20¢ Shepard Hall	1.75	.65	1.00

SCOTT NO.	DESCRIPTION	FIRST DAY COVER	MINT	USED

UX281

UX282

| UX281 | 20¢ Bugs Bunny | 1.75 | 1.85 | 2.50 |
| UX282 | 20¢ Golden Gate Bridge | 1.75 | .45 | 1.00 | 1.00 |

UX283

UX284

| UX283 | 50¢ Golden Gate Bridge at Sunset | 1.95 | 1.60 | 3.00 |
| UX284 | 20¢ Fort McHenry | 1.75 | .75 | .85 |

UX285

Classic Movie Monsters
UX285 *Lon Chaney as The Phantom of the Opera*
UX286 *Bela Lugosi as Dracula*
UX287 *Boris Karloff as Frankenstein's Monster*
UX288 *Boris Karloff as The Mummy*
UX289 *Lon Chaney Jr. as The Wolfman*

UX291

| UX285 | 20¢ Classic Movie Monsters, set of 5 | 8.75 | 12.00 | 12.00 |
| UX289a | same, bklt of 20 (4 of each) | .... | 44.00 | .... |

UX290

UX292

1998

UX290	20¢ University of Mississippi	1.75	.65	.85
UX291	20¢ Sylvester & Tweety	1.75	1.75	3.00
UX291a	same, bklt of 10	....	18.00	....
UX292	20¢ Girard College, Philadelphia, PA	1.75	.65	.85

UX293

UX297

UX298

UX293-96	20¢ Tropical Birds, set of 4	7.00	6.50	7.50
UX296a	same, bklt of 20 (5 of each)	....	32.00	....
UX297	20¢ Ballet	1.75	1.75	1.50
UX297a	same, bklt of 10	....	17.00	....
UX298	20¢ Kerr Hall, Northeastern University	1.75	.65	.85

UX299

UX300

UX301

| UX299 | 20¢ Usen Castle, Brandeis University | 1.75 | .65 | .85 |

1999

| UX300 | 20¢ Love, Victorian | 1.75 | 1.75 | 2.50 |
| UX301 | 20¢ University of Wisc.-Madison-Bascom Hill | 1.75 | .65 | .75 |

UX302

UX303

| UX302 | 20¢ Washington and Lee University | 1.75 | .65 | .60 |
| UX303 | 20¢ Redwood Library & Anthenaum, Newport, RI | 1.75 | .65 | .60 |

UX304

UX305

UX304	20¢ Daffy Duck	1.75	1.75	1.50
UX304a	same, bklt of 10	....	17.00	....
UX305	20¢ Mount Vernon	1.75	.85	.85

UX306

UX307

Famous Trains
UX307 *Super Chief*
UX308 *Hiawatha*
UX309 *Daylight*
UX310 *Congressional*
UX311 *20th Century Limited*

1999

UX306	20¢ Block Island Lighthouse	1.75	.65	.50
UX307-11	20¢ Famous Trains, set of 5	8.75	9.00	6.00
UX311a	same, bklt of 20 (4 of each)	....	33.00	....

UX312

UX313

UX315

UX316

2000

UX312	20¢ University of Utah	1.75	.65	.70
UX313	20¢ Ryman Auditorium, Nashville, Tennessee	1.75	.65	.70
UX314	20¢ Road Runner & Wile E. Coyote	1.75	1.85	1.50
UX314a	same, bklt of 10	....	18.00	....
UX315	20¢ Adoption	1.75	1.85	1.75
UX315a	same, bklt of 10	....	18.00	....
UX316	20¢ Old Stone Row, Middlebury College, Vermont	1.75	.65	.60

SCOTT NO.	DESCRIPTION	FIRST DAY COVER	MINT	USED

UX336

The Stars and Stripes

UX317	Sons of Liberty Flag, 1775	UX327	Star-Spangled Banner, 1814
UX318	New England Flag, 1775	UX328	Bennington Flag, c. 1820
UX319	Forster Flag, 1775	UX329	Great Star Flag, 1837
UX320	Continential Colors, 1776	UX330	29-Star Flag, 1847
UX321	Francis Hopkinson Flag, 1777	UX331	Fort Sumter Flag, 1861
UX322	Brandywine Flag, 1777	UX332	Centennial Flag, 1876
UX323	John Paul Jones Flag, 1779	UX333	38-Star Flag
UX324	Pierre L'Enfant Flag, 1783	UX334	Peace Flag, 1891
UX325	Indian Peace Flag, 1803	UX335	48-Star Flag, 1912
UX326	Easton Flag, 1814	UX336	50-Star Flag, 1960

UX317-36	The Stars and Stripes, set of 20	35.00	85.00	58.00

UX337

Legends of Baseball

UX337	Jackie Robinson	UX347	Lefty Grove
UX338	Eddie Collins	UX348	Tris Speaker
UX339	Christy Mathewson	UX349	Cy Young
UX340	Ty Cobb	UX350	Jimmie Foxx
UX341	George Sisler	UX351	Pie Traynor
UX342	Rogers Hornsby	UX352	Satchel Paige
UX343	Mickey Cochrane	UX353	Honus Wagner
UX344	Babe Ruth	UX354	Josh Gibson
UX345	Walter Johnson	UX355	Dizzy Dean
UX346	Roberto Clemente	UX356	Lou Gehrig

UX337-56	20¢ Legends of Baseball, set of 20	35.00	42.00	40.00

UX357-60

UX361

UX357-60	20¢ Christmas Deer, set of 4	7.00	6.50	5.50

2001

UX361	20¢ Connecticut Hall, Yale University	1.75	.65	.75

UX362

UX363

UX364

UX362	20¢ University of South Carolina	1.75	.65	.85
UX363	20¢ Northwestern University Sesquicentennial 1851-2001	1.75	.65	.85
UX364	20¢ Waldschmidt Hall, The University of Portland ...	1.75	.65	.75

Legendary Playing Fields

UX365	Ebbets Field	UX370	Forbes Field
UX366	Tiger Stadium	UX371	Fenway Park
UX367	Crosley Field	UX372	Comiskey Park
UX368	Yankee Stadium	UX373	Shibe Park
UX369	Polo Grounds	UX374	Wrigley Field

2001

UX365-74	21¢ Legendary Playing Fields, set of 10	35.00	55.00	58.00
UX374a	same, bklt of 10		55.00	

UX375

UX376

UX377

UX375	21¢ White Barn	1.75	.70	.70
UX376	21¢ That's All Folks	2.00	2.00	1.75
UX376a	same, bklt of 10		18.00	
UX377-80	21¢ Santas, set of 4	7.50	8.00	7.00
UX380a	same, complete bklt of 20		37.00	

UX381

UX382

UX386

2002

UX381	23¢ Carlsbad Caverns	1.75	.75	.75
UX382-85	23¢ Teddy Bears, set of 4	7.50	6.00	6.00
UX385a	same, complete bklt of 20		29.00	
UX386-89	23¢ Christmas Snowmen, set of 4	7.50	6.00	6.00
UX389a	same, complete bklt of 20		29.00	

UX390

UX395

UX400

2003

UX390-94	23¢ Old Glory, set of 5	8.75	9.75	9.25
UX394a	same, complete booklet of 20 cards		36.00	
UX395-99	23¢ Southern Lighthouses, set of 5	8.75	7.75	7.75
UX399a	same, complete booklet of 20		34.00	
UX400	23¢ Ohio University, 200th Anniversary	1.75	.75	.75
UX401-04	23¢ Christmas Music Makers, set of 4	7.50	7.00	7.00
UX404a	same, complete bklt of 20		34.00	

UX401

UX405

2004

UX405	23¢ Columbia University, 250th Anniversary	1.75	.75	.75

UX406

UX407

UX406	23¢ Harriton House, 300th Anniversary	1.75	.75	.70
UX407-10	23¢ Art of Disney, set of 4	7.00	7.50	8.50
UX410a	same, complete booklet of 20		38.00	

UX411

UX421

UX411-20	23¢ Art of the American Indian, set of 10	17.50	19.00	19.00
UX420a	same, complete booklet of 20		33.00	
UX421-35	23¢ Cloudscapes, set of 15	26.25	28.00	28.00
UX435a	same, complete booklet of 20		35.00	

SCOTT NO.	DESCRIPTION	FIRST DAY COVER	MINT	USED

UX440

UX449

UX501

2005

SCOTT NO.	DESCRIPTION	FIRST DAY COVER	MINT	USED
UX436-39	Disney Characters, set of 4	7.00	7.50	7.50
UX439a	same, complete booklet of 20	....	36.00	....
UX440-44	23¢ Sporty Cars, set of 4	7.00	8.00	8.00
UX444a	same, complete booklet of 20	....	30.00	....
UX445-48	23¢ Let's Dance, set of 4	7.00	65.00	6.50
UX448a	same, complete booklet of 20	....	31.00	....

2006

UX449	24¢ Zebulon Pike Expedition, Bicentennial	1.75	.80	.75

Star Wars

UX489	Darth Vader	UX496	Obi-Wan Kenobi
UX490	Luke Skywalker	UX497	Boba Fett
UX491	C-3PO	UX498	Darth Maul
UX492	Queen Padme Amidala	UX499	Yoda
UX493	Millennium Falcon	UX500	Princess Leia and R2-D2
UX494	Emperor Palpatine	UX501	Chewbacca and Han Solo
UX495	Anakin Skywalker and	UX502	X-wing Starfighter
	Obi-Wan Kenobi	UX503	Stormtroopers

UX489-503	26¢ Star Wars, set of 15	27.50	33.00	33.00

UX450

UX454

UX505

UX509-28　　UX529-32

SCOTT NO.	DESCRIPTION	FIRST DAY COVER	MINT	USED
UX450-53	24¢ Disney Characters, set of 4	7.00	6.50	6.50
UX453a	same, complete booklet of 20	....	30.00	....
UX454-57	24¢ Baseball Sluggers, set of 4	7.00	6.75	6.75
UX457a	same, complete booklet of 20	....	32.00	....

UX504-08	26¢ Pacific Coast Lighthouses, set of 5	8.00	8.00	8.00
UX508a	same, complete booklet of 20	....	31.00	....
UX509-28	26¢ Marvel Comic Book Heroes, set of 20	40.00	38.00	38.00
UX529-32	26¢ Disney Characters, set of 4	7.50	8.00	8.00
	same, complete booklet of 20	....	38.00	....

UX458

D.C. Comics Super Heroes

UX458	Superman Cover	UX468	The Flash Cover
UX459	Superman	UX469	The Flash
UX460	Batman Cover	UX470	Plastic Man Cover
UX461	Batman	UX471	Plastic Man
UX462	Wonder Woman Cover	UX472	Aquaman Cover
UX463	Wonder Woman	UX473	Aquaman
UX464	Green Lantern Cover	UX474	Supergirl Cover
UX465	Green Lantern	UX475	Supergirl
UX466	Green Arrow Cover	UX476	Hawkman Cover
UX467	Green Arrow	UX477	Hawkman

UX458-77	24¢ D.C. Comics Super Heroes, set of 20	40.00	38.00	38.00

UX533

UX534

2008

UX533	27¢ Mount St. Mary's University postal card	2.75	.85	.85
UX534	27¢ Corinthian Column postal card	2.75	.85	.85

Southern Florida Wetlands

UX478	Snail Kite	UX483	White Ibis
UX479	Cape Sable Seaside Sparrow	UX484	American Crocodile
UX480	Wood Storks	UX485	Everglades Mink
UX481	Florida Panthers	UX486	Roseate Spoonbills
UX482	Bald Eagle	UX487	American Alligators

UX483

UX478-87	39¢ Southern Florida Wetlands, set of 10	....	53.00	....

UX535

UX535-38	27¢ Art of Disney: Imagination, set of 4	7.00	7.75	7.75
UX538a	same, complete booklet of 20	....	38.00	....

UX488

2007

UX488	26¢ Pineapple	1.95	.95	.95

UX539

Great Lakes Dunes

UX539	Vesper Sparrow
UX540	Piping Plover
UX541	Easter Hognose Snake
UX542	Common Meransers
UX543	Piping Plover Nestlings
UX544	Red Fox
UX545	Tiger Beetle
UX546	White Footed Mouse
UX547	Spotted Sandpiper
UX548	Red Admiral Butterfly

UX539-48	42¢ Great Lakes Dunes postal cards	....	35.00	....

SCOTT NO.	DESCRIPTION	FIRST DAY COVER	MINT	USED

Automobiles of the 1950's

UX549	1957 Lincoln Premiere
UX550	1957 Chrysler 300C
UX551	1959 Cadillac Eldorado
UX552	1957 Studebaker Golden Hawk
UX553	1957 Pontiac Safari

UX549

| UX549-53 | 27¢ Automobiles of the 1950's, set of 5 | 9.75 | 9.50 | 9.50 |

UX554 **UX556**

2009

UX554	27¢ Miami University	2.75	.85	.85
UX555	28¢ Koi Fish Postal Card (white fish, orange & white fish)	1.75	.85	.85
UX556	28¢ Koi Fish Postal Card (black fish, red & white fish)	1.75	.85	.85

Simpsons

UX557	Homer
UX558	Marge
UX559	Bart
UX560	Lisa
UX561	Maggie

Gulf Coast Lighthouses

UX562	Matagorda Island
UX563	Sabine Pass
UX564	Biloxi
UX565	Sand Island
UX566	Fort Jefferson

UX559 **UX562**

| UX557-61 | 28¢ Simpsons Postal Card, set of 5 | 9.75 | 9.75 | 9.75 |
| UX562-66 | 28¢ Gulf Coast Lighthouses | 19.95 | 9.95 | 9.95 |

Early TV Memories

UX567	Alfred Hitchcock	UX577	Lassie
UX568	Burns & Allen	UX578	The Lone Ranger
UX569	Dinah Shore Show	UX579	Ozzie & Harriet
UX570	Dragnet	UX580	Perry Mason
UX571	Ed Sullivan Show	UX581	Phil Silvers Show
UX572	The Honeymooners	UX582	Red Skelton Show
UX573	Hopalong Cassidy	UX583	Texaco Star Theatre
UX574	Howdy Doody	UX584	The Tonight Show
UX575	I Love Lucy	UX585	The Twilight Zone
UX576	Kukla, Fran & Ollie	UX586	You Bet Your Life

UX575

| UX567-86 | 28¢ Early TV Memories, set of 20 | 60.00 | 39.00 | 39.00 |

Kelp Forest

UX587	Western Gull
UX588	Lion's Mane Nudibranch
UX589	Northern Kelp Crab
UX590	Vermillion Rockfish
UX591	Yellowtail Rockfish
UX592	Pacific Rock Crab
UX593	Harbor Seal
UX594	Brown Pelican
UX595	Treefish, Monterey Truban Snail
UX596	Copper Rockfish

UX587

| UX587-96 | 44¢ Kelp Forest, set of 10 postal cards | 32.50 | 25.00 | .... |

2010

Cowboys of the Silver Screen

UX597	Roy Rogers
UX598	Tom Mix
UX599	William S. Hart
UX600	Gene Autrey

UX597

| UX597-600 | 28¢ Cowboys of the Silver Screen Postal Cards | 9.75 | 8.50 | .... |

SCOTT NO.	DESCRIPTION	FIRST DAY COVER	MINT	USED

Scenic American Landscapes

UX601	Acadia
UX602	Badlands
UX603	Bryce Canyon
UX604	Grand Canyon
UX605	Great Smokey Mountains
UX606	Mount McKinley
UX607	Mount Rainier
UX608	St. John, U.S. Virgin Islands
UX609	Yosemite
UX610	Zion

UX606

| UX601-10 | 28¢ Scenic American Landscapes | 29.00 | 25.00 | .... |

2011

Hawaiian Rain Forest

UX611	Hawaii 'amakihi, Hawaii 'elepaio
UX612	'Akepa, 'ope'ape'a
UX613	'I'wi, haha
UX614	'Oma'o, kanawao, 'ohelo kau lau nui
UX615	'Oha
UX616	Pulehua, kelea lau nui, 'ilihia
UX617	Koele Mountain damselfly, 'akala
UX618	Apapane, Hawaiian Mint
UX619	Jewel Orchid
UX620	Happyface spider, 'ala'ala wai nui

UX614

| UX611-20 | 44¢ Hawaiian Rain Forest Postal Cards, set of 10 | 29.00 | 25.00 | .... |

Pixar: Send a Hello

UX622	Lightening McQueen & Mater
UX623	Remy the Rat & Linquini
UX624	Buzz Lightyear & Two Aliens
UX625	Carl Frederickson & Dug
UX626	Wall-E

UX621 **UX625**

| UX621 | 29¢ Common Terns | 2.75 | .75 | .75 |
| UX622-26 | 29¢ Pixar: Send a Hello Postal Cards | 15.00 | 10.00 | .... |

2012

Pixar: Mail a Smile

UX628	Flik and Dot
UX629	Bob & Dashiell Parr
UX630	Nemo & Squirt
UX631	Jessie, Woody and Bullseye
UX632	Boo, Mike Wazowskie & Sulley

UX627, UX633 **UX630**

UX627	32¢ Sailboat Postal Card	2.25	.75	.75
UX628-32	45¢ Pixar: Mail a Smile Postal Cards	15.00	9.50	....
UX633	32¢ Sailboat	2.25	.95	....
	same, sheet of 4	....	4.75	....

Scenic American Landscapes

UX634	13-Mile Woods
UX635	Glacier National Park
UX636	Grand Teton National Park
UX637	Hagatna Bay
UX638	Lancaster County, PA
UX639	Niagra Falls
UX640	Nine-Mile Prarie
UX641	Okefenokee Swamp
UX642	Rio Grande
UX643	Voyageurs National Park

UX639

| UX634-43 | 32¢ Scenic American Landscapes | .... | 17.50 | .... |

2013

UX644

| UX644 | 33¢ Deer | 2.25 | .95 | .95 |

SCOTT NO.	DESCRIPTION	FIRST DAY COVER	MINT	USED
	2014			
UX645	(34¢) Tree	2.50	.95	.95
	2015			
UX646	(35¢) Fanciful Flowers	3.00	.95	.95
	2017			
UX647	(34¢) Azulillo Chilean Blue Crocus	3.00	.95	0.95

AIR POST POSTAL CARDS

	1949			
UXC1	4¢ orange	2.50	.75	.90
	1958 No border on card			
UXC2	5¢ red	2.50	2.40	.90
	1960 **Type of 1958 re-engraved: with border on card**			
UXC3	5¢ red	2.50	7.95	4.75
	1963			
UXC4	6¢ red	2.50	1.25	3.00
	1966			
UXC5	11¢ SIPEX	1.75	.95	42.00
	1967			
UXC6	6¢ Virgin Islands	1.75	.95	12.50
UXC7	6¢ Boy Scout Jamboree	2.50	.95	18.00
UXC8	13¢ AAM Convention	1.75	1.75	46.00

SCOTT NO.	DESCRIPTION	FIRST DAY COVER	MINT	USED
	1968-71 Precancels			
UXC9	8¢ blue & red	1.75	.95	3.00
UXC9a	8¢ luminescent (1969)	20.00	3.00	4.00
UXC10	9¢ red & blue (1971)	1.75	.70	1.50
	1971 Inscribed U.S. Air Mail			
UXC11	15¢ Travel Service	1.75	2.25	57.00
	1972 **Issued with various designs on reverse**			
UXC12	9¢ Grand Canyon	1.75	.95	85.00
UXC13	15¢ Niagara Falls	1.75	.95	85.00
	1974			
UXC14	11¢ red & ultramarine	1.75	1.40	26.00
UXC15	18¢ Visit USA	1.75	1.40	34.00
	1975			
UXC16	21¢ Visit USA	1.75	1.00	41.00
	1978			
UXC17	21¢ Curtiss Jenny	1.75	1.40	41.00
	1979			
UXC18	21¢ Moscow Olympics	1.75	1.40	41.00
	1981			
UXC19	28¢ Pacific Flight	1.75	1.40	31.00
	1982			
UXC20	28¢ Gliders	1.75	1.40	36.00

SCOTT NO.	DESCRIPTION	FIRST DAY COVER	MINT	USED

UXC21

UXC22

1983

| UXC21 | 28¢ Olympics .... | 1.75 | 1.80 | 32.00 |

1985

| UXC22 | 33¢ China Clipper .... | 1.75 | 1.80 | 32.00 |

UXC23

UXC24

1986

| UXC23 | 33¢ Ameripex '86 .... | 1.75 | 1.35 | 32.00 |

1988

| UXC24 | 36¢ DC-3 .... | 1.75 | 1.25 | 32.00 |

UXC25

1991

| UXC25 | 40¢ Yankee Clipper .... | 1.75 | 1.35 | 32.00 |

UXC26

1995

| UXC26 | 50¢ Soaring Eagle .... | 1.75 | 1.25 | 22.50 |

UXC27

UXC28

1999

| UXC27 | 55¢ Mount Rainier, Washington .... | 1.75 | 1.75 | 32.00 |

2001

| UXC28 | 70¢ Badlands National Park, South Dakota............. | 2.25 | 2.25 | 22.50 |

SCOTT NO.	DESCRIPTION	MINT	UNUSED	USED

PAID REPLY POSTAL CARDS

UY1m, UY3m

UY2m, UY11m

UY4m

UY1r, UY3r

UY2r, UY11r

UY4r

PAID REPLY CARDS: Consist of two halves—one for your message and one for the other party to use to reply.

1892 Card Framed

UY1	1¢ & 1¢ unsevered	70.00	19.00	9.00
UY1m	1¢ black ....(Message)	8.00	4.00	2.00
UY1r	1¢ black .... (Reply)	8.00	4.00	2.00

1893

UY2	2¢ & 2¢ unsevered	32.00	18.00	22.00
UY2m	2¢ blue ....(Message)	7.00	5.00	6.50
UY2r	2¢ blue .... (Reply)	7.00	5.00	6.50

1898 Designs of 1892 Card Unframed

UY3	1¢ & 1¢ unsevered	115.00	18.00	15.00
UY3m	1¢ black ....(Message)	15.50	7.00	3.00
UY3r	1¢ black .... (Reply)	15.50	7.00	3.00

1904

UY4	1¢ & 1¢ unsevered	75.00	15.00	7.00
UY4m	1¢ black ....(Message)	12.00	6.00	1.20
UY4r	1¢ black .... (Reply)	12.00	6.00	1.20

UY5m, UY6m, UY7m, UY13m

UY8m

UY12m

UY5r, UY6r, UY7r, UY13r

UY8r

UY12r

1910

UY5	1¢ & 1¢ unsevered	275.00	55.00	26.00
UY5m	1¢ blue ....(Message)	16.00	10.00	4.00
UY5r	1¢ blue .... (Reply)	16.00	10.00	4.00

1911 Double Line Around Instructions

UY6	1¢ & 1¢ unsevered	270.00	90.00	25.00
UY6m	1¢ green ....(Message)	32.00	14.00	7.00
UY6r	1¢ green .... (Reply)	32.00	14.00	7.00

1915 Single Frame Line Around Instruction

UY7	1¢ & 1¢ unsevered	1.85	.95	.60
UY7m	1¢ green ....(Message)	.40	.30	.25
UY7r	1¢ green .... (Reply)	.40	.30	.25

1918

UY8	2¢ & 2¢ unsevered	155.00	42.00	45.00
UY8m	2¢ red ....(Message)	36.00	12.00	9.00
UY8r	2¢ red .... (Reply)	36.00	12.00	9.00

SCOTT NO.	DESCRIPTION	MINT	UNUSED	USED
	1920 UY8 Surcharged			
UY9	1¢/2¢ & 1¢/2¢ unsevered	34.00	14.00	12.00
UY9m	1¢ on 2¢ red .... (Message)	8.00	3.00	4.00
UY9r	1¢ on 2¢ red .... (Reply)	8.00	3.00	4.00
	1924 Designs of 1893			
UY11	2¢ & 2¢ unsevered	3.25	1.75	37.00
UY11m	2¢ red ....(Message)	1.00	.65	15.00
UY11r	2¢ red .... (Reply)	1.00	.65	15.00
	1926			
UY12	3¢ & 3¢ unsevered	16.50	8.00	30.00
UY12m	3¢ red ....(Message)	4.00	1.75	7.00
UY12r	3¢ red .... (Reply)	4.00	1.75	7.00

SCOTT NO.	DESCRIPTION	FIRST DAY COVER	MINT	USED
	1951 Design of 1910 Single Line Frame			
UY13	2¢ & 2¢ unsevered	2.50	2.50	2.25
UY13m	2¢ carmine ....(Message)	....	.70	1.00
UY13r	2¢ carmine .... (Reply)	....	.70	1.00
	1952			
	UY7 Surcharged by cancelling machine, light green			
UY14	2¢/1¢ & 2¢/1¢ unsevered	....	2.50	2.75
UY14m	2¢ on 1¢ green .... (Message)	....	.50	1.00
UY14r	2¢ on 1¢ green .... (Reply)	....	.50	1.00
	1952 UY7 Surcharge Typographed, dark green			
UY15	2¢/1¢ & 2¢/1¢ unsevered	....	164.00	50.00
UY15m	2¢ on 1¢ green .... (Message)	....	20.00	12.00
UY15r	2¢ on 1¢ green .... (Reply)	....	20.00	12.00
	1956 Design of UX45			
UY16	4¢ & 4¢ unsevered	1.75	1.60	80.00
UY16m	4¢ carmine ....(Message)	....	.55	40.00
UY16r	4¢ carmine .... (Reply)	....	.55	40.00
	1958 Design of UX46			
UY17	3¢ & 3¢ purple, unsevered	1.75	6.00	2.50
	1962 Design of UX48			
UY18	4¢ & 4¢ red violet, unsevered	1.75	7.00	2.75
	1963 Design of UX49			
UY19	7¢ & 7¢ unsevered	1.75	5.50	65.00
UY19m	7¢ blue & red .... (Message)	....	1.75	40.00
UY19r	7¢ blue & red .... (Reply)	....	1.75	40.00
	1967 Design of UX54			
UY20	8¢ & 8¢ unsevered	1.75	4.50	60.00
UY20m	8¢ blue & red .... (Message)	....	1.75	40.00
UY20r	8¢ blue & red .... (Reply)	....	1.75	40.00
	1968 Design of UX55			
UY21	5¢ & 5¢ emerald	1.75	2.50	2.00
	1971 Design of UX58			
UY22	6¢ & 6¢ brown	1.75	1.50	2.00
	1972 Design of UX64			
UY23	6¢ & 6¢ blue	1.75	1.60	2.00
	1973 Design of UX66			
UY24	8¢ & 8¢ orange	1.75	1.35	2.00
	1975			
UY25	7¢ & 7¢ design of UX68	1.75	1.35	9.00
UY26	9¢ & 9¢ design of UX69	1.75	1.35	2.00
	1976			
UY27	9¢ & 9¢ design of UX70	1.75	1.35	2.00
	1977			
UY28	9¢ & 9¢ design of UX72	1.75	1.75	2.00
	1978			
UY29	(10¢ & 10¢) design of UX74	3.00	9.00	10.00
UY30	10¢ & 10¢ design of UX75	1.75	1.75	.40

SCOTT NO.	DESCRIPTION	FIRST DAY COVER	MINT	USED
UY31	(12¢ & 12¢) "B" Eagle, design of UX88	1.75	1.75	2.05
UY32	12¢ & 12¢ light blue, design of UX89	1.75	5.75	2.05
UY33	(13¢ & 13¢) buff, design of UX92	1.75	3.75	2.05
UY34	13¢ & 13¢ buff, design of UX93	1.75	2.00	.25
	1985			
UY35	(14¢ & 14¢) Carroll, design of UX105	1.75	4.75	2.05
UY36	14¢ & 14¢ Carroll, design of UX106	1.75	1.85	2.05
UY37	14¢ & 14¢ Wythe, design of UX108	1.75	1.50	2.05
	1987 -1988			
UY38	14¢ & 14¢ Flag, design of UX117	1.75	1.65	2.25
UY39	15¢ & 15¢ America the Beautiful, design of UX120	1.75	1.50	1.60
	1991			
UY40	19¢ & 19¢ Flag, design of UX153	1.75	1.65	1.50
	1995			
UY41	20¢ & 20¢ Red Barn, design of UX198	1.75	1.65	1.25
	1999			
UY42	20¢ & 20¢ Block Island Lighthouse, design of UX306	1.75	1.65	1.25
	2001-09			
UY43	21¢ & 21¢ White Barn, design of UX375	1.75	1.85	1.50
UY44	23¢ & 23¢ Carlsbad Caverns, design of UX381	1.75	1.85	1.50
UY45	24¢ & 24¢ Zebulon Pike Expedition, design of UX449	1.75	1.85	1.50
UY46	26¢ & 26¢ Pineapple, design of UX488	1.75	1.85	1.50
UY47	27¢ Corinthian Column double-reply postal card	3.75	1.75	1.50
UY48	28¢ Koi Fish reply card	3.50	1.75	1.40
	2011-2012			
UY49	29¢+29¢ Common Terns Postal Reply Card	4.50	1.75	1.75
UY50	32¢+32¢ Sailboat Postal & Reply Card	4.75	1.60	1.75
	2013-2014			
UY51	33¢+33¢ Deer Postal Reply Card	4.75	1.75	1.75
UY52	34¢ + 34¢ tree	4.75	1.75	2.50
	2015			
UY53	35¢ Fanciful Flowers Reply Card	4.75	1.95	2.00
	2017			
UY54	(34¢)+(34¢) Azulillo Chilean Blue Crocus	4.75	1.95	2.00

OFFICIAL POSTAL CARDS

UZ1

UZ2

UZ3

SCOTT NO.	DESCRIPTION	FIRST DAY COVER	MINT	USED
	1913			
UZ1	1¢ black (Printed Address)	......	755.00	495.00
	1983			
UZ2	13¢ Great Seal	1.75	.95	100.00
	1985			
UZ3	14¢ Great Seal	1.75	.95	90.00

UZ4

UZ5

UZ6

SCOTT NO.	DESCRIPTION	FIRST DAY COVER	MINT	USED
	1988			
UZ4	15¢ Great Seal	1.75	.95	100.00
	1991			
UZ5	19¢ Great Seal	1.75	1.10	100.00
	1995			
UZ6	20¢ Great Seal	1.75	1.10	100.00

SCOTT NO.	DESCRIPTION	IMPERFORATE (a) F	AVG	PART PERF. (b) F	AVG	PERFORATED (c) F	AVG

1862-71 First Issue

When ordering from this issue be sure to indicate whether the "a", "b" or "c" variety is wanted. Example: R27c. Prices are for used singles.

R1-R4   R5-R15   R16-R42

Scott	Description	Imperf F	Imperf AVG	Part Perf F	Part Perf AVG	Perf F	Perf AVG
R1	1¢ Express	75.00	58.00	48.00	35.00	1.50	1.15
R2	1¢ Playing Cards	2200.00	1700.00	1600.00	1100.00	195.00	120.00
R3	1¢ Proprietary	1100.00	900.00	275.00	200.00	.60	.40
R4	1¢ Telegraph	600.00	425.00	....	....	18.00	14.00
R5	2¢ Bank Check, blue	1.50	1.15	5.00	2.50	.60	.40
R6	2¢ Bank Check, orange	....	....	60.00	41.25	.30	.20
R7	2¢ Certificate, blue	15.00	11.00	....	....	31.00	22.00
R8	2¢ Certificate, orange	....	....	....	....	43.00	25.00
R9	2¢ Express, blue	15.00	11.00	30.00	28.00	.50	.35
R10	2¢ Express, orange	....	....	1800.00	1200.00	13.00	10.00
R11	2¢ Playing Cards, blue	1500.00	....	270.00	175.00	5.00	3.00
R12	2¢ Playing Cards, orange	....	....	....	....	50.00	38.00
R13	2¢ Proprietary, blue	975.00	610.00	315.00	185.00	.50	.40
R14	2¢ Proprietary, orange	....	....	....	....	60.00	40.00
R15	2¢ U.S. Internal Revenue	....	....	....	....	.40	.35
R16	3¢ Foreign Exchange	....	....	800.00	550.00	5.00	3.25
R17	3¢ Playing Cards	40,000	....	....	....	165.00	115.00
R18	3¢ Proprietary	....	....	800.00	500.00	8.00	6.50
R19	3¢ Telegraph	85.00	63.00	28.00	19.50	3.00	2.10
R20	4¢ Inland Exchange	....	....	....	....	2.25	1.45
R21	4¢ Playing Cards	....	....	....	....	705.00	430.00
R22	4¢ Proprietary	....	....	525.00	325.00	8.00	6.75
R23	5¢ Agreement	....	....	....	....	.50	.40
R24	5¢ Certificate	3.50	2.25	14.00	9.00	.50	.40
R25	5¢ Express	6.50	3.75	7.00	5.50	.50	.40
R26	5¢ Foreign Exchange	....	....	....	....	.50	.40
R27	5¢ Inland Exchange	8.50	6.50	6.50	4.50	.60	.40
R28	5¢ Playing Cards	....	....	....	....	36.00	26.00
R29	5¢ Proprietary	....	....	....	....	24.00	16.00
R30	6¢ Inland Exchange	....	....	....	....	2.00	1.35
R32	10¢ Bill of Lading	50.00	38.00	400.00	325.00	1.75	1.25
R33	10¢ Certificate	300.00	210.00	815.00	540.00	.35	.25
R34	10¢ Contract, blue	....	....	495.00	295.00	.60	.40
R35	10¢ Foreign Exchange	....	....	....	....	12.00	9.00
R36	10¢ Inland Exchange	395.00	250.00	5.00	3.25	.40	.25
R37	10¢ Power of Attorney	895.00	560.00	28.00	19.00	1.00	.65
R38	10¢ Proprietary	....	....	....	....	18.00	12.00
R39	15¢ Foreign Exchange	....	....	....	....	15.00	12.00
R40	15¢ Inland Exchange	38.00	27.00	13.00	9.00	2.00	1.50
R41	20¢ Foreign Exchange	80.00	55.00	....	....	65.00	48.00
R42	20¢ Inland Exchange	16.00	10.00	21.00	15.00	.50	.35

R43-R53   R54-R65   R66-R76

Scott	Description	Imperf F	Imperf AVG	Part Perf F	Part Perf AVG	Perf F	Perf AVG
R43	25¢ Bond	245.00	185.00	7.00	5.00	3.75	2.85
R44	25¢ Certificate	11.00	8.00	7.00	5.00	.60	.40
R45	25¢ Entry of Goods	21.00	12.50	235.00	150.00	1.40	1.10
R46	25¢ Insurance	12.00	9.00	15.00	12.00	.35	.25
R47	25¢ Life Insurance	47.00	35.00	800.00	600.00	10.00	7.00
R48	25¢ Power of Attorney	8.00	5.50	35.00	25.00	1.25	.75
R49	25¢ Protest	35.00	25.00	860.00	625.00	8.00	6.00
R50	25¢ Warehouse Receipt	50.00	35.00	850.00	670.00	45.00	35.00
R51	30¢ Foreign Exchange	175.00	95.00	8200.00	5000.00	55.00	39.00
R52	30¢ Inland Exchange	65.00	52.00	75.00	50.00	9.00	7.75
R53	40¢ Inland Exchange	2300.00	1500.00	9.00	6.50	8.00	4.75
R54	50¢ Conveyance, blue	18.00	12.00	3.50	2.75	.40	.30
R55	50¢ Entry of Goods	....	....	15.00	10.00	.50	.35
R56	50¢ Foreign Exchange	60.00	40.00	110.00	80.00	7.00	5.00
R57	50¢ Lease	30.00	21.00	170.00	110.00	10.00	7.00
R58	50¢ Life Insurance	45.00	30.00	155.00	95.00	2.00	1.40
R59	50¢ Mortgage	22.00	16.00	5.00	4.00	.70	.50
R60	50¢ Original Process	6.00	4.00	600.00	400.00	1.10	.90
R61	50¢ Passage Ticket	110.00	85.00	400.00	255.00	2.25	1.55
R62	50¢ Probate of Will	52.00	42.00	200.00	135.00	20.00	13.00
R63	50¢ Surety Bond, blue	275.00	185.00	3.00	2.10	.40	.25
R64	60¢ Inland Exchange	110.00	75.00	95.00	55.00	9.00	7.25
R65	70¢ Foreign Exchange	575.00	450.00	165.00	125.00	13.00	9.00

Scott	Description	Imperf F	Imperf AVG	Part Perf F	Part Perf AVG	Perf F	Perf AVG
R66	$1 Conveyance	26.00	20.00	2200.00	1350.00	27.50	18.50
R6	$1 Entry of Goods	44.00	32.00	....	....	2.50	2.10
R68	$1 Foreign Exchange	85.00	60.00	....	....	.90	.50
R69	$1 Inland Exchange	16.00	10.00	3200.00	1700.00	.75	.60
R70	$1 Lease	43.00	32.00	....	....	4.00	3.00
R71	$1 Life Insurance	200.00	165.00	....	....	10.00	8.00
R72	$1 Manifest	49.50	33.00	....	....	38.00	26.50
R73	$1 Mortgage	28.00	19.00	....	....	225.00	155.00
R74	$1 Passage Ticket	310.00	210.00	....	....	275.00	210.00
R75	$1 Power of Attorney	85.00	65.00	....	....	3.00	2.00
R76	$1 Probate of Will	85.00	65.00	....	....	55.00	42.50

R77-R80   R81-R87

Scott	Description	Imperf F	Imperf AVG	Part Perf F	Part Perf AVG	Perf F	Perf AVG
R77	$1.30 Foreign Exchange	8000.00	....	....	....	82.00	59.00
R78	$1.50 Inland Exchange	30.00	21.00	....	....	6.50	5.00
R79	$1.60 Foreign Exchange	1250.00	950.00	....	....	120.00	85.00
R80	$1.90 Foreign Exchange	10000.00	....	....	....	115.00	86.00
R81	$2 Conveyance	195.00	135.00	2100.00	1500.00	4.00	3.00
R82	$2 Mortgage	135.00	95.00	....	....	7.00	5.00
R83	$2 Probate of Will	6000.00	4800.00	....	....	75.00	64.00
R84	$2.50 Inland Exchange	8000.00	6500.00	....	....	22.00	18.00
R85	$3 Charter Party	185.00	125.00	....	....	11.00	9.00
R86	$2 Manifest	165.00	105.00	....	....	52.00	38.00
R87	$3.50 Inland Exchange	7000.00	....	....	....	70.00	53.00

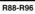

R88-R96   R97-R101

Scott	Description	Imperf F	Imperf AVG	Part Perf F	Part Perf AVG	Perf F	Perf AVG
R88	$5 Charter Party	300.00	225.00	....	....	10.00	8.00
R89	$5 Conveyance	42.00	35.00	....	....	11.00	8.00
R90	$5 Manifest	185.00	125.00	....	....	90.00	65.00
R91	$5 Mortgage	160.00	135.00	....	....	25.00	17.50
R92	$5 Probate of Will	675.00	550.00	....	....	25.00	17.50
R93	$10 Charter Party	750.00	550.00	....	....	35.00	25.00
R94	$10 Conveyance	125.00	95.00	....	....	75.00	50.00
R95	$10 Mortgage	750.00	550.00	....	....	35.00	25.00
R96	$10 Probate of Will	2100.00	1600.00	....	....	42.00	32.00
R97	$15 Mortgage, blue	2300.00	2100.00	....	....	255.00	180.00
R98	$20 Conveyance	150.00	100.00	....	....	115.00	85.00
R99	$20 Probate of Will	2100.00	1500.00	....	....	2100.00	1500.00
R100	$25 Mortgage	1825.00	1250.00	....	....	185.00	125.00
R101	$50 U.S. Internal Revenue	275.00	195.00	....	....	175.00	150.00

R102

Scott	Description	Imperf F	Imperf AVG	Part Perf F	Part Perf AVG	Perf F	Perf AVG
R102	$200 U.S. Internal Revenue	2350.00	1850.00	....	....	2250.00	800.00

SCOTT NO.	DESCRIPTION	F	USED AVG

R103, R104, R134, R135, R151

R112-R114

R115-R117, R142-R143

R105-R111, R136-R139

1871 SECOND ISSUE

NOTE: The individual denominations vary in design from the illustrations shown which are more typical of their relative size.

Scott No.	Description	F	AVG
R103	1¢ blue and black	82.00	72.00
R104	2¢ blue and black	2.50	2.25
R105	3¢ blue and black	52.00	37.00
R106	4¢ blue and black	140.00	90.00
R107	5¢ blue and black	1.75	1.00
R108	6¢ blue and black	205.00	130.00
R109	10¢ blue and black	1.60	1.20
R110	15¢ blue and black	90.00	55.00
R111	20¢ blue and black	10.00	8.00
R112	25¢ blue and black	1.50	.85
R113	30¢ blue and black	130.00	75.00
R114	40¢ blue and black	110.00	70.00
R115	50¢ blue and black	1.35	.85
R116	60¢ blue and black	200.00	155.00
R117	70¢ blue and black	90.00	75.00

R118-R122, R144

R123-R126, R145-R147

Scott No.	Description	F	AVG
R118	$1 blue and black	9.25	7.00
R119	$1.30 blue and black	625.00	525.00
R120	$1.50 blue and black	20.00	14.00
R121	$1.60 blue and black	650.00	525.00
R122	$1.90 blue and black	410.00	300.00
R123	$2.00 blue and black	21.00	15.00
R124	$2.50 blue and black	50.00	30.00
R125	$3.00 blue and black	65.00	40.00
R126	$3.50 blue and black	440.00	325.00

R127, R128, R148, R149

R129-R131, R150

SCOTT NO.	DESCRIPTION	F	USED AVG
R127	$5 blue and black	32.50	20.00
R128	$10 blue and black	225.00	155.00
R129	$20 blue and black	875.00	525.00
R130	$25 blue and black	925.00	650.00
R131	$50 blue and black	1050.00	660.00

1871-72 THIRD ISSUE

Scott No.	Description	F	AVG
R134	1¢ claret and black	58.00	40.00
R135	2¢ orange and black	.40	.25
R135b	2¢ orange and black (center inverted)	500.00	450.00
R136	4¢ brown and black	77.00	57.00
R137	5¢ orange and black	.40	.25
R138	6¢ orange and black	85.00	64.00
R139	15¢ brown and black	22.00	17.00
R140	30¢ orange and black	32.00	26.00
R141	40¢ brown and black	80.00	65.00
R142	60¢ orange and black	110.00	85.00
R143	70¢ green and black	85.00	60.00
R144	$1 green and black	3.75	2.50
R145	$2 vermillion and black	40.00	30.00
R146	$2.50 claret and black	100.00	70.00
R147	$3 green and black	80.00	65.00
R148	$5 vermillion and black	40.00	30.00
R149	$10 green and black	310.00	185.00
R150	$20 orange and black	800.00	635.00

1874 on greenish paper

Scott No.	Description	F	AVG
R151	2¢ orange and black	.40	.25
R151a	2¢ orange and black (center inverted)	650.00	600.00

SCOTT NO.	DESCRIPTION	UNUSED F	AVG	USED F	AVG

R152 *Liberty*

R153 surcharge

R154, R155 surcharge

1875-78

Scott No.	Description	Unused F	AVG	Used F	AVG
R152a	2¢ blue on blue silk paper	....	....	.50	.40
R152b	2¢ watermarked ("USIR") paper	....	....	.40	.30
R152c	2¢ watermarked, rouletted	....	....	35.00	24.00

1898 Postage Stamps 279 & 267 Surcharged

Scott No.	Description	Unused F	AVG	Used F	AVG
R153	1¢ green, small I.R.	5.00	3.50	3.00	2.10
R154	1¢ green, large I.R.	.40	.30	.40	.30
R155	2¢ carmine, large I.R.	.40	.30	.40	.30

DOCUMENTARY STAMPS
Newspaper Stamp PR121 Surcharged

INT. REV.
$5.
DOCUMENTARY.

Scott No.	Description	Unused F	AVG	Used F	AVG
R159	$5 dark blue, red surcharge reading down	475.00	350.00	210.00	175.00
R160	$5 dark blue, red surcharge reading up	150.00	110.00	115.00	95.00

R161-R172

R173-R178, R182, R183

1898 Battleships Inscribed "Documentary"

Scott No.	Description	Unused F	AVG	Used F	AVG
R161	1/2¢ orange	4.00	3.00	20.00	15.00
R162	1/2¢ dark gray	.40	.30	.35	.30
R163	1¢ pale blue	.40	.30	.35	.30
R164	2¢ carmine	.40	.30	.45	.35
R165	3¢ dark blue	3.95	2.10	.45	.35
R166	4¢ pale rose	2.00	1.40	.45	.35
R167	5¢ lilac	.65	.45	.40	.45
R168	10¢ dark brown	2.00	1.40	.35	.30
R169	25¢ purple brown	4.35	4.00	.50	.40
R170	40¢ blue lilac (cut cancel .40)	125.00	90.00	1.50	1.00
R171	50¢ slate violet	36.00	18.00	.35	.30
R172	80¢ bistre (cut cancel .25)	110.00	80.00	.40	.30
R173	$1 dark green	22.00	16.00	.30	.25
R174	$3 dark brown (cut cancel .25)	40.00	28.00	1.00	.70
R175	$5 orange red (cut cancel .25)	66.00	48.00	2.00	1.40
R176	$10 black (cut cancel .70)	145.00	90.00	4.00	2.75
R177	$30 red (cut cancel 50.00)	460.00	350.00	160.00	110.00
R178	$50 gray brown (cut cancel 2.50)	260.00	210.00	6.00	3.95

SCOTT NO.	DESCRIPTION	UNUSED F	AVG	USED F	AVG

R179, R225, R246, R248   R180, R226, R249   R181, R224, R227, R247, R250

1899 Various Portraits Inscribed "Series of 1898"

R179	$100 yellow brown & black ..... (cut cancel 25.00)	260.00	200.00	39.00	28.50
R180	$500 carmine lake & black.... (cut cancel 325.00)	1400.00	1100.00	850.00	550.00
R181	$1000 green & black .... (cut cancel 150.00)	1300.00	675.00	385.00	300.00

1900

R182	$1 carmine .... (cut cancel .40)	38.00	29.00	.75	.50
R183	$3 lake .... (cut cancel 9.00)	300.00	225.00	55.00	42.00

R184-R189   R190-R194

Designs of R173-78 surcharged

R184	$1 gray...................................... (cut cancel .25)	31.00	21.00	.40	.25
R185	$2 gray...................................... (cut cancel .25)	31.00	21.00	.40	.25
R186	$3 gray...................................... (cut cancel 5.00)	130.00	85.00	16.00	12.00
R187	$5 gray...................................... (cut cancel 1.50)	75.00	55.00	10.00	7.50
R188	$10 gray.................................... (cut cancel 4.00)	200.00	120.00	22.00	15.00
R189	$50 gray............................... (cut cancel 130.00)	1875.00	1400.00	550.00	375.00

1902

R190	$1 green................................... (cut cancel .35)	44.00	33.00	4.00	3.00
R191	$2 green................................... (cut cancel .35)	44.00	33.00	2.00	1.25
R191a	$2 surcharged as R185	125.00	85.00	85.00	60.00
R192	$5 green................................... (cut cancel 5.00)	200.00	140.00	38.00	29.00
R192a	$5 surcharge omitted	250.00	170.00	......	......
R193	$10 green............................. (cut cancel 50.00)	450.00	300.00	145.00	95.00
R194	$50 green........................... (cut cancel 275.00)	2500.00	1900.00	1100.00	795.00

R195-R216   R217-R223

1914 Inscribed "Series of 1914"
Single Line Watermark "USPS"

R195	1/2¢ rose..	14.00	10.00	5.00	3.50
R196	1¢ rose..	2.50	1.75	.40	.25
R197	2¢ rose..	4.00	3.00	.40	.25
R198	3¢ rose..	77.00	55.00	35.00	25.00
R199	4¢ rose..	23.00	17.00	2.25	1.50
R200	5¢ rose..	10.00	7.00	.50	.35
R201	10¢ rose..	8.00	6.00	.35	.25
R202	25¢ rose..	48.00	34.00	.70	.45
R203	40¢ rose..	32.00	24.00	3.00	2.00
R204	50¢ rose..	13.00	10.00	.35	.25
R205	80¢ rose..	210.00	160.00	15.50	12.00

1914 Double Line Watermark "USIR"

R206	1/2¢ rose..	2.00	1.40	.65	.45
R207	1¢ rose..	.35	.25	.30	.20
R208	2¢ rose..	.40	.25	.30	.25
R209	3¢ rose..	2.00	1.40	.35	.25
R210	4¢ rose..	4.50	3.00	.60	.40
R211	5¢ rose..	2.00	1.40	.40	.25
R212	10¢ rose..	.90	.60	.30	.25
R213	25¢ rose..	8.00	6.00	1.75	1.20
R214	40¢ rose.............................. (cut cancel .60)	120.00	85.00	15.00	10.00
R215	50¢ rose..	26.00	18.00	.35	.25
R216	80¢ rose.............................. (cut cancel 1.25)	175.00	115.00	28.00	21.00
R217	$1 green............................... (cut cancel .30)	62.00	48.00	.55	.40
R218	$2 carmine........................... (cut cancel .25)	82.00	58.00	.85	.60
R219	$3 purple.............................. (cut cancel 1.00)	110.00	80.00	4.00	2.75
R220	$5 blue.................................. (cut cancel .60)	95.00	70.00	4.00	2.75
R221	$10 orange............................ (cut cancel 1.00)	210.00	155.00	6.00	4.00
R222	$30 vermillion....................... (cut cancel 5.50)	675.00	500.00	20.00	14.00
R223	$50 violet .... (cut cancel 375.00)	1700.00	1275.00	1100.00	800.00

SCOTT NO.	DESCRIPTION	UNUSED F	AVG	USED F	AVG

1914-15 Various Portraits Inscribed "Series of 1914" or "Series of 1915"

R224	$60 brown ....(cut cancel 70.00)	200.00	140.00	150.00	100.00
R225	$100 green.............................(cut cancel 17.00)	68.00	50.00	45.00	30.00
R226	$500 blue ....(cut cancel 275.00)	......	......	650.00	450.00
R227	$1000 orange.......................(cut cancel 300.00)	......	......	700.00	400.00

R228-239, 251-256, R260-263

1917 Perf. 11

R228	1¢ carmine rose	.40	.30	.25	.20
R229	2¢ carmine rose	.30	.25	.25	.20
R230	3¢ carmine rose	1.85	1.35	.50	.35
R231	4¢ carmine rose	.85	.70	.30	.25
R232	5¢ carmine rose	.40	.35	.25	.20
R233	8¢ carmine rose	2.75	2.00	.40	.25
R234	10¢ carmine rose	2.00	1.60	.40	.30
R235	20¢ carmine rose	.80	.55	.30	.25
R236	25¢ carmine rose	1.50	1.00	.30	.25
R237	40¢ carmine rose	2.50	1.50	.50	.35
R238	50¢ carmine rose	2.75	1.75	.25	.20
R239	80¢ carmine rose	8.00	6.00	.30	.25

R240-245, R257-259

Same design as issue of 1914-15 Without dates.

R240	$1 yellow green.......................................	8.50	6.50	.30	.25
R241	$2 rose	14.00	10.00	.25	.20
R242	$3 violet .... (cut cancel .30)	55.00	43.00	1.25	.85
R243	$4 yellow brown .... (cut cancel .30)	38.00	28.00	2.00	1.40
R244	$5 dark blue .... (cut cancel .30)	23.00	17.00	.50	.35
R245	$10 orange.............................. (cut cancel .30)	48.00	38.00	1.50	1.00

Types of 1899 Various Portraits Perf. 12

R246	$30 deep orange, Grant............(cut cancel 2.50)	50.00	35.00	15.00	10.00
R247	$60 brown, Lincoln..................(cut cancel 1.00)	60.00	40.00	8.00	5.50
R248	$100 green, Washington............(cut cancel .45)	40.00	27.00	1.25	.80
R249	$500 blue, Hamilton ....(cut cancel 15.00)	325.00	225.00	40.00	28.00
R249a	$500 Numerals in orange	400.00	275.00	60.00	40.00
R250	$1000 orange, Madison (Perf. In. 3.00) ....(cut cancel 3.50)	160.00	100.00	13.00	8.00

1928-29 Perf. 10

R251	1¢ carmine rose	2.25	1.50	1.80	1.20
R252	2¢ carmine rose	.75	.55	.40	.30
R253	4¢ carmine rose	8.00	5.00	5.00	3.50
R254	5¢ carmine rose	1.80	1.20	.75	.50
R255	10¢ carmine rose	2.75	1.85	1.50	1.00
R256	20¢ carmine rose	7.00	5.00	6.00	4.00
R257	$1 green............................... (cut cancel 2.00)	175.00	120.00	40.00	27.00
R258	$2 rose	75.00	50.00	3.00	2.00
R259	$10 orange............................ (cut cancel 7.00)	250.00	175.00	50.00	35.00

1929-30 Perf. 11 x 10

R260	2¢ carmine rose	4.00	2.75	3.00	2.00
R261	5¢ carmine rose	3.00	2.00	2.25	1.60
R262	10¢ carmine rose	10.50	7.00	8.00	5.00
R263	20¢ carmine rose	17.00	11.00	9.00	6.00

SCOTT NO.	DESCRIPTION	PLATE BLOCK F/NH	UNUSED F/NH	USED F

R733, R734

1962 CENTENNIAL INTERNAL REVENUE. Inscribed "Established 1862"

R733	10¢ violet blue & green...............	19.50	1.35	.50

1964 Without Inscription Date

R734	10¢ violet blue & green...............	34.00	5.00	.75

SCOTT NO.	DESCRIPTION	VIOLET PAPER (a) F	AVG	GREEN PAPER (b) F	AVG

PROPRIETARY STAMPS

RB1-2

RB3-7

1871-74 Perforated 12

SCOTT NO.	DESCRIPTION	VIOLET PAPER (a) F	AVG	GREEN PAPER (b) F	AVG
RB1	1¢ green & black	7.00	5.00	13.00	8.00
RB2	2¢ green & black	8.00	6.00	28.00	20.00
RB3	3¢ green & black	25.00	17.00	65.00	40.00
RB4	4¢ green & black	15.00	10.00	24.00	16.00
RB5	5¢ green & black	160.00	110.00	195.00	120.00
RB6	6¢ green & black	60.00	40.00	125.00	85.00
RB7	10¢ green & black	240.00	165.00	65.00	45.00
RB8	50¢ green & black (large)	900.00	600.00	750.00	550.00

SCOTT NO.	DESCRIPTION	SILK PAPER (a) F	AVG	WMKD PERF. (b) F	AVG	ROULETTE (c) F	AVG

RB11-12

RB13-19

SCOTT NO.	DESCRIPTION	SILK PAPER (a) F	AVG	WMKD PERF. (b) F	AVG	ROULETTE (c) F	AVG
RB11	1¢ green	2.50	1.90	.50	.35	135.00	100.00
RB12	2¢ brown	2.75	1.85	1.70	1.00	155.00	95.00
RB13	3¢ orange	14.00	10.00	4.50	3.50	130.00	95.00
RB14	4¢ red brown	11.00	8.00	10.00	6.00		
RB15	4¢ red			7.00	4.00	260.00	200.00
RB16	5¢ black	180.00	140.00	130.00	90.00		1800.00
RB17	6¢ violet blue	38.00	29.00	26.00	19.00	495.00	275.00
RB18	6¢ violet			37.00	28.00	500.00	350.00
RB19	10¢ blue			350.00	250.00		

SCOTT NO.	DESCRIPTION	UNUSED F	AVG	USED F	AVG

RB20-31

RB32-64

RB65-73

1898 Battleship Inscribed "Proprietary"

SCOTT NO.	DESCRIPTION	UNUSED F	AVG	USED F	AVG
RB20	1/8¢ yellow green	.35	.25	.35	.25
RB21	1/4¢ brown	.35	.25	.25	.20
RB22	3/8¢ deep orange	.30	.25	.50	.40
RB23	5/8¢ deep ultramarine	.30	.25	.30	.25
RB24	1¢ dark green	2.25	1.50	.30	.25
RB25	1-1/4¢ violet	.30	.25	.30	.25
RB26	1-7/8¢ dull blue	16.00	12.00	2.25	1.80
RB27	2¢ violet brown	1.50	1.00	.40	.30
RB28	2-1/2¢ lake	4.50	3.15	.30	.25
RB29	3-3/4¢ olive gray	45.00	30.00	16.00	12.00
RB30	4¢ purple	17.00	12.00	1.60	1.10
RB31	5¢ brown orange	17.00	12.00	1.60	1.10

1914 Watermarked "USPS"

SCOTT NO.	DESCRIPTION	UNUSED F	AVG	USED F	AVG
RB32	1/8¢ black	.30	.25	.30	.25
RB33	1/4¢ black	3.30	2.55	1.60	1.00
RB34	3/8¢ black	.40	.30	.30	.25
RB35	5/8¢ black	6.50	5.00	3.00	2.75
RB36	1-1/4¢ black	5.00	3.50	2.00	1.25
RB37	1-7/8¢ black	60.00	48.00	21.00	15.00
RB38	2-1/2¢ black	14.00	10.00	4.00	2.75
RB39	3-1/8¢ black	130.00	90.00	65.00	45.00
RB40	3-3/4¢ black	62.00	35.00	26.00	19.00
RB41	4¢ black	77.00	55.00	42.00	32.00
RB43	5¢ black	155.00	115.00	105.00	85.00

1914 Watermarked "USIR"

SCOTT NO.	DESCRIPTION	UNUSED F	AVG	USED F	AVG
RB44	1/8¢ black	.40	.30	.30	.25
RB45	1/4¢ black	.30	.25	.30	.25
RB46	3/8¢ black	.80	.60	.50	.40
RB47	1/2¢ black	4.00	2.75	3.50	2.50
RB48	5/8¢ black	.30	.25	.30	.25
RB49	1¢ black	6.00	9.50	6.00	4.50
RB50	1-1/4¢ black	.75	.60	.45	.35
RB51	1-1/2¢ black	4.50	3.50	3.00	2.00
RB52	1-7/8¢ black	1.40	1.00	1.00	.80
RB53	2¢ black	7.00	5.50	6.00	4.00

SCOTT NO.	DESCRIPTION	UNUSED F	AVG	USED F	AVG
RB54	2-1/2¢ black	1.80	1.30	2.00	1.40
RB55	3¢ black	5.50	4.00	4.00	3.00
RB56	3-1/8¢ black	7.00	5.00	5.00	4.00
RB57	3-3/4¢ black	17.00	11.00	11.00	8.00
RB58	4¢ black	.60	.50	.30	.25
RB59	4-3/8¢ black	19.00	13.00	11.00	8.00
RB60	5¢ black	4.50	3.50	4.00	3.00
RB61	6¢ black	72.00	60.00	48.00	35.00
RB62	8¢ black	26.00	16.00	15.00	11.00
RB63	10¢ black	17.00	13.00	10.00	7.00
RB64	20¢ black	33.00	23.00	22.00	16.00

1919 Offset Printing

SCOTT NO.	DESCRIPTION	UNUSED F	AVG	USED F	AVG
RB65	1¢ dark blue	.35	.25	.25	.20
RB66	2¢ dark blue	.40	.30	.30	.25
RB67	3¢ dark blue	1.60	1.20	.85	.65
RB68	4¢ dark blue	2.50	2.00	.80	.60
RB69	5¢ dark blue	3.25	2.00	1.40	1.00
RB70	8¢ dark blue	22.00	16.00	14.00	11.00
RB71	10¢ dark blue	10.00	8.00	4.00	2.75
RB72	20¢ dark blue	15.00	12.00	6.00	4.00
RB73	40¢ dark blue	58.00	45.00	15.00	11.00

FUTURE

FUTURE DELIVERY STAMPS

Documentary Stamps of 1917 Overprinted

DELIVERY — Type I   **DELIVERY** — Type II

1918-34 Perforated 11, Type I Overprint Lines 8mm. Apart

SCOTT NO.	DESCRIPTION	UNUSED F	AVG	USED F	AVG
RC1	2¢ carmine rose	8.00	5.00	.30	.25
RC2	3¢ carmine rose (cut cancel 13.50)	42.00	32.00	35.00	29.00
RC3	4¢ carmine rose	13.00	9.00	.30	.25
RC3A	5¢ carmine rose	95.00	60.00	4.00	2.75
RC4	10¢ carmine rose	22.00	15.00	.30	.25
RC5	20¢ carmine rose	35.00	25.00	.30	.25
RC6	25¢ carmine rose (cut cancel .25)	65.00	45.00	.75	.55
RC7	40¢ carmine rose (cut cancel .25)	75.00	50.00	.75	.55
RC8	50¢ carmine rose	16.00	11.00	.30	.25
RC9	80¢ carmine rose (cut cancel 1.00)	145.00	95.00	10.00	7.00
RC10	$1 green (cut cancel .25)	60.00	45.00	.30	.25
RC11	$2 rose (cut cancel .25)	65.00	45.00	.30	.25
RC12	$3 violet (cut cancel .30)	185.00	145.00	4.00	3.25
RC13	$5 dark blue (cut cancel .25)	110.00	90.00	.75	.50
RC14	$10 orange (cut cancel .25)	135.00	95.00	1.50	1.00
RC15	$20 olive bistre (cut cancel .75)	350.00	220.00	8.00	6.00

Perforated 12

SCOTT NO.	DESCRIPTION	UNUSED F	AVG	USED F	AVG
RC16	$30 vermillon (cut cancel 2.00)	110.00	85.00	7.00	5.00
RC17	$50 olive green (cut cancel 2.00)	90.00	75.00	6.00	5.00
RC18	$60 brown (cut cancel 1.25)	120.00	90.00	9.00	7.00
RC19	$100 yellow green (cut cancel 8.00)	200.00	180.00	40.00	30.00
RC20	$500 blue (cut cancel 6.00)	225.00	130.00	16.00	12.00
RC21	$1000 orange (cut cancel 1.75)	185.00	150.00	8.00	6.00
RC22	1¢ carmine rose (lines 2mm apart)	1.20	.75	.30	.25
RC23	80¢ carmine rose (lines 2mm apart) (cut cancel .40)	190.00	150.00	3.50	2.00

1925-34 Perforated 11 Type II Overprint

SCOTT NO.	DESCRIPTION	UNUSED F	AVG	USED F	AVG
RC25	$1 green (cut cancel .10)	82.00	60.00	2.00	1.00
RC26	$10 orange (cut cancel 5.75)	220.00	170.00	26.00	22.00

STOCK

STOCK TRANSFER STAMPS

Documentary Stamps Overprinted

TRANSFER — Type I   **STOCK TRANSFER** — Type II

1918-22 Perforated 11 Type I Overprint

SCOTT NO.	DESCRIPTION	UNUSED F	AVG	USED F	AVG
RD1	1¢ carmine rose	1.00	.70	.30	.25
RD2	2¢ carmine rose	.30	.25	.30	.25
RD3	4¢ carmine rose	.30	.25	.30	.25
RD4	5¢ carmine rose	.35	.30	.30	.25
RD5	10¢ carmine rose	.35	.30	.30	.25
RD6	20¢ carmine rose	.65	.45	.30	.25
RD7	25¢ carmine rose (cut cancel .25)	2.25	1.75	.30	.25
RD8	40¢ carmine rose	2.25	1.15	.30	.25
RD9	50¢ carmine rose	.80	.50	.30	.25
RD10	80¢ carmine rose (cut cancel .25)	9.00	7.00	.50	.35
RD11	$1 green (red ovverprint) (cut cancel 4.00)	150.00	120.00	28.00	23.00
RD12	$1 green (black overprint)	3.00	2.00	.40	.25
RD13	$2 rose	3.00	2.00	.30	.25
RD14	$3 violet (cut cancel .25)	26.00	19.00	7.00	5.00
RD15	$4 yellow brown (cut cancel .25)	12.00	8.00	.30	.25
RD16	$5 dark blue (cut cancel .25)	8.00	5.00	.30	.25
RD17	$10 orange (cut cancel .25)	27.00	20.00	.50	.45
RD18	$20 olive bistre (cut cancel 3.50)	120.00	95.00	20.00	14.00

Perforated 12

SCOTT NO.	DESCRIPTION	UNUSED F	AVG	USED F	AVG
RD19	$30 vermillion (cut cancel 1.20)	39.00	33.00	6.00	4.00
RD20	$50 olive green (cut cancel 26.00)	130.00	110.00	65.00	55.00
RD21	$60 brown (cut cancel 10.00)	300.00	230.00	28.00	22.00
RD22	$100 green (cut cancel 3.50)	45.00	35.00	7.00	5.00
RD23	$500 blue (cut cancel 80.00)	500.00	450.00	160.00	120.00
RD24	$1000 orange (cut cancel 33.00)	400.00	350.00	100.00	85.00

SCOTT NO.	DESCRIPTION	UNUSED F	AVG	USED F	AVG
	1928 Perforated 10 Type I Overprint				
RD25	2¢ carmine rose	5.00	4.00	.40	.35
RD26	4¢ carmine rose	5.00	4.00	.40	.35
RD27	10¢ carmine rose	5.00	4.00	.40	.35
RD28	20¢ carmine rose	6.00	5.00	.40	.35
RD29	50¢ carmine rose	10.00	8.00	.60	.45
RD30	$1 green	40.00	28.00	.40	.30
RD31	$2 carmine rose	40.00	28.00	.35	.30
RD32	$10 orange ....(cut cancel .25)	40.00	28.00	.50	.35
RD33	2¢ carmine rose	11.00	6.00	1.00	.70
RD34	10¢ carmine rose	3.00	2.00	.40	.35
RD35	20¢ carmine rose	6.00	4.00	.30	.25
RD36	50¢ carmine rose	5.00	4.00	.30	.25
RD37	$1 green ....(cut cancel .30)	70.00	50.00	13.00	9.00
RD38	$2 rose ....(cut cancel .30)	90.00	70.00	13.00	9.00
	1920-28 Perforated 10 Type II overprint				
RD39	2¢ carmine rose	11.00	9.00	1.00	.70
RD40	10¢ carmine rose	4.00	2.00	.60	.40
RD41	20¢ carmine rose	6.00	4.00	.30	.25

SILVER TAX STAMPS

Documentary Stamps of 1917 Overprinted

1934-36

SCOTT NO.	DESCRIPTION	UNUSED F	AVG	USED F	AVG
RG1	1¢ carmine rose	1.70	1.25	1.00	.70
RG2	2¢ carmine rose	2.25	1.50	.75	.50
RG3	3¢ carmine rose	2.40	1.25	.90	.60
RG4	4¢ carmine rose	2.40	1.40	1.75	1.25
RG5	5¢ carmine rose	3.60	2.50	1.50	1.00
RG6	8¢ carmine rose	4.85	3.00	3.50	2.50
RG7	10¢ carmine rose	5.25	3.50	4.00	2.50
RG8	20¢ carmine rose	7.75	5.00	4.00	2.50
RG9	25¢ carmine rose	7.75	5.00	5.00	3.50
RG10	40¢ carmine rose	8.50	6.00	6.50	4.50
RG11	50¢ carmine rose	10.00	7.00	8.00	5.00

SCOTT NO.	DESCRIPTION	UNUSED F	AVG	USED F	AVG
RG12	80¢ carmine rose	18.00	12.00	11.00	7.00
RG13	$1 green	42.00	35.00	18.00	13.00
RG14	$2 rose	50.00	45.00	27.00	18.00
RG15	$3 violet	82.00	65.00	40.00	28.00
RG16	$4 yellow brown	80.00	50.00	35.00	17.00
RG17	$5 dark blue	82.00	60.00	33.00	20.00
RG18	$10 orange	115.00	90.00	25.00	17.00
RG19	$30 vermillion ....(cut cancel 20.00)	245.00	140.00	60.00	40.00
RG20	$60 brown ....(cut cancel 30.00)	280.00	150.00	85.00	60.00
RG21	$100 green	275.00	185.00	35.00	22.50
RG22	$500 blue ....(cut cancel 110.00)	600.00	400.00	235.00	160.00
RG23	$1000 orange ....(cut cancel 70.00)	......	......	120.00	77.50
RG26	$100 green, 11mm spacing	600.00	400.00	85.00	55.00
RG27	$1000 orange, 11mm spacing	......	......	1700.00	1450.00

TOBACCO SALE TAX STAMPS

Documentary Stamps of 1917 Overprinted

1934

SCOTT NO.	DESCRIPTION	UNUSED F	AVG	USED F	AVG
RJ1	1¢ carmine rose	.40	.35	.25	.20
RJ2	2¢ carmine rose	.45	.30	.25	.20
RJ3	5¢ carmine rose	1.40	.90	.45	.30
RJ4	10¢ carmine rose	1.75	1.15	.45	.30
RJ5	25¢ carmine rose	4.75	3.00	1.85	1.20
RJ6	50¢ carmine rose	4.75	3.00	1.85	1.20
RJ7	$1 green	12.00	8.00	1.85	1.20
RJ8	$2 rose	20.00	14.00	2.15	1.40
RJ9	$5 dark blue	25.00	17.00	4.75	3.00
RJ10	$10 orange	40.00	27.00	12.00	7.75
RJ11	$20 olive bistre	100.00	70.00	15.00	9.75

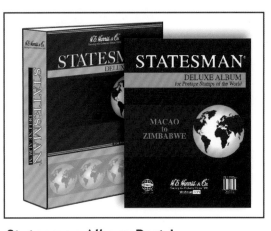

HUNTING PERMIT

SCOTT NO.	DESCRIPTION	UNUSED VF	F	AVG	USED VF	F	AVG

RW1

RW2

RW3

RW4

RW5

1934-1938 Inscribed: DEPARTMENT OF AGRICULTURE (NH + 75%)

Scott No.	Year	Description	VF	F	AVG	VF	F	AVG
RW1	1934	$1 Mallards	650.00	475.00	400.00	160.00	125.00	110.00
RW2	1935	$1 Canvasbacks	575.00	425.00	375.00	185.00	150.00	125.00
RW3	1936	$1 Canada Geese	350.00	250.00	200.00	85.00	70.00	60.00
RW4	1937	$1 Scaup Ducks	290.00	225.00	160.00	65.00	55.00	40.00
RW5	1938	$1 Pintail Drake	450.00	300.00	225.00	65.00	55.00	40.00

RW6

RW7

RW8

RW9

RW10

Note: NH premiums RW6-9 (75%) RW10-16 (50%) RW17-25 (40%)
1939-1958 Inscribed: DEPARTMENT OF INTERIOR

Scott No.	Year	Description	VF	F	AVG	VF	F	AVG
RW6	1939	$1 Green-Winged Teal	200.00	165.00	135.00	55.00	45.00	38.00
RW7	1940	$1 Black Mallards	200.00	165.00	135.00	55.00	45.00	38.00
RW8	1941	$1 Ruddy Ducks	200.00	165.00	135.00	55.00	45.00	38.00
RW9	1942	$1 Baldpates	210.00	175.00	140.00	55.00	45.00	35.00
RW10	1943	$1 Wood Ducks	115.00	85.00	77.00	55.00	42.00	30.00

RW11

RW12

RW13

RW14

RW15

Scott No.	Year	Description	VF	F	AVG	VF	F	AVG
RW11	1944	$1 White Fronted Geese	130.00	90.00	82.00	47.00	37.00	27.00
RW12	1945	$1 Shoveller Ducks	95.00	72.00	62.00	36.00	28.00	22.00
RW13	1946	$1 Redhead Ducks	50.00	35.00	25.00	20.00	15.00	10.00
RW14	1947	$1 Snow Geese	50.00	35.00	25.00	20.00	15.00	10.00
RW15	1948	$1 Buffleheads	50.00	35.00	25.00	20.00	15.00	10.00

RW16

RW17

RW18

RW19

RW20

Scott No.	Year	Description	VF	F	AVG	VF	F	AVG
RW16	1949	$2 Goldeneye Ducks	60.00	40.00	35.00	18.00	15.00	10.00
RW17	1950	$2 Trumpeter Swans	75.00	55.00	45.00	15.00	12.00	9.00
RW18	1951	$2 Gadwall Ducks	75.00	55.00	45.00	15.00	12.00	9.00
RW19	1952	$2 Harlequin Ducks	75.00	55.00	45.00	15.00	12.00	9.00
RW20	1953	$2 Blue-Winged Teal	80.00	60.00	50.00	15.00	12.00	9.00

Notes on Hunting Permit Stamps
1. Unused stamps without gum (uncancelled) are priced at one-half gummed price.
2. The date printed on the stamp is one year later than the date of issue listed above.
3. #RW1-RW25 and RW31 are plate blocks of 6.

SCOTT NO.	DESCRIPTION	UNUSED VF	F	AVG	USED VF	F	AVG

RW21

RW22

RW23

RW24

RW25

RW21	1954 $2 Ringed-Necked Ducks	85.00	60.00	50.00	13.00	10.00	7.50
RW22	1955 $2 Blue Geese	85.00	60.00	50.00	12.00	9.00	7.50
RW23	1956 $2 American Merganser	85.00	60.00	50.00	12.00	9.00	7.50
RW24	1957 $2 Americacn Eider	85.00	60.00	50.00	12.00	9.00	7.50
RW25	1958 $2 Canada Geese	85.00	60.00	50.00	12.00	9.00	7.50

PLATE BLOCKS RW1-RW25

SCOTT NO.	UNUSED NH F	AVG	UNUSED OG F	AVG	SCOTT NO.	UNUSED NH F	AVG	UNUSED OG F	AVG
	PLATE BLOCKS OF 6					PLATE BLOCKS OF 6			
RW1	16000.00	12000.00	13500.00	9500.00	RW14	475.00	375.00	350.00	325.00
RW2	12000.00	9000.00	9500.00	7500.00	RW15	500.00	425.00	425.00	375.00
RW3	5200.00	4300.00	4500.00	3200.00	RW16	575.00	450.00	450.00	400.00
RW4	4600.00	3500.00	4200.00	3300.00	RW17	795.00	650.00	650.00	550.00
RW5	5100.00	4200.00	4400.00	3300.00	RW18	795.00	650.00	650.00	550.00
RW6	4700.00	3800.00	3600.00	2900.00	RW19	795.00	650.00	650.00	550.00
RW7	4700.00	3800.00	3700.00	3100.00	RW20	825.00	675.00	675.00	575.00
RW8	4300.00	3800.00	3700.00	3100.00	RW21	795.00	675.00	675.00	600.00
RW9	4300.00	3600.00	3500.00	2900.00	RW22	795.00	675.00	675.00	600.00
RW10	1075.00	850.00	925.00	775.00	RW23	840.00	725.00	725.00	640.00
RW11	1200.00	875.00	925.00	775.00	RW24	795.00	675.00	650.00	575.00
RW12	900.00	650.00	675.00	550.00	RW25	795.00	675.00	650.00	575.00
RW13	500.00	400.00	350.00	325.00					

RW26

RW27

RW28

RW29

RW30

RW31

1959-1971 (NH + 40%)

RW26	1959 $3 Dog & Mallard	185.00	135.00	12.00	9.00
RW27	1960 $3 Redhead Ducks	135.00	110.00	12.00	9.00
RW28	1961 $3 Mallard Hen & Ducklings	135.00	110.00	12.00	9.00
RW29	1962 $3 Pintail Drakes	150.00	115.00	12.00	9.00
RW30	1963 $3 Brant Ducks Landing	150.00	115.00	12.00	9.00
RW31	1964 $3 Hawaiian Nene Goose	145.00	115.00	12.00	9.00

Notes on Hunting Permit Stamps
1. Unused stamps without gum (uncancelled) are priced at one-half gummed price.
2. The date printed on the stamp is one year later than the date of issue listed above.
3. #RW1-RW25 and RW31 are plate blocks of 6.

SCOTT NO.	DESCRIPTION	UNUSED VF	F	USED VF	F

RW32

RW33

RW34

RW35

RW32	1965 $3 Canvasback Drakes	145.00	115.00	12.00	9.00
RW33	1966 $3 Whistling Swans	145.00	115.00	12.00	9.00
RW34	1967 $3 Old Squaw Ducks	170.00	125.00	12.00	9.00
RW35	1968 $3 Hooded Mergansers	100.00	72.00	12.00	9.00

RW36

RW37

RW38

RW39

RW36	1969 $3 White-Winged Scoters	98.00	72.00	12.00	9.00
RW37	1970 $3 Ross's Geese	98.00	72.00	12.00	9.00
RW38	1971 $3 Three Cinnamon Teal	689.00	48.00	12.00	9.00
RW39	1972 $5 Emperor Geese	42.00	32.00	9.00	7.50

RW40

RW41

RW42

RW43

RW44

RW45

1973-1978

RW40	1973 $5 Steller's Eider	32.00	24.00	9.00	7.50
RW41	1974 $5 Wood Ducks	32.00	24.00	9.00	7.50
RW42	1975 $5 Canvasbacks	29.00	22.00	9.00	7.50
RW43	1976 $5 Canada Geese	29.00	22.00	9.00	7.50
RW44	1977 $5 Pair of Ross's Geese	29.00	23.00	9.00	7.50
RW45	1978 $5 Hooded Merganser Drake	29.00	23.00	9.00	7.50

SCOTT NO.	DESCRIPTION	UNUSED NH VF	F	USED VF	F

RW46

RW47

RW48

RW49

1979-1986

SCOTT NO.	DESCRIPTION	UNUSED NH VF	F	USED VF	F
RW46	1979 $7.50 Green-Winged Teal	29.00	23.00	10.00	9.00
RW47	1980 $7.50 Mallards.	29.00	23.00	10.00	9.00
RW48	1981 $7.50 Ruddy Ducks	29.00	23.00	10.00	9.00
RW49	1982 $7.50 Canvasbacks.	29.00	23.00	10.00	9.00

PLATE BLOCKS RW26-RW63					
SCOTT NO.	UNUSED NH F	UNUSED OG F	SCOTT NO.	UNUSED NH F	UNUSED OG F
RW26	740.00	550.00	RW45	90.00	....
RW27	700.00	525.00	RW46	90.00	....
RW28	700.00	550.00	RW47	90.00	....
RW29	750.00	550.00	RW48	90.00	....
RW30	725.00	485.00	RW49	90.00	....
RW31	2800.00	2400.00	RW50	90.00	....
RW32	750.00	573.00	RW51	90.00	....
RW33	750.00	573.00	RW52	90.00	....
RW34	750.00	573.00	RW53	90.00	....
RW35	395.00	300.00	RW54	110.00	....
RW36	395.00	300.00	RW55	110.00	....
RW37	270.00	300.00	RW56	120.00	....
RW38	155.00	220.00	RW57	120.00	....
RW39	125.00	....	RW58	150.00	....
RW40	115.00	....	RW59	150.00	....
RW41	100.00	....	RW60	150.00	....
RW42	90.00	....	RW61	150.00	....
RW43	90.00	....	RW62	150.00	....
RW44	90.00	....	RW63	150.00	....

RW50

RW51

RW52

RW53

RW50	1983 $7.50 Pintails	29.00	23.00	10.00	9.00
RW51	1984 $7.50 Widgeon.	29.00	23.00	10.00	9.00
RW52	1985 $7.50 Cinnamon Teal	29.00	23.00	10.00	9.00
RW53	1986 $7.50 Fulvous Whistling	29.00	23.00	10.00	9.00

RW54

RW55

RW56

RW57

1987-1993

RW54	1987 $10.00 Redhead Ducks	35.00	25.00	13.00	11.00
RW55	1988 $10.00 Snow Goose	35.00	27.00	13.00	11.00
RW56	1989 $12.50 Lesser Scaup	35.00	27.00	13.00	11.00
RW57	1990 $12.50 Black Bellied Whistling Duck	35.00	27.00	13.00	11.00

RW58

RW59

RW60

RW61

RW58	1991 $15.00 King Eiders	55.00	40.00	18.00	15.00
RW59	1992 $15.00 Spectacled Eider	50.00	35.00	17.00	14.00
RW60	1993 $15.00 Canvasbacks	50.00	35.00	17.00	14.00
RW61	1994 $15.00 Red-Breasted Merganser	50.00	38.00	17.50	12.50

RW62

RW63

RW64

RW65

RW66

RW67

1992-2000

RW62	1995 $15.00 Mallards	50.00	38.00	17.50	12.50
RW63	1996 $15.00 Surf Scoters	50.00	38.00	17.50	12.50
RW64	1997 $15.00 Canada Goose	50.00	38.00	17.50	12.50
RW65	1998 $15.00 Barrow's Goldeneye	75.00	57.00	32.00	24.00
RW65a	1998 $15.00 Barrow's Goldeneye, self-adhesive, pane of 1	42.00	39.00	18.00	....
RW66	1999 $15.00 Greater Scaup	58.00	47.00	31.00	....
RW66a	1999 $15.00 Greater Scaup, self-adhesive, pane of 1	40.00	34.00	18.00	....
RW67	2000 $15.00 Mottled Duck	40.00	33.00	28.00	....
RW67a	2000 $15.00 Mottled Duck, self-adhesive, pane of 1	37.00	31.00	18.00	....

SCOTT NO.	DESCRIPTION	UNUSED NH VF	F	USED VF	F

RW68

RW69

2001-2003

RW68	2001 $15.00 Northern Pintail	38.00	31.00	26.00	....
RW68a	2001 $15.00 Northern Pintail, self-adhesive, pane of 1	37.00	32.00	18.00	....
RW69	2002 $15.00 Black Scoters	38.00	34.00	26.00	....
RW69a	2002 $15.00 Black Scoters, self-adhesive, pane of 1	37.00	....	18.00	....

RW70

RW71

RW72

RW73

2004-2006

RW70	2003 $15.00 Snow Geese	40.00	32.00	26.00	....
RW70a	2003 $15.00 Snow Geese, self-adhesive, pane of 1	37.00	....	18.00	....
RW71	2004 $15.00 Redheads	38.00	32.00	23.00	....
RW71a	2004 $15.00 Redheads, self-adhesive, pane of 1	37.00	....	18.00	....
RW72	2005 $15.00 Hooded Mergansers	38.00	32.00	23.00	....
RW72a	2005 $15.00 Hooded Mergansers, self-adhesive, pane of 1	37.00	....	20.00	....
RW73	2006 $15.00 Ross's Goose	38.00	32.00	23.00	....
RW73a	2006 $15.00 Ross's Goose, self-adhesive, pane of 1	37.00	....	20.00	....

RW74

RW75

RW76   **RW77**

2007-2010

RW74	2007 $15.00 Ringed-Necked Ducks	38.00	32.00	23.00	....
RW74a	2007 $15.00 Ringed-Necked Ducks, self-adhesive, pane of 1	37.00	....	22.00	....
RW75	2008 $15 Northern Pintail Ducks	38.00	32.00	26.00	....
RW75a	2008 $15 Pintail Ducks, self-adhesive	37.00	....	22.00	....
RW76	2009 $15 Long-Tailed Duck	38.00	32.00	26.00	....
RW76a	2009 $15 Long-Tailed Duck, self-adhesive	37.00	....	22.00	....
RW77	2010 $15 American Widgeon	38.00	32.00	26.00	....
RW77a	2010 $15 American Widgeon, self-adhesive	37.00	....	19.00	....

SCOTT NO.	DESCRIPTION	UNUSED NH VF	F	USED VF	F

RW78

RW79

RW80

RW81

2011-2014

RW78	2011 $15 White-Fronted Geese	38.00	32.00	26.00	....
RW78a	2011 $15 White-Fronted Geese, self-adhesive	35.00	....	19.00	....
RW79	2012 $15 Wood Duck	38.00	....	25.50	
RW79a	2012 $15 Wood Duck, self-adhesive	35.00	....	19.50	
RW80	2013 $15 Common Goldeneye	35.00	....	25.00	
RW80a	2013 $15 Common Goldeneye, self-adhesive	35.00	....	25.00	
RW81	2014 $15 Canvasbacks	35.00	....	25.00	
RW81a	2014 $15 Canvasbacks, Self-Adhesive	35.00	....	25.00	

RW82

RW83

RW84

RW85

RW86

RW87

2015-2020

RW82	2015 $25 Ruddy Ducks	45.00	....	30.00	....
RW82a	2015 $25 Ruddy Ducks, self-adhesive	45.00	....	30.00	....
RW83	2016 $25 Trumpeter Swans	45.00	....	30.00	....
RW83a	2016 $25 Trumpeter Swans, self-adhesive	45.00	....	30.00	....
RW84	2017 $25 Canada Geese	45.00	....	30.00	....
RW84a	2017 $25 Canada Geese, self-adhesive	45.00	....	30.00	....
RW85	2018 $25 Mallards	45.00	....	30.00	....
RW85A	2018 $25 Mallards, self-adhesive	45.00	....	30.00	....
RW86	2019 $25 Wood Duck and Decoy	45.00	....	30.00	....
RW86a	2019 $25 Wood Duck and Decoy, self-adhesive	45.00	....	30.00	....
RW87	2020 $25 Black-bellied Whistling Ducks	45.00	....	30.00	....
RW87a	2020 $25 Black-bellied Whistling Ducks, self adhesive	45.00	....	30.00	....

PLATE BLOCKS RW64-RW87

SCOTT NO.	UNUSED NH F	UNUSED OG F	SCOTT NO.	UNUSED NH F	UNUSED OG F
RW64	150.00	....	RW76	150.00	....
RW65	260.00	....	RW77	150.00	....
RW66	150.00	....	RW78	150.00	....
RW67	150.00	....	RW79	150.00	....
RW68	150.00	....	RW80	150.00	....
RW69	150.00	....	RW81	150.00	....
RW70	150.00	....	RW82	200.00	....
RW71	150.00	....	RW83	200.00	....
RW72	150.00	....	RW84	200.00	....
RW73	150.00	....	RW85	200.00	....
RW74	150.00	....	RW86	200.00	....
RW75	150.00	....	RW87	200.00	....

STATE HUNTING PERMIT

NO.	DESCRIPTION	F-VF NH

AL7

ALABAMA

NO.	DESCRIPTION	F-VF NH
AL1	'79 $5 Wood Ducks	16.00
AL2	'80 $5 Mallards	14.00
AL3	'81 $5 Canada Geese	14.00
AL4	'82 $5 Green-Winged Teal	14.00
AL5	'83 $5 Widgeons	14.00
AL6	'84 $5 Buffleheads	24.00
AL7	'85 $5 Wood Ducks	17.00
AL8	'86 $5 Canada Geese	17.00
AL9	'87 $5 Pintails	18.00
AL10	'88 $5 Canvasbacks	12.50
AL11	'89 $5 Hooded Mergansers	12.50
AL12	'90 $5 Wood Ducks	12.50
AL13	'91 $5 Redheads	12.50
AL14	'92 $5 Cinnamon Teal	12.50
AL15	'93 $5 Green-Winged Teal	12.50
AL16	'94 $5 Canvasbacks	13.00
AL17	'95 $5 Canada Geese	13.00
AL18	'96 $5 Wood Ducks	13.00
AL19	'97 $5 Snow Geese	13.00
AL20	'98 $5 Barrows Goldeneye	13.00
AL21	'99 $5 Redheads	13.00
AL22	'00 $5 Buffleheads	13.00
AL23	'01 $5 Ruddy Duck	13.00
AL24	'02 $5 Pintail	13.00
AL25	'03 $5 Wood Duck	13.00
AL26	'04 $5 Ring-Necked Duck	13.00
AL27	'05 $5 Canada Geese	13.00
AL28	'06 $5 Canvasbacks	13.00
AL29	'07 $5 Blue-Winged Teal	13.00
AL30	'08 $5 Hooded Mergansers	13.00
AL31	'09 $5 Wood Duck	13.00
AL32	'10 $5 Pintail	13.00
AL33	'11 $5 Wigeon	11.00
AL34	'12 $6 Ring-necked Duck	11.00
AL35	'13 $5 Canvasbacks	11.00
AL36	'14 $5 Pintails	11.00
AL37	'15 $5 Mallards	11.00
AL38	'16 $10 Wigeons	18.00
AL39	'17 $10 Canada Geese	18.00
AL40	'18 $10 Blue-winged Teal	18.00
AL41	'19 $10 Wood Duck	18.00

AK1

ALASKA

NO.	DESCRIPTION	F-VF NH
AK1	'85 $5 Emperor Geese	14.00
AK2	'86 $5 Steller's Eiders	13.00
AK3	'87 $5 Spectacled Eiders	15.00
AK4	'88 $5 Trumpeter Swans	11.00
AK5	'89 $5 Barrow's Goldeneyes	11.00
AK6	'90 $5 Old Squaws	12.00
AK7	'91 $5 Snow Geese	14.00
AK8	'92 $5 Canvasbacks	14.00
AK9	'93 $5 Tule White Front Geese	14.00
AK10	'94 $5 Harlequin Ducks	25.00
AK11	'95 $5 Pacific Brant	28.00
AK12	'96 $5 Aleutian Canada Geese	30.00
AK13	'97 $5 King Eiders	22.00
AK14	'98 $5 Barrows Goldeneye	18.00
AK15	'99 $5 Pintail	18.00
AK16	'00 $5 Common Eiders	18.00
AK17	'01 $5 Buffleheads	15.00
AK18	'02 $5 Black Scoter	14.00
AK19	'03 $5 Canada Geese	14.00
AK20	'04 $5 Lesser Scaup	14.00
AK21	'05 $5 Hooded Merganser	14.00
AK22	'06 $5 Pintails, Mallard, green-winged teal	14.00
AK23	'07 $5 Northern Shoveler	14.00
AK24	'08 $5 Pintail	14.00
AK25	'09 $5 Mallards	14.00
AK26	'10 $5 Pintails	14.00
AK27	'11 $5 Canada Geese	13.00
AK28	'12 $5 Harlequin Ducks	11.00
AK29	'13 $5 White-fronted geese	10.00
AK30	'14 $5 White-winged Scoter	10.00
AK31	'15 $5 Northern Pintail	10.00
AK32	'16 $5 Pacific Brant	10.00
AK33	'17 $10 American Wigeon	18.00
AK34	'18 $10 Bufflehead	18.00
AK35	'19 $10 Emperor Goose	18.00

AZ1

ARIZONA

NO.	DESCRIPTION	F-VF NH
AZ1	'87 $5.50 Pintails	13.00
AZ2	'88 $5.50 Green-Winged Teal	13.00
AZ3	'89 $5.50 Cinnamon Teal	13.00
AZ4	'90 $5.50 Canada Geese	15.00
AZ5	'91 $5.50 Blue-Winged Teal	13.00
AZ6	'92 $5.50 Buffleheads	13.00
AZ7	'93 $5.50 Mexican Ducks	15.00
AZ8	'94 $5.50 Mallards	15.00
AZ9	'95 $5.50 Widgeon	15.00
AZ10	'96 $5.50 Canvasback	15.00
AZ11	'97 $5.50 Gadwall	15.00
AZ12	'98 $5.50 Wood Duck	15.00
AZ13	'99 $5.50 Snow Geese	15.00
AZ14	'00 $7.50 Ruddy Ducks	22.00
AZ15	'01 $7.50 Redheads	18.00
AZ16	'02 $7.50 Ring-necked ducks	18.00
AZ17	'03 $7.50 Northern Shoveler	18.00
AZ18	'04 $7.50 Lesser Scaup	18.00
AZ19	'05 $7.50 Pintails	18.00
AZ20	'06 $7.50 Canada Geese	18.00
AZ21	'07 $8.75 Wood Duck	18.00
AZ22	'08 $8.75 Canvasback	18.00
AZ23	'09 $8.75 Hooded Mergansers	18.00
AZ24	'10 $8.75 Green-winged teal.	18.00
AZ25	'11 $8.75 Bufflehead	18.00
AZ26	'12 $8.75 American Widgeon	18.00
AZ27	'13 $8.75 Pintail	18.00

AR5

ARKANSAS

NO.	DESCRIPTION	F-VF NH
AR1	'81 $5.50 Mallards	50.00
AR2	'82 $5.50 Wood Ducks	40.00
AR3	'83 $5.50 Green-Winged Teal	55.00
AR4	'84 $5.50 Pintails	20.00
AR5	'85 $5.50 Mallards	12.00
AR6	'86 $5.50 Black Swamp Mallards	12.00
AR7	'87 $7 Wood Ducks	12.00
AR8	'88 $7 Pintails	12.00
AR9	'89 $7 Mallards	12.00
AR10	'90 $7 Black Ducks & Mallards	12.00
AR11	'91 $7 Sulphur River Widgeons	12.00
AR12	'92 $7 Shirey Bay Shovelers	12.00
AR13	'93 $7 Grand Prairie Mallards	15.00
AR14	'94 $7 Canada Goose	19.00
AR15	'95 $7 White River Mallards	19.00
AR16	'96 $7 Black Lab	22.00
AR17	'97 $7 Chocolate Lab	18.00
AR18	'98 $7 Labrador retriever, mallards	18.00
AR19	'99 $7.00 Wood Duck	18.00
AR20	'00 $7 Mallards and Golden Retriever	21.00
AR21	'01 $7 Canvasback	18.00
AR22	'02 $7 Mallards	18.00
AR23	'03 $7 Mallards & Chesapeake Bay Retriever	18.00
AR24	'04 $7 Mallards	15.00
AR24a	'04 $20 Mallards	35.00
AR25	'05 $7 Mallards and Labrador Retriever	16.00
AR25a	'05 $20 Mallards and Labrador Retriever	35.00
AR26	'06 $7 Mallards	16.00
AR26a	'06 $20 Mallards	35.00
AR27	'07 $7 Mallards, Labrador Retriever	16.00
AR27a	'07 $20 Mallards, Labrador Retriever	35.00
AR28	'08 $7 Mallards, Labrador Retriever	16.00
AR28a	'08 $20 Mallards, Labrador Retriever	35.00
AR29	'09 $7 Hooded Merganwers	16.00
AR29a	'09 $20 Hooded Merganwers	35.00
AR30	'10 $7 Mallards and Black Labrador Retriever	16.00
AR30a	'10 $20 Mallards and Black Labrador Retriever	40.00
AR31	'11 $7 Mallards	16.00
AR31a	'11 $20 Mallards	35.00
AR32	'12 $7 Green Winged Teal	16.00
AR32a	'12 $20 Green Winged Teal	35.00
AR32b	'$35.00 Green-winged Teal.	60.00
AR33	'13 $7 Mallards	16.00
AR33a	'13 $35 Mallards	55.00
AR34	'14 $7 Mallards	16.00
AR34a	'14 $35 Mallards	55.00
AR35	'15 $7 Snow Geese	16.00
AR35a	'15 $35 Snow Geese	55.00
AR36	'16 $7 Mallards	16.00
AR36a	'16 $35 Mallards	55.00
AR37	'17 $7 Mallards	16.00
AR37a	'17 $35 Mallards	55.00
AR38	'18 $7 Ring-necked Ducks	16.00
AR38	'18 $35 Ring-necked Ducks	55.00
AR39	'19 $7 Mallards	16.00
AR39a	'19 $35 Mallards	55.00

CA16

CALIFORNIA

NO.	DESCRIPTION	F-VF NH
CA1	'71 $1 Pintails	500.00
CA2	'72 $1 Canvasbacks	1400.00
CA3	'73 $1 Mallards	15.00
CA4	'74 $1 White-Fronted Geese	4.50
CA5	'75 $1 Green-Winged Teal	150.00
CA6	'76 $1 Widgeons	30.00
CA7	'77 $1 Cinnamon Teal	45.00
CA8	'78 $5 Cinnamon Teal	45.00
CA9	'78 $5 Hooded Mergansers	100.00
CA10	'79 $5 Wood Ducks	12.00
CA11	'80 $5 Pintails	12.00
CA12	'81 $5 Canvasbacks	12.00
CA13	'82 $5 Widgeons	12.00
CA14	'83 $5 Green-Winged Teal	15.00
CA15	'84 $7.50 Mallard Decoy	15.00
CA16	'85 $7.50 Ring-Necked Ducks	15.00
CA17	'86 $7.50 Canada Goose	15.00
CA18	'87 $7.50 Redheads	15.00
CA19	'88 $7.50 Mallards	15.00
CA20	'89 $7.50 Cinnamon Teal	16.00
CA21	'90 $7.50 Canada Goose	19.00
CA22	'91 $7.50 Gadwalls	19.00
CA23	'92 $7.90 White-Fronted Goose	21.00
CA24	'93 $10.50 Pintails	21.00
CA25	'94 $10.50 Wood Duck	23.00
CA26	'95 $10.50 Snow Geese	23.00
CA27	'96 $10.50 Mallard	20.00
CA28	'97 $10.50 Pintails	22.00
CA29	'98 $10.50 Green-Winged Teal (pair)	42.00
CA30	'99 $10.50 Wood Duck (pair)	42.00
CA31	'00 $10.50 Canada geese, mallard, widgeon	20.00
CA32	'01 $10.50 Redheads	20.00
CA33	'02 $10.50 Pintails	20.00
CA34	'03 $10.50 Mallards	20.00
CA35	'04 $13.90 Cinnamon Teal	22.00
CA36	'05 $14.20 Pintails	22.00
CA37	'06 $14.95 White-Fronted Goose	24.00
CA38	'07 $16 Pintails	24.00
CA39	'08 $16.80 Mallards	27.00
CA40	'09 $17.50 Shovelers	28.00
CA41	'10 $18.10 Redheads	25.00
CA42	'11 $18.93 Barrow's Goldeneyes	25.00
CA43	'12 $19.44 Canada Geese	28.00
CA44	'13 $20.01 Widgeons	30.00
CA45	'14 $20.26 Lesser Scaup	30.00
CA46	'15 $20.52 Green-winged Teal	30.00
CA47	'16 $20.52 Lesser Snow Geese	30.00
CA48	'17 $20.52 Ruddy Duck	30.00
CA49	'18 $20.52 Black Brants	30.00

CO1

COLORADO

NO.	DESCRIPTION	F-VF NH
CO1	'90 $5 Canada Geese	17.00
CO2	'91 $5 Mallards	23.00
CO3	'92 $5 Pintails	13.00
CO4	'93 $5 Green-Winged Teal	13.00
CO5	'94 $5 Wood Ducks	13.00
CO6	'95 $5 Buffleheads	13.00
CO7	'96 $5 Cinnamon Teal	13.00
CO8	'97 $5 Widgeon	13.00
CO9	'98 $5 Redhead	13.00
CO10	'99 $5 Blue-winged Teal	13.00
CO11	'00 $5 Gadwalls	13.00
CO12	'01 $5 Ruddy Duck	13.00
CO13	'02 $5 Common Goldeneyes	13.00
CO14	'03 $5 Canvasbacks	13.00
CO15	'04 $5 Snow Geese	13.00
CO16	'05 $5 Shovelers	13.00
CO17	'06 $5 Ring-Necked Ducks	13.00
CO18	'07 $5 Hooded Mergansers	13.00
CO19	'08 $5 Lesser Scaup	13.00
CO20	'09 $5 Barrows's Goldeneye	13.00
CO21	'10 $5 Pintails	13.00
CO22	'11 $5 Green Winged Teal.	13.00
CO23	'12 $5 Ross's geese	10.00
CO24	'13 $5 Greater Scaups	10.00
CO25	'14 $5 Canada Geese	10.00
CO26	'15 $7.50 Wood Ducks	12.00
CO27	'16 $10 Marsh Mallards	15.00
CO28	'17 $10 Redheads	15.00
CO29	'18 $5 Ring-necked Ducks	10.00
CO30	'19 $5 Northern Pintails	10.00

CT7

CONNECTICUT

NO.	DESCRIPTION	F-VF NH
CT1	'93 $5 Black Ducks	15.00
CT2	'94 $5 Canvasbacks	18.00
CT3	'95 $5 Mallards	18.00
CT4	'96 $5 Old Squaw	23.00
CT5	'97 $5 Green Winged Teal	15.00
CT6	'98 $5 Mallards	15.00
CT7	'99 $5 Canada Geese	28.00
CT8	'00 $5 Wood Duck	15.00
CT9	'01 Bufflehead	15.00
CT10	'02 Greater Scaups	18.00
CT11	'03 $5 Black Duck	15.00
CT12	'04 $5 Wood Duck	15.00
CT13	'05 $10 Mallards	21.00
CT14	'06 $10 Buffleheads	21.00
CT15	'07 $10 Black Duck Decoy	21.00
CT16	'08 $10 Common Goldeneyes	21.00
CT17	'09 $10 Black Duck	21.00
CT18	'10 $13 Common Goldeneyes	23.00
CT19	'12 $13 Pintail	25.00
CT20	'13 $13 Wood ducks	25.00
CT21	'14 $13 Hooded Mergansers	25.00
CT22	'15 $13 Canvasbacks	25.00
CT23	'16 $13 Atlantic Brant	25.00
CT24	'17 $17 Canvasbacks and Lighthouse	28.00
CT25	'18 $17 Black Scoter and Lighthouse	28.00
CT26	'19 $17 Buffleheads	28.00

NO.	DESCRIPTION	F-VF NH

DE1

DELAWARE

NO.	DESCRIPTION	F-VF NH
DE1	'80 $5 Black Ducks	70.00
DE2	'81 $5 Snow Geese	55.00
DE3	'82 $5 Canada Geese	55.00
DE4	'83 $5 Canvasbacks	40.00
DE5	'84 $5 Mallards	15.00
DE6	'85 $5 Pintail	12.00
DE7	'86 $5 Widgeons	12.00
DE8	'87 $5 Redheads	12.00
DE9	'88 $5 Wood Ducks	10.00
DE10	'89 $5 Buffleheads	10.00
DE11	'90 $5 Green-Winged Teal	10.00
DE12	'91 $5 Hooded Merganser	10.00
DE13	'92 $5 Blue-Winged Teal	10.00
DE14	'93 $5 Goldeneye	10.00
DE15	'94 $5 Blue Goose	14.00
DE16	'95 $5 Scaup	14.00
DE17	'96 $6 Gadwall	15.00
DE18	'97 $6 White Winged Scoter	15.00
DE19	'98 $6 Blue Winged Teal	14.00
DE20	'99 $6 Tundra Swan	14.00
DE21	'00 $6 American brant	14.00
DE22	'01 $6 Old Squaw	15.00
DE23	'02 $6 Ruddy Ducks	15.00
DE24	'03 $9 Ring Necked Duck	18.00
DE25	'04 $9 Black Scoter	20.00
DE26	'05 $9 Common Merganser and Lighthouse	18.00
DE27	'06 $9 Red-Breasted Mergansers	18.00
DE28	'07 $9 Surf Scooters, Lighthouse	18.00
DE29	'08 $9 Greater Scaup, Lighthouse	18.00
DE30	'09 $9 Black Ducks	18.00
DE31	'10 $9 Canvasback	18.00
DE32	'11 $9 Hooded Mergansers	18.00
DE33	'12 $9 Lesser Scaup	14.00
DE34	'13 $9 Wigeon	14.00
DE35	'14 $9 Blue-winged teal	14.00
DE36	'15 $9 Black Duck	14.00
DE37	'16 $9 Green-winged Teal	14.00
DE38	'17 $15 Canvasbacks and Retriever	25.00
DE39	'18 $15 Pintails and Golden Retriever	25.00
DE40	'19 $15 Long-tailed Duck and Retriever	25.00

FL8

FLORIDA

NO.	DESCRIPTION	F-VF NH
FL1	'79 $3.25 Green-Winged Teal	160.00
FL2	'80 $3.25 Pintails	18.00
FL3	'81 $3.25 Widgeon	18.00
FL4	'82 $3.25 Ring-Necked Ducks	18.00
FL5	'83 $3.25 Buffleheads	55.00
FL6	'84 $3.25 Hooded Merganser	20.00
FL7	'85 $3.25 Wood Ducks	18.00
FL8	'86 $3 Canvasbacks	14.00
FL9	'87 $3.50 Mallards	13.00
FL10	'88 $3.50 Redheads	12.00
FL11	'89 $3.50 Blue-Winged Teal	12.00
FL12	'90 $3.50 Wood Ducks	13.00
FL13	'91 $3.50 Northern Pintails	12.00
FL14	'92 $3.50 Ruddy Duck	12.00
FL15	'93 $3.50 American Widgeon	12.00
FL16	'94 $3.50 Mottled Duck	12.00
FL17	'95 $3.50 Fulvous Whistling Duck	13.00
FL18	'96 $3.50 Goldeneyes	23.00
FL19	'97 $3.50 Hooded Mergansers	19.00
FL20	'98 $3.50 Shoveler	36.00
FL21	'99 $3 Pintail	18.00
FL22	'00 $3.50 Rin-necked duck	18.00
FL23	'01 $3.50 Canvasback	18.00
FL24	'02 $3.50 Mottled Duck	66.00
FL25	'03 $3.50 Green-Winged Teal	135.00

GA1

GEORGIA

NO.	DESCRIPTION	F-VF NH
GA1	'85 $5.50 Wood Ducks	19.00
GA2	'86 $5.50 Mallards	12.00
GA3	'87 $5.50 Canada Geese	12.00
GA4	'88 $5.50 Ring-Necked Ducks	12.00
GA5	'89 $5.50 Duckling & Golden Retriever Puppy	22.00
GA6	'90 $5.50 Wood Ducks	12.00
GA7	'91 $5.50 Green-Winged Teal	12.00
GA8	'92 $5.50 Buffleheads	18.00

NO.	DESCRIPTION	F-VF NH
GA9	'93 $5.50 Mallards	18.00
GA10	'94 $5.50 Ring-Necked Ducks	18.00
GA11	'95 $5.50 Widgeons, Labrador Retriever	42.00
GA12	'96 $5.50 Black Ducks	35.00
GA13	'97 $5.50 Lesser Scaup	58.00
GA14	'98 $5.50 Black Lab with Ringnecks	37.00
GA15	'99 $5.50 Pintails	35.00

HI1

HAWAII

NO.	DESCRIPTION	F-VF NH
HI1	'96 $5 Nene Geese	13.00
HI2	'97 $5 Hawaiian Duck	13.00
HI3	'98 $5 Wild Turkey	15.00
HI4	'99 $5 Ring-necked Pheasant	18.00
HI5	'00 $5 Erckesls Francolin	15.00
HI6	'01 $5 Japanese Green Pheasant	15.00
HI7	'02 $10 Chukar Partridge	19.00
HI8	'03 $10 Nene Geese	19.00
HI9	'04 $10 Nene Geese	19.00
HI10	'05 $10 California Quail	19.00
HI11	'06 $10 Black Francolin	19.00
HI12	'07 $10 Gray Francolin	19.00
HI13	'08 $10 Chukar Partridge	19.00
HI14	'09 $10 California Quail	19.00
HI15	'11 $10 Green Pheasant	17.50
HI16	'11 $10 Wild Turkey	17.50
HI17	'12 $10 Mouflon Sheep	17.50
HI18	'15 $10 Mouflon Sheep	17.50
HI19	'16 $10 Axis Deer	17.50
HI20	'17 $10 Pheasant and Wild Sheep	17.50
HI21	'18 $10 Boar	17.50
HI22	'19 $10 Mouflon Sheep	17.50

ID1

IDAHO

NO.	DESCRIPTION	F-VF NH
ID1	'87 $5.50 Cinnamon Teal	20.00
ID2	'88 $5.50 Green-Winged Teal	16.00
ID3	'89 $6 Blue-Winged Teal	14.00
ID4	'90 $6 Trumpeter Swans	28.00
ID6	'91 $6 Widgeons	12.00
ID7	'92 $6 Canada Geese	18.00
ID8	'93 $6 Common Goldeneye	17.00
ID9	'94 $6 Harlequin Ducks	19.00
ID10	'95 $6 Wood Ducks	20.00
ID11	'96 $6 Mallard	28.00
ID12	'97 $6.50 Shovelers	20.00
ID13	'98 $6.50 Canada Geese	20.00

IL11

ILLINOIS

NO.	DESCRIPTION	F-VF NH
IL1	'75 $5 Mallard	400.00
IL2	'76 $5 Wood Ducks	175.00
IL3	'77 $5 Canada Goose	125.00
IL4	'78 $5 Canvasbacks	125.00
IL5	'79 $5 Pintail	85.00
IL6	'80 $5 Green-Winged Teal	85.00
IL7	'81 $5 Widgeons	85.00
IL8	'82 $5 Black Ducks	60.00
IL9	'83 $5 Lesser Scaup	75.00
IL10	'84 $5 Blue-Winged Teal	60.00
IL11	'85 $5 Redheads	21.00
IL12	'86 $5 Gadwalls	21.00
IL13	'87 $5 Buffleheads	18.00
IL14	'88 $5 Common Goldeneyes	16.00
IL15	'89 $5 Ring-Necked Ducks	16.00
IL16	'90 $10 Lesser Snow Geese	21.00
IL17	'91 $10 Labrador Retriever & Canada Goose	21.00
IL18	'92 $10 Retriever & Mallards	35.00
IL19	'93 $10 Pintail Decoys & Puppy	43.00
IL20	'94 $10 Canvasbacks & Retrievers	43.00
IL21	'95 $10 Retriever, Green-Winged Teal, Decoys	43.00
IL22	'96 $10 Wood Ducks	26.00
IL23	'97 $10 Canvasbacks	25.00
IL24	'98 $10 Canvasbacks	25.00
IL25	'99 $10 Canada Geese, black labrador retriever	35.00
IL27	'01 $10 Canvasback, yellow labrador	35.00
IL28	'02 $10 Canvasbacks, Chesapeake Retriever	35.00
IL29	'03 $10 Chocolate Lab, Green-winged Teal	32.00
IL30	'04 $10 Wood Ducks	24.00
IL31	'05 $10 Green-winged Teal	24.00
IL32	'06 $10 Northern Pintails	24.00

NO.	DESCRIPTION	F-VF NH
IL33	'07 $10 Bufflehead	25.00
IL34	'08 $10 Greater Scaup	45.00
IL35	'09 $10 Common Goldeneye	85.00
IL36	'10 $15 Blue Winged Teal	45.00

IN10

INDIANA

NO.	DESCRIPTION	F-VF NH
IN1	'76 $5 Green-Winged Teal	13.00
IN2	'77 $5 Pintail	13.00
IN3	'78 $5 Canada Geese	13.00
IN4	'79 $5 Canvasbacks	13.00
IN5	'80 $5 Mallard Ducklings	13.00
IN6	'81 $5 Hooded Mergansers	13.00
IN7	'82 $5 Blue-Winged Teal	13.00
IN8	'83 $5 Snow Geese	13.00
IN9	'84 $5 Redheads	13.00
IN10	'85 $5 Pintail	13.00
IN11	'86 $5 Wood Duck	13.00
IN12	'87 $5 Canvasbacks	13.00
IN13	'88 $6.75 Redheads	13.00
IN14	'89 $6.75 Canada Goose	13.00
IN15	'90 $6.75 Blue-Winged Teal	13.00
IN16	'91 $6.75 Mallards	13.00
IN17	'92 $6.75 Green-Winged Teal	13.00
IN18	'93 $6.75 Wood Ducks	13.00
IN19	'94 $6.75 Pintail	13.00
IN20	'95 $6.75 Goldeneyes	13.00
IN21	'96 $6.75 Black Ducks	13.00
IN22	'97 $6.75 Canada Geese	13.00
IN23	'98 $6.75 Widgeon	13.00
IN24	'99 $6.75 Bluebills	13.00
IN25	'00 $6.75 Ring-necked Duck	13.00
IN26	'01 $6.75 Green-winged Teal	13.00
IN27	'02 $6.75 Green-winged Teal	13.00
IN28	'03 $6.75 Shoveler	13.00
IN29	'04 $6.75 Hooded Mergansers	13.00
IN30	'05 $6.75 Buffleheads	13.00
IN31	'06 $6.75 Gadwalls	13.00
IN32	'07 $6.75 Pintails	13.00
IN33	'08 $6.75 Shovelers	13.00
IN34	'09 $6.75 Snow Geese	13.00
IN35	'10 $6.75 Black Duck	20.00
IN36	'11 $6.75 Wigeon	13.00
IN37	'12 $6.75 Canada geese	20.00
IN38	'13 $6.75 Wood ducks	11.25
IN39	'14 $6.75 Blue-winged teal	11.25

IA14

IOWA

NO.	DESCRIPTION	F-VF NH
IA1	'72 $1 Mallards	125.00
IA2	'73 $1 Pintails	40.50
IA3	'74 $1 Gadwalls	95.00
IA4	'75 $1 Canada Geese	100.00
IA5	'76 $1 Canvasbacks	31.00
IA6	'77 $1 Lesser Scaup	28.00
IA7	'78 $1 Wood Ducks	55.00
IA8	'79 $5 Buffleheads	275.00
IA9	'80 $5 Redheads	30.00
IA10	'81 $5 Green-Winged Teal	30.00
IA11	'82 $5 Snow Geese	22.00
IA12	'83 $5 Widgeons	22.00
IA13	'84 $5 Wood Ducks	40.00
IA14	'85 $5 Mallard & Mallard Decoy	22.00
IA15	'86 $5 Blue-Winged Teal	14.00
IA16	'87 $5 Canada Goose	14.00
IA17	'88 $5 Pintails	14.00
IA18	'89 $5 Blue-Winged Teal	14.00
IA19	'90 $5 Canvasbacks	14.00
IA20	'91 $5 Mallards	14.00
IA21	'92 $5 Labrador Retriever & Ducks	14.00
IA22	'93 $5 Mallards	14.00
IA23	'94 $5 Green-Winged Teal	14.00
IA24	'95 $5 Canada Geese	14.00
IA25	'96 $5 Canvasbacks	14.00
IA 26	'97 $5 Canada Geese	14.00
IA27	'98 $5 Pintails	14.00
IA28	'99 $5 Trumpeter Swan	19.00
IA29	'00 $5.50 Hooded Merganser	16.00
IA30	'01 $6 Snow Geese	15.00
IA31	'02 $8.50 Northern Shoveler	27.00
IA32	'03 $8.50 Ruddy Duck	20.00
IA33	'04 $8.50 Wood Ducks	18.00
IA34	'05 $8.50 Green-winged Teals	18.00
IA35	'06 Ring-Necked Duck	18.00
IA36	'07 $8.50 Wigeon	18.00
IA37	'08 $8.50 Wood Duck	18.00
IA38	'09 $10.00 Pintail	23.00
IA39	'10 $8.50 Green-winged teal	31.00
IA40	'11 Hooded Merganser	22.00

NO.	DESCRIPTION	F-VF NH
IA41	'12 Blue-winged teal	17.50
IA42	'13 Wood ducks	22.50
IA43	'14 Redhead	17.50
IA44	'15 Canada Geese	25.00

KS1

KANSAS

NO.	DESCRIPTION	F-VF NH
KS1	'87 $3 Green-Winged Teal	15.00
KS2	'88 $3 Canada Geese	11.00
KS3	'89 $3 Mallards	11.00
KS4	'90 $3 Wood Ducks	11.00
KS5	'91 $3 Pintail	10.00
KS6	'92 $3 Canvasbacks	10.00
KS7	'93 $3 Mallards	12.00
KS8	'94 $3 Blue-Winged Teal	12.00
KS9	'95 $3 Barrow's Goldeneye	12.00
KS10	'96 $3 Widgeon	13.00
KS11	'97 $3 Mallard (blue)	13.00
KS12	'98 $3 Mallard (green)	13.00
KS13	'99 $3 Mallard (red)	13.00
KS14	'00 $3 Mallard (purple)	13.00
KS15	'01 $3 Mallard (orange)	13.00
KS16	'02 $5 Pintail (blue)	13.00
KS17	'03 $5 Pintail (green)	16.00
KS18	'04 $5 Pintail (red)	16.00

KS1

KENTUCKY

NO.	DESCRIPTION	F-VF NH
KY1	'85 $5.25 Mallards	19.00
KY2	'86 $5.25 Wood Ducks	13.00
KY3	'87 $5.25 Black Ducks	14.00
KY4	'88 $5.25 Canada Geese	14.00
KY5	'89 $5.25 Retriever & Canvasbacks	19.00
KY6	'90 $5.25 Widgeons	12.00
KY7	'91 $5.25 Pintails	13.00
KY8	'92 $5.25 Green-Winged Teal	18.00
KY9	'93 $5.25 Canvasbacks & Decoy	25.00
KY10	'94 $5.25 Canada Goose	21.00
KY11	'95 $7.50 Retriever, Decoy, Ringnecks	29.00
KY12	'96 $7.50 Blue-Winged Teal	18.00
KY13	'97 $7.50 Shovelers	18.00
KY14	'98 $7.50 Gadwalls	19.00
KY15	'99 $7.50 Common Goldeneyes	19.00
KY16	'00 $7.50 Hooded Merganser	26.00
KY17	'01 $7.50 Mallard	18.00
KY18	'02 $7.50 Pintails	18.00
KY19	'03 $7.50 Snow Goose	18.00
KY20	'04 $7.50 Black Ducks	19.00
KY21	'05 $7.50 Canada Geese	18.00
KY22	'06 $7.50 Mallards	18.00
KY23	'07 $7.50 Green-Winged Teal	18.00
KY24	'08 $7.50 Pintails	18.00
KY25	'09 $7.50 Snow Geese	18.00

LA1

LOUISIANA

NO.	DESCRIPTION	F-VF NH
LA1	'89 $5 Blue-Winged Teal	15.00
LA1a	'89 $7.50 Blue-Winged Teal	20.00
LA2	'90 $5 Green-Winged Teal	12.00
LA2a	'90 $7.50 Green-Winged Teal	15.00
LA3	'91 $5 Wood Ducks	12.00
LA3a	'91 $7.50 Wood Ducks	18.00
LA4	'92 $5 Pintails	15.00
LA4a	'92 $7.50 Pintails	18.00
LA5	'93 $5 American Widgeon	15.00
LA5a	'93 $7.50 American Widgeon	18.00
LA6	'94 $5 Mottled Duck	16.00
LA6a	'94 $7.50 Mottled Duck	18.00
LA7	'95 $5 Speckle Bellied Goose	16.00
LA7a	'95 $7.50 Speckle Bellied Goose	18.00
LA8	'96 $5 Gadwall	15.00
LA8a	'96 $7.50 Gadwell	18.00
LA9	'97 $5.00 Ring Necked Duck	16.00
LA9a	'97 $13.50 Ring Necked Duck	30.00
LA10	'98 $5.50 Mallards	15.00
LA10a	'98 $13.50 Mallards	30.00
LA11	'99 $5.50 Snow Geese	15.00
LA11a	'99 $13.50 Snow Geese	30.00
LA12	'00 $5.50 Lesser Scaup	15.00

NO.	DESCRIPTION	F-VF NH
LA12a	'00 $13.50 Lesser Scaup	45.00
LA13	'01 $5.50 Northern Shoveler	15.00
LA13a	'01 $13.50 Northern Shoveler	45.00
LA14	'02 $5.50 Canvasbacks	15.00
LA14a	'02 $25 Canvasbacks	45.00
LA15	'03 $5.50 Redhead	15.00
LA15a	'03 $25.00 Redhead	45.00
LA16	'04 $5.50 Hooded Merganser	15.00
LA16a	'04 $25 Hooded Merganser	45.00
LA17	'05 $5.50 Pintails and Labrador Retriever	15.00
LA17a	'05 $25 Pintails and Labrador Retriever	45.00
LA18	'06 $5.50 Mallards, Labrador Retriever	15.00
LA18a	'06 $25 Mallards, Labrador Retriever	45.00
LA19	'07 $5.50 Mallards, Labrador Retriever	15.00
LA19a	'07 $25 Mallards, Labrador Retriever	40.00
LA20	'08 $5.50 Wood Ducks, Golden Retriever	13.00
LA20a	'08 $25 Wood Ducks, Golden Retriever	62.50
LA21	'09 $5.50 Ducks, Chesapeake Bay Retriever	11.00
LA21a	'09 $25 Ducks, Chesapeake Bay Retriever	40.00
LA22	'10 $5.50 Pintails	10.00
LA22a	'10 $25 Pintails	40.00
LA23	'11 $5.50 Wood Ducks	10.00
LA23a	'11 $25 Wood Ducks	41.00
LA24	'12 $5.50 Wigeons	10.00
LA24a	'12 $25 Wigeons	32.50
LA25	'13 $5.50 Mallards	10.00
LA25a	'13 $25 Mallards	35.00
LA26	'14 $5.50 White-fronted Geese	10.00
LA26a	'14 $25 White-fronted Geese	32.50
LA27	'15 5.50 Blue-winged Teal	10.00
LA27a	'15 $25 Blue-winged Teal	35.00
LA28	'16 $5.50 Gadwalls	12.00
LA28a	'16 $25 Gadwalls	35.00
LA29	'17 $5.50 Green-winged Teal	10.00
LA29a	'17 $25 Green-tailed Teal	35.00
LA30	'18 $5.50 Canvasbacks	10.00
LA30a	'18 $25 Canvasbacks	35.00
LA31	'19 $5.50 Shovelers	10.00
LA31a	'19 $25 Shovelers	35.00

ME2

MAINE

NO.	DESCRIPTION	F-VF NH
ME1	'84 $2.50 Black Ducks	25.00
ME2	'85 $2.50 Common Eiders	45.00
ME3	'86 $2.50 Wood Ducks	13.00
ME4	'87 $2.50 Buffleheads	11.00
ME5	'88 $2.50 Green-Winged Teal	11.00
ME6	'89 $2.50 Common Goldeneyes	10.00
ME7	'90 $2.50 Canada Geese	10.00
ME8	'91 $2.50 Ring-Necked Duck	10.00
ME9	'92 $2.50 Old Squaw	10.00
ME10	'93 $2.50 Hooded Merganser	10.00
ME11	'94 $2.50 Mallards	13.00
ME12	'95 $2.50 White-Winged Scoters	15.00
ME13	'96 $2.50 Blue-Winged Teal	15.00
ME14	'97 $2.50 Greater Scaup	15.00
ME15	'98 $2.50 Surf Scoters	15.00
ME16	'99 $2.50 Black Duck	12.00
ME17	'00 $2.50 Common Eider	10.00
ME18	'01 $2.50 Wood Duck	10.00
ME19	'02 $2.50 Bufflehead	10.00
ME20	'03 $5.50 Green-winged Teal	18.00
ME21	'04 $5.50 Barrows Goldeneyes	18.00
ME22	'05 $8.50 Canada Goose	18.00
ME23	'06 $7.50 Ring-Necked Ducks	18.00
ME24	'07 $7.50 Long-Tailed Ducks	18.00
ME25	'08 Hooded Mergansers	18.00
ME26	'09 $7.50 Mallards	18.00
ME27	'10 $7.50 Harlequin Ducks	18.00
ME28	'11 $7.50 Wood Ducks	13.00
ME29	'12 $7.50 Ringed-necked ducks	13.00
ME30	'13 $7.50 Greater Scaup	13.00
ME31	'14 $7.50 Wigeon	13.00
ME32	'15 $7.50 Canvasbacks	13.00
ME33	'16 $7.50 Blue-winged Teal	13.00
ME34	'17 $7.50 Common Eiders	13.00
ME35	'18 $7.50 Northern Pintails	13.00
ME36	'19 $7.50 Canada Goose	13.00

MD1

MARYLAND

NO.	DESCRIPTION	F-VF NH
MD1	'74 $1.10 Mallards	15.00
MD2	'75 $1.10 Canada Geese	15.00
MD3	'76 $1.10 Canvasbacks	15.00
MD4	'77 $1.10 Greater Scaup	15.00
MD5	'78 $1.10 Redheads	15.00
MD6	'79 $1.10 Wood Ducks	15.00
MD7	'80 $1.10 Pintail Decoy	15.00

NO.	DESCRIPTION	F-VF NH
MD8	'81 $3 Widgeon	12.00
MD9	'82 $3 Canvasback	12.00
MD10	'83 $3 Wood Duck	17.00
MD11	'84 $6 Black Ducks	18.00
MD12	'85 $6 Canada Geese	18.00
MD13	'86 $6 Hooded Mergansers	18.00
MD14	'87 $6 Redheads	18.00
MD15	'88 $6 Ruddy Ducks	18.00
MD16	'89 $6 Blue-Winged Teal	18.00
MD17	'90 $6 Lesser Scaup	18.00
MD18	'91 $6 Shovelers	18.00
MD19	'92 $6 Bufflehead	18.00
MD20	'93 $6 Canvasbacks	18.00
MD21	'94 $6 Redheads	18.00
MD22	'95 $6 Mallards	40.00
MD23	'96 $6 Canada Geese	50.00
MD24	'97 $6 Canvasbacks	18.00
MD25	'98 $6 Pintails	18.00
MD26	'99 $6 Wood Ducks	18.00
MD27	'00 $6 Oldsquaws	24.00
MD28	'01 $6 American Widgeon	18.00
MD29	'02 $9 Black Scoters	24.00
MD30	'03 $9 Lesser Scaup	24.00
MD31	'04 $9 Pintails	24.00
MD32	'05 $9 Ruddy Duck	24.00
MD33	'06 $9 Canada Geese	24.00
MD34	'07 $9 Wood Ducks	24.00
MD35	'08 $9 Canvasbacks	18.00
MD36	'09 $9 Blue-Winged Teal	18.00
MD37	'10 $9 Hooded Merganser	18.00
MD38	'11 $9 Canada Geese	18.00
MD39	'12 $9 Wigeons	18.00
MD40	'13 $9 Lesser Scaup	18.00
MD41	'14 $9 Ring-necked duck	18.00
MD42	'15 $9 Canvasback	18.00
MD43	'16 $9 Shovelers	18.00
MD44	'17 $9 Black Ducks	18.00
MD45	'18 $9 Green-winged Teal	18.00
MD46	'19 $9 Green Ducks	18.00

MA12

MASSACHUSETTS

NO.	DESCRIPTION	F-VF NH
MA1	'74 $1.25 Wood Duck Decoy	19.00
MA2	'75 $1.25 Pintail Decoy	16.00
MA3	'76 $1.25 Canada Goose Decoy	16.00
MA4	'77 $1.25 Goldeneye Decoy	16.00
MA5	'78 $1.25 Black Duck Decoy	18.00
MA6	'79 $1.25 Ruddy Turnstone Duck Decoy	24.00
MA7	'80 $1.25 Old Squaw Decoy	19.00
MA8	'81 $1.25 Red-Breasted Merganser Decoy	19.00
MA9	'82 $1.25 Greater Yellowlegs Decoy	19.00
MA10	'83 $1.25 Redhead Decoy	19.00
MA11	'84 $1.25 White-Winged Scoter Decoy	19.00
MA12	'85 $1.25 Ruddy Duck Decoy	19.00
MA13	'86 $1.25 Preening Bluebill Decoy	18.00
MA14	'87 $1.25 American Widgeon Decoy	18.00
MA15	'88 $1.25 Mallard Decoy	18.00
MA16	'89 $1.25 Brant Decoy	18.00
MA17	'90 $1.25 Whistler Hen Decoy	18.00
MA18	'91 $5 Canvasback Decoy	15.00
MA19	'92 $5 Black-Bellied Plover Decoy	15.00
MA20	'93 $5 Red-Breasted Merganser Decoy	15.00
MA21	'94 $5 White-Winged Scoter Decoy	15.00
MA22	'95 $5 Female Hooded Merganser Decoy	15.00
MA23	'96 $5 Eider Decoy	15.00
MA24	'97 $5 Curlew Shorebird	15.00
MA25	'98 $5 Canada Goose	15.00
MA26	'99 $5 Oldsquaw Decoy	15.00
MA27	'00 $5 Merganser Hen decoy	15.00
MA28	'01 $5 Black Duck decoy	15.00
MA29	'02 $5 Bufflehead decoy	15.00
MA30	'03 $5 Green-winged Teal decoy	14.00
MA31	'04 $5 Wood Duck Decoy	14.00
MA32	'05 $5 Oldsquaw Drake Decoy	14.00
MA33	'06 $5 Long-Bellied Curlew Decoy	14.00
MA34	'07 $5 Goldeneye Decoy	14.00
MA35	'08 $5 Black Duck Decoy	14.00
MA36	'09 $5 White-Winged Scoter Decoy	14.00
MA37	'10 $5 Canada Goose Decoy	14.00
MA38	'11 $5 Brant Decoy	14.00

MI10

MICHIGAN

NO.	DESCRIPTION	F-VF NH
MI1	'76 $2.10 Wood Duck	7.00
MI2	'77 $2.10 Canvasbacks	355.00
MI3	'78 $2.10 Mallards	32.00

NO.	DESCRIPTION	F-VF NH
MI4	'79 $2.10 Canada Geese	.77.00
MI5	'80 $3.75 Lesser Scaup	.25.00
MI6	'81 $3.75 Buffleheads	.31.00
MI7	'82 $3.75 Redheads	.31.00
MI8	'83 $3.75 Wood Ducks	.31.00
MI9	'84 $3.75 Pintails	.31.00
MI10	'85 $3.75 Ring-Necked Ducks	.31.00
MI11	'86 $3.75 Common Goldeneyes	.28.00
MI12	'87 $3.85 Green-Winged Teal	.15.00
MI13	'88 $3.85 Canada Geese	.12.00
MI14	'89 $3.85 Widgeons	.13.00
MI15	'90 $3.85 Wood Ducks	.13.00
MI16	'91 $3.85 Blue-Winged Teal	.13.00
MI17	'92 $3.85 Red-Breasted Merganser	.11.00
MI18	'93 $3.85 Hooded Merganser	.11.00
MI19	'94 $3.85 Black Duck	.11.00
MI20	'95 $4.35 Blue Winged Teal	.11.00
MI21	'96 $4.35 Canada Geese	.11.00
MI22	'97 $5 Canvasbacks	.30.00
MI23	'98 $5 Pintail	.11.00
MI24	'99 $5 Shoveler	.13.00
MI25	'00 $5 Mallards	.48.00
MI26	'01 $5 Ruddy Duck	.12.00
MI27	'02 $5 Wigeons	.12.00
MI28	'03 $5 Redhead	.12.00
MI29	'04 $5 Wood Duck	.12.00
MI30	'05 $5 Blue-winged Teals	.12.00
MI31	'06 $5 Widgeon	.12.00
MI32	'07 $5 Pintails	.12.00
MI33	'08 $5 Wood Ducks	.12.00
MI34	'09 $5 Canvasbacks	.12.00
MI35	'10 $5 Buffleheads	.12.00
MI36	'11 $5 Mallard	.10.00
MI37	'12 $5 Ring-necked ducks	.10.00
MI38	'13 $5 Black duck	.10.00
MI39	'14 $5 Long-tailed ducks	.10.00
MI40	'15 $6 Common Goldeneyes	.10.00
MI41	'16 $6 Green-winged Teal	.10.00
MI42	'17 $6 Shovelers	.10.00
MI43	'18 $6 Wingeons and Black Labrador	.10.00
MI44	'19 $6 Pintails	.10.00

MINNESOTA

NO.	DESCRIPTION	F-VF NH
MN1	'77 $3 Mallards	.18.00
MN2	'78 $3 Lesser Scaup	.15.00
MN3	'79 $3 Pintails	.15.00
MN4	'80 $3 Canvasbacks	.18.00
MN5	'81 $3 Canada Geese	.18.00
MN6	'82 $3 Redheads	.18.00
MN7	'83 $3 Blue Geese & Snow Goose	.18.00
MN8	'84 $3 Wood Ducks	.18.00
MN9	'85 $3 White-Fronted Geese	.12.00
MN10	'86 $5 Lesser Scaup	.12.00
MN11	'87 $5 Common Goldeneyes	.15.00
MN12	'88 $5 Buffleheads	.12.00
MN13	'89 $5 Widgeons	.12.00
MN14	'90 $5 Hooded Mergansers	.25.00
MN15	'91 $5 Ross's Geese	.12.00
MN16	'92 $5 Barrow's Goldeneyes	.12.00
MN17	'93 $5 Blue-Winged Teal	.12.00
MN18	'94 $5 Ringneck Duck	.12.00
MN19	'95 $5 Gadwall	.12.00
MN20	'96 $5 Greater Scaup	.14.00
MN21	'97 $5 Shoveler with Decoy	.14.00
MN22	'98 $5 Harlequin Ducks	.14.00
MN23	'99 $5 Green-winged Teal	.14.00
MN24	'00 $5 Red-Breasted Merganser	.25.00
MN25	'01 $5 Black Duck	.30.00
MN26	'02 $5 Ruddy Duck	.18.00
MN27	'03 $5 Long Tailed Duck	.18.00
MN28	'04 $7.50 Common Merganser	.18.00
MN29	'05 $7.50 White-winged Scoters and Lighthouse	.18.00
MN30	'06 $7.50 Mallard	.18.00
MN31	'07 $7.50 Lesser Scaups	.18.00
MN32	'08 $7.50 Ross's Geese	.18.00
MN33	'09 $7.50 Common Goldeneye	.18.00
MN34	'10 $7.50 Wood Duck	.18.00
MN35	'11 $7.50 Red-Breasted Merganser	.18.00
MN36	'12 $7.50 Ruddy Duck	.18.00
MN37	'13 $7.50 Pintail	.18.00
MN38	'14 $7.50 Canada Geese	.18.00
MN39	'15 $7.50 Harlequin Duck	.25.00
MN40	'16 $7.50 Wigeon	.18.00
MN41	'17 $7.50 Redheads	.18.00
MN42	'18 $7.50 White-winged Scoter	.16.00
MN43	'19 $7.50 Gadwall	.16.00

MISSISSIPPI

NO.	DESCRIPTION	F-VF NH
MS1	'76 $2 Wood Duck	.27.00

NO.	DESCRIPTION	F-VF NH
MS2	'77 $2 Mallards	.13.00
MS3	'78 $2 Green-Winged Teal	.13.00
MS4	'79 $2 Canvasbacks	.12.00
MS5	'80 $2 Pintails	.12.00
MS6	'81 $2 Redheads	.12.00
MS7	'82 $2 Canada Geese	.19.00
MS8	'83 $2 Lesser Scaup	.12.00
MS9	'84 $2 Black Ducks	.12.00
MS10	'85 $2 Mallards	.20.00
MS11	'86 $2 Widgeons	.12.00
MS12	'87 $2 Ring-Necked Ducks	.12.00
MS13	'88 $2 Snow Geese	.12.00
MS14	'89 $2 Wood Ducks	.9.00
MS15	'90 $2 Snow Geese	.17.00
MS16	'91 $2 Labrador Retriever & Canvasbacks	.11.00
MS17	'92 $2 Green-Winged Teal	.10.00
MS18	'93 $2 Mallards	.11.00
MS19	'94 $2 Canvasbacks	.15.00
MS20	'95 $5 Blue-Winged Teal	.17.00
MS21	'96 $5 Hooded Merganser	.23.00
MS22	'97 $5 Wood Duck	.30.00
MS23	'98 $5 Pintails	.15.00
MS24	'99 $5 Ring-necked Duck	.15.00
MS24a	'99 $5 Ring-necked Duck, S/A, die-cut	.15.00
MS25	'00 $5 Mallards	.15.00
MS25a	'00 $5 Mallards, S/A, die cut	.450.00
MS26	'01 $10 Gadwall	.15.00
MS26a	'01 $10 Gadwall, S/A, die cut	.15.00
MS27	'02 $10 Wood Duck	.15.00
MS27a	'02 $10 Wood Duck, S/A, die cut	.15.00
MS28	'03 $10 Pintail	.15.00
MS28a	'03 $10 Pintail, S/A, die cut	.15.00
MS29	'04 $10 Wood Ducks	.15.00
MS29a	'04 $10 Wood Ducks, S/A, die cut	.15.00
MS30	'05 $10 Blue-Winged Teal	.15.00
MS30a	'05 $10 Blue-Winged Teal, S/A, die cut	.15.00
MS30b	'05 $15 Blue-Winged Teal, non-resident	.24.00
MS31	'06 $10 Labrador Retriever	.15.00
MS31a	'06 $10 Labrador Retriever, S/A, die-cut	.15.00
MS31b	'06 $15 Labrador Retriever, non-resident	.24.00
MS32	'07 $10 Wood Ducks	.15.00
MS32a	'07 $15 Wood Duck, S/A, die-cut	.15.00
MS32b	'07 $15 Wood Ducks, non-resident	.24.00
MS33	'08 $10 Green-winged Teal	.15.00
MS33a	'08 $10 Green-winged Teal, S/A, die-cut	.15.00
MS33b	'08 $15 Green-winged Teal, non-resident	.24.00
MS34	'09 $10 Blue-winged Teal	.15.00
MS34a	'09 $10 Blue-winged Teal, S/A, die-cut	.15.00
MS34b	'09 $15 Blue-winged Teal, non-resident	.24.00
MS35	'10 $10 Mallards	.15.00
MS35a	'10 $10 Mallards, S/A, die-cut	.15.00
MS35b	'10 $15 Mallards, non-resident	.24.00
MS36	'11 $10 Wood Duck	.15.00
MS36a	'11 $10 Wood Duck S/A, die-cut	.15.00
MS36b	'11 $15 Wood Duck, non-resident	.24.00
MS37	'12 $10 Green-winged teal	.15.00
MS37a	'12 $10 Green-winged teal, S/A, die-cut	.15.00
MS37b	'12 $15 Green-winged teal, non-resident	.24.00
MS38	'13 $10 Mallard	.15.00
MS38a	'13 $10 Mallard, S/A, die-cut	.15.00
MS38b	'13 $15 Mallard, non-resident	.24.00
MS39	'14 $10 Wood Ducks	.17.00
MS39a	'14 $10 Wood Ducks, S/A, die-cut	.17.00
MS39b	'14 $15 Wood Ducks, non-resident	.24.00
MS40	'15 $10 Pintail	.17.00
MS40a	'15 $10 Pintail, S/A, die-cut	.17.00
MS40b	'15 $10 Pintail, non-resident	.24.00
MS41	'16 $10 Pintail	.17.00
MS41a	'16 $10 Pintail, S/A, die-cut	.17.00
MS41b	'16 $10 Pintail, non-resident	.24.00
MS42	'17 $10 Gadwall	.17.00
MS42a	'17 $10 Gadwall, S/A, die-cut	.17.00
MS42b	'17 $15 Gadwall, non-resident	.24.00
MS43	'18 $10 Canvasback	.17.00
MS43a	'18 $10 Canvasback, S/A, die-cut	.17.00
MS43b	'18 $15 Canvasback, non-resident	.24.00
MS44	'19 $10 Redheads	.17.00
MS44a	'19 $10 Redheads, S/A, die-cut	.17.00
MS44b	'19 $15 Redheads, non-resident	.24.00

MISSOURI

NO.	DESCRIPTION	F-VF NH
MO1	'79 $3.40 Canada Geese	.400.00
MO2	'80 $3.40 Wood Ducks	.90.00
MO3	'81 $3 Lesser Scaup	.55.00
MO4	'82 $3 Buffleheads	.55.00
MO5	'83 $3 Blue-Winged Teal	.57.00
MO6	'84 $3 Mallards	.55.00
MO7	'85 $3 American Widgeons	.28.00
MO8	'86 $3 Hooded Mergansers	.18.00
MO9	'87 $3 Pintails	.15.00
MO10	'88 $3 Canvasback	.14.00
MO11	'89 $3 Ring-Necked Ducks	.11.00
MO12	'90 $5 Redheads	.10.00
MO13	'91 $5 Snow Geese	.10.00
MO14	'92 $5 Gadwalls	.10.00
MO15	'93 $5 Green-Winged Teal	.10.00
MO16	'94 $5 White-Fronted Goose	.10.00

NO.	DESCRIPTION	F-VF NH
MO17	'95 $5 Goldeneyes	.12.00
MO18	'96 $5 Black Duck	.16.00

MONTANA

NO.	DESCRIPTION	F-VF NH
MT34	'86 $5 Canada Geese	.15.00
MT35	'87 $5 Redheads	.18.00
MT36	'88 $5 Mallards	.15.00
MT37	'89 $5 Black Labrador Retriever & Pintail	.15.00
MT38	'90 $5 Blue-Winged & CinnamonTeal	.10.00
MT39	'91 $5 Snow Geese	.10.00
MT40	'92 $5 Wood Ducks	.10.00
MT41	'93 $5 Harlequin Ducks	.10.00
MT42	'94 $5 Widgeons	.10.00
MT43	'95 $5 Tundra Swans	.10.00
MT44	'96 $5 Canvasbacks	.10.00
MT45	'97 $5 Golden Retriever	.10.00
MT46	'98 $5 Gadwalls	.10.00
MT47	'99 $5 Barrow's Goldeneye	.10.00
MT48	'00 $5 Mallard decoy, Chesapeake retriever	.10.00
MT49	'01 $5 Canada Geese, Steamboat	.10.00
MT50	'02 ($5) Sandhill crane	.10.00
MT51	'03 $5 Mallards	.80.00

NEBRASKA

NO.	DESCRIPTION	F-VF NH
NE1	'91 $6 Canada Geese	.12.00
NE2	'92 $6 Pintails	.12.00
NE3	'93 $6 Canvasbacks	.12.00
NE4	'94 $6 Mallards	.12.00
NE5	'95 $5 Wood Ducks	.12.00
NE6	'06 $5 Wood Ducks	.12.00
NE7	'07 $5 Canvasbacks	.12.00
NE8	'08 $5 Swans	.12.00
NE9	'09 $5 Northern Pintail	.12.00

NEVADA

NO.	DESCRIPTION	F-VF NH
NV1	'79 $2 Canvasbacks & Decoy	.50.00
NV2	'80 $2 Cinnamon Teal	.10.00
NV3	'81 $2 Whistling Swans	.12.00
NV4	'82 $2 Shovelers	.12.00
NV5	'83 $2 Gadwalls	.12.00
NV6	'84 $2 Pintails	.12.00
NV7	'85 $2 Canada Geese	.26.00
NV8	'86 $2 Redheads	.26.00
NV9	'87 $2 Buffleheads	.23.00
NV10	'88 $2 Canvasbacks	.15.00
NV11	'89 $2 Ross's Geese	.21.00
NV12	'90 $5 Green-Winged Teal	.21.00
NV13	'91 $5 White-Faced Ibis	.15.00
NV14	'92 $5 American Widgeon	.14.00
NV15	'93 $5 Common Goldeneye	.14.00
NV16	'94 $5 Mallards	.14.00
NV17	'95 $5 Wood Duck	.14.00
NV18	'96 $5 Ring Necked Duck	.24.00
NV19	'97 $5 Ruddy Duck	.14.00
NV20	'98 $5 Hooded Merganser	.19.00
NV21	'99 $5 Canvasback Decoy	.19.00
NV22	'00 $5 Canvasbacks	.19.00
NV23	'01 $5 Lesser Scaup	.19.00
NV24	'02 $5 Cinnamon Teal	.15.00
NV25	'03 $5 Green-winged Teal	.15.00
NV26	'04 $10 Redhead	.19.00
NV27	'05 $10 Gadwalls	.19.00
NV28	'06 $10 Tundra Swans	.19.00
NV29	'07 $10 Wood Ducks	.19.00
NV30	'08 $10 Pintail	.19.00
NV31	'09 $10 Canada Goose	.19.00
NV32	'10 $10 Shovelers	.19.00
NV33	'11 $10 Green Winged Teal	.18.00
NV34	'12 $10 Wigeon	.18.00
NV35	'13 $10 Snow Goose	.18.00
NV36	'14 $10 American Coots	.18.00
NV37	'15 $10 White-footed Goose	.18.00
NV38	'16 $10 Buffleheads	.18.00
NV39	'17 $10 Ruddy Duck	.18.00

NO.	DESCRIPTION	F-VF NH

NH2

NEW HAMPSHIRE

NO.	DESCRIPTION	F-VF NH
NH1	'83 $4 Wood Ducks	130.00
NH2	'84 $4 Mallards	100.00
NH3	'85 $4 Blue-Winged Teal	130.00
NH4	'86 $4 Hooded Mergansers	25.00
NH5	'87 $4 Canada Geese	12.00
NH6	'88 $4 Buffleheads	12.00
NH7	'89 $4 Black Ducks	12.00
NH8	'90 $4 Green-Winged Teal	12.00
NH9	'91 $4 Golden Retriever & Mallards	16.00
NH10	'92 $4 Ring-Necked Ducks	12.00
NH11	'93 $4 Hooded Mergansers	12.00
NH12	'94 $4 Common Goldeneyes	12.00
NH13	'95 $4 Northern Pintails	12.00
NH14	'96 $4 Surf Scoters	16.00
NH15	'97 $4 Old Squaws	12.00
NH16	'98 $4 Canada Goose	12.00
NH17	'99 $4 Mallards	12.00
NH18	'00 $4 Black Ducks	12.00
NH19	'01 $4 Blue-winged Teal	12.00
NH20	'02 $4 Pintails	12.00
NH21	'03 $4 Wood Ducks	12.00
NH22	'04 $4 Wood Ducks	12.00
NH23	'05 $4 Oldsquaw and Lighthouse	12.00
NH24	'06 $4 Common Elders	12.00
NH25	'07 $4 Black Ducks	12.00

NJ1

NEW JERSEY

NO.	DESCRIPTION	F-VF NH
NJ1	'84 $2.50 Canvasbacks	45.00
NJ1a	'84 $5 Canvasbacks	65.00
NJ2	'85 $2.50 Mallards	20.00
NJ2a	'85 $5 Mallards	24.00
NJ3	'86 $2.50 Pintails	23.00
NJ3a	'86 $5 Pintails	16.00
NJ4	'87 $2.50 Canada Geese	24.00
NJ4a	'87 $5 Canada Geese	22.00
NJ5	'88 $2.50 Green-Winged Teal	17.00
NJ5a	'88 $5 Green-Winged Teal	14.00
NJ6	'89 $2.50 Snow Geese	16.00
NJ6a	'89 $5 Snow Geese	16.00
NJ7	'90 $2.50 Wood Ducks	18.00
NJ7a	'90 $5 Wood Ducks	12.00
NJ8	'91 $2.50 Atlantic Brant	18.00
NJ8a	'91 $5 Atlantic Brant	16.00
NJ9	'92 $2.50 Bluebills	16.00
NJ9a	'92 $5 Bluebills	14.00
NJ10	'93 $2.50 Buffleheads	14.00
NJ10a	'93 $5 Buffleheads	14.00
NJ11	'94 $2.50 Black Ducks	16.00
NJ11a	'94 $5 Black Ducks	16.00
NJ12	'95 $2.50 Widgeon, Lighthouse	16.00
NJ12a	'95 $5 Widgeon, Lighthouse	16.00
NJ13	'96 $2.50 Goldeneyes	15.00
NJ13a	'96 $5 Goldeneyes	18.00
NJ14	'97 $5 Oldsquaws	16.00
NJ14a	'97 $10 Oldsquaws	22.00
NJ15	'98 $5 Mallards	17.00
NJ15a	'98 $10.00 Mallards	20.00
NJ16	'99 $5 Redheads	17.00
NJ16a	'99 $10 Redheads	20.00
NJ17	'00 $5 Canvasbacks	18.00
NJ17a	'00 $10 Canvasbacks	20.00
NJ18	'01 $5 Tundra Swans	16.00
NJ18a	'01 $10 Tundra Swans	20.00
NJ19	'02 $5 Wood Ducks	16.00
NJ19a	'02 $10 Wood Ducks	20.00
NJ20	'03 $5 Pintails & Black Lab	15.00
NJ20a	'03 $10 Pintails & Black Lab	20.00
NJ21	'04 $5 Merganser/Puppy	13.00
NJ21a	'04 $10 Merganser/Puppy	20.00
NJ22	'05 $5 Canvasback Decoys and Retriever	15.00
NJ22a	'05 $10 Canvasback Decoys and Retriever	20.00
NJ23	'06 $5 Wood Duck Decoy, Golden Retriever	15.00
NJ23a	'06 $10 Wood Duck Decoy, Golden Retriever	20.00
NJ24	'07 $5 Green-Winged Teal, Labrador Retriever	12.00
NJ24a	'07 $10 Green-Winged Teal, Labrador Retriever	18.00
NJ25	'08 $5 Canvasbacks	12.00
NJ25a	'08 $10 Canvasbacks	18.00

NM1

NEW MEXICO

NO.	DESCRIPTION	F-VF NH
NM1	'91 $7.50 Pintails	18.00
NM2	'92 $7.50 American Widgeon	18.00
NM3	'93 $7.50 Mallard	18.00
NM4	'94 $7.50 Green-Winged Teal	25.00

NY3

NEW YORK

NO.	DESCRIPTION	F-VF NH
NY1	'85 $5.50 Canada Geese	14.00
NY2	'86 $5.50 Mallards	10.00
NY3	'87 $5.50 Wood Ducks	10.00
NY4	'88 $5.50 Pintails	10.00
NY5	'89 $5.50 Greater Scaup	10.00
NY6	'90 $5.50 Canvasbacks	10.00
NY7	'91 $5.50 Redheads	12.00
NY8	'92 $5.50 Wood Ducks	12.00
NY9	'93 $5.50 Blue-Winged Teal	12.00
NY10	'94 $5.50 Canada Geese	12.00
NY11	'95 $5.50 Common Goldeneye	12.00
NY12	'96 $5.50 Common Loon	12.00
NY13	'97 $5.50 Hooded Merganser	12.00
NY14	'98 $5.50 Osprey	12.00
NY15	'99 $5.50 Buffleheads	15.00
NY16	'00 $5.50 Wood Ducks	20.00
NY17	'01 $5.50 Pintails	12.00
NY18	'02 $5.50 Canvasbacks	12.00

NC1

NORTH CAROLINA

NO.	DESCRIPTION	F-VF NH
NC1	'83 $5.50 Mallards	60.00
NC2	'84 $5.50 Wood Ducks	45.00
NC3	'85 $5.50 Canvasbacks	25.00
NC4	'86 $5.50 Canada Geese	25.00
NC5	'87 $5.50 Pintails	18.00
NC6	'88 $5 Green-Winged Teal	12.00
NC7	'89 $5 Snow Geese	18.00
NC8	'90 $5 Redheads	18.00
NC9	'91 $5 Blue-Winged Teal	18.00
NC10	'92 $5 American Widgeon	18.00
NC11	'93 $5 Tundra Swans	18.00
NC12	'94 $5 Buffleheads	18.00
NC13	'95 $5 Brant, Lighthouse	18.00
NC14	'96 $5 Pintails	18.00
NC15	'97 $5 Wood Ducks	18.00
NC15a	'97 $5 Wood Ducks, self-adhesive	45.00
NC16	'98 $5 Canada Geese	15.00
NC16a	'98 $5 Canada Geese, self-adhesive	36.00
NC17	'99 $5 Green-winged Teal	22.00
NC17a	'99 $5 Green-winged Teal, self-adhesive	25.00
NC18	'00 $10 Green-winged Teal	24.00
NC18a	'00 $10 Green-winged Teal, self-adhesive	36.00
NC19	'01 $10 Black Duck, lighthouse	23.00
NC19a	'01 $10 Black Duck, lighthouse, self-adhesive	25.00
NC20	'02 $10 Pintails, Hunters, Dog	23.00
NC20a	'02 $10 Pintails, Hunters, Dog, self-adhesive	35.00
NC21	'03 $10 Ringneck & Brittney Spaniel	20.00
NC21a	'03 $10 Ringneck & Brittney Spaniel, self-adhesive	30.00
NC22	'04 $10 Mallard	20.00
NC22a	'04 $10 Mallard, self-adhesive	25.00
NC23	'05 $10 Green-winged Teals	24.00
NC23a	'05 $10 Green-winged Teals, self-adhesive	25.00
NC24	'06 $10 Lesser Scaups, perf.	23.00
NC24a	'06 $10 Lesser Scaups, self-adhesive, die-cut	25.00
NC25	'07 $10 Wood Ducks	23.00
NC25a	'07 $10 Wood Ducks, self-adhesive, die cut	25.00
NC26	'08 $10 Surf Scooters	20.00
NC26a	'08 $10 Surf Scooters, self-adhesive, die cut	25.00
NC27	'09 $10 Wigeons, perf.	18.00
NC27a	'09 $10 Wigeons, self-adhesive	24.00
NC28	'10 $10 Snow Geese	19.00
NC28a	'10 $10 Snow Geese, self-adhesive, die-cut	24.00
NC29	'11 $10 Canada Geese	18.00
NC29a	'11 $10 Canada Geese S/A	19.00
NC30	'12 $10 Redheads	17.00
NC30a	'12 $10 Redheads, S/A	18.00
NC31	'13 $10 Shovelers	17.00
NC31a	'13 $10 Shovelers, self-adhesive	18.00

NO.	DESCRIPTION	F-VF NH
NC32	'14 $10 Hooded Mergansers, W/A	17.00
NC32a	'14 $10 Hooded Mergansers, S/A	18.00
NC33	'15 $10 Black Ducks	17.00
NC33a	'15 $10 Black Ducks, S/A, die-cut	18.00
NC34	'16 $13 Atlantic Brant and Lighthouse	20.00
NC34a	'16 $13 Atlantic Brant and Lighthouse, S/A	20.00
NC35	'17 $13 Gadwalls	20.00
NC35a	'17 $13 Gadwalls, S/A	20.00
NC36	'18 $13 Canvasbacks	20.00
NC36a	'18 $13 Canvasbacks, S/A	20.00
NC37	'19 $13 Ring-necked Ducks	20.00
NC37a	'19 $13 Ring-necked Ducks, S/A	20.00

ND35

NORTH DAKOTA

NO.	DESCRIPTION	F-VF NH
ND32	'82 $9 Canada Geese	120.00
ND35	'83 $9 Mallards	70.00
ND38	'84 $9 Canvasbacks	50.00
ND41	'85 $9 Greater Scaup	25.00
ND44	'86 $9 Pintails	25.00
ND47	'87 $9 Snow Geese	18.00
ND50	'88 $9 White-Winged Scoters	16.00
ND53	'89 $6 Redheads	12.00
ND56	'90 $6 Labrador Retriever & Mallard	12.00
ND59	'91 $6 Green-Winged Teal	12.00
ND62	'92 $6 Blue-Winged Teal	12.00
ND65	'93 $6 Wood Ducks	12.00
ND67	'94 $6 Canada Geese	12.00
ND69	'95 $6 Widgeon	12.00
ND71	'96 $6 Mallards	12.00
ND73	'97 $6 White Fronted Geese	12.00
ND75	'98 $6 Blue Winged Teal	12.00
ND77	'99 $6 Gadwalls	12.00
ND79	'00 $6 Pintails	12.00
ND81	'01 $6 Canada Geese	12.00
ND83	'02 $6 Text, black on green	18.00
ND84	'03 $6 Text, black on green	18.00
ND85	'04 $6 Text, black on green	18.00
ND86	'05 $6 Text, black on green	15.00
ND87	'06 $6 black, green	13.00
ND88	'07 $6 Text, black on green	13.00
ND89	'08 $6 Text, black on green	13.00
ND90	'09 $6 Text, black on green	13.00
ND91	'10 $6 black, green	13.00
ND92	'11 $6 Black	10.00
ND93	'12 $6 Black, green	10.00
ND94	'13 $6 Black, green	10.00
ND95	'14 $10 Black, green	14.00
ND96	'15 $10 Black, green	14.00

OH4

OHIO

NO.	DESCRIPTION	F-VF NH
OH1	'82 $5.75 Wood Ducks	60.00
OH2	'83 $5.75 Mallards	40.00
OH3	'84 $5.75 Green-Winged Teal	40.00
OH4	'85 $5.75 Redheads	35.00
OH5	'86 $5.75 Canvasback	35.00
OH6	'87 $6 Blue-Winged Teal	15.00
OH7	'88 $6 Common Goldeneyes	12.00
OH8	'89 $6 Canada Geese	12.00
OH9	'90 $9 Black Ducks	18.00
OH10	'91 $9 Lesser Scaup	18.00
OH11	'92 $9 Wood Duck	18.00
OH12	'93 $9 Buffleheads	18.00
OH13	'94 $11 Mallards	22.00
OH14	'95 $11 Pintails	25.00
OH15	'96 $11 Hooded Mergansers	25.00
OH16	'97 $11 Widgeons	22.00
OH17	'98 $11 Gadwall	22.00
OH18	'99 $11 Mallard	20.00
OH19	'00 $11 Buffleheads	20.00
OH20	'01 $11 Canvasback	20.00
OH21	'02 $11 Ring Neck	20.00
OH22	'03 $11 Hooded Merganser	20.00
OH23	'04 $15 Tundra Swans	20.00
OH24	'05 $15 Wood Duck	24.00
OH25	'06 $15 Pintail	24.00
OH26	'07 $15 Canada Geese	45.00
OH27	'08 $15 Green-Winged Teal	24.00
OH28	'09 $15 Common Goldeneye	24.00
OH29	'10 $10 Ruddy Ducks	24.00
OH30	'11 $15 Red-Breasted Merganser	40.00
OH31	'12 $15 Mallards	24.00

NO.	DESCRIPTION	F-VF NH
OH32	'13 $15 Blue-winged teal	24.00
OH33	'14 $15 Pintail	24.00
OH34	'15 $15 Shoveler	24.00
OH35	'16 $15 Wood Ducks	24.00
OH36	'17 $15 Wigeons	24.00
OH37	'18 $15 Ring-necked Ducks	24.00
OH38	'19 $15 Black Duck	24.00

OK4

OKLAHOMA

NO.	DESCRIPTION	F-VF NH
OK1	'80 $4 Pintails	50.00
OK2	'81 $4 Canada Goose	20.00
OK3	'82 $4 Green-Winged Teal	12.00
OK4	'83 $4 Wood Ducks	12.00
OK5	'84 $4 Ring-Necked Ducks	12.00
OK6	'85 $4 Mallards	12.00
OK7	'86 $4 Snow Geese	12.00
OK8	'87 $4 Canvasbacks	11.00
OK9	'88 $4 Widgeons	10.00
OK10	'89 $4 Redheads	10.00
OK11	'90 $4 Hooded Merganser	10.00
OK12	'91 $4 Gadwalls	10.00
OK13	'92 $4 Lesser Scaup	10.00
OK14	'93 $4 White-Fronted Geese	10.00
OK15	'94 $4 Blue-Winged Teal	10.00
OK16	'95 $4 Ruddy Ducks	10.00
OK17	'96 $4 Buffleheads	10.00
OK18	'97 $4 Goldeneyes	10.00
OK19	'98 $4 Shoveler	10.00
OK20	'99 $4 Canvasbacks	10.00
OK21	'00 $4 Pintails	12.00
OK22	'01 $4 Canada Goose	12.00
OK23	'02 $4 Green-winged Teal	12.00
OK24	'03 $10 Wood Duck	18.00
OK25	'04 $10 Mallard	18.00
OK26	'05 $10 Snow Geese	18.00
OK27	'06 $10 Widgeons	18.00
OK28	'07 $10 Redheads	18.00
OK29	'08 $10 Mallards, Labrador Retriever	18.00
OK30	'09 $10 Gadwells	18.00
OK31	'10 $10 Ringed-neck Duck	18.00
OK32	'11 $10 Blue Winged Teal	18.00
OK33	'12 $10 White-Fronted Goose	18.00
OK34	'13 $10 Common Goldeneye	18.00
OK35	'14 $10 Canvasback	18.00
OK36	'15 $10 Pintails	18.00
OK37	'16 $10 Mallard	18.00
OK38	'17 $10 Green-winged Teal	18.00
OK39	'18 $10 Shovelers	17.00
OK40	'19 $10 Wood Duck	17.00

OR1

OREGON

NO.	DESCRIPTION	F-VF NH
OR1	'84 $5 Canada Geese	25.00
OR2	'85 $5 Lesser Snow Goose	35.00
OR3	'86 $5 Pacific Brant	18.00
OR4	'87 $5 White-Fronted Geese	16.00
OR5	'88 $5 Great Basin Canada Geese	16.00
OR6	'89 $5 Black Labrador Retriever & Pintails	16.00
OR7	'89 $5 Black Labrador Retriever & Pintails	16.00
OR8	'90 $5 Mallards & Golden Retriever	16.00
OR9	'91 $5 Buffleheads & Chesapeake Bay Retriever	16.00
OR10	'92 $5 Green-Winged Teal	16.00
OR11	'93 $5 Mallards	16.00
OR12	'94 $5 Pintails	16.00
OR14	'95 $5 Wood Ducks	16.00
OR16	'96 $5 Mallard/Widgeon/Pintail	16.00
OR18	'97 $5 Canvasbacks	16.00
OR20	'98 $5 Pintail	16.00
OR22	'99 $5 Canada Geese	16.00
OR24	'00 $7.50 Canada Geese, Mallard, Widgeon	16.00
OR25	'01 $7.50 Canvasbacks	16.00
OR26	'02 $7.50 American Wigeon	16.00
OR27	'03 $7.50 Wood Duck	16.00
OR28	'04 $7.50 Ross' Goose	16.00
OR29	'05 $7.50 Hooded Merganser	16.00
OR30	'06 $7.50 Pintail, Mallard	16.00
OR31	'07 $7.50 Wood Ducks	16.00
OR32	'08 $7.50 Pintails	16.00
OR33	'09 $7.50 Mallards	16.00
OR34	'10 $9.50 Wood Duck	18.00
OR35	'11 $9.50 Canvasback	18.00
OR36	'12 $9.50 Mallard	18.00
OR37	'13 $9.50 Wigeons	18.00
OR38	'14 $9.50 Canada geese	18.00
OR39	'15 $9.50 Pintail	18.00
OR40	'16 $10.50 Common Mergansers	20.00
OR41	'17 $10.50 Gadwalls	20.00
OR42	'18 $11 Buffleheads	20.00
OR43	'19 $11 White Geese	20.00

PA1

PENNSYLVANIA

NO.	DESCRIPTION	F-VF NH
PA1	'83 $5.50 Wood Ducks	14.00
PA2	'84 $5.50 Canada Geese	10.00
PA3	'85 $5.50 Mallards	12.00
PA4	'86 $5.50 Blue-Winged Teal	12.00
PA5	'87 $5.50 Pintails	12.00
PA6	'88 $5.50 Wood Ducks	12.00
PA7	'89 $5.50 Hooded Mergansers	10.00
PA8	'90 $5.50 Canvasbacks	10.00
PA9	'91 $5.50 Widgeons	10.00
PA10	'92 $5.50 Canada Geese	10.00
PA11	'93 $5.50 Northern Shovelers	10.00
PA12	'94 $5.50 Pintails	10.00
PA13	'95 $5.50 Buffleheads	10.00
PA14	'96 $5.50 Black Ducks	10.00
PA15	'97 $5.50 Hooded Merganser	10.00
PA16	'98 $5.50 Wood Duck	10.00
PA17	'99 $5.50 Ring-necked Ducks	10.00
PA18	'00 $5.50 Green-winged Teal	10.00
PA19	'01 $5.50 Pintails	10.00
PA20	'02 $5.50 Snow Geese	10.00
PA21	'03 $5.50 Canvasbacks	10.00
PA22	'04 $5.50 Hooded Mergansers	10.00
PA23	'05 $5.50 Red-breasted Mergansers	10.00
PA24	'06 $5.50 Pintails	10.00
PA25	'07 $5.50 Wood Ducks	10.00
PA26	'08 $5.50 Redheads	10.00
PA27	'09 $5.50 Hooded Merganser	10.00
PA28	'10 $5.50 Canvasbacks	10.50
PA29	'11 $5.50 Wigeons	10.50
PA30	'12 $5.50 Ruddy Ducks	10.00
PA31	'13 $5.50 Black Ducks	10.00
PA32	'14 $5.50 Shoveler	10.00
PA33	'15 $5.50 Green-winged Teal	10.00
PA34	'16 $5.50 Pintail	10.00
PA35	'17 $5.50 Bufflehead	9.50
PA36	'18 $5.50 Mallards	9.50
PA37	'19 $5.50 Long-tailed Duck	9.50

RI1

RHODE ISLAND

NO.	DESCRIPTION	F-VF NH
RI1	'89 $7.50 Canvasbacks	15.00
RI2	'90 $7.50 Canada Geese	15.00
RI3	'91 $7.50 Wood Ducks & Labrador Retriever	25.00
RI4	'92 $7.50 Blue-Winged Teal	18.00
RI5	'93 $7.50 Pintails	18.00
RI6	'94 $7.50 Wood Ducks	22.00
RI7	'95 $7.50 Hooded Mergansers	18.00
RI8	'96 $7.50 Harlequin	24.00
RI9	'97 $7.50 Black Ducks	18.00
RI10	'98 $7.50 Black Ducks	18.00
RI11	'99 $7.50 Common Eiders	18.00
RI12	'00 $7.50 Canvasbacks	18.00
RI13	'01 $7.50 Canvasbacks, Mallard, Lighthouse	18.00
RI14	'02 $7.50 White-winged Scoter	17.00
RI15	'03 $7.50 Oldsquaw	15.00
RI16	'04 $7.50 Canvasbacks	15.00
RI17	'05 $7.50 Black Ducks and Lighthouse	15.00
RI18	'06 $7.50 Canvasbacks, Lighthouse	15.00
RI19	'07 $7.50 Harlequin Decoy	15.00
RI20	'08 $7.50 Mallard Decoys	15.00
RI21	'09 $7.50 Hooded Merganser	15.00
RI22	'10 $7.50 Red-breasted Merganser	15.00
RI23	'11 $7.50 Barrow's Goldeneye	15.00
RI24	'12 $7.50 Mallard	15.50
RI25	'13 $7.50 Canvasbacks	15.00
RI26	'14 $7.50 Canvasbacks	15.00
RI27	'15 $7.50 Canvasbacks	15.00
RI28	'16 $7.50 Wood Duck	15.00
RI29	'17 $7.50 Lesser Scaup	15.00
RI30	'18 $7.50 Harlequin, S/A	13.50
RI31	'19 $7.50 Long-tailed Duck	13.50

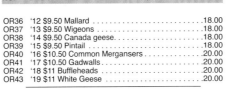

SC5

SOUTH CAROLINA

NO.	DESCRIPTION	F-VF NH
SC1	'81 $5.50 Wood Ducks	65.00
SC2	'82 $5.50 Mallards	100.00
SC3	'83 $5.50 Pintails	100.00
SC4	'84 $5.50 Canada Geese	65.00
SC5	'85 $5.50 Green-Winged Teal	60.00
SC6	'86 $5.50 Canvasbacks	25.00
SC7	'87 $5.50 Black Ducks	20.00
SC8	'88 $5.50 Widgeon & Spaniel	18.00
SC9	'89 $5.50 Blue-Winged Teal	12.00
SC10	'90 $5.50 Wood Ducks	12.00
SC11	'91 $5.50 Labrador Retriever, Pintails & Decoy	12.00
SC12	'92 $5.50 Buffleheads	17.00
SC13	'93 $5.50 Lesser Scaup	17.00
SC14	'94 $5.50 Canvasbacks	17.00
SC15	'95 $5.50 Shovelers, Lighthouse	17.00
SC16	'96 $5.50 Redheads, Lighthouse	18.00
SC17	'97 $5.50 Old Squaws	18.00
SC18	'98 $5.50 Ruddy Ducks	18.00
SC19	'99 $5.50 Barrow's goldeneye	18.00
SC20	'00 $5.50 Wood Ducks, boykin spaniel	18.00
SC21	'01 $5.50 Mallard, yellow labrador,decoy	16.00
SC22	'02 $5.50 Widgeon, Chocolate Labrador	16.00
SC23	'03 $5.50 Green-winged Teal	16.00
SC24	'04 $5.50 Black Labrador	16.00
SC25	'05 $5.50 Canvasbacks	12.00
SC26	'06 $5.50 Black Ducks	12.00
SC27	'07 $5.50 Redheads, Golden Retriever	12.00
SC28	'08 $5.50 Blue-Winged Teal, Labrador Retriever	12.00
SC29	'09 $5.50 Ring-Necked Duck, Labrador Retriever	12.00
SC30	'10 $Wood Duck and Boykin	12.00
SC31	'11 $5.50 Blue Winged Teal & Chocolate Laborador Retriever	12.00
SC32	'12 $5.50 Green-Winged Teal and Golden Retriever	12.00
SC33	'13 $5.50 Black Duck and Boykin Spaniel	12.00
SC34	'14 $5.50 Wood Ducks	12.00
SC35	'15 $5.50 Hooded Mergansers	15.00
SC36	'16 $5.50 Mottled Ducks	12.00
SC37	'17 $5.50 Wigeons	12.00
SC38	'18 $5.50 Pintail	12.00
SC39	'19 $5.50 Canvasbacks and Spaniel	12.00

SD6

SOUTH DAKOTA

NO.	DESCRIPTION	F-VF NH
SD3	'76 $1 Mallards	30.00
SD4	'77 $1 Pintails	75.00
SD5	'78 $1 Canvasbacks	30.00
SD6	'86 $2 Canada Geese	15.00
SD7	'87 $2 Blue Geese	10.00
SD8	'88 $2 White-Fronted Geese	10.00
SD9	'89 $2 Mallards	8.00
SD10	'90 $2 Blue-Winged Teal	8.00
SD11	'91 $2 Pintails	8.00
SD12	'92 $2 Canvasbacks	8.00
SD13	'93 $2 Lesser Scaup	8.00
SD14	'94 $2 Redheads	8.00
SD15	'95 $2 Wood Ducks	8.00
SD16	'96 $2 Canada Goose	8.00
SD17	'97 $2 Widgeons	8.00
SD18	'98 $2 Green Winged Teal	8.00
SD19	'99 $2 Tundra Swam	10.00
SD20	'00 $3 Buffleheads	10.00
SD21	'01 $3 Mallards	10.00
SD22	'02 $3 Canvasbacks	10.00
SD23	'03 $3 Pintail	10.00
SD24	'04 $3 Text, purple	10.00
SD25	'05 $5 Text, magenta	10.00
SD26	'06 $5 Brown, Orange	10.00
SD27	'07 $5 Text (Brown)	10.00

TN9

TENNESSEE

NO.	DESCRIPTION	F-VF NH
TN1	'79 $2 Mallards	95.00
TN2	'79 $5 Mallards, Non-Resident	550.00
TN3	'80 $2 Canvasbacks	55.00
TN4	'80 $5 Canvasbacks, Non-Resident	185.00
TN5	'81 $2 Wood Ducks	50.00

NO.	DESCRIPTION	F-VF NH
TN6	'82 $6 Canada Geese	60.00
TN7	'83 $6 Pintails	60.00
TN8	'84 $6 Black Ducks	60.00
TN9	'85 $6 Blue-Winged Teal	25.00
TN10	'86 $6 Mallard	15.00
TN11	'87 $6 Canada Geese	15.00
TN12	'88 $6 Canvasbacks	15.00
TN13	'89 $6 Green-Winged Teal	15.00
TN14	'90 $13 Redheads	15.00
TN15	'91 $13 Mergansers	20.00
TN16	'92 $14 Wood Ducks	20.00
TN17	'93 $14 Pintails & Decoy	25.00
TN18	'94 $16 Mallard	30.00
TN19	'95 $16 Ring-Necked Duck	35.00
TN20	'96 $18 Black Ducks	45.00
TN21	'99 $10 Mallard	18.00
TN22	'00 $10 Bufflehead	18.00
TN23	'01 $10 Wood Ducks	18.00
TN24	'02 $10 Green-winged Teal	18.00
TN25	'03 $10 Canada Geese	18.00
TN26	'04 $10 Wood Ducks	18.00
TN27	'05 $10 Mallards	18.00
TN28	'06 $10 Canada Goose	18.00
TN29	'07 $10 Harlequin	18.00
TN30	'08 $10 Wood Ducks	18.00
TN31	'09 $10 Mallards	18.00
TN32	'10 $10 Wood Ducks	18.00
TN33	'11 $10 Wood Ducks	18.00
TN34	'12 $10 Cinnamon Teal	18.00
TN35	'13 $10 King Elders	18.00
TN36	'14 $10 Wood Ducks	18.00
TN37	'15 $10 Green-winged Teal	18.00
TN38	'16 $10 Northern Shoveler	18.00
TN39	'17 $10 Cinnamon Teal	18.00
TN40	'18 $10 Pintails	18.00
TN41	'19 $10 Shovelers	18.00

TX5

TEXAS

NO.	DESCRIPTION	F-VF NH
TX1	'81 $5 Mallards	35.00
TX2	'82 $5 Pintails	25.00
TX3	'83 $5 Widgeons	100.00
TX4	'84 $5 Wood Ducks	30.00
TX5	'85 $5 Snow Geese	11.00
TX6	'86 $5 Green-Winged Teal	11.00
TX7	'87 $5 White-Fronted Geese	11.00
TX8	'88 $5 Pintails	11.00
TX9	'89 $5 Mallards	11.00
TX10	'90 $5 American Widgeons	14.00
TX11	'91 $7 Wood Duck	14.00
TX12	'92 $7 Canada Geese	14.00
TX13	'93 $7 Blue-Winged Teal	14.00
TX14	'94 $7 Shovelers	14.00
TX15	'95 $7 Buffleheads	14.00
TX16	'96 $3 Gadwalls	75.00
TX17	'97 $3 Cinnamon Teal	65.00
TX18	'98 $3 Pintail, Labrador Retriever	65.00
TX19	'99 $3 Canvasbacks	42.00
TX20	'00 $3 Hooded Merganser	35.00
TX21	'01 $3 Snow Goose	25.00
TX22	'02 $3 Redheads	25.00
TX23	'03 $3 Mottled Duck	25.00
TX24	'04 $3 American Goldeneye	18.00
TX25	'05 $7 Mallards	18.00
TX26	'06 $7 Green-Winged Teals	24.00
TX27	'07 $7 Wood Duck	14.00
TX28	'08 $7 Pintails	14.00
TX29	'09 $7 Blue-Winged Teal	14.00
TX30	'10 $7 Wigeons	14.00
TX31	'11 $7 White-Fronted Geese	14.00
TX32	'12 $7 Canada Geese	22.00
TX33	'13 $7 Wood Ducks	14.00
TX34	'14 $7 Cinnamon Teal	14.00
TX35	'15 $7 Ring-necked Duck	14.00

UT1

UTAH

NO.	DESCRIPTION	F-VF NH
UT1	'86 $3.30 Whistling Swans	12.00
UT2	'87 $3.30 Pintails	10.00
UT3	'88 $3.30 Mallards	10.00
UT4	'89 $3.30 Canada Geese	10.00
UT5	'90 $3.30 Canvasbacks	10.00
UT6	'91 $3.30 Tundra Swans	13.00
UT7	'92 $3.30 Pintails	13.00
UT8	'93 $3.30 Canvasbacks	13.00
UT9	'94 $3.30 Chesapeake Retriever & Ducks	100.00

NO.	DESCRIPTION	F-VF NH
UT10	'95 $3.30 Green-Winged Teal	13.00
UT11	'96 $7.50 White-Fronted Goose	18.00
UT12	'97 $7.50 Redheads, pair	95.00

VT1

VERMONT

NO.	DESCRIPTION	F-VF NH
VT1	'86 $5 Wood Ducks	14.00
VT2	'87 $5 Common Goldeneyes	14.00
VT3	'88 $5 Black Ducks	14.00
VT4	'89 $5 Canvasbacks	14.00
VT5	'90 $5 Green-Winged Teal	14.00
VT6	'91 $5 Hooded Mergansers	14.00
VT7	'92 $5 Snow Geese	14.00
VT8	'93 $5 Mallards	14.00
VT9	'94 $5 Ring-Necked Duck	14.00
VT10	'95 $5 Bufflehead	14.00
VT11	'96 $5 Bluebills	14.00
VT12	'97 $5 Pintail	14.00
VT13	'98 $5 Blue-Winged Teal	14.00
VT14	'99 $5 Canvasbacks	14.00
VT15	'00 $5 Widgeons	12.00
VT16	'01 $5 Old Squaw	12.00
VT17	'02 $5 Greater Scaups	12.00
VT18	'03 $5 Mallard	12.00
VT19	'04 $5 Pintails	12.00
VT20	'05 $5 Canvasbacks	12.00
VT21	'06 $5 Canada Goose	12.00
VT22	'07 $5 Ring-Necked Duck	12.00
VT23	'08 $7.50 Harlequin	12.00
VT24	'09 $7.50 Harlequin	12.00
VT25	'10 $7.50 Wood Duck	12.00
VT26	'11 $7.50 Black and Numbered Sticker	12.00
VT27	'12 $7.50 Black and Numbered Sticker	12.00
VT28	'13 $7.50 Black	12.00

VA1

VIRGINIA

NO.	DESCRIPTION	F-VF NH
VA1	'88 $5 Mallards	15.00
VA2	'89 $5 Canada Geese	14.00
VA3	'90 $5 Wood Ducks	10.00
VA4	'91 $5 Canvasbacks	10.00
VA5	'92 $5 Buffleheads	10.00
VA6	'93 $5 Black Ducks	10.00
VA7	'94 $5 Lesser Scaup	10.00
VA8	'95 $5 Snow Geese	10.00
VA9	'96 $5 Hooded Mergansers	10.00
VA10	'97 $5 Pintail, Labrador Retriever	10.00
VA11	'98 $5 Mallards	14.00
VA12	'99 $5 Green-winged Teal	14.00
VA13	'00 $5 Mallards	14.00
VA14	'01 $5 Blue-winged Teal	12.00
VA15	'02 $5 Canvasbacks	12.00
VA16	'03 $5 Mallard	12.00
VA17	'04 $5 Goldeneyes	12.00
VA18	'05 $9.75 Wood Ducks, perforated	18.00
VA18a	'05 $9.75 Wood Ducks, rouletted	18.00
VA18b	'05 $9.75 Wood Ducks, S/A, die cut	18.00
VA19	'06 $9.75 Black Ducks, perforated	18.00
VA19a	'06 $9.75 Wood Ducks, S/A, die cut	18.00
VA20	'07 $10 Canada Geese	18.00
VA20a	'07 $10 Canada Geese, S/A, die cut	18.00
VA21	'08 $10 Widgeons	18.00
VA21a	'08 $10 Widgeons, S/A, die cut.	18.00
VA22	'09 $10 Ringed-Neck Duck, perf.	18.00
VA22a	'09 $10 Ring-Neck Duck, S/A	18.00
VA23	'10 $10 Green-winged Teal	18.00
VA23a	'10 $10 Green-winged Teal, S/A, die cut	18.00
VA24	'11 $10 Redheads	18.00
VA24a	'11 $10 Redheads S/A	18.00
VA25	'12 $10 Buffleheads	18.00
VA25a	'12 $10 Buffleheads, S/A	18.00
VA26	'13 $10 Hooded Mergansers	18.00
VA26a	'13 $10 Hooded Mergansers, S/A.	18.00
VA27	'14 $10 Canvasbacks, W/A	18.00
VA27a	'14 $10 Canvasbacks, S/A	18.00
VA28	'15 $10 Tundra Swans	18.00
VA28a	'15 $10 Tundra Swans, S/A, die-cut	18.00
VA29	'16 $10 Pintails	18.00
VA29a	'16 $10 Pintails, S/A, die-cut	18.00
VA30	'17 $10 Ring-necked Ducks	18.00
VA30a	'17 $10 Ring-necked Ducks, S/A, die-cut	18.00
VA31	'18 $10 Canada Goose	15.00
VA31a	'18 $10 Canada Goose, S/A, die-cut	15.00
VA32	'19 $10 Shoveler	15.00
VA32a	'19 $10 Shoveler, S/A, die-cut	15.00

WA1

WASHINGTON

NO.	DESCRIPTION	F-VF NH
WA1	'86 $5 Mallards	10.00
WA2	'87 $5 Canvasbacks	14.00
WA3	'88 $5 Harlequin	11.00
WA4	'89 $5 American Widgeons	11.00
WA5	'90 $5 Pintails & Sour Duck	11.00
WA6	'91 $5 Wood Duck	13.00
WA8	'92 $6 Labrador Puppy & Canada Geese	13.00
WA9	'93 $6 Snow Geese	13.00
WA10	'94 $6 Black Brant	15.00
WA11	'95 $6 Mallards	14.00
WA12	'96 $6 Redheads	24.00
WA13	'97 $6 Canada Geese	14.00
WA14	'98 $6 Goldeneye	18.00
WA15	'99 $6 Bufflehead	18.00
WA16	'00 $6 Canada Geese, Mallard, Widgeon	30.00
WA17	'01 $6 Mallards	22.00
WA18	'02 $10 Green-winged Teal	22.00
WA19	'03 $10 Pintail	22.00
WA20	'04 $10 Canada Goose	18.00
WA21	'05 $10 Barrow's Goldeneyes	18.00
WA22	'06 $10 Widgeons, Mallard	18.00
WA23	'07 $10 Ross's Goose	18.00
WA24	'08 $10 Wood Ducks	18.00
WA25	'09 $11 Canada Goose	18.00
WA26	'10 $10 Pintail	40.00
WA27	'11 $10 Ruddy Duck	18.00
WA28	'12 $15 Brant	24.00
WA29	'13 $15 Shovelers	24.50
WA30	'14 $15 Redheads	24.00
WA31	'15 $15 Canvasbacks	24.00
WA32	'16 $15 Wooded Merganser	24.00
WA33	'17 $15 Cinnamon Teal and Labrador	24.00
WA34	'18 $15 Wood Ducks	22.00
WA35	'19 $15 Ring-necked Duck and Labrador	22.00

WV1

WEST VIRGINIA

NO.	DESCRIPTION	F-VF NH
WV1	'87 $5 Canada Geese	18.00
WV2	'87 $5 Canada Geese, Non-Resident	18.00
WV3	'88 $5 Wood Ducks	12.00
WV4	'88 $5 Wood Ducks, Non-Resident	14.00
WV5	'89 $5 Decoys	14.00
WV6	'89 $5 Decoys, Non-Resident	20.00
WV7	'90 $5 Labrador Retriever & Decoy	22.00
WV8	'90 $5 Labrador Retriever & Decoy, Non-Resident	24.00
WV9	'91 $5 Mallards	14.00
WV10	'91 $5 Mallards, Non-Resident	14.00
WV11	'92 $5 Canada Geese	14.00
WV12	'92 $5 Canada Geese, Non-Resident	14.00
WV13	'93 $5 Pintails	14.00
WV14	'93 $5 Pintails, Non-Resident	14.00
WV15	'94 $5 Green-Winged Teal	14.00
WV16	'94 $5 Green-Winged Teal, Non-Resident	14.00
WV17	'95 $5 Mallards	14.00
WV18	'95 $5 Mallards, Non-Resident	14.00
WV19	'96 $5 American Widgeons	14.00
WV20	'96 $5 Widgeon, Non-Resident	14.00

WI3

WISCONSIN

NO.	DESCRIPTION	F-VF NH
WI1	'78 $3.25 Wood Ducks	80.00
WI2	'79 $3.25 Buffleheads	25.00
WI3	'80 $3.25 Widgeons	12.00
WI4	'81 $3.25 Lesser Scaup	12.00
WI5	'82 $3.25 Pintails	11.00
WI6	'83 $3.25 Blue-Winged Teal	11.00
WI7	'84 $3.25 Hooded Merganser	12.00
WI8	'85 $3.25 Lesser Scaup	14.00
WI9	'86 $3.25 Canvasbacks	16.00
WI10	'87 $3.25 Canada Geese	11.00
WI11	'88 $3.25 Hooded Merganser	11.00
WI12	'89 $3.25 Common Goldeneye	11.00

NO.	DESCRIPTION	F-VF NH
WI13	'90 $3.25 Redheads	11.00
WI14	'91 $5.25 Green-Winged Teal	12.00
WI15	'92 $5.25 Tundra Swans	12.00
WI16	'93 $5.25 Wood Ducks	12.00
WI17	'94 $5.25 Pintails	12.00
WI18	'95 $5.25 Mallards	12.00
WI19	'96 $5.25 Green-Winged Teal	12.00
WI20	'97 $7 Canada Geese	18.00
WI21	'98 $7 Snow Geese	18.00
WI22	'99 $7 Greater Scaups	14.00
WI23	'00 $7 Canvasbacks	14.00
WI24	'01 $7 Common Goldeneye	16.00
WI25	'02 $7 Shovelers	12.00
WI26	'03 $7 Canvasbacks	12.00
WI27	'04 $7 Pintail	12.00
WI28	'05 $7 Wood Ducks	14.00
WI29	'06 $7 Green-Winged Teals	14.00
WI30	'07 $7 Redheads	14.00
WI31	'08 $7 Canvasbacks	14.00
WI32	'09 $7 Wigeons	14.00
WI33	'10 $7 Wood Ducks	14.00
WI34	'11 $7 Shovelers	14.00
WI35	'12 $7 Redhead	14.00
WI36	'13 $7 Long-Tailed Ducks	14.00
WI37	'14 $7 Wood Duck	12.00
WI38	'15 $7 Blue-winged Teal	14.00
WI39	'16 $7 Ring-necked Duck	14.00
WI40	'17 $7 Canvasbacks and Lighthouse	14.00
WI41	'18 $7 Canada Geese	13.00
WI42	'19 $7 Redheads	13.00

WY10

WYOMING

NO.	DESCRIPTION	F-VF NH
WY1	'84 $5 Meadowlark	72.00
WY2	'85 $5 Canada Geese	64.00
WY3	'86 $5 Antelope	115.00
WY4	'87 $5 Grouse	115.00
WY5	'88 $5 Fish	120.00
WY6	'89 $5 Deer	185.00
WY7	'90 $5 Bear	55.00
WY8	'91 $5 Rams	50.00
WY9	'92 $5 Bald Eagle	40.00
WY10	'93 $5 Elk	25.00
WY11	'94 $5 Bobcat	25.00
WY12	'95 $5 Moose	25.00
WY13	'96 $5 Turkey	25.00
WY14	'97 $5 Rocky Mountain Goats	25.00
WY15	'98 $5 Thunder Swans	25.00
WY16	'99 $5 Brown Trout	25.00

NO.	DESCRIPTION	F-VF NH
WY17	'00 $5 Buffalo	25.00
WY18	'01 $10 Whitetailed Deer	25.00
WY19	'02 $10 River Otters	25.00
WY20	'03 $10 Mountain Bluebird	25.00
WY21	'04 $10 Cougar	25.00
WY22	'05 $10 Burrowing Owls	25.00
WY23	'06 $10.50 Cut-Throat Trout	25.00
WY24	'07 $10.50 Blue Grouses	25.00
WY25	'08 $12.50 Black-footed Ferret	25.00
WY26	'09 $12.50 Great Gray Owl	25.00
WY27	'10 $12.50 Cinnamon Teal	25.00
WY28	'11 $12.50 Wolverine	20.00
WY29	'12 $12.50 Black Bear	20.00
WY30	'13 $12.50 Greater Short-Horned Lizard	20.00
WY31	'14 $12.50 Ruffled Grouse	20.00
WY32	'15 $12.50 Sauger	20.00
WY33	'16 $12.50 Swift Fox	20.00
WY34	'17 $12.50 Mallard	20.00
WY35	'18 $12.50 Badger	20.00
WY36	'19 $12.50 Mule Deer	20.00

CANAL ZONE

SCOTT NO.	DESCRIPTION	UNUSED NH F	AVG	UNUSED OG F	AVG	USED F	AVG

CANAL ZONE

PANAMA

1904

U.S. Stamp 300, 319, 304, 306-07 overprinted

SCOTT NO.	DESCRIPTION	UNUSED NH F	AVG	UNUSED OG F	AVG	USED F	AVG
4	1¢ blue green	115.00	72.00	50.00	35.00	25.00	20.00
5	2¢ carmine..................	95.00	65.00	43.00	25.00	25.00	20.00
6	5¢ blue......................	325.00	200.00	150.00	100.00	65.00	50.00
7	8¢ violet black.............	575.00	350.00	270.00	175.00	95.00	75.00
8	10¢ pale red brown.....	500.00	350.00	270.00	175.00	100.00	80.00

CANAL

ZONE

1924-25

U.S. Stamps 551-54, 557, 562, 564-66, 569-71 overprinted

Type 1 Flat Tops on Letters "A". Perf. 11

SCOTT NO.	DESCRIPTION	UNUSED NH F	AVG	UNUSED OG F	AVG	USED F	AVG
70	1/2¢ olive brown	3.50	2.50	1.75	1.40	.75	.65
71	1¢ deep green	3.50	2.50	1.75	1.25	1.10	.70
71e	same, bklt pane of 6 ...	300.00	200.00	170.00	125.00	....	....
72	1-1/2¢ yellow brown ...	5.00	3.50	2.50	1.85	1.60	1.35
73	2¢ carmine..................	20.00	15.00	10.00	7.00	1.75	1.25
73a	same, bklt pane of 6 ...	400.00	315.00	250.00	185.00	....	....
74	5¢ dark blue...............	50.00	40.00	25.00	20.00	9.00	6.50
75	10¢ orange	110.00	80.00	55.00	40.00	24.00	17.00
76	12¢ brown violet	100.00	75.00	50.00	40.00	27.00	19.50
77	14¢ dark blue..............	75.00	55.00	40.00	30.00	20.00	16.00
78	15¢ gray	125.00	80.00	65.00	45.00	35.00	30.00
79	30¢ olive brown	100.00	65.00	48.00	35.00	25.00	20.00
80	50¢ lilac	210.00	135.00	100.00	70.00	42.00	35.00
81	$1 violet brown	575.00	395.00	300.00	200.00	100.00	85.00

CANAL

ZONE

1925-28

U.S. Stamps 554-55, 557, 564-66, 623, 567, 569-71, overprinted

Type II Pointed Tops on Letters "A"

SCOTT NO.	DESCRIPTION	UNUSED NH F	AVG	UNUSED OG F	AVG	USED F	AVG
84	2¢ carmine..................	80.00	60.00	40.00	30.00	10.00	6.25
84d	same, bklt pane of 6 ...	450.00	350.00	300.00	260.00	....	....
85	3¢ violet	10.00	8.50	5.00	3.75	2.75	1.75
86	5¢ dark blue...............	10.00	8.50	5.00	3.75	2.75	1.75
87	10¢ orange	92.00	70.00	47.00	35.00	10.00	9.00
88	12¢ brown violet	60.00	50.00	30.00	24.00	14.00	10.00
89	14¢ dark blue..............	67.00	50.00	36.00	25.00	16.00	13.00
90	15¢ gray	22.00	16.00	11.00	8.00	4.00	2.50
91	17¢ black	11.00	8.00	6.00	4.00	3.00	2.25
92	20¢ carmine rose........	20.00	15.00	11.00	8.00	4.00	3.00
93	30¢ olive brown	15.00	12.00	9.00	6.00	4.00	3.00
94	50¢ lilac	635.00	475.00	310.00	250.00	150.00	135.00
95	$1 violet brown	310.00	250.00	180.00	140.00	50.00	45.00

1926

Type II overprint on U.S. Stamp 627

96	2¢ carmine rose..........	10.00	7.00	6.00	4.00	3.75	2.50

1927

Type II overprint on U.S. Stamp 583-84, 591

Rotary Press Printing, Perf. 10

97	2¢ carmine..................	150.00	110.00	80.00	70.00	10.50	8.50
98	3¢ violet	25.00	20.00	12.00	10.00	5.00	4.00
99	10¢ orange	50.00	35.00	30.00	20.00	6.75	5.50

SCOTT NO.	DESCRIPTION	PLATE BLOCK F/NH	F	AVG	UNUSED F/NH	F	AVG	USED F	AVG
100	1¢ green	35.00	25.00	22.00	4.25	2.75	2.00	1.30	1.00
101	2¢ carmine.............	45.00	30.00	26.00	4.75	3.00	2.00	.90	.80
101a	same, bklt pane of 6	....	....	....	275.00	175.00	150.00	....	....
102	3¢ violet (1931).....	125.00	90.00	80.00	6.50	4.50	3.00	3.50	2.50
103	5¢ dark blue........	280.00	200.00	190.00	60.00	40.00	35.00	11.00	9.00
104	10¢ orange (1930)	260.00	180.00	160.00	30.00	23.00	18.00	12.00	10.00

VERY FINE QUALITY: To determine the Very Fine price, add the difference between the Fine and Average prices to the Fine quality price. For example: if the Fine price is $10.00 and the Average price is $6.00, the Very Fine price would be $14.00. From 1935 to date, add 20% to the Fine price to arrive at the Very Fine price.

105,160

106

107

108, 161

109

110

111

112

113

114

1928-40 Builders Issue

SCOTT NO.	DESCRIPTION	PLATE BLOCK F/NH	F	AVG	UNUSED F/NH	F	AVG	USED F	AVG
105-14	1¢-50¢ complete, 10 varieties.........	....	....	....	10.40	8.05	4.95	5.70	3.45
105	1¢ Gorgas.........	3.75	3.00	2.50	.55	.40	.30	.30	.25
106	2¢ Goethals.........	4.50(6)	3.25	2.50	.35	.30	.25	.30	.25
106a	same, bklt pane of 6	....	....	....	22.00	20.00	16.00	....	....
107	5¢ Gaillard Cut (1929).................	24.00(6)	18.00	16.00	1.65	1.40	1.20	.55	.45
108	10¢ Hodges (1932)	8.00(6)	6.00	4.50	.40	.30	.25	.30	.25
109	12¢ Gaillard (1929)	18.00(6)	15.00	12.00	1.50	1.00	.80	.85	.50
110	14¢ Sibert (1937)	25.00(6)	16.00	14.00	1.40	1.25	.95	1.10	.75
111	15¢ Smith (1932).	15.00(6)	12.00	8.00	.80	.65	.45	.50	.40
112	20¢ Rousseau (1932).................	15.00(6)	12.00	8.00	1.25	.75	.65	.30	.25
113	30¢ Williamson (1940).................	19.00(6)	15.00	12.00	1.25	1.15	.85	.95	.75
114	50¢ Blackburn (1929).................	28.00(6)	17.00	13.50	2.75	1.90	1.50	.85	.70

1933

Type II overprint on U.S. Stamps 720 & 695

Rotary Press Printing, Perf. 11 x 10-1/2

115	3¢ Washington	56.00	40.00	35.00	4.00	3.50	2.50	.40	.35
116	14¢ Indian............	90.00	70.00	46.00	8.00	6.00	4.00	3.35	2.75

117, 153

1934

117	3¢ Goethals.........	1.75(6)	1.25	1.00	.40	.35	.25	.25	.25
117a	same, bklt pane of 6	....	....	....	100.00	60.00	50.00	....	....

SCOTT NO.	DESCRIPTION	PLATE BLOCK F/NH	F/OG	UNUSED F/NH	F/OG	USED F

1939 U.S. Stamps 803, 805 overprint

118	1/2¢ red orange............	3.75	3.00	.35	.25	.25
119	1-1/2¢ bistre brown	3.25	2.75	.35	.25	.25

FOR YOUR CONVENIENCE,

COMPLETE SETS ARE LISTED

BEFORE SINGLE STAMP LISTINGS!

SCOTT NO.	DESCRIPTION	PLATE BLOCK F/NH	PLATE BLOCK F/OG	UNUSED F/NH	UNUSED F/OG	USED F

120
Balboa—Before

121
Balboa—After

122	*Gaillard Cut—Before*	**123**	*After*
124	*Bas Obispo—Before*	**125**	*After*
126	*Gatun Locks—Before*	**127**	*After*
128	*Canal Channel—Before*	**129**	*After*
130	*Gamboa—Before*	**131**	*After*
132	*Pedro Miguel Locks—Before*	**133**	*After*
134	*Gatun Spillway—Before*	**135**	*After*

1939 25th ANNIVERSARY ISSUE

SCOTT NO.	DESCRIPTION	PLATE BLOCK F/NH	PLATE BLOCK F/OG	UNUSED F/NH	UNUSED F/OG	USED F
120-35	1¢-50¢ complete, 16 varieties	....	....	155.00	135.00	89.50
120	1¢ yellow green	20.00(6)	16.00	1.25	.95	.45
121	2¢ rose carmine	20.00(6)	16.00	1.25	.85	.50
122	3¢ purple	20.00(6)	16.00	1.25	.85	.25
123	5¢ dark blue	32.00(6)	28.00	2.75	2.00	1.30
124	6¢ red orange	80.00(6)	67.00	5.50	3.75	3.25
125	7¢ black	80.00(6)	67.00	6.00	4.00	3.25
126	8¢ green	88.00(6)	74.00	7.75	5.50	3.50
127	10¢ ultramarine	88.00(6)	74.00	7.00	5.00	5.00
128	11¢ blue hreen	180.00(6)	160.00	12.00	9.00	8.00
129	12¢ brown carmine	160.00(6)	135.00	12.00	9.00	7.00
130	14¢ dark violet	180.00(6)	160.00	12.00	9.00	7.00
131	15¢ olive green	210.00(6)	165.00	16.00	12.00	6.00
132	18¢ rose pink	200.00(6)	160.00	17.00	13.00	8.00
133	20¢ brown	240.00(6)	200.00	18.00	14.00	8.00
134	25¢ orange	425.00(6)	350.00	27.00	22.00	18.00
135	50¢ violet brown	475.00(6)	360.00	35.00	27.00	6.00

136   **137**   **138**

139   **140**

1945-49

SCOTT NO.	DESCRIPTION	PLATE BLOCK F/NH	PLATE BLOCK F/OG	UNUSED F/NH	UNUSED F/OG	USED F
136-40	1/2¢-25¢ complete 5 varieties	....	....	3.50	2.50	1.75
136	1/2¢ Major General Davis (1948)	3.50(6)	2.75	.55	.45	.25
137	1-1/2¢ Gov. Magoon (1948)	3.50(6)	2.75	.55	.45	.25
138	2¢ T. Roosevelt (1948)	2.00(6)	1.50	.35	.25	.25
139	5¢ Stevens	3.75(6)	3.00	.50	.40	.25
140	25¢ J.F. Wallace (1948)	12.50(6)	11.00	1.60	1.25	.85

141

1948 CANAL ZONE BIOLOGICAL AREA

141	10¢ Map & Coat-mundi	11.00(6)	8.50	1.95	1.50	1.20

142   **143**   **144**   **145**

1949 CALIFORNIA GOLD RUSH

SCOTT NO.	DESCRIPTION	PLATE BLOCK F/NH	PLATE BLOCK F/OG	UNUSED F/NH	UNUSED F/OG	USED F
142-45	3¢-18¢ complete 4 varieties	....	....	5.15	4.25	3.35
142	3¢ "Forty Niners"	7.00(6)	5.00	.70	.55	.35
143	6¢ Journey–Las Cruces	8.25(6)	6.00	.80	.65	.40
144	12¢ Las Cruces–Panama Trail	23.00(6)	19.00	1.75	1.40	1.10
145	18¢ Departure–San Francisco	28.00(6)	23.00	2.60	2.25	2.75

146   **147**   **148**

149   **150**

1951-58

146	10¢ West Indian Labor.	28.00(6)	23.00	3.25	2.75	2.25
147	3¢ Panama R.R.(1955)	8.00(6)	7.00	1.10	.80	.80
148	3¢ Gorgas Hospital (1957)	6.00	5.00	.60	.50	.45
149	4¢ S.S. Ancon (1958)	5.00	4.00	.55	.50	.40
150	4¢ T. Roosevelt (1958)	5.00	4.00	.60	.55	.45

151   **152, 154**

1960-62

151	4¢ Boy Scout Badge	7.00	5.00	.60	.50	.45
152	4¢ Adminstration Building	1.75	1.35	.35	.25	.25

LINE PAIR

153	3¢ G.W. Goethals, coil	1.40	1.25	.30	.25	.25
154	4¢ Adminstration Building, coil	1.40	1.25	.30	.25	.25
155	5¢ J.F. Stevens, coil (1962)	1.55	1.25	.40	.30	.25

156   **157**

PLATE BLOCK

156	4¢ Girl Scout Badge (1962)	4.75	3.50	.45	.40	.35
157	4¢ Thatcher Ferry Bridge (1962)	5.00	4.00	.40	.35	.30
157a	same, silver omitted (bridge)	....	....	8500.00	....	....

158   **159**

SCOTT NO.	DESCRIPTION	PLATE BLOCK F/NH	F/OG	UNUSED F/NH	F/OG	USED F
	1968-78					
158	6¢ Goethals Memorial..	3.50	....	.40	....	.25
159	8¢ Fort San Lorenzo (1971)	3.00	....	.50	....	.25
	LINE PAIR					
160	1¢ W.C. Gorgas, coil (1975)	1.50	....	.35	....	.25
161	10¢ H.F. Hodges, coil (1975)	6.00	....	.90	....	.55
162	25¢ J.F. Wallace, coil (1975)	26.00	....	3.25	....	3.00

163

165

PLATE BLOCK

SCOTT NO.	DESCRIPTION	PLATE BLOCK F/NH	F/OG	UNUSED F/NH	F/OG	USED F
163	13¢ Cascades Dredge (1976)	2.50	....	.50	....	.30
163a	same, bklt pane of 4.....	....	....	3.50	....	
164	5¢ J.F. Stevens (#139) Rotary Press (1977).....	7.00	....	.90	....	1.00
165	15¢ Locomotive (1978)	2.50	....	.60	....	.40

SCOTT NO.	DESCRIPTION	PLATE BLOCK F/NH	F	AVG	UNUSED F/NH	F	AVG	USED F	AVG

AIR POST

AIR MAIL

105 & 106 Surcharged

25 CENTS 25

1929-31

C1	15¢ on 1¢ green, Type I..................	225.00(6)	150.00	110.00	15.50	12.00	10.00	6.25	4.50
C2	15¢ on 1¢ yellow green, Type II (1931)......	....	....	....	120.00	110.00	85.00	75.00	68.00
C3	25¢ on 2¢ carmine	200.00	150.00	140.00	7.00	5.00	4.00	2.50	1.85

AIR MAIL

114 & 106 Surcharged

≡10c

1929

C4	10¢ on 50¢ lilac ...	220.00(6)	170.00	150.00	14.00	13.00	8.00	7.00	6.00
C5	20¢ on 2¢ carmine	175.00(6)	135.00	125.00	8.00	7.00	5.00	2.00	1.50

C6-C14

1931-49

C6-14	4¢-$1 complete, 9 varieties...........	....	....	....	28.00	21.00	16.00	7.60	5.00
C6	4¢ Gaillard Cut, red violet (1949).........	11.00(6)	8.00	6.00	1.25	1.00	.75	1.00	.85
C7	5¢ yellow green ...	5.50(6)	4.50	2.75	.75	.55	.40	.45	.35
C8	6¢ yellow brown (1946)..................	9.00(6)	8.00	5.00	1.00	.85	.65	.40	.30
C9	10¢ orange	12.50(6)	9.50	6.00	1.30	1.00	.85	.40	.30
C10	15¢ blue..............	13.50(6)	10.50	7.00	1.60	1.35	1.00	.40	.30
C11	20¢ red violet......	22.00(6)	17.00	13.00	2.85	2.20	1.85	.40	.30
C12	30¢ rose lake (1941).............	40.00(6)	36.00	28.00	4.50	3.25	2.75	1.30	.80
C13	40¢ yellow	40.00(6)	30.00	24.00	4.50	3.50	3.00	1.30	.100
C14	$1 black..............	105.00(6)	82.50	70.00	12.00	9.00	8.00	2.75	2.25

C15   C16

C17   C18

C19   C20

1939 25th ANNIVERSARY ISSUE

C15-20	5¢-$1 complete 6 varieties	....	....	95.00	75.00	52.00
C15	5¢ Plane over Sosa Hill	50.00(6)	40.00	5.00	4.00	2.75
C16	10¢ Map of Central America........................	65.00(6)	50.00	5.00	4.00	3.50
C17	15¢ Scene near Fort Amador	70.00(6)	60.00	7.50	6.00	1.50
C18	25¢ Clippper at Cristobal Harbor	325.00(6)	250.00	22.00	18.00	9.00
C19	39¢ Clipper over Gaillard Cut	170.00(6)	110.00	21.00	17.00	8.00
C20	$1 Clipper Alighhting	600.00(6)	450.00	50.00	42.00	29.00

C21-31, C34

1951

C21-26	4¢-80¢ complete 6 varieties	....	....	29.25	25.50	13.00
C21	4¢ Globe & Wing, red violet	9.00(6)	7.00	1.00	.85	.50
C22	6¢ light brown..............	8.00(6)	6.00	.85	.60	.40
C23	10¢ light red orange	11.00(6)	8.50	1.25	1.10	.50
C24	21¢ light blue...............	100.00(6)	85.00	12.00	10.00	5.00
C25	31¢ cerise	100.00(6)	85.00	13.00	11.00	5.00
C26	80¢ Light gray black.....	65.00(6)	48.00	7.75	6.50	2.00

1958

C27-31	5¢-35¢ complete 5 varieties	....	....	30.75	25.00	9.70
C27	5¢ Globe & Wing, yellow green	8.00	6.00	1.20	1.00	.65
C28	7¢ olive........................	8.00	6.00	1.20	1.00	.60
C29	15¢ brown violet..........	47.00	39.00	5.50	4.75	3.25
C30	25¢ orange yellow........	120.00	90.00	14.00	12.00	3.25
C31	35¢ dark blue	70.00	65.00	12.00	10.00	3.25

C32   C33

 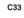

C35

1961-63

C32	15¢ Emblem Caribbean School	16.00	13.00	1.50	1.40	1.00
C33	7¢ Anti-Malaria (1962)..	3.50	3.00	.60	.40	.50
C34	8¢ Globe & Wing carmine (1968)	8.00	6.00	.85	.60	.40
C35	15¢ Alliance for Progress (1963)	16.00	13.00	1.60	1.35	1.35

SCOTT NO.	DESCRIPTION	PLATE BLOCK F/NH	F/OG	UNUSED F/NH	F/OG	USED F

C36

C37

C38

C39

C40

C41

1964 50th ANNIVERSARY ISSUE

C36-41	6¢-80¢ complete 6 varieties	....	....	12.75	10.00	9.90
C36	6¢ Cristobal	3.85	3.25	.65	.55	.60
C37	8¢ Gatun Locks	4.25	3.50	.65	.55	.55
C38	15¢ Madden Dam	9.50	8.00	1.25	1.60	1.60
C39	20¢ Gaillard Cut	12.50	10.00	2.00	1.60	1.20
C40	30¢ Miraflores Locks	20.00	16.00	3.50	2.50	3.00
C41	80¢ Balboa	28.00	26.00	6.00	5.50	4.50

C42-C53

1965

C42-47	6¢-80¢ complete 6 varieties	....	....	6.40	....	2.55
C42	6¢ Gov. Seal, green & black	3.50	....	.65	....	.40
C43	8¢ rose red & black	3.50	....	.65	....	.30
C44	15¢ blue & black	7.25	....	.85	....	.35
C45	20¢ lilac & black	5.00	....	.85	....	.40
C46	30¢ reddish brown & black	5.25	....	1.25	....	.40
C47	80¢ bistre & balck	19.00	....	2.85	....	1.00

1968-76

C48-53	10¢-35¢ complete 6 varieties	....	....	4.60	....	5.50
C48	10¢ Gov. Seal, dull orange& black	3.75	....	.40	....	.25
C48a	same, bklt pane of 4	....	....	4.50	....	....
C49	11¢ Seal, olive & black (1971)	3.75	....	.40	....	.30
C49a	same, bklt pane of 4	....	....	3.50	....	....
C50	13¢ Seal, emerald & black (1974)	5.50	....	1.00	....	.35
C50a	same, bklt pane of 4	....	....	7.00	....	....
C51	22¢ Seal, violet & black (1976)	6.50	....	1.00	....	2.50
C52	25¢ Seal, pale yellow green & black	6.00	....	.90	....	.75
C53	35¢ Seal, salmon & black (1976)	11.00	....	1.35	....	2.20

AIR MAIL OFFICIAL STAMPS

C7-14 Overprinted
1941-42 Overprint 19 to 20-1/2 mm. long

OFFICIAL
PANAMA CANAL

CO1-7	5¢-$1 complete 7 varieties	....	....	132.00	93.00	40.00
CO1	5¢ Gaillard Cut, yellow green (C7)	....	....	7.50	5.75	2.50
CO2	10¢ orange (C9)	....	....	12.00	9.00	3.00
CO3	15¢ blue (C10)	....	....	15.00	12.00	3.00
CO4	20¢ red violet (C11)	....	....	23.00	15.00	5.00
CO5	30¢ rose lake (1942) (C12)	....	....	24.00	20.00	7.00
CO6	40¢ yellow (C13)	....	....	24.00	20.00	10.00
CO7	$1 black (C14)	....	....	28.00	21.00	14.00

1947 Overprint 19 to 20-1/2mm. long

CO14	6¢ yellow brown (C8)	....	....	25.00	15.00	6.25

SCOTT NO.	DESCRIPTION	UNUSED NH F	AVG	UNUSED OG F	AVG	USED F	AVG

POSTAGE DUE STAMPS

1914
U.S. Postage Due Stamps
J45-46, 49 overprint

CANAL ZONE

J1	1¢ rose carmine	155.00	125.00	85.00	70.00	18.00	14.00
J2	2¢ rose carmine	425.00	350.00	225.00	200.00	55.00	45.00
J3	10¢ rose carmine	1700.00	1400.00	925.00	850.00	55.00	45.00

1924
Type I overprint on U.S. Postage Due Stamps J61-62, 65

J12	1¢ carmine rose	185.00	145.00	95.00	85.00	30.00	23.00
J13	2¢ deep claret	125.00	85.00	60.00	55.00	15.00	12.50
J14	10¢ deep claret	425.00	350.00	220.00	185.00	55.00	48.00

1925
Canal Zone Stamps
71, 73, 75 overprinted

POSTAGE DUE

J15	1¢ deep green	150.00	140.00	85.00	75.00	17.00	14.00
J16	2¢ carmine	45.00	35.00	25.00	20.00	7.50	5.50
J17	10¢ orange	85.00	70.00	50.00	40.00	12.50	10.00

1925
Type II overprint on U.S. Postage Due Stamps J61-62, 65

J18	1¢ carmine rose	18.00	16.00	8.00	6.50	3.00	2.25
J19	2¢ carmine rose	32.00	27.00	15.00	13.00	5.00	4.00
J20	10¢ carmine rose	350.00	300.00	155.00	140.00	20.00	17.00

POSTAGE DUE
-1-

1929-39
107 Surcharged

J21	1¢ on 5¢ blue	10.00	8.00	5.50	4.50	2.20	1.85
J22	2¢ on 5¢ blue	17.00	14.00	9.75	8.00	3.50	2.50
J23	5¢ on 5¢ blue	17.00	14.00	9.75	8.00	4.00	3.00
J24	10¢ on 5¢ blue	17.00	14.00	9.75	8.00	4.00	3.00

J25

1932-41

J25-29	1¢-15¢ complete, 5 varieties	5.40	4.50	4.20	3.00	3.60	2.55
J25	1¢ claret	.50	.40	.40	.30	.30	.25
J26	2¢ claret	.50	.40	.40	.30	.30	.25
J27	5¢ claret	.90	.70	.70	.50	.30	.40
J28	10¢ claret	2.50	1.75	1.75	1.40	1.75	1.40
J29	15¢ claret (1941)	1.95	1.50	1.50	1.00	1.30	.90

SCOTT NO.	DESCRIPTION		UNUSED F/NH	F	USED F

OFFICIAL STAMPS

1941
105, 107, 108, 111, 112, 114, 117, 139 overprinted

OFFICIAL
PANAMA
CANAL

"PANAMA" 10mm. Long

OFFICIAL
PANAMA CANAL

O1/9	1¢-50¢ (O1-2, O4-7, O9) 7 varieties		132.50	96.75	21.25
O1	1¢ yellow green (105)		3.50	2.75	.60
O2	3¢ deep violet (117)		7.50	5.50	1.00
O3	5¢ blue (107)		....	....	40.00
O4	10¢ orange (108)		12.00	10.00	2.25
O5	15¢ gray black (111)		20.00	16.00	3.00
O6	20¢ olive brown (112)		25.00	18.00	3.50
O7	50¢ lilac (114)		60.00	50.00	7.50

1947

O9	5¢ deep blue (139)		15.00	13.00	4.50

ORDER BY MAIL, PHONE (800) 546-2995
OR FAX (256) 246-1116

SCOTT NO.	DESCRIPTION	MINT ENTIRES

CANAL ZONE MINT POSTAL STATIONERY ENTIRES

ENVELOPES

U16	1934, 3¢ purple	1.50
U17	1958, 4¢ blue	1.65
U18	1969, 4¢ + 1¢ blue	1.65
U19	1969, 4¢ + 2¢ blue	3.25
U20	1971, 8¢ Gaillard Cut	1.00
U21	1974, 8¢ + 2¢ Gaillard Cut	1.35
U22	1976, 13¢ Gaillard Cut	1.00
U23	1978, 13¢ + 2¢ Gaillard Cut	1.00

AIR MAIL ENVELOPES

UC3	1949, 6¢ DC-4 Skymaster	4.75
UC4	1958, 7¢ DC-4 Skymaster	5.25
UC5	1963, 3¢ + 5¢ purple	7.25
UC6	1964, 8¢ Tail Assembly	3.00
UC7	1965, 4¢ + 4¢ blue	5.25
UC8	1966, 8¢ Tail Assembly	5.75
UC9	1968, 8¢ + 2¢ Tail Assembly	3.50
UC10	1968, 4¢ + 4¢ + 2¢ Tail Assembly	2.75
UC11	1969, 10¢ Tail Assembly	4.75
UC12	1971, 4¢ + 5¢ + 2¢ blue	4.75
UC13	1971, 10¢ + 1¢ Tail Assembly	4.75
UC14	1971, 11¢ Tail Assembly	1.50
UC15	1974, 11¢ + 2¢ Tail Assembly	2.00
UC16	1975, 8¢ + 2¢ + 3¢ emerald	1.75

POSTAL CARDS

UX10	1935, 1¢ overprint on U.S. #UX27	2.25
UX11	1952, 2¢ overprint on U.S. #UX38	2.75
UX12	1958, 3¢ Ship in Lock	2.50
UX13	1963, 3¢ + 1¢ Ship in Lock	4.75
UX14	1964, 4¢ Ship in Canal	4.25
UX15	1965, 4¢ Ship in Lock	1.50
UX16	1968, 4¢ + 1¢ Ship in Lock	1.50
UX17	1969, 5¢ Ship in Lock	1.50
UX18	1971, 5¢ + 1¢ Ship in Lock	1.00
UX19	1974, 8¢ Ship in Lock	1.25
UX20	1976, 8¢ + 1¢ Ship in Lock	1.00
UX21	1978, 8¢ + 2¢ Ship in Lock	1.25

AIR MAIL POSTAL CARDS

UXC1	1958, 5¢ Plane, Flag & Map	4.25
UXC2	1963, 5¢ + 1¢ Plane, Flag & Map	11.00
UXC3	1965, 4¢ + 2¢ Ship in Lock	4.75
UXC4	1968, 4¢ + 4¢ Ship in Lock	3.50
UXC5	1971, 5¢ + 4¢ Ship in Lock	1.50

SCOTT NO.	DESCRIPTION	UNUSED OG F	AVG	UNUSED F	AVG	USED F	AVG

CONFEDERATE STATES

1, 4
Jefferson Davis

2, 5
Thomas Jefferson

(Confederate States 1-14 + 40% for VF Centering)

1861

1	5¢ green	275.00	180.00	150.00	100.00	150.00	100.00
2	10¢ blue	300.00	210.00	150.00	105.00	180.00	120.00

3
Andrew Jackson

6, 7
Jefferson Davis
6: Fine Print
7: Coarse Print

1862

3	2¢ green	950.00	900.00	600.00	550.00	800.00	700.00
4	5¢ blue	200.00	175.00	125.00	100.00	125.00	80.00
5	10¢ rose	1500.00	1000.00	1100.00	900.00	450.00	425.00
6	5¢ light blue, London Print	16.00	13.00	9.00	7.50	30.00	25.00
7	5¢ blue, Local Print	18.50	15.00	13.50	11.00	21.00	18.00

8
Andrew Jackson

1863

8	2¢ red brown	75.00	50.00	55.00	40.00	400.00	295.00

9

10, 11 (Die A)
Jefferson Davis

12 (Die B)

9	10¢ blue (TEN)	975.00	675.00	600.00	475.00	550.00	500.00
10	10¢ blue (with frame line)	....	....	5500.00	4000.00	1850.00	1650.00
11	10¢ blue (no frame)	16.00	12.00	9.00	8.00	23.00	19.00
12	10¢ blue, filled corner	19.00	16.00	9.00	8.00	23.00	19.00

13
George Washington

14
John C. Calhoun

13	20¢ green	49.00	35.00	35.00	25.00	375.00	325.00

1862

14	1¢ orange	110.00	80.00	75.00	50.00	....	....

SCOTT NO.	DESCRIPTION	UNUSED NH F	AVG	UNUSED OG F	AVG	USED F	AVG

CUBA

U.S. Administration

CUBA

1899
U.S. Stamps of 267, 279, 279B, 268, 281, 282C surcharged

1 c. de PESO.

221	1¢ on 1¢ yellow green	10.00	8.50	5.50	5.00	.65	.55
222	2¢ on 2¢ carmine........	19.00	15.00	10.00	8.00	.85	.70
223	2-1/2¢ on 2¢ carmine .	12.00	10.00	5.50	5.00	1.00	.75
224	3¢ on 3¢ purple	27.00	19.00	15.00	13.00	2.00	1.50
225	5¢ on 5¢ blue.............	27.00	19.00	15.00	13.00	2.50	2.00
226	10¢ on 10¢ brown.......	65.00	55.00	28.00	23.00	8.00	7.00

227   228   229

230   231

Republic under U.S. Military Rule Watermarked US-C

227	1¢ Columbus	7.50	5.50	4.00	3.00	.35	.25
228	2¢ Coconut Palms......	7.50	5.50	4.00	3.00	.35	.25
229	3¢ Allegory "Cuba"......	7.50	5.50	4.00	3.00	.35	.25
230	5¢ Ocean Liner...........	9.50	8.00	6.00	4.75	.35	.25
231	10¢ Cane Field	25.00	17.00	15.00	12.00	.75	.55

SPECIAL DELIVERY
1899
Surcharged of 1899 on U.S. E5

E1	10¢ on 10¢ blue..........	270.00	200.00	140.00	95.00	110.00	90.00

E2
Special Delivery Messenger

Republic under U.S. Military Rule
Watermarked US-C Inscribed "Immediate"

E2	10¢ orange	115.00	85.00	45.00	30.00	18.00	14.00

POSTAGE DUE STAMPS
1899
Surcharge of 1899 on U.S. J38-39, J41-42

J1	1¢ on 1¢ deep claret...	90.00	80.00	45.00	40.00	7.00	5.00
J2	2¢ on 2¢ deep claret...	90.00	80.00	45.00	40.00	7.00	5.00
J3	5¢ on 5¢ deep claret...	95.00	75.00	45.00	40.00	7.00	5.00
J4	10¢ on 10¢ deep claret	60.00	50.00	25.00	20.00	3.00	2.00

GUAM

1899
U.S. Stamps of 279, 267, 268, 272, 280-82C, 284, 275, 276 overprinted

GUAM

1	1¢ deep green	40.00	30.00	20.00	13.00	30.00	22.00
2	2¢ red	38.00	30.00	19.00	13.00	29.00	22.00
3	3¢ purple	250.00	200.00	130.00	90.00	160.00	120.00
4	4¢ lilac brown	220.00	190.00	130.00	90.00	160.00	120.00
5	5¢ blue.....................	60.00	40.00	30.00	20.00	50.00	35.00
6	6¢ lake......................	220.00	170.00	120.00	90.00	180.00	130.00
7	8¢ violet brown	220.00	170.00	120.00	90.00	180.00	130.00
8	10¢ brown (Type I)	80.00	60.00	40.00	20.00	50.00	30.00
10	15¢ olive green	250.00	170.00	140.00	100.00	130.00	100.00
11	50¢ orange	650.00	500.00	300.00	200.00	310.00	220.00
12	$1 black (Type I)........	650.00	500.00	300.00	200.00	370.00	200.00

SPECIAL DELIVERY
U.S. Stamp E5 overprint

GUAM

E1	10¢ blue.....................	275.00	200.00	140.00	100.00	200.00	150.00

SCOTT NO.	DESCRIPTION	UNUSED OG F	AVG	UNUSED F	AVG	USED F	AVG

HAWAII

23, 24   25, 26

1864 Laid Paper

23	1¢ black	300.00	200.00	230.00	150.00	2000.00	1400.00
24	2¢ black	350.00	220.00	240.00	160.00	920.00	620.00

1865 Wove Paper

25	1¢ dark blue...............	375.00	220.00	250.00	170.00	....	....
26	2¢ dark blue...............	375.00	220.00	250.00	170.00	....	....

27-29, 50-51
King Kamehame-ha IV

1861-63

27	2¢ pale rose, horizontal laid paper...................	400.00	275.00	275.00	185.00	275.00	185.00
28	2¢ pale rose, vertical laid paper...................	400.00	275.00	275.00	185.00	275.00	185.00

1869 Engraved

29	2¢ red, thin wove paper	50.00	35.00	40.00	35.00		....

30
Princess Kamamalu

31
King Kamehameha IV

32, 39, 52C
King Kamehameha V

33
King Kamehameha V

34
Mataia Kekuanaoa

1864-71 Wove Paper

30	1¢ purple	12.00	9.00	9.00	7.00	8.50	6.00
31	2¢ rose vermillion	70.00	55.00	52.00	43.00	10.00	7.00
32	5¢ blue......................	200.00	140.00	150.00	95.00	35.00	25.00
33	6 yellow green	45.00	30.00	30.00	20.00	10.00	7.00
34	18¢ dull rose	105.00	70.00	80.00	50.00	40.00	28.00

35, 38, 43
King David Kalakaua

36, 46
Prince William Pitt Leleichoku

1875

35	2¢ brown....................	15.00	9.00	6.00	4.00	3.25	2.10
36	12¢ black	110.00	85.00	60.00	38.00	42.00	28.00

SCOTT NO.	DESCRIPTION	UNUSED OG F	AVG	UNUSED F	AVG	USED F	AVG

37, 42
Princess Likelike

40, 44, 45
King David Kalakaua

41
Queen Kapiolani

47
Statue of King Kamehameha I

48
King William Lunalilo

49
Queen Emma Kaleleonalani

1882

SCOTT NO.	DESCRIPTION	UNUSED OG F	AVG	UNUSED F	AVG	USED F	AVG
37	1¢ blue	22.00	11.00	8.00	6.50	7.00	5.00
38	2¢ lilac rose	280.00	110.00	95.00	75.00	45.00	40.00
39	5¢ ultramarine	30.00	14.00	14.00	10.00	4.00	2.75
40	10¢ black	80.00	60.00	40.00	25.00	22.00	18.00
41	15¢ red brown	110.00	75.00	45.00	32.00	26.00	20.00

1883-86

42	1¢ green	6.00	4.00	3.00	2.00	2.10	1.50
43	2¢ rose	10.00	6.00	3.50	2.50	1.25	.85
44	10¢ red brown	70.00	50.00	25.00	20.00	11.00	7.00
45	10¢ vermillion	75.00	55.00	27.00	22.00	15.00	10.00
46	12¢ red lilac	160.00	85.00	58.00	50.00	35.00	30.00
47	25¢ dark violet	290.00	180.00	120.00	100.00	70.00	55.00
48	50¢ red	300.00	210.00	125.00	100.00	90.00	75.00
49	$1 rose red	500.00	200.00	185.00	155.00	250.00	200.00
50	2¢ Orange Vermillion	150.00	95.00	120.00	90.00	....	....
51	2¢ Carmine	30.00	20.00	25.00	20.00	....	....

52
Queen Liliuokalani

1890-91

52	2¢ dull violet	12.00	8.00	5.00	3.25	2.00	1.40
52C	5¢ deep indigo	220.00	110.00	77.00	50.00	150.00	100.00

Provisional GOVT. 1893

1893 Provisional Government
Red Overprint

53	1¢ purple	14.00	10.00	6.00	4.25	15.00	11.00
54	1¢ blue	14.00	10.00	6.00	4.25	15.00	11.00
55	1¢ green	3.00	2.00	1.50	1.00	4.00	2.75
56	2¢ brown	20.00	14.00	9.00	6.00	25.00	20.00
57	2¢ dull violet	3.00	2.00	1.50	1.00	1.50	1.00
58	5¢ deep indigo	22.00	15.00	11.00	7.00	30.00	22.00
59	5¢ ultramarine	10.00	8.00	6.00	4.00	3.25	1.95
60	6¢ green	26.00	16.00	13.00	9.00	30.00	20.00
61	10¢ black	20.00	17.00	11.00	8.00	17.00	14.00
62	12¢ black	20.00	17.00	9.00	7.00	18.00	14.00
63	12¢ red lilac	300.00	225.00	130.00	95.00	225.00	170.00
64	25¢ dark violet	55.00	35.00	20.00	15.00	50.00	40.00

Black Overprint

65	2¢ rose vermillion	140.00	80.00	40.00	30.00	85.00	60.00
66	2¢ rose	2.00	1.50	1.20	.80	3.00	2.00
67	10¢ vermillion	38.00	25.00	16.00	10.00	35.00	28.00
68	10¢ red brown	14.00	11.00	7.00	5.00	15.00	10.00
69	12¢ red lilac	510.00	425.00	250.00	175.00	600.00	425.00
70	15¢ red brown	35.00	25.00	17.00	13.00	35.00	25.00
71	18¢ dull rose	55.00	40.00	28.00	22.00	40.00	28.00
72	50¢ red	125.00	90.00	55.00	40.00	100.00	70.00
73	$1 rose red	210.00	170.00	105.00	80.00	190.00	130.00

74, 80
Coat of Arms

75, 81
View of Honolulu

76
Statue of King Kamehameha I

1894

SCOTT NO.	DESCRIPTION	UNUSED OG F	AVG	UNUSED F	AVG	USED F	AVG
74	1¢ yellow	4.50	3.25	2.25	1.55	1.40	1.00
75	2¢ brown	4.50	3.25	2.25	1.55	.80	.55
76	5¢ rose lake	10.00	8.50	4.00	2.75	2.00	1.40

77
Star and Palm

78
S.S."Arawa"

79
Pres. S.B. Dole

77	10¢ yellow green	12.00	9.00	7.00	5.00	6.00	4.00
78	12¢ blue	28.00	23.00	12.00	8.00	18.00	12.00
79	25¢ deep blue	35.00	29.00	15.00	10.00	16.00	11.00

82
Statue of King Kamehameha I

1899

80	1¢ dark green	3.50	2.00	1.50	1.00	1.50	1.00
81	2¢ rose	3.50	2.00	1.50	1.00	1.50	1.00
82	5¢ blue	13.00	10.00	6.00	4.00	4.00	2.80

O1
Lorrin A. Thurston

1896 OFFICIAL STAMPS

O1	2¢ green	72.00	50.00	40.00	28.00	20.00	14.00
O2	5¢ black brown	72.00	50.00	40.00	28.00	20.00	14.00
O3	6¢ deep ultramarine	90.00	80.00	40.00	28.00	20.00	14.00
O4	10¢ bright rose	75.00	55.00	40.00	28.00	20.00	14.00
O5	12¢ orange	120.00	90.00	40.00	28.00	20.00	14.00
O6	25¢ gray violet	155.00	110.00	50.00	33.00	20.00	14.00

MARSHALL ISLANDS

The Marshall Islands are a part of the U.S. administered Trust Territories of the Pacific formed in 1947.
They were granted postal autonomy in 1984 on their way to independence.

SCOTT NO.	DESCRIPTION	UNUSED F/NH
	1984 COMMEMORATIVES	
31-34	20¢ Postal Independence, attached.......................	2.75
	1984-85 MAPS & NAVIGATION	
35-49A	**1¢-$1, 16 varieties**	**13.00**
35	1¢ Mili Atoll	
36	3¢ Likiep Atoll	
37	5¢ Ebon Atoll	
38	10¢ Jaluit Atoll	
39	13¢ Alinginae Atoll	
40	14¢ Wotho Atoll (1985)	
41	20¢ Kwajalein Atoll	
42	22¢ Enewetok (1985)	
43	28¢ Ailinglaplap Atoll	
44	30¢ Majuro Atoll	
45	33¢ Namu Atoll (1985)	
46	37¢ Rongelap Atoll	
47	39¢ Utirik & Taka (1985)	
48	44¢ Ujelang Atoll (1985)	
49	50¢ Maloelap & Aur (1985)	
49A	$1.00 Arno Atoll	
	1984-85 BOOKLET PANES	
39a	13¢ Ailingingae (10)	11.00
40a	14¢ Wotho Atoll (10)	11.00
41a	20¢ Kwajalein (10)	12.00
41b	13¢ (5) & 20¢ (5)	13.00
42a	22¢ Eniwetok (10)	12.00
42b	14¢ (5) & 22¢ (5)	13.00
	1984 COMMEMORATIVES	
50-53	40¢ U.P.U.—Hamburg, attached.......................	3.50
54-57	20¢ Dolphins, attached	2.25
58	20¢ Christmas, strip of 4	4.50
59-62	20¢ Constitution, attached	2.50
	1985 COMMEMORATIVES	
63-64	22¢ Audubon Birds, attached...........................	1.65
65-69	22¢ Seashells, attached..................................	2.75
70-73	22¢ Decade for Women, attached	2.45

SCOTT NO.	DESCRIPTION	UNUSED F/NH
74-77	22¢ Reef Fish, attached	2.40
78-81	22¢ Youth Year, attached	2.40
82-85	14¢-44¢ Christmas, 4 varieties	2.40
86-90	22¢ Halley's Comet, strip of 5	6.00
91-94	22¢ Medicinal Plants, attached	2.40
	1986-87 MAPS & NAVIGATION	
107	$2 Wotje & Erikub	6.50
108	$5 Bikini Atoll...	12.50
109	$10 Stick Chart (1987)	22.50
	1986 COMMEMORATIVES	
110-13	14¢ Marine Invertebrates, attached	3.00
114	$1 AMERIPEX '86 Souvenir Sheet	4.00
115-18	22¢ Operation Crossroads, Atomic Tests, attached	2.90
119-23	22¢ Seashells, designs as #65-69, attached	2.75
124-27	22¢ Game Fish, attached.	2.50
128-31	22¢ Christmas, Peace, attached.....................	3.00
	1987 COMMEMORATIVES	
132-35	22¢ Whaling Ships, attached	2.75
136-41	33¢, 39¢, 44¢ Historic Aircraft, 3 attached pairs	5.50
142	$1 CAPEX '87 Souvenir Sheet.........................	3.00

SCOTT NO.	DESCRIPTION	UNUSED F/NH

143

152

157

160

143-51	14¢-44¢ U.S. Constitution, 3 attached strips of 3	5.25
152-56	22¢ Seashells, attached	2.75
157-59	44¢ Copra Industry, attached	3.00
160-63	14¢-44¢ Christmas	2.90

164

168

1988

| 164-67 | 44¢ Marine Birds | 4.50 |

1988-89 Definitives

| 168-83 | 1¢-$5 Fish, 16 singles complete set | 26.00 |
| 184 | $10 Blue Jack (1989) | 20.00 |

Booklet Panes 1987-89

170a	14¢ Hawkfish pane (10)	3.80
171a	15¢ Balloonfish pane (10)	6.00
173a	22¢ Lyretail wrasse pane (10)	7.50
173b	5 (14¢) & 5 (22¢) pane (10)	6.00
174a	25¢ Parrotfish pane (10)	8.00
174b	5 (15¢) & 5 (25¢) pane (10)	8.00

188

| 188-89 | 15¢-25¢ Olympics 2 attached strip of 5 | 5.00 |

190a

191

| 190 | 25¢ Stevenson, sheetlet of 9 | 7.00 |
| 191-94 | 25¢ Ships & Flags, attached | 2.75 |

SCOTT NO.	DESCRIPTION	UNUSED F/NH

195

202

205

195-99	25¢ Christmas, strip of 5	3.00
200-04	25¢ J.F.K. Tribute, strip of 5	3.50
205-08	25¢ Space Shuttle, strip of 4	3.00

209

1989 COMMEMORATIVES

| 209-12 | 45¢ Links to Japan, attached | 4.00 |

213

216

213-15	45¢ Alaska Anniv., strip of 3	3.75
216-20	25¢ Seashells, strip of 5	3.00
221	$1 Japanese Art Souvenir Sheet	2.60

222

226

230a

232

222-25	45¢ Migrant Birds, attached	4.90
226-29	45¢ Postal Service, attached	4.80
230	$1.50 PHILEX-FRANCE Souv. Sheet	12.00
231	$1.00 Postal Service Centenary Souvenir Sheet	12.00
232-38	25¢-$1 20th Anniversary First Moon Landing	20.00
238a	booklet pane of 232-38	20.00

239

248

SCOTT NO.	DESCRIPTION	UNUSED F/NH

1989 WWII Anniversary Issues

239	25¢ Invasion of Poland	1.00
240	45¢ Sinking of HMS Royal Oak	1.65
241	45¢ Invasion of Finland	1.65
242-45	45¢ Battle of River Plate, 4 attached	5.00

1990 WWII Anniversary Issues

246-47	25¢ Invasion of Denmark and Norway	1.75
248	25¢ Katyn Forest Massacre	1.00
249-50	25¢ Bombing of Rotterdam/25¢ Invasion of Belgium	1.75
251	45¢ Winston Churchill	1.65
252-53	45¢ Evacuation at Dunkirk, 2 attached	3.50
254	45¢ Occupation of Paris	1.65
255	25¢ Battle of Mers-el-Kebir	1.00
256	25¢ Battles for Burma Road	1.00
257-60	45¢ U.S. Destroyers, 4 attached	6.00
261-64	45¢ Battle for Britain, 4 attached	6.00
265	45¢ Tripartite Pact 1940	1.65
266	25¢ Roosevelt Reelected	.90
267-70	25¢ Battle of Taranto, 4 attached	4.00

1991 WWII Anniversary Issues

271-74	30¢ Roosevelt's Four Freedoms of Speech, 4 attached	4.00
275	30¢ Battle of Beda Fomm	.95
276-77	29¢ Invasion of Greece and Yugoslavia, 2 attached	1.80
278-81	50¢ Sinking of the Bismarck, 4 attached	7.00
282	30¢ Germany Invades Russia	1.00
283-84	29¢ Atlantic Charter, 2 attached	1.80
285	29¢ Siege of Moscow	1.00
286-87	29¢ Sinking of the USS Reuben James, 2 attached	1.80
288-91	50¢ Japanese Attack Pearl Harbor, 4 attached	7.00
288-91b	same, 2nd printing (1 title corrected)	30.00
292	29¢ Japanese Capture Guam	1.00
293	29¢ Fall of Singapore	1.00
294-95	50¢ Flying Tigers, 2 attached	3.50
296	29¢ Fall of Wake Island	1.00

1992 WWII Anniversary Issues

297	29¢ Arcadia Conference	1.00
298	50¢ Fall of Manila	1.50
299	29¢ Japanese take Rabaul	1.00
300	29¢ Battle of Java Sea	1.00
301	50¢ Fall of Rangoon	1.50
302	29¢ Japanese on New Guinea	1.00
303	29¢ MacArthur evacuated from Corregidor	1.00
304	29¢ Raid on Saint-Nazaire	1.00
305	29¢ Bataan/Death March	1.00
306	50¢ Doolittle Raid on Tokyo	1.50
307	29¢ Fall of Corregidor	1.00
308-11	50¢ Battle of the Coral Sea, 4 attached	7.25
308-11b	same, 2nd printing (4 titles corrected)	27.00
312-15	50¢ Battle of Midway, 4 attached	7.25
316	29¢ Village of Lidice destroyed	1.00
317	29¢ Fall of Sevastopol	1.00
318-19	29¢ Convoy PQ 17 Destroyed, 2 attached	2.55
320	29¢ Marines on Guadalcanal	1.00
321	29¢ Battle of Savo Island	1.00
322	29¢ Dieppe Raid	1.00
323	50¢ Battle of Stalingrad	1.90
324	29¢ Battle of Eastern Solomons	1.00
325	50¢ Battle of Cape Esperance	1.90
326	29¢ Battle of El Alamein	1.00
327-28	29¢ Battle of Barents Sea, 2 attached	2.70

1993 WWII Anniversary Issues

329	29¢ Casablanca Conference	1.00
330	29¢ Liberation of Kharkov	1.00
331-34	50¢ Battle of Bismarck Sea, 4 attached	7.25
335	50¢ Interception of Admiral Yamamoto	1.50
336-37	29¢ Battle of Kursk, 2 attached	2.70

341   **345a**   **346**

1989

341-44	25¢ Christmas 1989, 4 attached	4.70
345	45¢ Milestones in space (25)	35.00

1990

346-65A	1¢/$2 Birds (21)	35.00
361a	Essen '90 Germany, miniature sheet of 4 (347, 350, 353, 361)	5.70

366   **370**

377

366-69	25¢ Children's Games, 4 attached	5.00
370-76	25¢, $1 Penny Black, singles	18.00
376a	booklet pane of 370-76	18.50
377-80	25¢ Endangered Wildlife, 4 attached	6.00

381   **382**

383   **387**

381	25¢ Joint Issue (US & Micronesia)	1.25
382	45¢ German Reunification	1.45
383-86	25¢ Christmas 1990, 4 attached	4.50
387-90	25¢ Breadfruit, 4 attached	4.00

395

1991

391-94	50¢ 10th Anniversaary of Space Shuttle, 4 attached	5.00
395-98	52¢ Flowers, 4 attached	6.25
398a	52¢ Phila Nippon, sheet of 4	6.25

399   **400**

399	29¢ Operation Desert Storm	1.25
400-06	29¢, $1 Birds, set of 7 singles	25.00
406a	same, booklet pane of 7	25.00

407   **411**

407-10	12¢-50¢ Air Marshall Islands Aircraft, set of 4	5.00
411	29¢ Admission to the United Nations	1.00

SCOTT NO.	DESCRIPTION	UNUSED F/NH

412

413

| 412 | 30¢ Christmas 1991, Dove | 1.20 |
| 413 | 29¢ Peace Corps | 1.20 |

414

418

425

1992

414-17	29¢ Ships, strip of 4	5.00
418-24	50¢, $1 Columbus, set of 7 singles	19.00
424a	same, booklet pane of 7	19.00
425-28	29¢ Handicrafts, 4 attached	3.25

429

430

| 429 | 29¢ Christmas, 1992 | 1.00 |
| 430-33 | 9-45¢ Birds, set of 4 | 4.50 |

441

466A

478

1993

| 434-40 | 50¢, $1 Reef Life, set of 7 singles | 24.00 |
| 440a | same, booklet pane of 7 | 24.50 |

1993-95

| 441-66B | 10¢-$10 Ships & Sailing Vessels, 28 varieties | 79.75 |
| 466C | "Hong Kong '94" miniature sheet of 4 (#464d-64g) | 5.00 |

1993 WWII Anniversary Issues (continued)

467-70	52¢ Invasion of Sicily, 4 attached	8.00
471	50¢ Bombing of Schweinfurt	1.75
472	29¢ Liberation of Smolensk	1.00
473	29¢ Landings at Bougainville	1.00
474	50¢ Invasion of Tarawa	1.75
475	52¢ Teheran Conference, 1943	1.75
476-77	29¢ Battle of North Cape, 2 attached	2.50

1994 WWII Anniversary Issues

478	29¢ Gen. Dwight D. Eisenhower	1.00
479	50¢ Invasion of Anzio	1.75
480	52¢ Siege of Leningrad lifted	1.75
481	29¢ US Liberates Marshall Islands	1.00
482	29¢ Japanese Defeated at Truk	1.00
483	52¢ US Bombs Germany	1.75

484	50¢ Lt. Gen. Mark Clark, Rome Falls to the Allies	1.75
485-88	75¢ D-Day—Allied Landings at Normandy, 4 attached	11.00
485-88b	same, 2nd printing (3 titles corrected)	29.00
489	50¢ V-1 Bombardment of England Begins	1.75
490	29¢ US Marines Land on Saipan	1.00
491	50¢ 1st Battle of Philippine Sea	1.75
492	29¢ US Liberates Guam	1.00
493	50¢ Warsaw Uprising	1.75
494	50¢ Liberation of Paris	1.75
495	29¢ US Marines land on Peliliu	1.75
496	52¢ MacArthur returns to the Philippines	1.75
497	52¢ Battle of Leyte Gulf	1.75
498-99	50¢ Battleship Tirpitz Sunk, 2 attached	4.70
500-03	50¢ Battle of the Bulge, 4 attached	11.00

1995 WWII Anniversary Issues

504	32¢ Yalta Conference Begins	1.25
505	55¢ Bombing of Dresden	3.80
506	$1 Iwo Jima Invaded by US Marines	4.50
507	32¢ Remagen Bridge Taken by US Forces	1.25
508	55¢ Okinawa Invaded by US Forces	2.25
509	50¢ Death of F.D.R.	2.25
510	32¢ US/USSR troops meet at Elbe River	1.50
511	60¢ Russian troops capture Berlin	2.25
512	55¢ Allies liberate concentration camps, 1945	2.25
513-16	75¢ VE Day, 4 attached	18.00
517	32¢ UN Charter signed	1.40
518	55¢ Potsdam Conference convenes	2.50
519	60¢ Churchill resigns	2.50
520	$1 Enola Gay drops atomic bomb on Hiroshima, 1945	5.00
521-24	75¢ VJ Day, 4 attached	17.60

1994 WWII Anniversary Issues (continued)

| 562 | $1 MacArthur returns to the Philippines, souvenir sheet | 5.20 |
| 563 | $1 Harry S. Truman/UN Charter souvenir sheet | 4.95 |

567

1993 (continued)

| 567-70 | 29¢ New Capitol | 2.50 |

572

576

571	50¢ Super Tanker "Eagle" souvenir sheet	1.35
572-75	29¢ Life in the 1800s, 4 attached	3.00
576	29¢ Christmas 1993	1.00

1994

| 577 | $2.90 15th Anniversary Constitution souvenir sheet | 6.80 |
| 578 | 29¢ 10th Anniversary Postal Service souvenir sheet | 1.00 |

579

583

582a

579-80	50¢ World Cup Soccer, 2 attached	5.80
582	50¢ Solar System, Planets, sheetlet of 12	20.00
583-86	75¢ 25th Anniversary of First Moon Landing, 4 attached	7.00
586b	$3 25th Anniversary of First Moon Landing, souvenir sheet	7.00

SCOTT NO.	DESCRIPTION	UNUSED F/NH

587a   588

| 587 | "PHILAKOREA '94" souvenir sheet of 3 | 5.50 |
| 588 | 29¢ Christmas 1994 | 1.00 |

590a   591a   592a

1995

589	50¢ New Year 1995 (Year of the Boar)	1.80
590	55¢ Marine Life, 4 attached	8.80
591	55¢ John F. Kennedy, strip of 6	8.00
592	75¢ Marilyn Monroe, 4 attached	8.00

593a   594a   595a

593	32¢ Cats, 4 attached	3.80
594	75¢ Space Shuttle, 4 attached	6.80
595	60¢ Pacific Game Fish, 8 attached	17.00

596a   597a

596	32¢ Island Legends, 4 attached, plus 4 labels	3.80
597	32¢ Orchids (Singapore '95), miniature sheet of 4	3.50
598	50¢ Suzhou Gardens souvenir sheet	1.10

599   600a   601

599	32¢ Christmas 1995	1.00
600	32¢ Jet Fighter Planes, sheetlet of 25	19.00
601	32¢ Yitzhak Rabin	1.00

SCOTT NO.	DESCRIPTION	UNUSED F/NH

603a   604a

1996

602	50¢ New Year 1996 (Year of the Rat)	1.25
603	32¢ Native Birds, 4 attached	7.80
604	55¢ Wild Cats, 4 attached	6.50

605a   606a   607a   608

605	32¢ Sailing Ships, sheetlet of 25	18.00
606	60¢ Olympic Games Centenary, 4 attached	6.50
607	55¢ History of the Marshall Islands, sheetlet of 12	16.00
608	32¢ Elvis Presley First #1 Hit 40th Anniversary	2.00
609	50¢ The Palance Museum, Shenyang souvenir sheet	1.50

610   611a   612a

610	32¢ James Dean	1.85
611	60¢ Automobiles, sheet of 8	13.00
612	32¢ Island Legends 1996, 4 attached	3.20

613a

614a   615

613	55¢ Steam Locomotives, sheet of 12	16.00
614	32¢ Marine Life (Taipei '96), miniature sheet of 4	3.20
615	$3 Stick Chart, Canoe & Flag of the Republic	7.35

SCOTT NO.	DESCRIPTION	UNUSED F/NH

616   **617a**   **618a**

616	32¢ Christmas 1996	1.00
617	32¢ World's Legendary Biplanes, sheet of 25	18.00
618	32¢ Native Crafts, 4 attached	3.20

620   **622a**

623

1997

619	60¢ New Year 1997 (Year of the Ox)	1.45
620-21	32¢-60¢ Amata Kabua, President of Marshall Islands, set of 2	2.50
622	32¢ Elvis Presley, strip of 3	2.80
623-24	32¢ Hong Kong '97, 2 sheets of 2	2.80

625a   **627a**   **628**

625	60¢ The Twelve Apostles, sheet of 12	17.75
626	$3 Rubens "The Last Supper", souvenir sheet	7.50
627	60¢ First Decade of the 20th Century, sheet of 15	22.50
628	60¢ Deng Xiaoping (1904-97), Chinese Leader	1.55
629	32¢ Native Crafts (1996), 4 attached, self-adhesive, Die-Cut	4.65
630	32¢ Native Crafts (1996), 4 attached, self-adhesive, perf.	5.25
631-37	50¢-$1 Anniv. 1st US & Marshall Islands Stamps, booklet of 7	11.40

638   **640a**   **641a**

638	16¢ Bristle-Thighed Curlew, strip of 4	3.80
639	50¢ Bank of China, Hong Kong, souvenir sheet	1.80
640	32¢ Canoes, strip of 4	3.80
641	32¢ Legendary Aircraft, sheet of 25	20.00

642a   **643a**   **646a**

642	32¢ "Old Ironsides" Bicentennial	.95
643	32¢ Island Legends, 4 attached	3.50
644	60¢ Marine Life, 4 attached	6.00
645	60¢ Princess Diana, strip of 3	5.00
646	60¢ Events of the 20th Century, 1910-19, sheetlet of 15	22.00

647-48   **649a**

647-48	32¢ Christmas, Angel, pair	1.85
649	20¢ US State-Named Warships, sheet of 50	30.00
650	50¢ Treasure Ship, Shanghai '97, souvenir sheet	1.45

652a   **653a**

654a   **655a**

1998

651	60¢ Year of the Tiger, souvenir sheet	1.80
652	32¢ Elvis Presley's 1968 Television Special, strip of 3	2.90
653	32¢ Sea Shells, strip of 4	3.00
654	60¢ Events of the 20th Century, 1920-29, sheetlet of 15	22.00
655	32¢ Canoes of the Pacific, sheetlet of 8	7.00

665   **667a**   **670**

656	60¢ Berlin Airlift, 4 attached	6.00
657	60¢ Events of the 20th Century, 1930-39, sheetlet of 15	24.00
658-64	60¢-$3 Tsar Nicholas II, bklt of 7 (60¢ x 6, $3 x 1)	17.00
665	32¢ Babe Ruth	.95
666	32¢ Legendary Aircraft of the US Navy, sheet of 25	19.00
667	60¢ Chevrolet Automobiles, sheetlet of 8	12.00
668	33¢ Marshalese Language and Alphabet, sheetlet of 24	18.00
669	33¢ New Buildings in Marshall Islands, strip of 3	2.80
670	32¢ Midnight Angel	.95
671-77	60¢-$3 John Glenn's Return to Space, bklt of 7 (60¢ x 6, $3 x 1)	17.00
678	$3.20 Airplane delivering supplies, souvenir sheet	7.80
679	60¢ Events of the 20th Century, 1940-49, sheetlet of 15	23.00
680	33¢ Warships, sheetlet of 25	20.00

SCOTT NO.	DESCRIPTION	UNUSED F/NH

682 **701a** **699a**

1999

681	60¢ Year of the Rabbit, souvenir sheet	2.50
682-89	1¢-¢10 Birds (8)	28.80
690	33¢ Canoes of the Pacific, sheetlet of 8	7.00
691-98	same, self-adhesive, block of 10 (691-97 x 1, 698 x 3)	8.00
699	60¢ Great American Indian Chiefs, sheetlet of 12	18.00
700	33¢ Marshall Islands National Flag	.95
701	33¢ Flowers of the Pacific, 6 attached	5.50
702	60¢ Events of the 20th Century, 1950-59, sheetlet of 15	23.00
703	$1.20 HMAS Australia, souvenir sheet	3.00
704	33¢ Elvis Presley	1.00
705	60¢ IBRA '99 Exhibition, sheetlet of 4	6.00

706 **707a**

713a **714**

706	33¢ Marshall Islands Constitution, 20th Anniversary	.95
707	33¢ Marshall Islands Postal Service, 15th Anniversary, 4 attached	4.50
708	33¢ Legendary Aircraft, sheetlet of 25	20.00
709	$1 PHILEXFRANCE '99, souvenir sheet	2.80
710	60¢ Tanker Alrehab, souvenir sheet	1.75
711	60¢ Events of the 20th Century, 1960-69, sheetlet of 15	22.00
712	33¢ 1st Manned Moonlanding, 30th Anniversary, sheetlet of 3	2.80
713	33¢ Ships, 4 attached	3.75
714-21	5¢-$5 Birds, set of 8	30.00

722 **728a** **729a**

722	33¢ Christmas	.95
723	60¢ Events of the 20th Century, 1970-79, sheetlet of 15	22.00
724-25	33¢ Millenium, 2 attached	1.85

2000

726	60¢ Events of the 20th Century, 1980-89, sheetlet of 15	22.00
727	60¢ New Year 2000 (Year of the Dragon), souvenir sheet	1.75
728	33¢ Legendary Aircraft, sheetlet of 25	20.00
729	33¢ Roses, 6 attached	5.80
730	60¢ Events of the 20th Century, 1990-99, sheetlet of 15	22.50

SCOTT NO.	DESCRIPTION	UNUSED F/NH

731a **739a**

731	33¢ Pandas, 6 attached	5.80
732-38	1¢-42¢ American Presidents, 7 sheetlets of 6	20.00
739	33¢ First Zepplin Flight, 4 attached	3.50

740 **747a**

740-46	60¢-$1 Sir Winston Churchill, bklt of 7 (60¢ x 6, $1 x 1)	14.00
747	33¢ US Military 225th Anniversary, 3 attached	2.80

748a **750a**

748	33¢ National Government, 4 attached	3.50
749	60¢ Ships, 6 attached	9.00
750	60¢ Queen Mother's 100th birthday, 4 attached	7.00

752a **754a**

751	33¢ Reef Life, sheetlet of 8	6.95
752	60¢ Butterflies, sheetlet of 12	18.00
753	33¢ Reunification of Germany, 10th Anniversary	.95
754	33¢ Submarines, 4 attached	3.80
755	33¢ Christmas	.85
756	60¢-$1 Sun Yat-sen, bklt of 7 (60¢ x 6, $1 x 1)	12.00

758

2001

757	80¢ Year of the Snake, souvenir sheet	2.80
758	34¢ Carnations, stamp + label	1.00
759	34¢ Violets, stamp + label	1.00
760	34¢ Jonquil, stamp + label	1.00
761	34¢ Sweet Pea, stamp + label	1.00
762	34¢ Lily of the Valley, stamp + label	1.00
763	34¢ Rose, stamp + label	1.00
764	34¢ Larkspur, stamp + label	1.00
765	34¢ Poppy, stamp + label	1.00
766	34¢ Aster, stamp + label	1.00
767	34¢ Marigold, stamp + label	1.00
768	34¢ Chrysanthemum, stamp + label	1.00
769	34¢ Poinsettia, stamp + label	1.00

SCOTT NO.	DESCRIPTION	UNUSED F/NH

770

772

770-71	$5-$10 Sailing Canoes	39.00
772-75	34¢-$1 Famous People, set of 4	8.00
776	80¢ Butterflies, sheetlet of 12	24.00

777a

778a

777	34¢ Fairy Tales, 7 varieties attached	7.00
778	34¢ Watercraft Racing, 4 attached	3.80
779	80¢ Manned Spacecraft 40th Anniv, 4 attached	8.50

780a

783a

780	34¢ Stamp Day	1.00
781	80¢ American Achievements in Space, 4 attached	8.80
782	34¢ Marine Life, 4 attached	3.75
783	34¢ Sports, 4 attached	5.75
784	57¢ Atlan Anien	1.20

785a

788a

798a

785	34¢ Zodiac Signs, sheetlet of 12	12.00
786	80¢ Phila Nippon 2001, sheetlet of 12	24.00
787	80¢ US Naval Heroes in WWII Pacific Theater, sheetlet of 9	18.50
788	34¢ Classic Cars, 8 attached	8.00
789	34¢-$1 Remembrance of Victims of Sept. 11, bklt of 7 (34¢ x 6, $1 x 1)	9.00
790	34¢ Christmas, 4 attached	3.75
791	80¢ Airplanes, 10 attached	20.00

2002

792	80¢ Year of the Horse, souvenir sheet	2.00
793	34¢ Shells, 6 attached	5.50
794	80¢ Reign of Queen Elizabeth, 50th Anniv., souvenir sheet	2.00
795	34¢ United We Stand	1.00
796	34¢ Classic Cars, 8 attached	7.50
797	34¢ Corals, 4 attached	4.00
798	80¢ Butterflies, sheet of 12	24.00

802a

804

SCOTT NO.	DESCRIPTION	UNUSED F/NH

799	34¢ Horses in Art, sheet of 12	10.00
800	80¢ Horses in Art, souvenir sheet	1.80
801	37¢ Russian Fairy Tale The Frog Princess, sheet of 12	12.80
802	80¢ Carousel Figures, 4 attached	8.00
803	37¢ Birds, sheet of 16	15.80
804	80¢ Benjamin Franklin, 2 attached	4.00
805	37¢ Sea Turtles, 4 attached	4.00
806	80¢ Intl. Federation of Stamp Dealers, 50 Anniv., 6 attached	12.50
807	37¢ U.S. Navy Ships, 6 attached	5.80

808a

812a

808	23¢ Insects and Spiders, sheet of 20	12.00
809	80¢ Classic Cars, 8 attached	16.00
810	80¢ Queen Mother, redrawn, 4 attached	8.50
811	80¢ Regal Princess Cruise Ship, souvenir sheet	1.80
812	80¢ World War I Heroes, 8 attached	16.00
813	37¢ Snowman cookies, 2 attached	1.80

815

817

2003

814	80¢ Year of the Ram, souvenir sheet	2.25
815	60¢ UN Membership, 12th Anniv.	1.75
816	50¢ Folktales, block of 4	5.50
817-19	37¢-$13.65 Famous People	40.00
820	37¢ Marshallese Culture, block of 8	7.00

821a

821	80¢ Butterflies, sheetlet of 12	30.00
822	37¢ Powered Flight Centenary, blk of 10	14.00
823	37¢ Classic Cars, 8 attached	7.50
824	37¢ Marshallese Culture, part 2, 8 attached	7.50
825	37¢ Christmas Ornaments, 4 attached	3.80

827a

833a

2004

826	$1 Year of the Monkey, souvenir sheet	2.80
827	37¢ Ships, type of 2002, strip of 3	2.80
828	37¢ Classic Cars, type of 2001, 8 attached	7.50
829	37¢ Greetings, sheet of 8	7.50
830-32	37¢ Marshall Islands Postal Service 20th Anniv., set of 3	8.00
833	37¢ Lewis & Clark Expedition, strip of 3	3.75

SCOTT NO.	DESCRIPTION	UNUSED F/NH

834a

837a **841**

834	37¢ D-Day, 60th Anniversary, 4 attached	4.35
835	37¢ Marine Life, 2 attached	2.00
836	60¢ President Ronald Reagan	2.00
837	37¢ First Manned Moon Landing, 35th Anniv., 4 attached	3.80
838	37¢ Festival of the Arts, sheet of 12	11.80
839	23¢ Aircraft, sheet of 50	29.50
840	37¢ Lewis & Clark Expedition, type of 2004, strip of 3	4.75

842a **844a**

841	37¢ John Wayne	1.75
842	$1 23rd UPU Congress, Bucharest, Romania, sheet of 4	10.00
843	37¢ Marine Life, sheet of 10	10.00
844	37¢ Christmas, sheet of 9	8.00
845	37¢ Lewis & Clark Expedition, type of 2004, strip of 3	3.75
846	37¢ Battle of the Bulge, 60th Anniv., block of 4	5.75

847a

849

2005

847	1¢-$1 United States Presidents, sheet of 45	39.00
848	$1 Year of the Rooster, souvenir sheet	3.82
849	37¢ Rotary International, Centennial	1.80
850-53	37¢-$1 Hibiscus Varieties, set of 4	8.25

854a

856

854	$1.56 Turtles souvenir sheet of 2	7.25
855	Lewis & Clark Expedition, type of 2004, strip 0f 3	3.85
856	37¢ American First Day Cover Society, 50th Anniversary, 4 attached	4.75

857a

858a

860

857	37¢ VE Day, 60th Anniversary, 4 attached	5.00
858	37¢ Pope John Paul II, 5 attached	5.75
859	37¢-80¢ United Nations, 60th Anniversary, 2 attached	3.80
860-63	1¢-$4 Hibiscus Varieties, set of 4	14.00

864a **865a**

| 864 | 37¢ Space Shuttles, 5 attached | 5.75 |
| 865 | 37¢ Classic Cars Type of 2001, 8 attached | 9.00 |

866a **867a**

866	37¢ VJ Day, 60th Anniv., 4 attached	6.00
867	37¢ Lewis & Clark Expedition, type of 2004, strip of 3	4.00
868	37¢ Battle of Trafalgar, Bicentennial, sheet of 25	34.00
869	37¢ Battle of Trafalgar, souvenir sheet	2.00

870a **871a** **872a**

870	37¢ Christmas, 4 attached	5.00
871	37¢ Lewis & Clark Expedition, type of 2004, strip of 3	3.75
872	37¢ Marshallese Culture, 5 attached	5.50

877

873a **875**

| 873 | 48¢ Benjamin Franklin, sheet of 9 | 13.50 |

2006

874	$1 Year of the Dog, souvenir sheet	3.95
875	39¢ Love	1.50
876	84¢ Butterflies, sheet of 12	25.50
877	39¢ First Spaceflight by Yuri Gagarin	1.75

880 **883a**

878-81	10¢-$4.05 Hibiscus Varieties, set of 4	17.00
882	1/2¢-50¢ Washington 2006 World Philatelic Exhibition, souvenir sheet of 20	9.00
883	39¢ Sharks, 4 attached	5.80
884	39¢ Operations Crossroads, sheet of 6 stamps + 6 labels	7.50
885	39¢ Lewis and Clark, 2 attached	3.00
886	39¢ Marshallese Culture, 5 attached	7.00
887	39¢ Ships, sheet of 10	10.00
888	39¢ Christmas	1.10

2007

889	39¢ Greetings, 4 attached	5.00
890	$1 Year of the Pig, souvenir sheet	4.00
891	39¢ Railway Passenger Trains, 6 attached	7.00
892	39¢ Dolphins, block of 4	5.50
893-96	26¢-61¢ Fish	4.75
897	41¢ Space Age miniature sheet of 10	14.00
898	41¢ Scouting block of 4	5.25
899	41¢ Purple Heart	1.75
900	41¢ United States Air Force, sheet of 25	31.00
901	41¢ Marshallese Culture strip of 5	6.25

SCOTT NO.	DESCRIPTION	UNUSED F/NH

902c

903a

| 902 | 41¢ Yacht Registry, sheet of 10 | 11.50 |
| 903 | 41¢ Santa Claus block of 4 | 5.25 |

2008

904	41¢ Bouquets, sheet of 25	25.00
905	26¢ Chinese New Year, sheet of 12	7.50
906	41¢ U.S. Lighthouses, block of 6	16.50
907	41¢ Wild Cats, sheet of 12	13.00
908	41¢ Ships, sheet of 12	13.00
909	41¢ Constellations, sheet of 20	20.00
910	42¢ U.S. Marine Corps, sheet of 10	10.00

919

906a

928d

911-23	1¢-$16.50 Tropical Fish, set of 13	75.00
	911	1¢ Banded Butterflyfish
	912	3¢ Damselfish
	913	5¢ Pink Skunk Clownfish
	914	27¢ Copperband Butterflyfish
	915	42¢ Threadfin Butterflyfish
	916	60¢ Beau Gregory Damselfish
	917	61¢ Porkfish
	918	63¢ Goatfish
	919	94¢ Common Longnose Butterflyfish
	920	$1 Royal Gramma
	921	$4.80 Longfin Bannerfish
	922	$5 Blue-Striped Blenny
	923	$16.50 Emperor Butterflyfish
924	42¢ Birds, sheet of 25	24.00
925	42¢ Dinosaurs, sheet of 12	13.00
926	42¢ Fishing Flies, sheet of 5	5.15
927	42¢ Wild West Portraits, sheet of 16	20.00
928	42¢ Endangered Species, block of 6	6.75
929	42¢ Marshallese Culture Horiz., strip of 5	5.00
930	42¢ Spacecraft and the Solar System, sheet of 10	11.00
931	42¢ Christmas, sheet of 8	8.00

932a

934b

| 932 | 42¢ Owls, block of 6 | 6.25 |
| 933 | $1 First U.S. Airmail Stamp Souvenir Sheet | 2.50 |

2009

934	42¢ Flower Bouquets, sheet of 25	26.00
935	$ Abraham Lincoln, block of 4	9.50
936	42¢ Arctic Explorers, block of 4	4.50

937L

938g

| 937 | 44¢ Famous American Indians, sheet of 12 | 13.00 |
| 938 | 44¢ US Military Air Heroes, sheet of 16 | 18.00 |

939

945e

949c

939	44¢ Marshall Islands Postal Service, souvenir sheet	1.25
940-44	28¢-$1.22 Marine Life	10.00
945	44¢ Constellations, sheet of 20	23.00
946	44¢ Rose Varieties, strip of 5	5.75
947	44¢ Hot Air Balloons, strip of 5	5.75
948	44¢ 2009 Solar Eclipse, strip of 3	3.75
949	44¢ Steam Locomotives, block of 6	7.00
950	44¢ Marshallese Culture, horiz. strip of 5	5.75
951	44¢ Birds of Prey, block of 8	11.00
952	44¢ Dogs, strip of 5	6.00
953	98¢ Dogs, sheet of 4	11.00
954	44¢ Christmas Wreaths, horiz. strip of 5	6.00
955	44¢ Endangered Species, sheet of 8	16.00
956	44¢ Prehistoric Animals, strip of 5	6.00
957	44¢ Shells, block of 4	5.80

2010

958	44¢ Signs of the Zodiac, sheet of 12	16.00
959	44¢ Waterfowl, sheet of 8	10.00
960	44¢ Famous American Indiana, sheet of 12	16.00
961	44¢ Boy Scouts of America, block of 4	5.00
962	98¢ Shells, block of 4	10.00
963	44¢ Astronomers, strip of 5	5.25
964	44¢ Constellations, sheet of 20	25.00
965	28¢ Mandarin Goby	1.80
966	44¢ Marshallese Alphabet, sheet of 24	27.00
967	44¢ Statue of Liberty, sheet of 9	8.00
968	44¢ Classic Cars, sheet of 5	5.50
969	44¢ Carousel Horses, block of 6	6.50

965

969b

970	44¢ US Warships of WWII, sheet of 15	14.00
971-972	28¢ -98¢ Shells	2.80
973	44¢ Marshallese Culture Strip of 5	4.00
974	44¢ Santa Claus, strip of 4	3.80
975	44¢ President John F. Kennedy, sheet of 6	6.50
976	44¢ Orchids, sheet of 9	8.50
977	44¢ Butterflies, sheet of 12	12.00

986

2011

978	44¢ Tulips, block of 6	6.50
979	98¢ Year of the Rabbit, sheet of 4	9.50
980	44¢ Ronald Reagan, strip of 5	5.50
981	44¢ Firsts in Flight, strip of 5	5.50
982-85	1¢-$10 Turtles	25.00
986	29¢ Corals and Fish, Horizontal Strip of 5	3.75
987	44¢ Famous American Indians, sheet of 12	13.00
988	44¢ Firsts in Flight, strip of 5	5.50
989	$1 First Man in Space, strip of 3	7.50
990	44¢ Wedding of Prince William, sheet of 15	16.00
991	44¢ Apostles of Jesus, sheet of 12	13.00
992	44¢ Garden Life, sheet of 12	13.00
993	98¢ Antartic Treaty, sheet of 9	22.00
994	44¢ Firsts in Flights, strip of 5	5.50
995	$4.95 Outrigger Canoes	12.00
996	$10.95 Plumeria Flowers	26.00
997	$13.95 Marshall Island Flag	34.00
998	$14.95 Coconut Palm Trees and Coconuts	36.00
999	$18.30 Micronesian Pigeons	44.00
1000	$29.95 Triton's Trumpet	73.00
1001	44¢ End of Space Shuttle Missions, sheet of 7	8.00
1002	44¢ Marshallese Culture, strip of 5	5.50
1003	44¢ Fish, sheet of 12	13.00

SCOTT NO.	DESCRIPTION	UNUSED F/NH
1004	44¢ Firsts in Flight, horizontal strip of 5	5.50
1005-08	64¢ National Buildings & Symbols, set of 4	6.50
1009	$4.95 Anniversary UN Admission S/S	12.00

1010I

1013a

| 1010 | Christmas, sheet of 12 | 19.00 |
| 1011 | 98¢ Compact of Free Association, sheet of 3 | 7.50 |

1018a

1026a

2012

1012	44¢ Firsts in Flight, horizontal strip of 5	5.50
1013	44¢ Hanukkah, block of 8	8.75
1014	44¢ American Entry into WWII, sheet of 10 + labels	11.00
1015	44¢ Stained Glass Windows, sheet of 9	9.75
1016	45¢ Rhododendrens, sheet of 9	10.00
1017	45¢ Marine Life	1.25
1018	$1.05 Year of the Dragon, sheet of 4	10.00
1019	32¢ Whales, strip of 4	3.25
1020-25	Priority & Express Mail Stamps	240.00
1020	$5.15 Chuuk War Canoe	12.00
1021	$11.35 Cymbidium Orchid	26.00
1022	$15.45 Arrival of Early Inhabitants	36.00
1023	$16.95 Mandarinfish	39.00
1024	$18.95 Hibiscus Rosa-sinensis	45.00
1025	$38 Seahorses	89.00
1026	$1.05 Queen Elizabeth II, sheet of 6	16.00
1027-28	85¢ - $1.05 Birds	4.75

1041a

1043h

1046

1029	45¢ Chinese Terra Cotta Warriors, block of 6	6.50
1030	45¢ Inuits, block of 6	6.50
1031	45¢ Creation of Tobolar Coconut Twine and Rope, strip of 4	4.50
1032	45¢ Scientists, sheet of 20	22.00
1033	45¢ Clouds, sheet of 15	16.50
1034	45¢ Birds, block of 10	11.50
1035	45¢ WWII, sheet of 10	11.50
1036	45¢ Introduction of Euro Currency, sheet of 10	13.50
1037	45¢ Civil War, sheet of 5	6.75
1038	45¢ American Indian Dances, block of 6	6.75
1039	$4.95 USSS Constitution and HMS Guerrire S/S	13.50
1040	45¢ Twelve Days of Christmas, sheet of 12	12.00
1041	45¢ Locomotives, sheet of 50	56.00
1042	$5.15 Chuuk War Canoe	13.00

2013

1043	45¢ Birds of the World, sheet of 10	10.00
1044	46¢ Australia 225th Anniversary, sheet of 10	11.00
1045-53	33¢-$44.95 Marine Life	265.00

1055g

1056c

1054	$1.10 Year of the Snake sheet of 4	10.00
1055	46¢ Camellias block of 8	8.00
1056	46¢ Birds, sheet of 10	10.00

1059a

1060a

1063a

1057	46¢ Birds, sheet of 10	10.00
1058	46¢ Birds, sheet of 10	10.00
1059	33¢ Cats strip of 6	4.50
1060	46¢ Presidential Medals sheet of 45	45.00
1061	$2 "Ich Bin Ein Berliner" speech by Pres. Kennedy	4.50
1062	46¢ British Steam Locomotives sheet of 10	10.00
1063	46¢ Indian Headressses strip of 5	5.50
1064	46¢ American Civil Rights Movement sheet of 10	10.00
1065	46¢ World War II sheet of 10	10.00
1066	46¢ Traditional Marshallese Children's Games	4.50
1067	46¢ Restarting Space Shittle Program sheet of 6	6.50
1068	46¢ WWII Aircraft sheet of 25	25.00
1069	46¢ Christmas Block of 6	6.50
1070	46¢ Gettysburg Address sheet of 5	5.50
1071	$2 Thanksgiving S/S	4.75

1070a

1074

2014

1072	46¢ Military Aircraft Diagrams sheet of 15	15.00
1073	$5.60 Marshall Islands Postal Service Authority S/S	12.50
1074-76	34¢-$1.15 Shells set of 3	5.00
1077	$1.15 Year of the Horse Sheet of 4	11.00
1078	49¢ Garden Insects Block of 10	11.00
1079	$1.15 Castles in Great Britain, Strip of 4	10.50
1080	49¢ Historic Flags of US, Sheet of 15 with Labels	16.00
1081	49¢ Traditional Eurpoean Costumes, Sheet of 20	22.00
1082	49¢ Military Aircraft Diagrams, Sheet of 15	16.00
1083	4¢ Hawkwinged Conch	0.50
1084	$19.99 Filled Dogwinkle	42.00
1085	49¢ Trees, Block of 6	7.00
1086	$5.50 Opening of Panama Canal, S/S	12.50
1087	49¢ Amphibians and Reptiles, Sheet of 12	13.00

1088

1100c

1029	45¢ Chinese Terra Cotta Warriors, block of 6	6.50
1030	45¢ Inuits, block of 6	6.50
1031	45¢ Creation of Tobolar Coconut Twine and Rope, strip of 4	4.50
1032	45¢ Scientists, sheet of 20	22.00
1033	45¢ Clouds, sheet of 15	16.50
1034	45¢ Birds, block of 10	11.50
1035	45¢ WWII, sheet of 10	11.50
1036	45¢ Introduction of Euro Currency, sheet of 10	13.50
1037	45¢ Civil War, sheet of 5	6.75
1038	45¢ American Indian Dances, block of 6	6.75
1039	$4.95 USSS Constitution and HMS Guerrire S/S	13.50
1040	45¢ Twelve Days of Christmas, sheet of 12	12.00
1041	45¢ Locomotives, sheet of 50	56.00
1042	$5.15 Chuuk War Canoe	13.00

2015

1101	49¢ Greetings, Block of 6	7.00
1102	34¢ Dinosaurs, Strip of 4	3.25
1103	$1-$2.50 Reef Life, Miniature Sheet of 7	18.00
1104	49¢ Berries, Strip of 5	6.00
1105	$1.15 Year of the Ram, Sheet of 4	10.50

SCOTT NO.	DESCRIPTION	UNUSED F/NH

1023a

1124f

1106-09	49¢ Rays, Set of 4 Singles	4.00
1110	49¢ Seashells, Strip of 4	4.25
1111	49¢ Canoes, Strip of 4	4.25
1112	49¢ Early European Navigators, Strip of 4	4.25
1113	49¢ Sea Wonders, Sheet of 15	15.00
1114	$5.60 Penny Black, Souvenir Sheet	12.00
1115	$5.60 End of the Civil War, Souvenir Sheet	12.00
1116	49¢ Postal Relics, Sheet of 12	12.75
1117	49¢ Winged Wonders, Sheet of 15	15.25
1118a	$3 Apollo & Soyuz Joint Mission, Souvenir Sheet	6.75
1119-22	$1.20 National Icons, Set of 4	10.25
1123	49¢ WWII 70th Anniversary, 1945, Sheet of 10	10.50
1124	$1.00 Best of Marshall Islands, Souvenir Pane of 7	14.75

1127a

1130a

1133b

1125	$5.60 25th Anniversary of German Reunification, Souvenir Sheet	12.00
1126	49¢ Land Wonders, Sheet of 15	16.00
1127	49¢ Christmas Snowflakes, Sheet of 10	10.50
1128	$1.20 Christmas Snowflakes, Sheet of 4	10.25
1129	49¢ Marshall Islands Legends, Sheet of 16	15.25

1138b

1142d

1148f

2016

1130	49¢ The Art of Haiku, Sheet of 20	21.25
1131	$4 First Concorde Commercial Flight, Souvenir Sheet	8.75
1132	$1.20 Year of the Monkey, Souvenir Sheet	10.25
1133	49¢ Wildlife, Sheet of 10	10.50
1134	49¢ Great Seals of the U.S. I, sheet of 10	10.50
1135	49¢ Great Seals of the U.S. II, sheet of 10	10.50
1136	49¢ Great Seals of the U.S. III, sheet of 10	10.50
1137	49¢ Great Seals of the U.S. IV, sheet of 10	10.50
1138	49¢ Great Seals of the U.S. V, sheet of 10	10.50
1139	90¢ Queen Elizabeth II 90th Birthday, sheet of 6	11.25
1140	49¢ Semaphore Signals, sheet of 30	30.00
1141	49¢ Art of Howard Koslow, sheet of 20	21.25
1142	49¢ Peace Doves, block of 6	6.00
1143	98¢ Marshall Islands Constitution Commemorative, souvenir sheet	2.00
1144	$3 Marshall Islands Sovereignty 30th Anniversary, souvenir sheet	6.25
1145	49¢ Christmas Ornaments, sheet of 10	10.50
1146	$1.20 Christmas Ornaments, sheet of 4	10.00
1147	$5.75 Pearl Harbor, 75th Anniversary, souvenir sheet	12.00
1148	49¢ U.S. National Parks, sheet of 10	10.00

1169a

1166a

1149a

1151a

1165a

2017

1149	$1.20 Year of the Rooster, souvenir sheet of 4	10.00
1150	49¢ Celebration Photography, sheet of 10	10.25
1151	49¢ The Art of Haiku II, sheet of 20	21.25
1152	49¢ Flora, sheet of 10	10.00
1153	49¢ China Clipper, sheet of 6	6.00
1154	49¢ Natural Majesties, sheet of 10	10.25
1155	49¢ Jazz and Blues Instruments, sheet of 10	10.25
1156	49¢ U.S. National Parks II, sheet of 10	10.00
1157	$1 100th Anniversary of John F. Kennedy's birth, souvenir sheet	2.10
1158	$1.50 150th Anniversary of Frank Lloyd Wright's birth, souvenir sheet	3.10
1159	49¢ World Youth, sheet of 20	21.25
1160	49¢ Atolls of Marshall Islands, sheet of 10	10.25
1161	49¢ Honoring the Art of Paul Calle, sheet of 20	21.25
1162	49¢ Steamships, sheet of 10	10.25
1163	49¢ Fire Dancers, sheet of 6	6.00
1164	$5 Launch of QE2, souvenir sheet	10.50
1165	49¢ Eyes of Nature, sheet of 10	10.25
1166	49¢ Christmas Nativity, sheet of 6	6.00
1167	$1.20 Christmas International, sheet of 4	10.25
1168	49¢ U.S. National Parks II, sheet of 10	10.00
1169	49¢ Recovered Birds, sheet of 10	10.00

1172

1175a

1179c

2018

1170-72	1¢-$10 Marine Life, set of 3	21.25
1173	$18.90 Shortin Mako Shark	38.00
1174	$7 The Royal Engagement, souvenir sheet 2	26.00
1175	50¢-$3.50 Year of the Dog, sheet of 4	16.50
1176	$2 Winter Olympics, South Korea, sheet of 6	25.00
1177	50¢-$1.75 Shark Sanctuary, sheet of 6	19.50
1178	$1-$3 Queen Elizabeth II Sapphire Jubilee, sheet of 4	16.50
1179	$1.35 Grand Canyon Centennial, sheet of 6	16.50
1180	$4 Grand Canyon, souvenir sheet	8.00
1181	$2 Cats, sheet of 4	16.50
1182	$4 Cats, souvenir sheet	8.00
1183	$1-$2 Visit to Israel President Trump, sheet of 6	18.50
1184	$2 Elvis Presley, sheet of 3	12.50
1185	$2 Elvis Presley, sheet of 4	16.50
1186-89	$4 Elvis Presley, set of 4 souvenir sheets	34.00

1191

1202f

1199d

1190-95	50¢-$24.90 Butterflies, set of 6	135.00
1196	$1-$4 The Louve Museum, sheet of 4	21.25
1197	50¢-$2 Seabirds of the Pacific, sheet of 4	15.00
1198	$2 Birth of Prince Louis, sheet of 4	16.50
1199	$2 Whales, sheet of 4	16.50
1200	$4 Whales, souvenir sheet	8.00
1201	$1.60 First Ladies of the U.S., Barbara Bush, sheet of 5	16.50
1202	$1.40 Transcontinental Railroad, sheet of 6	18.00
1203	$4 Transcontinental Railroad, souvenir sheet	8.00
1204	$1-$3 Royal Wedding Prince Harry & Meghan Markle, sheet of 4	16.50
1205	$5 Royal Wedding, souvenir sheet	10.50

SCOTT NO.	DESCRIPTION	UNUSED F/NH

1206a

1211d

1212a

1206	$2 Celestial Wonders-Comets, sheet of 3	12.50
1207	$2 Peace Summit of President Trump & Kim Jong Un, sheet of 3	12.50
1208-09	50¢-$2 Star Trek Cats, set of 2 sheets of 6	30.00
1210	$2 Praga 2018 World Stamp Expo, sheet of 4	16.50
1211	$2 Praga 2018 World Stamp Expo, Synagogues, sheet of 4	16.50
1212	10¢-$1.20 Happy Lunar New Year, sheet of 12	16.50
1213	$2 Year of the Boar, souvenir sheet	4.00
1214	$5 20 Years of Diplomatic Relations, sheet of 4	41.00
1215-16	$10 Diplomatic Relations, set of 2 souvenir sheets of 2	82.00
....	50¢-$18.90 Christmas Toys, set of 4	41.00

1219d

1225d

1219	50¢-$1.75 Owls of the World, sheet of 6	14.50
1220-21	$1-$2 WWI Razzle Dazzle Ships, set of 2 sheets of 3	33.00
1222	$2 Gandhi, 150th Birthday Anniv., sheet of 4	16.50
1223	$2 Leonardo Da Vinci., sheet of 4	16.50
1224	$4 Leonardo Da Vinci., souvenir sheet	8.00
1225	$1.50 Birds of Marshall Islands, sheets of 6	18.50
1226	$5 Birds of Marshall Islands, souvenir sheet	10.50

1233

1254d

1227-28	$1.20-$1.50 Colorful Fish, set of 2 sheets of 6	35.00
1229-33	5¢-$1.05 Marine Life, set of 5	4.50
1234	$1.20 Star Trek Key Comics, sheets of 6	15.00
1235	$2 Jellyfish, sheet of 3	12.50
1236	$5 Jellyfish, souvenir sheet	10.50
1237	$1.10 Apollo 11, sheet of 5	12.00
1238	$4 Apollo 11, souvenir sheet	8.00

1239

1239	$2 Sacred Kingfisher, sheet of 4	16.50
1240	$5 Sacred Kingfisher, souvenir sheet	10.50
1241	$2 Queen Victoria, 200th, sheet of 4	16.50
1242	$5 Queen Victoria, 200th, souvenir sheet	10.50
1243	$2 D-Day, 75th Anniversary, sheet of 4	16.50
1244	$7.50 D-Day, 75th Anniversary, souvenir sheet	16.00
1245	$2 Abdication of Japanese Emperor, sheet of 4	16.50
1246	$2 Birth of Archie Mountbatten-Windsor, sheet of 4	16.50
1247	$1-$2 Sites & Scenes of Singapore, sheet of 4	13.00
1248	$5 Sites & Scenes of Singapore, souvenir sheet	10.50

1249

1249	$1.50 Dorje Chang Buddha II, single from sheet of 4	3.50
1250	$2 Plumeria, sheet of 4	16.50
1251	$5 Plumeria, souvenir sheet	10.50
1252	$2 Morning Glory, sheet of 4	16.50
1253	$5 Morning Glory, souvenir sheet	10.50
1254	$2 Clownfish, sheet of 4	16.50
1255	$7 Clownfish, souvenir sheet	15.00
1256	$2 Pres. Donald Trump Visits Japan, sheet of 4	16.50
1257	$5 Pres. Donald Trump Visits Japan, souvenir sheet	10.50

SEMI-POSTAL

1996

B1	32¢+8¢ 50th Anniv. of Nuclear Testing, sheet of 6	7.00

AIR POST

1985

C1-2	44¢ Audubon Birds, attached	3.00

C9

C13

1986-89

C3-6	44¢ AMERIPEX '86, attached	4.75
C7	44¢ Operation Crossroads, souvenir sheet	6.00
C8	44 Statue of Liberty, Peace	1.40
C9-12	44¢ Girl Scouts, attached	4.65
C13-16	44¢ Marine Birds, attached	4.65

C17

C22

C17-20	44¢ CAPEX '87, attached	4.80
C21	45¢ Space Shuttle	1.25
C22-25	12¢-45¢ Aircraft	4.50

Booklet Panes

C22a	12¢ Dornier DO288, pane (10)	5.00
C23a	36¢ Boeing 737, pane (10)	12.00
C24a	39¢ Hawker 748, pane (10)	13.00
C25a	45¢ Boeing 727, pane (10)	14.00
C25b	5 (36¢) & 5 (45¢), pane (10)	13.00

POSTAL STATIONERY

UX1

UX1	20¢ Elvis Presley, postal card (1996)	4.95
UX2-5	20¢ Canoes, set of 4	6.00
UX6	20¢ Heavenly Angels, Christmas (1996)	2.00
UX7	32¢ Turtle (1997)	2.00

FEDERATED STATES OF MICRONESIA

Micronesia, formed from the major portion of the Caroline Islands, became postally autonomous in 1984.
It forms part of the U.S. administered Trust Territories of the Pacific.

SCOTT NO.	DESCRIPTION	UNUSED F/NH

1984 COMMEMORATIVES

| 1-4 | 20¢ Postal Service, attached .... | 2.90 |

1984 DEFINITIVES

5-20	1¢-$5 16 varieties, singles, complete set...............................	28.50
5	1¢ Pedro de Quiros	
6	2¢ Louis Duperrey	
7	3¢ Fyedor Lutke	
8	4¢ Dumont d'Urville	
9	5¢ Men's House, Yap	
10	10¢ Sleeping Lady Hill	
11	13¢ Liduduhriab Waterfall	
12	17¢ Tonachau Peak	
13	19¢ Pedro de Quiros	
14	20¢ Louis Duperrey	
15	30¢ Fyedor Lutke	
16	37¢ Dumont d'Urville	
17	50¢ Devil Mask, Truk	
18	$1 Sokeh's Rock	
19	$2 Canoes	
20	$5 Stone Money	

1984 COMMEMORATIVES

| 21 & C4-6 | 20¢-40¢ AUSIPEX '84, 4 varieties .... | 4.00 |

| 22 & C7-9 | 20¢-40¢ Christmas '84, 4 varieties................................. | 5.75 |

1985 COMMEMORATIVES

| 23 & C10-12 | 22¢-44¢ Ships, 4 varieties................................. | 4.00 |
| 24 & C13-14 | 22¢-44¢ Christmas '85, 3 varieties............................. | 4.00 |

| 25-28 & C15 | 22¢ Audubon, booklet of 4 attached, & 44¢ airmail................. | 4.50 |

1985-88 DEFINITIVES

31-39 & C34-36	12 varieties, singles, complete set...............................	30.00
31	3¢ Long-billed	
32	14¢ Truk Monarch	
33	15¢ Waterfall	
34	22¢ Tall Ship Senyavin	
35	22¢ Pohnpei Mountain starling	
36	25¢ Tonachau Peak	
37	36¢ Tall Ship	
38	45¢ Sleeping Lady	
39	$10 National Seal	
C34	33¢ Great truk white-eye	
C35	44¢ Blue-faced parrotfinch	
C36	$1 Yap monarch	

Booklet Panes 1988

33a	15¢ booklet pane of (10)	9.00
36a	25¢ booklet pane of (10)	10.00
36b	booklet pane of (10), 5—15¢ & 5—25¢....................	11.70

1985 COMMEMORATIVES & AIR MAILS

| 45 & C16-18 | 22¢-44¢ Nan Mandol Ruins, 4 varieties........................ | 4.65 |

1986 COMMEMORATIVES & AIRMAILS

46 & C19-20	22¢, 44¢ Peace Year	5.00
48-51	22¢ on 20¢ Postal Service, block of 4 attached...........	2.90
52 & C21-24	22¢-44¢ AMERIPEX '86, 5 varieties.....................	6.50
53	22¢ Passport..................................	.80

| 54-55 & C26-27 | 5¢-44¢ Christmas, 4 varieties .... | 4.7h5 |

SCOTT NO.	DESCRIPTION	UNUSED F/NH

56   58

1987 COMMEMORATIVES & AIR MAILS

Scott	Description	Price
56 & C28-30	22¢-44¢ Shelter for Homeless, 4 varieties..............................	5.20
57	$1 CAPEX '87 souvenir sheet	4.75
58 & C31-33	22¢-44¢ Christmas, 4 varieties...	4.00

59   63   67

1988 COMMEMORATIVES & AIR MAILS

Scott	Description	Price
59-62 & C37-38	22¢, 44¢ Colonial Flags, 7 varieties...	5.65
63-66	25¢ & 45¢ Summer Olympics, 2 pairs	2.80
67-70	25¢ Christmas, block of 4 attached	2.80
71	25¢ Truk Lagoon, souvenir sheet of 18 varieties..........................	12.00

72   77

1989 COMMEMORATIVES

Scott	Description	Price
72-75	45¢ Flowers, block of 4 attached	4.75
76	$1 Japanese Art souvenir sheet..	2.90
77-80	25¢, 45¢ Sharks, attached, 2 pairs	4.75
81	25¢ Space Achievements souvenir sheet of 9	7.00

82   83

Scott	Description	Price
82	$2.40 Priority Mail	6.65
83-102	1¢-$5 Seashells (12)..	24.00
85a	15¢ Commercial trochus pane (10)..	9.00
88a	25¢ Triton's trumpet pane (10)..	14.00
88b	5 (15¢) + 5 (25¢) pane 10	14.00

103a   104

Scott	Description	Price
103	25¢ Fruits & Flowers, sheet of 18	12.00
104-05	Christmas	2.50

106   110

1990 COMMEMORATIVES

Scott	Description	Price
106-09	World Wildlife Fund (4 varieties)	7.50
110-13	45¢ Whaling Ships & Artifacts, 4 attached	4.75
114	$1 Whaling Souvenir Sheet...	2.90
115	$1 Penny Black Anniversary Souvenir Sheet...............................	2.90

116   122

Scott	Description	Price
116-20	25¢ P.A.T.S. strip of 5...	3.75
121	$1 Expo '90 Souvenir Sheet..	2.90
122-23	25¢ & 45¢ Loading Mail	2.50

124   127

Scott	Description	Price
124-26	25¢ Joint Issue, 3 attached	3.00
127-30	45¢ Moths, 4 attached..	4.75

131a

Scott	Description	Price
131	25¢ Christmas, sheetlet of 9	7.00

134   138   143a

1991

Scott	Description	Price
132	25¢+45¢ Government bldgs., Souvenir Sheet of 2	1.80
133	$1 New Capitol Souvenir Sheet	2.90
134-37	29¢+50¢ Turtles, 2 pairs	7.50
138-41	29¢ Operation Desert Storm, 4 attached	3.00
142	$2.90 Operation Desert Storm Priority Mail	7.20
142a	$2.90 Operation Desert Storm Souvenir Sheet............................	7.00
143	29¢ Phila Nippon Souvenir Sheet of 3	2.60
144	50¢ Phila Nippon Souvenir Sheet of 3	4.35
145	$1 Phila Nippon Souvenir Sheet	2.75

146

149a

1991 (continued)

146-48	29¢ Christmas 1991 set of 3	3.50
149	29¢ Pohnpei Rain Forest, sheetlet of 18	17.20

150a

151a

1992

150	29¢ Peace Corps/Kennedy, strip of 5	4.05
151	29¢ Columbus, strip of 3	6.00

152

154

152-53	29¢, 50¢ UN Membership Anniversary	5.20
153a	same, Souvenir Sheet of 2	6.00
154	29¢ Christmas, 1992	2.95

155a

156

1993

155	29¢ Pioneers of Flight I, 8 attached	6.00

1993-94

156-67	10¢-$2.90, Fish, 16 varieties	25.00

168a

172

173

177a

179

182

1993

168	29¢ Sailing Ships, sheetlet of 12	18.00
172	29¢ Thomas Jefferson	1.00
173-76	29¢ Canoes, 4 attached	3.80
177	29¢ Local Leaders I, strip of 4	3.00
178	50¢ Pioneers of Flight II, 8 attached	10.00
179-80	29¢, 50¢ Tourist Attractions, Pohnpei	2.80
181	$1 Tourist Attractions, Souvenir Sheet	2.80
182-83	29¢, 50¢ Butterflies, 2 pairs	4.50

184

186a

184-85	29¢-50¢ Christmas 1993	2.60
186	29¢ Micronesia Culture, sheetlet of 18	15.00

192a

193a

194

1994

187-89	29¢-50¢ Tourist Attractions, Kosrae	3.00
190	"Hong Kong '94" miniature sheet of 4 (#182a, 182b, 183a, 183b)	5.80
191	29¢ Pioneers of Flight III, 8 attached	7.80
192	29¢ 1994 Micronesian Games, 4 attached	3.70
193	29¢ Native Costumes, 4 attached	3.70
194	29¢ Constitution, 15th Anniversary	2.00

195a

198a

196

195	29¢ Flowers, strip of 4	3.80
196-97	50¢ World Cup Soccer, pair	5.75
198	29¢ 10th Anniv. Inauguration Postal Service, 4 attached	5.85

SCOTT NO.	DESCRIPTION	UNUSED F/NH

199a

201a

202

199	"PHILAKOREA '94" Dinosaur, miniature sheet of 3	6.50
200	50¢ Pioneers of Flight IV, 8 attached	10.00
201	29¢ Migratory Birds, 4 attached	6.20
202-03	29¢, 50¢ Christmas 1994	4.90
204-07	32¢ Local Leaders II, set of 4	6.50

208

1995

| 208 | 50¢ New Year 1995 (Year of the Boar) | 1.75 |

209a

211a

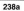
228a

209	32¢ Chuuk Lagoon, 4 attached	8.00
210	32¢ Pioneers of Flight V, 8 attached	7.20
211	32¢ Dogs, 4 attached	4.00
213-26	32¢-$5.00 Fish, set of 7	30.00
227	32¢ Fish, sheetlet of 25 (1996)	25.00
228	32¢ Flowers II, strip of 4	3.50
229	$1 UN 50th Anniversary Souvenir Sheet	2.80

230a

231a

230	32¢ Orchids (Singapore '95), min. sheet of 4	3.75
231	60¢ US Warships, 4 attached	6.65
232	50¢ Temple of Heaven Souvenir Sheet	1.45
233	60¢ Pioneers of Flight VI, 8 attached	12.50

SCOTT NO.	DESCRIPTION	UNUSED F/NH

234

236

| 234-35 | 32¢-60¢ Christmas Poinsettias | 2.55 |
| 236 | 32¢ Yitzhak Rabin | 1.10 |

238a

239a

240a

241a

1996

237	50¢ New Year 1996 (Year of the Rat)	1.75
238	32¢ Pioneers of Flight VII, 8 attached	8.25
239	32¢ Tourism in Yap, 4 attached	4.00
240	55¢ Sea Stars, 4 attached	6.25
241	60¢ Olympic Games Centenary, 4 attached	7.80
242	50¢ The Tarrying Garden, Suzhou Souvenir Sheet	2.00

243

245a

| 243-44 | 32¢ Marine Vessels, 2 attached | 3.50 |
| 245 | 55¢ Automobile, sheet of 8 | 12.00 |

247

249a

248a

247	32¢ Police Drug Enforcement Dog	1.50
248	32¢ Citrus Fruit, strip of 4	7.25
249	60¢ Pioneers of Flight VIII, 8 attached	16.00

SCOTT NO.	DESCRIPTION	UNUSED F/NH

250a

251

253

1996 (continued)

250	32¢ Fish (Taipei '96), miniature sheet of 4	4.25
251-52	32¢-60¢ Christmas 1996, set of 2	2.55
253	$3 Canoe & Flag of Micronesia	8.00

257, 258

1997

254	60¢ Deng Xiaoping, sheet of 4	7.50
255	$3 Deng Xiaoping, souvenir sheet	8.50
256	$2 Bridge to the Future, salute to Hong Kong, souvenir sheet	6.50
257	32¢ Year of the Ox	1.25
258	$2 Year of the Ox, souvenir sheet	5.00

259

259	60¢ Return of Hong Kong to China, sheet of 6	10.50
260	$3 Return of Hong Kong to China, souvenir sheet	8.75
261	32¢ Sea Goddesses of the Pacific, sheet of 6	4.50
262-64	20¢-60¢ Hiroshige, 3 sheetlets of 3	11.00
265-66	$2 Hiroshige, souvenir sheets(2)	12.00

267a

268a

269a

267	32¢ 2nd Federated States of Micronesia Games, 4 attached	3.50
268	50¢ Elvis Presley, sheetlets of 6	10.00
269	32¢ Undersea Exploration, sheetlet of 9	8.50
270-72	$2 Undersea Exploration, souvenir sheets (3)	16.00

SCOTT NO.	DESCRIPTION	UNUSED F/NH

273a

274a

273	60¢ Princess Diana	1.50
274	50¢ World Wildlife Fund, Butterly Fish, 4 attached	7.50

275-76

275-76	32¢ Christmas Paintings, Fra Angelico, pair	1.80
277-78	60¢ Christmas Paintings, Simon Marmion, pair	3.00

1998

279-80	50¢ Year of the Tiger, souvenir sheets (2)	3.00
281	$1 Micronesia's Admission to the UN, souvenir sheet	2.75
282	32¢ Disney's Winnie the Pooh, sheetlet of 8	11.00
283-84	$1 Disney's Winnie the Pooh, souvenir sheets (2)	12.50

285a

285	32¢ 1998 World Cup Soccer Championships, sheetlet of 8	7.00
286-87	$2 1998 World Cup, souvenir sheets (2)	11.00
288	$3 Olympics, souvenir sheet	9.50
289-91	32¢-60¢ Old Testament Bible Stories, 3 sheetlets of 3	9.50
292-94	$2 Old Testament Bible Stories, souvenir sheets (3)	15.50

295a

299a

295	32¢ International Year of the Ocean, sheetlet of 9	7.00
296-98	$2 International Year of the Ocean, souvenir sheets (3)	15.00
299	50¢ Native Birds, 4 attached	5.00
300	$3 Native Birds, souvenir sheet	7.50

319a

320a

301-19A	1¢-$10.75 Fish, 20 varieties	59.00
320	32¢ Fala, FDR's Dog, sheetlet of 6	4.80
321-22	32¢-60¢ Christmas, 20th Century Art, 2 sheetlets of 3	7.00
323	$2 Christmas, 20th Century Art, souvenir sheet	5.00
324-25	60¢ John Glenn's Return to Space 2 sheets of 6	24.00
326-27	$2 John Glenn's Return to Space 2 souvenir sheets	10.00

SCOTT NO.	DESCRIPTION	UNUSED F/NH

328

334a

342a

1999

328-33	33¢-$11.75 Fish, 6 varieties	40.00
334	33¢ Russian Space Exploration, sheetlet of 20	17.00
335-36	$2 Russian Space Exploration 2 souvenir sheets	10.00
337-38	33¢-50¢ "Romance of the 3 Kingdoms" by Lo Kuan-chung, 2 sheetlets of 5	15.00
339	$2 "Romance of the 3 Kingdoms", souvenir sheet	10.00
340-41	55¢ IBRA '99 Exhibition, set of 2	3.00
342	$2 IBRA '99 Exhibition, souvenir sheet	5.50
343	33¢ Voyages of the Pacific, sheetlet of 20	16.00

344a

347a

344	33¢ Space Achievements, sheetlet of 20	17.00
345-46	$2 Space Achievements, 2 souvenir sheets	10.50
347	33¢ Earth Day-Endangered Species, sheetlet of 20	17.00
348-49	$2 Earth Day-Endangered Species, 2 souvenir sheets	11.00

356a

358

362a

350-51	33¢ Hokusai Paintings, 2 sheetlets of 6	10.00
352-53	$2 Hokusai Paintings, 2 souvenir sheets	10.00
354	50¢ Flowers, photomosaic of Princess Diana, sheetlet of 8	10.00
355	20¢ Highlights of the 12th Century, sheetlet of 17	9.50
356	33¢ Science & Technology of Ancient China, sheetlet of 17	16.00
357	33¢ Costumes, sheetlet of 20	17.00
358-60	33¢-$2 Christmas-Van Dyck Paintings	7.50
361	$2 Christmas-Van Dyck Paintings, souvenir sheet	5.50
362	33¢ Millenium-Airplanes, sheetlet of 15	15.00
363-64	$2 Millenium-Airplanes, 2 souvenir sheets	11.00

365a

372a

2000

365-67	33¢ Orchids, 3 sheetlets of 6	15.00
368-69	$1 Orchids, 2 souvenir sheets	10.00
370	33¢ Leaders of the 20th Century, sheetlet of 12	9.25
371	$2 New Year 2000 (Year of the Dragon), souvenir sheet	6.00
372-73	20¢-55¢ Butterflies, 2 sheetlets of 6	12.00
374-76	$2 Butterflies, 3 souvenir sheets	17.00
377	20¢ Highlights of the 1920's, sheetlet of 17	9.00

378

385a

378	33¢ Millennium 2000	1.10
379	33¢ Peacemakers, sheetlet of 24	18.00
380	33¢ Philantropists, sheetlet of 16	14.00
381-82	33¢ Mushrooms, 2 sheetlets of 6	10.00
383-34	$2 Mushrooms, 2 souvenir sheets	10.00
385	33¢ Flowers of the Pacific, sheetlet of 6	5.00
386	33¢ Wildflowers, sheetlet of 6	5.00
387	$2 Flowers of the Pacific, souvenir sheet	5.00
388	$2 Wildflowers, souvenir sheet	5.00

389a

390a

389	33¢ 2000 Summer Olympics, Sydney, souvenir sheet of 4	3.00
390	33¢ Zeppelins & Airships, sheetlet of 6	5.00
391-92	$2 Zeppelins & Airships, 2 souvenir sheets	10.25
393	33¢ Queen Mother Flower Photomosaic, sheet of 8	6.00
394	33¢-$1 2000 Summer Olympics, Sydney, souvenir sheet of 3	4.50

395

395-98	33¢ Fish, set of 4	3.00
399-400	33¢ Fish, 2 sheetlets of 9	15.00
401-02	$2 Fish, 2 souvenir sheets	10.00
403	50¢ Pope John Paul II Photomosaic, sheet of 8	11.00

404

408a

404-07	20¢-$3.20 2000 Christmas, set of 4	11.50
408-09	33¢ Dogs & Cats, 2 sheetlets of 6	10.00
410-11	$2 Dogs & Cats, 2 souvenir sheets	10.00

414a

416a

2001

412-13	60¢ Year of the Snake, 2 souvenir sheets	3.00
414	50¢ Pokemon, sheet of 6	7.50
415	$2 Farfetch'd, souvenir sheet	5.50
416-17	50¢-60¢ Whales, 2 sheetlets of 6	16.00
418-19	$2 Whales, 2 souvenir sheets	10.00

SCOTT NO.	DESCRIPTION	UNUSED F/NH

420a   424

420	34¢ Ecology, sheetlet of 6	5.00
421	60¢ Ecology, sheetlet of 4	6.00
422-23	$2 Ecology, 2 souvenir sheets	11.00
424-28	11¢-$3.50 Fish, set of 5	14.40
429	$12.25 Blue-spotted boxfish	29.00
430-35	34¢ Japanese Art, set of 6	5.00
436	34¢ Japanese Art, sheetlet of 6	5.00
437-38	$2 Japanese Art, 2 imperf sheets	10.00
439	60¢ Toulouse-Lautrec Paintings, sheetlets of 3	4.50
440	$2 Toulouse-Lautrec Paintings, souvenir sheet	5.00
441	60¢ Queen Victoria, sheetlet of 6	9.00
442	$2 Queen Victoria, souvenir sheet	5.00
443	60¢ Queen Elizabeth II, 75th Birthday, sheet of 6	9.00
444	$2 Queen Elizabeth II, 75th Birthday, souvenir sheet	5.00

445   457a

445-46	60¢ Marine Life, 2 sheetlets of 6	18.00
447-48	$2 Marine Life, 2 souvenir sheets	10.00
449-52	60¢ Prehistoric Animals, set of 4	6.00
453-54	60¢ Prehistoric Animals, 2 sheetlets of 6	18.00
455-56	$2 Prehistoric Animals, 2 souvenir sheets	10.50
457-58	50¢ Shells, 2 sheetlets of 6	15.00
459-60	$2 Shells, 2 souvenir sheets	10.50

461   469a   473

461-64	5¢-$2.10 Birds, set of 4	6.50
465-66	60¢ Birds, 2 sheetlets of 6	18.00
467-68	$2 Birds, 2 souvenir sheets	10.50
469-70	60¢ Nobel Prizes Cent., 2 sheetlets of 6	18.00
471-72	$2 Nobel Prizes Cent., 2 souvenir sheets	10.50
473-76	22¢-$1 Christmas, set of 4	5.00
477	$2 Christmas, souvenir sheet	5.00
478-79	60¢ Attack on Pearl Harbor, 60th Anniv., 2 sheetlets of 6	18.00
480-81	$2 Attack on Pearl Harbor, 60th Anniv., 2 souvenir sheets	10.50

485   492a   494a

2002

482	60¢ Year of the Horse, sheetlet of 5	7.75
483	80¢ Reign of Queen Elizabeth II, 50th Anniv., sheetlet of 4	8.00
484	$2 Reign of Queen Elizabeth II, 50th Anniv., souvenir sheet	5.00
485	$1 United We Stand	2.25
486-87	$1 2002 Winter Olympics, set of 2	5.00
488-89	60¢ Japanese Art, 2 sheetlets of 6	18.00
490-91	$2 Japanese Art, 2 souvenir sheets	10.50
492	80¢ Intl. Year of Mountains, sheet of 4	8.00
493	$2 Intl. Year of Mountains, souvenir sheet	5.00
494	60¢ President John F. Kennedy, sheet of 4	6.50
495	$2 President John F. Kennedy, souvenir sheet	5.00
496	60¢ Princess Diana, sheetlet of 6	9.00
497	$2 Princess Diana, souvenir sheet	5.00

498a   502   504

498	80¢ International Year of Eco-Tourism, sheet of 6	12.75
499	$2 International Year of Eco-Tourism, souvenir sheet	5.00
500	$1 20th World Boy Scout Jamboree, Thailand, sheet of 3	8.00
501	$2 20th World Boy Scout Jamboree, Thailand, souvenir sheet	5.00
502-03	$1 2002 Winter Olympics, redrawn smaller rings, set of 2	5.00
503a	$2 2002 Winter Olympics, redrawn smaller rings, souvenir sheet	5.00
504	37¢ Xavier High School, 50th Anniversary	1.00
505	80¢ Queen Elizabeth Memorial, souvenir sheet of 4	8.00
506	$2 Queen Elizabeth Memorial, souvenir sheet	5.00

507a   509   525

507	80¢ Teddy Bear Centennial, sheet of 4	10.00
508	37¢ Elvis Presley (1935-77), sheetlet of 6	5.25
509-13	15¢-$1 Christmas, set of 5	10.25
514	$2 Christmas, souvenir sheet	5.00
515-19	37¢-80¢ Flora, Fauna & Mushrooms, set of 5 sheets of 6	48.00
520-24	$2 Flora, Fauna & Mushrooms, set of 5 souvenir sheets	25.00
525-37	3¢-$13.65 Bird Definitives, set of 13	70.00

538a   539a   543a

2003

538	60¢ 1st Non-Stop Solo Transatlantic Flight 75th Anniversary, sheet of 6	9.00
539	37¢ Year of the Ram, sheet of 6	6.00
540	37¢ Astronauts Killed in Shuttle Columbia, In Memorium, sheet of 7	6.50
541	$1 Coronation of Queen Elizabeth II, 50th Anniversary, sheet of 3	7.75
542	$2 Coronation of Queen Elizabeth II, 50th Anniversary, souvenir sheet	5.00
543	$1 Prince Williams, 21st Birthday, sheet of 3	7.75
544	$2 Prince Williams, 21st Birthday, souvenir sheet	5.00

545a   551a

545-46	37¢ Operation Iraqi Freedom, set of 2 sheets of 6	11.50
547	60¢ Tour de France Bicycle Race, Centenary, sheet of 4	6.50
548	$2 Tour de France Bicycle Race, Centenary, souvenir sheet	5.00
549	$1 International Year of Freshwater, sheet of 3	7.75
550	$2 International Year of Freshwater, souvenir sheet	5.00
551	55¢ Powered Flight Centenary, sheet of 6	8.00
552	$2 Powered Flight Centenary, souvenir sheet	5.00
553-54	80¢ Circus Performers, set of 2 sheets of 4	16.00
555	80¢ Paintings of Boy Scouts by Norman Rockwell, sheet of 4	8.00
556	$2 Paintings of Boy Scouts by Norman Rockwell, souvenir sheet, imperf	5.00

SCOTT NO.	DESCRIPTION	UNUSED F/NH

557a

565

578

557	80¢ Paintings by Paul Gauguin, sheet of 4	8.00
558	$2 Paintings by Paul Gauguin, souvenir sheet, imperf.	5.00
559-62	37¢-80¢ Paintings by James McNeill Whistler, set of 4	6.00
563	$1 Paintings by James McNeill Whistler, sheet of 3	7.75
564	$2 Paintings by James McNeill Whistler, souvenir sheet, imperf.	5.00
565-68	37¢-80¢ Christmas, set of 4	6.50
569	$2 Christmas, souvenir sheet	5.00
570-73	80¢ Cats, Dogs, Birds & Amphibians, set of 4 sheets of 4	30.00
574-77	$2 Cats, Dogs, Birds & Amphibians, set of 4 souvenir sheets	20.00

2004

578	37¢ President Bailey Olter	1.00

581

586

579	80¢ Paintings by Pablo Picasso, sheet of 4	8.00
580	$2 Painting by Pablo Picasso, souvenir sheet, imperf.	5.00
581-84	22¢-$1 Paintings in the Hermitage Museum, set of 4	6.00
585	$2 Painting in the Hermitage Museum, souvenir sheet, imperf.	5.00
586	50¢ Year of the Monkey	1.75
587	$1 Year of the Monkey, souvenir sheet	2.50

588a

591a

588	80¢ Election of Pope John Paul II, 25th Anniv., sheet of 4	8.00
589	80¢ 2004 European Soccer Championships, sheet of 4	8.00
590	$2 2004 European Soccer Championships, souvenir sheet	5.00
591	50¢ D-Day, 60th Anniversary, sheet of 6	7.50
592	$2 D-Day, 60th Anniversary, souvenir sheet	5.00
593	$2 Deng Xiaoping, souvenir seet	5.00

594a

607a

594-96	80¢ Locomotives, 3 sheets of 4	25.00
597-99	$2 Locomotives, 3 souvenir sheets	16.00

SCOTT NO.	DESCRIPTION	UNUSED F/NH

600-01	2¢-10¢ Birds, Type of 2002, set of 2	.65
602	80¢ International Year of Peace, sheet of 3	6.65
603-06	37¢-$1 2004 Summer Olympics, Athens, set of 4	7.50
607-08	80¢ Elvis Presley's First Recording, 50th Anniv., 2 sheets of 4	16.00
609	55¢ Flowers, sheet of 6	9.20
610	$2 Flowers, souvenir sheet	5.50
611	80¢ FIFA, Centennial, sheet of 4	8.95
612	$2 FIFA, Centennial, souvenir sheet	5.50
613-14	20¢ National Basketball Assoc. Players, set of 2	2.00

615a

625a

623a

615-17	80¢ Prehistoric Animals, 3 sheets of 4	26.00
618-20	$2 Preshistoric Animals, 3 souvenir sheets	16.50
621	55¢ Fish and Coral, sheet of 6	9.20
622	$2 Fish and Coral, Great barracuda, souvenir sheet	5.50
623	55¢ Reptiles and Amphibians, sheet of 6	9.20
624	$2 Reptiles and Amphibians, Loggerhead turtle, souvenir sheet	5.50
625	55¢ Birds of the Pacific, sheet of 6	9.20
626	2¢ Birds of the Pacific, Golden whistler, souvenir sheet	5.50
627-30	37¢-$1 Christmas, set of 4	8.95
631	$2 Chirstmas, souvenir sheet	5.50

632

634a

2005

632	50¢ Year of the Rooster	4.00
633	20¢ National Basketball Assoc. Player, Luke Walton	.85
634	55¢ Pres. Ronald Reagan, 2 attached	3.50

635a

638a

635-36	60¢ Elvis Presley, 2 sheets of 6	19.00
637-38	60¢ End of World War II, 60th Anniv., 2 sheets of 5	16.00

639a

643

639	$1 Friedrich von Schiller, sheet of 3	7.75
640	$2 Friedrich von Schiller, souvenir sheet	5.25
641-44	37¢-$1 Battle of Trafalgar, Bicent., set of 4	8.00
645	$2 Battle of Trafalgar, Bicent., souvenir sheet	5.25

SCOTT NO.	DESCRIPTION	UNUSED F/NH

646   647a   649a

Scott No.	Description	Unused F/NH
646	$1 Pope John Paul II	2.60
647	$1 Rotary International, Cent., sheet of 3	7.75
648	$2 Rotary International, Cent., souvenir sheet	5.25
649	$1 Jules Verne, sheet of 3	7.75
650	$2 Jules Verne, souvenir sheet	5.25

651a   652a

Scott No.	Description	Unused F/NH
651	80¢ Nature's Wisdom, Expo 2005, Aichi, Japan, sheet of 4	8.50
652	37¢-$1 Boats, sheet of 4	7.00
653	$2 Boats, sovenir sheet	5.25

654   658

Scott No.	Description	Unused F/NH
654-57	4¢-37¢ Kosrae Government Building Complex, set of 4	1.95
658	37¢ Vatican City No. 67	1.35

659e   661

Scott No.	Description	Unused F/NH
659	50¢ Worldwide Fund for Nature, 4 attached	5.50
659e	Souvenir Sheet, Worldwide Fund for Nature	11.00
660	$1 Albert Einstein, sheet of 4	10.50
661-64	4¢-37¢ Bananas, set of 4	2.00

665a   668

Scott No.	Description	Unused F/NH
665	80¢ Hans Christian Anderson, sheet of 3	6.75
666	$2 Hans Christian Anderson, souvenir sheet	5.25
667	80¢ Pope Benedict XVI	2.75
668-71	37¢-$1 Christmas, set of 4	7.25
672	$2 Christmas, souvenir sheet	5.25
673-78	4¢-$1 Flowers, set of 6	6.35
679	80¢ Flowers, sheet of 4	7.75
680-81	$2 Flowers, set of 2 souvenir sheets	10.50

682   730   731

2006

Scott No.	Description	Unused F/NH
682	50¢ Year of the Dog	1.40
683	$1 Year of the Dog, souvenir sheet	3.75
684-90	24¢-$4.05 Birds, set of 7	18.00
691	39¢ vice President Petrus Tun	1.05
692	$1 Rembrandt, sheet of 4	10.25
693	$2 Rembrandt, souvenir sheet	5.25
694	84¢ Queen Elizabeth II, sheet of 4	8.75
695	$2 Queen Elizabeth II, souvenir sheet	5.25
696	75¢ Space Achievements, sheet of 6	11.00
697-98	$1 Space Achievements, 2 sheets of 4	21.00
699-701	$2 Space Achievements, 3 souvenir sheets	16.00
702-15	1¢-$10 Butterflies	58.00
716-20	22¢-84¢ Christmas, set of 5	6.50
721-22	75¢ Concorde, set of 2 pairs	7.75

2007

Scott No.	Description	Unused F/NH
723	75¢ Year of the Pig	2.00
724	$2 Mozart souvenir sheet	5.50
725	$1 Ludwig Durr souvenir sheet	7.75
726	Marilyn Monroe sheet of 4	11.00
727	$1 Scouting Centenary	8.00
728	$2 Scouting souvenir sheet	5.25
729	50¢ Pope Benedict	1.25
730	60¢ Wedding of Queen Elizabeth II 60th Anniversary sheet of 6	9.50
731	90¢ Princess Diana sheet of 4	9.50
732	$2 Princess Diana souvenir sheet	5.25
733-40	22¢-$4.60 Bananas, set of 8	23.00
741	75¢ Elvis sheet of 6	11.50
742	90¢ Fish sheet of 4	9.25
743	$2 Fish souvenir sheet	5.25
744	90¢ Flowers sheet of 4	9.25
745	$2 Flowers souvenir sheet	5.25
746	90¢ Peace Corp sheet of 4	9.25
747	$1 Gerald Ford miniature sheet of 6	16.00
748	75¢ Penguins sheet of 6	11.50
749	$3.50 Penguins souvenir sheet	9.00
750	90¢ Red Cross sheet of 4	9.50
751-54	22¢-90¢ Cats set of 4	5.75
755	$2 Cats souvenir sheet	5.25
756-59	22¢-90¢ Christmas, churches set of 4	5.00
760	26¢-$2 America's Cup strip of 4	10.00
761	$1 sheet of 4 Helicopters	14.00
762	$2.50 Helicopters souvenir sheet	9.00
763	Princess Diana Sheet	24.00

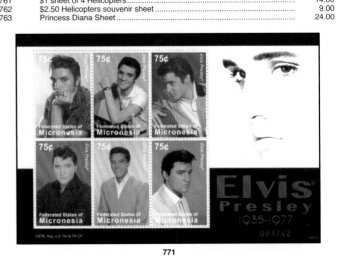

771

2008

Scott No.	Description	Unused F/NH
764	90¢ John F. Kennedy sheet of 4	12.00
765	90¢ Year of the Rat	4.75
766	50¢ 2008 Olympic Games, Beijing, sheet of 4	5.25
767	$2 Breast Cancer Awareness, souvenir sheet	5.25
768	90¢ Hummer, sheet of 4	9.50
769	$2 Hummer, souvenir sheet	5.00
770	$3 World Stamp Championship, Israel	8.00
771	75¢ Elvis Presley, sheet of 6	12.00

SCOTT NO.	DESCRIPTION	UNUSED F/NH

772e

773a

772	42¢ Phoenix Suns, sheet of 9	9.00
773	90¢ Royal Air Force, sheet of 4	9.00
774	94¢ Pope Benedict, sheet of 4	9.50
775	75¢ Muhammad Ali, sheet of 6	10.50
776	94¢ Muhammad Ali, sheet of 4	10.00

777

| 777 | 75¢ Star Trek, sheet of 6 | 11.00 |
| 778 | 94¢ Star Trek, sheet of 4 | 10.50 |

779

784b

| 779-82 | 22¢-94¢ Christmas, set of 4 | 5.00 |
| 783 | 94¢ Famous Men, attached pair | 5.25 |

2009

| 784 | Inauguration of Barak Obama, sheet of 6 | 8.75 |

785c

800a

785	94¢ Marilyn Monroe, sheet of 4	9.50
786-99	Ocean Waves & Surfers	66.00
800	94¢ Year of the Ox, sheet of 4	9.50

SCOTT NO.	DESCRIPTION	UNUSED F/NH

801

803b

801	42¢ Peonies	1.15
802	59¢ Olympic Sports, sheet of 4	5.75
803	59¢ Tang Dynasty Art, sheet of 4	5.75

813

806

830

804	$2.50 Elvis with Stethescope S/S	6.50
805	$2.50 Elvis with Guitar S/S	6.50
806	$2.50 Elvis, strip of film S/S	6.50
807	$2.50 Elvis "Hope" S/S	6.50
808	Michael Jackson, horizontal S/S	5.00
809	Michael Jackson, vertical S/S	5.00
810	75¢ Apollo 11, sheet of 6	9.95
811	98¢ Apollo 11, sheet of 4	9.50
812-15	Butterflies, set of 4	7.00
816	Butterflies, sheet of 6	11.00
817-22	Fish, set of 6	13.00
823	Fish, sheet of 4	9.50
824-27	Dolphins, set of 4	12.00
828	75¢ Dolphins, sheet of 6	11.00

842

847b

829-32	Sea Shells, set of 4	10.00
833	75¢ Sea Shells, sheet of 6	11.00
834-37	Corals, set of 4	6.50
838	98¢ Corals, sheet of 4	10.00
839	98¢ Corals, sheet of 2	4.75
840	98¢ Abraham Lincoln, sheet of 4	10.00
841	75¢ Chinese Aviation, sheet of 4	7.75
842	$2 Chinese Aviation, souvenir sheet	5.25
843-46	Christmas, set of 4	16.00
847	98¢ Visit of Pope Benedict, sheet of 4	10.00
848	Mandarin Fish, block or strip of 4	5.25

858

849

862a

849-52	Turtles, set of 4	12.50
853	98¢ Turtles, sheet of 4	11.00
854	$1.56 Turtles S/S of 2	8.00
855-58	Birds, set of 4	7.00
859	98¢ Birds, sheet of 4	10.00
860	$1.56 Birds, souvenir sheet of 2	8.00
860c-h	44¢ Diplomatic Relations Between Micronesia and PRC	......
860I	'09 44¢ Diplomatic Relations Between Micronesia and PRC	....
860J	'09 44¢ Diplomatic Relations Between Micronesia and PRC	....
860k	'09 44¢ Diplomatic Relations Between Micronesia and PRC	....
860l	'09 44¢ Diplomatic Relations Between Micronesia and PRC	....

2010

| 861 | 22¢ Chinese Zodiac Animals, sheet of 12 | 7.25 |
| 862 | $2 Year of the Tiger, souvenir sheet | 10.00 |

SCOTT NO.	DESCRIPTION	UNUSED F/NH
863	75¢ Darwin, sheet of 6	11.00
864	75¢ Pope John Paul, sheet of 4	7.75

870

873

865-68	Mushrooms, set of 4	6.00
869	75¢ Mushrooms, sheet of 6	11.00
870	80¢ Pre/Nakayama, sheet of 4	8.00
871	$2 Pres/Nakayama, souvenir sheet	5.00
872	94¢ Girl Guides, sheet of 4	9.25
873	$2.50 Girl Guides, souvenir sheet	6.25
874-89	1¢-$4.80 Flowers and Fruits	40.00
890	75¢ British Monarchs, sheet of 6	11.00
891	75¢ Botticelli, sheet of 6	11.00
892	94¢ Henri Durant, Red Cross Founder, sheet of 4	11.00
893	$2.50 Henri Durant, souvenir sheet	7.00
894	75¢ Princess Diana, sheet of 4	7.50
895	$2 Issuance of the Penny Black, sheet of 2	10.00
896-900	22¢-$4.95 Christmas, set of 5	15.50
901	75¢ Pope John Paul II	2.00
902	75¢ Pope Benedict XVI, sheet of 4	7.75
903	75¢ Abraham Lincoln, sheet of 4	7.75
904-05	'10 World Cup Soccer Championship, 2 sheets of 6	18.00

2011

906	'11 Year of the Rabbit S/S of 2	7.50
907	75¢ John F. Kennedy, sheet of 4	7.50
908	75¢ Elvis, sheet of 4	7.50
909	95¢ Mohandas K. Gandi	2.50
910	$2.50 Gandhi Souvenir Sheet	6.25
911	75¢ Three Gorges Dam, sheet of 4	7.50
912	$2 Terra Cotta Warriors Souvenir Sheet	5.00
913	94¢ Royal Wedding, sheet of 4	9.75
914	94¢ Royal Wedding, sheet of 4	9.75
915-16	$1.50 Royal Wedding, set of 2 souvenir sheets	19.00
917	75¢ President Obama, sheet of 4	7.25
918	75¢ President Obama, sheet of 4	7.25
919	75¢ President Obama, sheet of 4	7.25
920	98¢ South Pole, sheet of 4	9.75
921-22	98¢ Civil War, 2 sheets of 4	20.00
923	75¢ Abraham Lincoln	1.95
924	$2.50 Abraham Lincoln souvenir sheet	6.75
925	75¢ Pope John Paul II, sheet of 4	7.25
926	$2.50 Pope John Paul II souvenir sheet	6.00
927	75¢ Elvis, sheet of 6	11.00
928	75¢ Elvis, sheet of 6	11.00
929	$2.50 Elvis souvenir sheet	6.50

945

950

930	$2.50 Elvis Souvenir Sheet	6.50
931	$2.50 Elvis Souvenir Sheet	6.50
932	$2.50 Elvis Souvenir Sheet	6.50
933-34	98¢ Royal Wedding, 2 sheets of 4	19.75
935	$2.50 Royal Wedding Souvenir Sheet	6.25
936	98¢ Princess Diana, sheet of 4	10.00
937	98¢ Princess Diana, sheet of 4	10.00
938	50¢ Reptiles of Micronesia, sheet of 4	6.25
939	$2.50 Reptiles of Micronesia Souvenir Sheet of 2	6.25
940	98¢ 9/11 sheet of 4	10.00
941	$2.50 World Trade Center Souvenir Sheet	6.25
942	50¢ Women's World Cup, sheet of 8	10.00
943	98¢ Women's World Cup, sheet of 4	10.00
944	$1 Whales, sheet of 3	7.50
945	$2.50 Whales souvenir sheet	6.25
946	63¢ Sun Yat-Sen, attached pair	3.25
947	63¢ Sun Yat-Sen, attached pair	3.25
947c	$2 Sr. Sun Yat-Sen Souvenir Sheet of 2	9.00
948	75¢ Sharks, sheet of 4	7.50
949	$2.50 Sharks Souvenir Sheet	6.25
950	$1 Game Fish, sheet of 3	7.25
951-52	$2.50 Game Fish, set of 2 souvenir sheets	12.50
953-56	22¢ - $4.95 Christmas, set of 4	16.00
957	$1.25 Chinese Pottery, sheet of 4	12.50
958	$3.50 Chinese Pottery souvenir sheet	8.75
959	$8 Year of the Dragon	19.75
960	44¢ Peace Corps, sheet of 4	7.50
961	44¢ Erhart Aten, Governor	1.25

2012

962	25¢ 25th Anniversary of Independence	.65
963	$1.25 Pope Benedict Horizontal Pair	5.75

SCOTT NO.	DESCRIPTION	UNUSED F/NH
964	$3.50 Pope Benedict S/S	7.75
965	$1.25 President Ronald Reagan	2.75
966	$3.50 Ronald Reagan, Souvenir Sheet	7.75
967	$1.25 Queen Elizabeth II sheet of 4	12.50
968	$3.50 Queen Elizabeth II souvenir sheet	8.75
969	$1.25 Sinking of the Titanic, sheet of 3	9.25
970	$3.50 Sinking of the Titanic, S/S	8.75
971	$1.50 Hindenburg Disaster, sheet of 3	11.00
972	$3.50 Hindenburg Disaster S/S	8.75
973	$1.25 Hybrid Dogs, sheet of 4	12.50
974	$3.50 Hybrid Dogs Souvenir Sheet	8.75
975	$1.25 Mother Teresa	3.25
976	$3.50 Mother Teresa Souvenir Sheet	8.75
977	$1 Three Stooges, sheet of 5	12.50
978	$3.50 Three Stooges Souvenir Sheet	8.75

989

993

990

979	80¢ Summer Olympics sheet of 4	8.00
980	$1.25 Turtles sheet of 4	13.00
981	$1.25 Turtles S/S of 2	6.50
982-86	$3.50 Elvis set of 5 S/S	43.00
987-88	$1.25 Pope Benedict set of 2 sheets of 4	24.00
989-90	$1.25 JFK Space Flight Speech set of 2 sheets of 4	24.00
991-92	$1.25 Ranger Moon Program set of 2 sheets of 4	24.00
993	$1.25 Carnivorous Plants sheet of 4	12.75

996

1002

1000

994	$1.25 Carnivorous Plants S/S of 2	6.25
995-98	25¢-45¢ Christmas set of 4	3.25
999	$1 Octopus sheet of 5	12.75
1000	$1 Raphael Paintings sheet of 4	10.00
1001	$3.50 Raphael Paintings S/S	9.00
1002	18¢ Year of the Snake sheet of 20	9.00

1003

1005

2013

1003	$1.25 Michelangelo sheet of 4	13.00
1004	$1.25 Michelangelo Sheet of 3	10.00
1005	$1.25 World Radio Day sheet of 4	11.00
1006	$3.50 World Radio Day S/S	8.00

1007

1012

1007-08	$1.20 Vincent van Gohn set of 2 sheets of 4	19.00
1009	$3.50 Vincent van Gohn S.S	8.00
1010	$1.20 Sarah Bernhardt sheet of 4	11.00
1011	$3.50 Sarah Bernhardt S/S	8.00
1012	$1.20 John F. Kennedy sheet of 4	11.00
1013	$3.50 John F. Kennedy S/S	8.00

SCOTT NO.	DESCRIPTION	UNUSED F/NH

1014

1017

1014	$1.20 Louis Comfort Tiffany Sheet of 4	11.00
1015	$3.50 Louis Comfort Tiffany S/S	8.00
1016-17	$1.50 Art History set of 2 sheets 3	20.00
1018-19	$3.50 Art History set of 2 S/S	16.00

1021

1028

1020-21	$1.20 Pope Benedict set of 2 Sheets of 4	21.00
1022-23	$3.50 Pope Benedict set of 2 S/S	16.00
1024-25	$1.20 Dolphins set of 2 sheets of 4	22.00
1026-27	$3.50 Dolphins set of 2 S/S	16.00
1028-29	$1.20 Fish of Oceania set of 2 sheets of 4	22.00

1035

1038

1030-31	$3.50 Fish of Oceania set of 2 S/S	16.00
1032	$1.20 Dr. Lois Engelberger	2.75
1033	$3.50 Dr. Lois Engelberger S/S	7.75
1034-35	$1.25 Mushroom set of 2 sheets of 4	22.00
1036-37	$3.50 Mushrooms set of 2 S/S	16.00
1038	46¢ John De Avila	1.25

1041

1039

1045

1039	$1 Sheels sheet of 6	13.00
1040	$3.50 Shells S/S	8.00
1041	75¢ Wildlife of Thailand sheet of 8	13.00
1042	$1.75 Wildlife of Thailand sheet of 2	8.00
1043	$1.50 Internet 30th Anniversary sheet of 3	10.00
1044	$3.50 Internet S/S	7.75
1045	$10 Elvis Presley Foil S/S	22.00

2014

1046	$1.20 Dogs, Sheet of 4	10.50
1047	$3.50 Dogs, S/S	8.00
1048	$1 Parrots, Sheet of 6	13.00
1049	$3.50 Parrots, S/S	8.00
1050-51	$1.20 World War I, 2 Sheets of 4	21.00
1052-53	$2 World War I, Set of 2 S/S	17.00
1054-55	$1.50 Paintings, 2 Sheets of 3	19.00
1056-57	$4 Paintings, Set of 2 S/S	17.00
1058	$1.75 Pope Francis, Horizontal Pair	7.50

1046

1059	$1.75 Pope Wearing Zucchetto	4.00
1059a	Horizontal Pair,	
1060	$3.50 Pope Francis, Sheet of 2	15.00
1061	$3.50 Pope Francis, Sheet of 2	15.00
1062-63	49¢ College of Micronesia, Set of 2	3.00

1065

| 1064 | $1.20 Birth of Prince George, Sheet of 4 | 10.50 |
| 1065 | $4 Birth of Prince George Souvenir Sheet | 9.00 |

1067

1073

1066-73	1¢ - $1 Birds, Set of 8	5.25
1074-75	$1.20 Canonization of Pope John Paul II, 2 Sheets of 4	21.00
1076-77	$2 Canonization of Pope John Paul II, 2 S/S of 2	17.00
1078	$1.75 Nelson Mandela, Sheet of 4	15.00
1079	$1.75 Nelson Mandela, Sheet of 4	15.00
1080-81	$7 Nelson Mandela, Set of 2 Souvenir Sheets	29.00
1082-84	$1 Keitani Graham, Wrestler, Set of 3	6.75
1085	$1.20 South Korean Tourist Attractions, Sheet of 4	10.50
1086	$2 South Korean Tourist Attractions, S/S of 2	9.00
1087	$1.20 Caroline Kennedy, Sheet of 4	10.50
1088	$1.20 Caroline Kennedy, Sheet of 4	10.50
1089	$2 Caroline Kennedy, Souvenir Sheet of 2	9.00
1090	$2 Caroline Kennedy, Souvenir Sheet of 2	9.00
1091	75¢ Fruit, Sheet of 9	14.50
1092	75¢ Polar Bears, Sheet of 4	7.00
1093	$2.50 Polar Bears, S/S	6.00
1094-95	75¢ Tropical Fish, 2 Sheets of 4	13.00

1096

1113

1096-97	$2 Tropical Fish, 2 S/S of 2	17.00
1098	$2 Bodyboarding	4.50
1099	75¢ Seaglass, Sheet of 4	7.00
1100	75¢ Seaglass, Sheet of 6	10.00
1101-02	$4 Seaglass, 2 Souvenir Sheets	17.00
1103	$1.20 Paintings by Oi Baishi, Sheet of 4	10.50
1104	$1.20 Paintings by Oi Baishi, Sheet of 4	10.50
1105-06	$4 Paintings by Oi Baishi, Set of 2 Souvenir Sheets	17.00
1107-08	$1 Alphonse Mucha 75th Anniversary, set of 2 sheets	18.50
1109-10	$1 Sharks, set of 2 sheets	18.50
1113-14	$1 Butterflies, set of 2 sheets	28.75
1115-16	$3.50 Butterflies, set of 2 souvenir sheets	16.75

SCOTT NO.	DESCRIPTION	UNUSED F/NH

1134　　　　　　　　　1126

1117-20	$4 Elvis Presley, set of 4 souvenir sheets	39.00
1121	40¢ Orbicular Batfish, strip of 4	3.25
1122	90¢ Orbicular Batfish, strip of 4	7.50
1123-26	49¢-$2 Christmas, set of 4	8.50
1127	90¢ Year of the Ram, sheet of 4	8.50
1128	$8 Year of the Ram, gold souvenir sheet	18.00
1129	$1 Trans-Siberian Railway, sheet of 4	9.25
1130	$3.50 Trans-Siberian Railway, souvenir sheet	8.25
1131-32	$1 Coral Reefs, set of 2 sheets	18.50
1133-34	$3.50 Coral Reefs, set of 2 souvenir sheets	16.75

1158

1159

1160

2015

1135-38	29¢ - $3 Sharks, set of 4	11.00
1139	75¢ Pope John Paul II, sheet of 4	6.25
1140	$1 Duke of Cambridge and President Obama, sheet of 4	8.50
1141	$1.75 Duke of Cambridge, souvenir sheet	7.75
1142	$1 WWI Airships, sheet of 6	12.50
1143	$3.50 WWI Airships, souvenir sheet	8.00
1144	$1 Extreme Sports, BMX, sheet of 6	12.50
1145	$3.50 Extreme Sports, BMX, souvenir sheet	8.00
1146-50	1¢ - 10¢ Marine Life, set of 5	.65
1151-54	20¢ - 27¢ Hibiscus Flowers, set of 4	2.75
1155	50¢ Hibiscus Flowers, strip of 5	5.75
1156	$1 Hibiscus Flowers, strip of 5	10.50
1157	$1 London Stamp Expo, British Warbler, sheet of 6	12.50
1158	$3.50 London Stamp Expo, souvenir sheet	8.00
1159	$1 Queen Elizabeth II and World Leaders, sheet of 6	12.50
1160	$3.50 Queen Elizabeth II and President Obama	8.00
1161	$1 Mask Artifacts, sheet of 6	12.50
1162	$3.50 Mask Artifacts, souvenir sheet	8.00
1163-64	$1 Submarines, set of 2 sheets	18.50
1165	$1 Sir Winston Churchill, sheet of 6	12.50
1166	$1.75 Sir Winston Churchill, souvenir sheet	7.50

1168　　　　　　　　　1170

1167	$1 Birth of Princess Charlotte, sheet of 4	9.00
1168	$3.50 Birth of Princess Charlotte, souvenir sheet	8.00
1169	$1 Birds of Micronesia, sheet of 6	12.50
1170	$3.50 Birds of Micronesia, souvenir sheet	8.00

SCOTT NO.	DESCRIPTION	UNUSED F/NH

1179b　　　　　　　　　1181a

......	$1 First stamps of U.N. Member States, 8 sheets of 6	......
......	$3.50 First stamps of U.N. Members, U.S., souvenir sheet	......
1179	$1 Pope Benedict, sheet of 5	10.75
1180	$3.50 Pope Benedict, souvenir sheet	8.00
1181	$1 Space Anniversary, sheet of 4	9.00
1182	$3.50 Space Anniversary, souvenir sheet	8.00
1183	$1 Vincent van Gogh, sheet of 6	13.50

1185b

1191a

1193

1184	$3.50 Vincent van Gogh, souvenir sheet	8.00
1185	$1 Orchids, sheet of 4	9.00
1186	$3.50 Orchids, souvenir sheet	8.00
1187	$1 Plants and Flowers, sheet of 6	13.50
1188	$3.50 Plants and Flowers, souvenir sheet	8.00
1189	$1 Marine Mammels, sheet of 6	13.50
1190	$3.50 Marine Mammals, souvenir sheet	8.00
1191	$1 Battle of Waterloo, sheet of 6	13.50
1192	$3.50 Battle of Waterloo, souvenir sheet	8.00
1193-96	34¢-$2 Christmas Paintings, set of 4	9.00

C1　　　　　　　　　C39

1984-94 AIR MAIL

C1-3	28¢-40¢ Aircraft, set of 3	2.75
C25	$1 Ameripex '86 Souvenir Sheet	4.90
C39-42	45¢ State Flags, block of 4 attached	4.90
C43-46	22¢-45¢ Aircraft Serving Micronesia (4 varieties)	7.50
C47-48	40¢, 50¢ Aircraft and Ships	5.75
C49	$2.90 25th Anniv. First Moon Landing, souvenir sheet	7.50

Postal Stationery

U1	20¢ National Flag	17.00
U2	22¢ Tail Ship Senyavin	12.00
U3	29¢ on 30¢ New Capitol	5.00

Postal Cards

| UX1-4 | 20¢ Scenes, set of 4 | 7.50 |

REPUBLIC OF PALAU

Palau is a Strategic Trust of the United States; a designation granted by the United Nations after World War II. It is the first Trust Territory to be granted postal independence, which became effective November 1, 1982. The first stamps were issued March 10, 1983.

SCOTT NO.	DESCRIPTION	UNUSED F/NH

1983 COMMEMORATIVES

1-4	20¢ Art and Preamble, attached	3.50
5-8	20¢ Birds, attached	2.60

1983-84 DEFINITIVES

9-21	1¢-$5, 13 varieties, singles, complete set	26.50
9	1¢ Sea Fan	
10	3¢ Map Cowrie	
11	5¢ Jellyfish	
12	10¢ Hawksbill Turtle	
13	13¢ Giant Clam	
14	20¢ Parrotfish	
15	28¢ Chambered Nautilus	
16	30¢ Dappled Sea Cucumber	
17	37¢ Sea Urchin	
18	50¢ Starfish	
19	$1 Squid	
20	$2 Dugong (1984)	
21	$5 Pink Sponge (1984)	

1983-84 Booklet Panes

13a	13¢ Giant Clam (10)	13.50
13b	13¢ (5) & 20¢ (5)	16.50
14b	20¢ Parrotfish (10)	14.75

1983 COMMEMORATIVES

24-27	20¢ Whales, attached	6.25
28-32	20¢ Christmas, strip of 5	4.05
33-40	20¢ When Different Worlds Meet, attached	5.50

1984 COMMEMORATIVES

41-50	20¢ Seashells, attached	5.75
51-54	40¢ Explorer Ships, attached	4.75
55-58	20¢ Fishing, attached	2.50
59-62	20¢ Christmas, Flowers, attached	3.25

1985 COMMEMORATIVES

63-66	22¢ Audubon—Birds, attached	4.65
67-70	22¢ Canoes, attached	2.80

1985 DEFINITIVES

75-85	14¢-$10, 7 varieties, singles complete set	32.00
75	14¢ Trumpet Triton	....
76	22¢ Parrotfish	....
77	25¢ Damsel Fish	....
79	33¢ Clownfish	....
80	39¢ Sea Turtle	....
81	44¢ Sailfish	....
85	$10 Spinner Dolphins	....

1985 Booklet Panes

75a	14¢ Trumpet Triton (10)	12.00
76a	22¢ Parrotfish (10)	15.00
76b	14¢ (5) & 22¢ (5)	16.00

1985 COMMEMORATIVES

86-89	44¢ Youth Year, attached	5.20
90-93	14¢-44¢ Christmas, 4 varieties	4.05
94	$1 Trans-Pacific, souvenir sheet	3.75
95-98	44¢ Halley's Comet, attached	4.75

SCOTT NO.	DESCRIPTION	UNUSED F/NH

99   104

1986 COMMEMORATIVES

99-102	44¢ Songbirds, attached	4.75
103	14¢ World of Sea and Reef, Ameripex '86 sheet of 40	51.00
104-08	22¢ Seashells, strip of 5	3.75

109   113   117

109-12, C17	22¢ International Peace Year, 4 attached, 44¢ Airmail	6.50
113-16	22¢ Reptiles, attached	3.70
117-21	22¢ Christmas, attached	3.50

121B   122   142

1987 COMMEMORATIVES

| 121B-E | 44¢ Butterflies, attached | 5.50 |
| 122-25 | 44¢ Fruit Bats, attached | 5.50 |

1987-88 FLOWER DEFINITIVES

126-42	1¢-$5, 17 varieties, single complete set	52.00
126	1¢ Kerdeu	......
127	3¢ Ngemoel	......
128	5¢ Uror	......
129	10¢ Woody Vine	......
130	14¢ Rur	......
131	15¢ Jaml (1988)	......
132	22¢ Denges	......
133	25¢ Ksid (1988)	......
134	36¢ Meldii (1988)	......
135	39¢ Emeridesh	......
136	44¢ Eskeam	......
137	45¢ Shrub (1988)	......
138	50¢ Rriu	......
139	$1 Koranges	......
140	$2 Meliin	......
141	$5 Orchid	......
142	$10 Flower Bouquet (1988)	......

1987 Booklet Panes

130a	14¢ Bikkia Palauensis (10)	5.80
132a	22¢ Bruguiera Gymnorhiza (10)	9.50
132b	14¢ (5) and 22¢ (5)	9.50

1988 Booklet Panes

131a	15¢ Limnophila (10)	7.00
133a	25¢ Ksid (10)	7.50
133b	15¢ (5) 25¢ (5)	7.20

SCOTT NO.	DESCRIPTION	UNUSED F/NH

146   155

1987 COMMEMORATIVES (continued)

146-49	22¢ Capex '87, attached	2.80
150-54	22¢ Seashells, strip of 5	3.75
155-63	14¢-44¢ U.S. Bicentennial 3 attached, strips of 3	6.50
164-67	12¢-44¢ Japan Links	3.20
168	$1 Japan souvenir sheet	3.20

173   178

| 173-77 | 22¢ Christmas, attached | 3.50 |
| 178-82 | 22¢ Marine Species, attached | 4.75 |

187   196a   198

1988 COMMEMORATIVES

183-86	44¢ Butterflies, attached	4.55
187-90	44¢ Birds, attached	4.55
191-95	25¢ Seashells, strip of 5	3.75
196	25¢ Finlandia sheetlet of 6	4.25
197	45¢ PRAGA '88, sheetlet of 6	7.00
198-202	25¢ Christmas, strip of 5	3.75
203	25¢ Chambered Nautilus, sheetlet of 5	4.40

204   208

1989 COMMEMORATIVES

204-07	45¢ Endangered Birds, attached	5.20
208-11	45¢ Mushrooms, attached	5.20
212-16	25¢ Seashells, attached	3.95
217	$1 Japanese Art souvenir sheet	3.30
218	25¢ Apollo 11 mission, sheetlet of 25	16.00

SCOTT NO.	DESCRIPTION	UNUSED F/NH

219

220a

222

1989 COMMEMORATIVES (continued)

219	$2.40 Priority Mail	6.25
220	25¢ Literacy (block of 10)	6.50
221	25¢ Stilt Mangrove Fauna, sheetlet of 20	16.00
222-26	25¢ Christmas (strip of 5)	4.00

227

231

1990 COMMEMORATIVES

227-30	25¢ Soft Coral (4 attached)	3.20
231-34	45¢ Forest Birds (4 attached)	5.20

235a

237

235	Prince Boo Visit (sheet of 9)	6.50
236	$1 Penny Black Ann.	2.90
237-41	45¢ Tropical Orchids (strip of 5)	6.50

242

249

254

242-45	45¢ Butterflies II (4 attached)	5.00
246	25¢ Lagoon Life, sheet of 25	17.00
247-48	45¢ Pacifica, pair	4.50
249-53	25¢ Christmas, strip of 5	3.75
254-57	45¢ U.S. Forces in Palau, attached	6.00
258	$1 U.S. Peleliu, souvenir sheet	3.75

SCOTT NO.	DESCRIPTION	UNUSED F/NH

259

263a

267

1991

259-62	30¢ Hard Corals, attached	4.00
263	30¢ Angaur—The Phosphate Island sheet of 16	14.00

1991-92

266-83	1¢-$10 Birds, 18 varieties	56.00

1991 Booklet Panes

269b	19¢ Palau fantail booklet pane (10)	5.25
272a	Booklet pane of 10, 19¢ (5) + 29¢ (5)	7.00
272b	29¢ Palau fruit dove booklet pane (10)	6.00

288a

289a

290a

294a

1991 (continued)

288	29¢ Christianity in Palau, sheetlet of 6	4.90
289	29¢ Marine Life, sheetlet of 20	16.50
290	20¢ Operation Desert Storm, sheetlet of 9	5.50
291	$2.90 Operation Desert Storm Priority Mail	8.00
292	$2.90 Operation Desert Storm Souvenir Sheet	8.00
293	29¢ 10th Anniversary of Independence sheetlet of 8	6.75
294	50¢ Giant Clams, Souvenir Sheet of 5	7.00

295a

Peace Corps Palau

297a

295	29¢ Japanese Heritage in Palau, sheet of 6	5.00
296	$1.00 Phila Nippon, Souvenir Sheet	4.00
297	29¢ Peace Corps, sheetlet of 6	5.00

299a

298	29¢ Christmas, 1991, strip of 5	5.00
299	29¢ Pearl Harbor/WWII, sheetlet of 10	11.50

SCOTT NO.	DESCRIPTION	UNUSED F/NH

300a

301a

302a

1992

300	50¢ Butterflies, attached	5.50
301	29¢ Shells, strip of 5	4.00
302	29¢ Columbus & Age of Discovery, sheetlet of 20	16.00
303	29¢ World Environment, sheetlet of 24	18.00
304-09	50¢ Olympians, set of 6 Souvenir Sheets	8.00

310e

312a

310	29¢ Elvis Presley, sheetlet of 9	9.50
311	50¢ WWII Aircraft, sheet of 10	12.00
312	29¢ Christmas, strip of 5	4.75

313a

314a

1993

313	50¢ Fauna, 4 attached	5.75
314	29¢ Seafood, 4 attached	3.50

315a

316a

315	50¢ Sharks, 4 attached	5.75
316	29¢ WWII in the Pacific, sheetlet of 10	11.00
317	29¢ Christmas 1993, strip of 5	4.50
318	29¢ Prehistoric Sea Creatures, sheet of 25	19.50
319	29¢ International Year of Indigeneous People, sheet of 2	3.25
320	$2.90 Quarrying of Stone Money, souvenir sheet	8.50
321	29¢ Jonah and the Whale, sheet of 25	19.50

322a

323a

1994

322	40¢ Rays "Hong Kong '94", 4 attached	4.55
323	20¢ Estuarine Crocodile, 4 attached	4.75

SCOTT NO.	DESCRIPTION	UNUSED F/NH

324a

327

324	50¢ Large Seabirds, 4 attached	5.80
325	29¢ Action in the Pacific, 1944, sheet of 10	11.00
326	50¢ D-Day, sheet of 10	15.00
327	29¢ Pierre de Coubertin	1.05
328-33	50¢-$2 Winter Olympic medalists, souvenir sheet of 1 (6)	15.50

334a

340a

338a

334	29¢ PHILAKOREA '94 (Fish), sheetlet of 8	8.35
335	40¢ PHILAKOREA '94 (Mammals), sheetlet of 8	11.85
336	50¢ PHILAKOREA '94 (Birds), sheetlet of 8	13.85
337	29¢ 25th Anniversary First Manned Moon Landing, sheet of 20	16.00
338	29¢ Independence Day, strip of 5	4.25
339	$1 50th Anniv. of Invasion of Peleliu, souvenir sheet	3.75
340	29¢ Disney Characters Visit Palau, sheetlet of 9	8.50
341-42	$1 Mickey, Donald visiting Palau, souvenir sheet of 1 (2)	6.95
343	$2.90 Pluto, Mickey in Boat, souvenir sheet	8.65

344a

345a

351

344	20¢ Int. Year of the Family, sheetlet of 12	6.50
345	29¢ Christmas, strip of 5	4.35
346-48	29¢-50¢ World Cup '94, 3 sheetlets of 12	35.00

1995

350	32¢ Elvis Presley, sheetlet of 9	9.25
351-65	1¢-$10 Palau Fishes, set of 15	55.00

1995 Booklet Panes

366a	20¢ Magenta dottyback (10)	5.50
367a	32¢ Reef Lizardfish (10)	8.95
367b	same, 20¢ (5) & 32¢ (5)	7.25

368a

369a

370a

372a

SCOTT NO.	DESCRIPTION	UNUSED F/NH

765a

769a

765-66	26¢-37¢ Marine Life, 2 sheets of 6	10.00
767-68	$2 Marine Life, 2 souvenir sheets	10.00
769	$3 International Year of Peace, sheet of 3	22.00
770	$2 International Year of Peace, souvenir sheet	5.50

771

777a

771-74	37¢-$1 2004 Summer Olympics, set of 4	7.20
775	80¢ Election of Pope John Paul II, 25th Anniv., Sheet of 4	11.00
776	$2 Deng Xiaoping, Chinese Leader, souvenir sheet	5.50
777	50¢ D-Day, 60th Anniversary, sheet of 6	8.35
778	$2 D-Day, 60th Anniversary, souvenir sheet	5.50

779a

781

779	80¢ European Soccer Championships, sheet of 4	8.95
780	$2 European Soccer Championships, souvenir sheet	5.50
781-82	37¢ Babe Ruth, set of 2	3.00

783a

787a

783-84	26¢-37¢ Trains, Bicentennial, 2 sheets of 4	8.35
785-86	$2 Trains, Bicentennial, 2 souvenir sheets	10.50
787-89	80¢ Butterflies, Reptiles, Amphibians, and Birds, 3 sheets of 4	26.80
790-92	$2 Butterflies, Reptiles, Amphibians, and Birds, 3 souvenir sheets	16.45
793-95	26¢-80¢ Dinosaurs, 3 sheets of 4	20.00
796-98	$2 Dinosaurs, 3 souvenir sheets	16.00

799a

| 799 | 80¢ FIFA, Centennial, sheet of 4 | 8.95 |
| 800 | $2 FIFA, souvenir sheet | 5.50 |

SCOTT NO.	DESCRIPTION	UNUSED F/NH

804

801

809a

801-03	26¢ National Basketball Assoc. Players, set of 3	3.25
804-07	$1 Christmas, set of 4	7.80
808	$2 Christmas, souvenir sheet	5.50
809	80¢ Palau-Rep. of China Diplomatic Relations, 5th Anniv., sheet of 4	10.00

2005

811

812a

810	50¢ Year of the Rooster, sheet of 4	5.50
811	80¢ Rotary International, Centennial, sheet of 4	8.50
812	$1 Friedrich von Schiller, sheet of 3	7.75
813	$2 Friedrich von Schiller, souvenir sheet	5.25

814a

816

814	$1 Hans Christian Anderson, sheet of 3	7.75
815	$2 Hans Christian Anderson, souvenir sheet	5.25
816-19	37¢-$1 Battle of Trafalgar, Bicent., set of 4	7.50
820	$2 Battle of Trafalgar, Bicent., souvenir sheet	5.25

821a

825a

821-22	80¢ End of World War II, 60th Anniv., 2 sheets of 4	17.50
823-24	$2 End of World War II, 60th Anniv., 2 souvenir shts	11.50
825	$1 Jules Verne, sheet of 3	7.75
826	$2 Jules Verne, souvenir sheet	5.25

827

830a

827	$1 Pope John Paul II	2.75
828	80¢ Elvis Presley	3.75
829	80¢ Elvis Presley, sheet of 4	9.50
830	80¢ Trains, sheet of 4	8.00
831	$2 Trains, souvenir sheet	5.25

SCOTT NO.	DESCRIPTION	UNUSED F/NH

832a

834a

832	80¢ VJ Day, 60th Anniv., sheet of 4	8.50
833	$2 VJ Day, 60th Anniv., souvenir sheet	5.25
834	80¢ Expo 2005, Aichi, Japan, sheet of 4	8.50

853a

854a

853	63¢ WWF, 4 attached	6.35
853e	63¢ WWF, souvenir sheet	13.50
854	18¢ World of Sea and Reef, sheet of 40	19.00
855	$2 Mozart, souvenir sheet	5.25

835a

837a

835	80¢ Sailing, sheet of 4	8.50
836	$2 Sailing, souvenir sheet	5.25
837-38	$1 World cup Soccer Championships, 75th Anniv., 2 sheets of 3	15.50
839	$1 Sepp Herberger, souvenir sheet	5.75
840	$1 Franz Beckenbauer, souvenir sheet	5.00
841	37¢ Vatican City No. 61	1.00

856a

858a

856	84¢ Queen Elizabeth II, sheet of 4	8.75
857	$2 Queen Elizabeth II, souvenir sheet	5.50
858	$1 Rembrandt, sheet of 4	10.50
859	$2 Rembrandt, souvenir sheet	5.50

842a

843a

| 842 | 80¢ Taipei 2005 Intl. Stamp Exhibition, sheet of 4 | 8.00 |
| 843 | 37¢ Items from the National Museum, sheet of 10 | 9.50 |

860a

861a

860	$1 International Space Station, sheet of 4	10.50
861-62	75¢ Space Achievements, 2 sheets of 6	24.00
863-65	$2 Space Achievements, 3 souvenir sheets	16.00
866	$7 Elvis Presley Gold	24.00
867	75¢ Peace Corps, souvenir sheet of 4	11.00
868-69	75¢ Concorde, set of 2 pairs	6.00
870	84¢ Christmas, sheet of 4	9.00

844

845

844	80¢ Pope Benedict XVI	2.10
845-48	37¢-$1 Christmas, set of 4	7.25
849	$2 Christmas, souvenir sheet	5.25

872c

879

2007

871	75¢ Year of the Pig	1.95
872	84¢ Marilyn Monroe, sheet of 4	8.75
873	39¢ Elvis, sheet of 9	11.00
874	75¢ Elvis, sheet of 6	12.00
875	$1 Scouting sheet of 3	7.75
876	$2 Scouting souvenir sheet	5.25
877	$1 Mushrooms sheet of 4	10.00
878	$2 Mushrooms souvenir sheet	5.25
879-885	10¢-$1 Helicopters, set of 7	9.00
886	$2 Helicopters souvenir sheet	5.25
887	$2 Triton Horn Shell souvenir sheet	5.25

850

851

2006

| 850 | 50¢ Year of the Dog | 1.75 |
| 851-52 | 24¢-39¢ Birds, set of 2 | 1.85 |

888

890a

SCOTT NO.	DESCRIPTION	UNUSED F/NH
888-889	50¢ Birds sheets of 6, set of 2	16.00
890	60¢ Wedding Anniversary of Queen Elizabeth II attached pair	3.25

891a — **892a**

891	$1 Crabs, souvenir sheet of 4	10.00
892	$1 Flowers sheet of 4	10.00
893	$2 Flowers souvenir sheet	5.25

894 — **895b** — **896**

894	41¢ Pope Benedict	1.25
895	90¢ Princess Diana, sheet of 4	9.00
896	$2 Princess Diana souvenir sheet	5.25

897 — **920a**

897-916	2¢-$1 Butterflies definitives, set of 20	69.00
917	50¢ Udoud Money Beads, sheet of 6	7.75
918	50¢ Cowries, sheet of 6	7.75
919	75¢ Children & Wildlife, sheet of 4	7.75
920	80¢ Birds of Southeast Asia, sheet of 4	8.00
921	$2 Birds souvenir sheet	5.25

922d — **931d**

922	80¢ Tropical Fish, sheet of 4	8.25
923	$2 Tropical Fish souvenir sheet	5.25
924	50¢ Holocaust Rememberance, sheet of 8	10.75
925-28	22¢-90¢ Christmas, set of 4	4.75
929	25¢-$2 America's Cup, strip of 4	10.50

2008

930	50¢ Year of the Rat	1.75
931	90¢ Kennedy, sheet of 4	9.50
932	50¢ 2008 Summer Olympics, sheet of 4	5.50

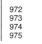

933d — **934**

933	50¢ Taiwan Tourist Attractions, sheet of 4	5.50
934	$2 Illuminated Temple Souvenir Sheet	5.50

937 — **939c**

935	$3 2008 World Stamp Championships Sheet	7.50
936	90¢ Sir Edmund Hillary, sheet of 4	9.25
937	75¢ Elvis, sheet of 6	12.00

942f — **949**

938	90¢ Pope Benedict, sheet of 4	8.75
939	75¢ Muhammad Ali, sheet of 6	12.00
940	94¢ Muhammad Ali, sheet of 4	10.00
941-42	75¢ Space, set of 2 sheets of 6	23.00
943-44	94¢ Space, set of 2 sheets of 4	20.00
945	75¢ Star Trek The Next Generation, sheet of 6	10.75
946	94¢ Star Trek The Next Generation, sheet of 4	10.00
947-50	22¢-94¢ Christmas Angels	4.75

957f — **970**

2009

951	94¢ Inauguration of Barak Obama, sheet of 4	9.50
952	$2 President Obama, souvenir sheet	5.25
953	94¢ Year of the Ox, horizontal pair	5.00
954	94¢ Teenage Mutant Ninja Turtles, sheet of 4	9.50
955	44¢ Michael Jackson, sheet of 4	4.50
956	28¢-75¢ Michael Jackson sheet of 4	5.00
957	26¢ Palau Pacific Resort, sheet of 6	4.00
958-61	28¢-$1.05 Dolphins, set of 4	7.00
962	75¢ Dolphins, sheet of 6	12.00
963-66	28¢-$1.05 Shells, set of 6	7.00
967	75¢ Shells, sheet of 6	12.00
968	75¢ Cats, sheet of 6	11.00
969	94¢ Cats, sheet of 4	11.50
970-71	$2 Cats, souvenir sheets (set of 2)	11.00

973 — **978**

972	75¢ Fish, sheet of 6	12.00
973	44¢ Abraham Lincoln, sheet of 4	4.75
974	98¢-$2 Pope Benedict, sheet of 3	10.00
975	$2.50 Elvis, Steve Grayson	7.00

SCOTT NO.	DESCRIPTION	UNUSED F/NH
976	$2.50 Elvis, with Guitar	7.00
977	$2.50 Elvis, Smooth Fast & In Gear	7.00
978	$2.50 Elvis, Speedway Film Clips	7.00
979-991	1¢-$10 Fish	63.00
992	53¢ Worldwide Fund for Nature, block of 4	5.50
992a	53¢ Worldwide Fund for Nature, sheet of 8	10.00
993	98¢ First Man on the Moon, sheet of 4	10.00
994-97	26¢-$2 Christmas, set of 4	9.00

1010a   1010b

2010

SCOTT NO.	DESCRIPTION	UNUSED F/NH
998	75¢ Charles Darwin, sheet of 6	11.00
999-1002	26¢-$1.05 Reptiles and Amphibians, set of 4	7.50
1003	75¢ Reptiles and Amphibians, sheet of 6	11.00
1004	75¢ Pope John Paul II	2.00
1005	75¢ Abraham Lincoln, sheet of 4	8.00
1006	75¢ Elvis, sheet of 4	8.00
1007	94¢ Girl Guides, sheet of 4	9.75
1008	$2.50 Girl Guides, souvenir sheet	6.50
1009	$1 Palau Governmental Buildings, sheet of 3	7.50
1010	75¢ Princess Diana, pair	3.75
1011	94¢ Mother Theresa, sheet of 4	10.00
1012	94¢ Henri Dunant, sheet of 4	10.00
1013	$2.50 Henri Dunant, souvenir sheet	6.00
1014	94¢ Botticelli Paintings, sheet of 4	9.00
1015	$2.50 Botticelli Paintings, souvenir sheet	6.00
1016	$2 Issuance of the Penny Black, sheet of 2	10.00
1017-20	26¢-$2 Christmas, set of 4	9.50
1021-22	World Cup Soccer, set of 2 sheets of 6	17.50
1023	94¢ Michelangelo, sheet of 4	9.50
1024	$2.50 Michlangelo, souvenir sheet	6.00
1025	75¢ Pope Benedict XVI	2.00
1026	98¢ Napoleon Wrasses, sheet of 3	7.75
1027	98¢ Sharks, sheet of 3	7.75
1028	98¢ Sea Turtles, sheet of 3	7.75
1029	98¢ Dugongs, sheet of 3	7.75

1028b   1028c

2011

SCOTT NO.	DESCRIPTION	UNUSED F/NH
1030	75¢ Lincoln, sheet of 4	7.50
1031	75¢ John Kennedy, sheet of 4	7.50
1032	75¢ President Barack Obama, sheet of 4	7.75
1033	50¢ Indipex 2011, sheet of 6	7.75
1034	$2.50 Indipex Gandhi Souvenir Sheet	6.50
1035	75¢ Whales, sheet of 6	11.00
1036	$2.50 Whales Souvenir Sheet	6.50
1037	94¢ Pope Benedict XVI visit to Spain	9.50
1038	$2.50 Pope Benedict Souvenir Sheet	6.50
1039	98¢ Ronald Reagan, sheet of 4	9.75
1040	75¢ Elvis, sheet of 4	7.50
1041	75¢ Elvis, sheet of 4	7.50
1042-45	$2.50 Elvis, sheet of 4 Souvenir Sheets	24.00

1048   1055

SCOTT NO.	DESCRIPTION	UNUSED F/NH
1046	75¢ Pope John Paul II, sheet of 4	7.50
1047	$2.50 Pope John Paul II, Souvenir Sheet	6.25
1048	98¢ Royal Wedding	2.50
1049-50	$2 Royal Wedding S/S set of 2	9.75
1051-21	75¢ Princess Diana, set of 2 sheets of 4	14.75
1053	29¢ Taro plant & Inscription, sheet of 30	19.00
1054	$2 President Remeliik Souvenir Sheet	5.00
1055-56	98¢ Birds of Palau, set of 2 sheets of 4	19.00
1057-58	$2 Birds of Palau, set of 2 souvenir sheets	9.75
1059	60¢ Abraham Lincoln, sheet of 5	7.50
1060	$2.50 Abraham Lincoln Souvenir Sheet	6.50
1061	50¢ Peace Corps, sheet of 4	5.00
1062	75¢ Tenth Anniversary of 9/11, sheet of 4	7.50

SCOTT NO.	DESCRIPTION	UNUSED F/NH
1063	$2.50 World Trade Center Souvenir Sheet	6.50
1064-65	98¢ World Cup Soccer, 2 sheets of 4	19.00
1066	98¢ Barack Obama 50th Birthday, sheet of 4	10.00
1067	$2.50 President Obama Souvenir Sheet	6.50
1068-69	$1.25 Crustaceans, set of 2 sheets of 4	24.00
1070-71	$3 Crustacians, set of 2 Souvenir Sheets	14.75
1072	75¢ Dangerous Creatures & Coral Reefs, sheet of 5	9.00
1073	$1 Dangerous Creatures & Coral Reefs, sheet of 3	7.50
1074	$2.50 Jolly Fish Souvenir Sheet	6.50
1075	$2.50 Barra Cuda Souvenir Sheet	6.50

1087a   1103a

2012

SCOTT NO.	DESCRIPTION	UNUSED F/NH
1076-79	26¢ - $4.25 Christmas	15.00
1080-81	98¢ Lizards, 2 sheets of 4	20.00
1082-83	$2.50 Lizards, 2 Souvenir Sheets	12.50
1084	50¢ Japan/Palau Friendship Bridge, sheet of 4	5.00
1085	$1.25 Michelangelo, sheet of 3	9.25
1086	$3.50 Michelangelo, Souvenir Sheet	9.00
1087	$1 Titanic, sheet of 4	10.00
1088	$3 Titanic, Souvenir Sheet	7.50
1089	$1.25 Amelia Earhart, sheet of 4	13.00
1090	$1.25 Amelia Earhart, Souvenir Sheet of 2	6.50
1091	80¢ Summer Olympics, sheet of 4	8.00
1092	$1 Blossoms of Flowering Trees, sheet of 6	15.00
1093	$3.50 National Cherry Blossom Festival S/S	9.00
1094	98¢ Elvis, sheet of 4	10.00
1095	98¢ Elvis, sheet of 4	10.00
1096	$1.25 Stingrays, sheet of 4	13.00
1097	$3.50 Stingrays, Souvenir Sheet	9.00
1098-02	$3.50 Elvis Presley, set of 5	44.00
1103	$1.25 Peter Pan, sheet of 4	13.00
1104	$1.25 Televised Tour of the White House, sheet of 4	13.00
1105	$1.25 Pope Benedict, Horizontal Pair	6.50
1106-07	$1.25 Apollo Moon Missions, set of 2 sheets of 4	24.00
1108	$1 Raphael, sheet of 4	10.00
1109	$3 Raphael, Souvenir Sheet	7.50

1110a   1111

SCOTT NO.	DESCRIPTION	UNUSED F/NH
1110	$1.25 Dog Breeds, sheet of 4	12.50
1111	$3.50 Dog Breeds, Souvenir Sheet	9.00
1112-15	$3.50 Famous Speeches, set of 4	33.00
1116	$1.25 Carnivorous Plants, sheet of 4	12.00
1117	$3.50 Carnivorous Plants, Souvenir Sheets	9.00
1118-23	29¢-$1.05 Christmas, set of 6	9.00
1124	$3.50 Christmas, Souvenir Sheet	9.00

1125

SCOTT NO.	DESCRIPTION	UNUSED F/NH
1111	$3.50 Dog Breeds, Souvenir Sheet	9.00
1112-15	$3.50 Famous Speeches, set of 4	33.00
1116	$1.25 Carnivorous Plants, sheet of 4	12.00
1117	$3.50 Carnivorous Plants, Souvenir Sheets	9.00
1118-23	29¢-$1.05 Christmas, set of 6	9.00
1124	$3.50 Christmas, Souvenir Sheet	9.00
1125	$1.20 Hindenburg	12.00
1126	$3.50 Hindenburg, Souvenir Sheet	9.00

1127   1133

SCOTT NO.	DESCRIPTION	UNUSED F/NH

2013

1127	$1.20 World Radio Day Sheet of 4	11.00
1128	$3.50 World Radio Day Souvenir Sheet	8.00
1129	$1.50 Paintings by Paul Signac sheet of 3	10.00
1130	$3.50 Women at the Well Souvenir Sheet	7.75
1131	$1.20 Queen Elizabeth II sheet of 4	10.50
1132	$3.50 Queen Elizabeth II Souvenir Sheet	7.75
1133	$1.20 Seashells sheet of 4	10.50

1136

1145

1134	$3.50 Seashells Souvenir Sheet	7.75
1135-36	$1.20 Cats set of 2 sheets of 4	21.00
1137-38	$3.50 Cats set of 2 souvenir sheets	16.00
1139-40	$1.50 History of Art set of 2 sheets of 3	20.00
1141-42	$3.50 History of Art set of 2 souvenir sheets	16.00
1143	$1 Grand Central Terminal sheet of 6	13.50
1144	$3.50 Grand Central Terminal Souvenir sheet	7.75
1145-46	$1.20 John F. Kennedy set of 2 sheets of 4	22.00

1149

1155

1147-48	$3.50 John F. Kennedy set of 2 souvenir sheets	16.00
1149	$1.20 Pope Francis sheet of 4	11.00
1150	$3.50 Pope Francis souvenir sheet	7.75
1151	$1.25 Margaret Thatcher sheet of 4	11.00
1152	$3.50 Margaret Thatcher souvenir sheet	7.75
1153	$1.20 Henry Ford sheet of 4	10.50
1154	$3.50 Henry Ford Souvenir sheet	7.75
1155-56	$1.20 Tropical Fish set of 2 sheets of 4	21.00
1157-58	$3.50 Tropical Fish set of 2 souvenir sheets	15.00

1161

1163

1159	$1.20 2013 World Stamp Exhibition sheet of 4	10.50
1160	$3.50 2013 World Stamp Exhibition souvenir sheet	7.75
1161	$1.20 Butterflies sheet of 4	10.50
1162	$3.50 Butterflies souvenir sheet	7.75
1163	$2 Pearls sheet of 4	17.50

1174

1175

1164	$4 Pearls souvenir sheet	9.00
1165	$1.20 Birth of Prince George sheet of 4	10.50
1166	$3.50 Birth of Prince George souvenir sheet	7.75
1167-73	$1.10 Sea Life Photos by Kevin Davidson, set of 7 sheets of 6	99.50
1167	$1.10 Sea Life Photos by Kevin Davidson, Sheet of 6, a-f	15.00
1168	$1.10 Sea Life Photos by Kevin Davidson, Sheet of 6, a-f	15.00
1169	$1.10 Sea Life Photos by Kevin Davidson, Sheet of 6, a-e, 1168f	15.00
1170	$1.10 Sea Life Photos by Kevin Davidson, Sheet of 6, a-f	15.00
1171	$1.10 Sea Life Photos by Kevin Davidson, Sheet of 6, a-f	15.00
1172	$1.10 Sea Life Photos by Kevin Davidson, Sheet of 6, a-e, 1171d	15.00
1173	$1.10 Sea Life Photos by Kevin Davidson, Sheet of 6, a-f	15.00
1174	$10 Elvis Presley foil souvenir sheet	22.50
1175	$1.20 Queen Elizabeth II sheet of 4	10.50

1184

1197

1218

1176	$3.50 Queen Elizabeth II souvenir sheet	7.75
1177	$1.20 World Water Day	2.75
1178	$3.50 World Water Day souvenir sheet	7.75
1179-82	29C-$3.50 Christmas set of 4	12.00
1183	$1.20 Nelson Mandella vertical strip of 3	7.75
	same, mint sheet of 6	16.50
1184	$1.20 Nelson Mandella sheet of 6	16.00
1185-86	$3.50 Nelson Mandella souvenir sheets	15.00
1187	$1 Orchids sheet of 6	13.00
1188	$3.50 Orchids Souvenir sheet	7.75
1189	$1.20 Chess in Art sheet of 4	10.50
1190	$3.50 Chess in art souvenir sheet	7.75

2014

1191-92	$1.50 Modern Art, Set of 2 Sheets of 3	19.50
1193-94	$3.50 Modern Art, Set of 2 S/S	15.00
1195-96	$1.75 Seashells, Set of 2 Sheets of 4	29.50
1197-98	$3.50 Set of 2 Souvenir Sheets of 2	29.50

1228

1237

1238

1199	$1.50 Caroline Kennedy, Sheet of 4	13.00
1200	$4 Caroline Kennedy, S/S	9.00
1201	$1.20 Winter Sports, Sheet of 4	10.50
1202	$1.20 Winter Sports, Sheet of 6	15.50
1203-04	$1.20 Pope Francis, Set of 2 Souvenir Sheets	22.00
1205-06	$2 Pope Francis, Set of 2 Souvenir Sheets of 2	18.00
1207-08	$2.50 World War I, Set of 2 Sheets of 4	42.00
1209-10	$2 World War I, Set of 2 Souvenir Sheets of 2	18.00
1211	$1 South Koreans Stamp Sheet of 8	18.00
1212-13	$3.50 Reptiles, Set of 2 Sheets of 4	58.00
1214-15	$3.50 Set of 2 Souvenir Sheets	16.00
1216-17	$1 Seagulls, Set of 2 Sheets of 6	26.00
1218	75¢ Prince George, Horizontal Strip of 3	5.00
1219	$1 Prince George Attached Pair	4.50
1220-21	Prince George Set of 2 Souvenir Sheets	18.00
1222	45¢ Fish, Sheet of 6	6.00
1223-24	$1.75 Alice in Wonderland, Set of 2 Sheets of 4	30.00
1225-26	$2.50 Alice in Wonderland, 2 Souvenir Sheets of 2	22.00
1227	$1.50 Tourist Attractions in Russia, 2 Sheets of 4	9.75
1228	$2 Tourist Attractions in Russia, Souvenir Sheet of 2	8.75
1229	$1 Owls, Sheet of 4	8.75
1230	$3 Owls Souvenir Sheet	6.50
1231	$4 Owls Souvenir Sheet	8.75
1232-39	2¢ - $1 Marine Life, Set of 8	6.00
1240	$1.20 Trains, Sheet of 4	10.75
1241	$3.50 Trains, Souvenir Sheet	7.50
1242-43	$1.50 Paintings, Set of 2 Sheets of 3	19.00
1244-45	$4 Paintings, Set of 2 Souvenir Sheets	17.00

1249

1263

1246-47	$1.20 Frogs and Toads, 2 Sheet of 4	22.00
1248-49	$4 Frogs and Toads, Set of 2 Souvenir Sheets	18.00
1252-55	34¢ - $3.50 Raphael Christmas Paintings, Set of 4	13.00
1250-51	$1.20 Characters *Downtown Abbey*, set of 2 S/S	26.00
1256	40¢ Lagoon Jellyfish, sheet of 4	4.00
1257	90¢ Lagoon Jellyfish, strip of 4	9.00
1258	$1.20 Pope Benedict XVI, sheet of 4	11.00
1259	$4.00 Pope Benedict XVI, souvenir sheet	8.50
1260-61	$1.20 Dinosaurs, set of 2 souvenir sheets	24.00
1262-63	$4.00 Dinosaurs, set of 2 souvenir sheets	20.00

SCOTT NO.	DESCRIPTION	UNUSED F/NH

1274　　　　　　　1267　　　　　　　1287d

2015

1264	$1.20 Taipei 2015, Bubble Tea, sheet of 6	16.00
1265	$4.00 Taipei 2015, Bubble Tea, souvenir sheet	8.50
1266	75¢ Pope John Paul II	1.60
1267	$1.20 Camouflage of WWI, sheet of 5	12.50
1268	$4.00 Camouflage of WWI, souvenir sheet	8.50
1269	$1.20 World Heritage Sites, South Pacific, sheet of 5	12.50
1270	$4.00 World Heritage Sites, South Pacific, S/S	9.00
1271-72	45¢ 1940 Evacuation of Dunkirk, set of 2 sheets	30.50
1273	$1.20 Queen Elizabeth II, sheet of 6	15.25
1274	$4.00 Queen Elizabeth II, souvenir sheet	8.50
1275	65¢ Battle of Britain, sheet of 6	8.25
1276	$4.00 Battle of Britain, souvenir sheet	8.50
1277	$1.00 Pope Benedict XVI, sheet of 4	8.25
1278	$3.50 Pope Benedict XVI, souvenir sheet	7.50
1279	65¢ Birds of the South Pacific, sheet of 6	8.25
1280	$4.00 Birds of the South Pacific, souvenir sheet	8.50
1281	$1.20 Birth of Princess Charlotte, sheet of 4	10.00
1282	$4.00 Birth of Princess Charlotte, souvenir sheet	8.50
1283	65¢ Visit of Pope Francis, sheet of 6	8.25
1284	$4.00 Visit of Pope Francis, souvenir sheet	8.50
1285	65¢ President Dwight D. Eisenhower, sheet of 6	8.25
1286	$4.00 President Dwight D. Eisenhower, S/S	8.50
1287	$1.20 Sir Winston Churchill, sheet of 4	10.00
1288	$4.00 Sir Winston Churchill, souvenir sheet	8.50
1289	65¢ William Shakespeare, sheet of 6	8.25
1290	$4.00 William Shakespeare, souvenir sheet	8.50

1295a　　　　　　　　　1297b

1291-94	34¢-$2 Christmas Paintings, set of 4	9.50
1295	$1.20 German Reunification, sheet of 4	10.00
1296	$4.00 German Reunification, souvenir sheet	8.50
1297	65¢ Star Trek Spacecraft, sheet of 6	9.00
1298	$4.00 Star Trek Spacecraft, souvenir sheet	9.00
1299	$1.20 Marine Mollusks, sheet of 4	10.00
1300	$4.00 Marine Mollusks, souvenir sheets	8.50
1301	65¢ Coral Reef Snakes, sheet of 6	8.50
1302	$4.00 Coral Reef Snakes, souvenir sheets	8.50
1303	65¢ WWII Submarines, sheet of 6	8.25
1304	$4.00 WWI Submarines, souvenir sheet	8.50

1313　　　　　　　1322b　　　　　　　1327a

2016

1305	65¢ Flowers and Plants of Palau, sheet of 6	9.00
1306	$4.00 Flowers and Plants of Palau, souvenir sheet	8.50
1307	$1.20 The 2016 Olympic Champions, sheet of 4	10.50
1308	$4 Olympic Champions, Yoshiyuki Tsuruta, souvenir sheet	8.50
1309	65¢ Vincent van Gogh Paintings, sheet of 6	8.25
1310	$4 Vincent van Gogh Paintings, souvenir sheet	8.50
1311-12	65¢ Jimi Hendrix, set of 2 sheets	16.50
1313	$4 Jimi Hendrix, souvenir sheet	8.50
1314-17	$4 Elvis Presley, set of 4 souvenir sheets	34.00
1318	$1.50 Queen Elizabeth II, 90th Birthday, sheet of 3	9.00
1319	$5 Queen Elizabeth II, 90th Birthday, souvenir sheet	10.25
1320	$1.25 New York City, sites and scenes, sheet of 4	10.50
1321	$3 New York City, skyline, souvenir sheet	6.25
1322	$1 Nancy Reagan, sheet of 6	12.50
1323	$1.20 Nancy Reagan, sheet of 4	10.50

SCOTT NO.	DESCRIPTION	UNUSED F/NH
1324	$2.50 Nancy Reagan, souvenir sheet of 2	10.50
1325	$5 Nancy Reagan, souvenir sheet	10.50
1326	47¢ Palau World of Sea and Reef, sheet of 40	39.00
1327	$1 Star Trek, sheet of 6	12.50
1328	$3 Star Trek, souvenir sheet	6.25
1329	$1.50 Rare Birds of Palau, sheet of 4	12.50
1330	$5 Rare Birds of Palau, souvenir sheet	10.50

1339f　　　　　　　　1340a

1331	$1.50 Ngardmau Waterfall, sheet of 4	12.50
1332	$5 Ngardmau Waterfall, souvenir sheet	10.50
1333	$1 Obama Visits UK, sheet of 6	12.50
1334	$2 Obama Visits UK, sheet of 3	12.50
1335	$2.50 Obama Visits U.N., souvenir sheet of 2	10.50
1336	$1 William Shakespeare, sheet of 6	12.50
1337	$1.50 William Shakespeare, sheet of 4	12.00
1338	$5 William Shakespeare, souvenir sheet	10.50
1339	$1.20 Jellyfish Lake, sheet of 6	15.00
1340	$1.20 Giant Clams, sheet of 6	15.00
1341	$1.25 ABAI Mens Meeting Place, sheet of 4	10.75
1342	$1.50 The Rock Islands, sheet of 4	12.50
1343	$1.75 Manta Ray and Devil Ray, sheet of 4	15.00
1344	$1.75 Remembering World War II, sheet of 4	15.00
1345	$1.50 Protected Species, sheet of 3	9.25

1346b　　　　　　　　1350a

1346	$1.75 Crabs, sheet of 3	11.75
1347	$1.35 Pearl Harbor, 75th Anniversary, Vintage Posters, sheet of 6	19.00
1348	$3 Pearl Harbor, 75th Anniversary, souvenir sheet	12.50
1349	$1 Palauan Fish, sheet of 6	12.50
1350	$2.50 Palauan Fish, souvenir sheet of 2	10.50
1351	75¢-$1 Summer Olympics, sheet of 7	11.75
1352	75¢-$1 Festival of Pacific Arts, sheet of 11	15.00

1353　　　　　　1359　　　　　　1367

2017

1353	$1 Legends of the Wild West, sheet of 6	12.50
1354	$5 Legends of the Wild West, Buffalo Bill, souvenir sheet	10.50
1355	$1-$1.50 Princess Diana's World Travels, sheet of 7	15.00
1356	$1.80 Princess Diana, 20 Years in Memoriam	15.00
1357	$1.35 John F. Kennedy, 100th Birthday, sheet of 6	15.75
1358	$1.60 John F. Kennedy, 100th Birthday, sheet of 4	16.50
1359	$1.25 Seals of the World, sheet of 6	15.75
1360	$4.50 Seals of the World, souvenir sheet	9.50
1361	$2.00 National Geographic Animals, sheet of 4	17.00
1362	$4.00 National Geographic Animals, souvenir sheet	8.50
1363	$1.60 Gustav Klimt Paintings, sheet of 4	13.50
1364	$4.00 Gustav Klimt Paintings, souvenir sheet	8.50
1365-68	$4.00 Elvis Presley, set of 4 souvenir sheet	34.00
1369	50¢ PCAA, 50th Anniversary, sheet of 15	16.00

1372b　　　　　　　　1379a

UNITED NATIONS (NEW YORK)

SCOTT NO.	DESCRIPTION	FIRST DAY COVERS SING	INSC. BLK	INSRIP BLK-4	UNUSED F/NH	USED F
1, 6						
2, 10, UX1-2						
3, 11						
4, 7, 9						
5						
8						
12						
13-14						

1951

| 1-11 | 1¢ to $1 Definitives | 85.00 | 150.00 | 70.00 | 15.50 | 10.00 |

1952-1953

| 12-22 | 1952-53 Issues, complete (11) | ...... | ...... | ...... | 15.50 | ...... |

1952

| 12 | 5¢ United Nations Day | 1.75 | 3.50 | 3.75 | .85 | .35 |
| 13-14 | 3¢ & 5¢ Human Rights Day | 2.50 | 7.00 | 7.75 | 1.75 | .75 |

1953

15-16	3¢ & 5¢ Refugee Issue	1.80	4.50	6.00	1.50	.95
17-18	3¢ & 5¢ U.P.U. Issue	3.00	7.50	13.00	3.00	1.85
19-20	3¢ & 5¢ Technical Assistance	1.75	4.40	6.00	1.75	1.00
21-22	3¢ & 5¢ Human Rights Day	7.75	18.50	9.50	2.15	1.85

1954

23-30	1954 Issues, complete (8)	......	......		24.00	......
23-24	3¢ & 8¢ Food & Agriculture	2.05	5.15	6.00	1.50	1.00
25-26	3¢ & 8¢ International Labor	2.75	6.85	12.00	3.00	2.50
27-28	3¢ & 8¢ Geneva	4.00	10.00	11.00	3.00	2.00
29-30	3¢ & 8¢ Human Rights Day	7.75	18.50	85.00	19.00	5.60

1955

31/40	1955 Issues, (9) (No #38)	......	......		8.00	......
31-32	3¢ & 8¢ Int. Civil Aviation Org	3.95	10.00	13.00	3.00	2.00
33-34	3¢ & 8¢ UNESCO	2.00	5.00	5.00	1.25	1.00
35-37	3¢ to 8¢ United Nations	3.25	17.50	14.00	3.50	2.50
38	same, souvenir sheet	85.00	......		175.00	60.00

15-16						
17-18						
19-20						
21-22						
23-24						
25-26						
27-28						
57-58						
59-60						
61-62						
63-64						
65-66						

SETS ONLY: Prices listed are for complete sets as indicated. We regrettably cannot supply individual stamps from sets.

SCOTT NO.	DESCRIPTION	FIRST DAY COVERS SING	INSC. BLK	INSRIP BLK-4	UNUSED F/NH	USED F
38 var	Second print, retouched	......	......	......	180.00	65.00
39-40	3¢ & 8¢ Human Rights Day	2.00	5.00	6.25	1.40	.90

1956

41-48	1956 Issues, complete (8)	......	......	......	3.40	......
41-42	3¢ & 8¢ International Telecommunications	2.00	5.00	5.00	1.30	.90
43-44	3¢ & 8¢ World Health Org.	2.00	5.00	5.00	1.30	.90
45-46	3¢ & 8¢ United Nations Day	1.25	3.15	2.25	.55	.30
47-48	3¢ & 8¢ Human Rights Day	1.25	3.15	2.10	.50	.30

1957

49-58	1957 Issues, complete (10)	......	......	......	2.40	......
49-50	3¢ & 8¢ Meteorological Org.	1.25	3.15	1.35	.35	.30
51-52	3¢ & 8¢ Emergency Force	1.25	3.15	1.35	.35	.30
53-54	same, re-engraved	......	......	6.00	1.40	.45
55-56	3¢ & 8¢ Security Council	1.25	3.15	1.35	.35	.30
57-58	3¢ & 8¢ Human Rights Day	1.25	3.15	1.35	.35	.30

67-68						
69-70						
71-72						
73-74						
75-76						
77-78						
79-80						
81-82						
83-85						
86-87						

1958

59-68	1958 Issues, complete (10	......	......	......	1.65	......
59-60	3¢ & 8¢ Atomic Energy Agency	1.25	3.15	1.35	.35	.30
61-62	3¢ & 8¢ Central Hall	1.25	3.15	1.35	.35	.30
63-64	4¢ & 8¢ U.N. Seal	1.25	3.15	1.35	.35	.30
65-66	4¢ & 8¢ Economic & Social Council	1.25	3.15	1.35	.35	.30
67-68	4¢ & 8¢ Human Rights Day	1.21	3.15	1.35	.35	.30

1959

69-76	1959 Issues, complete (8)	......	......	......	1.35	......
69-70	4¢ & 8¢ Flushing Meadows	1.25	3.15	1.40	.35	.30
71-72	4¢ & 8¢ Economic Commission Europe	1.25	3.15	1.60	.35	.50
73-74	4¢ & 8¢ Trusteeship Council	1.25	3.15	1.90	.40	.30
75-76	4¢ & 8¢ World Refugee Year	1.25	3.15	1.40	.35	.30

1960

77/87	1960 Issues, (10) (No #85)	......	......	......	1.65	...
77-78	4¢ & 8¢ Palais de Chaillot	1.25	3.15	1.40	.35	.30
79-80	4¢ & 8¢ Economic Commission Asia	1.25	3.15	1.40	.35	.30
81-82	4¢ & 8¢ 5th World Forestry Congress	1.25	3.15	1.40	.35	.30
83-84	4¢ & 8¢ 15th Anniversary	1.25	3.15	1.40	.35	.30
85	same, souvenir sheet	4.25	......	......	2.10	1.80
85 var	Broken "V" Variety	135.00	......	......	72.50	67.50
86-87	4¢ & 8¢ International Bank	1.25	3.15	1.40	.35	.30

FIRST DAY COVERS: Prices for United Nations First Day Covers are for cacheted, unaddressed covers with each variety in a set mounted on a separate cover. Complete sets mounted on one cover do exist and sell for a slightly lower price.

UNITED NATIONS (NEW YORK)

SCOTT NO.	DESCRIPTION	FIRST DAY COVERS SING	INSC. BLK	INSRIP BLK-4	UNUSED F/NH	USED F

88-89

90-91

92

93-94

95-96

97-99

100-101

102-103

1961

SCOTT NO.	DESCRIPTION	SING	INSC. BLK	BLK-4	F/NH	F
88-99	**1961 Issues, complete (12)**	.....	.....	.....	2.65	.....
88-89	4¢ & 8¢ International Court of Justice	1.25	3.15	1.35	.35	1.25
90-91	4¢ & 7¢ Int. Monetary Fund	1.25	3.15	1.35	.35	1.25
92	30¢ Abstract Flags	1.25	3.15	3.00	.75	.60
93-94	4¢ & 11¢ Economic Commission Latin America	1.25	3.15	2.70	.60	.50
95-96	4¢ & 11¢ Economic Commission Africa	1.25	3.15	1.25	.35	.35
97-99	3¢, 4¢ & 13¢ Children's Fund	1.25	3.50	2.55	.55	.50

1962

100-13	**1962 Issues, complete (14)**	.....	.....	.....	3.05	.....
100-01	4¢ & 7¢ Housing & Community Development	1.25	3.15	1.40	.35	.30
102-03	4¢ & 11¢ Malaria Eradication	1.25	3.15	2.35	.50	.35
104-07	1¢ to 11¢ Definitives	2.00	4.00	3.30	.75	.65
108-09	5¢ & 15¢ Memorial Issue	1.25	3.15	3.40	.75	.55
110-11	4¢ & 11¢ Operation in the Congo	1.25	3.15	3.30	.75	.55
112-13	4¢ & 11¢ Peaceful Uses of Outer Space	1.25	3.15	2.40	.55	.30

104

105

106

107

108-09

110-11

112-13

114-15

116-17

118

119-20

121-22

123-24

1963

114-22	**1963 Issues, complete (9)**	.....	.....	.....	2.10	.....
114-15	5¢ & 11¢ Science & Technology	1.25	3.15	1.85	.40	.35
116-17	5¢ & 11¢ Freedom From Hunger	1.25	3.15	1.85	.40	.35
118	25¢ UNTEA	1.10	3.00	3.00	.70	.60
119-20	5¢ & 11¢ General Assem. Bldg.	1.25	3.15	1.85	.40	.35
121-22	5¢ & 11¢ Human Rights	1.25	3.15	1.85	.40	.35

1964

123-36	**1964 Issues, complete (14)**	.....	.....	.....	3.30	.....
123-24	5¢ & 11¢ Maritime Organization (IMCO)	1.25	3.15	1.85	.40	.35
125-28	2¢ to 50¢ Definitives	3.25	7.75	7.00	1.60	1.50
129-30	5¢ & 11¢ Trade & Development	1.25	3.15	1.85	.40	.35
131-32	5¢ & 11¢ Narcotics Control	1.25	3.45	1.85	.40	.35
133	5¢ Cessation of Nuclear Testing	.60	1.30	.65	.25	.25
134-36	4¢ to 11¢ Education for Progress	1.30	3.25	2.90	.70	.50

125, UX3

126

127

128, U3-4

129-30

131-32

133

134-36

137-38

139-40

141-42

143-45

SCOTT NO.	DESCRIPTION	SING	INSC. BLK	BLK-4	F/NH	F
137/53	**1965 Issues, (15) (No #145 or 150)**	.....	.....	.....	2.90	.....
137-38	5¢ & 11¢ United Nations Special Fund	1.25	3.15	1.65	.35	.30
139-40	5¢ & 11¢ United Nations Forces in Cyprus	1.25	3.15	1.65	.35	.30
141-42	5¢ & 11¢ I.T.U. Centenary	1.25	3.15	1.65	.35	.30
143-44	5¢ & 15¢ Int'l Cooperation Year	1.25	3.15	1.85	.40	.35
145	same, souvenir sheet	1.75	.....	.....	.60	.50
146-49	1¢ to 25¢ Definitive	3.50	8.75	7.65	1.20	.95

1966

150	$1 Definitive	3.10	7.75	9.50	2.50	2.00

1965

151-53	4¢ to 11¢ Population Trends	1.60	3.75	2.40	.55	.50

1966

154-63	**1966 Issues, complete (10)**	.....	.....	.....	1.90	.....
154-55	5¢ & 15¢ World Federation (WFUNA)	1.25	3.15	2.00	.50	.30
156-57	5¢ & 11¢ World Health Organization	1.25	3.15	1.85	.45	.30
158-59	5¢ & 11¢ Coffee Agreement	1.25	3.15	1.85	.45	.30
160	15¢ Peace Keeping Observers	.60	1.50	1.85	.40	.40
161-63	4¢ to 11¢ UNICEF	1.60	3.75	2.25	.50	.45

1967

164/80	**1967 Issues, (16) (No #179)**	.....	.....	.....	3.20	.....
164-65	5¢ & 11¢ Development	1.25	3.15	1.80	.35	.30
166-67	1-1/2 ¢ & 5¢ Definitives	1.25	3.15	1.35	.35	.30
168-69	5¢ & 11¢ Independence	1.25	3.15	1.75	.40	.30
170-74	4¢ to 15¢ Expo '67 Canada	3.00	7.50	4.20	.95	.85

146

147

148

149

150

151-53

154-55

156-57

158-59

160

161-63

164-65

166

UNITED NATIONS (NEW YORK)

SCOTT NO.	DESCRIPTION	FIRST DAY COVERS SING	INSC. BLK	INSRIP BLK-4	UNUSED F/NH	USED F
175-76	5¢ & 15¢ International Tourist Year	1.25	3.15	1.90	.40	.35
177-78	6¢ & 13¢ Towards Disarmament	1.25	3.15	1.90	.40	.35
179	36¢ Chagall Window souvenir sheet	1.25	......	......	.80	.75
180	6¢ Kiss of Peace	.60	......	.90	.25	.25
	1968					
181-91	**1968 Issues, complete (11)**	......	......	......	4.00	......
181-82	6¢ & 13 ¢ Secretariat	1.25	3.15	1.90	.40	.35
183-84	6¢ & 75¢ H. Starcke	6.25	15.00	8.00	1.85	1.65
185-86	6¢ & 13¢ Industrial Development	1.25	3.15	1.90	.45	.25
187	6¢ Definitive	.60	1.50	.90	.25	.25
188-89	6¢ & 20¢ Weather Watch	1.25	3.15	2.70	.60	.40
190-91	6¢ & 13¢ International Year—Human Rights	1.25	3.15	2.30	.50	.40
	1969					
192-202	**1969 Issues (11)**	......	......	......	2.45	......
192-93	6¢ & 13¢ Institute Training Research	1.25	3.15	2.00	.45	.35
194-95	6¢ & 15¢ U.N. Building—Chile	1.25	3.15	2.15	.45	.40
196	13¢ Definitive	.60	1.50	1.55	.35	.25
197-98	6¢ & 13¢ Peace Through International Law	1.25	3.15	1.95	.40	.35
199-200	6¢ & 20¢ Labor & Development	1.25	3.15	2.55	.60	.45
201-02	6¢ & 13¢ Tunisian Mosaics	1.25	3.15	2.25	.50	.35
	1970					
203/14	**1970 Issues, (11) (No #212)**	......	......	......	3.25	......
203-04	6¢ & 25¢ Japanese Peace Bell	1.25	3.15	3.00	.70	.50
205-06	6¢ & 13¢ L. Mekong Delta Devel	1.25	3.15	2.10	.50	.35
207-08	6¢ & 13¢ Fight Cancer	1.25	3.15	2.10	.50	.35
209-11	6¢ to 25¢ Peace & Progress	1.70	4.25	4.10	.95	.80
212	same, souvenir sheet	1.40	......	......	.95	.85
213-14	6¢ & 13¢ Peace, Justice & Prog	1.25	3.15	2.25	.50	.35
	1971					
215-25	**1971 Issues (11)**	......	......	......	3.25	......
215	6¢ Peaceful Uses Sea-Bed	.60	1.50	.90	.25	.25
216-17	6¢ & 13¢ Support Refugees	1.25	3.15	2.10	.50	.30
218	13¢ World Food Programme	.60	1.50	1.40	.35	.30
219	20¢ Universal Postal Union Building	.70	1.75	1.90	.45	.35
220-21	8¢ & 13¢ Anti-Discrimination	1.25	3.15	2.25	.45	.35
222-23	8¢ & 60¢ Definitives	2.50	6.25	6.75	1.50	1.10
224-25	8¢ & 21¢ International School	1.25	3.15	3.00	.70	.55

SETS ONLY: Prices listed are for complete sets as indicated. We regrettably cannot supply individual stamps from sets.

INSCRIPTION BLOCKS: Each corner of United Nations complete sheets contains the U.N. Emblem plus the name of the issue in the selvage. These are offered as Inscription Blocks of Four.

UNITED NATIONS (NEW YORK)

SCOTT NO.	DESCRIPTION	FIRST DAY COVERS SING	INSC. BLK	INSRIP BLK-4	UNUSED F/NH	USED F
	1972					
226-33	1972 Issues, complete (8)	......	......	......	3.85	......
226	95¢ Definitive	2.75	6.85	9.25	2.00	1.90
227	8¢ Non-Proliferation	.60	1.50	1.00	.25	.25
228	15¢ World Health Org.	.60	1.50	1.75	.40	.25
229-30	8¢ & 15¢ Environment	1.25	3.15	2.35	.55	.40
231	21¢ Economic Commission Europe	.75	1.85	2.10	.45	.40
232-33	8¢ & 15¢ Art—Sert Ceiling	1.25	3.15	2.25	.50	.40
	1973					
234-43	1973 Issues, complete (10)	......	......	......	2.60	......
234-35	8¢ & 15¢ Disarmament Decade	1.25	3.15	2.25	.55	.50
236-37	8¢ & 15¢ Drug Abuse	1.25	3.15	2.50	.55	.50
238-39	8¢ & 21¢ Volunteers Programme	1.25	3.15	2.85	.60	.50
240-41	8¢ & 15¢ Namibia	1.25	3.15	2.75	.55	.50
242-43	8¢ & 21¢ Human Rights	1.25	3.15	3.00	.60	.55
	1974					
244-55	1974 Issues, complete (12)	......	......	......	3.25	......
244-45	10¢ & 21¢ ILO Headquarters	1.30	3.25	3.25	.70	.65
246	10¢ Universal Postal Union	.60	1.50	.95	.25	.25
247-48	10¢ & 18¢ Brazil Peace Mural	1.25	3.15	2.85	.65	.60
249-51	2¢ to 18¢ Definitives	1.65	4.15	3.00	.65	.60
252-53	10¢ & 18¢ World Population Year	1.35	3.35	3.25	.70	.75
254-55	10¢ & 26¢ Law of the Sea	1.35	3.35	3.50	1.50	.80

231

232-33

234-35

236-37

238-39

240-41

242-43

244-45

246

SCOTT NO.	DESCRIPTION	FIRST DAY COVERS SING	INSC. BLK	INSRIP BLK-4	UNUSED F/NH	USED F

265-66

267

268

269

270

271

272-73

274-75

276-77

280

278-79

281-82

283-84

289-90

285-86

287-88

SCOTT NO.	DESCRIPTION	FIRST DAY COVERS SING	INSC. BLK	INSRIP BLK-4	UNUSED F/NH	USED F
272-73	13¢ & 26¢ World Federation	1.50	3.75	3.75	.85	.65
274-75	13¢ & 31¢ Conf. on Trade & Dev.	1.45	3.65	4.70	.95	.75
276-77	13¢ & 25¢ Conference on Human Settlements	1.25	3.15	4.00	.85	.75
278-79	13¢ & 31¢ Postal Admin.	9.50	23.50	13.00	4.00	2.25
280	13¢ World Food Council	.60	1.50	1.50	.30	.30
	1977					
281-90	Issues, complete (10)	......	......	......	3.85	......
281-82	13¢ & 31¢ WIPO	1.40	3.50	4.20	.90	.80
283-84	13¢ & 25¢ Water Conference	1.35	3.40	3.95	.85	.75
285-86	13¢ & 31¢ Security Council	1.50	3.75	4.25	.95	.75
287-88	13¢ & 25¢ Combat Racism	1.35	3.40	3.85	.95	.70
289-90	13¢ & 18¢ Atomic Energy	1.25	3.15	3.00	.65	.70
	1978					
291-303	1978 Issues, complete (13)	......	......	......	6.25	......
291-93	1¢, 25¢ & $1 Definitives	4.00	10.00	11.00	2.50	2.00
294-95	13¢ & 31¢ Smallpox Eradication	1.40	3.50	4.40	.95	.85
296-97	13¢ & 18¢ Namibia	1.25	3.15	3.00	.70	.60
298-99	13¢ & 25¢ ICAO	1.30	3.25	3.75	.85	.70
300-01	13¢ & 18¢ General Assembly	1.25	3.15	3.25	.70	.65
302-03	13¢ & 31¢ TCDC	1.50	3.75	4.00	.95	.90

	1975					
256/66	1975 Issues, (10) (No #262)	......	......	......	4.10	......
256-57	10¢ & 26¢ Peaceful Uses of Space	1.35	3.35	3.45	.75	.70
258-59	10¢ & 18¢ Int'l. Women's Year	1.25	3.15	3.25	.65	.65
260-61	10¢ & 26¢ Anniversary	1.30	3.35	3.25	.80	.75
262	same, souvenir sheet	1.55	......	......	1.00	.80
263-64	10¢ & 18¢ Namibia	1.25	3.15	3.10	.65	.65
265-66	13¢ & 26¢ Peacekeeping	1.35	3.35	3.85	.85	.85
	1976					
267-80	1976 Issues, complete (14)	......	......	......	7.90	......
267-71	3¢ to 50¢ Definitives	3.10	7.75	9.50	2.10	1.85

247-48

249

250, U6

251

252-53

254-55

256-57

258-59

260-62

263-64

291

292

293

294-95

296-97

298-99

300-01

302-03

304

305

306

307

UNITED NATIONS (NEW YORK)

SCOTT NO.	DESCRIPTION	FIRST DAY COVERS SING	INSC. BLK	INSRIP BLK-4	UNUSED F/NH	USED F
	1979					
304-15	1979 Issues, complete (12)	......	......	......	4.25	......
304-07	5¢, 14¢, 15¢ & 20¢ Definitives	2.00	5.00	5.25	1.10	1.10
308-09	15¢ & 20¢ UNDRO..........................	1.35	3.40	3.50	.75	.65
310-11	15¢ & 31¢ I.Y.C.	3.75	9.40	4.95	1.10	.95
312-13	15¢ & 31¢ Namibia........................	1.55	3.85	4.40	1.00	.85
314-15	15¢ & 20¢ Court of Justice	1.40	3.50	3.75	.85	.75

1980 World Flags

326 Luxembourg
327 Fiji
328 Viet Nam
329 Guinea
330 Surinam
331 Bangladesh
332 Mali
333 Yugoslavia
334 France
335 Venezuela
336 El Salvador
337 Madagascar
338 Cameroon
339 Rwanda
340 Hungary

325
308-09
310-11

312-13
314-15
316
317

SCOTT NO.	DESCRIPTION	FIRST DAY COVERS SING	INSC. BLK	INSRIP BLK-4	UNUSED F/NH	USED F
	1980					
316/42	1980 Issues, (26) (No #324)	......	......	......	7.95	......
316-17	15¢ & 31¢ Economics	1.65	4.15	4.25	.95	.95
318-19	15¢ & 20¢ Decade for Women	1.35	3.40	3.50	.75	.70
320-21	15¢ & 31¢ Peacekeeping	1.60	4.00	4.25	.90	.90
322-23	15¢ & 31¢ Anniversary	1.55	3.90	4.25	.90	.75
324	same, souvenir sheet	1.45	......	......	.95	.90
325-40	15¢ 1980 World Flags, 16 varieties....	10.00	......	22.00	5.00	3.75
341-42	15¢ & 20¢ Economic & Social Council....	1.30	3.25	4.00	.85	.75

318-19
320
321
322
323
341
342
343
344
345
346-47
348
349
366
367

1981 World Flags

350 Djibouti
351 Sri Lanka
352 Bolivia
353 Equatorial Guinea
354 Malta
355 Czechoslovakia
356 Thailand
357 Trinidad
358 Ukraine
359 Kuwait
360 Sudan
361 Egypt
362 United States
363 Singapore
364 Panama
365 Costa Rica

368
369

370
371
372
373
390-91

SCOTT NO.	DESCRIPTION	FIRST DAY COVERS SING	INSC. BLK	INSRIP BLK-4	UNUSED F/NH	USED F
	1981					
343-67	1981 Issues, complete (25)	......	......	......	11.00	......
343	15¢ Palestinian People.................	.75	1.85	1.60	.35	.30
344-45	20¢ & 35¢ Disabled Persons............	1.70	4.25	5.50	1.25	1.00
346-47	20¢ & 31¢ Fresco	1.60	4.00	5.50	1.25	1.00
348-49	20¢ & 40¢ Sources of Energy	1.90	4.75	5.75	1.20	1.00
350-65	20¢ 1981 World Flags, 16 varieties....	13.50	......	28.00	7.00	5.50
366-67	18¢ & 28¢ Volunteers Program	1.55	3.85	5.50	1.20	.95
	1982					
368-91	1982 Issues, complete (24)	......	......	......	11.50	......
368-70	17¢, 28¢ & 49¢ Definitives	2.50	6.25	9.25	2.00	1.80
371-72	20¢ & 40¢ Human Environment	1.95	4.85	7.00	1.40	1.25
373	20¢ Space Exploration	.90	2.25	3.25	.70	.60
374-89	20¢ World Flags, 16 varieties...........	13.00	......	29.00	7.00	5.50
390-91	20¢ & 28¢ Nature Conservation........	1.75	4.35	5.75	1.20	1.00

1982 World Flags

374 Austria
375 Malaysia
376 Seychelles
377 Ireland
378 Mozambique
379 Albania
380 Dominica
381 Solomon Islands
382 Philippines
383 Swaziland
384 Nicaragua
385 Burma
386 Cape Verde
387 Guyana
388 Belgium
389 Nigeria

392
393
394
395
396
397
398

1983 World Flags

399 United Kingdom
400 Barbados
401 Nepal
402 Israel
403 Malawi
404 Byelorussian SSR
405 Jamaica
406 Kenya
407 China
408 Peru
409 Bulgaria
410 Canada
411 Somalia
412 Senegal
413 Brazil
414 Sweden

415
416
417-18

SCOTT NO.	DESCRIPTION	FIRST DAY COVERS SING	INSC. BLK	INSRIP BLK-4	UNUSED F/NH	USED F
	1983					
392-416	1983 Issues, complete (25)	......	......	......	12.50	......
392-93	20¢ & 40¢ World Communications Year..	2.05	5.15	6.00	1.40	1.25
394-95	20¢ & 37¢ Safety at Sea	1.95	4.75	6.00	1.40	1.25
396	20¢ World Food Program	.85	2.10	3.95	.85	.50
397-98	20¢ & 28¢ Trade & Development	1.60	4.00	7.25	1.60	1.25
399-414	20¢ World Flags, 16 varieties...........	13.00	......	29.00	6.50	7.00
415-16	20¢ & 40¢ Human Rights	2.50	6.25	7.00	2.00	1.50

419
420
421
423
422
424

1984 World Flags

425 Burundi
426 Pakistan
427 Benin
428 Italy
429 Tanzania
430 United Arab Emirates
431 Ecuador
432 Bahamas
433 Poland
434 Papua New Guinea
435 Uruguay
436 Chile
437 Paraguay
438 Bhutan
439 Central African Republic
440 Australia

UNITED NATIONS (NEW YORK)

SCOTT NO.	DESCRIPTION	FIRST DAY COVERS SING	INSC. BLK	INSRIP BLK-4	UNUSED F/NH	USED F
417-42	**1984 Issues, complete (25)**	......	......	......	20.40	
417-18	20¢ & 40¢ Population	2.10	5.25	6.50	1.75	1.25
419-20	20¢ & 40¢ Food Day	2.10	5.25	6.50	2.00	1.25
421-22	20¢ & 50¢ Heritage	2.25	5.50	8.00	2.25	1.50
423-24	20¢ & 50¢ Future for Refugees	2.25	5.50	8.00	2.00	1.35
425-40	20¢ 1984 World Flags, 16 varieties	13.00	......	39.00	11.50	10.00
441-42	20¢ & 35¢ Youth Year	2.10	5.25	9.00	2.00	1.70

1985 World Flags

450 Grenada	458 Liberia
451 Germany-West	459 Mauritius
452 Saudi Arabia	460 Chad
453 Mexico	461 Dominican Republic
454 Uganda	462 Oman
455 Sao Tome & Principie	463 Ghana
456 U.S.S.R.	464 Sierra Leone
457 India	465 Finland

444

443

445

1985

SCOTT NO.	DESCRIPTION	FIRST DAY COVERS SING	INSC. BLK	INSRIP BLK-4	UNUSED F/NH	USED F
443/67	**1985 Issues, (24) (No #449)**	......	......	......	25.00	......
443	23¢ ILO—Turin Centre	1.00	2.50	3.50	.85	.60
444	50¢ United Nations University in Japan	1.65	4.15	6.75	1.65	1.25
445-46	22¢ & $3 Definitives	8.00	20.00	29.00	6.50	5.25
447-48	22¢ & 45¢ 40th Anniversary	2.30	5.75	7.75	1.75	1.50
449	same, souvenir sheet	2.50	......	......	2.50	1.50
450-65	22¢ 1985 World Flags, 16 varieties	14.00	......	44.00	12.50	10.00
466-67	22¢ & 33¢ Child Survival	2.25	5.65	6.75	1.50	1.20

1986 World Flags

477 New Zealand	485 Iceland
478 Lao PDR	486 Antigua & Barbuda
479 Burkina Faso	487 Angola
480 Gambia	488 Botswana
481 Maldives	489 Romania
482 Ethiopia	490 Togo
483 Jordan	491 Mauritania
484 Zambia	492 Colombia

446

447

448

466

441

468

469

473

475

476

1986

SCOTT NO.	DESCRIPTION	FIRST DAY COVERS SING	INSC. BLK	INSRIP BLK-4	UNUSED F/NH	USED F
468-92	**1986 Issues (25)**	......	......	......	24.50	......
468	22¢ African Crisis	1.05	2.60	3.25	.70	.60
469-72	22¢ Development, 4 varieties, attached	2.50	3.25	7.00	6.00	5.00
473-74	22¢ & 44¢ Philately	2.30	5.75	7.50	1.75	1.00
475-76	22¢ & 33¢ Peace Year	2.25	5.65	10.50	2.25	1.00
477-92	22¢ 1986 World Flags, 16 varieties	14.00	......	44.00	12.50	10.00

493a

494

495

497

1987 World Flags

499 Comoros	507 Argentina
500 Democratic Yemen	508 Congo
501 Mongolia	509 Niger
502 Vanuatu	510 St. Lucia
503 Japan	511 Bahrain
504 Gabon	512 Haiti
505 Zimbabwe	513 Afghanistan
506 Iraq	514 Greece

515

517

573-74

1986

SCOTT NO.	DESCRIPTION	FIRST DAY COVERS SING	INSC. BLK	INSRIP BLK-4	UNUSED F/NH	USED F
493	22¢ to 44¢ World Federation of United Nations Associations Souvenir sheet of 4	4.00	......	......	5.50	4.00

1987

SCOTT NO.	DESCRIPTION	FIRST DAY COVERS SING	INSC. BLK	INSRIP BLK-4	UNUSED F/NH	USED F
494-518	**1987 Issues (25)**	......	......	......	19.00	......
494	22¢ Trygve Lie	1.05	2.60	5.00	1.00	.75
495-96	22¢ & 44¢ Shelter Homeless	2.25	5.65	8.50	1.85	1.75
497-98	22¢ & 33¢ Anti-Drug Campaign	2.25	5.65	8.25	1.85	1.75
499-514	22¢ 1987 World Flags, 16 varieties	14.00	......	44.00	12.50	10.00
515-16	22¢ & 39¢ United Nations Day	2.30	5.75	7.50	1.50	1.30
517-18	22¢ & 44¢ Child Immunization	2.35	5.70	14.00	3.25	3.00

519

521

524

1988 World Flags

528 Spain
529 St. Vincent & Grenadines
530 Ivory Coast
531 Lebanon
532 Yemen
533 Cuba
534 Denmark
535 Libya
536 Qatar
537 Zaire
538 Norway
539 German Democratic Republic
540 Iran
541 Tunisia
542 Samoa
543 Belize

526

544-45

546

548

549

550

1988

SCOTT NO.	DESCRIPTION	FIRST DAY COVERS SING	INSC. BLK	INSRIP BLK-4	UNUSED F/NH	USED F
519/44	**1988 Issues (24) (No #522-23)**	......	......	......	19.25	......
519-20	22¢ & 33¢ World without Hunger	2.25	5.65	8.50	2.35	1.75
521	3¢ For a Better World	.90	2.25	.90	.25	.25
	Sheetlets					
522-23	25¢ & 44¢ Forest Conservation (set of 6, includes Geneva and Vienna)	15.00	40.00	130.00	27.50	25.00
524-25	25¢ & 50¢ Volunteer Day	2.60	6.50	10.50	2.25	2.00
526-27	25¢ & 38¢ Health in Sports	2.30	5.75	12.00	2.75	2.00
528-43	25¢ 1988 World Flags, 16 varieties	14.50	......	44.00	12.50	10.00
544	25¢ Human Rights	1.75	4.25	4.00	.75	.75
545	$1 Human Rights souvenir sheet	2.75	......	......	2.50	2.00

552

553

570-71

1989 World Flags

554 Indonesia
555 Lesotho
556 Guatamala
557 Netherlands
558 South Africa
559 Portugal
560 Morocco
561 Syrian Arab Republic
562 Honduras
563 Kampuchea
564 Guinea-Bissau
565 Cyprus
566 Algeria
567 Brunei
568 St. Kitts & Nevis
569 United Nations

572

UNITED NATIONS (NEW YORK)

SCOTT NO.	DESCRIPTION	FIRST DAY COVERS SING	INSC. BLK	INSRIP BLK-4	UNUSED F/NH	USED F
	1989					
546-71	**1989 Issues (26)**........................	......	......	......	30.00	......
546-47	25¢ & 45¢ World Bank	2.60	6.50	12.00	2.75	2.00
548	25¢ Nobel Peace Prize......................	1.10	1.65	3.75	1.10	.95
549	45¢ United Nations Definitive..........	1.40	2.10	5.75	1.10	.95
550-51	25¢ & 36¢ Weather Watch...............	2.30	5.75	12.00	3.50	2.50
552-53	25¢ & 90¢ U.N. Offices in Vienna....	3.75	9.25	24.00	6.25	5.50
554-69	25¢ 1989 World Flags, 16 varieties...	14.50	......	50.00	13.50	11.00
	Sheetlets (12)					
570-71	25¢ & 45¢ Human Rights 40th Ann.					
	(strips of 3 with tabs)	2.60	6.50	21.00	5.00	......
	1990					
572/83	**1990 Issues (11) (No #579)**...........	......	......	......	25.50	......
572	25¢ International Trade Center.........	1.75	2.95	8.00	2.10	1.80
573-74	25¢ & 40¢ AIDS...............................	2.60	6.50	11.00	2.75	2.25
575-76	25¢ & 90¢ Medicinal Plants..............	3.75	9.25	12.00	3.50	2.50
577-78	25¢ & 45¢ United Nations 45th Anniversary	2.60	6.50	16.50	4.00	3.50
579	25¢ & 45¢ United Nations 45th Anniversary Souvenir Sheet...............	2.10			8.00	8.00
580-81	25¢ & 36¢ Crime Prevention	2.30	5.75	15.00	4.00	3.00
	Sheetlets (12)					
582-83	25¢ & 45¢ Human Rights					
	(strips of 3 with tabs)	2.60	6.50	23.00	5.00	......

575-76

577-78

580-81

584

588

590

591

592

593

595

597

603

605

609

SCOTT NO.	DESCRIPTION	FIRST DAY COVERS SING	INSC. BLK	INSRIP BLK-4	UNUSED F/NH	USED F
	1991					
584-600	**1991 Issues (17)**........................	......	......	......	29.00	......
584-87	30¢ Econ. Comm. for Europe, 4 varieties, attached	4.50	7.50	7.00	5.75	5.50
588-89	30¢ & 50¢ Namibia—A New Nation ...	3.50	8.75	12.00	2.75	2.75
590-91	30¢ & 50¢ Definitives	4.00	10.00	10.50	2.35	2.25
592	$2 Definitive...................................	5.50	13.50	21.00	4.75	4.00
593-94	30¢ & 70¢ Children's Rights..............	4.00	10.00	17.00	4.00	4.00
595-96	30¢ & 90¢ Banning of Chemical........	4.25	10.50	21.00	5.00	5.00
597-98	30¢ & 40¢ 40th Anniversary of UNPA ...	3.50	8.75	12.00	2.50	2.50
	Sheetlets (12)					
599-600	30¢ & 50¢ Human Rights (strips of 3 with tabs)	3.00	7.50	31.50	7.00	......

611

613

614

618

620

624

626

629

633

SCOTT NO.	DESCRIPTION	FIRST DAY COVERS SING	INSC. BLK	INSRIP BLK-4	UNUSED F/NH	USED F
	1992					
601-17	**1992 Issues (17)**........................	......	......	......	23.00	......
601-02	29¢-50¢ World Heritage—UNESCO ...	3.60	9.00	10.00	2.50	2.00
603-04	29¢ Clean Oceans, 2 varieties, attached	2.50	4.95	4.95	1.70	1.50
605-08	29¢ Earth Summit, 4 varieties, attached .	3.50	4.25	6.00	5.00	4.50
609-10	29¢ Mission to Planet Earth, 2 varieties, attd	2.50	4.95	15.00	6.75	6.50
611-12	29¢-50¢ Science and Technology	3.60	9.00	8.75	1.95	1.75
613-15	4¢-40¢ Definitives............................	3.40	8.50	9.75	2.00	1.95
	Sheetlets (12)					
616-17	20¢-50¢ Human Rights (strips of 3 with tabs)	3.00	9.50	25.00	7.50	......
	1993					
618-36	**1993 Issues (19)**........................	......	......	......	22.75	......
618-19	29¢-52¢ Aging	3.00	9.50	11.00	3.00	3.00
620-23	29¢ Endangered Species, 4 attached	3.50	4.25	3.50	3.00	3.00
624-25	29¢-50¢ Health Environment..................	3.60	9.00	10.00	2.50	2.35
626	5¢ Definitive...................................	2.00	4.00	1.00	.25	.25
	Sheetlets (12)					
627-28	29¢-35¢ Human Rights (strips of 3 with tabs)	3.00	9.50	20.00	6.75	......
629-32	29¢ Peace, 4 attached	3.50	8.00	12.00	11.00	10.00
633-36	29¢ Environment—Climate, strip of 4.....	3.50	7.00	12.00(8)	5.00	4.75

637

643

644

645

646

647

651

653

655

SCOTT NO.	DESCRIPTION	FIRST DAY COVERS SING	INSC. BLK	INSRIP BLK-4	UNUSED F/NH	USED F
	1994					
637-54	**1994 Issues (18)**........................	......	......	......	21.50	......
637-38	29¢-45¢ International Year of the Family	2.25	8.50	13.00	3.00	3.00
639-42	29¢ Endangered Species, 4 attached	3.00	4.25	3.50	3.00	2.50
643	50¢ Refugees..................................	1.75	5.75	8.00	1.50	1.50
644-46	10¢-$1 Definitives (3).......................	3.50	12.50	13.00	3.25	3.00
647-50	29¢ International Decade for Natural Disaster Reduction, 4 attached	3.00	4.25	12.50	10.50	10.00
651-52	29¢-52¢ Population and Development	2.25	9.00	11.00	2.50	2.25
653-54	29¢-50¢ Development through Partnership	2.25	9.00	8.75	1.75	1.50

UNITED NATIONS (NEW YORK)

SCOTT NO.	DESCRIPTION	FIRST DAY COVERS SING	INSC. BLK	INSRIP BLK-4	UNUSED F/NH	USED F

661

663
656

1995

SCOTT NO.	DESCRIPTION	SING	INSC. BLK	BLK-4	F/NH	F
655/69	1995 Issues (14) (No #665)...................	....	....	....	34.00	....
655	32¢ 50th Anniversary of the UN	1.75	4.00	6.75	2.00	1.50
656	50¢ Social Summit	1.75	5.75	6.50	1.40	1.25
657-60	29¢ Endangered Species, 4 attached	3.00	4.25	3.50	3.00	3.00
661-62	32¢-55¢ Youth: Our Future.....................	2.50	11.00	12.00	3.00	3.00
663-64	32¢-50¢ 50th Anniversary of the UN	2.50	11.00	12.00	3.50	3.00

666

668

665	82¢ 50th Anniversary of the UN, Souvenir Sheet..	2.50	....	....	4.50	4.25
666-67	32¢-40¢ 4th World Conference on Women.	2.50	9.00	10.50	2.40	2.25
668	20¢ UN Headquarters	1.75	....	2.25	.45	.45

669a

669	32¢ 50th Anniversary, Miniature Sheet of 12	....	....	....	18.00	....
669a-l	32¢ 50th Anniversary of the UN, booklet single	1.75	....	....	.75	.25
670	same, souvenir booklet of 4 panes of 3...	....	....	....	22.00	....

671

672

1996

671/89	1996 Issues (18) (No #685).....................	....	....	....	19.00	....
671	32¢ WFUNA 50th Anniversary.................	1.75	4.00	3.75	.85	.75
672-73	32¢-60¢ Definitives.................................	2.50	9.00	9.00	2.25	2.10
674-77	32¢ Endangered Species, 4 attached	3.00	4.25	4.50	3.50	3.00
678-82	32¢ City Summit (Habitat II), strip of 5.....	3.75	5.00	17.00	8.00	7.00
683-84	32¢-50¢ Sport & the Environment..........	2.50	9.00	15.00	3.50	3.00
685	82¢ Sport & the Environment souvenir sheet	2.50	....	....	3.50	3.50

686

688

| 686-87 | 32¢-60¢ A Plea for Peace........................ | 2.50 | 9.00 | 9.75 | 2.25 | 2.00 |
| 688-89 | 32¢-60¢ UNICEF 50th Anniversary .... | 2.50 | 9.00 | 24.00 | 2.40 | 2.25 |

1997 World Flags

690	Tadjikistan	694	Liechtenstein
691	Georgia	695	South Korea
692	Armenia	696	Kazakhstan
693	Namibia	697	Latvia

698

1997

SCOTT NO.	DESCRIPTION	SING	INSC. BLK	BLK-4	F/NH	F
690/717	1997 Issues (27) (No. #708, 708A)........	....	....	26.00	....	....
690-97	1997 World Flags, 8 varieties..................	12.50	....	41.00	11.00	10.00
698-99	8¢-55¢ Flowers, UN headquarters	2.25	8.00	8.00	1.85	1.50

700-03

704-07

700-03	32¢ Endangered Species, 4 attached	3.00	4.25	4.00	3.30	3.10
704-07	32¢ Earth Summit +5, 4 attached............	3.00	4.25	6.50	5.25	5.00
708	$1 Earth Summit +5, souvenir sheet.......	2.50	....	....	4.75	4.50
708a	$1 1997 Pacific '97 overprint on #708.....	15.00	....	....	23.00	23.00

709-13

| 709-13 | 32¢ Transporation, strip of 5................... | 3.75 | 5.00 | 11.00(10) | 5.00 | 5.00 |

714

716

714-15	32¢-50¢ Tribute to Philately....................	2.50	9.00	18.00	4.50	4.25
716-17	32¢-60¢ Terracota Warriors....................	2.50	9.00	11.50	2.75	2.50
718	same, Souvenir bklt of 6 panes of 4........	....	....	....	13.00	....

1998 World Flags

719	Micronesia
720	Slovakia
721	Dem. People's Rep. of Korea
722	Azerbaijan
723	Uzbekistan
724	Monaco
725	Czeh Republic
726	Estonia

730-33

1998

719-26	1998 World Flags, 8 varieties..................	12.50	....	33.00	8.75	8.00
727-29	1¢-21¢ Definitives...................................	4.50	10.00	4.50	1.00	.95
730-33	32¢ Endangered Species, 4 attached	3.00	4.25	4.50	3.75	3.00

UNITED NATIONS (NEW YORK)

SCOTT NO.	DESCRIPTION	FIRST DAY COVERS SING	INSC. BLK	INSRIP BLK-4	UNUSED F/NH	USED F

734a

734	32¢ Intl. Year of the Ocean, sheetlet of 12	15.00	....	....	15.00	....
735	32¢ Rain Forest, Jaguar...........................	1.75	4.25	4.00	.85	.75
736	$2 Rain Forest, Jaguar, souvenir sheet...	7.00	....	....	5.00	4.75
737-38	32¢-40¢ 50 Year of Peacekeeping..........	3.75	9.00	8.50	1.85	1.75
739-40	32¢-50¢ 50th of the Dec. of Human Rights	4.00	9.50	9.00	2.25	2.00
741-42	32¢-60¢ Schonbrunn Castle....................	4.25	10.00	11.00	2.40	2.25
743	same, souvenir bklt of 6 panes................	....	....	....	23.00	....

1999 World Flags

744	Lithuania	748	Moldova
745	San Marino	749	Kyrgyzstan
746	Turkmenistan	750	Bosnia & Herzegovia
747	Marshall Islands	751	Eritrea

754

1999

744-51	1999 World Flags, 8 varieties..................	12.50	....	36.00	9.50	9.00
752-53	33¢-$5 Definitives.....................................	12.00	30.00	58.00	13.00	12.00
754-55	33¢-60¢ World Heritage Sites, Australia .	4.25	10.00	12.00	2.50	2.40
756	same, souvenir bklt of 6 panes................	....	....	....	18.00	....

757-60

| 757-60 | 33¢ Endangered Species, 4 attached ..... | 3.00 | 4.25 | 4.00 | 3.50 | 3.25 |

761-62

764-67

761-62	33¢ Unispace III Conference...................	1.75	4.25	6.50	2.40	2.25
763	$2 Unispace III Conference, souvenir sheet	7.00	....	....	5.50	5.00
764-67	33¢ Universal Postal Union.....................	1.75	4.25	4.75	3.75	3.50

770-71

768	33¢ In Memorium	1.75	4.25	7.50	1.65	1.50
769	$1 In Memorium, souvenir sheet.............	3.25	....	....	2.75	2.75
770-71	33¢-60¢ Education-Keystone to the 21st Century..	4.25	10.00	11.00	2.40	2.40

772

773-76

2000

| 772 | 33¢ International Year of Thanksgiving ... | 1.75 | 4.25 | 4.25 | 1.00 | .85 |
| 773-76 | 33¢ Endangered Species, 4 attached ..... | 3.00 | 4.25 | 4.25 | 3.50 | 3.00 |

777

787

782

777-78	33¢-60¢ Our World 2000........................	4.25	10.00	11.00	2.50	2.25
779-80	33¢-55¢ 55th Anniversary of the UN	4.25	10.00	11.00	2.25	2.00
781	same, 33¢-55¢ souvenir sheet................	....	....	....	3.75	3.50
782	33¢ International Flag of Peace	1.75	4.25	4.00	.90	.90
783	33¢ United Nations in the 21st Century, sheet of 6.....	5.00	4.25	11.00	11.00	11.00
784-85	33¢-60¢ World Heritage Sites, Spain	4.25	10.00	14.00	3.00	3.00
786	same, souvenir bklt of 6 panes of 4........	....	....	....	13.00	....
787	33¢ Respect for Refuges.......................	1.75	4.25	4.50	.95	.95
788	$1 Respect for Refuges, souvenir sheet ..	3.25	....	....	3.50	3.50

793

789-92

2001

789-92	34¢ Endangered Species, 4 attached	3.00	4.25	4.00	3.50	3.00
793-94	34¢-80¢ Intl. Volunteers Year	4.50	10.00	12.00	2.75	2.50
795-802	2001 World Flags, 8 varieties..................	12.50	....	40.00	11.00	9.00
803-04	7¢-34¢ Definitives..................................	3.50	8.50	5.00	1.00	1.00
805-06	34¢-70¢ World Heritage Sites, Japan	4.50	10.00	11.00	2.50	2.40
807	same, souvenir bklt of 6 panes of 4........	....	....	....	16.00	....

808

816

809

808	80¢ Dag Hammarskjold.........................	2.50	4.00	9.25	1.95	1.85
809-10	34¢-80¢ 50th Anniv. of the UNPA...........	4.50	10.00	14.00	3.00	3.00
811	same, $2.40 souvenir sheet	6.50	....	....	8.00	8.00
812-15	34¢ Climate Change, strip of 4................	3.00	4.25	11.00	5.00	5.00
816	34¢ Nobel Peace Prize...........................	1.75	4.25	4.75	1.40	1.00

UNITED NATIONS (NEW YORK)

SCOTT NO.	DESCRIPTION	FIRST DAY COVERS SING	INSC. BLK	INSRIP BLK-4	UNUSED F/NH	USED F

817

822

2002

817	80¢ Children and Stamps	2.50	4.00	8.50	1.95	1.75
818-21	34¢ Endangered Species, 4 attached	3.00	4.25	4.00	3.50	3.50
822-23	34¢-57¢ Independence of East Timor	4.00	9.00	10.50	2.25	2.25
824-27	34¢-80¢ Intl. Year of Mountains, 2 pairs	5.00	11.00	7.00	9.00	8.50
828-31	37¢-60¢ Johannesburg Summit, 2 pairs	4.50	10.00	....	9.00	9.00

832

837

832-33	34¢-80¢ World Heritage Sites, Italy	4.50	10.00	14.50	3.75	3.50
834	same, souvenir bklt of 6 panes of 4	....	....	....	15.00	....
835	70¢ UNAIDS Awareness, semi postal	2.25	3.75	8.00	1.75	1.65

2003

836	37¢ Indigenous Art, sheet of 6	7.00	....	....	8.00	8.00
837-39	23¢-70¢ Definitives	3.50	4.50	14.00	3.50	3.50
840-41	23¢-70¢ Centenary of First Flight, 2 attach.	3.00	4.00	6.00	3.25	3.00

842-45

842-45	37¢ Endangered Species, 4 attached	3.50	4.50	4.50	3.75	3.50
846-47	23¢-37¢ Intl. Year of Freshwater, 2 attach.	2.25	3.75	6.00	2.25	2.25
848	37¢ Ralph Bunche	1.75	4.50	4.50	1.00	1.00
849	60¢ In Memoriam, UN Complex Bombing in Iraq	2.25	4.50	7.50	2.00	1.40
850-51	37¢-80¢ World Heritage Sites, United States	4.25	9.50	14.00	3.00	2.75
852	same, souvenir bklt of 6 panes of 4	....	....	....	12.00	....
853-57	37¢ UN Headquarters + labels, vert strip of 5	....	....	....	26.00	....
....	same, sheet of 4 (853-57)	....	....	....	100.00	....

863

865

2004

859-61	37¢ Endangered Species, 4 attached	4.00	6.00	4.75	4.00	3.75
862	37¢ Indigenous Art, sheet of 6	7.50	....	....	7.00	7.00
863-64	37¢-70¢ Road Safety	4.50	10.00	11.00	2.75	2.50
865	80¢ Japanese Peace Bell, 50th Anniv.	2.50	5.00	9.00	2.00	1.85

866

866-67	37¢-60¢ World Heritage Sites, Greece	4.25	9.50	11.00	2.50	2.25
868	same, souvenir bklt. of 6 panes of 4	....	....	....	19.00	....
869-70	37¢-80¢ My Dream for Peace	4.50	10.00	13.00	3.75	2.85
871-72	37¢-70¢ Human Rights	4.50	10.00	19.50(8)	2.75	2.50
873	37¢ Disarmament	1.75	4.50	4.25	.95	.95

874

876-79

2005

874	80¢ U.N. 60th Anniversary	2.50	5.00	9.00	2.00	2.00
875	$1 U.N. 60th Anniv., souvenir sheet	3.25	....	....	22.50	18.00
876-79	37¢ Orchids, 4 attached	4.00	6.00	4.75	3.75	3.75
880-84	80¢ Sculptures-personalized stamps, 5 attached	25.00	50.00	275.00	135.00	135.00
885-86	37¢ Nature's Wisdom	4.50	10.00	14.00	3.00	3.00
887-88	37¢-70¢ International Year of Sports	4.50	10.00	13.00	2.75	2.75
889-90	37¢-80¢ World Heritage Sites, Egypt	4.50	10.00	14.00	3.00	2.90
891	same, souvenir bklt. of 6 panes of 4	....	....	....	19.00	....
892-93	37¢-80¢ My Dream for Peace type of 2004	4.50	10.00	14.00	3.00	2.75
894-95	37¢-80¢ Food for Life	4.50	10.00	14.00	3.50	2.75

896

898

2006

896	25¢ Stylized Flags in Heart and Hands	1.75	4.25	3.00	.70	.65
897	37¢ Indigenous Art, sheet of 6	7.50	....	....	7.00	7.00
898-902	39¢ UN Headquarters + labels, strip of 5	7.00	....	....	11.00	....
....	same, sheet of 4	....	....	....	47.00	....

903

908-11

903-07	84¢ Sculptures + label, strip of 5	11.00	....	....	22.00	22.00
....	same, sheet of 2	....	....	....	35.00	....
908-11	39¢ Endangered Species, 4 attached	5.00	10.00	4.75	4.25	4.25

913

918

912	75¢ Peace personalized stamp	2.25	....	18.00	3.50	3.50
913-914	39¢-84¢ Day of Families	4.50	10.00	15.00	3.25	3.00
915-16	39¢-84¢ World Heritage Sites, France	4.50	10.00	15.00	3.25	3.00
917	same, bklt of 6 panes of 4	....	....	....	19.00	....
918-19	39¢-84¢ My Dream of Peace One Day	4.50	10.00	15.00	3.00	3.00
920	39¢ Flags and Coins, sheet of 8	10.00	....	....	9.00	9.00

UNITED NATIONS (NEW YORK)

SCOTT NO.	DESCRIPTION	FIRST DAY COVERS SING	INSC. BLK	INSRIP BLK-4	UNUSED F/NH	USED F

925-28

2007

921-24	39¢ Flags, 4 varieties	5.00	10.00	19.00	5.00	5.00
925-28	39¢ Endangered Species, 4 attached	5.00	10.00	5.50	4.50	4.50
929	84¢ UN Emblem + label	....	....	105.00	27.00	22.00
....	same, sheet of 10 + 10 labels	....	....	....	160.00	
930	39¢ Flags and Coins, sheet of 8..............	10.00	....	....	8.50	8.50
931	84¢ UN Emblem + label	....	....	19.00	3.50	3.00
....	same, sheet of 10 + 10 labels	....	....	....	60.00	
932-33	39¢-84¢ Peaceful Vision	4.50	10.00	13.00	3.25	3.25
934-38	UN symbols personalized stamps, strip of 5 attached....................................	....	....	....	11.00	....
	same sheet of 4....................................	....	....	....	42.00	....
939	90¢ UN Flag & Label..............................	....	....	25.00	5.50	....
	same sheet of 10...................................	....	....	....	48.00	....
940	90¢ UN Peacekeeping Helmet................	3.00	4.50	10.00	2.50	3.50
941-42	41¢-90¢ World Heritage Sites, South America	5.50	11.00	14.00	3.75	3.00
943	same, bklt panes of 6 panes of 4	....	....	....	23.00	
944	90¢ Universal Postal Union, joint issue with Swiss Post Humanitarian Mail	3.00	4.50	18.50	3.50	2.50
945-46	41¢-90¢ Space for Humanity.....................	5.50	11.00	19.00	4.00	3.00
947	$1 Space for Humanity souvenir sheet	3.25	....	....	3.50	3.50

948

2008

948	41¢ Holocaust Remeberance Day	2.00	....	4.50	1.00	1.00
	same, sheet of 9.....................................	....	....	....	9.00	....

949-52

949-52	41¢ Endangered Species........................	4.75	....	5.00	4.25	4.00
	same, sheet of 16....................................	....	....	....	18.00	....

961

953	41¢ Flags and Coins, sheet of 8..............	10.00	....	....	9.00	9.00
954-58	42¢ UN Personalized, strip of 5 w/labels	....	....	....	9.50	9.50
	same, sheet of 20...................................	....	....	....	38.00	75.00
959	94¢ UN Emblem + Label........................	3.50	....	....	4.00	4.00
960	42¢ Wheelchair Accessibility..................	3.50	....	4.00	1.25	1.25
961	94¢ "UN" In Braille................................	7.75	....	11.00	2.25	2.25

963

962	42¢ Sprinter...	3.50	....	5.00	1.25	1.25
963	94¢ Hurdler..	5.00	....	11.00	2.25	2.25
964	$1.25 Sprinter, souvenir sheet.................	5.75	....	....	3.25	3.25

965

967

965	94¢ Sport for Peace with label	7.75	....	4.00	4.00	
966	42¢ Children's Art, "We Can End Poverty"	3.00	....	5.00	1.25	1.25
967	94¢ Children's Art, "We Can End Poverty"	3.75	....	10.00	2.25	2.25
968	42¢ Climate Change, sheet of 4..............	4.75	....	....	5.00	5.00
968a	42¢ Climate Change, bklt pane of 4........	4.75	....	....	5.00	5.00
969	94¢ Climate Change, sheet of 4..............	10.00	....	....	10.00	10.00
970	Climate Change, souvenir booklet	....	....	....	21.00	....

2009

971-73	1¢-10¢ Flowers, set of 3..........................	3.50	....	3.50	.75	.75
974	94¢ U Thant...	3.50	....	11.00	3.00	3.00
975-78	42¢ Endangered Species, block of 4.......	7.75	....	5.00	4.50	4.50

985

990

979-80	44¢-98¢ World Heritage Sites, Germany	5.50	....	16.00	3.75	3.75
981	World Heritage Sites, souvenir booklet ...	....	....	....	22.00	
982-86	44¢ Personalized Stamps, vert. strip of 5 with labels...	....	....	....	8.50	8.50
	same, full sheet	....	....	....	35.00	....
987-91	98¢ Personalized Stamps, vert. strip of 5 with labels...	....	....	....	22.00	22.00
	same, full sheet	....	....	....	43.00	....
992-93	44¢-98¢ Economic & Social Council	4.75	....	16.00	4.00	4.00

994

995d

994	98¢ UN Emblem with label......................	....	....	....	4.50	....
	same, sheet..	....	....	....	48.00	....
995	44¢ Millennium Development Goals, sheet of 8..	10.00	....	....	9.00	9.00
996	$1 Mohandas K. Gandhi.........................	3.95	....	12.00	2.50	2.50
997	44¢ Indigenous People, sheet of 6...........	....	....	....	7.00	7.00

2010

998	44¢ Flags & Coins, sheet of 8	10.00	....	....	9.00	9.00

998a *Bahamas*		**998d** *Kuwait*		**998g** *St. Lucia*
998b *Jamaica*		**998e** *Panama*		**998h** *Yemen*
998c *Honduras*		**998f** *Guatemala*		

999-1002	44¢ Endangered Species........................	5.00	10.00	5.50	4.50	4.50

UNITED NATIONS (NEW YORK)

SCOTT NO.	DESCRIPTION	FIRST DAY COVERS SING	INSC. BLK	INSRIP BLK-4	UNUSED F/NH	USED F

1004b

1008

1003	44¢ One Planet, One Ocean, sheet of 4.				4.25	4.25
1004	98¢ One Planet, One Ocean, sheet of 4.				8.75	8.75
1005	One Planet, One Ocean, souvenir booklet				21.00	
1006-07	3¢-4¢ People of Different Cultures	3.75		2.00	.75	.50
1008-09	98¢ Expo 2010 Shanghi	6.50			7.25	7.25
1009a	Pane of 5, Expo 2010 Shanhi			42.00		
1010	98¢ UN 65th Anniversary	3.75		11.00	2.50	2.50
1011	UN 65th Anniversary S/S	6.25			5.00	5.00

1012-16

1019e

1012-16	44¢ UN Transport	3.25		12.00	5.50	5.50
1017-18	15¢ - $1.50 Int. Year of Biodiversity	7.75		19.00	4.00	4.00
1019	44¢ Indigenous People, sheet of 6	8.75			7.00	7.00
1020-21	11¢-$5 UN Headquarters	14.00		49.00	12.00	11.00
1022	44¢ Flags & Coins, sheet of 8	10.00			9.00	9.00
1023	98¢ UN Emblem Plus Label				3.50	
	Same, sheet of 10 + labels				32.50	
1024	44¢ 50th Anniversary of Human Space Flight, sheet of 16	19.00			15.50	
1025	Human Space Flight S/S sheet of 2	4.75			3.75	
1026-27	44¢-98¢ World Heritage Sites in Nordic Countries	6.00		13.50	4.00	
	same, 2 panes of 20				62.00	
1028	44¢ AIDS ribbon	3.75			1.20	
	same, pane of 4				3.75	
1029-30	44¢-98¢ Economic & Social Council	5.95		12.50	3.25	

1027

1031

1031-34	44¢ Endangered Species	5.95		4.75	4.00	4.00
1035-36	44¢-98¢ International Year of Forests	4.50		8.00	3.25	3.25
1037	$1.05 UN Emblem and Label				3.50	3.50
1038	Personalized sheet of 10 with labels				34.00	
1039	45¢ Flags & Coins, sheet of 8	12.50			8.00	
1040-41	$1.05 Autism Awareness	5.95		11.00	5.00	5.00

2012

1042-45	45¢ Endangered Species	5.75		5.00	4.00	3.75
1046-47	$1.05 Conservation with labels, vertical pair				6.75	6.75
	same, sheet of 10 with labels				32.50	
1048	$1.05 Conference on Stable Development	4.50		8.75	2.50	2.50
1049-50	45¢-$1.05 Sport for Peace			13.50	3.25	3.25
1050a	Sport for Peace, Souvenir Sheet				2.50	2.50
1051-52	42¢-$1.05 UNESCO World Heritage sites in Africa	4.75		13.00	3.25	3.25
1053	45¢ Indigenous People, sheet of 6	9.00			6.25	6.25

2013

1054	$1.10 UN Emblem and Label				3.00	3.00
1055	$1.10 Sheet of 10				32.50	
1056-57	46¢-$1.10 World Radio Day	5.75		14.00	3.50	3.50
1058-59	$1.10-$3.00 Circle of People and United Nations Headquarters	12.00		35.00	9.00	9.00

1058

1061

1060-61	46¢-$1.10 World Heritage Sites, China	5.00		13.50	3.50	
1062	World Heritage Sites, China, Souvenir Booklet				22.00	
1063-66	$1.10 Flags, pane of 16	36.00		10.00	9.50	9.50

1067a

1068-1069

1067	46¢ World Ocean's Day sheet of 12	15.00			15.00	
1068-69	$1.10 Nebulae	6.75		9.75	5.00	4.75
1070	46¢ Nebulae Souvenir sheet of 1	2.75			1.25	1.25
1071	$1.10 World Humanitarian Day sheet of 10				32.00	32.00
1072-73	46¢-$1.10 Works of Disable Artists	4.75		13.50	3.50	3.50
1074-77	$1.10 endangered Species	12.00		11.00	9.50	9.50
1078	46¢ Flags & Coins sheet of 8	12.00			8.50	8.50

2014

| 1079 | $1.15 UN emblem & label | 3.75 | | | 3.75 | 3.75 |
| 1080 | $1.15 Personalized sheet of 10 with labels | | | | 33.00 | 33.00 |

1082

1083

1081-82	47¢-$1.15 Int. Day of Happiness	4.50		15.00	4.25	4.25
1083-86	$1.15 Flags set of 4	12.00			11.50	11.50
1087	49¢ International Year of Jazz, Sheet of 12	16.00			13.50	15.00
1088-89	33¢ - $2 Definitives	7.00		20.00	5.50	5.50
1090-91	49¢ - $1.15 Taj Majal	5.75		15.00	4.25	4.25
1092	Taj Majah Souvenir Booklet			22.50		
1093-94	49¢ - $1.15 International Year of Family Farming, Set of 2	4.50		15.00	4.25	4.25

1093

1097

1095	$1.15 Global Education First Initiative	4.25		10.50	2.75	2.75
1096	$1.50 Global Education First Initiative Souvenir Sheet	6.00			3.75	3.75
1097-1100	$1.15 Endangered Species, Block of 4	12.00		10.50	10.50	10.50
1101	$1.15 ASDA 100th Anniversary Personalized Sheet of 10				32.00	

1107

1114

2015

1102	$1.15 UN emblem & label			30.00 (10)	3.50	3.50
1103	49¢ Flags & Coins, sheet of 8	12.00			8.50	
1104-05	49¢ and $1.20 World Poetry Day, 2 sheets of 8	27.00			22.00	
1106-09	$1.20 Endangered Species, set of 4	16.00		10.50	10.25	
1110-11	35¢ - 40¢ Definitives	4.50		7.00	1.75	
1112	$1.20 Greetings from New York, sheet of 10				30.00	
1113-14	49¢ - $1.20 World Heritage Sites, Southeast Asia	5.75		14.00	3.75	

UNITED NATIONS;
OFFICES IN GENEVA, SWITZERLAND
Denominations in Swiss Currency

NOTE: Unless illustrated, designs can be assumed to be similar to the equivalent New York or Vienna issues

SCOTT NO.	DESCRIPTION	FIRST DAY COVERS SING	FIRST DAY COVERS INSC. BLK	INSRIP BLK-4	UNUSED F/NH	USED F
	1969-70					
1-14	5¢ to 10fr Definitives	45.00	110.00	85.00	18.00	12.00
	1971					
15-21	**1971 Issues, complete (7)**	......	......	......	4.25	......
15	30¢ Peaceful Uses Sea Bed	.95	2.40	1.40	.30	.30
16	50¢ Support for Refugees	1.10	2.75	2.40	.55	.40
17	50¢ World Food Programme	1.40	3.50	2.65	.55	.45
18	75¢ U.P.U. Building	2.75	6.85	4.25	.90	.80
19-20	30¢ & 50¢ Anti-Discrimination	2.25	5.65	4.25	.90	.60
21	1.10fr International School	3.65	9.00	6.25	1.35	1.15
	1972					
22-29	**1972 Issues, complete (8)**	......	......	......	5.95	......
22	40¢ Definitive	1.10	2.75	1.90	.40	.35
23	40¢ Non Proliferation	2.15	5.40	3.50	.75	.75
24	80¢ World Health Day	2.15	5.40	3.75	.85	.85
25-26	40¢ & 80¢ Environment	3.75	9.50	7.00	1.75	1.40
27	1.10fr Economic Committee Europe	3.25	8.15	7.00	1.60	1.35
28-29	40¢ & 80¢ Art—Sert Ceiling	3.50	8.75	7.00	1.70	1.00
	1973					
30-36	**1973 Issues, complete (6)**	......	......	......	5.50	......
30-31	60¢ & 1.10fr Disarmament Decade	3.50	8.75	8.00	2.00	1.50
32	60¢ Drug Abuse	2.00	5.00	3.25	.70	.65
33	80¢ Volunteer	2.50	6.25	4.00	.95	.75
34	60¢ Namibia	2.05	5.15	3.00	.75	.75
35-36	40¢ & 80¢ Human Rights	2.65	6.65	6.50	1.40	1.00
	1974					
37-45	**1974 Issues, complete (9)**	......	......	......	7.15	......
37-38	60¢ & 80¢ ILO Headquarters	2.75	6.85	7.50	1.50	1.25
39-40	30¢ & 60¢ U.P.U. Centenary	2.25	5.65	6.00	1.25	1.00
41-42	60¢ & 1fr Brazil Peace Mural	3.00	7.50	8.50	1.75	1.45
43-44	60¢ & 80¢ World Population Year	2.50	6.25	8.00	1.70	1.85
45	1.30fr Law of the Sea	2.25	5.65	7.00	1.50	1.15
	1975					
46-56	**1975 Issues, (10) (No #52)**	......	......	......	9.25	......
46-47	60¢ & 90¢ Peaceful Use of Space	2.40	6.00	8.75	1.90	1.40
48-49	60¢ & 90¢ International Women's Year	2.75	6.85	8.00	1.75	1.40
50-51	60¢ & 90¢ 30th Anniversary	2.25	5.65	8.00	1.75	1.25
52	same, souvenir sheet	2.50	......	......	1.75	1.40
53-54	50¢ & 1.30fr Namibia	2.50	6.25	8.00	2.00	1.40
55-56	60¢ & 70¢ Peacekeeping	2.10	5.25	7.00	1.50	1.25
	1976					
57-63	**1976 Issues, (7)**	......	......	......	8.95	......
57	90¢ World Federation	1.80	4.50	5.75	1.25	1.20
58	1.10fr Conference T.& D.	2.10	5.25	6.00	1.25	1.20
59-60	40¢ & 1.50fr Human Settlement	3.00	7.50	9.00	2.00	1.50
61-62	80¢ & 1.10fr Postal Administration	12.00	29.50	14.00	5.00	4.50
63	70¢ World Food Council	1.40	3.50	4.00	.85	.65

SCOTT NO.	DESCRIPTION	FIRST DAY COVERS SING	FIRST DAY COVERS INSC. BLK	INSRIP BLK-4	UNUSED F/NH	USED F
	1977					
64-72	**1977 Issues, complete (9)**	......	......	......	7.50	......
64	80¢ WIPO	1.40	3.50	4.00	.90	.70
65-66	80¢ & 1.10fr Water Conference	3.00	7.50	9.00	2.00	1.45
67-68	80¢ & 1.10fr Security Council	3.00	7.50	9.00	2.00	1.45
69-70	40¢ & 1.10fr Combat Racism	2.50	6.25	7.00	1.75	1.40
71-72	80¢ & 1.10fr Atomic Energy	3.00	7.50	9.00	2.00	1.45
	1978					
73-81	**1978 Issues, complete (9)**	......	......	30.95	7.20	......
73	35¢ Definitive	.95	2.40	2.20	.45	.40
74-75	80¢ & 1.10fr Smallpox Eradication	2.95	7.50	10.75	2.00	1.70
76	80¢ Namibia	1.50	3.75	5.00	1.25	1.00
77-78	70¢ & 80¢ ICAO	2.25	5.65	8.00	1.65	1.25
79-80	70¢ & 1.10fr General Assembly	3.00	7.50	9.00	2.00	1.65
81	80¢ TCDC	1.40	3.50	4.25	.95	.90
	1979					
82-88	**1979 Issues, complete (7)**	......	......	......	7.50	......
82-83	80¢ & 1.50fr UNDRO	3.10	7.75	10.00	2.75	1.95
84-85	80¢ & 1.10fr I.Y.C.	4.75	11.85	7.00	2.00	1.40
86	1.10fr Namibia	1.90	4.75	5.00	1.25	.95
87-88	80¢ & 1.10fr Court of Justice	3.00	7.50	8.00	2.00	1.55
	1980					
89-97	**1980 Issues, (8) (No #95)**	......	......	......	5.40	......
89	80¢ Economics	1.50	4.75	5.25	1.15	1.15
90-91	40¢ & 70¢ Decade for Women	1.95	6.00	5.50	1.25	1.10
92	1.10fr Peacekeeping	1.85	6.00	5.25	1.25	1.00
93-94	40¢ & 70¢ 35th Anniversary	2.00	6.00	5.50	1.25	1.15
95	Same, Souvenir Sheet	2.75	......	......	1.40	1.25
96-97	40¢ & 70¢ Economic & Social Council	1.85	6.00	6.00	1.25	1.25
	1981					
98-104	**1981 Issues, complete (7)**	......	......	......	6.00	......
98	80¢ Palestinian People	1.70	4.25	4.00	1.00	.70
99-100	40¢ & 1.50fr Disabled People	2.75	6.85	9.00	2.00	1.70
101	80¢ Fresco	1.50	3.75	4.50	1.00	1.00
102	1.10fr Sources of Energy	1.50	3.75	5.00	1.25	1.00
103-04	40¢ & 70¢ Conservation	1.75	4.50	8.00	1.70	1.70
	1982					
105-12	**1982 Issues, complete (8)**	......	......	......	7.00	......
105-06	30¢ & 1fr Definitives	2.10	5.25	7.50	1.50	1.40
107-08	40¢ & 1.20fr Human Environment	2.40	6.00	9.00	1.85	1.70
109-10	80¢ & 1fr Space Exploration	2.65	6.65	9.50	2.00	1.70
111-12	40¢ & 1.50fr Conservation	2.75	6.95	10.00	2.25	1.75

SCOTT NO.	DESCRIPTION	FIRST DAY COVERS SING	INSC. BLK	INSRIP BLK-4	UNUSED F/NH	USED F
		1983				
113-20	1983 Issues, complete (8)	......	......	......	8.35	......
113	1.20fr World Communications	1.75	4.40	7.25	1.55	1.35
114-15	40¢ & 80¢ Safety at Sea	1.75	4.40	7.25	1.55	1.45
116	1.50fr World Food Program	2.25	5.65	8.50	1.70	1.45
117-18	80¢ & 1.10fr Trade & Development.......	2.75	6.95	9.75	1.95	1.70
119-20	40¢ & 1.20fr Human Rights....................	3.50	8.75	9.00	2.05	1.80
		1984				
121-28	1984 Issues, complete (8)	......	......	......	9.20	......
121	1. 20fr Population	1.75	4.50	7.00	1.50	1.25
122-23	50¢ & 80¢ Food Day	1.75	4.50	7.00	1.75	1.25
124-25	50¢ & 70¢ Heritage	1.75	4.50	8.00	2.25	1.25
126-27	35¢ & 1.50fr Future for Refugees...........	2.75	6.95	9.00	2.25	1.75
128	1.20fr Youth Year.................................	1.75	4.50	8.00	1.95	1.25
		1985				
129/39	1985 Issues, (10) (No #137)	......	......	......	11.50	......
129-30	80¢-1.20fr Turin Centre	2.75	6.95	9.00	2.25	1.75
131-32	50¢-80¢ U.N. University	2.00	5.00	8.00	1.95	1.50
133-34	20¢-1.20fr Definitives	2.25	5.65	9.00	2.00	1.60
135-36	50¢-70¢ 40th Anniversary	2.00	5.80	8.00	1.95	1.60
137	same, souvenir sheet	2.75	......	......	2.50	2.50
138-39	50¢-1.20fr Child Survival.........................	5.75	14.50	10.00	2.00	2.50
		1986				
140-49	1986 Issues (10)...................................	......	......	......	17.25	......
140	1.40fr Africa in Crisis	2.00	5.00	8.00	2.50	1.40
141-44	35¢ Development, 4 varieties, attached ..	2.00	2.75	12.00	10.50	9.50
145	5¢ Definitive	1.10	2.75	1.00	.25	.25
146-47	50¢ & 80¢ Philately	1.85	4.65	9.50	2.00	1.80
148-49	45¢ & 1.40fr Peace Year	2.75	6.95	12.50	3.00	2.25
150	35¢-70¢ WFUNA, souvenir sheet...........	2.75	......	......	5.50	4.00
		1987				
151-61	1987 Issues (11)	......	......	......	13.00	......
151	1.40fr Trygve Lie..................................	2.00	5.00	8.00	2.00	1.75
152-53	90¢-1.40fr Definitive..............................	3.50	8.75	11.00	2.50	1.75
154-55	50¢-90¢ Shelter Homeless.....................	2.00	5.00	9.50	1.95	1.75
156-57	80¢-1.20fr Anti-Drug Campaign..............	2.75	6.95	11.00	2.50	1.75
158-59	35¢-50¢ United Nations Day	3.50	8.75	8.50	1.50	1.45
160-61	90¢-1.70fr Child Immunization	1.85	4.65	20.00	4.25	4.00

120

122 123 124

125 126 127 128 145

130 133 134 148

149 152 153 164 178

183 184 185 179

201 202 203 204 213

205 206 255 256

SCOTT NO.	DESCRIPTION	FIRST DAY COVERS SING	INSC. BLK	INSRIP BLK-4	UNUSED F/NH	USED F
		1988				
162/172	1988 Issues, (8) (No #165-66, 172)	......	......	......	9.00	......
162-63	35¢-1.40fr World without Hunger	2.50	6.25	11.00	2.75	2.00
164	50¢ For a Better World	1.25	3.15	4.00	.85	.85
				Sheetlets (12)		
165-66	50¢-1.10fr Forest Conservation..............	15.00	40.00	14.00	8.00	7.50
	(set of 6, includes NY and Vienna).........			130.00	27.50	25.00
167-68	80¢-90¢ Volunteer Day..........................	2.50	6.25	10.00	2.40	2.25
169-70	50¢-1.40fr Health in Sports	2.75	6.95	11.00	2.25	2.00
171	90¢ Human Rights 40th Anniversary	2.00	5.00	6.00	1.25	1.00
172	2fr Human Rights 40th Anniversary souvenir sheet......................................	2.75	....	....	3.25	3.00
		1989				
173-81	1989 Issues (9).....................................	......	......	......	19.50	......
173-74	80¢ & 1.40fr. World Bank	2.75	6.95	17.00	4.00	3.25
175	90¢ Nobel Peace Prize	1.50	3.75	8.00	1.40	1.10
176-77	90¢ & 1.10fr World Weather Watch........	2.75	6.95	19.25	5.25	5.25
178-79	50¢ & 2fr UN Offices in Vienna	4.00	10.00	24.50	5.25	5.25
				Sheetlets (12)		
180-81	35¢ & 80¢ Human Rights 40th Ann. .... (strips of 3 w/tabs)	1.85	4.65	24.00	7.00	....
		1990				
182/94	1990 Issues, No #190 (12)	......	......	......	33.50	......
182	1.50fr International Trade	2.15	5.40	14.00	3.00	2.75
183	5fr Definitive	7.75	19.50	25.00	6.00	5.25
184-85	50¢ & 80¢ SIDA (AIDS)..........................	2.15	5.50	15.50	3.25	3.25
186-87	90¢ & 1.40fr Medicinal Plants................	3.60	9.00	17.00	3.50	3.50
188-89	90¢ & 1.10fr Anniversary of U.N............	3.00	7.50	19.00	4.00	4.00
190	same, souvenir sheet	3.00	....	....	7.00	7.00
191-92	50¢ & 2fr Crime Prevention	4.15	10.50	22.00	4.50	4.50
193-94	35¢ & 90¢ Human Rights .... (strips of 3 w/tabs)	1.95	4.95	30.00	7.50	....
		1991				
195-210	1991 Issues (17)...................................	......	......	......	31.00	......
195-98	90¢ Econ. Comm. for Europe, 4 varieties, attached	5.75	6.75	7.75	6.75	6.75
199-200	70¢ & 90¢ Namibia—A New Nation	3.85	9.60	19.50	4.25	4.25
201-02	80¢ & 1.50fr Definitives	5.00	12.50	19.50	4.25	4.25
203-04	80¢ & 1.10fr Children's Rights................	4.50	11.25	19.50	4.25	4.25
205-06	80¢ & 1.40fr Banning of Chemical Weapons..	5.00	12.50	29.00	7.00	7.00
207-08	50¢ & 1.60fr 40th Anniv. of the UNPA.....	4.75	11.95	19.50	4.25	4.25
				Sheetlets (12)		
209-10	50¢ & 90¢ Human Rights (strips of 3 w/tabs)................................	2.75	7.50	38.00	9.50	....
		1992				
211-25	1992 Issues (15)...................................	......	......	......	38.00	......
211-12	50¢-1.10fr. World Heritage—UNESCO ...	3.60	9.00	19.00	4.25	4.25
213	3fr Definitive	6.00	15.00	19.00	4.75	4.75
214-15	80¢ Clean Oceans, 2 varieties, attached	2.75	5.35	7.50	2.50	2.50
216-19	75¢ Earth Summit, 4 varieties, attached .	4.00	4.95	9.00	7.00	7.00
220-21	1.10fr Mission to Planet Earth, 2 varieties, attached	4.00	6.95	13.00	5.75	5.75
222-23	90¢-1.60fr Science and Technology........	4.75	11.75	25.00	6.00	6.00
224-25	50¢-90¢ Human Rights (strips of 3 w/tabs)	2.75	6.50	38.00	9.50	
		1993				
226-43	1993 Issues (18)...................................	......	......	......	36.00	......
226-27	50¢-1.60fr Aging	3.60	9.00	19.00	4.00	3.75
228-31	80¢ Endangered Species, 4 attached	4.00	5.00	6.50	5.25	5.25
232-33	60¢-1fr Healthy Environment..................	3.00	8.00	19.00	4.25	4.25
234-35	50¢-90¢ Human Rights (strips of 3 w/tabs)................................	3.00	7.00	38.00	9.50	....
236-39	60¢ Peace, 4 attached	3.50	4.50	11.00	9.50	7.50
240-43	1.10fr Environment—Climate, strip of 4 ..	3.50	8.00	20.00(8)	9.75	9.75

279

277

294

280-83

284-88

1994

SCOTT NO.	DESCRIPTION	FIRST DAY COVERS SING	INSC. BLK	INSRIP BLK-4	UNUSED F/NH	USED F
244-61	1994 Issues (18)................................	....	....	.... 33.50		....
244-45	80¢-1fr Intl. Year of the Family	3.50	12.50	17.50	3.75	3.75
246-49	80¢ Endangered Species, 4 attached	4.50	5.00	7.00	5.75	5.75
250	1.20fr Refugees....................................	2.50	9.25	16.00	3.50	4.85
251-54	60¢ Intl. Decade for Natural Disaster Reduction, 4 attached	3.50	4.25	10.00	9.00	8.00
255-57	60¢-1.80fr Definitives (3)	5.00	17.50	26.00	5.50	5.50
258-59	60¢-80¢ Population and Development....	4.00	10.00	16.00	4.00	3.50
260-61	80¢-1fr Development through Partnership	3.50	12.50	18.00	3.75	3.75

1995

262/75	1995 Issues (13) (No #272).................	....	....	.... 40.00		....
262	80¢ 50th Anniversary of the UN	1.75	6.50	7.00	1.75	1.75
263	1fr Social Summit	2.25	7.50	9.00	2.00	2.00
264-67	80¢ Endangered Species, 4 attached	4.50	5.00	7.50	6.50	6.50
268-69	80¢-1fr Youth: Our Future.......................	3.50	12.50	24.00	5.25	5.25
270-71	60¢-1.80fr 50th Anniversary of the UN....	4.75	15.50	24.00	5.25	5.25
272	2.40fr 50th Anniversary of the UN, souvenir sheet......................................	4.50	....	....	6.00	6.00
273-74	60¢-1fr 4th Conference on Women	3.00	10.00	23.00	5.25	5.25
275	60¢ 50th Anniversary, min. sheet of 12 ..	....	....	....	21.00	....
276	same, souvenir booklet of 4 panes of 3...	....	....	....	23.00	....

1996

277/95	1996 Issues (18) (No #291).................	....	....	.... 31.00		....
277	80¢ WFUNA 50th Anniversary...............	1.75	6.50	8.00	1.75	1.75
278-79	40¢-70¢ Definitives.............................	2.75	10.00	10.00	2.25	2.25
280-83	80¢ Endangered Species, 4 attached	4.50	5.00	7.00	6.50	6.00
284-88	80¢ City Summit (Habitat II), strip of 5 ..	5.00	15.00	22.00	11.00	9.50
289-90	70¢-1.10fr Sport & the Environment.......	3.50	12.50	16.50	3.50	3.50
291	1.80fr Sport & the Environment souvenir sheet......................................	3.50	....	....	4.00	4.00
292-93	80¢-1fr A Plea for Peace	3.50	12.50	20.00	4.25	4.25
294-95	80¢-1fr UNICEF 50th Anniversary..........	3.50	12.50	13.50	4.25	4.25

302-05

312

296

314

1997

296/315	1997 Issues (19) (No.# 306)...................	....	....	.... 26.50		....
296-97	10¢-$1 10fr. Definitives.........................	2.75	10.00	11.75	2.75	2.00
298-301	80¢ Endangered Species, 4 attached	4.50	5.00	7.00	5.50	5.00
302-05	45¢ Earth Summit +5, 4 attached............	2.50	2.75	6.50	5.50	5.00
306	1.10Fr Earth Summit, souvenir sheet......	2.40	....	....	4.25	3.75
307-11	70¢ Transporation, strip of 5.................	5.50	13.50	16.00(10)	7.00	6.75
312-13	70¢-1.10Fr Tribute to Philately	3.50	12.50	18.50	4.00	3.50
314-15	45¢-70¢ Terracota Warriors....................	2.75	10.00	18.50	4.00	3.50
316	same, Souvenir bklt of 6 pane of 4..........	....	....	....	15.00	....

317

322a

318-21

1998

SCOTT NO.	DESCRIPTION	FIRST DAY COVERS SING	INSC. BLK	INSRIP BLK-4	UNUSED F/NH	USED F
	1998 Issues (12) (No #322, 321, 331)....	....	....	.... 24.50		....
317	2fr Definitive	4.00	9.00	15.50	3.25	3.25
318-21	80¢ Endangered Species, 4 attached	4.50	5.00	6.50	5.75	5.75
322	45¢ Intl. Year of the Ocean, sheetlet of 12	15.00	....	....	15.00	....
323	70¢ Rain Forests, Orangutans	2.00	4.50	6.00	1.50	1.50
324	3fr Rain Forests, Orangutans, souvenir sheet	7.00	....	....	6.00	6.00
325-26	70¢-90¢ 50 Years of Peacekeeping	4.00	9.00	14.00	3.25	3.25
327-28	90¢-1.80fr 50th of the Dec. of Human Rights	6.75	15.00	18.00	5.50	5.00
329-30	70¢-1.10fr Schonbrunn Castle	4.50	10.00	14.50	3.65	3.25
331	same, souvenir bklt of 6 panes..............	....	....	....	18.00	....

332

333

1999

	1999 Issues (16) (No #355, 342, 348)....	....	....	.... 25.50		....
332	1.70fr Denfinitive	4.00	9.00	13.00	3.25	2.75
333-34	90¢-1.10fr World Heritage Sites, Australia	4.50	10.00	15.00	3.85	3.25
335	same, souvenir bklt of 6 panes..............	....	....	....	13.00	....

336-39

347

336-39	90¢ Endangered Species, 4 attached	4.50	5.00	7.50	6.50	6.00
340-41	45¢ Unispace III Conference..................	1.95	4.00	6.00	2.50	2.50
342	2fr Unispace III Conference, souvenir sheet	6.00	....	....	5.50	5.50
343-46	70¢ Universal Postal Union....................	2.00	4.50	6.00	5.25	4.75
347	1.10fr In Memorium	2.40	5.00	8.50	2.00	2.00
348	2fr In Memoriam, souvenir sheet.............	3.75	....	....	3.75	3.75

349

351

349-50	70¢-1.80fr Education-Keystone to the 21st Century...	6.50	14.00	21.00	5.00	4.50

2000

351	90¢ International Year of Thanksgiving ...	1.95	4.00	7.25	1.65	1.65
352-55	90¢ Endangered Species, 4 attached	4.50	5.00	8.75	7.50	7.50
356-57	90¢-1.10fr Our World 2000.....................	4.50	10.00	16.00	3.85	3.50
358-59	90¢-1.40fr 55th Anniversary of the UN....	4.75	11.00	19.00	4.00	4.00
360	same, 90¢-1.40fr souvenir sheet............	....	....	....	5.00	4.50
361	50¢ United Nations in the 21st Century...	7.50	7.50	....	10.00	10.00
362-63	1fr-1.20fr World Hertitage Sites, Spain...	5.25	11.50	19.00	4.50	4.50
364	same, souvenir bklt of 6 panes..............	....	....	....	13.00	....
365	80¢ Respect for Regugees.....................	1.75	6.50	7.00	1.50	1.50
366	1.80fr Respect for Refugees, souvenir sheet	3.50	....	....	3.25	3.25

SCOTT NO.	DESCRIPTION	FIRST DAY COVERS SING	INSC. BLK	INSRIP BLK-4	UNUSED F/NH	USED F

371

384

2001

367-70	90¢ Endangered Species, 4 attached	4.50	5.00	7.25	6.25	6.25
371-72	90¢-1.10fr Intl. Volunteers Year	4.50	10.00	17.00	3.85	3.85
373-74	1.20fr-1.80fr World Hertiage Sites, Japan	6.00	12.50	22.00	5.50	5.00
375	same, souvenir bklt of 6 panes	....	....	....	14.00	....
376	2fr Dag Hammarskjold	3.50	7.50	15.50	3.50	3.50
377-78	90¢-1.30fr 50th Anniv. of UNPA	4.50	10.00	20.00	5.00	5.00
379	same, 3.50fr souvenir sheet	4.50	....	....	8.00	8.00
380-83	90¢ Climate Change, strip of 4	4.50	5.00	14.00	6.25	6.25
384	90¢ Nobel Peace Prize	1.95	4.00	7.00	1.65	1.65

385

400

2002

385	1.30fr Palais des Nations	2.75	6.00	10.00	2.50	2.35
386-89	90¢ Endangered Species, 4 attached	4.50	5.00	7.00	6.00	5.95
390-91	90¢-1.30fr Independence of East Timor ..	4.50	7.50	17.50	5.75	3.75
392-95	70¢-1.20fr Intl. Year of Mountains, 2 pairs	4.50	5.00	11.00	7.00	7.00
396-99	90¢-1.80fr Johannesburg Summit, 2 pairs	6.00	7.00	32.00	13.00	12.00
400-01	90¢-1.30fr World Heritage Sites, Italy	4.50	7.50	17.00	3.50	3.50
402	same, souvenir bklt of 6 panes of 4	....	....	....	32.00	....
403	1.30fr UNAIDS Awareness, semi postal ..	2.75	6.00	10.00	2.50	2.50
404	3fr Entry of Switzerland into United Nations	7.00	15.00	25.00	5.50	5.50
B1	90¢+30¢ UNAIDS Awareness, souvenir sheet	2.40	....	....	5.00	5.00

406

413

2003

405	90¢ Indigenous Art, sheet of 6	11.00	....	....	12.00	12.00
406	90¢ Interparliamentary Union	1.95	4.00	8.25	2.00	1.75
407-10	90¢ Endangered Species, 4 attached	4.50	5.00	9.00	7.50	7.00
411-12	70¢-1.30fr Intl. Year of Freshwater, 2 attached	4.25	9.50	14.00	4.00	4.00
413	1.80fr Ralph Bunche	3.75	9.50	16.00	3.50	3.50
414	85¢ In Memorium of Victims	4.50	5.00	9.00	1.75	1.75
415-16	90¢-1.30fr World Heritage Sites, United States	4.50	7.50	19.00	4.40	4.40
417	same, souvenir bklt of 6 panes of 4	....	....	....	13.00	....

429

433

2004

418-21	1fr Endangered Species, 4 attached	8.00	10.00	9.00	8.25	8.25
422	1fr Indigenous Art, sheet of 6	12.00	....	....	13.00	....
423-24	85¢-1fr Road Safety	4.25	8.00	18.00	4.00	3.80
425	1.30fr Japanese Peace Bell, 50th Anniv ..	3.00	7.75	12.00	2.75	2.50
426-27	1fr-1.30fr World Heritage Sites, Greece ..	4.50	7.50	22.00	5.00	4.50
428	same, souvenir bklt of 6 panes of 4	....	....	....	18.50	....
429-30	85¢-1.20fr My Dream for Peace	4.25	8.00	19.00	4.00	3.75
431-32	85¢-1.30fr Human Rights	5.00	9.00	35.00(8)	4.50	4.50
433	180¢ Sports	4.50	8.50	16.00	4.00	4.00

434

2005

440

434	1.30fr U.N. 60th Anniv.	3.00	7.75	12.00	3.00	3.00
435	3fr U.N. 60th Anniv., souvenir sheet	7.00	....	....	8.00	8.00
436-39	1fr Orchids, 4 attached	8.00	10.00	9.50	8.00	8.00
440-41	1fr-1.30fr Nature's Wisdom	4.50	7.50	22.00	5.00	4.50
442-43	1fr-1.30fr International Year of Sports	4.50	7.50	22.00	5.00	4.50

444

449

444-45	1fr-1.30fr World Heritage Sites, Egypt	4.50	7.50	24.00	5.50	5.00
446	same, souvenir bklt of 6 panes	....	....	....	18.50	....
447-48	1fr-1.30fr My Dream for Peace type of 2004	4.50	7.50	22.00	5.00	4.50
449-50	1fr-1.30fr Food for life	4.50	7.50	22.00	5.00	4.50

451

453-56

2006

451	1.30fr Armillary Sphere, Palais des Nations	3.50	6.50	12.00	2.75	2.60
452	1.20fr Indigenous Art, sheet of 6	15.00	....	....	15.00	15.00
453-56	1fr Endangered Species, 4 attached	8.00	10.00	9.75	8.50	8.00

457

462

457-58	1fr-1.30fr Day of Families	4.50	7.50	22.00	5.00	4.50
459-60	1fr-1.30fr World Heritage Sites, France	4.50	7.50	22.00	5.00	4.00
461	same, 20¢-50¢ souvenir bklt of 6 panes .	....	....	....	18.50	....
462-63	85¢-1.20fr My Dream of Peace One Day	4.25	8.00	20.00	4.50	4.50
464	85¢ Flags and Coins, sheet of 8	15.00	....	....	18.50	18.50

465-68

2007

465-68	1fr Endangered Species, 4 attached	8.00	10.00	10.00	8.50	8.00
469	85¢ Flags and Coins, sheet of 8	15.00	....	....	16.00	16.00
470-71	1.20fr-1.80fr Peaceful Visions	6.00	8.00	31.00	8.00	8.00
472-73	1fr-1.80fr World Heritage Series, South America	6.00	8.00	24.00	5.50	5.50
474	same, 20¢-50¢ souvenir bklt of 6 panes .	....	....	....	22.50	....
475	1.80fr Universal Postal Union, joint issue with Swiss Post Humanitarian Mail	4.00	7.00	11.00	4.00	4.00
476-77	1.00fr-1.80fr Space for Humanity	5.00	8.00	15.00	6.00	6.00
478	3fr Space for Humanity souvenir sheet ...	6.50	....	....	7.00	....

SCOTT NO.	DESCRIPTION	FIRST DAY COVERS SING	INSC. BLK	INSRIP BLK-4	UNUSED F/NH	USED F

479

480-83

2008

479	85¢ Holocaust Remembrance Day	2.75	....	10.00	2.50	2.50
	same, sheet of 9	....	....		19.00	
480-83	1fr Endangered Species block of 4	9.00	....	10.00	9.50	9.00
	same, pane of 16	....	....		35.00	

485

487

491

484	85¢ Flags and Coins, sheet of 8	18.00	....	....	16.50	16.50
485	1 fr Handshake	3.50	....	11.00	2.50	2.50
486	1.80 fr Sign Language	6.00	....	18.00	4.50	4.50
487	1 fr Gymnast	3.50	....	11.00	3.00	3.00
488	1.80 fr Tennis Player	6.00	....	18.00	4.50	4.50
489	3 fr Gymnast, souvenir sheet	7.75	....		8.00	8.00
490	1 fr Childrens' Art "We Can End Poverty"	3.50	....	11.00	2.75	2.75
491	1.80 fr Childrens' Art "We Can End Poverty"	7.75	....	18.00	4.25	4.25

492

492	1.20 fr Climate Change, sheet of 4	12.00	....	....	12.00	12.00
493	1.80 fr Climate Change, sheet of 4	17.00	....	....	17.00	17.00
494	Climate Change, souvenir booklet	....	....	....	24.00	....

2009

| 495 | 1.30 fr U Thant | .... | .... | 14.00 | 3.50 | 3.50 |
| 496-99 | 1 fr Endangered Species, block of 4 | 3.75 | .... | 10.00 | 9.00 | 8.50 |

503a

505e

500-01	1 fr-1.30fr World Heritage, Germany	6.75	....	27.00	6.00	6.00
502	World Heritage Sites, souvenir booklet	....	....	....	23.00	
	1 fr-180 fr Economic and Social Council	5.75	....	24.00	8.00	7.00
503-04	85¢-1.80 fr Economic and Social Council	7.50	....	29.00	7.00	6.75
505	1.30 fr UN Millennium Goals, sheet of 8	21.00	....	....	23.00	
506-10	1 fr 40th Anniversary UNPA in Geneva,					
	strip of 5 with labels	....	....		35.00	35.00
	same, sheet of two strips	....	....		68.00	
511	1.30 fr Indigenous People, sheet of 6	....	....		19.00	....

2010

| 512 | 85¢ Flags & Coins, sheet of 8 | .... | .... | | 16.00 | 16.00 |

512a	*Equatorial Guinea*	**512e**	*Argentina*
512b	*Loas*	**512f**	*Morocco*
512c	*Seychelles*	**512g**	*Sudan*
512d	*Mauritania*	**512h**	*Brunei*

513-16	1fr Endangered Species	8.00	11.00	12.00	9.00	9.00
517	1.60fr Arachnid	4.75	15.00	16.00	4.25	1.25
518	1.90fr Starfish	5.75	17.00	18.00	4.75	4.75

520

519	85¢ One Planet, One Ocean, Sheet of 4	....	....		10.00	10.00
520	1 fr One Planet, One Ocean, sheet of 4	....	....		11.00	11.00
521	One Planet, One Ocean, souvenir bklt	....	....		23.00	....
522	1.90fr UN 65th Anniversary	....	....		4.50	4.50
522a	UN 65th Anniversary S/S	....	....		10.00	10.00

523-27

523-27	1fr UN Transport	12.75	....	22.00	12.00	12.00
528	1.90 fr Campaign Against Child Labor, sheet of 10	....	....		36.00	36.00
529	1.30 fr Indigenous People, sheet of 6	....	....		20.00	20.00

2011

| 530-31 | 10¢-50¢ UN Headquarters | 5.75 | .... | 6.75 | 1.65 | 1.65 |
| 532 | 85¢ Flag & Coins, sheet of 8 | 17.50 | .... | | 16.00 | 16.00 |

533

533	Anniversary of Human Space Flight, sheet of 16	22.50	....		20.00	....
534	Anniversary of Human Space Flight, S/S of 2	5.75	....		4.75	
535-536	85¢-1fr World Heritage Sites in Nordic Countries	....	....	22.00	5.00	5.00
	same, sheet of 20	....	....		88.00	
537	1.30fr Aids Ribbon	6.75	....		3.75	
	same, pane of 4	....	....		14.50	
538-39	1fr-1.30fr Economic & Social Counsil	7.50	....	26.00	6.50	
540-43	1fr Endangered Species	12.50	....	11.50	10.75	
544-45	85¢-1.40fr Intl. Year of Forests	7.25	....	12.00	6.75	6.00

2013

546	85¢ Flags & Coins, sheet of 8	19.50	....		18.00	....
547-548	1.40fr Autism Awareness	8.00	....	16.00	7.50	7.00
549-552	1 fr Endangered Species	10.75	....			
553	1.40fr Conference on Sustainable Development	5.50	....	15.00	4.50	4.50
554-555	1fr-1.40fr Sport for Peace	....	....		6.75	6.75
555a	Sport for Peace, Souvenir Sheet	....	....		4.50	4.50
556-557	85¢-1fr UNESCO World Heritage sites in Africa	5.75	....	19.00	4.95	4.95

SCOTT NO.	DESCRIPTION	FIRST DAY COVERS SING	INSC. BLK	INSRIP BLK-4	UNUSED F/NH	USED F

561

562

558	85¢ Indigenous People, sheet of 6	9.00	....	....	12.75	....
559-560	1.40fr-1.90fr World Radio Day	9.75	....	34.00	9.00	9.00
561-562	1fr-1.40fr People and Dove	8.95	....	25.50	6.75	6.75

563

564

| 563-64 | 1.40fr-1.90fr World Heritage Sites, China | .... | 33.00 | 8.50 | 8.50 |
| 565 | World HeritageSites, China, Souvenir Booklet | .... | .... | 25.00 | .... |

566k-566l

567   568

566	World Oceans' Day sheet of 12	27.00	....	....	26.00	26.00
566	World Oceans' Day sheet of 12	27.00	....	....	26.00	26.00
567-68	1.40fr Nebulae	8.00	....	15.00	7.50	7.50
569	1fr Nebulae Souvenir sheet of 1	3.75	....	....	2.75	2.75
570-71	1.40fr-1.90fr Works of disable artists	11.00	....	34.00	8.50	8.50
572-75	1.40fr Endangered Species	14.50	....	14.00	13.50	13.50
576	1.40fr Flags & Coins sheet of 8	29.00	....	....	27.00	27.00

577

583

2014

577-78	1fr-1.40fr International Day of Happiness	7.00	....	25.00	6.50	6.50
579	1fr International Year of Jazz, Sheet of 12	35.00	....	....	31.00	....
580-81	2.20fr-2.60fr Definitives	14.00	....	50.00	13.00	13.00
582-83	1.40fr-1.90fr Taj Majal, Set of 2	9.75	....	35.00	9.50	9.50
584	Taj Mahal Souvenir Booklet	....	....	....	26.00	....

585

593

585-86	1.30fr - 1.60fr International Year of Family Farming	8.75	....	31.00	8.50	8.50
587	1.30fr Personalized Sheet of 10 with Labels	....	....	....	39.00	....
588	1.90fr Global Education First Initiative	6.75	....	20.00	5.50	5.50
589	1.90fr Global Education First Initiative Souvenir Sheet	6.75	....	....	5.50	5.50
590-93	1.40fr Endangered Species	16.00	....	15.00	14.50	....

598

601

2015

594	90¢ Flags and Coins, sheet of 8	19.00	....	....	17.00	....
595-96	1fr - 1.40fr World Poetry Day, 2 sheets of 6	39.00	....	....	35.00	....
597-600	1.40fr Endangered Species	15.00	....	14.50	14.00	....
601-02	1.40fr-1.90fr World Heritage Sites, Southeast Asia	10.50	....	32.00	8.25	....
603	World Heritage Souvenir Booklet	....	....	....	24.50	....

604   605

604-05	1fr - 1.40fr End Violence Against Children	8.75	....	24.00	5.95	....
606	Greetings from the United Nations, sheet of 10 plus Labels	....	....	....	39.00	....
607-10	1fr - 1.90fr UN Building	16.00	....	29.00	15.50	....

611

607-10	1fr - 1.90fr UN Building	16.00	....	29.00	15.50	....
611	1.40fr Souvenir Sheet	4.75	....	....	3.75	....
612	1.40fr UN Climate Change Conference	4.75	....	14.00	3.75	....

613

619

2016

613-14	1fr-1.50fr LGBT Equality	....	....	24.00	6.00	....
615-16	1fr-2fr U.N. Women-HeforShe	....	....	29.00	6.50	....
617-18	1fr-1.50fr International Dance Day, 2 sheets of 6	....	....	38.00(2)	....	....
619-20	1fr-1.50fr U.N Peacekeepers	....	....	24.00	6.00	....

628b

SCOTT NO.	DESCRIPTION	FIRST DAY COVERS SING	INSC. BLK	INSRIP BLK-4	UNUSED F/NH	USED F
621-24	1fr-2fr Sports for Peace & Development, 2 pairs			28.00	15.00	
625-26	1fr-1.50fr World Heritage Sites, Czech Republic			24.00	6.00	
627	9.60fr World Heritage Sites, souvenir booklet				27.00	
628	2fr Eye on Africa, sheet of 4				17.00	
629	1fr Sustainable Development Goals, sheet of 17			40.00	40.00	

635   **637**

644

2017

SCOTT NO.	DESCRIPTION	FIRST DAY COVERS SING	INSC. BLK	INSRIP BLK-4	UNUSED F/NH	USED F
630-31	1fr-1.50fr International Dance Day, 2 sheets of 6			38.00(2)		
632-35	1.50fr Endangered Species, block of 4			15.00	13.00	
636-37	1fr-2fr World Environment Day			24.00	6.00	
638-39	1fr-1.50fr World Heritage Sites, Along the Silk Road			24.00	6.00	
640	9.60fr World Heritage Sites, souvenir booklet				27.00	
641-42	1fr-2fr International Day of Peace			24.00	6.00	
643	2fr International Day of Peace				6.00	
644-45	1fr-1.50fr World Food Day			24.00	6.00	

650   **656**

2018

SCOTT NO.	DESCRIPTION	FIRST DAY COVERS SING	INSC. BLK	INSRIP BLK-4	UNUSED F/NH	USED F
646-49	1.50fr Endangered Species, block of 4			15.00	13.00	
650-51	1fr-2fr World Health Day			30.00	7.00	
652	1.50fr NABA Lugano 2018, sheet 10			38.00		
653-54	1fr-1.50fr UNISPACE, 50th Anniv.			27.00	7.00	
655	2fr UNISPACE, souvenir sheet				5.00	
656	2fr Nelson Mandela				5.00	
657-58	1fr-1.50fr World Heritage Sites, United Kingdom			24.00	6.00	
659	9.60fr World Heritage Sites, prestige booklet				27.00	
660	1fr Music Day 2018, sheet of 12				26.00	

663   **673**

2019

SCOTT NO.	DESCRIPTION	FIRST DAY COVERS SING	INSC. BLK	INSRIP BLK-4	UNUSED F/NH	USED F
661	1fr International Languages, sheet of 6				13.00	
662	1.50fr Sexual Equality, single			17.00	4.25	
663-66	1.50fr Endangered Species, block of 4			38.00	15.00	
667	2.60fr World Bee Day, souvenir sheet				6.00	
668-72	1fr International Labour Organization, strip of 5			25.00	12.00	
673-74	1fr-1.50fr Climate Change			25.00	6.00	
675	2fr Climate Change, souvenir sheet				5.00	
676	1.50fr UNPA 50th Anniv., personalized sheet of 10				36.00	
677-78	1fr-1.50fr World Heritage Sites, Cuba			25.00	6.00	
679	9.60fr World Heritage Sites, Cuba, prestige booklet				27.00	

AIR LETTER SHEETS & POSTAL CARDS

1969

SCOTT NO.	DESCRIPTION	FIRST DAY COVERS SING	INSC. BLK	INSRIP BLK-4	UNUSED F/NH	USED F
UC1	65¢ ultramarine & light blue				4.50	1.90

1969

| UX1 | 20¢ olive green & black | | | | 1.65 | .50 |
| UX2 | 30¢ violet blue, blue, light & dark green | | | | 1.65 | .70 |

UX3   **UX4**

1977

| UX3 | 40¢ multicolored | | | | 1.25 | .75 |
| UX4 | 70¢ multicolored | | | | 1.65 | 1.35 |

UX5   **UX6**

1985

| UX5 | 50¢ Six languages | | | | 1.25 | 6.00 |
| UX6 | 70¢ Birds & Rainbow | | | | 1.65 | 5.25 |

UX7   **UX10**

1986

| UX7 | 70¢+10¢ Surcharge on UX6 | | | | 8.00 | 3.65 |

1992-93

UX8	90¢ U.N. Buildings				1.75	3.00
UX9	50¢ + 10¢ Surcharge on UX5				1.75	3.00
UX10	80¢ Postal Card				1.75	3.50

UX11   **UX12**

1997

| UX11 | 50¢+20¢ Surcharge on UX5 | | | | 1.75 | 3.75 |
| UX12 | 80¢+30¢ Surcharge on UX10 | | | | 2.00 | 3.75 |

UX13   **UX14**

1998

| UX13 | 70¢ Assembly Hall | | | | 2.00 | 3.25 |
| UX14 | 1.10fr Palais des Nations | | | | 2.50 | 3.50 |

2001

UX15	1.30fr Palais des Nations				2.75	3.50
UX16	70¢+15¢ Surcharge on UX13				2.10	2.25
UX17	90¢+10¢ Surcharge on UX8				2.50	2.50
UX18	1.10fr+10¢ Surcharge on UX14				2.75	3.75
UX19	85¢ Ceiling Sculpture				2.95	2.50
UX20	1 fr Broken Chair Memorial				2.95	3.00
UX21	1.80 fr League of Nations Building				3.95	5.00

UNITED NATIONS:
OFFICES IN VIENNA, AUSTRIA
Denominations in Austrian Currency

NOTE: Unless illustrated, designs can be assumed to be similar to the equivalent New York or Geneva issue

SCOTT NO.	DESCRIPTION	FIRST DAY COVERS SING	INSC. BLK	INSRIP BLK-4	UNUSED F/NH	USED F

(illustrations of stamps labeled 3, 5, 9, 19, 24, 37, 38, 40, 41, 42, 43)

1979

| 1-6 | 50g to 10s Definitives | 6.75 | 16.95 | 10.00 | 2.25 | 2.50 |

1980

7/16	1980 Issues, (9) (No #14)	......	......	......	6.50	......
7	4s International Economic Order	3.75	9.50	11.50	1.25	1.20
8	2.50s International Economic Definitive	1.85	2.15	(B)8.75	.80	.70
9-10	4s & 6s Decade for Women	3.10	7.75	6.50	1.50	1.40
11	6s Peacekeeping	1.95	4.85	5.25	1.15	1.05
12-13	4s & 6s 35th Anniversary	3.15	7.85	6.50	1.25	1.40
14	same, souvenir sheet	3.85			1.40	1.40
15-16	4s & 6s Economic and Social Council	2.35	5.85	6.50	1.40	1.20

1981

17-23	1981 Issues, complete (7)	......	......	......	5.65	......
17	4s Palestinian People	1.55	3.85	3.75	.85	.75
18-19	4s & 6s Disabled Persons	2.40	6.00	5.50	1.50	1.50
20	6s Fresco	1.45	3.65	4.40	1.50	1.50
21	7.50s Sources of Energy	1.95	4.85	3.95	1.00	1.00
22-23	5s & 7s Volunteers Program	2.75	6.85	7.75	1.75	1.75

1982

24-29	1982 Issues, complete (6)	......	......	......	4.85	......
24	3s Definitive	.85	2.15	3.00	.65	.45
25-26	5s & 7s Human Environment	2.50	6.25	9.00	1.95	1.75
27	5s Space Exploration	1.25	3.15	3.95	.85	.85
28-29	5s & 7s Nature Conservation	2.50	6.25	7.75	1.75	1.75

1983

30-38	1983 Issues, complete (9)	......	......	......	7.00	......
30	4s World Communications	.85	2.15	3.95	.85	.55
31-32	4s & 6s Safety at Sea	2.15	5.35	6.15	1.40	1.40
33-34	5s & 7s World Food Program	2.60	6.50	7.00	1.75	1.65
35-36	4s & 8.50s Trade & Develop	2.75	6.95	8.95	1.95	1.85
37-38	5s & 7s Human Rights	3.15	7.85	8.95	1.95	1.85

1984

39-47	1984 Issues, complete (9)	......	......	......	8.55	......
39	7s Population	1.40	3.50	4.50	1.00	.95
40-41	4.50s & 6s Food Day	1.85	4.65	7.25	1.50	1.50
42-43	3.50s & 15s Heritage	3.50	8.75	10.50	2.50	2.25
44-45	4.50s & 8.50s Future for Refugees	2.25	5.65	10.50	2.25	1.75
46-47	3.50s & 6.50s Youth Year	1.80	4.50	9.00	2.00	1.65

1985

48/56	1985 Issues, (8) (No #54)	......	......	......	10.90	......
48	7.50s I.L.O. Turin Centre	1.25	3.15	5.50	1.40	1.00
49	8.50s U.N. University	1.35	3.40	5.50	1.50	1.10
50-51	4.50s & 15s Definitives	3.15	7.95	13.75	3.25	2.35
52-53	6.50s & 8.50s 40th Anniversary	2.50	6.25	12.00	3.00	3.50
54	Same, Souvenir Sheet	3.25	......	......	3.00	2.90
55-56	4s-6s Child Survival	2.15	5.40	13.00	3.00	2.85

1986

57-65	1986 Issues (9)	......	......	......	17.00	......
57	8s Africa in Crisis	1.35	3.40	6.00	1.50	.90
58-61	4.50s Development, 4 varieties, attached	3.05	7.65	13.00	12.00	2.25
62-63	3.50s & 6.50s Philately	1.95	4.95	9.75	2.00	1.15
64-65	5s & 6s Peace Year	2.25	5.65	12.00	2.50	1.95
66	4s to 7s WFUNA, souvenir sheet	3.05	......	......	5.50	5.00

1987

67-77	1987 Issues (11)	......	......	......	13.40	......
67	8s Trygve Lie	1.35	3.40	6.00	1.10	1.00
68-69	4s & 9.50s Shelter Homeless	2.35	5.95	10.00	2.25	2.00
70-71	5s & 8s Anti-Drug Campaign	2.25	5.65	8.00	2.25	2.00
72-73	2s & 17s Definitives	3.45	8.65	11.00	2.75	2.25
74-75	5s & 6s United Nations Day	2.25	5.65	10.00	2.75	2.50
76-77	4s & 9.50s Child Immunization	2.35	5.95	14.00	3.00	3.00

1988

78/86	1988 Issues, (7) (No #80-81, 87)	......	......	......	13.00	......
78-79	4s & 6s World Without Hunger	2.25	5.65	8.00	2.00	1.50
					Sheetlets	
80-81	4s & 5s Forest Conservation	22.50	65.00	18.00	8.00	8.00
	(set of 6, includes NY and Geneva)	......	......	130.00	35.00	25.00
82-83	6s & 7.50s Volunteer Day	2.35	5.95	12.00	2.75	2.00
84-85	6s & 8s Health in Sports	2.50	6.25	14.50	3.25	2.00
86	5s Human Rights 40th Anniversary	1.00	2.50	4.00	1.50	1.50
87	11s Human Rights 40th Anniversary souvenir sheet	1.75	......	......	3.00	2.25

1989

88-96	1989 Issues (9)	......	......	......	18.75	......
88-89	5.50s & 8s World Bank	2.35	5.95	16.50	3.50	3.00
90	6s Nobel Peace Prize	1.25	3.15	6.75	1.35	1.00
91-92	4s & 9.50s World Weather Watch	2.35	5.95	19.50	4.00	3.50
93-94	5s & 7.50s UN Office in Vienna	2.25	5.65	24.00	5.50	5.00
					Sheetlets(12)	
95-96	4s & 6s Human Rights, 40th Ann. (strips of 3 w/tabs)	2.25	5.65	25.00	5.50	......

1990

97/109	1990 Issues, (12) (No #105)	......	......	......	27.95	......
97	12s Int'l. Trade Center	2.15	5.40	8.00	2.00	1.50
98	1.50s Definitive	.85	2.15	1.80	.40	.30
99-100	5s & 11s AIDS	2.75	6.95	18.00	4.25	3.00
101-02	4.50s & 9.50s Medicinal Plants	2.50	6.25	21.00	4.50	3.00
103-04	7s & 9s 45th Anniv. of U.N.	2.75	6.95	21.00	4.50	3.50
105	same, souvenir sheet	2.75	......	......	7.75	6.00
106-07	6s & 8s Crime Prevention	2.50	6.25	18.00	4.00	3.25
					Sheetlets(12)	
108-09	4.50s & 7s Human Rights (strips of 3 w/tabs)	2.35	5.95	30.00	7.00	......

(illustrations of stamps labeled 44, 45, 46, 50, 51, 64, 72, 73, 93, 94, 98, 116, 117, 137, 118, 119, 120, 138)

SCOTT NO.	DESCRIPTION	FIRST DAY COVERS SING	INSC. BLK	INSRIP BLK-4	UNUSED F/NH	USED F

149

167

168

169

193

194

195

196-99

200-04

1991

SCOTT NO.	DESCRIPTION	SING	INSC. BLK	BLK-4	F/NH	F
110-24	1991 Issues, (15)	....	....	....	29.50	....
110-13	5s Econ. Comm. for Europe, 4 varieties, attached	5.50	13.75	6.50	5.75	5.50
114-15	6s & 9.50s Namibia—A New Nation	4.50	11.25	23.00	5.00	5.00
116	20s Definitive Issue	4.75	11.85	16.00	3.75	4.00
117-18	7s & 9s Children's Rights	4.50	11.25	18.00	4.00	3.00
119-20	5s & 10s Chemical Weapons	4.75	11.95	22.00	5.00	5.00
121-22	5s & 8s 40th Anniv. of U.N.P.A.	4.15	10.35	15.00	3.50	3.00
				Sheetlets (12)		
123-24	4.50s & 7s Human Rights (strips of 3 w/tabs)	2.50	6.25	39.00	8.50	
....						

1992

125-40	1992 Issues, (17)	....	....	....	32.00	....
125-26	5s-9s World Heritage—UNESCO	4.25	10.75	18.00	3.50	3.00
127-28	7s Clean Oceans, 2 varieties, attached...	4.25	5.50	7.50	3.00	2.50
129-32	5.50s Earth Summit, 4 varieties, attached		4.25	8.95	8.50	7.00
5.00						
133-34	10s Mission to Planet Earth, 2 varieties, attached	4.25	5.50	16.00	7.00	6.50
135-36	5.50s-7s Science & Technology	4.00	10.25	13.00	2.75	2.25
137-38	5.50s-7s Definitives	4.00	10.25	13.00	2.75	2.50
				Sheetlets (12)		
139-40	6s-10s Human Rights (strips of 3 w/tabs)	2.75	6.95	38.00	10.00	....

1993

141-59	1993 Issues, (19)	....	....	....	35.00	....
141-42	5.50s-7s Aging	4.00	10.25	12.00	2.50	2.25
143-46	7s Endangered Species, 4 attached	5.00	6.00	7.50	6.00	5.50
147-48	6s-10s Healthy Environment	4.00	11.50	17.50	4.00	3.00
149	13s Definitive	4.00	10.25	12.50	3.50	3.50
				Sheetlets (12)		
150-51	5s-6s Human Rights	3.00	7.00	40.00	10.00	....
152-55	5.50s Peace, 4 attached (strips of 3 w/tabs)	2.50	6.00	11.00	9.00	9.00
156-59	7s Environment—Climate, strip of 4	4.00	7.00	22.00(8)	9.75	9.75

1994

160-77	1994 Issues (18)	....	....	....	33.00	....
160-61	5.50s-8s Intl. Year of the Family	3.00	10.75	16.00	3.50	3.25
162-65	7s Endangered Species, 4 attached	6.25	7.50	7.50	6.50	6.50
166	12s Refugees	3.50	12.00	9.00	2.25	1.75
167-69	50g-30s Definitives (3)	8.50	33.50	32.50	7.00	7.00
170-73	6s Intl. Decade for Natural Disaster Reduction, 4 attached	5.50	6.50	10.00	9.00	8.50
174-75	5.50s-7s Population and Development	3.00	10.25	17.00	4.00	3.50
176-77	6s-7s Development through Partnership.	3.50	10.25	16.00	3.50	3.50

1995

178/91	1995 Issues (13) (No #188)	....	....	....	53.95	....
178	7s 50th Anniversary of the UN	2.00	7.25	8.00	1.75	1.75
179	14s Social Summit	3.50	12.50	14.00	3.00	3.00
180-83	7s Endangered Species, 4 attached	6.25	7.50	8.00	7.00	6.50
184-85	6s-7s Youth: Our Future	3.50	10.25	18.00	4.00	4.00
186-87	7s-10s 50th Anniversary of the UN	4.00	11.50	19.00	4.00	4.00
188	17s 50th Anniversary of the UN, souvenir sheet	3.50	....	....	6.00	6.00
189-90	5.50s-6s 4th World Conference on Women..	3.25	10.50	19.00	4.00	4.00
191	3s 50thAnniversary, min. sheet of 12	....	....	....	23.00	....
192	same, souvenir booklet of 4 panes of 3...	....	....	....	28.00	....

1996

193/211	1996 Issues (18) (No 207)	....	....	....	27.50	....
193	7s WFUNA 50th Anniversary	2.00	7.25	8.00	1.60	1.35
194-95	1s-10s Definitives	3.25	10.50	10.50	2.50	2.25
196-99	7s Endangered Species, 4 attached	6.25	7.50	8.00	7.00	6.00
200-04	6s City Summit (Habitat II), strip of 5	6.75	16.50	28.00	10.00	10.00
205-06	6s-7s Sport & the Environment	3.50	10.25	16.00	3.00	3.00
207	13s Sport & theEnvrinronment souvenir sheet	3.25	....	....	3.50	3.00
208-09	7s-10s A Plea for Peace	4.00	11.50	18.00	3.50	5.50
210-11	5.5s-8s UNICEF 50th Anniversary	3.50	10.25	11.50	3.00	3.00

207

208

209

210

211

214-17

218-21

212

228

230

223-27

1997

212/31	1997 Issues (19) (No. #222)	....	....	....	27.50	....
212-13	5s-6s Definitives	3.25	10.50	10.50	2.50	2.25
214-17	7s Endangered Species, 4 attached	6.25	7.50	8.00	7.00	6.00
218-21	3.5s Earth Summit +5, 4 attached	3.25	3.75	7.00	5.50	5.00
222	11s Earth Summit +5, souvenir sheet	2.50	....	....	3.50	3.50
223-27	7s Transportation, strip of 5	6.75	9.50	16.00(10)	7.00	7.00
228-29	6.50s-7s Tribute to Philately	3.50	10.25	15.00	3.50	3.00
230-31	3s-6s Terracota Warriors	2.75	8.25	16.00	3.50	3.50
232	same, Souvenir bklt of 6 panes of 4	....	....	....	14.00	....

SCOTT NO.	DESCRIPTION	FIRST DAY COVERS SING	INSC. BLK	INSRIP BLK-4	UNUSED F/NH	USED F

239a

233

1998

233-34	6.50-9s Definitives	3.75	8.00	15.00	3.00	3.00
235-38	7s Endangered Species, 4 attached	6.25	7.50	7.00	6.00	5.50
239	3.50s Intl. Year of the Ocean, sheetlet of 12	15.00		16.00	16.00	
240	6.50s Rain Forest, Ocelot	2.00	4.50	6.75	1.50	1.25
241	22s Rain Forests, Ocelot, souvenir sheet	6.50		4.50	4.50	4.00
242-43	4s-7.50s 50 Years of Peacekeeping	3.25	7.00	11.00	2.50	2.25
244-245	4.40s-7s 50th of the Dec. of Human Rights	3.25	7.00	11.00	2.50	2.25
246-47	3.50s-7s Schonbrunn Palace	3.25	7.00	8.25	1.95	1.95
248	33s Schonbrunn Palace booklet				18.00	

249

253-56

1999

249	8s Definitives	2.50	6.75	9.50	2.25	2.25
250-51	4.50s-6.50s World Heritage Sites, Australia	3.00	6.50	11.00	2.50	2.35
252	same, souvenir bklt of 6 panes				10.50	
253-56	7s Endangered Species, 4 attached	6.25	7.50	7.00	6.00	5.50
257-58	3.50s Unispace III Conference	1.95	4.50	5.50	2.00	2.00
259	13s Unispace III Conference, souvenir sheet	3.50			5.00	5.00
260-63	6.50s Universal Postal Union	2.00	4.50	6.75	5.00	5.00

264

266

264	3.50s In Memorium	1.95	4.50	5.50	1.25	1.25
265	14s In Memorium	3.50			3.00	3.00
266-67	7s-13s Education-Keystone to the 21st Century	5.00	11.50	18.00	4.75	4.00

268

273

2000

268	7s International Year of Thanksgiving	1.95	4.50	7.00	1.50	1.50
269-72	7s Endangered Species, 4 attached	6.25	7.50	7.00	6.00	5.50
273-74	7s-8s Our World 2000	4.50	10.50	15.00	4.00	3.00

275

288

275-76	7s-9s 55th Anniversary of the UN	4.50	10.50	15.00	4.00	4.00
277	same, 7s-9s souvenir sheet				4.00	4.00
278	3.50s United Nations in the 21st Century	1.75	4.50		6.75	6.75
279-80	4.50s-6.50s World Heritage Series, Spain	3.00	6.50	10.00	2.35	2.25
281	same, souvenir bklt of 6 panes				11.00	
282	7s Respect for Refugees	1.95	4.50	6.50	1.50	1.50
283	25s Respect for Refugees, souvenir sheet	7.00			5.50	5.50

2001

284-87	7s Endangered Species, 4 attached	6.25	7.50	7.00	6.00	5.50
288-89	10s-12s Intl. Volunteers Year	5.50	12.50	21.00	5.00	5.00
290-91	7s-15s World Heritage Sites, Japan	5.50	12.50	22.00	5.00	5.00

293

294

292	36s World Heritage Sites, Japan Prestige Booklet				14.00	
293	7s Dag Hammarskjold	1.95	4.50	6.50	1.50	1.50
294-95	7s-8s 50th Anniv. of the UNPA	4.50	10.50	12.00	4.00	3.00
296	same, 28s souvenir sheet	7.50			5.50	5.00
297-300	7s Climate Change, strip of 4	6.25	7.50	12.50	6.00	5.50
301	7s Nobel Peace Prize	1.95	4.50	6.00	1.25	1.25

302

312

2002

302-07	e0.07-e2.03 Austrian Tourist Attractions	5.50	15.00	52.00	11.00	11.00
308-11	e0.51 Endangered Species, 4 attached	5.00	6.00	7.00	6.00	6.00
312-13	e0.51-1.09 Independence of East Timor	3.50	8.00	19.00	4.00	4.00
314-17	e0.22-0.51 Intl. Year of Mountains, 2 pairs	3.50	4.50	19.00	5.50	5.50
318-21	e0.51-0.58 Johannesburg Summit, 2 pairs	4.50	5.50	8.00	7.00	6.50

322

322-23	e0.51-0.58 World Heritage Sites, Italy	2.25	7.00	14.00	3.00	3.50
324	same, souvenir bklt of 6 panes of 4				20.00	
325	e0.51-0.25 UNAIDS Awareness, souvenir sheet	2.25			5.00	5.00

SCOTT NO.	DESCRIPTION	FIRST DAY COVERS SING	INSC. BLK	INSRIP BLK-4	UNUSED F/NH	USED F

327

333-34

2003

326	e0.51 Indigenous Art, sheet of 6..............	9.50	....	....	10.00	10.00
327-28	e0.25-e1.00 Austrian Tourist Attractions..	2.50	7.50	16.00	3.50	3.50
329-32	e0.51 Endangered Species, 4 attached ..	5.00	6.00	7.00	6.00	6.00
333-34	e0.55-e0.75 Intl. Year of Freshwater, 2 attach	2.50	8.00	12.00	5.50	5.50

335

341

335	e0.04 Schloss Eggenberg, Graz	1.75	4.50	4.50	1.00	.75
336	e2.10 Ralphe Bunche.............................	3.75	9.50	28.00	6.00	6.00
337	e2.10 In Memoriam , UN Complex Bomding in Iraq	3.75	9.50	28.00	6.00	6.00
338-39	e0.51-e0.75 World Heritage Sites, United States	2.50	17.00	18.00	4.00	4.00
340	same, souvenir bklt of 6 panes of 4.........	....	....	....	14.00	....

353

355

2004

341	e0.55 Schloss Schonbrunn, Vienna	2.10	4.00	7.50	1.75	.85
342-45	e0.55 Endangered Species, 4 attached ..	7.00	9.00	7.00	6.50	6.50
346	e0.55 Indigenous Art, sheet of 6..............	10.50	....	....	11.00	11.00
347-48	e0.55-e0.75 Road Safety	2.50	8.00	18.00	4.00	4.00
349	e2.10 Japanese Peace Bell, 50th Anniv..	3.75	9.50	29.00	6.75	6.75
350-51	e0.55-e0.75 World Heritage Sites, Greece	2.50	8.00	17.50	4.00	4.00
352	same, souvenir bklt of 6 panes of 4.........	....	....	....	21.00	....
353-54	e0.55-e1.00 My Dream for Peace	2.75	8.50	22.00	4.50	4.50
355-56	e0.55-e1.25 Human Rights	3.25	....	....	5.75	5.50

357

2005

357	e0.55 U.N. 60th Anniv.............................	2.10	4.00	10.00	2.25	2.25
358	e2.10 U.N. 60th Anniv.............................	3.75	....	....	6.75	6.75
359	e0.75 Definitive......................................	2.35	5.00	11.00	2.50	2.50

360-63

| 360-63 | e0.55 Orchids, 4 attached .... | 7.00 | 9.00 | 7.75 | 7.00 | 6.50 |
| 364-65 | e0.55-e0.75 Nature's Wisdom................. | 2.50 | 8.00 | 19.00 | 4.00 | 4.00 |

366

368

366-67	e0.55-e1.10 International Year of Sports.	2.75	8.50	27.00	6.00	6.00
368-69	e0.55-e0.75 World Heritage Sites, Egypt	2.50	8.00	21.00	4.00	5.00
370	same, souvenir bklt of 6 panes of 4.........	....	....	....	23.00	....

371

373

| 371-72 | e0.55-e1.00 My Dream for Peace, type of 2004... | 2.75 | 8.50 | 22.50 | 5.00 | 5.00 |
| 373-74 | e0.55-e1.25 Food for Life .... | 2.75 | 8.50 | 26.50 | 6.00 | 6.00 |

376-79

2006

| 375 | e0.55 Indigenous Art, sheet of 6.............. | 11.50 | .... | .... | 11.00 | 11.00 |
| 376-79 | e0.55 Endangered Species, 4 attached .. | 7.00 | 9.00 | 8.50 | 7.25 | 6.75 |

380

382

380-81	e0.55-e1.25 Day of Families	2.75	8.50	28.00	6.00	6.00
382-83	e0.55-e0.75 World Heritage Sites, France	2.50	8.00	20.00	4.50	4.00
384	same, souvenir bklt of 6 panes of 4.........	....	....	....	22.00	....

385

387a

| 385-86 | e0.55-e1.00 My Dream for Peace One Day | 2.75 | 8.50 | 24.00 | 5.75 | 5.75 |
| 387 | e0.55 Flags and Coins, sheet of 8........... | 15.00 | .... | .... | 18.00 | 18.00 |

388-91

2007

388-91	e0.55 Endangered Species, 4 attached ..	7.00	9.00	8.00	7.00	6.50
392	e0.55 Flags and Coins, sheet of 8...........	15.00	....	....	14.00	14.00
393-97	e0.55 UN Headquarters + labels, strip of 5	....	....	....	48.00	....
....	same, sheet of 2 (393-97)	....	....	....	100.00	....
398-99	e0.55-e1.25 Peaceful Visions.................	5.00	6.25	31.00	8.00	8.00

SCOTT NO.	DESCRIPTION	FIRST DAY COVERS SING	INSC. BLK	INSRIP BLK-4	UNUSED F/NH	USED F
400-01	e0.55-e0.75 World Heritage Sites, South America	2.50	8.00	22.00	5.00	5.00
....	e0.75 Universal Postal Union, joint issue with					
402	same, booklet of 6 panes of 4	....	....	....	24.00	....
403	e0.75 UPU, joint issue with Swiss Post Humanitarian Mail	2.50	5.00	9.00	2.00	2.00
404-08	Space, vert. strip of 5 + labels	....	....	....	48.00	....
	same, sheet of 10 + labels	....	....	....	100.00	....
409-10	65¢+e1.15 Space for Humanity, set of 2	12.75	....	24.00	8.00	8.00
	same, 2 sheets of 6	....	....	....	38.00	....
411	e2.10 Space for Humanity souvenir sheet	7.25	....	....	7.00	7.00

412

2008

412	65¢ International Holocaust Remembrance Day	3.25	....	11.00	2.50	2.50
	same, sheet of 9	....	....	....	22.00	....

414   **415**

413-16	Sculptures	....	....	42.00	9.00	9.00
413	10¢ Johann Strauss Memorial, Vienna	1.25	....	1.50	.60	.60
	same, pane of 20	....	....	....	7.50	....
414	15¢ Pallas Athene Fountain, Vienna	1.25	....	2.50	.95	.95
	same, pane of 20	....	....	....	11.00	....
415	65¢ Pegasus Fountain, Saizburg	3.50	....	9.50	3.00	3.00
	same, pane of 20	....	....	....	46.00	....
416	e1.40 Statue, Beledere Palace Gardens, Vienna	7.50	....	20.00	6.00	6.00
	same, pane of 20	....	....	....	97.00	....

417-20

417-20	65¢ Endangered Species block of 4	9.00	....	12.00	9.00	9.00
	same, pane of 16	....	....	....	45.00	....

428   **429**   **433**

421	65¢ Flags and Coins, sheet of 8	21.00	....	....	4.00	21.00
422-26	UN Personalized, strip of 5 w/labels	....	....	....	45.00	....
427-428	55¢-1.40e Disabled Persons and Sport for Peace	12.00	....	35.00	8.00	8.50
429-430	65¢-1.30e Man On Rings and Swimmer	12.00	....	31.00	7.50	7.50
431	2.10e Man On Rings, souvenir sheet	9.00	....	....	9.00	9.00
432-433	65¢- 75¢ Childrens' Art "We Can End Poverty"	8.00	....	24.00	6.00	6.00

435

434	65¢ Climate Change, sheet of 4	10.00	....	....	11.00	11.00
435	1.15e Climate Change, sheet of 4	18.00	....	....	18.00	18.00
436	Climate Change, souvenir booklet	....	....	....	30.00	....

444b   **446**

2009

437	1.15e U Thant	....	....	15.00	3.75	3.75
438-41	65¢ Endangered Species, block of 4	4.50	....	10.00	8.50	8.50
442-43	65¢-1.40e World Heritage Sites, Germany	7.95	....	32.00	7.00	7.00
444	World Heritage Sites, souvenir booklet	....	....	....	28.00	....
445-449	65¢ Personalized Stamp, strip of 5 with labels	....	....	....	17.00	17.00
	same, sheet	....	....	....	35.00	....
450-51	55¢-75¢ Economic/Social Council	7.95	....	20.00	4.50	4.50

454   **457h**

452-56	e1.40 Personalized, strip of 5 with labels	....	....	....	38.00	....
	same, sheet of 10	....	....	....	80.00	....
457	65¢ UN Millennium Goals, sheet of 8	19.50	....	....	17.00	....
458	65¢ Indigenous People, sheet of 6	....	....	....	15.00	....

2010

459	65¢ Flags & Coins, sheet of 8	....	....	....	19.00	19.00

459a Romania   **459b** Slovenia   **459c** Azerbaijan   **459d** Bangladesh
459e Belarus   **459f** Malta   **459g** Swaziland   **459h** Jordan

460-64	65¢ Human Trafficking, vertical strip of 5 with labels	....	....	....	26.00	26.00
	same, sheet of 2 strips	....	....	....	52.00	....
465-68	65¢ Endangered Species	9.75	11.75	10.50	9.75	9.75
469	5¢ Colonial Algae	2.25	3.75	1.00	0.35	0.35
470	20¢ Boxfish	2.75	4.5	3.25	0.85	0.85

471

471-72	55¢-65¢ One Planet, One Ocean Miniature Sheet of 4 (2)	....	....	....	21.00	21.00
473	7.80 One Planet, One Ocean, One Prestige Booklet	....	....	....	26.00	....
474	75¢ UN 60th Anniversary	....	....	12.50	3.00	3.00
474a	75¢ UN 60th Anniversary S/S of 2	....	....	....	6.00	6.00

475-79

475-79	e0.65 UN Transport	11.00	....	19.50	10.00	10.00
480	e0.65 Indigenous People, sheet of 6	14.50	....	....	14.00	14.00

2011

481-82	e1.25 - e2.85 UN Headquarters	12.50	....	62.00	13.50	13.50
483	e0.65 Flag and Coins, sheet of 8	17.50	....	....	16.00	16.00
484	Anniversary of Human Space Flight, sheet of 16	22.50	....	....	19.50	....
485	Anniversary of Human Space Flight, S/S of 2	6.50	....	....	5.00	....

SCOTT NO.	DESCRIPTION	PLATE BLOCK F/NH	UNUSED F/NH	USED F

284, 289, 295, 297 — 285, 290, 298, 305, 309 — 286, 291, 296, 299 — 287, 292, 300, 306, 310 — 288, 293

King George VI

1949 (with "Postes-Postage")

Scott	Description	Plate Block	Unused	Used
284-88	1¢-5¢ complete, 5 varieties...............	10.70	2.70	1.00
284	1¢ green............................	1.25	.30	.25
284a	same, booklet pane of 3....................	......	1.25	......
285	2¢ sepia............................	1.60	.35	.25
286	3¢ rose violet............................	2.00	.45	.25
286a	same, booklet pane of 3....................	......	2.80	......
286b	same, booklet pane of 4....................	......	3.50	......
287	4 dark carmine	3.00	.65	.25
287a	same, booklet pane of 3....................	......	13.50	......
287b	same, booklet pane of 6....................	......	19.00	......
288	5¢ deep blue........................	7.25	1.40	.25

1950 Type of 1949
(without "Postes-Postage")

Scott	Description	Plate Block	Unused	Used
289-93	1¢-5¢ complete, 5 varieties	9.50	2.90	1.95
289	1¢ green..............................	1.30	.30	.25
290	2¢ sepia..............................	3.00	.45	.25
291	3¢ rose violet..........................	2.00	.45	.25
292	4¢ dark carmine	2.00	.45	.25
293	5¢ deep blue..........................	7.75	1.55	1.25
294	50¢ Oil Wells, Alberta.........................	60.50	12.65	1.65

Coil Stamps Perf. 9-1/2 Vertically

Scott	Description	Plate Block	Unused	Used
295-300	1¢-4¢ complete, 6 vars.....................	......	25.50	3.75

(without "Postes-Postage")

Scott	Description	Plate Block	Unused	Used
295	1¢ green.............................	......	.70	.35
296	3¢ rose violet.........................	......	1.25	.65

(with "Postes-Postage")

Scott	Description	Plate Block	Unused	Used
297	1¢ green..............................	......	.45	.25
298	2¢ sepia..............................	......	3.60	1.80
299	3¢ rose violet..........................	......	2.40	.25
300	4¢ dark carmine	......	19.00	.95
301	10¢ Fur Resources	6.00	1.15	.25
302	$1 Fishing	275.00	65.00	14.00

294 — 301 — 302 — 303

304 — 311 — 314 — 315

1951

1951-52 COMMEMORATIVES

Scott	Description	Plate Block	Unused	Used
303/19	(303-04, 311-15, 317-19) complete, 10 vars....	26.40	9.25	3.70
303	3¢ Sir Robert L. Borden	1.85	.30	.25
304	4¢ William L.M. King	1.85	.35	.25

(with "Postes-Postage")

Scott	Description	Plate Block	Unused	Used
305	2¢ olive green	1.35	.25	.25
306	4¢ orange vermillion.........................	1.85	.40	.25
306a	same, booklet pane of 3.........................	......	6.00	......
306b	same, booklet pane of 6.........................	......	5.50	......

Coil Stamps Perf. 9-1/2 Vertically

Scott	Description	Plate Block	Unused	Used
309	2¢ olive green	......	1.55	.80
310	4¢ orange vermillion.........................	......	3.25	.95

1951 "CAPEX" Exhibition

Scott	Description	Plate Block	Unused	Used
311	4¢ Trains of 1851 & 1951.....................	3.50	.70	.25
312	5¢ Steamships	11.00	2.25	1.80
313	7¢ Stagecoach & Plane	6.50	1.35	.45
314	15¢ "Three Pence Beaver"....................	7.00	1.50	.30
315	4¢ Royal Visit..................................	1.30	.35	.25

SCOTT NO.	DESCRIPTION	PLATE BLOCK F/NH	UNUSED F/NH	USED F

317 — 318 — 1952 319 — 316

Scott	Description	Plate Block	Unused	Used
316	20¢ Paper Production	10.00	1.85	.25
317	4¢ Red Cross................................	1.50	.36	.25
318	3¢ J.J.C. Abbott.............................	1.35	.30	.25
319	4¢ A. Mackenzie.............................	1.55	.35	.25

1952-53

Scott	Description	Plate Block	Unused	Used
320	7¢ Canada Goose..........................	2.40	.50	.25
321	$1 Indian House & Totem Pole (1953)........................	55.00	12.00	1.15

1953-54 COMMEMORATIVES

Scott	Description	Plate Block	Unused	Used
322/50	(322-24, 330, 335-36, 349-50) complete, 8 varieties	8.95	1.90	1.60
322	2¢ Polar Bear...............................	1.35	.30	.25
323	3¢ Moose..................................	1.40	.30	.25
324	4¢ Bighorn Sheep	1.75	.30	.25

320 — 321 — 322 — 323 — 324

1953

Scott	Description	Plate Block	Unused	Used
325-29	1¢-5¢ complete, 5 vars...................	4.50	1.25	.95
325	1¢ violet brown..............................	1.35	.25	.25
325a	same, booklet pane of 3........................	......	1.50	
326	2¢ green....................................	1.35	.25	.25
327	3¢ carmine rose	1.40	.25	.25
327a	same, booklet pane of 3........................	1.85	......	
327b	same, booklet pane of 4........................	2.50	......	
328	4¢ violet....................................	1.40	.25	.25
328a	same, bklt. pane of 3.........................	......	2.50	......
328b	same, bklt. pane of 6.........................	......	2.25	......
329	5¢ ultramarine	3.00	.40	.25
330	4¢ Queen Elizabeth II	1.35	.40	.25

Coil Stamps Perf. 9-1/2 Vertically

Scott	Description	Plate Block	Unused	Used
331-33	2¢-4¢ complete, 3 vars.....................	......	8.00	3.60
331	2¢ green....................................	......	1.60	1.25
332	3¢ carmine rose	......	1.60	1.25
333	4¢ violet....................................	......	3.30	1.90
334	50¢ Textile Industry	23.00	4.70	.25

325-29, 331-33 — 330 — 334 — 335

336 — 337-342, 345-348 — 343

1954

Scott	Description	Plate Block	Unused	Used
335	4¢ Walrus..................................	1.85	.30	.25
336	5¢ Beaver..................................	2.25	.35	.25
336a	same, booklet pane of 5........................	......	1.95	......
337-43	1¢-15¢ cpl., 7 vars.	11.75	2.75	1.50
337	1¢ violet brown..............................	1.40	.25	.25
337a	same, booklet pane of 5........................	......	1.40	......
338	2¢ green....................................	1.40	.25	.25
338a	mini pane of 25	......	4.40	......
338a	sealed pack of 2.............................	......	9.50	......
339	3¢ carmine rose	1.40	.25	.25
340	4¢ violet....................................	1.40	.25	.25
340a	same, booklet pane of 5........................	......	1.65	......
340b	same, booklet pane of 6........................	......	5.50	......
341	5¢ bright blue...............................	1.75	.25	.25
341a	same, booklet pane of 5........................	......	1.65	......
341b	mini sheet of 20.............................	......	8.25	......
342	6¢ orange..................................	2.75	.55	.25
343	15¢ Gannet	7.75	1.60	.25

SCOTT NO.	DESCRIPTION	PLATE BLOCK F/NH	UNUSED F/NH	USED F

349   350   351   352   353

Coil Stamps Perf. 9-1/2 Vertically

Scott	Description	PB	Unused	Used
345-48	2¢-4¢ complete, 3 vars	......	4.50	.75
345	2¢ green	......	.65	.25
347	4¢ violet	......	1.60	.25
348	5¢ bright blue	......	2.50	.25
349	4¢ J.S.D. Thompson	1.85	.35	.25
350	5¢ M. Bowell	1.85	.35	.25

1955

351	10¢ Eskimo in Kayak	2.25	.40	.20

1955-56 COMMEMORATIVES

352/64	(352-61, 364 (complete, 11 varieties	26.00	3.75	2.10
352	4¢ Musk Ox	1.85	.40	.25
353	5¢ Whooping Cranes	2.00	.45	.25

1955

354	5¢ Intl. Civil Aviation Org.	2.40	.50	.25
355	5¢ Alberta-Saskatchewan	2.40	.50	.25
356	5¢ Boy Scout Jamboree	2.40	.50	.25
357	4¢ R.B. Bennett	2.40	.50	.25
358	5¢ C. Tupper	2.40	.50	.25

1956

359	5¢ Hockey Players	2.25	.50	.25
360	4¢ Caribou	2.40	.50	.25
361	5¢ Mountain Goat	2.40	.50	.25
362	20¢ Paper Industry	9.50	1.55	.25
363	25¢ Chemical Industry	10.75	1.85	.25
364	5¢ Fire Prevention	1.85	.40	.25

354   355   356   357

358   359   360   361

362   363   364   365

1957 COMMEMORATIVES

365-74	complete, 10 varieties	20.50(7)	6.20	4.50
365-68	Recreation, attached	2.95	2.10	1.60
365	5¢ Fishing	......	.40	.25
366	5¢ Swimming	......	.40	.25
367	5¢ Hunting	......	.40	.25
368	5¢ Skiing	......	.40	.25
369	5¢ Loon	1.75	.40	.25
370	5¢ D. Thompson, Explorer	1.75	.40	.25
371	5¢ Parliament Building	1.75	.40	.25
372	15¢ Posthorn & Globe	12.50	2.50	2.25
373	5¢ Coal Miner	1.75	.35	.25
374	5¢ Royal Visit	1.75	.35	.25

1958 COMMEMORATIVES

375-82	complete, 8 varieties	13.75(6)	2.75	1.80
375	5¢ Newspaper	......	.35	.25
376	5¢ Int'l. Geophysical Year	......	.35	.25
377	5¢ Miner Panning Gold	3.25	.35	.25
378	5¢ La Verendrye, Explorer	2.50	.35	.25
379	5¢ S. deChamplain	5.25	.35	.25
380	5¢ National Health	2.30	.35	.25
381	5¢ Petroleum Industry	2.30	.35	.25
382	5¢ Speaker's Chair & Mace	2.30	.35	.25

369   370   371   372

373   374   375   376

377   378   379

380   381   382

1959 COMMEMORATIVES

383-88	complete, 6 varieties	14.65	2.00	1.25
383	5¢ Old & Modern Planes	2.40	.35	.25
384	5¢ NATO Anniversary	2.40	.35	.25
385	5¢ Woman Tending Tree	2.40	.35	.25
386	5¢ Royal Tour	2.40	.35	.25
387	5¢ St. Lawrence Seaway	5.25	.35	.25
387a	same, center inverted	...	9800.00	8000.00
388	5¢ Plains of Abraham	2.40	.35	.25

1960-62 COMMEMORATIVES

389-400	complete, 12 varieties	17.50	4.00	2.25
389	5¢ Girl Guides Emblem	1.85	.45	.25
390	5¢ Battle of Long Sault	1.85	.45	.25

1961

391	5¢ Earth Mover	1.85	.45	.25
392	5¢ E.P. Johnson	1.85	.45	.25

383   384   385

386   387   388   389

390   391   392

SCOTT NO.	DESCRIPTION	PLATE BLOCK F/NH	UNUSED F/NH	USED F
393	5¢ A. Meighen	1.85	.40	.25
394	5¢ Colombo Plan	1.85	.40	.25
395	5¢ Natural Resources	1.85	.40	.25

1962

396	5¢ Education	1.85	.40	.25
397	5¢ Red River Settlement	1.85	.40	.25
398	5¢ Jean Talon	1.85	.40	.25
399	5¢ Victoria, B.C.	1.85	.40	.25
400	5¢ Trans-Canada	1.85	.40	.25

393 / 395 / 396 / 394 / 397 / 398 / 399 / 400 / 401-09

1962-63

401-05	1¢-5¢ complete, 5 varieties	7.00	1.00	.85
401	1¢ deep brown (1963)	1.10	.30	.25
401a	same, booklet pane of 5	......	3.30	......
402	2¢ green (1963)	3.60	.30	.25
402a	mini pane of 25	......	8.00	......
402a	same, sealed pack of 2	......	18.50	......
403	3¢ purple (1963)	1.25	.30	.25
404	4¢ carmine (1963)	1.25	.30	.25
404a	same, booklet pane of 5	......	3.70	......
404b	mini pane of 25	......	13.00	......
405	5¢ violet blue	1.50	.30	.25
405a	same, booklet pane of 5	......	5.00	......
405b	mini pane of 20	......	15.00	......

1963-64 Coil Stamps, Perf. 9-1/2 Horiz.

406-09	2¢-5¢ complete, 4 varieties	......	15.50	6.00
406	2¢ green	......	4.65	2.25
407	3¢ purple (1964)	......	3.00	1.75
408	4¢ carmine	......	4.65	2.15
409	5¢ violet blue	......	4.65	.85

1963-64 COMMEMORATIVES

410/35	(410, 412-13, 416-17, 431-35) 10 varieties	10.20	2.50	1.60
410	5¢ Sir Casimir S. Gzowski	1.60	.35	.25
411	$1 Export Trade	74.25	15.00	2.50
412	5¢ Sir M. Frobisher, Explorer	1.60	.35	.25
413	5¢ First Mail Routes	1.60	.35	.25

1963-64

414	7¢ Jet Takeoff (1964)	2.75	.60	.55
415	15¢ Canada Geese	11.00	2.20	.25

1964

416	5¢ World Peace	1.50	.35	.25
417	5¢ Canadian Unity	1.50	.35	.25

410 / 411 / 412 / 413 / 414, 430, 436 / 415 / 416 / 417

COATS OF ARMS & FLORAL EMBLEMS

419	Quebec & White Garden Lily
420	Nova Scotia & Mayflower
421	New Brunswick & Purple Violet (1965)
422	Manitoba & Prairie Crocus (1965)
423	British Columbia & Dogwood (1965)
424	Prince Edward Island & Lady's Slipper (1965)
425	Saskatchewan & Prairie Lily (1966)
426	Alberta & Wild Rose (1966)
427	Newfoundland & Pitcher Plant (1966)
428	Yukon & Fireweed (1966)
429	Northwest Territories & Mountain Avens (1966)

418
Ontario & White Trillium

429A
Canada & Maple Leaf

1964-66

SCOTT NO.	DESCRIPTION	PLATE BLOCK F/NH	UNUSED F/NH	USED F
418-29A	complete, 13 varieties	15.00	3.55	2.75
418	5¢ red brown, buff & green	1.60	.35	.25
419	5¢ green, yellow & orange	1.60	.35	.25
420	5¢ blue, pink & green	1.60	.35	.25
421	5¢ carmine, green & violet	1.60	.35	.25
422	5¢ red brown, lilac & green	2.75	.35	.25
423	5¢ lilac, green & bistre	1.60	.35	.25
424	5¢ violet, green & deep rose	1.60	.35	.25
425	5¢ sepia, orange & green	1.60	.35	.25
426	5¢ green, yellow & carmine	1.60	.35	.25
427	5¢ black, green & carmine	1.60	.35	.25
428	5¢ dark blue, rose & green	2.75	.35	.25
429	5¢ olive, yellow & green	1.60	.35	.25
429A	5¢ dark blue & red (1966)	1.60	.35	.25

1964
Surcharged on 414

430	8¢ on 7¢ Jet Takeoff	......	.50	.40
431	5¢ Charlottetown Conference	1.60	.35	.25
432	5¢ Quebec Conference	1.60	.35	.25
433	5¢ Queen Elizabeth's Visit	1.60	.35	.25
434	3¢ Christmas	1.60	.35	.25
434a	mini sheet of 25	......	8.25	......
434a	same, sealed pack of 2	......	17.50	......
435	5¢ Christmas	1.60	.35	.25

Jet Type of 1964

436	8¢ Jet Takeoff	2.30	.50	.25

1965 COMMEMORATIVES

437-44	8 varieties	9.00	2.50	1.65
437	5¢ I.C.Y.	1.65	.35	.25

431 / 432 / 433 / 434, 435 / 437 / 438 / 439 / 440 / 441 / 442 / 443-44

438	5¢ Sir Wilfred Grenfell	1.60	.35	.25
439	5¢ National Flag	1.60	.35	.25
440	5¢ Winston Churchill	1.60	.35	.25
441	5¢ Inter-Parliamentary	1.60	.35	.25
442	5¢ Ottawa, National Capital	1.60	.35	.25
443	3¢ Christmas	1.60	.35	.25
443a	mini pane of 25	......	7.00	......
443a	same, sealed pack of 2	......	15.00	......
444	5¢ Christmas	1.60	.35	.25

SCOTT NO.	DESCRIPTION	PLATE BLOCK F/NH	UNUSED F/NH	USED F

1966 COMMEMORATIVES

445-52	8 varieties	11.50	2.35	1.70
445	5¢ Alouette II Satellite	1.60	.35	.25
446	5¢ La Salle Arrival	1.60	.35	.25
447	5¢ Highway Safety	1.60	.35	.25
448	5¢ London Conference	1.60	.35	.25
449	5¢ Atomic Reactor	1.60	.35	.25
450	5¢ Parliamentary Library	1.60	.35	.25
451	3¢ Christmas	1.60	.35	.25
451a	mini pane of 25	......	5.25	......
451a	same, sealed pack of 2	......	11.00	......
452	5¢ Christmas	1.60	.35	.25

445 446 447 448

449 451, 452 450 453

1967 COMMEMORATIVES

453/77	(453, 469-77) complete, 10 varieties	10.00	2.70	2.10
453	5¢ National Centennial	1.60	.35	.25

454 455 456, 466 457, 467

458, 468 459-460F, 468A-B, 543-49 461 465B

Regional Views & Art Designs
1967-72 Perf.12 except as noted

454-65B	1¢-$1 complete, 14 varieties	95.50	18.25	3.60
454-64	1¢-20¢, 11 varieties	21.00	3.35	1.85
454	1¢ brown	1.35	.30	.25
454a	same, booklet pane of 5	......	1.35	......
454b	booklet pane, 1¢(1), 6¢(4)	......	3.30	......
454c	booklet pane, 1¢(5), 5¢(5)	......	3.85	......

NOTE: #454d, 454e, 456a, 457d, 458d, and 460h are Booklet Singles

454d	1¢ perf. 10 (1968)	......	.35	.25
454e	1¢ 12-1/2 x 12 (1969)	......	.45	.25
455	2¢ green	1.40	.30	.25
455a	booklet pane 2¢(4), 3¢(4)	......	1.80	......
456	3¢ dull purple	2.10	.30	.25
456a	3¢ 12-1/2 x 12 (1971)	......	2.20	1.20
457	4¢ carmine rose	2.10	.30	.25
457a	same, booklet pane 5	......	1.50	......
457b	miniature pane of 25	......	26.00	......
457c	same, booklet pane of 25	......	9.00	......
457d	4¢ perf.10 (1968)	......	.70	.30
458	5¢ blue	1.55	.30	.25
458a	same, booklet pane of 5	......	6.50	......
458b	miniature pane of 20	......	34.00	......
458c	booklet pane of 20, perf.10	......	8.50	......
458d	5¢ perf. 10 (1968)	......	.70	.30
459	6¢ orange, perf. 10 (1968)	3.85	.35	.25
459a	same, booklet pane of 25	......	10.00	......
459b	6¢ orange 12-1/2x12 (1969)	3.30	.35	.25
460	6¢ black, 12-1/2x12 (1970)	2.30	.30	.25
460a	booklet pane of 25, perf.10	......	15.85	......
460b	booklet pane of 25, 12-1/2x12	......	18.50	......
460c	6¢ black, 12-1/2x12 (1970)	2.20	.35	.25
460d	booklet pane of 4, 12-1/2x12	......	5.50	......
460e	booklet pane of 4, perf.10	......	12.00	......
460f	6¢ black, perf. 12 (1972)	2.50	.50	.35
460g	6¢ black, perf. 10 (I)	......	1.75	.40
460h	6¢ black, perf. 10 (II)	......	4.00	1.25

460, 460a, b,& g: Original Die. Weak shading lines around 6.
460 c, d, e, & h: Reworked plate lines strengthened, darker.
460f: Original Die. Strong shading lines, similar to 468B, but Perf 12x12 .

461	8¢ "Alaska Highway"	3.00	.35	.25
462	10¢ "The Jack Pine"	1.80	.35	.25
463	15¢ "Bylot Island"	3.55	.55	.25
464	20¢ "The Ferry, Quebec"	3.55	.70	.25
465	25¢ "The Solemn Land"	7.60	1.50	.25
465A	50¢ "Summer Stores"	22.00	4.40	.25
465B	$1 "Imp. Wildcat No. 3"	49.50	9.90	.80

1967-70 Coil Stamps

466-68B	3¢-6¢ complete, 5 varieties	......	7.40	3.35

Perf. 9-1/2 Horizontally

466	3¢ dull purple	......	4.00	1.10
467	4¢ carmine rose	......	1.25	.65
468	5¢ blue	......	2.75	.85

Perf. 10 Horizontally

468A	6¢ orange (1969)	......	.50	.25
468B	6¢ black (1970)	......	.45	.25

NOTE: See #543-50 for similar issues

469 470 471

472 473 474

1967

469	5¢ Expo '67	1.60	.35	.25
470	5¢ Women's Franchise	1.60	.35	.25
471	5¢ Royal Visit	1.60	.35	.25
472	5¢ Pan-American Games	1.60	.35	.25
473	5¢ Canadian Press	1.60	.35	.25
474	5¢ George P. Vanier	1.60	.35	.25
475	5¢ View of Toronto	1.60	.35	.25
476	3¢ Christmas	1.30	.35	.25
476a	miniature pane of 25	......	4.25	......
476a	same, sealed pack of 2	......	8.50	......
477	5¢ Christmas	1.30	.20	.25

475 476, 477 478 479

480 481 482

483 484 485 486

1968 COMMEMORATIVES

478-89	complete, 12 varieties	22.00	5.25	3.75
478	5¢ Gray Jays	4.40	.55	.25
479	5¢ Weather Map & Inst	1.55	.35	.25
480	5¢ Narwhal	1.55	.35	.25
481	5¢ Int'l Hydro. Decade	1.55	.35	.25
482	5¢ Voyage of "Nonsuch"	1.55	.35	.25
483	5¢ Lacrosse Players	1.55	.35	.25
484	5¢ G. Brown, Politician	1.55	.35	.25
485	5¢ H. Bourassa, Journalist	1.55	.35	.25
486	15¢ W.W.I Armistice	11.00	2.25	1.70

NOTE: Beginning with #478, some issues show a printer's inscription with no actual plate number.

SCOTT NO.	DESCRIPTION	PLATE BLOCK F/NH	UNUSED F/NH	USED F

487	5¢ J. McCrae		1.60	.35	.25
488	5¢ Eskimo Family		1.20	.25	.25
488a	same, booklet pane of 10		.....	3.15	.....
489	6¢ Mother & Child		1.20	.25	.25

1969 COMMEMORATIVES

490-504	complete, 15 varieties	48.25	12.50	9.00
490	6¢ Game of Curling	1.55	.35	.25
491	6¢ V. Massey	1.55	.35	.25
492	50¢ A. deSuzor-Cote, Artist	20.00	3.85	3.30
493	6¢ I.L.O.	1.55	.35	.25
494	15¢ Vickers Vimy Over Atlantic	9.50	2.85	1.80
495	6¢ Sir W. Osler	1.55	.35	.25
496	6¢ White Throated Sparrows	2.00	.45	.25
497	10¢ Ipswich Sparrow	3.85	.75	.50
498	25¢ Hermit Thrush	9.60	2.10	2.00
499	6¢ Map of Prince Edward Island	1.55	.30	.25
500	6¢ Canada Games	1.55	.30	.25
501	6¢ Sir Isaac Brock	1.55	.30	.25
502	5¢ Children of Various Races	1.55	.30	.25
502a	booklet pane of 10	.....	4.00	.....
503	6¢ Children Various Races	1.35	.35	.25
504	6¢ Stephen Leacock	1.55	.35	.25

1970 COMMEMORATIVES

505/31	(505-18, 531) 15 varieties	26.00	13.75	12.00
505	6¢ Manitoba Cent	1.55	.35	.25
506	6¢ N.W. Territory Centenary	1.55	.35	.25
507	6¢ International Biological	1.55	.35	.25
508-11	Expo '70 attached	12.00	9.75	9.75
508	25¢ Emblems	.....	2.50	2.50
509	25¢ Dogwood	.....	2.50	2.50
510	25¢ Lily	.....	2.50	2.50
511	25¢ Trillium	.....	2.50	2.50

512	6¢ H. Kelsey—Explorer	1.55	.35	.25
513	10¢ 25th U.N. Anniversary	3.85	.80	.65
514	15¢ 25th U.N. Anniversary	6.25	1.25	1.10
515	6¢ L. Riel—Metis Leader	1.55	.35	.25
516	6¢ Sir A. Mackenzie-Explorer	1.55	.35	.25
517	6¢ Sir O. Mowat Confederation Father	1.55	.35	.25
518	6¢ Isle of Spruce	1.55	.35	.25

519-30	5¢-15¢ complete, 12 varieties	18.00	5.50	3.50
519-23	5¢ Christmas, attached	7.95(10)	3.10	2.80
519	5¢ Santa Claus	.....	.45	.25
520	5¢ Sleigh	.....	.45	.25
521	5¢ Nativity	.....	.45	.25
522	5¢ Skiing	.....	.45	.25
523	5¢ Snowman & Tree	.....	.45	.25
524-28	6¢ Christmas, attached	10.00(10)	3.55	3.25
524	6¢ Christ Child	.....	.55	.25
525	6¢ Tree & Children	.....	.55	.25
526	6¢ Toy Store	.....	.55	.25
527	6¢ Santa Claus	.....	.55	.25
528	6¢ Church	.....	.55	.25

NOTE: We cannot supply blocks or pairs of the 5¢ & 6¢ Christmas designs in varying combinations of designs.

529	10¢ Christ Child	2.20	.60	.40
530	15¢ Snowmobile & Trees	4.80	1.25	1.00
531	6¢ Sir Donald A. Smith	1.55	.35	.25

1971 COMMEMORATIVES

532/58	(532-42, 552-58) complete, 18 varieties	31.00	8.50	7.95
532	6¢ E. Carr—Painter & Writer	1.55	.35	.25
533	6¢ Discovery of Insulin	1.55	.35	.25
534	6¢ Sir E. Rutherford—Physicist	1.55	.35	.25
535-38	6¢-7¢ Maple Leaves	6.75	1.20	.80
535	6¢ Maple Seeds	1.75	.35	.25
536	6¢ Summer Leaf	1.75	.35	.25
537	Autumn Leaf	1.75	.35	.25
538	7¢ Winter Leaf	1.75	.35	.25
539	6¢ L. Papineau—Polit. Reform	1.55	.35	.25
540	6¢ Copper Mine Expedition	1.55	.35	.25
541	15¢ Radio Canada Int'l	9.95	2.00	1.50
542	6¢ Census Centennial	1.55	.35	.25

Stamp illustrations with identifying numbers:
487, 488, 490, 491, 492, 493, 494, 495, 496, 500, 501, 499, 502, 503, 504, 505, 506, 507, 508, 509, 512, 513-514, 515, 516, 517, 518, 519, 524, 529, 530, 531, 532, 533, 534, 535, 539, 540, 541, 542, 543, 549, 544, 550

SCOTT NO.	DESCRIPTION	PLATE BLOCK F/NH	UNUSED F/NH	USED F

552

553

554-55

556-57

558

559

560

561

1971

543	7¢ Trans. & Communication.............................	3.70	.40	.20
543a	bklt. pane, 7¢(3), 3¢(1), 1¢(1)	......	4.50	......
543b	bklt. pane 7¢(12), 3¢(4), 1¢(4)	......	8.50	......
544	8¢ Parliamentary Library................................	2.95	.50	.20
544a	bklt. pane 8¢(2), 6¢(1), 1¢(3)	......	2.55	......
544b	bklt. pane 8¢(11), 6¢(1), 1¢(6)	......	6.95	......
544c	bklt. pane 8¢(5), 6¢(1), 1¢(4)	......	3.85	......

1971 Coil Stamps Perf.10 Horizontally

549	7¢ Trans. & Communication.............................	......	.40	.25
550	8¢ Parliamentary Library................................	......	.35	.25
552	7¢ B.C. Centennial	1.55	.35	.25
553	7¢ Paul Kane	3.20	.50	.25
554-57	6¢-15¢ Christmas..	8.00	1.65	1.50
554	6¢ Snowflake, dark blue................................	1.25	.35	.25
555	7¢ same, bright green....................................	1.25	.35	.25
556	10¢ same, deep carmine & silver...................	2.20	.45	.40
557	15¢ same, light ultramarine, deep carmine & silver........	4.00	.85	.85
558	7¢ P. Laporte	2.70	.35	.25

1972 COMMEMORATIVES

559/610	(559-61, 582-85, 606-10) 12 varieties	47.85(9)	10.40	8.60
559	8¢ Figure Skating..	1.55	.35	.25
560	8¢ W.H.O. Heart Disease...............................	1.80	.40	.25
561	8¢ Frontenac & Ft. St. Louis	1.55	.35	.25

VERY FINE QUALITY: From 1935 to date, add 20% to the Fine price. Minimum of 3¢ per stamp.

1972-76 INDIAN PEOPLES OF CANADA

562-81	complete, 20 varieties.....................................	17.25	7.35	4.40
562-63	Plains, attached	2.15	.90	.60
562	8¢ Buffalo Chase	......	.45	.30
563	8¢ Indian Artifacts..	......	.45	.30
564-65	Plains, attached	2.15	.90	.60
564	8¢ Thunderbird Symbolism.............................	......	.45	.30
565	8¢ Sun Dance Costume..................................	......	.45	.30
566-67	Algonkians, attached (1973)	2.15	.90	.60
566	8¢ Algonkian Artifacts....................................	......	.45	.30
567	8¢ Micmac Indians...	......	.45	.30
568-69	Algonkians, attached (1973)	2.00	.80	.75
568	8¢ Thunderbird Symbolism.............................	......	.45	.30
569	8¢ Costume	......	.45	.30
570-71	Pacific, attached (1974)	2.00	.80	.60
570	8¢ Nootka Sound House................................	......	.45	.30
571	8¢ Artifacts	......	.45	.30
572-73	Pacific, attached (1974)	2.00	.80	1.00
572	8¢ Chief in Chilkat Blanket............................	......	.45	.30
573	8¢ Thunderbird—Kwakiutl.............................	......	.45	.30
574-75	Subarctic, attached (1975)............................	1.70	.70	.60
574	8¢ Canoe & Artifacts.....................................	......	.35	.25
575	8¢ Dance—Kutcha-Kutchin............................	......	.35	.25
576-77	Subarctic, attached (1975)............................	1.70	.70	.65
576	8¢ Kutchin Costume......................................	......	.35	.25
577	8¢ Ojibwa Thunderbird..................................	......	.35	.25
578-79	Iroquois, attached (1976)..............................	1.70	.70	.60
578	10¢ Masks..	......	.35	.25
579	10¢ Camp	......	.35	.25
580-81	Iroquois, attached (1976)..............................	1.70	.70	.60
580	10¢ Iroquois Thunderbird..............................	......	.35	.25
581	10¢ Man & Woman	......	.35	.25

562

564

582

1972 EARTH SCIENCES

582-85	Sciences, attached............................	38.50(16)	8.25	8.00
582	15¢ Geology...................................	......	2.00	1.75
583	15¢ Geography	......	2.00	1.75
584	15¢ Photogrammetry	......	2.00	1.75
585	15¢ Cartography..............................	......	2.00	1.75

NOTE: Plate Block Price is for a miniature pane of 16 Stamps.

1973-76 DEFINITIVE ISSUE PERF. 12 x 12-1/2

586-93A	1¢-10¢, 9 varieties		8.85	1.85	1.60
586	1¢ Sir J. Macdonald	1.30	.25	.25
586a	bklt. pane 1¢(3), 6¢(1), 8¢(2)	......	1.25	......
586b	bklt. pane 1¢(6), 6¢(1), 8¢(11)	......	3.00	......
586c	bklt. pane 1¢(2), 2¢(4), 8¢(4)	......	1.70	......
587	2¢ Sir W. Laurier...	1.30	.30	.25
588	3¢ Sir R.L. Borden...	1.30	.30	.25
589	4¢ W.L. Mackenzie King	1.30	.30	.25
590	5¢ R.B. Bennett...	1.30	.30	.25
591	6¢ L.B. Pearson	1.30	.30	.25
592	7¢ L. St. Laurent (1974)................................	1.30	.30	.25
593	8¢ Queen Elizabeth	1.30	.30	.25
593b	same (pf. 13x13-1/2) (1976).........................	4.95	1.00	.50
593A	10¢ Queen Elizabeth (perf 13x13-1/2) (1976) ...	1.55	.35	.50
593c	10¢ same, perf 12x12-1/2 booklet single..........	......	.50	.50

586

593, 593b, 593A, 604-605

594, 594a, 594B

599, 599a, 600

1972-73 Photogravure & Engraved Perf. 12-1/2x12

594-99	10¢-$1, 6 varieties		26.00	5.10	6.45
594	10¢ Forests	1.80	.40	.25
595	15¢ Mountain Sheep.......................................	1.90	.45	.25
596	20¢ Prairie Mosaic	3.30	.60	.25
597	25¢ Polar Bears	3.30	.65	.25
598	50¢ Seashore..	5.95	1.25	.25
599	$1 Vancouver Skyline(1973)...........................	13.75	2.80	.75

NOTE: #594-97 exist with 2 types of phosphor tagging. Prices are for Ottawa tagged.

1976-77 Perf. 13

594a	10¢ Forests	1.80	.40	.25
595a	15¢ Mountain Sheep.......................................	13.00	.65	.25
596a	20¢ Prairie Mosaic	3.25	.65	.25
597a	25¢ Polar Bears	3.60	.75	.25
598a	50¢ Seashore..	9.50	1.90	.25
599a	$1 Vancouver Skyline(1977)...........................	13.75	2.80	.45

1972 Lithographed & Engraved Perf. 11

600	$1 Vancouver Skyline	29.00	6.00	2.30
601	$2 Quebec Buildings.....................................	25.00	5.00	3.25

1974-76 Coil Stamps

604	8¢ Queen Elizabeth	......	.30	.25
605	10¢ Queen Elizabeth (1976)...........................	......	.40	.25

1972

606-09	6¢-15¢ Christmas..	8.40	1.70	1.45
606	6¢ Five candles...	1.30	.40	.25
607	8¢ same	1.55	.40	.25
608	10¢ Six candles...	2.30	.45	.25
609	15¢ same	3.50	.80	.80
610	8¢ C.Krieghoff—Painter	2.60	.40	.25

606, 607

608, 609

610

611

SCOTT NO.	DESCRIPTION	PLATE BLOCK F/NH	UNUSED F/NH	USED F

1973 COMMEMORATIVES

611-28	18 varieties, complete	28.40	6.70	5.40
611	8¢ Monseignor De Laval	1.55	.25	.25
612	8¢ G.A. French & Map	1.55	.30	.25
613	10¢ Spectrograph	2.00	.45	.35
614	15¢ "Musical Ride"	3.95	.75	.70
615	8¢ J. Mance—Nurse	1.55	.35	.25
616	8¢ J. Howe	1.55	.35	.25
617	15¢ "Mist Fantasy" Painting	3.30	.70	.65
618	8¢ P.E.I. Confederation	1.55	.35	.25
619	8¢ Scottish Settlers	1.55	.35	.25
620	8¢ Royal Visit	1.55	.35	.25
621	15¢ same	3.25	.70	.60
622	8¢ Nellie McClung	1.55	.35	.25
623	8¢ 21st Olympic Games	1.55	.35	.25
624	15¢ same	3.30	.70	.60
625-28	6¢ to 15¢ Christmas	5.75	1.30	1.25
625	6¢ Skate	1.30	.25	.25
626	8¢ Bird Ornament	1.30	.25	.25
627	10¢ Santa Claus	1.55	.30	.30
628	15¢ Shepherd	3.30	.65	.65

1974 COMMEMORATIVES

629-55	complete, 27 varieties	22.40(16)	11.25	7.50
629-32	Summer Olympics, attached	2.00	1.65	1.35
629	8¢ Children Diving	......	.45	.25
630	8¢ Jogging	......	.45	.25
631	8¢ Bicycling	......	.45	.25
632	8¢ Hiking	......	.45	.25
633	8¢ Winnipeg Centenary	1.55	.25	.25
634-39	Postal Carriers, attached	4.60(6)	3.85	3.85
634	8¢ Postal Clerk & Client	......	.75	.50
635	8¢ Mail Pick-up	......	.75	.50
636	8¢ Mail Handler	......	.75	.50
637	8¢ Sorting Mail	......	.75	.50
638	8¢ Letter Carrier	......	.75	.50
639	8¢ Rural Delivery	......	.75	.35
640	8¢ Agriculture Symbol	1.55	.35	.25
641	8¢ Antique to Modern Phones	1.55	.35	.25
642	8¢ World Cycling Championship	1.55	.35	.25
643	8¢ Mennonite Settlers	1.55	.35	.25
644-47	Winter Olympics, attached	2.00	1.75	1.40
644	8¢ Snowshoeing	......	.40	.25
645	8¢ Skiing	....	.40	.25
646	8¢ Skating	....	.40	.25
647	8¢ Curling	......	.40	.25
648	8¢ U.P.U. Cent.	1.55	.35	.25
649	15¢ same	4.80	1.00	.70
650-53	6¢ to 15¢ Christmas	8.00	1.55	1.40
650	6¢ Nativity	1.30	.25	.25
651	8¢ Skaters in Hull	1.30	.25	.25
652	10¢ The Ice Cone	2.00	.45	.35
653	15¢ Laurentian Village	3.60	.60	.50
654	8¢ G. Marconi—Radio Inventor	1.55	.35	.25
655	8¢ W.H. Merritt & Welland Canal	1.55	.35	.25

1975 COMMEMORATIVES

656-80	complete, 25 varieties	67.50(18)	16.60	15.00
656	$1 "The Sprinter"	11.75	2.85	2.75
657	$2 "The Plunger"	25.35	5.75	5.50
658-59	Writers, attached	1.55	.90	.50
658	8¢ L.M. Montgomery—Author	......	.35	.25
659	8¢ L. Hemon—Author	......	.35	.25
660	8¢ M. Bourgeoys—Educator	1.55	.35	.25
661	8¢ A. Desjardins—Credit Union	1.55	.35	.25
662-63	Religious, attached	1.55	.70	.70
662	8¢ S Chown & Church	......	.30	.25
663	8¢ J. Cook & Church	......	.30	.25
664	20¢ Pole Vaulter	3.30	.75	.50
665	25¢ Marathon Runner	3.85	.85	.55
666	50¢ Hurdler	7.75	1.50	1.40
667	8¢ Calgary Centenary	1.55	.35	.25
668	8¢ Int'l. Women's Year	1.55	.35	.25
669	8¢ "Justice"	1.55	.35	.25
670-73	Ships, attached	2.75	2.20	1.85
670	8¢ W.D. Lawrence	......	.55	.35
671	8¢ Beaver	......	.55	.35
672	8¢ Neptune	......	.55	.35
673	8¢ Quadra	......	.55	.35
674-79	6¢ to 15¢ Christmas	5.60(4)	1.75	1.50
674-75	Christmas, attached	1.35	.60	.35
674	6¢ Santa Claus	......	.30	.25
675	6¢ Skater	......	.30	.25
676-77	Christmas, attached	1.50	.55	.45
676	8¢ Child	......	.30	.25
677	8¢ Family & Tree	......	.30	.25
678	10¢ Gift	1.55	.35	.25
679	15¢ Trees	2.40	.55	.55
680	8¢ Horn & Crest	1.55	.35	.25

SCOTT NO.	DESCRIPTION	PLATE BLOCK F/NH	UNUSED F/NH	USED F

674

676

679

680

681

687

684

689   690   691

1976 COMMEMORATIVES

681-703	complete, 23 varieties	75.00(18)	21.25	16.90
681	8¢ Olympic Flame	1.50	.35	.25
682	20¢ Opening Ceremony	3.70	.85	.70
683	25¢ Receiving Medals	4.95	1.10	.85
684	20¢ Communication Arts	6.95	1.35	.70
685	25¢ Handicraft Tools	8.25	1.65	.75
686	50¢ Performing Arts	12.50	2.50	1.65
687	$1 Notre Dame & Tower	17.00	3.50	2.75
688	$2 Olympic Stadium	28.00	5.80	5.35
689	20¢ Olympic Winter Games	5.00	1.00	.85
690	20¢ "Habitat"	2.95	.65	.65
691	10¢ Benjamin Franklin	1.85	.40	.25
692-93	Military College, attached	1.55	.70	.50
692	8¢ Color Parade	......	.30	.25
693	8¢ Wing Parade	......	.30	.25
694	20¢ Olympiad—Phys. Disabled	3.25	.65	.60
695-96	Authors, attached	1.55	.60	.50
695	8¢ R.W. Service—Author	......	.30	.25
696	8¢ G. Guevremont—Author	......	.30	.25
697	8¢ Nativity Window	1.30	.30	.25
698	10¢ same	1.55	.30	.25
699	20¢ same	2.80	.65	.65
700-03	Inland Vessels, attached	2.30	1.85	1.75
700	10¢ Northcote	......	.45	.40
701	10¢ Passport	......	.45	.40
702	10¢ Chicora	......	.45	.40
703	10¢ Athabasca	......	.45	.40

692-93

694

695

696   697

700

704

1977 COMMEMORATIVES

704/51	(704, 732-51) complete, 21 varieties	20.85(14)	7.25	5.50
704	25¢ Silver Jubilee	3.85	.80	.70

705, 781, 781a

713, 713a, 716, 716a, 789, 789a, 791, 792

714, 715, 729, 730, 790, 797, 800, 806

1977-79 Definitives
Perf. 12x12-1/2

705-27	1¢ to $2 complete, 22 varieties	66.50	19.50	6.40
705	1¢ Bottle Gentian	1.10	.25	.25
707	2¢ Western Columbine	1.10	.25	.25
708	3¢ Canada Lily	1.10	.25	.25
709	4¢ Hepatica	1.10	.25	.25
710	5¢ Shooting Star	1.10	.25	.25
711	10¢ Lady's Slipper	1.10	.25	.25
711a	same, perf.13 (1978)	1.35	.25	.25
712	12¢ Jewelweed, perf 13x13-1/2 (1978)	3.80	.30	.25
713	12¢ Queen Elizabeth II, perf.13x13-1/2	1.55	.35	.25
713a	same, perf.12x12-1/2	......	.35	.25
714	12¢ Parliament, perf.13	1.55	.25	.25
715	14¢ same, perf.13 (1978)	1.80	.30	.25
716	14¢ Queen Elizabeth II perf. 13x13-1/2	1.80	.30	.25
716a	14¢ same, perf 12x12-1/2	......	.30	.25
716b	same, booklet pane of 25	......	6.25	......

NOTE: 713a and 716a are from booklet panes. 713a will have one or more straight edges, 716a may or may not have straight edges.

717

723, 723A

726

Perforated 13-1/2

717	15¢ Trembling Aspen	2.50	.50	.25
718	20¢ Douglas Fir	2.65	.55	.25
719	25¢ Sugar Maple	3.30	.70	.25
720	30¢ Oak Leaf	3.70	.80	.25
721	35¢ White Pine (1979)	4.20	.90	.35
723	50¢ Main Street (1978)	6.85	1.40	.30
723A	50¢ same, 1978 Lic. Plate	6.50	1.25	.45
723C	60¢ Ontario House	7.75	1.55	.45
724	75¢ Row Houses (1978)	9.00	1.90	.70
725	80¢ Maritime (1978)	9.75	1.95	.90
726	$1 Fundy Park (1979)	12.00	2.50	.70
727	$2 Kluane Park (1979)	26.00	5.25	1.60

1977-78 Coil Stamps Perf. 10 Vert.

729	12¢ Parliament	......	.30	.25
730	14¢ same (1978)	......	.40	.25

732

733

735

736   737

1977 COMMEMORATIVES

732	12¢ Cougar	1.55	.35	.25
733-34	Thomson, attached	1.55	.70	.45
733	12¢ Algonquin Park	......	.35	.25
734	12¢ Autumn Birches	......	.35	.25
735	12¢ Crown & Lion	1.55	.35	.25
736	12¢ Badge & Ribbon	1.55	.35	.25
737	12¢ Peace Bridge	1.55	.35	.25

SCOTT NO.	DESCRIPTION	PLATE BLOCK F/NH	UNUSED F/NH	USED F

738-39   740   741

738-39	Pioneers, attached	1.60	.70	.45
738	12¢ Bernier & CGS Arctic	......	.30	.25
739	12¢ Fleming & RR Bridge	......	.30	.25
740	25¢ Peace Tower	3.85	.75	.75
741	10¢ Braves & Star	1.20	.25	.20
742	12¢ Angelic Choir	1.55	.25	.20
743	25¢ Christ Child	3.55	.80	.60
744-47	Sailing Ships	1.55	1.35	1.15
744	12¢ Pinky	......	.35	.25
745	12¢ Tern	......	.35	.25
746	12¢ Five Masted	......	.35	.25
747	12¢ Mackinaw	......	.35	.25
748-49	Inuit, attached	1.55	.60	.50
748	12¢ Hunting Seal	......	.35	.25
749	12¢ Fishing	......	.35	.25
750-51	Inuit, attached	1.55	.60	.50
750	12¢ Disguised Archer	......	.35	.25
751	12¢ Hunters of Old	......	.35	.25

1978 COMMEMORATIVES

752/79	(No #756a)28 varieties	33.00(19)	13.45	8.65
752	12¢ Peregrine Falcon	1.55	.35	.25
753	12¢ CAPEX Victoria	1.55	.35	.25
754	14¢ CAPEX Cartier	1.80	.35	.25
755	30¢ CAPEX Victoria	3.75	.70	.55
756	$1.25 CAPEX Albert	15.50	3.25	1.40
756a	$1.69 CAPEX sheet of 3		4.50	4.50
757	14¢ Games Symbol	1.80	.40	.25
758	30¢ Badminton Players	3.70	.80	.50
759-60	Comm. Games, attached	1.80	.80	.55
759	14¢ Stadium	......	.40	.25
760	14¢ Runners	......	.40	.25
761-62	Comm. Games, attached	3.70	1.65	1.35
761	30¢ Edmonton	......	.85	.60
762	30¢ Bowls	......	.85	.60
763-64	Captain Cook, attached	1.80	.80	.45
763	14¢ Captain Cook	......	.35	.25
764	14¢ Nootka Sound	......	.35	.25
765-66	Resources, attached	1.80	.80	.45
765	14¢ Miners	......	.35	.25
766	14¢ Tar Sands	......	.35	.25
767	14¢ CNE 100th Anniversary	1.80	.35	.25
768	14¢ Mere d'Youville	1.80	.35	.25
769-70	Inuit, attached	1.80	.85	.45
769	14¢ Woman Walking	......	.35	.25
770	14¢ Migration	......	.35	.25
771-72	Inuit, attached	1.80	.85	.45
771	14¢ Plane over Village	......	.35	.25
772	14¢ Dog Team & Sled	......	.35	.25

744   748-49   763

752   753   757   764

759   765-66

767   768   769-70

773   780   813   815

773	12¢ Mary & Child w/pea	1.60	.35	.25
774	14¢ Mary & Child w/apple	1.80	.40	.25
775	30¢ Mary & Child w/goldfinch	3.85	.80	.35
776-79	Ice Vessels, attached	1.80	1.60	1.40
776	14¢ Robinson	......	.40	.25
777	14¢ St. Roch	......	.40	.25
778	14¢ Northern Light	......	.40	.25
779	14¢ Labrador	......	.40	.25

1979 COMMEMORATIVES

780/846	(780, 813-20, 833-46) complete, 23 varieties	36.00(16)	9.75	4.55
780	14¢ Quebec Winter Carnival	1.75	.40	.25

1977-83 Definitives Perf 13x131/2

781-92	1¢-32¢ complete, 11 varieties	16.00	4.15	2.00
781	1¢ Gentian (1979)	1.00	.25	.25
781a	1¢ same, perf 12x12-1/2	......	.25	.25
781b	booklet pane, 1¢ (2—781a), 12¢ (4—713a)	......	1.75	......
782	2¢ Western Columbine (1979)	1.00	.25	.25
782a	booklet pane, 2¢ (4—782b), 12¢ (3—716a)	......	1.75	......
782b	2¢ same, perf 12x121/2 (1978)	......	.25	.25
783	3¢ Canada Lily (1979)	1.00	.25	.25
784	4¢ Hepatica (1979)	1.00	.25	.25
785	5¢ Shooting Star (1979)	1.00	.25	.25
786	10¢ Lady's-Slipper (1979)	1.25	.30	.25
787	15¢ Violet (1979)	2.00	.40	.25
789	17¢ Queen Elizabeth II (1979)	2.00	.75	.65
789a	17¢ same, 12x12-1/2 (1979)	......	.40	.25
789b	booklet pane of 25	......	11.00	......
790	17¢ Parliament Bldg. (1979)	2.00	.45	.25
791	30¢ Queen Elizabeth II (1982)	3.25	.75	.25
792	32¢ Queen Elizabeth II (1983)	3.60	.80	.25

NOTE: 781a, 782b, 797 & 800 are from booklet panes and will have one or more straight edges. 789a may or may not have straight edges.

1979 Perf 12x12-1/2

797	1¢ Parliament Building	......	.75	.30
797a	booklet pane 1¢ (1—797), 5¢ (3—800), 17¢ (2—789a)	......	2.60	......
800	5¢ Parliament Building	......	.35	.25

1979 Coil Stamps Perf 10 Vertical

806	17¢ Parliament Building, slate green	......	.50	.25

1979

813	17¢ Turtle	2.00	.45	.25
814	35¢ Whale	4.60	.95	.35
815-16	Postal Code, attached	2.00	.90	.45
815	17¢ Woman's Finger	......	.50	.25
816	17¢ Man's Finger	......	.50	.25
817-18	Writers, attached	2.00	.90	.60
817	17¢ "Fruits of the Earth"	......	.50	.25
818	17¢ "The Golden Vessel"	......	.50	.25
819-20	Colonels, attached	2.00	.90	.60
819	17¢ Charles de Salaberry	......	.50	.25
820	17¢ John By	......	.50	.25

817-18

819-20   821 Ontario

SCOTT NO.	DESCRIPTION	PLATE BLOCK F/NH	UNUSED F/NH	USED F

PROVINCIAL FLAGS

821 *Ontario*	**822** *Quebec*	**823** *Nova Scotia*
824 *New Brunswick*	**825** *Manitoba*	**826** *British Columbia*
827 *Prince Edward Island*	**828** *Saskatchewan*	**829** *Alberta*
830 *Newfoundland*	**831** *Northern Teritories*	**832** *Yukon Territory*

SCOTT NO.	DESCRIPTION	PLATE BLOCK F/NH	UNUSED F/NH	USED F
832a	17¢ Sheet of 12 varieties, attached	......	5.00	......
821-32	set of singles	......	4.90	3.30
Any	17¢ single	......	.45	.25
833	17¢ Canoe—kayak	2.00	.45	.25
834	17¢ Field Hockey	2.00	.45	.25
835-36	Inuit, attached	2.00	.90	.60
835	17¢ Summer Tent	......	.40	.25
836	17¢ Igloo	......	.40	.25
837-38	Inuit, attached	2.00	.90	.60
837	17¢ The Dance	......	.40	.25
838	17¢ Soapstone Figures	......	.40	.25
839	15¢ Wooden Train	1.75	.40	.25
840	17¢ Horse Pull Toy	2.00	.55	.25
841	35¢ Knitted Doll	4.50	.90	.55
842	17¢ I.Y.C.	2.00	.45	.25
843-44	Flying Boats, attached	2.00	.90	.60
843	17¢ Curtiss, HS2L	......	.45	.25
844	17¢ Canadair CL215	......	.45	.25
845-46	Flying Boats, attached	4.50	1.85	1.75
845	35¢ Vichers Vedette	......	.85	.60
846	35¢ Consolidated Canso	......	.85	.60

833

834

839

835-36

842

843

847

848

1980 COMMEMORATIVES

847-77	complete, 31 varieties	5250(23)	15.95	10.25
847	17¢ Arctic Islands Map	2.00	.45	.25
848	35¢ Olympic Skiing	4.40	.90	.60
849-50	Artists, attached	2.00	.90	.55
849	17¢ School Trustees	......	.40	.25
850	17¢ Inspiration	......	.40	.25
851-52	Artists, attached	4.40	1.85	1.50
851	35¢ Parliament Bldgs	......	.90	.70
852	35¢ Sunrise on the Saguenay	......	.90	.70
853	17¢ Atlantic Whitefish	2.25	.40	.25
854	17¢ Greater Prairie Chicken	2.25	.40	.25

849

853

855

856

857-58

859

870

860

862

863

865

873

866-67

878

877

855	17¢ Gardening	2.00	.45	.25
856	17¢ Rehabilitation	2.00	.45	.25
857-58	"O Canada", attached	2.00	.90	.55
857	17¢ Bars of Music	......	.45	.25
858	17¢ Three Musicians	......	.45	.25
859	17¢ John Diefenbaker	2.00	.45	.25
860-61	Musicians, attached	2.00	.90	.55
860	17¢ Emma Albani	......	.45	.25
861	17¢ Healy Willan	......	.45	.25
862	17¢ Ned Hanlan	2.00	.45	.25
863	17¢ Saskatchewan	2.00	.45	.25
864	17¢ Alberta	2.00	.45	.25
865	35¢ Uranium Resources	4.40	.90	.35
866-67	Inuit, attached	2.00	.90	.50
866	17¢ Sedna	......	.45	.20
867	17¢ Sun	......	.45	.20
868-69	Inuit, attached	4.40	1.85	1.50
868	35¢ Bird Spirit	......	.90	.45
869	35¢ Shaman	......	.90	.45
870	15¢ Christmas	1.75	.35	.25
871	17¢ Christmas	2.00	.40	.25
872	35¢ Christmas	4.40	.90	.45
873-74	Aircraft	2.00	.90	.65
873	17¢ Avro Canada CF-100	......	.45	.20
874	17¢ Avro Lancaster	......	.45	.20
875-76	Aircraft, attached	4.40	1.85	1.65
875	35¢ Curtiss JN-4	......	.85	.65
876	35¢ Hawker Hurricane	......	.85	.65
877	17¢ Dr. Lachapelle	2.00	.45	.25

1981 COMMEMORATIVES

878-906	complete, 29 varieties	37.00(19)	13.50	8.75
878	17¢ Antique Instrument	2.00	.45	.25
879-82	Feminists, attached	2.25	1.90	1.70
879	17¢ Emily Stowe	......	.50	.30
880	17¢ Louise McKinney	......	.50	.30
881	17¢ Idola Saint-Jean	......	.50	.30
882	17¢ Henrietta Edwards	......	.50	.30
883	17¢ Marmot	2.00	.45	.25
884	35¢ Bison	4.40	.90	.80
885-86	Women, attached	2.00	.85	.70
885	17¢ Kateri Tekakwitha	......	.45	.25
886	17¢ Marie de L'Incarnation	......	.45	.25
887	17¢ "At Baie Saint-Paul"	2.00	.45	.25
888	17¢ Self-Portrait	2.00	.45	.25
889	35¢ Untitled No. 6	4.40	.90	.80

879

883

885

887

SCOTT NO.	DESCRIPTION	PLATE BLOCK F/NH	UNUSED F/NH	USED F

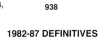

890

894

896

897

898

899

900

903

SCOTT NO.	DESCRIPTION	PLATE BLOCK F/NH	UNUSED F/NH	USED F
890-93	Canada Day, attached	3.85(8)	1.85	1.80
890	17¢ Canada in 1867	......	.55	.50
891	17¢ Canada in 1873	......	.55	.50
892	17¢ Canada in 1905	......	.55	.50
893	17¢ Canada in 1949	......	.55	.50
894-95	Botanists, attached	2.00	.75	.60
894	17¢ Frere Marie Victorin	......	.45	.25
895	17¢ John Macoun	......	.45	.25
896	17¢ Montreal Rose	2.00	.45	.25
897	17¢ Niagara-on-the-Lake	2.00	.45	.25
898	17¢ Acadians	2.00	.45	.25
899	17¢ Aaron Mosher	2.00	.45	.25
900	15¢ Christmas Tree in 1781	2.00	.45	.25
901	15¢ Christmas Tree in 1881	2.00	.45	.25
902	15¢ Christmas Tree in 1981	2.00	.45	.25
903-04	Aircraft, attached	2.00	.90	.50
903	17¢ Canadair CL-41 Tutor	......	.45	.25
904	17¢ de Havilland Tiger Moth	......	.45	.25
905-06	Aircraft, attached	4.40	1.85	1.55
905	35¢ Avro Canada C-102	......	.85	.70
906	35¢ de Havilland Canada Dash-7	......	.85	.70
907	(30¢) "A" Maple Leaf	7.75	1.75	.25
908	(30¢) "A" Maple Leaf, Coil	......	1.90	.25

907, 908

909

914

915

1982 COMMEMORATIVES

SCOTT NO.	DESCRIPTION	PLATE BLOCK F/NH	UNUSED F/NH	USED F
909/75	(909-16, 954, 967-75) 18 varieties, complete	51.25(16)	15.25	8.00
909	30¢ 1851 Beaver	3.30	.75	.25
910	30¢ 1908 Champlain	3.30	.75	.25
911	35¢ 1935 Mountie	4.15	.90	.75
912	35¢ 1928 Mt. Hurd	4.15	.90	.75
913	60¢ 1929 Bluenose	6.90	1.50	1.25
913a	$1.90 Phil. Exhib. sheet of 5	......	4.85	......
914	30¢ Jules Leger	3.30	.75	.25
915	30¢ Terry Fox	3.30	.75	.25
916	30¢ Constitution	3.30	.75	.25

916

917

925/952, 1194, 1194A

938

939

926

1982-87 DEFINITIVES

SCOTT NO.	DESCRIPTION	PLATE BLOCK F/NH	UNUSED F/NH	USED F
917-37	1¢-$5 complete, 23 varieties	135.00	36.00	11.00
917a-21a	1¢-10¢, 5 varieties	4.10	1.00	.70
917	1¢ Decoy	1.00	.25	.25
917a	1¢ perf.13x13-1/2 (1985)	1.25	.25	.25
918	2¢ Fishing Spear	1.00	.25	.25
918a	2¢ perf.13x13-1/2 (1985)	1.00	.25	.25
919	3¢ Stable Lantern	1.00	.25	.25

SCOTT NO.	DESCRIPTION	PLATE BLOCK F/NH	UNUSED F/NH	USED F
919a	3¢ perf.13x13-1/2 (1985)	1.25	.25	.25
920	5¢ Bucket	1.00	.25	.25
920a	5¢ perf.13x13-1/2 (1984)	1.25	.25	.25
921	10¢ Weathercock	1.55	.25	.25
921a	10¢ perf.13x13-1/2 (1985)	1.55	.35	.25
922	20¢ Ice Skates	2.25	.50	.25
923	30¢ Maple Leaf, blue & red, perf.13x13-1/2	3.30	.75	.25
923a	30¢ booklet pane (20) perf 12x12-1/2	......	17.00	
923b	as above, single	......	1.65	1.65
924	32¢ Maple Leaf, red & brown, perf.13x13-1/2 (1983)	3.50	.75	.25
924a	32¢ booklet pane (25) perf. 12x12-1/2	......	19.00	
924b	as above, single	......	1.35	1.00
925	34¢ Parliament (multicolored, perf.13x13-1/2 (1985)	3.85	.75	.25
925a	34¢ booklet pane (25) perf.13x13-1/2	......	18.00	
925b	34¢ single, perf 13-1/2x14	......	1.65	1.00
926	34¢ Elizabeth II (1985), perf.13x13-1/2	3.80	.85	.25
926A	36¢ Elizabeth II (1987) perf. 13x13-1/2	20.00	4.00	2.75
926B	36¢ Parliament Library (1987)	4.00	.85	.25
926Bc	as above, booklet pane (10)	......	8.75	......
926Bd	as above, booklet pane (25)	......	22.00	......
926Be	Booklet single (perf. 13-1/2x14)	......	.95	......
927	37¢ Plow (1983)	4.30	.95	.30
928	39¢ Settle bed (1985)	4.55	1.15	.30
929	48¢ Cradle (1983)	5.25	1.15	.35
930	50¢ Sleigh (1985)	5.50	1.10	.30
931	60¢ Ontario Street (1985)	5.50	1.40	.40
932	64¢ Stove (1983)	7.00	1.55	.40
933	68¢ Spinning Wheel (1985)	7.50	1.65	.40
934	$1 Glacier Park (1984)	11.00	2.25	.65
935	$1.50 Waterton Lakes (1985)	18.00	4.00	.80
936	$2 Banff Park (1985)	21.00	4.50	1.40
937	$5 Point Pelee (1983)	53.00	12.00	2.50

1982-87 BOOKLET SINGLES

SCOTT NO.	DESCRIPTION	PLATE BLOCK F/NH	UNUSED F/NH	USED F
938-948	1¢-36¢ complete, 11 varieties	......	6.45	4.95
938	1¢ East Block (1987)	......	.35	.30
939	2¢ West Block (1985)	......	.35	.30
940	5¢ Maple Leaf (1982)	......	.35	.30
941	5¢ East Block (1985)	......	.30	.25
942	6¢ West Block (1987)	......	.30	.25
943	8¢ Maple Leaf (1983)	......	.60	.60
944	10¢ Maple Leaf (1982)	......	.45	.45
945	30¢ Maple Leaf, red perf. 12x12-1/2 (1982)	......	.75	.80
945a	booklet pane 2# 940, 1 #944, 1 #945	......	1.65	......
946	32¢ Maple Leaf, brown on white, perf.12x12-1/2 (1983)	......	.65	.75
946b	booklet pane 2 #941, 1 #943, 1 #946	......	1.65	......
947	34¢ Library, slate blue, perf.12x12-1/2 (1985)	......	1.40	.95
947a	booklet pane, 3 #939, 2 #941, 1 #947	......	2.80	......
948	36¢ Parliament Library (1987)	......	1.50	.95
948a	booklet pane, 2 #938, 2 #942, #948	......	2.40	......

1982-1987 COILS

SCOTT NO.	DESCRIPTION	PLATE BLOCK F/NH	UNUSED F/NH	USED F
950-53	30¢-36¢ complete, 4 varieties	......	3.50	.85
950	30¢ Maple Leaf (1982)	......	.95	.25
951	32¢ Maple Leaf (1983)	......	.85	.25
952	34¢ Parliament (1985)	......	.90	.25
953	36¢ Parliament (1987)	......	.95	.25

954

955 *Yukon Territories*

Paintings

956 *Quebec*
959 *Prince Edward Island*
962 *Ontario*
965 *British Columbia*

957 *Newfoundland*
960 *Nova Scotia*
963 *New Brunswick*
966 *Manitoba*

958 *Northwest Territories*
961 *Saskatchewan*
964 *Alberta*

1982 COMMEMORATIVES

SCOTT NO.	DESCRIPTION	PLATE BLOCK F/NH	UNUSED F/NH	USED F
954	30¢ Salvation Army	3.30	.75	.25
955-66	set of singles	......	9.75	8.50
......	same, any 30¢ single	......	.95	.50
966a	sheet of 12 varieties, attached	......	10.00	
967	30¢ Regina	3.30	.75	.25
968	30¢ Henley Regatta	3.30	.75	.25
969-70	30¢ Aircraft, attached	4.30	1.80	1.25
969	30¢ Fairchild FC-2W1	......	.70	.30

967

968

969

SCOTT NO.	DESCRIPTION	PLATE BLOCK F/NH	UNUSED F/NH	USED F
970	30¢ De Havilland Canada Beaver	....	.85	.25
971-72	Aircraft, attached	6.75	3.00	2.40
971	60¢ Noorduyn Norseman	....	1.50	.95
972	60¢ Fokker Super Universal	....	1.50	.95
973	30¢ Joseph, Mary & Infant	3.50	.70	.25
974	35¢ Shepherds	4.25	.90	.60
975	60¢ Wise Men	7.00	1.45	1.00

973

976

978

977

1983 COMMEMORATIVES

976/1008 (976-82, 993-1008) complete, 23 varieties	80.25(20)		26.75	12.40
976	32¢ World Comm. Year	3.60	.80	.25
977	$2 Commonwealth Day	46.00	10.00	4.75
978-79	Poet/Author, attached	3.60	1.75	1.10
978	32¢ Laure Conan	....	.80	.25
979	32¢ E.J. Pratt	....	.80	.25
980	32¢ St.John Ambulance	3.50	.75	.25
981	32¢ University Games	3.50	.75	.25
982	64¢ University Games	7.25	1.50	1.00

Forts

984 Ft. William		**989** Ft. Chambly	
985 Ft. Rodd Hill		**990** Ft. No. 1 Pt. Levis	
986 Ft. Wellington		**991** Ft. at Coteau-du-Lac	
987 Fort Prince of Wales		**992** Fort Beausejour	
988 Halifax Citadel			

992a	32¢ Forts, pane of 10	....	9.50	9.00
983-92	set of singles	....	8.40	8.00
......	Any 32¢ single Fort	....	.75	.60
993	32¢ Boy Scouts	3.55	.80	.60
994	32¢ Council of Churches	3.55	.80	.60
995	32¢ Humphrey Gilbert	3.55	.80	.60
996	32¢ Nickel	3.55	.80	.60
997	32¢ Josiah Henson	3.55	.80	.60
998	32¢ Fr. Antoine Labelle	3.55	.80	.60

980

981

983 Ft. Henry

993

994

995

996

997

998

999

1003

1004

1007

1009

1010

1011

1012

1013

1014

1015

999-1000	Steam Trains, attached	14.00	3.85	2.50
999	32¢ Toronto 4-4-0	....	.85	.65
1000	32¢ Dorchester 0-4-0	....	.85	.65
1001	37¢ Samson 0-6-0	4.40	.95	.75
1002	64¢ Adam Brown 4-4-0	7.25	1.60	1.25
1003	32¢ Law School	3.55	.80	.25
1004	32¢ City Church	3.55	.80	.25
1005	37¢ Family	4.40	.95	.65
1006	64¢ County Chapel	6.45	1.55	1.50
1007-08	Army Regiment, attached	3.55	1.60	1.50
1007	32¢ Canada & Br.Reg.	.....	.75	.30
1008	32¢ Winn. & Dragoons	.....	.75	.30

1984 COMMEMORATIVES

1009/44 (1009-15, 1028-39, 1040-44) complete, 24 varieties	60.15(20)		19.75 8.50	
1009	32¢ Yellowknife	3.60	.80	.25
1010	32¢ Year of the Arts	3.60	.80	.25
1011	32¢ Cartier	3.60	.80	.25
1012	32¢ Tall Ships	3.60	.80	.25
1013	32¢ Canadian Red Cross	3.60	.80	.25
1014	32¢ New Brunswick	3.60	.80	.25
1015	32¢ St. Lawrence Seaway	3.60	.80	.25

PROVINCIAL LANDSCAPES BY JEAN PAUL LEMIEUX

1016 New Brunswick	
1017 British Columbia	
1018 Yukon Territory	
1019 Quebec	
1020 Manitoba	
1021 Alberta	
1022 Prince Edward Island	
1023 Saskatchewan	
1024 Nova Scotia	
1025 Northwest Territories	
1026 Newfoundland	
1027 Ontario	

1016

1027a	sheet of 12 varieties attached	....	11.00	9.00
1016-27	set of singles	....	9.55	5.75
.....	Any 32¢ single Provinces	....	.85	.50
1028	32¢ Loyalists	3.60	.70	.25
1029	32¢ Catholicism	3.60	.70	.25
1030	32¢ Papal Visit	3.60	.70	.25
1031	64¢ Papal Visit	7.25	1.45	.90

1028

1029

1030

1032

SCOTT NO.	DESCRIPTION	PLATE BLOCK F/NH	UNUSED F/NH	USED F

1036

1040

1043

1044

1045

1046

Scott	Description	Plate Block	Unused	Used
1032-35	Lighthouses, attached	3.80	3.50	1.75
1032	32¢ Louisbourg	......	.75	.25
1033	32¢ Fisgard	......	.75	.25
1034	32¢ Ile Verte	......	.75	.25
1035	32¢ Gilbraltar Point	......	.75	.25
1036-37	Locomotives, attached	3.60	1.65	1.20
1036	32¢ Scotia 0-6-0	......	.75	.30
1037	32¢ Countess of Dufferin 4-4-0	......	.75	.30
1038	37¢ Grand Trunk 2-6-0	4.70	.95	.80
1039	64¢ Canadian Pacific 4-6-0	7.25	1.65	1.15
1039a	32¢-64¢ Locomotive S/S	......	4.25	4.25
1040	32¢ Christmas	3.60	.80	.25
1041	37¢ Christmas	4.40	.95	.75
1042	64¢ Christmas	7.25	1.55	1.00
1043	32¢ Royal Air Force	3.60	.75	.25
1044	32¢ Newspaper	3.60	.75	.25

1985 COMMEMORATIVES

Scott	Description	Plate Block	Unused	Used
1045/76	(1045-49, 1060-66, 1067-76) complete, 21 varieties	49.40(16)	19.00	8.25
1045	32¢ Youth Year	3.60	.80	.30
1046	32¢ Canadian Astronaut	3.60	.80	.30
1047-48	Women, attached	3.60	1.65	1.25
1047	32¢ T. Casgrain	......	.80	.25
1048	32¢ E. Murphy	......	.80	.25
1049	32¢ G. Dumont	3.60	.80	.25
1059a	34¢ Forts pane of 10	......	16.00	15.00
1050-59	set of singles	......	11.00	9.00
......	any Fort single	......	.95	.65
1060	34¢ Louis Hebert	3.80	.85	.25
1061	34¢ Inter-Parliamentary	3.80	.85	.25
1062	34¢ Girl Guides	3.80	.85	.25
1063-66	Lighthouses, attached	3.80	3.75	2.95
1063	34¢ Sisters Islets	......	.90	.30
1064	34¢ Pelee Passage	......	.90	.30
1065	34¢ Haut-fond Prince	......	.90	.30
1066	34¢ Rose Blanche	......	.90	.30
1066b	Lighthouse Souvenir Sheet	......	5.00	5.00
1067	34¢ Christmas	3.75	.85	.25
1068	39¢ Christmas	4.25	.95	.70
1069	68¢ Christmas	7.50	1.65	1.15
1070	32¢ Christmas, booklet single	......	1.25	.50
1070a	same, booklet pane of 10	......	13.00	......
1071-72	Locomotives, attached	4.75	1.90	1.25
1071	34¢ GT Class K2	......	.95	.65
1072	34¢ CP Class P2a	......	.95	.65
1073	39¢ CMoR Class 010a	4.50	.85	.85
1074	68¢ CGR Class H4D	7.75	1.60	1.35
1075	34¢ Royal Navy	3.85	.85	.25
1076	34¢ Montreal Museum	3.85	.85	.25

1047-48

1049

1050

1060

1061

1062

FORTS

1050 Lower Ft. Garry	**1051** Fort Anne	**1052** Fort York
1053 Castle Hill	**1054** Fort Whoop Up	**1055** Fort Erie
1056 Fort Walsh	**1057** Fort Lennox	**1058** York Redoubt
1059 Fort Frederick		

1063

1067

1075

1076

1077

1078

1986 COMMEMORATIVES

Scott	Description	Plate Block	Unused	Used
1077/1121	(1077-79, 1090-1107,1108-16, 1117-21) complete, 35 varieties	70.50	29.50	15.00
1077	34¢ Computer Map	3.80	.85	.25
1078	34¢ Expo '86	3.80	.85	.25
1079	39¢ Expo '86	4.40	.95	.60

1987 HERITAGE ARTIFACTS

Scott	Description	Plate Block	Unused	Used
1080	25¢ Butter Stamp	3.30	.75	.30
1081	42¢ Linen Chest	5.25	1.10	.35
1082	55¢ Iron Kettle	7.25	1.55	.45
1083	72¢ Hand-drawn Cart	8.75	1.85	.60

1986-87 Definitive

Scott	Description	Plate Block	Unused	Used
1084	$5 La Mauricie	58.00	12.50	3.50

1090

1091

1092

1094

1103

1104

1095

1099

1986 COMMEMORATIVES

Scott	Description	Plate Block	Unused	Used
1090	34¢ Philippe Aubert de Gaspe	3.85	.85	.25
1091	34¢ Molly Brant	3.85	.85	.25
1092	34¢ Expo '86	3.85	.85	.25
1093	68¢ Expo '86	7.75	1.65	.75
1094	34¢ Canadian Forces Postal Service	3.80	.75	.20
1095-98	Birds, attached	4.75	3.80	3.25
1095	34¢ Great Blue Heron	......	1.10	.45
1096	34¢ Snow Goose	......	1.10	.45
1097	34¢ Great Horned Owl	......	1.10	.45
1098	34¢ Spruce Grouse	......	1.10	.45
1099-1102	Science & Technology, attached	4.85	4.25	3.25
1099	34¢ Rotary Snowplow	......	.85	.30
1100	34¢ Canadarm	......	.85	.30
1101	34¢ Anti-gravity Flight Suit	......	.85	.30
1102	34¢ Variable-pitch Propeller	......	.85	.30
1103	34¢ CBC	3.70	.85	.20
1104-07	Exploration, attached	4.65	3.75	3.00
1104	34¢ Continent	......	.85	.30
1105	34¢ Vikings	......	.85	.30
1106	34¢ John Cabot	......	.85	.30
1107	34¢ Hudson Bay	......	.85	.30
1107b	CAPEX souvenir sheet	......	3.75	3.50

SCOTT NO.	DESCRIPTION	PLATE BLOCK F/NH	UNUSED F/NH	USED F
1108-09	Frontier Peacemakers, attached	3.85	1.75	1.25
1108	34¢ Crowfoot	......	.85	.30
1109	34¢ J.F. Macleod	......	.85	.30
1110	34¢ Peace Year..................	3.85	.85	.25
1111-12	Calgary, attached	3.85	1.75	1.25
1111	34¢ Ice Hockey	......	.85	.25
1112	34¢ Biathlon	......	.85	.25
1113	34¢ Christmas Angels..................	3.85	.85	.25
1114	39¢ Christmas Angels..................	4.30	.95	.55
1115	68¢ Christmas Angels..................	7.65	1.65	1.15
1116	29¢ Christmas Angels, booklet singles	......	1.65	1.45
1116a	same, booklet pane of 10.	......	15.00	......

1108

1110

1111

1113

1117

1122

1117	34¢ John Molson.......................	4.00	.85	.25
1118-19	Locomotive, attached	4.50	1.95	1.40
1118	34¢ CN V1a.....................	......	.95	.30
1119	34¢ CP T1a.....................	......	.95	.30
1120	39¢ CN U2a.....................	4.75	.95	.90
1121	68¢ CP H1c.....................	7.75	1.65	1.40

1987 COMMEMORATIVES

1122/54	(1122-25, 1126-54) complete, 33 varieties	68.75	28.50	13.25
1122	34¢ Toronto P.O.	3.70	.75	.25

1987 CAPEX EXHIBITION

1123	36¢ Nelson-Miramichi: Post Office...................	3.95	.90	.30
1124	42¢ Saint Ours P.O.	4.95	1.05	.40
1125	72¢ Battleford P.O.	8.25	1.75	1.40
1125A	CAPEX Souvenir Sheet	......	4.50	4.25
1126-29	Exploration, attached	4.00	3.50	3.25
1126	34¢ Brule	......	.95	.45
1127	34¢ Radisson	......	.95	.45
1128	34¢ Jolliet	......	.95	.45
1129	34¢ Wilderness	......	.95	.45
1130	36¢ Calgary Olympics.....................	3.95	.90	.30
1131	42¢ Calgary Olympics.....................	4.95	1.00	.75
1132	36¢ Volunteers.....................	4.00	.90	.30
1133	36¢ Charter of Freedom.....................	4.00	.90	.30
1134	36¢ Engineering.....................	4.00	.90	.30

1987 COMMEMORATIVES

1135-38	Science & Tech., attached	4.40	3.80	2.80
1135	36¢ Reginald A. Fessenden.....................	......	.90	.40
1136	36¢ Charles Fenerty.....................	......	.90	.40
1137	36¢ Desbarats & Leggo.....................	......	.90	.40
1138	36¢ Frederick N. Gisborne.....................	......	.90	.40
1139-40	Steamships, attached.....................	4.25	1.75	1.25
1139	36¢ Segwun.....................	......	.90	.35
1140	36¢ Princess Marguerite.....................	......	.90	.35
1141-44	Historic Shipwrecks, att'd.....................	4.40	3.80	3.25
1141	36¢ Hamilton & Scourge.....................	......	.90	.35
1142	36¢ San Juan.....................	......	.90	.35
1143	36¢ Breadalbane.....................	......	.90	.35
1144	36¢ Ericsson.....................	......	.90	.35
1145	36¢ Air Canada.....................	3.95	.90	.30

1132

1133

1134

1135

1139

1141

1145

1146

1147

1148

1154

1155

1162

1163

1165

1166

1169

1146	36¢ Quebec Summit.....................	3.95	.90	.30
1147	36¢ Commonwealth Mtg.....................	3.95	.90	.30
1148	36¢ Christmas.....................	3.95	.90	.30
1149	42¢ Christmas.....................	3.95	.90	.40
1150	72¢ Christmas.....................	8.00	1.75	1.25
1151	31¢ Christmas booklet single.....................	......	.85	.50
1151a	same, booklet pane of 10.....................	......	7.75	......
1152-53	Calgary Olympics, attached.....................	3.95	1.85	1.10
1152	36¢ Cross-Country Skiing.....................	......	.90	.30
1153	36¢ Ski Jumping.....................	......	.90	.30
1154	36¢ Grey Cup.....................	3.95	.90	.30

1987-91 DEFINITIVE ISSUES

1155	1¢ Flying Squirrel.....................	1.00	.25	.25
1156	2¢ Porcupine.....................	1.00	.25	.25
1157	3¢ Muskrat.....................	1.00	.25	.25
1158	5¢ Hare.....................	1.00	.25	.25
1159	6¢ Red Fox.....................	1.00	.25	.25
1160	10¢ Skunk.....................	1.25	.25	.25
1160a	same, perf. 13x12-1/2.....................	......	9.00	.60
1161	25¢ Beaver.....................	2.80	.65	.20
1162	37¢ Elizabeth II.....................	4.40	.95	.30
1163	37¢ Parliament.....................	4.40	.95	.30
1163a	same, bklt. pane of 10 (1988).....................	......	9.00	7.50
1163b	same, bklt. pane of 25 (1988).....................	......	23.00	16.00
1163c	37¢, perf. 13-1/2x14 (1988).....................	1.20	......	
1164	38¢ Elizabeth II (1988).....................	4.40	.95	.30
1164a	38¢, perf. 13x13-1/2.....................	1.65	.75	
1164b	same, booklet pane of 10.....................	......	11.00	8.00
1165	38¢ Clock Tower (1988).....................	4.40	1.00	.25
1165a	same, booklet pane of 10.....................	......	10.00	6.00
1165b	same, booklet pane of 25.....................	......	24.00	22.00
1166	39¢ Flag & Clouds.....................	4.60	1.00	.20
1166a	same, booklet pane of 10.....................	......	9.50	7.50
1166b	same, booklet pane of 25.....................	......	28.00	22.50
1166c	same, perf. 12-1/2x13.....................	......	27.00	1.00
1167	39¢ Elizabeth II.....................	4.40	1.00	.25
1167a	same, booklet pane of 10.....................	......	9.50	9.00
1167b	39¢, perf. 13 (1990).....................	94.00	19.00	.90
1168	40¢ Elizabeth II (1990).....................	4.40	1.00	.25
1168a	same, booklet pane of 10.....................	......	9.00	8.00
1169	40¢ Flag and Mountains (1990).....................	4.40	1.00	.25
1169a	same, booklet pane of 25.....................	......	33.00	28.00
1169b	same, booklet pane of 10.....................	......	10.00	9.00
1170	43¢ Lynx.....................	6.00	1.25	.45
1171	44¢ Walrus (1989).....................	8.25	1.75	.25
1171a	44¢, perf. 12-1/2x13.....................	3.00	1.75	
1171b	same, booklet pane of 5.....................	....	15.00	
1171c	perf., 13-1/2x13.....................	560.00	65.00	
1172	45¢ Pronghorn (1990).....................	4.95	1.15	.30
1172b	same, booklet pane of 5.....................	......	15.00	12.00
1172d	45¢, perf. 13.....................	135.00	26.00	1.40
1172f	Perf. 12-1/2x13.....................	......	2.75	.50
1172A	46¢, Wolverine (1990).....................	5.25	1.15	.35
1172Ac	46¢, perf. 12-1/2x13.....................	1.50	.60	
1172Ae	same, booklet pane of 5.....................	......	7.50	5.25
1172Ag	same, perf. 14-1/2x14.....................	31.00	6.75	.50
1173	57¢ Killer Whale.....................	6.50	1.40	.45
1174	59¢ Musk-ox (1989).....................	7.00	1.55	.45
1174a	same, perf. 13.....................	60.00	14.00	8.00
1175	61¢ Timber Wolf (1990).....................	7.00	1.50	.50
1175a	61¢, perf. 13.....................	450.00	90.00	8.50
1176	63¢ Harbor Porpoise.....................	17.00	3.50	.50
1176a	63¢, perf. 13.....................	60.00	14.00	5.75
1177	74¢ Wapiti (1988).....................	10.00	2.00	.95
1178	76¢ Grizzly Bear (1989).....................	10.00	2.25	.75
1178a	76¢, perf. 12-1/2x13.....................	......	3.50	2.80
1178b	same, booklet pane of 5.....................	......	17.00	......
1178c	same, perf. 13.....................	210.00	45.00	20.00
1179	78¢ Beluga (1990).....................	12.00	2.50	.95
1179a	same, booklet pane of 5.....................	......	17.00	......
1179b	78¢, perf. 13.....................	195.00	40.00	8.50
1179c	same, perf. 12-1/2x13.....................	......	3.30	2.75
1180	80¢ Peary caribou (1990).....................	9.75	2.00	.95
1180a	80¢, perf. 12-1/2x13.....................	......	3.50	1.25
1180b	same, booklet pane of 5.....................	......	17.50	......
1180c	80¢, perf. 14-1/2x14.....................	33.00	6.50	3.00

SCOTT NO.	DESCRIPTION	PLATE BLOCK F/NH	UNUSED F/NH	USED F

1181

1184

1191, 1192, 1193

1203

Scott	Description	Plate Block	Unused	Used
1181	$1 Runnymede Library	11.00	2.40	.80
1182	$2 McAdam Train Station	23.00	4.80	1.50
1183	$5 Bonsecours Market	62.00	13.00	4.00

BOOKLET STAMPS

Scott	Description	Plate Block	Unused	Used
1184	1¢ Flag, booklet single (1990)		.30	.25
1184a	same, perf. 12-1/2 x 13		15.00	15.00
1185	5¢ Flag, booklet single (1990)		.30	.25
1185a	same, perf. 12-1/2x13		10.00	10.00
1186	6¢ Parliament East (1989)		.75	.30
1187	37¢ Parliament booklet single		1.10	.75
1187a	booklet pane (4), 1 #938, 2 #942, 1 #1187		1.90	
1188	38¢ Parliament Library booklet single (1989)		1.10	.45
1188a	booklet pane (5), 3 #939a, 1 #1186, 1 #1188		2.25	
1189	39¢ Flag booklet single (1990)		1.15	.45
1189b	perf. 12-1/2x13		20.00	20.00
1189c	booklet pane (4) #11896		62.00	
1189a	booklet pane (4), 1 #1184, 2 #1185, 1 #1189		2.00	
1190	40¢ Flag booklet single (1990)		1.75	.65
1190a	booklet pane (4) 2 #1184, 1 #1185, 1 #1190		2.50	

1204

1206

1210

1216

1214

1215

1217-20

1221

SELF-ADHESIVE BOOKLET STAMPS

Scott	Description	Plate Block	Unused	Used
1191	38¢ Flag, forest (1989)		1.75	.95
1191a	same, booklet pane of 12		19.00	
1192	39¢ Flag field (1990)		1.55	.95
1192a	same, booklet pane of 12		17.00	
1193	40¢ Flag, seacoast (1991)		1.70	.95
1193a	same, booklet pane of 12		18.00	

COIL STAMPS

Scott	Description	Plate Block	Unused	Used
1194	37¢ Parliament Library (1988)		.95	.25
1194A	38¢ Parliament Library (1989)		1.25	.25
1194B	39¢ Flag (1990)		1.00	.25
1194C	40¢ Flag (1990)		1.00	.25

1988 COMMEMORATIVES

Scott	Description	Plate Block	Unused	Used
1195/1236	(1195-1225, 1226-36) complete, 39 varieties	74.75	38.25	15.75
1195-96	Calgary Olympics, att'd	4.50	2.00	1.15
1195	37¢ Alpine Skiing		.95	.35
1196	37¢ Curling		.95	.35
1197	43¢ Figure Skating	5.00	1.10	.85
1198	74¢ Luge	8.35	1.85	1.10
1199-1202	Explorers, attached	4.60	3.85	3.10
1199	37¢ Anthony Henday		.90	.45
1200	37¢ George Vancouver		.90	.45
1201	37¢ Simon Fraser		.90	.45
1202	37¢ John Palliser		.90	.45
1203	50¢ Canadian Art	5.75	1.25	1.15
1204-05	Wildlife Conservation, att'd	4.40	1.95	1.15
1204	37¢ Ducks Unlimited		.95	.35
1205	37¢ Moose		.95	.35
1206-09	Science & Technology, att'd	4.40	3.85	3.40
1206	37¢ Kerosene		.95	.40
1207	37¢ Marquis Wheat		.95	.40
1208	37¢ Electron Microscope		.95	.40
1209	37¢ Cancer Therapy		.95	.40
1210-13	Butterflies, attached	4.40	3.80	3.40
1210	37¢ Short-tailed Swallowtail		.90	.45
1211	37¢ Northern Blue		.90	.45
1212	37¢ Macoun's Arctic		.90	.45
1213	37¢ Tiger Swallowtail		.90	.45
1214	37¢ Harbor Entrance	4.40	.95	.25
1215	37¢ 4-H Club Anniv.	4.40	.95	.25
1216	37¢ Les Forges Du St. Maurice	4.40	.95	.25
1217-20	Dogs, attached	5.25	4.50	4.25

1222

1226

1227

1228

1229-32

Scott	Description	Plate Block	Unused	Used
1217	37¢ Tahltan Bear Dog		1.20	.45
1218	37¢ Nova Scotia Retriever		1.20	.45
1219	37¢ Canadian Eskimo Dog		1.20	.45
1220	37¢ Newfoundland Dog		1.20	.45
1221	37¢ Baseball	4.25	.95	.25
1222	37¢ Christmas Nativity	4.40	.95	.25
1223	43¢ Virgin & Child	4.80	1.10	.75
1224	74¢ Virgin & Child	8.30	1.85	1.15
1225	32¢ Christmas Icons booklet single		1.15	.95
1225a	same, booklet pane of 10		10.00	9.50
1226	37¢ Charles Inglis	4.40	.95	.30
1227	37¢ Ann Hopkins	4.40	.95	.30
1228	37¢ Angus Walters	4.40	.95	.30
1229-32	Small Craft Series, attached	4.40	3.85	3.25
1229	37¢ Chipewyan Canoe		.95	.45
1230	37¢ Haida Canoe		.95	.45
1231	37¢ Inuit Kayak		.95	.45
1232	37¢ Micmac Canoe		.95	.45
1233-36	Explorers, attached	4.40	3.85	3.75
1233	38¢ Matonabbee		.95	.45
1234	38¢ Sir John Franklin		.95	.45
1235	38¢ J.B.Tyrrell		.95	.45
1236	38¢ V. Stefansson		.95	.45

1237

1243

1245

1249

1251

1256, 1256a

1259, 1259a

1260

1252

1989 COMMEMORATIVES

Scott	Description	Plate Block	Unused	Used
1237/63	(1237-56, 1257, 1258, 1259, 1260-63) complete, 26 varieties		25.00	12.00
1237-40	Canadian Photography, att'd	4.40	3.80	3.50
1237	38¢ W. Notman		.95	.45
1238	38¢ W.H. Boorne		.95	.45
1239	38¢ A. Henderson		.95	.45
1240	38¢ J.E. Livernois		.95	.45
1241	50¢ Canadian Art	6.00	1.35	.95
1243-44	19th Century Poets, att'd	4.40	1.95	1.50
1243	38¢ L.H.Frechette		.95	.45
1244	38¢ A. Lampman		.95	.45
1245-48	Mushrooms, attached	4.40	3.85	3.40
1245	38¢ Cinnabar Chanterelle		.95	.45
1246	38¢ Common Morel		.95	.45
1247	38¢ Spindell Coral		.95	.45
1248	38¢ Admirable Boletus		.95	.45
1249-50	Canadian Infantry, attached	225.00	1.95	1.70
1249	38¢ Light Infantry		.95	.45
1250	38¢ Royal 22nd Regiment		.95	.45
1251	38¢ International Trade	4.40	.95	.30
1252-55	Performing Arts, attached	4.40	3.95	3.40
1252	38¢ Dance		.95	.45
1253	38¢ Music		.95	.45
1254	38¢ Film		.95	.45
1255	38¢ Theatre		.95	.45
1256	38¢ Christmas 1989	4.40	.95	.45
1256a	same, booklet single		4.95	
1256b	same, booklet pane of 10 perf., 13x12-1/2		53.00	
1257	44¢ Christmas 1989	4.95	1.10	.75
1257a	same, booklet single		4.50	.75
1257a	same, booklet pane of 5		22.50	
1258	76¢ Christmas 1989	8.75	1.85	1.40
1258a	same, booklet single		7.25	7.25
1258a	same, booklet pane of 5		34.00	
1259	33¢ Christmas, booklet single		1.15	1.65
1259a	same, booklet pane of 10		15.00	
1260-63	WWII 50th Anniversary, att'd	4.95	4.10	4.00
1260	38¢ Declaration of War		.95	.65
1261	38¢ Army Mobilization		.95	.65
1262	38¢ Navy Convoy System		.95	.65
1263	38¢ Commonwealth Training		.95	.65

SCOTT NO.	DESCRIPTION	PLATE BLOCK F/NH	UNUSED F/NH	USED F

1264   1270   1272-73   1274

1990 COMMEMORATIVES

Scott	Description	Plate Block	Unused	Used
1264/1301	(1264-73, 1274-94, 1295, 1296, 1297, 1298-1301) complete, 38 vars.	62.25	35.50	17.50
1264-65	Norman Bethune, attached	7.75	2.50	1.85
1264	39¢ Bethune in Canada	.....	1.25	.50
1265	39¢ Bethune in China		1.25	.50
1266-69	Small Craft Series, att'd.	4.70	3.95	3.50
1266	39¢ Dory	.....	1.00	.45
1267	39¢ Pointer	.....	1.00	.45
1268	39¢ York Boat	.....	1.00	.45
1269	39¢ North Canoe	.....	1.00	.45
1270	39¢ Multiculturalism	4.40	1.00	.25
1271	50¢ Canadian Art,"The West Wind"	5.95	1.30	1.15
1272-73	Canada Postal System 39¢ booklet pair	.....	2.40	2.40
1273a	same, booklet pane of 8	.....	8.25	.....
1273b	same, booklet pane of 9	.....	13.00	.....
1274-77	Dolls of Canada, attached	4.70	4.00	3.60
1274	39¢ Native Dolls	.....	.95	.40
1275	39¢ Settlers' Dolls	.....	.95	.40
1276	39¢ Four Commercial Dolls	.....	.95	.40
1277	39¢ Five Commercial Dolls	.....	.95	.40

1278   1279   1283   1287

1288   1289   1293   1294   1297

Scott	Description	Plate Block	Unused	Used
1278	39¢ Canada/Flag Day	4.50	.90	.25
1279-82	Prehistoric Life, attached	4.70	3.95	3.50
1279	39¢ Trilobite	.....	.95	.40
1280	39¢ Sea Scorpion	.....	.95	.40
1281	39¢ Fossil Algae	.....	.95	.40
1282	39¢ Soft Invertebrate	.....	.95	.40
1283-86	Canadian Forests, attached	4.70	3.95	3.50
1283	39¢ Acadian	.....	.95	.40
1284	39¢ Great Lakes—St.Lawrence	.....	.95	.40
1285	39¢ Coast	.....	.95	.40
1286	39¢ Boreal	.....	.95	.40
1287	39¢ Climate Observations	4.50	.95	.40
1288	39¢ Int'l. Literacy Year	4.50	.95	.40
1289-92	Can. Lore & Legend, attached	5.25	4.40	3.85
1289	39¢ Sasquatch	.....	1.00	.75
1290	39¢ Kraken	.....	1.00	.75
1291	39¢ Werewolf	.....	1.00	.75
1292	39¢ Ogopogo	.....	1.00	.75
1293	39¢ Agnes Macphail	4.40	.95	.25
1294	39¢ Native Mary & Child	4.40	.95	.25
1294a	same, booklet pane of 10	.....	10.00	.....
1295	45¢ Inuit, Mother & Child	5.40	1.25	.85
1295a	same, booklet pane of 5	.....	9.70	.....
1296	78¢ Raven Children	9.60	2.00	1.40
1296a	same, booklet pane of 5	.....	15.00	.....
1297	34¢ Christmas sgl	.....	1.25	.50
1297a	same, booklet pane of 10	.....	9.60	.....
1298-1301	World War II—1940, att'd	5.00	4.25	4.00
1298	39¢ Home Front	.....	1.10	.95
1299	39¢ Communal War Efforts	.....	1.10	.95
1300	39¢ Food Production	.....	1.10	.95
1301	39¢ Science and War	.....	1.10	.95

1302   1311   1316   1321

1991 COMMEMORATIVES

Scott	Description	Plate Block	Unused	Used
	1302-43, 1345-48, 46 varieties	41.75	45.00	21.00
1302-05	Canadian Doctors, att'd.	4.75	4.00	3.25
1302	40¢ Jennie Trout	.....	1.00	.45
1303	40¢ Wilder Penfield	.....	1.00	.45
1304	40¢ Sir Frederick Banting	.....	1.00	.45
1305	40¢ Harold Griffith	.....	1.00	.45
1306-09	Prehistoric Life, attached	4.75	4.25	3.25
1306	40¢ Microfossils	.....	1.00	.45
1307	40¢ Early tree	.....	1.00	.45
1308	40¢ Early fish	.....	1.00	.45
1309	40¢ Land reptile	.....	1.00	.45
1310	50¢ Canadian Art, "Forest, British Columbia"	6.25	1.35	1.15
1311	40¢ The Butchart Gardens, attached booklet single.	.....	1.10	.45
1312	40¢ International Peace Garden, booklet single	.....	1.10	.45
1313	40¢ Royal Botanical Garden, booklet single	.....	1.10	.45
1314	40¢ Montreal Botanical Garden, booklet single	.....	1.10	.45
1315	40¢ Halifax Public Gardens, booklet single	.....	1.10	.45
1315a	Public Gardens, strip of 5	.....	4.75	3.00
1315b	Public Gardens, attached booklet pane of 10	.....	9.75	.....
1316	40¢ Canada Day	4.60	.95	.45
1317-20	Small Craft Series, attached	4.60	4.10	3.30
1317	40¢ Verchere Rowboat	.....	.95	.45
1318	40¢ Touring Kayak	.....	.95	.45
1319	40¢ Sailing Dinghy	.....	.95	.45
1320	40¢ Cedar Strip Canoe	.....	.95	.45
1321	40¢ South Nahanni River	.....	.95	.45
1322	40¢ Athabasca River	.....	.95	.45
1323	40¢ Voyageur Waterway	.....	.95	.45
1324	40¢ Jacques Cartier River	.....	.95	.45
1325	40¢ Main River	.....	.95	.45
1325a	Canadian Rivers, strip of 5	.....	4.75	4.00
1325b	Canadian Rivers, attached booklet pane of 10	.....	9.75	.....
1326-29	Arrival of the Ukrainians, attached	4.75	4.10	3.25
1326	40¢ Leaving	.....	.95	.45
1327	40¢ Winter in Canada	.....	.95	.45
1328	40¢ Clearing Land	.....	.95	.45
1329	40¢ Growing Wheat	.....	.95	.45
1330-33	Dangerous Public Service Occupations, attached.	6.60	5.60	4.75
1330	40¢ Ski Patrol	.....	1.25	.45
1331	40¢ Police	.....	1.25	.45
1332	40¢ Firefighters	.....	1.25	.45
1333	40¢ Search & Rescue	.....	1.25	.45
1334-37	Folktales, attached	4.75	4.20	3.25
1334	40¢ Witched Canoe	.....	.95	.45
1335	40¢ Orphan Boy	.....	.95	.45
1336	40¢ Chinook Wind	.....	.95	.45
1337	40¢ Buried Treasure	.....	.95	.45
1338	40¢ Queen's University, booklet, single	.....	.95	.75
1338a	Same booklet pane of 10	.....	9.50	.....
1339	40¢ Santa at Fireplace	4.75	1.00	.25
1339a	Same, booklet pane of 10	.....	9.50	.....
1340	46¢ Santa with White horse, tree	5.25	1.15	.80
1340a	Same, booklet pane of 5	.....	5.50	.....
1341	80¢ Sinterklaas, girl	8.60	1.95	1.25
1341a	Same, booklet pane of 5	.....	9.55	.....
1342	35¢ Santa with Punchbowl, booklet, single	.....	.95	.25
1342a	Same, booklet pane of 10	.....	9.00	.....
1343	40¢ Basketball Centennial	4.40	.95	.35
1344	40¢-80¢ Basketball Souvenir Sheet of 3	.....	6.00	.....
1345-48	World War II—1941, att'd	5.00	4.00	3.75
1345	40¢ Women's Armed Forces	.....	1.10	.95
1346	40¢ War Industry	.....	1.10	.95
1347	40¢ Cadets and Veterans	.....	1.10	.95
1348	40¢ Defense of Hong Kong	.....	1.10	.95

1326   1330   1334   1338

1343   1349   1339   1342

SCOTT NO.	DESCRIPTION	PLATE BLOCK F/NH	UNUSED F/NH	USED F
	1991-96 Regular Issue			
1349	1¢ Blueberry (1992)	.95	.25	.25
1350	2¢ Wild Strawberry (1992)	.95	.25	.25
1351	3¢ Black Crowberry (1992)	.95	.25	.25
1352	5¢ Rose Hip (1992)	.95	.25	.25
1353	6¢ Black Raspberry (1992)	.95	.25	.25
1354	10¢ Kinnikinnick (1992)	1.25	.30	.25
1355	25¢ Saskatoon berry (1992)	2.90	.65	.25
1356	42¢ Flag + Rolling Hills	4.75	1.00	.25
1356a	Same, booklet pane of 10	......	11.00	8.00
1356b	Same, booklet pane of 50	......	112.00	......
1356c	Same, booklet pane of 25	......	23.00	......
1357	42¢ Queen Elizabeth II (Karsh)	4.75	1.05	.25
1357a	Same, booklet pane of 10	......	10.00	9.50
1358	43¢ Queen Elizabeth II (Karsh) (1992)	5.50	1.25	.25
1358a	Same, booklet pane of 10	......	12.00	8.50
1359	43¢ Flag + Prairie (1992)	5.50	1.10	.25
1359a	Same, booklet pane of 10	......	11.00	8.50
1359b	Same, booklet pane of 25	......	33.00	......
1360	45¢ Queen Elizabeth II (Karsh) (1995)	6.65	1.30	.25
1360a	Same, booklet pane of 10	......	13.00	9.50
1361	45¢ Flag & Building (1995)	5.95	1.10	.25
1361a	Same, booklet pane of 10	......	12.00	11.50
1361b	Same, booklet pane of 25	......	33.00	......
1362	45¢ Flag & Building, perf. 13 1/2 x 13	5.25	1.25	.25
1362a	Same, booklet pane of 10	......	11.00	9.00
1362b	Same, booklet pane of 30	......	33.00	......
1363	48¢ McIntosh Apple Tree, perf. 13	5.50	1.20	.25
1363a	Same, perf. 14 1/2 x 14	......	1.75	.40
1363b	Same, booklet pane of 5	......	8.75	......
1364	49¢ Delicious Apple perf.13 (1992)	5.60	1.25	.25
1364a	Same, perf. 14 1/2 x 14	......	3.00	.40
1364b	Same, booklet pane of 5	......	16.00	......
1365	50¢ Snow Apple (1994)	5.75	1.25	.45
1365a	Same, perf. 14 1/2 x 14	......	7.75	......
1365b	Same, perf. 14 1/2 x 14	......	3.00	.50
1365c	Same, booklet pane of 5	......	15.00	......
1366	52¢ Gravenstein apple (1995)	7.50	1.70	.45
1366a	Same, booklet pane of 5	......	9.00	6.00
1366b	Same, Gravenstein apple, perf. 14 1/2 x 14	12.00	2.50	.55
1366c	Same, booklet pane of 5	......	12.00	......
1367	65¢ Black Walnut Tree	7.60	1.65	.45
1368	67¢ Beaked Hazelnut (1992)	7.60	1.65	.45
1369	69¢ Shagbark Hickory (1994)	8.00	1.65	.45
1370	71¢ American Chestnut (1995)	8.25	1.65	.45
1371	84¢ Stanley Plum Tree, perf. 13	9.75	2.25	.45
1371a	Same, perf. 14 1/2 x 14	......	2.75	.50
1371b	Same, booklet pane of 5	......	13.50	......
1372	86¢ Bartlett Pear, perf. 13 (1992)	12.00	2.65	.75
1372a	Same, perf. 14 1/2 x 14	13.15	3.50	1.65
1372b	Same, booklet pane of 5 (perf. 14-1/2x14)	......	16.00	......
1372c	Same, booklet pane of 5	......	19.00	......
1373	88¢ Westcot Apricot (1994)	10.00	2.15	.60
1373b	Same, perf. 14 1/2 x 14	......	4.75	2.35
1363c	Same, booklet pane of 5	......	24.50	......
1374	90¢ Elberta Peach (1995)	11.00	2.40	.65
1374a	Same, booklet pane of 5	......	12.00	......
1374b	perf. 14 1/2 x 14	......	4.25	1.75
1374c	Same, booklet pane of 5	......	22.00	......
1375	$1 Yorkton Court House (1994)	11.50	2.50	.65
1375b	perf. 13-1/2x13	12.00	2.50	.65
1376	$2 Provincial Normal School, Nova Scotia (1994)	23.00	5.00	1.25
1378	$5 Carnegie Public Library, Victoria	58.00	12.00	2.75
1388	42¢ Flag and Mountains, quick-stick (1992)	......	1.65	.85
1388a	Same, booklet pane of 12	......	19.00	......
1389	43¢ Flag, estuary shore (1993)	......	1.65	.85
1394	42¢ Canadian Flag + Rolling Hills, coil	......	1.00	.30
1395	43¢ Canadian Flag, coil (1992)	......	1.00	.30
1396	45¢ Canadian Flag, coil (1995)	......	1.15	.30

1363

1399

1404

1992 COMMEMORATIVES

SCOTT NO.	DESCRIPTION	PLATE BLOCK F/NH	UNUSED F/NH	USED F
1399-1455, 57 varieties		44.15	56.10	22.25
1399	42¢ Ski Jumping	......	1.10	.45
1400	42¢ Figure Skating	......	1.10	.45
1401	42¢ Hockey	......	1.10	.45
1402	42¢ Bobsledding	......	1.10	.45
1403	42¢ Alpine Skiing	......	1.10	.45
1403a	Olympic Winter Games, Strips of 5	......	5.50	4.75
1403b	Olympic Winter Games, booklet pane of 10	......	11.00	10.00
1404-05	350th Anniversary of Montreal, attached	4.75	2.25	1.00
1404	42¢ Modern Montreal	......	1.00	.40
1405	42¢ Early Montreal	......	1.00	.40
1406	48¢ Jaques Cartier	5.50	1.20	.85
1407	84¢ Columbus	9.50	2.10	1.10
1407a	42¢-84¢ Canada '92, Souvenir Sheet of 4	......	5.75	5.75
1408	42¢ The Margaree River	......	1.00	.40
1409	42¢ Eliot or West River	......	1.00	.40
1410	42¢ Ottowa River	......	1.00	.40
1411	42¢ Niagara River	......	1.00	.40
1412	42¢ South Saskatchewan River	......	1.00	.40
1412a	Canadian Rivers II, Strip of 5	......	5.25	4.00
1412b	Canadian Rivers II, booklet pane of 10	......	10.00	......

1413

1420

SCOTT NO.	DESCRIPTION	PLATE BLOCK F/NH	UNUSED F/NH	USED F
1413	42¢ 50th Anniversary of the Alaska Highway	4.80	1.00	.35
1414	42¢ Gymnastics	......	1.00	.35
1415	42¢ Track and Field	......	1.00	.35
1416	42¢ Diving	......	1.00	.35
1417	42¢ Cycling	......	1.00	.35
1418	42¢ Swimming	......	1.00	.35
1418a	Olympic Summer Games, Strip of 5, attached	......	5.50	8.50
1418b	Olympic Summer Games, booklet pane of 10	......	11.00	10.00
1419	50¢ Canadian Art "Red Nasturtiums"	5.95	1.20	1.50
1420	Nova Scotia	......	2.10	1.50
1421	Ontario	......	2.10	1.50
1422	Prince Edward Island	......	2.10	1.50
1423	New Brunswick	......	2.10	1.50
1424	Quebec	......	2.10	1.50
1425	Saskatchewan	......	2.10	1.50
1426	Manitoba	......	2.10	1.50
1427	Northwest Territories	......	2.10	1.50
1428	Alberta	......	2.10	1.50
1429	British Columbia	......	2.10	1.50
1430	Yukon	......	2.10	1.50
1431	Newfoundland	......	2.10	1.50
1431a	42¢ 125th Anniversary of Canada, 12 various attached	......	24.00	22.00

1432

1436

SCOTT NO.	DESCRIPTION	PLATE BLOCK F/NH	UNUSED F/NH	USED F
1432-35	Canadian Folk Heroes, attached	4.95	4.25	3.50
1432	42¢ Jerry Potts	......	1.00	.35
1433	42¢ Capt. William Jackman	......	1.00	.35
1434	42¢ Laura Secord	......	1.00	.35
1435	42¢ Joseph Montferrand	......	1.00	.35
1436	42¢ Copper	......	1.00	.45
1437	42¢ Sodalite	......	1.15	.45
1438	42¢ Gold	......	1.15	.45
1439	42¢ Galena	......	1.15	.45
1440	42¢ Grossular	......	1.15	.45
1440a	Minerals, Strip of 5	......	5.50	4.25
1440b	Minerals, booklet pane of 10	......	11.50	9.50

1441

1443a

SCOTT NO.	DESCRIPTION	PLATE BLOCK F/NH	UNUSED F/NH	USED F
1441-42	Canadian Space Exploration, attached	4.95	2.25	2.25
1441	42¢ Anik E2 Satellite	......	1.00	.75
1442	42¢ Earth, Space Shuttle	......	1.10	1.00
1443-45	National Hockey League, booklet singles	......	3.25	.95
1443a	Skates, Stick, booklet pane of 8	......	8.00	......
1444a	Team Emblems, booklet pane of 8	......	8.00	......
1445a	Goalie's Mask, booklet pane of 9	......	10.00	......

SCOTT NO.	DESCRIPTION	PLATE BLOCK F/NH	UNUSED F/NH	USED F

1446-47

1452

Scott No.	Description	Plate Block	Unused	Used
1446-47	Order of Canada + D. Michener, attached	5.25	2.25	1.50
1446	42¢ Order of Canada	....	1.10	.35
1447	42¢ Daniel Roland Michener..........................	....	1.10	.35
1448-51	World War II —1942, att'd	4.95	4.25	3.30
1448	42¢ War Reporting	....	1.10	.50
1449	42¢ Newfoundland Air Bases.........................	....	1.10	.50
1450	42¢ Raid on Dieppe	....	1.10	.50
1451	42¢ U-boats offshore	....	1.10	.50
1452	42¢ Jouluvana—Christmas...........................	4.50	1.00	.25
1452a	Same, perf. 13½	....	1.15	.25
1452b	Same, booklet pane of 10............................	....	11.00	....
1453	48¢ La Befana—Christmas..........................	6.00	1.35	.75
1453a	Same, booklet pane of 5.............................	....	6.75	....
1454	84¢ Weihnachtsmann	9.25	2.00	.85
1454a	Same, booklet pane of 5.............................	....	11.00	....
1455	37¢ Santa Claus	....	1.00	.95
1455a	Same, booklet pane of 10............................	....	9.75	....

1455

1456

1460

1993 COMMEMORATIVES

Scott No.	Description	Plate Block	Unused	Used
1456-89, 1491-1506, 50 varieties..		41.00	42.50	19.50
1456-59	Canadian Women, attached....	5.50	4.80	3.50
1456	43¢ Adelaide Sophia Hoodless	....	1.10	.35
1457	43¢ Marie-Josephine Gerin-Lajoie..................	....	1.10	.35
1458	43¢ Pitseolak Ashoona	....	1.10	.35
1459	43¢ Helen Kinnear	....	1.10	.35
1460	43¢ Stanley Cup Centennial	5.25	1.10	.35

1461

1467

Scott No.	Description	Plate Block	Unused	Used
1461	43¢ Coverlet "Bed Rugg", New Brunswick.........	....	1.10	.35
1462	43¢ Pieced Quilt, Ontario............................	....	1.10	.35
1463	43¢ Doukhobor Bedcover, Saskatchewan..........	....	1.10	.35
1464	43¢ Kwakwaka'wakw ceremonial robe, British Columbia....	....	1.10	.35
1465	43¢ Boutonne coverlet, Quebec	....	1.10	.35
1465a	Handcrafted Textiles, Strip of 5	....	5.75	3.00
1465b	Handcrafted Textiles, booklet pane of 10...........	....	11.50	7.00
1461-65	Same, set of 5 singles...............................	....	5.00	...
1466	86¢ Canadian Art—"Drawing for the Owl".........	9.75	2.25	1.25
1467	43¢ Empress Hotel, Victoria, B.C.	....	1.15	.35
1468	43¢ Banff Springs Hotel, Banff, Alberta	....	1.15	.35
1469	43¢ Royal York Hotel, Toronto, Ontario.............	....	1.15	.35
1470	43¢ Chateau Frontenac, Quebec City, Quebec .	....	1.15	.35
1471	43¢ Algonquin Hotel, St. Andrews, N.B............	....	1.15	.35
1471a	Canadian Pacific Hotels, strip of 5.................	....	6.25	4.00
1471b	Canadian Pacific Hotels, booklet pane of 10	....	12.50	....

1472

1490a

1484

Scott No.	Description	Plate Block	Unused	Used
1472	43¢ Algonquin Park, Ontario............................	....	1.25	1.10
1473	43¢ De la Gaspesie Park,Quebec	....	1.25	1.10
1474	43¢ Cedar Dunes Park, P.E.I.	....	1.25	1.10
1475	43¢ Cape St. Mary's Reserve, Newfoundland ...	....	1.25	1.10
1476	43¢ Mount Robson Park, B.C.	....	1.25	1.10
1477	43¢ Writing-On-Stone Park, Alberta................	....	1.25	1.10
1478	43¢ Spruce Woods Park, Manitoba..................	....	1.25	1.10
1479	43¢ Herschel Island Park, Yukon....................	....	1.25	1.10
1480	43¢ Cypress Hills Park, Saskatchewan	....	1.25	1.10
1481	43¢ The Rocks Park, New Brunswick...............	....	1.25	1.10
1482	43¢ Blomidon Park, Nova Scotia....................	....	1.25	1.10
1483	43¢ Katannilik Park, Northwest Territories.........	....	1.25	1.10
1483a	100th Anniversary of Territorial Parks, 12 varieties attached....................................	....	18.00	18.00
1484	43¢ Toronto Bicentennial	5.25	1.10	.40
1485	43¢ Fraser River	....	1.10	.40
1486	43¢ Yukon River	....	1.10	.40
1487	43¢ Red River	....	1.10	.40
1488	43¢ St. Lawrence River...............................	....	1.10	.40
1489	43¢ St. John River	....	1.10	.40
1489a	Canadian Rivers III, strip of 5.........................	...	6.00	4.25
1489b	Canadian Rivers III, booklet pane of 10.............	...	11.00	8.50

1491

1495

1499

Scott No.	Description	Plate Block	Unused	Used
1490	43¢-86¢ Canadian Motor Vehicles souvenir sheet of 6 ...		9.50	9.00
1491-94	Canadian Folklore—Folk Songs, attached....	5.50	4.50	3.50
1491	43¢ The Alberta Homesteader	...	1.10	.35
1492	43¢ Les Raftmans.....................................	...	1.10	.35
1493	43¢ I'se the B'y that Builds the Boat	...	1.10	.35
1494	43¢ Bear Song...	...	1.10	.35

1502

1507

Scott No.	Description	Plate Block	Unused	Used
1495-98	Dinosaurs, attached..................................	5.50	4.75	3.50
1495	43¢ Massospondylus (Jurassic period)	...	1.20	.35
1496	43¢ Styracosaurus (Cretaceous period)	...	1.20	.35
1497	43¢ Albertosaurus (Cretaceous period)	...	1.20	.35
1498	43¢ Platecarpus (Cretaceous period)	...	1.20	.35
1499	43¢ Santa Claus—Poland............................	4.85	1.10	.25
1499a	same, booklet pane of 10............................	...	11.00	...
1500	49¢ Santa Claus—Russia............................	6.00	1.25	.55
1500a	same, booklet pane of 5..............................	...	6.75	...
1501	86¢ Father Christmas, Australia......................	10.00	2.40	.65
1501a	same, booklet pane of 5..............................	...	11.00	...
1502	38¢ Santa Claus	...	1.00	.65
1502a	same, booklet pane of 10............................	...	9.00	...
1503-06	World War II —1943..................................	5.30	4.50	4.00
1503	43¢ Aid to Allies......................................	...	1.15	.65
1504	43¢ Canada's Bomber Force	...	1.15	.65
1505	43¢ Battle of the Atlantic	...	1.15	.65
1506	43¢ Invasion of Italy	...	1.15	.65

1994

Scott No.	Description	Plate Block	Unused	Used
1507-08	43¢ Greeting booklet (10 stamps w/35 stickers)	...	11.00	...

SCOTT NO.	DESCRIPTION	PLATE BLOCK F/NH	UNUSED F/NH	USED F

1509

1510

1517

1994 COMMEMORATIVES

SCOTT NO.	DESCRIPTION	PLATE BLOCK F/NH	UNUSED F/NH	USED F
	1509-22, 1524-26, 1528-40, 41 varieties	...	34.00	13.75
1509	43¢ Jeanne Sauve	5.50	1.10	.40
1510	43¢ T. Eaton Prestige	...	1.10	.40
1510a	43¢ T. Eaton Prestige, booklet of 10	...	11.00	...
1511	43¢ Saguenay River	...	1.25	.35
1512	43¢ French River	...	1.25	.35
1513	43¢ Mackenzie River	...	1.25	.35
1514	43¢ Churchill River	...	1.25	.35
1515	43¢ Columbia River	...	1.25	.35
1515a	Canadian Rivers IV, strip of 5	...	5.75	5.00
1515b	Canadian Rivers IV, booklet pane of 10	...	12.00	...
1516	88¢ Canadian Art "Vera"	10.50	2.25	1.25

1523a

1524a

1525

SCOTT NO.	DESCRIPTION	PLATE BLOCK F/NH	UNUSED F/NH	USED F
1517-18	Commonwealth Games, attached	5.25	2.25	1.50
1517	43¢ Lawn Bowls	...	1.10	.35
1518	43¢ Lacrosse	...	1.10	.35
1519-20	Commonwealth Games, attached	5.25	2.25	1.50
1519	43¢ Wheelchair Marathon	...	1.10	.35
1520	43¢ High Jump	...	1.10	.35
1521	50¢ Commonwealth Games (Diving)	5.60	1.25	.80
1522	88¢ Commonwealth Games (Cycling)	9.75	2.25	1.15
1523	43¢ Intl. Year of the Family, souvenir sheet of 5	...	6.00	5.50
1524	Canada Day—Maple Trees, 12 varieties, attached	...	14.00	13.00
1525-26	Famous Canadians, attached	5.25	2.25	1.15
1525	43¢ Billy Bishop, Fighter Ace	...	1.10	.35
1526	43¢ Mary Travers, Folk Singer	...	1.10	.35
1527	43¢-88¢ Historic Motor Vehicles, souvenir sheet of 6	...	8.75	8.50

1528

1533

1536

SCOTT NO.	DESCRIPTION	PLATE BLOCK F/NH	UNUSED F/NH	USED F
1528	43¢ 50th Anniversary of ICAO	6.00	1.35	.35
1529-32	Dinosaurs, attached	5.35	4.75	3.75
1529	43¢ Coryphodon	...	1.20	.35
1530	43¢ Megacerops	...	1.20	.35
1531	43¢ Short-Faced Bear	...	1.20	.35
1532	43¢ Woolly Mammoth	...	1.20	.35
1533	43¢ Family Singing Carols	5.25	1.10	.25
1533a	same, booklet pane of 10	...	11.00	...
1534	50¢ Choir	5.75	1.25	.65
1534a	same, booklet pane of 5	...	6.75	...
1535	88¢ Caroling	9.75	2.25	1.15
1535a	same, booklet pane of 5	...	11.00	...
1536	38¢ Caroling Soloist, booklet single	...	1.00	.65
1536a	same, booklet pane of 10	...	9.75	...
1537-40	World War II—1944, attached	5.60	4.75	3.75
1537	43¢ D-Day Beachhead	...	1.15	.45
1538	43¢ Artillery—Normandy	...	1.15	.45
1539	43¢ Tactical Air Forces	...	1.15	.45
1540	43¢ Walcheren and Scheldt	...	1.15	.45

1995 COMMEMORATIVES

SCOTT NO.	DESCRIPTION	PLATE BLOCK F/NH	UNUSED F/NH	USED F
	1541-51, 1553-58, 1562-67, 1570-90, 47 varieties	...	48.75	17.75
1541-44	World War II—1945, attached	5.35	4.75	3.75
1541	43¢ Veterans Return Home	...	1.10	.45
1542	43¢ Freeing the POW	...	1.10	.45
1543	43¢ Liberation of Civilians	...	1.10	.45
1544	43¢ Crossing the Rhine	...	1.10	.45
1545	88¢ Canadian Art "Floraison"	9.50	2.25	1.25
1546	(43¢) Canada Flag over Lake	5.25	1.15	.35
1547	(43¢) Louisbourg Harbor, ships near Dauphin Gate	...	1.15	.35
1548	(43¢) Walls, streets & buildings of Louisbourg...	...	1.15	.35
1549	(43¢) Museum behind King's Bastion	...	1.15	.35
1550	(43¢) Drawing of King's Garden, Convent, Hospital & barracks	...	1.15	.35
1551	(43¢) Partially eroded fortifications	...	1.15	.35
1551a	(43¢) Fortress of Louisbourg, strip of 5	...	6.00	4.75
1551b	(43¢) Fortress of Louisbourg, booklet pane of 10	...	11.00	9.00
1552	43¢-88¢ Historic Land Vehicles/Farm and Frontier souvenir sheet of 6	...	9.00	9.00
1553	43¢ Banff Springs Golf Club	...	1.20	.35
1554	43¢ Riverside Country Club	...	1.20	.35
1555	43¢ Glen Abbey Golf Club	...	1.20	.35
1556	43¢ Victoria Golf Club	...	1.20	.35
1557	43¢ Royal Montreal Golf Club	...	1.20	.35
1557a	43¢ Royal Canadian Golf Assoc., strip of 5	...	6.50	5.00
1557b	43¢ Royal Canadian Golf Assoc., booklet pane of 10	...	12.50	11.00
1558	43¢ Lunenberg Academy Centennial	5.00	1.20	.35
1559-61	43¢ Group of Seven 75th Anniv. 3 souv. sheets (2 w/3 stamps and 1 w/4 stamps)	...	11.75	11.50
1562	43¢ Winnipeg, Manitoba 125th Anniversary	5.00	1.10	.35
1563-66	Migratory Wildlife, attached	5.50	4.75	3.00
1563, 65-67	Migratory Wildlife, attached (revised inscription)	6.00	5.25	5.25
1563	45¢ Monarch Butterfly	...	1.10	.40
1564	45¢ Belted Kingfisher	...	1.10	.40
1565	45¢ Northern Pintail	...	1.10	.40
1566	45¢ Hoary Bat	...	1.10	.40
1568-69	45¢ Canadian Memorial College, Toronto, Greetings Booklet (10 stamps w/15 stickers)	...	12.75	...
1570-73	45¢ Canadian Bridges, attached	5.50	4.75	3.75
1570	45¢ Quebec Bridge, Quebec	...	1.15	.40
1571	45¢ Highway 403-401-410 interchange, Ontario	...	1.15	.40
1572	45¢ Hartland Covered Wooden Bridge, New Brunswick	...	1.15	.40
1573	45¢ Alex Fraser Bridger, British Columbia	...	1.15	.40

1546

1547

1553

1558

1559a

1562

1563

1570

1574

SCOTT NO.	DESCRIPTION	PLATE BLOCK F/NH	UNUSED F/NH	USED F
1574	45¢ Polar bear, caribou	......	1.15	.40
1575	45¢ Arctic poppy, cargo canoe	......	1.15	.40
1576	45¢ Inuk man, igloo, sled dogs	......	1.15	.40
1577	45¢ Dog-sled team, ski plane	......	1.15	.40
1578	45¢ Children	......	1.15	.40
1578a	45¢ Canadian Arctic, strip of 5	......	6.00	5.50
1578b	45¢ Canadian Arctic, booklet pane of 10	......	11.00	11.00
1579	45¢ Superman	......	1.45	.40
1580	45¢ Johnny Canuck	......	1.45	.40
1581	45¢ Nelvana	......	1.45	.40
1582	45¢ Captain Canuck	......	1.45	.40
1583	45¢ Fleur de Lys	......	1.45	.40
1583a	45¢ Comic Book Characters, strip of 5	......	7.00	3.00
1583b	45¢ Comic Book Characters, booklet pane of 10	......	13.50	12.00
1584	45¢ United Nations, 50th Anniversary	6.50	1.40	.40
1585	45¢ The Nativity	5.00	1.15	.40
1585a	same, booklet pane of 10	......	11.00	......
1586	52¢ The Annunciation	6.25	1.35	.65
1586a	same, booklet pane of 5	......	6.75	......
1587	90¢ Flight to Egypt	9.75	2.25	.70
1587a	same, booklet pane of 5	......	11.00	......
1588	40¢ Holly, booklet single	......	1.00	.70
1588a	same, booklet pane of 10	......	9.75	......
1589	45¢ La Francophonie's Agency, 25th Anniversary	5.10	1.15	.35
1590	45¢ End of the Holocaust, 50th Anniversary	5.10	1.15	.35

1996 COMMEMORATIVES

SCOTT NO.	DESCRIPTION	PLATE BLOCK F/NH	UNUSED F/NH	USED F
	1591-98, 1602-03, 1606-14, 1617-21, 1622-29, 36 varieties.	......	44.50	16.75
1591-94	Birds, attached	......	5.00	4.25
1591	45¢ American Kestrel	......	1.15	.35
1592	45¢ Atlantic Puffin	......	1.15	.35
1593	45¢ Pileated Woodpecker	......	1.15	.35
1594	45¢ Ruby-throated Hummingbird	......	1.15	.35
1595-98	High Technology Industries, attached	......	5.25	4.25
1595	45¢ Ocean technology	......	1.25	.45
1596	45¢ Aerospace technology	......	1.25	.45
1597	45¢ Information technology	......	1.25	.45
1598	45¢ Biotechnology	......	1.25	.45
1598b	Booklet pane of 12	......	14.50	......
1600-01	45¢ Special Occasions, Greetings Booklet (10 stamps w/35 stickers)	......	18.00	......
1602	90¢ Canadian Art—"The Spirit of Haida Gwaii"	10.00	2.25	1.25
1603	45¢ AIDS Awareness	5.25	1.15	.25
1604	45¢-90¢ Historic Canadian Industrial & Commercial Vehicles souvenir sheet of 6	......	10.00	9.50
1605	5¢-45¢ CAPEX '96 souvenir pane of 25 vehicle stamps	......	10.00	9.50
1606	45¢ Yukon Gold Rush centennial, strip of 5	......	6.75	6.00
1606a	45¢ Jim Mason's discovery on Rabbit Creek, 1896	......	1.25	.65
1606b	45¢ Miners trekking to gold fields, boats on Lake Laberge	......	1.25	.65
1606c	45¢ Supr. Sam Steele, North West Mounted Police	......	1.25	.65
1606d	45¢ Dawson, boom town, city of entertainment	......	1.25	.65
1606e	45¢ Klondike gold fields	......	1.25	.65
1607	45¢ Canada Day (Maple Leaf), self-adhesive	......	1.15	.35
1607a	same, pane of 12	......	13.00	......
1608	45¢ Ethel Catherwood, high jump, 1928	......	1.30	.90
1609	45¢ Etienne Desmarteau, 56 lb. weight throw, 1904	......	1.30	.90
1610	45¢ Fanny Rosenfeld, 100m, 400m relay, 1928	......	1.30	.90
1611	45¢ Gerald Ouellette, smallbore, fifle, prone, 1956	......	1.30	.90
1612	45¢ Percy Williams, 100m, 200m, 1928	......	1.30	.90
1612a	45¢ Canadian Gold Medalists, strip of 5	......	6.50	4.75
1612b	45¢ Canadian Gold Medalists, booklet pane of 10	......	13.00	......
1613	45¢ 125th Anniv. of British Columbia's Entry into Confederation	5.25	1.15	.35
1614	45¢ Canadian Heraldy	5.25	1.15	.35
1615	45¢ Motion Pictures Centennial, self-adhesive, sheet of 5	......	6.00	5.50
1615a	45¢ L'arrivee d'un train en gate, Lumiere cinematography, 1896	......	1.25	1.10
1615b	45¢ Back to God's Country, Nell & Ernest Shipman, 1919	......	1.25	1.10
1615c	45¢ Hen Hop, Norman McLaren, 1942	......	1.25	1.10
1615d	45¢ Pour la suite du monde, Pierre Perrault, Michel Brault, 1963	......	1.25	1.10
1615e	45¢ Goin' Down the Road, Don Shebib, 1970	......	1.25	1.10

1579

1585

1584

1588

1589

1590

1591

1595

1600

1602

1603

1604a   1607

1606a

1608

1613

1614

1615a

1617

SCOTT NO.	DESCRIPTION	PLATE BLOCK F/NH	UNUSED F/NH	USED F

1618

1622

1627

1616	45¢ Motion Pictures Centennial, self-adhesive, sheet of 5	......	6.00	5.50
1616a	45¢ Mon oncle Antoine, Claude Jutra, 1971	......	1.25	1.10
1616b	45¢ The Apprenticeship of Duddy Kravitz, Ted Kotcheff, 1974		1.25	1.10
1616c	45¢ Les Ordres, Michel Brault, 1974		1.25	1.10
1616d	45¢ Les Bons Debarras, Francis Mankiewicz, 1980		1.25	1.10
1616e	45¢ The Grey Fox, Phillip Borsos, 1982	......	1.25	1.10
1617	45¢ Edouard Montpetit, Educator	2.25	1.15	.50
1618-21	Winnie the Pooh, attached	....	5.25	5.25
1618	45¢ Winnie, Lt. Colebourne, 1914		1.25	.80
1619	45¢ Winnie, Christopher Robin, 1925		1.25	.80
1620	45¢ Milne and Shepard's Winnie the Pooh, 1926		1.25	.80
1621	45¢ Winnie the Pooh at Walt Disney World, 1996		1.25	.80
1621b	same, souvenir sheet of 4 (#1618-21)		9.25	9.25
1621c	same, booklet pane of 16		20.00	
	same, 2 booklet panes plus souvenir book		24.00	......
1622	45¢ Margaret Laurence (1926-1987)	......	1.25	.45
1623	45¢ Donald G. Creighton (1902-1979)	......	1.25	.45
1624	45¢ Gabrielle Roy (1909-1983)	......	1.25	.45
1625	45¢ Felix-Antoine Savard (1896-1982)	......	1.25	.45
1626	45¢ Thomas C. Halliburton (1796-1865)	......	1.25	.45
1626a	45¢ Canadian Authors, strip of 5		7.25	6.75
1626b	45¢ Canadian Authors, booklet pane of 10	......	14.00	14.00
1627	45¢ Children on snowshoes, sled	5.25	1.15	.25
1627a	same, booklet pane of 10	......	11.00	
1628	52¢ Santa Claus skiing	6.00	1.30	.40
1628a	same, booklet pane of 5		7.00	......
1629	90¢ Children skating	9.50	2.25	.65
1629a	same, booklet pane of 5	......	12.00	......

1630

1631

1635

1636

1637

1638

1639

1640

1641

1659

1661

1665

1645

1647

1650

1997 COMMEMORATIVES

1630, 1631-48, 1649-72, 43 varieties			39.00	18.00
1630	45¢ New Year 1997 (Year of the Ox)	5.50	1.25	.60
1630a	same, souvenir sheet of 2	......	3.25	3.25
	same, souvenir sheet of 2, with Hong Kong '97 overprint	......	10.00	......
1631-34	Birds of Canada, attached	5.50	4.75	3.75
1631	45¢ Mountain bluebird		1.20	.35
1632	45¢ Western grebe		1.20	.35
1633	45¢ Northern gannet		1.20	.35
1634	45¢ Scarlet tanager		1.20	.35
1635	90¢ Canadian Art "York Boat on Lake Winnipeg"	10.00	2.30	1.25
1636	45¢ Canadian Tire, 75th Anniv.	5.00	1.15	.35
1637	45¢ Father Charles-Emile Gadbois (1906-1981)	5.00	1.15	.35
1638	45¢ Blue poppy		1.15	.35
1638a	same, booklet pane of 12	......	13.00	......
1639	45¢ Victorian Order of Nurses	5.00	1.15	.35
1640	45¢ Law Society of Upper Canada	5.00	1.15	.35
1641-44	45¢ Ocean Fish, attached	5.25	4.75	3.25
1641	45¢ Great White Shark		1.15	.35
1642	45¢ Pacific Halibut		1.15	.35
1643	45¢ Atlantic Sturgeon		1.15	.35
1644	45¢ Bluefin Tuna		1.15	.35
1645-46	45¢ Confederation Bridge, attached	5.35	2.75	1.50
1645	45¢ Lighthouse and Bridge		1.15	.35
1646	45¢ Bridge and Bird	......	1.15	.35
1647	45¢ Gilles Villeneuve, Formula 1 driver	5.15	1.15	.35
1648	90¢ Gilles Villeneuve, Formula 1 d iver	10.00	2.25	1.15
1648b	45¢-90¢ Gilles Villeneuve, souvenir sheet of 8	......	14.00	......
1649	45¢ John Cabot	5.10	1.15	.35
1650-53	45¢ Canada's scenic highways (Canada Day), attached	5.35	4.75	3.75
1650	45¢ Sea to Sky Highway, British Columbia	......	1.20	.75
1651	45¢ The Cabot Trail, Nova Scotia	......	1.20	.75
1652	45¢ The Wine Route, starting in Ontario	......	1.20	.75
1653	45¢ The Big Muddy, Saskatchewan	......	1.20	.75
1654	45¢ Industrial Design	5.10	1.20	.75
1654v	same, sheet of 24 w/12 different Labels	......	30.00	......
1655	45¢ Highland Games	5.10	1.20	.35
1656	45¢ Knights of Columbus in Canada	5.10	1.20	.35
1657	45¢ World Congress of the PTT	5.10	1.20	.35
1658	45¢ Canada's Year of Asia Pacific	5.10	1.20	.35
1659-60	45¢ Ice Hockey "Series of the Century", bklt singles	......	2.25	1.30
1660a	same, bklt pane of 10 (5 of each)	......	11.00	......
1661-64	Famous Politicians, attached	5.25	4.75	3.75
1661	45¢ Martha Black		1.15	.75
1662	45¢ Lionel Chevrier		1.15	.75
1663	45¢ Judy LaMarsh		1.15	.75
1664	45¢ Real Caouette		1.15	.75
1665-68	Supernatural, 4 attached	5.25	4.75	3.75
1665	45¢ Vampire		1.15	.35
1666	45¢ Werewolf		1.15	.35
1667	45¢ Ghost		1.15	.35
1668	45¢ Goblin		1.15	.35
1669	45¢ Christmas, Stained Glass Window	5.25	1.15	.30
1669a	same, bklt pane of 10	......	11.00	......
1670	52¢ Christmas, Stained Glass Window	6.25	1.25	.50
1670a	same, bklt pane of 5	......	7.00	......
1671	90¢ Christmas, Stained Glass Window	9.75	2.25	.75
1671a	same, bklt pane of 5	......	11.00	......
1672	45¢ 75th Royal Agriculture Winter Fair, Toronto	5.25	1.15	.35

1997-2000 Regular Issues

1673	1¢ Bookbinding	.95	.25	.25
1674	2¢ Ironwork	.95	.25	.25
1675	3¢ Glass blowing	.95	.25	.25
1676	4¢ Oyster farmer	.95	.25	.25
1677	5¢ Weaving	.95	.25	.25
1678	9¢ Quilting	1.25	.30	.25
1679	10¢ Artistic woodworking	1.25	.30	.25
1680	25¢ Leatherworking	2.85	.65	.25
1681	46¢ Queen Elizabeth II	5.00	1.15	.25
1682	46¢ Flags Over Icebergs	5.25	1.15	.25
1682a	same, booklet pane of 10	......	11.50	......
1684	55¢ Maple Leaf	6.25	1.35	.40
1684a	same, booklet pane of 5 + label	......	6.30	......
1685	73¢ Maple Leaf	8.50	1.85	.60
1686	95¢ Maple Leaf	11.00	2.40	.95
1686a	same, booklet pane of 5 + label	......	12.00	......
1687	$1 Loon	11.00	2.40	.70
1688-89	$1 Atlantic Walrus & White Tailed Deer	11.00	4.75	3.00
1688	$1 White-Tailed Deer		2.50	1.25
1689	$1 Atlantic Walrus		2.50	1.25
1689b	Souvenir Sheet Deer and Walrus		10.00	10.00
1690	$2 Polar Bear	22.00	5.00	2.25
1691-92	$2 Peregrine Falcons & Sable Island Horses	22.00	10.00	5.50
1691	$2 Peregrine Falcons		4.75	2.25
1692	$2 Sable Island Horses		4.75	2.25
1692b	Souvenir Sheet, 2 each 1691-92		20.00	20.00
1693	$5 Moose		13.00	2.25
1694	$8 Grizzly Bear		18.50	5.50
1695	46¢ Flag, coil		1.15	.35
1696	45¢ Maple Leaf		1.65	1.50
1696b	same, booklet pane of 18		38.00	
1697	45¢ Maple Leaf		1.40	.75
1698	46¢ Flags Over Icebergs		1.40	.75
1698a	same, booklet pane of 30		35.00	
1699	46¢ Maple Leaf		3.00	2.85
1699a	same, booklet pane of 18		58.00	
1700	47¢ Flag and Inukshuk		1.20	.25
1700a	same, booklet pane of 10		11.00	
1700b	same, booklet pane of 30		32.00	......

SCOTT NO.	DESCRIPTION	PLATE BLOCK F/NH	UNUSED F/NH	USED F

1708

1709a

1710

1714

1715

1721

1722

1723

1725

 image N5
1735

1736

1739

1750

1756

1761

1764

1998 COMMEMORATIVES

1708,1710-13,1715-20,1721-24,1735-37,1738-42, 1750-54,1760-61,1761-66 set of 40 1998 commemoratives		....	43.00	19.00
1708	45¢ Year of the Tiger	5.25	1.15	.35
1708a	same, souvenir sheet of 2		2.40	2.00
1709	45¢ Provincial Leaders. sheetlet of 10	....	14.00	12.00
1710-13	Birds, attached	5.20	4.75	3.75
1710	45¢ Hairy Woodpecker		43.00	19.00
1711	45¢ Great Crested Flycatcher		1.25	.45
1712	45¢ Eastern Screech Owl		1.25	.45
1713	45¢ Gray Crowned Rosy-Finch		1.25	.45
1714	45¢ Maple Leaf, self-adhesive, bklt single		1.75	1.50
1714a	same, bklt pane of 18		25.00	....
1714B	45¢ Maple Leaf, self-adhesive, die cut perf. 13 .		1.55	.92
1715-20	Fly Fishing, strip of 6, from bklt pane		7.75	5.75
1715	45¢ Coquihalla orange, steelhead trout		1.15	.55
1716	45¢ Steelhead bee, steelhead trout		1.15	.55
1717	45¢ Dark Montreal, brook trout		1.15	.55
1718	45¢ Lady Amherst, Atlantic salmon		1.15	.55
1719	45¢ Coho blue, coho salmon		1.15	.55
1720	45¢ Cosseboom special, Atlantic salmon		1.15	.55
1720a	same, bklt pane of 12		13.75	....
1721	45¢ Canadian Inst. of Mining Centennial	5.25	1.25	.35
1722	45¢ Imperial Penny Post Centennial	5.25	1.25	.35
1723-24	Sumo Wrestling Tournament, attached	5.25	2.50	2.50
1723	45¢ Rising sun, Mapleleaf and two wrestlers		1.15	.35
1724	45¢ Rising sun, Mapleleaf and Sumo champion		1.15	.35
1724b	45¢ Sumo Wrestling Tournament, souvenir sheet of 2		4.25	4.25
1725	45¢ St. Peters Canal, Nova Scotia		1.50	.75
1726	45¢ St. Ours Canal, Quebec		1.50	.75
1727	45¢ Port Carling Lock, Ontario		1.50	.75
1728	45¢ Locks, Rideau Canal, Onrtario		1.50	.75
1729	45¢ Peterborough lift lock, Trent-Severn Waterway, Ontario		1.50	.75
1730	45¢ Chambly Canal, Quebec		1.50	.75
1731	45¢ Lachine Canal, Quebec		1.50	.75
1732	45¢ Ice skating on Rideau Canal, Ottawa		1.50	.75
1733	45¢ Boat on Big Chute Marine Railway, Trent-Severn Waterway		1.50	.75
1734	45¢ Sault Ste. Marie Canal, Ontario		1.50	.75
1734a	45¢ Canals of Canada, bklt pane of 10 plus labels		16.00	....
1735	45¢ Health Professionals	5.25	1.15	.35
1736-37	Royal Canadian Mounted Police 125th Anniv. attd.	5.40	2.50	1.50
1736	45¢ Male mountie, native horse		1.15	.35
1737	45¢ Female mountie, helicopter, cityscape		1.15	.3
1737b	same, souvenir sheet of 2		3.00	2.75
1737c	same, souvenir sheet of 2 with signature		4.00	3.50
1737d	same, souvvenir sheet of 2 with Portugal '98 emblem		4.50	3.50
1737e	same, souvenir sheet of 2 with Italia '98 emblem	....	4.50	3.50
1738	45¢ William Roue, designer of Bluenose	5.25	1.15	.35

1739-42	Scenic Highways, 4 attached	5.75	4.75	3.75
1739	45¢ Dempster Highway, Yukon	....	1.15	.45
1740	45¢ Dinosaur Trail, Alberta	....	1.15	.45
1741	45¢ River Valley, Scenic Drive, New Burnswick	....	1.15	.45
1742	45¢ Blue Heron Route, Prince Edward Isalnd ...	....	1.15	.45
1743	45¢ "Peinture", Jean-Paul Riopelle, self-adhesive	....	1.25	.45
1744	45¢ "La demiere campagne de Napolean", Fernand Leduc, self-adhesive		1.25	.65
1745	45¢ "Jet fuligineux sur noir torture", Jean -Paul Monusseau, self-adhesive		1.25	.65
1746	45¢ "Le fond du garde-robe", Pierre Gauvreau, self-adhesive		1.25	.65
1747	45¢ "Jean lacustre", Paul-Emile Borduas, self-adhesive		1.25	.65
1748	45¢ "Syndicat des gens de met", Marcelle Ferron, self-adhesive		1.25	.65
1749	45¢ "Le tumulte a la machoire crispee", Marcel Barbeau, self-adhesive		1.25	.65
1749a	45¢ The Automatists, 50th Anniversary, self-adhesive, bklt pane of 7		10.00	9.50
1750-53	Canadian Legendary Heroes, 4 attached	5.75	4.75	3.50
1750	45¢ Napoleon-Alexandre Comeau (1848-1923) outdoorsman		1.15	.45
1751	45¢ Phyllis Munday (1894-1990), mountaineer .		1.15	.45
1752	45¢ Bill Mason (1929-1988), film maker		1.15	.45
1753	45¢ Harry "Red" Foster (1905-1985), sports enthusiast		1.15	.45
1754	90¢ Canadian Art "The Farmer's Family"	10.00	2.25	1.10
1755	45¢ Housing in Canada, sheetlet of 9	....	14.00	14.00
1756	45¢ University of Ottawa, 150th Anniversary	5.25	1.15	.30
1757	45¢ Elephant, bear performing tricks		1.15	.30
1758	45¢ Women standing on horse, aerial act		1.15	.30
1759	45¢ Lion tamer		1.15	.30
1760	45¢ Contortionists, acrobats		1.15	.30
1760a	45¢ The Circus, bklt pane of 12		14.00	....
1760b	same, souvenir sheet of 4		5.65	5.00
1761	45¢ John Peters Humphrey, Human Rights author	5.25	1.15	.35
1762-63	Canadian Naval Reserve, 75th Anniversary, attached	5.25	2.50	1.75
1762	45¢ HMCS Sackville		1.15	.35
1763	45¢ HMCS Shawinigan		1.15	.35
1764	45¢ Christmas, Sculpted wooden angels	5.25	1.15	.30
1764a	same, bklt pane of 10		43.00	....
1765	52¢ Christmas, Sculpted wooden angels	5.75	1.35	.55
1765a	same, bklt pane of 5		20.00	....
1766	90¢ Christmas, Sculpted wooden angels	10.00	2.20	.85
1766a	same, bklt pane of 5		43.00	

1767

image
1770

1999 COMMEMORATIVES

1767	46¢ New Year 1999, Year of the Rabbit	5.25	1.15	.40
1768	same, souvenir sheet of 2	....	2.75	2.50
1769	46¢ Le Theatre du Rideau Vert, 50th Anniversary	5.25	1.15	.40
1770-73	Birds, 4 attached	5.95	4.75	2.50
1770	46¢ Northern goshawk		1.15	.45
1771	46¢ Red-winged blackbird		1.15	.45
1772	46¢ American goldfinch		1.15	.45
1773	46¢ Sandhill crane		1.15	.45
1774	46¢ Northern goshawk, self-adhesive		1.20	.55
1775	46¢ Red-winged blackbird, self-adhesive		1.20	.55
1776	46¢ American goldfinch, self-adhesive		1.20	.55
1777	46¢ Sandhill crane, self-adhesive		1.20	.55
1777a	same, bklt pane of 6 (1774 x 2, 1775 x 2, 1776 x 2, 1777x 1), self-adhesive		7.50	....
1777b	same, bklt pane of 6 (1774 x 1, 1775 x 1, 1776 x 2, 1777 x 2), self-adhesive		7.50	....

SCOTT NO.	DESCRIPTION	PLATE BLOCK F/NH	UNUSED F/NH	USED F

1778

1779

1999 COMMEMORATIVES (continued)

SCOTT NO.	DESCRIPTION	PLATE BLOCK F/NH	UNUSED F/NH	USED F
1778	46¢ Univ. of British Columbia Museum of Anthropology. 50th Anniversary	5.26	1.15	.35
1779	46¢ Sailing Ship Marco Polo	5.26	1.15	.35
1779a	same, souvenir sheet of 2 (1779 x 1, Australia 1631 x 1)	....	3.50	3.50
1780-83	Canada's Scenic Highways, 4 attached	5.95	4.75	3.75
1780	46¢ Gaspe Peninsula, Highway 132, Quebec	....	1.25	.45
1781	46¢ Yellowhead Highway (PTH 16), Manitoba	....	1.25	.45
1782	46¢ Dempster Highway 8, Northwest Territories	....	1.25	.45
1783	46¢ Discovery Trail, Route 230N, Newfoundland	....	1.25	.45
1784	46¢ Creation of the Nunavnt Territory	5.25	1.15	.35
1785	46¢ International Year of Older Persons	5.25	1.15	.35
1786	46¢ Baisakhi, Religious Holiday of Sikh Canadians, 300 th Anniversary	9.25	2.25	.35
1787	46¢ Canadian orchid, Arethusa bulbosa, self-adhesive	....	1.25	.45
1788	46¢ Canadian orchid, Amerorchis rotundifolia, self-adhesive	....	1.25	.45
1789	46¢ Canadian orchid, Platanthera psycodes, self-adhesive	....	1.25	.45
1790	46¢ Canadian orchid, Cypripedium pubescens, self-adhesive	....	1.25	.45
1790a	same, bklt pane of 12 (1787-90 x 3)	....	15.00	....
1790b	same, souvenir sheet of 4 w/ China '99 emblem	....	4.95	4.95

1791

1799

SCOTT NO.	DESCRIPTION	PLATE BLOCK F/NH	UNUSED F/NH	USED F
1791-94	Horses, 4 attached	5.95	4.95	4.25
1791	46¢ Northern Dancer, thorough-bred race horse	....	1.25	.45
1792	46¢ Kingsway Skoal, bucking horse	....	1.25	.45
1793	46¢ Big Ben, show horse	....	1.25	.45
1794	46¢ Ambro Flight, harness race horse	....	1.25	.45
1795	46¢ Northern Dancer, thorough-bred race horse, self-adhesive	....	1.25	.45
1796	46¢ Kingsway Skoal, bucking horse, self-adhesive	....	1.25	.45
1797	46¢ Big Ben, show horse, self-adhesive	....	1.25	.45
1798	46¢ Ambro Flight, harness race horse, self-adhesive	....	1.25	.45
1798a	same, bklt of 12 (1795-98 x 3)	....	15.75	....
1799	46¢ Quebec Bar Association, 150th Anniversary	5.25	1.15	.35

1800

1801

SCOTT NO.	DESCRIPTION	PLATE BLOCK F/NH	UNUSED F/NH	USED F
1800	95¢ Canadian Art "Unicorn Rooster"	10.50	2.40	1.35
1801-04	46¢ Pan-American Games XIII, 4 attached	5.95	4.75	3.50
1801	46¢ Track & Field	....	1.25	.50
1802	46¢ Cycling, weight lifting, gymnastics	....	1.25	.50
1803	46¢ Swimming, sailboarding, kayaking	....	1.25	.50
1804	46¢ Soccer, tennis, medals winners	....	1.25	.50

1805

1806

SCOTT NO.	DESCRIPTION	PLATE BLOCK F/NH	UNUSED F/NH	USED F
1805	46¢ World Rowing Championships	5.25	1.15	.35
1806	46¢ Universal Postal Union	5.25	1.15	.35

1807a

1808a

SCOTT NO.	DESCRIPTION	PLATE BLOCK F/NH	UNUSED F/NH	USED F
1807	46¢ Canadian Int. Air Show, 50th Anniv., sheetlet of 4	....	6.50	6.50
1807a	46¢ Fokker DR-1, CT-114 Tutors	....	1.50	1.25
1807b	46¢ Tutors, H101 Salto sailplane	....	1.50	1.25
1807c	46¢ De Havilland DH100 Vampire MKIII	....	1.50	1.25
1807d	46¢ Stearman A-75	....	1.50	1.25
1808	46¢ Royal Canadian Air Force, 75th Anniv, sheetlet of 16	....	24.00	24.00
1808a	46¢ De Havilland Mosquito FVBI	....	1.25	1.25
1808b	46¢ Sopwith F1 Camel	....	1.25	1.25
1808c	46¢ De Havilland Canada DHC-3 Otter	....	1.25	1.25
1808d	46¢ De Havilland Canada CC-108 Caribou	....	1.25	1.25
1808e	46¢ Canadair DL-28 Argus MK 2	....	1.25	1.25
1808f	46¢ North American F86 Sabre 6	....	1.25	1.25
1808g	46¢ McDonnell Douglas CF-18 Hornet	....	1.25	1.25
1808h	46¢ Sopwith SF-1 Dolphin	....	1.25	1.25
1808i	46¢ Armstrong Whitworth Siskin IIIA	....	1.25	1.25
1808j	46¢ Canadian Vickers (Northrop) Delta II	....	1.25	1.25
1808k	46¢ Sikorsky CH-124A Sea King Helicopter	....	1.25	1.25
1808l	46¢ Vickers-Armstrong Wellington MKII	....	1.25	1.25
1808m	46¢ Avro Anson MKI	....	1.25	1.25
1808n	46¢ Canadair (Lockheed) CF-104G Starfighter	....	1.25	1.25
1808o	46¢ Burgess-Dunne seaplane	....	1.25	1.25
1808p	46¢ Avro 504K	....	1.25	1.25

1809

1810

SCOTT NO.	DESCRIPTION	PLATE BLOCK F/NH	UNUSED F/NH	USED F
1809	46¢ NATO, 50th Anniversary	5.25	1.15	.35
1810	46¢ Frontier College, 100th Anniversary	5.25	1.15	.35

1811a

1813

SCOTT NO.	DESCRIPTION	PLATE BLOCK F/NH	UNUSED F/NH	USED F
1811	33¢ Kites, bklt pane of 8	....	10.50	....
1811a	33¢ Master Control, sport kite by Lam Hoac (triangular)	....	2.50	.50
1811b	33¢ Indian Garden Flying Carpet, edo kite by Skye Morrison (trapezoidal)	....	2.50	.50
1811c	33¢ Gibson Girl, Manufactured box kite (rectangular)	....	2.50	.50
1811d	33¢ Dragon centipede kite by Zhang tian Wei (oval)	....	2.50	.50
1812	Holographic Dove & 2000	....	1.25	.50
....	same, pane of 4	....	6.50	6.50
1813	55¢ Girl & Dove	....	1.50	.95
....	same, pane of 4	....	6.50	6.50

1814

1815

SCOTT NO.	DESCRIPTION	PLATE BLOCK F/NH	UNUSED F/NH	USED F
1814	95¢ Millenium Dove	....	2.50	1.95
....	same, pane of 4	....	8.00	....
1815	46¢ Christmas, Angel, drum	5.25	1.15	.35
1815a	same, bklt pane of 10	....	11.00	....
1816	55¢ Christmas, Angel, toys	6.25	1.40	.50
1816a	same, bklt pane of	....	6.75	....
1817	95¢ Christmas, Angel, candle	10.50	2.50	1.25
1817a	same, bklt pane of 5	....	12.00	....

SCOTT NO.	DESCRIPTION	PLATE BLOCK F/NH	UNUSED F/NH	USED F

1818a   **1819a**   **1820a**

SCOTT NO.	DESCRIPTION	PLATE BLOCK F/NH	UNUSED F/NH	USED F
1818	46¢ Millenium Collection-Media Tech. sheet of 4	....		9.50
1818a	46¢ IMAX Movies	....	2.50	2.00
1818b	46¢ Softimage animation software	....	2.50	2.00
1818c	46¢ Ted Rogers Sr. (1900-39) and radio tube	....	2.50	2.00
1818d	46¢ Invention of radio facsimile device by Sir William Stephenson (1896-1989)	....	2.50	2.00
1819	46¢ Millenium Collection-Canadian Entertainment, sheet of 4		9.50	....
1819a	46¢ Calgary Stampede	....	2.50	2.00
1819b	46¢ Performers from Cirque du Soleil	....	2.50	2.00
1819c	46¢ Hockey Night in Canada	....	2.50	2.00
1819d	46¢ La Soiree du Hockey	....	2.50	2.00
1820	46¢ Millenium Collection-Entertainers, sheet of 4		....	9.50
1820a	46¢ Portia White (1911-68), singer	....	2.50	2.00
1820b	46¢ Glenn Gould (1932-82), pianist	....	2.50	2.00
1820c	46¢ Guy Lombardo (1902-77), band leader	....	2.50	2.00
1820d	46¢ Felix Leclerc (1914-88), singer, guitarist	....	2.50	2.00

1821a   **1822a**   **1823a**

SCOTT NO.	DESCRIPTION	PLATE BLOCK F/NH	UNUSED F/NH	USED F
1821	46¢ Millenium Collection-Fostering Canadian Talent, sheet of 4	....	9.50	....
1821a	46¢ Royal Canadian Academy of Arts (men viewing painting)	....	2.50	2.00
1821b	46¢ Canada Council (sky, musical staff, "A")	....	2.50	2.00
1821c	46¢ National Film Board of Canada	....	2.50	2.00
1821d	46¢ Canadian Broadcasting Corp.	....	2.50	2.00
1822	46¢ Millenium Collection-Medical Innovators, sheet of 4		9.50	....
1822a	46¢ Sir Frederic Banting (1891-1941), co-discoverer of insulin, syringe and dog		2.50	2.00
1822b	46¢ Dr. Armand Frappier (1904-91), microbiologist, holding flask		2.50	2.00
1822c	46¢ Dr. Hans Selye (1907-82), endocrinologist and molecular diagram		2.50	2.00
1822d	46¢ Maude Abbott (1869-1940), pathologist, and roses		2.50	2.00
1823	46¢ Millenium Collection-Social Progress, sheet of 4	....	9.50	....
1823a	46¢ Nun, doctor, hospital	....	2.50	2.00
1823b	46¢ Statue of women holding decree	....	2.50	2.00
1823c	46¢ Alphonse Desjardins (1854-1920) and wife, credit union founders		2.50	2.00
1823d	46¢ Father Moses Coady (1882-1959), educator of adults	....	2.50	2.00

1824a   **1825a**

SCOTT NO.	DESCRIPTION	PLATE BLOCK F/NH	UNUSED F/NH	USED F
1824	46¢ Millenium Collection-Charity, sheet of 4	....	9.50	....
1824a	46¢ Canadian Inter. Development Agency (hand and tools)	....	2.50	2.00
1824b	46¢ Dr. Lucille Teasdale (1929-96), hospital administrator in Uganda		2.50	2.00
1824c	46¢ Marathon of Hope inspired by Terry Fox (1958-81)		2.50	2.00
1824d	46¢ Meals on Wheels program	....	2.50	2.00

SCOTT NO.	DESCRIPTION	PLATE BLOCK F/NH	UNUSED F/NH	USED F
1825	46¢ Millenium Collection-Humanitarians and Peacekeepers, sheet of 4	....	9.50	....
1825a	46¢ Raoul Dandurand (1861-1942)	....	2.50	2.00
1825b	46¢ Pauline Vanier (1898-1991), Elizabeth Smellie (1884-1968) nurses		2.50	2.00
1825c	46¢ Lester B. Pearson (1897-1972), prime minister and Nobel Peace Prize winner	....	2.50	2.00
1825d	46¢ Amputee and shadow (Ottawa Convention on Land Mines)		2.50	2.00

1826a   **1827a**   **1828a**

2000 COMMEMORATIVES

SCOTT NO.	DESCRIPTION	PLATE BLOCK F/NH	UNUSED F/NH	USED F
1826	46¢ Millenium Collection-Canada's First People, sheet of 4	....	9.50	....
1826a	46¢ Chief Pontiac (c.1720-69)	....	2.50	2.00
1826b	46¢ Tom Longboat (1887-1949), marathon runner	....	2.50	2.00
1826c	46¢ Inuit sculpture of shaman	....	2.50	2.00
1826d	46¢ Medicine man	....	2.50	2.00
1827	46¢ Millenium Collection-Canada's Cultural Fabric, sheet of 4	....	9.50	....
1827a	46¢ Norse boat, L'Anse aux Meadows	....	2.50	2.00
1827b	46¢ Immigrants on Halifax Pier 21	....	2.50	2.00
1827c	46¢ Neptune Theater, Halifax (head of Neptune)	....	2.50	2.00
1827d	46¢ Stratford Festival (actor and theater)	....	2.50	2.00
1828	46¢ Millenium Collection-Literary Legends, sheet of 4	....	9.50	....
1828a	46¢ W.O. Mitchell (1914-98), novelist, and prairie scene		2.50	2.00
1828b	46¢ Gratien Gelinas (1909-99), actor and playwright, and stars		2.50	2.00
1828c	46¢ Le Cercle du Livre de France book club	....	2.50	2.00
1828d	46¢ Harlequin paperback books	....	2.50	2.00

1829a   **1830a**   **1831a**

SCOTT NO.	DESCRIPTION	PLATE BLOCK F/NH	UNUSED F/NH	USED F
1829	46¢ Millenium Collection-Great Thinkers, sheet of 4	....	9.50	....
1829a	46¢ Marshall McLuhan (1911-80), philosopher, and television set		2.50	2.00
1829b	46¢ Northrop Frye (1912-91), literary critic, and word "code"		2.50	2.00
1829c	46¢ Roger Lemelin (1919-92), novelist, and cast of "The Plouffe Family" TV series	....	2.50	2.00
1829d	46¢ Hilda Marion Neatby (1904-75), historian, and farm scene		2.50	2.00
1830	46¢ Millenium Collection-A Tradition of Generosity, sheet of 4		9.50	....
1830a	46¢ Hart Massey (1823-96), Hart House, University of Toronto		2.50	2.00
1830b	46¢ Dorothy (1899-1965) & Izaak Killam (1885-1955), philanthropists		2.50	2.00
1830c	46¢ Eric Lafferty Harvive (1892-1975), philanthropist, and mountain scene		2.50	2.00
1830d	46¢ Macdonald Stewart Foundation	....	2.50	2.00
1831	46¢ Millenium Collection-Engineering and Tech. Marvels, sheet of 4		9.50	....
1831a	46¢ Map of Rogers Pass, locomotive and tunnel diggers	....	2.50	2.00
1831b	46¢ Manic Dams	....	2.50	2.00
1831c	46¢ Canadian satellites, Remote Manipulator Arm	....	2.50	2.00
1831d	46¢ CN Tower	....	2.50	2.00

SCOTT NO.	DESCRIPTION	PLATE BLOCK F/NH	UNUSED F/NH	USED F

1994

1998

1994-97	48¢ National Library, 50th Anniv. 4 attached......	....	4.95	3.50
1994	48¢ Anne Hebert (1916-2000)		1.25	.50
1995	48¢ Hector de Saint-Denys Garneau (1912-43)		1.25	.50
1996	48¢ Morley Callaghan (1903-90)		1.25	.50
1997	48¢ Susanna Moodie (1803-85), Catharine Parr Trail (1802-99).......		1.25	.50
1997b	same, bklt pane of 8 (1994-97 x 2)		9.50	....
1998	48¢ World Road Cycling Championships, Hamilton, Ont.		1.25	.60
1998a	same, bklt pane of 8...............................		9.50	....
1999	48¢ Canadian Astronauts, self-adhesive, sheet of 8		12.00	
1999a	48¢ Marc Garneau, self-adhesive......................		1.50	1.10
1999b	48¢ Roberta Bondar, self-adhesive.................		1.50	1.10
1999c	48¢ Steve MacLean, self-adhesive.................		1.50	1.10
1999d	48¢ Chris Hadfield, self-adhesive		1.50	1.10
1999e	48¢ Robert Thrisk, self-adhesive		1.50	1.10
1999f	48¢ Bjarni Tryggvason, self-adhesive		1.50	1.10
1999g	48¢ Dave Williams, self-adhesive		1.50	1.10
1999h	48¢ Julie Payette, self-adhesive		1.50	1.10

2000-01

2002a

2000-01	48¢ Trees of Canada and Thailand, 2 attached.	5.75	2.75	1.75
2000	48¢ Acer Saccharum leaves (Canada)	....	1.25	.45
2001	48¢ Cassia fistula (Thailand)	....	1.25	.45
2001b	48¢ Trees of Canada and Thailand, souvenir sheet of 2		9.50	9.50
2002	48¢ L'Hommage a Rosa Luxemburg by Jean-Paul Riopelle, sheet of 6.........................		9.00	9.00
2002a	48¢ Red & Blue dots between birds at LR........		1.50	1.15
2002b	48¢ Bird with yellow beak at center		1.50	1.15
2002c	48¢ Three birds in circle at R		1.50	1.15
2002d	48¢ Sun at UR		1.50	1.15
2002e	48¢ Birds with purple outlines ar L................		1.50	1.15
2002f	48¢ Birds with red outline in circle at R..............		1.50	1.15
2003	$1.25 Pink bird in red circle at R, souvenir sheet	....	3.75	3.75

2004

2004	48¢ Gift boxes and Ice skates............................	....	1.25	.35
2004a	same, bklt pane of 6...................................		7.00	....
2005	65¢ Gift boxes and Teddy bear		1.75	.75
2005a	same, bklt pane of 6...................................		10.00	....
2006	$1.25 Gift boxes and Toy duck.........................		3.25	1.25
2006a	same, bklt pane of 6...................................		18.00	....
2008	49¢ Maple Leaf and Samara, self-adhesive, coil		1.25	.40
2009	80¢ Maple Leaf on Twig, self-adhesive, coil ...		1.95	.75
2010	$1.40 Maple Leaf on Twig, self-adhesive, coil ...		3.40	1.25
2011	49¢ Flag over Edmonton, Alberta, self-adhesive		1.25	.40
2011a	same, bklt pane of 10.................................		12.00	....
2012	49¢ Queen Elizabeth II, self-adhesive		1.25	.40
2012a	same, bklt pane of 10.................................		12.00	....
2013	80¢ Maple Leaf on Twig, self-adhesive		2.00	.75
2013a	same, bklt pane of 6...................................		12.00	....
2014	$1.40 Maple Leaf Twig, self-adhesive...............		3.50	1.25
2014a	same, bklt pane of 6...................................		19.50	....

2015

2024

2026

2004 COMMEMORATIVES

2015	49¢ Year of the Monkey	5.75	1.25	.40
2016	$1.40 Year of the Monkey souvenir sheet..........		3.75	3.75
2016a	same, with 2004 Hong Kong overprint.............		7.75	7.75
2017	49¢ National Hockey League Stars, sheet of 6..		10.00	10.00
2017a	49¢ Larry Robinson..		2.00	.95
2017b	49¢ Marcel Dionne..		2.00	.95
2017c	49¢ Ted Lindsay..		2.00	.95
2017d	49¢ Johnny Bower		2.00	.95
2017e	49¢ Brad Park		2.00	.95
2017f	49¢ Milt Schmidt..		2.00	.95
2018	49¢ National Hockey League Stars, sheet of 6, self-adhesive......................................		18.00	....
2018a	49¢ Larry Robinson, self-adhesive		3.00	1.10
2018b	49¢ Marcel Dionne, self-adhesive....................		3.00	1.10
2018c	49¢ Ted Lindsay, self-adhesive........................		3.00	1.10
2018d	49¢ Johnny Bower, self-adhesive		3.00	1.10
2018e	49¢ Brad Park, self-adhesive		3.00	1.10
2018f	49¢ Milt Schmidt, self-adhesive		3.00	1.10
2019	49¢ Quebec Winter Carnival, self-adhesive.......		1.25	.50
2019a	same, bklt pane of 6....................................		7.50	....
2020	49¢ St. Joseph's Oratory, Montreal, self-adhesive		1.25	.50
2020a	same, bklt pane of 6....................................		7.50	....
2021	49¢ International Jazz Festival		1.25	.50
2021a	same, booklet pane of 6...............................		7.50	....
2022	49¢ Traversee Internationale Swimming Marathon		1.25	.50
2022a	same, booklet pane of 6...............................		7.50	....
2023	49¢ Canadian National Exhibition		1.25	.50
2023a	same, booklet pane of 6...............................		7.50	....
2024	49¢ Governor General Ramon John Hnatyshyn	5.75	1.25	.40
2025	49¢ Royal Canadian Army Cadets, 125th Anniv, self-adhesive......................................		1.25	.40
2025a	same, bklt pane of 4....................................		5.00	....
2026	49¢ The Farm, Ship of Otto Sverdrup, Arctic Explorer	5.75	1.25	.40
2027	$1.40 The Farm, Ship of Otto Sverdrup, Arctic Explorer, souvenir sheet.....................................		5.75	5.75
2028-31	49¢ Urban Transit & Light Rail Systems, 4 attached	11.00	4.95	4.00
2028	49¢ Toronto Transit Commission.......................		1.25	.45
2029	49¢ Translink Skytrain, Vancouver.....................		1.25	.45
2030	49¢ Societe de Transport de Montreal...............		1.25	.45
2031	49¢ Calgary Transit Light Rail............................		1.25	.45

2035

2043

2032	49¢ Home Hardware, 40th Anniv., self-adhesive	....	1.25	.40
2032a	same, bklt pane of 10.................................		12.00	....
2033	49¢ University of Sherbrooke, 50th Anniv.	....	1.25	.40
2033a	same, bklt pane of 8...................................		9.75	....
2034	49¢ University of Prince Edwards Island, Bicenn	....	1.25	.40
2034a	same, bklt pane of 8...................................		9.75	....
2035	49¢ Montreal Children's Hospital Centenary, self-adhesive......................................		1.25	.40
2035a	same, bklt pane of 4....................................		5.00	....
2036-39	49¢ Bird Paintings by John James Audubon, 4 attached	5.75	4.95	4.25
2036	49¢ Ruby-crowned Kinglet...............................		1.25	.45
2037	49¢ White-winged Crossbill		1.25	.45
2038	49¢ Bohemian Waxwing		1.25	.45
2039	49¢ Boreal Chickadee.....................................		1.25	.45
2040	80¢ Lincoln's Sparrow by J.J. Audubon, self-adhesive.......		1.95	.95
2040a	same, bklt pane of 6...................................		11.50	....
2041-42	49¢ Pioneers of Trans Mail Service, 2 attached	5.75	2.50	1.75
2041	49¢ Sir Samuel Cunard		1.25	.40
2042	49¢ Sir Hugh Allan	....	1.25	.40
2043	49¢ D-Day 60th Anniversary............................	5.75	1.25	.40
2044	49¢ Pierre Dugua de Mons, Leader of First French Settlement in Acadia	5.75	1.25	.40

SCOTT NO.	DESCRIPTION	PLATE BLOCK F/NH	UNUSED F/NH	USED F
2045	(49¢) Butterfly and Flower, self-adhesive...........	....	15.00	15.00
2045a	same, bklt pane of 2..	....	30.00	....
....	complete bklt, 2045a + phonecard in greeting card	....	60.00	....
2046	(49¢) Children on Beach, self-adhesive............	....	15.00	15.00
2046a	same, bklt pane of 2..	....	50.00	....
....	complete bklt, 2046a + phonecard in greeting card	....	60.00	....
2047	(49¢) Rose, self-adhesive................................	....	15.00	15.00
2047a	same, bklt pane of 2..	....	30.00	....
....	complete bklt, 2047a + phonecard in greeting card	....	60.00	....
2048	(49¢) Dog, self-adhesive.................................	....	15.00	15.00
2048a	same bklt pane of 2..	....	30.00	....
....	complete bklt, 2048a + phonecard in greeting card	....	60.00	....

2049-50

2049-50	49¢ 2004 Summer Olympics , Athens, 2 attached	5.75	2.50	1.50
2049	49¢ Spyros Louis 1896 Marathon Gold Medalist	....	1.25	.45
2050	49¢ Soccer net inscribed "Canada" girls soccer	....	1.25	.45

2051   **2056**

2051-52	49¢ Canadian Open Golf Championship, self-adhesive, set of 2	....	2.50	.85
2051	49¢ Canadian Open Golf Championship, 'finishing swing'	....	1.25	.45
2052	49¢ Canadian Open Golf Championship, "ready to putt"	....	1.25	.45
2053	49¢ Maple Leaf and Samara, self-adhesive, coil	....	1.25	.40
2054	80¢ Maple Leaf on Twig, self-adhesive, die-cut 8.25, coil	....	2.50	.75
2055	$1.40 Maple Leaf on Twig, self-adhesive, die-cut 8.25, coil	....	6.00	1.40
2056	49¢ Montreal Heart Institute, 50th Anniversary..	....	1.35	.40
2056a	same, booklet pane of 4...........................	....	5.25	....
2057	49¢ Pets – Fish	....	1.25	.45
2058	49¢ Pets – Cats	....	1.25	.45
2059	49¢ Pets – Rabbit	....	1.25	.45
2060	49¢ Pets – Dog	....	1.25	.45
2060a	same, booklet pane of 4...........................	....	5.25	....

2061   **2065**

2061-62	49¢ Nobel Laureates in chemistry, 2 attached...	5.75	2.50	1.50
2061	49¢ Gerhard Herzberg, 1971 laureate & molecular structures..................................	....	1.25	.50
2062	49¢ Michael Smith, 1993 laureate & DNA double helix	....	1.25	.50
2063-64	(49¢) Ribbon Frame & Picture Album Frame, self-adhesive, 2 attached	....	2.50	1.60
2063	(49¢) Ribbon Frame, self-adhesive..................	....	1.50	.50
2064	(49¢) Picture Album Frame, self-adhesive.........	....	1.50	.50
2065-66	49¢ Victoria Cross 150th Anniv., 2 attached	4.00	2.50	1.50
2065	49¢ Victoria Cross......................................	....	1.25	.50
2066	49¢ Design for Victoria Cross approved w/ QEII's signature........	....	1.25	.50

2068   **2069**

SCOTT NO.	DESCRIPTION	PLATE BLOCK F/NH	UNUSED F/NH	USED F
2067	47¢ "Self-Portrait" by Jean Paul Lemieux, perf 13 x 13.24	4.00	1.25	.40
2067a	Same, perf. 13...............................4.00		2.75	2.75
2068	47¢ – $1.40 Paintings of Jean Paul Lemieux, souvenir sheet of 3..		9.50	
2069	49¢ Santa Claus and Sleigh, self-adhesive		1.25	.40
2069a	same, booklet pane of 6..............................		7.75	
2070	80¢ Santa Claus and Automobile, self-adhesive		1.95	.75
2070a	same, booklet pane of 6..............................		12.00	
2071	$1.40 Santa Claus and Train, self-adhesive.......		3.40	1.25
2071a	same, booklet pane of 6..............................		19.50	

2072   **2075**   **2080**

2072	50¢ Red Calla Lilies, self-adhesive, coil	....	1.25	.40
2072a	same, serpentine die cut 6.75......................	....	1.25	.40
2072b	same, serpentine die cut 7.25......................	....	7.50	.40
2073	85¢ Yellow Calla Lilies, self-adhesive, coil........	....	2.25	.75
2073a	same, serpentine die cut 6.75......................	....	6.50	.75
2074	$1.45 Iris, self-adhesive, coil.......................	....	3.75	1.25
2074a	same, serpentine die cut 6.75......................	....	7.75	3.75
2075	50¢ Queen Elizabeth II, self-adhesive	....	1.25	.40
2075a	same, booklet pane of 10............................	....	12.00	....
2076	50¢ Flag and Saskatoon, Saskatchewan, self-adhesive	....	1.55	.40
2077	50¢ Flag and Durrell, Newfoundland, self-adhesive	....	1.55	.40
2078	50¢ Flag and Shannon Falls, British Columbia, self-adhesive	....	1.55	.40
2079	50¢ Flag and Mont-Saint-Hillaire, Quebec, self-adhesive	....	1.55	.40
2080	50¢ Flag and Toronto, self-adhesive.................	....	1.25	.40
2080a	same, booklet pane of 10 (#2076-80 x 2)	....	12.00	....
2081	85¢ Yellow Calla Lilies, self-adhesive	....	2.25	.50
2081a	same, booklet pane of 6..............................	....	14.00	....
2082	$1.45 Iris, self-adhesive..............................	....	3.75	1.25
2082a	same, booklet pane of 6..............................	....	22.00	....

2083   **2086a**

2005 COMMEMORATIVES

2083	50¢ Year of the Rooseter	5.75	1.25	.40
2084	$1.45 Year of the Rooster, souvenir sheet.........		4.25	4.25
2084a	same, with dates, Canadian and Chinese flags in sheet margin..................................		7.00	7.00
2085	50¢ National Hockey League Stars, sheet of 6..		10.00	
2085a	50¢ Henri Richard.......................................		1.75	1.00
2085b	50¢ Grant Fuhr..		1.75	1.00
2085c	50¢ Allan Stanley		1.75	1.00
2085d	50¢ Pierre Pilote..		1.75	1.00
2085e	50¢ Bryan Trottier		1.75	1.00
2085f	50¢ John Bucyk...		1.75	1.00
2086	50¢ National Hockey League Stars, self-adhesive, pane of 6........		10.00	
2086a	50¢ Henri Richard, self-adhesive....................		1.75	.80
2086b	50¢ Grant Fuhr, self-adhesive.......................		1.75	.80
2086c	50¢ Allen Stanley, self-adhesive		1.75	.80
2086d	50¢ Pierre Pilote, self-adhesive		1.75	.80
2086e	50¢ Bryan Trottier, self-adhesive		1.75	.80
2086f	50¢ John Bucyk, self-adhesive		1.75	.80

2087a, 2088a   **2089**

2087	50¢ Fishing Flies, sheet of 4...........................	....	9.00	9.00
2087a	50¢ Alevin..	....	2.25	1.75
2087b	50¢ Jock Scott...	....	2.25	1.75
2087c	50¢ P.E.I. Fly...	....	2.25	1.75
2087d	50¢ Mickey Finn...	....	2.25	1.75
2088	50¢ Fishing Flies, self-adhesive, bklt pane of 4.	....	5.25	5.25
2088a	50¢ Alevin, self-adhesive	....	1.40	.45
2088b	50¢ Jock Scott, self-adhesive	....	1.40	.45
2088c	50¢ P.E.I. Fly, self-adhesive	....	1.40	.45
2088d	50¢ Mickey Finn, self-adhesive......................	....	1.40	.45
2089	50¢ Nova Scotia Agricultural College, self-adhesive	....	1.40	.45
2089a	same, booklet pane of 4..............................	....	5.00	....

SCOTT NO.	DESCRIPTION	PLATE BLOCK F/NH	UNUSED F/NH	USED F

2090

2092

2090	50¢ EXPO 2005, Aichi, Japan........................	5.75	1.25	.40
2091	50¢ Daffodils, souvenir sheet of 2.....................	....	3.50	3.50
2092	50¢ Yellow Daffodils, self-adhesive...................	....	1.50	1.00
2093	50¢ White Daffodils, self-adhesive....................	....	1.50	1.00
2093a	50¢ Daffodils, self-adhesive, bklt pane of 10	....	12.00	....

2094

2099

2094	50¢ TD Bank Financial Group, 150th Anniv., self-adhesive..	....	1.25	.45
2094a	same, booklet pane of 10.................................	....	12.50	....
2095-98	50¢ Bird Paintings by John James Audubon, 4 attached	5.75	5.00	3.75
2095	50¢ Horned lark	....	1.25	.45
2096	50¢ Piping plover	....	1.25	.45
2097	50¢ Stilt sandpiper	....	1.25	.45
2098	50¢ Willow ptarmigan	....	1.25	.45
2099	85¢ Double-crested Cormorant by John James Audubon, self-adhesive	....	2.25	.75
2099a	same, booklet pane of 6.................................	....	12.50	....

2100

2104

2100-03	50¢ Bridges, self-adhesive, 4 attached..............	5.75	5.00	3.50
2100	50¢ Jacques Cartier Bridge, Quebec.................	....	1.25	.45
2101	50¢ Souris Swinging Bridge, Manitoba...............	....	1.25	.45
2102	50¢ Angus L. MacDonald Bridge, Nova Scotia..	....	1.25	.45
2103	50¢ Canso Causeway, Nova Scotia..................	....	1.25	.45
2104	50¢ Maclean's Magazine	5.75	1.25	.45

2105-06

2105-06	50¢ Biosphere Reserves of Canada and Ireland, 2 attached	5.75	2.50	1.75
2105	50¢ Saskatoon Berries, Waterton Lakes National Park	....	1.25	.40
2106	50¢ Deer, Killarney National Park	....	1.25	.40
2106b	Souvenir Sheet	....	2.95	2.95

2107

2108

2107	50¢ Battle of the Atlantic, World War II	5.75	1.25	.40
2108	50¢ Opening of Canadian War Museum, Ottawa, self-adhesive..	....	1.25	.40
2108a	same, booklet pane of 4..................................	....	5.00	....

2109

2112

2109	50¢ Paintings by Homer Watson	5.75	1.30	.40
2109a	perf. 13-1/2x13...	....	3.50	1.25
2110	$1.35 Paintings by Homer Watson, souvenir sheet of 2	....	6.50	6.50
2111	50¢ Search and Rescue, sheet of 8...................	....	12.00	12.00
2112	50¢ Ellen Fairclough	5.75	1.25	.40
2113-14	50¢ 9th FINA World Championships, Montreal, 2 attached	....	2.50	1.00
2113	50¢ Diver..	....	1.25	.40
2114	50¢ Swimmer	....	1.25	.40

2115

2117

2115	50¢ Founding of Port Royal, Nova Scotia, 400th Anniv.	5.75	1.25	.40
2116	50¢ Province of Alberta, Centennial, self-adhesive	5.75	1.25	.40
2117	50¢ Province of Saskatchewan, Centennial	5.75	1.25	.40

2118

2120

2118	50¢ Oscar Peterson, Pianist, 80th Birthday.......	5.75	1.25	.40
2118a	same, souvenir sheet of 4...............................	....	4.75	....
2119	50¢ Acadiaan Deportation, 250th Anniversary...	5.75	1.25	.40
2120	50¢ Mass Polio Vaccinations in Canada, 50th Anniv.	5.75	1.25	.40
2121	50¢ Youth Sports, self-adhesive, complete booklet of 8 (2121a-d X2)...	....	9.95	....
2121a	50¢ Wall Climbing, self-adhesive......................	....	1.25	.50
2121b	50¢ Skateboarding, self-adhesive.....................	....	1.25	.50
2121c	50¢ Mountain biking, self-adhesive....................	....	1.25	.50
2121d	50¢ Snowboarding, self-adhesive.....................	....	1.25	.50

SCOTT NO.	DESCRIPTION	PLATE BLOCK F/NH	UNUSED F/NH	USED F

2122-23

2122-23	50¢ Wildcats, 2 attached....................................	5.75	2.50	1.65
2122	50¢ Puma concolor.....................................	....	1.25	.50
2123	50¢ Panthera pardus orientalis........................	....	1.25	.50
2123b	Souvenir Sheet		2.60	2.60

2124

2125

2124	50¢ Snowmen, self-adhesive............................	....	1.25	.40
2124a	same, booklet pane of 6..................................	7.25		....
2125	50¢ Creche Figures, St. Joseph Oratory, Montreal, self-adhesive..	....	1.25	.40
2125a	same, booklet pane of 6..................................	7.25		....
2126	85¢ Creche Figures, St. Joseph Oratory, Montreal, self-adhesive..	2.25		.75
2126a	same, booklet pane of 6..................................	14.00		....
2127	$1.45 Creche Figures, St. Joseph Oratory, Montreal, self-adhesive..	3.75		....
2127a	same, booklet pane of 6..................................	21.00		....

2128

2131, 2134

2128	51¢ Red bergamot flower, self-adhesive, coil	....	1.35	.40
2129	89¢ Yellow lady's slipper, self-adhesive, coil......	....	2.25	.90
2130	$1.05 Pink fairy slipper, self-adhesive, coil	....	2.60	1.00
2131	$1.49 Himalayan blue poppy, self-adhesive, coil	....	3.75	1.35
2132	89¢ Yellow lady's slipper, self-adhesive	....	2.40	.90
2132a	same, booklet pane of 6..................................	13.50		....
2133	$1.05 Pink fairy slipper, self-adhesive................	....	2.75	1.00
2133a	same, booklet pane of 6..................................	15.50		....
2134	$1.49 Himalayan blue poppy, self-adhesive	....	3.75	1.35
2134a	same, booklet pane of 6..................................	21.00		....

2135

2135	51¢ Flag and Houses, New Glasgow, Prince Edward Island, self-adhesive	....	1.25	.40
2136	51¢ Flag and Bridge, Bouctouche, New Brunswick, self-adhesive..	....	1.25	.40
2137	51¢ Flag and Windmills, Pincher Creek, Alberta self-adhesive..	....	1.25	.40
2138	51¢ Flag and Lower Fort Garry, Manitoba, self-adhesive........	....	1.25	.40
2139	51¢ Flag and Dogsled, Yukon Territory, self-adhesive	....	1.25	.40
2139a	Flags, booklet pane of 10 (2135-39 x 2)	....	12.00	....

2140

2142

2006 COMMEMORATIVES

2140	51¢ Year of the Dog	6.00	1.35	.40
2141	$1.49 Year of the Dog, Dog and pup, souvenir sheet	....	5.00	5.00
2142	51¢ Queen Elizabeth II, 80th Birthday, self-adhesive	....	1.35	.40
....	same, bookelt pane of 10...............................	....	12.50	....

2143

2146

2143-44	51¢ 2006 Winter Olympics, Turin, Italy, 2 attached	6.00	2.75	1.35
2143	51¢ Team pursuit speed skating	....	1.25	.45
2144	51¢ Skeleton	....	1.25	.45
2145	51¢ Gardens, complete booklet of 8..................	....	10.50	
2145a	51¢ Shade garden	....	1.25	.50
2145b	51¢ Flower garden	....	1.25	.50
2145c	51¢ Water garden	....	1.25	.50
2145d	51¢ Rock garden	....	1.25	.50
2146	51¢ Party Balloons, self-adhesive......................	....	1.40	.50
2146a	same, booklet pane of 6..................................	....	7.50	....

2147

2149

2147	51¢ Paintings by Dorothy Knowles	6.00	1.40	.45
2147a	same, single from souvenir sheet, perf. 12.75 X 12.5	....	2.25	2.25
2148	51¢-89¢ Paintings by Dorothy Knowles, souvenir sheet	....	5.25	5.25
2148a	89¢ single from souvenir sheet	....	3.25	3.25
2149	51¢ Canadian Labor Congress, 50th Anniversary	6.00	1.40	.45
2150	$1.49 Queen Elizabeth 80th Birthday, souvenir sheet of 2	....	7.75	....
2150a	single from souvenir sheet...............................	....	4.00	4.00

2151

2152

2151	51¢ McClelland & Stewart Publishing, self-adhesive	....	1.40	.45
....	same, booklet pane of 8..................................	....	10.00	....
2152	89¢ Canadian Museum of Civilization, self-adhesive	....	2.25	1.00
....	same, booklet pane of 8..................................	....	17.00	....

SCOTT NO.	DESCRIPTION	PLATE BLOCK F/NH	UNUSED F/NH	USED F

2154c

2155, 2156a

2153	51¢ Canadians in Hollywood, souvenir sheet of 4	....	6.75	....
2154	same, booklet pane of 4		6.00	....
2154a	51¢ John Candy, self-adhesive		1.50	1.00
2154b	51¢ Mary Pickford, self-adhesive		1.50	1.00
2154c	51¢ Fay Wray, self adhesive		1.50	1.00
2154d	51¢ Lorne Greene, self-adhesive		1.50	1.00
2154e	same, booklet of 8, Wray on cover		9.95	....
2154f	same, booklet of 8, Pickford on cover		9.95	....
2154g	same, booklet of 8, Greene on cover		9.95	....
2154h	same, booklet of 8, Candy on cover		9.95	....
2155	51¢ Champlain Surveys the East Coast		1.40	.50
2156	2-39¢ and 2-51¢ Champlain, souvenir sheet sheet of 4, joint issue with the U.S.		8.95	....
2156a	51¢ single from souvenir sheet	....	1.95	1.95

2157

2160

2157	51¢ Vancouver Aquarium, 50th Anniv., self-adhesive	....	1.40	.50
2157a	same, booklet pane of 10	....	12.00	....
2158-59	51¢ Canadian Forces Snowbirds, 2 attached	6.00	2.75	1.75
2158	51¢ view from cockpit	....	1.40	.75
2159	51¢ three C-114 Tutor jets		1.40	.75
2159b	same, souvenir sheet of 2		3.50	....
2160	51¢ Atlas of Canada	....	1.35	.50

2161

2162

2161	51¢ 2006 World Lacrosse Championship, self-adhesive	....	1.35	.45
2161a	same, booklet pane of 8	....	10.00	....
2162	51¢ Mountaineering, self-adhesive	....	1.35	.45
2162a	same, booklet pane of 8	....	10.00	....
....				

2163-66

2163-2166	51¢ Duck decoys	6.00	5.25	....
2163	51¢ Barrow's Golden Eye decoy	....	1.25	.60
2164	51¢ Mallard decoy	....	1.25	.60
2165	51¢ Red Breasted Merganser decoy	....	1.25	.60
2166	51¢ Black Duck decoy	....	1.25	.60
2166b	same, souvenir sheet of 4	....	5.95	....

2167

2168

2167	51¢ Society of Graphic Designers	6.00	1.40	.50
2168	51¢ Three glasses of wine, self-adhesive	....	1.25	.50
2169	51¢ Wine taster, self-adhesive		1.25	.50
2170	51¢ Various cheeses, self-adhesive		1.25	.50
2171	51¢ Woman with tray of cheeses, self-adhesive		1.25	.50
2171a	same, booklet of 8, 2 each 2168-2171		9.95	....

2172

2174

2172	51¢ MacDonald College, self-adhesive	....	1.35	.50
2172a	same, booklet pane of 4	....	5.00	....
2173	51¢ Endangered Species, souvenir sheet of 4 + 4 labels		7.00	....
2174	51¢ Newfoundland Marten		1.25	.60
2175	51¢ Blotched Tiger Salamander		1.25	.60
2176	51¢ Blue Racer		1.25	.60
2177	51¢ Swift Fox		1.25	.60
2177b	same, booklet of 8 (2174-2177 x 2)		10.00	....

2178

2183

2178-82	51¢ Opera singers, strip of 5	....	6.50	5.00
2178	51¢ Maureen Forrester		1.25	.50
2179	51¢ Raorel Jobin		1.25	.50
2180	51¢ Simoneau and Alarie		1.25	.50
2181	51¢ Jon Vickers		1.25	.50
2182	51¢ Edward Johnson		1.25	.50
2183	51¢ Madonna and Child, self-adhesive		1.35	.50
2183	same, booklet of pane of 12		14.75	....
2184	51¢ Snowman, self-adhesive		1.35	.40
2184a	same, booklet pane of 12		14.75	....
2185	89¢ Winter Joys, self-adhesive		2.25	.90
2185a	same, booklet pane of 6		12.75	....
2186	$1.49 Contemplation, self-adhesive		3.75	1.50
2186a	same, booklet pane of 6		21.00	....

2187

2188

2187	"P" Spotted coalroot flower, self-adhesive, coil	....	1.35	.50
2188	Nondenominated "P" Queen Elizabeth II, self-adhesive		1.35	.50
2188a	same, booklet pane of 10		12.75	....

SCOTT NO.	DESCRIPTION	PLATE BLOCK F/NH	UNUSED F/NH	USED F

2192

2195

2196

2197

SCOTT NO.	DESCRIPTION	PLATE BLOCK F/NH	UNUSED F/NH	USED F
2189	"P" Flag and Sirmilik National Park Nunaunt, self-adhesive	....	1.50	.50
2190	"P" Flag and Cliff near Chemainus, British Columbia self-adhesive	....	1.50	.50
2191	"P" Flag and Polar bears near Churchill, Manitoba self-adhesive	....	1.50	.50
2192	"P" Flag and Bras d'Or Lake, Nova Scotia, self-adhesive.......	....	1.50	.50
2193	"P" Flag and Tuktut Nogait National Park, Northwest Territories, self-adhesive	....	1.50	.50
2193a	same, booklet pane of 10 (2189-2193 x 2)	....	13.00	....
2193b	same, booklet of 30 (2189-2193 x 6)	....	38.00	....
2194	Flowers souvenir sheet of 4	....	10.50	....
2195	93¢ Flat-leaved Bladderwort, self-adhesive, coil	....	2.40	.85
2196	$1.10 March Skullcap, self-adhesive, coil..........	....	2.75	1.00
2197	$1.55 Little Larkspur, self-adhesive, coil............	....	4.00	1.50
2198	93¢ Flat-leaved Bladderwort, self-adhesive........	....	2.40	.85
2198a	same, booklet pane of 6.........................	....	13.50	....
2199	$1.10 March Skullcap, self-adhesive	....	3.00	1.00
2199a	same, booklet pane of 6.........................	....	16.00	....
2200	$1.55 Little Larkspur, self-adhesive	....	4.00	1.50
2200a	same, booklet pane of 6.........................	....	22.00	....

2201

2203

2007 COMMEMORATIVES

SCOTT NO.	DESCRIPTION	PLATE BLOCK F/NH	UNUSED F/NH	USED F
2201	52¢ Year of the Pig...........................	6.00	1.35	.50
2202	$1.55 Year of the Pig, souvenir sheet	....	5.25	5.25
2203	52¢ Celebration...............................	....	1.35	.50
2203a	same, booklet pane of 6........................	....	7.50	....

2204-05

SCOTT NO.	DESCRIPTION	PLATE BLOCK F/NH	UNUSED F/NH	USED F
2204-05	52¢ International Polar Year, 2 attached...........	....	2.75	1.75
2204	52¢ Somateria spectabilis................................	....	1.35	.50
2205	52¢ Crossota millsaeare................................	....	1.35	.50
2205b	52¢ International Polar Year, souvenir sheet of 2	....	3.25	3.25
2206	52¢ Lilacs, souvenir sheet of 2	....	3.25	3.25
2207	52¢ White lilacs, self-adhesive........................	....	1.40	.60
2208	52¢ Purple lilacs, self-adhesive.......................	....	1.40	.60
2208a	same, booklet pane of 10 (2207-08 x 2)	....	13.00	....

2209

2211

SCOTT NO.	DESCRIPTION	PLATE BLOCK F/NH	UNUSED F/NH	USED F
2209	52¢ HEC Montreal College, self-adhesvie	....	1.40	.50
2209a	same, booklet pane of 4..........................	....	4.95	....
2210	52¢ University of Saskatchewan, self-adhesive	....	1.40	.50
2210a	same, booklet pane of 4..........................	....	5.25	....
2211	52¢ Jelly Shelf by Mary Pratt	6.00	1.40	.50
2212	52¢-$1.55 Art by Mary Pratt, souvenir sheet......	....	6.50	....
2212a	$1.55 Iceberg in North Atlantic by Mary Pratt	....	5.50	5.00

2214

2215

SCOTT NO.	DESCRIPTION	PLATE BLOCK F/NH	UNUSED F/NH	USED F
2213	52¢-$1.55 Ottawa 150th Anniversary souvenir sheet of 2.........................	....	5.50	....
2213a	52¢ Ottawa 150th Anniversary...........................	....	2.00	1.50
2213b	$1.55 Ottawa 150th Anniversary........................	....	3.50	3.00
2214	52¢ Ottawa 150th Anniversary, self-adhesive....	....	1.35	.45
2214a	same, booklet pane of 4........................	....	5.25	....
2215-18	52¢ Royal Architectural Institute, strip of 4........	....	5.25	3.50
2215	52¢ University of Lethbridge	....	1.25	.65
2216	52¢ St. Mary's Church	....	1.25	.65
2217	52¢ Ontario Science Center........................	....	1.25	.65
2218	52¢ National Gallery of Canada........................	....	1.25	.65

2219

2220

SCOTT NO.	DESCRIPTION	PLATE BLOCK F/NH	UNUSED F/NH	USED F
2219	$1.55 Captain George Vancouver......................	17.75	4.00	1.75
2219a	same, souvenir sheet of 1........................	....	4.00	3.25
2220	52¢ FIFA World Youth Championship	6.00	1.35	.55
2221	52¢ Canadian Recording Artists, souvenir sheet	....	....	7.75
2222	same, booklet of 8.........................	....	14.00	....
	same, booklet of 4.........................	....	7.50	....
2222a	52¢ Gordon Lightfoot, self-adhesive.................	....	1.75	.60
2222b	52¢ Joni Mitchell, self-adhesive.......................	....	1.75	.60
2222c	52¢ Anne Murray, self-adhesive......................	....	1.75	.60
2222d	52¢ Paul Anka, self-adhesive........................	....	1.75	.60

2223

2234

2242

SCOTT NO.	DESCRIPTION	PLATE BLOCK F/NH	UNUSED F/NH	USED F
2223	52¢ Terra Nova National Park, self-adhesive.....	....	1.40	.55
2223a	same, booklet pane of 5...........................	....	6.00	....
2223BOOK	same, booklet of 10................................	....	15.00	....
2224	52¢ Jasper National Park, self-adhesive	....	1.40	.55
2224a	same, booklet pane of 5...........................	....	7.75	....
2224BOOK	same, booklet of 10................................	....	15.00	....
2225	52¢ 100 Years of Scouting, self-adhesive..........	....	1.40	.55
2225a	same, booklet of 8...............................	....	11.00	....
2226	52¢ Henri Membertou	6.00	1.40	.55
2227	52¢ Law Society of Saskatchewan	....	1.90	.85
2228	52¢ Law Society of Alberta, Canada.................	6.00	1.40	.55
2229	52¢ Endangered Animals sheet of 4 + 4 lables .	....	6.00	6.00
2229a	52¢ North Atlantic Right Whale	....	1.50	.65
2229b	52¢ Northern Cricket Frog	....	1.50	.65
2229c	52¢ White Sturgeon	....	1.50	.65
2229d	52¢ Leatherback Turtle	....	1.50	.65
2230-33	52¢ Endangered Animals block of 4	....	6.00	....
2230	52¢ North Atlantic Right Whale bklt single	....	1.50	.65
2231	52¢ Northern Cricket Frog bklt single	....	1.50	.65
2232	52¢ White Sturgeon bklt single	....	1.50	.65
2233	52¢ Leatherback Turtle bklt single	....	1.50	.65
2233b	bklt pane of 8................................	....	11.00	....
2234-38	1¢-25¢ Beneficial Insects	7.00	1.50	1.25
2234	1¢ Convergent Lady Beetle	.80	.30	.25
2235	3¢ Golden-Eyed Lacewing.............................	.90	.30	.25
2235b	3¢ Golden-Eyed Lacewing, dated 2012.............	....	.30	.25
2236	5¢ Northern Bumblebee...............................	1.00	.30	.25
2237	10¢ Canada Darner	1.20	.30	.25
2238	25¢ Cecropia Moth..................................	3.25	.60	.30
2238a	souvenir sheet of 5................................	....	1.50	1.50
2239	52¢ Reindeer & Snowflakes..........................	....	1.35	.60
2239a	same bklt pane of 6...............................	....	7.50	....
2240	52¢ Holy Family	....	1.40	.60
2240a	same bklt pane of 6...............................	....	7.50	....
2241	93¢ Angel Over Town	....	2.40	1.25
2241	same bklt pane of 6...............................	....	14.50	....
2242	$1.55 Dove...	....	4.00	1.85
2242a	same bklt pane of 6...............................	....	23.00	....

SCOTT NO.	DESCRIPTION	PLATE BLOCK F/NH	UNUSED F/NH	USED F

2248a   2249   2261   2287

Scott	Description	Plate Block	Unused	Used
2243	$1.60 Orchids sheet of 4	....	11.00	11.00
2244-47	$1.60 Orchids coils	....	11.00	8.00
2244	Odontioda Island Red Orchid coil		1.35	.60
2244a	Odontioda Island Red Orchid coil, die-cut 9.1 .		2.50	....
2245	95¢ Potinara Janet Elizabeth "Fire Dancer" Orchid coil..	....	2.40	1.00
2246	$1.15 Laeliocattieya Memorial Evelyn Light Orchid coil..		2.95	1.25
2247	$1.60 Masdevallia Kaleidoscope "Conni" Orchid coil.....		4.00	1.75
2248	Queen Elizabeth II		1.35	.60
2248a	same bklt pane of 10		12.50	....
2249	Flag & Sambro Island Lighthouse, Nova Scotia		1.40	.60
2250	Flag & Point Clark Lighthouse, Ontario		1.40	.60
2251	Flag & Cap-des-Rosiars		1.40	.60
2252	Flag & Warren Landing Lighthouse, Manitoba...		1.40	.60
2253	Flag & Panchena Point Lighthouse, British Columbia .		1.40	.60
2253a	bklt pane of 10, 2 each 2249-2253		12.50	....
2253b	Flag & Pachena Point Lighthouse, British Columbia		1.40	.65
2253c	same bklt pane of 10, 2 ea. 2249-52, 2253b		13.00	....
2253d	same bklt pane of 40, 6 ea. 2249-52, 2253b		38.00	....
2254	95¢ Potinara Janet Elizabeth "Fire Dancer" Orchid ...		2.45	1.10
2254a	same bklt pane of 6		14.00	....
2255	$1.15 Laeliocattieya Memorial Evelyn Light Orchid ...		3.00	1.35
2255a	same bklt pane of 6		17.00	....
2256	$1.60 Masdevallia Kaleidoscope "Conni" Orchid ...		4.00	1.75
2256a	same bklt pane of 6		23.00	....

2008

Scott	Description	Plate Block	Unused	Used
2257	52¢ Year of the Rat	5.75	1.25	.60
2258	$1.60 Year of the Rat souvenir sheet	....	4.00	4.00
2259	Fireworks		1.25	.60
2259a	same bklt pane of 6		7.50	....
2260	52¢ Peonies sheet of 2		3.25	2.50
2261-62	52¢ Peonies bklt singles		3.25	1.25
2262b	bklt pane of 10, 5 each of 2261 & 2262		12.00	....
2263	52¢ University of Alberta		1.25	.60
2263a	same bklt pane of 8		9.50	....

2273   2280d

Scott	Description	Plate Block	Unused	Used
2264	52¢ University of British Columbia	....	1.25	.60
2264a	same bklt pane of 8	....	9.25	....
2264b	gutter pane, 4 each of 2263-64		21.00	....
2265	52¢ Int. Ice Hockey Federation Championships	....	1.25	....
2265a	same bklt pane of 10		13.00	....
2266	52¢ Guide Dog		1.25	.60
2266a	same bklt pane of 10		13.00	....
2267-68	52¢ Canadian Oil & Gas Industries attached pair	....	2.50	2.25
2267	Transcanada Pipeline Completion		1.25	.60
2268	First Commercial Oil Well		1.25	.60
2268a	52¢ Canadian Industries bklt pane of 10	....	12.00	....
2269	Founding of Quebec City	5.75	1.25	.60
2270	52¢ Yousuf Karsh self-portrait	5.75	1.25	.60
2271	Souvenir sheet of 3, 2270, 2271a, 2271b	....	7.50	7.25
2271a	96¢ Audrey Hepburn		2.50	1.00
2271b	$1.60 Winston Churchill		3.75	1.75
2272	96¢ Audry Hepburn		2.50	1.00
2272a	same bklt pane of 4		9.00	....
2273	$1.60 Winston Churchill		3.75	1.75
2273a	same bklt pane of 4		15.00	....
2274	52¢ Royal Canadian Mint		1.25	.65
2275	52¢ Canadian Nurses Association		1.25	.65
2275a	same, booklet pane of 10		12.00	....
2276	Anne of Green Gables, sheetlet of 2		4.50	4.50
2276a	52¢ Anne Holding Buttercups		3.75	.95
2276b	52¢ Green Gables House		1.75	.95
2277	52¢ Anne Holding Buttercups, booklet single		1.50	.65
2278	52¢ Green Gables House, booklet single		1.50	.65
2278a	Anne of Green Gables, bklt pane of 10		12.00	....
2279	Canadians in Hollywood, souvenir sheet of 4		8.00	....
2279a	Norma Shearer		2.00	1.25
2279b	Chief Dan George		2.00	1.25
2279c	Marie Dressler		2.00	1.25
2279d	Raymond Burr		2.00	1.25
2280	Canadians in Hollywood, booklet pane of 4		6.25	....
	same, complete booklet		12.00	....
2280a	Marie Dressler, booklet single		1.60	1.25
2280b	Chief Dan George, booklet single		1.60	1.25
2280c	Norma Shearer, booklet single		1.60	1.25
2280d	Raymond Burr, booklet single		1.60	1.25

Scott	Description	Plate Block	Unused	Used
2281	52¢ Beijing Summer Olympics	....	1.25	.65
2281a	same, booklet pane of 10	....	12.00	....
2282	52¢ Lifesaving Society		1.25	.65
2282a	same, booklet pane of 10		12.00	....
2283	52¢ British Columbia 150th Anniversary	5.75	1.25	.65
2284	52¢ R. Samuel McLaughlin, Buick Automobile ..	5.75	1.25	.65
2285	Endangered Animal, sheet of 4 + labels		5.25	5.25
2285a	Prothonotary Warbler		1.25	.65
2285b	Taylor's Checkerspot Butterfly		1.25	.65
2285c	Roseate Tern		1.25	.65
2285d	Burrowing Owl		1.25	.65
2286	Prothonotary Warbler, booklet single		1.25	.65
2287	Taylor's Checkerspot Butterfly, booklet single....		1.25	.65
2288	Roseate Tern, booklet single		1.25	.65
2289	Burrowing Owl, booklet single		1.25	.65
2289a	Endangered Animal, bklt pane of 4, #2286-89...		5.00	....
2289b	Endangered Animal, bklt pane, 2 of #2289a		9.75	....
2290	52¢ 12th Francophone Summit	5.45	1.25	.50
2291	Winter Scenes, sheet of 3		7.75	....
2291a	Making Snow Angel		1.50	1.15
2291b	95¢ Skiing		2.50	1.85
2291c	$1.60 Tobogganing		3.75	3.00
2292	Christmas		1.25	.50
2292a	same, booklet pane of 6		7.25	....
	same, complete booklet, #2292a		13.95	....
2293	Making Snow Angle, booklet single		1.25	.50
2293a	same, booklet pane of 6		7.25	....
	same, complete bklt, 2 of #2293a		13.95	....
2294	95¢ Skiing, booklet single		2.25	.90
2294a	same, booklet pane of 6		13.00	....
2295	$1.60 Tobogganing, booklet single		3.85	1.50
2295a	same, booklet pane of 6		22.00	....
2295b	same, gutter pane, #2294a, 2295a		39.00	....

2300   2301   2303

2009 COMMEMORATIVES

Scott	Description	Plate Block	Unused	Used
2296	Year of the Ox	5.50	1.25	.50
2297	$1.65 Year of the Ox, souvenir sheet	....	4.25	4.25
2297a	same, w/China 2009 emblem overprinted in gold	....	4.75	4.75
2298	Queen Elizabeth II		1.25	.50
2298a	same, booklet pane of 10		12.50	....
2299	Sports of the Winter Olympics, sheet of 5		7.00	4.75
2299a	Curling		1.50	1.00
2299b	Bobsledding		1.50	1.00
2299c	Snowboarding		1.50	1.00
2299d	Freestyle Skiing		1.50	1.00
2299e	Ice-Sled Hockey		1.50	1.00
2299f	#2299, "Vancouver/2010" overprinted in sheet margin in silver		11.00	9.75
2300	Freestyle Skiing, booklet single		1.25	1.00
2301	Ice-Sled Hockey, booklet single		1.25	1.00
2302	Bobsledding, booklet single		1.25	1.00
2303	Curling, booklet single		1.25	1.00
2304	Snowboarding, booklet single		1.25	1.00
2304a	booklet pane of 10, 2 ea. 2300-2304		12.00	....
2304b	booklet pane of 30, 6 ea. 2300-2304		36.00	....
2305	Olympics, sheet of 5		11.00	11.00
2306	"P" 2010 Winter Olympics Emblem, die cut 9 1/4, rounded tips		2.25	1.75
2307	"P" 2010 Vancouver Winter Paralympics Emblem, die cut 9 1/4, rounded tips		2.25	1.75
2307a	"P" 2010 Winter Olympics Emblem, die cut 9-9 1/4, sawtooth tips		2.25	1.75
2307b	"P" 2010 Vancouver Winter Paralympics Emblem, die cut 9-9 1/4, sawtooth tips		2.25	1.75
2308	98¢ MIGA, Winter Olympics Mascot, die cut 8 1/4 - 9 1/4, sawtooth tips		3.25	1.75
2309	$1.18 SUMI, Paralympics Mascot, die cut 8 1/4 - 9 1/4, sawtooth tips		4.50	1.75
2310	$1.65 Quatchi, Winter Olympics Mascot, die cut 8 1/4 - 9 1/4, sawtooth tips		4.50	1.75
2311	98¢ MIGA, Winter Olympics Mascot, die cut 9 1/4, rounded tips		2.75	1.75
2312	$1.18 SUMI, Paralympics Mascot, die cut 9 1/4, rounded tips		3.25	1.75
2313	$1.65 Quatchi, Winter Olympics Mascot, die cut 9 1/4, rounded tips		4.25	1.75

SCOTT NO.	DESCRIPTION	PLATE BLOCK F/NH	UNUSED F/NH	USED F

2316

2321

2314	Celebration..................................	....	1.25	.50
2314a	same, booklet pane of 6.................................	....	7.25	5.75
2315	54¢ Rosemary Brown..................................	....	1.25	.90
2316	54¢ Abraham Doras Shadd..........................	....	1.25	.90
2316a	pair, 2315-16..................................	....	2.50	1.00
2317	"P" First Airplane Flight in Canada....................	....	1.25	.50
2318	54¢ Rhododendrons, sheet of 2....................	....	3.25	2.50
2319	54¢ White and Pink Rhododendrons................	....	1.25	.50
2320	54¢ Pink Rhododendrons..............................	....	1.25	.50
2320a	54¢ Rhododendrons, bklt pane of 10..............	....	12.50	....
2321	54¢ Jack Bush Painting, striped column, per 13 x 13 1/4..................................	....	1.25	.50
2321a	54¢ Jack Bush Painting, striped column, per 12 1/2 x 13 1/4..................................	....	1.75	1.75
2322	54¢ - $1.65 souvenir sheet, Paintings by Jack Bush..................................	....	5.75	5.75

2326

2334a

2323	54¢ Astronomy, souvenir sheet of 2....................	....	3.25	3.25
2323c	same as 2323, w/buff bkgrnd behind product code	....	5.00	5.00
2324	54¢ Canada-France-Hawaii Telescope..............	....	1.25	.50
2325	54¢ Horsehead Nebula..................................	....	1.25	.50
2325a	booklet pane of 10, each 2324 & 2325	....	13.00	....
2326	54¢ Polar Bear..................................	....	1.25	.50
2327	54¢ Arctic Tern..................................	....	1.25	.50
2327b	souvenir sheet, 1 ea. 2326-2327....................	....	3.50	....
2328	2¢ Caterpillar..................................	....	.25	.25
2329	54¢ Canadian Horse..................................	....	1.25	.50
2330	54¢ Newfoundland Pony..................................	....	1.25	.50
2330a	booklet pane of 10, 5 ea. 2329-2330	....	12.50	....
2331	54¢ Boundary Water Treaty..........................	....	1.25	.60
2333	54¢ Popular Singers, sheet of 4....................	....	6.50	5.75
2333a	54¢ Robert Charlebois..................................	....	1.75	1.25
2333b	54¢ Edith Butler..................................	....	1.75	1.25
2333c	54¢ Stompin' Tom Connors..........................	....	1.75	1.25
2333d	54¢ Bryan Adams..................................	....	1.75	1.25
2334	54¢ Popular Singers, booklet pane of 4............	....	6.00	5.00
	same, complete booklet..................................	....	12.00	....
2334a	54¢ Bryan Adams..................................	....	1.50	.50
2334b	54¢ Stompin' Tom Connors..........................	....	1.50	.50
2334c	54¢ Edith Butler..................................	....	1.50	.50
2334d	54¢ Robert Charlebois..................................	....	1.50	.50

2337

2338a

2335	54¢ Roadside Attractions, sheet of 4	....	5.75	5.15
2335a	54¢ Mr. PG, Prince George..........................	....	1.50	.85
2335b	54¢ Sign Post Forest	....	1.50	.85
2335c	54¢ Inukshuk..................................	....	1.50	.85
2335d	54¢ Pysanka..................................	....	1.50	.85
2336	54¢ Roadside Attractions, booklet pane of 4	....	5.00	5.00
	same, complete booklet..................................	....	9.75	....
2336a	54¢ Mr. PG, Prince George..........................	....	1.25	1.00
2336b	54¢ Sign Post Forest	....	1.25	1.00
2336c	54¢ Inukshuk..................................	....	1.25	1.00
2336d	54¢ Pysanka..................................	....	1.25	1.00
2337	54¢ Captain Robert Abram Bartlett....................	....	1.25	1.00
2338	54¢ Sports, booklet pane of 4....................	....	5.00	5.00
	same, complete booklet..................................	....	9.75	....
2338a	54¢ Five Pin Bowling	....	1.50	.75
2338b	54¢ Ringette..................................	....	1.50	.75
2338c	54¢ Lacrosse..................................	....	1.50	.75
2338d	54¢ Basketball..................................	....	1.50	.75

2339

2341

2339	P Montreal Canadians Hockey Jersey...............	....	1.25	.55
2339a	same, booklet pane of 10..................................	....	12.50	....
2340	$3 500 Goal Scorers of the Montreal Canadians	....	25.00	....
2340a	$3 Maurice Richard	....	8.50	6.00
2340b	$3 Jean Beliveau	....	8.50	6.00
2340c	$3 Guy Lafleur	....	8.50	6.00
2341	P National War Memorial	....	2.50	2.25
2341a	P National War Memorial Souvenir Sheet of 2...	....	3.25	3.25
2342	P National War Memorial, booklet single	....	1.25	.55
2342a	same, booklet pane of 10..................................	....	12.50	....
2343	Christmas, sheet of 4 + 6 labels	....	9.50	....
2343a	P Christmas	....	1.50	.55

2343b

2359

2343b	P Madonna & Child..	....	2.00	2.00
2343c	98¢ Magus	....	3.50	3.25
2343d	$1.65 Shepherd & Lamb	....	5.00	4.75
2344	P Christmas Tree	....	1.25	.55
2344a	same, booklet pane of 6..................................	....	7.25	....
	complete booklet..................................	....	14.50	....
2345	P Madonna & child, booklet stamp	....	1.25	.55
2345a	same, booklet pane of 6..................................	....	7.50	....
	complete booklet..................................	....	14.50	....
2346	98¢ Magus booklet stamp	....	2.50	1.10
2346a	same, booklet pane of 6..................................	....	13.50	....
2347	$1.65 Shepherd & Lamb booklet stamp..........	....	3.75	1.75
2347a	booklet pane of 6	....	22.50	....
2347b	booklet pane of 12, 6 each 2346-2347	....	42.00	....
2348	P Tiger in circle	....	1.25	.65
2349	$1.70 Sculpted Tiger Seal..........................	....	4.50	3.00

2356a

2373a

2010 COMMEMORATIVES

2350	Souvenir sheet of 5	....	7.50	....
2350a	P Flag over Watson's Mill..........................	....	1.50	1.00
2350b	P Flag over Keremeos Grist Mill	....	1.50	1.00
2350c	P Flag over Old Stone Mill	....	1.50	1.00
2350d	P Flag over Riordon Grist Mill	....	1.50	1.00
2350e	P Flag over Cornell Mill	....	1.50	1.00
2351	P Flag over Watson's Mill S/A booklet single	....	1.50	1.00
2352	P Flag over Keremeos Grist Mill S/A bklt single.	....	1.50	1.00
2353	P Flag over Old Stone Mill S/A booklet single	....	1.50	1.00
2354	P Flag over Riordon Grist Mill S/A bklt single	....	1.50	1.00
2355	P Flag over Cornell Mill S/A booklet single	....	1.50	1.00
2355a	Booklet pane of 10, 2 each 2351-55	....	13.50	....
2355b	Booklet pane of 30, 6 each 2351-55	....	42.00	....
2356	Orchids souvenir sheet of 4	....	11.00	....
2356a	P Striped Coralroot Orchid..........................	....	1.50	1.25
2356b	$1 Giant Helleborine Orchid	....	2.50	2.00
2356c	$1.22 Rose Pogonia Orchid	....	3.00	2.50
2356d	$1.70 Grass Pink Orchid..............................	....	4.00	3.50
2357	P Striped Coralroot Orchid S/A coil (sawtooth tips)	....	1.35	.60
2358	$1 Giant Helleborine Orchid S/A coil (sawtooth tips)	....	2.50	1.10
2359	$1.22 Rose Pogonia Orchid S/A coil (sawtooth tips)	....	3.00	1.35
2360	$1.70 Grass Pink Orchid S/A coil (sawtooth tips)	....	4.00	1.75
2361	P Striped Coralroot Orchid S/A coil (rounded tips)	....	1.75	.60
2362	$1 Giant Helleborine Orchid booklet stamps	....	2.50	1.00
2363	$1.22 Rose Pogonia Orchid booklet stamps......	....	3.00	1.00
2363a	booklet pane of 6	....	17.00	....
2364	$1.70 Grass Pink Orchid booklet stamp	....	4.00	1.75
2364a	booklet pane of 6	....	24.00	....
2365	P Queen Elizabeth II	....	1.25	.60
2365a	same, booklet pane of 10..................................	....	13.00	....

SCOTT NO.	DESCRIPTION	PLATE BLOCK F/NH	UNUSED F/NH	USED F
2366	57¢ souvenir sheet of 2............	....	3.25	2.50
2366a	57¢ Whistler, B.C.	....	1.50	.75
2366b	57¢ Vancouver	....	1.50	.75
2366c	#2366 with "Vancouver/2010" overprinted in sheet margin in gold...............	....	5.50	5.00
2367	57¢ Whistler, B.C.	....	1.25	.75
2368	57¢ Vancouver	....	1.25	.75
2368a	Booklet pane of 10, 5 each 2367-2368..............	....	13.00	....
2369	57¢ William Hall	....	1.25	.75
2370	57¢ Romeo LeBlanc	....	1.25	.75
2371	57¢ Gold Medal sheet of 2.........	....	4.00	4.00
2371a	57¢ Gold Medal single stamp	....	1.25	.75
2372	57¢ Gold Medal S/S booklet stamp	....	1.25	.75
2372a	same, booklet pane of 10............	....	13.00	.75
2373	57¢ Winter Olympics souvenir sheet of 2	....	3.50	3.50
2373a	57¢ Woman with painted face at left........	....	1.50	.60
2373b	57¢ Woman with painted face at right........	....	1.50	.60
2374	57¢ Woman with painted face at left S/A booklet stamp	....	1.25	.60

2377

2378

2375	57¢ Woman with painted face at right S/A bklt stamp	....	1.25	.60
2375a	Booklet pane of 10, 5 each 2374-2375............	....	12.50	....
2376	African Violet Hybrids, souvenir sheet of 2	....	3.50	3.50
2377	P red African violet	....	1.50	.75
2378	P purple african violet	....	1.50	.75
2378a	same, booklet pane of 10...........	....	12.50	....

2383

2387b

2379	$1.70 Canada-Israel Friendship..........	....	3.75	1.95
2379a	same, booklet pane of 3 + label........	....	11.50	....
2380-83	57¢ Indian Kings	....	5.50	5.00
2380	57¢ Tee Yee Neen Ho Ga Row	....	1.40	0.75
2381	57¢ Sa Ga Yeath Qua Pieth Tow	....	1.40	0.75
2382	57¢ Ho Nee Yeath Taw No Row	....	1.40	0.75
2383	57¢ Etow Oh Koam	....	1.40	0.75
2383b	Souvenir sheet of 4	....	6.75	6.75
2383c	Souvenir sheet of 4 with London 2010, emblem on sheet margin.....	....	9.00	9.00
2384	57¢ Canadian Navy Cent, sheet of 2.....	....	3.50	3.50
2384a	57¢ Male Sailor	....	1.50	.85
2384b	57¢ Female Sailor	....	1.50	.85
2385	57¢ Male Sailor	....	1.50	.85
2386	57¢ Female Sailor	....	1.50	.85
2386a	same, bklt pane of 10................	....	12.50	....
2387	57¢ Mammals, sheet of 2............	....	3.60	3.60
2387a	57¢ Hasrbor porpoise	....	1.25	.85
2387b	57¢ Sea Otter	....	1.25	.85
2387c	57¢ Hasrbor porpoise, perf 13x12.75 syncopated	....	1.25	.85
2387d	57¢ Sea Otter, perf 13x12.75 sycopated	....	1.25	.85
2387e	same, booklet pane of 8.............	....	10.00	....

2394

2395

2388	57¢ Canadian Geographic wildlife photography, sheet of 5	7.75	7.75	
2388a	57¢ Ardia Herodias	1.70	1.30	
2388b	57¢ Vulpees Vulpees	1.70	1.30	
2388c	57¢ Tetigonlidae	1.70	1.30	
2388d	57¢ Tachycineta bicolor	1.70	1.30	
2388e	57¢ Selaphorus rufus	1.70	1.30	
2389-93	57¢ Canadian Geographic wildlife photography, d/c 13.25	7.50	7.50	
2389	57¢ Ardia Herodias	1.50	1.50	
2390	57¢ Vulpees Vulpees	1.50	1.50	
2391	57¢ Tetigonlidae, die cut 13.25	1.50	1.50	
2392	57¢ Tachycineta bicolor, die cut 13.25	1.50	1.50	
2393	57¢ Selaphorus rufus, die cut 13.25	1.50	1.50	
2393a	57¢ Canadian Geographic wildlife photography, bklt pane of 10	12.50	....	
2394	57¢ Rotary International	1.35	.65	
2394a	same, bklt pane of 8..................	10.00	....	
2395	57¢ Rollande	1.30	.65	

2410

2397d

2414

2396	57¢, $1.70 Paintings by Prudence Heward, souvenir sheet of 2.....	....	6.50	6.50
2396a	$1.70 At the Theatre	....	5.50	4.50
2397	Roadside Attractions, sheet of 4	....	6.50	6.50
2397a	P Coffee Pot	....	1.50	1.00
2397b	P Happy Rock	....	1.50	1.00
2397c	P Wawa Goose	....	1.50	1.00
2397d	P Puffin	....	1.50	1.00
2398	P Coffee Pot, booklet single	....	1.40	1.00
2399	P Happy Rock, booklet single	....	1.40	1.00
2400	P Wawa Goose, booklet single	....	1.40	1.00
2401	P Puffin, booklet single	....	1.40	1.00
2401a	Booklet pane of 4	....	5.50	....
	Complete Booklet......................	....	11.00	....
2402	P Girl Guides	....	1.35	.65
2402a	same, bklt pane of 10................	....	12.50	....
2403	57¢ Founding of Cupids, Newfoundland...........	....	1.35	.65
2404	57¢ Year of British Home Children	....	1.35	.65
2405	$10 Blue Whale	....	22.00	13.00
2406	4¢ Paper Wasp	....	.25	.25
2406a	4¢ Paper Wasp, added microprinting and small design features	....	.30	.25
2407	6¢ Assassin Bug	....	.25	.25
2408	7¢ Large Milkweed Bug	....	.25	.25
2409	8¢ Margined Leatherwing	....	.25	.25
2409a	8¢ Margined Leathewing, added microprinting and small design features	....	.30	.25
2409b	Souvenir sheet of 3, #2235b, 2406a, 2409a......	....	.45	.45
2410	9¢ Dogbane Beetle	....	.25	.25
2410a	Souvenir sheet of 5 Beneficial Insects..............	....	1.05	.95
2411	Souvenir sheet of 3 Christmas Ornaments	....	8.25	8.25
2411a	P Christmas Ornament	....	1.50	.75
2411b	$1 Christmas Ornament..............	....	2.25	1.25
2411c	$1.70 Christmas Ornament..........	....	3.75	2.00
2412	(57¢) P Madonna & Child............	....	1.40	.75
2412a	same, booklet pane of 6.............	....	7.75	....
2413	P Christmas Ornament	....	1.35	.75
2413a	same, booklet pane of 6.............	....	7.75	....
2414	$1 Christmas Ornament..............	....	2.25	1.25
2414a	same, booklet pane of 6.............	....	13.50	....
2415	$1.70 Christmas Ornament	....	3.75	2.00
2415a	same, booklet pane of 6.............	....	23.50	....
2415b	Gutter pane, #2414a, 2415a........	....	40.00	....

2416

2428

2433

2011 COMMEMORATIVES

2416	P Year of the Rabbit	....	1.50	.75
2417	$1.75 Year of the Rabbit Souvenir Sheet...........	....	4.50	4.25
2418	P Canadian Flag, sheet of 5	....	7.75	6.75
2418a	P Canadian Flag on Soldier's Uniform	....	1.50	.65
2418b	P Canadian Flag on Hot Air Balloon	....	1.50	.65
2418c	P Canadian Flag of Search & Rescue Team's Uniform.......	....	1.50	.65
2418d	P Canadian Flag on Canadarm	....	1.50	.65
2418e	P Canadian Flag on Backpack	....	1.50	.65
2419	P Canadian Flag on Soldier's Uniform	....	1.50	.65
2420	P Canadian Flag on Hot Air Balloon	....	1.50	.65
2421	P Canadian Flag of Search & Rescue Team's Uniform.....	....	1.50	.65
2422	P Canadian Flag on Canadarm	....	1.50	.65
2423	P Canadian Flag on Backpack	....	1.50	.65
2423a	Booklet Pane of 10, 2 each #2419-23...............	....	13.00	....
2423b	Booklet Pane of 30, 6 each #2419-23...............	....	39.00	....
2424	Juvenile Wildlife, sheet of 4	....	10.50	10.50
2424a	P Arctic hare leverets	....	1.35	.75
2424b	$1.05 Red Fox Kit in hollow log	....	2.25	1.25
2424c	$1.25 Canada goslings	....	2.75	1.50
2424d	$1.75 Polar Bear Cub	....	3.75	2.00
2425	P Arctic hare leverets coil, D/C 9.25	....	1.90	1.55
2426	P Arctic hare leverets coil, D/C 8.25	....	1.90	.75
2427	$1.03 Red Fox Kit in hollow log coil, D/C 8.25...	....	2.50	1.25
2428	$1.25 Canada goslings coil D/C 8.50..............	....	2.90	1.50
2429	$1.75 Polar Bear Cub coil D/C 8.25	....	3.95	2.00
2430	$1.03 Red Fox Kit in hollow log bklt single	....	2.25	1.25
2430a	same, booklet pane of 6.............	....	13.50	....
2431	$1.25 Canada goslings bklt single	....	2.75	1.50
2431a	same, booklet pane of 6.............	....	17.00	....
2432	$1.75 Polar Bear Cub bklt single	....	4.00	2.00
2432a	Same, booklet pane of 6.............	....	23.50	....
2433	59¢ Carrie Best, Order of Canada Recipient	....	1.35	.75
2433a	same, bklt pane of 10................	....	13.50	....

SCOTT NO.	DESCRIPTION	PLATE BLOCK F/NH	UNUSED F/NH	USED F

2434

2436

2434	59¢ Ferguson Jenkins, order of Canada Recipient		1.35	.75
2434a	same, bklt pane of 10		13.50	....
2435	P Gift Box		1.35	.75
2435a	Same, bklt pane of 6		8.00	....
2436	59¢ Pow-wow Dancer		1.35	.75
2437	Paintings of Daphne Odjig, sheet of 3		8.50	8.25
2437a	$1.03 Pow-wow		2.25	1.25
2437b	$1.75 Spiritual Renewal		4.00	2.00
2438	$1.03 Pow-wow		2.25	1.25
2438a	same, booklet pane of 6		13.50	....
2439	$1.75 Spiritual Renewal		3.75	2.00
2439a	same, booklet pane of 6		24.00	....
2440	P Sunflower, sheet of 2		3.00	2.75
2440A	P Prado Red		1.40	.75
2440B	P Sunbright		1.40	.75

2442

2448b

2441-42	P Sunflower, coil pair		3.00	....
2441	P Prado Red, coil		1.35	.75
2442	P Sunbright, coil		1.35	.75
2443	P Prado Red, booklet single		1.35	.75
2444	P Sunbright, booklet single		1.35	.75
2444A	P Sunflower, booklet pane of 10		13.50	....
2445	Signs of the Zodiac, sheet of 4		6.25	6.00
2446	Signs of the Zodiac, sheet of 4		6.25	6.00
2446a	P Leo		1.50	.95
2446b	P Virgo		1.50	.95
2446c	P Libra		1.50	.95
2446d	P Scorpio		1.50	.95
2447	Signs of the Zodiac, sheet of 4		6.25	5.50
2447a	P Sagittarius		1.50	.95
2447b	P Capricorn		1.50	.95
2447c	P Aquarius		1.50	.95
2447d	P Pisces		1.50	.95
2448	Signs of the Zodiac, sheet of 12		18.00	18.00
2448a	P Aries		1.50	.75
2448b	P Taurus		1.50	.75
2448c	P Gemini		1.50	.75
2448d	P Cancer		1.50	.75
2448e	P Leo		1.50	.75
2448f	P Virgo		1.50	.75
2448g	P Libra		1.50	.75
2448h	P Scorpio		1.50	.75
2448i	P Sagittarius		1.50	.75
2448j	P Capricorn		1.50	.75
2448k	P Aquarius		1.50	.75
2448l	P Pisces		1.50	.75
2449	P Aries, booklet single		1.50	.75
2449a	same, booklet pane of 10		13.50	....
2450	P Taurus, booklet single		1.50	.75
2450a	same, booklet pane of 10		13.50	....
2450b	Gutter pane of 12, 6 each 2449-50		17.50	....
2451	P Gemini, booklet single		1.50	.75
2451a	same, booklet pane of 10		13.50	....
2452	P Cancer, booklet single		1.50	.75
2452a	same, booklet pane of 10		13.50	....
2452b	gutter pane of 12, 6 each 2451-52		17.00	....
2453	P Leo Booklet Single		1.50	.75
2453a	same, booklet pane of 10		13.50	....
2454	P Virgo Booklet Single		1.50	.75
2454a	same, booklet pane of 10		13.50	....
2455	P Libra Booklet Single		1.50	.75
2455a	same, booklet pane of 10		13.50	....
2456	P Scorpio Booklet Single		1.50	.75
2456a	same, booklet pane of 10		13.50	....
2457	P Sagittarius Booklet Single		1.50	.75
2457a	same, booklet pane of 10		13.50	....
2458	P Capricorn Booklet Single		1.50	.75
2458a	same, booklet pane of 10		13.50	....
2459	P Aquarius Booklet Single		1.50	.75
2459a	same, booklet pane of 10		13.50	....
2460	P Pisces Booklet Single		1.50	.75
2460a	same, booklet pane of 10		13.50	....
2461	P International Year of the Forest, sheet of 2		2.75	2.75
2461a	P Tree		1.35	.75
2461b	P Mushroom and Plants on Forest Floor		1.35	.75
2462	P Tree, booklet single		1.35	.75
2463	P Mushroom & Plants on Forest Floor, bklt single		1.35	.75
2463a	Booklet pane of 8, 4 each of 2462 & 2463		11.00	....

2462

2463

2464-65

2464-65	59¢ - $1.75 Royal Wedding, pair		5.50	5.00
2464	P Couple with Prince William at right		1.35	1.00
2465	$1.75 Couple with Prince William at right		4.00	2.00
2465b	same, souvenir sheet of 2		5.75	5.75
2465c	same, souvenir sheet of 2 with coat of arms overprint		7.00	7.00
2466	59¢ Royal Wedding, booklet single		1.25	.75
2466a	Same, booklet pane of 10		13.50	10.00
2467	$1.75 Royal Wedding, booklet single		3.75	3.25
2467a	Same, booklet pane of 10		39.00	....
2467b	Gutter pane, 6 #2466, 4 #2467		27.50	....

2468-2469

2468-69	59¢ Mail Delivery Pair		2.75	2.25
2468	59¢ Ponchon		1.35	.75
2469	59¢ Dog Sled		1.35	.75
2470	59¢ Canada Parks Centennial		1.35	.75
2470a	same, booklet pane of 10		13.50	....
2471	P Art Deco, sheet of 5		7.00	7.00
2471a	P Burrard Bridge		1.50	.75
2471b	P Cormier House		1.50	.75
2471c	P R.C. Water House Treatment Plant		1.50	.75
2471d	P Supreme Court of Canada		1.50	.75
2471e	P Dominion Building		1.50	.75
2472	P Burrard Bridge, booklet single		1.50	.75
2473	P Cormier House, booklet single		1.50	.75
2474	P R.C. Water House Treatment Plant, bklt single		1.50	.75
2475	P Supreme Court of Canada, booklet single		1.50	.75
2476	P Dominion Building, booklet single		1.50	.75
2476a	Art Deco Structures, booklet pane of 10		13.50	....
2477	Royal Wedding, sheet of 2		2.75	2.75
2477b	same, with Royal Tour Emblem, overprinted in sheet margin		3.00	3.00
2478	P Royal Wedding, booklet single		1.50	.75
2478a	same, booklet pane of 10		13.50	....
2479	P Ginette Reno		1.50	.75
2479a	P Ginette Reno, perf 12.5x13		1.50	.75

2483b

2486a

2480	P Bruce Cockburn		1.50	.75
2480a	P Bruce Cockburn, perf 12.5x13		1.50	.75
2481	P Robbie Robertson		1.50	.75
2481a	P Robbie Robertson, perf 12.5x13		1.50	.75
2482	P Kate and Anna McGarrigle		1.50	.75
2482a	P Kate and Anna McGarrigle, perf 12.5x13		1.50	.75
2482b	Popular Singers Souvenir Sheet of 4		6.00	....
2483	Popular Singers, booklet pane of 4		6.00	....
2483a	P Bruce Cockburn, booklet single		1.50	.75
2483b	P Kate and Anna McGarrigle, booklet single		1.50	.75
2483c	P Ginette Reno, booklet single		1.50	.75
2483d	P Robbie Robertson, booklet single		1.50	.75

SCOTT NO.	DESCRIPTION	PLATE BLOCK F/NH	UNUSED F/NH	USED F
2484	P Roadside Attractions Sheet of 4	....	6.00	2.75
2484a	P World's Largest Lobster.................................		1.50	.75
2484b	P Wild Blueberry		1.50	.75
2484c	P Big Potato..		1.50	.75
2484d	P Giant Squid...		1.50	.75
2485	P Roadside Attractions, booklet pane of 4		6.00	....
2485a	P World's Largest Lobster, booklet single.........		1.50	.75
2485b	P Wild Blueberry, booklet single		1.50	.75
2485c	P Big Potato, booklet single		1.50	.75
2485d	P Giant Squid, booklet single........................		1.50	.75
2486	Miss Supertest S/S of 2		5.50	5.25
2486a	P Miss Supertest III....................................		1.50	.75
2486b	$1.75 Miss Supertest III		3.75	1.95
2487	P Miss Supertest, booklet single....................		1.50	.75
2487a	same, booklet pane of 10.............................		13.50	

2488b   **2490c**   **2495**

SCOTT NO.	DESCRIPTION	PLATE BLOCK F/NH	UNUSED F/NH	USED F
2488	Canadian Inventions, booklet pane of 4............	....	5.75	....
2488a	59¢ Pacemaker, Dr. John Hopps		1.35	.75
2488b	59¢ Blackberry, Research in Motion		1.35	.75
2488c	59¢ Electric Oven, Thomas Ahern		1.35	.75
2488d	59¢ Electric Wheelchair, George J. Klein..........		1.35	.75
2489	P Dr. John Charles Polanyi		1.35	.75
2489a	same, booklet pane of 10.............................		13.50	....
2490	Christmas, sheet of 3		7.50	7.50
2490a	P Angel...		1.50	.75
2490b	$1.03 Nativity..		2.25	1.25
2490c	$1.75 Epiphany..		3.75	2.25
2491	P Christmas		1.35	.65
2491a	same, booklet pane of 6..............................		7.75	....
2492	P Angel, booklet single...............................		1.50	.75
2492a	same, booklet pane of 6..............................		7.75	....
2493	$1.03 Nativity, booklet single		2.25	1.25
2493a	$1.75 Epiphany..		13.50	....
2494	$1.75 Epiphany, booklet single		3.75	2.25
2494a	$1.75 Epiphany..		24.00	....

2498   **2505**   **2508**

2012 COMMEMORATIVES

SCOTT NO.	DESCRIPTION	PLATE BLOCK F/NH	UNUSED F/NH	USED F
2495	P Year of the Dragon....................................	....	1.50	.75
2496	$1.80 Year of the Dragon..............................		4.00	2.00
2496a	Year of the Dragon souvenir sheet of 2		7.50	4.25
2497	$1.80 Year of the Dragon, booklet single		4.00	2.00
2497a	same, booklet pane of 6...............................		25.00	....
2498	P Flag, souvenir sheet of 5		6.75	....
2498a	P Flag on Coast Guard Ship		1.35	.65
2498b	P Flag in Van Window..................................		1.35	.65
2498c	P Oympic Athlete Carrying Flag		1.35	.65
2498d	P Flag on Bobsled.......................................		1.35	.65
2498e	P Inuit Child waving Flag		1.35	.65
2499	P Flag on Coast Guard Ship, booklet single		1.35	.65
2499a	P Flag on Coast Guard Ship, "Canada" visible on reverse of stamp		1.50	.75
2500	P Flag in Van Window, booklet single		1.35	.65
2500a	P Flag in Van window, "Canada" visible on reverse of stamps		1.50	.75
2501	P Olympic Athlete Carrying Flag, booklet single		1.35	.65
2501a	P Olympic athlete carrying flag, "Canada" visible on reverse of stamps		1.50	.75
2502	P Flag on Bobsled, booklet single...................		1.35	.65
2502a	P Flag on Bobsled, microprinting with corrected spelling "Lueders"		1.50	.75
2502b	P Flag on Bobsled, microprinting with "Canada" visible on reverse of stamp		1.50	.75
2503c	booklet pane of 10, 2 each, 2499-2502, 2502a, 2503............................		13.50	....
2503d	P Inuit child waving flag, "Canada" visible on reverse of stamp		1.50	.75
2503e	booklet pane of 10, 2 each, 2499a, 2500a, 2501a, 2502b, 2503d...........................		13.50	....
2504	Juvenile Wildlife Souvenir Sheet of 4...............		10.50	10.50
2504a	P Three Raccoon Kits		1.40	.70
2504b	$1.05 Two Caribou Calves		2.30	1.25
2504c	$1.29 Adult Loon and Two Chicks...................		2.75	1.50
2504d	$1.80 Moose Calves		4.25	2.25
2505	P Three Raccoon Kits Coil, D/C 9.25...............		1.40	.70
2506	P Three Raccoon Kits Coil, D/C 8.25...............		1.40	.70
2507	$1.05 Two Caribou Calves Coil, D/C 8.25		2.30	1.25
2508	$1.29 Adult Loon and Two Chicks Coil, D/C 8.25		2.75	1.50
2509	$1.80 Moose Calves Coil, D/C 8.25.................		4.25	2.25

2520

2527

SCOTT NO.	DESCRIPTION	PLATE BLOCK F/NH	UNUSED F/NH	USED F
2510	$1.05 Two Caribou Calves, booklet single.........	....	2.25	1.25
2510a	same, booklet pane of 6..............................		14.00	....
2511	$1.29 Adult Loon and Two Chicks, booklet single		2.75	1.50
2511a	same, booklet pane of 6..............................		17.00	....
2512	$1.80 Moose Calves, booklet single		3.95	2.00
2512a	same, booklet pane of 6..............................		23.00	....
2513	P Crown, Canada #330.................................		1.40	.70
2514	P Map of Canada, Canada #471		1.40	.70
2515	P Reign of Queen Elizabeth II, 60th Anniversary		1.40	.70
2516	P Queen Elizabeth II Flowers, Canada #1168		1.40	.70
2517	P Queen Elizabeth II Tiara, Canada #1932		1.40	.70
2518	P Queen Elizabeth II...................................		1.35	.65
2519	P Queen Elizabeth II Wearing Robe and Tiara ..		1.40	.70
2519A	same, booklet pane of 10.............................		14.00	....
2520	P John Ware		1.40	.70
2520a	booklet pane of 10.....................................		14.00	
2521	P Viola Desmond		1.40	.70
2521a	booklet pane of 10.....................................		14.00	
2521b	gutter pane of 12, 6 each 2519, 2520		16.00	
2522	P Smoothly She Shifted, by Joe Fafard............		1.40	.70
2523	Souvenir sheet, Sculptures by Joe Fafard........		7.50	7.50
2523a	$1.05 Dear Vincent		2.25	1.25
2523b	$1.80 Capillery		4.25	2.25
2524	$1.05 Dear Vincent, booklet single		2.25	1.25
2524a	same, booklet pane of 6..............................		13.75	....
2525	$1.80 Capillary, booklet single		4.25	2.25
2525a	same, booklet pane of 6..............................		23.50	....
2526	Daylilies Souvenir Sheet of 2		2.75	2.75
2526a	P Orange Daylily		1.50	.65
2526b	P Purple Daylily..		1.50	.65
2527-28	P Daylilies Coil Pair		2.75	....
2527	P Orange Daylily Coil		1.50	.65
2528	P Purple Daylily Coil		1.50	.65
2529	P Orange Daylily, booklet single		1.50	.65
2530	P Purple Daylily, booklet single.....................		1.50	.65
2530a	same, booklet pane of 10.............................		13.50	....

2536   **2537**

SCOTT NO.	DESCRIPTION	PLATE BLOCK F/NH	UNUSED F/NH	USED F
2531-34	P Sinking of the Titanic	....	5.50	5.50
2531	P White Star Line Flag & Bow of Titanic, map showing Halifax....................................		1.35	.65
2532	P Bow of Titanic & Map showing Southhampton, England ...		1.35	.65
2533	P Propellers of Titanic, three men..................		1.35	.65
2534	P Propellers of Titanic, six men.....................		1.35	.65
2535	$1.80 Titanic Souvenir Sheet		4.50	4.50
2536	P White Star Line Flag & Titanic map showing Halifax, booklet single		1.35	.65
2537	P Bow of Titanic & map showing Southampton, England, bklt single		1.35	.65
2537a	P Titanic, booklet pane of 10........................		13.00	....
2538	$1.80 White Star Line Flag & Titanic................		4.25	2.25
2538a	same, booklet pane of 6...............................		23.50	....

2539   **2542**

SCOTT NO.	DESCRIPTION	PLATE BLOCK F/NH	UNUSED F/NH	USED F
2539	P Thomas Douglas, 5th Earl of Selkirk	....	1.35	.70
2540	$2 Reign of Queen Elizabeth II.......................		4.50	2.50
2540a	$2 Reign of Queen Elizabeth II, souvenir sheet		4.50	4.50
2541	P Franklin the Turtle, miniature sheet of 4		5.50	5.50
2541a	P Franklin, Beaver and Teddy Bear		1.40	.70
2541b	P Franklin helping young turtle to read book		1.40	.70
2541c	P Franklin and snail		1.40	.70
2541d	P Franklin watching bear feed fish in bowl........		1.40	.70
2542	P Franklin, beaver & teddy bear, booklet single.		1.40	.70
2543	P Franklin helping young turtle to read, bklt single.....		1.40	.70
2544	P Franklin and snail, booklet single		1.40	.70
2545	P Franklin watching bear feed fish in bowl, bklt single ...		1.40	.70
2545a	P Franklin the turtle booklet pane of 12		16.00	....

SCOTT NO.	DESCRIPTION	PLATE BLOCK F/NH	UNUSED F/NH	USED F

2547

2557

2546	P Calgary Stampede Centennial Souvenir Sheet of 2		4.00	4.00
2546a	P Saddle on Rodeo Horse		1.50	.70
2546b	$1.05 Commemorative Belt Buckle		2.50	1.25
2547	P Saddle on Rodeo Horse, booklet single		1.50	.70
2547a	same, booklet pane of 10		13.00	....
2548	$1.05 Commemorative Belt Buckle, bklt single		2.50	1.25
2548a	same, booklet pane of 10		24.00	....
2549	P Order of Canada Recipients Miniature sheet of 4		5.50	5.50
2549a	P Louise Arbour		1.50	.70
2549b	P Rick Hansen		1.50	.70
2549c	P Sheila Watt-Cloutier		1.50	.70
2549d	P Michael J. Fox		1.50	.70
2550	P Louise Arbour booklet single		1.50	.70
2550a	same, booklet pane of 10		13.50	....
2551	P Rick Hansen booklet single		1.50	.70
2551a	same, booklet pane of 10		13.50	....
2552	P Sheila Watt-Cloutier booklet single		1.50	.70
2552a	same, booklet pane of 10		13.50	....
2553	P Michael J. Fox		1.50	.70
2553A	same, booklet pane of 10		13.50	....
2554-55	P War of 1812 Bicentennial		2.75	2.75
2554	P Sir Isaac Brock		1.50	.70
2555	P Tecumseh		1.50	.70
2556	P 2012 Summer Olympics		1.50	.75
2556a	same, booklet pane of 10		13.50	....
2557	P Tommy Douglas		1.50	.75

2559

2566

2558	P Canadian Football League Sheet of 8		12.50	....
2558a	P British Columbia Lions		1.50	.75
2558b	P Edmonton Eskimos		1.50	.75
2558c	P Calgary Stampeders		1.50	.75
2558d	P Saskatchewan Roughriders		1.50	.75
2558e	P Winnipeg Blue Bombers		1.50	.75
2558f	P Hamilton-Tiger-Cats		1.50	.75
2558g	P Toronto Argonauts		1.50	.75
2558h	P Montreal Alouettes		1.50	.75
2559-66	P Canadian Football Leagues Coil		12.80	....
2559	P British Columbia Lions Coil Single		1.50	.75
2560	P Edmonton Eskimos Coil Single		1.50	.75
2561	P Calgary Stampeders Coil Single		1.50	.75
2562	P Saskatchewan Roughriders Coil Single		1.50	.75
2563	P Winnipeg Blue Bombers Coil Single		1.50	.75
2564	P Hamilton-Tiger-Cats Coil Single		1.50	.75
2565	P Toronto Argonauts Coil Single		1.50	.75
2566	P Montreal Alouettes Coil Single		1.50	.75

2568

2578

2567	P Grey Cup Centennial, sheet of 9		12.50	12.50
2567a	P Two football players and cup		1.50	.75
2567b	P British Columbia Lions player Geroy Simon		1.50	.75
2567c	P Edmonton Eskimos play Tom Wilkinson		1.50	.75
2567d	P Calgary Stampeders player "Thumper" Wayne Harris		1.50	.75
2567e	P Saskatchewan Roughriders player George Reed		1.50	.75
2567f	P Winnipeg Blue Bombers player Ken Pipen		1.50	.75
2567g	P Hamilton-Tiger-Cats player Danny McMannus		1.50	.75
2567h	P Toronto Argonauts player Michael "Pinball" Cannon		1.50	.75
2567i	P Montreal Alouettes player Anthony Calvillo		1.50	.75
2568	P Two football players and cup booklet single		1.50	.75
2568a	same, booklet pane of 10		13.50	....
2569	P British Columbia Lions player Geroy Simon, booklet single		1.50	.75
2569a	same, booklet pane of 10		13.50	....

2570

2582

2570	P Edmonton Eskimos player Tom Wilkinson, booklet single		1.50	.75
2570a	same, booklet pane of 10		13.50	....
2571	P Calgary Stampeders player "Thumper" Wayne Harris		1.50	.75
2571a	same, booklet pane of 10		13.50	....
2572	P Saskatchewan Roughriders player George Reed, booklet single		1.50.	.75
2572a	same, booklet pane of 10		13.50	....
2573	P Winnipeg Blue Bombers player Ken Pipen, booklet single		1.50	.75
2573a	same, booklet pane of 10		13.50	....
2574	P Hamilton-Tiger-Cats player Danny McMannus, booklet single		1.50	.75
2574a	same, booklet pane of 10		13.50	....
2575	P Toronto Argonauts player Michael "Pinball" Cannon, booklet single		1.50	.75
2575a	same, booklet pane of 10		13.50	....
2576	P Montreal Alouettes player Anthony Calvillo, booklet single		1.50	.75
2576a	same, booklet pane of 10		13.50	....
2577	P Military Regiments, souvenir sheet of 3		4.25	4.25
2577a	P Black Watch (Royal Highland) Regiment of Canada, perf 13x13.5		1.35	.75
2577b	P Royal Hamilton Light Infantry (Wentworth Regiment), perf 13x13.5		1.35	.75
2577c	P Royal Regiment of Canada, perf 13x13.5		1.35	.75
2578	P Black Watch (Royal Highland) Regiment of Canada, perf 13.25x13		1.35	.75
2578a	same, booklet pane of 10		13.50	....

2581a, 2583

2581b, 2584

2581c, 2585

2579	P Royal Hamilton Light Infantry (Wentworth Regiment), perf 13.25x13		1.35	.75
2579a	same, booklet pane of 10		13.50	....
2580	P Royal Regiment of Canada, perf 13.25x13		1.35	.75
2580a	same, booklet pane of 10		13.50	....
2581	Gingerbread Cookies Souvenir Sheet of 3		7.75	7.75
2581a	P Man and Woman Gingerbread Cookies		1.50	.75
2581b	$1.05 Five-Pointed Star Gingerbread Cookie		2.25	1.25
2581c	$1.80 Snowfake Gingerbread Cookie		4.25	2.25
2582	Stained Glass Window		1.50	.75
2582a	same, booklet pane of 12		15.50	....
2583	P Man and Woman Gingerbread Cookies, bklt single		1.50	.75
2583a	same, booklet pane of 12		15.50	....
2584	$1.05 Five-Pointed Star Gingerbread Cookie, bklt single		2.25	1.25
2584a	same, booklet pane of 6		13.50	....
2585	$1.80 Snowflake Gingerbread Cookie, bklt single		4.25	2.25
2585a	same, booklet pane of 6		23.00	....
2586	P Gray Dots		1.50	1.50
2586a	P Gray Dots, personalized issue		1.50	1.50
2587	P Gray Frame		1.50	1.50
2587a	P Gray Frame, personalized issue		....	1.50
2588	P Gray and Red Hearts		1.50	1.50
2588a	P Gray and Red Hearts, personalized issue		1.50	1.50
2589	P Multicolored Creatures		1.50	1.50
2589a	P Multicolored Creatures, personalized issue		1.50	1.50
2590	P Multicolored Butterflies		1.50	1.50
2590a	P Multicolored Butterflies, personalized issue		1.50	1.50
2591	P Multicolored Maple Leaves		1.50	1.50
2591a	P Multicolored Maple Leaves, personalized issue		1.50	1.50
2592	P Multicolored Flowers		1.50	1.50
2592a	P Multicolored Flowers, personalized issue		1.50	1.50
2593	P Multicolored Snowflakes		1.50	1.50
2593a	P Multicolored Snowflakes, personalized issue		1.50	1.50
2594	P Gray and Black Wedding Bells		1.50	1.50
2594a	P Gray and Black Wedding Bells, personalied issue		1.50	1.50
2595	P Gray Doves and Flowers		1.50	1.50
2595a	P Gray Doves and Flowers, personalized issue		1.50	1.50
2596	P Multicolored Balloons, Stars, Party		1.50	1.50
2596a	P Multicolored Balloons, Stars, Party, personalized issue		1.50	1.50
2597	P Multicolored Holly		1.50	1.50
2597a	P Multicolored Holly, personalized issue		1.50	1.50
2598	P Gray Cup Victory of Toronto Argonauts		1.35	.65
2598a	same, booklet pane of 10		13.00	....

SCOTT NO.	DESCRIPTION	PLATE BLOCK F/NH	UNUSED F/NH	USED F

2599

2602b, 2605, 2608

2632

2635

2013 COMMEMORATIVES

SCOTT NO.	DESCRIPTION	PLATE BLOCK F/NH	UNUSED F/NH	USED F
2599	P Year of the Snake		1.50	.75
2600	$1.85 Snake's Head		4.25	4.25
2600a	Year of the Snake Souvenir Sheet of 2		8.25	8.25
2601	$1.85 Snake's Head Booklet Single		4.25	4.25
2601a	same, booklet pane of 6		23.50	
2602	Juvenile Wildlife Souvenir Sheet of 4		11.00	11.00
2602a	P Four Woodchuck Pups		1.35	.75
2602b	$1.10 Pocupette		2.50	1.25
2602c	$1.34 Fawn		3.00	1.50
2602d	$1.85 Bear Cub		4.25	2.00
2603	P Four Woodchuck Pups coil D/C 9.25 horizontal		1.35	.75
2604	P Four Woodchuck Pups coil D/C 8.25 horizontal		1.35	.75
2605	$1.10 Pocupette Coil		2.50	1.25
2606	$1.34 Fawn coil		3.00	1.50
2607	$1.85 Bear Cub Coil		4.25	2.00
2608	$1.10 Porcupette booklet single		2.50	1.25
2608a	same, booklet pane of 6		14.50	
2609	$1.34 Fawn booklet single		3.00	1.50
2609a	same, booklet pane of 6		17.50	
2610	$1.85 Bear Cub Booklet Single		4.25	2.00
2610a	same, booklet pane of 6		24.00	

2612 **2613** **2614** **2615** **2616**

SCOTT NO.	DESCRIPTION	PLATE BLOCK F/NH	UNUSED F/NH	USED F
2611	P Flags, souvenir sheet of 5		6.75	6.75
2611a	P Flag design on chairs		1.35	.75
2611b	P Flag on hay roll		1.35	.75
2611c	P Flag Design onSpinnaker		1.35	.75
2611d	P Flag in flower bed		1.35	.75
2611e	P Flag design on hut		1.35	.75
2612	P Flag design on chairs booklet single		1.35	.75
2612a	P Flag design on chairs booklet single, "Canada" visible on reverse of stamp		1.35	.75
2613	P Flag on hay roll booklet single		1.35	.75
2613a	P Flag on hay roll booklet single, "Canada" visible on reverse of stamp		1.35	.75
2614	P Flag design onSpinnaker booklet single		1.35	.75
2614a	P Flag design onSpinnaker booklet single, "Canada" visible on reverse of stamp		1.35	.75
2615	P Flag in flower bed booklet single		1.35	.75
2615a	P Flag in flower bed booklet single, "Canada" visible on reverse of stamps		1.35	.75
2616	P Flag design on Hut, booklet single		1.35	.75
2616a	P Flag design on Hut booklet single, "Canada" visible on reverse of stamp		1.35	.75
2616b	Booklet pane of 10, 2 each, 2612-2616		13.50	
2616c	Booklet pane of 10, 2 each, 2612a-2616a		13.50	
2616d	Booklet pane of 30, 6 each of 2612-2616		38.50	
2616e	Booklet pane of 30, 6 each of 2612a-2616a		38.50	
2617	P Queen Elizabeth II, booklet single		1.35	.75
2617a	same, booklet pane of 10		13.50	
2617b	same, Canada visible on reverse of stamp		1.50	.75
2617c	same, booklet pane of 10		13.50	
2618	$1.85 Raoul Wallenberg		4.25	2.25
2618a	same, booklet pane of 6		23.50	

2619

2620

2624

SCOTT NO.	DESCRIPTION	PLATE BLOCK F/NH	UNUSED F/NH	USED F
2619	P Oliver Jones booklet single		1.35	.75
2619a	same, booklet pane 10		13.50	
2620	P Joe Fortes booklet single		1.35	.75
2620a	same, booklet pane of 10		13.50	
2621	Magnolias Souvenir sheet of 2		2.75	3.75
2621a	P Yellow Flower		1.35	.75
2621b	P White Flower		1.35	.75
2622-23	Magnolias Coils		2.75	
2622	P Yellow Flower Coil		1.35	.75
2623	P White Flower Coil		1.35	
2624	P Yellow Flower Booklet Single		1.35	.75

SCOTT NO.	DESCRIPTION	PLATE BLOCK F/NH	UNUSED F/NH	USED F
2625	P White Flower Booklet Single		1.35	.75
2625a	same, booklet pane of 10, 2 each 2624-2625		13.50	
2626	P Photography sheet of 3		4.00	4.00
2627	P Photography sheet of 4		8.75	8.75
2628	P Hot Properties #1, by Jim Bruekelman		1.50	.75
2629	P Louis-Joseph Papineau by Thomas Coffin Doane		1.50	.75
2630	P The Kitchen Sink, by Margaret Watkins		1.50	.75
2631	P Andor Pasztor by Gabor Szilasi		1.50	.75
2632	P Koo-tuck-tuck by Geraldine Moodie		1.50	.75
2632a	Booklet pane of 10, 2 each #2628-32		13.50	
2633	$1.10 basement Camera Shop circa 1937		2.50	1.25
2633a	same, booklet pane of 6		14.50	
2634	$1.85 Yousuf Karsh by Arnaud Maggs		4.25	2.25
2634a	same, booklet pane of 6		24.00	
2635	P The Prince of Wales Own Regiment		1.50	.75
2635a	same, booklet pane of 10		13.50	

2640 **2644** **2645**

SCOTT NO.	DESCRIPTION	PLATE BLOCK F/NH	UNUSED F/NH	USED F
2636	P Pet Adoption sheet of 5		6.50	6.50
2637	P Cat with bird on branch in background		1.50	.75
2638	P Parrot on perch		1.50	.75
2639	P Dog with squirrel, butterfly, flower and ball in background		1.50	.75
2640	P Dog with fireplace, dog bed and bone in background		1.50	.75
2641	P Cat with cat toys in background		1.50	.75
2641a	same, booklet pane of 10		13.50	
2642	P Chinatown Gares sheet of 8		11.00	
2642a	P Toronto		1.50	.75
2642b	P Montreal		1.50	.75
2642c	P Winnipeg		1.50	.75
2642d	P Edmonton		1.50	.75
2642e	P Vancouver		1.50	.75
2642f	P Ottawa		1.50	.75
2642g	P Mississauga		1.50	.75
2642h	P Victoria		1.50	.75
2643	P Chinatown Gares booklet pane of 8		11.00	
2643a	P Toronto		1.50	.75
2643b	P Montreal		1.50	.75
2643c	P Winnipeg		1.50	.75
2643d	P Edmonton		1.50	.75
2643e	P Vancouver		1.50	.75
2643f	P Ottawa		1.50	.75
2643g	P Mississauga		1.50	.75
2643h	P Victoria		1.50	.75
2644	P Coronation of Queen Elizabeth II		1.50	.75
2644a	same, booklet pane of 10		13.50	

2647 - 2648

2650

SCOTT NO.	DESCRIPTION	PLATE BLOCK F/NH	UNUSED F/NH	USED F
2645	P Big Brothers, Big Sisters		1.50	.75
2645a	same, booklet page of 10		13.50	
2646	Motorcyles sheet of 2		3.00	3.00
2646a	P 1908 CCM		1.50	.70
2646b	P 1914 Indian		1.50	.70
2647	P 1908 CCM bklt single		1.50	.70
2648	P 1914 Indian bklt single		1.50	.70
2648a	same, booklet pane of 10		13.50	
2649	P Benjamin Franklin and Quebec Harbor		1.50	.70
2649a	same, booklet pane of 10		13.50	

SCOTT NO.	DESCRIPTION	PLATE BLOCK F/NH	UNUSED F/NH	USED F

2653-2654

2650	P Lieutenant Colonel Charles de Salaberry	....	1.50	.70
2651	P Laura Secord	....	1.50	.70
2651a	attached pair, 2650-51		3.25	3.25
2652	P Children's Literature Souvenir Sheet of 2		2.75	2.75
2652a	P Stella hanging by legs from tree		1.50	.70
2652b	P Stella, brother Sam, and dog, Fred		1.50	.70
2653	P Stella hanging by legs from tree, booklet single	....	1.50	.70
2654	P Stella, brother Sam, and dog, Fred, booklet single	....	1.50	.70
2654a	Same, booklet pane of 10, 5 each of 2653 & 2654	....	13.5	....

2655

2655	P Canadian Bands Souvenir Sheet of 4	....	5.50	5.50
2655a	P The Tragically Hip		1.50	.70
2655b	P Rush		1.50	.70
2655c	P Beau Dommage		1.50	.70
2655d	P The Guess Who		1.50	.70
2656	P The Tragically Hip, booklet single	....	1.50	.70
2656a	same, booklet pane of 10		13.50	....
2657	P Rush, booklet single		1.50	.70
2657a	same, booklet pane of 10		13.50	....
2658	P Beau Dommage, booklet single		1.50	.70
2658a	same, booklet pane of 10		13.50	....
2659	P The Guess Who, booklet single		1.50	.70
2659a	same, booklet pane of 10		13.50	....

2660 **2662** **2672**

2660	63¢ Robertson Davies	....	1.50	.70
2660a	same, booklet pane of 10		13.50	....
2661	63¢ Pucks with Canadian National Hockey League Team Emblems	9.25		9.25
2661a	63¢ Vancouver Canucks		1.50	.70
2661b	63¢ Edmonton Oilers		1.50	.70
2661c	63¢ Toronto Maple Leafs		1.50	.70
2661d	63¢ Montreal Canadians		1.50	.70
2661e	63¢ Calgary Flames		1.50	.70
2661f	63¢ Winnipeg Jets		1.50	.70
2661g	63¢ Ottawa Senators		1.50	.70
2662-68	63¢ Pucks with Canadian NHL Team Emblems Coil Stamps	9.75		5.75
2662	63¢ Vancouver Canucks Coil		1.50	.70
2663	63¢ Edmonton Oilers coil		1.50	.70
2664	63¢ Toronto Maple Leafs coil		1.50	.70
2665	63¢ Montreal Canadians coil		1.50	.70
2666	63¢ Calgary Flames coil		1.50	.70
2667	63¢ Winnipeg Jets coil		1.50	.70
2668	63¢ Ottawa Senators coil		1.50	.70
2669	63¢ Home and Away Uniforms of Canadian NHL teams Sheet of 7	9.75		9.75
2669a	63¢ Vancouver Canucks Player and Fan	....	1.50	.70
2669b	63¢ Edmonton Oilers Player and Fan		1.50	.70
2669c	63¢ Toronto Maple Leafs Player and Fan		1.50	.70
2669d	63¢ Montreal Canadians Player and Fan		1.50	.70
2669e	63¢ Calgary Flames Player and Fan		1.50	.70
2669f	63¢ Winnipeg Jets Player and Fan		1.50	.70
2669g	63¢ Ottawa Senators Player and Fan		1.50	.70
2670	63¢ Vancouver Canucks Player and Fan booklet single	....	1.50	.70
2670a	same, booklet pane of 10		13.50	....
2671	63¢ Edmonton Oilers Player and Fan booklet single	....	1.50	.70
2671a	same, booklet pane of 10		13.50	....
2672	63¢ Toronto Maple Leafs Player and Fan booklet single	....	1.50	.70
2672a	same, booklet pane of 10		13.50	....
2673	63¢ Montreal Canadians Player and Fan booklet single		1.50	.70
2673a	same, booklet pane of 10		13.50	....
2674	63¢ Calgary Flames Player and Fan booklet single	....	1.50	.70
2674a	same, booklet pane of 10		13.50	....
2675	63¢ Winnipeg Jets Player and Fan booklet single	....	1.50	.70
2675a	same, booklet pane of 10		13.50	....
2676	63¢ Ottawa Senators Player and Fan booklet single		1.50	.70
2676a	same, booklet pane of 10		13.50	....

2677

2677	P Superman Sheet of 5	....	7.25	7.25
2677a	P Superman leaping tall buildings		1.50	.70
2677b	P Superman and lightening bolts		1.50	.70
2677c	P Superman breaking chanins		1.50	.70
2677d	P Superman over Daily Planet		1.50	.70
2677e	P Superman in stormy sky		1.50	.70
2678	P Superman Comics 75th Anniversary		1.50	.70
2679	P Superman leaping tall buildings booklet single		1.50	.70
2680	P Superman and lightening bolts booklet single		1.50	.70
2681	P Superman breaking chanins booklet single		1.50	.70
2682	P Superman over Daily Planet booklet single		1.50	.70
2683	P Superman in stormy sky booklet single		1.50	.70
2683a	Same, booklet pane of 10, 2 each of 2679-83		13.50	....
2684	P Hastings and Prince Edward Regiment	....	1.50	.70
2684a	same, bklt pane of 10		13.50	....
2685	P Birth of Prince George sheet of 2		3.00	3.00
2685a	P Birth of Prince George single from sheet		1.50	.70
2686	P Birth of Prince George booklet single		1.50	.70
2686a	same, bklt pane of 10		13.50	....

2678 **2686**

2687	Christmas sheet of 3		7.75	....
2687a	63¢ Christmas horn single from sheet		1.50	.70
2687b	$1.10 Cross-Stitched reindeer		2.50	1.50
2687c	$1.85 Cross-stitched Christmas Tree		3.75	2.00
2688	63¢ Cross-stitched Horn bklt single, D/C		1.50	.70
2688a	Same, bklt pane of 12		16.00	....
2689	63¢ Cross-stitched Horn bklt single, D/C 13.25 x 13		1.50	.70
2689a	Same, bklt pane of 12		16.00	....
2690	$1.10 Cross-Stitched reindeer		2.50	1.25
2690a	Same, bklt pane of 6		14.00	....
2691	$1.85 Cross-stitched Christmas Tree		3.75	2.00
2691a	Same, bklt pane of 6		22.00	....
2692	63¢ four woodchuck pups coil D/C		1.50	1.50
2692a	63¢ four woodchuck pups coil D/C 8.25 horiz.		1.50	1.50
2693	63¢ Flag Design on Chairs, bklt single D/C		1.50	1.50
2694	63¢ Flag on Hay Roll, bklt single D/C		1.50	1.50
2695	63¢ Flag Design on Spinnaker, bklt single, D/C		1.50	1.50
2696	63¢ Flag in Flower Bed, bklt single, D/C		1.50	1.50
2697	63¢ Flag Design on Hut, bklt single, D/C		1.50	1.50
2697a	same, bklt pane of 10, 2 each 2693-97		13.50	....
2698	63¢ Queen Elizabeth II, bklt single D/C		1.50	1.50
2698a	same, bklt pane of 10		13.50	....

2699 **2704c** **2705**

2014 COMMEMORATIVES

2699	$1.85 Year of the Horse		1.50	1.50
2700	$1.85 Year of the Horse		3.75	3.75
2700a	$1.85 Year of the Horse S/S of 2, #2600 & #2700	....	7.50	7.50
2701	$1.85 Year of the Horse bklt single D/C		3.95	....
2701a	same, bklt pane of 6		25.00	....
2702	63¢ Africville, Halifax, Nova Scotia bklt single D/C	....	1.50	1.50
2702a	same, bklt pane of 10		13.50	....
2703	63¢ Hogan's Alley, Vancouver, BC bklt single D/C13.25		1.50	1.50
2703a	same, bklt pane of 10		13.50	....
2704	63¢ Female Athletes, sheet of 3		4.50	4.50
2704a	63¢ Barbara Ann Scott, figure skater		1.50	1.50
2704b	63¢ Sandra Schmirler, curler		1.50	1.50
2704c	63¢ Sarah Burke, freestyle skier		1.50	1.50
2705	63¢ Barbara Ann Scott, figure skater, bklt single D/C 13.25		1.50	1.50
2705a	same, bklt pane of 10		13.50	....
2706	63¢ Sandra Schmirler, curler, bklt single D/C 13.25	....	1.50	1.50
2706a	same, bklt pane of 10		13.50	....

SCOTT NO.	DESCRIPTION	PLATE BLOCK F/NH	UNUSED F/NH	USED F

2711   **2714**

2707	63¢ Sarah Burke, freestyle skier, bklt single D/C	....	1.50	1.50
2707a	same, bklt pane of 10		13.50	....
2708	22¢ Monarch butterfly, perf 13.25 x 13		.50	.35
2709	Juvenile Wildlife S/S of 5		15.00	15.00
2709a	P Beaver Kits		1.75	.90
2709b	$1.00 Burrowing Owl Chicks		2.15	1.00
2709c	$1.20 Mountain Goat Kid		2.50	1.25
2709d	$1.80 Puffin chicks		3.50	1.75
2709e	$2.50 Newborn wapiti		4.75	2.50
2710	$1 Burrowing Owl Chicks coil, D/C 13.50		2.15	1.00
2710a	P Beaver Kits		1.75	.85
2711	P Beaver Kits coil D/C 8.25		1.75	.90
2712	$1.20 Mountain Goat Kid coil D/C 8.25		2.50	1.25
2713	$1.80 Puffin chicks coil, D/C 8.25		3.50	1.75
2714	$2.50 Newborn wapiti coil, D/C 8.25		4.75	2.50
2715	$1.20 Mountain Goat Kid, bklt single D/C 9.25		2.50	1.25
2715a	same, bklt pane of 6		14.50	....
2716	$1.80 Puffin chicks, bklt single D/C 9.25		3.50	1.75
2716a	same, bklt pane of 6		21.00	....
2717	$2.50 Newborn wapiti, bklt single, D/C 9.25		4.75	2.50
2717a	same, bklt pane of 6		28.00	....
2718	P National Parks souvenir sheet of 5		9.00	9.00
2718a	P Gros Morne National Park		1.75	.95
2718b	P Joggins Fossil Cliffs		1.75	.95
2718c	P Canadian Rocky Mountains Park		1.75	.95
2718d	P Nahinni National Park		1.75	.95
2718e	Miguasha National Park		1.75	.95
2719	P Gros Morne Nat. Park bklt single, D/C 13.25	....	1.75	.95
2720	P Nahinni National Park bklt single D/C 13.25	....	1.75	.95
2721	P Joggins Fossil Cliffs bklt single d/c 13.25	....	1.75	.95
2722	Miguasha National Park bklt single D/C 13.25	....	1.75	.95

2725   **2727a-b**

2723	P Canadian Rocky Mtns. Park bklt single D/C13.25	....	1.75	.95
2723a	same, bklt pane of 10, 2 each 2719-23		18.00	....
2723b	same, Booklet Pane of 30		49.00	....
2724	P Unesco World Heritage Sites sheet of 2		3.75	3.75
2724a	P Shiva Natajara Sculpture, mummified cat & bison		1.75	1.00
2724b	P Hadrasaur skeleton & Luohan Chinese sculpture		1.75	1.00
2725	P Shiva Natajara Sculpture, mummified cat & bison bklt single		1.75	1.00
2726	P Hadrasaur skeleton & Luohan Chinese sculpture bklt single		1.75	1.00
2726a	same, bklt pane of 10, 5 each 2725-26		18.00	....
2727	P Roses, Sheet of 2		3.25	3.25
2727a	P Konrad Henkel (Red) Rose		1.75	.95
2727b	P Maid of Honor (White) Rose		1.75	.95
2728-29	P Roses Coil Pair		3.50	....
2728	P Maid of Honor (White)Coil Rose		1.75	.95
2729	P Konrad Henkel (Red) Coil Rose		1.75	.95
2730	P Konrad Henkel (Red) Rose Booklet Single		1.75	.95
2731	P Maid of Honor (White) Rose Booklet Single	....	1.75	.95
2731a	Same, Booklet pane of 10		17.50	....
2732	$2.50 Komagata Maru Incident Booklet Single		5.00	3.50
2732a	Same, Booklet Pane of 6		32.50	....
2733	National Film Board, Sheet of 5 + Label		8.50	8.50
2733a	P Flamenco at 5:15		1.75	.95
2733b	P The Railrodder		1.75	.95
2733c	P Mon Oncle Antoine		1.75	.95
2733d	P Log Driver's Waltz		1.75	.95
2733e	P Neighbours		1.75	.95
2734	P Flamenco at 5:15 Booklet Single		1.75	.95
2735	P The Railrodder Booklet Single		1.75	.95
2736	P Mon Oncle Antoine Booklet Single		1.75	.95
2737	P Log Driver's Waltz Booklet Single		1.75	.95
2738	P Neighbours Booklet Single		1.75	.95
2738a	National Film Board, Sheet of 5		17.50	....
2739	UNESCO World Heritage Sites Miniature Sheet		17.50	17.50
2739a	$1.20 Head-Smashed-In Buffalo Jump		2.50	1.25
2739b	$1.20 Old Town Lunenburg		2.50	1.25
2739c	$1.20 Landscape of Grand Pre		2.50	1.25
2739d	$2.50 SGang Gwaay		5.00	2.50
2739e	$2.50 Rideau Canal		5.00	2.50
2740	$1.20 Old Town Lunenburg Booklet Single		2.50	1.25
2741	$1.20 Head-Smashed-In Buffalo Jump Bklt Single		2.50	1.25
2742	$1.20 Landescape of Grand Pre Booklet Single		2.50	1.25
2742a	Booklet Pane of 6		14.50	....
2743	$2.50 SGang Gwaay Booklet Single		5.00	2.50
2744	$2.50 Rideau Canal Booklet Single		5.00	2.50
2744a	Booklet Pane of 6		29.50	....

2746   **2748c**

2745	P Empress of Ireland		1.75	.95
2746	$2.50 Empress of Ireland Souvenir Sheet	....	5.00	2.50
2747	P Empress of Ireland Booklet Single		1.75	.95
2747a	Same, Booklet Pane of 10		17.50	....
2748	P Haunted Canada, Sheet of 5		8.50	8.50
2748a	P Ghost Bride		1.75	.95
2748b	P Ghost Train		1.75	.95
2748c	P Apparitions of Fort George		1.75	.95
2748d	P Count of Frontenac Hotel		1.75	.95
2748e	P Phantom Ship		1.75	.95
2749	P Ghost Bride Booklet Single		1.75	.95
2750	P Phantom Ship Booklet Single		1.75	.95
2751	P Ghost Train Booklet Single		1.75	.95
2752	P Count of Frontenac Hotel Booklet Single		1.75	.95
2753	P Apparitions of Fort George Booklet Single		1.75	.95
2753a	Booklet Pane of 10		17.50	....

2758   **2765c**

2757c	P Bogner's Grocery	....	1.75	.95
2757d	$2.50 Rallcuts #1		5.50	2.75
2758	P Bogner's Grocery Booklet Single		1.75	.95
2759	P St. Joseph's Convenant School Booklet Single		1.75	.95
2760	P La Ville de Quebec en Hiver		1.75	.95
2761	P Untitled by Lynne Cohen, Booklet Single		1.75	.95
2762	P Unidentified Chinese Man		1.75	.95
2762a	Booklet pane of 10, 2 each of 2758-62		17.50	....
2763	$1.20 Sitting Bull and Buffalo Bill Booklet Single	....	2.50	1.25
2763a	Booklet Pane of 6		14.50	....
2764	$2.50 Rallcuts #1 Booklet Single		5.25	2.75
2764a	Same, Booklet Pane of 6		31.00	....
2765	Country Music Recording Artists, Sheet of 5		9.00	9.00
2765a	P Hand Snow		1.75	.95
2765b	P Renee Martel		1.75	.95
2765c	P Shania Twain		1.75	.95
2765d	P Tommy Hunter		1.75	.95
2765e	P K. D. Lang		1.75	.95
2754	P Russ Jackson in Ottawa Rough Riders Uniform		1.75	.95
2755	P Russ Jackson in Ottawa Rough Riders Uniform Booklet Single		1.75	.95
2755a	Same, Booklet pane of 10		17.50	....

2771

2756	Photography, Sheet of 3		5.75	5.75
2756a	P Unidentified Chinese Man		1.75	.95
2756b	P St. Joseph's Covenant School		1.75	.95
2756c	$1.20 Sitting Bull and Buffalo Bill		3.25	1.50
2757	Photography, Sheet of 4		10.50	10.50
2757a	P Untitled by Lynne Cohen		1.75	.95
2757b	P La Ville de Quebec en Hiver		1.75	.95
2766	P Hank Snow Booklet Single		1.75	.95
2766a	Same, Booklet of 10		17.50	....
2767	P Renee Martel Booklet Single		1.75	.95
2767a	Same, Booklet Pane of 10		17.50	....
2768	P Shania Twain Booklet Single		1.75	.95
2768a	Same, Booket Pane of 10		17.50	....
2769	P Tommy Hunter Booket Single		1.75	.95
2769a	Same, Booklet Pane of 10		17.50	....
2770	P K. D. Lang Booklet Single		1.75	.95
2770a	Same, Booklet Pane of 10		17.50	....
2771	P Canadian Museum for Human Rights		1.75	.95
2771a	Same, Booklet Pane of 10		17.50	....

SCOTT NO.	DESCRIPTION	PLATE BLOCK F/NH	UNUSED F/NH	USED F

2772b   **2772e**

SCOTT NO.	DESCRIPTION	PLATE BLOCK F/NH	UNUSED F/NH	USED F
2772	P Comedians, Sheet of 5		9.00	
2772a	P Mike Myers		1.75	.95
2772b	P Martin Short		1.75	.95
2772c	P Catherine O'Hara		1.75	.95
2772d	P Olivier Guimond		1.75	.95
2772e	P Jim Carrey		1.75	.95
2773	P Mike Myers Booklet Single		1.75	
2773a	Booklet pane of 10, 6 of 2773, 1 each of 2774-77		17.50	
2774	P Martin Short Booklet Single		1.75	.95
2774a	Booklet pane of 10, 6 of 2774, 1 each of 2773, 2775-77		17.50	
2775	P Catherine O'Hara Booklet Single		1.75	.95
2775a	Booklet pane of 10, 6 of 2775, 1 each of 2773-74, 2776-77		17.50	
2776	P Olivier Guimond Booklet Single		1.75	.95
2776a	Booklet pane of 10, 6 of 2776, 1 each of 2773-75, 2777		17.50	
2777	P Jim Carrey Booklet Single		1.75	.95
2777a	Booklet pane of 10, 6 of 2777, 1 each of 2773-76		17.50	

2779   **2787a**

SCOTT NO.	DESCRIPTION	PLATE BLOCK F/NH	UNUSED F/NH	USED F
2778	P Canadian NHL Zambonis Sheet of 7		12.00	12.00
2778a	P Winnipeg Jets		1.75	.95
2778b	P Ottawa Senators		1.75	.95
2778c	P Toronto Maple Leafs		1.75	.95
2778d	P Montreal Canadians		1.75	.95
2778e	P Vancouver Canucks		1.75	.95
2778f	P Calgary Flames		1.75	.95
2778g	P Edmonton Oilers		1.75	.95
2779-85	P Canadian NHL Zambonis Coil		12.00	
2779	P Winnipeg Jets Coil		1.75	.95
2780	P Ottawa Senators Coil		1.75	.95
2781	P Toronto Maple Leafs Coil		1.75	.95
2782	P Montreal Canadians Coil		1.75	.95
2783	P Vancouver Canucks Coil		1.75	.95
2784	P Calgary Flames Coil		1.75	.95
2785	P Edmonton Oilers Coil		1.75	.95
2786	P NHL Hall of Fame Defensemen, Sheet of 6		10.50	10.50
2786a	P Tim Horton		1.75	.95
2786b	P Doug Harvey		1.75	.95
2786c	P Bobby Orr		1.75	.95
2786d	P Harry Howell		1.75	.95
2786e	P Pierre Pilote		1.75	.95
2786f	P Red Kelly		1.75	.95
2787	P NHL Hall of Fame Defensemen, Bklt Pane of 6		10.50	
2787a	P Tim Horton Booklet Single		1.75	.95
2787b	P Doug Harvey Booklet Single		1.75	.95
2787c	P Bobby Orr Booklet Single		1.75	.95
2787d	P Harry Howell Booklet Single		1.75	.95
2787e	P Pierre Pilote Booklet Single		1.75	.95
2787f	P Red Kelly Booklet Single		1.75	.95
2788	$2.50 Tim Horton Souvenir Sheet		5.00	2.50
2789	$2.50 Doug Harvey Souvenir Sheet		5.00	2.50
2790	$2.50 Bobby Orr Souvenir Sheet		5.00	2.50
2791	$2.50 Harry Howell Souvenir Sheet		5.00	2.50
2792	$2.50 Pierre Pilote Souvenir Sheet		5.00	2.50
2793	$2.50 Red Kelly Souvenir Sheet		5.00	2.50

2794   **2797**

SCOTT NO.	DESCRIPTION	PLATE BLOCK F/NH	UNUSED F/NH	USED F
2794	P "Wait for me Daddy"		1.75	.95
2795	P "Wait for me Daddy" Booklet Single		1.75	.95
2795a	Same, Booklet Pane of 10		17.50	
2796	Santa Claus, Sheet of 3		9.00	9.00
2796a	P Santa Writing Letter		1.75	.95
2796b	$1.20 Santa Carrying Sack		1.75	.95
2796c	$2.50 Santa with Dove		1.75	.95
2797	P Virgin & Child with John the Baptist		1.75	.95
2797a	Same, Booklet Pane of 12		19.00	
2798	P Santa Writing Letter, Booklet Single		1.75	.95
2798a	Same, Booklet Pane of 12		19.00	

2799   **2801**   **2804**

SCOTT NO.	DESCRIPTION	PLATE BLOCK F/NH	UNUSED F/NH	USED F
2799	$1.20 Santa Carrying Sack, Booklet Single		2.50	1.25
2799a	Same, Booklet Pane of 6		14.50	
2800	$2.50 Santa with Dove, Booklet Single		5.00	2.50
2800a	Same, Booklet Pane of 6		29.50	

2015 COMMEMORATIVES

SCOTT NO.	DESCRIPTION	PLATE BLOCK F/NH	UNUSED F/NH	USED F
2801	P Year of the Ram		1.75	.95
2802	$2.50 Year of the Ram, Souvenir Sheet		4.50	4.50
2802a	Year of the Ram, Souvenir Sheet of 2, #2700, 2802		7.75	7.75
2803	$2.50 Year of the Ram, Booklet Single		4.50	2.50
2803a	Same, Booklet Pane of 6		26.50	
2804	P Sir John A MacDonald, First Prime Minister		1.75	.95
2804a	Same, Booklet Pane of 10		17.50	
2805	$2.50 Nelson Mandela Souvenir Sheet		4.50	4.50
2806	P Nelson Mandela		1.65	.85
2806a	Same, Booklet Pane of 10		16.50	
2807	P Canadian Flag		1.65	.85
2807a	Same, Booklet Pane of 10		16.50	
2808	$5 Canadian Flag, 50th Anniversary Souvenir Sheet		9.50	9.50
2809	P Pansies Souvenir Sheet of 2		3.00	3.00
2809a	P Delta Premium Pure Light Blue Pansy (blue and yellow flower)		1.50	.85
2809b	P Midnight Glow Pansy (purple and yellow flower)		1.50	.85

2823c   **2831**   **2833**

SCOTT NO.	DESCRIPTION	PLATE BLOCK F/NH	UNUSED F/NH	USED F
2810-11	P Pansies Attached Pair		3.00	
2810	P Delta Premium Pure Light Blue Pansy Coil		1.50	.85
2811	P Midnight Glow Pansy Coil		1.50	.85
2812	P Delta Premium Pure Light Blue Pansy Booklet Single		1.50	.85
2813	P Midnight Glow Pansy Booklet Single		1.50	.85
2813a	Same, Booklet Pane of 10, 5 each of 2812-13		15.50	
2814	Photography sheet of 3		7.75	7.75
2814a	P Shoeshine Stand		1.75	.85
2814b	P Southan Sisters		1.75	.85
2814c	$2.50 La Voie Lactee		4.50	2.50
2815	Photography sheet of 4		7.00	7.00
2815a	P Angels		1.75	.85
2815b	P Isaac's First Swim		1.75	.85
2815c	P Friends and Family and Trips		1.75	.85
2815d	$1.20 Alex Colville		2.25	1.25
2816	P Angels booklet single		1.75	.85
2817	P Southan Sisters booklet single		1.75	.85
2818	P Friends and Family and Trips booklet single		1.75	.85
2819	P Isaac's First Swim booklet single		1.75	.85
2820	P Shoeshine Stand booklet single		1.75	.85
2820a	P Photography, booklet pane of 10		16.00	
2821	$1.20 Photography		2.25	1.25
2821a	same, booklet pane of 6		13.50	
2822	$2.50 Photography		4.50	2.50
2822a	same, booklet pane of 6		27.00	
2823	P Dinosaurs, sheet of 5		8.50	
2823a	P Euplocephalus Tutus		1.75	.85
2823b	P Chasmosaurus Belli		1.75	.85
2823c	P Tyrannosaurus Rex		1.75	.85
2823d	P Ornithomimus Edmontonicus		1.75	.85
2823e	P Tylosaurus Pembinensis		1.75	.85
2824	P Tyrannosaurus Rex booklet single		1.75	.85
2825	P Tylosaurus Pembinensis booklet single		1.75	.85
2826	P Chasmosaurus Belli booklet single		1.75	.85
2827	P Euplocephalus Tutus booklet single		1.75	.85
2828	P Ornithomimus Edmontonicus booklet single		1.75	.85
2828a	same, booklet pane of 10		17.50	
2829	P Love Your Pet, sheet of 5		8.50	
2829a	P Cat in Head Cone Sniffing Flowers		1.65	.85
2829b	P Dog Chasing Snowball		1.65	.85
2829c	P Veterinarian Examining Cat		1.65	.85
2829d	P Dog Drinking Water from Bowl		1.65	.85
2829e	P Cat on Leash Wearing ID Tags		1.65	.85
2830	P Cat in Head Cone Sniffing Flowers, bklt single		1.65	.85
2831	P Dog Chasing Snowball, booklet single		1.65	.85

SCOTT NO.	DESCRIPTION	PLATE BLOCK F/NH	UNUSED F/NH	USED F
2832	P Veterinarian Examining Cat, booklet single....	....	1.65	.85
2833	P Cat on Leash Wearing ID Tags, booklet single	....	1.65	.85
2834	P Dog Drinking Water from Bowl, booklet single	....	1.65	.85
2834a	P Love Your Pet, booklet of 10..........................	....	16.50	

2838b   **2838d**

SCOTT NO.	DESCRIPTION	PLATE BLOCK F/NH	UNUSED F/NH	USED F
2835	P In Flander's Field..............................	....	1.65	.85
2836	P In Flander's Field, booklet single	....	1.65	.85
2836a	same, booklet pane of 10.......................	....	16.50	....
2837	P Woman's World Cup Soccer Championships.	....	1.65	.85
2837a	same, booklet pane of 10.......................	....	16.50	....
2838	P Weather Phenomena, sheet of 5 plus label....	....	7.50	7.50
2838a	P Lightening	....	1.50	.75
2838b	P Double Rainbow	....	1.50	.75
2838c	P Sun Dog Over Iqaluit, Nunavut........	....	1.50	.75
2838d	P Fog near Cape Spear Lighthouse	....	1.50	.75
2838e	P Hoar Frost on Tree	....	1.50	.75
2839	P Lightening	....	1.50	.75
2840	P Hoar Frost on Tree	....	1.50	.75
2841	P Fog near Cape Spear Lighthouse	....	1.50	.75
2842	P Sun Dog Over Iqaluit, Nunavut........	....	1.50	.75
2843	P Double Rainbow	....	1.50	.75
2843a	same, booklet pane of 10.......................	....	15.00	....

2844b, 2847   **2844e, 2849**

SCOTT NO.	DESCRIPTION	PLATE BLOCK F/NH	UNUSED F/NH	USED F
2844	UNESCO World Heritage Sites, sheet of 5........	....	....	....
2844a	$1.20 Hoodoos, Alberta	....	....	....
2844b	$1.20 Woods Buffalo National Park...............	....	....	....
2844c	$1.20 Red Bay Basque Whaling Station...........	....	....	....
2844d	$2.50 Waterton Glacier International Peace Park	....	....	....
2844e	$2.50 Kluane National Park, Yukon	....	....	....
2845	$1.20 Hoodoos, Alberta	....	....	....
2846	$1.20 Red Bay Basque Whaling Station...........	....	....	....
2847	$1.20 Woods Buffalo National Park...............	....	....	....
2847a	$1.20 Canada Sites, booklet pane of 6............	....	....	....
2848	$2.50 Waterton Glacier International Peace Park	4.50	2.50	
2849	$2.50 Kluane National Park, Yukon	4.50	2.50	
2849a	same, booklet pane of 6...........................	26.00	....	

2851   **2860a**

SCOTT NO.	DESCRIPTION	PLATE BLOCK F/NH	UNUSED F/NH	USED F
2850	P Alice Munro, 2013 Nobel Literature Laureate........................	....	1.50	.75
2850a	same, booklet pane of 10........................	....	15.00	....
2851-52	P Franklin Expedition, set of 2	....	3.00	1.50
2851	P HMS Erebus Trapped in Ice	....	1.50	.75
2852	P Map of Northern Canadian Islands..........	....	1.50	.75
2853	$2.50 Franklin Expedition, souvenir sheet.........	....	4.00	2.00
2854	P HMS Erebus Trapped in Ice	....	1.50	.75
2855	P Map of Northern Canadian Islands..........	....	1.50	.75
2855a	same, booklet pane of 10, 5 each 2853-54....	....	15.00	....
2856	$2.50 Wreckage and Diagram of HMS Erebus..	....	4.25	2.25
2856a	same, booklet pane of 6...........................	....	23.50	....
2857	UNESCO World Heritage Sites, sheet of 5, Reissue	....	16.00	....
2846-47, 58	$1.20-$2.50 Reissue singles, set of 3..............	....	7.75	....
2858a	same, booklet pane of 6...........................	....	12.50	....
2859	P Queen Elizabeth II.............................	....	1.50	.75
2859a	same, booklet pane of 10........................	....	15.00	....
2860	P Haunted Canada, sheet of 5.............	....	7.50	7.50
2860a	P Brakeman Ghost, Vancouver, BC.............	....	1.50	.75
2860b	P Red River Trail Oxcart, Winnepeg............	....	1.50	.75
2860c	P Gray Lady of the Citadel, Halifax...........	....	1.50	.75
2860d	P Ghost of Marie-Josephte Corriveau, Levis.....	....	1.50	.75
2860e	P Ghost of Caribou Hotel, Carcross, Yukon.....	....	1.50	.75
2861	P Brakeman Ghost, Vancouver, BC.............	....	1.50	.75
2862	P Ghost of Marie-Josephte Corriveau, Levis.....	....	1.50	.75
2863	P Gray Lady of the Citadel, Halifax...........	....	1.50	.75
2864	P Red River Trail Oxcart, Winnepeg............	....	1.50	.75
2865	P Ghost of Caribou Hotel, Carcross, Yukon......	....	1.50	.75
2865a	same, booklet pane of 10, 2 each.................	....	15.00	....

2866a   **2879**

SCOTT NO.	DESCRIPTION	PLATE BLOCK F/NH	UNUSED F/NH	USED F
2866	P Hockey Goaltenders, sheet of 6	....	7.75	7.75
2866a	P Ken Dryden	....	1.50	.75
2866b	P Tony Esposito	....	1.50	.75
2866c	P Johnny Bower	....	1.50	.75
2866d	P Gump Worsley	....	1.50	.75
2866e	P Bernie Parent	....	1.50	.75
2866f	P Martin Brodeur	....	1.50	.75
2867	P Ken Dryden, booklet single...............	....	1.50	.75
2868	P Tony Esposito, booklet single	....	1.50	.75
2869	P Johnny Bower, booklet single	....	1.50	.75
2870	P Gump Worsley, booklet single	....	1.50	.75
2871	P Bernie Parent, booklet single	....	1.50	.75
2872	P Martin Brodeur, booklet single	....	1.50	.75
2872a	same, booklet pane of 6...........................	....	9.00	....
2873	P Ken Dryden, souvenir sheet...............	....	3.25	....
2874	P Tony Esposito, souvenir sheet...........	....	3.25	....
2875	P Johnny Bower, souvenir sheet...........	....	3.25	....
2876	P Gump Worsley, souvenir sheet...........	....	3.25	....
2877	P Bernie Parent, souvenir sheet...........	....	3.25	....
2878	P Martin Brodeur, souvenir sheet.........	....	3.25	....
2879	P $1.20-$2.50 Christmas, sheet of 3	....	9.50	....
2879a	P Moose	....	1.50	....
2879b	$1.20 Beaver	....	2.25	....
2879c	$2.50 Polar Bear................................	....	4.50	....

2880   **2884**   **2888**

SCOTT NO.	DESCRIPTION	PLATE BLOCK F/NH	UNUSED F/NH	USED F
2880	P Adoration of the Magi.......................		1.50	
2880a	same, booklet pane of 12.......................		17.50	
2881	P Moose, booklet single.......................		1.50	
2881a	same, booklet pane of 12.......................		17.50	
2882	$1.20 Beaver, booklet single...............		2.25	
2882a	same, booklet pane of 6........................		12.50	
2883	$2.50 Polar Bear, booklet single		4.50	
2883a	same, booklet pane of 6........................		12.50	

2896a - 2896b   **2901**

2016 COMMEMORATIVES

SCOTT NO.	DESCRIPTION	PLATE BLOCK F/NH	UNUSED F/NH	USED F
2884	P Year of the Monkey..........................		1.50	....
2885	$2.50 Year of the Monkey, souvenir sheet..........		4.50	....
2885a	$2.50 souvenir sheet of 2, 2885 and 2802b..........		7.75	....
2886	P Year of the Monkey, booklet single		1.50	....
2886a	same, booklet pane of 10........................		13.00	....
2887	$2.50 Year of the Monkey, booklet single		4.50	....
2887a	same, booklet pane of 6.........................		23.50	....
2888	P Queen Elizabeth II............................		1.50	....
2888a	same, booklet pane of 10........................		13.00	....
2889	UNESCO World Heritage Sites, sheet of 5............		6.50	....
2889a	P Landscape of Grand Pre, Nova Scotia		1.50	....
2889b	P Rideau Canal, Ontario		1.50	....
2889c	P Sgang Gwaay, British Columbia		1.50	....
2889d	P Head-Smashed-in Buffalo Jump, Alberta		1.50	....
2889e	P Old Town Lunenburg, Nova Scotia		1.50	....
2890	P Landscape of Grand Pre, Nova Scotia, bklt single		1.50	....
2891	P Sgang Gwaay, British Columbia, bklt single		1.50	....
2892	P Old Town Lunenburg, Novia Scotia, bklt single		1.50	....
2893	P Rideau Canal, Ontario, booklet single		1.50	....
2894	P Head-Smashed-in Buffalo Jump, Alberta, booklet single		1.50	....
2894a	same, booklet pane of 10........................		13.00	....
2894b	same, booklet pane of 30........................		39.00	....
2895	P Organization of No. 2 Construction Battalion		1.50	....
2895a	same, booklet page of 10........................		13.50	....
2896	P Hydrangeas, sheet of 2, water activated		3.00	....
2896a	P Hydrangea Macrophylia.........................		1.50	....
2896b	P Hydrangea Arborescens		1.50	....
2897-98	P Hydrangea coil pair, self-adhesive...........		3.00	....
2897	P Hydrangea Macrophylia coil, 8.25 vert...........		1.50	....
2898	P Hydrangea Arborescens coil, 8.25 vert...........		1.50	....
2899	P Hydrangea Macrophylia, booklet single..........		1.50	....
2900	P Hydrangea Arborescens, booklet single		1.50	....
2900a	same, booklet pane of 10, 5 each 2899 and 2900.....		13.00	....

SCOTT NO.	DESCRIPTION	UNUSED F/NH	USED F

2910   **2912a, 2917**

Scott	Description	Unused	Used
2901	P Woman's Suffrage Centennial	1.50	......
2901a	same, booklet pane of 10	13.00	......
2902	P Photography, sheet of 4	7.00	......
2903	P-$2.50 Photography, sheet of 3	8.00	......
2904	P Toronto, booklet single	1.50	......
2905	P Window, booklet single	1.50	......
2906	P Freighter's Boat on Banks of Red River, booklet single	1.50	......
2907	P Victoria Bridge, Grand Trunk Railway, booklet single	1.50	......
2908	P Sans Titre 0310/La Chambre Noire, booklet single	1.50	......
2908a	same, booklet pane of 10	14.00	......
2909	$1.20 Climbing Mt. Habel, booklet single	2.25	......
2909a	same, booklet pane of 6	12.50	......
2910	$2.50 Grey Owl, booklet single	4.50	......
2910a	same, booklet pane of 6	26.00	......

2911a, 2913   **2911b, 2914**

Scott	Description	Unused	Used
2911	P Star Trek Ships, sheet of 2	3.00	......
2912	P-$2.50 Star Trek, sheet of 5	14.00	......
2912a	P Captain James T. Kirk	1.50	......
2912b	$1 Klingon Commander Kor	2.00	......
2912c	$1.20 Dr. Leonard "Bones" McCoy	2.25	......
2912d	$1.80 Montgomery "Scotty" Scott	3.50	......
2912e	$2.50 Commander Spock	4.50	......
2913-14	P Star Trek Ships, coil pair	3.00	......
2913	P U.S.S. Enterprise, coil single, die cut 8.25	1.50	......
2914	P Klingon Battle Cruiser, coil single, die cut 8.25	1.50	......
2915	P U.S.S. Enterprise, booklet single, die cut 13.75	1.50	......
2916	P Klingon Battle Cruiser, booklet single, die cut 13.75	1.50	......
2916V	P-$2.50 Star Trek Prestige Booklet Complete	35.00	......
2917	P Captain James T. Kirk, booklet single	1.50	......
2918	P Montgomery "Scotty" Scott, booklet single	1.50	......
2919	P Klingon Commander Kor, booklet single	1.50	......
2920	P Commander Spock, booklet single	1.50	......
2921	P Dr. Leonard "Bones" McCoy, booklet single	1.50	......
2921a	same, booklet pane of 6	14.00	......
2922	$5 Star Trek, three-dimensional souvenir sheet of 2	20.00	......

2929b, 2931   **2923b, 2926**   **2935a, 2940**

Scott	Description	Unused	Used
2923	P Dinosaurs, sheet of 5	8.00	......
2923a	P Troodon Inequalis	1.50	......
2923b	P Dimetrodon Borealis	1.50	......
2923c	P Comox Valley Elasmosaur	1.50	......
2923d	P Cypretherium Coarctatum	1.50	......
2923e	P Acrotholus Audeti	1.50	......
2924	P Troodon Inequalis, booklet single	1.50	......
2925	P Cypretherium Coarctatum	1.50	......
2926	P Dimetrodon Borealis	1.50	......
2927	P Acrotholus Audeti	1.50	......
2928	P Comox Valley Elasmosaur	1.50	......
2928a	same, booklet of 10	14.00	......
2929	P Birds of Canada, sheet of 5	8.00	......
2929a	P Rock Ptarmigan (Lagopus Muta)	1.50	......
2929b	P Great Horned Owl (Bubo Virginianus)	1.50	......
2929c	P Common Raven (Corvus Corax)	1.50	......
2929d	P Atlantic Puffin (Fratercula Arctica)	1.50	......
2929e	P Sharp-tailed Grouse (Tympanuchus Phasianellus)	1.50	......
2930	P Sharp-tailed Grouse (Tympanuchus Phasianellus)	1.50	......
2931	P Great Horned Owl (Bubo Virginianus)	1.50	......
2932	P Atlantic Puffin (Fratercula Arctica)	1.50	......
2933	P Common Raven (Corvus Corax)	1.50	......
2934	P Rock Ptarmigan (Lagopus Muta)	1.50	......
2934a	same, booklet pane of 10	14.00	......
2935	P Haunted Canada, sheet of 5	8.00	......
2935a	P Bell Island Hag	1.50	......
2935b	P Dungarvon Whooper	1.50	......
2935c	P Winter Garden Theatre Ghost	1.50	......
2935d	P Lady in White	1.50	......
2935e	P Phantom Bell Ringers	1.50	......
2936	P Bell Island Hag, booklet single	1.50	......
2937	P Dungarvon Whooper, booklet single	1.50	......
2938	P Lady in White, booklet single	1.50	......
2939	P Winter Garden Theatre Ghost, booklet single	1.50	......
2940	P Phantom Bell Ringers, booklet single	1.50	......
2940a	same, booklet pane of 10	14.00	......

2941e, 2946   **2955**

2957   **2958**

Scott	Description	Unused	Used
2941	P National Hockey League Forwards, sheet of 6	9.25	......
2941a	P Sidney Crosby	1.50	......
2941b	P Phil Esposito	1.50	......
2941c	P Guy Lafleur	1.50	......
2941d	P Steve Yzerman	1.50	......
2941e	P Mark Messier	1.50	......
2941f	P Darryl Sittler	1.50	......
2942	P Sidney Crosby, booklet single	1.50	......
2943	P Phil Esposito, booklet single	1.50	......
2944	P Guy Lafleur, booklet single	1.50	......
2945	P Steve Yzerman, booklet single	1.50	......
2946	P Mark Messier, booklet single	1.50	......
2947	P Darryl Sittler, booklet single	1.50	......
2947a	same, booklet pane of 6	9.25	......
2948	$1.80 Sidney Crosby, souvenir sheet	3.50	......
2949	$1.80 Phil Esposito, souvenir sheet	3.50	......
2950	$1.80 Guy Lafleur, souvenir sheet	3.50	......
2951	$1.80 Steve Yzerman, souvenir sheet	3.50	......
2952	$1.80 Mark Messier, souvenir sheet	3.50	......
2953	$1.80 Darryl Sittler, souvenir sheet	3.50	......
2954	P-$2.50 Christmas Trees, sheet of 3	8.00	......
2955	P Virgin and Child, booklet single	1.50	......
2955a	same, booklet pane of 12	18.00	......
2956	P Santa & Christmas Tree, booklet single	1.50	......
2956a	same, booklet pane of 12	18.00	......
2957	$1.20 Christmas Tree in Hat, booklet single	2.25	......
2957a	same, booklet pane of 6	12.25	......
2958	$2.50 Dove & Christmas Tree, booklet single	4.50	......
2958a	same, booklet pane of 6	26.00	......

2959, 2959a, 2961   **2963a, 2966**

2017 COMMEMORATIVES

Scott	Description	Unused	Used
2959	P Year of the Rooster, perf. 12.5 x 13.25	1.50	......
2959a	same, perf. 13.25 x 12.5	1.50	......
2960	$2.50 Year of the Rooster, souvenir sheet	4.50	......
2960a	$2.50 Souvenir Sheet of 2, 2885a, 2960	11.00	......
2961	P Year of the Rooster, booklet single	1.50	......
2961a	same, booklet pane of 10	14.00	......
2962	$2.50 Year of the Rooster, booklet single	4.50	......
2962a	same, booklet pane of 6	27.00	......
2963	P UNESCO World Heritage Sites, sheet of 5	8.00	......
2963a	P Dinosaur Provincial Park	1.50	......
2963b	P Mistaken Point	1.50	......
2963c	P Historic District of Old Quebec	1.50	......
2963d	P L'Anse aux Meadows	1.50	......
2963e	P Red Bay Basque Whaling Station	1.50	......
2964	P Dinosaur Provincial Park, booklet single	1.50	......
2965	P Historic District of Old Quebec, booklet single	1.50	......
2966	P Red Bay Basque Whaling Station, booklet single	1.50	......
2967	P Mistaken Point, booklet single	1.50	......
2968	P L'Anse aux Meadows, booklet single	1.50	......
2968a	same, booklet pane of 10	14.00	......
2968b	same, booklet pane of 30	44.00	......

2969   **2970c, 2973**

SCOTT NO.	DESCRIPTION	UNUSED F/NH	USED F
2969	P Matieu Da Costa, booklet single	1.50	.....
2969a	same, booklet pane of 10	14.00	.....
2970	P Canadian Opera, sheet of 5	8.00	.....
2970a	P *Filumena*	1.50	.....
2970b	P Gerald Finley	1.50	.....
2970c	P Adrianne Pieczonka	1.50	.....
2970d	P Irving Guttman	1.50	.....
2970e	P *Louis Riel*	1.50	.....
2971	P *Filumena*, booklet single	1.50	.....
2972	P Gerald Finley, booklet single	1.50	.....
2973	P Adrianne Pieczonka, booklet single	1.50	.....
2974	P Irving Guttman, booklet single	1.50	.....
2975	P *Louis Riel*, booklet single	1.50	.....
2975a	same, booklet pane of 10	14.00	.....

| | **2979** | **2982** | **2980** |

2976	P Daisies, sheet of 2	3.25	.....
2977-78	P Daisies, coil pair	3.00	.....
2977	P Purple Daisy, coil single	1.50	.....
2978	P Yellow Daisy, coil single	1.50	.....
2979-80	P Daisies, booklet pair	3.00	.....
2979	P Purple Daisy, booklet single	1.50	.....
2980	P Yellow Daisy, booklet single	1.50	.....
2980a	same, booklet pane of 10	14.00	.....
2981	$2.50 Battle of Vimy Ridge, sheet of 2	10.00	.....
2982	P Battle of Vimy, booklet single	1.50	.....
2982a	same, booklet pane of 10	14.00	.....

| | **2983c, 2989** | **2983e, 2987** |

2983	P-$2.50 Star Trek II, sheet of 5	14.00	.....
2983a	P Admiral James T. Kirk	1.50	.....
2983b	$1 Captain Jonathan Archer	2.00	.....
2983c	$1.20 Captain Kathryn Janeway	2.25	.....
2983d	$1.80 Captain Benjamin Sisko	3.50	.....
2983e	$2.50 Captain Jean-Luc Picard	4.50	.....

| | **2984** | **12991** |

2984	$5 Borg Cube, booklet single	11.00	.....
2984V	P-$5 Star Trek II, Prestige Booklet Complete	36.00	.....
2985	P Galileo Shuttle, coil single, die cut 8	1.50	.....
2986	P Admiral James T. Kirk	1.50	.....
2987	P Captain Jean-Luc Picard	1.50	.....
2988	P Captain Benjamin Sisko	1.50	.....
2989	P Captain Kathryn Janeway	1.50	.....
2990	P Captain Jonathan Archer	1.50	.....
2990a	same, booklet pane of 10	14.00	.....
2991	P Galileo Shuttle, bklt single, die cut 13.75	2.75	.....

| | **2992c, 2995** | **2999c, 3002** |

2992	P Formula 1 Race Car Drivers, sheet of 5	8.00	.....
2992a	P Sir Jackie Stewart	1.50	.....
2992b	P Gilles Villeneuve	1.50	.....
2992c	P Ayrton Senna	1.50	.....
2992d	P Micheal Schumacher	1.50	.....
2992e	P Lewis Hamilton	1.50	.....

SCOTT NO.	DESCRIPTION	UNUSED F/NH	USED F
2993	P Sir Jackie Stewart, booklet single	1.50	.....
2994	P Gilles Villeneuve, booklet single	1.50	.....
2995	P Ayrton Senna, booklet single	1.50	.....
2996	P Micheal Schumacher, booklet single	1.50	.....
2997	P Lewis Hamilton, booklet single	1.50	.....
2997a	same, booklet pane of 10	14.50	.....
2998	P EID, booklet single	1.50	.....
2998a	same, booklet pane of 10	14.50	.....
2999	P Canadian Confederation, 150th Anniv., sheet of 10	14.50	.....
2999a	P Habitat 67 at Expo'67	1.50	.....
2999b	P Route Marker Trans-Canada Hwy.	1.50	.....
2999c	P Summit Series	1.50	.....
2999d	P Terry Fox Marathon of Hope	1.50	.....
2999e	P Canadarm in Space	1.50	.....
2999f	P Canadian Constitution	1.50	.....
2999g	P Woman of Nunavut	1.50	.....
2999h	P Rainbow Flag	1.50	.....
2999i	P Canadian Olympic Athlete	1.50	.....
2999j	P Paralympic Skiier	1.50	.....
3000	P Habitat 67 at Expo'67, booklet single	1.50	.....
3001	P Route Marker Trans-Canada Hwy., booklet single	1.50	.....
3002	P Summit Series, booklet single	1.50	.....
3003	P Terry Fox Marathon of Hope, booklet single	1.50	.....
3004	P Canadarm in Space, booklet single	1.50	.....
3005	P Canadian Constitution, booklet single	1.50	.....
3006	P Woman of Nunavut, booklet single	1.50	.....
3006a	P Woman of Nunavut, booklet pane of 8	11.50	.....
3007	P Rainbow Flag, booklet single	1.50	.....
3007a	P Rainbow Flag, booklet pane of 8	11.50	.....
3008	P Canadian Olympic Athlete, booklet single	1.50	.....
3009	P Paralympic Skiier, booklet single	1.50	.....
3009a	same, 3000-09 one each, booklet pane of 10	14.50	.....

| | **3017c, 3021** | **3012** |

3010	P Photography, sheet of 2	3.00	.....
3011	P Photography, sheet of 3	4.50	.....
3012	P Ti-Noir Lajeunesse, Violinist, booklet single	1.50	.....
3013	P Enlacees, booklet single	1.50	.....
3014	P Ontario, Canada, booklet single	1.50	.....
3015	P Construction of the Parliament Buildings, booklet single	1.50	.....
3016	P Sir John A. Macdonald, booklet single	1.50	.....
3016a	same, booklet pane of 10	14.50	.....
3017	P Birds of Canada, sheet of 5	8.00	.....
3017a	P Cyanocitta Cristata	1.50	.....
3017b	P Falco Rusticolus	1.50	.....
3017c	P Strix Nebulosa	1.50	.....
3017d	P Pandion Haliaetus	1.50	.....
3017e	P Gavia Immer	1.50	.....
3018	P Pandion Haliaetus, booklet single	1.50	.....
3019	P Falco Rusticolus, booklet single	1.50	.....
3020	P Cyanocitta Cristata, booklet single	1.50	.....
3021	P Strix Nebulosa, booklet single	1.50	.....
3022	P Gavia Immer, booklet single	1.50	.....
3022a	same, 3018-22 two each, booklet pane of 10	14.50	.....
3023	$2.50 - $25.00 Diwali - India Joint Issue, sheet of 2	5.25	.....
3024	P Diwali, floral flame, booklet single	1.50	.....
3025	P Diwali, single flame, booklet single	1.50	.....
3025a	P Diwali, 3024-25 five each, booklet of 10	14.50	.....

| | **3026f, 3032** | **3044** |

3026	P National Hockey League, Ultimate Six, sheet of 6	9.25	.....
3026a	P Maurice Richard	1.50	.....
3026b	P Jean Beliveau	1.50	.....
3026c	P Gordie Howe	1.50	.....
3026d	P Bobby Orr	1.50	.....
3026e	P Mario Lemieux	1.50	.....
3026f	P Wayne Gretzky	1.50	.....
3027	P Maurice Richard, booklet single	1.50	.....
3028	P Jean Beliveau, booklet single	1.50	.....
3029	P Gordie Howe, booklet single	1.50	.....
3030	P Bobby Orr, booklet single	1.50	.....
3031	P Mario Lemieux, booklet single	1.50	.....
3032	P Wayne Gretzky, booklet single	1.50	.....
3032a	same, booklet pane of 6	9.25	.....
3033	$1.80 Maurice Richard, souvenir sheet	3.50	.....
3034	$1.80 Jean Beliveau, souvenir sheet	3.50	.....
3035	$1.80 Gordie Howe, souvenir sheet	3.50	.....
3036	$1.80 Bobby Orr, souvenir sheet	3.50	.....
3037	$1.80 Mario Lemieux, souvenir sheet	3.50	.....
3038	$1.80 Wayne Gretzky, souvenir sheet	3.50	.....
3039	P History of Hockey - U.S. Joint Issue, sheet of 2	3.00	.....

SCOTT NO.	DESCRIPTION	UNUSED F/NH	USED F

3047

3048

3049

3040	P Hockey Player in Gear, booklet single	1.50	....
3041	P Hockey Player in Hat & Scarf, booklet single	1.50	....
3041a	same, 3040-41 five each, booklet pane of 10	14.50	....
3042	$5 Emblem of Toronto Maple Leafs, souvenir sheet	8.75	....
3043	P Emblem of Toronto Maple Leafs, coil single	1.50	....
3044	P Maple Leaf and 100, booklet single	1.50	....
3044a	same, booklet pane of 10	14.50	....
3045	P-$2.50 Christmas Animals, souvenir sheet of 3	8.00	....
3046	P Adoration of the Shepherds, booklet single	1.50	....
3046a	same, booklet pane of 12	18.00	....
3047	P Polar Bear, booklet single	1.50	....
3047a	same, booklet pane of 12	18.00	....
3048	$1.20 Cardinal, booklet single	2.25	....
3048a	same, booklet of 6	12.25	....
3049	$2.50 Caribou, booklet single	4.50	....
3049a	same, booklet of 6	26.00	....
3050	P Halifax Harbor Cent., booklet single	1.50	....
3050a	same, booklet pane of 10	14.50	....
3051	P Hanukkah, booklet single	1.50	....
3051a	same, booklet pane of 10	14.50	....

3057, 3062, 3071

3085

2018 COMMEMORATIVES

3052	P Year of the Dog	1.50	....
3053	$2.50 Year of the Dog, souvenir sheet	4.50	....
3053a	$2.50 Year of the Dog and Rooster, souvenir sheet	11.50	....
3054	P Year of the Dog, booklet single	1.50	....
3054a	same, booklet pane of 10	14.50	....
3054b	same, booklet pane of 30	44.00	....
3055	$2.50 Year of the Dog, booklet single	4.50	....
3055a	same, booklet pane of 6	27.00	....
3056	P-$2.50 From Far and Wide, souvenir sheet of 9	20.00	....
3057-61	P From Far and Wide, horiz. coil strip of 5, die-cut 9.25	8.00	....
3057	P St. John's, coil single, die-cut 9.25	1.50	....
3058	P Hopewell Rocks, coil single, die-cut 9.25	1.50	....
3059	P MacMillan Provincial Park, coil single, die-cut 9.25	1.50	....
3060	P Prince Edwards National Park, coil single, die-cut 9.25	1.50	....
3061	P Parc National de l'Ile-Bonaventure-et-du-Rocher-Perce, coil single, die-cut 9.25	1.50	....
3062-66	P From Far and Wide, vert. coil strip of 5, die-cut 8.5	8.00	....
3062	P St. John's, coil single, die-cut 8.5	1.50	....
3063	P Hopewell Rocks, coil single, die-cut 8.5	1.50	....
3064	P MacMillan Provincial Park, coil single, die-cut 8.5	1.50	....
3065	P Prince Edwards National Park, coil single, die-cut 8.5	1.50	....
3066	P Parc National de l'Ile-Bonaventure-et-du-Rocher-Perce, coil single, die-cut 8.5	1.50	....
3067	$1.20 Point Pelle, coil single	2.25	....
3068	$1.80 Naats'jhch'oh National Park, coil single	3.50	....
3069	$2.50 Arctic Bay, coil single	4.50	....
3070	$1 Pisew Falls Park, coil single	2.00	....
3071	P St. John's, booklet single	1.50	....
3072	P Hopewell Rocks, booklet single	1.50	....
3073	P MacMillan Provincial Park, booklet single	1.50	....
3074	P Prince Edwards National Park, booklet single	1.50	....
3075	P Parc National de l'Ile-Bonaventure-et-du-Rocher-Perce, booklet single	1.50	....
3075a	same, booklet pane of 10	14.50	....
3075b	same, booklet pane of 30	44.00	....
3076	$1.20 Point Pelle, booklet single	2.25	....
3076a	same, booklet of 6	12.25	....
3077	$1.80 Naats'jhch'oh National Park, booklet single	3.50	....
3077a	same, booklet of 6	21.00	....
3078	$2.50 Arctic Bay, booklet single	4.50	....
3078a	same, booklet of 6	27.00	....
3079	P Canadian Women in Winter Sports, sheet of 5	8.00	....
3079a	P Nancy Greene	1.50	....
3079b	P Sharon and Shirley Firth	1.50	....
3079c	P Danielle Goyette	1.50	....
3079d	P Clara Hughes	1.50	....
3079e	P Sonja Gaudet	1.50	....
3080	P Nancy Greene, booklet single	1.50	....
3081	P Sharon and Shirley Firth, booklet single	1.50	....
3082	P Danielle Goyette, booklet single	1.50	....
3083	P Clara Hughes, booklet single	1.50	....
3084	P Sonja Gaudet, booklet single	1.50	....
3084a	same, 3080-84 two each, booklet pane of 10	14.50	....
3085	P Kay Livingstone, booklet single	1.50	....
3085a	same, booklet pane of 10	14.50	....
3086	P Lincoln Alexander, booklet single	1.50	....
3086a	same, booklet pane of 10	14.50	....

3088, 3090   **3089, 3091**

3087	P Lotus Flowers, souvenir sheet of 2	3.25	....
3088-89	P Lotus Flowers, coil pair	3.00	....
3088	P Pink Lotus, coil single	1.50	....
3089	P Yellow Lotus, coil single	1.50	....
3090-91	P Lotus Flowers, booklet pair	3.00	....
3090	P Pink Lotus, booklet single	1.50	....
3091	P Yellow Lotus, booklet single	1.50	....
3091a	same, booklet pane of 10	14.50	....
3092	P Canadian Illustrators, souvenir sheet of 5	8.00	....
3092a	P Anita Kunz	1.50	....
3092b	P Will Davies	1.50	....
3092c	P Blair Drawson	1.50	....
3092d	P Gerard Dubois	1.50	....
3092e	P James Hill	1.50	....
3093	P Anita Kunz, booklet single	1.50	....
3094	P Will Davies, booklet single	1.50	....
3095	P Blair Drawson, booklet single	1.50	....
3096	P Gerard Dubois, booklet single	1.50	....
3097	P James Hill, booklet single	1.50	....
3097a	same, 3093-97 two each, booklet pane of 10	14.50	....

3098

3098	P Queen Elizabeth II, 65th Coronation Anniv., booklet single	1.50	....
3098a	same, booklet pane of 10	14.50	....
3099-3100	P Bees, booklet pair	3.00	....
3099	P Rusty-patched bee, booklet single	1.50	....
3100	P Metallic green bee, booklet single	1.50	....
3100a	same, booklet pane of 10	14.50	....
3101	P Memorial Cup, 100th Anniv., booklet single	1.50	....
3101a	same, booklet pane of 10	14.50	....

3102b
3105a, 3110

3102	P Royal Astronomical Society, souvenir sheet of 2	3.25	....
3103-04	P Royal Astronomical Society, pair	3.00	....
3103	P Milky Way, booklet single	1.50	....
3104	P Northern Lights, booklet single	1.50	....
3104a	same, booklet pane of 10	14.50	....
3105	P Sharks, souvenir sheet of 5	8.00	....
3105a	P Isurus Oxyrinchus	1.50	....
3105b	P Cetorhimus	1.50	....
3105c	P Carcharodon	1.50	....
3105d	P Somniosus	1.50	....
3105e	P Prionace Glauca	1.50	....
3106	P Carcharodon, booklet single	1.50	....
3107	P Cetorhinus, booklet single	1.50	....
3108	P Somniosus, booklet single	1.50	....
3109	P Prionace Glauca, booklet single	1.50	....
3110	P Isurus Oxyrinchus, booklet single	1.50	....
3110a	same, booklet of 10	14.50	....

3117a, 3118

3117c, 3122

3111c, 3115

SCOTT NO.	DESCRIPTION	UNUSED F/NH	USED F
3111	P Weather Wonders, souvenir sheet of 5	8.00	.....
3111a	P Steam Fog	1.50	.....
3111b	P Waterspout	1.50	.....
3111c	P Lenticular Clouds	1.50	.....
3111d	P Light Pillars	1.50	.....
3111e	P Moon Halo	1.50	.....
3112	P Steam Fog, booklet single	1.50	.....
3113	P Waterspout, booklet single	1.50	.....
3114	P Lenticular Clouds, booklet single	1.50	.....
3115	P Light Pillars, booklet single	1.50	.....
3116	P Moon Halo, booklet single	1.50	.....
3116a	same, booklet pane of 10	14.50	.....
3117	P Birds of Canada, souvenir sheet of 5	8.00	.....
3117a	P Poecile Atricapillus	1.50	.....
3117b	P Bubo Scandiacus	1.50	.....
3117c	P Cyanocitta Stelleri	1.50	.....
3117d	P Branta Canadensis	1.50	.....
3117e	P Grus Americana	1.50	.....
3117f	P Birds of Canada, Overprint, souvenir sheet of 5	8.00	.....
3118	P Poecile Atricapillus, booklet singles	1.50	.....
3119	P Grus Americana, booklet singles	1.50	.....
3120	P Branta Canadensis, booklet single	1.50	.....
3121	P Bubo Scandiacus, booklet single	1.50	.....
3122	P Cyanocitta Stelleri, booklet single	1.50	.....
3122a	same, booklet pane of 10	14.50	.....

3123d, 3127

SCOTT NO.	DESCRIPTION	UNUSED F/NH	USED F
3123	P Emergency Responders, souvenir sheet of 5	8.00	.....
3123a	P Canadian Armed Forces and Raft	1.50	.....
3123b	P Paramedics, Ambulances and Helicopter	1.50	.....
3123c	P Firefighters	1.50	.....
3123d	P Police Officers and Skyline	1.50	.....
3123e	P Search and Rescue Crew and Helicopter	1.50	.....
3124	P Canadian Armed Forces and Raft, booklet single	1.50	.....
3125	P Firefighters, booklet single	1.50	.....
3126	P Paramedics, Ambulances and Helicopter, bklt single	1.50	.....
3127	P Police Officers and Skyline, booklet single	1.50	.....
3128	P Search and Rescue Crew and Helicopter, bklt single	1.50	.....
3128a	same, booklet pane of 10	14.50	.....

3130, 3131

3134

SCOTT NO.	DESCRIPTION	UNUSED F/NH	USED F
3129	$4 Rocky Mountain Bighorn Sheep	7.50	.....
3130	P WWI Armistice	1.50	.....
3131	P WWI Armistice, booklet single	1.50	.....
3131a	same, booklet pane of 10	14.50	.....
3132	P $2.50 Christmas, Warm & Cozy, souvenir sheet 3	8.00	.....
3133	P Nativity Scene, booklet single	1.50	.....
3133a	same, booklet pane of 12	18.00	.....
3134	P Socks, booklet single	1.50	.....
3134a	same, booklet pane of 12	18.00	.....
3135	$1.20 Cap, booklet single	2.25	.....
3135b	same, booklet pane of 6	12.25	.....
3136	$2.50 Mittens, booklet single	4.50	.....
3136a	same, booklet pane of 6	26.00	.....

3137 **3152**

2019 COMMEMORATIVES

SCOTT NO.	DESCRIPTION	UNUSED F/NH	USED F
3137	P (90c) Queen Elizabeth II	1.60	.....
3137a	same, booklet pane of 10	15.50	.....
3138	P $2.50 From Far and Wide, souvenir sheet of 9	21.00	.....
3139-43	P From Far and Wide, booklet single	8.50	.....
3139	P Tombstone Terri. Park, coil single, die cut 9	1.60	.....
3140	P Athabasca Falls, coil single, die-cut 9	1.60	.....
3141	P Quttinirpaaq National Park, coil single, die-cut 9	1.60	.....
3142	P Mahone Bay, coil single, die-cut 9	1.60	.....
3143	P Little Limestone Lake Provincial Park, coil single, die-cut 9	1.60	.....
3144-48	P From Far and Wide, vert. coil strip of 5, die-cut 8	8.50	.....
3144	P Tombstone Terri. Park, coil single, die-cut 8	1.60	.....
3145	P Athabasca Falls, coil single, die-cut 8	1.60	.....

SCOTT NO.	DESCRIPTION	UNUSED F/NH	USED F
3146	P Quttinirpaaq National Park, coil single, die-cut 8	1.60	.....
3147	P Mahone Bay, coil single, die-cut 8	1.60	.....
3148	P Little Limestone Lake Provincial Park, coil single, die-cut 8	1.60	.....
3149	$1.05 Castle Butte, coil single, die-cut 13.25	2.25	.....
3150	$1.27 Algonquin Provi. Park, coil single, die-cut 8.25	2.50	.....
3151	$1.90 Mingan Archipelago, coil single, die-cut 8.25	3.75	.....
3152	$2.65 Iceburg Alley, coil single, die-cut 8.25	4.75	.....
3153	P Tombstone Terri. Park, booklet single	1.60	.....
3154	P Quttinirpaaq National Park, booklet single	1.60	.....
3155	P Little Limestone Lake Provincial Park, booklet single	1.60	.....
3156	P Athabasca Falls, booklet single	1.60	.....
3157	P Mahone Bay, booklet single	1.60	.....
3157a	same, booklet pane of 10	15.50	.....
3158	$1.27 Algonquin Provi. Park, booklet single	2.50	.....
3158a	same, booklet pane of 6	15.00	.....
3159	$1.90 Mingan Archipelago, booklet single	3.75	.....
3159a	same, booklet pane of 6	24.00	.....
3160	$2.65 Iceburg Alley, booklet single	4.75	.....
3160a	same, booklet pane of 6	28.50	.....

3161

SCOTT NO.	DESCRIPTION	UNUSED F/NH	USED F
3161	P Year of the Pig 2019	1.50	.....
3162	$2.65 Year of the Pig, souvenir sheet	4.75	.....
3162a	$2.65+$2.50 Year of the Pig & Dog (3053b), sheet of 2	9.00	.....
3163	P Year of the Pig, booklet single	1.60	.....
3163a	same, booklet pane of 10	15.50	.....
3164	$2.65 Year of the Pig, booklet single	4.75	.....
3164a	same, booklet pane of 6	28.50	.....

3167-68, 3169-70

SCOTT NO.	DESCRIPTION	UNUSED F/NH	USED F
3165	P Albert Jackson, Black History, booklet single	1.60	.....
3165a	same, booklet pane of 10	15.50	.....
3166	P Gardenia, souvenir sheet of 2	3.50	.....
3166a	P Pink Gardenia	1.60	.....
3166b	P Blue Green Gardenia	1.60	.....
3167-68	P Gardenia, coil pair	3.50	.....
3167	P Pink Gardenia, coil single	1.60	.....
3168	P Blue Green Gardenia, coil single	1.60	.....
3169-70	P Gardenia, booklet pair	3.50	.....
3169	P Pink Gardenia, booklet single	1.60	.....
3170	P Blue Green Gardenia, booklet single	1.60	.....
3170a	same, booklet pane of 10	15.50	.....
3171	P Canadians in Flight, sheet of 5	8.50	.....
3171a	P Elizabeth MacGill	1.60	.....
3171b	P Ultraflight Lazair Aircraft	1.60	.....
3171c	P Avro CF-105	1.60	.....
3171d	P C.H. Dickins	1.60	.....
3171e	P William George Barker	1.60	.....
3172	P Elizabeth MacGill, booklet single	1.60	.....
3173	P William George Barker, booklet single	1.60	.....
3174	P C.H. Dickins, booklet single	1.60	.....
3175	P Avro CF-105, booklet single	1.60	.....
3176	P Ultraflight Lazair Aircraft, booklet single	1.60	.....
3176a	same, booklet pane of 10	15.50	.....

3176

3178

3179a

SCOTT NO.	DESCRIPTION	UNUSED F/NH	USED F
3177	P Canada Sweets, sheet of 5	8.50	.....
3177a	P Sugar Pie	1.60	.....
3177b	P Butter Tart	1.60	.....
3177c	P Saskatoon Berry Pie	1.60	.....
3177d	P Nanaimo Bar	1.60	.....
3177e	P Blue-berry Grunt	1.60	.....
3177f	same, booklet pane of 10	15.50	.....
3178	P 1940 Vancouver Asahi Baseball	1.60	.....
3178a	same, booklet pane of 10	15.50	.....

SCOTT NO.	DESCRIPTION	PLATE BLOCK F/NH	UNUSED F/NH	USED F
3179	P Endangered Turtles, souvenir sheet of 2		3.25	.....
3179a	P Clemmys Guttatta		1.60	.....
3179b	P Emydoidea Blandingii		1.60	.....
3179c	same, booklet pane of 10		15.50	.....
3180	P Historic Covered Bridges, sheet of 5		8.50	.....
3180a	P Hartland, New Brunswick		1.60	.....
3180b	P Powerscourt, Quebec		1.60	.....
3180c	P Felix-Gabriel-Marchand, Quebec		1.60	.....
3180d	P West Montrose, Ontario		1.60	.....
3180e	P Ashnola No.1, British Columbia		1.60	.....
3181	P Hartland, New Brunswick, booklet single		1.60	.....
3182	P Powerscourt, Quebec, booklet single		1.60	.....
3183	P Felix-Gabriel-Marchand, Quebec, booklet single		1.60	.....
3184	P West Montrose, Ontario, booklet single		1.60	.....
3185	P Ashnola No.1, British Columbia, booklet single		1.60	.....
3185a	same, booklet pane of 10		15.50	.....
3186	P Command and Service Modules, Earth		1.60	.....
3187	P Lunar Module and Moon		1.60	.....
3186-87	P Apollo 11, 50th Anniv. pair		3.50	.....
3188-89	P Apollo 11, 50th Anniv., booklet pair		3.50	.....
3188	P Command and Service Modules, Earth, booklet single		1.60	.....
3189	P Lunar Module and Moon, booklet single		1.60	.....
3189a	same, booklet pane of 10		15.50	.....

3190a

SCOTT NO.	DESCRIPTION	PLATE BLOCK F/NH	UNUSED F/NH	USED F
3190	P Bears, sheet of 4		7.50	.....
3190a	P Grizzly Bear		1.60	.....
3190b	P Polar Bear		1.60	.....
3190c	P American Black Bear		1.60	.....
3190d	P Kermode Bear		1.60	.....
3191	P American Black Bear, booklet single		1.60	.....
3192	P Polar Bear, booklet single		1.60	.....
3193	P Kermode Bear, booklet single		1.60	.....
3194	P Grizzly Bear, booklet single		1.60	.....
3194a	same, booklet pane of 8		13.50	.....
3195	P, $1.27, $1.90, $2.65 Leonard Cohen, sheet of 6		15.00	.....
3196	P Leonard Cohen, squatting, booklet single		1.60	.....
3197	P Leonard Cohen, standing, booklet single		1.60	.....
3198	P Leonard Cohen, holding eyeglasses, booklet single		1.60	.....
3198a	same, booklet pane of 8		14.50	.....
3199	P, $1.27, $2.65 Shiney and Bright, sheet of 3		8.50	.....

3200

3204

SCOTT NO.	DESCRIPTION	PLATE BLOCK F/NH	UNUSED F/NH	USED F
3200	P Magi, booklet single		1.60	.....
3200a	same, booklet pane of 12		18.50	.....
3201	P Reindeer, booklet single		1.60	.....
3201a	same, booklet pane of 12		18.50	.....
3202	$1.27 Dancers, booklet single		2.25	.....
3202a	same, booklet pane of 6		12.50	.....
3203	$2.65 Patridge and Pears, booklet single		4.50	.....
3203a	same, booklet pane of 6		27.00	.....
3204	P Red River Resistance, booklet single		1.60	.....
3204a	same, booklet pane of 10		15.50	.....
3205	P Hanukkah, booklet single		1.60	.....
3205a	same, booklet pane of 10		15.50	.....

3207, 3212

3208, 3213

3209, 3214

3210, 3115   **3211, 3216**

2020 COMMEMORATIVES

SCOTT NO.	DESCRIPTION	PLATE BLOCK F/NH	UNUSED F/NH	USED F
3206	P(92c)-$2.71 From Far and Wide, souvenir sheet of 9		21.00	.....
3207-11	P From Far and Wide, coil strip of 5, die-cut 9.25		8.50	.....
3207	P Abraham Lake, coil single, die-cut 9.25		1.60	.....
3208	P Athabaska Sand Dunes, coil single, die-cut 9.25		1.60	.....
3209	P Herschel Island-Qikiqtaruk, coil single, die-cut 9.25		1.60	.....
3210	P French River, coil single, die-cut 9.25		1.60	.....
3211	P Magdalen Islands, coil single, die-cut 9.25		1.60	.....
3212-16	P From Far and Wide, coil strip of 5, die-cut 8.5		8.50	.....
3212	P Abraham Lake, coil single, die cut 8.5		1.60	.....
3213	P Athabaska Sand Dunes, coil single, die-cut 8.5		1.60	.....
3214	P Herschel Island-Qikiqtaruk, coil single, die-cut 8.5		1.60	.....
3215	P French River, coil single, die-cut 8.5		1.60	.....
3216	P Magdalen Islands, coil single, die-cut 8.5		1.60	.....
3217	$1.30 Kootenay National Park, coil single, die-cut 8.25		2.50	.....
3218	$1.94 Swallowtail Lighthouse, coil single, die-cut 8.25		3.75	.....
3219	$2.71 Cabot Trail, coil single, die-cut 8.25		4.75	.....
3220	$1.07 Carcajou Falls, coil single, die-cut 13.25		2.25	.....
3221	P Abraham Lake, booklet single		1.60	.....
3222	P Herschel Island-Qikiqtaruk, booklet single		1.60	.....
3223	P Magdalen Islands, booklet single		1.60	.....
3224	P Athabaska Sand Dunes, booklet single		1.60	.....
3225	P French River, booklet single		1.60	.....
3225a	same, booklet pane of 10		15.50	.....
3226	$1.30 Kootenay National Park, booklet single, die-cut 9.25		2.50	.....
3226a	same, booklet pane of 6		15.00	.....
3227	$1.94 Swallowtail Lighthouse, booklet single, die-cut 9.25		3.75	.....
3227a	same, booklet pane of 6		24.00	.....
3228	$2.71 Cabot Trail, booklet single, die-cut 9.25		4.75	.....
3228a	same, booklet pane of 6		28.50	.....

3229

SCOTT NO.	DESCRIPTION	PLATE BLOCK F/NH	UNUSED F/NH	USED F
3229	P(92c) Year of the Rat, 2020		1.60	.....
3230	$2.71 Year of the Rat, souvenir sheet		4.75	.....
3230a	$2.71 + $2.65 Year of the Rat & Pig (3162a), sheet of 2		9.75	.....
3231	P Year of the Rat, booklet single		1.60	.....
3231a	same, booklet pane of 10		15.75	.....
3232	$2.75 Year of the Rat, booklet single		4.75	.....
3232a	same, booklet pane of 6		28.50	.....

3233

3239

SCOTT NO.	DESCRIPTION	PLATE BLOCK F/NH	UNUSED F/NH	USED F

3235-3236, 3237-3238

3233	P Colored Hockey Championship, booklet single		1.60	.....
3233a	same, booklet pane of 10		15.75	.....
3234	P Dahlias, souvenir sheet of 2		3.50	.....
3235-36	P Dahlias, coil pair		3.50	.....
3235	P Dahlias, without background, coil single		1.60	.....
3236	P Dahlias, light blue background, coil single		1.60	.....
3237-38	P Dahlias, booklet pair		3.50	.....
3237	P Dahlias without background, booklet single		1.60	.....
3238	P Dahlias, light blue background, booklet single		1.60	.....
3238a	same, booklet pane of 10		15.50	.....
3239	P EID, booklet single		1.60	.....
3239a	same, booklet pane of 10		15.50	.....

3240-3241

3240-41	P Victory in Europe, 75th Anniv., booklet pair		3.50	.....
3240	P Leo Major, booklet single		1.60	.....
3241	P Veronica Foster, booklet single		1.60	.....
3241a	same, booklet pane of 10		15.50	.....
3242	P Paintings by Group Seven, sheet of 7		1.60	.....
3243	same, booklet pane of 7		12.50	.....

3244-3245

3244-45	P Radio History Canada, booklet pair		3.50	.....
3244	P Microphone, booklet single		1.60	.....
3245	P Radio Receiver, booklet single		1.60	.....
3245a	same, booklet pane of 10		15.50	.....

SCOTT NO.	DESCRIPTION		UNUSED F/NH

CANADA PHOSPHOR TAGGED ISSUES
Overprinted with barely visible phosphorescent ink

TYPES OF TAGGING

I = Wide Side Bars
II = Wide Bar in Middle
III = Bar at Right or Left
IV = Narrow Bar in Middle
V = Narrow Side Bars

1962-63 Queen Elizabeth II

337-41p	1¢-5¢ Elizabeth	(5)	52.50	10.60
401-5p	1¢-5¢ Elizabeth	(5)	10.75	1.75
404pIV	4¢ Carmine—IV		6.00	1.25
404pII	4¢ Carmine—II		17.50	4.00
405q	5¢ Elizabeth, mini. pane of 25		......	41.25

1964-67

434-35p	3¢-5¢ 1964 Christmas	(2)	13.00	2.25
434q	3¢ mini. pane of 25		......	12.10
434q	same, sealed pack of 2		......	25.00
443-44p	3¢-5¢ 1965 Christmas	(2)	3.50	.65
443q	3¢ mini. pane of 25		......	7.70
443q	same, sealed pack of 2		......	15.75
451-52p	3¢-5¢ 1966 Christmas	(2)	3.50	.80
451q	3¢ mini. pane of 25		......	5.15
451q	same, sealed pack of 2		......	10.50
453p	5¢ Centennial		2.25	.45

1967-72 Queen Elizabeth II

454-58pI	1¢-5¢—I	(4)	12.50	1.75
454-58pII	1¢-5¢—II	(4)	12.50	1.65
454-57pV	1¢-5¢—V	(4)	7.75	.95
454ep	1¢ booklet single—V		......	.25
457p	4¢ carmine—III		2.75	.35
458q	5¢ mini. pane of 20		......	65.00
459p	6¢ orange, perf.10—I		4.50	.65
459bp	6¢ orange, perf.12-1/2x12—I		4.50	.65
460p	6¢ black, perf 12-1/2x12—I		5.50	.40
460cp	6¢ black, perf 12-1/2x12—II		4.25	.50
460gp	6¢ black, booklet single, perf.10—V		......	.75
460pII	6¢ black, perf. 12—II		4.00	.55
460pV	6¢ black, perf. 12—V		4.00	.50

1967 Views

462-65pI	10¢-25¢—I	(4)	45.00	9.00
462-63pV	10¢-15¢—V	(2)	12.50	2.00

1967-69

476-77p	3¢-5¢ 1967 Christmas	(2)	3.50	.65
476q	3¢ mini. pane of 25		......	3.30
476q	same, sealed pack of 2		......	7.00
488-89p	5¢-6¢ 1968 Christmas	(2)	3.75	.70
488q	5¢ booklet pane of 10		......	4.15
502-3p	5¢-6¢ 1969 Christmas	(2)	3.50	.60
502q	5¢ booklet pane of 10		......	3.85

1970-71

505p	6¢ Manitoba		1.75	.35
508-11p	25¢ Expo '70	(4)	12.50	11.00
513-14p	10¢-15¢ U.N.	(2)	20.00	3.15
519-30p	5¢-15¢ Christmas	(12)	23.50	6.05
541p	15¢ Radio Canada		17.25	3.05

1971 Queen Elizabeth II

543-44p	7¢-8¢—I	(2)	9.25	1.05
544q	booklet pane, 8¢(2), 6¢(1), 1¢(3)		......	2.20
544r	booklet pane, 8¢(11), 6¢(1), 1¢(6)		......	6.05
544s	booklet pane, 8¢(5), 6¢(1), 1¢(4)		......	2.75
544pV	8¢ slate—V		4.25	.60
550p	8¢ slate, coil		......	.30

1971-72

554-57p	6¢-15¢ Christmas	(4)	11.00	2.50
560p	8¢ World Health Day		3.25	.65
561p	8¢ Frontenac		5.75	.95
562-63p	8¢ Indians	(2)	3.75	1.20
564-65p	8¢ Indians	(2)	3.75	1.20
582-85p	15¢ Sciences	(4)	16.00	13.20

1972 Pictorials

594-97	10¢-25¢—V	(4)	10.50	2.25
594-97p I	10¢-25¢—I	(4)	35.00	7.50

1972

606-09p	6¢-15¢ Christmas—V	(4)	12.75	2.65
606-09pI	6¢-15¢ Christmas—I	(4)	15.00	3.50
610p	8¢ Krieghoff		3.50	.40

SCOTT NO.	DESCRIPTION	PLATE BLOCK F/NH	UNUSED F/NH	USED F

B20   B24   B22

SEMI-POSTAL STAMPS

1974-76

B1-12	Olympics, 12 varieties	28.50	6.25	6.25

1974

B1-3	Emblems, 3 varieties	7.50	1.95	1.95
B1	8¢ + 2¢ Olympic Emblem	1.95	.55	.55
B2	10¢ + 5¢ same	2.65	.65	.65
B3	15¢ + 5¢ same	3.85	.95	.95

1975

B4-6	Water Sports, 3 varieties	7.25	1.95	1.95
B4	8¢ + 2¢ Swimming	1.85	.45	.50
B5	10¢ + 5¢ Rowing	2.75	.65	.65
B6	15¢ + 5¢ Sailing	3.85	.85	.85
B7-9	Combat Sports, 3 varieties	7.25	1.75	1.50
B7	8¢ + 2¢ Fencing	1.75	.45	.45
B8	10¢ + 5¢ Boxing	2.75	.65	.65
B9	15¢ + 5¢ Judo	3.85	.95	.95

1976

B10-12	Team Sports, 3 varieties	8.75	2.00	2.00
B10	8¢ + 2¢ Basketball	1.85	.45	.45
B11	10¢ + 5¢ Gymnastics	2.75	.65	.65
B12	20¢ + 5¢ Soccer	4.75	1.15	1.15

1997-2015

B13	45¢ + 5¢ Literacy	......	1.40	.75
B13a	same, booklet pane of 10	......	13.50	....
B14	Mental Health	......	1.40	1.40
B14a	same, booklet pane of 10	......	13.50	....
B15	P + 10¢ Mental Health semi-postal	......	1.40	1.40
B15a	same, booklet pane of 10	......	14.50	....
B16	P + 10¢ Mental Health semi-postal	......	1.60	1.60
B16a	same, booklet pane of 10	......	15.50	....
B17	Mental Health Souvenir Sheet of 2	......	2.95	2.95
B17a	P + 10¢ Mental Health Semi-postal	......	1.50	1.50
B18	P + 10¢ Mental Health Semi-postal S/A booklet single	......	1.50	1.50
B18a	same, booklet pane of 10	......	16.00	....
B19	P+10¢, Hands and Heart	......	1.65	1.65
B19a	same, booklet pane of 10	......	16.50	....
B20	63¢ +10¢ Children's Art by Ezra Peters	......	1.75	1.75
B20a	same, booklet pane of 10	......	1.75	
B21	P +10¢ Children in Paper Boat, single	......	1.75	
B21a	same, booklet pane of 10	......	16.50	....
B22	P +10¢ Children Reading Story Under Tented Bedsheet	......	1.75	
B22a	same, booklet pane of 10	......	16.50	....
B23-24	P+10¢ Stylized Bird, pair	......	3.00	17.00
B24a	same, booklet pane of 10	......	17.00	

2017-2019

B25-26	P+10c Stylized Cats, pair	8.75	2.50	2.00
B26a	same, B25-B26 five each, booklet pane of 10	1.85	17.50	.45
B27	P+10c Child on Hill	2.75	1.75	
B27a	same, booklet pane of 10	2.75	17.50	
B28-29	P+10c Ice Cream Cone & Ice Pop	......	1.75	
B29a	same, booklet pane of 10	......	17.50	

SCOTT NO.	DESCRIPTION	UNUSED NH VF F AVG	UNUSED OG VF F AVG	USED VF F AVG

AIR POST STAMPS

C2   C5

1928

C1	5¢ brown olive	33.00	22.00	17.00	18.00	14.00	12.00	4.50	3.50	2.75

1930

C2	5¢ olive brown	165.00	125.00	100.00	92.00	70.00	55.00	28.00	21.00	16.00

1932

C3	6¢ on 5¢ brown olive	23.00	17.00	12.00	14.00	11.00	7.50	3.50	2.60	1.50
C4	6¢ on 5¢ olive brown	82.00	60.00	50.00	48.00	38.00	32.00	11.50	8.75	5.50

SCOTT NO.	DESCRIPTION	PLATE BLOCK F/NH F/OG	UNUSED F/NH F/OG	USED F

C6   C7   C9

1935

| C5 | 6¢ red brown | 40.00 | 25.00 | 5.50 | 4.00 | 1.25 |

1938

| C6 | 6¢ blue | 25.00 | 16.00 | 4.50 | 3.25 | .45 |

1942-43

| C7 | 6¢ deep blue | 33.00 | 23.00 | 7.50 | 5.00 | 1.00 |
| C8 | 7¢ deep blue (1943) | 6.50 | 4.50 | 1.50 | 1.00 | .25 |

1946

| C9 | 7¢ deep blue | 6.00 | 4.00 | 1.25 | .90 | .25 |
| C9a | same, booklet pane of 4 | … | …… | 4.00 | … | … |

AIR POST SPECIAL DELIVERY

CE1   CE3

1942-43

| CE1 | 16¢ bright ultramarine | 14.00 | 10.00 | 3.50 | 2.50 | 1.85 |
| CE2 | 17¢ bright ultramarine (1943) | 19.00 | 14.00 | 4.50 | 3.00 | 2.75 |

1946

| CE3 | 17¢ bright ultramarine (circumflex "E") | 31.00 | 22.00 | 6.00 | 4.25 | 4.00 |

1947

| CE4 | 17¢ bright ultramarine (grave "E") | 31.00 | 22.00 | 6.00 | 4.75 | 4.00 |

SCOTT NO.	DESCRIPTION	UNUSED NH VF F AVG	UNUSED O.G. VF F AVG	USED VF F AVG

SPECIAL DELIVERY STAMPS

E1   E2   E3

1898

| E1 | 10¢ blue green | 415.00 | 250.00 | 190.00 | 150.00 | 75.00 | 48.00 | 11.00 | 7.50 | 5.00 |

1922

| E2 | 20¢ carmine | 330.00 | 210.00 | 150.00 | 140.00 | 90.00 | 60.00 | 9.00 | 7.00 | 4.50 |

1927

| E3 | 20¢ orange | 110.00 | 70.00 | 48.00 | 49.00 | 30.00 | 18.00 | 12.50 | 9.00 | 6.75 |

1930

| E4 | 20¢ henna brown | 138.00 | 95.00 | 75.00 | 82.00 | 60.00 | 45.00 | 16.50 | 12.50 | 8.75 |

1933

| E5 | 20¢ henna brown | 140.00 | 90.00 | 75.00 | 85.00 | 60.00 | 44.00 | 19.00 | 14.00 | 10.00 |

E4   E6

SCOTT NO.	DESCRIPTION	PLATE BLOCK F/NH F/OG	UNUSED F/NH F/OG	USED F

E7   E10

1935

| E6 | 20¢ dark carmine | 105.00 | 75.00 | 19.00 | 14.00 | 7.00 |

1938-39

E7	10¢ dark green(1939)	50.00	38.00	11.00	8.00	3.75
E8	20¢ dark carmine	265.00	178.25	45.00	30.00	27.00
E9	10¢ on 20¢ dark carmine (#E8) (1939)	50.00	35.00	10.00	7.00	5.50

1942

| E10 | 10¢ green | 22.50 | 16.00 | 5.00 | 3.75 | 2.00 |

1946

| E11 | 10¢ green | 22.00 | 15.00 | 4.00 | 3.00 | 1.25 |

SCOTT NO.	DESCRIPTION	UNUSED NH F AVG	UNUSED F AVG	USED F AVG

WAR TAX STAMPS

MR1   MR3

2¢ + 1¢ Die I. Below large letter "T" there is a clear horizontal line of color.
Die II. Right side of line is replaced by two short lines and five dots.

1915

| MR1 | 1¢ green | 52.00 | 42.00 | 33.00 | 16.50 | .30 | .25 |
| MR2 | 2¢ carmine | 55.00 | 42.00 | 33.00 | 16.50 | .30 | .25 |

1916 Perf 12

MR3	2¢ + 1¢ carmine (I)	75.00	65.00	48.00	31.00	.30	.25
MR3a	2¢ + 1¢ carmine(II)	375.00	275.00	160.00	95.00	5.00	3.60
MR4	2¢ + 1¢ brown (II)	42.00	34.00	18.00	10.00	.35	.30
MR4a	2¢ + 1¢ brown(I)	950.00	750.00	550.00	350.00	10.00	8.00

Perf 12 x 8

| MR5 | 2¢ + 1¢ carmine | 125.00 | 85.00 | 75.00 | 48.00 | 28.00 | 20.00 |

Coil Stamps Perf. 8 Vertically

MR6	2¢ + 1¢ carmine (I)	275.00	200.00	190.00	115.00	8.50	6.50
MR7	2¢ + 1¢ brown (II)	85.00	60.00	58.00	35.00	1.25	.90
MR7a	2¢ + 1¢ brown (I)	350.00	280.00	230.00	140.00	8.00	6.00

SCOTT NO.	DESCRIPTION	UNUSED O.G. VF F AVG	UNUSED VF F AVG	USED VF F AVG

REGISTRATION STAMPS

F2

1875-88 Perf. 12 (NH+50%)

| F1 | 2¢ orange | 95.00 | 75.00 | 55.00 | 70.00 | 46.75 | 28.50 | 4.00 | 3.50 | 2.75 |
| F1a | 2¢ vermillion | 130.00 | 80.00 | 50.00 | 82.50 | 55.00 | 33.00 | 9.50 | 6.35 | 3.40 |

SCOTT NO.	DESCRIPTION	UNUSED NH F	AVG	UNUSED F	AVG	USED F	AVG
F1b	2¢ rose carmine	285.00	210.00	150.00	165.00	110.00	66.00	110.00	72.50	40.00
F1d	2¢ orange, perf 12x11-1/2	365.00	308.00	220.00	305.00	203.50	132.50	88.00	58.85	32.50
F2	5¢ dark green...................	100.00	85.00	60.00	82.50	55.00	34.50	4.50	3.25	1.95
F2d	5¢ dark green, perf 12x11-1/2	1140.00	960.00	500.00	950.00	800.00	450.00	185.00	125.00	90.00
F3	8¢ blue..........................	550.00	365.00	245.00	455.00	305.00	205.00	410.00	275.00	148.50

POSTAGE DUE STAMPS

J1

J11

J6

J15

J21

1906-28

J1	1¢ violet....................................35.00	20.00	14.50	9.25	4.50	2.75
J2	2¢ violet....................................35.00	20.00	14.50	9.25	.90	.65
J3	4¢ violet (1928)...........................105.00	80.00	62.00	48.00	22.00	16.00
J4	5¢ violet....................................35.00	17.50	14.50	9.25	1.75	1.25
J5	10¢ violet (1928)..........................135.00	110.00	75.00	55.00	13.00	9.50

1930-32

J6	1¢ dark violet...............................22.00	18.00	12.00	8.50	4.00	3.00
J7	2¢ dark violet...............................12.00	9.00	7.00	5.50	1.00	.70
J8	4¢ dark violet...............................35.00	28.00	20.00	15.00	5.75	4.00
J9	5¢ dark violet...............................42.00	34.00	23.00	18.00	6.75	5.25
J10	10¢ dark violet (1932)....................175.00	140.00	100.00	75.00	10.00	7.75

1933-34

J11	1¢ dark violet (1934).....................23.00	18.00	15.00	11.00	6.75	5.25
J12	2¢ dark violet...............................15.00	11.00	14.00	8.00	1.25	.75
J13	4¢ dark violet...............................24.00	17.00	14.00	11.00	7.25	5.75
J14	10¢ dark violet.............................45.00	32.50	40.00	28.00	5.75	4.50

SCOTT NO.	DESCRIPTION	UNUSED NH F	AVG	UNUSED F	AVG	USED F

1935-65

J15-20	1¢-10¢ complete, 7 varieties....................	6.50	5.25	5.50	4.95	3.35
J15	1¢ dark violet...................................	.80	.55	.35	.25	.25
J16	2¢ dark violet...................................	.80	.55	.35	.25	.25
J16B	3¢ dark violet (1965)...........................	2.25	1.75	1.95	1.35	1.00
J17	4¢ dark violet...................................	.50	.40	.35	.25	.25
J18	5¢ dark violet (1948)..........................	.50	.40	.40	.30	.40
J19	6¢ dark violet (1957)..........................	2.25	1.70	1.95	1.35	1.50
J20	10¢ dark violet.................................	.50	.40	.35	.25	.25

POSTAGE DUES

1967 Perf. 12
Regular Size Design 20mm X 17mm

SCOTT NO.	DESCRIPTION	PLATE BLOCK F/NH	UNUSED F/NH	USED F
J21-27	1¢-10¢ cpl., 7 vars.	22.00	3.50	3.40
J21	1¢ carmine rose	8.25	.25	.25
J22	2¢ carmine rose	1.40	.25	.25
J23	3¢ carmine rose	1.40	.25	.25
J24	4¢ carmine rose	2.75	.45	.25
J25	5¢ carmine rose	10.00	1.65	1.35
J26	6¢ carmine rose	3.00	.40	.25
J27	10¢ carmine rose	3.00	.45	.25

1969-78 Perf. 12 (White or Yellow Gum)
Modular Size Design 20mm x 15-3/4 mm

J28/37 (J28-31, J33-37) 9 vars.		14.00	2.95	1.90
J28	1¢ carmine rose (1970).........	3.00	.55	.45
J29	2¢ carmine rose (1972).........	2.25	.45	.35
J30	3¢ carmine rose (1974).........	1.70	.30	.25
J31	4¢ carmine rose (1969).........	1.75	.35	.25
J32a	5¢ carmine rose (1977).........	125.00	24.75	24.75
J33	6¢ carmine rose (1972).........	1.50	.30	.25
J34	8¢ carmine rose	1.50	.30	.25
J35	10¢ carmine rose (1969)........	1.50	.65	.25
J36	12¢ carmine rose (1969)........	5.00	.85	.65
J37	16¢ carmine rose (1974)........	2.00	.40	.35

1977-78
Perf. 12-1/2 X 12

J28a-40 1¢-50¢ cpl., 9 vars.		22.00	5.05	4.75
J28a	1¢ carmine rose	.95	.25	.25
J31a	4¢ carmine rose	.95	.25	.25
J32	5¢ carmine rose	.95	.25	.25
J34a	8¢ carmine rose (1978).........	2.50	.40	.25
J35a	10¢ carmine rose	1.35	.30	.25
J36a	12¢ carmine rose	11.00	2.25	1.40
J38	20¢ carmine rose	2.60	.55	.45
J39	24¢ carmine rose	3.25	.65	.45
J40	50¢ carmine rose	4.60	1.25	1.00

OFFICIAL STAMPS
1949-50
#249, 250, 252, 254, 269-73
overprinted O.H.M.S.

O1-10	1¢-$1 complete, 9 vars.	......	315.00	165.00
O1-8	1¢-20¢, 7 varieties	......	47.50	18.50
O1	1¢ green........................	12.00	2.50	1.85
O2	2¢ brown.......................	110.00	15.40	8.00
O3	3¢ rose violet..................	12.00	2.50	1.35
O4	4¢ dark carmine................	17.50	3.30	.70
O6	10¢ olive.......................	22.00	5.55	.65
O7	14¢ black brown................	32.00	7.50	2.25
O8	20¢ slate black................	85.00	18.50	3.00
O9	50¢ dark blue green............	1100.00	203.50	100.00
O10	$1 red violet..................	450.00	73.00	40.00

1950 #294 overprinted O.H.M.S.

O11	50¢ dull green.................	300.00	39.00	26.50

1950 #284-88 overprinted O.H.M.S.

O12-15A 1¢-5¢ cpl., 5 vars.		26.75	6.95	3.25
O12	1¢ green........................	3.50	.75	.40
O13	2¢ sepia........................	5.00	1.50	.75
O14	3¢ rose violet..................	5.25	1.50	.60
O15	4¢ dark carmine................	5.25	1.50	.20
O15A	5¢ deep blue...................	11.00	2.40	1.60

1950 #284-88, 269-71, 294, 273 overprinted G

O16-25	1¢-$1 complete, 10 vars.	......	148.00	85.00
O16-24	1¢-50¢, 9 varieties	......	37.00	8.00
O16	1¢ green........................	4.25	.90	.25
O17	2¢ sepia........................	7.00	1.75	.85
O18	3¢ rose violet..................	7.00	1.75	.25
O19	4¢ dark carmine................	7.00	1.75	.25
O20	5¢ deep blue...................	14.00	2.75	.95
O21	10¢ olive.......................	17.00	3.75	.50
O22	14¢ black brown................	38.00	7.15	2.25
O23	20¢ slate black................	90.00	16.50	1.05
O24	50¢ dull green.................	60.00	11.00	5.75
O25	$1 red violet..................	475.50	112.00	82.00

1950-51 #301, 302 overprinted G

O26	10¢ black brown................	8.00	1.30	.30
O27	$1 bright ultramarine..........	450.00	100.00	85.00

SCOTT NO.	DESCRIPTION	PLATE BLOCK F/NH	UNUSED F/NH	USED F
	1951-53 #305-06, 316, 320-21 overprinted G			
O28	2¢ olive green	3.50	.70	.25
O29	4¢ orange vermillion ('52)	4.95	.95	.25
O30	20¢ gray (1952)	17.00	3.75	.25
O31	7¢ blue (1952)	19.75	4.10	1.25
O32	$1 gray (1953)	90.00	16.25	10.25
	1953 #325-29, 334 overprinted G			
O33-37	1¢-5¢ complete, 5vars.	8.40	2.40	1.15
O33	1¢ violet brown	2.00	.40	.25
O34	2¢ green	2.00	.40	.25
O35	3¢ carmine	2.00	.40	.25
O36	4¢ violet	3.00	.50	.25
O37	5¢ ultramarine	3.00	.50	.25
O38	50¢ lightgreen	27.00	5.25	1.00
	1955 #351 overprinted G			
O39	10¢ violet brown	6.50	1.40	.25

SCOTT NO.	DESCRIPTION	PLATE BLOCK F/NH	UNUSED F/NH	USED F
	1955-56 #337, 338, 340, 341, 362 overprinted G			
O40-45	1¢-20¢ cpl., 5vars.	17.00	6.50	1.35
O40	1¢ violet brown(1956)	3.00	.85	.45
O41	2¢ green (1956)	3.00	.85	.25
O43	4¢ violet(1956)	7.00	1.85	.25
O44	5¢ bright blue	3.00	.85	.25
O45	20¢ green(1956)	9.95	2.25	.25
	1963 #401, 402, 404, 405 overprinted G			
O46-49	1¢-5¢ cpl., 4 vars.	14.60	4.30	2.95
O46	1¢ deep brown	4.00	1.20	.85
O47	2¢ green	4.00	1.20	.85
O48	4¢ carmine	8.00	1.40	.85
O49	5¢ violet blue	2.75	.85	.55
	1949-50 AIR POST OFFICIAL STAMPS			
CO1	7¢ deep blue, O.H.M.S.(C9)	45.00	10.00	4.50
CO2	7¢ deep blue, G (C9)	90.00	18.15	13.75
	1950 SPECIAL DELIVERY OFFICIAL STAMPS			
EO1	10¢ green, O.H.M.S.(E11)	99.00	16.00	12.25
EO2	10¢ green, G (E11)	185.00	25.00	25.00

British Columbia & Vancouver Island #1-18

1

Queen Victoria

2

Queen Victoria

4

7

Seal

SCOTT NO.	DESCRIPTION	UNUSED O.G. VF	F	AVG	UNUSED VF	F	AVG	USED VF	F	AVG
	1860 Imperforate									
1	2-1/2p dull rose	...	...	...	...	21,000.00	15000.00	...	...	...
	1860 Perforated 14									
2	2-1/2p dull rose	950.00	650.00	425.00	475.00	375.00	240.00	300.00	225.00	150.00
	VANCOUVER ISLAND									
	1865 Imperforate									
3	5¢ rose	....	....	....	....	....	....	....	....	....
4	10¢ blue	4500.00	2450.00	1650.00	3000.00	1975.00	1200.00	1350.00	725.00	450.00
	Perforated 14									
5	5¢ rose	1050.00	700.00	450.00	700.00	530.00	340.00	525.00	430.00	270.00
6	10¢ blue	1050.00	700.00	450.00	700.00	530.00	340.00	525.00	430.00	270.00
	BRITISH COLUMBIA									
	1865									
7	3p blue	350.00	220.00	110.00	170.00	110.00	70.00	300.00	160.00	95.00
	New Values surcharged on 1865 design									
	1867-69 Perforated 14									
8	2¢ brown	400.00	225.00	150.00	250.00	165.00	95.00	240.00	160.00	95.00
9	5¢ bright red	625.00	375.00	225.00	400.00	272.00	160.00	400.00	320.00	185.00
10	10¢ lilac rose	4500.00	2450.00	1300.00	2450.00	1300.00	700.00	...	...	...
11	25¢ orange	800.00	550.00	325.00	450.00	325.00	190.00	410.00	320.00	185.00
12	50¢ violet	2400.00	1225.00	850.00	1500.00	975.00	575.00	1450.00	995.00	570.00
13	$1 green	3800.00	2250.00	1500.00	2400.00	1600.00	980.00	...	...	...
	1869 Perforated 12-1/2									
14	5¢ bright red	5200.00	2800.00	1675.00	3600.00	2250.00	1350.00	2550.00	1950.00	990.00
15	10c lilac rose	3000.00	1900.00	1050.00	1700.00	1250.00	795.00	1650.00	1295.00	770.00
16	25¢ orange	1950.00	1400.00	800.00	1250.00	810.00	500.00	900.00	825.00	500.00
17	50¢ violet	3150.00	1550.00	950.00	1400.00	795.00	775.00	1450.00	825.00	650.00
18	$1 green	4750.00	2800.00	1550.00	2400.00	1155.00	1150.00	2875.00	1950.00	1175.00

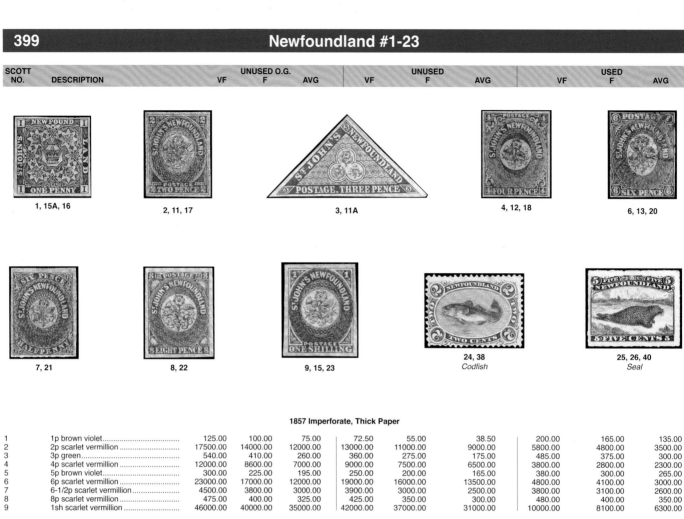

1, 15A, 16	2, 11, 17	3, 11A	4, 12, 18	6, 13, 20

7, 21	8, 22	9, 15, 23	24, 38 *Codfish*	25, 26, 40 *Seal*

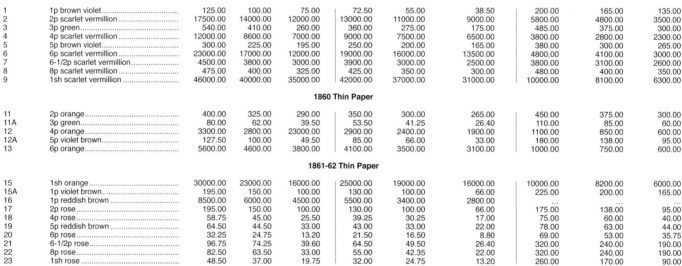

SCOTT NO.	DESCRIPTION	UNUSED O.G. VF	F	AVG	UNUSED VF	F	AVG	USED VF	F	AVG
	1857 Imperforate, Thick Paper									
1	1p brown violet	125.00	100.00	75.00	72.50	55.00	38.50	200.00	165.00	135.00
2	2p scarlet vermillion	17500.00	14000.00	12000.00	13000.00	11000.00	9000.00	5800.00	4800.00	3500.00
3	3p green	540.00	410.00	260.00	360.00	275.00	175.00	485.00	375.00	300.00
4	4p scarlet vermillion	12000.00	8600.00	7000.00	9000.00	7500.00	6500.00	3800.00	2800.00	2300.00
5	5p brown violet	300.00	225.00	195.00	250.00	200.00	165.00	380.00	300.00	265.00
6	6p scarlet vermillion	23000.00	17000.00	12000.00	19000.00	16000.00	13500.00	4800.00	4100.00	3000.00
7	6-1/2p scarlet vermillion	4500.00	3800.00	3000.00	3900.00	3000.00	2500.00	3800.00	3100.00	2600.00
8	8p scarlet vermillion	475.00	400.00	325.00	425.00	350.00	300.00	480.00	400.00	350.00
9	1sh scarlet vermillion	46000.00	40000.00	35000.00	42000.00	37000.00	31000.00	10000.00	8100.00	6300.00
	1860 Thin Paper									
11	2p orange	400.00	325.00	290.00	350.00	300.00	265.00	450.00	375.00	300.00
11A	3p green	80.00	62.00	39.50	53.50	41.25	26.40	110.00	85.00	60.00
12	4p orange	3300.00	2800.00	23000.00	2900.00	2400.00	1900.00	1100.00	850.00	600.00
12A	5p violet brown	127.50	100.00	49.50	85.00	66.00	33.00	180.00	138.00	95.00
13	6p orange	5600.00	4600.00	3800.00	4100.00	3500.00	3100.00	1000.00	750.00	600.00
	1861-62 Thin Paper									
15	1sh orange	30000.00	23000.00	16000.00	25000.00	19000.00	16000.00	10000.00	8200.00	6000.00
15A	1p violet brown	195.00	150.00	100.00	130.00	100.00	66.00	225.00	200.00	165.00
16	1p reddish brown	8500.00	6000.00	4500.00	5500.00	3400.00	2800.00	...	...	...
17	2p rose	195.00	150.00	100.00	130.00	100.00	66.00	175.00	138.00	95.00
18	4p rose	58.75	45.00	25.50	39.25	30.25	17.00	75.00	60.00	40.00
19	5p reddish brown	64.50	44.50	33.00	43.00	33.00	22.00	78.00	63.00	44.00
20	6p rose	32.25	24.75	13.20	21.50	16.50	8.80	69.00	53.00	35.75
21	6-1/2p rose	96.75	74.25	39.60	64.50	49.50	26.40	320.00	240.00	190.00
22	8p rose	82.50	63.50	33.00	55.00	42.35	22.00	320.00	240.00	190.00
23	1sh rose	48.50	37.00	19.75	32.00	24.75	13.20	260.00	170.00	90.00

27
Prince Albert

28, 29
Queen Victoria

30
Fishing Ship

31
Queen Victoria

32, 32A, 37
Prince of Wales

35, 36
Queen Victoria

SCOTT NO.	DESCRIPTION	UNUSED O.G.		UNUSED		USED	
		F	AVG	F	AVG	F	AVG
	1920						
127	2¢ on 30¢ slate..	9.00	6.75	8.25	5.75	5.50	4.00
	Bars 10-1/2mm apart						
128	3¢ on 15¢ scarlet...	325.00	265.00	280.00	195.00	225.00	170.00
	Bars 13-1/2mm apart						
129	3¢ on 15¢ scarlet...	26.00	20.00	23.00	16.00	11.00	8.55
130	3¢ on 35¢ red	17.00	13.00	15.00	11.00	9.50	7.50

141

142

143

144

145, 163, 172
Map of Newfoundland

146, 164, 173
S.S. Caribou

1923-24 PICTORIAL ISSUE

SCOTT NO.	DESCRIPTION	UNUSED O.G.		UNUSED		USED	
131-44	1¢-24¢ complete, 14 varieties...........................	210.00	135.00	140.00	80.00	85.00	62.00
131	1¢ gray green	3.50	2.35	2.25	1.60	.25	.20
132	2¢ carmine	3.50	2.35	2.25	1.55	.25	.20
133	3¢ brown..	4.75	3.00	2.85	1.95	.25	.20
134	4¢ brown violet	5.50	3.50	3.25	2.25	1.85	1.25
135	5¢ ultramarine	10.00	8.00	6.00	3.75	2.25	1.70
136	6¢ gray black	9.00	7.50	6.00	4.00	5.30	3.95
137	8¢ dull violet	7.25	6.00	6.00	4.00	4.25	3.25
138	9¢ slate green..	52.00	45.00	48.00	35.00	28.00	20.00
139	10¢ dark violet	6.25	5.00	6.00	4.50	2.50	1.90
140	11¢ olive green..	10.50	8.00	9.75	7.00	7.00	4.75
141	12¢ lake...	10.50	8.00	9.75	7.00	7.75	5.75
142	15¢ deep blue	13.00	9.00	12.00	8.00	8.00	5.75
143	20¢ red brown (1924)...	19.00	16.00	17.50	12.00	7.50	6.00
144	24¢ black brown (1924).....................................	82.00	60.00	77.00	48.00	45.00	38.00

147, 165, 174
Queen Mary and King George

148, 166, 175
Prince of Wales

149, 167, 176
Express Train

150, 168, 177
Newfoundland Hotel, St. John's

151, 178
Town of Heart's Content

152
Cabot Tower, St. John's

153, 169, 179
War Memorial, St. John's

154, 158
Post Office, St. John's

156, 170, 180
First Airplane to Cross Atlantic Non-Stop

157, 171, 181
House of Parliament, St. John's

159, 182
Grand Falls, Labrador

SCOTT NO.	DESCRIPTION	UNUSED O.G. F	AVG	UNUSED F	AVG	USED F	AVG

1928 Tourist Publicity Issue
Unwatermarked. Thin paper, dull colors

SCOTT NO.	DESCRIPTION	UNUSED O.G. F	AVG	UNUSED F	AVG	USED F	AVG
145-59	1¢-30¢ complete, 15 varieties........140.00	90.00	99.00	70.00	68.00	44.00	
145	1¢ deep green 2.10	1.55	1.25	.95	.75	.60	
146	2¢ deep carmine 4.25	3.25	2.50	1.85	.65	.50	
147	3¢ brown 4.25	3.25	4.00	2.00	.50	.32	
148	4¢ lilac rose 5.25	5.00	5.00	3.50	1.85	1.20	
149	5¢ slate green 12.25	11.75	9.50	7.50	4.50	2.80	
150	6¢ ultramarine 8.25	7.75	7.75	5.00	5.00	4.00	
151	8¢ light red brown 10.25	8.50	8.75	6.50	4.50	3.50	
152	9¢ myrtle green 10.25	8.50	10.00	7.00	7.00	5.00	
153	10¢ dark violet 12.50	11.00	12.00	7.50	4.50	3.25	
154	12¢ brown carmine 8.25	7.00	7.75	6.00	5.00	5.00	
155	14¢ red brown 17.00	13.00	16.00	12.00	7.00	6.00	
156	15¢ dark blue.....................12.00	11.00	12.00	7.50	7.00	6.00	
157	20¢ gray black 17.00	15.00	16.00	12.00	6.75	4.00	
158	28¢ gray green 40.00	36.00	38.00	28.00	24.00	18.00	
159	30¢ olive brown 21.00	17.50	19.00	15.00	7.75	5.75	

1929

| 160 | 3¢ on 6¢ gray black ....5.50 | 4.00 | 5.00 | 3.25 | 3.35 | 2.85 | |

1929-31 Tourist Publicity Issue
Types of 1928 re-engraved
Unwatermarked. Thicker paper, brighter colors

163-71	1¢-20¢ complete, 9 varieties..........155.00	115.00	135.00	90.00	64.90	50.00	
163	1¢ green 3.00	2.50	2.75	2.00	.65	.50	
164	2¢ deep carmine 3.00	2.50	2.75	2.00	.35	.25	
165	3¢ deep red brown 3.00	2.50	2.75	2.00	.35	.25	
166	4¢ magenta 5.25	4.00	5.00	3.50	1.50	.75	
167	5¢ slate green.....................11.00	9.00	10.00	8.00	1.50	.75	
168	6¢ ultramarine 15.00	13.00	12.00	7.00	9.00	7.00	
169	10¢ dark violet 12.50	9.00	12.00	8.00	2.50	1.75	
170	15¢ deep blue (1930) 72.00	60.00	65.00	45.00	38.00	33.00	
171	20¢ gray black (1931).........110.00	90.00	97.00	65.00	28.00	22.00	

1931 Tourist Publicity Issue
Types of 1928 re-engraved, watermarked, coat of arms
Thicker paper, brighter colors

172-82	1¢-30¢ complete, 11 varieties........250.00	180.00	225.00	140.00	105.00	75.00	
172	1¢ green 4.25	3.00	3.95	2.00	1.25	.85	
173	2¢ red 11.00	8.00	10.00	7.50	1.30	.90	
174	3¢ red brown 5.25	4.00	5.00	3.00	1.30	.85	
175	4¢ rose 6.25	5.00	5.75	4.00	2.75	1.85	
176	5¢ greenish gray 19.00	14.00	15.00	12.00	7.00	6.00	
177	6¢ ultramarine 30.00	25.00	29.00	18.00	16.00	13.00	
178	8¢ light red brown 30.00	25.00	29.00	18.00	16.00	13.00	
179	10¢ dark violet 21.00	16.00	19.00	16.00	9.00	7.50	
180	15¢ deep blue.....................59.00	50.00	56.00	40.00	28.00	21.00	
181	20¢ gray black 75.00	60.00	65.00	45.00	18.00	14.00	
182	30¢ olive brown 60.00	48.00	56.00	39.00	26.00	21.00	

THREE CENTS

160
136 surcharged in red

183, 253
Codfish

185, 186
King George

187
Queen Mary

188, 189
Prince of Wales

190, 191, 257
Caribou

192
Princess Elizabeth

193, 260
Salmon

194, 261
Newfoundland Dog

195, 262
Northern Seal

196, 263
Trans-Atlantic Beacon

1932-37 RESOURCES ISSUE Perf. 13-1/2

183-99	1¢-48¢ complete, 17 varieties..........97.25	70.50	85.00	60.00	48.50	36.50	
183	1¢ green 3.85	2.50	3.50	2.75	.55	.40	
184	1¢ gray black 1.35	.90	.90	.70	.25	.20	
185	2¢ rose 3.75	3.50	2.75	2.00	.35	.30	
186	2¢ green 2.00	1.50	1.50	.85	.25	.20	
187	3¢ orange brown 2.00	.95	1.50	.70	.35	.30	
188	4¢ deep violet 8.50	7.00	8.00	6.00	1.40	.90	
189	4¢ rose lake 1.00	.80	.90	.50	.30	.30	
190	5¢ violet brown (I) 14.00	11.00	13.00	10.00	1.40	.30	
191	5¢ deep violet (II) 2.00	1.50	1.75	1.00	.25	.20	
191a	5¢ deep violet (I)...............14.00	11.00	13.00	10.00	1.00	.60	
192	6¢ dull blue 14.00	11.00	13.00	10.00	11.00	8.00	
193	10¢ olive black 1.90	1.40	1.75	1.25	.85	.60	
194	14¢ black 4.75	3.50	4.90	3.00	2.50	2.00	
195	15¢ magenta 3.95	2.75	5.50	2.50	2.00	1.75	
196	20¢ gray green 4.00	3.00	3.60	2.50	1.00	.70	
197	25¢ gray 3.95	3.00	3.60	2.50	2.25	1.75	
198	30¢ ultramarine 36.00	30.00	33.00	28.00	24.00	19.00	
199	48¢ red brown (1937).............14.85	10.00	13.00	8.00	5.00	3.75	

197, 265
Sealing Fleet

198, 266
Fishing Fleet

208
The Duchess of York

209, 259
Corner Brook Paper Mills

210, 264
Loading Iron Ore, Bell Island

1932 Perf. 13-1/2

208-10	7¢-24¢ complete, 3 varieties 7.25	5.50	6.00	4.50	5.00	3.95	
208	7¢ red brown 1.90	1.35	1.75	1.15	1.25	1.00	
209	8¢ orange red 1.90	1.35	1.75	1.15	1.25	1.00	
210	24¢ light blue 3.85	2.50	3.60	2.25	3.25	2.25	

1933 LAND & SEA OVERPRINT

| 211 | 15¢ brown..........................15.50 | 13.00 | 14.00 | 12.00 | 9.50 | 7.55 | |

L. & S. Post.

211
No. C9 with Overprint and Bars

212
Sir Humphrey Gilbert

213
Compton Castle, Devon

214
The Gilbert Arms

216
Token to Gilbert from Queen Elizabeth

215
Eton College

217
Gilbert Commissioned by Queen Elizabeth

218
Gilbert's Fleet Leaving Plymouth

219
The Fleet Arriving at St. John's

220
Annexation of Newfoundland

221
Coat of Arms of England

SCOTT NO.	DESCRIPTION	UNUSED O.G. F	AVG	UNUSED F	AVG	USED F	AVG

1933 SIR HUMPHREY GILBERT ISSUE

SCOTT NO.	DESCRIPTION	UNUSED O.G. F	AVG	UNUSED F	AVG	USED F	AVG
212-25	1¢-32¢ complete, 14 varieties........	185.00	155.00	150.00	138.00	104.00	96.00
212	1¢ gray black...........................	1.65	1.40	1.25	1.00	.75	.70
213	2¢ green.................................	1.75	1.40	1.25	1.00	.75	.70
214	3¢ yellow brown........................	3.25	2.50	2.60	2.00	.95	.70
215	4¢ carmine...............................	2.75	2.25	2.25	2.00	.75	.70
216	5¢ dull violet...........................	4.25	3.50	3.50	3.00	1.00	.75
217	7¢ blue...................................	26.00	21.00	22.00	19.00	12.65	12.00
218	8¢ orange red...........................	11.00	9.00	10.00	9.00	6.50	6.00
219	9¢ ultramarine..........................	12.00	9.50	10.00	9.00	7.00	5.75
220	10¢ red brown..........................	12.00	9.50	10.00	9.00	7.00	5.50
221	14¢ black.................................	23.00	16.00	20.00	17.00	15.00	14.00
222	15¢ claret................................	21.00	16.00	20.00	17.00	15.00	14.00
223	20¢ deep green.........................	19.00	14.00	15.00	14.00	11.00	9.00
224	24¢ violet brown........................	35.00	26.00	28.00	20.00	23.00	20.00
225	32¢ gray..................................	35.00	26.00	28.00	20.00	23.00	20.00

222
Gilbert on the
"Squirrel"

223
1624 Map of Newfoundland

224
Queen Elizabeth I

225
Gilbert Statue at Truro

226
Windsor Castle and King George

SCOTT NO.	DESCRIPTION	UNUSED F/NH	F	USED F

1935 SILVER JUBILEE

SCOTT NO.	DESCRIPTION	UNUSED F/NH	F	USED F
226-29	4¢-24¢ complete, 4 varieties	23.00	19.90	10.00
226	4¢ bright rose..	3.00	2.75	.75
227	5¢ violet..	3.50	3.00	.90
228	7¢ dark blue...	6.50	4.50	3.50
229	24¢ olive green.......................................	13.00	10.00	7.50

1937 CORONATION ISSUE

SCOTT NO.	DESCRIPTION	UNUSED F/NH	F	USED F
230-32	2¢-5¢ complete, 3 varieties	9.75	5.50	2.60
230	2¢ deep green..	2.75	1.75	.75
231	4¢ carmine rose......................................	2.75	1.75	.75
232	5¢ dark violet..	5.25	3.50	1.50

230
King George VI and Queen Elizabeth

233

234
Die I: Fine Impression
Die II: Coarse Impression

235

SCOTT NO.	DESCRIPTION	UNUSED F/NH	F	USED F

236

237

238

239

240

241

242

245, 254
King George VI

243

1937 LONG CORONATION ISSUE

SCOTT NO.	DESCRIPTION	UNUSED F/NH	F	USED F
233-43	1¢-48¢ complete, 11 varieties..........................	45.00	41.00	25.10
233	1¢ Codfish...	.85	.50	.35
234	3¢ Map, die I..	3.75	3.25	1.10
234a	3¢ same, die II..	2.60	2.75	1.00
235	7¢ Caribou..	3.75	3.25	2.60
236	8¢ Paper Mills..	3.75	3.25	2.60
237	10¢ Salmon..	6.00	5.50	4.25
238	14¢ Newfoundland Dog	6.00	5.50	3.50
239	15¢ Northern Seal.....................................	5.25	4.75	3.50
240	20¢ Cape Race..	4.00	3.50	2.50
241	24¢ Bell Island..	5.25	4.25	3.50
242	25¢ Sealing Fleet......................................	5.25	4.25	3.50
243	48¢ Fishing Fleet......................................	8.00	7.25	3.50

249

2
▲ CENTS ▲

250
249 surcharged

1938 ROYAL FAMILY Perf. 13-1/2

SCOTT NO.	DESCRIPTION	UNUSED F/NH	F	USED F
245-48	2¢-7¢ complete, 4 varieties	7.25	5.10	2.65
245	2¢ green..	2.50	1.75	.25
246	3¢ dark carmine	2.50	1.75	.25
247	4¢ light blue..	3.00	2.25	.25
248	7¢ dark ultramarine..................................	2.25	2.00	1.20
249	5¢ violet blue...	1.75	1.50	1.15

249 SURCHARGED

SCOTT NO.	DESCRIPTION	UNUSED F/NH	F	USED F
250	2¢ on 5¢ violet blue..................................	1.65	1.25	.95
251	4¢ on 5¢ violet blue..................................	1.25	.95	.95

SCOTT NO.	DESCRIPTION	UNUSED F/NH	F	USED F

252   **267**

1941 GRENFELL ISSUE

| 252 | 5¢ dull blue | .65 | .50 | .35 |

1941-44 RESOURCES ISSUE
Designs of 1931-38. Perf. 12-1/2

253-66	1¢-48¢ complete, 14 varieties	22.00	20.00	11.40
253	1¢ dark gray	.50	.35	.25
254	2¢ deep green	.50	.35	.25
255	3¢ rose carmine	.75	.35	.25
256	4¢ blue	1.20	.95	.25
257	5¢ violet	1.20	.95	.25
258	7¢ violet blue (1942)	1.60	1.40	1.00
259	8¢ red	1.85	1.40	.70
260	10¢ brownish black	1.85	1.40	.65
261	14¢ black	2.60	2.40	2.00
262	15¢ pale rose violet	2.60	2.25	1.45
263	20¢ green	2.60	2.25	1.20
264	24¢ deep blue	3.30	2.80	2.00
265	25¢ slate	3.30	2.80	2.00
266	48¢ red brown (1944)	5.00	4.00	1.80

SCOTT NO.	DESCRIPTION	UNUSED F/NH	F	USED F

TWO CENTS
268

269

270

1943-47

267	30¢ Memorial University	2.20	1.60	1.10
268	2¢ on 30¢ University (1946)	.45	.35	.30
269	4¢ Princess Elizabeth (1947)	.45	.35	.25
270	5¢ Cabot (1947)	.45	.35	.25

AIR POST STAMPS

SCOTT NO.	DESCRIPTION	UNUSED O.G. VF	F	AVG	UNUSED VF	F	AVG	USED VF	F	AVG

Trans-Atlantic AIR POST, 1919. ONE DOLLAR.
C2
70 surcharged

AIR MAIL to Halifax, N.S. 1921
C3

Air Mail DE PINEDO 1927
C4
74 overprinted

Trans-Atlantic AIR MAIL By B. M. "Columbia" September 1930 Fifty Cents
C5
126 surcharged

C6, C9
Airplane and Dog Team

1919

| C2 | $1 on 15¢ scarlet | 275.00 | 195.00 | 165.00 | 225.00 | 170.00 | 135.00 | 225.00 | 185.00 | 165.00 |
| C2a | same without comma after "POST" | 310.00 | 270.00 | 190.00 | 250.00 | 200.00 | 170.00 | 260.00 | 205.00 | 165.00 |

1921

| C3 | 35¢ red | 195.00 | 165.00 | 125.00 | 140.00 | 105.00 | 78.75 | 185.00 | 150.00 | 125.00 |
| C3a | same with period after "1921" | 225.00 | 175.00 | 135.00 | 175.00 | 131.25 | 98.00 | 205.00 | 160.00 | 140.00 |

C7, C10
First Trans-atlantic Airmail

C8, C11
Routes of Historic Trans-atlantic Flights

TRANS-ATLANTIC WEST TO EAST Per Dornier DO-X May, 1932. One Dollar and Fifty Cents
C12
C11 surcharged

C13

1931 Unwatermarked

C6	15¢ brown	15.00	13.00	11.00	12.50	10.75	9.00	8.50	6.60	4.40
C7	50¢ green	48.00	34.00	26.00	42.00	31.00	27.00	26.00	20.00	16.00
C8	$1 blue	110.00	85.00	60.00	90.00	78.00	56.00	60.00	46.75	31.35

Watermarked Coat of Arms

C9	15¢ brown	16.00	13.00	9.00	13.00	11.00	7.00	7.75	6.00	4.00
C10	50¢ green	90.00	72.00	63.00	85.00	65.00	40.00	36.00	29.00	22.00
C11	$1 blue	155.00	118.00	72.00	120.00	90.00	65.00	92.00	77.00	58.00

1932 TRANS-ATLANTIC FLIGHT

| C12 | $1.50 on $1 blue | 470.00 | 360.00 | 225.00 | 375.00 | 295.00 | 195.00 | 360.00 | 275.00 | 181.50 |

SCOTT NO.	DESCRIPTION	UNUSED O.G. VF	F	AVG	UNUSED VF	F	AVG	USED VF	F	AVG

C14

C15

1933 LABRADOR ISSUE

SCOTT NO.	DESCRIPTION	UNUSED O.G. VF	F	AVG	UNUSED VF	F	AVG	USED VF	F	AVG
C13-17	5¢-75¢ complete, 5 varieties	206.00	172.50	103.50	150.00	112.50	75.00	156.00	135.50	100.00
C13	5¢ "Put to Flight"	15.85	13.20	7.95	11.00	9.00	7.00	10.50	9.00	7.25
C14	10¢ "Land of Heart's Delight"	23.75	19.80	11.85	16.00	12.00	8.00	18.00	16.00	14.00
C15	30¢ "Spotting the Herd"......................	39.50	33.00	19.75	30.50	22.00	17.00	31.00	27.00	21.00
C16	60¢ "News from Home".......................	71.00	59.00	36.00	60.00	40.00	29.00	58.00	52.00	38.00
C17	75¢ "Labrador, The Land of Gold".......	71.00	59.00	36.00	60.00	40.00	30.00	58.00	52.00	38.00

C16

C17

1933
GEN. BALBO
FLIGHT.
$4.50

C18
C17 Surcharged

C19

1933 BALBOA FLIGHT ISSUE

SCOTT NO.	DESCRIPTION	UNUSED O.G. VF	F	AVG	UNUSED VF	F	AVG	USED VF	F	AVG
C18	$4.50 on 75¢ bistre	650.00	545.00	330.00	460.00	385.00	302.50	460.00	385.00	302.50

1943

C19	7¢ St. John's	.55	.45	.40	.50	.40	.35	.35	.30	.25

POSTAGE DUE STAMPS

SCOTT NO.	DESCRIPTION	UNUSED F/NH	F	USED F	SCOTT NO.	DESCRIPTION	UNUSED F/NH	F	USED F
						1946-49 **Unwatermarked, Perf. 11**			
					J1a	1¢ yellow green.................................	9.50	6.00	5.50
	J1								
	1939 Unwatermarked, Perf. 10-1/2x10					**Unwatermarked, Perf. 11x9**			
J1	1¢ yellow green.................................	7.50	4.00	5.25	J2a	2¢ vermillion...................................	10.00	7.00	5.50
J2	2¢ vermillion...................................	11.00	7.00	5.25	J3a	3¢ ultramarine................................	10.00	7.00	7.50
J3	3¢ ultramarine................................	11.00	7.50	6.00	J4a	4¢ yellow orange.............................	17.00	15.00	15.00
J4	4¢ yellow orange.............................	15.00	12.00	10.00					
J5	5¢ pale brown	18.00	14.00	5.00		**Watermarked, Perf. 11**			
J6	10¢ dark violet.................................	12.00	8.00	5.00	J7	10¢ dark violet.................................	18.00	12.00	14.00

SCOTT NO.	DESCRIPTION	UNUSED O.G.			UNUSED			USED		
		VF	F	AVG	VF	F	AVG	VF	F	AVG

1

Crown of Great Britain surrounded by Heraldic Flowers of the United Kingdom

6 **7** **8** **9** **10** **11**

1851 PENCE ISSUE. Imperforate

SCOTT NO.	DESCRIPTION	VF	F	AVG	VF	F	AVG	VF	F	AVG
1	3p red.....................................	5200.00	3900.00	2850.00	2600.00	2100.00	1600.00	450.00	350.00	300.00
2	6p olive yellow........................	7000.00	5000.00	2900.00	3700.00	3000.00	2200.00	850.00	700.00	600.00
3	1sh bright red violet...............	30500.00	26000.00	19000.00	16000.00	13000.00	10000.00	6600.00	5000.00	4500.00
4	1sh dull violet	35500.00	30000.00	22000.00	23000.00	18000.00	13500.00	7600.00	6300.00	4600.00

1860-63 CENTS ISSUE
(NH + 50%)

SCOTT NO.	DESCRIPTION	VF	F	AVG	VF	F	AVG	VF	F	AVG
6	1¢ Locomotive........................	40.00	30.00	22.50	30.00	22.50	17.00	38.00	32.00	28.00
7	2¢ Queen Victoria, orange (1863).......	16.00	14.00	12.00	12.50	9.50	7.00	14.00	10.50	7.75
8	5¢ same, yellow green..............	31.00	25.00	18.00	16.00	13.00	11.00	23.00	16.00	11.00
9	10¢ same, vermillion................	60.00	45.00	33.00	42.00	31.50	23.75	48.00	39.00	33.00
10	12-1/2¢ Ships	100.00	75.00	60.00	60.00	45.00	33.75	80.00	64.00	54.00
11	17¢ Prince of Wales...............	55.00	44.00	32.00	42.00	31.50	23.75	67.00	54.00	47.00

Nova Scotia #1-13

SCOTT NO.	DESCRIPTION	UNUSED O.G.			UNUSED			USED		
		VF	F	AVG	VF	F	AVG	VF	F	AVG

1

2, 3

Royal Crown and Heraldic Flowers of the United Kingdom

1851-53 PENCE ISSUE
Imperf. Blue Paper

SCOTT NO.	DESCRIPTION	VF	F	AVG	VF	F	AVG	VF	F	AVG
1	1p Queen Victoria	3600.00	3100.00	2700.00	3200.00	2300.00	1800.00	675.00	530.00	485.00
2	3p blue	1450.00	1200.00	900.00	1100.00	950.00	800.00	250.00	210.00	185.00
3	3p dark blue	1775.00	1350.00	1000.00	1200.00	1000.00	850.00	315.00	255.00	200.00
4	6p yellow green.....................	5100.00	4000.00	3100.00	3700.00	2900.00	2450.00	695.00	540.00	430.00
5	6p dark green	10000.00	7000.00	5600.00	6600.00	5100.00	4100.00	1800.00	1550.50	1400.00
6	1sh reddish violet..................	26000.00	21000.00	18000.00	19000.00	15000.00	13000.00	5400.00	4100.00	3400.00
7	1sh dull violet	26000.00	21000.00	18000.00	19000.00	15000.00	13000.00	6600.00	5300.00	4800.00

8

11

Queen Victoria

12

1860-63 CENTS ISSUE
White or Yellowish Paper, Perf. 12
(NH + 50%)

SCOTT NO.	DESCRIPTION	VF	F	AVG	VF	F	AVG	VF	F	AVG
8	1¢ black................................	13.00	10.00	7.00	8.00	6.50	4.95	8.50	6.50	5.50
9	2¢ lilac..................................	12.50	10.00	7.00	8.00	6.00	4.50	13.00	9.00	7.00
10	5¢ blue	410.00	310.00	250.00	285.00	210.00	165.00	11.50	8.00	6.00
11	8-1/2¢ green	13.00	11.00	9.50	9.00	8.00	7.00	19.75	15.00	11.00
12	10¢ vermillion	13.00	11.00	9.75	9.00	8.00	6.50	12.00	9.00	6.00
13	12-1/2¢ black	38.00	28.00	23.00	28.00	21.00	16.00	38.00	30.00	22.00

SCOTT NO.	DESCRIPTION	UNUSED O.G. VF	F	AVG	UNUSED VF	F	AVG	VF	USED F	AVG

1, 5   2, 6   3, 7

Queen Victoria

1861 PENCE ISSUE, Perf. 9

No.	Description	VF	F	AVG	VF	F	AVG	VF	F	AVG
1	2p dull rose	975.00	775.00	575.00	525.00	450.00	310.00	325.00	260.00	185.00
2	3p blue	2000.00	1600.00	1100.00	950.00	725.00	575.00	725.00	595.00	560.00
3	6p yellow green	2300.00	1975.00	1600.00	1500.00	1200.00	1050.00	1200.00	1050.00	875.00

4   8   9   10

1862-65 PENCE ISSUE, Perf. 11 to 12
(NH + 50%)

No.	Description	VF	F	AVG	VF	F	AVG	VF	F	AVG
4	1p yellow orange	58.00	41.00	34.00	30.00	23.00	19.00	36.00	30.00	24.00
5	2p rose	9.00	7.50	5.25	6.00	5.00	4.00	7.75	6.00	4.50
6	3p blue	13.00	9.00	6.00	10.00	7.00	5.00	16.00	13.00	11.00
7	6p yellow green	115.00	85.00	68.00	80.00	70.00	55.00	96.00	70.00	58.00
8	9p violet	96.00	80.00	65.00	68.00	54.00	49.00	81.00	66.00	55.00

1868-70 PENCE ISSUE
(NH + 50%)

No.	Description	VF	F	AVG	VF	F	AVG	VF	F	AVG
9	4p black	10.25	7.85	5.40	7.85	6.05	4.15	19.25	14.85	9.35
10	4-1/2p brown (1870)	62.00	53.00	47.00	51.00	42.00	32.000	62.00	52.00	38.00

11   12   13   14   15   16

Queen Victoria

1872 CENTS ISSUE
(NH + 40%)

No.	Description	VF	F	AVG	VF	F	AVG	VF	F	AVG
11	1¢ brown orange	6.00	4.60	3.00	5.00	3.85	2.50	9.30	7.15	4.70
12	2¢ ultramarine	25.00	21.00	18.00	22.00	18.00	16.00	31.00	27.00	21.00
13	3¢ rose	25.00	19.00	16.00	17.25	13.20	10.00	23.00	20.00	16.00
14	4¢ green	10.00	7.75	6.00	6.50	5.00	4.50	26.50	20.35	13.75
15	6¢ black	8.00	6.00	4.00	7.00	5.00	3.50	23.50	18.15	12.10
16	12¢ violet	9.00	6.50	4.00	8.00	6.00	3.75	35.75	27.50	20.35

HOW TO WRITE YOUR ORDER

PLEASE USE ORDER FORM

1.) Please use black or blue ink (NO PENCIL) and print all requested information (name, address, etc.)
2.) Indicate quantity, country (U.S., UN, Canada or province), catalog number, item description (single, plate block, etc.)
3.) Specify condition (F, VF, NH, etc.) and check whether it is mint or used
4.) Enter price as listed in this catalog
5.) Total all purchases, adding shipping/handling charge from table below. Alabama residents (only) also add sales tax.
6.) Payment may be made by check, money order, or credit card (VISA, Discover, American Express or Mastercard are accepted). ORDERS FROM OUTSIDE THE UNITED STATES MUST BE PAID WITH A CREDIT CARD and all payments must be made in U.S. funds.

SHIPPING AND HANDLING CHARGES*
Safe delivery is guaranteed. We assume all losses.

If ordering STAMPS ONLY Orders under $150.00 .... add $4.95
If order includes supply items and totals
Orders under $50.00 .... add $5.95
Orders from $50.00 to $149.99 .... add $7.95
Orders from $150.00 to $299.99 .... add $9.95
Orders over $300 .... add $12.95

The following charges may not fully cover the actual postage or freight, insurance and handling cost for foreign orders, and additional charges may be added.

RETURN POLICY

H.E. Harris offers a 60 day money-back guarantee on every item. The customer has 60 days to examine, grade (at customer's expense) and evaluate every stamp to insure customer satisfaction. If the customer is not completely satisfied with their purchase, they can return it for a full refund or exchange:

- Call 1-800-546-2995, for a Return Authorization Number. You will not receive a credit for the product returned unless you have a Return Authorization Number. The Return Authorization Number must be written on the outside of all boxes returned.
- Please keep a list of the products being sent back.

The credit will be processed after we receive your return. Please allow 4 weeks for the return to show on the account. Sorry, we cannot accept C.O.D. freight or refund the original or return shipping costs. If you have questions about returning a Whitman Publishing product, please contact our customer service department at 1-800-546-2995 during normal business hours, 8 a.m. to 5 p.m. Central Standard Time.

H.E. HARRIS PERFORMANCE PLEDGE

- All stamps are genuine, exactly as described, and have been inspected by our staff experts.
- H.E. Harris & Co. upholds the standards set forth by the
American Philatelic Society and the American Stamp Dealers Association.
- If you have any problem with your order, please call our customer service department at 1-800-546-2995.
We will handle it to your complete satisfaction.

H.E. Harris & Co.
Serving the Collector Since 1916

TEN DOLLARS OFF COUPON

THIS COUPON IS WORTH $10.00, WITH ANY ORDER OF $50.00 OR MORE FROM THE 2021 H.E. HARRIS US/BNA CATALOG

H.E. Harris & Co.®
Serving the Collector Since 1916

THIS COUPON IS WORTH $10.00, WITH ANY ORDER OF $50.00 OR MORE FROM THE 2021 H.E. HARRIS US/BNA CATALOG

10

TEN DOLLARS OFF COUPON

10   10

Note: Coupon ONLY valid with order of $50.00 or more from the H.E. Harris 2021 US/BNA Catalog. Copies of coupon will not be accepted. Please include this coupon with order and payment. **If placing order by phone, please mention code US**. Coupon expires December 31, 2021.

THIRTY DOLLARS OFF COUPON

THIS COUPON IS WORTH $30.00, WITH ANY ORDER OF $300.00 OR MORE FROM THE 2021 H.E. HARRIS US/BNA CATALOG

H.E. Harris & Co.®
Serving the Collector Since 1916

THIS COUPON IS WORTH $30.00, WITH ANY ORDER OF $300.00 OR MORE FROM THE 2021 H.E. HARRIS US/BNA CATALOG

30

THIRTY DOLLARS OFF COUPON

30   30

Note: Coupon ONLY valid with order of $300.00 or more from the H.E. Harris 2021 US/BNA Catalog. Copies of coupon will not be accepted. Please include this coupon with order and payment. **If placing order by phone, please mention code US**. Coupon expires December 31, 2021.

ONE-HUNDRED DOLLARS OFF COUPON

THIS COUPON IS WORTH $100.00, WITH ANY ORDER OF $1000.00 OR MORE FROM THE 2021 H.E. HARRIS US/BNA CATALOG

H.E. Harris & Co.®
Serving the Collector Since 1916

THIS COUPON IS WORTH $100.00, WITH ANY ORDER OF $1000.00 OR MORE FROM THE 2021 H.E. HARRIS US/BNA CATALOG

100

ONE-HUNDRED DOLLARS OFF COUPON

100   100

Note: Coupon ONLY valid with order of $1000.00 or more from the H.E. Harris 2021 US/BNA Catalog. Copies of coupon will not be accepted. Please include this coupon with order and payment. **If placing order by phone, please mention code US**. Coupon expires December 31, 2021.

NOTES

H.E. Harris & Co.®
Serving the Collector Since 1916
4001 Helton Drive, Bldg. A · Florence, AL 35630
www.whitman.com
You may also order by phone 1-800-546-2995 or Fax 1-256-246-1116

RUSH SHIPMENT TO:

Name _____

Address _____

City/State/Zip _____

Phone *(in case of question about your order)* _____

FAST CREDIT CARD ORDERING

☐ VISA   ☐ mastercard   ☐ DISCOVER   ☐ AMERICAN EXPRESS

Card # _____

Expiration Date _____ CVV _____

Signature _____

Catalog or Stock No.	Qty.	Description	Mint	Used	Unit Price	Total Price

Shipping & Handling

If ordering STAMPS ONLY Orders under $150.00.................add $4.95
If order includes supply items and totals
    Orders under $50.00....................................add $5.95
    Orders from $50.00 to $149.99 ....add $7.95
    Orders from $150.00 to $299.99 ....add $9.95
    Orders over $300.....................................add $12.95
Foreign orders: S&H will be added separately.
Please apply your tax rate if you live in the following states:
GA, AL, IL, IN, KY, MD, MI, MN, NC, NJ, NY, VA, WI

For Office Use Only

2021-USBNA

TOTAL FRONT	
TOTAL REVERSE	
DISCOUNTS–If applicable	
SUBTOTAL	
SHIPPING CHARGE	
SALES TAX IF APPLICABLE	
TOTAL PURCHASE	

Catalog or Stock No.	Qty.	Description	Mint	Used	Unit Price	Total Price
				TOTAL THIS SIDE			

H.E. Harris & Co.®
Serving the Collector Since 1916

4001 Helton Drive, Bldg. A · Florence, AL 35630
www.whitman.com
You may also order by phone 1-800-546-2995 or Fax 1-256-246-1116

See Page 411 for Return Policy.
Sorry, no CODs.

Make payment in U.S. dollars by personal check, money order, Visa, Master Card, Discover or American Express. Please do not send cash.

Orders for shipment outside the U.S. must be paid by credit card and shipping charges will be added.

We Thank You For Your Order!

RUSH SHIPMENT TO:

Name _____

Address _____

City/State/Zip _____

Phone *(in case of question about your order)* _____

FAST CREDIT CARD ORDERING

☐ VISA ☐ mastercard ☐ DISCOVER ☐ AMERICAN EXPRESS

Card # _____

Expiration Date _____ CVV _____

Signature _____

Catalog or Stock No.	Qty.	Description	Mint	Used	Unit Price	Total Price

Shipping & Handling

If ordering STAMPS ONLY Orders under $150.00.................add $4.95
If order includes supply items and totals
    Orders under $50.00.......................................add $5.95
    Orders from $50.00 to $149.99 ....add $7.95
    Orders from $150.00 to $299.99 ....add $9.95
    Orders over $300...add $12.95
Foreign orders: S&H will be added separately.

Please apply your tax rate if you live in the following states:
GA, AL, IL, IN, KY, MD, MI, MN, NC, NJ, NY, VA, WI

For Office Use Only

TOTAL FRONT	
TOTAL REVERSE	
DISCOUNTS–If applicable	
SUBTOTAL	
SHIPPING CHARGE	
SALES TAX IF APPLICABLE	
TOTAL PURCHASE	

2021-USBNA

Catalog or Stock No.	Qty.	Description	Mint	Used	Unit Price	Total Price
				TOTAL THIS SIDE		

H.E. Harris & Co.®

Serving the Collector Since 1916

4001 Helton Drive, Bldg. A · Florence, AL 35630
www.whitman.com
You may also order by phone 1-800-546-2995 or Fax 1-256-246-1116

See Page 411 for Return Policy.
Sorry, no CODs.

Make payment in U.S. dollars by personal check, money order, Visa, Master Card, Discover or American Express. Please do not send cash.

Orders for shipment outside the U.S. must be paid by credit card and shipping charges will be added.

We Thank You For Your Order!

RUSH SHIPMENT TO:

Name _____

Address _____

City/State/Zip _____

Phone *(in case of question about your order)* _____

FAST CREDIT CARD ORDERING

☐ VISA ☐ mastercard ☐ DISCOVER ☐ AMERICAN EXPRESS

Card # _____

Expiration Date _____ CVV _____

Signature _____

Catalog or Stock No.	Qty.	Description	Mint	Used	Unit Price	Total Price

Shipping & Handling

If ordering STAMPS ONLY Orders under $150.00.................add $4.95
If order includes supply items and totals
    Orders under $50.00...add $5.95
    Orders from $50.00 to $149.99 ....add $7.95
    Orders from $150.00 to $299.99 ....add $9.95
    Orders over $300.. add $12.95
Foreign orders: S&H will be added separately.
Please apply your tax rate if you live in the following states:
GA, AL, IL, IN, KY, MD, MI, MN, NC, NJ, NY, VA, WI

For Office Use Only

TOTAL FRONT	
TOTAL REVERSE	
DISCOUNTS–If applicable	
SUBTOTAL	
SHIPPING CHARGE	
SALES TAX IF APPLICABLE	
TOTAL PURCHASE	

2021-USBNA

Catalog or Stock No.	Qty.	Description	Mint	Used	Unit Price	Total Price
			TOTAL THIS SIDE			

H.E. Harris & Co.®
Serving the Collector Since 1916
4001 Helton Drive, Bldg. A · Florence, AL 35630
www.whitman.com
You may also order by phone 1-800-546-2995 or Fax 1-256-246-1116

See Page 411 for Return Policy.
Sorry, no CODs.

Make payment in U.S. dollars by personal check, money order, Visa, Master Card, Discover or American Express. Please do not send cash.

Orders for shipment outside the U.S. must be paid by credit card and shipping charges will be added.

We Thank You For Your Order!

RUSH SHIPMENT TO:

Name _____

Address _____

City/State/Zip _____

Phone *(in case of question about your order)* _____

FAST CREDIT CARD ORDERING

☐ VISA ☐ mastercard ☐ DISCOVER ☐ AMERICAN EXPRESS

Card # _____

Expiration Date _____ CVV _____

Signature _____

Catalog or Stock No.	Qty.	Description	Mint	Used	Unit Price	Total Price

Shipping & Handling

If ordering STAMPS ONLY Orders under $150.00..................add $4.95
If order includes supply items and totals
    Orders under $50.00..add $5.95
    Orders from $50.00 to $149.99 ....add $7.95
    Orders from $150.00 to $299.99 ....add $9.95
    Orders over $300...add $12.95
Foreign orders: S&H will be added separately.
Please apply your tax rate if you live in the following states:
GA, AL, IL, IN, KY, MD, MI, MN, NC, NJ, NY, VA, WI

For Office Use Only

2021-USBNA

TOTAL FRONT	
TOTAL REVERSE	
DISCOUNTS–If applicable	
SUBTOTAL	
SHIPPING CHARGE	
SALES TAX IF APPLICABLE	
TOTAL PURCHASE	

Catalog or Stock No.	Qty.	Description	Mint	Used	Unit Price	Total Price
		TOTAL THIS SIDE				